LOCATION OF VIDEONOTES IN THE TEXT

VideoNote

(continued on next page)

LOCATION OF VIDEONOTES IN THE TEXT *(continued)*

VideoNote

Eighth Edition

Starting Out with C++ Early Objects

Tony Gaddis
Judy Walters
Godfrey Muganda

PEARSON

Boston Columbus Indianapolis New York San Francisco Upper Saddle River
Amsterdam Cape Town Dubai London Madrid Milan Munich Paris Montreal Toronto
Delhi Mexico City Sao Paulo Sydney Hong Kong Seoul Singapore Taipei Tokyo

Editorial Director, ECS: Marcia Horton
Executive Editor: Matt Goldstein
Editorial Assistant: Jenah Blitz-Stoehr
Director of Marketing: Christy Lesko
Marketing Manager: Yezan Alayan
Senior Senior Marketing Coordinator: Kathryn Ferranti
Director of Production: Erin Gregg
Senior Managing Editor: Scott Disanno
Production Project Manager: Kayla Smith-Tarbox
Manufacturing Buyer: Lisa McDowell
Art Director: Anthony Gemmellaro
Cover Designer: Joyce Wells
Manager, Rights and Permissions: Michael Joyce
Text Permission Coordinator: Jackie Bates, GEX inc.
Cover Image: Svetlana Kuznetsova / Shutterstock
Media Project Manager: Renata Butera
Full-Service Project Management: Mohinder Singh/ Aptara®, Inc.
Composition: Aptara®, Inc.
Printer/Binder: Edwards Brothers Malloy
Cover Printer: Lehigh-Phoenix Color/Hagerstown
Text Font: Sabon

Credits and acknowledgments borrowed from other sources and reproduced, with permission, in this textbook appear on appropriate page within text.

Credits: Figure 1-1a: Microsoft Powerpoint and Microsoft Word, Microsoft Corporation. 2010.
Reference: The most commonly used method for encoding characters is ASCII...(cont.)The American Standard Code for Information Interchange. American National Standards Institute. 2012.
Reference: "QuickSort is a recursive sorting algorithm that was invented in 1960 by C. A. R. Hoare." Hoare, C.A.R. "QuickSort". Oxford University Press. 1960.

Library of Congress Cataloging-in-Publication Data

Gaddis, Tony.
Starting out with C++ : early objects / Tony Gaddis, Judy Walters, Godfrey Muganda.—Eighth edition.
pages cm
ISBN-13: 978-0-13-336092-9
ISBN-10: 0-13-336092-X
1. C++ (Computer program language) I. Walters, Judy. II. Muganda, Godfrey. III. Title.
QA76.73.C153G33 2014
005.13'3—dc23 2012045400

10 9 8 7 6 5 4 3 2 1

ISBN 10: 0-13-336092-X
ISBN 13: 978-0-13-336092-9

Contents

Additional Appendices

The following appendices are located on the book's companion web site.

Preface

Welcome to *Starting Out with C++: Early Objects*, 8th Edition. This book is intended for use in a two-term or three-term C++ programming sequence, or an accelerated one-term course. Students new to programming, as well those with prior course work in other languages, will find this text beneficial. The fundamentals of programming are covered for the novice, while the details, pitfalls, and nuances of the C++ language are explored in-depth for both the beginner and more experienced student. The book is written with clear, easy-to-understand language and it covers all the necessary topics for an introductory programming course. This text is rich in example programs that are concise, practical, and real world oriented, ensuring that the student not only learns how to implement the features and constructs of C++, but why and when to use them.

What's New in the Eighth Edition

This book's pedagogy and clear writing style remain the same as in the previous edition. However, many improvements have been made to make it even more student-friendly and to keep it state of the art for introductory programming using the C++ programming language.

- **Updated Material**
  Material has been updated throughout the book to reflect changes in technology, operating systems, and software development environments, as well as to improve clarity and incorporate best practices in object-oriented programming.

- **New Material**
  New material has been added on a number of topics including expanded coverage on using files. Chapter 5 now brings together, adds to, and better organizes the material on files formerly found in Chapters 3, 4, and 5.

- **Reorganized Chapters**
  Several chapters have been reorganized to improve student learning. Chapter 2, Introduction to C++, now covers integer and floating-point data types before introducing characters and strings. Chapter 5, Looping, now discusses how looping structures are used before introducing the mechanics of creating them. Chapter 7, Introduction to Classes and Objects, now revisits a class students already know and have been using, the `string` class, before introducing how to create and use their own classes and objects.

- **Greater Focus on Object-Oriented Programming**
  Many examples throughout the text have been rewritten to incorporate appropriate use of classes and objects.
- **Improved Sample Programs**
  Sample programs have been revised where appropriate to incorporate current best programming practices. For example, throughout the book functions receiving objects or arrays whose values should not be changed now use the `const` keyword to protect them.
- **Improved Diagrams**
  Many diagrams have been improved and new diagrams added to better illustrate important concepts.
- **New Programming Challenges**
  New Programming Challenges have been added in many chapters, including a number of Challenges that ask students to develop object-oriented solutions and to create solutions that reuse, modify, and build on previously written code.
- **Answers in the Book**
  Answers to all the Checkpoint questions throughout the book and to the odd-numbered review questions at the end of every chapter are now conveniently located at the back of the book in Appendices C and D.

Organization of the Text

This text teaches C++ in a step-by-step fashion. Each chapter covers a major set of topics and builds knowledge as the student progresses through the book. Although the chapters can be easily taught in their existing sequence, flexibility is provided. The following dependency diagram (Figure P-1) suggests possible sequences of instruction.

Chapter 1 covers fundamental hardware, software, and programming concepts. The instructor may choose to skip this chapter if the class has already mastered those topics. Chapters 2 through 6 cover basic C++ syntax, data types, expressions, selection structures, repetition structures, and functions. Each of these chapters builds on the previous chapter and should be covered in the order presented.

Chapter 7 introduces object-oriented programming. It can be covered any time after Chapter 6, but before Chapter 11. Instructors who prefer to introduce arrays before classes can cover Chapter 8 before Chapter 7. In this case it is only necessary to postpone Section 8.12 (Arrays of Objects) until Chapter 7 has been covered.

As Figure P-1 illustrates, in the second half of the book Chapters 11, 12, 13, and 14 can be covered in any order. Chapters 11, 15, and 16, however, should be done in sequence. Instructors who wish to introduce data structures at an earlier point in the course, without having first covered advanced C++ and OOP features, can cover Chapter 17 (Linked Lists), followed by Chapters 18 and 19 (Stacks & Queues and Binary Trees), any time after Chapter 14 (Recursion). In this case it is necessary to simply omit the sections in Chapters 17–19 that deal with templates and the Standard Template Library.

Figure P-1

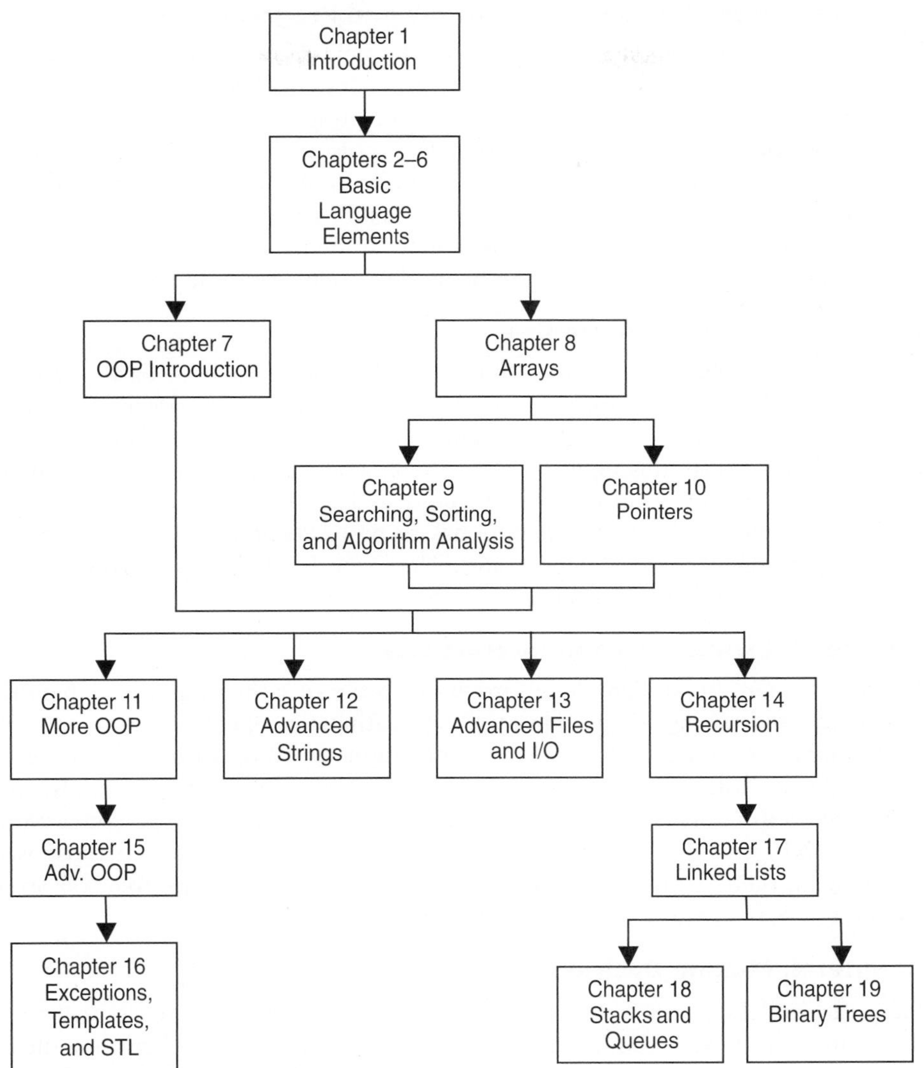
Chapter 1
Introduction
Chapters 2–6
Basic
Language
Elements
Chapter 7
OOP Introduction
Chapter 8
Arrays
Chapter 9
Searching, Sorting,
and Algorithm Analysis
Chapter 10
Pointers
Chapter 11
More OOP
Chapter 12
Advanced
Strings
Chapter 13
Advanced Files
and I/O
Chapter 14
Recursion
Chapter 15
Adv. OOP
Chapter 17
Linked Lists
Chapter 16
Exceptions,
Templates,
and STL
Chapter 18
Stacks and
Queues
Chapter 19
Binary Trees

Brief Overview of Each Chapter

Chapter 1: Introduction to Computers and Programming

This chapter provides an introduction to the field of computer science and covers the fundamentals of hardware, software, operating systems, programming, problem solving, and software engineering. The components of programs, such as key words, variables, operators, and punctuation are covered. The tools of the trade, such as hierarchy charts and pseudocode, are also presented. The *Tying It All Together* section shows students how to use the `cout` statement to create a personalized output message. Programming Challenges at the end of the chapter help students see how the same basic input, processing, and output structure can be used to create multiple programs.

Chapter 2: Introduction to C++

This chapter gets the student started in C++ by introducing the basic parts of a C++ program, data types, the use of variables and literals, assignment statements, simple arithmetic operations, program output, and comments. The C++ `string` class is presented and `string` objects are used from this point on in the book as the primary method of handling strings. Programming style conventions are introduced, and good programming style is modeled here, as it is throughout the text. An optional section explains the difference between ANSI standard and prestandard C++ programs. The *Tying It All Together* section lets the student play with simple text-based graphics.

Chapter 3: Expressions and Interactivity

In this chapter the student learns to write programs that input and handle numeric, character, and string data. The use of arithmetic operators and the creation of mathematical expressions are covered, with emphasis on operator precedence. Debugging is introduced, with a section on hand tracing a program. Sections are also included on using random numbers, on simple output formatting, on data type conversion and type casting, and on using library functions that work with numbers. For those who wish to cover them, there is also a section on C-strings. The *Tying It All Together* section shows students how to create a simple interactive word game.

Chapter 4: Making Decisions

Here the student learns about relational expressions and how to control the flow of a program with `if`, `if/else`, and `if/else if` statements. Logical operators, the conditional operator, and the `switch` statement are also covered. Applications of these constructs, such as menu-driven programs, are illustrated. This chapter also continues the theme of debugging with a section on validating output results. The *Tying It All Together* section uses random numbers and branching statements to create a fortune telling game.

Chapter 5: Looping

This chapter introduces, C++'s repetitive control mechanisms. The `while` loop, `do-while` loop, and `for` loop are presented, along with a variety of methods to control them. These include using counters, user input, end sentinels, and end-of-file testing. Applications utilizing loops, such as keeping a running total and performing data validation, are also covered. An extensive new section on working with files has been added, and the emphasis on testing and debugging continues, with a section on creating good test data. The chapter's *Tying It All Together* section introduces students to Windows commands to create colorful output and uses a loop to create a multi-colored display.

Chapter 6: Functions

In this chapter the student learns how and why to modularize programs, using both `void` and value-returning functions. Parameter passing is covered, with emphasis on when arguments should be passed by value versus when they need to be passed by reference. Scope of variables is covered and sections are provided on local versus global variables and on static local variables. Overloaded functions are also introduced and demonstrated. The *Tying It All Together* section includes a modular, menu-driven program that emphasizes the versatility of functions, illustrating how their behavior can be controlled by the arguments sent to them.

Chapter 7: Introduction to Classes and Objects

In this chapter the text begins to focus on the object-oriented paradigm. Students have used provided C++ classes since the beginning of the text, but now they learn how to define their own classes and to create and use objects of these classes. Careful attention is paid to illustrating which functions belong in a class versus which functions belong in a client program that uses the class. Good object-oriented practices are discussed and modeled, such as protecting member data through carefully constructed accessor and mutator functions and hiding class implementation details from client programs. Once students are comfortable working with classes and objects, the chapter provides a brief introduction to the topic of object-oriented analysis and design. The chapter also introduces structures and uses them in the *Tying It All Together* section, where students learn to use screen control techniques to create an animation that simulates the motion of a yoyo.

Chapter 8: Arrays

In this chapter the student learns to create and work with single and multidimensional arrays. Many examples of array processing are provided, including functions to compute the sum, average, highest and lowest values in an array. Students also learn to create tables using two-dimensional arrays, and to analyze the array data by row or by column. Programming techniques using parallel arrays are also demonstrated, and the student is shown how to use a data file as an input source to populate an array. STL vectors are introduced and compared to arrays. A section on arrays of objects and structures is located at the end of the chapter, so it can be covered now or saved for later if the instructor wishes to cover this chapter before Chapter 7. The *Tying It All Together* section uses arrays to create a game of *Rock*, *Paper*, *Scissors* between a human player and the computer.

Chapter 9: Searching, Sorting, and Algorithm Analysis

Here the student learns the basics of searching for information stored in arrays and of sorting arrays, including arrays of objects. The chapter covers the Linear Search, Binary Search, Bubble Sort, and Selection Sort algorithms and has an optional section on sorting and searching STL vectors. A brief introduction to algorithm analysis is included, and students are shown how to determine which of two algorithms is more efficient. This chapter's *Tying It All Together* section uses both a table lookup and a searching algorithm to encode and decode secret messages.

Chapter 10: Pointers

This chapter explains how to use pointers. Topics include pointer arithmetic, initialization of pointers, comparison of pointers, pointers and arrays, pointers and functions, dynamic memory allocation, and more. The *Tying It All Together* section demonstrates the use of pointers to access library data structures and functions that return calendar and wall clock time.

Chapter 11: More About Classes and Object-Oriented Programming

This chapter continues the study of classes and object-oriented programming. It covers object aggregation and composition, as well as inheritance, and illustrates the difference between is-a and has-a relations. Constant member functions, static members, friends, memberwise assignment, copy constructors, object type conversion operators, convert constructors, and operator overloading are also included. The *Tying It All Together* section brings together the concepts of inheritance and convert constructors to build a program that formats the contents of an array to form an HTML table for display on a Web site.

Chapter 12: More on C-Strings and the `string` Class

This chapter covers standard library functions for working with characters and C-strings, covering topics such as passing C-strings to functions and using the C++ `sstream` classes to convert between numeric and string forms of numbers. Additional material about the C++ `string` class and its member functions and operators is presented, with a program illustrating how to write your own string class. The *Tying It All Together* section shows students how to access string-based program environments to obtain information about the computer and the network on which the program is running.

Chapter 13: Advanced File and I/O Operations

This chapter introduces more advanced topics for working with sequential access text files and introduces random access and binary files. Various modes for opening files are discussed, as well as the many methods for reading and writing their contents. The *Tying It All Together* program applies many of the techniques covered in the chapter to merge two text files into an HTML document for display on the Web, with different colors used to illustrate which file each piece of data came from.

Chapter 14: Recursion

In this chapter recursion is defined and demonstrated. A visual trace of recursive calls is provided, and recursive applications are discussed. Many recursive algorithms are presented, including recursive functions for computing factorials, finding a greatest common denominator (GCD), performing a binary search, sorting using QuickSort, and solving the famous Towers of Hanoi problem. For students who need more challenge, there is a section on exhaustive and enumeration algorithms. The *Tying It All Together* section uses recursion to evaluate prefix expressions.

Chapter 15: Polymorphism and Virtual Functions

The study of classes and object-oriented programming continues in this chapter with the introduction of more advanced concepts such as polymorphism and virtual functions. Information is also presented on abstract base classes, pure virtual functions, type compatibility within an inheritance hierarchy, and virtual inheritance. The *Tying It All Together* section illustrates the use of inheritance and polymorphism to display and animate graphical images.

Chapter 16: Exceptions, Templates, and the Standard Template Library (STL)

Here the student learns to develop enhanced error trapping techniques using exceptions. Discussion then turns to using function and class templates to create generic code. Finally, the student is introduced to the containers, iterators, and algorithms offered by the Standard Template Library (STL). The *Tying It All Together* section uses various containers in the Standard Template Library to create an educational children's game.

Chapter 17: Linked Lists

This chapter introduces concepts and techniques needed to work with lists. A linked list ADT is developed, and the student learns how to create and destroy a list, as well as to write functions to insert, append, and delete nodes, to traverse the list, and to search for a specific node. A linked list class template is also demonstrated. The *Tying It All Together* section brings together many of the most important concepts of OOP by using objects, inheritance, and polymorphism in conjunction with the STL list class to animate a collection of images.

Chapter 18: Stacks and Queues

In this chapter the student learns to create and use static and dynamic stacks and queues. The operations of stacks and queues are defined, and templates for each ADT are demonstrated. The static array-based stack uses exception-handling to handle stack overflow and underflow, providing a realistic and natural example of defining, throwing, and catching exceptions. The *Tying It All Together* section discusses strategies for evaluating postfix expressions and uses a stack to convert a postfix expression to infix.

Chapter 19: Binary Trees

This chapter covers the binary tree ADT and demonstrates many binary tree operations. The student learns to traverse a tree, insert, delete, and replace elements, search for a particular element, and destroy a tree. The *Tying It All Together* section introduces a tree structure versatile enough to create genealogy trees.

Appendices in the Book

Appendix A: The ASCII Character Set A list of the ASCII and extended ASCII characters and their codes.

Appendix B: Operator Precedence and Associativity A list of the C++ operators with their precedence and associativity.

Appendix C: Answers to Checkpoints A tool students can use to assess their understanding by comparing their answers to the Checkpoint exercises found throughout the book. The answers to all Checkpoint exercises are included.

Appendix D: Answers to Odd-Numbered Review Questions Another tool students can use to gauge their understanding and progress.

Additional Appendices on the Book's Companion Website

Appendix E: A Brief Introduction to Object-Oriented Programming An introduction to the concepts and terminology of object-oriented programming.

Appendix F: Using UML in Class Design A brief introduction to the Unified Modeling Language (UML) class diagrams with examples of their use.

Appendix G: Multi-Source File Programs A tutorial on how to create, compile, and link programs with multiple source files. Includes the use of function header files, class specification files, and class implementation files.

Appendix H: Multiple and Virtual Inheritance A self-contained discussion of the C++ concepts of multiple and virtual inheritance for anyone already familiar with single inheritance.

Appendix I: Header File and Library Function Reference A reference for the C++ library functions and header files used in the book.

Appendix J: Namespaces An explanation of namespaces and their purpose, with examples provided on how to define a namespace and access its members.

Appendix K: C++ Casts and Run-Time Type Identification An introduction to different ways of doing type casting in C++ and to run-time type identification.

Appendix L: Passing Command Line Arguments An introduction to writing C++ programs that accept command-line arguments. This appendix will be useful to students working in a command-line environment, such as UNIX or Linux.

Appendix M: Binary Numbers and Bitwise Operations A guide to the binary number system and the C++ bitwise operators, as well as a tutorial on the internal storage of integers.

Appendix N: Introduction to Flowcharting A tutorial that introduces flowcharting and its symbols. It includes handling sequence, selection, case, repetition, and calls to other modules. Sample flowcharts for several of the book's example programs are presented.

Features of the Text

Concept Statements — Each major section of the text starts with a concept statement. This statement summarizes the key idea of the section.

Example Programs — The text has over 350 complete example programs, each designed to highlight the topic currently being studied. In most cases, these are practical, real-world examples. Source code for these programs is provided so that students can run the programs themselves.

Program Output — After each example program there is a sample of its screen output. This immediately shows the student how the program should function.

Tying It All Together — This special section, found at the end of every chapter, shows the student how to do something clever and fun with the material covered in that chapter.

VideoNote

VideoNotes — A series of online videos, developed specifically for this book, are available for viewing at `http://www.pearsonhighered.com/gaddis/`. VideoNote icons appear throughout the text, alerting the student to videos about specific topics.

Checkpoints — Checkpoints are questions placed throughout each chapter as a self-test study aid. Answers for all Checkpoint questions are provided in Appendix C at the back of the book so students can check how well they have learned a new topic.

Notes — Notes appear at appropriate places throughout the text. They are short explanations of interesting or often misunderstood points relevant to the topic at hand.

Warnings — Warnings caution the student about certain C++ features, programming techniques, or practices that can lead to malfunctioning programs or lost data.

Case Studies — Case studies that simulate real-world applications appear in many chapters throughout the text, with complete code provided for each one. Additional case studies are provided on the book's companion website. These case studies are designed to highlight the major topics of the chapter in which they appear.

Review Questions and Exercises — Each chapter presents a thorough and diverse set of review questions, such as fill-in-the-blank and short answer, that check the student's mastery of the basic material presented in the chapter. These are followed by exercises requiring problem solving and analysis, such as the *Algorithm Workbench*, *Predict the Output*, and *Find the Errors* sections. Each chapter ends with a *Soft Skills* exercise that focuses on communication and group process skills. Answers to the odd-numbered review questions and review exercises are provided in Appendix D at the back of the book.

Programming Challenges — Each chapter offers a pool of programming exercises designed to solidify the student's knowledge of the topics currently being studied. In most cases the assignments present real-world problems to be solved.

Group Projects	There are several group programming projects throughout the text, intended to be constructed by a team of students. One student might build the program's user interface, while another student writes the mathematical code, and another designs and implements a class the program uses. This process is similar to the way many professional programs are written and encourages teamwork within the classroom.
C++ Quick Reference Guide	For easy access, a quick reference guide to the C++ language is printed on the inside back cover.

Supplements

Student Resources

The following items are available on the Gaddis Series resource page at www.pearsonhighered.com/gaddis:

- Complete source code for every program included in the book
- Additional case studies, complete with source code
- Serendipity Booksellers ongoing software development project
- A full set of appendices (including several tutorials) that accompany the book
- Access to the book's companion VideoNotes
- Links to download numerous programming environments and IDEs, including MinGW C++ Compiler and wxDev-C++ IDE

Instructor Resources

The following supplements are available to qualified instructors only.

- Answers to all Review Questions in the text
- Solutions for all Programming Challenges in the text
- PowerPoint presentation slides for every chapter
- A computerized test bank
- A collection of lab materials
- Source code files

Visit the Pearson Education Instructor Resource Center (http://www.pearsonhighered.com/irc) for information on how to access them.

Practice and Assessment with MyProgrammingLab

MyProgrammingLab helps students fully grasp the logic, semantics, and syntax of programming. Through practice exercises and immediate, personalized feedback, *MyProgrammingLab* improves the programming competence of beginning students who often struggle with the basic concepts and paradigms of popular high-level programming languages. A self-study and homework tool, a *MyProgrammingLab* course consists of hundreds of small practice exercises organized around the structure of this textbook. For students, the system automatically detects errors in the logic and syntax of their code submissions and offers targeted hints that enable them to figure out what went wrong. For instructors, a comprehensive gradebook tracks correct and incorrect answers and stores the code input by students for review.

MyProgrammingLab is offered to users of this book in partnership with Turing's Craft, the makers of the CodeLab interactive programming exercise system. For a full demonstration, to see feedback from instructors and students, or to get started using *MyProgrammingLab* in your course, visit MyProgrammingLab.com.

Integrated Development Environment (IDE) Resource Kits

Instructors who adopt this text for their students can also order an accompanying kit that contains the following popular C++ development environments:

- Microsoft® Visual Studio 2010 Express Edition
- Dev C++
- NetBeans
- Eclipse
- CodeLite

The kit also provides access to a website containing written and video tutorials for getting started in each IDE. For ordering information, please contact your Pearson Education Representative or visit www.pearsonhighered.com/cs.

Acknowledgments

There have been many helping hands in the development and publication of this text. We would like to thank the following faculty reviewers for their helpful suggestions and expertise.

Reviewers of the Eighth Edition or Its Previous Versions

Ahmad Abuhejleh
University of Wisconsin, River Falls

David Akins
El Camino College

Steve Allan
Utah State University

Ijaz A. Awan
Savannah State University

John Bierbauer
North Central College

Don Biggerstaff
Fayetteville Technical Community College

Paul Bladek
Spokane Falls Community College

Chuck Boehm
Dean Foods, Inc.

Bill Brown
Pikes Peak Community College

Richard Cacace
Pensacola Junior College

Randy Campbell
Morningside College

Stephen P. Carl
Wright State University

Wayne Caruolo
Red Rocks Community College

Thomas Cheatham
Middle Tennessee State University

James Chegwidden
Tarrant County College

John Cigas
Rockhurst University

John Cross
Indiana University of Pennsylvania

Fred M. D'Angelo
Pima Community College

Joseph DeLibero
Arizona State University

Dennis Fairclough
Utah Valley State College

Larry Farrer
Guilford Technical Community College

Richard Flint
North Central College

Sheila Foster
California State University Long Beach

David E. Fox
American River College

Cindy Fry
Baylor University

Peter Gacs
Boston University

Cristi Gale
Sterling College

James Gifford
University of Wisconsin, Stevens Point

Leon Gleiberman
Touro College

Simon Gray
Ashland University—Ohio

Margaret E. Guertin
Tufts University

Jamshid Haghighi
Guilford Technical Community College

Ranette H. Halverson
Midwestern State University,
Wichita Falls, TX

Dennis Heckman
Portland Community College

Ric Heishman
Northern Virginia Community College

Patricia Hines
Brookdale Community College

Mike Holland
Northern Virginia Community College

Lister Wayne Horn
Pensacola Junior College

Richard Hull
Lenoir-Rhyne College

Norman Jacobson
University of California, Irvine

Eric Jiang
San Diego State University

Yinping Jiao
South Texas College

Neven Jurkovic
Palo Alto College

David Kaeli
Northeastern University

Chris Kardaras
North Central College

Eugene Katzen
Montgomery College—Rockville

Willard Keeling
Blue Ridge Community College

A. J. Krygeris
Houston Community College

Ray Larson
Inver Hills Community College

Stephen Leach
Florida State University

Parkay Louie
Houston Community College

Zhu-qu Lu
University of Maine, Presque Isle

Tucjer Maney
George Mason University

Bill Martin
Central Piedmont Community College

Svetlana Marzelli
Atlantic Cape Community College

Debbie Mathews
J. Sargeant Reynolds

Ron McCarty
Penn State Erie, The Behrend College

Robert McDonald
East Stroudsburg University

James McGuffee
Austin Community College

M. Dee Medley
Augusta State University

Cathi Chambley-Miller
Aiken Technical College

Sandeep Mitra
SUNY Brockport

Frank Paiano
Southwestern Community College

Theresa Park
Texas State Technical College

Mark Parker
Shoreline Community College

Robert Plantz
Sonoma State University

Tino Posillico
SUNY Farmingdale

Mahmoud K. Quweider
University of Texas at Brownsville

M. Padmaja Rao
Francis Marion University

Timothy Reeves
San Juan College

Ronald Robison
Arkansas Tech University

Caroline St. Clair
North Central College

Dolly Samson
Weber State University

Kate Sanders
Rhode Island College

Lalchand Shimpi
Saint Augustine's College

Sung Shin
South Dakota State University

Barbara A. Smith
University of Dayton

Garth Sorenson
Snow College

Donald Southwell
Delta College

Daniel Spiegel
Kutztown University

Ray Springston
University of Texas at Arlington

Kirk Stephens
Southwestern Community College

Cherie Stevens
South Florida Community College

Joe Struss
Des Moines Area Community College

Hong Sung
University of Central Oklahoma

Sam Y. Sung
South Texas College

Mark Swanson
Red Wing Technical College

Martha Tillman
College of San Mateo

Delores Tull
Itawamba Community College

Rober Tureman
Paul D. Camp Community College

Jane Turk
LaSalle University

Sylvia Unwin
Bellevue Community College

Stewart Venit
California State University, Los Angeles

David Walter
Virginia State University

Doug White
University of Northern Colorado

Chris Wild
Old Dominion University

Catherine Wyman
DeVry Institute of Technology, Phoenix

Sherali Zeadally
University of the District of Columbia

Chaim Ziegler
Brooklyn College

The authors would like to thank their students at Haywood Community College and North Central College for inspiring them to write student-friendly books. They would also like to thank their families for their tremendous support throughout this project, as well as North Central College for providing Prof. Walters and Muganda with the sabbatical term during which they worked on this book. An especially big thanks goes to our terrific editorial, production, and marketing team at Addison-Wesley. In particular we want to thank our editor Matt Goldstein and our production project manager Kayla Smith-Tarbox, who have been instrumental in guiding the production of this book. We also want to thank our project manager, Mohinder Singh, who helped everything run smoothly, and our meticulous and knowledgable copyeditor, Linthoingambi Khaidem, who dedicated many hours to making this book the best book it could be. You are great people to work with!

About the Authors

Tony Gaddis is the principal author of the Starting Out With . . . series of textbooks. He is a highly acclaimed instructor with twenty years of experience teaching computer science courses at Haywood Community College. Tony was previously selected as the North Carolina Community College "Teacher of the Year" and has received the Teaching Excellence award from the National Institute for Staff and Organizational Development. The Starting Out With . . . series includes introductory books covering C++, Java™, Microsoft® Visual Basic®, Microsoft® C#, Python, Programming Logic and Design, and Alice, all published by Pearson/Addison-Wesley.

Judy Walters is an Associate Professor of Computer Science at North Central College in Naperville, Illinois, where she teaches courses in both Computer Science and Interactive Media Studies. She is also very involved with International Programs at her college and has spent two semesters teaching in Costa Rica, where she hopes to retire some day.

Godfrey Muganda is an Associate Professor of Computer Science at North Central College. He teaches a wide variety of courses at both the undergraduate and graduate levels, including courses in Algorithms, Computer Organization, Web Applications, and Web Services. His primary research interests are in the area of Fuzzy Sets and Systems.

CHAPTER 1

Introduction to Computers and Programming

TOPICS

1.1 Why Program?

CONCEPT: Computers can do many different jobs because they are programmable.

Think about some of the different ways that people use computers. In school, students use computers for tasks such as writing papers, searching for articles, sending e-mail, and participating in online classes. At work, people use computers to analyze data, make presentations, conduct business transactions, communicate with customers and coworkers, control machines in manufacturing facilities, and do many other things. At home, people use computers for tasks such as paying bills, shopping online, social networking, and playing games. And don't forget that smart phones, iPods®, car navigation systems, and many other devices are computers as well. The uses of computers are almost limitless in our everyday lives.

Computers can do such a wide variety of things because they can be programmed. This means that computers are not designed to do just one job, but to do any job that their programs tell them to do. A *program* is a set of instructions that a computer follows to perform a task. For example, Figure 1-1 shows screens using Microsoft Word and PowerPoint, two commonly used programs.

Figure 1-1 A Word Processing Program and a Presentation Program

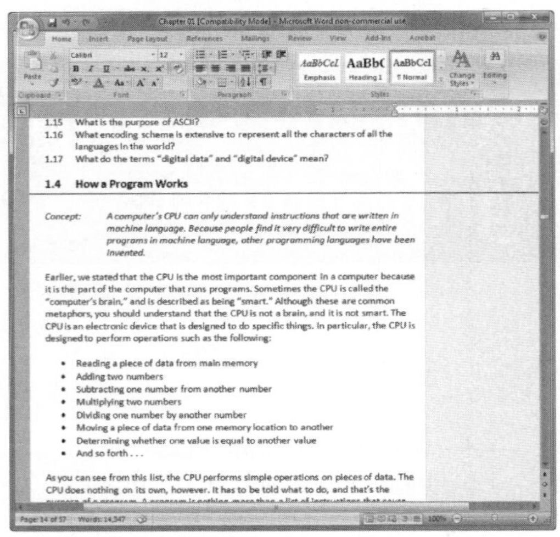

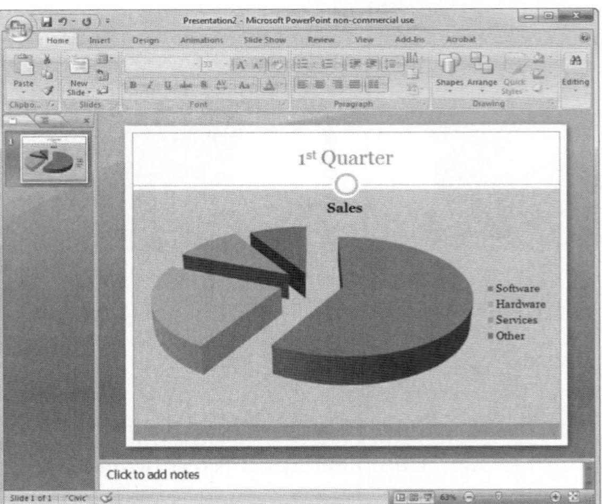

Programs are commonly referred to as *software*. Software is essential to a computer because without software, a computer can do nothing. All of the software that we use to make our computers useful is created by individuals known as programmers or software developers. A *programmer*, or *software developer*, is a person with the training and skills necessary to design, create, and test computer programs. Computer programming is an exciting and rewarding career. Today you will find programmers working in business, medicine, government, law enforcement, agriculture, academics, entertainment, and almost every other field.

Computer programming is both an art and a science. It is an art because every aspect of a program should be designed with care and judgment. Listed below are a few of the things that must be designed for any real-world computer program:

- The logical flow of the instructions
- The mathematical procedures
- The appearance of the screens
- The way information is presented to the user
- The program's "user-friendliness"
- Manuals and other forms of written documentation

There is also a scientific, or engineering side to programming. Because programs rarely work right the first time they are written, a lot of experimentation, correction, and redesigning is required. This demands patience and persistence of the programmer. Writing software demands discipline as well. Programmers must learn special languages like C++ because computers do not understand English or other human languages. Languages such as C++ have strict rules that must be carefully followed.

Both the artistic and scientific nature of programming makes writing computer software like designing a car. Both cars and programs should be functional, efficient, powerful, easy to use, and pleasing to look at.

1.2 Computer Systems: Hardware and Software

CONCEPT: All computer systems consist of similar hardware devices and software components. This section provides an overview of standard computer hardware and software organization.

Hardware

Hardware refers to the physical components that a computer is made of. A computer, as we generally think of it, is not an individual device, but a system of devices. Like the instruments in a symphony orchestra, each device plays its own part. A typical computer system consists of the following major components:

1. The central processing unit (CPU)
2. Main memory (random-access memory, or RAM)
3. Secondary storage devices
4. Input devices
5. Output devices

The organization of a computer system is depicted in Figure 1-2.

Figure 1-2

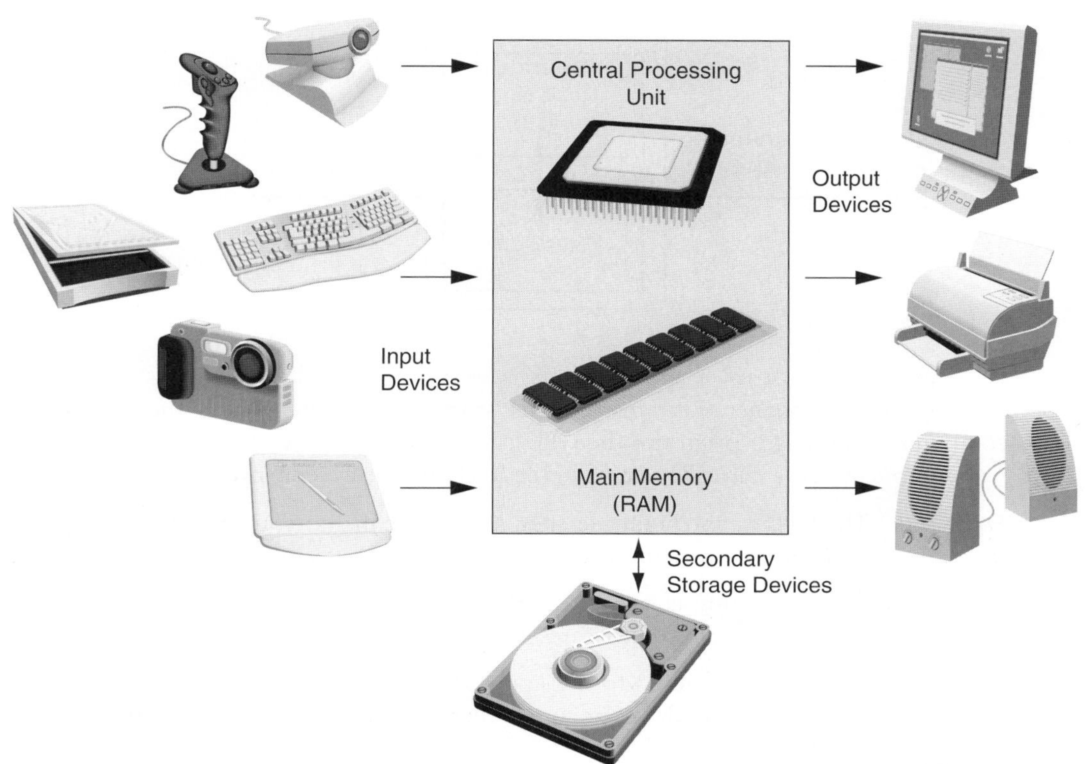

The CPU

When a computer is performing the tasks that a program tells it to do, we say that the computer is *running* or *executing* the program. The *central processing unit*, or *CPU*, is the part of a computer that actually runs programs. The CPU is the most important component in a computer because without it, the computer could not run software.

In the earliest computers, CPUs were huge devices that weighed tons. They were made of electrical and mechanical components such as vacuum tubes and switches. Today, CPUs are small chips known as *microprocessors* that can be held in the palm of your hand. In addition to being much smaller than the old electromechanical CPUs in early computers, today's microprocessors are also much more powerful.

The CPU's job is to fetch instructions, follow the instructions, and produce some result. Internally, the central processing unit consists of two parts: the *control unit* and the *arithmetic and logic unit (ALU)*. The control unit coordinates all of the computer's operations. It is responsible for determining where to get the next instruction and regulating the other major components of the computer with control signals. The arithmetic and logic unit, as its name suggests, is designed to perform mathematical operations. The organization of the CPU is shown in Figure 1-3.

Figure 1-3

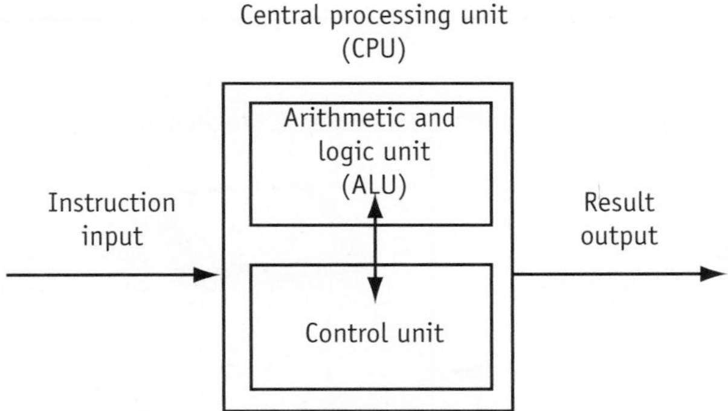

A program is a sequence of instructions stored in the computer's memory. When a computer is running a program, the CPU is engaged in a process known formally as the *fetch/decode/execute cycle*. The steps in the fetch/decode/execute cycle are as follows:

Fetch The CPU's control unit fetches, from main memory, the next instruction in the sequence of program instructions.

Decode The instruction is encoded in the form of a number. The control unit decodes the instruction and generates an electronic signal.

Execute The signal is routed to the appropriate component of the computer (such as the ALU, a disk drive, or some other device). The signal causes the component to perform an operation.

These steps are repeated as long as there are instructions to perform.

Main Memory

You can think of main memory as the computer's work area. This is where the computer stores a program while the program is running, as well as the data that the program is working with. For example, suppose you are using a word processing program to write an essay for one of your classes. While you do this, both the word processing program and the essay are stored in main memory.

Main memory is commonly known as *random-access memory* or *RAM*. It is called this because the CPU is able to quickly access data stored at any random location in this memory. RAM is usually a *volatile* type of memory that is used only for temporary storage while a program is running. When the computer is turned off, the contents of RAM are erased. Inside your computer, RAM is stored in small chips.

A computer's memory is divided into tiny storage cells known as *bytes*. One byte is enough memory to store just a single letter of the alphabet or a small number. In order to do anything meaningful, a computer has to have lots of bytes. Most computers today have millions, or even billions, of bytes of memory.

Each byte is divided into eight smaller storage locations known as bits. The term *bit* stands for *binary digit*. Computer scientists usually think of bits as tiny switches that can be either on or off. Bits aren't actual "switches," however, at least not in the conventional sense. In most computer systems, bits are tiny electrical components that can hold either a positive or a negative charge. Computer scientists think of a positive charge as a switch in the *on* position and a negative charge as a switch in the *off* position.

Each byte is assigned a unique number known as an address. The addresses are ordered from lowest to highest. A byte is identified by its address, in much the same way a post office box is identified by an address, so that the data stored there can be located. Figure 1-4 shows a group of memory cells with their addresses. The number 149 is stored in the cell with the address 16, and the number 72 is stored at address 23.

Figure 1-4

0	1	2	3	4	5	6	7	8	9
10	11	12	13	14	15	16 149	17	18	19
20	21	22	23 72	24	25	26	27	28	29

Secondary Storage

Secondary storage is a type of memory that can hold data for long periods of time—even when there is no power to the computer. Frequently used programs are stored in secondary memory and loaded into main memory as needed. Important information, such as word processing documents, payroll data, and inventory figures, is saved to secondary storage as well.

The most common type of secondary storage device is the disk drive. A *disk drive* stores data by magnetically encoding it onto a circular disk. Most computers have a disk drive mounted inside their case. External disk drives, which connect to one of the computer's communication ports, are also available. External disk drives can be used to create backup copies of important data or to move data to another computer.

In addition to external disk drives, many types of devices have been created for copying data and for moving it to other computers. For many years floppy disk drives were popular. A *floppy disk drive* records data onto a small, flexible ("floppy") disk, which can be removed from the drive. The use of floppy disk drives has declined dramatically in recent years, in favor of superior devices such as USB flash drives. *USB flash drives* are small devices that plug into the computer's USB (universal serial bus) port and appear to the system as a disk drive. These drives, which use *flash memory* to store data, are inexpensive, reliable, and small enough to be carried in your pocket.

Optical devices such as the *CD* (compact disc) and the *DVD* (digital versatile disc) are also popular for data storage. Data is not recorded magnetically on an optical disc, but rather is encoded as a series of pits on the disc surface. CD and DVD drives use a laser to detect the pits and thus read the encoded data. Optical discs hold large amounts of data, and because recordable CD and DVD drives are now commonplace, they are good media for creating backup copies of data.

Input Devices

Input is any information the computer collects from the outside world. The device that collects the information and sends it to the computer is called an *input device*. Common input devices are the keyboard, mouse, scanner, digital camera, and microphone. Disk drives, CD/DVD drives, and USB flash drives can also be considered input devices because programs and information are retrieved from them and loaded into the computer's memory.

Output Devices

Output is any information the computer sends to the outside world. It might be a sales report, a list of names, or a graphic image. The information is sent to an *output device,* which formats and presents it. Common output devices are computer screens, printers, and speakers. Output sent to a computer screen is sometimes called *soft copy,* while output sent to a printer is called *hard copy.* Disk drives, USB flash drives, and CD/DVD recorders can also be considered output devices because the CPU sends information to them so it can be saved.

Software

If a computer is to function, software is needed. Everything that a computer does, from the time you turn the power switch on until you shut the system down, is under the control of software. There are two general categories of software: system software and application software. Most computer programs clearly fit into one of these two categories. Let's take a closer look at each.

System Software

The programs that control and manage the basic operations of a computer are generally referred to as *system software*. System software typically includes the following types of programs:

- *Operating Systems*
  An *operating system* is the most fundamental set of programs on a computer. The operating system controls the internal operations of the computer's hardware, manages all the devices connected to the computer, allows data to be saved to and retrieved from storage devices, and allows other programs to run on the computer.

- *Utility Programs*
  A *utility program* performs a specialized task that enhances the computer's operation or safeguards data. Examples of utility programs are virus scanners, file-compression programs, and data-backup programs.

- *Software Development Tools*
  The software tools that programmers use to create, modify, and test software are referred to as *software development tools*. Compilers and integrated development environments, which we discuss later in this chapter, are examples of programs that fall into this category.

Application Software

Programs that make a computer useful for everyday tasks are known as *application software*, or *application programs*. These are the programs that people normally spend most of their time running on their computers. Figure 1-1, at the beginning of this chapter, shows screens from two commonly used applications Microsoft Word, a word processing program, and Microsoft PowerPoint, a presentation program. Some other examples of application software are spreadsheet programs, e-mail programs, Web browsers, and game programs.

Checkpoint

1.1 Why is the computer used by so many different people, in so many different professions?

1.2 List the five major hardware components of a computer system.

1.3 Internally, the CPU consists of what two units?

1.4 Describe the steps in the fetch/decode/execute cycle.

1.5 What is a memory address? What is its purpose?

1.6 Explain why computers have both main memory and secondary storage.

1.7 What are the two general categories of software?

1.8 What fundamental set of programs controls the internal operations of the computer's hardware?

1.9 What do you call a program that performs a specialized task, such as a virus scanner, a file-compression program, or a data-backup program?

1.10 Word processing programs, spreadsheet programs, e-mail programs, Web browsers, and game programs belong to what category of software?

1.3 Programs and Programming Languages

CONCEPT: A program is a set of instructions a computer follows in order to perform a task. A programming language is a special language used to write computer programs.

What Is a Program?

Computers are designed to follow instructions. A computer program is a set of instructions that tells the computer how to solve a problem or perform a task. For example, suppose we want the computer to calculate someone's gross pay. Here is a list of things the computer might do:

1. Display a message on the screen asking "How many hours did you work?"
2. Wait for the user to enter the number of hours worked. Once the user enters a number, store it in memory.
3. Display a message on the screen asking "How much do you get paid per hour?"

4. Wait for the user to enter an hourly pay rate. Once the user enters a number, store it in memory.
5. Multiply the number of hours by the amount paid per hour, and store the result in memory.
6. Display a message on the screen that tells the amount of money earned. The message must include the result of the calculation performed in step 5.

Collectively, these instructions are called an algorithm. An *algorithm* is a set of well-defined steps for performing a task or solving a problem. Notice these steps are ordered sequentially. Step 1 should be performed before step 2, and so forth. It is important that these instructions be performed in their proper sequence.

Although a person might easily understand the instructions in the pay-calculating algorithm, it is not ready to be executed on a computer. A computer's CPU can only process instructions that are written in *machine language*. A machine language program consists of a sequence of *binary numbers* (numbers consisting of only 1s and 0s), which the CPU interprets as commands. Here is an example of what a machine language instruction might look like:

```
1011010000000101
```

As you can imagine, the process of encoding an algorithm in machine language is very tedious and difficult. In addition, each different type of CPU has its own machine language. If you wrote a machine language program for computer *A* and then wanted to run it on a computer *B* that has a different type of CPU, you would have to rewrite the program in computer *B*'s machine language.

Programming languages, which use words instead of numbers, were invented to ease the task of programming. A program can be written in a programming language such as C++, which is much easier to understand than machine language. Programmers save their programs in text files, and then use special software to convert their programs to machine language.

Program 1-1 shows how the pay-calculating algorithm might be written in C++.

NOTE: The line numbers shown in Program 1-1 are *not* part of the program. This book shows line numbers in all program listings to help point out specific parts of the program.

Program 1-1

```
// This program calculates the user's pay.
#include <iostream>
using namespace std;

int main()
{
   double hours, rate, pay;

   // Get the number of hours worked.
   cout << "How many hours did you work? ";
   cin  >> hours;

```

(program continues)

Program 1-1 *(continued)*

```
    // Get the hourly pay rate.
    cout << "How much do you get paid per hour? ";
    cin  >> rate;

    // Calculate the pay.
    pay = hours * rate;

    // Display the pay.
    cout << "You have earned $" << pay << endl;
    return 0;
}
```

Program Output with Example Input Shown in Bold

```
How many hours did you work? 10 [Enter]
How much do you get paid per hour? 15 [Enter]
You have earned $150
```

The "Program Output with Example Input Shown in Bold" shows what the program will display on the screen when it is running. In the example, the user enters 10 for the number of hours worked and 15 for the hourly pay. The program displays the earnings, which are $150.

Programming Languages

In a broad sense, there are two categories of programming languages: low-level and high-level. A *low-level language* is close to the level of the computer, which means it resembles the numeric machine language of the computer more than the natural language of humans. The easiest languages for people to learn are *high-level languages*. They are called "high-level" because they are closer to the level of human-readability than computer-readability. Figure 1-5 illustrates the concept of language levels.

Figure 1-5

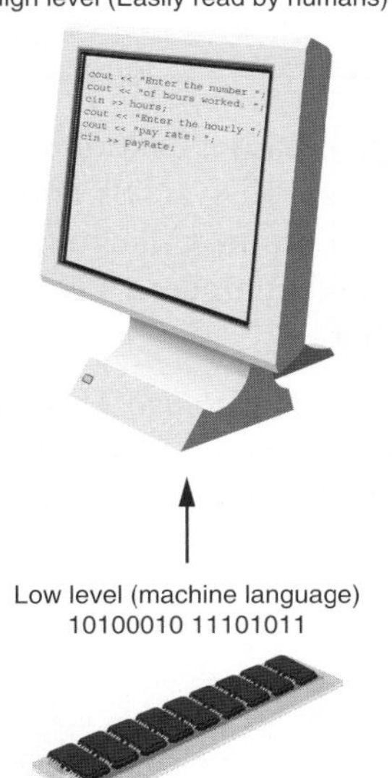

Many high-level languages have been created. Table 1-1 lists a few of the well-known ones.

Table 1-1 Well-Known High-Level Programming Languages

Language	Description
BASIC	Beginners All-purpose Symbolic Instruction Code. A general programming language originally designed to be simple enough for beginners to learn.
C	A structured, general-purpose language developed at Bell Laboratories. C offers both high-level and low-level features.
C++	Based on the C language, C++ offers object-oriented features not found in C. Also invented at Bell Laboratories.
C#	Pronounced "C sharp." A language invented by Microsoft for developing applications based on the Microsoft .NET platform.
COBOL	Common Business-Oriented Language. A language designed for business applications.
FORTRAN	Formula Translator. A language designed for programming complex mathematical algorithms.
Java	An object-oriented language invented at Sun Microsystems. Java may be used to develop programs that run over the Internet in a Web browser.
JavaScript	A language used to write small programs that run in Web pages. Despite its name, JavaScript is not related to Java.
Pascal	A structured, general-purpose language designed primarily for teaching programming.
Python	A general purpose language created in the early 1990s. It has become popular for both business and academic applications.
Ruby	A general purpose language created in the 1990s. It is becoming increasingly popular for programs that run on Web servers.
Visual Basic	A Microsoft programming language and software development environment that allows programmers to quickly create Windows-based applications.

C++ is a widely used language because, in addition to the high-level features necessary for writing applications such as payroll systems and inventory programs, it also has many low-level features. C++ is based on the C language, which was invented for purposes such as writing operating systems and compilers. Because C++ evolved from C, it carries all of C's low-level capabilities with it.

C++ is also popular because of its *portability.* This means that a C++ program can be written on one type of computer and then run on many other types of systems. This usually requires that the program is recompiled on each type of system, but the program itself may need little or no change.

NOTE: Programs written for specific *graphical* environments often require significant changes when moved to a different type of system. Examples of such graphical environments are Windows, the X-Window System, and the Mac OS operating system.

Source Code, Object Code, and Executable Code

When a C++ program is written, it must be typed into the computer and saved to a file. A *text editor*, which is similar to a word processing program, is used for this task. The statements written by the programmer are called *source code*, and the file they are saved in is called the *source file*.

After the source code is saved to a file, the process of translating it to machine language can begin. During the first phase of this process, a program called the *preprocessor* reads the source code. The preprocessor searches for special lines that begin with the `#` symbol. These lines contain commands, or *directives*, that cause the preprocessor to amend or process the source code in some way. During the next phase the *compiler* steps through the preprocessed source code, translating each source code instruction into the appropriate machine language instruction. This process will uncover any *syntax errors* that may be in the program. Syntax errors are illegal uses of key words, operators, punctuation, and other language elements. If the program is free of syntax errors, the compiler stores the translated machine language instructions, which are called *object code*, in an *object file*.

Although an object file contains machine language instructions, it is not a complete program. Here is why. C++ is conveniently equipped with a library of prewritten code for performing common operations or sometimes-difficult tasks. For example, the library contains hardware-specific code for displaying messages on the screen and reading input from the keyboard. It also provides routines for mathematical functions, such as calculating the square root of a number. This collection of code, called the *run-time library*, is extensive. Programs almost always use some part of it. When the compiler generates an object file, however, it does not include machine code for any run-time library routines the programmer might have used. During the last phase of the translation process, another program called the *linker* combines the object file with the necessary library routines. Once the linker has finished with this step, an *executable file* is created. The executable file contains machine language instructions, or *executable code*, and is ready to run on the computer.

Figure 1-6 illustrates the process of translating a C++ source file into an executable file. The entire process of invoking the preprocessor, compiler, and linker can be initiated with a single action. For example, on a Linux system, the following command causes the C++ program named `hello.cpp` to be preprocessed, compiled, and linked. The executable code is stored in a file named `hello`.

```
g++ -o hello hello.cpp
```

Figure 1-6

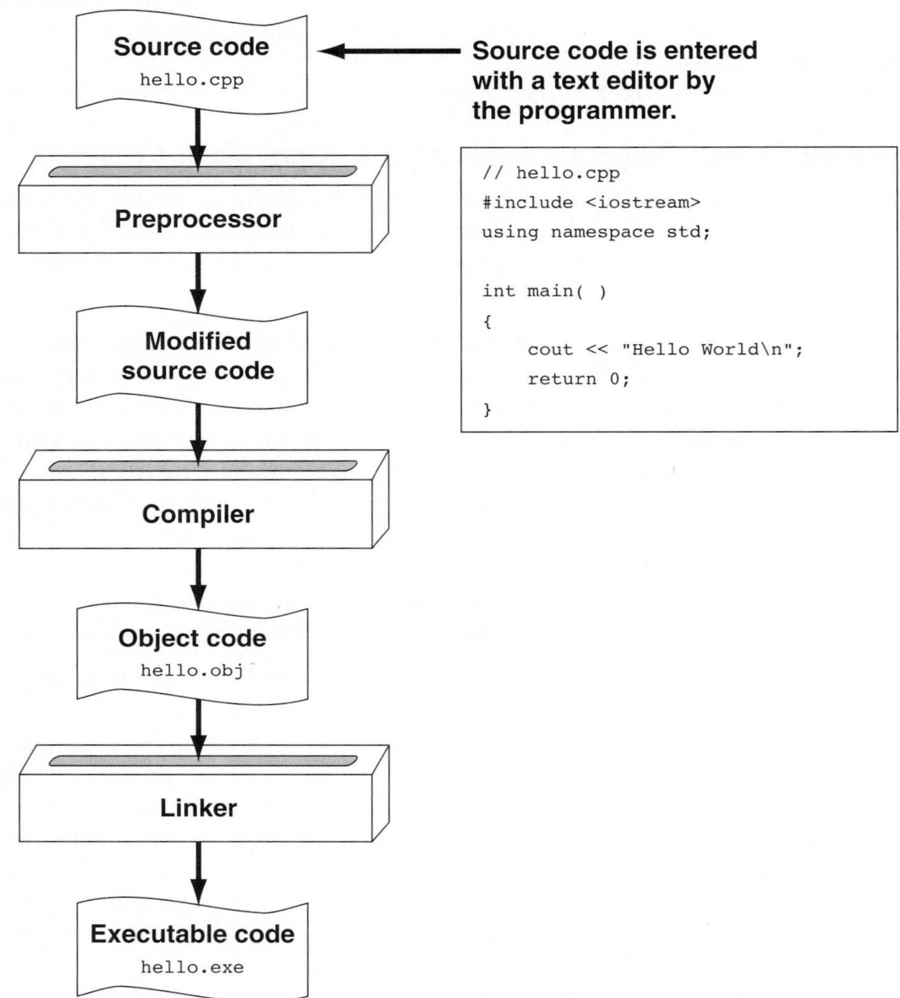

Many development systems, particularly those on personal computers, have *integrated development environments (IDEs)*. These environments consist of a text editor, compiler, debugger, and other utilities integrated into a package with a single set of menus. Preprocessing, compiling, linking, and even executing a program is done with a single click of a button, or by selecting a single item from a menu. Figure 1-7 shows a screen from the Microsoft Visual Studio IDE.

Figure 1-7

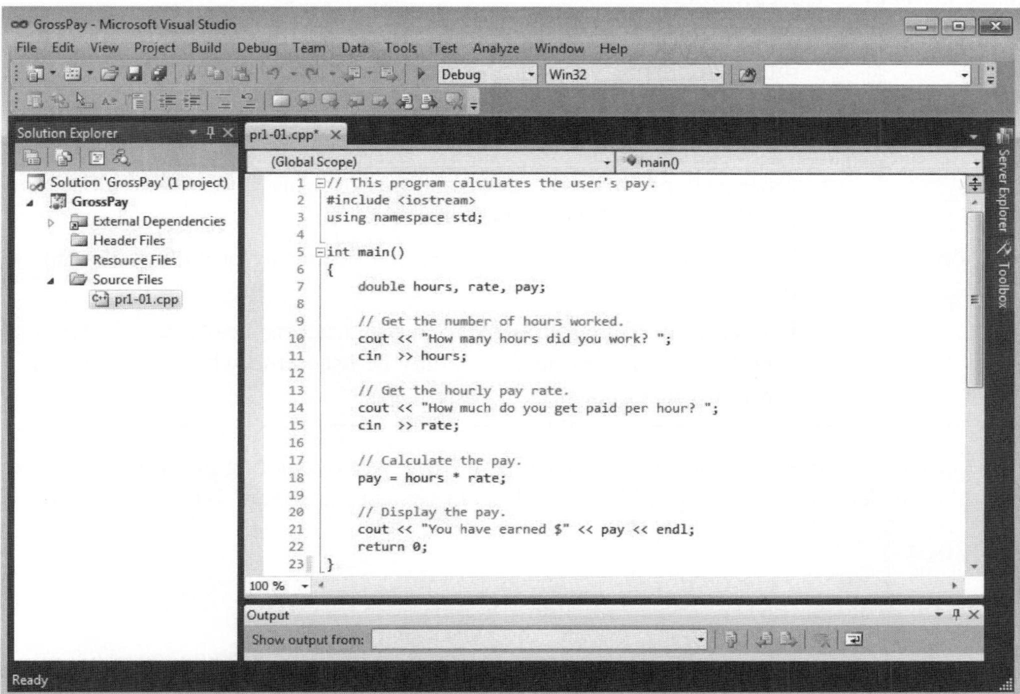

Checkpoint

1.11 What is an algorithm?

1.12 Why were computer programming languages invented?

1.13 What is the difference between a high-level language and a low-level language?

1.14 What does *portability* mean?

1.15 Explain the operations carried out by the preprocessor, compiler, and linker.

1.16 Explain what is stored in a source file, an object file, and an executable file.

1.17 What is an integrated development environment?

1.4 What Is a Program Made of?

CONCEPT: **There are certain elements that are common to all programming languages.**

Language Elements

All programming languages have a few things in common. Table 1-2 lists the common elements found in almost every language.

Table 1-2 Programming Language Elements

Language Element	Description
Key Words	Words that have a special meaning. Key words may only be used for their intended purpose. Key words are also known as reserved words.
Programmer-Defined Identifiers	Words or names defined by the programmer. They are symbolic names that refer to variables or programming routines.
Operators	Operators perform operations on one or more operands. An operand is usually a piece of data, like a number.
Punctuation	Punctuation characters that mark the beginning or ending of a statement, or separate items in a list.
Syntax	Rules that must be followed when constructing a program. Syntax dictates how key words and operators may be used, and where punctuation symbols must appear.

Let's look at some specific parts of Program 1-1 (the pay-calculating program) to see examples of each element listed in the table above. For convenience, Program 1-1 is listed again.

Program 1-1

```
 1 // This program calculates the user's pay.
 2 #include <iostream>
 3 using namespace std;
 4
 5 int main()
 6 {
 7    double hours, rate, pay;
 8
 9    // Get the number of hours worked.
10    cout << "How many hours did you work? ";
11    cin  >> hours;
12
13    // Get the hourly pay rate.
14    cout << "How much do you get paid per hour? ";
15    cin  >> rate;
16
17    // Calculate the pay.
18    pay = hours * rate;
19
20    // Display the pay.
21    cout << "You have earned $" << pay << endl;
22    return 0;
23 }
```

Key Words (reserved words)

Three of C++'s key words appear on lines 3 and 5: `using`, `namespace`, and `int`. The word `double`, which appears on line 7, is also a C++ key word. These words, which are always written in lowercase, each have a special meaning in C++ and can only be used for their intended purposes. As you will see, the programmer is allowed to make up his or her own names for certain things in a program. Key words, however, are reserved and cannot be used for anything other than their designated purposes. Part of learning a programming language is learning what the key words are, what they mean, and how to use them.

NOTE: The `#include <iostream>` statement in line 2 is a preprocessor directive.

NOTE: In C++, key words are written in all lowercase.

Programmer-Defined Identifiers

The words `hours`, `rate`, and `pay` that appear in the program on lines 7, 11, 15, 18, and 21 are programmer-defined identifiers. They are not part of the C++ language but rather are names made up by the programmer. In this particular program, these are the names of variables. As you will learn later in this chapter, variables are the names of memory locations that may hold data.

Operators

On line 18 the following statement appears:

```
pay = hours * rate;
```

The `=` and `*` symbols are both operators. They perform operations on pieces of data, known as operands. The `*` operator multiplies its two operands, which in this example are the variables `hours` and `rate`. The `=` symbol is called the *assignment operator.* It takes the value of the expression on the right and stores it in the variable whose name appears on the left. In this example, the `=` operator stores in the `pay` variable the result of the `hours` variable multiplied by the `rate` variable. In other words, the statement says, "Make the `pay` variable equal to `hours` times `rate`" or "`pay` is assigned the value of `hours` times `rate`."

Punctuation

Notice that many lines end with a semicolon. A semicolon in C++ is similar to a period in English. It marks the end of a complete sentence (or statement, as it is called in programming). Semicolons do not appear at the end of every line in a C++ program, however. There are rules that govern where semicolons are required and where they are not. Part of learning C++ is learning where to place semicolons and other punctuation symbols.

Lines and Statements

Often, the contents of a program are thought of in terms of lines and statements. A *line* is just that—a single line as it appears in the body of a program. Program 1-1 is shown with each of its lines numbered. Most of the lines contain something meaningful; however, some of the lines are empty. The blank lines are only there to make the program more readable.

A *statement* is a complete instruction that causes the computer to perform some action. Here is the statement that appears in line 10 of Program 1-1:

```
cout << "How many hours did you work? ";
```

It causes the computer to display the message “How many hours did you work?” on the screen. Statements can be a combination of key words, operators, and programmer-defined symbols. Statements usually occupy only one line in a program, but sometimes they are spread out over more than one line.

Variables

A *variable* is a named storage location in the computer’s memory for holding a piece of data. The data stored in variables may change while the program is running (hence the name “variable”). Notice that in Program 1-1 the words `hours`, `rate`, and `pay` appear in several places. All three of these are the names of variables. The `hours` variable is used to store the number of hours the user worked. The `rate` variable stores the user’s hourly pay rate. The `pay` variable holds the result of `hours` multiplied by `rate`, which is the user’s gross pay.

NOTE: Notice the variables in Program 1-1 have names that reflect their purpose. In fact, it would be easy to guess what the variables were used for just by reading their names. This is discussed further in Chapter 2.

Variables are symbolic names that represent locations in the computer’s random-access memory (RAM). When information is stored in a variable, it is actually stored in RAM. Assume a program has a variable named `length`. Figure 1-8 illustrates the way the variable name represents a memory location.

Figure 1-8

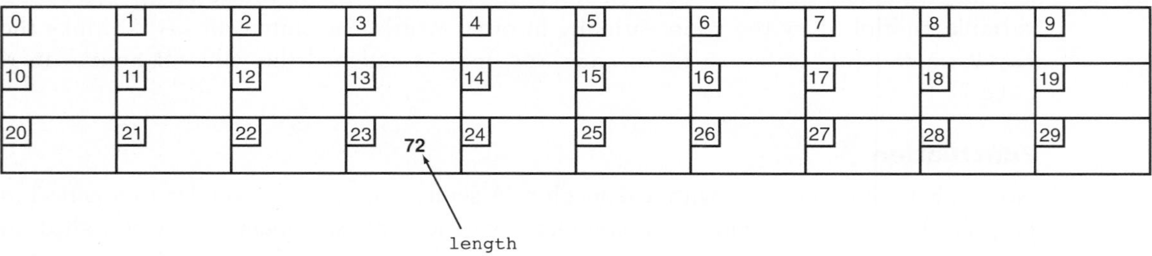

In Figure 1-8 the variable `length` is holding the value 72. The number 72 is actually stored in RAM at address 23, but the name `length` symbolically represents this storage location. You can think of a variable as a box that holds information. In Figure 1-8, the number 72 is stored in the box named `length`. Only one item may be stored in the box at any given time. If the program stores another value in this box, it will take the place of the number 72.

Variable Definitions

In programming, there are two general types of data: numbers, such as 3, and characters, such as the letter ‘A’. Numbers are used to perform mathematical operations, and characters are used to print information on the screen or on paper.

Numeric data can be categorized even further. For instance, the following are all whole numbers, or integers:

```
5
7
-129
32154
```

The following are real, or floating-point, numbers:

```
3.14159
6.7
1.0002
```

When creating a variable in a C++ program, you must know what type of data the program will be storing in it. Look at line 7 of Program 1-1:

```
double hours, rate, pay;
```

The word `double` in the statement indicates that the variables `hours`, `rate`, and `pay` will be used to hold double precision floating-point numbers. This statement is called a *variable definition*. In C++, all variables must be defined before they can be used because the variable definition is what causes the variables to be created in memory. If you review the listing of Program 1-1, you will see that the variable definitions come before any other statements using those variables.

1.5 Input, Processing, and Output

CONCEPT: **The three primary activities of a program are input, processing, and output.**

Computer programs typically perform a three-step process of gathering input, performing some process on the information gathered, and then producing output. Input is information a program collects from the outside world. It can be sent to the program by the user, who is entering data at the keyboard or using the mouse. It can also be read from disk files or hardware devices connected to the computer. Program 1-1 allows the user to enter two items of information: the number of hours worked and the hourly pay rate. Lines 11 and 15 use the `cin` (pronounced "see in") object to perform these input operations:

```
cin >> hours;
cin >> rate;
```

Once information is gathered from the outside world, a program usually processes it in some manner. In Program 1-1, the hours worked and hourly pay rate are multiplied in line 18 to produce the value assigned to the variable `pay`:

```
pay = hours * rate;
```

Output is information that a program sends to the outside world. It can be words or graphics displayed on a screen, a report sent to the printer, data stored in a file, or information sent to any device connected to the computer.

Lines 10, 14, and 21 in Program 1-1 all use the `cout` (pronounced "see out") object to display messages on the computer's screen.

```
cout << "How many hours did you work? ";
cout << "How much do you get paid per hour? ";
cout << "You have earned $" << pay << endl;
```

You will learn more about objects later in the book and about the `cin` and `cout` objects in Chapters 2 and 3.

Checkpoint

1.18 Describe the difference between a key word and a programmer-defined symbol.

1.19 Describe the difference between operators and punctuation symbols.

1.20 Describe the difference between a program line and a statement.

1.21 Why are variables called "variable"?

1.22 What happens to a variable's current contents when a new value is stored there?

1.23 What must take place in a program before a variable is used?

1.24 What are the three primary activities of a program?

1.6 The Programming Process

CONCEPT: The programming process consists of several steps, which include design, creation, testing, and debugging activities.

Designing and Creating a Program

Now that you have been introduced to what a program is, it's time to consider the process of creating a program. Quite often, when inexperienced students are given programming assignments, they have trouble getting started because they don't know what to do first. If you find yourself in this dilemma, the steps listed in Figure 1-9 may help. These are the steps recommended for the process of writing a program.

Figure 1-9

1. Define what the program is to do.
2. Visualize the program running on the computer.
3. Use design tools to create a model of the program.
4. Check the model for logical errors.
5. Write the program source code.
6. Compile the source code.
7. Correct any errors found during compilation.
8. Link the program to create an executable file.
9. Run the program using test data for input.
10. Correct any errors found while running the program.
    Repeat steps 4 through 10 as many times as necessary.
11. Validate the results of the program.

The steps listed in Figure 1-9 emphasize the importance of planning. Just as there are good ways and bad ways to paint a house, there are good ways and bad ways to create a program. A good program always begins with planning.

With the pay-calculating program as our example, let's look at each step in more detail.

1. Define what the program is to do.

This step requires that you clearly identify the purpose of the program, the information that is to be input, the processing that is to take place, and the desired output. Here are the requirements for the example program:

Purpose	To calculate the user's gross pay.
Input	Number of hours worked, hourly pay rate.
Processing	Multiply number of hours worked by hourly pay rate. The result is the user's gross pay.
Output	Display a message indicating the user's gross pay.

2. Visualize the program running on the computer.

Before you create a program on the computer, you should first create it in your mind. Step 2 is the visualization of the program. Try to imagine what the computer screen looks like while the program is running. If it helps, draw pictures of the screen, with sample input and output, at various points in the program. For instance, here is the screen produced by the pay-calculating program:

```
How many hours did you work? 10
How much do you get paid per hour? 15
You earned $ 150
```

In this step, you must put yourself in the shoes of the user. What messages should the program display? What questions should it ask? By addressing these issues, you will have already determined most of the program's output.

3. Use design tools to create a model of the program.

While planning a program, the programmer uses one or more design tools to create a model of the program. Three common design tools are hierarchy charts, flowcharts, and pseudocode. A *hierarchy chart* is a diagram that graphically depicts the structure of a program. It has boxes that represent each step in the program. The boxes are connected in a way that illustrates their relationship to one another. Figure 1-10 shows a hierarchy chart for the pay-calculating program.

A hierarchy chart begins with the overall task and then refines it into smaller subtasks. Each of the subtasks is then refined into even smaller sets of subtasks, until each is small enough to be easily performed. For instance, in Figure 1-10, the overall task "Calculate Gross Pay" is listed in the top-level box. That task is broken into three subtasks. The first subtask, "Get Payroll Data from User," is broken further into two subtasks. This process of "divide and conquer" is known as *top-down design*.

Figure 1-10

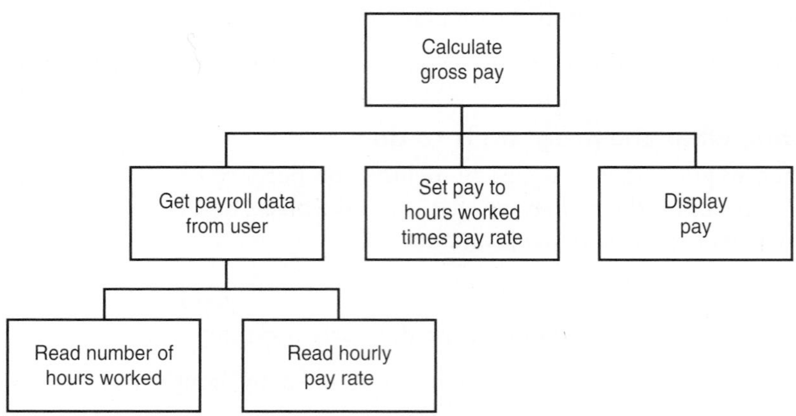

A *flowchart* is a diagram that shows the logical flow of a program. It is a useful tool for planning each operation a program must perform and the order in which the operations are to occur. For more information see Appendix N, Introduction to Flowcharting.

Pseudocode is a cross between human language and a programming language. Although the computer can't understand pseudocode, programmers often find it helpful to write an algorithm using it. This is because pseudocode is similar to natural language, yet close enough to programming language that it can be easily converted later into program source code. By writing the algorithm in pseudocode first, the programmer can focus on just the logical steps the program must perform, without having to worry yet about syntax or about details such as how output will be displayed.

Pseudocode can be written at a high level or at a detailed level. Many programmers use both forms. High level pseudocode simply lists the steps a program must perform. Here is high level pseudocode for the pay-calculating program.

```
Get payroll data
Calculate gross pay
Display gross pay
```

High level pseudocode can be expanded to produce detailed pseudocode. Here is the detailed pseudocode for the same program. Notice that it even names variables and tells what mathematical operations to perform.

VideoNote
Designing a Program with Pseudocode

```
Ask the user to input the number of hours worked
Input hours
Ask the user to input the hourly pay rate
Input rate
Set pay equal to hours times rate
Display pay
```

4. Check the model for logical errors.

Logical errors, also called *logic errors*, are mistakes that cause a program to produce erroneous results. Examples of logical errors would be using the wrong variable's value in a computation or performing order-dependent actions in the wrong order. Once a model of the program has been created, it should be checked for logical errors. The programmer should trace through the charts or pseudocode, checking the logic of each step. If an error is found, the model can be corrected before the actual program source code is written. In general, the earlier an error is detected in the programming process, the easier it is to correct.

5. Write the program source code.

Once a model of the program (hierarchy chart, flowchart, or pseudocode) has been created, checked, and corrected, the programmer is ready to write the source code, using an actual computer programming language, such as C++. Many programmers write the code directly on the computer, typing it into a text editor. Some programmers, however, prefer to write the program on paper first, then enter it into the computer. Once the program has been entered, the source code is saved to a file.

6. Compile the source code.

Next the saved source code is ready to be compiled. The compiler will translate the source code to machine language.

7. Correct any errors found during compilation.

If the compiler reports any errors, they must be corrected and the code recompiled. This step is repeated until the program is free of compile-time errors.

8. Link the program to create an executable file.

Once the source code compiles with no errors, it can be linked with the libraries specified by the program `#include` statements to create an executable file. If an error occurs during the linking process, it is likely that the program has failed to include a needed library file. The needed file must be included and the program relinked.

9. Run the program using test data for input.

Once an executable file is generated, the program is ready to be tested for run-time and logic errors. A run-time error occurs when the running program asks the computer to do something that is impossible, such as divide by zero. Normally a run-time error causes the program to abort. If the program runs, but fails to produce correct results, it likely contains one or more logic errors. To help identify such errors, it is important that the program be executed with carefully selected sample data that allows the correct output to be predicted.

10. Correct any errors found while running the program.

When run-time or logic errors occur in a program, they must be corrected. You must identify the step where the error occurred and determine the cause.

Desk-checking is a process that can help locate these types of errors. The term desk-checking means the programmer starts reading the program, or a portion of the program, and steps through each statement. A sheet of paper is often used in this process to jot down the current contents of all variables and sketch what the screen looks like after each output operation. When a variable's contents change, or information is displayed on the screen, this is noted. By stepping through each statement in this manner, many errors can be located and corrected.

If the error is a result of incorrect logic (such as an improperly stated math formula), you must correct the statement or statements involved in the logic. If the error is due to an incomplete understanding of the program requirements, then you must restate the program's purpose and modify all affected charts, pseudocode, and source code. The program must then be saved, recompiled, relinked, and retested. This means steps 4 though 10 must be repeated until the program reliably produces satisfactory results.

11. Validate the results of the program.

When you believe you have corrected all errors, enter test data to verify that the program solves the original problem.

What Is Software Engineering?

The field of software engineering encompasses the complete process of crafting computer software. It includes designing, writing, testing, debugging, documenting, modifying, and maintaining complex software development projects. Like traditional engineers, software engineers use a number of tools in their craft. Here are a few examples:

- Program specifications
- Charts and diagrams of screen output
- Hierarchy charts
- Pseudocode
- Examples of expected input and desired output
- Special software designed for testing programs

Most commercial software applications are very large. In many instances one or more teams of programmers, not a single individual, develop them. It is important that the program requirements be thoroughly analyzed and divided into subtasks that are handled by individual teams or individuals within a team.

In step 3 of the programming process, you were introduced to the hierarchy chart as a tool for top-down design. When the subtasks identified in a top-down design are long or complex, they can be developed as modules, or separate components, of a program. If the program is very large or complex, a team of software engineers can be assigned to work on the individual modules. As the project develops, the modules are coordinated to become a single software application.

Checkpoint

1.25 What four items should you identify when defining what a program is to do?

1.26 What does it mean to "visualize a program running"? What is the value of doing this?

1.27 What is a hierarchy chart?

1.28 What is pseudocode?

1.29 What is the difference between high level pseudocode and detailed pseudocode?

1.30 Describe what a compiler does with a program's source code.

1.31 What is a logic error?

1.32 What is a run-time error?

1.33 Describe the process of desk-checking.

1.7 Tying It All Together: *Hi! It's Me*

Most programs, as you have learned, have three primary activities: input, processing, and output. But it is possible to write a program that has only output. Program 1-2, shown below, displays the message:

```
Hi! It's me.
I'm learning to program!
```

Program 1-2 can be found in the Chapter 1 folder on the book's companion website. Open the program in whatever C++ development environment your class is using. Then compile it and run it. Your instructor will show you how to do this.

Program 1-2

```
1  //This program prints a message with your name in it.
2  #include <iostream>
3  using namespace std;
4
5  int main()
6  {
7      cout << "Hi! It\'s me.\n";
8      cout << "I\'m learning to program!\n";
9      return 0;
10 }
```

Once you have run it, change the word `me` on line 7 to *your* name to personalize the message. Then recompile and rerun the program.

In the next chapter you will learn what the `\'` and `\n` do.

Review Questions and Exercises

Fill-in-the-Blank and Short Answer

1. Computers can do many different jobs because they can be __________.
2. The job of the __________ is to fetch instructions, carry out the operations commanded by the instructions, and produce some outcome or resultant information.
3. Internally, the CPU consists of the __________ and the __________.
4. A(n) __________ is an example of a secondary storage device.
5. The two general categories of software are __________ and __________.
6. A program is a set of __________.
7. Since computers can't be programmed in natural human language, algorithms must be written in a(n) __________ language.
8. __________ is the only language computers really process.
9. __________ languages are close to the level of humans in terms of readability.

10. __________ languages are close to the level of the computer.
11. A program's ability to run on several different types of computer systems is called __________.
12. Words that have special meaning in a programming language are called __________ words.
13. Words or names defined by the programmer are called __________.
14. __________ are characters or symbols that perform operations on one or more operands.
15. __________ characters or symbols mark the beginning or ending of programming statements, or separate items in a list.
16. The rules that must be followed when constructing a program are called __________.
17. A(n) __________ is a named storage location.
18. A variable must be __________ before it can be used in a program.
19. The three primary activities of a program are __________, __________, and __________.
20. __________ is information a program gathers from the outside world.
21. __________ is information a program sends to the outside world.
22. A(n) __________ is a diagram that graphically illustrates the structure of a program.
23. Both main memory and secondary storage are types of memory. Describe the difference between the two.
24. What is the difference between system software and application software?
25. What is the difference between a syntax error and a logical error?

Algorithm Workbench

26. **Available Credit**

    Design a hierarchy chart for a program that calculates a customer's available credit. The program should carry out the following steps:

    1. Display the message "Enter the customer's maximum credit."
    2. Wait for the user to enter the customer's maximum credit.
    3. Display the message "Enter the amount of credit used by the customer."
    4. Wait for the user to enter the customer's credit used.
    5. Subtract the used credit from the maximum credit to get the customer's available credit.
    6. Display a message that shows the customer's available credit.

27. **Account Balance**

    Write high-level and detailed pseudocode for a program that calculates the current balance in a bank account. The program must ask the user for

    - The starting balance
    - The total dollar amount of deposits made
    - The total dollar amount of withdrawals made

    Once the program calculates the current balance, it should be displayed on the screen.

VideoNote
Designing the Account Balance Program

28. **Sales Tax**

    Write high-level and detailed pseudocode for a program that calculates the total of a retail sale. The program should ask the user for

    - The retail price of the item being purchased
    - The sales tax rate

    Once these items have been entered, the program should calculate and display

    - The sales tax for the purchase
    - The total of the sale

Predict the Output

Questions 29–32 are programs expressed as English statements. What would each display on the screen if they were actual programs?

29. The variable `sum` starts with the value 0.
    Add 10 to `sum`.
    Add 15 to `sum`.
    Add 20 to `sum`.
    Display the value of `sum` on the screen.

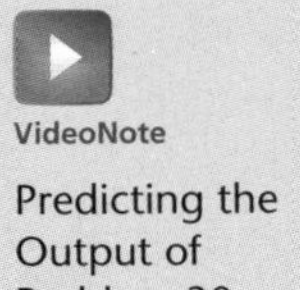

VideoNote

Predicting the Output of Problem 30

30. The variable `x` starts with the value 0.
    The variable `y` starts with the value 5.
    Add 1 to `x`.
    Add 1 to `y`.
    Add `x` and `y`, and store the result in `y`.
    Display the value in `y` on the screen.

31. The variable `j` starts with the value 10.
    The variable `k` starts with the value 2.
    The variable `l` starts with the value 4.
    Store the value of `j` times `k` in `j`.
    Store the value of `k` times `l` in `l`.
    Add `j` and `l`, and store the result in `k`.
    Display the value in `k` on the screen.

32. The variable `a` starts with the value 1.
    The variable `b` starts with the value 10.
    The variable `c` starts with the value 100.
    The variable `x` starts with the value 0.
    Store the value of `c` times 3 in `x`.
    Add the value of `b` times 6 to the value already in `x`.
    Add the value of `a` times 5 to the value already in `x`.
    Display the value in `x` on the screen.

Find the Error

33. The following pseudocode algorithm has an error. It is supposed to use values input for a rectangular room's length and width to calculate and display its area. Find the error.

```
area = width × length.
Display "What is the room's width?".
Input width.
Display "What is the room's length?".
Input length.
Display area.
```

Soft Skills

Before a programmer can design a program he or she must have some basic knowledge about the domain, or area, the program will deal with and must understand exactly what it is that the client wants the program to do. Otherwise the final program may not work correctly or may not meet the client's needs.

34. Suppose one of your friends, who paints the insides of houses, has asked you to develop a program that determines and displays how much paint is needed to paint a room if the length and width of the room is input. What information are you lacking that you need to write this program? Write at least three questions that you would need to ask your friend before starting the project.

Programming Challenges

VideoNote
Solving the Candy Bar Sales Problem

1. Candy Bar Sales

Using Program 1-1 as an example, write a program that calculates how much a student organization earns during its fund raising candy sale. The program should prompt the user to enter the number of candy bars sold and the amount the organization earns for each bar sold. It should then calculate and display the total amount earned.

2. Baseball Costs

Using Program 1-1 as an example, write a program that calculates how much a little league baseball team spent last year to purchase new baseballs. The program should prompt the user to enter the number of baseballs purchased and the cost of each baseball. It should then calculate and display the total amount spent to purchase the baseballs.

CHAPTER

2 Introduction to C++

TOPICS

2.1 The Parts of a C++ Program

CONCEPT: C++ programs have parts and components that serve specific purposes.

Every C++ program has an anatomy. Unlike human anatomy, the parts of C++ programs are not always in the same place. Nevertheless, the parts are there and your first step in learning C++ is to learn what they are. We will begin by looking at Program 2-1.

Program 2-1

```
// A simple C++ program
#include <iostream>
using namespace std;

int main()
{
   cout << "Programming is great fun!";
   return 0;
}
```

Program Output

```
Programming is great fun!
```

Let's examine the program line by line. Here's the first line:

```
// A simple C++ program
```

The `//` marks the beginning of a *comment*. The compiler ignores everything from the double-slash to the end of the line. That means you can type anything you want on that line, and the compiler will never complain! Although comments are not required, they are very important to programmers. Most programs are much more complicated than the example in Program 2-1, and comments help explain what's going on.

Line 2 looks like this:

```
#include <iostream>
```

When a line begins with a `#` it indicates it is a *preprocessor directive*. The preprocessor reads your program before it is compiled and only executes those lines beginning with a `#` symbol. Think of the preprocessor as a program that "sets up" your source code for the compiler.

The `#include` directive causes the preprocessor to include the contents of another file in the program. The word inside the brackets, `iostream`, is the name of the file that is to be included. The `iostream` file contains code that allows a C++ program to display output on the screen and read input from the keyboard. Because the `cout` statement (on line 7) prints output to the computer screen, we need to include this file. Its contents will be placed in the program at the point the `#include` statement appears. The `iostream` file is called a *header file*, so it should be included at the head, or top, of the program.

Line 3 reads

```
using namespace std;
```

Programs usually contain various types of items with unique names. In this chapter you will learn to create variables. In Chapter 6 you will learn to create functions. In Chapter 7 you will learn to create objects. Variables, functions, and objects are examples of program entities that must have names. C++ uses *namespaces* to organize the names of program entities. The statement `using namespace std;` declares that the program will be accessing entities whose names are part of the namespace called `std`. (Yes, even namespaces have names.) The program needs access to the `std` namespace because every name created by the `iostream` file is part of that namespace. In order for a program to use the entities in `iostream`, it must have access to the `std` namespace. More information on namespaces can be found in Appendix J, which is available on the book's companion Web site.

Line 5 reads

```
int main()
```

This marks the beginning of a function. A *function* can be thought of as a group of one or more programming statements that has a name. The name of this function is `main`, and the set of parentheses that follows the name indicates that it is a function. The word `int` stands for "integer." It indicates that the function sends an integer value back to the operating system when it is finished executing.

Although most C++ programs have more than one function, every C++ program must have a function called `main`. It is the starting point of the program. If you're ever reading someone else's program and want to find where it starts, just look for the function called `main`.

NOTE: C++ is a case-sensitive language. That means it regards uppercase letters as being entirely different characters than their lowercase counterparts. In C++, the name of the function `main` must be written in all lowercase letters. C++ doesn't see "main" the same as "Main" or "MAIN."

Line 6 contains a single, solitary character:

```
{
```

This is called a left-brace, or an opening brace, and it is associated with the beginning of the function `main`. All the statements that make up a function are enclosed in a set of braces. If you look at the third line down from the opening brace you'll see the closing brace. Everything between the two braces is the contents of the function `main`.

WARNING! Make sure you have a closing brace for every opening brace in your program.

After the opening brace you see the following statement in line 7:

```
cout << "Programming is great fun!";
```

This line displays a message on the screen. You will read more about `cout` and the << operator later in this chapter. The message "Programming is great fun!" is printed without the quotation marks. In programming terms, the group of characters inside the quotation marks is called a *string literal,* a *string constant,* or simply a *string.*

NOTE: This is the only line in the program that causes anything to be printed on the screen. The other lines, like `#include <iostream>` and `int main()`, are necessary for the framework of your program, but they do not cause any screen output. Remember, a program is a set of instructions for the computer. If something is to be displayed on the screen, you must use a programming statement for that purpose.

Notice that line 7 ends with a semicolon. Just as a period marks the end of a sentence, a semicolon is required to mark the end of a complete statement in C++. But many C++ lines, such as comments, preprocessor directives, and the beginning of functions, are not complete statements. These do not end with semicolons. Here are some examples of when to use, and not use, semicolons.

```
// Semicolon examples        // This is a comment
# include <iostream>         // This is a preprocessor directive
int main()                   // This begins a function
cout << "Hello";             // This is a complete statement
```

As you spend more time working with C++ you will get a feel for where you should and should not use semicolons. For now don't worry about it. Just concentrate on learning the parts of a program.

Line 8 reads

```
return 0;
```

This sends the integer value 0 back to the operating system when the program finishes running. The value 0 usually indicates that a program executed successfully.

The last line of the program, line 9, contains the closing brace:

```
}
```

This brace marks the end of the `main` function. Because `main` is the only function in this program, it also marks the end of the program.

In the sample program you encountered several sets of special characters. Table 2-1 provides a short summary of how they were used.

Table 2-1 Special Characters

Character	Name	Description
`//`	Double slash	Marks the beginning of a comment.
`#`	Pound sign	Marks the beginning of a preprocessor directive.
`< >`	Opening and closing brackets	Encloses a filename when used with the `#include` directive.
`( )`	Opening and closing parentheses	Used in naming a function, as in `int main()`.
`{ }`	Opening and closing braces	Encloses a group of statements, such as the contents of a function.
`" "`	Opening and closing quotation marks	Encloses a string of characters, such as a message that is to be printed on the screen.
`;`	Semicolon	Marks the end of a complete programming statement.

Checkpoint

2.1 The following C++ program will not compile because the lines have been mixed up.

```
int main()
}
// A crazy mixed up program
#include <iostream>
return 0;
cout << "In 1492 Columbus sailed the ocean blue.";
{
using namespace std;
```

When the lines are properly arranged the program should display the following on the screen:

```
In 1492 Columbus sailed the ocean blue.
```

Rearrange the lines in the correct order. Test the program by entering it on the computer, compiling it, and running it.

2.2 On paper, write a program that will display your name on the screen. Use Program 2-1 as your guide. Place a comment with today's date at the top of the program. Test your program by entering, compiling, and running it.

2.2 The cout Object

CONCEPT: cout is used to display information on the computer's screen.

In this section you will learn to write programs that produce output on the screen. The simplest type of screen output that a program can display is *console output*, which is merely plain text. The word *console* is an old computer term. It comes from the days when a computer operator interacted with the system by typing on a terminal. The terminal, which consisted of a simple screen and keyboard, was known as the console.

On modern computers, running graphical operating systems such as Windows or Mac OS, console output is usually displayed in a window such as the one shown in Figure 2-1. C++ provides an object named cout that is used to produce console output. (You can think of the word cout as meaning console **out**put.)

Figure 2-1 A Console Window

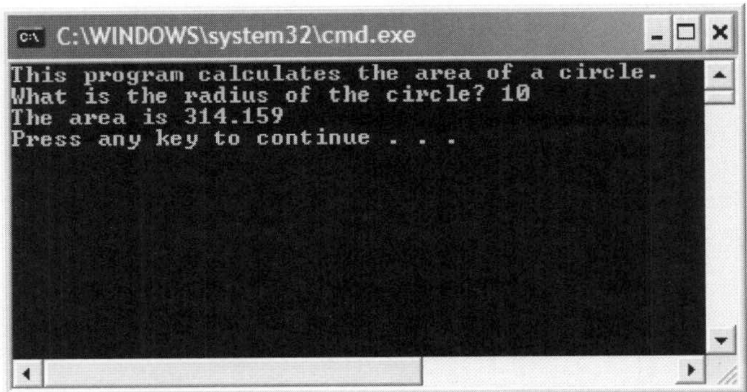

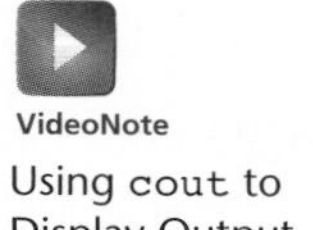

Using cout to Display Output

cout is classified as a *stream object*, which means it works with streams of data. To print a message on the screen, you send a stream of characters to cout. Let's look at line 7 from Progam 2-1:

```
cout << "Programming is great fun!";
```

The << operator is used to send the string "Programming is great fun!" to cout. When the << symbol is used this way, it is called the *stream-insertion operator.* The item immediately to the right of the operator is *inserted* into the output stream that is sent to cout to be displayed on the screen.

> **NOTE:** The stream insertion operator is always written as two less-than signs with no space between them. Because you are using it to send a stream of data to the cout object, you can think of the stream insertion operator as an arrow that must point toward cout, as shown here.
>
> ```
> cout << "Hello";
> cout ← "Hello";
> ```

Program 2-2 shows another way to write the same program.

Program 2-2

```
// A simple C++ program
#include <iostream>
using namespace std;

int main()
{
   cout << "Programming is " << "great fun!";
   return 0;
}
```

Program Output

```
Programming is great fun!
```

As you can see, the stream-insertion operator can be used to send more than one item to cout. The output of this program is identical to Program 2-1. Program 2-3 shows yet another way to accomplish the same thing.

Program 2-3

```
// A simple C++ program
#include <iostream>
using namespace std;

int main()
{
   cout << "Programming is ";
   cout << "great fun!";
   return 0;
}
```

Program Output

```
Programming is great fun!
```

An important concept to understand about Program 2-3 is that although the output is broken into two programming statements, this program will still display the message on a single line. Unless you specify otherwise, the information you send to cout is displayed in a continuous stream. Sometimes this can produce less-than-desirable results. Program 2-4 illustrates this.

Program 2-4

```
// An unruly printing program
#include <iostream>
using namespace std;

int main()
{
   cout << "The following items were top sellers";
   cout << "during the month of June:";
   cout << "Computer games";
   cout << "Coffee";
   cout << "Aspirin";
   return 0;
}
```

Program Output

```
The following items were top sellersduring the month of June:Computer
gamesCoffeeAspirin
```

The layout of the actual output looks nothing like the arrangement of the strings in the source code. First, notice there is no space displayed between the words "sellers" and "during," or between "June:" and "Computer." cout displays messages exactly as they are sent. If spaces are to be displayed, they must appear in the strings.

Second, even though the output is broken into five lines in the source code, it comes out as one long line of output. Because the output is too long to fit on one line of the screen, it wraps around to a second line when displayed. The reason the output comes out as one long line is that cout does not start a new line unless told to do so. There are two ways to instruct cout to start a new line. The first is to send cout a *stream manipulator* called endl (pronounced "end-line" or "end-L"). Program 2-5 does this.

Program 2-5

```
// A well-adjusted printing program
#include <iostream>
using namespace std;

int main()
{
   cout << "The following items were top sellers" << endl;
   cout << "during the month of June:" << endl;
   cout << "Computer games" << endl;
   cout << "Coffee" << endl;
   cout << "Aspirin" << endl;
   return 0;
}
```

(program continues)

Program 2-5 *(continued)*

Program Output

```
The following items were top sellers
during the month of June:
Computer games
Coffee
Aspirin
```

NOTE: The last character in `endl` is the lowercase letter L, *not* the number one.

Every time `cout` encounters an `endl` stream manipulator it advances the output to the beginning of the next line for subsequent printing. The manipulator can be inserted anywhere in the stream of characters sent to `cout`, as long as it is outside the double quotes. Notice that an `endl` is also used at the end of the last line of output.

Another way to cause subsequent output to begin on a new line is to insert a `\n` inside a string that is being output. Program 2-6 does this.

Program 2-6

```
// Another well-adjusted printing program
#include <iostream>
using namespace std;

int main()
{
   cout << "The following items were top sellers\n";
   cout << "during the month of June:\n";
   cout << "Computer games\nCoffee";
   cout << "\nAspirin\n";
   return 0;
}
```

Program Output

```
The following items were top sellers
during the month of June:
Computer games
Coffee
Aspirin
```

`\n` is an example of an *escape sequence*. Escape sequences are written as a backslash character (`\`) followed by a control character and are used to control the way output is displayed. There are many escape sequences in C++. The newline escape sequence (`\n`) is just one of them.

When `cout` encounters `\n` in a string, it doesn't print it on the screen. Instead it interprets it as a special command to advance the output cursor to the next line. You have probably noticed that inserting the escape sequence requires less typing than inserting `endl`. That's why some programmers prefer it.

Escape sequences give you the ability to exercise greater control over the way information is output by your program. Table 2-2 lists a few of them.

Table 2-2 Common Escape Sequences

Escape Sequence	Name	Description
`\n`	Newline	Causes the cursor to go to the next line for subsequent printing.
`\t`	Horizontal tab	Causes the cursor to skip over to the next tab stop.
`\a`	Alarm	Causes the computer to beep.
`\b`	Backspace	Causes the cursor to back up, or move left one position.
`\r`	Return	Causes the cursor to go to the beginning of the current line, not the next line.
`\\`	Backslash	Causes a backslash to be printed.
`\'`	Single quote	Causes a single quotation mark to be printed.
`\"`	Double quote	Causes a double quotation mark to be printed.

A common mistake made by beginning C++ students is to use a forward slash (/) instead of a back slash (\) when trying to write an escape sequence. This will not work. For example, look at the following line of code.

```
cout << "Four score/nAnd seven/nYears ago./n";   // Error!
```

Because the programmer accidentally wrote `/n` instead of `\n`, `cout` will simply display the `/n` characters on the screen, rather than starting a new line of output. This code will create the following output:

```
Four score/nAnd seven/nYears ago./n
```

Another common mistake is to forget to put the `\n` inside quotation marks. For example, the following code will not compile.

```
cout << "Good" << \n;           // Error!
cout << "Morning" << \n;        // This code will not compile.
```

We can correct the code by placing the `\n` sequences inside the string literals, as shown here:

```
cout << "Good\n";               // This will work.
cout << "Morning\n";
```

It is important not to confuse the backslash (\) with the forward slash (/). An escape sequence must start with a backslash, be placed inside quotation marks, and have no spaces between the backslash and the control character.

When you type an escape sequence in a string, you type two characters (a backslash followed by another character). However, an escape sequence is stored in memory as a single character. For example, consider the following string literal:

```
"One\nTwo\nThree\n"
```

The diagram in Figure 2-2 breaks this string into its individual characters. Notice how each \n escape sequence is considered just one character.

Figure 2-2

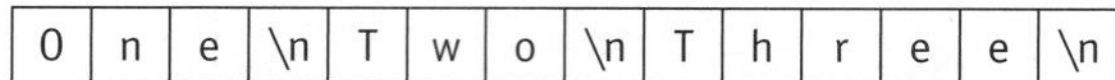

The #include Directive

CONCEPT: The `#include` directive causes the contents of another file to be inserted into the program.

Now is a good time to expand our discussion of the `#include` directive. The following line has appeared near the top of every example program.

```
#include <iostream>
```

As previously mentioned, the `iostream` header file must be included in any program that uses the `cout` object. This is because `cout` is not part of the "core" of the C++ language. Specifically, it is part of the *input-output stream library*. The `iostream` header file contains information describing `iostream` objects. Without it, the compiler will not know how to properly compile a program that uses `cout`.

Preprocessor directives are not C++ statements. They are commands to the preprocessor, which runs prior to the compiler (hence the name "preprocessor"). The preprocessor's job is to set programs up in a way that makes life easier for the programmer.

For example, any program that uses the `cout` object must contain the extensive setup information found in the `iostream` file. The programmer could type all this information into the program, but it would be very time consuming. An alternative would be to use an editor to "cut and paste" it into the program, but that would still be inefficient. The solution is to let the preprocessor insert the contents of `iostream` automatically.

WARNING! Do not use semicolons at the end of preprocessor directives. Because preprocessor directives are not C++ statements, they do not require them. In fact, in many cases an error will result if a preprocessor directive is terminated with a semicolon.

An `#include` directive must contain the name of the file you wish to include in the program. The preprocessor inserts the entire contents of this file into the program at the point it encounters the `#include` directive. The compiler doesn't actually see the `#include` directive. Instead it sees the code that was inserted by the preprocessor, just as if the programmer had typed it there.

The code contained in header files is C++ code. Typically it describes complex objects like `cout`. Later you will learn to create your own header files.

Checkpoint

2.3 The following `cout` statement contains errors.

```
cout << "red /n" << "blue \ n" << "yellow" \n << "green";
```

Correct it so that it will display a list of colors, with one item per line.

2.4 What output will the following lines of code display on the screen?

```
cout << "The works of Wolfgang\ninclude the following";
cout << "\nThe Turkish March" << endl;
cout << "and Symphony No. 40 ";
cout << "in G minor." << endl;
```

2.5 On paper, write a program that will display your name on the first line, your street address on the second line, your city, state, and ZIP code on the third line, and your telephone number on the fourth line. Test your program by entering, compiling, and running it.

2.4 Standard and Prestandard C++

CONCEPT: C++ programs written before the language became standardized may appear slightly different from programs written today.

C++ is now a standardized programming language, but it hasn't always been. The language has evolved over the years, and as a result, there is a "newer style" and an "older style" of writing C++ code. The newer style is the way programs are written with standard C++, while the older style is the way programs were typically written using prestandard C++. Although the differences between the older and newer styles are subtle, it is important that you recognize them. When you go to work as a computer science professional, it is likely that you will see programs written in the older style. Here are some of the most noticeable differences between prestandard and standard C++.

Older Style Header Files

In older style C++, all header files end with the ".h" extension. For example, in a prestandard C++ program the statement that includes the `iostream` header file is written as

```
#include <iostream.h>
```

Absence of `using namespace std;`

Another difference between the newer and older styles is that older style programs typically do not use the `using namespace std;` statement. In fact, some older compilers do not support namespaces at all and will produce an error message if a program has that statement.

No `return 0;`

Still another difference is that older style C++ programs do not end the `main` function with a `return 0;` statement. Therefore the line that begins the `main` function says `void main()` or `void main(void)` instead of `int main()` to indicate that the function does not return anything back to the operating system when the program finishes executing.

An Older Style Program

To illustrate these differences, look at the following program. It is a modification of Program 2-1, written in the older style.

```
// A simple C++ program
#include <iostream.h>

void main(void)
{
   cout << "Programming is great fun!";
}
```

Some standard C++ compilers do not support programs written in the older style, and prestandard compilers normally do not support programs written in the newer style.

2.5 Variables, Literals, and the Assignment Statement

CONCEPT: Variables represent storage locations in the computer's memory. Literals are constant values that can be assigned to variables.

The concept of a variable in computer programming is somewhat different from the concept of a variable in mathematics. In programming, as you learned in Chapter 1, a variable is a named storage location for holding data. Variables allow you to store and work with data in the computer's memory. They provide an "interface" to RAM. Part of the job of programming is to determine how many variables a program will need and what type of information each will hold. Program 2-7 is an example of a C++ program with a variable.

Program 2-7

```
// This program has a variable.
#include <iostream>
using namespace std;

int main()
{
   int number;

   number = 5;
   cout << "The value of number is " << "number" << endl;
   cout << "The value of number is " <<  number  << endl;

   number = 7;
   cout << "Now the value of number is " << number << endl;

   return 0;
}
```

Program Output

```
The value of number is number
The value of number is 5
Now the value of number is 7
```

Let's look more closely at this program. Start by looking at line 7.

```
int number;
```

This is called a *variable definition*. It tells the compiler the variable's name and the type of data it will hold. Notice that the definition gives the data type first, then the name of the variable, and ends with a semicolon. This variable's name is `number`. The word `int` stands for integer, so `number` may only be used to hold integer numbers.

NOTE: You must have a definition for every variable you use in a program. In C++, a variable definition can appear at any point in the program as long as it occurs before the variable is ever used. Later in this chapter, and throughout the book, you will learn the best places to define variables.

Now look at line 9.

```
number = 5;
```

This is called an *assignment statement* and the = sign is called the *assignment operator.* This operator copies the value on its right (5) into the variable named on its left (`number`). This line does not print anything on the computer's screen. It runs silently behind the scenes, storing a value in RAM. After this line executes, `number` will be set to 5.

NOTE: The item on the left-hand side of an assignment statement *must* be a variable. It would be incorrect to say `5 = number;`

Now look at lines 10 and 11. Notice that in line 10 the word `number` has double quotation marks around it and in line 11, it does not.

```
cout << "The value of number is " << "number" << endl;
cout << "The value of number is " <<  number  << endl;
```

Now compare these two lines with the output they produce. When double quotation marks are placed around the word `number` it becomes a string literal and is no longer a variable name. So in the first `cout` statement the word `"number"` is inserted into the output stream, producing the following output.

```
The value of number is number
```

In the second `cout` statement there are no quotation marks around the word `number`, so it is the variable name `number` that is inserted into the output stream. When you send a variable name to `cout` it prints the variable's contents, so the following line is displayed.

```
The value of number is 5
```

Recall from Chapter 1 that variables are called variables because their values can change. The assignment statement on line 13 replaces the previous value stored in `number` with a 7.

```
number = 7;
```

Therefore the final `cout` statement on line 14

```
cout << "Now the value of number is " << number  << endl;
```

causes the following output to print.

```
Now the value of number is 7
```

Sometimes a Number Isn't a Number

As shown in Program 2-7, placing quotation marks around a variable name makes it a string literal. When string literals are sent to `cout`, they are printed exactly as they appear inside the quotation marks. You've probably noticed by now that the `endl` stream manipulator is written with no quotation marks around it. If we put the following line in a program, it would print out the word `endl`, rather than cause subsequent output to begin on a new line.

```
cout << "endl";     // Wrong!
```

In fact, placing double quotation marks around anything that is not intended to be a string will create an error of some type. For example, in Program 2-7 the number 5 was assigned to the variable `number`. It would have been incorrect to write the assignment this way:

```
number = "5";       // Wrong!
```

In this line, 5 is no longer an integer. It is a string. Because `number` was defined to be an integer variable, you can only store integers in it. The integer 5 and the string "5" are not the same thing.

The fact that numbers can be represented as strings frequently confuses people who are new to programming. Just remember that strings are intended for humans to read. They are to be printed on computer screens or paper. Numbers, however, are intended primarily for mathematical operations. You cannot perform math on strings, and you cannot display numbers on the screen without first converting them to strings. Fortunately, `cout` handles this conversion automatically when you send a number to it.

Literals

A variable is called a "variable" because its value may be changed. A literal, on the other hand, is a value that cannot change during the program's execution. For this reason, literals are also called constants. Many programmers refer to them as literals when they hold strings or characters and as constants when they hold numbers, such as integers. Program 2-8 contains integer constants, string literals, and a variable.

Program 2-8

```
// This program uses integer constants, string literals, and a variable.
#include <iostream>
using namespace std;

int main()
{
   int apples;

   apples = 20;
   cout << "On Sunday we sold " << apples << " bushels of apples. \n";

   apples = 15;
   cout << "On Monday we sold " << apples << " bushels of apples. \n";
   return 0;
}
```

Program 2-8 *(continued)*

Program Output
```
On Sunday we sold 20 bushels of apples.
On Monday we sold 15 bushels of apples.
```

Of course, the variable is `apples`. Table 2-3 lists the literals found in the program.

Table 2-3 Program 2-8 Literals

Integer Constants	String Literals
`20`	`"On Sunday we sold"`
`15`	`"On Monday we sold"`
`0`	`"bushels of apples. \n"`

What are literals used for? As you can see from Program 2-8, they are commonly used to store known values in variables and to display messages on the screen.

Checkpoint

2.6 Which of the following are legal C++ assignment statements?

```
a.  a = 7;
b.  7 = a;
c.  7 = 7;
```

2.7 List all the variables and literals that appear below.

```
int main()
{
   int little;
   int big;
   little = 2;
   big = 2000;
   cout << "The little number is " << little << endl;
   cout << "The big number is " << big << endl;
   return 0;
}
```

2.8 When the above main function runs, what will display on the screen?

2.9 When the following main function runs, what will display on the screen?

```
int main()
{
   int number;

   number = 712;
   cout << "The value is " << "number" << endl;
   return 0;
}
```

2.6 Identifiers

CONCEPT: A variable name should indicate what the variable is used for.

An *identifier* is a programmer-defined name that represents some element of a program. Variable names are examples of identifiers. You may choose your own variable names in C++, as long as you do not use any of the C++ *key words*. The key words make up the "core" of the language and have specific purposes. Table 2-4 shows a complete list of the C++ key words. Note that they are all lowercase.

Table 2-4 C++ Key Words

and	continue	goto	public	try
and_eq	default	if	register	typedef
asm	delete	inline	reinterpret_cast	typeid
auto	do	int	return	typename
bitand	double	long	short	union
bitor	dynamic_cast	mutable	signed	unsigned
bool	else	namespace	sizeof	using
break	enum	new	static	virtual
case	explicit	not	static_cast	void
catch	export	not_eq	struct	volatile
char	extern	operator	switch	wchar_t
class	false	or	template	while
compl	float	or_eq	this	xor
const	for	private	throw	xor_eq
const_cast	friend	protected	true	

You should always choose names for your variables that indicate what the variables are used for. You may be tempted to give variables names like this:

```
int x;
```

However, the rather nondescript name, x, gives no clue as to the variable's purpose. Here is a better example.

```
int itemsOrdered;
```

The name itemsOrdered gives anyone reading the program an idea of the variable's use. This way of coding helps produce self-documenting programs, which means you can get an understanding of what the program is doing just by reading its code. Because real-world programs usually have thousands of lines, it is important that they be as self-documenting as possible.

You probably have noticed the mixture of uppercase and lowercase letters in the variable name itemsOrdered. Although all of C++'s key words must be written in lowercase, you may use uppercase letters in variable names.

The reason the O in itemsOrdered is capitalized is to improve readability. Normally "items ordered" is two words. However, you cannot have spaces in a variable name, so the two words must be combined into one. When "items" and "ordered" are stuck together you get a variable definition like this:

```
int itemsordered;
```

Capitalization of the first letter of the second word and any succeeding words makes variable names like `itemsOrdered` easier to read and is the convention we use for naming variables in this book. However, this style of coding is not required. You are free to use all lowercase letters, all uppercase letters, or any combination of both. In fact, some programmers use the underscore character to separate words in a variable name, as in the following.

```
int items_ordered;
```

Legal Identifiers

Regardless of which style you adopt, be consistent and make your variable names as sensible as possible. Here are some specific rules that must be followed with all C++ identifiers.

- The first character must be one of the letters a through z, A through Z, or an underscore character (_).
- After the first character you may use the letters a through z or A through Z, the digits 0 through 9, or underscores.
- Uppercase and lowercase characters are distinct. This means `ItemsOrdered` is not the same as `itemsordered`.

Table 2-5 lists variable names and indicates whether each is legal or illegal in C++.

Table 2-5 Some C++ Variable Names

Variable Name	Legal or Illegal
`dayOfWeek`	Legal.
`3dGraph`	Illegal. Variable names cannot begin with a digit.
`_employee_num`	Legal.
`June1997`	Legal.
`Mixture#3`	Illegal. Variable names may only use letters, digits, and underscores.

2.7 Integer Data Types

CONCEPT: There are many different types of data. Variables are classified according to their data type, which determines the kind of information that may be stored in them. Integer variables can only hold whole numbers.

Computer programs collect pieces of data from the real world and manipulate them in various ways. There are many different types of data. In the realm of numeric information, for example, there are whole numbers and fractional numbers. There are negative numbers and positive numbers. Then there is textual information. Names and addresses, for instance, are stored as groups of characters. When you write a program you must determine what types of information it will be likely to encounter.

If you are writing a program to calculate the number of miles to a distant star, you'll need variables that can hold very large numbers. If you are designing software to record microscopic dimensions, you'll need to store very small and precise numbers. Additionally, if you are writing a program that must perform thousands of intensive calculations, you'll want data stored in variables that can be processed quickly. The data type of a variable determines all of these factors.

Although C++ offers many data types, in the very broadest sense there are only two: numeric and character. Numeric data types are broken into two additional categories: integer and floating-point, as shown in Figure 2-3.

Figure 2-3 Basic C++ Data Types

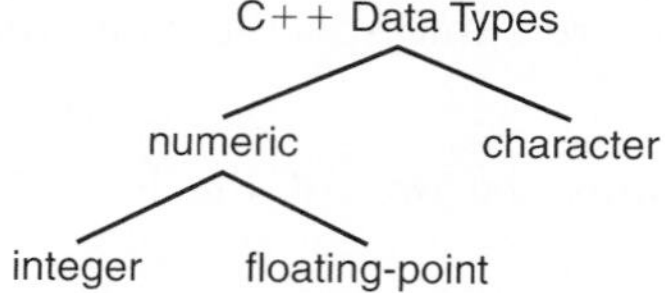

Integers are whole numbers like –2, 19, and 24. Floating-point numbers have a decimal point like –2.35, 19.0, and 0.024. Additionally, the integer and floating-point data types are broken into even more classifications.

Your primary considerations for selecting the best data type for a numeric variable are the following:

- whether the variable needs to hold integers or floating-point values,
- the largest and smallest numbers that the variable needs to be able to store,
- whether the variable needs to hold signed (both positive and negative) or only unsigned (just zero and positive) numbers, and
- the number of decimal places of precision needed for values stored in the variable.

Let's begin by looking at integer data types. C++ has six different data types for storing integers. On most computers each of these has either two or four bytes of memory. The number of bytes a data type can hold is called its *size*. Typically, the larger the size a data type is, the greater the range of values it can hold.

Recall from Chapter 1 that a byte is made up of 8 bits. So a data type that stores data in two bytes of memory can hold 16 bits of information. This means it can store 2^{16} *bit patterns*, which is 65,536 different combinations of zeros and ones. A data type that uses 4 bytes of memory has 32 bits, so it can hold 2^{32} different bit patterns, which is 4,294,967,296 different combinations. What these different combinations are used for depends on the data type. For example, the `unsigned short` data type, which is for storing non-negative integers such as ages or weights, uses its 16 bits to represent the values 0 through +65,535. The `short` data type, on the other hand, stores both positive and negative numbers, so it uses its 16 bits to represent the values from –32,768 to +32,767. Figure 2-4 shows how numbers are stored in an `unsigned short` variable.

Figure 2-4 Unsigned Short Data Type Storage

Example value = binary 25

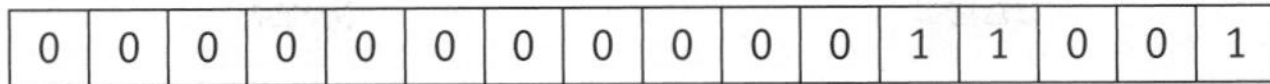
0	0	0	0	0	0	0	0	0	0	0	1	1	0	0	1

Smallest value that can be stored = binary 0

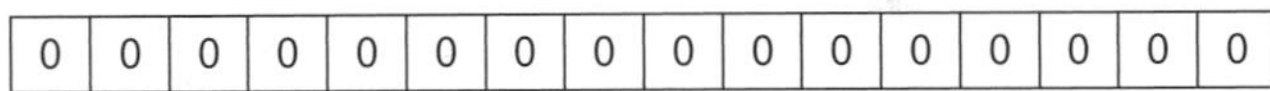
0	0	0	0	0	0	0	0	0	0	0	0	0	0	0	0

Largest value that can be stored = binary 65,535

1	1	1	1	1	1	1	1	1	1	1	1	1	1	1	1

Table 2-6 shows all six C++ integer data types with their typical sizes and ranges. Depending on your operating system, the sizes and ranges may be different.

Table 2-6 Integer Data Types, Sizes, and Ranges

Data Type	Size	Range
`short`	2 bytes	–32,768 to +32,767
`unsigned short`	2 bytes	0 to +65,535
`int`	4 bytes	–2,147,483,648 to +2,147,483,647
`unsigned int`	4 bytes	0 to 4,294,967,295
`long`	4 bytes	–2,147,483,648 to +2,147,483,647
`unsigned long`	4 bytes	0 to 4,294,967,295

Here are some examples of integer variable definitions. Notice that an `unsigned int` variable can also be defined using only the word `unsigned`, as shown below.

```
short  count;
unsigned short age;
int speed;
unsigned int days;      // These two definitions
unsigned days;          // are equivalent.
long deficit;
unsigned long insects;
```

Notice also that in Table 2-6 the `int` and `long` data types have the same sizes and ranges, and the `unsigned int` data type has the same size and range as the `unsigned long` data type. This is not always true because the size of integers is dependent on the type of system you are using. Here are the only guarantees:

- Integers are at least as big as short integers.
- Long integers are at least as big as integers.
- Unsigned short integers are the same size as short integers.
- Unsigned integers are the same size as integers.
- Unsigned long integers are the same size as long integers.

Later in this chapter you will learn to use the `sizeof` operator to determine how large all the data types are on your computer.

Program 2-9 uses integer, unsigned integer, and long integer variables.

Program 2-9

```
// This program has variables of several of the integer types.
#include <iostream>
using namespace std;

int main()
{
   int checking;
   unsigned int miles;
   long days;

   checking = -20;
   miles = 4276;
   days = 190000;

   cout << "We have made a long journey of " << miles << " miles.";
   cout << "\nOur checking account balance is " << checking;
   cout << "\nAbout " << days << " days ago Columbus ";
   cout << "stood on this spot.\n";
   return 0;
}
```

Program Output

```
We have made a long journey of 4276 miles.
Our checking account balance is -20
About 190000 days ago Columbus stood on this spot.
```

Notice in Program 2-9 that the variable `days` is assigned 190000 rather than 190,000. There are no commas in the number. This is because C++ does not allow commas inside numeric constants.

In most programs you will need many variables. If a program uses more than one variable of the same data type, for example the two integers `length` and `width`, they can be defined separately, like this

```
int length;
int width;
```

or, alternatively, both variable definitions can be placed in a single statement, like this

```
int length, width;
```

Many instructors, however, prefer that each variable be placed on its own line:

```
int length,
    width;
```

Whether you place multiple variables on the same line or each variable on its own line, when you define several variables of the same type in a single statement, simply separate their names with commas. A semicolon is used at the end of the entire definition. Program 2-10 illustrates this. This program also shows how it is possible to give an initial value to a variable at the time it is defined.

Program 2-10

```
// This program defines three variables in the same statement.
// They are given initial values at the time they are defined.
#include <iostream>
using namespace std;

int main()
{
   int floors =  15,
       rooms  = 300,
       suites =  30;

   cout << "The Grande Hotel has " << floors << " floors\n";
   cout << "with " << rooms << " rooms and " << suites;
   cout << " suites.\n";
   return 0;
}
```

Program Output

```
The Grande Hotel has 15 floors
with 300 rooms and 30 suites.
```

Integer and Long Integer Constants

Look at the following statement from Program 2-10:

```
int floors = 15,
    rooms = 300,
    suites = 30;
```

This statement contains three integer literals, or constants. In C++, integer constants are normally stored in memory just as an `int`.

One of the pleasing characteristics of the C++ language is that it allows you to control almost every aspect of your program. If you need to change the way something is stored in memory, the tools are provided to do that. For example, what if you are in a situation where you have an integer constant, but you need it to be stored in memory as a long integer? (Rest assured, this is a situation that does arise.) C++ allows you to force an integer constant to be stored as a long integer by placing the letter L at the end of the number. Here is an example:

```
32L
```

On a computer that uses 2-byte integers and 4-byte long integers, this constant will use 4 bytes. This is called a long integer literal, or long integer constant.

NOTE: Although C++ allows you to use either an uppercase or lowercase L, the lowercase l looks too much like the number 1, so you should always use the uppercase L.

Hexadecimal and Octal Constants (enrichment)

Programmers commonly express values in numbering systems other than decimal (or base 10). Hexadecimal (base 16) and octal (base 8) are popular because they make certain programming tasks more convenient than decimal numbers do.

By default, C++ assumes that all integer constants are expressed in decimal. You express hexadecimal numbers by placing `0x` in front of them. (This is zero-x, not oh-x.) Here is how the hexadecimal number F4 would be expressed in C++:

```
0xF4
```

Octal numbers must be preceded by a 0 (zero, not oh). For example, the octal 31 would be written

```
031
```

NOTE: You will not be writing programs for some time that require this type of manipulation. However, good programmers develop the skills for reading other people's source code. You may find yourself reading programs that use items like long integer, hexadecimal, or octal constants.

Checkpoint

2.10 Which of the following are illegal C++ variable names, and why?

```
x
99bottles
july97
theSalesFigureForFiscalYear98
r&d
grade_report
```

2.11 Is the variable name `Sales` the same as `sales`? Why or why not?

2.12 Refer to the data types listed in Table 2-6 for these questions.

A) If a variable needs to hold numbers in the range 32 to 6,000, what data type would be best?

B) If a variable needs to hold numbers in the range –40,000 to +40,000, what data type would be best?

C) Which of the following integer constants use more memory, `20` or `20L`?

2.13 Which integer data types can only hold non-negative values?

2.14 How would you combine the following variable definition and assignment statement into a single statement?

```
int apples;
apples = 20;
```

2.15 How would you combine the following variable definitions into a single statement?

```
int xCoord = 2;
int yCoord = -4;
int zCoord = 6;
```

2.8 Floating-Point Data Types

CONCEPT: Floating-point data types are used to define variables that can hold real numbers.

Whole numbers are not adequate for many jobs. If you are writing a program that works with dollar amounts or precise measurements, you need a data type that allows fractional values. In programming terms, these are called *floating-point* numbers.

Internally, floating-point numbers are stored in a manner similar to *scientific notation.* Take the number 47,281.97. In scientific notation this number is 4.728197×10^4. (10^4 is equal to 10,000, and $4.728197 \times 10{,}000$ is 47,281.97.) The first part of the number, 4.728197, is called the *mantissa*. The mantissa is multiplied by a power of 10.

Computers typically use *E notation* to represent floating-point values. In E notation, the number 47,281.97 would be 4.728197E4. The part of the number before the E is the mantissa, and the part after the E is the power of 10. When a floating-point number is stored in memory, it is stored as the mantissa and the power of 10.

Table 2-7 shows other numbers represented in scientific and E notation.

Table 2-7 Floating-Point Representations

Decimal Notation	Scientific Notation	E Notation
247.91	2.4791×10^2	2.4791E2
0.00072	7.2×10^{-4}	7.2E–4
2,900,000	2.9×10^6	2.9E6

In C++ there are three data types that can represent floating-point numbers. They are

```
float
double
long double
```

The `float` data type is considered *single precision*. The `double` data type is usually twice as big as `float`, so it is considered *double precision*. As you've probably guessed, the `long double` is intended to be larger than the `double`. The exact sizes of these data types is dependent on the computer you are using. The only guarantees are

- A `double` is at least as big as a `float`.
- A `long double` is at least as big as a `double`.

Table 2-8 shows the sizes and ranges of floating-point data types usually found on PCs.

Table 2-8 Floating-Point Data Types on PCs

Data Type	Key Word	Size	Range	Significant Digits
Single precision	`float`	4 bytes	Numbers between ±3.4E-38 and ±3.4E38	7
Double precision	`double`	8 bytes	Numbers between ±1.7E-308 and ±1.7E308	16
Long double precision	`long double`	8 bytes*	Numbers between ±1.7E-308 and ±1.7E308	16

*Some compilers use more than 8 bytes for `long doubles`. These allow greater ranges.

You will notice there are no unsigned floating-point data types. On all machines, variables of the `float`, `double`, and `long double` data type can store both positive and negative numbers. Program 2-11 uses floating-point data types.

Program 2-11

```
// This program uses two floating-point data types, float and double.
#include <iostream>
using namespace std;

int main()
{
   float distance = 1.496E8;          // in kilometers
   double mass = 1.989E30;            // in kilograms

   cout << "The Sun is " << distance << " kilometers away.\n";
   cout << "The Sun\'s mass is " << mass << " kilograms.\n";
   return 0;
}
```

Program Output

```
The Sun is 1.496e+008 kilometers away.
The Sun's mass is 1.989e+030 kilograms.
```

Floating-Point Constants

Floating-point literals, commonly referred to as floating-point constants, may be expressed in a variety of ways. As shown in Program 2-11, E notation is one method. When you are writing numbers that are extremely large or extremely small, this will probably be the easiest way. E notation numbers may be expressed with an uppercase E or a lowercase e. Notice in the source code the constants were written as 1.496E8 and 1.989E30, but the program printed them as 1.496e+008 and 1.989e+030. The uppercase E and lowercase e are equivalent. The plus sign in front of the exponent is also optional.

You can also express floating-point constants in decimal notation. The constant 1.496E8 could have been written as

```
149600000.0
```

Obviously the E notation is more convenient for lengthy numbers; but for numbers like 47.39, decimal notation is preferable to 4.739E1.

All of the following floating-point constants are equivalent:

```
1.496E8
1.496e8
1.496E+8
1.496e+8
149600000.0
```

Floating-point constants are normally stored in memory as `doubles`. Just in case you need to force a constant to be stored as a `float`, you can append the letter `F` or `f` to the end of it. For example, the following constants would be stored as `float` numbers:

```
1.2F
45.907f
```

NOTE: Because floating-point constants are normally stored in memory as `doubles`, some compilers issue a warning message when you assign a floating-point constant to a `float` variable. For example, if `num` is a `float`, the following statement might cause the compiler to generate a warning message:

```
num = 14.725;
```

You can suppress the error message by appending the `f` suffix to the floating-point constant, as shown here:

```
num = 14.725f;
```

If you want to force a value to be stored as a `long double`, append an `L` to it, as shown here:

```
1034.56L
```

The compiler won't confuse this with a long integer because of the decimal point. A lowercase letter `l` can also be used to define a floating-point constant to be a `long double`, but an uppercase `L` is preferable, as the lowercase letter `l` is easily confused with the digit `1`.

Assigning Floating-Point Values to Integer Variables

When a floating-point value is assigned to an integer variable, the fractional part of the value (the part after the decimal point) is discarded. This occurs because an integer variable cannot hold any value containing decimals. For example, look at the following code.

```
int number;
number = 7.8;                // Assigns 7 to number
```

This code attempts to assign the floating-point value 7.8 to the integer variable `number`. Because this is not possible, the value 7 is assigned to `number`, and the fractional part is discarded. When part of a value is discarded in this manner, the value is said to be *truncated*.

Assigning a floating-point variable to an integer variable has the same effect. For example, look at the following code.

```
int intVar;
double doubleVar = 7.8;
intVar = doubleVar;          // Assigns 7 to intVar
                             // doubleVar remains 7.8
```

WARNING! Floating-point variables can hold a much larger range of values than integer variables can. If a floating-point value is stored in an integer variable, and the whole part of the value (the part before the decimal point) is too large for the integer variable, an invalid value will be stored in the integer variable.

Checkpoint

2.16 How would the following number in scientific notation be represented in E notation?

6.31×10^{17}

2.17 What will the following code display?

```
int number;
number = 3.625:
cout << number;
```

2.18 Write a program that defines an integer variable named `age` and a `double` variable named `weight`. Store your age and weight as constants (i.e., literals) in the variables. The program should display these values on the screen in a manner similar to the following:

Program Output
My age is 26 and my weight is 168.5 pounds.

(Feel free to lie to the computer about your age and weight. It will never know!)

2.9 The `char` Data Type

CONCEPT: A variable of the `char` data type holds only a single character.

You learned earlier in this chapter that there are two basic kinds of data types, numeric and character. The previous two sections examined numeric data types. Now let's take a look at character data types.

The simplest character data type is the `char` data type. It can hold only a single character and, on most systems, uses just one byte of memory. Here is an example. Notice that the character literal holding the value being assigned to the variable is enclosed in single quotes.

```
char letter = 'A';
```

Program 2-12 uses a `char` variable and several character literals.

Program 2-12

```
// This program uses a char variable and several character literals.
#include <iostream>
using namespace std;

int main()
{
   char letter;

   letter = 'A';
   cout << letter << endl;

   letter = 'B';
   cout << letter << endl;
   return 0;
}
```

Program Output

```
A
B
```

Interestingly, characters are closely related to integers because internally they are stored as integers. Each printable character, as well as many nonprintable characters, is assigned a unique number. The most commonly used method for encoding characters is ASCII, which stands for the American Standard Code for Information Interchange. When a character is stored in memory, it is actually its numeric code that is stored. When the computer is instructed to print the value on the screen, it displays the character that corresponds to the numeric code. Appendix A shows the entire ASCII character set so you can see which integer value is used to represent each character. Notice that the number 65 is the code for capital A, 66 is the code for capital B, and so on.

Program 2-13 illustrates this relationship between characters and how they are stored.

Program 2-13

```
// This program demonstrates that characters are actually
// stored internally by their ASCII integer value.
#include <iostream>
using namespace std;

int main()
{
   char letter;

   letter = 65;              // 65 is the ASCII code for the character A
   cout << letter << endl;

   letter = 66;              // 66 is the ASCII code for the character B
   cout << letter << endl;
   return 0;
}
```

(program continues)

Program 2-13 *(continued)*

Program Output
```
A
B
```

Figure 2-5 further illustrates that when you think of characters, such as A, B, and C, being stored in memory, it is really the numbers 65, 66, and 67 that are stored.

Figure 2-5

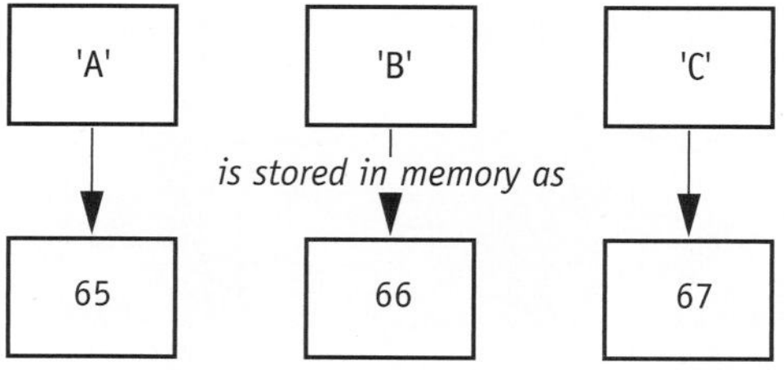

Character and String Literals

Character literals and `char` variables can only hold a single character. If you want to store more than one character in a literal or variable, you need to use a more complex character data type, a string. String literals and variables can hold a whole series of characters. In the next section we will examine string variables in more detail. For now, let's look at string literals and compare them to character literals.

In the following example, 'H' is a character literal and "Hello" is a string literal. Notice that while a character literal is enclosed in single quotation marks, a string literal is enclosed in double quotation marks.

```
cout << 'H' << endl;        // This displays a character literal.
cout << "Hello" << endl;    // This displays a string literal.
```

Because a string literal can be virtually any length, there must be some way for the program to know how long it is. In C++ this is done by appending an extra byte to its end and storing the number 0 in it. This is called the *null terminator* or *null character* and marks the end of the string.

Don't confuse the null terminator with the character `'0'`. If you look at Appendix A you will see that the character `'0'` has ASCII code 48, whereas the null terminator has ASCII code 0. If you want to print the character `0` on the screen, you use ASCII code 48. If you want to mark the end of a string, you use ASCII code 0.

Let's look at an example of how a string literal is stored in memory. Figure 2-6 depicts the way the string `"Sebastian"` would be stored.

Figure 2-6

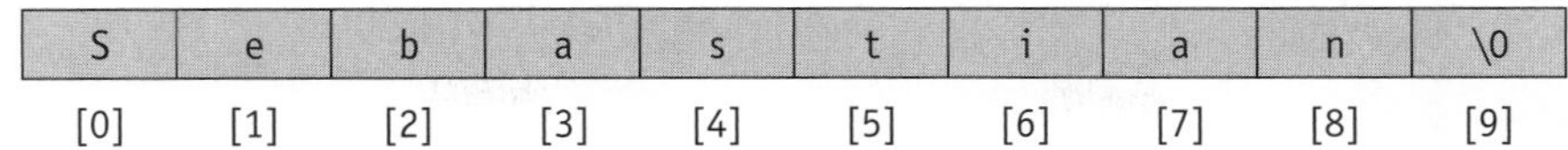

First, notice that the characters in the string are stored in consecutive memory locations. Second, notice that the quotation marks are not stored with the string. They simply mark the beginning and end of the string in your source code. Finally, notice the very last byte of the string. It contains the null terminator, which is represented by the \0 character. The addition of this last byte means that although the string `"Sebastian"` is 9 characters long, it occupies 10 bytes of memory.

The null terminator is another example of something that sits quietly in the background. It doesn't print on the screen when you display a string, but nevertheless, it is there silently doing its job.

NOTE: C++ automatically places the null terminator at the end of string literals.

Now let's compare the way character and string literals are stored. Suppose you have the literals `'A'` and `"A"` in a program. Figure 2-7 depicts their internal storage.

Figure 2-7

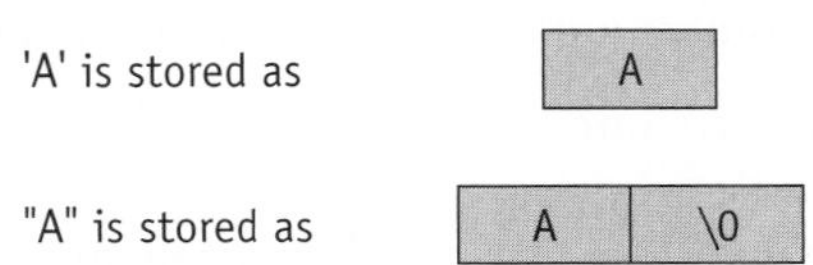

As you can see, `'A'` is a 1-byte element and `"A"` is a 2-byte element. Since characters are really stored as ASCII codes, Figure 2-8 shows what is actually being stored in memory.

Figure 2-8

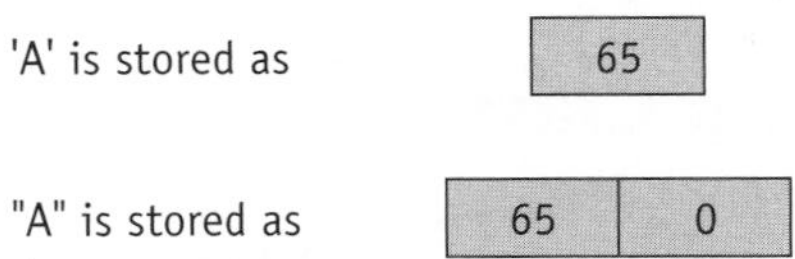

Because a `char` variable can only hold a single character, it can be assigned the character `'A'`, but not the string `"A"`.

```
char letterOne = 'A';          // This will work.
char letterTwo = "A";          // This will NOT work!
```

You have learned that some strings look like a single character but really aren't. It is also possible to have a character that looks like a string. An example is the newline character, `\n`. Although it is represented by two characters, a slash and an `n`, it is internally represented as one character. In fact, all escape sequences, internally, are just 1 byte.

Program 2-14 shows the use of `\n` as a character literal, enclosed in single quotation marks. If you refer to the ASCII chart in Appendix A, you will see that ASCII code 10 is the linefeed character. This is the code C++ uses for the newline character.

Program 2-14

```
// This program uses character literals.
#include <iostream>
using namespace std;

int main()
{
   char letter;

   letter = 'A';
   cout << letter << '\n';

   letter = 'B';
   cout << letter << '\n';
   return 0;
}
```

Program Output

```
A
B
```

Let's review some important points regarding characters and strings:

- Printable characters are internally represented by numeric codes. Most computers use ASCII codes for this purpose.
- Characters normally occupy a single byte of memory.
- Strings are consecutive sequences of characters that occupy consecutive bytes of memory.
- String literals have a null terminator at the end. This marks the end of the string.
- Character literals are enclosed in single quotation marks.
- String literals are enclosed in double quotation marks.
- Escape sequences such as `'\n'` are stored internally as a single character.

2.10 The C++ `string` Class

CONCEPT: Standard C++ provides a special data type for storing and working with strings.

Because a `char` variable can store only one character in its memory location, another data type is needed for a variable able to hold an entire string. While C++ does not have a built-in data type able to do this, Standard C++ provides something called the `string` class that allows the programmer to create a string type variable.

Using the `string` Class

The first step in using the `string` class is to `#include` the `string` header file. This is accomplished with the following preprocessor directive:

```
#include <string>
```

The next step is to define a string type variable, called a string object. Defining a string object is similar to defining a variable of a primitive type. For example, the following statement defines a string object named movieTitle.

```
string movieTitle;
```

You can assign a string literal to movieTitle with the assignment operator, like this.

```
movieTitle = "Wheels of Fury";
```

And you can use cout to display the value of the movieTitle object, as shown here.

```
cout << "My favorite movie is " << movieTitle << endl;
```

Program 2-15 is a complete program that demonstrates the preceding statements.

Program 2-15

```
// This program demonstrates the string class.
#include <iostream>
#include <string>            // Required for the string class.
using namespace std;

int main()
{
   string movieTitle;

   movieTitle = "Wheels of Fury";
   cout << "My favorite movie is " << movieTitle << endl;
   return 0;
}
```

Program Output

```
My favorite movie is Wheels of Fury
```

As you can see, working with string objects is similar to working with variables of other types. Throughout this text we will continue to discuss string class features and capabilities.

Checkpoint

2.19 What are the ASCII codes for the following characters? (Refer to Appendix A)

```
C
F
W
```

2.20 Which of the following is a character literal?

```
'B'
"B"
```

2.21 Assuming the `char` data type uses 1 byte of memory, how many bytes do each of the following literals use?

```
'Q'
"Q"
"Sales"
'\n'
```

2.22 What is wrong with the following program statement?

```
char letter = "Z";
```

2.23 What header file must you include in order to use `string` objects?

2.24 Write a program that stores your name, address, and phone number in three separate `string` objects. Then display their contents on the screen.

2.11 The `bool` Data Type

CONCEPT: Boolean variables are set to either **`true`** or **`false`**.

Expressions that have a `true` or `false` value are called *Boolean* expressions, named in honor of English mathematician George Boole (1815–1864).

The `bool` data type allows you to create variables that hold `true` or `false` values. Program 2-16 demonstrates the definition and use of a `bool` variable. Although it appears that it is storing the *words* true and false, it is actually an integer variable that stores `0` for false and `1` for true, as you can see from the program output.

Program 2-16

```
// This program uses Boolean variables.
#include <iostream>
using namespace std;

int main()
{
   bool boolValue;

   boolValue = true;
   cout << boolValue << endl;

   boolValue = false;
   cout << boolValue << endl;
   return 0;
}
```

Program Output

```
1
0
```

2.12 Determining the Size of a Data Type

CONCEPT: **The `sizeof` operator may be used to determine the size of a data type on any system.**

Chapter 1 discussed the portability of the C++ language. As you have seen in this chapter, one of the problems of portability is the lack of common sizes of data types on all machines. If you are not sure what the sizes of data types are on your computer, C++ provides a way to find out.

A special operator called `sizeof` will report the number of bytes of memory used by any data type or variable. Program 2-17 illustrates its use. The first line that uses the operator is line 9.

```
cout << "The size of an integer is " << sizeof(int);
```

The name of the data type or variable is placed inside the parentheses that follow the operator. The operator "returns" the number of bytes used by that item. This operator can be used anywhere you can use an unsigned integer, including in mathematical operations.

Program 2-17

```
1  // This program displays the size of various data types.
2  #include <iostream>
3  using namespace std;
4
5  int main()
6  {
7     long double apple;
8
9     cout << "The size of an integer is " << sizeof(int);
10    cout << " bytes.\n";
11    cout << "The size of a long integer is " << sizeof(long);
12    cout << " bytes.\n";
13    cout << "An apple can be eaten in " << sizeof(apple);
14    cout << " bytes!\n";
15    return 0;
16 }
```

Program Output

```
The size of an integer is 4 bytes.
The size of a long integer is 4 bytes.
An apple can be eaten in 8 bytes!
```

2.13 More on Variable Assignments and Initialization

CONCEPT: **An assignment operation assigns, or copies, a value into a variable. When a value is assigned to a variable as part of the variable's definition, it is called an initialization.**

VideoNote

Assignment Statements

As you have already seen in several examples, a value is stored in a variable with an *assignment statement*. For example, the following statement copies the value 12 into the variable `unitsSold`.

```
unitsSold = 12;
```

The = symbol, as you recall, is called the *assignment operator.* Operators perform operations on data. The data that operators work with are called *operands*. The assignment operator has two operands. In the previous statement, the operands are `unitsSold` and `12`.

It is important to remember that in an assignment statement, C++ requires the name of the variable receiving the assignment to appear on the left side of the operator. The following statement is incorrect.

```
12 = unitsSold;  // Incorrect!
```

In C++ terminology, the operand on the left side of the = symbol must be an lvalue. An *lvalue* is something that identifies a place in memory whose contents may be changed, so a new value can be stored there. Most of the time the lvalue will be a variable name. It is called an lvalue because it is a value that may appear on the left-hand side of an assignment operator.

The operand on the right side of the = symbol must be an rvalue. An *rvalue* is any expression that has a value. This could be a single number, like 12, or the result of a calculation, such as 4 + 8. The assignment statement evaluates the expression on the right-hand side to get the value of the rvalue and then puts it in the memory location identified by the lvalue. Both of the following statements assign the value 12 to the `unitsSold` variable.

```
unitsSold = 12;
unitsSold = 4 + 8;
```

You have also seen that it is possible to assign values to variables when they are defined. This is called *initialization*. When multiple variables are defined in the same statement, it is possible to initialize some of them without having to initialize all of them. Program 2-18 illustrates this.

Program 2-18

```
// This program shows variable initialization.
#include <iostream>
#include <string>
using namespace std;

int main()
{
   string month = "February";     // month is initialized to "February"
   int year,                      // year is not initialized
       days = 28;                 // days is initialized to 28

   year = 2007;                   // Now year is assigned a value

   cout << "In "   << year << " " << month
        << " had " << days << " days.\n";

   return 0;
}
```

Program Output

```
In 2007 February had 28 days.
```

2.14 Scope

CONCEPT: A variable's scope is the part of the program that has access to the variable.

Every variable has a *scope*. The scope of a variable is the part of the program where it may be used. The rules that define a variable's scope are complex, and we will just introduce the concept here. Later in the book we will cover this topic in more depth.

The first rule of scope is that a variable cannot be used in any part of the program before it is defined. Program 2-19 illustrates this.

Program 2-19

```
 1 // This program can't find its variable.
 2 #include <iostream>
 3 using namespace std;
 4
 5 int main()
 6 {
 7    cout << value;    // ERROR! value has not been defined yet!
 8
 9    int value = 100;
10    return 0;
11 }
```

The program will not work because line 7 attempts to send the contents of the variable `value` to `cout` before the variable is defined. The compiler reads a program from top to bottom. If it encounters a statement that uses a variable before the variable is defined, an error will result. To correct the program, the variable definition must be put before any statement that uses it.

2.15 Arithmetic Operators

CONCEPT: There are many operators for manipulating numeric values and performing arithmetic operations.

VideoNote
Arithmetic Operators

C++ provides many operators for manipulating data. Generally, there are three types of operators: unary, binary, and ternary. These terms reflect the number of operands an operator requires.

Unary operators only require a single operand. For example, consider the following expression: −5

Of course, we understand this represents the value negative five. The constant 5 is preceded by the minus sign. The minus sign, when used this way, is called the *negation operator.* Since it only requires one operand, it is a unary operator.

Binary operators work with two operands. *Ternary operators*, as you may have guessed, require three operands. C++ only has one ternary operator, which will be discussed in Chapter 4.

Arithmetic operations occur frequently in programming. Table 2-9 shows the common arithmetic operators in C++. All are binary operators.

Table 2-9 Fundamental Arithmetic Operators

Operator	Meaning	Example
+	Addition	`total = cost + tax;`
–	Subtraction	`cost = total - tax;`
*	Multiplication	`tax = cost * rate;`
/	Division	`salePrice = original / 2;`
%	Modulus	`remainder = value % 3;`

Here is an example of how each of these operators works.

The *addition operator* returns the sum of its two operands.

```
total = 4 + 8;          // total is assigned the value 12
```

The *subtraction operator* returns the value of its right operand subtracted from its left operand.

```
candyBars = 8 - 3;      // candyBars is assigned the value 5
```

The *multiplication operator* returns the product of its two operands.

```
points = 3 * 7;         // points is assigned the value 21
```

The *division operator* returns the quotient of its left operand divided by its right operand.

```
double points =  5.0 / 2;     // points is assigned the value 2.5
```

However, the division operator works differently depending on whether its operands are integer or floating-point numbers. When either operand is a floating-point number, it performs the "normal" type of division you are familiar with, as shown above. On the other hand, when both operands are integers, the result of the division will also be an integer. If the result has a fractional part, it will be thrown away. This type of division is known as *integer division*.

Here is an example of integer division.

```
double fullBoxes = 26 / 8;    // fullBoxes is assigned 3.0, not 3.25
```

The result of the integer divide is 3 because 8 goes into 26 three whole times with a remainder of 2. The remainder is discarded. When the 3 is assigned to the floating-point variable `fullBoxes`, it is changed into the floating-point value 3.0. The fractional part of the division is discarded even though the result is being assigned to a floating-point variable because the division takes place before the assignment.

If you want the division operator to perform regular division, you must make sure at least one of the operands is a floating-point number.

The *modulus operator* computes the *remainder* of doing an integer divide.

```
leftOver = 26 % 8;       // leftOver is assigned the value 2
```

Figure 2-9 illustrates the use of the integer divide and modulus operations.

Figure 2-9 Integer Divide and Modulus Operations

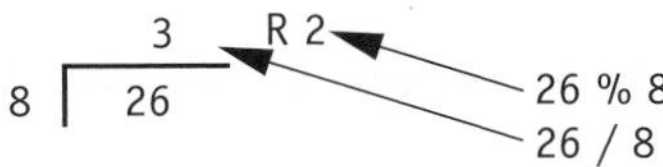

In Chapter 3 you will learn how to use these operators in more complex mathematical formulas. For now we will concentrate on their basic usage. Here is a program that does that. It uses two arithmetic operators, the addition operator and the multiplication operator.

Suppose we need to write a program that calculates and displays an employee's total wages for the week. The regular hours for the work week are 40, and any hours worked over 40 are considered overtime. The employee earns $18.25 per hour for regular hours and $27.38 per hour for overtime hours. The employee has worked 50 hours this week. The following pseudocode algorithm shows the program's logic.

```
Regular wages = base pay rate × regular hours
Overtime wages = overtime pay rate × overtime hours
Total wages = regular wages + overtime wages
Display the total wages
```

Program 2-20 shows the C++ code for the program.

Program 2-20

```
// This program calculates hourly wages, including overtime.
// It uses two arithmetic operators, the addition operator
// and the multiplication operator.
#include <iostream>
using namespace std;

int main()
{
   double basePayRate     = 18.25,    // Base pay rate
          overtimePayRate = 27.38,    // Overtime pay rate
          regularHours    = 40.0,     // Regular hours worked}
          overtimeHours   = 10,       // Overtime hours worked
          regularWages,               // Computed regular wages
          overtimeWages,              // Computed overtime wages
          totalWages;                 // Computed total wages

   // Calculate regular wages
   regularWages = basePayRate * regularHours;

   // Calculate overtime wages
   overtimeWages = overtimePayRate * overtimeHours;

```

(program continues)

Program 2-20 *(continued)*

```
    // Calculate total wages
    totalWages = regularWages + overtimeWages;

    // Display total wages
    cout << "Wages for this week are $" << totalWages << endl;
    return 0;
}
```

Program Output

```
Wages for this week are $1003.8
```

Notice that the output displays the wages as $1003.8, with just one digit after the decimal point. In Chapter 3 you will learn to format output so you can control how it displays.

Here is a program that illustrates two additional arithmetic operators. It uses integer division and the modulus operator to convert seconds into minutes and seconds.

Program 2-21

```
// This program converts seconds to minutes and seconds.
// It uses integer division and the modulus operator.
#include <iostream>
using namespace std;

int main()
{
   int totalSeconds = 125,      // Number of seconds to be converted
   minutes,                     // Number of minutes in totalSeconds
   seconds;                     // Number of seconds remaining

   // Calculate the number of minutes
   minutes = totalSeconds / 60;

   // Calculate the remaining seconds
   seconds = totalSeconds % 60;

   // Display the results
   cout << totalSeconds << " seconds is equivalent to ";
   cout << minutes << " minutes and " << seconds << " seconds. \n";

   return 0;
}
```

Program Output

```
125 seconds is equivalent to 2 minutes and 5 seconds.
```

Checkpoint

2.25 Is the following assignment statement valid or invalid? If it is invalid, why?

```
72 = amount;
```

2.26 What is wrong with the following program? How would you correct it?

```
#include <iostream>
using namespace std;
int main()
{
   critter = 62.7;
   double critter;
   cout << critter << endl;
   return 0;
}
```

2.27 What will be assigned to x in each of the following statements?

```
x = 8 + 3;
x = 8 - 3;
x = 8 * 3;
x = 8 % 3;
```

2.28 Is the following an example of integer division or floating-point division? What value will be displayed?

```
cout << 16 / 3;
```

2.16 Comments

CONCEPT: Comments are notes of explanation that document lines or sections of a program.

It may surprise you that one of the most important parts of a program has absolutely no impact on the way it runs. We are speaking, of course, of the comments. Comments are part of the program, but the compiler ignores them. They are intended for people who may be reading the source code.

Some programmers resist putting more than just a few comments in their source code. After all, it may seem like enough work to type the parts of the program that actually do something. It is crucial, however, that you develop the habit of thoroughly annotating your code with descriptive comments. It might take extra time now, but it will almost certainly save time in the future.

Imagine writing a program of medium complexity with about 8,000 to 10,000 lines of C++ code. Once you have written the code and satisfactorily debugged it, you happily put it away and move on to the next project. Ten months later you are asked to make a modification to the program (or worse, track down and fix an elusive bug). You pull out the massive pile of paper that contains your source code and stare at thousands of statements only to discover they now make no sense at all. You find variables with names like `z2`, and you can't remember what they are for. If only you had left some notes to yourself explaining all the program's nuances and oddities. But it's too late now. All that's left to do is decide what will take less time: figuring out the old program or completely rewriting it!

This scenario might sound extreme, but it's one you don't want to happen to you. Real-world programs are big and complex. Thoroughly documented programs will make your life easier, not to mention the work of other programmers who may have to read your code in the future. In addition to telling what the program does and describing the purpose of variables, comments can also be used to explain complex procedures in your code and to provide information such as who wrote the program and when it was written or last modified.

Single Line Comments

You have already seen one way to place comments in a C++ program. As illustrated in programs throughout this chapter, you simply place two forward slashes (`//`) where you want the comment to begin. The compiler ignores everything from that point to the end of the line. This is called a *single line comment*.

Multi-Line Comments

The second type of comment in C++ is the *multi-line comment*. Multi-line comments start with /* (a forward slash followed by an asterisk) and end with */ (an asterisk followed by a forward slash). Everything between these markers is ignored. Program 2-22 illustrates the use of both a multi-line comment and single line comments. The multi-line comment starts on line 1 with the /* symbol, and ends on line 6 with the */ symbol.

Program 2-22

```
 1 /*
 2    PROGRAM: Payroll.cpp
 3    Written by Herbert Dorfmann
 4    This program calculates company payroll
 5    Last modified: 8/20/2012
 6 */
 7 #include <iostream>
 8 using namespace std;
 9
10 int main()
11 {
12    int employeeID;     // Employee ID number
13    double payRate;     // Employees hourly pay rate
14    double hours;       // Hours employee worked this week

(The remainder of this program is left out.)
```

Notice that unlike a comment started with `//`, a multi-line comment can span several lines. This makes it more convenient to write large blocks of comments because you do not have to mark every line. On the other hand, the multi-line comment is inconvenient for writing single line comments because you must type both a beginning and ending comment symbol.

NOTE: Many programmers use a combination of single line comments and multi-line comments, as illustrated in the previous sample program. Convenience usually dictates which style to use.

When using multi-line comments:

- Be careful not to reverse the beginning symbol with the ending symbol.
- Be sure not to forget the ending symbol.

Both of these mistakes can be difficult to track down and will prevent the program from compiling correctly.

2.17 Programming Style

CONCEPT: Programming style refers to the way a programmer uses identifiers, spaces, tabs, blank lines, and punctuation characters to visually arrange a program's source code. These are some, but not all, of the elements of programming style.

In Chapter 1 you learned that syntax rules govern the way a language may be used. The syntax rules of C++ dictate how and where to place key words, semicolons, commas, braces, and other components of the language. The compiler's job is to check for syntax errors and, if there are none, to generate object code.

When the compiler reads a program it processes it as one long stream of characters. The compiler is not influenced by whether each statement is on a separate line, or whether spaces separate operators from operands. Humans, on the other hand, find it difficult to read programs that aren't written in a visually pleasing manner. Consider Program 2-23 for example.

Program 2-23

```
#include <iostream>
using namespace std;int main(){double shares=220.0;double
avgPrice=14.67;cout
<<"There were "<<shares<<" shares sold at $"<<avgPrice<<
" per share.\n";return 0;}
```

Program Output

```
There were 220 shares sold at $14.67 per share.
```

Although the program is syntactically correct (it doesn't violate any rules of C++), it is difficult to read. The same program is shown in Program 2-24, written in a clearer style.

Program 2-24

```
// This program is visually arranged to make it readable.
#include <iostream>
using namespace std;

```

(program continues)

Program 2-24 *(continued)*

```
int main()
{
   double shares = 220.0;
   double avgPrice = 14.67;

   cout << "There were " << shares << " shares sold at $";
   cout << avgPrice << " per share.\n";
   return 0;
}
```

Program Output

```
There were 220 shares sold at $14.67 per share.
```

Programming style refers to the way source code is visually arranged. Ideally, it is a consistent method of putting spaces and indentions in a program so visual cues are created. These cues quickly tell a programmer important information about a program.

For example, notice in Program 2-24 that the opening and closing braces of the `main` function align and inside the braces each line is indented. It is a common C++ style to indent all the lines inside a set of braces. You will also notice the blank line between the variable definitions and the `cout` statements. This is intended to visually separate the definitions from the executable statements.

NOTE: Although you are free to develop your own style, you should adhere to common programming practices. By doing so, you will write programs that visually make sense to other programmers and that minimize the likelihood of errors.

Another aspect of programming style is how to handle statements that are too long to fit on one line. Because C++ is a free-flowing language, it is usually possible to spread a statement over several lines. For example, here is a `cout` statement that uses four lines:

```
cout << "The Fahrenheit temperature is "
     << fahrenheit
     << " and the Celsius temperature is "
     << celsius << endl;
```

This statement works just as if it were typed on one line. You have already seen variable definitions treated similarly:

```
int fahrenheit,
    celsius,
    kelvin;
```

Other issues related to programming style will be presented throughout the book.

2.18 Tying It All Together: *Smile!*

With just the little bit of C++ covered so far, you can print pictures using `cout` statements. Here is the code to make a simple smiley face. Try it!

```
 ^   ^
   *
 \___/
```

Program 2-25

```
// This program prints a simple smiley face.
#include <iostream>
using namespace std;

int main()
{
   cout << "\n\n";
   cout << "      ^   ^   \n";
   cout << "        *     \n";
   cout << "      \\___/  \n";
   return 0;
}
```

Now try revising Program 2-25 to make faces like these.

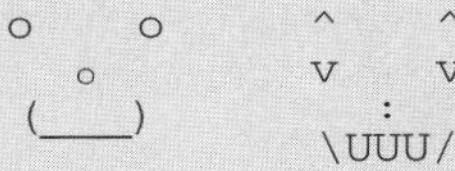

Review Questions and Exercises

Fill-in-the-Blank and Short Answer

1. Every complete statement ends with a __________.
2. To use `cout` statements you must include the __________ file in your program.
3. Every C++ program must have a function named __________.
4. Preprocessor directives begin with a __________.
5. A group of statements, such as the body of a function, must be enclosed in __________.
6. `72`, `'A'`, and `"Hello World"` are all examples of __________.

7. 978.65×10^{12} would be written in E notation as __________.

8. The character literal `'A'` requires __________ byte(s) of memory, whereas the string literal `"A"` requires __________ byte(s).

9. Which of the following are *not* valid assignment statements?

   A) `total = 9;`
   B) `72 = amount;`
   C) `yourAge = myAge;`

10. If the variable `letter` has been defined as a `char` variable, which of the following are *not* valid assignment statements?

    A) `letter = w;`
    B) `letter = 'w';`
    C) `letter = "w";`

11. Which of the following are *not* valid `cout` statements?

    A) `cout << "Hello" << endl;`
    B) `cout << "Hello" << \n;`
    C) `cout << Hello;`

12. Which of the following are *not* valid `cout` statements?

    A) `cout << "Hello world";`
    B) `cout << Hello world;`
    C) `cout << "Hello" << " world";`

13. Assume `x = 4`, `y = 7`, and `z = 2`. What value will be stored in integer variable `result` by each of the following statements?

    A) `result = x + y;`
    B) `result = y * 2;`
    C) `result = y / z;`

14. Assume `x = 2.5`, `y = 7.0`, and `z = 3`. What value will be stored in integer variable `result` by each of the following statements?

    A) `result = x + y;`
    B) `result = y * 2;`
    C) `result = y / z;`

15. Write a C++ statement that defines the `double` variables `temp`, `weight`, and `height` all in the same statement.

16. Write a C++ statement that defines the `int` variables `months`, `days`, and `years` all in the same statement, with `months` initialized to 2 and `years` initialized to 3.

17. Write assignment statements that perform the following operations with `int` variable `i`, `double` variables `d1` and `d2`, and `char` variable `c`.

    A) Add 2 to `d1` and store the result in `d2`.
    B) Multiply `d2` times 4 and store the result in `d1`.
    C) Store the character `'K'` in `c`.
    D) Store the ASCII code for the character `'K'` in `i`.
    E) Subtract 1 from `i` and store the result back in `i`.

18. Write assignment statements that perform the following operations with `int` variable `i`, `double` variables `d1` and `d2`, and `char` variable `c`.

    A) Subtract 8.5 from `d2` and store the result in `d1`.
    B) Divide `d1` by 3.14 and store the result in `d2`.
    C) Store the ASCII code for the character `'F'` in `c`.
    D) Add 1 to `i` and store the new value back in `i`.
    E) Add `d1` to the current value of `d2` and store the result back in `d2` as its new value.

19. Modify the following program segment so it prints two blank lines between each line of text.

```
cout << "Two mandolins like creatures in the";
cout << "dark";
cout << "Creating the agony of ecstasy.";
cout << "                    - George Barker";
```

20. Rewrite the follow statement to use the newline escape character, instead of an `endl`, each time subsequent output is to be displayed on a new line.

```
cout << "L" << endl
     << "E" << endl
     << "A" << endl
     << "F" << endl;
```

Algorithm Workbench

21. Create detailed pseudocode for a program that calculates how many days are left until Christmas, when given as an input how many weeks are left until Christmas. Use variables named `weeks` and `days`.

22. Create detailed pseudocode for a program that determines how many full 12-egg cartons of eggs a farmer can pack when given as an input the number of eggs he has collected on a given day. Use variables named `eggs` and `cartons`.

23. Create detailed pseudocode for a program that determines distance traveled when given inputs of speed and time. Use variables named `speed`, `time`, and `distance`.

24. Create detailed pseudocode for a program that determines miles per gallon a vehicle gets when given inputs of miles traveled and gallons of gas used. Use variables named `miles`, `gallons`, and `milesPerGallon`.

Predict the Output

25. What will the following programs print on the screen?

    A)
```
#include <iostream>
using namespace std;
int main()
{
    int freeze = 32, boil = 212;
    freeze = 0;
    boil = 100;
    cout << freeze << endl << boil << endl;
    return 0;
}
```

B)
```
#include <iostream>
using namespace std;
int main()
{
    int x = 0, y = 2;
    x = y * 4;
    cout << x << endl << y << endl;
    return 0;
}
```

C)
```
#include <iostream>
using namespace std;
int main()
{
    cout << "I am the incredible";
    cout << "computing\nmachine";
    cout << "\nand I will\namaze\n";
    cout << "you.\n";
    return 0;
}
```

26. A)
```
#include <iostream>
using namespace std;

int main()
{
    cout << "Be careful!\n";
    cout << "This might/n be a trick ";
    cout << "question.\n";
    return 0;
}
```

B)
```
#include <iostream>
using namespace std;

int main()
{
    int a, x = 23;

    a = x % 2;
    cout << x << endl << a << endl;
    return 0;
}
```

Find the Error

27. The following program contains syntax errors. Locate as many as you can.

```
*/ What's wrong with this program? /*
#include iostream
using namespace std;

int main();
}
   int a, b, c    \\ Three integers
   a = 3
   b = 4
   c = a + b
   Cout < "The value of c is %d" < C;
   return 0;
{
```

Soft Skills

Programmers need good communication skills as well as good analytical and problem-solving skills. Good communication can minimize misunderstandings that easily arise when expectations of different individuals involved in a project are not clearly enough articulated before the project begins. A detailed set of project specifications can clarify the scope of a project, what interaction will occur between the user and the program, and exactly what the program will and will not do.

28. Pair up with another student in the class. One of you is the client and the other is the software developer. Briefly discuss a simple program the client wants the programmer to create. Here are some possible ideas.
    - the paint problem described in the Chapter 1 Soft Skills exercise
    - a program that can halve the quantities of ingredients for a recipe
    - a program that determines how long it will take to drive from point A to point B

Once you have decided on a program, you should independently, with no further communication, each write down detailed specifications. The client writes down exactly what he wants the program to do and the developer writes down her understanding of exactly what the program will do. When you are done, compare what you have written. Rarely will the two agree.

Now discuss the discrepancies and see if you can come to a clear understanding of exactly what the program must do. Together create a program specification sufficiently detailed that both of you believe it leaves no room for misunderstanding.

Programming Challenges

1. Sum of Two Numbers

Write a program that stores the integers 62 and 99 in variables and stores the sum of these two in a variable named `total`. Display the total on the screen.

2. Sales Prediction

The East Coast sales division of a company generates 62 percent of total sales. Based on that percentage, write a program that will predict how much the East Coast division will generate if the company has $4.6 million in sales this year. Display the result on the screen.

3. Sales Tax

Write a program that computes the total sales tax on a $52 purchase. Assume the state sales tax is 4 percent and the county sales tax is 2 percent. Display the purchase price, state tax, county tax, and total tax amounts on the screen.

VideoNote
Solving the Restaurant Bill Problem

4. Restaurant Bill

Write a program that computes the tax and tip on a restaurant bill for a patron with a $44.50 meal charge. The tax should be 6.75 percent of the meal cost. The tip should be 15 percent of the total after adding the tax. Display the meal cost, tax amount, tip amount, and total bill on the screen.

5. Cyborg Data Type Sizes

You have been given a job as a programmer on a Cyborg supercomputer. In order to accomplish some calculations, you need to know how many bytes the following data types use: `char`, `int`, `float`, and `double`. You do not have any manuals, so you can't look up this information. Write a C++ program that will determine the amount of memory used by each of these types and display the information on the screen.

6. Miles per Gallon

A car holds 16 gallons of gasoline and can travel 350 miles before refueling. Write a program that calculates the number of miles per gallon the car gets. Display the result on the screen.

7. Distance per Tank of Gas

A car with a 20 gallon gas tank averages 21.5 miles per gallon when driven in town and 26.8 miles per gallon when driven on the highway. Write a program that calculates and displays the distance the car can travel on one tank of gas when driven in town and when driven on the highway.

8. Land Calculation

In the United States, land is often measured in square feet. In many other countries it is measured in square meters. One acre of land is equivalent to 43,560 square feet. A square meter is equivalent to 10.7639 square feet. Write a program that computes and displays the number of square feet and the number of square meters in $\frac{1}{4}$ acre of land.

Hint: Because a square meter is larger than a square foot, there will be fewer square meters in $\frac{1}{4}$ acre than there are square feet.

9. Circuit Board Price

An electronics company sells circuit boards at a 40 percent profit. Write a program that calculates the selling price of a circuit board that costs them $12.67 to produce. Display the result on the screen.

10. Personal Information

Write a program that displays the following information, each on a separate line:

Your name
Your address, with city, state, and zip code
Your telephone number
Your college major

Use only a single `cout` statement to display all of this information.

11. Triangle Pattern

Write a program that displays the following pattern on the screen:

```
   *
  ***
 *****
*******
```

12. Diamond Pattern

Write a program that displays the following pattern on the screen:

13. Pay Period Gross Pay

A particular employee earns $32,500 annually. Write a program that determines and displays what the amount of his gross pay will be for each pay period if he is paid twice a month (24 pay checks per year) and if he is paid bi-weekly (26 checks per year).

14. Basketball Player Height

The star player of a high school basketball team is 73 inches tall. Write a program to compute and display the height in feet / inches form.

Hint: Try using the modulus and integer divide operations.

15. Stock Loss

Kathryn bought 600 shares of stock at a price of $21.77 per share. A year later she sold them for just $16.44 per share. Write a program that calculates and displays the following:

- The total amount paid for the stock.
- The total amount received from selling the stock.
- The total amount of money she lost.

16. Energy Drink Consumption

A soft drink company recently surveyed 12,467 of its customers and found that approximately 14 percent of those surveyed purchase one or more energy drinks per week. Of those customers who purchase energy drinks, approximately 64 percent of them prefer citrus flavored energy drinks. Write a program that displays the following:

- The approximate number of customers in the survey who purchase one or more energy drinks per week.
- The approximate number of customers in the survey who prefer citrus flavored energy drinks.

17. Past Ocean Levels

The Earth's ocean levels have risen an average of 1.8 millimeters per year over the past century. Write a program that computes and displays the number of centimeters and number of inches the oceans rose during this time. One millimeter is equivalent to 0.1 centimeters. One centimeter is equivalent to 0.3937 inches.

18. Future Ocean Levels

During the past decade ocean levels have been rising faster than in the past, an average of approximately 3.1 millimeters per year. Write a program that computes how much ocean levels are expected to rise during the next 20 years if they continue rising at this rate. Display the answer in both centimeters and inches.

CHAPTER

3 Expressions and Interactivity

TOPICS

3.1 The `cin` Object

CONCEPT: `cin` can be used to read data typed at the keyboard.

So far you have written programs with built-in information. You have initialized the variables with the necessary starting values without letting the user enter his or her own data. These types of programs are limited to performing their task with only a single set of starting information. If you decide to change the initial value of any variable, the program must be modified and recompiled.

VideoNote
Using `cin` to Read Input

In reality, most programs ask for values that will be assigned to variables. This means the program does not have to be modified if the user wants to run it several times with different sets of information. For example, a program that calculates the area of a circle might ask the user to enter the circle's radius. When the circle area has been computed and printed, the program could be run again and a different radius could be entered.

Just as C++ provides the `cout` object to produce console output, it provides an object named `cin` that is used to read console input. (You can think of the word `cin` as meaning console **in**put.) Program 3-1 shows `cin` being used to read values input by the user. Notice that in line 2 there is a `#include` statement to include the `iostream` file. This file must be included in any program that uses `cin`.

Program 3-1

```
1 // This program calculates and displays the area of a rectangle.
2 #include <iostream>
3 using namespace std;
4
5 int main()
6 {
7    int length, width, area;
8
9    cout << "This program calculates the area of a rectangle.\n";
10
11   // Have the user input the rectangle's length and width
12   cout << "What is the length of the rectangle? ";
13   cin  >> length;
14   cout << "What is the width of the rectangle? ";
15   cin  >> width;
16
17   // Compute and display the area
18   area = length * width;
19   cout << "The area of the rectangle is " << area << endl;
20   return 0;
21 }
```

Program Output with Example Input Shown in Bold

```
This program calculates the area of a rectangle.
What is the length of the rectangle? 10[Enter]
What is the width of the rectangle? 20[Enter]
The area of the rectangle is 200.
```

Instead of calculating the area of one rectangle, this program can be used to compute the area of any rectangle. The values that are stored in the `length` and `width` variables are entered by the user when the program is running. Look at lines 12 and 13.

```
cout << "What is the length of the rectangle? ";
cin  >> length;
```

In line 12 `cout` is used to display the question "What is the length of the rectangle?" This is called a *prompt*. It lets the user know that an input is expected and prompts them as to what must be entered. When `cin` will be used to get input from the user, it should always be preceded by a prompt.

Line 13 uses `cin` to read a value from the keyboard. The >> symbol is the *stream extraction operator*, which *extracts* characters from the input stream so they can be used in the program. More specifically, the stream extraction operator gets characters from the stream object on its left and stores them in the variable whose name appears on its right. In this example line, the characters read in by `cin` are taken from the `cin` object and stored in the `length` variable.

Gathering input from the user is normally a two-step process:

1. Use `cout` to display a prompt on the screen.
2. Use `cin` to read a value from the keyboard.

The prompt should ask the user a question, or tell the user to enter a specific value. For example, the code we just examined from Program 3-1 displays the following prompt:

```
What is the length of the rectangle?
```

This tells the user to enter the rectangle's length. After the prompt displays, the program uses `cin` to read a value from the keyboard and store it in the `length` variable.

Notice that the << and >> operators appear to point in the direction that data is flowing. It may help to think of them as arrows. In a statement that uses `cout`, the << operator always points toward `cout`, as shown here. This indicates that data is flowing from a variable or a literal to the `cout` object.

```
cout << "What is the length of the rectangle? ";
cout ← "What is the length of the rectangle? ";
```

In a statement that uses `cin`, the >> operator always points toward the variable receiving the value. This indicates that data is flowing from the `cin` object to a variable.

```
cin >> length;
cin → length;
```

The `cin` object causes a program to wait until data is typed at the keyboard and the [Enter] key is pressed. No other lines will be executed until `cin` gets its input.

When the user enters characters from the keyboard, they are temporarily placed in an area of memory called the *input buffer*, or *keyboard buffer.* When `cin` reads them, it automatically converts them to the data type of the variable where the input data will be stored. For example, if the user types 10, it is read as the characters '1' and '0', but `cin` is smart enough to know this will have to be converted to the `int` value 10 before it is stored in `length`. If the user enters a floating-point number like 10.7, however, there is a problem. `cin` knows such a value cannot be stored in an integer variable, so it stops reading when it gets to the decimal point, leaving the decimal point and the rest of the digits in the input buffer. This can cause a problem when the next value is read in. Program 3-2 illustrates this problem.

Program 3-2

```
// This program illustrates what can happen when a
// floating-point number is entered for an integer variable.
#include <iostream>
using namespace std;

int main()
{
   int intNumber;
   double floatNumber;

   cout << "Input a number. ";
   cin  >> intNumber;
   cout << "Input a second number.\n";
   cin  >> floatNumber;
   cout << "You entered: " << intNumber
        << " and " << floatNumber << endl;
```

(program continues)

Program 3-2 *(continued)*

```

   return 0;
}
```

Program Output with Example Input Shown in Bold

```
Input a number. 12.3[Enter]
Input a second number.
You entered: 12 and 0.3
```

Let's look more closely at what occurred in Program 3-2. When prompted for the first number, the user entered 12.3 from the keyboard. However, because `cin` was reading a value into `intNumber`, an integer variable, it stopped reading when it got to the decimal point, and a 12 was stored in `intNumber`. When the second `cin` statement needed a value to read into `floatNumber`, it found that it already had a value in the input buffer, the .3 left over from the user's first input. Instead of waiting for the user to enter a second number, the .3 was read in and stored in `floatNumber`.

Later you will learn how to prevent something like this from happening, but for now this illustrates the need to provide the user with clear prompts. If the user had been specifically prompted to enter an integer for the first number, there would have been less chance of a problem occurring.

NOTE: Remember to include the `iostream` file in any program that uses `cout` or `cin`.

Entering Multiple Values

You can use `cin` to input multiple values at once. Program 3-3 is a modified version of Program 3-1 that does this.

Program 3-3

```
// This program calculates and displays the area of a rectangle.
#include <iostream>
using namespace std;

int main()
{
   int length, width, area;

   cout << "This program calculates the area of a rectangle.\n";

   // Have the user input the rectangle's length and width
   cout << "Enter the length and width of the rectangle ";
   cout << "separated by a space.\n";
   cin  >> length >> width;

```

(program continues)

Program 3-3 *(continued)*

```
16    // Compute and display the area
17    area = length * width;
18    cout << "The area of the rectangle is " << area << endl;
19    return 0;
20 }
```

Program Output with Example Input Shown in Bold

```
This program calculates the area of a rectangle.
Enter the length and width of the rectangle separated by a space.
```
10 20[Enter]
```
The area of the rectangle is 200
```

Line 14 waits for the user to enter two values. The first is assigned to `length` and the second to `width`.

```
cin >> length >> width;
```

In the example output, the user entered 10 and 20, so 10 is stored in `length` and 20 is stored in `width`.

Notice the user separates the numbers by spaces as they are entered. This is how `cin` knows where each number begins and ends. It doesn't matter how many spaces are entered between the individual numbers. For example, the user could have entered

```
10            20
```

NOTE: The **[Enter]** key must be pressed after the last number is entered.

You can also read multiple values of different data types with a single `cin` statement. This is shown in Program 3-4.

Program 3-4

```
// This program demonstrates how cin can read multiple values
// of different data types.
#include <iostream>
using namespace std;

int main()
{
   int whole;
   double fractional;
   char letter;

   cout << "Enter an integer, a double, and a character: ";
   cin  >> whole >> fractional >> letter;

   cout << "whole: " << whole << endl;
   cout << "fractional: " << fractional << endl;
   cout << "letter: " << letter << endl;
   return 0;
}
```

(program continues)

Program 3-4 *(continued)*

Program Output with Example Input Shown in Bold
```
Enter an integer, a double, and a character: 4 5.7 b[Enter]
whole: 4
fractional: 5.7
letter: b
```

As you can see in the example output, and in Figure 3-1, the values are stored in the order entered in their respective variables.

Figure 3-1

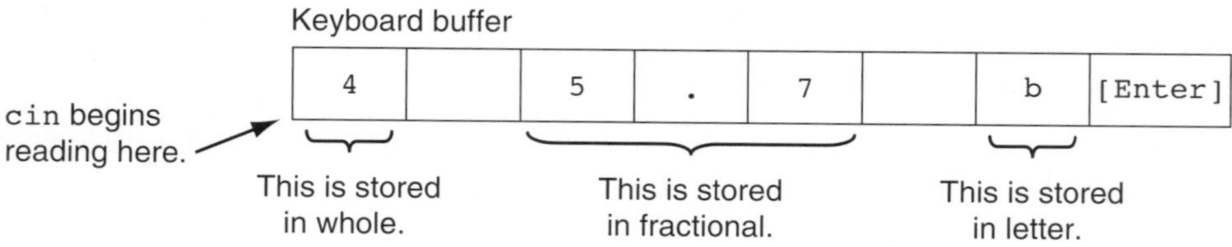

But what if the user had entered the values in the wrong order, as shown in the following sample run?

Program 3-4 Output with Different Example Input Shown in Bold
```
Enter an integer, a double, and a character: 5.7 4 b[Enter]
whole: 5
fractional: 0.7
letter: 4
```

Because the data was not entered in the specified order, there is a complete mix-up of what value is stored for each variable. Figure 3-2 illustrates what happens.

Figure 3-2

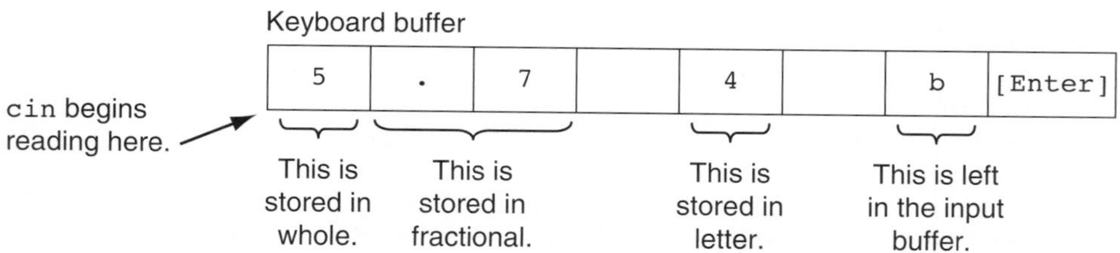

The `cin` statement on line 13 reads `5` for `int` variable `whole`, `.7` for `double` variable `fractional`, and `4` for `char` variable `letter`. The character `b` is left in the input buffer. For a program to function correctly it is important that the user enter data values in the order the program expects to receive them, and not enter a floating-point number when an integer is expected.

Checkpoint

3.1 What header file must be included in programs using cin?

3.2 What is the >> symbol called?

3.3 Where does cin read its input from?

3.4 True or False: cin requires the user to press the **[Enter]** key after entering data.

3.5 Assume value is an integer variable. If the user enters 3.14 in response to the following programming statement, what will be stored in value?

```
cin >> value;
```

3.6 A program has the following variable definitions.

```
long miles;
int feet;
double inches;
```

Write a single cin statement that reads a value into each of these variables.

3.7 The following program will run, but the user will have difficulty understanding what to do. How would you improve the program?

```
// This program multiplies two numbers and displays the result.
#include <iostream>
using namespace std;

int main()
{
   double first, second, product;
   cin >> first >> second;
   product = first * second;
   cout << product;
   return 0;
}
```

3.8 Complete the following program skeleton so it asks for the user's weight (in pounds) and displays the equivalent weight in kilograms.

```
#include <iostream>
using namespace std;

int main()
{
   double pounds, kilograms;

   // Write a prompt to tell the user to enter his or her weight
   // in pounds.
   // Write code here that reads in the user's weight in pounds.
   // The following line does the conversion.

   kilograms = pounds / 2.2;

   // Write code here that displays the user's weight in kilograms.

   return 0;
}
```

3.2 Mathematical Expressions

CONCEPT: C++ allows you to construct complex mathematical expressions using multiple operators and grouping symbols.

VideoNote
Evaluating Mathematical Expressions

In Chapter 2 you were introduced to the basic mathematical operators, which are used to build mathematical expressions. An *expression* is a programming statement that has a value. Usually, an expression consists of an operator and its operands. Look at the following statement:

```
sum = 21 + 3;
```

Since 21 + 3 has a value, it is an expression. Its value, 24, is stored in the variable `sum`. Expressions do not have to be in the form of mathematical operations. In the following statement, 3 is an expression.

```
number = 3;
```

Here are some programming statements where the variable `result` is being assigned the value of an expression. They are called assignment statements.

```
result = x;
result = 4;
result = 15 / 3;
result = 22 * number;
result = sizeof(int);
result = a + b + c;
```

In each of these statements, a number, variable name, or mathematical expression appears on the right side of the = symbol. A value is obtained from each of these and stored in the variable `result`. These are all examples of a variable being assigned the value of an expression.

Although some instructors prefer that you not perform mathematical operations within a `cout` statement, it is possible to do so. Program 3-5 illustrates how to do this.

Program 3-5

```
// This program displays the decimal value of a fraction.
#include <iostream>
using namespace std;

int main()
{
   double numerator, denominator;

   cout << "This program shows the decimal value of a fraction.\n";

   // Have the user enter the numerator and denominator
   cout << "Enter the numerator: ";
   cin  >> numerator;
   cout << "Enter the denominator: ";
   cin  >> denominator;
```

(program continues)

Program 3-5 *(continued)*

```

    // Compute and display the decimal value
    cout << "The decimal value is "<< (numerator / denominator) << endl;
    return 0;
}
```

Program Output with Example Input Shown in Bold

```
This program shows the decimal value of a fraction.
Enter the numerator: 3[Enter]
Enter the denominator: 16[Enter]
The decimal value is 0.1875
```

The `cout` object can display the value of any legal expression in C++. In Program 3-5 the value of the expression `numerator` / `denominator` is displayed.

NOTE: The Program 3-5 example input shows the user entering 3 and 16. Because these values are assigned to `double` variables, they are stored as 3.0 and 16.0.

NOTE: When sending an expression that includes an operator to `cout`, it is always a good idea to put parentheses around the expression. Some operators will yield unexpected results otherwise.

Operator Precedence

It is possible to build mathematical expressions with several operators. The following statement assigns the sum of 17, *x*, 21, and *y* to the variable `answer`.

```
answer = 17 + x + 21 + y;
```

Some expressions are not that straightforward, however. Consider the following statement:

```
outcome = 12 + 6 / 3;
```

What value will be stored in `outcome`? It could be assigned either 6 or 14, depending on whether the addition operation or the division operation takes place first. The answer is 14 because the division operator has higher *precedence* than the addition operator. This is exactly the same as the operator precedence found in algebra.

Mathematical expressions are evaluated from left to right. However, when there are two operators and one has higher precedence than the other, it is done first. Multiplication and division have higher precedence than addition and subtraction, so the example statement works like this:

- First, 6 is divided by 3, yielding a result of 2.
- Then, 12 is added to 2, yielding a result of 14.
- Finally, 14 is stored in the outcome variable.

These steps could be diagrammed in the following way:

```
outcome = 12  +  6 / 3
                 \___/
outcome = 12  +    2
          \________/
outcome =      14
```

Table 3-1 shows the precedence of the arithmetic operators. The operators at the top of the table have higher precedence than the ones below them.

Table 3-1 Precedence of Arithmetic Operators (Highest to Lowest)

`( )`		Expressions within parentheses are evaluated first
`-`	unary	Negation of a value, e.g., –6
`* / %`	binary	Multiplication, division, and modulus
`+ -`	binary	Addition and subtraction

The multiplication, division, and modulus operators have the same precedence. This is also true of the addition and subtraction operators. Table 3-2 shows some expressions with their values.

Table 3-2 Some Expressions

Expression	Value
`5 + 2 * 4`	13
`10 / 2 - 3`	2
`8 + 12 * 2 - 4`	28
`4 + 17 % 2 - 1`	4
`6 - 3 * 2 + 7 - 1`	6

Associativity

Associativity is the order in which an operator works with its operands. Associativity is either *left to right* or *right to left*. The associativity of the division operator is left to right, so it divides the operand on its left by the operand on its right. Table 3-3 shows the arithmetic operators and their associativity.

Table 3-3 Associativity of Arithmetic Operators

Operator	Associativity
`(unary negation) -`	Right to left
`* / %`	Left to right
`+ -`	Left to right

Grouping with Parentheses

Parts of a mathematical expression may be grouped with parentheses to force some operations to be performed before others. When a pair of parentheses is encountered, the expression inside the parentheses is evaluated before any expressions outside of it. Thus, in the following statement, a plus b is evaluated first. Then its sum is divided by 4.

```
average = (a + b) / 4;
```

Without the parentheses b would be divided by 4 **before** adding a to the result because the division operator has a higher precedence than the addition operator. Table 3-4 shows more expressions and their values.

Table 3-4 More Arithmetic Expressions

Expression	Value
`(5 + 2) * 4`	28
`10 / (5 - 3)`	5
`8 + 12 * (6 - 2)`	56
`(4 + 17) % 2 - 1`	0
`(6 - 3) * (2 + 7) / 3`	9

Converting Algebraic Expressions to Programming Statements

In algebra it is not always necessary to use an operator for multiplication. C++, however, requires an operator for any mathematical operation. Table 3-5 shows some algebraic expressions that perform multiplication and the equivalent C++ expressions.

Table 3-5 Algebraic and C++ Multiplication Expressions

Algebraic Expression	Operation	C++ Equivalent
6B	6 times B	`6 * B`
(3)(12)	3 times 12	`3 * 12`
4xy	4 times x times y	`4 * x * y`

When converting some algebraic expressions to C++, you may have to insert parentheses that do not appear in the algebraic expression. For example, look at the following expression:

$$x = \frac{a + b}{c}$$

To convert this to a C++ statement, $a + b$ will have to be enclosed in parentheses:

```
x = (a + b) / c;
```

Table 3-6 shows more algebraic expressions and their C++ equivalents.

Table 3-6 Algebraic and C++ Expressions

Algebraic Expression	C++ Expression
$y = 3\frac{x}{2}$	`y = x / 2 * 3;`
$z = 3bc + 4$	`z = 3 * b * c + 4;`
$a = \frac{3x + 2}{4a - 1}$	`a = (3 * x + 2) / (4 * a - 1)`

No Exponents Please!

Unlike many programming languages, C++ does not have an exponent operator. Raising a number to a power requires the use of a *library function*. The C++ library isn't a place where you check out books, but a collection of specialized functions. Think of a library function as a "routine" that performs a specific operation. One of the library functions is called pow, and its purpose is to raise a number to a power. Here is an example of how it's used:

```
area = pow(4.0, 2);
```

This statement contains a *call* to the pow function. The numbers inside the parentheses are *arguments*. Arguments are information being sent to the function. The pow function always raises the first argument to the power of the second argument. In this example, 4.0 is raised to the power of 2. The result is *returned* from the function and used in the statement where the function call appears. The pow function expects floating-point arguments. On some C++ compilers integer arguments will also work, but since many compilers require that at least the first argument be a `double`, that is the convention we use in this book. The value returned from the function is always a `double` number. In this case, 16.0 is returned from pow and assigned to the variable `area`. This is illustrated in Figure 3-3.

Figure 3-3

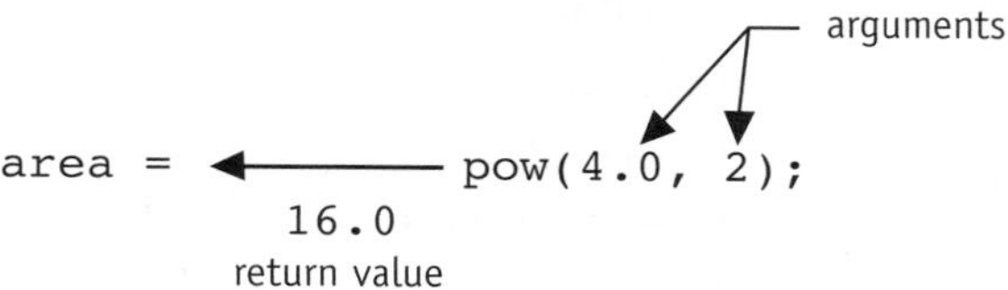

The statement `area = pow(4.0, 2)` is equivalent to the following algebraic statement:

area = 4^2

Here is another example of a statement using the pow function. It assigns 3 times 6^3 to x:

```
x = 3 * pow(6.0, 3);
```

And the following statement displays the value of 5 raised to the power of 4:

```
cout << pow(5.0, 4);
```

It might be helpful to think of pow as a "black box" that accepts two numbers and then sends a third number out. The number that comes out has the value of the first number raised to the power of the second number, as illustrated in Figure 3-4.

Figure 3-4

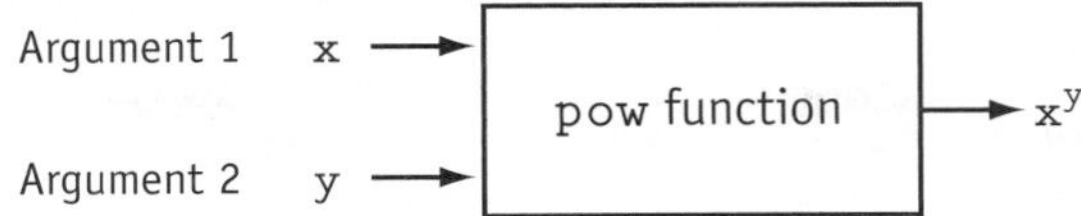

There are some guidelines that should be followed when the `pow` function is used. First, the program must include the `cmath` header file. Second, at least the first of the two arguments you pass to the function, if not both, should be a `double`. Third, because the `pow` function returns a `double` value, any variable that value is assigned to should also be a `double`. For example, in the following statement the variable `area` should be defined as a `double`:

```
area = pow(4.0, 2);
```

Program 3-6 solves a simple algebraic problem. It asks the user to enter the radius of a circle and then calculates the area of the circle. The formula is

$$\text{Area} = \pi r^2$$

which is expressed in the program as

```
area = 3.14159 * pow(radius, 2);
```

Program 3-6

```
// This program calculates the area of a circle. The formula for the
// area of a circle is PI times the radius squared. PI is 3.14159.
#include <iostream>
#include <cmath>      // Needed for the pow function
using namespace std;

int main()
{
   double area, radius;

   cout << "This program calculates the area of a circle.\n";

   // Get the radius
   cout << "What is the radius of the circle? ";
   cin  >> radius;

   // Compute and display the area
   area = 3.14159 * pow(radius, 2);
   cout << "The area is " << area << endl;
   return 0;
}
```

Program Output with Example Input Shown in Bold

```
This program calculates the area of a circle.
What is the radius of the circle? 10[Enter]
The area is 314.159
```

NOTE: Program 3-6 is presented as a demonstration of the pow function. In reality, there is no reason to use this function in such a simple operation. Line 18 could just as easily be written

```
area = 3.14159 * radius * radius;
```

The pow function is useful, however, in operations that involve larger exponents.

Checkpoint

3.9 In each of the following cases, tell which operator has higher precedence or whether they have the same precedence.

A) `+` and `*`

B) `*` and `/`

C) `/` and `%`

3.10 Complete the following table by writing the value of each expression in the Value column.

Expression	Value
6 + 3 * 5	
12 / 2 – 4	
9 + 14 * 2 – 6	
5 + 19 % 3 – 1	
(6 + 2) * 3	
14 / (11 – 4)	
9 + 12 * (8 – 3)	
(6 + 17) % 2 – 1	
(9 – 3) * (6 + 9) / 3	

3.11 Write C++ expressions for the following algebraic expressions:

$$y = 6x$$

$$a = 2b + 4c$$

$$y = x^3$$

$$g = \frac{x + 2}{z^2}$$

$$y = \frac{x^2}{z^2}$$

3.12 Study the following program code and then complete the table following it.

```
double value1, value2, value3;
cout << "Enter a number: ";
cin  >> value1;
value2 = 2 * pow(value1, 2);
value3 = 3 + value2 / 2 - 1;
cout << value3;
```

If the User Enters . . .	The Program Will Display What Number (Stored in `value3`)?
2	
5	
4.3	
6	

3.13 Complete the following program skeleton so it displays the volume of a cylindrical fuel tank. The formula for the volume of a cylinder is

Volume = $\pi r^2 h$

where
π is 3.14159
r is the radius of the tank
h is the height of the tank

```
#include <iostream>
#include <cmath>

int main()
{
   double volume, radius, height;
   cout << "This program will tell you the volume of\n";
   cout << "a cylinder-shaped fuel tank.\n";
   cout << "How tall is the tank? ";
   cin  >> height;
   cout << "What is the radius of the tank? ";
   cin  >> radius;

   // You must complete the program.
   return 0;
}
```

3.3 Data Type Conversion and Type Casting

CONCEPT: Sometimes it is necessary to convert a value from one data type to another. C++ provides ways to do this.

If a floating-point value is assigned to an `int` variable, what value will the variable receive? If an `int` is multiplied by a `float`, what data type will the result be? What if a `double` is divided by an `unsigned int`? Is there any way of predicting what will happen in these instances? The answer is yes. When an operator's operands are of different data types, C++ automatically converts them to the same data type. When it does this it follows a set of rules, and understanding these rules will help you prevent subtle errors from creeping into your programs.

Just like officers in the military, data types are ranked. One data type outranks another if it can hold a larger number. For example, a `float` outranks an `int` and a `double` outranks a `float`. Table 3-7 lists the data types in order of their rank, from highest to lowest.

Table 3-7 Data Type Ranking

`long double`
`double`
`float`
`unsigned long`
`long`
`unsigned int`
`int`

One exception to the ranking in Table 3-7 is when an `int` and a `long` are the same size. In that case, an `unsigned int` outranks `long` because it can hold a higher value.

When C++ is working with an operator, it strives to convert the operands to the same type. This implicit, or automatic, conversion is known as *type coercion*. When a value is converted to a higher data type, it is said to be *promoted*. To *demote* a value means to convert it to a lower data type. Let's look at the specific rules that govern the evaluation of mathematical expressions.

Rule 1: `char`, `short`, and `unsigned short` values are automatically promoted to `int` values.

You will notice that `char`, `short`, and `unsigned short` do not appear in Table 3-7. That's because anytime values of these data types are used in a mathematical expression, they are automatically promoted to an `int`.*

Rule 2: When an operator works with two values of different data types, the lower-ranking value is promoted to the type of the higher-ranking value.

In the following expression, assume that `years` is an `int` variable and `interestRate` is a `double` variable:

```
years * interestRate
```

Before the multiplication takes place, the value in `years` will be promoted to a `double`.

Rule 3: When the final value of an expression is assigned to a variable, it will be converted to the data type of that variable.

In the following statement, assume that `area` is a `long int` variable, while `length` and `width` are both `int` variables:

```
area = length * width;
```

Because the values stored in `length` and `width` are the same data type, neither one will be converted to any other data type. The result of the multiplication, however, will be promoted to `long` so it can be stored in `area`.

* The only exception to this rule is when an `unsigned short` holds a value larger than can be held by an `int`. This can happen on systems where a `short` is the same size as an `int`. In this case, the `unsigned short` is promoted to `unsigned int`.

But what if the variable receiving the value is of a lower data type than the value it is receiving? In this case the value will be demoted to the type of the variable. If the variable's data type does not have enough storage space to hold the value, part of the value will be lost, and the variable could receive an inaccurate result. As mentioned in Chapter 2, if the variable receiving the value is an integer and the value being assigned to it is a floating-point number, the floating-point value will be *truncated* when it is converted to an `int` and stored in the variable. This means everything after the decimal point will be discarded. Here is an example:

```
int x;
double y = 3.75;
x = y;                    // x is assigned 3 and y remains 3.75
```

It is important to understand, however, that when the data type of a variable's value is changed, it does not affect the variable itself. For example, look at the following code segment.

```
int quantity1 = 6;
double quantity2 = 3.7;
double total;

total = quantity1 + quantity2;
```

Before C++ performs the above addition, it moves a copy of `quantity1's` value into its workspace and converts it to a `double`. So 6.0 and 3.7 are added, and the resulting value, 9.7, is stored in `total`. However, the variable `quantity1` remains an `int`, and the value stored there in memory is untouched. It is still the integer 6.

Type Casting

Sometimes programmers want to change the data type of a value explicitly themselves. This can be done by using a type cast expression. A *type cast expression* lets you manually promote or demote a value. Its general format is

```
static_cast<DataType>(Value)
```

where *`Value`* is a variable or literal value that you wish to convert and *`DataType`* is the data type you wish to convert it to. Here is an example of code that uses a type cast expression:

```
double number = 3.7;
int val;
val = static_cast<int>(number);
```

This code defines two variables: `number`, a `double`, and `val`, an `int`. The type cast expression in the third statement returns a copy of the value in `number`, converted to an `int`. When a `double` or `float` is converted to an `int` the fractional part is truncated, so this statement stores 3 in `val`. The value of `number`, `3.7`, is not changed.

Type cast expressions are useful in situations where C++ will not perform the desired conversion automatically. Program 3-7 shows an example where a type cast expression is used to prevent integer division from taking place. The statement that uses the type cast expression is

```
booksPerMonth = static_cast<double>(books) / months;
```

Program 3-7

```
 1 // This program uses a type cast to avoid an integer division.
 2 #include <iostream>
 3 using namespace std;
 4 
 5 int main()
 6 {
 7    int    books,
 8           months;
 9    double booksPerMonth;
10 
11    // Get user inputs
12    cout << "How many books do you plan to read? ";
13    cin  >> books;
14    cout << "How many months will it take you to read them? ";
15    cin  >> months;
16 
17    // Compute and display books read per month
18    booksPerMonth = static_cast<double>(books) / months;
19    cout << "That is " << booksPerMonth << " books per month.\n";
20    return 0;
21 }
```

Program Output with Example Input Shown in Bold

```
How many books do you plan to read? 30[Enter]
How many months will it take you to read them? 7[Enter]
That is 4.28571 books per month.
```

The variable `books` is an integer, but a copy of its value is converted to a `double` before it is used in the division operation. Without the type cast expression in line 18, integer division would have been performed, resulting in an incorrect answer.

It is important to note that if we had written line 18 as shown in the following statement, integer division would still have occurred.

```
booksPerMonth = static_cast<double>(books / months);
```

Because operations inside parentheses are done before other operations, the division operator would perform integer division on its two integer operands, and the result of the expression `books / months` would be 4. The 4 would then be converted to the `double` value 4.0, and this would be the value assigned to `booksPerMonth`.

WARNING! To prevent the integer division from taking place, one of the operands should be converted to a `double` prior to the division operation. This forces C++ to automatically convert the value of the other operand to a `double`.

Program 3-8 shows another use of a type cast.

Program 3-8

```
1 // This program prints a character from its ASCII code.
2 #include <iostream>
3 using namespace std;
4
5 int main()
6 {
7    int number = 65;
8
9    // Display the value of the number variable
10   cout << number << endl;
11
12   // Use a type cast to display the value of number
13   // converted to the char data type
14   cout << static_cast<char>(number) << endl;
15   return 0;
16 }
```

Program Output

```
65
A
```

Let's take a closer look at this program. In line 7 the `int` variable `number` is initialized with the value 65. In line 10, `number` is sent to `cout`, causing 65 to be displayed. In line 14, a type cast expression is used to convert the value in `number` to the `char` data type before sending it to `cout`. Recall from Chapter 2 that characters are stored in memory as integer ASCII codes. Because the number 65 is the ASCII code for the letter 'A', the statement on line 14 causes the letter 'A' to be displayed.

NOTE: C++ provides several different type cast expressions. A `static_cast` is the most commonly used type cast expression, so it is the one we will primarily use in this book. Additional information on type casts is contained in Appendix K.

C-style and Prestandard C++ Type Cast Expressions

C++ also supports two older methods of creating type cast expressions: the C-style form and the prestandard C++ form. The C-style cast places the data type to be converted to, enclosed in parentheses, in front of the operand whose value is to be converted. Here are three examples.

```
cout << (int) 2.6;          // Displays integer 2

intVal = (int)number;       // Assigns intVal the value of
                            // number, converted to an int

booksPerMonth =             // Converts a copy of the value
  (double)books / months;   // stored in books to a double
                            // before performing the division
                            // operation
```

Because the typecast operator appears in parentheses preceding the operand, this form of type cast notation is called *prefix notation*.

The prestandard C++ form of the type cast expression also places the data type to be converted to before the operand whose value is to be converted, but it places the parentheses around the operand, rather than around the data type. Here are the same three examples as they would be written using the prestandard C++ form of type casting.

```
cout << int(2.6);
intVal = int(number);
booksPerMonth = double(books) / months;
```

This type cast notation is called *functional notation*.

The `static_cast` expression is recommended by the ANSI standard for this type of data type conversion and is now considered preferable to either the C-style or the prestandard C++ form of type casting. However, you will probably see code in the workplace that uses these older styles. Program 3-9 illustrates how Program 3-7 would be written using a prestandard C++ type cast.

Program 3-9

```
// This program illustrates the prestandard C++ form of type casting.
#include <iostream>
using namespace std;

int main()
{
   int    books,
          months;
   double booksPerMonth;

   // Get user inputs
   cout << "How many books do you plan to read? ";
   cin  >> books;
   cout << "How many months will it take you to read them? ";
   cin  >> months;

   // Compute and display books read per month
   booksPerMonth = double(books) / months;
   cout << "That is " << booksPerMonth << " books per month.\n";
   return 0;
}
```

The output is identical to that produced by Program 3-7.

Checkpoint

3.14 Assume the following variable definitions:

```
int a = 5, b = 12;
double x = 3.4, z = 9.1;
```

What are the values of the following expressions?

A) `b / a`

B) `x * a`

C) `static_cast<double>(b / a)`

D) `static_cast<double>(b) / a`

E) `b / static_cast<double>(a)`

F) `static_cast<double>(b) / static_cast<double>(a)`

G) `b / static_cast<int>(x)`

H) `static_cast<int>(x) * static_cast<int>(z)`

I) `static_cast<int>(x * z)`

J) `static_cast<double>(static_cast<int>(x) * static_cast<int>(z))`

3.15 What will the following program code display if a capital B is entered when the `cin` statement asks the user to input a letter?

```
char letter;

cout << "The ASCII values of uppercase letters are "
     << static_cast<int>('A') << " - "
     << static_cast<int>('Z') << endl;

cout << "The ASCII values of lowercase letters are "
     << static_cast<int>('a') << " - "
     << static_cast<int>('z') << endl << endl;

cout << "Enter a letter and I will tell you its ASCII code: ";
cin  >> letter;
cout << "The ASCII code for " << letter << " is "
     << static_cast<int>(letter) << endl;
```

3.16 What will the following program code display?

```
int    integer1 = 19,
       integer2 = 2;
double doubleVal;

doubleVal = integer1 / integer2;
cout << doubleVal << endl;
doubleVal = static_cast<double>(integer1) / integer2;
cout << doubleVal << endl;
doubleVal = static_cast<double>(integer1 / integer2);
cout << doubleVal << endl;
```

3.4 Overflow and Underflow

CONCEPT: When a value cannot fit in the number of bits provided by a variable's data type, overflow or underflow occurs.

Just as a bucket will overflow if you try to put more water in it than it can hold, a variable will experience a similar problem if you try to store a value in it that requires more bits than it has available. Let's look at an example. Suppose a `short int` that uses 2 bytes of memory has the following value stored in it.

0	1	1	1	1	1	1	1	1	1	1	1	1	1	1	1

This is the binary representation of 32,767, the largest value that will fit in this data type. Without going into the details of how negative numbers are stored, it is helpful to understand that for integer data types that store both positive and negative numbers, a number with a 0 in the *high order* (i.e., leftmost) *bit* is interpreted as a positive number, and a number with a 1 in the high order bit is interpreted as a negative number. If 1 is added to the value stored above, the variable will now be holding the following bit pattern.

1	0	0	0	0	0	0	0	0	0	0	0	0	0	0	0

But this is not 32,768. Instead, it is interpreted as a negative number, which was not what was intended. A binary 1 has "flowed" into the high bit position. This is called *overflow.*

Likewise, when an integer variable is holding the value at the far end of its data type's negative range and 1 is subtracted from it, the 1 in its high order bit will become a 0, and the resulting number will be interpreted as a positive number. This is another example of overflow.

In addition to overflow, floating-point values can also experience *underflow.* This occurs when a value is too close to zero, so small that more digits of precision are needed to express it than can be stored in the variable holding it. Program 3-10 illustrates both overflow and underflow.

Program 3-10

```
// This program demonstrates overflow and underflow.
#include <iostream>
using namespace std;

```

(program continues)

Program 3-10 *(continued)*

```
int main()
{
    // Set intVar to the maximum value a short int can hold
    short intVar = 32767;

    // Set floatVar to a number too small to fit in a float
    float floatVar = 3.0E-47;

    // Display intVar
    cout << "Original value of intVar     " << intVar << endl;

    // Add 1 to intVar to make it overflow
    intVar = intVar + 1;
    cout << "intVar after overflow        " << intVar << endl;

    // Subtract 1 from intVar to make it overflow again
    intVar = intVar - 1;
    cout << "intVar after 2nd overflow    " << intVar << endl;

    // Display floatVar
    cout << "Value of very tiny floatVar  " << floatVar;
    return 0}
}
```

Program Output

```
Original value of intVar     32767
intVar after overflow       -32768
intVar after 2nd overflow    32767
Value of very tiny floatVar 0
```

Although some systems display an error message when an overflow or underflow occurs, most do not. The variable simply holds an incorrect value now and the program keeps running. Therefore, it is important to select a data type for each variable that has enough bits to hold the values you will store in it.

3.5 Named Constants

CONCEPT: Literals may be given names that symbolically represent them in a program.

In Chapter 2 you learned that values which will not change when a program runs can be stored as literals. However, sometimes this is not ideal. For example, assume the following statement appears in a banking program that calculates data pertaining to loans:

```
amount = balance * 0.069;
```

In such a program, two potential problems arise. First, it is not clear to anyone other than the original programmer what 0.069 is. It appears to be an interest rate, but in some situations there are fees associated with loan payments. How can the purpose of this statement be determined without painstakingly checking the rest of the program?

The second problem occurs if this number is used in other calculations throughout the program and must be changed periodically. Assuming the number is an interest rate, what if the rate changes from 6.9 percent to 7.2 percent? The programmer will have to search through the source code for every occurrence of the number.

Both of these problems can be addressed by using named constants. A *named constant*, also called a *constant variable*, is like a variable, but its content is read-only and cannot be changed while the program is running. Here is a definition of a named constant:

```
const double INTEREST_RATE = 0.069;
```

It looks just like a regular variable definition except that the word `const` appears before the data type name. The key word `const` is a qualifier that tells the compiler to make the variable read-only. This ensures that its value will remain constant throughout the program's execution. If any statement in the program attempts to change its value, an error results when the program is compiled. A named constant can have any legal C++ identifier name, but many programmers use all uppercase letters in the name, as we have done here, to distinguish it from a regular variable.

When a named constant is defined it must be initialized with a value. It cannot be defined and then later assigned a value with an assignment statement.

```
const double INTEREST_RATE;      // illegal
INTEREST_RATE = 0.069;           // illegal
```

An added advantage of using named constants is that they make programs more self-documenting. Once the named constant `INTEREST_RATE` has been correctly defined, the program statement

```
newAmount = balance * 0.069;
```

can be changed to read

```
newAmount = balance * INTEREST_RATE;
```

A new programmer can read the second statement and better understand what is happening. It is evident that `balance` is being multiplied by the interest rate. Another advantage to this approach is that widespread changes can easily be made to the program. Let's say the interest rate appears in a dozen different statements throughout the program. If the rate changes, the initialization value in the definition of the named constant is the only value that needs to be modified. If the rate increases to 7.2 percent, the definition is simply changed to the following:

```
const double INTEREST_RATE = 0.072;
```

The program is then ready to be recompiled. Every statement that uses `INTEREST_RATE` will use the new value.

Named constants can also help prevent typographical errors in a program's code. For example, suppose you use the number 3.14159 as the value of PI in a program that performs various geometric calculations. Each time you type the number 3.14159 in the program's code, there is a chance that you will make a mistake with one or more of the digits. To help prevent a mistake such as this, you can define a named constant for PI, initialized with the correct value, and then use that constant in all of the formulas that require its value.

Program 3-11, which calculates the area of a circle, uses a named constant. It is defined on line 9 and used on line 19.

Program 3-11

```
 1 // This program calculates the area of a circle. The formula for the
 2 // area of a circle is PI times the radius squared. PI is 3.14159.
 3 #include <iostream>
 4 #include <cmath>                    // Needed for the pow function
 5 using namespace std;
 6
 7 int main()
 8 {
 9    const double PI = 3.14159;     // PI is a named constant
10    double area, radius;
11
12    cout << "This program calculates the area of a circle.\n";
13
14    // Get the radius
15    cout << "What is the radius of the circle? ";
16    cin  >> radius;
17
18    // Compute and display the area
19    area = PI * pow(radius, 2);
20    cout << "The area is " << area << endl;
21    return 0;
22 }
```

Program Output with Example Input Shown in Bold

```
This program calculates the area of a circle.
What is the radius of the circle? 10.0[Enter]
The area is 314.159
```

The `#define` Directive

The older C-style method of creating named constants is with the `#define` preprocessor directive. Although it is preferable to use the `const` modifier, there are programs still in use that contain the `#define` directive. In addition, the `#define` directive has other uses, so it is important to understand it. Program 3-12 shows how the preprocessor can be used to create a named constant.

Program 3-12

```
1 // This program calculates the area of a circle. The formula for the
2 // area of a circle is PI times the radius squared. PI is 3.14159.
3 #include <iostream>
4 #include <cmath>                     // Needed for the pow function
5 using namespace std;
6
7 #define PI 3.14159                   // PI is "defined" to be 3.14159
8
9 int main()
10 {
11    double area, radius;
12
13    cout << "This program calculates the area of a circle.\n";
14
15    // Get the radius
16    cout << "What is the radius of the circle? ";
17    cin  >> radius;
18
19    // Compute and display the area
20    area = PI * pow(radius, 2);
21    cout << "The area is " << area << endl;
22    return 0;
23 }
```

If the user enters 10.0, or 10, for the radius, the output will be the same as that produced by Program 3-11.

Remember, the preprocessor scans your program before it is compiled. It looks for directives, which are lines that begin with the # symbol. Preprocessor directives cause your source code to be modified prior to being compiled. Line 7 of Program 3-12 contains the following `#define` directive:

```
#define PI 3.14159
```

The word `PI` is a named constant, and 3.14159 is its value. Anytime `PI` is used in the program, it will be replaced by the value 3.14159. The code on line 20 that reads

```
area = PI * pow(radius, 2);
```

will be sent to the compiler as

```
area = 3.14159 * pow(radius, 2);
```

If there had been a line that read

```
cout << PI << endl;
```

it would be compiled as

```
cout << 3.14159 << endl;
```

It is important to realize the difference between constant variables created with the key word `const` and constants created with the `#define` directive. Constant variables are defined like regular variables. They have a data type and a specific storage location in memory. In fact, they are like regular variables in every way except that you cannot change their value while the program is running. Constants created with the `#define` directive, however, are not variables at all. They are text substitutions. Each occurrence of the named constant in your source code is removed and the value of the constant is written in its place when it is sent to the compiler.

Be careful not to put a semicolon at the end of a `#define` directive. If you used a semicolon it would actually become part of the value of the constant. If the `#define` directive in line 7 of Program 3-12 had read like this,

```
#define PI 3.14159;
```

the mathematical statement

```
area = PI * pow(radius, 2);
```

would have been modified to read

```
area = 3.14159; * pow(radius, 2);
```

Because of the semicolon, the preprocessor would have created a syntax error in the statement, and the compiler would have given an error message when trying to process this statement.

NOTE: `#define` directives are intended for the preprocessor, and C++ statements are intended for the compiler. The preprocessor does not look for semicolons to terminate directives.

Checkpoint

3.17 Write statements using the `const` qualifier to create named constants for the following literal values:

Constant Value	Description
`2.71828`	Euler's number (known in mathematics as *e*)
`5.256E5`	Number of minutes in a year
`32.2`	The gravitational acceleration constant (in feet per second^2)
`9.8`	The gravitational acceleration constant (in meters per second^2)
`1609`	Number of meters in a mile

3.18 Write `#define` directives for the literal values listed in question 3.17.

3.19 Assuming the user enters 6 in response to the question, what will the following program display on the screen?

```
#include <iostream>
using namespace std;

#define GREETING1 "This program calculates the number "
#define GREETING2 "of candy pieces sold."
#define QUESTION "How many jars of candy have you sold? "
#define RESULTS "The number of pieces sold: "
#define YOUR_COMMISSION "Candy pieces you get for commission: "
#define COMMISSION_RATE .20
```

```
int main()
{
   const int PIECES_PER_JAR = 1860;
   int jars, pieces;
   double commission;

   cout << GREETING1;
   cout << GREETING2 << endl;
   cout << QUESTION;
   cin  >> jars;

   pieces = jars * PIECES_PER_JAR;
   cout << RESULTS << pieces << endl;
   commission = pieces * COMMISSION_RATE;
   cout << YOUR_COMMISSION << commission << endl;
   return 0;
}
```

3.20 Complete the following program code segment so it properly converts a speed entered in miles per hour to feet per second. One mile per hour is 1.467 feet per second.

```
// Define a named constant called CONVERSION, whose value is 1.467.
double milesPerHour, feetPerSecond;

cout << "This program converts miles per hour to\n";
cout << "feet per second.\n";
cout << "Enter a speed in MPH: ";
cin  >> milesPerHour;
// Insert a mathematical statement here to
// calculate feet per second and assign the result
// to the feetPerSecond variable.
cout << "That is " << feetPerSecond << " feet per second.\n";
```

3.6 Multiple and Combined Assignment

CONCEPT: Multiple assignment means to assign the same value to several variables with one statement.

C++ allows you to assign a value to multiple variables at once. If a program has several variables, such as `a`, `b`, `c`, and `d`, and each variable needs to be assigned the same value, such as 12, the following statement may be written:

```
a = b = c = d = 12;
```

The value 12 will be assigned to each variable listed in the statement. This works because the assignment operations are carried out from right to left. First 12 is assigned to `d`. Then `d`'s value, now a 12, is assigned to `c`. Then `c`'s value is assigned to `b`, and finally `b`'s value is assigned to `a`.

Here is another example. After this statement executes, both `store1` and `store2` will hold the same value as `begInv`.

```
store1 = store2 = begInv;
```

Combined Assignment Operators

VideoNote
Combined Assignment Operators

Quite often programs have assignment statements of the following form:

```
number = number + 1;
```

The expression on the right side of the assignment operator gives the value of `number` plus 1. The result is then assigned to `number`, replacing the value previously stored there. Effectively, this statement adds 1 to `number`. In a similar fashion, the following statement subtracts 5 from `number`.

```
number = number - 5;
```

If you have never seen this type of statement before, it might cause some initial confusion because the same variable name appears on both sides of the assignment operator. Table 3-8 shows other examples of statements written this way.

Table 3-8 Assignment Statements that Change a Variable's Value (Assume x = 6)

Statement	What It Does	Value of x After the Statement
`x = x + 4;`	Adds 4 to x	10
`x = x - 3;`	Subtracts 3 from x	3
`x = x * 10;`	Multiplies x by 10	60
`x = x / 2;`	Divides x by 2	3
`x = x % 4`	Makes x the remainder of x / 4	2

Because these types of operations are so common in programming, C++ offers a special set of operators designed specifically for these jobs. Table 3-9 shows the *combined assignment operators*, also known as *compound operators* or *arithmetic assignment operators*.

Table 3-9 Combined Assignment Operators

Operator	Example Usage	Equivalent To
`+=`	`x += 5;`	`x = x + 5;`
`-=`	`y -= 2;`	`y = y - 2;`
`*=`	`z *= 10;`	`z = z * 10;`
`/=`	`a /= b;`	`a = a / b;`
`%=`	`c %= 3;`	`c = c % 3;`

As you can see, the combined assignment operators do not require the programmer to type the variable name twice. Also, they give a clear indication of what is happening in the statement.

Program 3-13 uses both a multiple assignment statement and a combined assignment operator.

Program 3-13

```
// This program tracks the inventory of two widget stores.
// It illustrates the use of multiple and combined assignment.
#include <iostream>
using namespace std;

int main()
{
   int begInv,     // Beginning inventory for both stores
       sold,       // Number of widgets sold
       store1,     // Store 1's inventory
       store2;     // Store 2's inventory

   // Get the beginning inventory for the two stores
   cout << "One week ago, 2 new widget stores opened\n";
   cout << "at the same time with the same beginning\n";
   cout << "inventory. What was the beginning inventory? ";
   cin  >> begInv;

   // Set each store's inventory
   store1 = store2 = begInv;

   // Get the number of widgets sold at each store
   cout << "How many widgets has store 1 sold? ";
   cin  >> sold;
   store1 -= sold;     // Adjust store 1's inventory

   cout << "How many widgets has store 2 sold? ";
   cin  >> sold;
   store2 -= sold;     // Adjust store 2's inventory

   // Display each store's current inventory
   cout << "\nThe current inventory of each store:\n";
   cout << "Store 1: " << store1 << endl;
   cout << "Store 2: " << store2 << endl;
   return 0;
}
```

Program Output with Example Input Shown in Bold

```
One week ago, 2 new widget stores opened
at the same time with the same beginning
inventory. What was the beginning inventory? 100[Enter]
How many widgets has store 1 sold? 25[Enter]
How many widgets has store 2 sold? 15[Enter]

The current inventory of each store:
Store 1: 75
Store 2: 85
```

More elaborate statements may be expressed with the combined assignment operators. Here is an example:

```
result *= a + 5;
```

In this statement, `result` is multiplied by the sum of `a + 5`. Notice that the precedence of the combined assignment operators is lower than that of the regular arithmetic operators. The above statement is equivalent to

```
result = result * (a + 5);
```

which is different from

```
result = result * a + 5;
```

Table 3-10 shows additional examples using combined assignment operators.

Table 3-10 Examples Using Combined Assignment Operators and Arithmetic Operators

Example Usage	Equivalent To
`x += b + 5;`	`x = x + (b + 5);`
`y -= a * 2;`	`y = y - (a * 2);`
`z *= 10 - c;`	`z = z * (10 - c);`
`a /= b + c;`	`a = a / (b + c);`
`c %= d - 3;`	`c = c % (d - 3);`

Checkpoint

3.21 Write a multiple assignment statement that assigns 0 to the variables `total`, `subtotal`, `tax`, and `shipping`.

3.22 Write statements using combined assignment operators to perform the following:

A) Add 6 to `x`.

B) Subtract 4 from `amount`.

C) Multiply `y` by 4.

D) Divide `total` by 27.

E) Store in `x` the remainder of `x` divided by 7.

F) Add `y * 5` to `x`.

G) Subtract `discount` times 4 from `total`.

H) Multiply `increase` by `salesRep` times 5.

I) Divide `profit` by `shares` minus 1000.

3.23 What will the following program segment display?

```
int unus, duo, tres;

unus = duo = tres = 5;
unus += 4;
duo *= 2;
tres -= 4;
unus /= 3;
duo += tres;
cout << unus << endl << duo << endl << tres << endl;
```

3.7 Formatting Output

CONCEPT: `cout` provides ways to format data as it is being displayed. This affects the way data appears on the screen.

The same data can be printed or displayed in several different ways. For example, all of the following numbers have the same value, although they look different:

```
720
720.0
720.00000000
7.2e+2
+720.0
```

The way a value is printed is called its *formatting*. The `cout` object has a standard way of formatting variables of each data type. Sometimes, however, you need more control over the way data is displayed. Consider Program 3-14, for example, which displays three rows of numbers with spaces between each one.

Program 3-14

```cpp
// This program displays three rows of numbers.
#include <iostream>
using namespace std;

int main()
{
   int num1 = 2897, num2 = 5,    num3 = 837,
       num4 = 34,   num5 = 7,    num6 = 1623,
       num7 = 390,  num8 = 3456, num9 = 12;

   // Display the first row of numbers
   cout << num1 << "  " << num2 << "  " << num3 << endl;

   // Display the second row of numbers
   cout << num4 << "  " << num5 << "  " << num6 << endl;

   // Display the third row of numbers
   cout << num7 << "  " << num8 << "  " << num9 << endl;

   return 0;
}
```

Program Output

```
2897  5  837
34  7  1623
390  3456  12
```

Unfortunately, the numbers do not line up in columns. This is because some of the numbers, such as 5 and 7, occupy one position on the screen, while others occupy two or three positions. `cout` uses just the number of spaces needed to print each number.

To remedy this, `cout` offers a way of specifying the minimum number of spaces to use for each number. A stream manipulator, `setw`, can be used to establish print fields of a specified width. Here is an example of how it is used:

```
value = 23;
cout << setw(5) << value;
```

The number inside the parentheses after the word `setw` specifies the field width for the value immediately following it. The *field width* is the minimum number of character positions, or spaces, on the screen to print the value in. In our example, the number 23 will be displayed in a field of five spaces.

To further clarify how this works, look at the following statements:

```
value = 23;
cout << "(" << setw(5) << value << ")";
```

This will produce the following output:

```
(   23)
```

Notice that the number occupies the last two positions in the field. Since the number did not use the entire field, `cout` filled the extra three positions with blank spaces. Because the number appears on the right side of the field with blank spaces "padding" it in front, it is said to be *right-justified*.

Program 3-15 shows how the numbers in Program 3-14 can be printed in columns that line up perfectly by using `setw`. In addition, because the program uses `setw(6)`, and the largest number has four digits, the numbers will be separated without having to print a string literal containing blanks between the numbers.

Program 3-15

```
// This program uses setw to display three rows of numbers so they align.
#include <iostream>
#include <iomanip>          // Header file needed to use setw
using namespace std;

int main()
{
   int num1 = 2897, num2 = 5,    num3 = 837,
       num4 = 34,   num5 = 7,    num6 = 1623,
       num7 = 390,  num8 = 3456, num9 = 12;
```

(program continues)

Program 3-15 *(continued)*

```
11
12     // Display the first row of numbers
13     cout << setw(6) << num1 << setw(6) << num2 << setw(6) << num3 << endl;
14
15     // Display the second row of numbers
16     cout << setw(6) << num4 << setw(6) << num5 << setw(6) << num6 << endl;
17
18     // Display the third row of numbers
19     cout << setw(6) << num7 << setw(6) << num8 << setw(6) << num9 << endl;
20
21     return 0;
22 }
```

Program Output

```
2897     5   837
  34     7  1623
 390  3456    12
```

NOTE: A new header file, iomanip, is named in the #include directive on line 3 of Program 3-15. This file must be included in any program that uses setw.

Notice that a setw manipulator is used with each value. This is because setw only establishes a field width for the value immediately following it. After that value is printed, cout goes back to its default method of printing.

You might wonder what will happen if the number is too large to fit in the field, as in the following statement:

```
value = 18397;
cout << setw(2) << value;
```

In cases like this, cout will print the entire number because setw only specifies the minimum number of positions in the print field. Any number requiring a larger field than the specified minimum will cause cout to override the setw value.

You may specify the field width for any type of data. Program 3-16 shows setw being used with an integer, a floating-point number, and a string object.

Program 3-16

```
// This program demonstrates the setw manipulator
// being used with variables of various data types.
#include <iostream>
#include <iomanip>        // Header file needed to use setw
#include <string>         // Header file needed to use string objects
using namespace std;

```

(program continues)

Program 3-16 *(continued)*

```
int main()
{
   int intValue = 3928;
   double doubleValue = 91.5;
   string stringValue = "Jill Q. Jones";

   cout << "(" << setw(5)  << intValue << ")"    << endl;
   cout << "(" << setw(8)  << doubleValue << ")" << endl;
   cout << "(" << setw(16) << stringValue << ")" << endl;
   return 0;
}
```

Program Output

```
( 3928)
(    91.5)
(   Jill Q. Jones)
```

Program 3-16 illustrates a number of important points:

- The field width of a floating-point number includes a position for the decimal point.
- The field width of a string includes all characters in the string, including spaces.
- The value printed in the field is right-justified by default. This means it is aligned with the right side of the print field, and any blanks that must be used to pad it are inserted in front of the value.

The `setprecision` Manipulator

Floating-point values may be rounded to a number of *significant digits*, or *precision*, which is the total number of digits that appear before and after the decimal point. You can control the number of significant digits with which floating-point values are displayed by using the `setprecision` manipulator. Program 3-17 shows the results of a division operation displayed with different numbers of significant digits.

Program 3-17

```
// This program demonstrates how the setprecision manipulator
// affects the way a floating-point value is displayed.
#include <iostream>
#include <iomanip>        // Header file needed to use setprecision
using namespace std;

int main()
{
   double, number1 = 132.364, number2 = 26.91;
   double quotient = number1 / number2;

   cout << quotient << endl;
   cout << setprecision(5) << quotient << endl;
```

(program continues)

Program 3-17 *(continued)*

```
14     cout << setprecision(4) << quotient << endl;
15     cout << setprecision(3) << quotient << endl;
16     cout << setprecision(2) << quotient << endl;
17     cout << setprecision(1) << quotient << endl;
18     return 0;
19 }
```

Program Output

```
4.91877
4.9188
4.919
4.92
4.9
5
```

NOTE: With prestandard compilers, your output may be different from that shown in Program 3-17.

The first value in Program 3-17 is displayed in line 12 without the `setprecision` manipulator. (By default, the system displays floating-point values with six significant digits.) The subsequent `cout` statements print the same value, but rounded to five, four, three, two, and one significant digits. Notice that, unlike `setw`, `setprecision` does not count the decimal point. When we used `setprecision(5)`, for example, the output contained five significant digits, which required six positions to print 4.9188.

If the value of a number is expressed in fewer digits of precision than specified by `setprecision`, the manipulator will have no effect. In the following statements, the value of `dollars` only has four digits of precision, so the number printed by both `cout` statements is 24.51.

```
double dollars = 24.51;
cout << dollars << endl;                        // displays 24.51
cout << setprecision(5) << dollars << endl;     // displays 24.51
```

Table 3-11 shows how `setprecision` affects the way various values are displayed. Notice that when fewer digits are to be displayed than the number holds, `setprecision` rounds, rather than truncates, the number. Notice also that trailing zeros are omitted. Therefore, for example, 21.40 displays as 21.4 even though `setprecision(5)` is specified.

Table 3-11 The `setprecision` Manipulator

Number	Manipulator	Value Displayed
`28.92786`	`setprecision(3)`	`28.9`
`21.40`	`setprecision(5)`	`21.4`
`109.50`	`setprecision(4)`	`109.5`
`34.78596`	`setprecision(2)`	`35`

Unlike field width, the precision setting remains in effect until it is changed to some other value. As with all formatting manipulators, you must include the header file `iomanip` to use `setprecision`.

Program 3-18 shows how the `setw` and `setprecision` manipulators may be combined to control the way floating-point numbers are displayed.

Program 3-18

```cpp
// This program asks for sales figures for three days.
// The total sales are calculated and displayed in a table.
#include <iostream>
#include <iomanip>        // Header file needed to use stream manipulators
using namespace std;

int main()
{
   double day1, day2, day3, total;

   // Get the sales for each day
   cout << "Enter the sales for day 1: ";
   cin  >> day1;
   cout << "Enter the sales for day 2: ";
   cin  >> day2;
   cout << "Enter the sales for day 3: ";
   cin  >> day3;

   // Calculate total sales
   total = day1 + day2 + day3;

   // Display the sales figures
   cout << "\nSales Figures\n";
   cout << "-------------\n";
   cout << setprecision(5);
   cout << "Day 1: " << setw(8) << day1 << endl;
   cout << "Day 2: " << setw(8) << day2 << endl;
   cout << "Day 3: " << setw(8) << day3 << endl;
   cout << "Total: " << setw(8) << total << endl;
   return 0;
}
```

Program Output with Example Input Shown in Bold

```
Enter the sales for day 1: 321.57[Enter]
Enter the sales for day 2: 269.60[Enter]
Enter the sales for day 3: 307.00[Enter]

Sales Figures
-------------
Day 1:   321.57
Day 2:    269.6
Day 3:      307
Total:   898.17
```

The output created by Program 3-18, as we directed, allows a maximum of five significant digits to be displayed and is printed right justified in a field width of eight characters. However, the result is clearly not what is desired. In just a moment, we'll look at another manipulator that provides additional control over the format of the output.

The `fixed` Manipulator

If a number is too large to print using the number of digits specified with `setprecision`, many systems print it in scientific notation. For example, here is the output of Program 3-18 with larger numbers being input.

```
Enter the sales for day 1: 145678.99[Enter]
Enter the sales for day 2: 205614.85[Enter]
Enter the sales for day 3: 198645.22[Enter]

Sales Figures
-------------
Day 1: 1.4568e+005
Day 2: 2.0561e+005
Day 3: 1.9865e+005
Total: 5.4994e+005
```

To prevent this, you can use another stream manipulator, `fixed`, which indicates that floating-point output should be printed in *fixed-point*, or decimal, *notation*.

```
cout << fixed;
```

What is perhaps most important about the `fixed` manipulator, however, is that when it is used in conjunction with the `setprecision` manipulator `setprecision` behaves in a new way. It specifies the number of digits to be displayed after the decimal point of a floating-point number, rather than the total number of digits to be displayed. This is usually what we want. For example, if we rewrite line 25 of Program 3-18 as

```
cout << fixed << setprecision(2);
```

and rerun the program using the same sample data, we get the following results:

```
Enter the sales for day 1: 321.57[Enter]
Enter the sales for day 2: 269.60[Enter]
Enter the sales for day 3: 307.00[Enter]

Sales Figures
-------------
Day 1:    321.57
Day 2:    269.60
Day 3:    307.00
Total:    898.17
```

By using `fixed` and `setprecision` together, we get the desired output. Notice in this case, however, we set the precision to 2, the number of decimal places we wish to see, not to 5.

The `showpoint` Manipulator

By default, floating-point numbers are displayed without trailing zeroes, and floating-point numbers with no fractional part are displayed without a decimal point. For example, this code

```
double x = 456.0;
cout << x << endl;
```

will just display 456, and nothing more.

Another useful manipulator, showpoint, allows these defaults to be overridden. When showpoint is used, it indicates that a decimal point and decimal digits should be printed for a floating-point number, even if the value being displayed has no decimal digits. Here is the same code with the addition of the showpoint manipulator.

```
double x = 456.0;
cout << showpoint << x << endl;
```

It displays the following output:

```
456.000
```

Three zeros are shown because six significant digits are displayed if we do not specify how many decimal digits we want. We can use the fixed, showpoint, and setprecision manipulators together, as shown below, for even more control over how the output looks.

```
double x = 456.0;
cout << fixed << showpoint << setprecision(2) << x << endl;
```

This version of the code produces the following output:

```
456.00
```

Program 3-19 further illustrates the use of these manipulators. As with setprecision, the fixed and showpoint manipulators remain in effect until the programmer explicitly changes them.

Program 3-19

```
// This program illustrates the how the showpoint, setprecision, and
// fixed manipulators operate both individually and when used together.
#include <iostream>
#include <iomanip>       // Header file needed to use stream manipulators
using namespace std;

int main()
{
   double x = 6.0;

   cout << x << endl;
   cout << showpoint << x << endl;
   cout << setprecision(2) << x << endl;
   cout << fixed << x << endl;

   return 0;
}
```

Program Output

```
6
6.00000
6.0
6.00
```

When `x` is printed the first time, in line 11, none of the manipulators have been set yet. Therefore, since the value being displayed requires no decimal digits, only the number 6 is displayed. When `x` is printed the second time, in line 12, the `showpoint` manipulator has been set, so a decimal point followed by zeroes is displayed. However, since the `setprecision` manipulator has not yet been set, we have no control over how many zeroes are to be printed, and `6.00000` is displayed. When `x` is printed the third time, in line 13, the `setprecision` manipulator has been set. However, because the `fixed` manipulator has not yet been set, `setprecision(2)` indicates that two significant digits should be shown, and 6.0 is displayed, Finally, when `x` is printed the final time, in line 14, the `fixed` and `setprecision` manipulators have both been set, specifying that exactly two decimal digits are to be printed, so 6.00 is displayed.

Actually, when the `fixed` and `setprecision` manipulators are both used, it is not necessary to use the `showpoint` manipulator. For example,

```
cout << fixed << setprecision(2);
```

will automatically display a decimal point before the two decimal digits. However, many programmers prefer to use it anyway as shown here:

```
cout << fixed << showpoint << setprecision(2);
```

The `left` and `right` Manipulators

Normally, as you have seen, output is right-justified. This means if the field it prints in is larger than the value being displayed, it is printed on the far right of the field, with leading blanks. There are times when you may wish to force a value to print on the left side of its field, padded by blanks on the right. To do this you can use the `left` manipulator. It remains in effect until you use a `right` manipulator to set it back. These manipulators can be used with any type of value, even a string. Program 3-20 illustrates the `left` and `right` manipulators. It also illustrates that the `fixed`, `showpoint`, and `setprecision` manipulators have no effect on integers, only on floating-point numbers.

Program 3-20

```
// This program illustrates the use of the left and right manipulators.
#include <iostream>
#include <iomanip>        // Header file needed to use stream manipulators
#include <string>         // Header file needed to use string objects
using namespace std;

int main()
{
   string month1 = "January",
          month2 = "February",
          month3 = "March";

   int days1 = 31,
       days2 = 28,
       days3 = 31;

   double high1 = 22.6,
          high2 = 37.4,
          high3 = 53.9;
```

(program continues)

Program 3-20 *(continued)*

```
    cout << fixed << showpoint << setprecision(1);
    cout << "Month        Days    High\n";

    cout << left  << setw(12) << month1
         << right << setw(4)  << days1 << setw(9) << high1 << endl;
    cout << left  << setw(12) << month2
         << right << setw(4)  << days2 << setw(9) << high2 << endl;
    cout << left  << setw(12) << month3
         << right << setw(4)  << days3 << setw(9) << high3 << endl;

    return 0;
}
```

Program Output

```
Month        Days    High
January       31     22.6
February      28     37.4
March         31     53.9
```

Chapter 13 introduces additional stream manipulators and output formatting methods. However, the manipulators we have covered in this chapter are normally sufficient to produce the output you desire. Table 3-12 summarizes these six manipulators.

Table 3-12 Output Stream Manipulators

Stream Manipulator	Description
`setw(n)`	Sets a minimum print field width of size *n* for the next value output.
`fixed`	Displays floating-point numbers in fixed point (i.e., decimal) form.
`showpoint`	Causes a decimal point and trailing zeroes to be displayed for floating-point numbers, even if there is no fractional part.
`setprecision(n)`	Sets the precision of floating-point numbers.
`left`	Causes subsequent output to be left-justified.
`right`	Causes subsequent output to be right-justified.

Checkpoint

3.24 Write `cout` statements with stream manipulators that perform the following:

A) Display the number 34.789 in a field of nine spaces with two decimal places of precision.

B) Display the number 7.0 in a field of five spaces with three decimal places of precision. The decimal point and any trailing zeroes should be displayed.

C) Display the number 5.789e+12 in fixed-point notation.

D) Display the number 67 left-justified in a field of seven spaces.

3.25 The following program skeleton asks for an angle in degrees and converts it to radians. The formatting of the final output is left to you.

```
#include <iostream>
#include <iomanip>
using namespace std;

int main()
{
   const double PI = 3.14159;
   double degrees, radians;

   cout << "Enter an angle in degrees and I will convert it\n";
   cout << "to radians for you: ";
   cin  >> degrees;
   radians = degrees * PI / 180;

   // Display the value in radians left-justified, in fixed-point
   // notation, with four decimal places of precision, in a field
   // seven spaces wide.
   return 0;
}
```

3.8 Working with Characters and Strings

CONCEPT: Special functions exist for working with characters and strings.

In Chapter 2 you were introduced to characters and to string objects. Let's review a few of their characteristics. A `char` variable can hold only one character, whereas a variable defined as a string can hold a whole set of characters. The following variable definitions and initializations illustrate this.

```
char letter1 = 'A',
     letter2 = 'B';
string name1 = "Mark Twain",
       name2 = "Samuel Clemens";
```

As with numeric data types, characters and strings can be assigned values.

```
letter2 = letter1;         // Now letter2's value is 'A'
name2 = name1;             // Now name2's value is "Mark Twain"
```

Like numeric data types, they can be displayed with the `cout` statement. The following line of code outputs a character variable, a string literal, and a `string` object.

```
cout << letter1 << ". " << name1 << endl;
```

The output produced is

```
A. Mark Twain
```

However, inputting characters and strings is a little trickier than reading in numeric values.

Inputting a String

Although it is possible to use `cin` with the >> operator to input strings, it can cause problems you need to be aware of. When `cin` reads data it passes over and ignores any leading *whitespace* characters (spaces, tabs, or line breaks). However, once it comes to the first nonblank character and starts reading, it stops reading when it gets to the next whitespace character. If we use the following statement

```
cin >> name1;
```

we can input "Mark" or "Twain", but not "Mark Twain" because `cin` cannot input strings that contain embedded spaces.

Program 3-21 illustrates this problem.

Program 3-21

```
// This program illustrates a problem that can occur if
// cin is used to read character data into a string object.
#include <iostream>
#include <string>       // Header file needed to use string objects
using namespace std;

int main()
{
   string name;
    string city;

    cout << "Please enter your name: ";
    cin  >> name;
    cout << "Enter the city you live in: ";
    cin  >> city;

    cout << "Hello, " << name << endl;
    cout << "You live in " << city << endl;
    return 0;
}
```

Program Output with Example Input Shown in Bold

```
Please enter your name. John Doe[Enter]
Enter the city you live in: Hello, John
You live in Doe
```

Notice that the user was never given the opportunity to enter the city. In the first input statement, when `cin` came to the space between `John` and `Doe`, it stopped reading, storing just `John` as the value of `name`. In the second input statement, `cin` used the leftover characters it found in the keyboard buffer and stored `Doe` as the value of `city`.

To solve this problem, you can use a C++ function called `getline`. This function reads in an entire line, including leading and embedded spaces, and stores it in a `string` object. The `getline` function looks like the following, where `cin` is the input stream we are reading from and `inputLine` is the name of the `string` variable receiving the input string.

```
getline(cin, inputLine);
```

Program 3-22 illustrates the getline function.

Program 3-22

```
// This program illustrates using the getline function
// to read character data into a string object.
#include <iostream>
#include <string>       // Header file needed to use string objects
using namespace std;

int main()
{
    string name;
    string city;

    cout << "Please enter your name: ";
    getline(cin, name);
    cout << "Enter the city you live in: ";
    getline(cin, city);

    cout << "Hello, " << name << endl;
    cout << "You live in " << city << endl;
    return 0;
}
```

Program Output with Example Input Shown in Bold

```
Please enter your name. John Doe[Enter]
Enter the city you live in: Chicago[Enter]
Hello, John Doe
You live in Chicago
```

Inputting a Character

Sometimes you want to read only a single character of input. For example, some programs display a menu of items for the user to choose from. Often the selections will be denoted by the letters A, B, C, and so forth. The user chooses an item from the menu by typing a character. The simplest way to read a single character is with `cin` and the >> operator, as illustrated in Program 3-23.

Program 3-23

```
// This program reads a single character into a char variable.
#include <iostream>
using namespace std;

int main()
{
   char ch;

   cout << "Type a character and press Enter: ";
   cin  >> ch;
   cout << "You entered " << ch << endl;
   return 0;
}
```

(program continues)

Program 3-23 *(continued)*

Program Output with Example Input Shown in Bold

```
Type a character and press Enter: A[Enter]
You entered A
```

Using `cin.get`

As with string input, however, there are times when using `cin >>` to read a character does not do what we want. For example, because it passes over all leading whitespace, it is impossible to input just a blank or [Enter] with `cin >>`. The program will not continue past the `cin` statement until some character other than the spacebar, the tab key, or the [Enter] key has been pressed. (Once such a character is entered, the [Enter] key must still be pressed before the program can continue to the next statement.) Thus, programs that ask the user to `"Press the enter key to continue."` cannot use the `>>` operator to read only the pressing of the [Enter] key.

In those situations, the `cin` object has a built-in function named `get` that is helpful. Because the `get` function is built into the `cin` object, we say that it is a *member function* of `cin`. The `get` member function reads a single character, including any whitespace character. If the program needs to store the character being read, the `get` member function can be called in either of the following ways. In both examples, assume that `ch` is the name of a `char` variable the character is being read into.

```
cin.get(ch);
ch = cin.get();
```

If the program is using the `get` function simply to pause the screen until the **`[Enter]`** key is pressed, and does not need to store the character, the function can also be called like this:

```
cin.get();
```

Notice that in all three of these programming statements the format of the `get` function call is actually the same. First comes the name of the object. In this case it is `cin`. Then comes a period, followed by the name of the member function being called. In this case it is `get`. The statement ends with a set of parentheses and a closing semicolon. This is the basic format for calling *any* member function and is illustrated in Figure 3-5

Figure 3-5

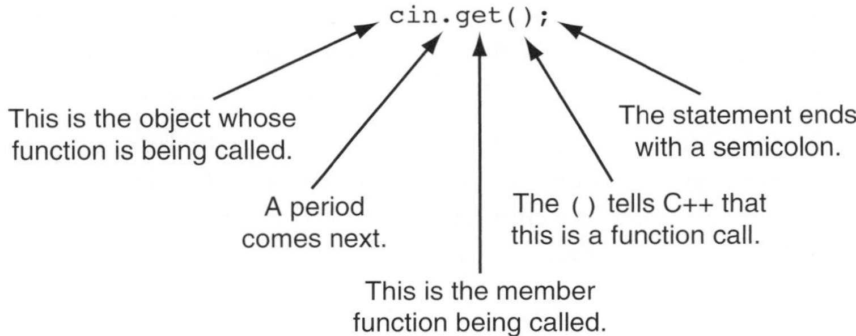

Program 3-24 illustrates all three ways to use the `get` member function.

Program 3-24

```
// This program demonstrates three ways to use cin.get()
// to pause a program.
#include <iostream>
using namespace std;

int main()
{
    char ch;

    cout << "This program has paused. Press Enter to continue.";
    cin.get(ch);
    cout << "It has paused a second time. Please press Enter again.";
    ch = cin.get();
    cout << "It has paused a third time.  Please press Enter again.";
    cin.get();
    cout << "Thank you!";
    return 0;
}
```

Program Output with Example Input Shown in Bold

```
This program has paused. Press Enter to continue.[Enter]
It has paused a second time. Please press Enter again.[Enter]
It has paused a third time.  Please press Enter again.[Enter]
Thank you!
```

Mixing `cin >>` and `cin.get`

Mixing `cin >>` with `cin.get` can cause an annoying and hard-to-find problem. For example, look at the following code segment. The lines are numbered for reference.

```
1 char ch;                          // Define a character variable
2 int number;                       // Define an integer variable
3 cout << "Enter a number: ";
4 cin  >> number;                   // Read an integer
3 cout << "Enter a character: ";
6 ch = cin.get();                   // Read a character
7 cout << "Thank You!\n";
```

These statements allow the user to enter a number, but not a character. It will appear that the `cin.get` statement on line 6 has been skipped. This happens because `cin >>` and `cin.get` use slightly different techniques for reading data.

In the example code segment, when line 4 is executed, the user enters a number and then presses the **`[Enter]`** key. Let's suppose the number 100 is entered. Pressing the **`[Enter]`** key causes a newline character (`'\n'`) to be stored in the keyboard buffer right after the 100, as shown in Figure 3-6.

Figure 3-6

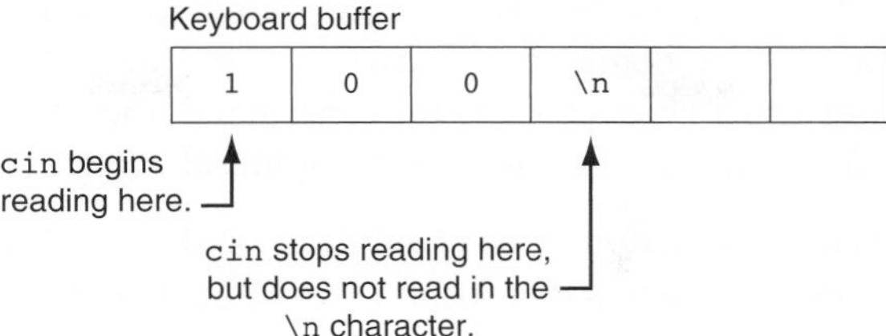

When the `cin >>` statement in line 4 reads the data the user entered, it stops when it comes to the newline character. The newline character is not read, but remains in the keyboard buffer. Input statements that read data from the keyboard only wait for the user to enter a value if the keyboard buffer is empty, but now it's not empty. When the `cin.get` function in line 6 executes, it begins reading the keyboard buffer from where the previous input operation stopped, and it finds the newline character. So it uses it and does not wait for the user to input another value. You can remedy this situation by using the `cin.ignore` function, described in the following section.

Using `cin.ignore`

The `cin.ignore` function tells the `cin` object to skip one or more characters in the keyboard buffer. Here is its general form:

```
cin.ignore(n, c);
```

The arguments shown in the parentheses are optional. If they are used, `n` is an integer and `c` is a character. They tell `cin` to skip `n` number of characters, or until the character `c` is encountered. For example, the following statement causes `cin` to skip the next 20 characters or until a newline is encountered, whichever comes first:

```
cin.ignore(20,'\n');
```

If no arguments are used, `cin` will only skip the very next character. Here's an example:

```
cin.ignore();
```

The problem that previously occurred when `cin >>` and `cin.get` statements were intermixed can be avoided by inserting a `cin.ignore` statement after the `cin >>` statement, as shown below. This causes the newline character left behind by `cin >>` to be bypassed, forcing `cin.get` to wait for the user to enter another character.

```
cout << "Enter a number: ";
cin  >> number;
cin.ignore();           // Skip the newline character
cout << "Enter a character: ";
cin.get(ch);
cout << "Thank You!" << endl;
```

Useful `string` Member Functions and Operators

C++ `string` objects also have a number of member functions. For example, if you want to know the length of the string that is stored in a `string` object, you can call the object's `length` member function. Here is an example of how to use it.

```
string state = "New Jersey";
int size = state.length();
```

The first statement creates a `string` object named `state`, and initializes it with the string `"New Jersey"`. The second statement defines an `int` variable named `size`, and initializes it with the length of the string in the `state` object. After this code executes, the `size` variable will hold the value 10. The blank space between `"New"` and `"Jersey"` is a character and is counted just like any other character. On the other hand, the `'\0'` null character you learned about in Chapter 2 that marks the end of a string literal is not counted.

Another useful member function is `assign`. One of the versions of this function lets you assign a set of repeated characters to a string without having to count the characters. Suppose, for example, you have declared a `string` object named `spaces`, and you want to assign it 22 blanks. You could do it by using a string literal like this:

```
spaces = "                      ";
```

However, counting the number of spaces to include in the string literal is tedious, and it is easy to miscount. It would be much easier to use the `string` class `assign` member function, as shown here.

```
spaces.assign(22, ' ');
```

The `string` class also has special operators for working with strings. One of them is the + operator.

You have already encountered the + operator to add two numeric quantities. Because strings cannot be added, when this operator is used with string operands it *concatenates* them, or joins them together. Assume we have the following definitions and initializations in a program.

```
string greeting1 = "Hello ",
       greeting2;
string word1     = "World";
string word2     = "People";
```

The following statements illustrate how string concatenation works.

```
greeting2 = greeting1 + word1; // greeting2 now holds "Hello World"
greeting1 = greeting1 + word2; // greeting1 now holds "Hello People"
```

Notice that the string stored in `greeting1` has a blank as its last character. If the blank were not there, `greeting2` would have been assigned the string `"HelloWorld"`.

The last statement could also have been written using the += combined assignment operator, like this:

```
greeting1 += word2;
```

Program 3-25 uses the `string` class member functions and the string concatenation operator we have just been looking at. You will learn about many other useful `string` class member functions and operators in later chapters.

Program 3-25

```
// This program displays the user's name surrounded by stars.
// It uses the + operator and several string class member functions.
#include <iostream>
#include <string>       // Header file needed to use string objects
using namespace std;
```

(program continues)

Program 3-25 *(continued)*

```
int main()
{
   string firstName, lastName, fullName;
   string stars;
   int numStars;

   cout << "Please enter your first name: ";
   getline(cin, firstName);

   cout << "Please enter your last name: ";
   getline(cin, lastName);

   fullName = firstName + " " + lastName;

   numStars = fullName.length();
   stars.assign(numStars, '*');

   cout << endl;
   cout << stars    << endl;
   cout << fullName << endl;
   cout << stars    << endl;
   return 0;
}
```

Program Output with Example Input Shown in Bold

```
Please enter your first name: Mary Lou[Enter]
Please enter your last name: St. Germaine[Enter]

*********************
Mary Lou St. Germaine
*********************
```

3.9 Using C-Strings

CONCEPT: C-strings provide another way to store and work with strings.

In C, and in C++ prior to the introduction of the `string` class, strings were stored as a set of individual characters. A group of contiguous 1-byte memory cells was set up to hold them, with each cell holding just one character of the string. A group of memory cells like this is called an *array*. You will learn more about arrays in Chapter 8, but for now all you need to know is how to set one up and use it to hold and work with the characters that make up a string.

Because this was the way to create a string variable in C, a string defined in this manner is called a *C-string*. Here is a statement that defines `word` to be an array of characters that will hold a C-string and initializes it to `"Hello"`.

```
char word[10] = "Hello";
```

Notice that the way we define `word` is similar to the way we define any other variable. The data type is specified first and then the variable name is given. The only difference is the `[10]` that follows the name of the variable. This is called a *size declarator.* It tells how many memory cells to set up to hold the characters in the C-string.

As with string literals, the null character is automatically appended to the end of a C-string to mark its end. Figure 3-7 shows what the contents of the `word` variable would look like in memory. Notice that the 10 memory cells are numbered 0–9.

Figure 3-7

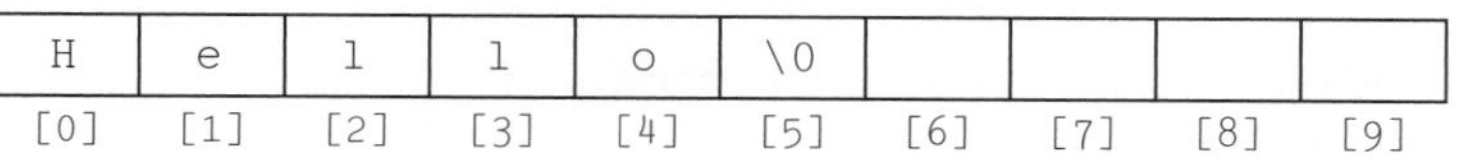

Because one space must be reserved for the null terminator, `word` can only hold a string of up to nine characters.

Like string objects, C-strings can have their contents input using `cin`, and they can have their contents displayed using `cout`. This is illustrated in Program 3-26. Because the variable `name` is defined in line 8 to have 12 memory cells, it can store a name of up to 11 characters. Notice that no special header file is needed to use C-strings.

Program 3-26

```
 1 // This program uses cin >> to read a word into a C-string.
 2 #include <iostream>
 3 using namespace std;
 4
 5 int main()
 6 {
 7    const int SIZE = 12;
 8    char name[SIZE];          // name is a set of 12 memory cells
 9
10    cout << "Please enter your first name: ";
11    cin  >> name;
12    cout << "Hello, " << name << endl;
13    return 0;
14 }
```

Program Output with Example Input Shown in Bold

```
Please enter your first name: Sebastian[Enter]
Hello, Sebastian
```

Except for inputting and displaying them with `cin >>` and `cout <<`, almost everything else about using `string` objects and C-strings is different. This is because the `string` class includes functions and operators that save the programmer having to worry about many of the details of working with strings. When using C-strings, however, it is the responsibility of the programmer to handle these things.

Because C-strings are harder to work with than `string` objects, you might be wondering why you are learning about them. There are two reasons. First, you are apt to encounter older programs that use them, so you need to understand them. Second, even though strings can now be declared as `string` objects in most cases, there are still times when only C-strings will work. You will be introduced to some of these cases later in the book.

Assigning a Value to a C-String

The first way in which using a C-string differs from using a `string` object is that, except for initializing it at the time of its definition, it cannot be assigned a value using the assignment operator. In Program 3-26 we could not, for example, replace the `cin` statement with the following line of code.

```
name = "Sebastian";                          // Wrong!
```

Instead, to assign a value to a C-string, we must use a function called `strcpy` (pronounced *string copy*) to copy the contents of one string into another. In the following line of code `Cstring` is the name of the variable receiving the value, and `value` is either a string literal or the name of another C-string variable.

```
strcpy(Cstring, value);
```

Program 3-27 shows how the `strcpy` function works.

Program 3-27

```
// This program uses the strcpy function to copy one C-string to another.
#include <iostream>
using namespace std;

int main()
{
   const int SIZE = 12;
   char name1[SIZE],
        name2[SIZE];

   strcpy(name1, "Sebastian");
   cout << "name1 now holds the string " << name1 << endl;

   strcpy(name2, name1);
   cout << "name2 now also holds the string " << name2 << endl;

   return 0;
}
```

Program Output

```
name1 now holds the string Sebastian
name2 now also holds the string Sebastian
```

Keeping Track of a How Much a C-String Can Hold

Another crucial way in which using a C-string differs from using a `string` object involves the memory allocated for it. With a `string` object, you do not have to worry about there being too little memory to hold a string you wish to place in it. If the storage space allocated to the `string` object is too small, the `string` class functions will make sure more memory is allocated to it. With C-strings this is not the case. The number of memory cells set aside to hold a C-string remains whatever size you originally set it to in the definition statement. It is the job of the programmer to ensure that the number of characters placed in it does not exceed the storage space. If the programmer uses `cin` to read a value into a C-string and the user types in more characters than it can hold, `cin` will store all the characters anyway. The ones that don't fit will spill over into the following memory cells, overwriting whatever was previously stored there. This type of error, known as a *buffer overrun*, can lead to serious problems.

One way to prevent this from happening is to use the `setw` stream manipulator. This manipulator, which we used earlier in this chapter to format output, can also be used to control the number of characters that `cin >>` inputs on its next read, as illustrated here:

```
char word[5];
cin >> setw(5) >> word;
```

Another way to do the same thing is by using the `cin width` function.

```
char word[5];
cin.width(5);
cin >> word;
```

In both cases the field width specified is 5 and `cin` will read, at most, one character less than this, leaving room for the null character at the end. Program 3-28 illustrates the use of the `setw` manipulator with `cin`, while Program 3-29 uses its `width` function. Both programs produce the same output.

Program 3-28

```
// This program uses setw with the cin object.
#include <iostream>
#include <iomanip>       // Header file needed to use stream manipulators
using namespace std;

int main()
{
   const int SIZE = 5;
   char word[SIZE];

   cout << "Enter a word: ";
   cin  >> setw(SIZE) >> word;
   cout << "You entered " << word << endl;

   return 0;
}
```

Program 3-29

```
// This program uses cin's width function.
#include <iostream>
#include <iomanip>       // Header file needed to use stream manipulators
using namespace std;

int main()
{
   const int SIZE = 5;
   char word[SIZE];
```

(program continues)

Program 3-29 *(continued)*

```

    cout << "Enter a word: ";
    cin.width(SIZE);
    cin  >> word;
    cout << "You entered " << word << endl;

    return 0;
}
```

Program Output for Programs 3-28 and 3-29 with Example Input Shown in Bold

```
Enter a word: Eureka[Enter]
You entered Eure
```

In Program 3-29, `cin` only reads and stores four characters into `word`. If the field width had not been specified, `cin` would have written the entire word "Eureka" into memory, overflowing the space set up to hold `word`. Figure 3-8 illustrates the way memory would have been affected by this. The shaded area is the 5 bytes of memory allocated to hold the C-string.

Figure 3-8

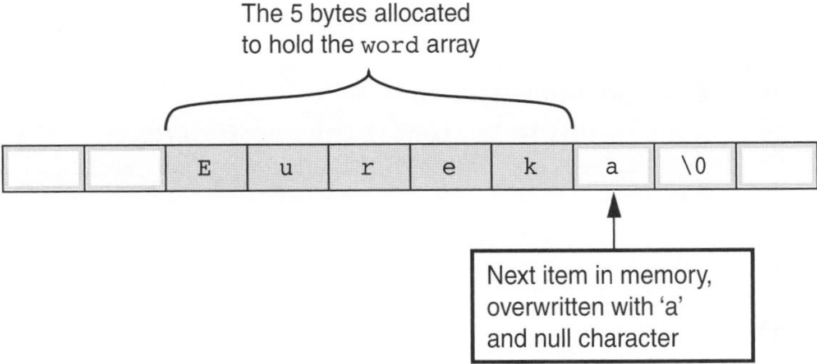

There are three important points to remember about the way `cin` handles field widths:

- The field width only pertains to the very next item entered by the user.
- To leave space for the '\0' character, the maximum number of characters read and stored will be one less than the size specified.
- If `cin` comes to a whitespace character before reading the specified number of characters, it will stop reading.

Reading a Line of Input

Still another way in which using C-strings differs from using string objects is that you must use a different set of functions when working with them. To read a line of input, for example, you must use `cin.getline` rather than `getline`. These two names look a lot alike, but they are two different functions and are not interchangeable. Like `getline`, `cin.getline` allows you to read in a string containing spaces. It will continue reading until it has read the maximum specified number of characters, or until the [Enter] key is pressed. Here is an example of how it is used:

```
cin.getline(sentence, 20);
```

The `getline` function takes two arguments separated by a comma. The first argument is the name of the array that the string is to be stored in. The second argument is the size of the array. When the `cin.getline` statement executes, `cin` will read up to one character less than this number, leaving room for the null terminator. This eliminates the need for using the `setw` manipulator or the `width` function. The statement above will read up to 19 characters. The null terminator will automatically be placed in the array after the last character. Program 3-30 shows the `getline` function being used to read a sentence of up to 80 characters.

Program 3-30

```
// This program demonstrates cin's getline function
// to read a line of text into a C-string.
#include <iostream>
using namespace std;

int main()
{
   const int SIZE = 81;
   char sentence[SIZE];

   cout << "Enter a sentence: ";
   cin.getline(sentence, SIZE);
   cout << "You entered " << sentence << endl;
   return 0;
}
```

Program Output with Example Input Shown in Bold

```
Enter a sentence: To be, or not to be, that is the question.[Enter]
You entered To be, or not to be, that is the question.
```

(In the printed output, "To be, or not to be, that is the question.[Enter]" on the first line is in bold.)

Later chapters cover more on C-strings and how they differ from `string` objects.

Checkpoint

3.26 Will the following string literal fit in the space allocated for `name`? Why or why not?

```
char name[4] = "John";
```

3.27 If a program contains the definition `string name;` indicate whether each of the following lettered program statements is legal or illegal.

A) `cin >> name;`

B) `cin.getline(name, 20);`

C) `cout << name;`

D) `name = "John";`

3.28 If a program contains the definition `char name[20];` indicate whether each of the following lettered program statements is legal or illegal.

A) `cin >> name;`

B) `cin.getline(name, 20);`

C) `cout << name;`

D) `name = "John";`

3.10 More Mathematical Library Functions

CONCEPT: The C++ run-time library provides functions for performing complex mathematical operations.

Earlier in this chapter you learned to use the pow function to raise a number to a power. The C++ library has numerous other functions that perform specialized mathematical operations. These functions are useful in scientific and special purpose programs. Table 3-13 shows some of the most common ones. They all require the `cmath` header file.

Table 3-13 Selected Mathematical Library Functions

Function	Example	Description
`abs`	`y = abs(x);`	Returns the absolute value of the argument. The argument and the return value are integers.
`cos`	`y = cos(x);`	Returns the cosine of the argument. The argument should be an angle expressed in radians. The return type and the argument are doubles.
`exp`	`y = exp(x);`	Computes the exponential function of the argument, which is `x`. The return type and the argument are doubles.
`fmod`	`y = fmod(x, z);`	Returns, as a double, the remainder of the first argument divided by the second argument. Works like the modulus operator, but the arguments are doubles. (The modulus operator only works with integers.) Take care not to pass zero as the second argument. Doing so would cause division by zero.
`log`	`y = log(x);`	Returns the natural logarithm of the argument. The return type and the argument are doubles.
`log10`	`y = log10(x);`	Returns the base-10 logarithm of the argument. The return type and the argument are doubles.
`round`	`y = round(x);`	Returns the argument rounded to the nearest whole number. The return value is an integer.
`sin`	`y = sin(x);`	Returns the sine of the argument. The argument should be an angle expressed in radians. The return type and the argument are doubles.
`sqrt`	`y = sqrt(x);`	Returns the square root of the argument. The return type and argument are doubles. The argument must be zero or greater.
`tan`	`y = tan(x);`	Returns the tangent of the argument. The argument should be an angle expressed in radians. The return type and the argument are doubles.

With the exception of the `abs` and `round` functions, all of the functions listed in Table 3-13 take one or more `double` arguments and return a `double` value. However, most C++ compilers allow them to be called with `int` arguments as well. So, for example, both of the following will work to print the square root of 30.

```
cout << sqrt(30.0);     // Displays 5.47723
cout << sqrt(30);       // Displays 5.47723
```

Program 3-31 shows the `sqrt` function being used to find the hypotenuse of a right triangle. The program uses the following formula, taken from the Pythagorean theorem:

$$c = \sqrt{a^2 + b^2}$$

In the formula, c is the length of the hypotenuse, and a and b are the lengths of the other sides of the triangle.

Program 3-31

```
 1 // This program inputs the lengths of the two sides of a right
 2 // triangle, then calculates and displays the length of the hypotenuse.
 3 #include <iostream>
 4 #include <cmath>          // Header file needed to use the sqrt function
 5 using namespace std;
 6
 7 int main()
 8 {
 9    double a, b, c;
10
11    // Get the length of the two sides
12    cout << "Enter the length of side a: ";
13    cin  >> a;
14    cout << "Enter the length of side b: ";
15    cin  >> b;
16
17    // Compute and display the length of the hypotenuse
18    c = sqrt(pow(a, 2.0) + pow(b, 2.0));
19
20    cout << "The length of the hypotenuse is ";
21    cout << c << endl;
22    return 0;
23 }
```

Program Output with Example Input Shown in Bold

```
Enter the length of side a: 5.0[Enter]
Enter the length of side b: 12.0[Enter]
The length of the hypotenuse is 13
```

The following statement, taken from line 18 of Program 3-31, calculates the square root of the sum of the squares of the triangle's two sides:

```
c = sqrt(pow(a, 2.0) + pow(b, 2.0));
```

Notice that the following mathematical expression is used as the `sqrt` function's argument:

```
pow(a, 2.0) + pow(b, 2.0)
```

This expression calls the `pow` function twice: once to calculate the square of `a` and again to calculate the square of `b`. These two squares are then added together, and the sum is sent to the `sqrt` function.

Random Numbers

Some programs need to use randomly generated numbers. The C++ library has a function called `rand()` for this purpose. To use the `rand()` function, you must include the `cstdlib` header file in your program. The number returned by the function is a non-negative integer. Here is an example of how it is used.

```
randomNum = rand();
```

However, the numbers returned by the function are really *pseudorandom*. This means they have the appearance and properties of random numbers, but in reality are not random. They are actually generated with an algorithm. The algorithm needs a starting value, called a *seed*, to generate the numbers. If it is not given one, it will produce the same stream of numbers each time it is run. Program 3-32 illustrates this.

Program 3-32

```
// This program demonstrates what happens in C++ if you
// try to generate random numbers without setting a "seed".
#include <iostream>
#include <cstdlib>        // Header file needed to use rand
using namespace std;

int main()
{
   // Generate and print three random numbers
   cout << rand() << "      " ;
   cout << rand() << "      " ;
   cout << rand() << endl;

   return 0;
}
```

Program Output from Run 1

```
41       18467       6334
```

Program Output from Run 2

```
41       18467       6334
```

To get a different stream of random numbers each time you run the program, you must provide a seed for the random number generator to start with. In C++ this is done by calling the `srand` function. Program 3-33 illustrates this. Notice that the `srand` function is called on line 16 before `rand` is ever called, and that `rand` is only called once for the whole program.

Notice also that the variable created in line 9 to hold the seed is declared to be `unsigned`. As you may recall, this data type holds only non-negative integers. This is the data type the `srand` function expects to receive when it is called, so making the variable `unsigned` guarantees that no negative numbers will be sent to `srand`.

Program 3-33

```
1 // This program demonstrates using random numbers when a
2 // "seed" is provided for the random number generator.
3 #include <iostream>
4 #include <cstdlib>       // Header file needed to use srand and rand
5 using namespace std;
6
7 int main()
8 {
9    unsigned seed;          // Random generator seed
10
11   // Get a "seed" value from the user
12   cout << "Enter a seed value: ";
13   cin  >> seed;
14
15   // Set the random generator seed before calling rand()
16   srand(seed);
17
18   // Now generate and print three random numbers
19   cout << rand() << "      " ;
20   cout << rand() << "      " ;
21   cout << rand() << endl;
22
23   return 0;
24 }
```

Program Output with Example Input Shown in Bold

Run 1:

```
Enter a seed value: 19[Enter]
100      15331      209
```

Run 2:

```
Enter a seed value: 171[Enter]
597      10689      28587
```

As you can see from the Program 3-33 output, each time the program is run with a different seed, a different stream of random numbers is generated. However, if we run the program a third time using 19 or 171 as the seed again, we will get exactly the same numbers we did the first time.

NOTE: The stream of random numbers generated on your computer system may be different.

Notice that on line 13 of Program 3-33 `cin` is used to get a value from the user for the random number generator seed. Another common practice for getting a seed value is to call the `time` function, which is part of the C++ standard library. This function returns the number of seconds that have elapsed since midnight, January 1, 1970, so it will provide a different seed value each time the program is run. Program 3-34 illustrates the use of the `time` function, which appears on line 13 of the program. Notice that when you call it, you must pass 0 as an argument. Notice also that Program 3-34 has a new header file, `ctime`, which is included on line 5. This header file is needed to use `time`.

Program 3-34

```
// This program demonstrates using the C++ time function
// to provide a "seed" for the random number generator.
#include <iostream>
#include <cstdlib>        // Header file needed to use srand and rand
#include <ctime>          // Header file needed to use time
using namespace std;

int main()
{
   unsigned seed;          // Random generator seed

   // Use the time function to get a "seed" value for srand
   seed = time(0);
   srand(seed);

   // Now generate and print three random numbers
   cout << rand() << "       " ;
   cout << rand() << "       " ;
   cout << rand() << endl;

   return 0;
}
```

Program Output

```
2961       21716       181
```

The above output was produced by one sample run. It will be different every time you run the program.

Limiting the Range of a Random Number

Sometimes a program needs a random number in a specific range. To limit the range of the random number to an integer between 1 and some maximum value `max`, you can use the following formula.

```
number = rand() % max + 1;
```

For example, to generate a random number in the range of 1 through 6 to represent the roll of a dice, you would use

```
dice = rand() % 6 + 1;
```

Here is how the statement works. Recall that the modulus operator gives us the remainder of an integer divide. When the positive integer returned by the `rand` function is divided by 6, the remainder will be a number between 0 and 5. Because we want a number between 1 and 6, we simply add 1 to it.

This idea can be extended to produce a random number in any range. For example, suppose a program needs a random number in the range of 10–18. Since that range includes 9 numbers, we could use the following line of code:

```
number = rand() % 9 + 10;
```

The operation `rand() % 9` gives us a number between 0 and 8. Adding 10 to it give us the desired result, a number in the range 10 to 18.

Checkpoint

3.29 Assume the variables `angle1` and `angle2` hold angles stored in radians. Write a statement that adds the sine of `angle1` to the cosine of `angle2` and stores the result in the variable `x`.

3.30 To find the cube root (the third root) of a number, raise it to the power of ⅓. To find the fourth root of a number, raise it to the power of ¼. Write a statement that will find the fifth root of the variable `x` and store the result in the variable `y`.

3.31 Write a statement that produces a random number between 1 and 100 and stores it in the variable `luckyNumber`.

3.11 Focus on Debugging: *Hand Tracing a Program*

Hand tracing is a debugging process where you pretend that you are the computer executing a program. You step through each of the program's statements one by one. As you look at a statement, you record the contents that each variable will have after the statement executes. This process is helpful in finding mathematical mistakes and other logic errors.

To hand trace a program you construct a chart with a column for each variable. The rows in the chart correspond to the lines in the program. For example, Program 3-35 is shown with a hand trace chart. The program uses the following four variables: `num1`, `num2`, `num3`, and `avg`. Notice that the hand trace chart has a column for each variable and a row for each line of code in function `main`.

Program 3-35 ***(with hand trace chart empty)***

```
// This program computes and displays the average of three numbers
// entered by the user. However, it contains a bug. Can you find it?
#include <iostream>
using namespace std;

int main()
{
   double num1, num2, num3, avg;

   cout << "Enter the first number: ";
   cin  >> num1;
   cout << "Enter the second number: ";
   cin  >> num2;
   cout << "Enter the third number: ";
   cin  >> num3;
   avg = num1 + num2 + num3 / 3;
   cout << "The average is " << avg << endl;
  return 0;
}
```

num1	num2	num3	avg

(program continues)

Program 3-35 ***(with hand trace chart empty)*** *(continued)*

Program Output with Example Input Shown in Bold

```
Enter the first number:  10[Enter]
Enter the second number: 20[Enter]
Enter the third number:  30[Enter]
The average is 40
```

Notice that the program runs, but it displays an incorrect average. The correct average of 10, 20, and 30 is 20, not 40. To find the error we will hand trace the program.

To hand trace a program, you step through each statement, observe the operation that is taking place, and then record the contents of the variables after the statement executes. After the hand trace is complete, the chart will appear as follows. We have written question marks in the chart where we do not yet know the contents of a variable.

Program 3-35 ***(with hand trace chart filled in)***

```
1 // This program computes and displays the average of three numbers
2 // entered by the user. However, it contains a bug. Can you find it?
3 #include <iostream>
4 using namespace std;
5
6 int main()
7 {
8    double num1, num2, num3, avg;
9
10   cout << "Enter the first number: ";
11   cin  >> num1;
12   cout << "Enter the second number: ";
13   cin  >> num2;
14   cout << "Enter the third number: ";
15   cin  >> num3;
16   avg = num1 + num2 + num3 / 3;
17   cout << "The average is " << avg << endl;
18   return 0;
19 }
```

num1	num2	num3	avg
?	?	?	?
?	?	?	?
10	?	?	?
10	?	?	?
10	20	?	?
10	20	?	?
10	20	30	?
10	20	30	40
10	20	30	40

Do you see the error? By examining the statement on line 16 that computes the average, we find a mistake. The division operation takes place before the addition operations, so we must rewrite that statement as

```
avg = (num1 + num2 + num3) / 3;
```

Hand tracing is a simple process that focuses your attention on each statement in a program. Often this helps you locate errors that are not obvious.

3.12 Green Fields Landscaping Case Study—Part 1

Problem Statement

One of the services provided by Green Fields Landscaping is the sale and delivery of mulch, which is measured and priced by the cubic yard. You have been asked to create a program that will determine the number of cubic yards of mulch the customer needs and the total price.

Program Design

Program Steps

The program must carry out the following general steps (this list of steps is sometimes called General Pseudocode):

1. Set the price for a cubic yard of mulch (currently 22.00).
2. Ask the user to input the number of square feet to be covered and the depth of the mulch to be spread over this area.
3. Calculate the number of cubic feet of mulch needed.
4. Calculate the number of cubic yards of mulch needed.
5. Calculate the total price for the mulch.
6. Display the results.

Variables whose values will be input

```
double squareFeet               // square feet of land to be covered
int    depth                    // how many inches deep the mulch is to be spread
```

Variables whose values will be output

```
double cubicYards               // number of cubic yards of mulch needed
double totalPrice               // total price for all the cubic yards ordered
```

Program Constants

```
double PRICE_PER_CUBIC_YD       // the price for 1 delivered cubic yard of mulch
```

Additional Variables

```
double cubicFeet                // number of cubic feet of mulch needed
```

Detailed Pseudocode (including actual variable names and needed calculations)

```
PRICE_PER_CUBIC_YD = 22.00
Input squareFeet              // with prompt
Input depth                   // with prompt
cubicFeet = squareFeet * (depth / 12.0)
cubicYards = cubicFeet / 27
totalPrice = cubicYards * PRICE_PER_CUBIC_YD
Display cubicYards, PRICE_PER_CUBIC_YD, and totalPrice
```

The Program

The next step, after the pseudocode has been checked for logic errors, is to expand the pseudocode into the final program. This is shown in Program 3-36.

Program 3-36

```
// This program is used by Green Fields Landscaping to compute the
// number of cubic yards of mulch a customer needs and its price.
#include <iostream>
#include <iomanip>
using namespace std;

const double PRICE_PER_CUBIC_YD = 22.00;

int main()
{
   double squareFeet;   // square feet of land to be covered
   int    depth;        // inches deep the mulch is to be spread
   double cubicFeet,    // number of cubic feet of mulch needed
          cubicYards,   // number of cubic yards of mulch needed
          totalPrice;   // total price for all the cubic yards ordered

   // Get inputs
   cout << "Number of square feet to be covered with mulch: ";
   cin  >> squareFeet;
   cout << "Number of inches deep: ";
   cin  >> depth;

   // Perform calculations
   cubicFeet = squareFeet * (depth / 12.0);
   cubicYards = cubicFeet / 27;
   totalPrice = cubicYards * PRICE_PER_CUBIC_YD;

   // Display outputs
   cout << "\n Number of cubic yards needed: " << cubicYards << endl;
   cout << fixed << showpoint << setprecision(2);
   cout << "Price per cubic yard: $" << setw(7)
        << PRICE_PER_CUBIC_YD << endl;
   cout << "Total price:          $" << setw(7)
        << totalPrice << endl << endl;

   return 0;
}
```

Program Output with Example Input Shown in Bold

```
Number of square feet to be covered with mulch: 270[Enter]
Number of inches deep: 12[Enter]

Number of cubic yards needed: 10
Price per cubic yard: $  22.00
Total price:          $ 220.00
```

(program output continues)

Program 3-36 *(continued)*

Program Output with Different Example Input Shown in Bold
```
Number of square feet to be covered with mulch: 800[Enter]
Number of inches deep: 3[Enter]

Number of cubic yards needed: 7.40741
Price per cubic yard: $  22.00
Total price:          $ 162.96
```

General Crates, Inc., Case Study

The following additional case study, which contains applications of material introduced in Chapter 3, can be found on the book's companion website.

This case study develops a program that accepts the dimensions on a crate to be built and outputs information on its volume, building cost, selling cost, and profit. The case study illustrates the major program development steps: initial problem statement, program design using hierarchy charts and pseudocode, development of the algorithm needed to create the outputs, source code for the final working program, and output created by running the program with several test cases.

3.13 Tying It All Together: *Word Game*

With the programming knowledge you have learned so far, you can start constructing simple games. Here is one that creates a program to play a word game. It will ask the player to enter the following:

- their name (`name`)
- the name of a city (`city`)
- a fun activity (`activity`)
- a type of animal (`animal`)
- a food or product you can buy (`product`)
- an adjective noun (`petname`)
- a number between 10 and 50 (`age`)
- a number between 0 and 15 (`kids`)

Then it will display a story using those words.

Program 3-37

```
// This program uses strings to play a word game.
#include <iostream>
#include <string>
using namespace std;

```

(program continues)

Program 3-37 *(continued)*

```
int main()
{  // Stored strings
   string s1 = "There once was a person named ",
          s2 = " who lived in ",
          s3 = "\nand who loved ",
          s4 = ". At the age of ",
          s5 = ", ",
          s6 = " graduated \nfrom high school and went to work in a ",
          s7 = " factory.\n",
          s8 = " got married and had ",
          s9 = " children and a pet ",
          s10= " named ",
          s11= ".\nEvery weekend the family and ",
          s12= " had fun ",
          s13= " together.";

   // Values input by the user
   string name, city, activity, animal, product, petName;
   int age, kids;

   cout << "Enter the following information and I\'ll "
        << "tell you a story.\n\n";
   cout << "Your name: ";
   getline(cin, name);

   cout << "The name of a city: ";
   getline(cin, city);

   cout << "A physical activity (e.g. jogging, playing baseball): ";
   getline(cin, activity);

   cout << "An animal: ";
   getline(cin, animal);

   cout << "A food or product you can buy: ";
   getline(cin, product);

   cout << "An adjective noun (e.g. blue car): ";
   getline(cin, petName);

   cout << "A number between 10 and 50: ";
   cin  >> age;

   cout << "A number between 0 and 15: ";
   cin  >> kids;

    cout << endl << s1 << name << s2 << city << s3 << activity;
    cout << s4 << age << s5 << name << s6 << product << s7;
    cout << name << s8 << kids << s9 << animal << s10 << petName;
    cout << s11 << petName << s12 << activity << s13 << endl;

   return 0;
}
```

(program continues)

Program 3-37 *(continued)*

Sample Run with User Input Shown in Bold

```
Enter the following information and I'll tell you a story.

Your name: Joe[Enter]
The name of a city: Honolulu[Enter]
A physical activity (e.g. jogging, playing baseball): scuba diving[Enter]
An animal: bear[Enter]
A food or product you can buy: potato chips[Enter]
An adjective noun (e.g. blue car): dish rag[Enter]
A number between 10 and 50: 20[Enter]
A number between 0 and 15: 10[Enter]

There once was a person named Joe who lived in Honolulu
and who loved scuba diving. At the age of 20, Joe graduated
from high school and went to work in a potato chips factory.
Joe got married and had 10 children and a pet bear named dish rag.
Every weekend the family and dish rag had fun scuba diving together.
```

Try running this program with a variety of inputs. Then try modifying it to make up new stories.

Review Questions and Exercises

Short Answer

1. Assume a string object has been defined as follows:

```
string description;
```

A) Write a `cin` statement that reads in a one word description.
B) Write a statement that reads in a description that can contain multiple words separated by blanks.

2. Write a definition statement for a character array large enough to hold any of the following strings:

```
"Billy Bob's Pizza"
"Downtown Auto Supplies"
"Betty Smith School of Architecture"
"ABC Cabinet Company"
```

3. Assume the array `name` is defined as follows:

```
char name[25];
```

A) Using a stream manipulator, write a `cin` statement that will read a string into `name`, but will read no more characters than `name` can hold.
B) Using the `getline` function, write a `cin` statement that will read a string into `name` but that will read no more characters than `name` can hold.

4. Assume the following variables are defined:

```
int age;
double pay;
char section;
```

Write a single `cin` statement that will read input into each of these variables.

5. What header files must be included in the following program?

```
int main()
{
   double amount = 89.7;
   cout << fixed << showpoint << setprecision(1);
   cout << setw(8) << amount << endl;
   return 0;
}
```

6. Write a definition statement for a character array named `city`. It should be large enough to hold a string 30 characters in length.

7. Assume the following preprocessor directive appears in a program:

```
#define SIZE 12
```

How will the preprocessor rewrite the following lines?

A) `price = SIZE * unitCost;`
B) `cout << setw(SIZE) << 98.7;`
C) `cout << SIZE;`

8. Complete the following table by writing the value of each expression in the Value column.

Expression	Value
`28 / 4 - 2`	
`6 + 12 * 2 - 8`	
`4 + 8 * 2`	
`6 + 17 % 3 - 2`	
`2 + 22 * (9 - 7)`	
`(8 + 7) * 2`	
`(16 + 7) % 2 - 1`	
`12 / (10 - 6)`	
`(19 - 3) * (2 + 2) / 4`	

9. Write C++ expressions for the following algebraic expressions:

A) $a = 12x$

B) $z = 5x + 14y + 6k$

C) $y = x^4$

D) $g = \dfrac{h + 12}{4k}$

E) $g = \dfrac{a^3}{b^2k^4}$

10. Assume a program has the following variable definitions

```
int units;
float mass;
double weight;
```

and the following statement:

```
weight = mass * units;
```

Which automatic data type conversions will take place?

11. Assume a program has the following variable definitions

```
int a, b = 2;
double c = 4.3;
```

and the following statement:

```
a = b * c;
```

What value will be stored in a?

12. Assume that qty and salesReps are both integers. Use a type cast expression to rewrite the following statement so it will no longer perform integer division.

```
unitsEach = qty / salesReps;
```

13. Rewrite the following variable definition so the variable is a named constant with the value 12.

```
int rate;
```

14. Complete the following table by writing statements with combined assignment operators in the right-hand column. The statements should be equivalent to the statements in the left-hand column.

Statements with Assignment Operator	Statements with Combined Assignment Operator
`x = x + 5;`	
`total = total + subtotal;`	
`dist = dist / rep;`	
`ppl = ppl * period;`	
`inv = inv - shrinkage;`	
`num = num % 2;`	

15. Write a multiple assignment statement that can be used instead of the following group of assignment statements:

```
east = 1;
west = 1;
north = 1;
south = 1;
```

16. Replace the following statements with a single statement that initializes `sum` to 0 at the time it is defined.

```
int sum;
sum = 0;
```

17. Is the following code legal? Why or why not?

```
const int DAYS_IN_WEEK;
DAYS_IN_WEEK = 7;
```

18. Write a `cout` statement so the variable `divSales` is displayed in a field of eight spaces, in fixed-point notation, with a decimal point and two decimal digits.

19. Write a `cout` statement so the variable `profit` is displayed in a field of 12 spaces, in fixed-point notation, with a decimal point and four decimal digits.

20. What header file must be included
    A) to perform mathematical functions like `sqrt`?
    B) to use `cin` and `cout`?
    C) to use stream manipluators like `setprecision`?

Algorithm Workbench

21. A bowling alley is offering a prize to the bowler whose average score from bowling three games is the lowest. Write a pseudocode algorithm for a program that inputs three bowling scores and calculates and displays their average.

22. Pet World offers a 15% discount to senior citizens. Write a pseudocode algorithm for a program that inputs the amount of a sale, then calculates and displays both the amount the customer saves and the amount they must pay.

23. A retail store grants its customers a maximum amount of credit. Each customer's available credit is his or her maximum amount of credit minus the amount of credit used. Write a pseudocode algorithm for a program that asks for a customer's maximum credit and amount of credit used, then calculates and displays the customer's available credit.

24. Little Italy Pizza charges $12.00 for a 12-inch diameter sausage pizza and $14.00 for a 14-inch diameter sausage pizza. Write the pseudocode for an algorithm that calculates and displays how much each of these earns the establishment per square inch of pizza sold. (Hint: you will need to first calculate how many square inches there are in each pizza.)

Predict the Output

25. Trace the following programs and tell what each will display. (Some require a calculator.)
    A) *(Assume the user enters 38711. Use a calculator.)*

```
#include <iostream>
using namespace std;
```

```
int main()
{
   double salary, monthly;

   cout << "What is your annual salary? ";
   cin  >> salary;
   monthly = static_cast<int>(salary) / 12;
   cout << "Your monthly wages are " << monthly << endl;
   return 0;
}
```

B)

```
#include <iostream>
using namespace std;

int main()
{
   long x, y, z;
   x = y = z = 4;
   x += 2;
   y -= 1;
   z *= 3;
   cout << x << " " << y << " " << z << endl;
   return 0;
}
```

C)

```
#include <iostream>
using namespace std;
#define WHO "Columbus"
#define DID "sailed"
#define WHAT "the ocean blue."

int main()
{
   const int WHEN = 1492;
   cout << "In " << WHEN << " " << WHO << " "
        << DID << " " << WHAT << endl;
   return 0;
}
```

26. A) *(Assume the user enters George Washington.)*

```
#include <iostream>
#include <iomanip>
#include <string>
using namespace std;
int main()
{
   string userInput;

   cout << "What is your name? ";
   cin  >> userInput;
   cout << "Hello " << userInput << endl;
   return 0;
}
```

B) *(Assume the user enters George Washington.)*

```
#include <iostream>
#include <iomanip>
#include <string>
using namespace std;

int main()
{
   string userInput;

   cout << "What is your name? ";
   getline(cin, userInput);
   cout << "Hello " << userInput << endl;
   return 0;
}
```

C) *(Assume the user enters 36720152. Use a calculator.)*

```
#include <iostream>
#include <iomanip>
using namespace std;

int main()
{
   long seconds;
   double minutes, hours, days, months, years;

   cout << "Enter the number of seconds that have\n";
   cout << "elapsed since some time in the past and\n";
   cout << "I will tell you how many minutes, hours,\n";
   cout << "days, months, and years have passed: ";
   cin  >> seconds;
   minutes = seconds / 60;
   hours = minutes / 60;
   days = hours / 24;
   years = days / 365;
   months = years * 12;

   cout << fixed << showpoint << setprecision(4) << left;
   cout << "Minutes: " << setw(6) << minutes << endl;
   cout << "Hours: "   << setw(6) << hours << endl;
   cout << "Days: "    << setw(6) << days << endl;
   cout << "Months: "  << setw(6) << months << endl;
   cout << "Years: "   << setw(6) << years << endl;
   return 0;
}
```

Find the Errors

27. Each of the following programs has some errors. Locate as many as you can.

A)
```
using namespace std;
int main()
{
   double number1, number2, sum;
```

```
    Cout << "Enter a number: ";
    Cin  << number1;
    Cout << "Enter another number: ";
    Cin  << number2;
    number1 + number2 = sum;
    Cout "The sum of the two numbers is " << sum
    return 0;
}
```

B)
```
#include <iostream>
using namespace std;
int main()
{
    int number1, number2;
    double quotient;
    cout << "Enter two numbers and I will divide\n";
    cout << "the first by the second for you.\n";
    cin  >> number1, number2;
    quotient = double<static_cast>(number1)/number2;
    cout << quotient
}
```

28. A)
```
#include <iostream>;
using namespace std;
int main()
{
    const int number1, number2, product;

    cout << "Enter two numbers and I will multiply\n";
    cout << "them for you.\n";
    cin  >> number1 >> number2;
    product = number1 * number2;
    cout << product
    return 0;
}
```

B)
```
#include <iostream>;
using namespace std;
main
{
    int number1, number2;

    cout << "Enter two numbers and I will multiply\n"
    cout << "them by 50 for you.\n"
    cin  >> number1 >> number2;
    number1 =* 50;
    number2 =* 50;
    return 0;
    cout << number1 << " " << number2;
}
```

29. A)
```
#include <iostream>;
using namespace std;
main
{
```

```
    double number, half;

    cout << "Enter a number and I will divide it\n"
    cout << "in half for you.\n"
    cin  >> number1;
    half =/ 2;
}
```

B)
```
#include <iostream>;
using namespace std;
int main()
{
    char name, go;

    cout << "Enter your name: ";
    cin.width(20);
    cin.getline >> name;
    cout << "Hi " << name << endl;
    cout "Press the ENTER key to end this program.";
    cin  >> go;
    return 0;
}
```

Soft Skills

Often programmers work in teams with other programmers to develop a piece of software. It is important that the team members be able to communicate clearly with one another.

30. Suppose you and a fellow student have been assigned to develop together the pizza cost program described in Problem 24. You have developed a pseudocode algorithm for the program and emailed it to your partner, but he does not understand how it works. Write a paragraph that you might email back clearly explaining how the algorithm works, what steps must be done, why they must be done in a particular order, and why the calculations you have specified in the pseudocode are the correct ones to use. Write your answer using full English sentences with correct spelling and grammar.

Programming Challenges

1. Miles per Gallon

Write a program that calculates a car's gas mileage. The program should ask the user to enter the number of gallons of gas the car can hold and the number of miles it can be driven on a full tank. It should then calculate and display the number of miles per gallon the car gets.

2. Stadium Seating

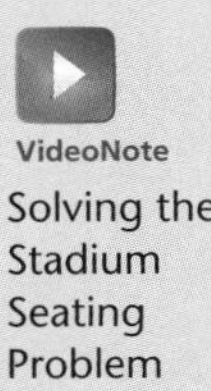

Solving the Stadium Seating Problem

There are three seating categories at a stadium. For a softball game, Class A seats cost $15, Class B seats cost $12, and Class C seats cost $9. Write a program that asks how many tickets for each class of seats were sold, then displays the amount of income generated from ticket sales. Format your dollar amount in a fixed-point notation with two decimal points and make sure the decimal point is always displayed.

3. Housing Costs

Write a program that asks the user to enter their *monthly* costs for each of the following housing related expenses:

- rent or mortgage payment
- utilities
- phones
- cable

The program should then display the total monthly cost of these expenses, and the total annual cost of these expenses.

4. How Much Insurance?

Many financial experts advise property owners to insure their homes or buildings for at least 80 percent of the amount it would cost to replace the structure. Write a program that asks the user to enter the replacement cost of a building and then displays the minimum amount of insurance that should be purchased for the property.

5. Batting Average

Write a program to find a baseball player's batting average. The program should ask the user to enter the number of times the player was at bat and the number of hits he got. It should then display his batting average to 4 decimal places.

6. Test Average

Write a program that asks for five test scores. The program should calculate the average test score and display it. The number displayed should be formatted in fixed-point notation, with one decimal point of precision.

7. Average Rainfall

Write a program that calculates the average monthly rainfall for three months. The program should ask the user to enter the name of each month, such as June or July, and the amount of rain (in inches) that fell that month. The program should display a message similar to the following:

```
The average monthly rainfall for June, July, and August was 6.72 inches.
```

8. Box Office

A movie theater only keeps a percentage of the revenue earned from ticket sales. The remainder goes to the distibutor. Write a program that calculates a theater's gross and net box office profit for a night. The program should ask for the name of the movie, and how many adult and child tickets were sold. (The price of an adult ticket is $6.00 and a child's ticket is $3.00.) It should display a report similar to the following:

Movie Name:	"Wheels of Fury"
Adult Tickets Sold:	382
Child Tickets Sold:	127
Gross Box Office Profit:	$ 2673.00
Amount Paid to Distributor:	– $ 2138.40
Net Box Office Profit:	$ 534.60

Assume the theater keeps 20 percent of the gross box office profit.

9. How Many Widgets?

The Yukon Widget Company manufactures widgets that weigh 9.2 pounds each. Write a program that calculates how many widgets are stacked on a pallet, based on the total weight of the pallet. The program should ask the user how much the pallet weighs by itself and with the widgets stacked on it. It should then calculate and display the number of widgets stacked on the pallet.

10. How many Calories?

A bag of cookies holds 40 cookies. The calorie information on the bag claims that there are 10 "servings" in the bag and that a serving equals 300 calories. Write a program that asks the user to input how many cookies they actually ate and then reports how many total calories were consumed.

11. Celsius to Fahrenheit

Write a program that converts Celsius temperatures to Fahrenheit temperatures. The formula is

$$F = \frac{9}{5}C + 32$$

where F is the Fahrenheit temperature and C is the Celsius temperature. The program should prompt the user to input a Celsius temperature and should display the corresponding Farenheit temperature.

12. Currency

Write a program that will convert U.S. dollar amounts to Japanese yen and to euros, storing the conversion factors in the constant variables YEN_PER_DOLLAR and EUROS_PER_DOLLAR. To get the most up-to-date exchange rates, search the Internet using the term "currency exchange rate" or "currency converter". If you cannot find the most recent exchange rates, use the following:

1 Dollar = 78.18 Yen
1 Dollar = .8235 Euros

13. Monthly Sales Tax

A retail company must file a monthly sales tax report listing the sales for the month and the amount of sales tax collected. Write a program that asks for the month, the year, and the total amount collected at the cash register (that is, sales plus sales tax). Assume the state sales tax is 4 percent and the county sales tax is 2 percent.

If the total amount collected is known and the total sales tax is 6 percent, the amount of product sales may be calculated as

$$S = \frac{T}{1.06}$$

where S is the product sales and T is the total income (product sales plus sales tax).

The program should display a report similar to the following:

```
Month: March 2008
--------------------
Total Collected:      $ 26572.89
Sales:                $ 25068.76
County Sales Tax:     $   501.38
State Sales Tax:      $  1002.75
Total Sales Tax:      $  1504.13
```

14. Property Tax

Madison County collects property taxes on the assessed value of property, which is 60 percent of its actual value. For example, if a house is valued at $158,000 its assessed value is $94,800. This is the amount the homeowner pays tax on. At last year's tax rate of $2.64 for each $100 of assessed value, the annual property tax for this house would be $2502.72. Write a program that asks the user to input the actual value of a piece of property and the current tax rate for each $100 of assessed value. The program should then calculate and report how much annual property tax the homeowner will be charged for this property.

15. Senior Citizen Property Tax

Madison County provides a $5000 homeowner exemption for senior citizens. For example, if their house is valued at $158,000 its assessed value would be $94,800, as explained above. However they would only pay tax on $89,800. At last year's tax rate of $2.64 for each $100 of assessed value, their property tax would be $2370.72. In addition to the tax break, senior citizens are allowed to pay their property tax in 4 equal payments. The quarterly payment due on this property would be $592.68. Write a program that asks the user to input the actual value of a piece of property and the current tax rate for each $100 of assessed value. The program should then calculate and report how much annual property tax a senior homeowner will be charged for this property and what their quarterly tax bill will be.

16. Math Tutor

Write a program that can be used as a math tutor for a young student. The program should display two random numbers between 1 and 9 to be added, such as

$$\begin{array}{r} 2 \\ \underline{+\,1} \end{array}$$

After the student has entered an answer and pressed the [Enter] key, the program should display the correct answer so the student can see if his or her answer is correct.

17. Interest Earned

Assuming there are no deposits other than the original investment, the balance in a savings account after one year may be calculated as

$$\text{Amount} = \text{Principal} * \left(1 + \frac{\text{Rate}}{\text{T}}\right)^{\text{T}}$$

where Principal is the balance in the account, Rate is the annual interest rate, and T is the number of times the interest is compounded during a year (e.g., T is 4 if the interest is compounded quarterly).

Write a program that asks for the principal, the interest rate, and the number of times the interest is compounded. It should display a report similar to the following:

```
Interest Rate:              4.25%
Times Compounded:             12
Principal:              $ 1000.00
Interest:               $   43.33
Final balance:          $ 1043.33
```

18. Monthly Payments

The monthly payment on a loan may be calculated by the following formula:

$$\text{Payment} = \frac{\text{Rate} * (1 + \text{Rate})^N}{(1 + \text{Rate})^N - 1} * L/;$$

Rate is the monthly interest rate, which is the annual interest rate divided by 12. (A 12 percent annual interest would be 1 percent monthly interest.) *N* is the number of payments and `L` is the amount of the loan. Write a program that asks for these values and displays a report similar to the following:

```
Loan Amount:                 $ 10000.00
Monthly Interest Rate:               1%
Number of Payments:                  36
Monthly Payment:             $   332.14
Amount Paid Back:            $ 11957.15
Interest Paid:               $  1957.15
```

19. Pizza Slices

Joe's Pizza Palace needs a program to calculate the number of slices a pizza of any size can be divided into. The program should perform the following steps:

A) Ask the user for the diameter of the pizza in inches.
B) Calculate the number of slices that may be taken from a pizza of that size if each slice has an area of 14.125 square inches.
C) Display a message telling the number of slices.

The number of square inches in the total pizza can be calculated with this formula:

$$\text{Area} = \pi r^2$$

where variable r is the radius of the pizza and π is the Greek letter PI. In your program make PI a named constant with the value 3.14. Display the number of slices as a whole number (i.e., with no decimals).

20. How Many Pizzas?

Modify the program you wrote in Programming Challenge 19 so that it reports the number of pizzas you need to buy for a party if each person attending is expected to eat an average of 4 slices. The program should ask the user for the number of people who will be at the party and for the diameter of the pizzas to be ordered. It should then calculate and display the number of pizzas to purchase. Because it is impossible to buy a part of a pizza, the number of required pizzas should be displayed as a whole number.

21. Angle Calculator

Write a program that asks the user for an angle, entered in radians. The program should then display the sine, cosine, and tangent of the angle. (Use the `sin`, `cos`, and `tan` library functions to determine these values.) The output should be displayed in fixed-point notation, rounded to four decimal places of precision.

22. Stock Transaction Program

Last month Joe purchased 100 shares of stock. Here are the details of the purchase:

- When Joe purchased the stock, he paid $32.87 per share.
- Joe paid his stock broker a commission that amounted to 2% of the amount he paid for the stock.

Two months later Joe sold the stock. Here are the details of the sale:

- He sold the stock for $33.92 per share.
- He paid his stock broker another commission that amounted to 2% of the amount he received for the stock.

Write a program that displays the following information:

- The amount of money Joe paid for the stock.
- The amount of commission Joe paid his broker when he bought the stock.
- The amount that Joe sold the stock for.
- The amount of commission Joe paid his broker when he sold the stock.
- The amount of profit or loss that Joe had after selling his stock and paying both broker commissions.

CHAPTER

4 Making Decisions

TOPICS

4.1 Relational Operators

CONCEPT: Relational operators allow you to compare numeric and `char` values and determine whether one is greater than, less than, equal to, or not equal to another.

So far, the programs you have written follow this simple scheme:

- Gather input from the user.
- Perform one or more calculations.
- Display the results on the screen.

Computers are good at performing calculations, but they are also quite adept at comparing values to determine if one is greater than, less than, or equal to, the other. These types of operations are valuable for tasks such as examining sales figures, determining profit and loss, checking a number to ensure it is within an acceptable range, and validating the input given by a user.

Numeric data is compared in C++ by using relational operators. Characters can also be compared with these operators, because characters are considered numeric values in C++. Each relational operator determines whether a specific relationship exists between two values. For example, the greater-than operator (>) determines if a value is greater than another. The equality operator (==) determines if two values are equal. Table 4-1 lists all of C++'s relational operators.

Table 4-1 Relational Operators

Relational Operators	Meaning
`>`	Greater than
`<`	Less than
`>=`	Greater than or equal to
`<=`	Less than or equal to
`==`	Equal to
`!=`	Not equal to

NOTE: All the relational operators are binary operators with left-to-right associativity. Recall that associativity is the order in which an operator works with its operands.

All of the relational operators are binary. This means they use two operands. Here is an example of an expression using the greater-than operator:

```
x > y
```

This expression is called a *relational expression*. It is used to determine whether `x` is greater than `y`. The following expression determines whether `x` is less than `y`:

```
x < y
```

The Value of a Relationship

So, how are relational expressions used in a program? Remember, all expressions have a value. Relational expressions are *Boolean expressions*, which means their value can only be *true* or *false*. If `x` is greater than `y`, the expression `x > y` will be true and the expression `x < y` will be false.

The == operator determines whether the operand on its left is equal to the operand on its right. If both operands have the same value, the expression is true. Assuming that `a` is 4, the following expression is true:

```
a == 4
```

and the following expression is false:

```
a == 2
```

WARNING! Notice the equality operator is two = symbols together. Don't confuse this operator with the assignment operator, which is one = symbol. The == operator determines if a variable is equal to another value, but the = operator assigns the value on the operator's right to the variable on its left. There will be more about this later in the chapter.

Two of the relational operators actually test for a pair of relationships. The >= operator determines whether the operand on its left is greater than *or* equal to the operand on the right. If a is 4, b is 6, and c is 4, both of the following expressions are true:

```
b >= a
a >= c
```

and the following expression is false:

```
a >= 5
```

The <= operator determines whether the operand on its left is less than *or* equal to the operand on its right. Once again, if a is 4, b is 6, and c is 4, both of the following expressions are true:

```
a <= c
b <= 10
```

and the following expression is false:

```
b <= a
```

The last relational operator is !=, which is the not-equal operator. It determines whether the operand on its left is different than (i.e., *not* equal to) the operand on its right, which is the opposite of the == operator. As before, if a is 4, b is 6, and c is 4, both of the following expressions are true:

```
a != b
b != c
```

These expressions are true because a is *not* equal to b and b is *not* equal to c. However, the following expression is false because a *is* equal to c:

```
a != c
```

Table 4-2 shows other relational expressions and their true or false values.

Table 4-2 Example Relational Expressions (Assume x is 10 and y is 7.)

Expression	Value
x < y	false, because x is not less than y.
x > y	true, because x is greater than y.
x >= y	true, because x is greater than or equal to y.
x <= y	false, because x is not less than or equal to y.
y != x	true, because y is not equal to x.

What Is Truth?

If a relational expression can evaluate to either true or false, how are those values represented internally in a program? How does a computer store *true* in memory? How does it store *false*?

As you saw in Program 2-16, those two abstract states are converted to numbers. This can be confusing, especially for new programmers, because in C++ zero is considered false, and any nonzero value is considered true. The C++ key word `false` is stored as 0, and the key word `true` is stored as 1. And when a relational expression is false it evaluates to 0. However, when a relational expression is true it does not always evaluate to 1. Though it usually does, it can actually evaluate to any nonzero value.

To illustrate this more fully, look at Program 4-1.

Program 4-1

```
// This program displays the values C++ uses to represent true and false.
#include <iostream>
using namespace std;

int main()
{
   bool trueValue, falseValue;
   int x = 5, y = 10;

   trueValue = (x < y);
   falseValue = (y == x);

   cout << "True  is " << trueValue << endl;
   cout << "False is " << falseValue << endl;
   return 0;
}
```

Program Output

```
True  is 1
False is 0
```

Let's examine the statements containing the relational expressions a little closer:

```
trueValue = (x < y);
falseValue = (y == x);
```

These statements may seem odd because they are assigning the value of a comparison to a variable. In the first statement, the variable `trueValue` is being assigned the result of `x < y`. Because `x` is less than `y`, the expression is true, and the variable `trueValue` is assigned a nonzero value. In the second statement, the expression `y == x` is false, so the variable `falseValue` is set to 0.

When writing statements such as these, most programmers enclose the relational expression in parentheses, as shown above, to make it clearer.

Parentheses are not actually required, however, because even without them the relational operation is carried out before the assignment operation is performed. This occurs because relational operators have a higher precedence than the assignment operator. Likewise, arithmetic operators have a higher precedence than relational operators.

The statement

```
result = x < y - 8;
```

is equivalent to the statement

```
result = x < (y - 8);
```

In both cases, `y - 8` is evaluated first. Then this value is compared to `x`. Notice, however, how much clearer the second statement is. It is always a good idea to place parentheses around an arithmetic expression when its result will be used in a relational expression.

Table 4-3 shows examples of other statements that include relational expressions.

Table 4-3 Statements that Include Relational Expressions (Assume `x` is 10, `y` is 7, and `z` is an `int` or `bool`.)

Statement	Outcome
`z = x < y`	`z` is assigned 0 because `x` is not less than `y`.
`cout << (x > y);`	Displays 1 because `x` is greater than `y`.
`z = (x >= y);`	`z` is assigned 1 because `x` is greater than or equal to `y`.
`cout << (x <= y);`	Displays 0 because `x` is not less than or equal to `y`.
`z = (y != x);`	`z` is assigned 1 because `y` is not equal to `x`.
`cout << (x == (y + 3));`	Displays 1 because `x` is equal to `y + 3`.

Relational operators also have a precedence order among themselves. The two operators that test for equality or lack of equality (== and `!=`) have the same precedence as each other. The four other relational operators, which test relative size, have the same precedence as each other. These four relative relational operators have a higher precedence than the two equality relational operators. Table 4-4 shows the precedence of relational operators.

Table 4-4 Precedence of Relational Operators (Highest to Lowest)

`>   >=   <   <=`
`==   !=`

Here is an example of how this is applied. If `a = 9`, `b = 24`, and `c = 0`, the following statement displays a 1.

```
cout << (c == a > b);
```

Because of the relative precedence of the operators in this expression, `a > b` is evaluated first. Since 9 is *not* greater than 24, it evaluates to false, or 0. Then `c == 0` is evaluated. Because `c` *does* equal 0, this evaluates to true, or 1. So a 1 is inserted into the output stream and printed.

In this chapter's remaining sections you will see how to get the most from relational expressions by using them in statements that take action based on the results of the comparison.

Checkpoint

4.1 Assuming `x` is 5, `y` is 6, and `z` is 8, indicate whether each of the following relational expressions is true or false:

A) `x == 5`
B) `7 <= (x + 2)`
C) `z > 4`
D) `(2 + x) != y`
E) `z != 4`
F) `x >= 0`
G) `x <= (y * 2)`

4.2 Indicate whether each of the following statements about relational expressions is correct or incorrect.

A) `x <= y` is the same as `y > x`.
B) `x != y` is the same as `y >= x`.
C) `x >= y` is the same as `y <= x`.

4.3 Answer the following questions with a yes or no.

A) If it is true that x > y and it is also true that `x < z`, does that mean `y < z` is true?
B) If it is true that `x >= y` and it is also true that `z == x`, does that mean that `z == y` is true?
C) If it is true that `x != y` and it is also true that `x != z`, does that mean that `z != y` is true?

4.4 What will the following program segment display?

```
int a = 0, b = 2, x = 4, y = 0;

cout << (a == b) << " " << (a != y) << " "
     << (b <= x) << " " << (y > a) << endl;
```

4.2 The `if` Statement

CONCEPT: The `if` statement can cause other statements to execute only under certain conditions.

VideoNote
Using an `if` Statement

You might think of the statements in a procedural program as individual steps taken as you are walking down a road. To reach the destination, you must start at the beginning and take each step, one after the other, until you reach the destination. The programs you have written so far are like a "path" of execution for the program to follow.

Figure 4-1

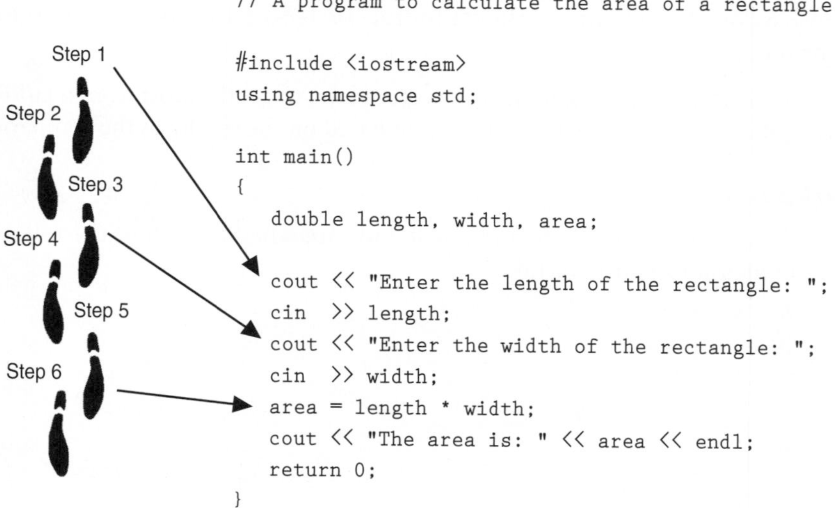
Step 1
Step 2
Step 3
Step 4
Step 5
Step 6
// A program to calculate the area of a rectangle
#include <iostream>
using namespace std;
int main()
{
double length, width, area;
cout << "Enter the length of the rectangle: ";
cin >> length;
cout << "Enter the width of the rectangle: ";
cin >> width;
area = length * width;
cout << "The area is: " << area << endl;
return 0;
}

The type of code in Figure 4-1 is called a *sequence structure* because the statements are executed in sequence, one after another, without branching off in another direction. Programs often need more than one path of execution, however. Many algorithms require a program to execute some statements only under certain circumstances. This can be accomplished with a *decision structure.*

In a decision structure's simplest form an action, or set of actions, is carried out only when a specific condition exists. If the condition does not exist, the actions are not performed. The flowchart in Figure 4-2 shows the logic of a decision structure. The diamond symbol represents a yes/no question or a true/false condition. If the answer to the question is yes (or if the condition is true), the program flow follows one path, which leads to the actions being performed. If the answer to the question is no (or the condition is false), the program flow follows another path, which skips the actions.

Figure 4-2

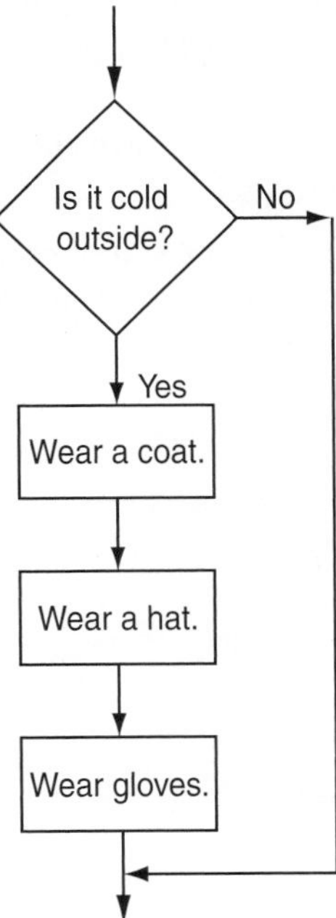

In the flowchart, the actions "Wear a coat", "Wear a hat", and "Wear gloves" are performed only when it is cold outside. If it is not cold outside, these actions are skipped. The actions are *conditionally executed* because they are performed only when a certain condition (cold outside) exists.

We perform mental tests like these every day. Here are some other examples:

> If the car is low on gas, stop at a service station and get gas.
> If it's raining outside, go inside.
> If you're hungry, get something to eat.

The most common way to code a decision structure in C++ is with the `if` statement. Figure 4-3 shows the general format of the `if` statement and a flowchart visually depicting how it works.

Figure 4-3

```
if (condition)
{
      statement 1;
      statement 2;
         .
         .
      statement n;
}
```

or

```
if (condition) {
      statement 1;
      statement 2;
         .
         .
      statement n;
}
```

condition
false
true
statement(s)

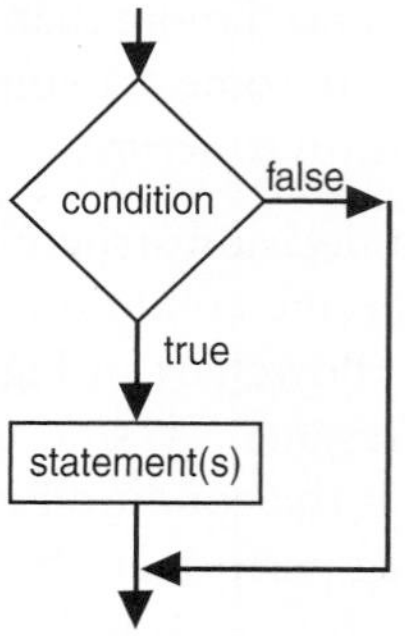

Notice that the statements inside the body of the `if` construct are contained within a set of curly braces. This creates what C++ calls a *block* and lets the compiler know which statements are associated with the `if`. The opening brace must be located after the `if` *condition* and before the first statement in the body. However, while following this requirement, different programmers choose different places to locate it. The two most common placements are shown in Figure 4-3. This book uses the form shown on the left. Your instructor will tell you what form he or she wants you to use.

Program 4-2 illustrates the use of an `if` statement. The user enters three test scores and the program calculates their average. If the average equals 100, the program congratulates the user on earning a perfect score.

Program 4-2

```
// This program correctly averages 3 test scores.
#include <iostream>
#include <iomanip>
using namespace std;

int main()
{
   int score1, score2, score3;
   double average;

   // Get the three test scores
   cout << "Enter 3 test scores and I will average them: ";
   cin  >> score1 >> score2 >> score3;

   // Calculate and display the average score
   average = (score1 + score2 + score3) / 3.0;
   cout << fixed << showpoint << setprecision(1);
   cout << "Your average is " << average << endl;

   // If the average equals 100, congratulate the user
   if (average == 100)
   {  cout << "Congratulations! ";
      cout << "That's a perfect score!\n";
   }
   return 0;
}
```

(program continues)

Program 4-2 *(continued)*

Program Output with Example Input Shown in Bold

```
Enter 3 test scores and I will average them: 80 90 70[Enter]
Your average is 80.0
```

Program Output with Other Example Input Shown in Bold

```
Enter 3 test scores and I will average them: 100 100 100[Enter]
Your average is 100.0
Congratulations! That's a perfect score!
```

Let's look more closely at lines 21–24 of Program 4-2, which cause the congratulatory message to be printed.

```
if (average == 100)
{   cout << "Congratulations! ";
    cout << "That's a perfect score!\n";
}
```

There are four important things to notice. First, the word `if`, which begins the statement, is a C++ key word and must be written in lowercase. Second, the condition to be tested (`average == 100`) must be enclosed inside parentheses. Third, there is *no* semicolon after the test condition, even though there *is* a semicolon after each action associated with the `if` construct. We will explain why shortly. And finally, the block of statements to be conditionally executed is surrounded by curly braces. This is required whenever two or more actions are associated with an `if` statement.

If there is only one statement to be conditionally executed, the braces can be omitted. For example, in Program 4-2 if the two `cout` statements were combined into one statement, they could be written as shown here.

```
if (average == 100)
   cout << "Congratulations! That's a perfect score!\n";
```

However, some instructors prefer that you *always* place braces around a conditionally executed block, even when it consists of only one statement.

Table 4-5 shows other examples of `if` statements and their outcomes.

Table 4-5 Example `if` Statements

Statements	Outcome

`if (hours > 40)`
`{   overTime = true;`
`    payRate *= 2;`
`}`
	Assigns `true` to Boolean variable `overTime` and doubles `payRate` only when `hours` is greater than 40. Because there is more than one statement in the conditionally executed block, braces `{}` are required.

`if (temperature > 32)` `    freezing = false;`	Assigns `false` to Boolean variable `freezing` only when `temperature` is greater than 32. Because there is only one statement in the conditionally executed block, braces `{}` are optional.

Programming Style and the `if` Statement

Even though `if` statements usually span more than one line, they are technically one long statement. For instance, the following `if` statements are identical except in style:

```
if (a >= 100)
   cout << "The number is out of range.\n";

if (a >= 100) cout << "The number is out of range.\n";
```

The first of these two `if` statements is considered to be better style because it is easier to read. By indenting the conditionally executed statement or block of statements, you cause it to stand out visually so you can tell at a glance what part of the program the `if` statement executes. This is a standard way of writing `if` statements and is the method you should use. Here are two important style rules for writing `if` statements:

- The conditionally executed statement(s) should begin on the line after the `if` statement.
- The conditionally executed statement(s) should be indented one "level" from the `if` statement.

NOTE: In most editors, each time you press the tab key, you are indenting one level.

Three Common Errors to Watch Out For

When writing `if` statements, there are three common errors you must watch out for.

1. Misplaced semicolons
2. Missing braces
3. Confusing = with ==

Be Careful with Semicolons

Semicolons do not mark the end of a line. They mark the end of a complete C++ statement. The `if` construct isn't complete without the one or more conditionally executed statements that come after it. So you must not put a semicolon after the `if (condition)` portion of an `if` statement.

```
if (condition)        <---- No semicolon goes here
{
      statement 1;    <--
      statement 2;    <--  Semicolons go here
         .
         .
      statement n;    <--
}
```

If you inadvertently put a semicolon after the `if` part, the compiler will assume you are placing a null statement there. The *null statement* is an empty statement that does nothing. This will prematurely terminate the `if` statement, which disconnects it from the block of statements that follows it. These statements will then always execute. For example, notice what would have happened in Program 4-2 if the `if` statement had been prematurely terminated with a semicolon, as shown here.

```
if (average == 100);      // Error. The semicolon terminates
{                         // the if statement prematurely.
    cout << "Congratulations! ";
    cout << "That's a perfect score!\n";
}
```

Output of Revised Program 4-2 with Example Input Shown in Bold

```
Enter 3 test scores and I will average them: 80 90 70[Enter]
Your average is 80.0
Congratulations! That's a perfect score!
```

Because the `if` statement ends when the premature semicolon is encountered, the `cout` statements inside the braces are no longer part of it. Therefore, they *always* execute, regardless of whether `average` equals 100 or not. This erroneous version of Program 4-2 can be found on the book's companion website as Program 4-2B.

NOTE: Indentation and spacing are for human readers of a program, not the computer. Even though the `cout` statements inside the braces in the above example are indented, the semicolon still terminates the `if` construct.

Don't Forget the Braces

If you intend to conditionally execute a block of statements rather than just one statement with an `if` statement, don't forget the braces. Without a set of braces, the `if` condition only determines whether or not the very next statement will be executed. Any following statements are considered to be outside the `if` statement and will *always* be executed. For example, notice what would have happened in the original Program 4-2 if the braces enclosing the two `cout` statements had been omitted.

```
if (average == 100)
    cout << "Congratulations! ";          // There are no braces.
    cout << "That's a perfect score!\n";  // This is outside the if.
```

Output of Program 4-2 Revised a Second Time with Example Input Shown in Bold

```
Enter 3 test scores and I will average them: 80 90 70[Enter]
Your average is 80.0
That's a perfect score!
```

With no braces around the set of statement to be conditionally executed, only the first of these statements belongs to the `if` construct. Because the condition in our test case (`average == 100`) was false, the `Congratulations!` message was skipped. However the `cout` statement that prints `That's a perfect score!` was executed, as it would be every time, regardless of whether `average` equals 100 or not. This erroneous version of Program 4-2 can be found on the book's companion website as Program 4-2C.

Don't Confuse == With =

Earlier you saw a warning not to confuse the equality operator (`==`) with the assignment operator (`=`), as in the following statement:

```
if (x = 2)          // Caution here!
    cout << "It is True!";
```

This statement does not determine whether `x` is equal to 2; instead it assigns `x` the value 2! Furthermore, the `cout` statement will *always* be executed because the expression `x = 2` evaluates to 2, which C++ considers true.

This occurs because the value of an assignment expression is the value being assigned to the variable on the left side of the = operator. Therefore the value of the expression `x = 2` is 2. Earlier you learned that C++ stores the value `true` as 1. However, it actually considers all nonzero values, not just 1, to be true. Thus 2 represents a true condition.

Let's examine this more closely by looking at yet another variation of the original Program 4-2. This time notice what would have happened if the equal-to relational operator in the `if` condition had been replaced by the assignment operator, as shown here.

```
if (average = 100)        // Error. This assigns 100 to average.
{
    cout << "Congratulations! ";
    cout << "That's a perfect score!\n";
}
```

Output of Program 4-2 Revised a Third Time with Example Input Shown in Bold

```
Enter 3 test scores and I will average them: 80 90 70[Enter]
Your average is 80.0
Congratulations! That's a perfect score!
```

Rather than comparing `average` to 100, the `if` statement *assigns* it the value 100. This causes the `if` test to evaluate to 100, which is considered true. Therefore the two `cout` statements will execute every time, regardless of what test scores are entered by the user. This erroneous version of Program 4-2 can be found on the book's companion website as Program 4-2D.

More About Truth

Now that you've gotten your feet wet with relational expressions and `if` statements, let's look further at the subject of truth. You have seen that a relational expression has the value 1 when it is true and 0 when false. You have also seen that while 0 is considered false, all values other than 0 are considered true. This means that any value, even a negative number, represents true as long as it is not 0.

Just as in real life, truth is a complicated thing. Here is a summary of the rules you have seen so far:

- When a relational expression is true, it has a nonzero value, which in most cases is represented by the value 1.
- When a relational expression is false, it has the value 0.

- An expression that has the value 0 is considered false by the `if` statement. This includes the `bool` value `false`, which is equivalent to 0.
- An expression that has *any* value other than 0 is considered true. This includes the `bool` value `true`, which is equivalent to 1.

The fact that the `if` statement considers any nonzero value as true opens many possibilities. Relational expressions are not the only conditions that may be tested. For example, if the variable value is an integer, the following is a legal `if` statement in C++:

```
if (value)
   cout << "It is True!";
```

If `value` contains any number other than 0, the `if` condition will evaluate to `true`, and the message "`It is True!`" will be displayed. If `value` is set to 0, however, the `if` condition will evaluate to `false`, and the `cout` statement will be skipped. Here is another example:

```
if (x + y)
   cout << "It is True!";
```

In this statement the sum of `x` and `y` is tested. If the sum is 0, the expression is considered false; otherwise it is considered true. You may also use the return value of a function call as a conditional expression. Here is an example that uses the `pow` function:

```
if (pow(a, b))
   cout << "It is True!";
```

This `if` statement uses the `pow` function to raise `a` to the power of `b`. If the result is anything other than 0, the `cout` statement will be executed.

Flags

A *flag* is a variable that signals whether or not some condition currently exists in a program. Because `bool` variables hold the values `true` and `false`, they are the perfect type of variables to use for flags. When the flag variable is set to `true`, it means the condition does exist. When the flag variable is set to `false`, it means that the condition does not exist, at least not yet.

For example, suppose a program that calculates sales commissions has a Boolean variable, defined and initialized as shown here:

```
bool salesQuotaMet = false;
```

In the program, the `salesQuotaMet` variable is used as a flag to indicate whether a salesperson has met the sales quota. When we define the variable, we initialize it with `false` because we do not yet know if the salesperson has met the quota. Assuming a variable named `sales` holds the amount of sales, code similar to the following might appear in the program.

```
if (sales >= QUOTA_AMOUNT)
    salesQuotaMet = true;
```

If the test condition is true (i.e., `sales` *is* greater than or equal to the `QUOTA_AMOUNT`), the flag `salesQuotaMet` is set to `true`. Otherwise, it remains `false`.

Later in the program we might test the flag in the following way:

```
if (salesQuotaMet)
   cout << "You have met your sales quota!\n";
```

This code displays "You have met your sales quota!" if the bool variable `salesQuotaMet` is `true`. Otherwise, it does not display anything. Notice that we did not have to use the == operator to explicitly compare the `salesQuotaMet` variable with the value `true`. The above code is equivalent to the following:

```
if (salesQuotaMet == true)
   cout << "You have met your sales quota!\n";
```

Integer Flags

Integer variables may also be used as flags. This is because in C++ the value 0 is considered false, and any nonzero value is considered true. In the sales commission program previously described, we could define the `salesQuotaMet` variable with the following statement:

```
int salesQuotaMet = 0;    // 0 means false
```

As before, we initialize the variable with 0, meaning false, because we do not yet know if the sales quota has been met. After the sales have been calculated, we can use code similar to the following:

```
if (sales >= QUOTA_AMOUNT)
   salesQuotaMet = 1;     // 1 means true
```

Later in the program we could test the flag like this:

```
if (salesQuotaMet)        // Any value other than 0 evaluates to true
   cout << "You have met your sales quota!\n";
```

This is equivalent to the following:

```
if (salesQuotaMet != 0)
   cout << "You have met your sales quota!\n";
```

Checkpoint

4.5 Write an `if` statement that performs the following logic: if the value of variable `price` is greater than 500, then assign 0.2 to the variable `discountRate`.

4.6 Write an `if` statement that multiplies `payRate` by 1.5 if `hours` is greater than 40.

4.7 Write an `if` statement that performs the following logic: if the variable `sales` is greater than 50,000, then assign 0.25 to the `commissionRate` variable, and assign 250 to the `bonus` variable.

4.8 TRUE or FALSE: Both of the following `if` statements perform the same operation.

```
if (calls == 20)                    if (calls = 20)
    rate *= 0.5;                        rate *= 0.5;
```

4.9 Write an `if` statement that performs the following logic: if the variable named `ticketsSold` is equal to 200, then set the Boolean flag variable `soldOut` to `true`;

4.10 Write an `if` statement that prints "The performance is sold out!" if the Boolean flag variable `soldOut` is set to `true`.

4.11 Although the following code segments are syntactically correct, each contains an error. Locate the error and indicate what is wrong.

A)
```
hours = 12;
if (hours > 40);
   cout << hours << " hours qualifies for over-time.\n";
```

B)
```
interestRate = .05;
if (interestRate = .07)
   cout << "This account is earning the maximum rate.\n";
```

C)
```
interestRate = .05;
if (interestRate > .07)
   cout << "This account earns a $10 bonus.\n";
   balance += 10.0;
```

4.3 The if/else Statement

CONCEPT: The `if/else` statement will execute one set of statements when the `if` condition is true, and another set when the condition is false.

VideoNote Using an if/else Statement

The `if/else` statement is an expansion of the `if` statement. Figure 4-4 shows the general format of this statement and a flowchart visually depicting how it works.

Figure 4-4

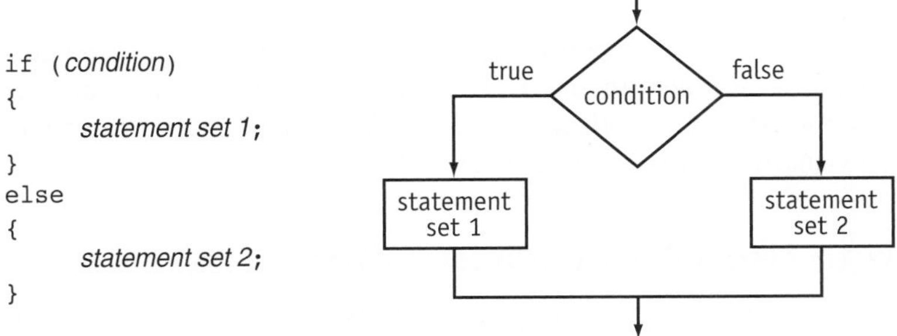

As with the `if` statement, a condition is tested. If the condition is true, a block containing one or more statements is executed. If the condition is false, however, a different group of statements is executed. Program 4-3 uses the `if/else` statement along with the modulus operator to determine if a number is odd or even.

Program 4-3

```
// This program uses the modulus operator to determine
// if a number is odd or even. If the number is evenly divisible
// by 2, it is an even number. A remainder indicates it is odd.
#include <iostream>
using namespace std;

int main()
{
   int number;

   cout << "Enter an integer and I will tell you if it\n";
   cout << "is odd or even. ";
   cin  >> number;

   if (number % 2 == 0)
       cout << number << " is even.\n";
   else
       cout << number << " is odd.\n";
   return 0;
}
```

Program Output with Example Input Shown in Bold

```
Enter an integer and I will tell you if it
is odd or even. 17[Enter]
17 is odd.
```

The `else` part at the end of the `if` statement specifies one or more statements that are to be executed when the condition is false. When `number % 2` does not equal 0, a message is printed indicating the number is odd. Note that the program will only take one of the two paths in the `if/else` statement. If you think of the statements in a computer program as steps taken down a road, consider the `if/else` statement as a fork in the road. It causes program execution to follow one of two mutually exclusive paths.

Notice the programming style used to construct the `if/else` statement. The word `else` is at the same level of indention as `if`. The statements whose execution are controlled by the `if` and by the `else` are both indented one level. This makes the two possible paths of execution visually clear to anyone reading the code.

When to Use `if` and When to Use `if/else`

Sometimes new programming students are unsure whether to use two separate `if` statements or a single `if/else` statement when two possible conditions exist. Here is the basic rule. If both conditions could be true or both could be false, use two separate `if` statements. Here is an example:

```
if (score >= 60)                  // Use 2 if statements here
    cout << "You passed. \n";
if (score >= 80)
    cout << "Good job. \n";
```

In this case two separate `if` statements are needed because with a score below 60 we do not want *either* message to be displayed, and with a score of 80 or higher we want *both* messages to be displayed.

On the other hand, if the two conditions are mutually exclusive, such that one *must* be true and the other false, an `if/else` statement should be used. Here is an example:

```
if (score >= 60)              // Do NOT use 2 if statements here
    cout << "You passed. \n";
if (score < 60)
    cout << "You failed. \n";
```

Here the two test conditions are mutually exclusive. Either it is true that the score is 60 or higher, in which case the first message should be displayed, or it is false and the score is below 60, in which case the second message should be displayed. Therefore these two statements should be combined into a single `if/else` construct, like this:

```
if (score >= 60)         // Use a single if/else statement instead
    cout << "You passed. \n";
else
    cout << "You failed. \n";
```

Program 4-3 used a single `if/else` statement to test the integer variable `number` to see if it was even or odd because these are mutually exclusive conditions. If a number is evenly divisible by 2, it is even. If not, it must be odd. Program 4-4 includes another case where `if/else` is the right construct to use. It shows how to make sure a program does not attempt to perform division by zero.

Division by zero is mathematically impossible to perform and it normally causes a program to crash. This means the program will prematurely stop running, sometimes with an error message. Program 4-4 shows a way to test the value of a divisor before the division takes place.

Program 4-4

```
// This program makes sure that the divisor is not
// equal to 0 before it performs a divide operation.
#include <iostream>
using namespace std;

int main()
{
   double num1, num2, quotient;

   // Get the two numbers
   cout << "Enter two numbers: ";
   cin  >> num1 >> num2;

   // If num2 is not zero, perform the division.
   if (num2 != 0)
   {
      quotient = num1 / num2;
      cout << "The quotient of " << num1 << " divided by "
           << num2 << " is " << quotient << ".\n";
   }
```

(program continues)

Program 4-4 *(continued)*

```
21    else
22    {
23       cout << "Division by zero is not possible.\n";
24       cout << "Please run the program again and enter "
25            << "a number other than zero.\n";
26    }
27    return 0;
28 }
```

Program Output with Example Input Shown in Bold

```
Enter two numbers: 10 0[Enter]
Division by zero is not possible.
Please run the program again and enter a number other than zero.
```

Notice how line 15 of Program 4-4 tests the value of `num2`. If the user enters anything other than zero, the lines controlled by the `if` are executed, allowing the division to be performed and the result to be displayed. But if the user enters a zero for `num2`, the lines controlled by the `else` are executed instead, causing an error message to be displayed. Notice also the braces on lines 22 and 26. As with the `if` part of an `if` construct, if you wish to execute more than one statement in the `else` part, these statements must be placed inside a set of braces. Otherwise the `else` only controls a single statement.

Comparing Floating-Point Numbers

Testing floating-point numbers for equality can sometimes give erroneous results. Because of a lack of precision or round-off errors, a number that should be mathematically equal to another might not be. In Program 4-5, the number 6 is multiplied by 0.666667, a decimal version of 2/3. Of course, 6 times 2/3 is 4. The program, however, disagrees.

Program 4-5

```
// This program demonstrates how a lack of precision in
// floating-point numbers can make equality comparisons unreliable.
#include <iostream>
using namespace std;

int main()
{
   double result = .666667 * 6.0;

   // 2/3 of 6 should be 4 and, if you print result, 4 is displayed.
   cout << "result = " << result << endl;

   // However, internally result is NOT precisely equal to 4.
   if (result == 4.0)
      cout << "result DOES equal 4!" << endl;
   else
      cout << "result DOES NOT equal 4!" << endl;

   return 0;
}
```

(program continues)

Program 4-5 *(continued)*

Program Output

```
result = 4
result DOES NOT equal 4!
```

Typically, the value in `result` will be a number just short of 4, like 3.999996. To prevent errors like this, it is wise to stick with greater-than and less-than comparisons when using floating-point numbers. For example, instead of testing if the result equals 4.0, you could test to see if it is very close to 4.0. Program 4-6 demonstrates this technique.

Program 4-6

```
1  // This program demonstrates how to safely test a floating-point number
2  // to see if it is, for all practical purposes, equal to some value.
3  #include <iostream>
4  #include <cmath>
5  using namespace std;
6
7  int main()
8  {
9     double result = .666667 * 6.0;
10
11    // 2/3 of 6 should be 4 and, if you print result, 4 is displayed.
12    cout << "result = " << result << endl;
13
14    // However, internally result is NOT precisely equal to 4.
15    // So test to see if it is "close" to 4.
16    if (abs(result - 4.0 < .0001))
17       cout << "result DOES equal 4!" << endl;
18    else
19       cout << "result DOES NOT equal 4!" << endl;
20
21    return 0;
22  }
```

Program Output

```
result = 4
result DOES equal 4!
```

Line 16 of the program uses the `abs` function introduced in Chapter 3. Recall that it returns the absolute value of the argument. By using it, we ensure that the test condition will be true if the difference between `result` and 4.0 is less than .0001, regardless of whether `result` is just a tiny bit smaller or a tiny bit larger than .0001.

Checkpoint

4.12 Write an `if/else` statement that assigns 0.10 to `commission` unless `sales` is greater than or equal to 50,000.00, in which case it assigns 0.20 to `commission`.

4.13 Write an `if/else` statement that assigns 1 to `x` if `y` is equal to 100. Otherwise it should assign 0 to `x`.

4.14 Write an `if/else` statement that assigns .10 to the variable `discount` if the Boolean flag variable `prepaid` is `true` and assigns 0.0 to `discount` if `prepaid` is `false`.

4.15 True or false: The following `if/else` statements cause the same output to display.

A)
```
if (x > y)
   cout << "x is greater than y.\n";
else
   cout << "x is not greater than y.\n";
```

B)
```
if (x <= y)
   cout << "x is not greater than y.\n";
else
   cout << "x is greater than y\n";
```

4.16 Will the `if/else` statement shown on the right below function exactly the same as the two separate `if` statements shown on the left?

```
if (x < y)              if (x < y)
   cout << 1;              cout << 1;
if (x > y)              else
   cout << 2;              cout << 2;
```

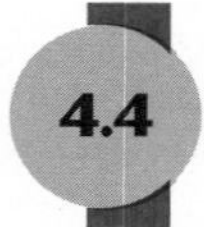

4.4 The `if/else if` Statement

CONCEPT: The `if/else if` statement is a chain of `if` statements. They perform their tests, one after the other, until one of them is found to be true.

We make certain mental decisions by using sets of different but related rules. For example, we might decide the type of coat or jacket to wear by consulting the following rules:

if it is very cold, wear a heavy coat,
else, if it is chilly, wear a light jacket,
else, if it is windy, wear a windbreaker,
else, if it is hot, wear no jacket.

The purpose of these rules is to determine which type of outer garment to wear. If it is cold, the first rule dictates that a heavy coat must be worn. All the other rules are then ignored. If the first rule doesn't apply, however (if it isn't cold), then the second rule is consulted. If that rule doesn't apply, the third rule is consulted, and so forth.

The way these rules are connected is very important. If they were consulted individually, we might go out of the house wearing the wrong jacket or, possibly, more than one jacket. For instance, if it is windy, the third rule says to wear a windbreaker. What if it is both windy and very cold? Will we wear a windbreaker? A heavy coat? Both? Because of the order that the rules are consulted in, the first rule will determine that a heavy coat is needed. The third rule will not be consulted, and we will go outside wearing the most appropriate garment.

VideoNote
Using an `if/else if` Statement

This type of decision making is also very common in programming. In C++ it can be accomplished through the `if/else if` statement. Figure 4-5 shows its format and a flowchart visually depicting how it works.

Figure 4-5

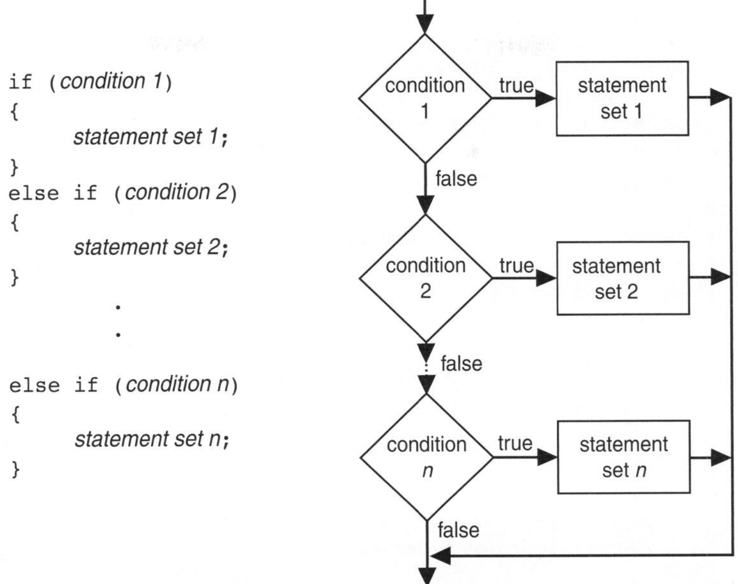
if (condition 1)
{
statement set 1;
}
else if (condition 2)
{
statement set 2;
}
.
.
else if (condition n)
{
statement set n;
}
condition 1
true
statement set 1
false
condition 2
true
statement set 2
false
condition n
true
statement set n
false

This construction is like a chain of `if/else` statements. The `else` part of one statement is linked to the `if` part of another. When put together this way, the chain of `if/else`s becomes one long statement. Program 4-7 shows an example. The user is asked to enter a numeric test score, and the program displays the letter grade earned.

Program 4-7

```
// This program uses an if/else if statement to assign a
// letter grade of A, B, C, D, or F to a numeric test score.
#include <iostream>
using namespace std;

int main()
{
   // Create named constants to hold minimum
   // scores required for each letter grade.
   const int MIN_A_SCORE = 90,
             MIN_B_SCORE = 80,
             MIN_C_SCORE = 70,
             MIN_D_SCORE = 60;

   int testScore;     // Holds a numeric test score
   char grade;        // Holds a letter grade

   // Get the numeric score
   cout << "Enter your numeric test score and I will\n";
   cout << "tell you the letter grade you earned: ";
   cin  >> testScore;
```

(program continues)

Program 4-7 *(continued)*

```
22
23     // Determine the letter grade
24     if (testScore >= MIN_A_SCORE)
25         grade = 'A';
26     else if (testScore >= MIN_B_SCORE)
27         grade = 'B';
28     else if (testScore >= MIN_C_SCORE)
29         grade = 'C';
30     else if (testScore >= MIN_D_SCORE)
31         grade = 'D';
32     else if (testScore >= 0)
33         grade = 'F';
34
35     // Display the letter grade
36     cout << "Your grade is " << grade << ".\n";
37
38     return 0;
39 }
```

Program Output with Example Input Shown in Bold

```
Enter your numeric test score and I will
tell you the letter grade you earned: 88[Enter]
Your grade is B.
```

As with other forms of the `if` statement, braces are required in an `if/else if` whenever there is more than one statement in a conditionally executed block. Otherwise they are optional. Because each of the conditionally executed blocks of code in Program 4-7 contains only one statement, braces were not used.

The `if/else if` statement has a number of notable characteristics. Let's analyze how it works in Program 4-7. First, the relational expression `testScore >= MIN_A_SCORE` is tested on line 24.

```
if (testScore >= MIN_A_SCORE)
    grade = 'A';
```

If `testScore` is greater than or equal to `MIN_A_SCORE`, which is 90, the letter 'A' is assigned to grade and the rest of the linked `if` statements are skipped. If `testScore` is not greater than or equal to `MIN_A_SCORE`, the `else` part takes over and causes the next `if` condition to be tested on line 26.

```
else if (testScore >= MIN_B_SCORE)
    grade = 'B';
```

The first `if` statement filtered out all of the grades of 90 or higher, so when this next `if` statement executes, `testScore` will have a value of 89 or less. If `testScore` is greater than or equal to `MIN_B_SCORE`, which is 80, the letter 'B' is assigned to grade and the rest of the `if` statements are skipped. This chain of events continues until one of the conditional expressions is found true or the end of the entire `if/else if` construct is encountered. In either case, the program resumes at the statement immediately following the `if/else if` statement. This is the `cout` statement on line 36 that prints the grade. Figure 4-6 shows the paths that may be taken by the `if/else if` statement.

Figure 4-6

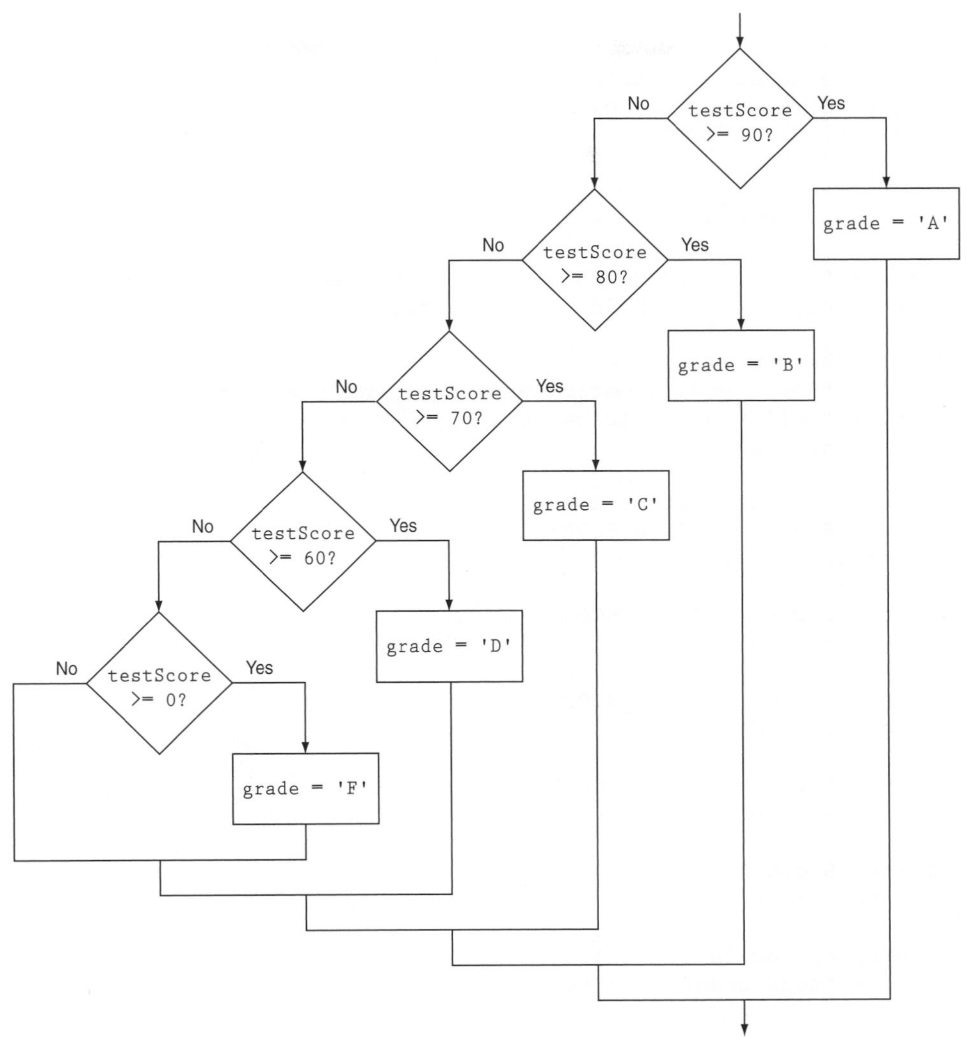

Each `if` condition in the structure depends on all the `if` conditions before it being false. The statements following a particular `else if` are executed when the conditional expression associated with that `else if` is true and all previous conditional expressions are false. To demonstrate how this interconnection works, let's look at Program 4-8, which uses independent `if` statements instead of an `if/else if` statement.

Program 4-8

```
// This program illustrates a bug that occurs when independent if/else
// statements are used to assign a letter grade to a numeric test score.
#include <iostream>
using namespace std;

```

(program continues)

Program 4-8 *(continued)*

```
 6 int main()
 7 {
 8    // Create named constants to hold minimum
 9    // scores required for each letter grade.
10    const int MIN_A_SCORE = 90,
11              MIN_B_SCORE = 80,
12              MIN_C_SCORE = 70,
13              MIN_D_SCORE = 60;
14
15    int testScore;     // Holds a numeric test score
16    char grade;        // Holds a letter grade
17
18    // Get the numeric score
19    cout << "Enter your numeric test score and I will\n";
20    cout << "tell you the letter grade you earned: ";
21    cin  >> testScore;
22
23    // Determine the letter grade
24    if (testScore >= MIN_A_SCORE)
25       grade = 'A';
26
27    if (testScore >= MIN_B_SCORE)
28       grade = 'B';
29
30    if (testScore >= MIN_C_SCORE)
31       grade = 'C';
32
33    if (testScore >= MIN_D_SCORE)
34       grade = 'D';
35
36    if (testScore >= 0)
37       grade = 'F';
38
39    // Display the letter grade
40    cout << "Your grade is " << grade << ".\n";
41
42    return 0;
43 }
```

Program Output with Example Input Shown in Bold

```
Enter your numeric test score and I will tell you
the letter grade you earned: 88[Enter]
Your grade is F.
```

In Program 4-8, *all* the `if` statements execute because they are individual statements. In the example output, `testScore` is assigned the value 88, yet the student receives an F. Here is what happens. First the program comes to the `if` statement on line 24. Because the student's score is *not* at least 90, the assignment statement on line 25 is skipped. Next the program comes to the `if` statement on line 27. Because the student's score *is* at least 80, the statement on line 28 executes and `grade` is assigned a 'B'. However, because none of the `if` statements are connected to the ones above them, the `if` statements on lines 30, 33, and 36 all execute as well. Because `testScore` is also at least 70, it causes 'C' to be assigned to grade, replacing the 'B' that was previously stored there. This continues until all the `if` statements have executed. The last one will cause 'F' to be assigned to grade. (Students will be very unhappy with this method since 'F' is the only grade it gives out!)

Using a Trailing `else`

A final `else`, placed at the end of an `if/else if` statement is called a *trailing* `else`. A trailing `else` provides a default action, or set of actions, when none of the `if` expressions are true and is often used to catch errors. This feature would be helpful, for example, in Program 4-7. What happens in the current version of that program if the user accidentally enters a test score that is less than zero? The `if/else if` statement handles all scores down through zero, but none lower. If the user enters –88, for example, the program does not assign any value to the variable `grade` because there is no code to handle a negative score. We can fix this problem by adding a trailing `else` to the `if/else if` statement. This is done in Program 4-9.

Program 4-9

```
// This program uses an if/else if statement to assign a letter
// grade of A, B, C, D, or F to a numeric test score. A trailing
// else is used to set a flag if a negative value is entered.
#include <iostream>
using namespace std;

int main()
{
   // Create named constants to hold minimum
   // scores required for each letter grade.
   const int MIN_A_SCORE = 90,
             MIN_B_SCORE = 80,
             MIN_C_SCORE = 70,
             MIN_D_SCORE = 60,
             MIN_POSSIBLE_SCORE = 0;

   int testScore;               // Holds a numeric test score
   char grade;                  // Holds a letter grade
   bool goodScore = true;

   // Get the numeric score
   cout << "Enter your numeric test score and I will\n";
   cout << "tell you the letter grade you earned: ";
   cin  >> testScore;

   // Determine the letter grade
   if (testScore >= MIN_A_SCORE)
      grade = 'A';
   else if (testScore >= MIN_B_SCORE)
      grade = 'B';
   else if (testScore >= MIN_C_SCORE)
      grade = 'C';
```

(program continues)

Program 4-9 *(continued)*

```
    else if (testScore >= MIN_D_SCORE)
        grade = 'D';
    else if (testScore >= MIN_POSSIBLE_SCORE)
        grade = 'F';
    else
        goodScore = false;      // The score was below 0

    // Display the letter grade
    if (goodScore)
        cout << "Your grade is " << grade << ".\n";
    else
        cout << "The score cannot be below zero. \n";

    return 0;
}
```

Program Output with Example Input Shown in Bold

```
Enter your numeric test score and I will tell you
the letter grade you earned: 88[Enter]
Your grade is B.
```

Program Output with Different Example Input Shown in Bold

```
Enter your numeric test score and I will
tell you the letter grade you earned: -88[Enter]
The score cannot be below zero.
```

Checkpoint

4.17 What will the following program segment display?

```
int funny = 1, serious;
if (funny != 1)
{   funny = serious = 1;
}
else if (funny == 2)
{   funny = serious = 3;
}
else
{   funny = serious = 5;
}
cout << funny << "  " << serious << endl;
```

4.18 The following program is used in a bookstore to determine how many discount coupons a customer gets. Complete the table that appears after the program.

```
#include <iostream>
using namespace std;
int main()
{
   int numBooks, numCoupons;
   cout << "How many books are being purchased? ";
   cin  >> numBooks;
```

```
    if (numBooks < 1)
        numCoupons = 0;
    else if (numBooks < 3)
        numCoupons = 1;
    else if (numBooks < 5)
        numCoupons = 2;
    else
        numCoupons = 3;
    cout << "The number of coupons to give is " << numCoupons << endl;
    return 0;
}
```

If the customer purchases this many books...	...This many coupons are given.
1	
2	
3	
4	
5	
10	

4.19 Write an `if/else if` statement that carries out the following logic. If the value of variable `quantityOnHand` is equal to 0, display the message "Out of stock". If the value is greater than 0, but less than 10, display the message "Reorder". If the value is 10 or more do not display anything.

4.20 Write an `if/else if` statement that performs the same actions as in the above question when the value of `quantityOnHand` is equal to 0 or is greater than 0, but less than 10. However, when the value is 10 or more it should display the message "Quantity OK".

4.5 Menu-Driven Programs

CONCEPT: A *menu* is a set of choices presented to the user. A *menu-driven program* allows the user to determine the course of action by selecting it from the menu.

A menu is a screen displaying a set of choices the user selects from. For example, a program that keeps a mailing list might give you the following menu:

1. Add a name to the list.
2. Remove a name from the list.
3. Change a name in the list.
4. Print the list.
5. Quit the program.

The user selects one of the operations by entering its number. Entering 4, for example, causes the mailing list to be printed, and entering 5 causes the program to end. The `if/else if` structure can be used to set up such a menu. After the user enters a number, it compares the number to the available selections and executes the statements that perform the requested operation.

Program 4-10 calculates the charges for membership in a health club. The club has three membership packages to choose from: standard adult membership, child membership, and senior citizen membership. The program presents a menu that allows the user to choose the desired package and then calculates the cost of the membership.

Program 4-10

```
// This menu-driven program uses an if/else statement to carry
// out the correct set of actions based on the user's menu choice.
#include <iostream>
#include <iomanip>
using namespace std;

int main()
{
   // Constants for membership rates
   const double ADULT_RATE  = 120.0;
   const double CHILD_RATE  =  60.0;
   const double SENIOR_RATE = 100.0;

   int choice;           // Menu choice
   int months;           // Number of months
   double charges;       // Monthly charges

   // Display the menu and get the user's choice
   cout << "    Health Club Membership Menu\n\n";
   cout << "1. Standard Adult Membership\n";
   cout << "2. Child Membership\n";
   cout << "3. Senior Citizen Membership\n";
   cout << "4. Quit the Program\n\n";
   cout << "Enter your choice: ";
   cin  >> choice;

   // Set the numeric output formatting
   cout << fixed << showpoint << setprecision(2);

   // Use the menu selection to execute the correct set of actions
   if (choice == 1)
   {  cout << "For how many months? ";
      cin  >> months;
      charges = months * ADULT_RATE;
      cout << "\nThe total charges are $" << charges << endl;
   }
   else if (choice == 2)
   {  cout << "For how many months? ";
      cin  >> months;
      charges = months * CHILD_RATE;
      cout << "\nThe total charges are $" << charges << endl;
   }
```

(program continues)

Program 4-10 *(continued)*

```
43     else if (choice == 3)
44     {  cout << "For how many months? ";
45        cin  >> months;
46        charges = months * SENIOR_RATE;
47        cout << "\nThe total charges are $" << charges << endl;
48     }
49     else if (choice != 4)
50     {  cout << "\nThe valid choices are 1 through 4.\n"
51             << "Run the program again and select one of those.\n";
52     }
53     return 0;
54 }
```

Program Output with Example Input Shown in Bold

```
   Health Club Membership Menu

1. Standard Adult Membership
2. Child Membership
3. Senior Citizen Membership
4. Quit the Program

Enter your choice: 3[Enter]
For how many months? 4[Enter]
The total charges are $400.00
```

Notice that three `double` constants `ADULT_RATE`, `CHILD_RATE`, and `SENIOR_RATE` are defined in lines 10 through 12. These constants hold the monthly membership rates for adult, child, and senior citizen memberships. Also notice that the program lets the user know when an invalid menu choice is made. If a number other than 1, 2, 3, or 4 is entered, an error message is printed. This is known as *input validation*.

4.6 Nested `if` Statements

CONCEPT: To test more than one condition, an `if` statement can be nested inside another `if` statement.

It is possible for one `if` statement or `if/else` statement to be placed inside another one. This construct, called a *nested if*, allows you to test more than one condition to determine which block of code should be executed. For example, consider a banking program that determines whether a bank customer qualifies for a special low interest rate on a loan. To qualify, two conditions must exist:

1. The customer must be currently employed.
2. The customer must have recently graduated from college (in the past two years).

Figure 4-7 shows a flowchart for an algorithm that could be used in such a program.

Figure 4-7

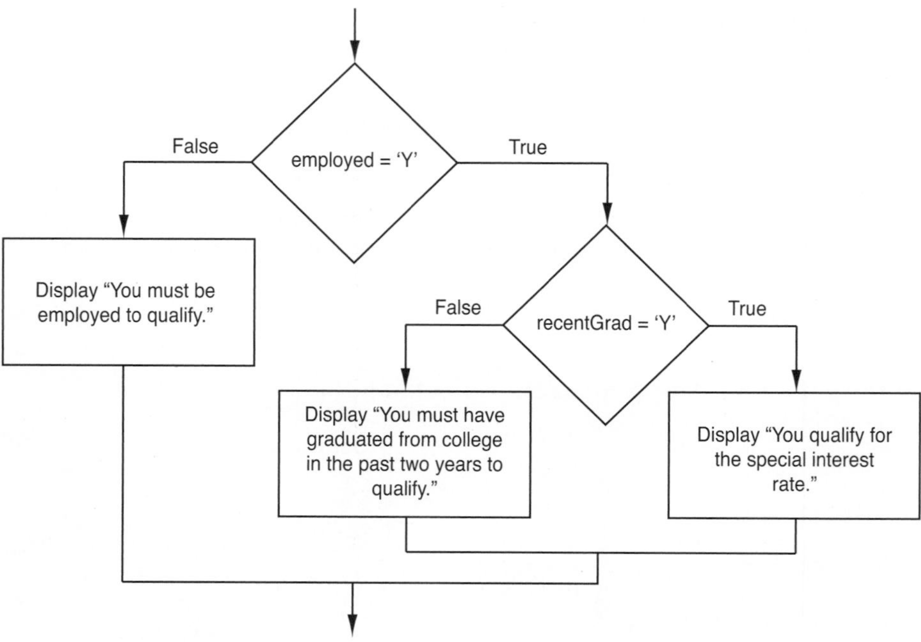

If we follow the flow of execution in this diagram, we see that first the expression `employed == 'Y'` is tested. If this expression is false, there is no need to perform any other tests. We know that the customer does not qualify for the special interest rate. If the expression is true, however, we need to test the second condition. This is done with a nested decision structure that tests the expression `recentGrad == 'Y'`. If this expression is also true, then the customer qualifies for the special interest rate. If this second expression is false, the customer does not qualify. Program 4-11 shows the code that corresponds to the logic of the flowchart. It nests one `if/else` statement inside another one.

Program 4-11

```
// This program determines whether a loan applicant qualifies for
// a special loan interest rate. It uses nested if/else statements.
#include <iostream>
using namespace std;

int main()
{
   char employed,          // Currently employed? (Y or N)
        recentGrad;        // Recent college graduate? (Y or N)

   // Is the applicant employed and a recent college graduate?
   cout << "Answer the following questions\n";
   cout << "with either Y for Yes or N for No.\n";

```

(program continues)

Program 4-11 *(continued)*

```
15      cout << "Are you employed? ";
16      cin  >> employed;
17      cout << "Have you graduated from college in the past two years? ";
18      cin  >> recentGrad;
19
20      // Determine the applicant's loan qualifications
21      if (employed == 'Y')
22      {
23         if (recentGrad == 'Y')         // Employed and a recent grad
24         {
25            cout << "You qualify for the special interest rate.\n";
26         }
27         else                           // Employed but not a recent grad
28         {
29            cout << "You must have graduated from college in the past\n";
30            cout << "two years to qualify for the special interest rate.\n";
31         }
32      }
33      else                              // Not employed
34      {
35         cout << "You must be employed to qualify for the "
36              << "special interest rate. \n";
37      }
38      return 0;
39   }
```

Program Output with Example Input Shown in Bold

```
Answer the following questions
with either Y for Yes or N for No.
Are you employed? N[Enter]
Have you graduated from college in the past two years? Y[Enter]
You must be employed to qualify for the special interest rate.
```

Program Output with Other Example Input Shown in Bold

```
Answer the following questions
with either Y for Yes or N for No.
Are you employed? Y[Enter]
Have you graduated from college in the past two years? N[Enter]
You must have graduated from college in the past
two years to qualify for the special interest rate.
```

Program Output with Other Example Input Shown in Bold

```
Answer the following questions
with either Y for Yes or N for No.
Are you employed? Y[Enter]
Have you graduated from college in the past two years? Y[Enter]
You qualify for the special interest rate.
```

Let's take a closer look at this program. The `if` statement that begins on line 21 tests the expression `employed == 'Y'`. If the expression is true, the inner `if` statement that begins on line 23 is executed. However, if the outer expression is false, the program jumps to line 33 and executes the statements in the outer `else` block instead.

When you are debugging a program with nested `if/else` statements, it's important to know which `if` statement each `else` goes with. The rule for matching each `else` with the proper `if` is this: An `else` goes with the closest previous `if` statement that doesn't already have its own `else`. This is easier to see when the statements are properly indented. Figure 4-8 shows lines similar to lines 21 through 37 of Program 4-11. It illustrates how each `else` should line up with the `if` it belongs to. These visual cues are important because nested `if` statements can be very long and complex.

Figure 4-8

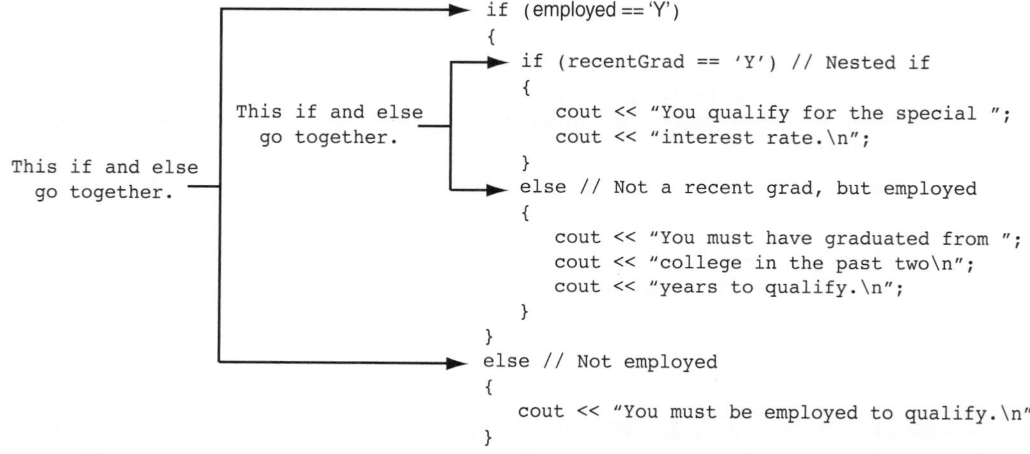

Checkpoint

4.21 If you execute the following code, what will it display if the user enters 5? 15? 30? –1?

```
int number;

cout << "Enter a number: ";
cin  >> number;
if (number > 0)
{   cout << "Zero   ";
    if (number > 10)
    {   cout << "Ten   ";
        if (number > 20)
        {   cout << "Twenty   ";
        }
    }
}
```

4.22 If you execute the following code, what will it display if the user enters 15 18? 15 10? 9 7?

```
int teamWins, teamLosses;

cout << " Enter the number of team wins and number of team losses: ";
cin  >> team Wins >> teamLosses;
if (teamWins > teamLosses)
{
   if(teamWins > 10)
      cout << "You are the champions. \n";
   else
      cout << "You have won more than 50% of your games. \n";
}
else
   cout << "Good luck in the rest of your games. ";
```

4.7 Logical Operators

CONCEPT: Logical operators connect two or more relational expressions into one or reverse the logic of an expression.

VideoNote
Using Logical Operators

In the previous section you saw how a program tests two conditions with two `if` statements. In this section you will see how to use logical operators to combine two or more relational expressions into one. Table 4-6 lists C++'s logical operators.

Table 4-6 Logical Operators

Operator	Meaning	Effect
`&&`	AND	Connects two expressions into one. Both expressions must be true for the overall expression to be true.
`||`	OR	Connects two expressions into one. One or both expressions must be true for the overall expression to be true. It is only necessary for one to be true, and it does not matter which.
`!`	NOT	Reverses the "truth" of an expression. It makes a true expression false, and a false expression true.

The && Operator

The `&&` operator is known as the logical AND operator. It takes two expressions as operands and creates an expression that is true only when both sub-expressions are true. Here is an example of an `if` statement that uses the `&&` operator:

```
if ((temperature < 20) && (minutes > 12))
   cout << "The temperature is in the danger zone.";
```

Notice that both of the expressions being ANDed together are complete expressions that evaluate to true or false. First `temperature < 20` is evaluated to produce a true or false result. Then `minutes > 12` is evaluated to produce a true or false result. Then, finally, these two results are ANDed together to arrive at a final result for the entire expression. The `cout` statement will only be executed if `temperature` is less than 20 AND `minutes` is greater than 12. If either relational test is false, the entire expression is false and the `cout` statement is not executed.

Table 4-7 shows a truth table for the `&&` operator. The truth table lists all the possible combinations of values that two expressions may have and the resulting value returned by the `&&` operator connecting the two expressions. As the table shows, both sub-expressions must be true for the `&&` operator to return a true value.

Table 4-7 Logical AND

Expression	Value of the Expression
`false && false`	`false (0)`
`false && true`	`false (0)`
`true && false`	`false (0)`
`true && true`	`true (1)`

NOTE: If the sub-expression on the left side of an `&&` operator is false, the expression on the right side will not be checked. Because the entire expression is false if even just one of the sub-expressions is false, it would waste CPU time to check the remaining expression. This is called *short circuit evaluation.*

The `&&` operator can be used to simplify programs that otherwise would use nested `if` statements. Program 4-12 is similar to Program 4-11, which determines if a bank customer qualifies for a special interest rate. However, Program 4-12 uses the logical `&&` operator instead of nested `if` statements.

Program 4-12

```
// This program determines whether a loan applicant qualifies for
// a special loan interest rate. It uses the && logical operator.
#include <iostream>
using namespace std;

int main()
{
   char  employed,      // Currently employed? (Y or N)
         recentGrad;    // Recent college graduate? (Y or N)

   // Is the applicant employed and a recent college graduate?
   cout << "Answer the following questions\n";
   cout << "with either Y for Yes or N for No.\n";

   cout << "Are you employed? ";
   cin  >> employed;
   cout << "Have you graduated from college in the past two years? ";
   cin  >> recentGrad;

```

(program continues)

Program 4-12 *(continued)*

```
    // Determine the applicant's loan qualifications
    if (employed == 'Y' && recentGrad == 'Y')    // Uses logical AND
        cout << "\nYou qualify for the special interest rate.\n";
    else
    {   cout << "\nYou must be employed and have graduated from college\n"
             << "in the past two years to qualify "
             << "for the special interest rate. \n";
    }
    return 0;
}
```

Program Output with Example Input Shown in Bold

```
Answer the following questions
with either Y for Yes or N for No.
Are you employed? Y[Enter]
Have you graduated from college in the past two years? N[Enter]

You must be employed and have graduated from college
in the past two years to qualify for the special interest rate.
```

Note that while this program is similar to Program 4-11, it is not the exact logical equivalent. In Program 4-12 the following message displays any time the applicant does not qualify for the special rate: "You must be employed and have graduated from college in the past two years to qualify for the special interest rate." Program 4-11, on the other hand, displays different messages when the loan applicant does not qualify depending on why they failed to qualify.

The || Operator

The || operator is known as the logical OR operator. It takes two expressions as operands and creates an expression that is true when either of the sub-expressions are true. Here is an example of an `if` statement that uses the || operator:

```
if ((temperature < 20) || (temperature > 100))
    cout << "The temperature is in the danger zone.";
```

The `cout` statement will be executed if `temperature` is less than 20 OR `temperature` is greater than 100. If either relational test is true, the entire expression is true and the `cout` statement is executed.

NOTE: The two things being ORed should both be logical expressions that evaluate to true or false. It would *not* be correct to write the `if` condition like this:

```
if (temperature < 20 || > 100)
```

NOTE: There is no || key on the computer keyboard. Use two | symbols. This symbol is on the backslash key. Press Shift and backslash to type it.

Table 4-8 shows a truth table for the || operator.

Table 4-8 Logical OR

<table>
<tr><th>Expression</th><th>Value of the Expression</th></tr>
<tr><td>false || false</td><td>false (0)</td></tr>
<tr><td>false || true</td><td>true (1)</td></tr>
<tr><td>true || false</td><td>true (1)</td></tr>
<tr><td>true || true</td><td>true (1)</td></tr>
</table>

All it takes for an OR expression to be true is for one of the sub-expressions to be true. It doesn't matter if the other sub-expression is false or true.

Program 4-13 performs different tests to qualify a person for a loan. This one determines if the customer earns at least $35,000 per year or has been employed for more than five years.

Program 4-13

```
// This program determines whether or not an applicant qualifies
// for a loan. It uses the logical || operator.
#include <iostream>
using namespace std;

int main()
{
    const double MIN_INCOME = 35000.0;
    const int MIN_YEARS = 5;

    double income;       // Annual income
    int years;           // Years at the current job

    // Get annual income and years on the job
    cout << "What is your annual income? ";
    cin  >> income;
    cout << "How many years have you worked at your current job? ";
    cin  >> years;

    // Determine if the applicant qualifies for a loan
    if (income >= MIN_INCOME || years > MIN_YEARS)    // Uses logical OR
        cout << "You qualify for a loan.\n";
    else
    {   cout << "\nYou must earn at least $" << MIN_INCOME
             << " or have been employed \n"
             << "for more than " << MIN_YEARS << " years "
             << "to qualify for a loan. \n";
    }
    return 0;
}
```

Program 4-13 *(continued)*

Program Output with Example Input Shown in Bold

```
What is your annual income? 40000[Enter]
How many years have you worked at your current job? 2[Enter]
You qualify for a loan.
```

Program Output with Other Example Input Shown in Bold

```
What is your annual income? 20000[Enter]
How many years have you worked at your current job? 7[Enter]
You qualify for a loan.
```

Program Output with Other Example Input Shown in Bold

```
What is your annual income? 30000[Enter]
How many years have you worked at your current job? 3[Enter]
You must earn at least $35000 or have been employed
for more than 5 years to qualify for a loan.
```

The message "You qualify for a loan." is displayed when either or both expressions `income >= MIN_INCOME` or `years > MIN_YEARS` are true. If both of these are false, the disqualifying message is printed.

NOTE: The `||` operator also performs short circuit evaluation. If the sub-expression on the left side of an `||` operator is true, the sub-expression on the right side will not be checked because it is only necessary for one of the sub-expressions to be true for the whole expression to evaluate to true.

The `!` Operator

The `!` operator performs a logical NOT operation. It takes an operand and reverses its truth or falsehood. In other words, if the expression is true, the `!` operator returns false, and if the expression is false, it returns true. Here is an `if` statement using the `!` operator:

```
if (!(temperature > 100))
   cout << "You are below the maximum temperature.\n";
```

First, the expression `(temperature > 100)` is tested to be true or false. Then the `!` operator is applied to that value. If the expression `(temperature > 100)` is true, the `!` operator returns false. If it is false, the `!` operator returns true. In the example, it is equivalent to asking "is the temperature not greater than 100?" or "is it false that the temperature is greater than 100?"

Table 4-9 shows a truth table for the `!` operator.

Table 4-9 Logical NOT

Expression	Value of the Expression
`!false`	`true (1)`
`!true`	`false (0)`

Program 4-14 performs the same task as Program 4-13. The `if` statement, however, uses the `!` operator to determine if it is false that the applicant makes at least $35,000 or has been on the job more than five years.

Program 4-14

```
// This program determines whether or not an applicant
// qualifies for a loan. It uses the ! logical operator
// to reverse the logic of the if statement.
#include <iostream>
using namespace std;

int main()
{
    const double MIN_INCOME = 35000.0;
    const int MIN_YEARS = 5;

    double income;       // Annual income
    int years;           // Years at the current job

    // Get annual income and years on the job
    cout << "What is your annual income? ";
    cin  >> income;
    cout << "How many years have you worked at your current job? ";
    cin  >> years;

    // Determine if the applicant qualifies for a loan
    if ( !(income >= MIN_INCOME || years > MIN_YEARS) )   // Uses logical NOT
    {   cout << "\nYou must earn at least $" << MIN_INCOME
             << " or have been employed \n"
             << "for more than " << MIN_YEARS << " years "
             << "to qualify for a loan. \n";
    }
    else
        cout << "You qualify for a loan.\n";
    return 0;
}
```

Program Output 4-14 is the same as that of Program 4-13.

Boolean Variables and the ! Operator

An interesting feature of a Boolean variable is that its value can be tested just by naming it. Suppose `moreData` is a Boolean variable. Then the test

```
if (moreData == true)
```

can be written simply as

```
if (moreData)
```

and the test

```
if (moreData == false)
```

can be written simply as

```
if (!moreData)
```

In fact, this second way of testing the value of a Boolean variable is preferable. This is because although the C++ constant `true` always has the value 1, a condition that evaluates to true may have *any* nonzero value. For example, C++ has a function called `isalpha()`, which tests whether or not a character is an alphabetic character. As you would expect, the test `isalpha('?')` evaluates to false and the test `isalpha('x')` evaluates to true. However, for some alphabetic characters, this function returns a value other than 1 to represent true. Program 4-15 illustrates this.

Program 4-15

```
1  // This program illustrates what can happen when a
2  // Boolean value is compared to the C++ constant true.
3  #include <iostream>
4  #include <cctype>         // Needed to use the isalpha function
5  using namespace std;
6
7  int main()
8  {
9      cout << "Is '?' an alphabetic character?  " << isalpha('?') << "\n";
10     cout << "Is 'X' an alphabetic character?  " << isalpha('X') << "\n";
11     cout << "Is 'x' an alphabetic character?  " << isalpha('x') << "\n\n";
12
13     cout << "Ask if(isalpha('x') == true) \n";
14     if (isalpha('x') == true)
15        cout << "The letter x IS an alphabetic character. \n\n";
16     else
17        cout << "The letter x is NOT an alphabetic character. \n\n";
18
19     cout << "Ask if(isalpha('x')) \n";
20     if (isalpha('x'))
21        cout << "The letter x IS an alphabetic character. \n";
22     else
23        cout << "The letter x is NOT an alphabetic character. \n";
24
25     return 0;
26 }
```

Program Output

```
Is '?' an alphabetic character?  0
Is 'X' an alphabetic character?  1
Is 'x' an alphabetic character?  2

Ask if(isalpha('x') == true
The letter x is NOT an alphabetic character

Ask if(isalpha('x'))
The letter x IS an alphabetic character
```

In line 14 when the condition `isalpha('x') == true` was tested, the program did not produce the desired result. The value 2 returned by the `isalpha` function was compared to the value 1, so the condition evaluated to false even though, in fact, both values being tested represent true. The code in line 20 worked correctly because the value 2, returned by the `isalpha` function, was correctly interpreted as true.

Precedence and Associativity of Logical Operators

Table 4-10 shows the precedence of C++'s logical operators, from highest to lowest.

Table 4-10 Precedence of Logical Operators

!
&&
||

The ! operator has a higher precedence than many of the C++ operators. Therefore, to avoid an error, it is a good idea always to enclose its operand in parentheses, unless you intend to apply it to a variable or a simple expression with no other operators. For example, consider the following expressions:

```
!(x > 2)
!x > 2
```

The first expression applies the ! operator to the expression x > 2. It is asking "is x not greater than 2?" The second expression, however, applies the ! operator to x only. It is asking "is the logical negation of x greater than 2?" Suppose x is set to 5. Since 5 is nonzero, it would be considered true, so the ! operator would reverse it to false, which is 0. The > operator would then determine if 0 is greater than 2. To avoid such an error, it is wise to always use parentheses.

The && and || operators rank lower in precedence than relational operators, which means that relational expressions are evaluated before their results are logically ANDed or ORed.

```
a > b && x < y    is the same as   (a > b) && (x < y)
a > b || x < y    is the same as   (a > b) || (x < y)
```

Thus you don't normally need parentheses when mixing relational operators with && and ||. However it is a good idea to use them anyway to make your intent clearer for someone reading the program.

Parentheses are even more strongly recommended anytime && and || operators are both used in the same expression. This is because && has a higher precedence than ||. Without parentheses to indicate which you want done first, && will always be done before ||, which might not be what you intended. Assume recentGrad, employed, and goodCredit are three Boolean variables. Then the expression

```
recentGrad || employed && goodCredit
```

is the same as

```
recentGrad ||(employed && goodCredit)
```

and *not* the same as

```
(recentGrad || employed)&& goodCredit
```

Checking Numeric Ranges with Logical Operators

Logical operators are effective for determining if a number is in or out of a range. To check if a number is inside a numeric range, it's best to use the && operator. For example, the following if statement checks the value in x to determine if it is in the range of 20 through 40.

```
if ((x >= 20) && (x <= 40))
   cout << x << " is in the acceptable range.\n";
```

The expression in the `if` statement will be true only when `x` is both greater than or equal to 20 AND less than or equal to 40. The value of `x` must be within the range of 20 through 40 for this expression to be true.

To check if a number is outside a range, the `||` operator is best to use. The following statement determines if the value of `x` is outside the range of 20 to 40:

```
if ((x < 20) || (x > 40))
   cout << x << " is outside the acceptable range.\n";
```

It's important not to get the logic of these logical operators confused. For example, the following `if` statement would never test true:

```
if ((x < 20) && (x > 40))
   cout << x << " is outside the acceptable range.\n";
```

Obviously, `x` can never be both less than 20 and greater than 40 at the same time.

NOTE: C++ does not allow you to check numeric ranges with expressions such as `5 < x < 20`. Instead you must use a logical operator to connect two relational expressions, as previously discussed.

Checkpoint

4.23 The following truth table shows various combinations of the values `true` and `false` connected by a logical operator. Complete the table by indicating if the result of such a combination is true or false.

Logical Expression	Result (true or false)
`true && false`	
`true && true`	
`false && false`	
`true || false`	
`true || true`	
`false || false`	
`!true`	
`!false`	

4.24 If `a = 2`, `b = 4`, and `c = 6`, indicate whether each of the following conditions is true or false:

A) `(a == 4) || (b > 2)`
B) `(6 <= c) && (a > 3)`
C) `(1 != b) && (c != 3)`
D) `(a >= -1) || (a <= b)`
E) `!(a > 2)`

4.25 If `a = 2`, `b = 4`, and `c = 6`, is the following expression true or false?

```
(b > a) || (b > c) && (c == 5)
```

4.26 Rewrite the following using the `!` operator so that the logic remains the same.

```
if (activeEmployee == false)
```

4.8 Validating User Input

CONCEPT: As long as the user of a program enters bad input, the program will produce bad output. Programs should be written to filter out bad input.

A famous saying of the computer world is "garbage in, garbage out." The integrity of a program's output is only as good as its input, so you should try to make sure garbage does not go into your programs. *Input validation* is the process of inspecting information given to a program by the user and determining if it is valid. A good program should give clear instructions about the kind of input that is acceptable, but still not assume the user has followed those instructions. Here are just a few examples of input validations performed by programs:

- Numbers are checked to ensure they are within a range of possible values. For example, there are 168 hours in a week. It is not possible for a person to be at work longer than 168 hours in one week.
- Values are checked for their "reasonableness." Although it might be possible for a person to be at work for 168 hours per week, it is not probable.
- Items selected from a menu or some other set of choices are checked to ensure they are available options.
- Variables are checked for values that might cause problems, such as division by zero.

Program 4-16 is a test scoring program that rejects any score less than 0 or greater than 100.

Program 4-16

```
// This test scoring program does not accept test
// scores that are less than 0 or greater than 100.
#include <iostream>
using namespace std;

int main()
{
   // Constants for grade thresholds
   const int A_SCORE = 90,
             B_SCORE = 80,
             C_SCORE = 70,
             D_SCORE = 60,
             MIN_SCORE = 0,     // Minimum valid score
             MAX_SCORE = 100;   // Maximum valid score

   int testScore;               // Holds the user entered numeric test score

   // Get the numeric test score
   cout << "Enter your numeric test score and I will\n"
        << "tell you the letter grade you earned: ";
   cin  >> testScore;

```

(program continues)

Program 4-16 *(continued)*

```
    // Check if the input is valid
    if (testScore >= MIN_SCORE && testScore <= MAX_SCORE)
    {
       // The score is valid, so determine the letter grade
       if (testScore >= A_SCORE)
         cout << "Your grade is A.\n";
       else if (testScore >= B_SCORE)
         cout << "Your grade is B.\n";
       else if (testScore >= C_SCORE)
         cout << "Your grade is C.\n";
       else if (testScore >= D_SCORE)
         cout << "Your grade is D.\n";
       else
         cout << "Your grade is F.\n";
    }
    else
    {
       // An invalid score was entered
       cout << "That is an invalid score. Run the program\n"
            << "again and enter a value in the range of\n"
            << MIN_SCORE << " through " << MAX_SCORE << ".\n";
    }
    return 0;
}
```

Program Output with Example Input Shown in Bold

```
Enter your numeric test score and I will
tell you the letter grade you earned: -1[Enter]

That is an invalid score. Run the program
again and enter a value in the range of
0 through 100.
```

Program Output with Different Example Input Shown in Bold

```
Enter your numeric test score and I will
tell you the letter grade you earned: 81[Enter]
Your grade is B.
```

In Chapter 5 you will learn an even better way to validate input data.

4.9 More About Blocks and Scope

CONCEPT: The scope of a variable is limited to the block in which it is defined.

C++ allows you to create variables almost anywhere in a program. It is a common practice to define all of a function's variables at the top of the function, right after the opening brace that marks the beginning of its body. However, especially in longer programs, variables are sometimes defined near the part of the program where they are used. This is permitted provided they are defined before they are used.

You learned earlier in this chapter that surrounding one or more programming statements with curly braces defines a block of code. The body of function `main`, which must be surrounded by braces, is a block of code. So is the set of statements associated with an `if` or an `else` in an `if/else` statement. Whenever a variable is defined inside a block, and you may define a variable inside *any* block, its scope is the part of the program between its definition and the block's closing brace. Thus the scope of a variable defined at the top of a function is, essentially, the entire function, while a variable defined in an inner block, is just that block.

Program 4-17 defines its variables later.

Program 4-17

```
// This program determines whether or not an applicant qualifies
// for a loan. It demonstrates late variable declaration, and
// even has a variable defined in an inner block.
#include <iostream>
using namespace std;

int main()
{
   // Constants for minimum income and years
   const double MIN_INCOME = 35000.0;
   const int MIN_YEARS = 5;

   // Get the annual income
   cout << "What is your annual income? ";

   double income;         // Variable definition
   cin >> income;

   if (income >= MIN_INCOME)
   {
      // Income is high enough, so get years at current job
      cout << "How many years have you worked at your current job? ";

      int years;          // Variable defined inside the if block
      cin >> years;

      if (years > MIN_YEARS)
         cout << "\nYou qualify.\n";
      else
         cout << "\nYou must have been employed for more than "
              << MIN_YEARS << " years to qualify.\n";
   }
   else                   // Income is too low
   {
      cout << "\nYou must earn at least $" << MIN_INCOME
           << " to qualify.\n";
   }
   return 0;
}
```

In Program 4-17 the `income` variable is defined on line 16, inside the braces marking the block of code that makes up the body of the `main` function. So its scope , the part of the program where it can be used, includes lines 16 through 38. Those are the lines from the point it is defined until the brace that closes the `main` function. The `years` variable is defined on line 24, inside the braces marking the block of code to be conditionally executed by the `if` statement. So its scope includes only lines 24 through 31. Those are the lines from the point it is defined until the brace that closes the `if` block. Variables like these that are defined inside a set of braces are said to have *local scope* or *block scope*. They are not visible and able to be used before their definition or after the closing brace of the block they are defined in.

NOTE: When a program is running and it enters the section of code that constitutes a variable's scope, it is said that the variable *comes into scope*. This simply means the variable is now visible and the program may reference it. Likewise, when a variable *leaves scope*, it may no longer be used.

Variables with the Same Name

When a block is nested inside another block, a variable defined in the inner block may have the same name as a variable defined in the outer block. This is generally not considered a good idea, as it can lead to confusion. However, it is permitted. When the variable in the inner block comes into scope, the variable in the outer block becomes "hidden" and cannot be used. This is illustrated by Program 4-18.

Program 4-18

```
// This program uses two variables with the same name.
#include <iostream>
using namespace std;

int main()
{
   int number;        // Define a variable named number

   cout << "Enter a number greater than 0: ";
   cin  >> number;

   if (number > 0)
   {  int number;     // Define another variable named number

      cout << "Now enter another number: ";
      cin  >> number;
      cout << "The second number you entered was ";
      cout << number << endl;
   }
   cout << "Your first number was " << number << endl;
   return 0;
}
```

(program continues)

Program 4-18 *(continued)*

Program Output with Example Input Shown in Bold
```
Enter a number greater than 0: 2[Enter]
Now enter another number: 7[Enter]
The second number you entered was 7
Your first number was 2
```

Program 4-18 has two separate variables named `number`. One is defined on line 7 in the outer block. The other is defined on line 13 in the inner block. The `cin` and `cout` statements in the inner block (belonging to the `if` statement) can only work with the `number` variable defined in that block. As soon as the program leaves that block, the inner `number` goes out of scope, revealing the outer `number` variable again.

WARNING! Although it's perfectly acceptable to define variables inside nested blocks, you should avoid giving them the same names as variables in the outer blocks. It's too easy to confuse one variable with another.

Checkpoint

4.27 Write an `if` statement that prints the message "The number is valid." if the variable `speed` is within the range 0 through 200.

4.28 Write an `if` statement that prints the message "The number is not valid." if the variable `speed` is outside the range 0 through 200.

4.29 Find and fix the errors in the following program.

```
#include <iostream>
using namespace std;

int main()
{
   cout << "This program calculates the area of a "
        << "rectangle. Enter the length: ";
   cin  >> length;
   cin  >> width;
   int length, width, area;
   area = length * width;
   cout << "The area is " << area << endl;
   return 0;
}
```

4.10 More About Characters and Strings

CONCEPT: Relational operators can also be used to compare characters and `string` objects.

Earlier in this chapter you learned to use relational operators to compare numeric values. They can also be used to compare characters and `string` objects.

Comparing Characters

As you learned in Chapter 3, characters are actually stored in memory as integers. On most systems, this integer is the ASCII value of the character. For example, the letter ‘A’ is represented by the number 65, the letter ‘B’ is represented by the number 66, and so on. Table 4-11 shows the ASCII numbers that correspond to some of the commonly used characters.

Table 4-11 ASCII Values of Commonly Used Characters

Character	ASCII Value
‘0’–‘9’	48–57
‘A’–‘Z’	65–90
‘a’–‘z’	97–122
blank	32
period	46

Every character, even the blank, has an ASCII code associated with it. Notice that the uppercase letters ‘A’–’Z’ have different codes than the lowercase letters ‘a’–’z’. Notice also that the ASCII code of a character representing a digit, such as `'1'` or `'2'`, is not the same as the value of the digit itself. A complete table showing the ASCII values for all characters can be found in Appendix A.

When two characters are compared, it is actually their ASCII values that are being compared. `'A' < 'B'` because the ASCII value of `'A'` (65) is less than the ASCII value of `'B'` (66). Likewise `'1' < '2'` because the ASCII value of `'1'` (49) is less than the ASCII value of `'2'` (50). However, as Table 4-11 shows, lowercase letters have higher numbers than uppercase letters, so `'a' > 'Z'`. Program 4-19 shows how characters can be compared with relational operators.

Program 4-19

```
// This program demonstrates how characters can
// be compared with the relational operators.
#include <iostream>
using namespace std;

int main()
{
   char ch;

   // Get a character from the user
   cout << "Enter a digit or a letter: ";
   ch = cin.get();

   // Determine what the user entered
   if (ch >= '0' && ch <= '9')
      cout << "You entered a digit.\n";
   else if (ch >= 'A' && ch <= 'Z')
      cout << "You entered an uppercase letter.\n";
   else if (ch >= 'a' && ch <= 'z')
```

(program continues)

Program 4-19 *(continued)*

```
        cout << "You entered a lowercase letter.\n";
    else
        cout << "That is not a digit or a letter.\n";

    return 0;
}
```

Program Output with Example Input Shown in Bold

```
Enter a digit or a letter: t[Enter]
You entered a lowercase letter.
```

Program Output with Different Example Input Shown in Bold

```
Enter a digit or a letter: V[Enter]
You entered an uppercase letter.
```

Program Output with Different Example Input Shown in Bold

```
Enter a digit or a letter: 5[Enter]
You entered a digit.
```

Program Output with Different Example Input Shown in Bold

```
Enter a digit or a letter: &[Enter]
That is not a digit or a letter.
```

Comparing `string` Objects

`string` objects can also be compared with relational operators. As with individual characters, when two `string` objects are compared, it is actually the ASCII value of the characters making up the strings that are being compared. For example, assume the following definitions exist in a program:

```
string str1 = "ABC";
string str2 = "XYZ";
```

The `string` object `str1` is considered less than the `string` object `str2` because the characters "ABC" alphabetically precede (have lower ASCII values than) the characters "XYZ". So the following `if` statement will cause the message "str1 is less than str2." to be displayed on the screen.

```
if (str1 < str2)
      cout << "str1 is less than str2.";
```

One by one, each character in the first operand is compared with the character in the corresponding position in the second operand. If all the characters in both `string` objects match, the two strings are equal. Other relationships can be determined if two characters in corresponding positions do not match. The first operand is less than the second operand if the first mismatched character in the first operand is less than its counterpart in the second operand. Likewise, the first operand is greater than the second operand if the first mismatched character in the first operand is greater than its counterpart in the second operand.

For example, assume a program has the following definitions:

```
string name1 = "Mary";
string name2 = "Mark";
```

The value in `name1`, "Mary", is greater than the value in `name2`, "Mark". This is because the first three characters in `name1` have the same ASCII values as the first three characters in `name2`, but the 'y' in the fourth position of "Mary" has a greater ASCII value than the 'k' in the corresponding position of "Mark".

Any of the relational operators can be used to compare two `string` objects. Here are some of the valid comparisons of `name1` and `name2`.

```
name1 > name2        // true
name1 <= name2       // false
name1 != name2       // true
```

`string` objects can also, of course, be compared to string literals:

```
name1 < "Mary Jane" // true
```

Program 4-20 further demonstrates how relational operators can be used with `string` objects.

Program 4-20

```
// This program uses relational operators to compare a string
// entered by the user with valid stereo part numbers.
#include <iostream>
#include <iomanip>
#include <string>
using namespace std;

int main()
{
   const double PRICE_A = 249.0,
                PRICE_B = 299.0;

   string partNum;             // Holds a stereo part number

   // Display available parts and get the user's selection
   cout << "The stereo part numbers are:\n";
   cout << "Boom Box   : part number S-29A \n";
   cout << "Shelf Model: part number S-29B \n";
   cout << "Enter the part number of the stereo you\n";
   cout << "wish to purchase: ";
   cin  >> partNum;

   // Set the numeric output formatting
   cout << fixed << showpoint << setprecision(2);

   // Determine and display the correct price
```

(program continues)

Program 4-20 *(continued)*

```
    if (partNum == "S-29A")
       cout << "The price is $" << PRICE_A << endl;
    else if (partNum == "S-29B")
       cout << "The price is $" << PRICE_B << endl;
    else
       cout << partNum << " is not a valid part number.\n";
    return 0;
}
```

Program Output with Example Input Shown in Bold

```
The stereo part numbers are:
Boom Box   : part number S-29A
Shelf Model: part number S-29B
Enter the part number of the stereo you
wish to purchase: S-29A[Enter]
The price is $249.00
```

NOTE: C-strings, unlike `string` objects, cannot be compared with relational operators. To compare C-strings, which you recall are strings defined as arrays of characters, you must use the `strcmp` function, which is discussed in Chapter 12.

Testing Characters

Program 4-19 compared a user entered character to certain character literals to test whether the entered character was a digit, an uppercase letter, or a lowercase letter. We can also test for these things, and more, by using character testing functions provided by the C++ library. These Boolean functions test the ASCII code of a character and return either `true` or `false`. For example, the following program segment uses the `isupper` function to determine if the character passed to it as an argument is an uppercase letter. If it is, the function returns `true`. Otherwise, it returns `false`[*]

```
char letter = 'a';
if (isupper(letter))
   cout << "Letter is uppercase.\n";
else
   cout << "Letter is not uppercase.\n";
```

Because the variable `letter`, in this example, contains a lowercase character, `isupper` returns `false`. The `if` statement will cause the message "Letter is not uppercase" to be displayed.

Table 4-12 lists some of the common character-testing functions C++ provides. To use these you need to include the `cctype` header file in your program.

* These functions actually return an `int` value. A non-zero value indicates `true` and a zero indicates `false`.

Table 4-12 Character Testing Functions

Character Function	Description
`isalpha`	Returns `true` if the argument is a letter of the alphabet. Otherwise, it returns `false`.
`isalnum`	Returns `true` if the argument is a letter of the alphabet or a digit. Otherwise, it returns `false`.
`isdigit`	Returns `true` if the argument is a digit from 0 to 9. Otherwise, it returns `false`.
`islower`	Returns `true` if the argument is a lowercase letter. Otherwise, it returns `false`.
`isprint`	Returns `true` if the argument is a printable character (including a space). Otherwise, it returns `false`.
`ispunct`	Returns `true` if the argument is a printable character other than a digit, letter, or space. Otherwise, it returns `false`.
`isupper`	Returns `true` if the argument is an uppercase letter. Otherwise, it returns `false`.

`isspace`	Returns `true` if the argument is a whitespace character. Otherwise it returns `false`. Whitespace characters are any of the following:
	`space ' '` `vertical tab '\v'`
	`newline '\n'` `tab '\t'`

Program 4-21 uses several of the functions shown in Table 4-12. It asks the user to input a character and then displays various messages, depending on the return value of each function.

Program 4-21

```
// This program demonstrates some of the available
// C++ character testing functions.
#include <iostream>
#include <cctype>        // Needed to use character testing functions
using namespace std;

int main()
{
   char input;

   cout << "Enter any character: ";
   cin.get(input);

   cout << "The character you entered is: " << input << endl;
   cout << "Its ASCII code is: " << static_cast<int>(input) << endl;

   if (isalpha(input))
      cout << "That's an alphabetic character.\n";

   if (isdigit(input))
      cout << "That's a numeric digit.\n";
```

(program continues)

Program 4-21 *(continued)*

```

    if (islower(input))
       cout << "The letter you entered is lowercase.\n";

    if (isupper(input))
       cout << "The letter you entered is uppercase.\n";

    if (isspace(input))
       cout << "That's a whitespace character.\n";

   return 0;
}
```

Program Output with Example Input Shown in Bold

```
Enter any character: A[Enter]
The character you entered is: A
Its ASCII code is: 65
That's an alphabetic character.
The letter you entered is uppercase.
```

Program Output with Other Example Input Shown in Bold

```
Enter any character: 7[Enter]
The character you entered is: 7
Its ASCII code is: 55
That's a numeric digit.
```

Checkpoint

4.30 Indicate whether each of the following relational expressions is true or false. Refer to the ASCII table in Appendix A if necessary.

A) 'a' < 'z'
B) 'a' == 'A'
C) '5' < '7'
D) 'a' < 'A'
E) '1' == 1
F) '1' == 49

4.31 Indicate whether each of the following relational expressions is true or false. Refer to the ASCII table in Appendix A if necessary.

A) "Bill" == "BILL"
B) "Bill" < "BILL"
C) "Bill" < "Bob"
D) "189" > "23"
E) "189" > "Bill"
F) "Mary" == " Mary"
G) "Mary" < "MaryEllen"
H) "MaryEllen" < "Mary Ellen"

4.32 Assume `str1` and `str2` are `string` objects that have been initialized with values. Write an `if/else if` statement that compares the two objects. If their values are the same, it should print a message saying so and display their value. Otherwise, it should display the values in alphabetical order.

4.33 Indicate whether each of these character testing functions will return true or false.

A) isalpha('B')
B) isalnum('B')
C) isdigit('B')
D) islower('B')
E) isprint('B')
F) ispunct('B')
G) isupper('B')
H) isspace('B')

4.11 The Conditional Operator

CONCEPT: You can use the conditional operator to create short expressions that work like `if/else` statements.

The conditional operator is powerful and unique. It provides a shorthand method of expressing a simple `if/else` statement. The operator consists of the question mark (?) and the colon(:). Its format is

```
expression ? expression : expression;
```

Here is an example of a statement using the conditional operator:

```
x < 0 ? y = 10 : z = 20;
```

This statement is called a *conditional expression* and consists of three sub-expressions separated by the `?` and `:` symbols. The expressions are `x < 0`, `y = 10`, and `z = 20`.

```
x < 0      ?      y = 10      :      z = 20;
```

The conditional expression above performs the same operation as this `if/else` statement:

```
if (x < 0)
   y = 10;
else
   z = 20;
```

The part of the conditional expression that comes before the question mark is the condition to be tested. It's like the expression in the parentheses of an `if` statement. If the condition is true, the part of the statement between the `?` and the `:` is executed. Otherwise, the part after the `:` is executed. Figure 4-9 illustrates the roles played by the three sub-expressions.

Figure 4-9

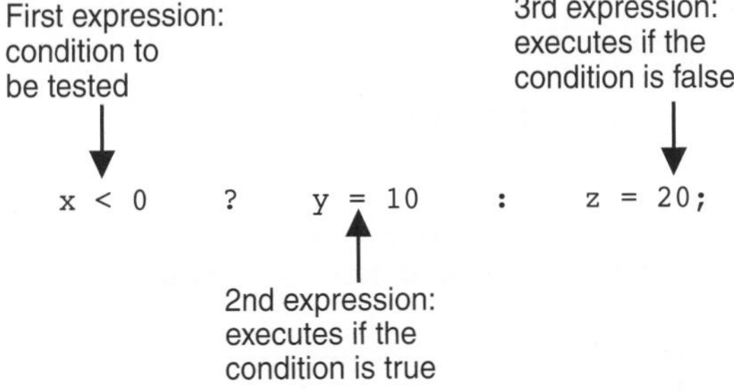

If it helps, you can put parentheses around the sub-expressions, as shown here:

```
(x < 0) ? (y = 10) : (z = 20);
```

NOTE: Because it takes three operands, the conditional operator is a *ternary* operator.

Using the Value of a Conditional Expression

Remember, in C++ all expressions have a value, and this includes the conditional expression. If the first sub-expression is true, the value of the conditional expression is the value of the second sub-expression. Otherwise it is the value of the third sub-expression. Here is an example of an assignment statement that uses the value of a conditional expression:

```
a = (x > 100) ? 0 : 1;
```

The value assigned to variable `a` will be either 0 or 1, depending upon whether `x` is greater than 100. This statement has the same logic as the following `if/else` statement:

```
if (x > 100)
    a = 0;
else
    a = 1;
```

Program 4-22 can be used to help a consultant calculate her charges. Her rate is $50.00 per hour, but her minimum charge is for five hours. The conditional operator is used in a statement that ensures the number of hours does not go below five.

Program 4-22

```
// This program calculates a consultant's charges at $50
// per hour, for a minimum of 5 hours. The ?: operator
// adjusts hours to 5 if fewer than 5 hours were worked.
#include <iostream>
#include <iomanip>
using namespace std;

int main()
{
   const double PAY_RATE = 50.0;  // Hourly pay rate
   const int MIN_HOURS = 5;       // Minimum billable hours
   double hours,                  // Hours worked
          charges;                // Total charges

   // Get the hours worked
   cout << "How many hours were worked? ";
   cin  >> hours;

   // Determine how many hours to charge for
   hours = hours < MIN_HOURS ? MIN_HOURS : hours;

   // Calculate and display the charges
   charges = PAY_RATE * hours;
   cout << fixed << showpoint << setprecision(2)
        << "The charges are $" << charges << endl;
   return 0;
}
```

(program continues)

Program 4-22 *(continued)*

Program Output with Example Input Shown in Bold

```
How many hours were worked? 10[Enter]
The charges are $500.00
```

Program Output with Other Example Input Shown in Bold

```
How many hours were worked? 2[Enter]
The charges are $250.00
```

Let's look more closely at the statement in line 20 that uses a conditional expression:

```
hours = hours < MIN_HOURS ? MIN_HOURS : hours;
```

If the value of the `hours` variable is less than `MIN_HOURS`, it stores `MIN_HOURS` in `hours`. Otherwise it assigns `hours` the value it already has. This ensures that `hours` will not have a value less than `MIN_HOURS` when it is used in line 23 to calculate the consultant's charges.

As you can see, the conditional operator gives you the ability to pack decision-making power into a concise line of code. With a little imagination it can be applied to many other programming problems. For instance, consider the following statement:

```
cout << "Your grade is: " << (score < 60 ? "Fail." : "Pass.");
```

If you were to use an `if/else` statement, this statement would be written as follows:

```
if (score < 60)
   cout << "Your grade is: Fail.";
else
   cout << "Your grade is: Pass.";
```

NOTE: The parentheses are placed around the conditional expression because the `<<` operator has higher precedence than the `?:` operator. Without the parentheses, just the value of the expression `score < 60` would be sent to `cout`.

Checkpoint

4.34 Rewrite the following `if/else` statements as conditional expressions.

A)
```
if (x > y)
     z = 1;
else
     z = 20;
```

B)
```
if (temp > 45)
     population = base * 10;
else
     population = base * 2;
```

C)
```
if (hours > 40)
     wages *= 1.5;
else
     wages *= 1;
```

D)
```
if (result >= 0)
     cout << "The result is positive\n";
else
     cout << "The result is negative.\n";
```

4.35 Rewrite the following conditional expressions as `if/else` statements.

A) `j = k > 90 ? 57 : 12;`
B) `factor = x >= 10 ? y * 22 : y * 35;`
C) `total += count == 1 ? sales : count * sales;`
D) `cout << ((num % 2) == 0) ? "Even\n" : "Odd\n");`

4.36 What will the following program segment display?

```
const int UPPER = 8, LOWER = 2;
int num1, num2, num3 = 12, num4 = 3;

num1 = num3 < num4 ? UPPER : LOWER;
num2 = num4 > UPPER ? num3 : LOWER;
cout << num1 << " " <<  num2 << endl;
```

4.12 The `switch` Statement

CONCEPT: The `switch` statement uses the value of a variable or expression to determine where the program will branch to.

A branch occurs when one part of a program causes another part to execute. The `if/else if` statement, introduced earlier in this chapter, allows your program to branch into one of several possible paths. It performs a series of tests (usually relational) and branches when one of these tests is true. The `switch` statement is a similar mechanism. It, however, tests the value of an integer expression and then uses that value to determine which set of statements to branch to. Here is the format of the `switch` statement:

```
switch (IntegerExpression)
{
   case ConstantExpression:   // Place one or more
                              // statements here

   case ConstantExpression:   // Place one or more
                              // statements here

   // case statements may be repeated
   // as many times as necessary

   default:                    // Place one or more
                               // statements here
}
```

The first line of the statement starts with the word `switch`, followed by an integer expression inside parentheses. This can be either of the following:

- A variable of any of the integer data types (including `char`).
- An expression whose value is of any of the integer data types.

On the next line is the beginning of a block containing several `case` statements. Each `case` statement is formatted in the following manner:

```
case ConstantExpression:    // Place one or more
                            // statements here
```

After the word `case` is a constant expression (which must be of an integer type such as an `int` or `char`), followed by a colon. The constant expression can be either an integer literal or an integer named constant. The expression cannot be a variable and it cannot be a Boolean expression such as `x < 22` or `n == 25`. The `case` statement marks the beginning of a section of statements that are branched to if the value of the `switch` expression matches that of the `case` expression. Notice that, unlike most blocks of statements, no braces are required around this set of statements.

WARNING! The expressions of each `case` statement in the block must be unique.

An optional `default` section comes after all the `case` statements. This section is branched to if none of the `case` expressions match the `switch` expression. Thus it functions like a trailing `else` in an `if/else if` statement.

Program 4-23 shows how a simple `switch` statement works.

Program 4-23

```
// This program demonstrates the use of a switch statement.
// The program simply tells the user what character they entered.
#include <iostream>
using namespace std;

int main()
{
   char choice;

   cout << "Enter A, B, or C: ";
   cin  >> choice;

   switch (choice)
   {
      case 'A':cout << "You entered A.\n";
               break;
      case 'B':cout << "You entered B.\n";
               break;
      case 'C':cout << "You entered C.\n";
               break;
      default: cout << "You did not enter A, B, or C!\n";
}
   return 0;

```

Program Output with Example Input Shown in Bold

```
Enter A, B, or C: B[Enter]
You entered B.
```

Program Output with Different Example Input Shown in Bold

```
Enter A, B, or C: F[Enter]
You did not enter A, B, or C!
```

The first case statement is `case 'A':`, the second is `case 'B':`, and the third is `case 'C':`. These statements mark where the program is to branch to if the variable `choice` contains the values 'A', 'B', or 'C'. (Remember, character variables and literals are considered integers.) The `default` section is branched to if the user enters anything other than A, B, or C.

Notice the `break` statements at the end of the `case 'A'`, `case 'B'`, and `case 'C'` sections.

```
switch (choice)
{
   case 'A':cout << "You entered A.\n";
            break; ←
   case 'B':cout << "You entered B.\n";
            break; ←
   case 'C':cout << "You entered C.\n";
            break; ←
   default:cout << "You did not enter A, B, or C!\n";
}
```

The `break` statement causes the program to exit the `switch` statement. The next statement executed after encountering a `break` statement will be whatever statement follows the closing brace that terminates the entire `switch` statement. A `break` statement is needed whenever you want to "break out of" a `switch` statement because it is not automatically exited after carrying out a set of statements the way an `if/else if` statement is.

The `case` statements show the program where to start executing in the block, and the `break` statements show the program where to stop. Without the `break` statements, the program would execute all of the lines from the matching `case` statement to the end of the block.

NOTE: The `default` section (or the last `case` section if there is no `default`) does not need a `break` statement. Some programmers prefer to put one there anyway for consistency.

Program 4-24 is a modification of Program 4-23 that demonstrates what happens if the `break` statements are omitted.

Program 4-24

```
// This program demonstrates how a switch statement
// works if there are no break statements.
#include <iostream>
using namespace std;

int main()
{
   char choice;

   cout << "Enter A, B, or C: ";
   cin  >> choice;

```

(program continues)

Program 4-24 *(continued)*

```
   // The following switch statement is missing its break statements!
   switch (choice)
   {
      case 'A':cout << "You entered A.\n";
      case 'B':cout << "You entered B.\n";
      case 'C':cout << "You entered C.\n";
      default :cout << "You did not enter A, B, or C!\n";
   }
   return 0;
}
```

Program Output with Example Input Shown in Bold

```
Enter A, B, or C: A[Enter]
You entered A.
You entered B.
You entered C.
You did not enter A, B, or C!
```

Program Output with Different Example Input Shown in Bold

```
Enter A, B, or C: C[Enter]
You entered C.
You did not enter A, B, or C!
```

Without the `break` statement, Program 4-24 “falls through” all of the statements below the one with the matching `case` expression. Sometimes this is what you want. Program 4-25 lists the features of three TV models a customer may choose from. Model 100 includes a 42" LCD flat screen. Model 200 includes 1080p high definition picture as well as a 42" LCD flat screen. Model 300 includes all of this as well as a built-in digital video recorder (DVR). The program uses a switch statement with carefully omitted breaks to print the features of the selected model.

Program 4-25

```
// This program is carefully constructed to use the
// "fall through" feature of the switch statement.
#include <iostream>
using namespace std;

int main()
{
   int modelNum;

   // Display available models and get the user's choice
   cout << "Our TVs come in three models: The 100, 200, and 300. \n";
   cout << "Which do you want? ";
   cin  >> modelNum;

```

(program continues)

Program 4-25 *(continued)*

```
    // Display the features of the selected model
    cout << "\nThat model has the following features:\n";

    switch (modelNum)
    {
       case 300: cout << "    Built-in DVR \n";
       case 200: cout << "    1080p high definition picture \n";
       case 100: cout << "    42\" LCD flat screen \n";
                 break;
       default : cout << "You can only choose the 100, 200, or 300. \n ";
    }
    return 0;
}
```

Program Output with Example Input Shown in Bold

```
Our TVs come in three models: The 100, 200, and 300.
Which do you want? 100[Enter]
That model has the following features:
    42" LCD flat screen
```

Program Output with Different Example Input Shown in Bold

```
Our TVs come in three models: The 100, 200, and 300.
Which do you want? 200[Enter]
That model has the following features:
    1080p high definition picture
    42" LCD flat screen
```

Program Output with Different Example Input Shown in Bold

```
Our TVs come in three models: The 100, 200, and 300.
Which do you want? 300[Enter]
That model has the following features:
    Built-in DVR
    1080p high definition picture
    42" LCD flat screen
```

Program Output with Different Example Input Shown in Bold

```
Our TVs come in three models: The 100, 200, and 300.
Which do you want? 500[Enter]

That model has the following features:
You can only choose the 100, 200, or 300.
```

Another example of how useful this "fall through" capability can be is when you want the program to branch to the same set of statements for multiple `case` expressions. For instance, Program 4-26 asks the user to select a grade of dog food. The available choices are A, B, and C. The `switch` statement will recognize either uppercase or lowercase letters.

Program 4-26

```
// The switch statement in this program uses the "fall through" feature
// to accept both uppercase and lowercase letters entered by the user.
#include <iostream>
using namespace std;

int main()
{
   char feedGrade;

   // Get the desired grade of feed
   cout << "Our dog food is available in three grades:\n";
   cout << "A, B, and C. Which do you want pricing for? ";
   cin  >> feedGrade;

   // Find and display the price
   switch(feedGrade)
   {
      case 'a':
      case 'A': cout << "30 cents per pound.\n";
                break;
      case 'b':
      case 'B': cout << "20 cents per pound.\n";
                break;
      case 'c':
      case 'C': cout << "15 cents per pound.\n";
                break;
      default : cout << "That is an invalid choice.\n";
   }
   return 0;
}
```

Program Output with Example Input Shown in Bold

```
Our dog food is available in three grades:
A, B, and C. Which do you want pricing for? b[Enter]
20 cents per pound.
```

Program Output with Different Example Input Shown in Bold

```
Our dog food is available in three grades:
A, B, and C. Which do you want pricing for? B[Enter]
20 cents per pound.
```

When the user enters `'a'` the corresponding `case` has no statements associated with it, so the program falls through to the next `case`, which corresponds with `'A'`.

```
case 'a':
case 'A':cout << "30 cents per pound.\n";
         break;
```

The same is technique is used for `'b'` and `'c'`.

Using `switch` in Menu-Driven Systems

The `switch` statement is a natural mechanism for building menu-driven systems like the one we built in Program 4-10. However in that program, once the user selects which health club package to purchase, the program uses an `if/else if` statement to calculate the charges. Program 4-27 is a modification of that program that uses a `switch` statement instead. Notice how the `switch` statement is nested inside an `if` statement that validates the user's menu choice before prompting for the number of months. This means that the prompt and input for the number of months only has to appear once. It also means that the user is never prompted to enter the number of months if the menu choice is invalid.

Program 4-27

```
// This menu-driven program uses a switch statement to carry out
// the appropriate set of actions based on the user's menu choice.
#include <iostream>
#include <iomanip>
using namespace std;

int main()
{
   // Constants for membership rates
   const double ADULT_RATE  = 120.0;
   const double CHILD_RATE  =  60.0;
   const double SENIOR_RATE = 100.0;

   int choice;             // Menu choice
   int months;             // Number of months
   double charges;         // Monthly charges

   // Display the menu and get the user's choice
   cout << "   Health Club Membership Menu\n\n";
   cout << "1. Standard Adult Membership\n";
   cout << "2. Child Membership\n";
   cout << "3. Senior Citizen Membership\n";
   cout << "4. Quit the Program\n\n";
   cout << "Enter your choice: ";
   cin  >> choice;

   // Validate and process the menu choice
   if (choice >= 1 && choice <= 3)
   {  cout << "For how many months? ";
      cin  >> months;

      // Set charges based on user input
      switch (choice)
      {
         case 1: charges = months * ADULT_RATE;
                 break;
         case 2: charges = months * CHILD_RATE;
                 break;
         case 3: charges = months * SENIOR_RATE;
      }
```

Program 4-27 *(continued)*

```
        // Display the monthly charges
        cout << fixed << showpoint << setprecision(2);
        cout << "The total charges are $" << charges << endl;
    }
    else if (choice != 4)
    {   cout << "The valid choices are 1 through 4.\n";
        cout << "Run the program again and select one of these.\n";
    }
    return 0;
}
```

Program Output with Example Input Shown in Bold

```
   Health Club Membership Menu

1. Standard Adult Membership
2. Child Membership
3. Senior Citizen Membership
4. Quit the Program

Enter your choice: 2[Enter]
For how many months? 6[Enter]
The total charges are $360.00
```

Program Output with Different Example Input Shown in Bold

```
   Health Club Membership Menu

1. Standard Adult Membership
2. Child Membership
3. Senior Citizen Membership
4. Quit the Program

Enter your choice: 5[Enter]
The valid choices are 1 through 4.
Run the program again and select one of these.
```

Checkpoint

4.37 Explain why you cannot convert the following `if/else if` statement into a `switch` statement.

```
if (temp == 100)
   x = 0;
else if (population > 1000)
   x = 1;
else if (rate < .1)
   x = -1;
```

4.38 What is wrong with the following `switch` statement?

```
switch (temp)
{
   case temp < 0 :  cout << "Temp is negative.\n";
                    break;
   case temp == 0:  cout << "Temp is zero.\n";
                    break;
   case temp > 0 :  cout << "Temp is positive.\n";
                    break;
}
```

4.39 What will the following program segment display?

```
int funny = 7, serious = 15;

funny = serious * 2;
switch (funny)
{  case 0 :  cout << "That is funny.\n";
             break;
   case 30:  cout << "That is serious.\n";
             break;
   case 32:  cout << "That is seriously funny.\n";
             break;
   default:  cout << funny << endl;
}
```

4.40 Complete the following program skeleton by writing a `switch` statement that displays `"one"` if the user has entered 1, `"two"` if the user has entered 2, and `"three"` if the user has entered 3. If a number other than 1, 2, or 3 is entered, the program should display an error message.

```
#include <iostream>
using namespace std;

int main()
{
   int userNum;

   cout << "Enter one of the numbers 1, 2, or 3: ";
   cin  >> userNum;

   // Write the switch statement here.

   return 0;
}
```

4.41 Rewrite the following program segment using a `switch` statement instead of the `if/else if` statement.

```
   int selection;

   cout << "Which formula do you want to see?\n\n";
   cout << "1. Area of a circle\n";
   cout << "2. Area of a rectangle\n";
   cout << "3. Area of a cylinder\n"
   cout << "4. None of them!\n";
   cin  >> selection;
```

```
if (selection == 1)
   cout << "Pi times radius squared\n";
else if (selection == 2)
   cout << "Length times width\n";
else if (selection == 3)
   cout << "Pi times radius squared times height\n";
else if (selection == 4)
   cout << "Well okay then, good-bye!\n";
else
   cout << "Not good with numbers, eh?\n";
```

4.13 Enumerated Data Types

CONCEPT: An enumerated data type in C++ is a programmer-defined data type whose legal values are a set of named integer constants.

So far we have used data types that are built into the C++ language, such as `int` and `double`, and object types, like `string`, which are provided by C++ classes. However, C++ also allows programmers to create their own data types. An *enumerated data type* is a programmer-defined data type that consists of values known as enumerators, which represent integer constants. Here is an example of an enumerated type declaration.

```
enum Roster { Tom, Sharon, Bill, Teresa, John };
```

This creates a data type named `Roster`. It is called an enumerated type because the legal set of values that variables of this data type can have are enumerated, or listed, as part of the declaration. A variable of the `Roster` data type may only have values that are in the list inside the braces.

It is important to realize that the example `enum` statement does not actually create any variables. It just defines the data type. It says that when we later create variables of this data type, this is what they will look like—integers whose values are limited to the integers associated with the symbolic names in the enumerated set. The following statement shows how a variable of the `Roster` data type would be defined.

```
Roster student;
```

The form of this statement is like any other variable definition: first the data type name, then the variable name. Notice that the data type name is `Roster`, not `enum Roster`.

Because `student` is a variable of the `Roster` data type, we may store any of the values `Tom`, `Sharon`, `Bill`, `Teresa`, or `John` in it. An assignment operation would look like this:

```
student = Sharon;
```

The value of the variable could then be tested like this:

```
if (student == Sharon)
```

Notice in the two examples that there are no quotation marks around `Sharon`. It is a named constant, not a string literal.

In Chapter 3 you learned that named constants are constant values that are accessed through their symbolic name. So what is the value of `Sharon`? The symbol `Tom` is stored as the integer 0. `Sharon` is stored as the integer 1. `Bill` is stored as the integer 2, and so forth.

Even though the values in an enumerated data type are actually stored as integers, you cannot always substitute the integer value for the symbolic name. For example, assuming that `student` is a variable of the `Roster` data type, the following assignment statement is illegal.

```
student = 2;    // Error!
```

You can, however, test an enumerated variable by using an integer value instead of a symbolic name. For example, the following two `if` statements are equivalent.

```
if (student == Bill)
if (student == 2)
```

You can also use relational operators to compare two enumerated variables. For example, the following `if` statement determines if the value stored in `student1` is less than the value stored in `student2`:

```
if (student1 < student2)
```

If `student1` equals `Bill` and `student2` equals `John`, this statement would be true. However, if `student1` equals `Bill` and `student2` equals `Sharon`, the statement would be false.

By default, the symbols in the enumeration list are assigned the integer values 0, 1, 2, and so forth. If this is not appropriate, you can specify the values to be assigned, as in the following example.

```
enum Department { factory = 1, sales = 2, warehouse = 4 };
```

Remember that if you do assign values to the enumerated symbols, they must be integers. The following value assignments would produce an error.

```
enum Department { factory = 1.1, sales = 2.2, warehouse = 4.4 };
                                                        // Error!
```

While there is no requirement that assigned integer values be placed in ascending order, it is generally considered a good idea to do this.

If you leave out the value assignment for one or more of the symbols, it will be assigned a default value, as illustrated here:

```
enum Colors { red, orange, yellow = 9, green, blue };
```

`red` will be assigned the value 0, `orange` will be 1, `yellow` will be 9, `green` will be 10, and `blue` will be 11.

One of the purposes of an enumerated data type is that the symbolic names help to make a program self-documenting. However, because these names are not strings, they are for use inside the program only. Using the `Roster` data type in our example, the following two statements would output a `2`, not the name `Sharon`.

```
Roster student1 = Sharon;
cout << student1;
```

Because the symbolic names of an enumerated data type are associated with integer values, they may be used in a switch statement, as shown in Program 4-28. This program also demonstrates that it is possible to use an enumerated data type without actually creating any variables of that type.

Program 4-28

```
// This program demonstrates an enumerated data type.
#include <iostream>
using namespace std;

// Declare the enumerated type
enum Roster { Tom = 1, Sharon, Bill, Teresa, John };
                    // Sharon – John will be assigned default values 2-5.
int main()
{
   int who;

   cout << "This program will give you a student's birthday.\n";
   cout << "Whose birthday do you want to know?\n";
   cout << "1 = Tom\n";
   cout << "2 = Sharon\n";
   cout << "3 = Bill\n";
   cout << "4 = Teresa\n";
   cout << "5 = John\n";
   cin  >> who;

   switch (who)
   {
      case Tom   :  cout << "\nTom's birthday is January 3.\n";
                    break;
      case Sharon:  cout << "\nSharon's birthday is April 22.\n";
                    break;
      case Bill  :  cout << "\nBill's birthday is December 19.\n";
                    break;
      case Teresa:  cout << "\nTeresa's birthday is February 2.\n";
                    break;
      case John  :  cout << "\nJohn's birthday is June 17.\n";
                    break;
      default    :  cout << "\nInvalid selection\n";
   }
   return 0;
}
```

(program continues)

Program 4-28 *(continued)*

Program Output with Example Input Shown in Bold

```
This program will give you a student's birthday.
Whose birthday do you want to know?
1 = Tom
2 = Sharon
3 = Bill
4 = Teresa
5 = John
2[Enter]

Sharon's birthday is April 22.
```

Checkpoint

4.42 Find all the things that are wrong with the following declaration.

```
Enum Pet = { "dog", "cat", "bird", "fish" }
```

4.43 Follow the instructions to complete the following program segment.

```
enum Paint { red, blue, yellow, green, orange, purple };
Paint color = green;

// Write an if/else statement that will print out "primary color"
// if color is red, blue, or yellow, and will print out
// "mixed color" otherwise. The if test should use a relational
// expression.
```

4.14 Focus on Testing and Debugging: *Validating Output Results*

CONCEPT: When testing a newly created or modified program, the output it produces must be carefully examined to ensure it is correct.

Once a program being developed has been designed, written in a programming language, and found to compile and link without errors, it is easy to jump to the conclusion that it works correctly. This is especially true if it runs without aborting and produces "reasonable" output. However, just because a program runs and produces output does not mean that it is correct. It may still contain logic errors that cause the output to be incorrect. To determine if a program actually works correctly it must be tested with data whose output can be predicted and the output examined to ensure it is accurate.

Program 4-29 runs and produces output that may initially appear reasonable. However, it contains a bug that causes it to produce incorrect output.

Program 4-29

```
// This program determines a client's total buffet luncheon cost
// when the number of guests and the per person cost are known.
// It contains a logic error.
#include <iostream>
#include <iomanip>
using namespace std;

const int ADULT_MEAL_COST = 6.25; // Child meal cost = 75% of this

int main()
{
   int      numAdults,          // Number of guests ages 12 and older
            numChildren;        // Number of guests ages 2-11
   double   adultMealTotal,     // Cost for all adult meals
            childMealTotal,     // Cost for all child meals
            totalMealCost;

   // Get number of adults and children attending
   cout << "This program calculates total cost "
        << "for a buffet luncheon.\n";
   cout << "Enter the number of adult guests (age 12 and over): ";
   cin  >> numAdults;
   cout << "Enter the number of child guests (age 2-11): ";
   cin  >> numChildren;

   // Calculate meal costs
   adultMealTotal = numAdults * ADULT_MEAL_COST;
   childMealTotal = numChildren * ADULT_MEAL_COST * .75;
   totalMealCost  = adultMealTotal + childMealTotal;

   // Display total meal cost
   cout << fixed << showpoint << setprecision(2);
   cout << "\nTotal buffet cost is $" << totalMealCost << endl;
   return 0;
}
```

Program Output with Example Input Shown in Bold

```
This program calculates total cost for a buffet luncheon.
Enter the number of adult guests (age 12 and over): 92[Enter]
Enter the number of child guests (age 2-11): 4[Enter]

Total buffet cost is $570.00
```

At first glance the program may appear to run correctly. The per person charge for adults is \$6.25, so if there were 100 adult guests the price would be \$625. But there are only 96 guests and four of them are children, so it should cost less. \$570 sounds "about right".

However, "about right" is not an a sufficient test of accuracy. If the program had been run with data whose output could have been more easily checked, the programmer would have quickly seen that there is an error. Here is the output from two more runs of the same program using more carefully selected sample data.

Program Output with Different Example Input Shown in Bold

```
This program calculates total cost for a buffet luncheon.
Enter the number of adult guests (age 12 and over): 1[Enter]
Enter the number of child guests (age 2-11): 0[Enter]

Total buffet cost is $6.00
```

Program Output with Still Different Example Input Shown in Bold

```
This program calculates total cost for a buffet luncheon.
Enter the number of adult guests (age 12 and over): 0[Enter]
Enter the number of child guests (age 2-11): 1[Enter]

Total buffet cost is $4.50
```

From this output we can see that the cost of a child meal is correctly being calculated as 75% of the cost of an adult meal, but the adult meal cost is wrong. For one adult, it is coming out as $6.00, when it should have been $6.25.

To find the problem, the programmer should determine which lines of code are most apt to have caused the problem. Most likely something is wrong either in the initialization or storage of `ADULT_MEAL_COST` on line 8, in the calculation or storage of `adultMealTotal` or `totalMealCost` on lines 14, 16, 27, and 29 or in the printing of `totalMealCost` on line 33. Because the cost for one adult meal is erroneously coming out as a whole dollar amount, even though it is formatted to appear as a floating-point number, one of the things to check is whether all the variables that need to hold floating-point values have been defined as type `float` or `double`. Sure enough, although `adultMealTotal` and `totalMealCost` have each been defined as a `double`, the named constant `ADULT_MEAL_COST` has been defined to be an `int`. So the 6.25 with which it is initialized is truncated to 6 when it is stored. When the definition of this named constant is rewritten as

```
const double ADULT_MEAL_COST = 6.25;
```

and the program is rerun, we get the following results.

Output of Revised Program with Example Input Shown in Bold

```
This program calculates total cost for a buffet luncheon.
Enter the number of adult guests (age 12 and over): 1[Enter]
Enter the number of child guests (age 2-11): 0[Enter]

Total buffet cost is $6.25
```

Now that this error has been found and fixed, the program is correct. However, additional testing with carefully developed test cases should be used to confirm this. The topic of how to develop good test cases will be dealt with further in the next chapter.

4.15 Green Fields Landscaping Case Study—Part 2

Problem Statement

Another of the services provided by Green Fields Landscaping is the sale of evergreen trees, which are priced by height. Customers have the choice of purchasing a tree on a "cash and carry" basis, of purchasing a tree and having it delivered, or of purchasing a tree and having it both delivered and planted. Table 4-13 shows the price for each of these. You have been asked to develop a program that uses the number of trees purchased, their height, and the delivery and planting information to create a customer invoice. To simplify the program you may assume that all trees purchased by a customer are the same height.

Table 4-13 Evergreen Tree Pricing Information

Under 3 feet tall	39.00 (tax included)
3 to 5 feet tall	69.00 (tax included)
6 to 8 feet tall	99.00 (tax included)
over 8 feet tall	199.00 (tax included)
delivery only (per tree)	20.00 (100.00 max. per order)
delivery + planting	50% of the cost of the tree

Program Design

Program Steps

The program must carry out the following general steps:

1. Have the user input the number of trees purchased and their height.
2. Have the user indicate if the trees will be planted by Green Fields.
3. If planting service is not desired, have the user indicate if they want delivery.
4. Calculate the total tree cost.
5. Calculate the planting and delivery charges.
6. Calculate the total of all charges.
7. Print a bill that displays the purchase information and all charges.

Named constants

```
double PRICE_1 =  39.00
double PRICE_2 =  69.00
double PRICE_3 =  99.00
double PRICE_4 = 199.00
double PER_TREE_DELIVERY = 20.00
double MAX_DELIVERY = 100.00
```

Variables whose values will be input

```
int  numTrees            // Number of evergreen trees purchased
int  height              // Tree height to the nearest foot
char planted             // Are trees to be planted?('Y'/'N')
char delivered           // Are trees to be delivered?('Y'/'N')
```

Variables whose values will be output

```
double treeCost          // Cost of each tree
double totalTreeCost     // Total price for all the trees
double deliveryCost      // Delivery cost for all the trees
double plantingCost      // Planting cost for all the trees
double totalCharges      // Total invoice amount
```

Detailed Pseudocode (including actual variable names and needed calculations)

```
Initialize deliveryCost and plantingCost to 0
Display screen heading
Input numTrees, height, planted
If planted = 'N'
   Input delivery
End If
If height < 3
   treeCost = PRICE_1
Else If height <= 5
   treeCost = PRICE_2
Else If height <= 8
   treeCost = PRICE_3
Else
   treeCost = PRICE_4
End If
totalTreeCost = numTrees * treeCost
If planted = 'Y'
   plantingCost = totalTreeCost / 2     // deliveryCost stays 0
Else If delivered = 'Y'
   If numTrees <= 5
      deliveryCost = PER_TREE_DELIVERY * numTrees
   Else
      deliveryCost = MAX_DELIVERY
   End If
End If
totalCharges = totalTreeCost + deliveryCost + plantingCost
Display invoice heading
Display numTrees, treeCost, totalTreeCost,
        deliveryCost, plantingCost, totalCharges
```

The Program

The next step, after the pseudocode has been checked for logic errors, is to expand the pseudocode into the final program. This is shown in Program 4-30.

Program 4-30

```
// This program is used by Green Fields Landscaping to
// create customer invoices for evergreen tree sales.
#include <iostream>
#include <iomanip>
using namespace std;

```

(program continues)

Program 4-30 *(continued)*

```
int main()
{
   const double PRICE_1 =  39.00,    // Set prices for different
                PRICE_2 =  69.00,    // size trees
                PRICE_3 =  99.00,
                PRICE_4 = 199.00;

   const double PER_TREE_DELIVERY = 20.00, // Set delivery fees
                MAX_DELIVERY = 100.00;

   int    numTrees,            // Number of evergreen trees purchased
          height;              // Tree height to the nearest foot
   char   planted,             // Are trees to be planted?('Y'/'N')
          delivered;           // Are trees to be delivered?('Y'/'N')
   double treeCost,            // Cost of a particular tree
          totalTreeCost,       // Total price for all the trees
          deliveryCost = 0.0,  // Delivery cost for all the trees
          plantingCost = 0.0,  // Planting cost for all the trees
          totalCharges;        // Total invoice amount

   // Display purchase screen and get purchase information
   cout << "           Green Fields Landscaping\n"
        << "           Evergreen Tree Purchase\n\n";
   cout << "Number of trees purchased: ";
   cin  >> numTrees;
   cout << "Tree height to the nearest foot: ";
   cin  >> height;
   cout << "Will Green Fields do the planting?(Y/N): ";
   cin  >> planted;

   if (!(planted == 'Y' || planted == 'y'))
   {   cout << "Do you want the trees delivered?  (Y/N): ";
       cin  >> delivered;
   }

   // Calculate costs
   if (height < 3)
      treeCost = PRICE_1;
   else if(height <= 5)
      treeCost = PRICE_2;
   else if(height <= 8)
      treeCost = PRICE_3;
   else
      treeCost = PRICE_4;

   totalTreeCost = numTrees * treeCost;

```

(program continues)

Program 4-30 *(continued)*

```
   if ((planted == 'Y') || (planted == 'y'))
      plantingCost = totalTreeCost / 2;
   else if((delivered == 'Y') || (delivered == 'y'))
      if (numTrees <= 5)
         deliveryCost = PER_TREE_DELIVERY * numTrees;
      else
         deliveryCost = MAX_DELIVERY;
   //else planting and delivery costs both remain 0.0

   totalCharges = totalTreeCost + deliveryCost + plantingCost;

   // Display information on the invoice
   cout << fixed << showpoint << setprecision(2);
   cout << "\n\n           Green Fields Landscaping\n"
        << "           Evergreen Tree Purchase\n\n";
   cout << setw(2) << numTrees << " trees @ $" << setw(6) << treeCost
        << " each =    $" << setw(8) << totalTreeCost << endl;
   cout << "Delivery charge             $"
        << setw(8) << deliveryCost << endl;
   cout << "Planting charge             $"
        << setw(8) << plantingCost << endl;
   cout << "                             ________" << endl;
   cout << "Total Amount Due            $"
        << setw(8) << totalCharges << endl << endl;
   return 0;
}
```

Program Output with Example Input Shown in Bold

```
           Green Fields Landscaping
           Evergreen Tree Purchase

Number of trees purchased: 4[Enter]
Tree height to the nearest foot: 7[Enter]
Will Green Fields do the planting?(Y/N): y[Enter]

           Green Fields Landscaping
           Evergreen Tree Purchase

 4 trees @ $ 99.00 each =    $  396.00
Delivery charge              $    0.00
Planting charge              $  198.00
                              ________
Total Amount Due             $  594.00
```

Crazy Al's Computer Emporium Case Study

The following additional case study, which contain applications of material introduced in Chapter 4, can be found on the book's companion website.

Crazy Al's is a retail seller of home computers whose sales staff work on commission. The commission rate varies depending on the amount of sales. This case study develops a program that computes monthly sales commission and then subtracts any pay already advanced to the salesperson to calculate how much remaining pay is due at the end of the month. The case study, which employs branching logic to determine the correct commission rate, includes problem definition, general and detailed pseudocode design, and a final running program with sample output.

4.16 Tying It All Together: *Fortune Teller*

With the `rand()` function you learned about in Chapter 3 and the `if/else if` statement you learned about in this chapter, you can now create a simple fortune telling game. Your program will start by asking users to enter three careers they would like to have some day. The program will then use random numbers to predict their future.

Program 4-31

```
// This program predicts the player's future using
// random numbers and an if/else if statement.
#include <iostream>
#include <string>             // Needed to use strings
#include <cstdlib>            // Needed for random numbers
using namespace std;

int main()
{
   // Strings to hold user entered careers
   string career1, career2, career3;

   int randomNum;    // Will hold the randomly generated integer

   // "Seed" the random generator
   unsigned seed = time(0);
   srand(seed);

```

(program continues)

Program 4-31 *(continued)*

```
    // Explain the game and get the player's career choices
    cout << "I am a fortune teller. Look into my crystal screen \n"
         << "and enter 3 careers you would like to have. Example: \n\n"
         << "      chef \n      astronaut \n      CIA agent \n\n"
         << "Then I will predict what you will be. \n\n";

    cout << "Career choice 1: ";
    getline(cin, career1);
    cout << "Career choice 2: ";
    getline(cin, career2);
    cout << "Career choice 3: ";
    getline(cin, career3);

    // Randomly generate an integer between 1 and 4.
    randomNum = 1 + rand() % 4;

    // Use branching logic to output the prediction
    if (randomNum == 1)
       cout << "\nYou will be a " << career1 << ". \n";
    else if (randomNum == 2)
       cout << "\nYou will be a " << career2 << ". \n";
    else if (randomNum == 3)
       cout << "\nYou will be a " << career3 << ". \n";
    else
       cout << "\nSorry. You will not be any of these. \n";
    return 0;
}
```

Sample Run with User Input Shown in Bold

```
I am a fortune teller. Look into my crystal screen
and enter 3 careers you would like to have. For example,

      chef
      astronaut
      CIA agent

Then I will predict what you will be.

Career choice 1: radio announcer[Enter]
Career choice 2: sky diving instructor[Enter]
Career choice 3: circus clown[Enter]

You will be a radio announcer.
```

Review Questions and Exercises

Fill-in-the-Blank and Short Answer

1. An expression using the greater-than, less-than, greater-than-or-equal-to, less-than-or-equal-to, equal, or not-equal operator is called a(n) __________ expression.
2. The value of a relational expression is 0 if the expression is __________ or 1 if the expression is __________.
3. The `if` statement regards an expression with the value 0 as __________ and an expression with a nonzero value as __________.
4. For an `if` statement to conditionally execute a group of statements, the statements must be enclosed in a set of __________.
5. In an `if/else` statement, the `if` part executes its statement(s) if the expression is __________, and the `else` part executes its statement(s) if the expression is __________.
6. The trailing `else` in an `if/else if` statement has a similar purpose as the __________ section of a `switch` statement.
7. If the sub-expression on the left of the `&&` logical operator is __________, the right sub-expression is not checked.
8. If the sub-expression on the left of the `||` logical operator is __________, the right sub-expression is not checked.
9. The __________ logical operator has higher precedence than the other logical operators.
10. Logical operators have __________ precedence than relational operators.
11. The __________ logical operator works best when testing a number to determine if it is within a range.
12. The __________ logical operator works best when testing a number to determine if it is outside a range.
13. A variable with __________ scope is only visible when the program is executing in the block containing the variable's definition.
14. The expression that is tested by a `switch` statement must have a(n) __________ value.
15. A program will "fall through" to the following `case` section if it is missing the __________ statement.
16. What value will be stored in the variable `t` after each of the following statements executes?

    A) `t = (12 > 1);`__________
    B) `t = (2 < 0);`__________
    C) `t = (5 == (3 * 2));`__________
    D) `t = (5 == 5);`__________
17. Write an `if` statement that assigns 100 to `x` when `y` is equal to 0.
18. Write an `if/else` statement that assigns 0 to `x` when `y` is equal to 10. Otherwise it should assign 1 to `x`.

19. Write an `if/else` statement that prints "Excellent" when `score` is 90 or higher, "Good" when `score` is between 80 and 89, and "Try Harder" when `score` is less than 80.

20. Write an `if` statement that sets the variable `hours` to 10 when the flag variable `minimum` is set to `true`.

21. Convert the following conditional expression into an `if/else` statement.

```
q = (x < y) ? (a + b) : (x * 2);
```

22. Convert the following `if/else if` statement into a `switch` statement:

```
if (choice == 1)
{
   cout << fixed << showpoint << setprecision(2);
}
else if ((choice == 2) || (choice == 3))
{
   cout << fixed << showpoint << setprecision(4);
}
else if (choice == 4)
{
   cout << fixed << showpoint << setprecision(6);
}
else
{
   cout << fixed << showpoint << setprecision(8);
}
```

23. Assume the variables `x = 5`, `y = 6`, and `z = 8`. Indicate if each of the following conditions is true or false:

    A) `(x == 5) || (y > 3)`
    B) `(7 <= x) && (z > 4)`
    C) `(2 != y) && (z != 4)`

24. Assume the variables `x = 5`, `y = 6`, and `z = 8`. Indicate if each of the following conditions is true or false:

    A) `(x >= 0) || (x <= y)`
    B) `(z - y) > y`
    C) `!((z - y) > x)`

Algorithm Workbench

25. Write a C++ statement that prints the message "The number is valid." if the variable `grade` is within the range 0 through 100.

26. Write a C++ statement that prints the message "The number is valid." if the variable `temperature` is within the range –50 through 150.

27. Write a C++ statement that prints the message "The number is not valid." if the variable `hours` is outside the range 0 through 80.

28. Write a C++ statement that displays the titles stored in the `string` objects `book1` and `book2` in alphabetical order.

29. Using the following chart, write a C++ statement that assigns .10, .15, or .20 to `commission`, depending on the value in `sales`.

Sales	Commission Rate
Up to \$10,000	10%
\$10,000 to \$15,000	15%
Over \$15,000	20%

30. Write one or more C++ statements that assign the correct value to `discount`, using the logic described here:

    Assign .20 to `discount` if `dept` equals 5 and `price` is \$100 or more.
    Assign .15 to `discount` if `dept` is anything else and `price` is \$100 or more.
    Assign .10 to `discount` if `dept` equals 5 and `price` is less than \$100.
    Assign .05 to `discount` if `dept` is anything else and `price` is less than \$100.

31. The following statement should determine if `x` is not greater than 20. What is wrong with it?

```
if (!x > 20)
```

32. The following statement should determine if `count` is within the range of 0 through 100. What is wrong with it?

```
if (count >= 0 || count <= 100)
```

33. The following statement should determine if `count` is outside the range of 0 through 100. What is wrong with it?

```
if (count < 0 && count > 100)
```

34. The following statement should determine if `x` has a value other than 1 or 2. What is wrong with it?

```
if (x! = 1 || x! = 2)
```

Find the Errors

35. Each of the following program segments has errors. Find as many as you can.

A)
```
cout << "Enter your 3 test scores and I will ";
     << "average them:";
int score1, score2, score3,
cin  >> score1 >> score2 >> score3;

double average;
average = (score1 + score2 + score3) / 3.0;
if (average = 100);
   perfectScore = true;// Set the flag variable
cout << "Your average is " << average << endl;
bool perfectScore;
if (perfectScore);
{
   cout << "Congratulations!\n";
   cout << "That's a perfect score.\n";
   cout << "You deserve a pat on the back!\n";
```

B)
```
double num1, num2, quotient;

cout << "Enter a number: ";
cin  >> num1;
cout << "Enter another number: ";
cin  >> num2;

if (num2 == 0)
   cout << "Division by zero is not possible.\n";
   cout << "Please run the program again ";
   cout << "and enter a number besides zero.\n";
else
   quotient = num1 / num2;
   cout << "The quotient of " << num1 <<
   cout << " divided by " << num2 << " is ";
   cout << quotient << endl;
```

C)
```
int testScore;

cout << "Enter your test score and I will tell you\n";
cout << "the letter grade you earned: ";
cin  >> testScore;

if (testScore < 60)
   cout << "Your grade is F.\n";
else if (testScore < 70)
   cout << "Your grade is D.\n";
else if (testScore < 80)
   cout << "Your grade is C.\n";
else if (testScore < 90)
   cout << "Your grade is B.\n";
else
   cout << "That is not a valid score.\n";
else if (testScore <= 100)
   cout << "Your grade is A.\n";
```

D)
```
double testScore;

cout << "Enter your test score and I will tell you\n";
cout << "the letter grade you earned: ";
cin  >> testScore;

switch (testScore)
{  case (testScore < 60.0):
            cout << "Your grade is F.\n";
            break;
   case (testScore < 70.0):
            cout << "Your grade is D.\n";
            break;
   case (testScore < 80.0):
            cout << "Your grade is C.\n";
            break;
   case (testScore < 90.0):
            cout << "Your grade is B.\n";
            break;
   case (testScore <= 100.0):
            cout << "Your grade is A.\n";
            break;
   default:  cout << "That score isn't valid\n"; }
```

Soft Skills

Programmers need to be able to look at alternative approaches to solving a problem and at different ways of implementing a solution, weighing the pros and cons of each. Further, they need to be able to clearly articulate to others why they recommend, or have chosen, a particular solution. Come to class prepared to discuss the following:

36. Sometimes either a `switch` statement or an `if/else if` statement can be used to implement logic that requires branching to different blocks of program code. But the two are not interchangeable.
    A) Under what circumstances would an `if/else if` statement be a more appropriate choice than a switch statement?
    B) Under what circumstances would a `switch` statement be a more appropriate choice than an `if/else if` statement?
    C) Under what circumstances would a set of nested `if/else` statements be more appropriate than either of the other two structures?

Try to come up with at least one example case for each of the three, where it is the best way to implement the desired branching logic.

Programming Challenges

1. Minimum/Maximum

Write a program that asks the user to enter two numbers. The program should use the conditional operator to determine which number is the smaller and which is the larger.

2. Roman Numeral Converter

Write a program that asks the user to enter a number within the range of 1 through 10. Use a switch statement to display the Roman numeral version of that number.

Input Validation: Decide how the program should handle an input that is less than 1 or greater than 10.

3. Magic Dates

The date June 10, 1960, is special because when we write it in the following format, the month times the day equals the year.

6/10/60

Write a program that asks the user to enter a month (in numeric form), a day, and a two-digit year. The program should then determine whether the month times the day is equal to the year. If so, it should display a message saying the date is magic. Otherwise, it should display a message saying the date is not magic.

Input Validation: Think about what legal values the program should accept for month and day.

4. Areas of Rectangles

The area of a rectangle is the rectangle's length times its width. Write a program that asks for the length and width of two rectangles. The program should then tell the user which rectangle has the greater area, or if the areas are the same.

5. Book Club Points

An online book club awards points to its customers based on the number of books purchased each month. Points are awarded as follows:

Books Purchased	Points Earned
0	0
1	5
2	15
3	30
4 or more	60

Write a program that asks the user to enter the number of books purchased this month and then displays the number of points awarded.

6. Change for a Dollar Game

Create a change-counting game that asks the user to enter what coins to use to make exactly one dollar. The program should ask the user to enter the number of pennies, nickels, dimes, and quarters. If the total value of the coins entered is equal to one dollar, the program should congratulate the user for winning the game. Otherwise, the program should display a message indicating whether the amount entered was more or less than one dollar. Use constant variables to hold the coin values.

7. Time Calculator

VideoNote
Solving the Time Calculator Problem

Write a program that asks the user to enter a number of seconds.

- There are 86400 seconds in a day. If the number of seconds entered by the user is greater than or equal to 86400, the program should display the number of days in that many seconds.
- There are 3600 seconds in an hour. If the number of seconds entered by the user is less than 86400, but is greater than or equal to 3600, the program should display the number of hours in that many seconds.
- There are 60 seconds in a minute. If the number of seconds entered by the user is less than 3600, but is greater than or equal to 60, the program should display the number of minutes in that many seconds.

8. Math Tutor Version 2

This is a modification of the math tutor problem in Chapter 3. Write a program that can be used as a math tutor for a young student. The program should display two random numbers between 10 and 50 that are to be added, such as:

```
   24
 + 12
  ——
```

The program should then wait for the student to enter the answer. If the answer is correct, a message of congratulations should be printed. If the answer is incorrect, a message should be printed showing the correct answer.

9. Software Sales

A software company sells a package that retails for $99. Quantity discounts are given according to the following table.

Quantity	Discount
10–19	20%
20–49	30%
50–99	40%
100 or more	50%

Write a program that asks for the number of units purchased and computes the total cost of the purchase.

Input Validation: Decide how the program should handle an input of less than 0.

10. Bank Charges

A bank charges $10 per month plus the following check fees for a commercial checking account:

$.10 each for fewer than 20 checks
$.08 each for 20–39 checks
$.06 each for 40–59 checks
$.04 each for 60 or more checks

Write a program that asks for the number of checks written during the past month, then computes and displays the bank's fees for the month.

Input Validation: Decide how the program should handle an input of less than 0.

11. Geometry Calculator

Write a program that displays the following menu:

```
Geometry Calculator

   1. Calculate the Area of a Circle
   2. Calculate the Area of a Rectangle
   3. Calculate the Area of a Triangle
   4. Quit

Enter your choice (1-4):
```

If the user enters 1, the program should ask for the radius of the circle and then display its area. Use 3.14159 for π. If the user enters 2, the program should ask for the length and width of the rectangle, and then display the rectangle's area. If the user enters 3, the program should ask for the length of the triangle's base and its height, and then display its area. If the user enters 4, the program should end.

Input Validation: Decide how the program should handle an illegal input for the menu choice or a negative value for any of the other inputs.

12. Running the Race

Write a program that asks for the names of three runners and the time it took each of them to finish a race. The program should display who came in first, second, and third place. Think about how many test cases are needed to verify that your problem works correctly. (That is, how many different finish orders are possible?)

> *Input Validation: Only allow the program to accept positive numbers for the times.*

13. Personal Best

Write a program that asks for the name of a pole vaulter and the dates and vault heights (in meters) of the athlete's three best vaults. It should then report in height order (best first), the date on which each vault was made, and its height.

> *Input Validation: Only allow the program to accept values between 2.0 and 5.0 for the heights.*

14. Body Mass Index

Write a program that calculates and displays a person's body mass index (BMI). The BMI is often used to determine whether a person with a sedentary lifestyle is overweight or underweight for his or her height. A person's BMI is calculated with the following formula:

$$\text{BMI} = \text{weight} \times 703/\text{height}^2$$

where weight is measured in pounds and height is measured in inches. The program should display a message indicating whether the person has optimal weight, is underweight, or is overweight. A sedentary person's weight is considered to be optimal if his or her BMI is between 18.5 and 25. If the BMI is less than 18.5, the person is considered to be underweight. If the BMI value is greater than 25, the person is considered to be overweight.

> *Input Validation: Determine what inputs the program needs the user to enter and what legal values the program should accept for these inputs.*

15. Fat Gram Calculator

Write a program that asks for the number of calories and fat grams in a food. The program should display the percentage of calories that come from fat. If the calories from fat are less than 30 percent of the total calories of the food, it should also display a message indicating the food is low in fat.

One gram of fat has 9 calories, so

```
Calories from fat = fat grams * 9
```

The percentage of calories from fat can be calculated as

```
Calories from fat ÷ total calories
```

> *Input Validation: The program should make sure that the number of calories is greater than 0, the number of fat grams is 0 or more, and the number of calories from fat is not greater than the total number of calories.*

16. The Speed of Sound

The speed of sound varies depending on the medium through which it travels. In general, sound travels fastest in rigid media, such as steel, slower in liquid media, such as water, and slowest of all in gases, such as air. The following table shows the approximate speed of sound, measured in feet per second, in air, water, and steel.

Medium	Speed (feet per sec.)
Air	1,100
Water	4,900
Steel	16,400

Write a program that displays a menu allowing the user to select air water, or steel. After the user has made a selection, the number of feet a sound wave will travel in the selected medium should be entered. The program will then display the amount of time it will take. (Round the answer to four decimal places.)

Input Validation: Decide how the program should handle an illegal input for the menu choice or a negative value for the distance.

17. The Speed of Sound in Gases

When traveling through a gas, the speed of sound depends primarily on the density of the medium. The less dense the medium, the faster the speed will be. The following table shows the approximate speed of sound at 0 degree celsius, measured in meters per second, when traveling through carbon dioxide, air, helium, and hydrogen.

Medium	Speed (meters per sec.)
Carbon dioxide	258.0
Air	331.5
Helium	972.0
Hydrogen	1270.0

Write a program that displays a menu allowing the user to select one of these 4 gases. After a valid selection has been made, the program should ask the user to enter the number of seconds (0 to 30) it took for the sound to travel in this medium from its source to the location at which it was detected. The program should then report how far away (in meters) the source of the sound was from the detection location.

Input Validation: The program should ensure that the user has selected one of the available menu choices and should only prompt for the number of seconds if the menu choice is legal.

18. Spectral Analysis

If a scientist knows the wavelength of an electromagnetic wave she can determine what type of radiation it is. Write a program that asks for the wavelength in meters of an electromagnetic wave and then displays what that wave is according to the following chart. (For example, a wave with a wavelength of 1E-10 meters would be an X-ray.)

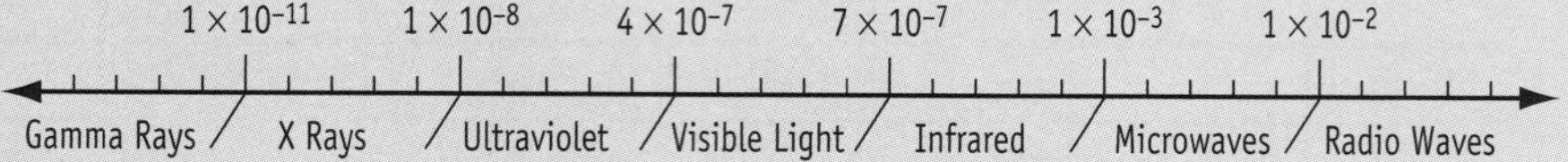

19. Long-Distance Calls

A long-distance carrier charges the following rates for telephone calls between the United States and Mexico:

Starting Time of Call	Rate per Minute
00:00–06:59	$0.12
07:00–19:00	0.55
19:01–23:59	0.35

Write a program that asks for the starting time and the number of minutes of the call, and displays the charges. The program should ask for the time to be entered as a floating-point number in the form HH.MM. For example, 07:00 hours should be entered as 07.00, and 16:28 hours should be entered as 16.28.

Hint: To find the fractional part of the entered number you can use the following expression:

```
startTime - static_cast<int>(startTime)
```

Input Validation: Figure out what inputs are valid for `startTime`, *and how the program will handle invalid inputs.*

20. Freezing and Boiling Points

The following table lists the freezing and boiling points of several substances. Write a program that asks the user to enter a temperature, and then shows all the substances that will freeze at that temperature and all that will boil at that temperature. For example, if the user enters –20 the program should report that water will freeze and oxygen will boil at that temperature.

Substance	Freezing Point (°F)	Boiling Point (°F)
Ethyl alcohol	–173	172
Mercury	–38	676
Oxygen	–362	–306
Water	32	212

21. Internet Service Provider Part 1

An International Internet phone company has three different subscription packages for its customers:

Package A: For $9.95 per month 5 hours of call time are provided. Additional usage costs $0.08 per minute.

Package B: For $14.95 per month 10 hours of call time are provided. Additional usage costs $0.06 per minute.

Package C: For $19.95 per month unlimited call time is provided.

Write a program that calculates a customer's monthly bill. It should input customer name, which package the customer has purchased, and how many hours were used. It should then create a bill that includes the input information and the total amount due. Wherever possible use named constants instead of numbers.

Input Validation: Be sure the user only selects package A, B, or C.

22. Internet Service Provider Part 2

Modify the program in problem 21 so it also displays how much money Package A customers would save if they purchased packages B or C, and how much money package B customers would save if they purchased package C. If there would be no savings, no message should be printed.

CHAPTER 5 Looping

TOPICS

5.1 Introduction to Loops: The `while` Loop

CONCEPT: A loop is part of a program that repeats.

Chapter 4 included several programs that report a student's letter grade based on his or her numeric test score. But what if we want to find out the letter grade for every student in a class of twenty students? We would have to run the program twenty times. Wouldn't it be easier if we could simply indicate that the code should be repeated twenty times in a single run? Fortunately there is a mechanism to do this. It is called a loop.

A *loop* is a control structure that causes a statement or group of statements to repeat. C++ has three looping control structures: the `while` loop, the `do-while` loop, and the `for` loop. The difference between each of these is how they control the repetition.

The `while` Loop

VideoNote

The `while` Loop

The `while` loop has two important parts: (1) an expression that is tested for a true or false value, and (2) a statement or block that is repeated as long as the expression is true. Figure 5-1 shows the general format of the `while` loop and a flowchart visually depicting how it works.

Figure 5-1

```
while (condition)
{
     statement;
     statement;
     // Place as many statements
     // here as necessary
}
```

Let's look at each part of the `while` loop. The first line, sometimes called the *loop header*, consists of the key word `while` followed by a *condition* to be tested enclosed in parentheses. The condition is expressed by any expression that can be evaluated as true or false. Next comes the *body* of the loop. This contains one or more C++ *statements*.

Here's how the loop works. The condition expression is tested, and if it is true, each statement in the body of the loop is executed. Then, the condition is tested again. If it is still true, each statement is executed again. This cycle repeats until the condition is false.

Notice that, as with an `if` statement, each statement in the body to be conditionally executed ends with a semicolon, but there is no semicolon after the condition expression in parentheses. This is because the `while` loop is not complete without the statements that follow it. Also, as with an `if` statement, when the body of the loop contains two or more statements, these statements must be surrounded by braces. When the body of the loop contains only one statement, the braces may be omitted. Essentially, the `while` loop works like an `if` statement that can execute over and over. As long as the expression in the parentheses is true, the conditionally executed statements will repeat.

Program 5-1 uses a `while` loop to print "Hello" five times.

Program 5-1

```
// This program demonstrates a simple while loop.
#include <iostream>
using namespace std;

int main()
{
```

(program continues)

Program 5-1 *(continued)*

```
 7     int number = 1;
 8
 9     while (number <= 5)
10     {
11        cout << "Hello   ";
12        number = number + 1;
13     }
14     cout << "\nThat's all!\n";
15     return 0;
16  }
```

Program Output

```
Hello   Hello   Hello   Hello   Hello
That's all!
```

Let's take a closer look at this program. In line 7 an integer variable `number` is defined and initialized with the value 1. In line 9 the `while` loop begins with this statement:

```
while (number <= 5)
```

This statement tests the variable `number` to determine whether its value is less than or equal to 5. Because it is, the statements in the body of the loop (lines 11 and 12) are executed:

```
cout << "Hello   ";
number = number + 1;
```

The statement in line 11 prints the word "Hello". The statement in line 12 adds one to `number`, giving it the value 2. This is the last statement in the body of the loop, so after it executes the loop starts over. It tests the expression `number <= 5` again, and because it is still true, the statements in the body of the loop are executed again. This cycle repeats until the value of `number` equals 6, making the expression `number <= 5` false. Then the loop is exited. This is illustrated in Figure 5-2.

Figure 5-2

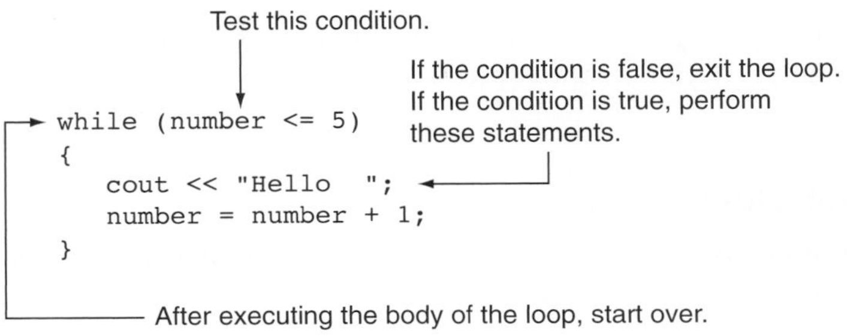

Test this condition.

If the condition is false, exit the loop.
If the condition is true, perform these statements.

```
while (number <= 5)
{
   cout << "Hello   ";
   number = number + 1;
}
```

After executing the body of the loop, start over.

Each execution of a loop is known as an *iteration*. This loop will perform five iterations before the expression `number <= 5` is tested and found to be false, causing the loop to terminate. The program then resumes execution at the statement immediately following the loop. A variable that controls the number of time a loop iterates is referred to as a *loop control variable*. In the example we have just seen, number is the loop control variable.

while Is a Pretest Loop

The while loop is a *pretest* loop. This means it tests its condition before each iteration. If the test expression is false to start with, the loop will never iterate. So if you want to be sure a while loop executes at least once, you must initialize the relevant data in such a way that the test expression starts out as true. For example, notice the variable definition of number in line 7 of Program 5-1:

```
int number = 1;
```

The number variable is initialized with the value 1. If number had been initialized with a value greater than 5, as shown in the following program segment, the loop would never execute:

```
int number = 6;
while (number <= 5)
{
   cout << "Hello   ";
   number = number + 1;
}
```

Infinite Loops

In all but rare cases, a loop must include a way to terminate. This means that something inside the loop must eventually make the test expression false. The loop in Program 5-1 stops when the expressions number <= 5 becomes false.

If a loop does not have a way of stopping, it is called an *infinite loop*. Infinite loops keep repeating until the program is interrupted. Here is an example:

```
int number = 1;
while (number <= 5)
{
   cout << "Hello   ";
}
```

This is an infinite loop because it does not contain a statement that changes the value of the number variable. Each time the expression number <= 5 is tested, number will still have the value 1.

Be Careful with Semicolons

It's also possible to create an infinite loop by accidentally placing a semicolon after the first line of the while loop. Here is an example:

```
int number = 1;
while (number <= 5);  // This semicolon is an ERROR!
{
   cout << "Hello   ";
   number = number + 1;
}
```

The semicolon at the end of the first line is interpreted as a null statement and disconnects the `while` statement from the block that comes after it. To the compiler, this loop looks like this:

```
while (number <= 5);
```

This `while` loop will continue executing the null statement, which does nothing, forever. The program will appear to have "gone into space" because there is nothing to display screen output or show any activity.

Don't Forget the Braces

If you write a loop that conditionally executes a block of statements, don't forget to enclose all of the statements in a set of braces. If the braces are accidentally left out, the `while` statement conditionally executes only the very next statement. For example, look at the following code.

```
int number = 1;
// This loop is missing its braces!
while (number <= 5)
   cout << "Hello   ";
   number = number + 1;
```

In this code, the body of the `while` loop ends with the `cout` statement. The statement that increases the value of `number` is not in the body of the loop, so the value of `number` remains 1, and the loop test condition remains true forever. The loop will print "Hello" over and over again, until the user stops the program.

Don't Confuse = with ==

Another common pitfall with loops is accidentally using the = operator when you intend to use the == operator. The following is an infinite loop because the test expression assigns 1 to `remainder` each time it is evaluated rather than testing if remainder is equal to 1:

```
while (remainder = 1)   // Error: Notice the assignment.
{
   cout << "Enter a number: ";
   cin  >> num;
   remainder = num % 2;
}
```

Remember, any nonzero value is evaluated as true.

Programming Style and the while Loop

It's possible to create loops that look like this:

```
while (number <= 5) { cout << "Hello   "; number = number + 1; }
```

Avoid this style of programming, however. The programming layout style you should use with the `while` loop is similar to that of the `if` statement:

- If there is only one statement repeated by the loop, it should appear on the line after the `while` statement and be indented one level.
- If the loop repeats a block of statements, the block should begin on the line after the `while` statement, and each line inside the braces should be indented.

In general, you'll find a similar layout style being used with the other types of loops presented in this chapter.

Now that you understand the `while` loop, let's see how it can be used in a useful situation. Program 5-2 revises Program 4-9 from the previous chapter to compute letter grades for multiple students.

Program 5-2

```
// This program uses a loop to compute letter grades for multiple students.
#include <iostream>
using namespace std;

int main()
{
    // Create named constants to hold minimum scores for each letter grade
    const int MIN_A_SCORE = 90,
              MIN_B_SCORE = 80,
              MIN_C_SCORE = 70,
              MIN_D_SCORE = 60,
              MIN_POSSIBLE_SCORE = 0;

    int numStudents,          // The total number of students
        student,              // The current student being processed
        testScore;            // Current student's numeric test score
    char grade;               // Current student's letter grade
    bool goodScore = true;

    // Get the number of students
    cout << "How many students do you have grades for? ";
    cin  >> numStudents;

    // Initialize the loop control variable
    student = 1;

    // Loop once for each student
    while (student <= numStudents)
    {
       // Get this student's numeric score
       cout << "\nEnter the numeric test score for student #"
            << student << ": ",
       cin  >> testScore;

       // Determine the letter grade
       if (testScore >= MIN_A_SCORE)
          grade = 'A';
       else if (testScore >= MIN_B_SCORE)
          grade = 'B';
       else if (testScore >= MIN_C_SCORE)
          grade = 'C';
       else if (testScore >= MIN_D_SCORE)
          grade = 'D';
       else if (testScore >= MIN_POSSIBLE_SCORE)
          grade = 'F';
       else
          goodScore = false;  // The score was below 0
```

(program continues)

Program 5-2 *(continued)*

```
48
49         // Display the letter grade
50         if (goodScore)
51            cout << "The letter grade is " << grade << ".\n";
52         else
53            cout << "The score cannot be below zero. \n";
54
55         // Set student to the next student
56         student = student + 1;
57      }
58      return 0;
59 }
```

Program Output with Example Input Shown in Bold

```
How many students do you have grades for? 3[Enter]

Enter the numeric test score for student #1: 88[Enter]
The letter grade is B.

Enter the numeric test score for student #2: 70[Enter]
The letter grade is C.

Enter the numeric test score for student #3: 93[Enter]
The letter grade is A.
```

Let's take a look at some of the key features of Program 5-2. The loop header for the `while` loop is on line 28. The body of the loop, which contains the statements to be executed each time the loop iterates, is contained between the braces on lines 29 and 57. The loop control variable is `student`, and it is initialized to 1 on line 25, before the loop. Notice that this variable is changed on line 56, inside the loop. This is very important. Because it is increased by one each time through the loop, it will eventually become greater than `numStudents`, and the loop will be exited. While the primary purpose of a loop control variable is to control the number of loop iterations, it can also be used for other purposes. Notice how Program 5-2 displays its current value as part of the prompt to the user on lines 31 and 32.

Checkpoint

5.1 How many lines will each of the following `while` loops display?

A)
```
int count = 1;
while (count < 5)
{  cout << "My favorite day is Sunday \n";
   count = count + 1;
}
```

B)
```
int count = 10;
while (count < 5)
{  cout << "My favorite day is Sunday \n";
   count = count + 1;
}
```
C)
```
int count = 1;
while (count < 5);
{  cout << "My favorite day is Sunday \n";
   count = count + 1;
}
```
D)
```
int count = 1;
while (count < 5)
   cout << "My favorite day is Sunday \n";
   count = count + 1;
```

5.2 Write a code segment that uses a `while` loop to display the odd numbers from 1 through 15.

5.2 Using the `while` Loop for Input Validation

CONCEPT: The `while` loop can be used to create input routines that repeat until acceptable data is entered.

Chapter 4 introduced the idea of data validation and showed how to use an `if` statement to validate data that is entered by the user. However, the `if` construct can only catch one bad value. If the user enters a second bad value after being prompted to reenter the original one, it will not be checked.

The `while` loop solves this problem, and is especially useful for validating input. If an invalid value is entered, a loop can require that the user re-enter it as many times as necessary until an acceptable value is received. For example, the following loop asks for a number in the range of 1 through 100:

```
cout << "Enter a number in the range 1 - 100: ";
cin  >> number;
while ((number < 1) || (number > 100))
{
   cout << "ERROR: Enter a value in the range 1 - 100: ";
   cin  >> number;
}
```

This code first allows the user to enter a number. This takes place just before the loop. If the input is valid, the `while` condition will be false, so the loop will not execute. If the input is invalid, however, the `while` condition will be true, so the statements in the body of the loop will be executed. They will display an error message and require the user to enter another number. The loop will continue to execute until the user enters a valid number. The general logic of performing input validation is shown in Figure 5-3.

Figure 5-3

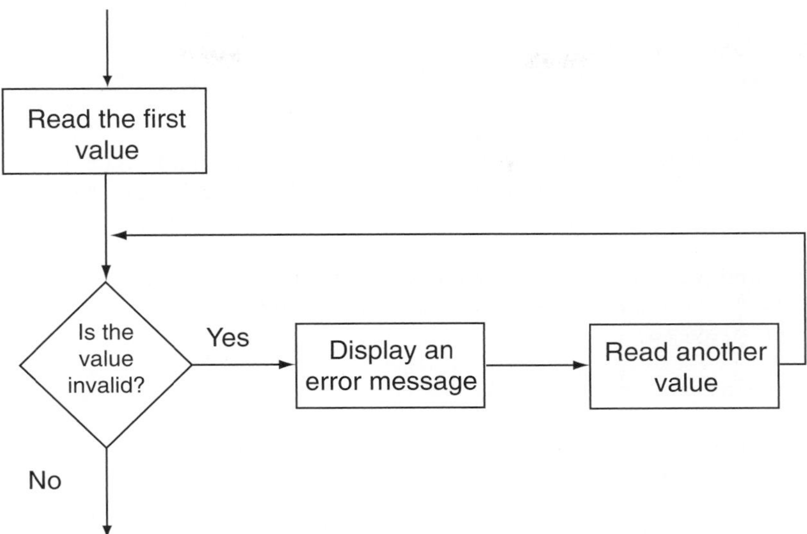

The read operation that takes place just before the loop is called a *priming read*. It provides the first value for the loop to test. Subsequent values, if required, are obtained by the loop.

Program 5-3 calculates the number of soccer teams a youth league may create, based on the given number of available players and a minimum and maximum number of players per team. The program uses `while` loops (in lines 26 through 32 and lines 37 through 41) to validate the user's input.

Program 5-3

```
 1 // This program calculates the number of soccer teams a
 2 // youth league can create from the number of available
 3 // players. It performs input validation using while loops.
 4 #include <iostream>
 5 using namespace std;
 6
 7 int main()
 8 {
 9    // Constants for minimum and maximum players per team
10    const int MIN_PLAYERS = 9,
11              MAX_PLAYERS = 15;
12
13    // Variables
14    int players,       // Number of available players
15        teamSize,      // Number of desired players per team
16        numTeams,      // Number of teams
17        leftOver;      // Number of players left over
18
19    // Get the number of players per team
20    cout << "How many players do you wish per team?\n";
21    cout << "(Enter a value in the range "
22         << MIN_PLAYERS << " - " << MAX_PLAYERS << "): ";
23    cin  >> teamSize;
```

(program continues)

Program 5-3 *(continued)*

```

    // Validate the input
    while (teamSize < MIN_PLAYERS || teamSize > MAX_PLAYERS)
    {
        cout << "\nTeam size should be "
             << MIN_PLAYERS << " to " << MAX_PLAYERS << " players.\n";
        cout << "How many players do you wish per team? ";
        cin  >> teamSize;
    }
    // Get and validate the number of players available
    cout << "\nHow many players are available? ";
    cin  >> players;

    while (players <= 0)
    {
        cout << "Please enter a positive number: ";
        cin  >> players;
    }
    // Calculate the number of teams and number of leftover players
    numTeams = players / teamSize;
    leftOver = players % teamSize;

    // Display the results
    cout << "\nThere will be " << numTeams << " teams with ";
    cout << leftOver << " players left over.\n";
    return 0;
}
```

Program Output with Example Input Shown in Bold

```
How many players do you wish per team?
(Enter a value in the range 9 - 15): 8[Enter]

Team size should be 9 to 15 players.
How many players do you wish per team? 12[Enter]

How many players are available? -138[Enter]
Please enter a positive number: 138[Enter]

There will be 11 teams with 6 players left over.
```

5.3 The Increment and Decrement Operators

CONCEPT: C++ provides a pair of operators for incrementing and decrementing variables.

To *increment* a value means to increase it, and to *decrement* a value means to decrease it. In the example below, `qtyOrdered` is incremented by 10 and `numSold` is decremented by 3.

```
qtyOrdered = qtyOrdered + 10;
numSold  =  numSold - 3;
```

Although the values stored in variables can be increased or decreased by any amount, it is particularly common to increment them or decrement them by 1. We did this in Programs 5-1 and 5-2 when we incremented the loop control variable by 1 each time the `while` loop iterated. In fact, increasing or decreasing a variable's value by 1 is so common that if we say a value is being incremented or decremented without specifying by how much, it is understood that it is being incremented or decremented by 1. C++ provides a pair of operators to do this. They are both unary operators. That means they operate on just one operand. The ++ operator increases its operand's value by 1. The –– operator decreases its operand's value by 1. For example, in the expression `num++`, the single operand is the variable `num`. The expression increases its value by 1.

NOTE: The expression `num++` is pronounced "num plus plus," and `num--` is pronounced "num minus minus."

Here are three different ways to increment the value of the variable `num` by 1.

```
num = num + 1;
num += 1;
num++;        // This statement uses the increment operator.
```

And here are three different ways to decrement it by 1:

```
num = num - 1;
num -= 1;
num--;        // This statement uses the decrement operator.
```

Notice that there is no space between the two plus signs in ++ or between them and the name of the variable being incremented. Likewise, there is no space between the two minus signs –– or between them and the name of the variable being decremented. Note also that unlike binary arithmetic operators, which can have either variables or literals as their operands, the ++ and –– operators cannot operate on literals. They can *only* operate on an lvalue, such as a variable. Here are some examples of legal and illegal expressions using ++ and ––.

```
count++;            // legal
count--             // legal
5++                 // illegal
5--                 // illegal
```

Program 5-4 illustrates the correct use of the ++ and –– operators. It uses each of them to change the value of a loop control variable.

Program 5-4

```
// This program has two loops. The first displays the numbers
// from 1 up to 5. The second displays the numbers from 5 down to 1.
// The program uses the ++ and -- operators to change the value
// of the loop control variables.
#include <iostream>
using namespace std;

```

(program continues)

Program 5-4 *(continued)*

```
 8 int main()
 9 {
10    int countUp = 1;     // Initialize the first loop control variable to 1
11    while (countUp < 6)
12    {
13       cout << countUp << "    ";
14       countUp++;          // The ++ operator increments countUp
15    }
16    cout << endl << endl;
17
18    int countDown = 5;   // Initialize the second loop control variable to 5
19    while (countDown > 0)
20    {
21       cout << countDown << "    ";
22       countDown--;        // The -- operator decrements countDown
23    }
24    return 0;
25 }
```

Program Output

```
1   2   3   4   5
5   4   3   2   1
```

Postfix and Prefix Modes

Our examples so far show the increment and decrement operators used in *postfix mode*, which means the operator is placed after the variable. The operators also work in *prefix mode*, where the operator is placed before the variable name. The statements on lines 14 and 22 of Program 5-4 could have been written like this:

```
++countUp;
--countDown;
```

In both prefix and postfix mode, these operators add 1 to, or subtract 1 from, their operand. What then is the difference between them?

In simple statements like those used in Program 5-4, there is no difference. The difference is important, however, when these operators are used in statements that do more than just increment or decrement a variable. For example, look at the following lines:

```
num = 4;
cout << num++;
```

This `cout` statement is doing two things: displaying the value of `num`, and incrementing `num`. But which happens first? `cout` will display a different value if `num` is incremented first than if it is incremented last. The answer depends on the mode of the increment operator.

Postfix mode causes the increment to happen after the value of the variable is used in the expression. In the example, `cout` will display 4, then `num` will be incremented to 5. Prefix mode, however, causes the increment to be done first. In the following statements, `num` will first be incremented to 5, and then `cout` will display 5:

```
num = 4;
cout << ++num;
```

Program 5-5 illustrates these dynamics further by placing increment and decrement operators in cout statements. This makes it easy to see the difference between using them in prefix and postfix mode. However, this should not normally be done. That is, in actual programming applications it is not recommended to place increment or decrement operators in cout statements.

Program 5-5

```
 1 // This program demonstrates the postfix and prefix
 2 // modes of the increment and decrement operators.
 3 #include <iostream>
 4 using namespace std;
 5
 6 int main()
 7 {
 8    int num = 4;
 9
10    // Illustrate postfix and prefix ++ operator
11    cout << num   << "  ";        // Displays 4
12    cout << num++ << "  ";        // Displays 4, then adds 1 to num
13    cout << num   << "  ";        // Displays 5
14    cout << ++num << "\n\n";      // Adds 1 to num, then displays 6
15
16    // Illustrate postfix and prefix -- operator
17    cout << num   << "  ";        // Displays 6
18    cout << num-- << "  ";        // Displays 6, then subtracts 1 from num
19    cout << num   << "  ";        // Displays 5
20    cout << --num << "\n\n";      // Subtracts 1 from num, then displays 4
21
22    return 0;
23 }
```

Program Output

```
4  4  5  6

6  6  5  4
```

Let's analyze the statements in this program. In line 8, num is initialized with the value 4, so the cout statement in line 11 displays 4. Then, line 12 sends the expression num++ to cout. Because the ++ operator is used in postfix mode, the value 4 is first sent to cout, and then 1 is added to num, making its value 5.

When line 13 executes, num will hold the value 5, so 5 is displayed. Then, line 14 sends the expression ++num to cout. Because the ++ operator is used in prefix mode, 1 is first added to num (making it 6), and then the value 6 is sent to cout. This same sequence of events happens in lines 17 through 20, except the -- operator is used.

For another example, look at the following code:

```
int x = 1;
int y
y = x++;      // Postfix increment
              // Assign x's old value to y and then increment x
```

The first statement defines the variable x (initialized with the value 1) and the second statement defines the variable y. The third statement does two things:

- It assigns the value of x to the variable y.
- The variable x is incremented.

Because the ++ operator is used in postfix mode, the old value of x (which is 1) is assigned to y before x is incremented. After the statement executes, y will contain 1, and x will contain 2.

Let's look at the same code, but with the ++ operator used in prefix mode:

```
int x = 1;
int y;
y = ++x;    // Prefix increment
```

In the third statement, the ++ operator is now used in prefix mode, causing variable x to be incremented before the assignment takes place. So, this code will store 2 in y. After the code has executed, x and y will both contain 2.

Using ++ and -- in Mathematical Expressions

The increment and decrement operators can also be used on variables in mathematical expressions. Consider the following program segment:

```
a = 2;
b = 5;
c = a * b++;
cout << a << " " << b << " " << c;
```

In the statement c = a * b++, c is assigned the value of a times b, which is 10. The variable b is then incremented. The cout statement will display

```
2 6 10
```

If the statement were changed to read

```
c = a * ++b;
```

the variable b would be incremented before it was multiplied by a. In this case c would be assigned the value of 2 times 6, so the cout statement would display

```
2 6 12
```

You can pack a lot of action into a single statement using the increment and decrement operators, but don't get too tricky with them. You might be tempted to try something like the following, thinking that c will be assigned 11:

```
a = 2;
b = 5;
c = ++(a * b);    // Error!
```

But this assignment statement simply will not work because, as previously mentioned, the operand of the increment and decrement operators must be an lvalue.

Using ++ and -- in Relational Expressions

The ++ and -- operators may also be used in relational expressions. Just as in arithmetic expressions, the difference between postfix and prefix mode is critical. Consider the following program segment:

```
x = 10;
if (x++ > 10)
   cout << "x is greater than 10.\n";
```

Two operations are taking place in this `if` statement: the value in `x` is tested to determine if it is greater than 10, and `x` is incremented. Because the increment operator is used in postfix mode, the comparison happens first. Since 10 is not greater than 10, the value of `x` before it is incremented, the `cout` statement won't execute. If the increment operator is used in prefix mode, however, `x` will be incremented before the `if` condition is tested, so the `if` statement will compare 11 to 10 and the `cout` statement will execute:

```
x = 10;
if (++x > 10)
   cout << "x is greater than 10.\n";
```

NOTE: Some instructors prefer that you only use the ++ and -- operators in statements whose sole purpose is to increment or decrement a variable. They may ask you not to use them in assignment statements, mathematical expressions, or relational expressions.

Checkpoint

5.3 What will each of the following program segments display?

A)
```
x = 2;
y = x++;
cout << x << " " << y;
```

B)
```
x = 2;
y = ++x;
cout << x << " " << y;
```

C)
```
x = 2;
y = 4;
cout << x++ << " " << --y;
```

D)
```
x = 2;
y = 2 * x++;
cout << x << " " << y;
```

E)
```
x = 99;
if (x++ < 100)
   cout "It is true!\n";
else
   cout << "It is false!\n";
```

F)
```
x = 0;
if (++x)
   cout << "It is true!\n";
else
   cout << "It is false!\n";
```

5.4 Counters

CONCEPT: **A counter is a variable that is regularly incremented or decremented each time a loop iterates.**

Sometimes it's important for a program to keep track of the number of iterations a loop performs. For example, Program 5-6 displays a table consisting of the numbers 1 through 5 and their squares, so its loop must iterate 5 times.

Program 5-6

```
// This program uses a while loop to display
// the numbers 1-5 and their squares.
#include <iostream>
#include <iomanip>
using namespace std;

int main()
{  int num = 1;

   cout << "Number  Square\n";
   cout << "--------------\n";
   while (num <= 5)
   {
      cout << setw(4) << num  << setw(7) << (num * num) << endl;
      num++;        // Increment counter
   }return 0;
}
```

Program Output

```
Number  Square
--------------
   1       1
   2       4
   3       9
   4      16
   5      25
```

In Program 5-6 the loop control variable `num` starts at `1` and is incremented each time through the loop. When `num` reaches `6`, the condition `num <= 5` becomes false, and the loop is exited. Variable `num` also acts as a *counter*, keeping count of how many times the loop has iterated so far. Notice how num is incremented in line 15 of the program. Because counters most often count by 1's, the increment operator is frequently used with them.

NOTE: It's important that num be properly initialized. Remember, variables defined inside a function have no guaranteed starting value.

Letting the User Control the Loop

Sometimes we want to let the user decide how many times a loop should iterate. Program 5-2 did this. Program 5-7, which is a revision of Program 5-6, also does this. It prompts the user to enter the maximum integer value to be displayed and squared. Then it has num, the loop counter, count up to that value.

Program 5-7

```
// This program displays integer numbers and their squares, beginning
// with one and ending with whatever number the user requests.
#include <iostream>
#include <iomanip>
using namespace std;

int main()
{
   int num,           // Counter telling what number to square
       lastNum;       // The final integer value to be squared

   // Get and validate the last number in the table
   cout << "This program will display a table of integer\n"
        << "numbers and their squares, starting with 1.\n"
        << "What should the last number be?\n"
        << "Enter an integer between 2 and 10: ";
   cin  >> lastNum;

   while ((lastNum < 2) || (lastNum > 10))
   {  cout << "Please enter an integer between 2 and 10: ";
      cin  >> lastNum;
   }
   // Display the table
   cout << "\nNumber  Square\n";
   cout << "--------------\n";

   num = 1;            // Set the counter to the starting value
   while (num <= lastNum)
   {
      cout << setw(4) << num  << setw(7) << (num * num) << endl;
      num++;           // Increment the counter
   }
   return 0;
}
```

Program 5-7 *(continued)*

Program Output with Example Input Shown in Bold

```
This program will display a table of integer
numbers and their squares, starting with 1.
What should the last number be?
Enter an integer between 2 and 10: 3[Enter]

Number  Square
--------------
   1       1
   2       4
   3       9
```

5.5 The do-while Loop

CONCEPT: The `do-while` loop is a post test loop, which means its expression is tested after each iteration.

In addition to the `while` loop, C++ also offers the `do-while` loop. The `do-while` loop looks similar to a `while` loop turned upside down. Figure 5-4 shows its format and a flowchart visually depicting how it works.

Figure 5-4

```
do
{    statement;
     statement;
     // Place as many statements
     // here as necessary.
} while (condition);
```

statement(s)
condition
true
false

As with the `while` loop, if there is only one conditionally executed statement in the loop body, the braces may be omitted.

NOTE: The `do-while` loop must be terminated with a semicolon after the closing parenthesis of the test expression.

Besides the way it looks, the difference between the `do-while` loop and the `while` loop is that `do-while` is a *post test* loop. This means it tests its expression at the end of the loop, after each iteration is complete. Therefore a `do-while` always performs at least one iteration, even if the test expression is false at the start. For example, in the following `while` loop the `cout` statement will not execute at all.

```
int x = 1;
while (x < 0)
    cout << x << endl;
```

But the `cout` statement in the following `do-while` loop will execute once because the `do-while` loop does not evaluate the expression `x < 0` until the end of the iteration.

```
int x = 1;
do
    cout << x << endl;
while (x < 0);
```

You should use the `do-while` loop when you want to make sure the loop executes at least once. For example, Program 5-8 computes and displays the average of a set of test scores before asking if the user wants to repeat the process with another set of scores. As with the `while` loop, a `do-while` loop can be written to iterate a set number of times or to allow the user to control how many times to loop. Program 5-8 illustrates another method for letting the user control the loop. It will repeat as long as the user enters a Y or y for yes.

Program 5-8

```
// This program averages 3 test scores. It uses a do-while loop
// that allows the code to repeat as many times as the user wishes.
#include <iostream>
using namespace std;

int main()
{
   int score1, score2, score3;    // Three test scores
   double average;                // Average test score
   char again;                    // Loop again? Y or N

   do
   {  // Get three test scores
      cout << "\nEnter 3 scores and I will average them: ";
      cin  >> score1 >> score2 >> score3;

      // Calculate and display the average
      average = (score1 + score2 + score3) / 3.0;
      cout << "The average is " << average << "\n\n";

      // Does the user want to average another set?
      cout << "Do you want to average another set? (Y/N) ";
      cin  >> again;
   } while (again == 'Y' || again == 'y');
   return 0;
}
```

(program continues)

Program 5-8 *(continued)*

Program Output with Example Input Shown in Bold

```
Enter 3 scores and I will average them: 80 90 70[Enter]
The average is 80

Do you want to average another set? (Y/N) y[Enter]

Enter 3 scores and I will average them: 60 75 88[Enter]
The average is 74.3333

Do you want to average another set? (Y/N) n[Enter]
```

The `toupper` Function

Let's take a closer look at the line containing the `do-while` loop test expression in Program 5-8.

```
while (again == 'Y' || again == 'y');
```

Notice how the logical OR operator is used to allow the user to enter either an uppercase or a lowercase 'Y' to do another iteration of the loop.

While this method works well to test both of these characters, it can be done more easily by using a C++ function named `toupper` (pronounced "to upper"). This function is passed a character and returns the integer ASCII code of a character. If the character it receives is a lowercase letter, it returns the ASCII code of its uppercase equivalent. If the character it receives is not a lowercase letter, it returns the ASCII code for the same character it was passed.

If the value returned by `toupper` were printed, it is the ASCII code that would print. However, if it is assigned to a `char` variable, which is then printed, the character itself will print. The following examples illustrate this.

```
char letter1, letter2, letter3;

letter1 = toupper('?');
cout << letter1;            // This displays ?

letter2 = toupper('A');
cout << letter2;            // This displays A

letter3 = toupper('b');
cout << letter3;            // This displays B

cout << toupper('c');       // This displays 67, the ASCII code for C
```

In the first example, the character passed to the `toupper` function is not a letter at all, so the ASCII code of the same character is returned and assigned to `letter1` for printing. In the second example, the character passed to `toupper` is already an uppercase letter so, again, the ASCII code of the same character it received is returned. In the third example, `toupper` receives a lowercase letter, so the ASCII code of its uppercase equivalent is returned. In the final example, `toupper` again receives a lowercase letter and returns the

ASCII code of its uppercase equivalent. However, this time the returned value is printed instead of being assigned to a `char` variable, so it is the integer value of the ASCII code itself that displays.

The value passed to `toupper` does not have to be a character literal. It can also be a character variable, as shown here:

```
char letter1 = 'b';
char letter2 = toupper(letter1);    // Now letter2's value is 'B'
```

The `toupper` function is especially useful when used in the test expression of a `do-while` loop. It can test the variable holding a user's input to see if the user has entered a 'Y' or a 'y' when asked whether or not the loop should iterate again. The following two `do-while` tests are logically equivalent:

```
while (again == 'Y' || again == 'y');
while (toupper(again) == 'Y');
```

It is important to understand that this last test expression does not change the value stored in the `again` variable. Rather, it compares the value returned by `toupper` to a character literal. To actually change the value stored in `again`, the value returned by the function would have to be *assigned* to it, as shown here:

```
again = toupper(again);
```

C++ provides a similar function to convert an uppercase letter to its lowercase equivalent. This function is named `tolower` (pronounced "to lower"). Here are two examples of its use:

```
while (tolower(again) == 'y');
again = tolower(again);
```

NOTE: To use `toupper` and `tolower` you must include the `cctype` file in your program. You can include it with the following statement:

```
#include <cctype>
```

Using `do-while` with Menus

The `do-while` loop is a good choice for repeating a menu. Recall Program 4-27, which displays a menu of health club packages. Program 5-9 is a modification of that program that uses a `do-while` loop to repeat the program until the user selects item 4 from the menu.

Program 5-9

```
// This menu-driven Health Club membership program carries out the
// appropriate actions based on the menu choice entered. A do-while loop
// allows the program to repeat until the user selects menu choice 4.
#include <iostream>
#include <iomanip>
using namespace std;
```

(program continues)

Program 5-9 *(continued)*

```

int main()
{
   // Constants for membership rates
   const double ADULT_RATE  = 120.0;
   const double CHILD_RATE  =  60.0;
   const double SENIOR_RATE = 100.0;

   int choice;       // Menu choice
   int months;       // Number of months
   double charges;   // Monthly charges

   do
   {  // Display the menu and get the user's choice
      cout << "\n   Health Club Membership Menu\n\n";
      cout << "1. Standard Adult Membership\n";
      cout << "2. Child Membership\n";
      cout << "3. Senior Citizen Membership\n";
      cout << "4. Quit the Program\n\n";
      cout << "Enter your choice: ";
      cin  >> choice;

      // Validate the menu selection
      while ((choice < 1) || (choice > 4))
      {
         cout << "Please enter 1, 2, 3, or 4: ";
         cin  >> choice;
      }
      // Process the user's choice
      if (choice != 4)
      {  cout << "For how many months? ";
         cin  >> months;

         // Compute charges based on user input
         switch (choice)
         {
            case 1: charges = months * ADULT_RATE;
                    break;
            case 2: charges = months * CHILD_RATE;
                    break;
            case 3: charges = months * SENIOR_RATE;
         }
         // Display the monthly charges
         cout << fixed << showpoint << setprecision(2);
         cout << "The total charges are $" << charges << endl;
      }
   } while (choice != 4); // Loop again if the user did not
                          // select choice 4 to quit
   return 0;
}
```

(program continues)

Program 5-9 *(continued)*

Program Output with Example Input Shown in Bold

```
   Health Club Membership Menu

1. Standard Adult Membership
2. Child Membership
3. Senior Citizen Membership
4. Quit the Program

Enter your choice: 1[Enter]
For how many months? 4[Enter]
The total charges are $480.00

   Health Club Membership Menu

1. Standard Adult Membership
2. Child Membership
3. Senior Citizen Membership
4. Quit the Program

Enter your choice: 4[Enter]
```

Checkpoint

5.4 What will the following program segments display?

A)
```
int count = 3;
do
    cout << "Hello World\n";
    count--;
while (count < 1);
```

B)
```
int val = 5;
do
   cout << val << " ";
while (val >= 5);
```

C)
```
int count = 0, number = 0, limit = 4;
do
{
   number += 2;
   count++;
} while (count < limit);
cout << number << "  " << count << endl;
```

5.5 Write a program segment with a `do-while` loop that displays whether a user-entered integer is even or odd. The code should then ask the user if he or she wants to test another number. The loop should repeat so long as the user enters Y or y. Use a logical OR operator in the `do-while` loop test expression.

5.6 Revise your answer to question 5.5 to use the `toupper` function in the `do-while` loop test expression.

5.6 The for Loop

CONCEPT: The for loop is a pretest loop that combines the initialization, testing, and updating of a loop control variable in a single loop header.

VideoNote
The for Loop

In general, there are two categories of loops: conditional loops and count-controlled loops. A *conditional loop* executes as long as a particular condition exists. For example, an input validation loop executes as long as the input value is invalid. When you write a conditional loop, you have no way of knowing the number of times it will iterate.

Sometimes you know the exact number of iterations that a loop must perform. A loop that repeats a specific number of times is known as a *count-controlled loop*. For example, if a loop asks the user to enter the sales amounts for each month in the year, it will iterate twelve times. In essence, the loop counts to twelve and asks the user to enter a sales amount each time it makes a count. A count-controlled loop must possess three elements:

1. It must initialize a counter variable to a starting value.
2. It must test the counter variable by comparing it to a final value. When the counter variable reaches its final value, the loop terminates.
3. It must update the counter variable during each iteration. This is usually done by incrementing the variable.

Count-controlled loops are so common that C++ provides a type of loop specifically for them. It is known as the `for` loop. The `for` loop is specifically designed to initialize, test, and update a counter variable. Here is the format of the `for` loop.

```
for (initialization; test; update)

{
   statement;
   statement;
  // Place as many statements
  // here as necessary.
}
```

As with the other loops you have used, if there is only one statement in the loop body, the braces may be omitted.

The first line of the `for` loop is the *loop header*. After the key word `for`, there are three expressions inside the parentheses, separated by semicolons. (Notice there is no semicolon after the third expression.) The first expression is the *initialization expression*. It is typically used to initialize a counter to its starting value. This is the first action performed by the loop and it is only done once.

The second expression is the *test expression*. It tests a condition in the same way the test expression in the `while` and `do-while` loop does, and controls the execution of the loop. As long as this condition is true, the body of the `for` loop will repeat. The `for` loop is a pretest loop, so it evaluates the test expression before each iteration.

The third expression is the *update expression*. It executes at the end of each iteration. Typically, this is a statement that increments the loop's counter variable.

Here is an example of a simple for loop that prints "Hello" five times:

```
for (count = 1; count <= 5; count++)
   cout << "Hello" << endl;
```

In this loop, the initialization expression is `count = 1`, the test expression is `count <= 5`, and the update expression is `count++`. The body of the loop has one statement, which is the `cout` statement. Figure 5-5 illustrates the sequence of events that take place during the loop's execution. Notice that Steps 2 through 4 are repeated as long as the test expression is `true`.

Figure 5-5

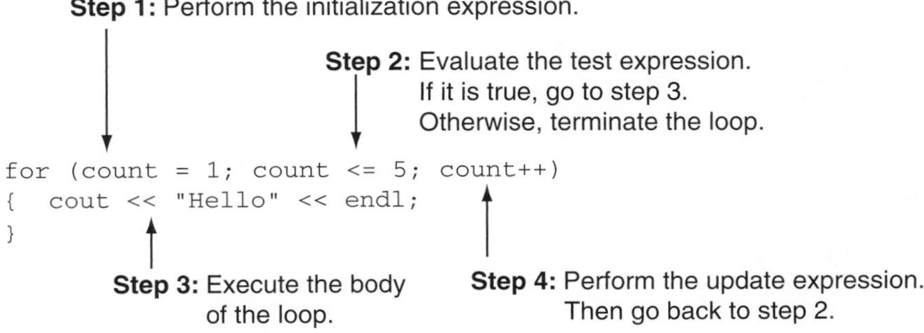

Figure 5-6 shows the loop's logic in the form of a flowchart.

Figure 5-6

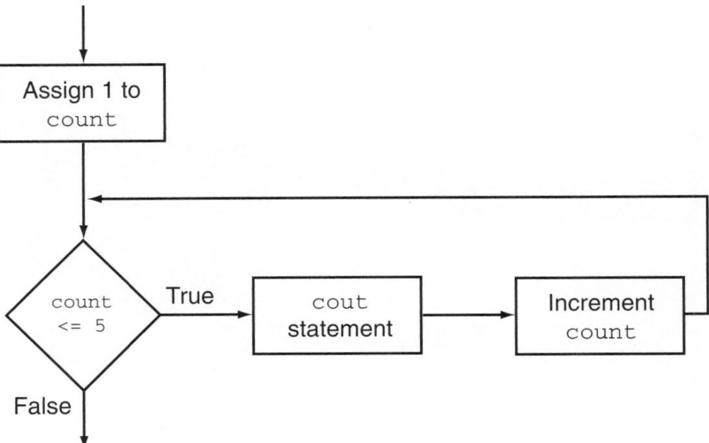

Notice how the counter variable `count` is used to control the number of times the loop iterates. During the execution of the loop, this variable takes on the values 1 through 5, and when the test expression `count <= 5` becomes `false`, the loop terminates. Also notice that in this example the `count` variable is used only in the loop header, to control the number of loop iterations. It is not used for any other purpose. However, it is also possible to use the counter variable within the body of a loop. For example, look at the following code:

```
for (number = 1; number <= 5; number++)
   cout << number << " ";
```

The counter variable in this loop is `number`. In addition to controlling the number of iterations, it is also used in the body of the loop. This loop will produce the following output:

```
1 2 3 4 5
```

As you can see, the loop displays the contents of the `number` variable during each iteration.

Program 5-10 is a new version of Program 5-6 that displays the numbers 1–5 and their squares by using a `for` loop instead of a `while` loop.

Program 5-10

```
// This program uses a for loop to display the numbers 1-5
// and their squares.
#include <iostream>
#include <iomanip>
using namespace std;

int main()
{  int num;

    cout << "Number  Square\n";
    cout << "--------------\n";

    for (num = 1; num <= 5; num++)
       cout << setw(4) << num  << setw(7) << (num * num) << endl;
    return 0;
}
```

Program Output

```
Number  Square
--------------
   1      1
   2      4
   3      9
   4     16
   5     25
```

The `for` Loop is a Pretest Loop

Because the `for` loop tests its test expression before it performs an iteration, it is possible to write a `for` loop in such a way that it will never iterate. Here is an example:

```
for (count = 11; count <= 10; count++)
   cout << "Hello" << endl;
```

Because the variable `count` is initialized to a value that makes the test expression false from the beginning, this loop terminates as soon as it begins.

Avoid Modifying the Counter Variable in the Body of the for Loop

Although it is okay to use the counter variable inside the body of the loop, as we did in Program 5-10, be careful not to place a statement there that modifies it. All modifications of the counter variable should take place in the update expression, which is automatically executed at the end of each iteration. If a statement in the body of the loop also modifies the counter variable, the loop will probably not terminate when you expect it to. The following loop, for example, increments x twice for each iteration:

```
for (x = 1; x <= 10; x++)
{
   cout << x << endl;
   x++;       // Wrong!
}
```

Other Forms of the Update Expression

You are not limited to incrementing the loop control variable by just 1 in the update expression. Here is a loop that displays all the even numbers from 2 through 100 by adding 2 to its counter:

```
for (num = 2; num <= 100; num += 2)
   cout << num << endl;
```

And here is a loop that counts backward from 10 down to 0:

```
for (num = 10; num >= 0; num--)
   cout << num << endl;
```

Defining a Variable in the for Loop's Initialization Expression

Not only may the counter variable be initialized in the initialization expression, it may be defined there as well. The following code shows an example. This is a modified version of the loop in Program 5-10.

```
for (int num = 1; num <= 5; num++)
   cout << setw(4) << num  << setw(7) << (num * num) << endl;
```

In this loop, the num variable is both defined and initialized in the initialization expression. If the counter variable is used only in the loop, it is considered good programming practice to define it in the loop header. This makes the variable's purpose clearer.

However, when a variable is defined in the initialization expression of a for loop, the scope of the variable is limited to the loop. This means you cannot access the variable in statements outside the loop. For example, the following program segment will not compile because the last cout statement cannot access the variable count.

```
for (int count = 1; count <= 10; count++)
   cout << count << endl;

cout << "count is now " << count << endl;   // ERROR!
```

Creating a User-Controlled for Loop

In Program 5-7 we allowed the user to control how many times a `while` loop should iterate. This can also be done with a `for` loop by having the user enter the final value for the counter variable. The following program segment illustrates this.

```
// Get the final counter value
cout << "How many times should the loop execute? ";
cin  >> finalValue;

for (int num = 1; num <= finalValue; num++)
{
   // Statements in the loop body go here.
}
```

Using Multiple Statements in the Initialization and Update Expressions

It is possible to execute more than one statement in the initialization expression and the update expression. When using multiple statements in either of these expressions, simply separate the statements with commas. For example, look at the loop in the following code, which has two statements in the initialization expression.

```
for (int x = 1, y = 1; x <= 5; x++)
{
   cout << x << " plus " << y << " equals " << (x + y) << endl;
}
```

The loop's initialization expression is

```
int x = 1, y = 1
```

This defines and initializes two `int` variables, `x` and `y`. The output produced by this loop is:

```
1 plus 1 equals 2
2 plus 1 equals 3
3 plus 1 equals 4
4 plus 1 equals 5
5 plus 1 equals 6
```

We can further modify the loop to execute two statements in the update expression. Here is an example:

```
for (int x = 1, y = 1; x <= 5; x++, y++)
{
   cout << x << " plus " << y << " equals " << (x + y) << endl;
}
```

The loop's update expression increments both the `x` and `y` variables.

```
x++, y++
```

The output produced by this loop is:

```
1 plus 1 equals 2
2 plus 2 equals 4
3 plus 3 equals 6
4 plus 4 equals 8
5 plus 5 equals 10
```

Connecting multiple statements with commas is allowed in the initialization and update expressions, but not in the test expression. If you wish to combine multiple expressions in the test expression, you must use the `&&` or `||` operators.

Here is an example of a `for` loop header that does this:

```
for (int count = 1; count <= 10 && moreData, count++)
```

This loop will execute only as long as `count <= 10` and Boolean variable `moreData` is true. As soon as either of these conditions becomes false, the loop will be exited.

Omitting the for Loop's Expressions or Loop Body

Although it is generally considered bad programming style to do so, one or more of the `for` loop's expressions, or even its loop body, can be omitted.

The initialization expression may be omitted from inside the `for` loop's parentheses if it has already been performed or if no initialization is needed. Here is an example a loop with the initialization being performed prior to the loop:

```
int num = 1;
for ( ; num <= maxValue; num++)
   cout << num << "        " << (num * num) << endl;
```

The update expression may be omitted if it is being performed elsewhere in the loop or if none is needed. Although this type of code is not recommended, the following `for` loop works just like a `while` loop:

```
int num = 1;
for ( ; num <= maxValue; )
{  cout << num << "        " << (num * num) << endl;
   num++;
}
```

It is also possible, though not recommended, to write a `for` loop that has no formal body. In this case, all the work of the loop is done by statements in the loop header. Here is an example that displays the numbers from 1 to 10. The combined increment operation and `cout` statement in the update expression perform the work of each iteration.

```
for (number = 1; number <= 10; cout << number++);
```

Checkpoint

5.7 What three expressions appear inside the parentheses of the `for` loop's header?

5.8 You want to write a `for` loop that displays "I love to program" 50 times. Assume that you will use a counter variable named `count`.
A) What initialization expression will you use?
B) What test expression will you use?
C) What update expression will you use?
D) Write the loop.

5.9 What will each of the following program segments display?

A)
```
for (int count = 0; count < 6; count++)
    cout << (count + count) << " ";
```

B)
```
for (int value = -5; value < 5; value++)
    cout << value << " ";
```

C)
```
int x
for (x = 3; x <= 10; x += 3)
   cout << x << "   ";
   cout << x << "   ";
```

5.10 Write a `for` loop that displays your name 10 times.

5.11 Write a `for` loop that displays all of the odd numbers, 1 through 49.

5.12 Write a `for` loop that displays every fifth number, 0 through 100.

5.7 Keeping a Running Total

CONCEPT: A running total is a sum of numbers that accumulates with each iteration of a loop. The variable used to keep the running total is called an accumulator.

Many programming tasks require you to add up a series of numbers. For example, if you want to find the average of a set of number, you must first add them up. Programs that add a series of numbers typically use two elements:

- A loop that reads each number in the series.
- A variable that accumulates the total of the numbers as they are read.

The variable that is used to accumulate the total of the numbers is called an *accumulator*. It is often said that the loop keeps a *running total* because it accumulates the total as it reads each number in the series. Figure 5-7 shows the general logic of a loop that calculates a running total.

Figure 5-7

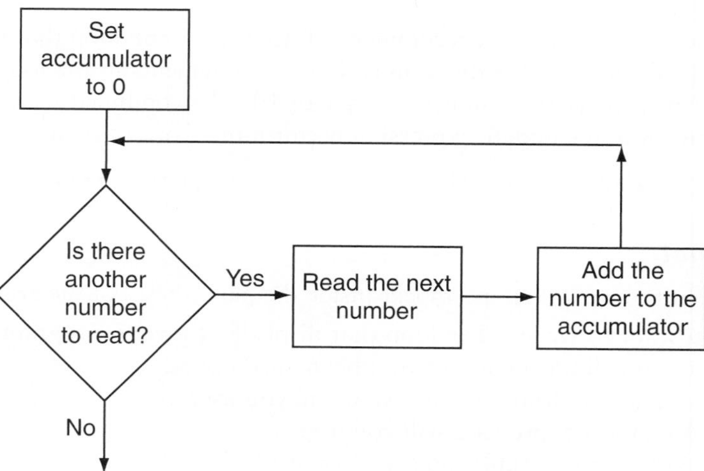

When the loop finishes, the accumulator will contain the total of the numbers read by the loop. Notice that the first step in the flowchart is to set the accumulator variable to 0. This is a critical step. Each time the loop reads a number, it adds it to the accumulator. If the accumulator starts with any value other than 0, it will not contain the correct total when the loop finishes.

Let's look at a program that keeps a running total. Program 5-11 calculates a company's total sales over a period of time by reading daily sales figures and adding them to an accumulator. It then uses this total to find the average sales per day.

Program 5-11

```
// This program takes daily sales figures over a period of time
// and calculates their total. It then uses this total to compute
// the average daily sales.
#include <iostream>
#include <iomanip>
using namespace std;

int main()
{
    int numDays;                 // Number of days
    double dailySales,           // The sales amount for a single day
           totalSales = 0.0,     // Accumulator, initialized with 0
           averageSales;         // The average daily sales amount

    // Get the number of days
    cout << "For how many days do you have sales figures? ";
    cin  >> numDays;

    // Get the sales for each day and accumulate a total
    for (int day = 1; day <= numDays; day++)  // day is the counter
    {
       cout << "Enter the sales for day " << day << ": ";
       cin  >> dailySales;
       totalSales += dailySales;    // Accumulate the running total
    }
    // Compute the average daily sales
    averageSales = totalSales / numDays;

    // Display the total sales and average daily sales
    cout << fixed << showpoint << setprecision(2);
    cout << "\nTotal sales:         $" << setw(8) << totalSales;
    cout << "\nAverage daily sales: $" << setw(8) << averageSales
         << endl;
    return 0;
}
```

Program Output with Example Input Shown in Bold

```
For how many days do you have sales figures? 5[Enter]
Enter the sales for day 1: 425.16[Enter]
Enter the sales for day 2: 397.20[Enter]
Enter the sales for day 3: 404.11[Enter]
Enter the sales for day 4: 468.43[Enter]
Enter the sales for day 5: 502.19[Enter]

Total sales:         $ 2197.09
Average daily sales: $  439.42
```

Let's take a closer look at a few of the key lines in this program. In line 12 the `totalSales` variable is defined. This is the accumulator. Notice that it is initialized with 0. In line 17 the user enters how many days of sales figures there are. This number is stored in the `numDays` variable and determines how many times the loop beginning in line 20 iterates. The variable `day`, which is defined in the loop's initialization expression, is initialized with 1. This variable is the counter that controls the loop and keeps track of which day's sales amount is currently being read in and processed. The test expression specifies the loop will repeat as long as `day` is less than or equal to `numDays`. The update expression increments `day` by one at the end of each loop iteration.

During each loop iteration, in line 23, the user enters the amount of sales for one specific day. This amount is stored in the `dailySales` variable. Then, in line 24, this amount is added to the existing value stored in the `totalSales` variable. Note that line 24 does not *assign* `dailySales` to `totalSales`, but rather *increases* the value stored in `totalSales` by the amount in `dailySales`. After the loop has finished, `totalSales` will contain the total of all the daily sales figures entered. In line 27, this total is used to calculate the average daily sales amount. To do this the value stored in `totalSales` is divided by the value stored in `numDays` and the result is placed in the variable `averageSales`. The program now has all the information needed to display the `totalSales` and `averageSales` in lines 31–33.

Sentinels

CONCEPT: A sentinel is a special value that marks the end of a list of values.

Program 5-11, in the previous section, requires the user to know in advance the number of days there are sales figures for. Sometimes the user has a list that is very long and doesn't know how many items there are.

A technique that can be used in a situation like this is to ask the user to enter a sentinel at the end of the list. A *sentinel* is a special value that cannot be mistaken for a member of the list and that signals that there are no more values to be entered. When the user enters the sentinel, the loop terminates.

Program 5-12 provides an example of using an end sentinel. This program calculates the total points earned by a soccer team over a series of games. It allows the user to enter the series of game points, then enter –1 to signal the end of the list.

Program 5-12

```
// This program illustrates the use of an end sentinel. It calculates
// the total number of points a soccer team has earned over a series
// of games. The user enters the point values, then -1 when finished.
#include <iostream>
using namespace std;

int main()
{
   int game = 1,          // Game counter
       points,            // Holds number of points for a specific game
       total = 0;         // Accumulates total points for all games
```

(program continues)

Program 5-12 *(continued)*

```
12
13     // Read in the points for game 1
14     cout << "Enter the number of points your team has earned\n";
15     cout << "so far this season. Then enter -1 when finished.\n\n";
16     cout << "Enter the points for game " << game << ": ";
17     cin  >> points;
18
19     // Loop as long as the end sentinel has not yet been entered
20     while (points != -1)
21     {  // Add point just read in to the accumulator
22        total += points;
23
24        // Enter the points for the next game
25        game++;
26        cout << "Enter the points for game " << game << ": ";
27        cin  >> points;
28     }
29     // Display the total points
30     cout << "\nThe total points are " << total << endl;
31     return 0;
32  }
```

Program Output with Example Input Shown in Bold

```
Enter the number of points your team has earned
so far this season. Then enter -1 when finished.

Enter the points for game 1: 2[Enter]
Enter the points for game 2: 1[Enter]
Enter the points for game 3: 3[Enter]
Enter the points for game 4: 2[Enter]
Enter the points for game 5: 1[Enter]
Enter the points for game 6: -1[Enter]

The total points are 9
```

Program Output with Different Example Input Shown in Bold

```
Enter the number of points your team has earned
so far this season. Then enter -1 when finished.

Enter the points for game 1: -1

The total points are 0
```

The value `-1` was chosen for the sentinel in this program because it is not possible for a team to score negative points. Notice that this program performs a priming read in line 17 to get the first value. This is done so the `while` loop will not try to test the value of `points` until a first value has been read in. It also makes it possible for the loop to immediately terminate if the user enters `-1` for the first value, as shown in the second sample run. Also note that the sentinel value is not included in the running total.

5.13 In the following program segment, which variable is the counter and which is the accumulator?

```
int number, x = 0, y = 0, maxNums;
cout << "How many numbers do you wish to enter? ";
cin >> maxNums;
while (x < maxNums)
{
   cout << "Enter a number: ";
   cin >> number;
   y += number;
   x++;
}
cout << "The sum of those numbers is " << y << endl;
```

5.14 Write a `for` loop that sums up the squares of the integers from 1 through 10.

5.15 Write a `for` loop that sums up the squares of the odd integers from 1 through 9.

5.16 Write a `for` loop that repeats seven times, asking the user to enter a number each time and summing the numbers entered.

5.17 Write a `for` loop that calculates the total of the following series of numbers:

$$\frac{1}{30} + \frac{2}{29} + \frac{3}{28} + \frac{4}{27} + \ldots \frac{30}{1}$$

5.18 Write a `for` loop that calculates the total of the following series of numbers:

$$\frac{1}{2} + \frac{1}{4} + \frac{1}{8} + \frac{1}{16} + \ldots \frac{1}{1024}$$

5.19 Write a sentinel controlled `while` loop that accumulates a series of test scores input by the user, until `-99` is entered. The code should then report how many scores were entered and the average of these scores. Do not count the end sentinel `-99` as a score.

5.9 Focus on Software Engineering: *Deciding Which Loop to Use*

CONCEPT: Although most repetitive algorithms can be written with any of the three types of loops, each works best in different situations.

Each of C++'s three loops are ideal to use in different situations. Here's a short summary of when each loop should be used.

The `while` Loop

The `while` loop is a pretest loop. It is ideal in situations where you do not want the loop to iterate if the test condition is false from the beginning. For example, validating input that has been read and reading lists of data terminated by a sentinel value are good applications of the `while` loop.

```
cout << "This program finds the square of any integer.\n";
cout << "\nEnter an integer, or -99 to quit: ";
cin  >> num;

while (num != -99)
{  cout << num << " squared is " << pow(num, 2.0) << endl;
   cout << "\nEnter an integer, or -99 to quit ";
   cin  >> num;
}
```

The do-while Loop

The do-while loop is a post test loop. It is ideal in situations where you always want the loop to iterate at least once. The do-while loop is a good choice for repeating a menu or for asking the user if they want to repeat a set of actions.

```
cout << "This program finds the square of any integer.\n";
do
{  cout << "\nEnter an integer: ";
   cin  >> num;
   cout << num << " squared is " << pow(num, 2.0) << endl;
   cout << "Do you want to square another number? (Y/N) ";
   cin  >> doAgain;
} while (doAgain == 'Y' || doAgain == 'y');
```

The for Loop

The for is a pretest loop with built-in expressions for initializing, testing, and updating a counter variable. The for loop is ideal in situations where the exact number of iterations is known.

```
cout << "This program finds the squares of the integers "
     << "from 1 to 8.\n\n";
for (num = 1; num <= 8; num++)
{
   cout << num << " squared is " << pow(num, 2.0) << endl;
}
```

A program containing the above code for all three types of loops can be found in the loop-examples.cpp file on the book's companion website, along with all the other programs in this chapter.

5.10 Nested Loops

CONCEPT: A loop that is inside another loop is called a *nested loop*.

VideoNote
Nested Loops

In Chapter 4 you saw how one if statement could be nested inside another one. It is also possible to nest one loop inside another loop. The first loop is called the *outer loop*. The one nested inside it is called the *inner loop*. This is illustrated by the following two while loops. Notice how the inner loop must be completely contained within the outer one.

```
while (condition1)       // Beginning of the outer loop
{  ---
   while (condition2)    // Beginning of the inner loop
   {  ---
      ---
   }                     // End of the inner loop
}                        // End of the outer loop
```

Nested loops are used when, for each iteration of the outer loop, something must be repeated a number of times. Here are some examples from everyday life:

- For *each* batch of cookies to be baked we must put *each* cookie on the cookie sheet.
- For *each* salesperson, we must add up *each* sale to determine total commission.
- For *each* teacher we must produce a class list for *each* of their classes.
- For *each* student we must add up *each* test score to find the student's test average.

Whatever the task, the inner loop will go through all its iterations each time the outer loop is executed. This is illustrated by Program 5-13, which handles this last task, finding student test score averages. Any kind of loop can be nested within any other kind of loop. This program uses two `for` loops.

Program 5-13

```
// This program averages test scores. It asks the user for the
// number of students and the number of test scores per student.
#include <iostream>
using namespace std;

int main()
{
   int numStudents,     // Number of students
       numTests;        // Number of tests per student
   double average;      // Average test score for a student

   // Get the number of students
   cout << "This program averages test scores.\n";
   cout << "How many students are there? ";
   cin  >> numStudents;

   // Get the number of test scores per student
   cout << "How many test scores does each student have? ";
   cin  >> numTests;
   cout << endl;

   // Read each student's scores and compute their average
   for (int snum = 1; snum <= numStudents; snum++)     // Outer loop
   {  double total = 0.0;    // Initialize accumulator

      for (int test = 1; test <= numTests; test++)     // Inner loop
      {  int score;

```

(program continues)

Program 5-13 *(continued)*

```
29          // Read a score and add it to the accumulator
30          cout << "Enter score " << test << " for ";
31          cout << "student " << snum << ": ";
32          cin  >> score;
33          total += score;  //
34       }                                                 // End inner loop
35       // Compute and display the student's average
36       average = total / numTests;
37       cout << "The average score for student " << snum;
38       cout << " is " << average << "\n\n";
39    }                                                    // End outer loop
40    return 0;
41 }
```

Program Output with Example Input Shown in Bold

```
This program averages test scores.
How many students are there? 2[Enter]
How many test scores does each student have? 3[Enter]

Enter score 1 for student 1: 84[Enter]
Enter score 2 for student 1: 79[Enter]
Enter score 3 for student 1: 97[Enter]
The average for student 1 is 86.6667
Enter score 1 for student 2: 92[Enter]
Enter score 2 for student 2: 88[Enter]
Enter score 3 for student 2: 94[Enter]
The average for student 2 is 91.3333
```

Let's trace what happened in Program 5-13, using the sample data shown. In this case, for each of two students, each of three scores were input and summed. First in line 23 the outer loop was entered and `snum` was set to 1. Then, once the `total` accumulator was initialized to zero for that student, the inner loop, which begins on line 26, was entered. While the outer loop was still on its first iteration and `snum` was still 1, the inner loop went through all of its iterations, handling tests 1, 2, and 3 for that student. It then exited the inner loop and in lines 36 through 38 calculated and output the average for student 1. Only then did the program reach the bottom of the outer loop and go back up to do its second iteration. The second iteration of the outer loop processed student 2. For *each* iteration of the outer loop, the inner loop did *all* its iterations.

It might help to think of each loop as a rotating wheel. The outer loop is a big wheel that is moving slowly. The inner loop is a smaller wheel that is spinning quickly. For every rotation the big wheel makes, the little wheel makes many rotations. Since, in our example, the outer loop was done twice, and the inner loop was done three times for each iteration of the outer loop, the inner loop was done a total of six times in all. This corresponds to the six scores input by the user. The following points summarize this.

- An inner loop goes through all of its iterations for each iteration of an outer loop.
- Inner loops complete their iterations faster than outer loops.
- To get the total number of iterations of an inner loop, multiply the number of iterations of the outer loop by the number of iterations done by the inner loop each time the outer loop is done.

5.11 Breaking Out of a Loop

CONCEPT: C++ provides ways to break out of a loop or out of a loop iteration early.

Sometimes it's necessary to stop a loop before it goes through all its iterations. The `break` statement, which was used with `switch` in Chapter 4, can also be placed inside a loop. When it is encountered, the loop immediately stops, and the program jumps to the statement following the loop.

Here is an example of a loop with a `break` statement. The `while` loop in the following program segment appears to execute 10 times, but the `break` statement causes it to stop after the fifth iteration.

```
int count = 1;
while (count <= 10)
{
   cout << count << endl;
   count++;
   if (count == 6)
      break;
}
```

This example is just to illustrate what a `break` statement inside a loop will do. However, you would not normally want to use one in this way because it violates the rules of structured programming and makes code more difficult to understand, debug, and maintain. The exit from a loop should be controlled by its condition test at the top of the loop, as in a `while` loop or `for` loop, or at the bottom, as in a `do-while` loop. Normally the only time a `break` statement is used inside a loop is to exit the loop early if an error condition occurs. Program 5-14 illustrates an example of this.

Program 5-14

```
// This program is supposed to find the square root of 5 numbers
// entered by the user. However, if a negative number is entered
// an error message displays and a break statement is used to
// stop the loop early.
#include <iostream>
#include <cmath>
using namespace std;

int main()
{
   double number;

   cout << "Enter 5 positive numbers separated by spaces and \n"
        << "I will find their square roots: ";

```

(program continues)

Program 5-14 *(continued)*

```
   for (int count = 1; count <= 5; count++)
   {
      cin >> number;
      if (number >= 0.0)
      {  cout << "\nThe square root of " << number << " is "
              << sqrt(number);
      }
      else
      {  cout << "\n\n" << number << " is negative. "
              << "I cannot find the square root \n"
              << "of a negative number. The program is terminating.\n";
         break;
      }
   }
   return 0;
}
```

Program Output with Example Input Shown in Bold

```
Enter 5 positive numbers separated by spaces and
I will find their square roots: 12 15 -17 19 31[Enter]

The square root of 12 is 3.4641
The square root of 15 is 3.87298

-17 is negative. I cannot find the square root
of a negative number. The program is terminating.
```

Using `break` in a Nested Loop

In a nested loop, the `break` statement only interrupts the loop it is placed in. The following program segment displays five rows of asterisks on the screen. The outer loop controls the number of rows, and the inner loop controls the number of asterisks in each row. The inner loop is designed to display 20 asterisks, but the `break` statement stops it during the 11th iteration.

```
for (row = 0; row < 3; row++)
{
   for (star = 0; star < 20; star++)
   {
      cout << '*';
      if (star == 10)
          break;
   }
   cout << endl;
}
```

The output of this program segment is

```
***********
***********
***********
```

WARNING! Use the `break` statement with great caution. Because it bypasses the loop condition to terminate a loop, it violates the rules of structured programming and makes code more difficult to understand, debug, and maintain. For this reason, we do ***not*** recommend using it to exit a loop. Because it is part of the C++ language, however, we have included it in this section.

The `continue` Statement

Sometimes you want to stay in a loop, but cause the current loop iteration to end immediately. This can be done with the `continue` statement. When `continue` is encountered, all the statements in the body of the loop that appear after it are ignored, and the loop prepares for the next iteration. In a `while` loop, this means the program jumps to the test expression at the top of the loop. If the expression is still true, the next iteration begins. Otherwise, the loop is exited. In a `do-while` loop, the program jumps to the test expression at the bottom of the loop, which determines if the next iteration will begin. In a `for` loop, `continue` causes the update expression to be executed, and then the test expression to be evaluated.

The following program segment demonstrates the use of `continue` in a `while` loop:

```
int testVal = 0;
while (testVal < 10)
{
   testVal++;
   if (testVal) == 4
      continue;        // Terminate this iteration of the loop
   cout << testVal << " ";
}
```

This loop looks like it displays the integers 1–10. However, here is the output:

```
1 2 3 5 6 7 8 9 10
```

Notice that the number 4 does not print. This is because when `testVal` is equal to 4, the `continue` statement causes the loop to skip the `cout` statement and begin the next iteration.

WARNING! As with the `break` statement, the `continue` statement violates the rules of structured programming and makes code more difficult to understand, debug, and maintain. For this reason, you should use `continue` with great caution.

There are some practical uses of the `continue` statement, however, and Program 5-15 illustrates one of these. The program calculates the charges for DVD rentals where current releases cost $3.50 and all others cost $2.50. If a customer rents several DVDs, every third one is free. The `continue` statement is used to skip the part of the loop that calculates the charges for every third DVD.

Program 5-15

```
// This program calculates DVD rental charges where every third DVD
// is free. It illustrates the use of the continue statement.
#include <iostream>
#include <iomanip>
using namespace std;

int main()
{
   int numDVDs;          // Number of DVDs being rented
   double total = 0.0;   // Accumulates total charges for all DVDs
   char current;         // Current release? (Y/N)

   // Get number of DVDs rented
   cout << "How many DVDs are being rented? ";
   cin  >> numDVDs;

   // Determine the charges
   for (int dvdCount = 1; dvdCount <= numDVDs; dvdCount++)
   {   if (dvdCount % 3 == 0)   // If it's a 3rd DVD it's free
       {
          cout << "DVD #" << dvdCount << " is free!\n";
          continue;
       }
       cout << "Is DVD #" << dvdCount << " a current release (Y/N)? ";
       cin  >> current;
       if ((current == 'Y') || (current == 'y'))
           total += 3.50;
       else
           total += 2.50;
   }
   // Display the total charges
   cout << fixed << showpoint << setprecision(2);
   cout << "The total is $" << total << endl;
   return 0;
}
```

Program Output with Example Input Shown in Bold

```
How many DVDs are being rented? 6[Enter]
Is DVD #1 a current release (Y/N)? y[Enter]
Is DVD #2 a current release (Y/N)? n[Enter]
DVD #3 is free!
Is DVD #4 a current release (Y/N)? n[Enter]
Is DVD #5 a current release (Y/N)? y[Enter]
DVD #6 is free!
The total is $12.00
```

Checkpoint

5.20 Which loop (`while`, `do-while`, or `for`) is best to use in the following situations?

A) The user must enter a set of exactly 14 numbers.
B) A menu must be displayed for the user to make a selection.
C) A calculation must be made an unknown number of times. (Maybe even no times.)
D) A series of numbers must be entered by the user, terminated by a sentinel value.
E) A series of values must be entered. The user specifies exactly how many.

5.21 How many total stars will be displayed by each of the following program segments?

A)
```
for (row = 0; row < 20; row++)
{   for (star = 0; star < 30; star++)
    {   cout << '*';
    }
    cout << endl;
}
```

B)
```
for (row = 0; row < 20; row ++)
{   for (star = 0; star < 30; star++)
    {   if (star > 10)
            break;
        cout << '*';
    }
    cout << endl;
}
```

5.22 What will the following program segment display?

```
int addOn = 0, subTotal = 0;
while (addOn < 5)
{
   addOn++;
   if (addOn == 3)
      continue;
   subTotal += addOn;
   cout << subTotal << "   ";
}
```

5.12 Using Files for Data Storage

CONCEPT: When a program needs to save data for later use, it writes the data in a file. The data can be read from the file at a later time.

The programs you have written so far require the user to reenter data each time the program runs because data kept in variables is stored in RAM and disappears once the program stops running. If a program is to retain data between the times it runs, it must have a way of saving it. Data written into a file, which is usually stored on a computer's disk, will remain there after the program stops running. That data can then be retrieved and used at a later time.

Most of the commercial software programs that you use on a day-to-day basis store data in files. The following are a few examples.

- **Word processors:** Word processing programs are used to write letters, memos, reports, and other documents. The documents are then saved in files so they can be viewed, edited, and printed at a later time.

- **Spreadsheets:** Spreadsheet programs are used to work with numerical data. Numbers and mathematical formulas can be inserted into the rows and columns of the spreadsheet. The spreadsheet can then be saved in a file for use later.
- **Image editors:** Image editing programs are used to draw graphics and edit images, such as the ones that you take with a digital camera. The images that you create or edit with an image editor are saved in files.
- **Business operations software:** Programs used in daily business operations rely extensively on files. Payroll programs keep employee data in files, inventory programs keep data about a company's products in files, accounting systems keep data about a company's financial operations in files, and so on.
- **Web browsers:** Sometimes when you visit a Web page, the browser stores a small file known as a *cookie* on your computer. Cookies typically contain information about the browsing session, such as the contents of a shopping cart.
- **Games:** Many computer games keep data stored in files. For example, some games keep a list of player names with their scores stored in a file. These games typically display the players' names in order of their scores, from highest to lowest. Some games also allow you to save your current game status in a file so you can quit the game and then resume playing it later without having to start from the beginning.

Programmers usually refer to the process of saving data in a file as *writing data* to the file. When a piece of data is written to a file, it is copied from a variable in RAM to the file. This is illustrated in Figure 5-8. The term *output file* is used to describe a file that data is written to. It is called an output file because the program stores output in it.

Figure 5-8 Writing data to a file

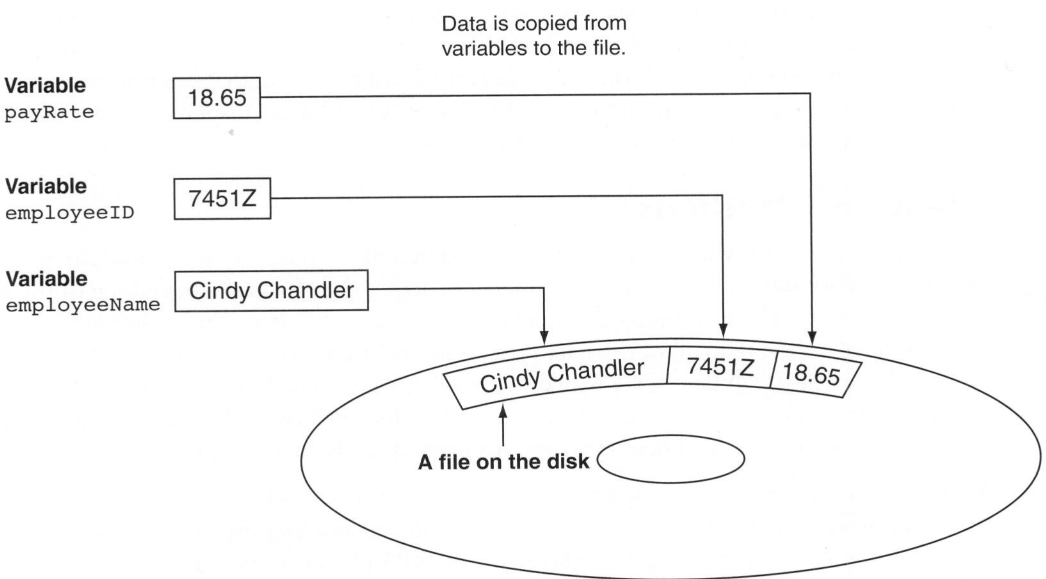

The process of retrieving data from a file is known as *reading data* from the file. When a piece of data is read from a file, it is copied from the file into a variable in RAM. Figure 5-9 illustrates this. The term *input file* is used to describe a file that data is read from. It is called an input file because the program gets input from the file.

Figure 5-9 Reading data from a file

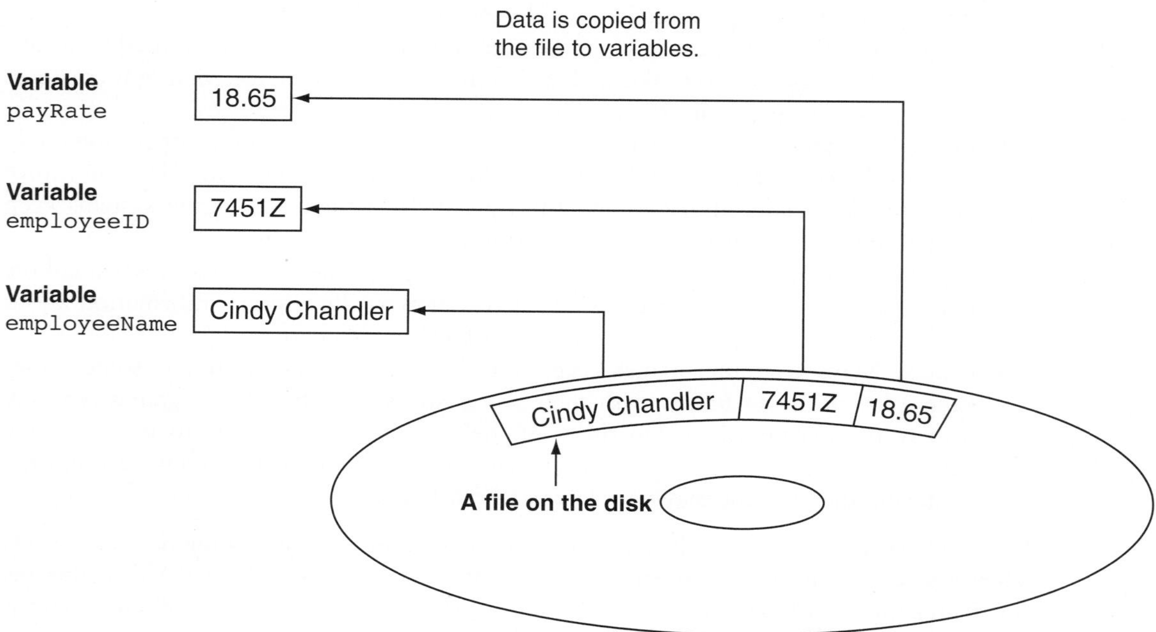

Types of Files

In general, there are two types of files: text and binary. A *text file* contains data that has been encoded as text, using a scheme such ASCII or Unicode. Even if the file contains numbers, those numbers are stored in the file as a series of characters. As a result, the file may be opened and viewed in a text editor such as Notepad. A *binary file* contains data that has not been converted to text. As a consequence, you cannot view the contents of a binary file with a text editor. In this chapter we will work only with text files. In Chapter 13 you will learn to work with binary files.

File Access Methods

There are two general ways to access data stored in a file: sequential access and direct access. When you work with a *sequential access file*, you access data from the beginning of the file to the end of the file. If you want to first read a piece of data that is stored at the very end of the file, you have to first read all of the data that comes before it. You cannot jump directly to the desired data. This is similar to the way cassette tape players work. If you want to listen to the last song on a cassette tape, you have to either fast-forward over all of the songs that come before it or listen to them. There is no way to jump directly to a specific song.

When you work with a *random access file* (which is also known as a *direct access file*), you can directly access any piece of data in the file without reading the data that comes before it. This is similar to the way a CD player or an MP3 player works. You can jump directly to any song that you want to listen to.

This chapter focuses on sequential access text files. These files are easy to work with, and you can use them to gain an understanding of basic file operations. In Chapter 13 you will learn to work with random access and binary files.

Filenames and File Stream Objects

Files on a disk are identified by a *filename*. For example, when you create a document with a word processor and then save the document in a file, you have to specify a filename. When you use a utility such as Windows Explorer to examine the contents of your disk, you see a list of filenames. Figure 5-10 shows how three files named `cat.jpg`, `notes.txt`, and `resume.doc` might be represented in Windows Explorer.

Figure 5-10 Three files

Each operating system has its own rules for naming files. Many systems, including Windows, support the use of *filename extensions*, which are short sequences of characters that appear at the end of a filename preceded by a period. The files depicted in Figure 5-10 have the extensions `.jpg`, `.txt`, and `.doc`. The period is called a "dot". So, for example, the filename `resume.doc` would be read "resume dot doc". The extension usually indicates the type of data stored in the file. For example, the `.jpg` extension usually indicates that the file contains a graphic image compressed according to the JPEG image standard. The `.txt` extension usually indicates that the file contains text. The `.doc` extension usually indicates that the file contains a Microsoft Word document.

In order for a program to work with a file on the computer's disk, the program must create a file stream object in memory. A *file stream object* is an object that is associated with a specific file and provides a way for the program to work with that file. It is called a "stream" object because a file can be thought of as a stream of data.

File stream objects work very much like the `cin` and `cout` objects. A stream of data may be sent to `cout`, which causes values to be displayed on the screen. A stream of data may be read from the keyboard by `cin` and stored in variables. Likewise, streams of data may be sent to a file stream object, which writes the data to the file it is associated with. When data is read from a file, the data flows from the file stream object associated with the file into variables.

Setting Up a Program for File Input/Output

There are five steps that must be taken when a file is used by a program:

1. Include the header file needed to perform file input/output.
2. Define a file stream object.
3. Open the file.
4. Use the file.
5. Close the file.

Let's examine each of these, beginning with step 1.

Just as you need to include the `iostream` file in your program to use `cin` and `cout`, you need another header file to use files. The `fstream` file contains all the declarations necessary for file operations. You can include it with the following statement:

```
#include <fstream>
```

The `fstream` header file defines the data types `ofstream`, `ifstream`, and `fstream`. Before a C++ program can work with a file, it must define an object of one of these data types. The object will be "linked" with an actual file on the computer's disk, and the operations that may be performed on the file depend on which of these three data types you pick for the file stream object. Table 5-1 lists and describes the file stream data types.

Table 5-1

File Stream Data Type	Description
`ofstream`	This stands for output file **`stream`** and is pronounced 'o' 'f' stream. An object of this data type can be used to create a file and write data to it.
`ifstream`	This stands for input file **`stream`** and is pronounced 'i' 'f' stream. An object of this data type can be used to open an existing file and read data from it.
`fstream`	This stands for file **`stream`** and is pronounced 'f' stream. An object of this data type can be used to open files for reading, writing, or both.

NOTE: In this chapter we only discuss the `ofstream` and `ifstream` data types. The `fstream` type is covered in Chapter 13.

Creating a File Stream Object and Opening a File

Before data can be written to or read from a file, two things must happen:

- A file stream object must be created.
- The file must be opened and linked to the file stream object.

The following code shows an example of opening a file for input (reading).

```
ifstream inputFile;
inputFile.open("Customers.txt");
```

The first statement defines an `ifstream` object named `inputFile`. The second statement calls the object's `open` member function, passing the string `"Customers.txt"` as an argument. In this statement, the `open` member function opens the `Customers.txt` file and links it with the `inputFile` object. After this code executes, you will be able to use `inputFile` to read data from the `Customers.txt` file.

The following code shows an example of opening a file for output (writing).

```
ofstream outputFile;
outputFile.open("Employees.txt");
```

The first statement defines an `ofstream` object named `outputFile`. The second statement then calls the object's `open` member function, passing it the string `"Employees.txt"` as an argument. This opens a file named `Employees.txt` and links it with `outputFile`. If the specified file did not previously exist, it will be created. If the specified file already exists, it will be erased and a new file with the same name will be created. After this code executes, you will be able to use `outputFile` to write data to the `Employees.txt` file.

Sometimes, when opening a file, you will need to specify its full path as well as its name. For example, on a Windows system the following statement opens the file `C:\data\inventory.txt` and links it with `inputFile`:

```
inputFile.open("C:\\data\\inventory.txt");
```

NOTE: Notice the use of two backslashes in the file's path. As mentioned before in this text, two backslashes are needed to represent one backslash in a string literal.

It is possible to define a file stream object and open a file all in one statement. Here is an example that defines an `ifstream` object named `inputFile`, opens the `Customers.txt` file, and associates `inputFile` with it:

```
ifstream inputFile("Customers.txt");
```

And here is an example that defines an `ofstream` object named `outputFile`, opens the `Employees.txt` file, and associates `outputFile` with it:

```
ofstream outputFile("Employees.txt");
```

Closing a File

The opposite of opening a file is closing it. Although a program's files are automatically closed when the program shuts down, it is a good programming practice to write statements that explicitly close them. Here are two reasons a program should close files when it is finished using them:

- Most operating systems temporarily store data in a *file buffer* before it is written to a file. A file buffer is a small "holding section" of memory that file-bound data is first written to. The data is not actually written to the file until the buffer is full. This is done to improve the system's performance because doing file I/O is much slower than processing data in memory. Closing a file causes any unsaved data still in a buffer to be written out to its file. This ensures that all the data the program intended to write to the file is actually in it if you need to read it back in later in the same program.
- Some operating systems limit the number of files that may be open at one time. When a program closes files that are no longer being used, it will not deplete more of the operating system's resources than necessary.

Calling the file stream object's `close` member function closes the file associated with it. Here is an example:

```
inputFile.close();
```

Writing Data to a File

You already know how to use the stream insertion operator (<<) with the `cout` object to write data to the screen. It can also be used with `ofstream` objects to write data to a file. Assuming `outputFile` is an `ofstream` object, the following statement demonstrates using the << operator to write a string literal to a file:

```
outputFile << "I love C++ programming\n";
```

This statement writes the string literal "I love C++ programming\n" to the file associated with `outputFile`. As you can see, the statement looks like a `cout` statement, except the name of the `ofstream` object name replaces `cout`. Here is a statement that writes both a string literal and the contents of a variable to a file:

```
outputFile << "Price: " << price << endl;
```

This statement writes the stream of data to `outputFile` exactly as `cout` would write it to the screen: It writes the string `"Price: "`, followed by the value of the `price` variable, followed by a newline character.

Program 5-16 demonstrates opening a file, writing data to the file, and closing the file. After this code has executed, we can open the `demofile.txt` file using a text editor, look at its contents, and, if we wish, print it.

Program 5-16

```
// This program writes data to a file.
#include <iostream>
#include <fstream>        // Needed to use files
using namespace std;

int main()
{
   ofstream outputFile;

   // Open the output file
   outputFile.open("demofile.txt");

   cout << "Now writing data to the file.\n";

   // Write four names to the file
   outputFile << "Bach\n";
   outputFile << "Beethoven\n";
   outputFile << "Mozart\n";
   outputFile << "Schubert\n";

   // Close the file
   outputFile.close();

   cout << "Done.\n";
   return 0;
}
```

Program Screen Output

```
Now writing data to the file.
Done.
```

Figure 5-11 shows how the file's contents appear in Notepad.

Figure 5-11

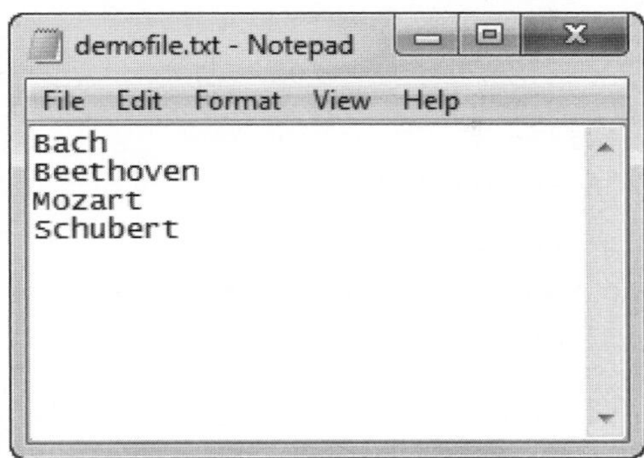

Notice that in lines 14 through 17 of Program 5-16, each string that was written to the file ends with a newline escape sequence (`\n`). The newline specifies the end of a line of text. Because a newline is written at the end of each string, the strings appear on separate lines when viewed in a text editor, as shown in Figure 5-11.

If we wrote the same four names without the `\n` escape sequence or an `endl` after each one, they would all appear on the same line of the file with no spaces between them, as shown in Figure 5-12 .

Figure 5-12

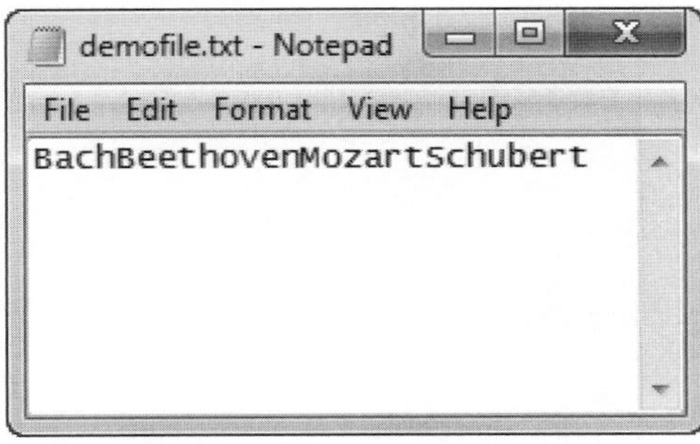

Program 5-17 also writes data to a file, but it gets its data from keyboard input when the program runs. This program asks the user to enter the first names of three friends, and then it writes those names to a file named `Friends.txt`.

Program 5-17

```
// This program writes user input to a file.
#include <iostream>
#include <fstream>         // Needed to use files
#include <string>
using namespace std;

```

(program continues)

Program 5-17 *(continued)*

```
int main()
{
   ofstream outputFile;
   string name1, name2, name3;

   // Open the output file
   outputFile.open("Friends.txt");

   // Get the names of three friends
   cout << "Enter the names of three friends.\n";
   cout << "Friend #1: ";
   cin  >> name1;
   cout << "Friend #2: ";
   cin  >> name2;
   cout << "Friend #3: ";
   cin  >> name3;

   // Write the names to the file
   outputFile << name1 << endl;
   outputFile << name2 << endl;
   outputFile << name3 << endl;

   // Close the file
   outputFile.close();

   cout << "The names were saved to a file.\n";
   return 0;
}
```

Program Screen Output with Example Input Shown in Bold

```
Enter the names of three friends.
Friend #1: Joe[Enter]
Friend #2: Chris[Enter]
Friend #3: Geri[Enter]
The names were saved to a file.
```

Figure 5-13 shows an example of the `Friends.txt` file opened in Notepad.

Figure 5-13

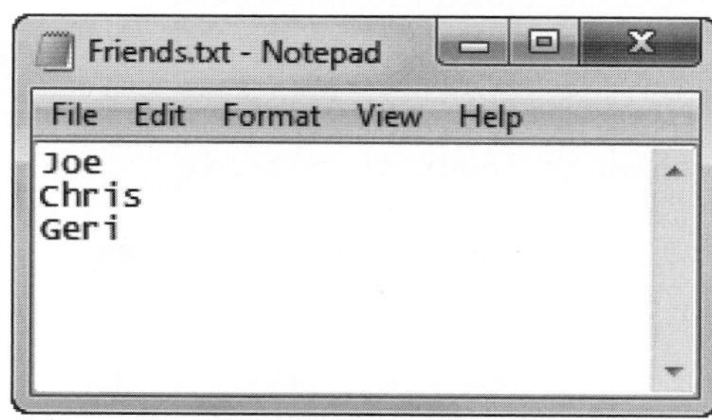

Reading Data from a File

In addition to viewing a text file with a text editor, you can also use the data in a text file as input for a program. This is easy to do because the >> operator can read data from a file as well as from the `cin` object. Assuming `inputFile` is an `fstream` or `ifstream` object, the following statement will read a string from the file and store it in the `string` variable `name`:

```
inputFile >> name;
```

Program 5-18 uses this statement. It opens the `Friends.txt` file holding the three names that we created by Program 5-17. It reads in the names and displays them on the screen. Then it closes the file.

Program 5-18

```
// This program reads data from a file.
#include <iostream>
#include <fstream>          // Needed to use files
#include <string>
using namespace std;

int main()
{
   ifstream inputFile;
   string name;

   // Open the input file
   inputFile.open("Friends.txt");

   cout << "Reading data from the file.\n";

   inputFile >> name;       // Read name 1 from the file and display it
   cout << name << endl;

   inputFile >> name;       // Read name 2 from the file and display it
   cout << name << endl;

   inputFile >> name;       // Read name 3 from the file and display it
   cout << name << endl;

   inputFile.close();       // Close the file
   return 0;
}
```

Program Output

```
Reading data from the file.
Joe
Chris
Geri
```

The Read Position

When a file has been opened for input, the file stream object internally maintains a special value known as a read position. A file's *read position* marks the location of the next byte that will be read from the file. When an input file is opened, its read position is initially set to the first byte in the file. So the first read operation extracts data starting at the first byte. As data is read from the file, the read position moves forward, toward the end of the file.

Let's see how this works with the example shown in Program 5-18. When the `Friends.txt` file is opened by the statement in line 13, the read position for the file will be positioned as shown in Figure 5-14.

Figure 5-14

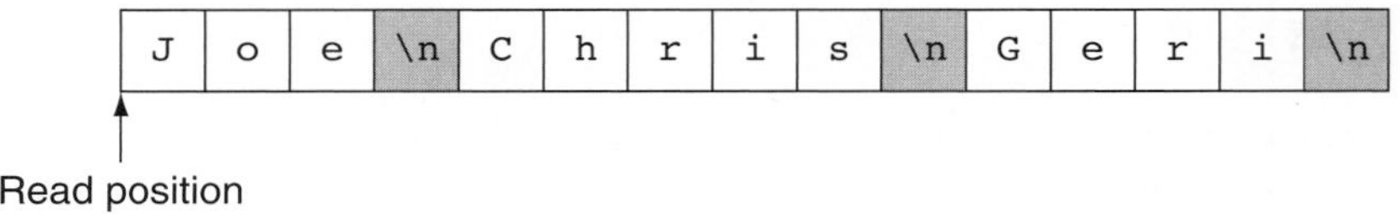

Keep in mind that when the >> operator extracts data from a file, it expects to read pieces of data that are separated by whitespace characters (spaces, tabs, or newlines). When the statement in line 17 executes, the >> operator reads data from the file's current read position, up to the `\n` character. The data that is read from the file is assigned to the `name` variable. The `\n` character is also read from the file, but it is not included as part of the data. So `name` will hold the value `"Joe"` after this statement executes. The file's read position will then be at the location shown in Figure 5-15.

Figure 5-15

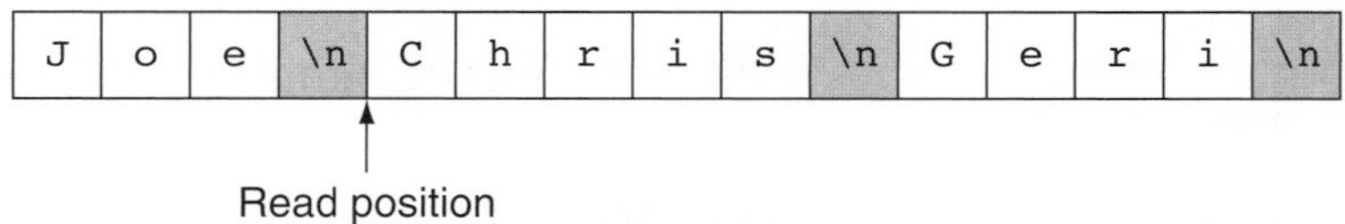

When the statement in line 20 executes, it reads the next item from the file, which is `"Chris"`, and assigns that value to the `name` variable. After this statement executes, the file's read position will be at the location shown in Figure 5-16.

Figure 5-16

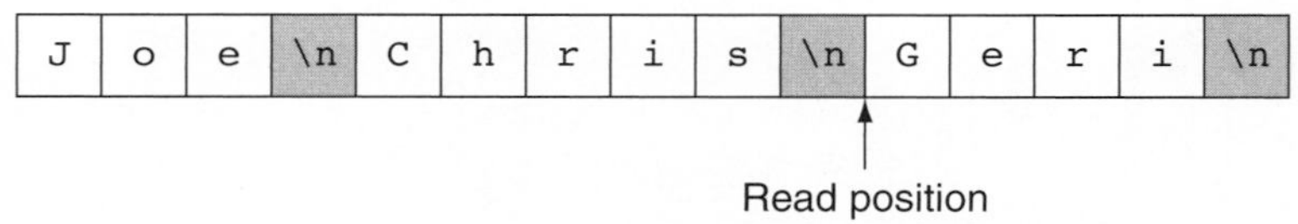

When the statement in line 23 executes, it reads the next item from the file, which is `"Geri"`, and assigns that value to the `name` variable. After this statement executes, the file's read position will be at the end of the file, as shown in Figure 5-17.

Figure 5-17

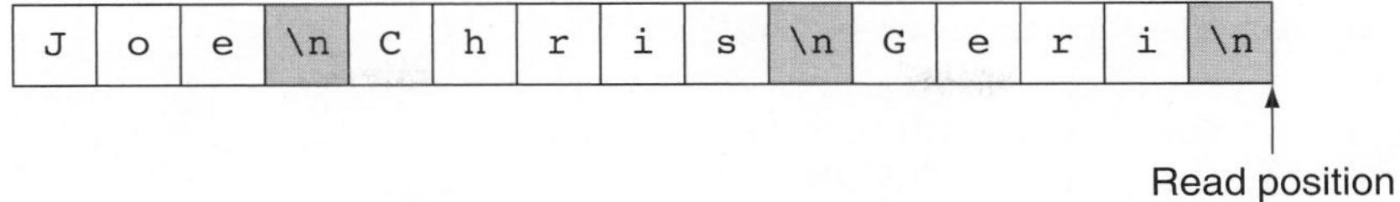

Using Loops to Process Files

Although some programs use files to store only small amounts of data, files are typically used to hold large collections of data. When a program uses a file to write or read a large amount of data, a loop is typically involved. For example, look at the code in Program 5-19. This program gets sales amounts for a series of days from the user and writes those amounts to a file named `Sales.txt`. The user specifies how many days of sales data will be entered. In the sample run of the program, the user enters sales amounts for five days.

Program 5-19

```
// This program uses a loop to write multiple values to a file.
#include <iostream>
#include <fstream>        // Needed to use files
using namespace std;

int main()
{
   ofstream outputFile;  // File stream object
   int numberOfDays;     // Number of days of sales
   double sales;         // Sales amount for a day

   // Get the number of days
   cout << "For how many days do you have sales? ";
   cin  >> numberOfDays;

   // Open the output file
   outputFile.open("Sales.txt");

   // Loop once for each day of sales
   for (int count = 1; count <= numberOfDays; count++)
   {
      // Get the sales amount for a day
      cout << "Enter the sales for day " << count << ": ";
      cin  >> sales;

      // Write the sales amount to the file
      outputFile << sales << endl;
   }
   // Close the file
   outputFile.close();

   cout << "Data written to Sales.txt\n";
   return 0;
}
```

(program continues)

Program 5-19 *(continued)*

Program Output (with Input Shown in Bold)

```
For how many days do you have sales? 5[Enter]
Enter the sales for day 1: 1000.00[Enter]
Enter the sales for day 2: 2000.00[Enter]
Enter the sales for day 3: 3000.00[Enter]
Enter the sales for day 4: 4000.00[Enter]
Enter the sales for day 5: 5000.00[Enter]
Data written to Sales.txt
```

Figure 5-18 shows the contents of the `Sales.txt` file containing the data entered by the user in the sample run.

Figure 5-18

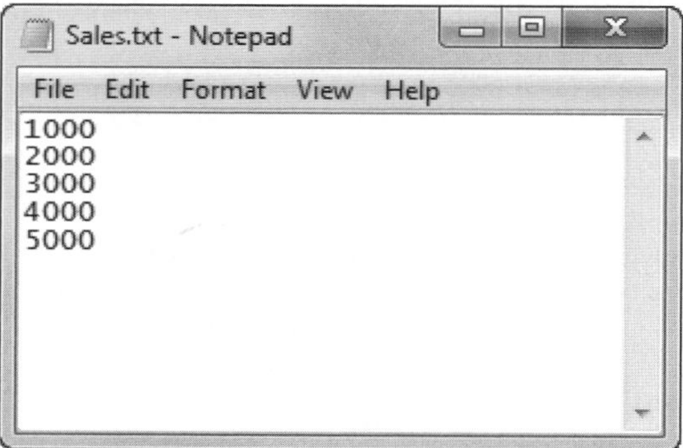

When data is stored in a text file, it is encoded as text, using a scheme such ASCII or Unicode. As previously mentioned, even numeric data is stored in the file as a series of characters. To read a numeric data value from a text file into a program you can use the >> operator. Just be sure to store the data in a numeric variable. The >> operator will then automatically convert the data to a numeric data type, just as it does when reading numeric data from the keyboard into a numeric variable. Program 5-20 uses the >> operator to read the data in the `Sales.txt` file and sum the values to find the total sales for the five days.

Program 5-20

```
// This program uses a loop to read in multiple values from a file.
#include <iostream>
#include <fstream>                  // Needed to use files
using namespace std;
```

(program continues)

Program 5-20 *(continued)*

```
int main()
{
   ifstream inputFile;          // File stream object
   int numberOfDays;            // Number of days of sales
   double sales,                // Sales amount for a day
          totalSales = 0.0;     // Accumulator

   // Get the number of days
   cout << "How many days of sales data are stored in your file? ";
   cin  >> numberOfDays;

   // Open the input file
   inputFile.open("Sales.txt");

   // Loop once for each piece of data to be read from the file
   for (int count = 1; count <= numberOfDays; count++)
   {
      // Read a sales figure from the file and add it to the sum
      inputFile >> sales;
      totalSales += sales;
   }
   // Close the file
   inputFile.close();

   cout << "Total sales for the " << numberOfDays << " days were $"
        << totalSales;

   return 0;
}
```

Program Output (with Input Shown in Bold)

```
How many days of sales data are stored in your file? 5[Enter]
Total sales for the 5 days were $15000
```

Detecting the End of the File

Program 5-20 asked the user how many values were in the file, and that is how many data items it read in. However, when reading data from a file, it is not necessary for the user to specify how many data values there are or where the data ends. This is because files have an end of file (EOF) mark at their end. You cannot see it, but it is there, and a program can test to see whether or not it has been reached. This test is important because an error will occur if the program attempts to read beyond the end of the file.

The easiest way to test if the end of the file has been reached is with the >> operator. This operator not only can read data from a file, but it also returns a true or false value indicating whether the data was successfully read or not. If the operator returns true, then a value was successfully read. If the operator returns false, it means that no value was read from the file. The EOF has been reached.

Program 5-21 revises Program 5-20 to read in the data from the `Sales.txt` file and sum the sales figures, without knowing how many numbers are in the file. It also counts the numbers as it reads them in.

Program 5-21

```
 1 // This program uses a loop to read in values
 2 // from a file until the end of file is reached.
 3 #include <iostream>
 4 #include <fstream>                 // Needed to use files
 5 using namespace std;
 6
 7 int main()
 8 {
 9     ifstream inputFile;            // File stream object
10     int numberOfDays = 0;          // Counts the records in the file
11     double sales,                  // Sales amount for a day
12     totalSales = 0.0;              // Accumulator
13
14     // Open the input file
15     inputFile.open("Sales.txt");
16
17     // Loop until the EOF is reached
18     while(inputFile >> sales)      // If a value was read
19     {   totalSales += sales;
20         numberOfDays++;
21     }
22     // Close the file
23     inputFile.close();
24
25     cout << "Total sales for the " << numberOfDays << " days were $"
26          << totalSales;
27
28     return 0;
29 }
```

Program Output

```
Total sales for the 5 days were $15000
```

Take a closer look at line 18:

```
while (inputFile >> sales)
```

Notice that the statement that extracts data from the file is used as a Boolean test expression in the `while` loop. It works like this:

- The expression `inputFile >> sales` executes.
- If an item is successfully read from the file, the item is stored in the `sales` variable, and the expression returns true to indicate that it succeeded. In that case, the statements in lines 19 and 20 execute and the loop repeats.
- When there are no more items to read from the file, the expression `inputFile >> sales` returns false, indicating that it did not read a value. In that case, the loop terminates.

Testing for File Open Errors

Under certain circumstances, the open member function will not work. For example, the following code will fail if the file `info.txt` does not exist or cannot be found in the expected directory:

```
fstream inputFile;
inputFile.open("info.txt");
```

Fortunately, there is a way to determine whether the open member function successfully opened the file. After you call the open member function, you can test the file stream object as if it were a Boolean expression. Program 5-22 shows how to do this.

Program 5-22

```
1 // This program tests for file open errors.
2 #include <iostream>
3 #include <fstream>        // Needed to use files
4 using namespace std;
5
6 int main()
7 {
8    ifstream inputFile;
9    int number;
10
11    // Attempt to open the input file
12    inputFile.open("ListOfNumbers.txt");
13
14    // If the file successfully opened, process it
15    if (inputFile)
16    {
17       // Read the numbers from the file and display them
18       while (inputFile  >> number)
19          cout << number << endl;
20
21       // Close the file
22       inputFile.close();
23    }
24    else // The file could not be found and opened
25    {
26       // Display an error message
27       cout << "Error opening the file.\n";
28    }
29    return 0;
30 }
```

Program Output (when ListOfNumbers.txt does not exist)

```
Error opening the file.
```

Let's take a closer look at certain parts of the code. Line 12 calls the open member function to open the file `ListOfNumbers.txt` and associate it with the `ifstream` object named `inputFile`. Then the `if` statement in line 15 tests the value of `inputFile` as if it were a Boolean expression. When tested this way, `inputFile` will give a true value if the file was successfully opened. Otherwise it will give a false value. As the example output shows, the program displays an error message if it could not open the file.

Another way to detect a failed attempt to open a file is with an `ifstream` class member function named `fail`, as shown in the following code:

```
ifstream inputFile;
inputFile.open("customers.txt");

if (inputFile.fail())
   cout << "Error opening file.\n";
else
{
   // Process the file
}
```

The `fail` member function returns true when an attempted file operation fails (i.e., is unsuccessful), and returns false otherwise. When using file I/O, it is good idea to always test the file stream object to make sure the file was opened successfully before attempting to use it. If the file could not be opened, the user should be informed and appropriate action taken by the program.

Letting the User Specify a Filename

In each of the previous examples, the name of the file being opened is hard-coded as a string literal into the program. In many cases, however, you will want to let the user specify the name of the file to be used.

In standard C++, a file stream object's `open` member function will not accept a `string` object as an argument. It requires you to pass it the name of the file as a C-string, which you recall is an array of characters terminated by the null character. String literals are stored in memory as C-strings (which explains why you can pass them to the `open` function), but `string` objects are not.

Fortunately, `string` objects have a member function named `c_str` that returns a copy of the object's contents formatted as a null-terminated C-string. You call the function like this:

```
stringObject.c_str()
```

where *`stringObject`* is the name of the `string` object. Program 5-23 shows an example of how to use the function. This is a modified version of Program 5-22 that prompts the user to enter the name of the file. In line 15, the name the user enters is stored in a `string` object named `filename`. In line 18, the value returned from `filename.c_str()` is passed as an argument to the open function.

Program 5-23

```
1 // This program lets the user enter a filename.
2 #include <iostream>
3 #include <string>
4 #include <fstream>        // Needed to use files
5 using namespace std;
6
```

(program continues)

Program 5-23 *(continued)*

```
int main()
{
   ifstream inputFile;
   string filename;
   int number;

   // Get the filename from the user
   cout << "Enter the filename: ";
   cin  >> filename;

   // Open the input file
   inputFile.open(filename.c_str());

   // If the file successfully opened, process it
   if (inputFile)
   {
      // Read the numbers from the file and display them
      while (inputFile >> number)
         cout << number << endl;

      // Close the file.
      inputFile.close();
   }
   else
   {
      // Display an error message
      cout << "Error opening the file.\n";
   }
   return 0;
}
```

Program Output with Example Input Shown in Bold

```
Enter the filename: myData.txt[Enter]
100
125
150
200
```

Checkpoint

5.23 A) What is an output file? B) What is an input file?

5.24 What header file must be included in a program to use files?

5.25 What five steps must be taken when a file is used by a program?

5.26 What is the difference between a text file and a binary file?

5.27 What is the difference between sequential access and random access?

5.28 What type of file stream object do you create if you want to write data to a file?

5.29 What type of file stream object do you create if you want to read data from a file?

5.30 Assuming `dataFile` is an `ofstream` object associated with a disk file named `payroll.dat`, which of the following statements would write the value of the `salary` variable to the file?

A) `cout << salary;`
B) `ofstream << salary;`
C) `dataFile << salary;`
D) `payroll.dat << salary;`

5.31 The following code has an error. Can you correct it?

```
ofstream outputFile;
string filename = "numbers.txt";
outputFile.open(filename);
```

5.32 Assume you have an output file named `numbers.txt` that is open and associated with an `ofstream` object named `outfile`. Write a program segment that uses a `for` loop to write the numbers 1 through 10 to the file.

5.13 Focus on Testing and Debugging: *Creating Good Test Data*

CONCEPT: Thorough testing of a program requires good test data.

Once a program has been designed, written in a programming language, and found to compile and link without errors, it must be thoroughly tested to find any logic errors and to ensure that it works correctly according to the original problem specification. When it comes to creating test data, quality is more important than quantity. That is, a small set of good test cases can provide more information about how a program works than twice as many cases that are not carefully thought out. Each test case should be designed to test a different aspect of the program, and you should always know what each test set you use is checking for. To illustrate this, look at Program 5-24. It uses a sentinel-controlled loop to average two test scores for each student in the class, where all test scores are between 0 and 100. The program compiles, links, and runs. But it contains several logic errors.

Program 5-24

```
// This program attempts to average 2 test scores for each
// student in a class. However, it contains logic errors.
#include <iostream>
#include <string>
#include <iomanip>
using namespace std;

int main()
{
   string name;                    // Student first name

   int count = 1,                  // Student counter
       score,                      // An individual score read in
       totalScore = 0;             // Total of a student's 2 scores
   double average;                 // Average of a student's 2 scores

```

(program continues)

Program 5-24 *(continued)*

```
    cout << fixed << showpoint << setprecision(1);
    cout << "Enter the first name of student " << count
         << " (or Q to quit): ";
    cin  >> name;

    while (name != "Q" && name != "q")
    {
       // Get and validate the first score
       cout << "Enter score 1: ";
       cin  >> score;
       if (score <= 0 || score >= 100)
       {  cout << "Score must be between 0 and 100. Please reenter: ";
          cin  >> score;
       }
       totalScore += score;      // Add the first score onto the total

       // Get and validate the second score
       cout << "Enter score 2: ";
       cin  >> score;
       if (score <= 0 || score >= 100)
       {  cout << "Score must be between 0 and 100. Please reenter: ";
          cin  >> score;
       }
       totalScore += score;     // Add the second score onto the total

       // Calculate and print average
       average = totalScore / 2;
       cout << name << setw(6) << average << endl;

       // Get the next student name
       cout << "Enter the first name of student " << count++
            << " (or Q to quit): ";
       cin  >> name;
    }
    return 0;
}
```

Table 5-2 Preliminary Test Plans for Program 5-24

	Name	Score 1	Score 2	Expected Outcome
Test 1:	Mary Q	80	80	80.0 program quits
Test 2:	Bill Q	70	80	75.0 program quits
Test 3:	Tom q	80	90	85.0 program quits
Test 4:	Sam q	–1 then 1	999 then 99	50.0 program quits

Try running the program using the four test cases shown in Table 5-2. The program contains five logic errors. However, if it is run with just these four test cases, none of the errors will be revealed. The test data is not designed carefully enough to catch them. Tests 1, 2, and 3 are really just three versions of the same test. They all simply check that the program can compute a correct average for a single student where the result has no decimal digits. The final test checks that the program can catch a single invalid value that is too small or too big, but does not check what will happen if a second invalid value is entered for the same input. Table 5-3 contains a better set of tests and illustrates some of the kinds of things you should check for when you test a program. These tests will reveal all five of the program's errors.

Table 5-3 Modified Test Plans for Program 5-24

Test	Name	Score 1	Score 2	Purpose	Expected Outcome
1	Mary Bill Tom Q	80 70 80	80 80 91	Program correctly handles both even results and ones with decimal values. Program can loop to handle multiple students. Program ends when Q is entered for the name.	80.0 75.0 85.5 program ends
2	Sam Ted q	–1 then 1 –1 then –2 then 1	101 then 99 200 then 500 then 99	Program correctly handles invalid scores, even when more than one bad score is entered in a row. Program catches bad inputs immediately outside the valid range (e.g., –1 & 101). Program ends when q is entered for the name.	50.0 50.0 program ends
3	Bob q	0	100	Program allows values at extreme ends of the valid range.	50.0 program ends

Rerun Program 5-24 using the test cases from Table 5-3 and examine the incorrect output to identify the errors. Then see if you can fix them. Do not rewrite the program. Just make the smallest changes necessary to correct the errors. Now test the program again using the test cases in Table 5-3. Continue making corrections and retesting until the program successfully passes all three of these test cases. A correct solution can be found on the book's companion website in the `pr5-24B.cpp` file of the Chapter 5 programs folder.

Central Mountain Credit Union Case Study

The manager of the Central Mountain Credit Union has asked you to write a loan amortization program that his loan officers can run on their laptops. Here is what it should do.

Problem Statement

When given the loan amount, annual interest rate, and number of years of a loan, the program must determine and display the monthly payment amount. It must then create and display an amortization table that lists the following information for each month of the loan:

- payment number
- amount of that month's payment that was applied to interest
- amount of that month's payment that was applied to principal
- balance after that payment.

The following report may be used as a model. It shows all the required information on a $2000 loan at 7.5% annual interest for .5 years (i.e., 6 months).

```
Monthly payment: $340.66

Month  Interest  Principal  Balance
-----------------------------------
   1      12.50     328.16  1671.84
   2      10.45     330.21  1341.62
   3       8.39     332.28  1009.34
   4       6.31     334.35   674.99
   5       4.22     336.44   338.55
   6       2.12     338.55     0.00
```

Calculations

The credit union uses the following formula to calculate the monthly payment of a loan:

$$\text{Payment} = \frac{\text{Loan} * \text{Rate}/12 * \text{Term}}{\text{Term} - 1}$$

where:

Loan = the amount of the loan
Rate = the annual interest rate
Term = $(1+ \text{Rate}/12)^{\text{Years}*12}$

Variables

Table 5-4 lists the variables needed in the program.

Table 5-4 Variables Used in the Central Mountain Credit Union Case Study

Variable	Description
`loan`	A `double`. Holds the loan amount.
`rate`	A `double`. Holds the annual interest rate.
`moInterestRate`	A `double`. Holds the monthly interest rate.
`years`	A `double`. Holds the number of years of the loan.
`balance`	A `double`. Holds the remaining balance to be paid.
`term`	A `double`. Used in the monthly payment calculation.
`payment`	A `double`. Holds the monthly payment amount.
`numPayments`	An `int`. Holds the total number of payments.
`month`	An `int`. Loop control variable that holds the current payment number.
`moInterest`	A `double`. Holds the monthly interest amount.
`principal`	A `double`. Holds the amount of the monthly payment that pays down the loan.

Program Design

Figure 5-19 shows a hierarchy chart for the program.

Figure 5-19

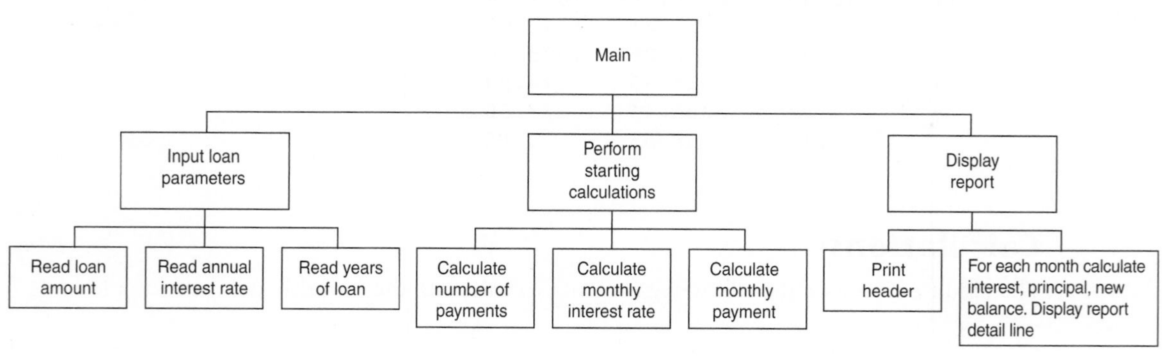

Detailed Pseudocode (including actual variable names and needed calculations)

```
Input loan, rate, years
numPayments = years * 12.0
moInterestRate = rate / 12.0
term = (1 + moInterestRate)numPayments
payment = (loan * moInterestRate * term) / (term – 1.0)
Display payment
Display a report header with column headings
balance = loan       // Remaining balance starts out as full loan amount
```

```
For each month of the loan
   moInterest = moInterestRate * balance // Calculate interest first
   If it's not the final month
      principal = payment – moInterest    // Rest of pmt goes to principal
   Else                                   // It's the last month so
      principal = balance                 // pay off exact final balance
      payment = balance + moInterest
   End If
   balance = balance – principal          // Only principal reduces the balance
   Display month, moInterest, principal, balance
End of loop
```

The Program

The next step, after the pseudocode has been checked for logic errors, is to expand the pseudocode into the final program. This is shown in Program 5-25.

Program 5-25

```
// This program produces a loan amortization table
// for the Central Mountain Credit Union.
#include <iostream>
#include <iomanip>
#include <cmath>          // Needed for the pow function
using namespace std;

int main()
{
   double loan,           // Loan amount
          rate,           // Annual interest rate
          moInterestRate, // Monthly interest rate
          years,          // Years of loan
          balance,        // Monthly balance
          term,           // Used to calculate payment
          payment;        // Monthly payment
   int    numPayments;    // Number of payments

   // Get loan information
   cout << "Loan amount: $";
   cin  >> loan;
   cout << "Annual interest rate (entered as a decimal): ";
   cin  >> rate;
   cout << "Years of loan: ";
   cin  >> years;

   // Calculate monthly payment
   numPayments = static_cast<int>(12 * years);
   moInterestRate = rate / 12.0;
   term = pow((1 + moInterestRate), numPayments);
   payment = (loan * moInterestRate * term) / (term - 1.0);

   // Display monthly payment
   cout << fixed << showpoint << setprecision(2);
   cout << "Monthly payment: $" << payment << endl;

```

(program continues)

Program 5-25 *(continued)*

```
   // Display report header
   cout << endl;
   cout << setw(5)  << "Month"     << setw(10) << "Interest";
   cout << setw(10) << "Principal" << setw(9)  << "Balance" << endl;
   cout << "----------------------------------\n";

   balance = loan;       // Remaining balance starts out as full loan amount

   // Produce a listing for each month
   for (int month = 1; month <= numPayments; month++)
   {
      double moInterest,          // Amount of pmt that pays interest
             principal;           // Amount of pmt that lowers the balance

      // Calculate amount paid for this month's interest and principal
      moInterest = moInterestRate * balance; // Calculate interest first
      if (month != numPayments)              // If not the final month
          principal = payment - moInterest;  // rest of pmt goes
                                             // to principal

      else                                   // It's the last month so
      {   principal = balance;               // pay exact final balance
          payment = balance + moInterest;
      }
      // Calculate new loan balance          // Only principal reduces the
      balance -= principal;                  // balance, not the whole pmt

      // Display this month's payment figures
      cout << setw(4)  << month     << setw(10) << moInterest;
      cout << setw(10) << principal << setw(10) << balance << endl;
   }
   return 0;
}
```

Program Output with Example Input Shown in Bold

```
Loan amount: $1200[Enter]
Annual interest rate (entered as a decimal): .08[Enter]
Years of loan: 1[Enter]
Monthly payment: $104.39
Month  Interest Principal  Balance
----------------------------------
   1      8.00     96.39   1103.61
   2      7.36     97.03   1006.59
   3      6.71     97.68    908.91
   4      6.06     98.33    810.58
   5      5.40     98.98    711.60
   6      4.74     99.64    611.96
   7      4.08    100.31    511.65
   8      3.41    100.98    410.68
   9      2.74    101.65    309.03
  10      2.06    102.33    206.70
  11      1.38    103.01    103.69
  12      0.69    103.69      0.00
```

> **NOTE:** You might have noticed in the output that for some months, such as months 5 and 6, the interest amount plus the principal amount does not add up to the monthly payment amount. Also, for some months, the previous balance minus the principal paid does not exactly equal the new balance. These problems are due to *round-off error*, which is caused by a disparity between the precision of a value the computer stores internally and the precision of the value it displays. Do not worry about this for now. You will learn later how to deal with this.

Testing the Program

Testing the program has been left as an exercise for you to do. Use what you learned in Section 5.13 about developing good test cases to develop a set of cases you can use to test Program 5-25. The program runs correctly except for one special case, where it fails. The program design failed to realize the need to handle this special case differently than it handles other data. Try to come up with input data for a test case that reveals the error. Then, once you have identified the problem, see if you can revise the program to fix it. A corrected version of Program 5-25 can be found in the `pr5-25B.cpp` file of the Chapter 5 programs folder on the book's companion website.

Lightening Lanes Case Study

The following additional case study, which contain applications of material introduced in Chapter 5, can be found on the book's companion website.

On Tuesday afternoons, Lightening Lanes Bowling Alley runs a special class to teach children to bowl. Each lane has an instructor who works with a team of four student bowlers and instructs them as they bowl three lines (i.e., games). The management of Lightening Lanes has asked you to develop a program that will report each student's three-game average score and compare it to the average score they bowled the previous week. In this way, the students can see how much they are improving. The program will use looping structures and data validation techniques learned in Chapter 5.

5.15 Tying It All Together: *What a Colorful World*

In Chapter 5's Tying It All Together section we'll take a look at how to use the looping constructs you learned about in this chapter, along with colorful output characters, to create interesting screen displays.

All the C++ programs you have seen so far produce output that is white on a black background. This is because they use the standard C++ `iostream` libraries, which can only display output in these two colors. However, C++ compilers provide other libraries you can use to call operating system functions that can display output in many colors. Because these libraries are tailored to specific operating systems, programs that use them will only run on the system they were written for.

Here is how to use Microsoft Windows functions to create programs with colorful output that can run on Windows 2000 and newer operating systems.

The first thing you need to do is include the following file in your program so you will be able to use the functions you need:

```
#include <windows.h>
```

Next, because programs can actually access more than one screen device at a time, you will need to indicate which screen you want the colors you set to appear on. The `cout` object writes to the standard output screen. You can set colors on this screen by providing a handle to it. A *handle* is an object of type `HANDLE`, which is defined by Microsoft Windows. Here is how to obtain a handle to the standard output screen:

```
HANDLE screen = GetStdHandle(STD_OUTPUT_HANDLE);
```

`GetStdHandle` is a Windows-specific library function and `STD_OUTPUT_HANDLE` is a Windows-specific constant.

The easiest way to set a color is to call the `SetConsoleTextAttribute` function and pass it the name of the handle to the output screen and a number that tells what color you want the output text to appear in. Table 5-5 shows the number that corresponds to each color.

Table 5-5 Windows Text Colors

Number	Text Color	Number	Text Color
0	Black	8	"Bright" Black
1	Blue	9	Bright Blue
2	Green	10	Bright Green
3	Cyan	11	Bright Cyan
4	Red	12	Bright Red
5	Purple	13	Bright Purple
6	Yellow	14	Bright Yellow
7	White	15	Bright White

Once you set a color it will remain in effect for all output text until you set a new one.

The following code segment shows how you can write the string "red" in red, "white" in white, "blue" in blue, and "bright yellow" in bright yellow.

```
SetConsoleTextAttribute(screen, 4);
cout << "Red" << endl;
SetConsoleTextAttribute(screen, 7);
cout << "White" << endl;
SetConsoleTextAttribute(screen, 1);
cout << "Blue" << endl;
SetConsoleTextAttribute(screen, 14);
cout << "Bright Yellow" << endl;
```

Here are two programs that use color. Neither one requires any input. Try running them to see their output displayed in color. Program 5-26 uses a loop to display `"Hello World"` on a black background in each of the 16 colors shown in Table 5-5.

Program 5-26

```
// This program demonstrates Windows functions to print colored
// text. It displays " Hello World!" in 16 different colors.
#include <iostream>
#include <windows.h>     // Needed to display colors and call Sleep
using namespace std;

int main()
{
   // Create a handle to the computer screen.
   HANDLE screen = GetStdHandle(STD_OUTPUT_HANDLE);

   // Write 16 lines in 16 different colors.
   for (int color = 0; color < 16; color++)
   {
      SetConsoleTextAttribute (screen, color);
      cout << " Hello World!" << endl;
      Sleep(400);   // Pause between lines to watch them appear
   }
   // Restore the normal text color)
    SetConsoleTextAttribute(screen, 7);
    return 0;
}
```

Notice in Program 5-26 that each `cout` statement ended with an `endl`. This is needed to "flush" the buffer to ensure that all the output has been written to the screen before you change to another color. A `'\n'` will not work because it causes output to go to the next line, but does not flush the output buffer.

Program 5-27 provides another example of creating colorful output. It uses a loop to print the ABCs in color, alternating between bright green, red, and yellow.

Program 5-27

```
// This program writes the ABCs in green, red, and yellow.
#include <iostream>
#include <windows.h>     // Needed to display colors and call sleep
using namespace std;

int main()
{
   // Bright Green = 10   Bright Red = 12   Bright Yellow = 14

   // Get the handle to standard output device (the console)
   HANDLE screen = GetStdHandle(STD_OUTPUT_HANDLE);

```

(program continues)

Program 5-27 *(continued)*

```
    // Write the ABCs using 3 colors
    int color = 10;      // Staring color = green
    for (char letter = 'A'; letter <= 'Z'; letter++)
    {
       SetConsoleTextAttribute (screen, color); // Set the color
       cout << letter << "  " << endl;          // Print the letter

       color +=2;                               // Choose next color
       if (color > 14)
          color = 10;

       Sleep(280);  // Pause between characters to watch them appear
    }
    // Restore normal text attribute (i.e. white)
    SetConsoleTextAttribute(screen, 7);
    return 0;
}
```

There are three important things to remember when working with colors:

- Include the `<windows.h>` header file.
- Follow each `cout` statement with an `endl`.
- Always set the text color back to normal (i.e., white) before quitting.

Review Questions and Exercises

Fill-in-the-Blank

1. To __________ a value means to increase it by one.
2. To __________ a value means to decrease it by one.
3. When the increment or decrement operator is placed before the operand (or to the operand's left), the operator is being used in __________ mode.
4. When the increment or decrement operator is placed after the operand (or to the operand's right), the operator is being used in __________ mode.
5. The statement or block that is repeated is known as the __________ of the loop.
6. Each repetition of a loop is known as a(n) __________.
7. A loop that evaluates its test expression before each repetition is a(n) __________ loop.
8. A loop that evaluates its test expression after each repetition is a(n) __________ loop.
9. A loop that does not have a way of stopping is a(n) __________ loop.
10. A(n)__________ is a variable that "counts" the number of times a loop repeats.

11. A(n) __________ is a sum of numbers that accumulates with each iteration of a loop.
12. A(n) __________ is a variable that is initialized to some starting value, usually zero, and then has numbers added to it in each iteration of a loop.
13. A(n) __________ is a special value that marks the end of a series of values.
14. The __________ loop is ideal for situations that require a counter.
15. The __________ loop always iterates at least once.
16. The __________ and __________ loops will not iterate at all if their test expressions are false to start with.
17. Inside the `for` loop's parentheses, the first expression is the __________ , the second expression is the __________ , and the third expression is the __________.
18. A loop that is inside another is called a(n) __________ loop.
19. The __________ statement causes a loop to terminate immediately.
20. The __________ statement causes a loop to skip the remaining statements in the current iteration.
21. What header file do you need to include in a program that performs file operations?
22. What data type do you use when you want to create a file stream object that can write data to a file?
23. What happens if you open an output file and the file already exists?
24. What data type do you use when you want to create a file stream object that can read data from a file?
25. What is a file's read position? Where is the read position when a file is first opened for reading?
26. Why should a program do when it is finished using a file?

Algorithm Workbench

27. Write code that lets the user enter a number. The number should be multiplied by 2 and printed until the number exceeds 50. Use a `while` loop.
28. Write a `do-while` loop that asks the user to enter two numbers. The numbers should be added and the sum displayed. The user should be asked if he or she wishes to perform the operation again. If so, the loop should repeat; otherwise it should terminate.
29. Write a `for` loop that displays the following set of numbers:

```
0, 10, 20, 30, 40, 50 . . . 1000
```

30. Write a loop that asks the user to enter a number. The loop should iterate 10 times and keep a running total of the numbers entered.
31. Write a nested loop that displays the following ouput:

```
*****
*****
*****
```

32. Write a nested loop that displays 10 rows of '#' characters. There should be 15 '#' characters in each row.

33. Rewrite the following code, converting the `while` loop to a `do-while` loop:

```
char doAgain = 'y';
int sum = 0;

cout << "This code will increment sum 1 or more times.\n";
while ((doAgain == 'y') || (doAgain == 'Y'))
{  sum++;
   cout << "Sum has been incremented. Increment it again(y/n)? ";
   cin  >> doAgain;
}
cout << "Sum was incremented " << sum << " times.\n";
```

34. Rewrite the following code, replacing the `do-while` loop with a `while` loop. When you do this you will no longer need an `if` statement.

```
int number;
cout << "Enter an even number: ";
do
{  cin >> number;
   if (number % 2 != 0)
      cout << "Number must be even. Reenter number: ";
} while (number % 2 != 0);
```

35. Convert the following `while` loop to a `for` loop:

```
int count = 0;
while (count < 50)
{
   cout << "count is " << count << endl;
   count++;
}
```

36. Convert the following `for` loop to a `while` loop:

```
for (int x = 50; x > 0; x--)
{
   cout << x << " seconds to go.\n";
}
```

37. Write a code segment that creates an `ofstream` object named `outfile`, opens a file named `numbers.txt`, and associates it with `outfile`. The code should then use a loop to write the numbers 1 through 100 to the file before closing it.

38. Write a code segment that creates an `ifstream` object named `infile`, opens the `numbers.txt` file created by the code in the previous question, and associates it with `infile`. The code should then use a loop to read and display all of the numbers in the file before closing it.

Predict the Output

What will each of the following program segments display?

39.
```
int x = 1;
while (x < 10);
    x++;
    cout << x;
```

40.
```
int x = 1;
while (x < 10)
    x++;
    cout << x;
```

41.
```
for (int count = 1; count <= 10; count++)
{  cout << ++count << "  ";    // This is a bad thing to do!
}
```

42.
```
for (int row = 1; row <= 3; row++)
{  cout << "\n$";
   for (int digit = 1; digit <= 4; digit++)
      cout << '9';
}
```

Find the Errors

43. Each of the program segments in this section has errors. Find as many as you can.

A)
```
int num1 = 0, num2 = 10, result;

num1++;
result = ++(num1 + num2);
cout << num1 << " " << num2 << " " << result;
```

B)
```
// This code should add two user-entered numbers.
int num1, num2;
char again;

while ((again == 'y') || (again == 'Y'))
   cout << "Enter two numbers: ";
   cin  >> num1 >> num2;
   cout << "Their sum is << (num1 + num2) << endl;
   cout << "Do you want to do this again? ";
   cin  >> again;
```

44. A)
```
// This code should use a loop to raise a number to a power.
int num, bigNum, power, count;

cout << "Enter an integer: ";
cin  >> num;
cout << "What power do you want it raised to? ";
cin  >> power;
bigNum = num;

while (count++ < power);
   bigNum *= num;

cout << "The result is << bigNum << endl;
```

B)
```
// This code should average a set of numbers.
int numCount, total;
double average;

cout << "How many numbers do you want to average? ";
cin  >> numCount;
for (int count = 0; count < numCount; count++)
{
   int num;
   cout << "Enter a number: ";
   cin  >> num;
   total += num;
   count++;
}
average = total / numCount;
cout << "The average is << average << endl;
```

45. A)
```
// This code should display the sum of two numbers.
int choice, num1, num2;

do
{
   cout << "Enter a number: ";
   cin  >> num1;
   cout << "Enter another number: ";
   cin  >> num2;
   cout << "Their sum is " << (num1 + num2) << endl;
   cout << "Do you want to do this again?\n";
   cout << "1 = yes, 0 = no\n";
   cin  >> choice;
} while (choice = 1)
```

B)
```
// This code should display the sum of the numbers 1 - 100.
int count = 1, total;

while (count <= 100)
   total += count;
   cout << "The sum of the numbers 1 - 100 is ";
   cout << total << endl;
```

Soft Skills

Programmers not only need to be able to analyze what is wrong with a faulty algorithm, but also need to be able to explain the problem to others.

46. Write a clear problem description for a simple program and create a pseudocode solution for it. The pseudocode should incorporate the logic, including all the calculations, needed in the program, but should purposely contain a subtle logic error. Then pair up with another student in the class who has done the same thing and swap your work. Each of you should trace the logic to find the error in the pseudocode you are given, then clearly explain to your partner what the problem is, why the "code" will not work as written, and what should be done to correct it.

    As an alternative, your instructor may wish to provide you with a problem description and an incorrect pseudocode solution. Again, the goal is not only for you to find the error, but also to clearly explain what the problem is, why the "code" will not work as written, and what should be done to correct it.

Programming Challenges

1. Characters for the ASCII Codes

Write a program that uses a loop to display the characters for each ASCII code 32 through 127. Display 16 characters on each line with one space between characters.

2. Sum of Numbers

Write a program that asks the user for a positive integer value and that uses a loop to validate the input. The program should then use a second loop to compute the sum of all the integers from 1 up to the number entered. For example, if the user enters 50, the loop will find the sum of 1, 2, 3, 4, ... 50.

3. Distance Traveled

The distance a vehicle travels can be calculated as follows:

```
distance = speed * time
```

For example, if a train travels 40 miles per hour for 3 hours, the distance traveled is 120 miles.

Write a program that asks the user for the speed of a vehicle (in miles per hour) and how many hours it has traveled. It should then use a loop to display the total distance traveled at the end of each hour of that time period. Here is an example of the output:

```
What is the speed of the vehicle in mph? 40
How many hours has it traveled? 3
Hour      Miles Traveled
--------------------------------
   1           40
   2           80
   3          120
```

4. Celsius to Fahrenheit Table

In one of the Chapter 3 Programming Challenges you were asked to write a program that converts a Celsius temperature to Fahrenheit. Modify that program so it uses a loop to display a table of the Celsius temperatures from 0 to 20 and their Fahrenheit equivalents.

$$F = 9/5C + 32$$

5. Speed Conversion Chart

Write a program that displays a table of speeds in kilometers per hour with their values converted to miles per hour. The table should display the speeds from 40 kilometers per hour through 120 kilometers per hour, in increments of 5 kilometers per hour. (In other words, it should display 40 kph, 45 kph, 50 kph and so forth, up through 120 kph.)

$$MPH = KPH * 0.6214$$

Solving the Ocean Levels Problem

6. Ocean Levels

Assuming the level of the Earth's oceans continues rising at about 3.1 millimeters per year, write a program that displays a table showing the total number of millimeters the oceans will have risen each year for the next 25 years.

7. Pennies for Pay

Write a program that calculates how much a person earns in a month if the salary is one penny the first day, two pennies the second day, four pennies the third day, and so on with the daily pay doubling each day the employee works. The program should ask the user for the number of days the employee worked during the month, validate that it is between 1 and 31, and then display a table showing how much the salary was for each day worked, as well as the total pay earned for the month. The output should be displayed in dollars with two decimal points, not in pennies.

8. Calories Burned

Running on a particular treadmill you burn 3.9 calories per minute. Write a program that uses a loop to display the number of calories burned after 10, 15, 20, 25, and 30 minutes.

9. Membership Fees Increase

A country club, which currently charges $2500 per year for membership, has announced it will increase its membership fee by 4% each year for the next six years. Write a program that uses a loop to display the projected rates for the next six years.

10. Random Number Guessing Game

Write a program that generates a random number between 1 and 100 and asks the user to guess what the number is. If the user's guess is higher than the random number, the program should display "Too high. Try again." If the user's guess is lower than the random number, the program should display "Too low. Try again." The program should use a loop that repeats until the user correctly guesses the random number. Then the program should display "Congratulations. You figured out my number."

11. Random Number Guessing Game Enhancement

Enhance the program that you wrote for Programming Challenge 10 so it keeps a count of the number of guesses the user makes. When the user correctly guesses the random number, the program should display the number of guesses along with the message of congratulations.

12. The Greatest and Least of These

Write a program with a loop that lets the user enter a series of integers, followed by −99 to signal the end of the series. After all the numbers have been entered, the program should display the largest and smallest numbers entered.

13. Student Line Up

A teacher has asked all her students to line up single file according to their first name. For example, in one class Amy will be at the front of the line and Yolanda will be at the end. Write a program that prompts the user to enter a number between 1 and 25 for the number of students in the class, then loops to read in that many names. Once all the names have been read in it reports which student would be at the front of the line and which one would be at the end of the line. You may assume that no two students have the same name.

14. Rate of Inflation

The annual rate of inflation is the rate at which money loses its value. For example, if the annual rate of inflation is 3.0%, then in one year it will cost $1030 to buy the goods that could have been purchased for $1000 today. Put another way, a year from now $1000 will only buy 1/1.03 * $1000, or $970.87, worth of goods. Two years from now $1000 will only buy only 1/1.03 of $970.87, or $942.59 worth of goods. Write a program that allows the user to enter an annual rate of inflation between 1% and 15%, and which then reports how much $1000 today will be worth each year for the next 10 years.

15. Population

Write a program that will predict the size of a population of organisms. The program should ask the user for the starting number of organisms, their average daily population increase (as a percentage of current population), and the number of days they will multiply. A loop should display the size of the population for each day.

> *Input Validation: The program should not accept a number less than two for the starting size of the population, a negative number for average daily population increase, or a number less than one for the number of days they will multiply.*

16. Math Tutor Version 3

This program started in Chapter 3 and was modified in Chapter 4. Starting with the version described in Chapter 4, modify the program again so it displays a menu allowing the user to select an addition, subtraction, or multiplication problem. The final selection on the menu should let the user quit the program. After the user has finished the math problem, the program should display the menu again. This process must repeat until the user chooses to quit the program. If the user selects an item not on the menu, the program should print an error message and then display the menu again.

17. Hotel Suites Occupancy

Write a program that calculates the occupancy rate of the 120 suites (20 per floor) located on the top 6 floors of a 15-story luxury hotel. These are floors 10–12 and 14–16 because, like many hotels, there is no 13th floor. Solve the problem by using a *single* loop that loops once for each floor between 10 and 16 and, on each iteration, asks the user to input the number of suites occupied on that floor. Use a nested loop loop to validate that the value entered is between 0 and 20. After all the iterations, the program should display how many suites the hotel has, how many of them are occupied, and what percentage of them are occupied.

18. Rectangle Display

Write a program that asks the user for two positive integers between 2 and 10 to use for the length and width of a rectangle. If the numbers are different, the larger of the two numbers should be used for the length and the smaller for the width. The program should then display a rectangle of this size on the screen using the character 'X'. For example, if the user enters either 2 5 or 5 2, the program should display the following:

```
XXXXX
XXXXX
```

19. Diamond Display

Write a program that uses nested loops to display the diamond pattern shown below.

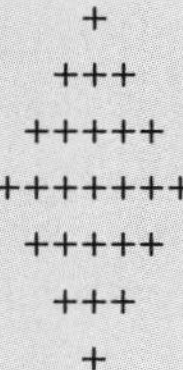

20. Triangle Display

Write a program that uses nested loops to display the triangle pattern shown below.

```
+
+++
+++++
+++++++
+++++
+++
+
```

21. Arrowhead Display

Write a program that uses nested loops to display the arrowhead pattern shown below.

```
      +
      +++
      +++++
+++++++++++++
      +++++
      +++
      +
```

22. Sales Bar Chart

Write a program that asks the user to enter today's sales rounded to the nearest $100 for each of three stores. The program should then display a bar graph comparing each store's sales. Create each bar in the graph by displaying a row of asterisks. Each asterisk should represent $100 of sales.

Here is an example of the program's output. User input is shown in bold.

```
Enter today's sales for store 1: 1000[Enter]
Enter today's sales for store 2: 1200[Enter]
Enter today's sales for store 3: 900[Enter]

    DAILY SALES
  (each * = $100)
Store 1: **********
Store 2: ************
Store 3: *********
```

23. Savings Account Balance

Write a program that calculates the balance of a savings account at the end of a three-month period. It should ask the user for the starting balance and the annual interest rate. A loop should then iterate once for every month in the period, performing the following steps:

A) Ask the user for the total amount deposited into the account during that month and add it to the balance. Do not accept negative numbers.

B) Ask the user for the total amount withdrawn from the account during that month and subtract it from the balance. Do not accept negative numbers or numbers greater than the balance after the deposits for the month have been added in.

C) Calculate the interest for that month. The monthly interest rate is the annual interest rate divided by 12. Multiply the monthly interest rate by the average of that month's starting and ending balance to get the interest amount for the month. This amount should be added to the balance.

After the last iteration, the program should display a report that includes the following information:

- starting balance at the beginning of the three-month period
- total deposits made during the three months
- total withdrawals made during the three months
- total interest posted to the account during the three months
- final balance

24. Using Files—Total and Average Rainfall

Write a program that reads in from a file a starting month name, an ending month name, and then the monthly rainfall for each month during that period. As it does this, it should sum the rainfall amounts and then report the total rainfall and average rainfall for the period. For example, the output might look like this:

During the months of March–June the total rainfall was 7.32 inches and the average monthly rainfall was 1.83 inches.

Data for the program can be found in the `Rainfall.txt` file.

Hint: After reading in the month names, you will need to read in rain amounts until the EOF is reached, and count how many pieces of rain data you read in.

25. Using Files—Population Bar Chart

Write a program that produces a bar chart showing the population growth of Prairieville, a small town in the Midwest, at 20 year intervals during the past 100 years. The program should read in the population figures (rounded to the nearest 1000 people) for 1910, 1930, 1950, 1970, 1990, and 2010 from a file. For each year it should display the date and a bar consisting of one asterisk for each 1000 people. The data can be found in the `People.txt` file.

Here is an example of how the chart might begin:

```
PRAIRIEVILLE POPULATION GROWTH
(each * represents 1000 people)

1910  **
1930  ****
1950  *****
```

26. Using Files—Student Line Up

Modify the Student Line Up program described in Programming Challenge 13 so that it gets the names from a data file. Names should be read in until there is no more data to read. Data to test your program can be found in the `LineUp.txt` file.

27. Using Files—Savings Account Balance Modification

Modify the Savings Account Balance program described in Programming Challenge 23 so that it writes the report to a file. After the program runs, print the file to hand in to your instructor.

CHAPTER

6 Functions

TOPICS

6.1 Modular Programming

CONCEPT: A program may be broken up into a set of manageable functions, or modules. This is called modular programming.

A function is a collection of statements that performs a specific task. So far you have used functions in two ways: 1) you have created a function called `main` in every program you've written, and 2) you have called library functions such as `pow` and `sqrt`. In this chapter you will learn how to create your own functions that can be used like library functions.

Functions are commonly used to break a problem down into small manageable pieces, or modules. Instead of writing one long function that contains all the statements necessary to solve a problem, several smaller functions can be written, with each one solving a specific part of the problem. These small functions can then be executed in the desired order to solve the problem. This approach is sometimes called *divide and conquer* because a large problem is divided into several smaller problems that are more easily solved. Figure 6-1 illustrates this idea by comparing two programs, one that uses a single module containing all of the statements necessary to solve a problem, and another that divides a problem into a set of smaller problems, each handled by a separate function.

Figure 6-1

This program has one long, complex function containing all of the statements necessary to solve a problem.
In this program the problem has been divided into smaller problems, each handled by a separate function.
main function
function 2
function 3

```
int main()
{
   statement;
   statement;
   statement;
   statement;
   statement;
   statement;
   statement;
   statement;
   statement;
   statement;
   statement;
   statement;
   statement;
   statement;
   statement;
   statement;
   statement;
   statement;
}
```

```
int main()
{
   statement;
   statement;
   statement;
}

void function2()
{
   statement;
   statement;
   statement;
}

void function3()
{
   statement;
   statement;
   statement;
}
```

Another reason to write functions is that they simplify programs. If a specific task is performed in several places in a program, a function can be written once to perform that task, and then be executed anytime it is needed. This benefit of using functions is known as *code reuse* because you are writing the code to perform a task once and then reusing it each time you need to perform the task.

6.2 Defining and Calling Functions

CONCEPT: A function call is a statement that causes a function to execute. A function definition contains the statements that make up the function.

When creating a function, you must write its *definition*. All function definitions have the following parts:

VideoNote
Defining and Calling Functions

Name — Every function must have a name. In general, the same rules that apply to variable names also apply to function names.

Parameter list — The program module that calls a function can send data to it. The parameter list is the list of variables that hold the values being passed to the function. If no values are being passed to the function, its parameter list is *empty*.

Body — The body of a function is the set of statements that carry out the task the function is performing. These statements are enclosed in a set of braces.

Return type A function can send a value back to the program module that called it. The return type is the data type of the value being sent back.

Figure 6-2 shows the definition of a simple function with the various parts labeled. Notice that the function's return type is actually listed first.

Figure 6-2

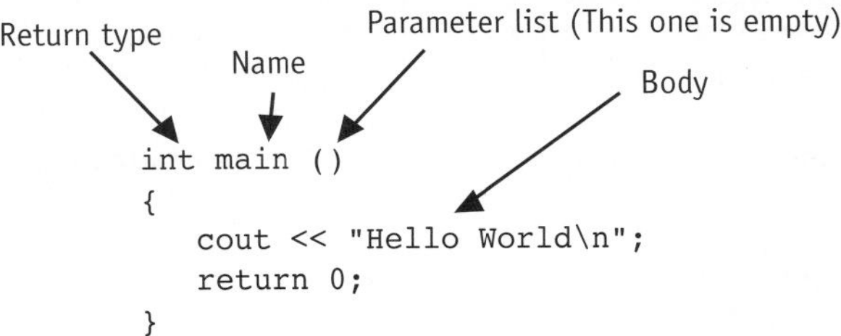

The line in the definition that reads `int main ()` is called the *function header.*

Void Functions

You already know that a function can return a value. The `main` function in all of the programs you have seen in this book is declared to return an `int` value to the operating system. The `return 0;` statement causes the value 0 to be returned when the `main` function finishes executing.

It isn't necessary for all functions to return a value, however. Some functions simply perform one or more statements and then return. In C++ these are called *void functions.* The `displayMessage` function shown here is an example:

```
void displayMessage()
{
   cout << "Hello from the function displayMessage.\n";
}
```

The function's name is `displayMessage`. This name is descriptive, as function names should be. It gives an indication of what the function does. It displays a message. Notice the function's return type is `void`. This means the function does not send back a value when it has finished executing and returns to the part of the program that invoked it. Because no value is being sent back, no `return` statement is required. When the statements in the function have finished executing and the right brace that ends the function is encountered, the program automatically returns.

Calling a Function

A function is executed when it is *called.* Function `main` is called automatically when a program starts, but all other functions must be executed by *function call* statements. When a function is called, the program branches to that function and executes the statements in its body. Let's look at Program 6-1, which contains two functions: `main` and `displayMessage`.

Program 6-1

```
 1 // This program has two functions: main and displayMessage.
 2 #include <iostream>
 3 using namespace std;
 4
 5 /*************************************
 6  *          displayMessage           *
 7  *  This function displays a greeting. *
 8  *************************************/
 9 void displayMessage()
10 {
11    cout << "Hello from the function displayMessage.\n";
12 }
13
14 /*************************************
15  *               main                *
16  *************************************/
17 int main()
18 {
19    cout << "Hello from main.\n";
20    displayMessage();        // Call displayMessage
21    cout << "Back in function main again.\n";
22    return 0;
23 }
```

Program Output

```
Hello from main.
Hello from the function displayMessage.
Back in function main again.
```

The function `displayMessage` is called by the following statement in line 20:

```
displayMessage();
```

This statement is the function call. It is simply the name of the function followed by a set of parentheses and a semicolon. Let's compare this with the function header:

```
Function Header ——————→ void displayMessage()
Function Call ——————→ displayMessage();
```

The function header is part of the function definition. It declares the function's return type, name, and parameter list. It must *not* be terminated with a semicolon because the definition of the function's body follows it.

The function call is a statement that executes the function, so it *is* terminated with a semicolon like all other C++ statements. Notice that the function call does not list the return type and, if the program is not passing data into the function, the parentheses are left empty.

NOTE: Later in this chapter you will see how data can be passed into a function by being listed inside the parentheses.

Even though the program starts executing at `main`, the function `displayMessage` is defined first. This is because before a function can be called, the compiler must know certain things about it. It must know the function's name, its return type, how many parameter variables it has, and what the data type of each of these variables is. One way to ensure the compiler will know this information is to place the function definition before all calls to that function. (Later you will see an alternative and preferred method of accomplishing this.)

> **NOTE:** You should always document your functions by writing comments that describe what they do. These comments should appear just before the function definition.

Notice how Program 6-1 flows. It starts, of course, in function `main`. When the call to `displayMessage` is encountered, the program branches to that function and performs its statements. Once `displayMessage` has finished executing, the program branches back to function `main` and resumes with the line that follows the function call. This is illustrated in Figure 6-3.

Figure 6-3

```
void displayMessage()
{
   cout << "Hello from the function displayMessage.\n";
}
```

1 2

```
int main()
{
   cout << "Hello from main.\n";
   displayMessage();
   cout << "Back in function main again.\n";
   return 0;
}
```

Function call statements may be used in control structures such as loops, `if` statements, and `switch` statements. Program 6-2 places the `displayMessage` function call inside a loop.

Program 6-2

```
// The function displayMessage is repeatedly called from within a loop.
#include <iostream>
using namespace std;

/***************************************
 *           displayMessage            *
 *  This function displays a greeting. *
 ***************************************/
void displayMessage()
{
   cout << "Hello from the function displayMessage.\n";
}

```

(program continues)

Program 6-2 *(continued)*

```
/*************************************
 *                main               *
 *************************************/
int main()
{
   cout << "Hello from main.\n";

   for (int count = 0; count < 3; count++)
       displayMessage();   // Call displayMessage

   cout << "Back in function main again.\n";
   return 0;
}
```

Program Output

```
Hello from main.
Hello from the function displayMessage.
Hello from the function displayMessage.
Hello from the function displayMessage.
Back in function main again.
```

It is possible to have many functions and function calls in a program. Program 6-3 has three functions: `main`, `first`, and `second`.

Program 6-3

```
// This program has three functions: main, first, and second.
#include <iostream>
using namespace std;

/*************************************
 *                first              *
 * This function displays a message. *
 *************************************/
void first()
{
   cout << "I am now inside the function first.\n";
}

/*************************************
 *                second             *
 * This function displays a message. *
 *************************************/
void second()
{
   cout << "I am now inside the function second.\n";
}

```

(program continues)

Program 6-3 *(continued)*

```
23 /*************************************
24  *                 main              *
25  *************************************/
26 int main()
27 {
28    cout << "I am starting in function main.\n";
29    first();     // Call function first
30    second();    // Call function second
31    cout << "Back in function main again.\n";
32    return 0;
33 }
```

Program Output

```
I am starting in function main.
I am now inside the function first.
I am now inside the function second.
Back in function main again.
```

In lines 29 and 30 of Program 6-3, function `main` contains a call to `first` and a call to `second`:

```
first();
second();
```

Each call statement causes the program to branch to a function and then back to `main` when the function is finished. Figure 6-4 illustrates the paths taken by the program.

Figure 6-4

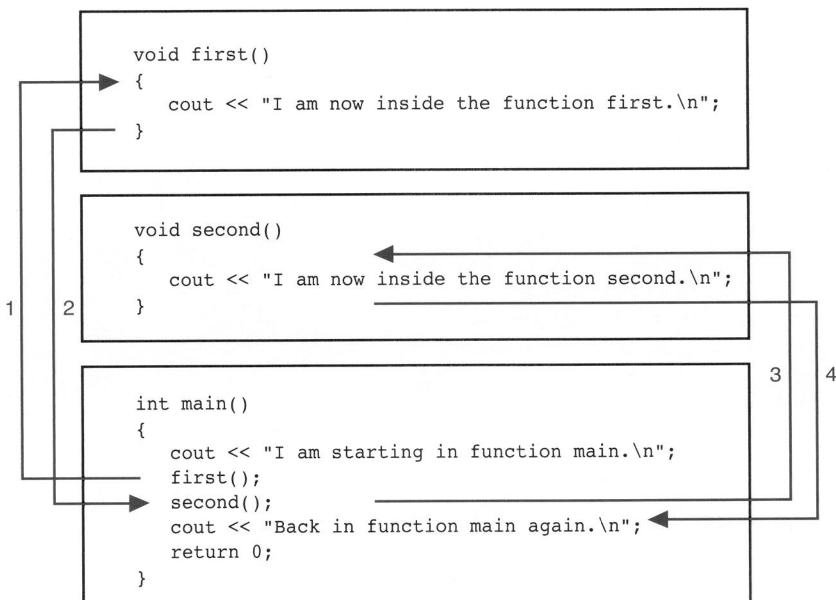

Functions may also be called in a hierarchical, or layered, fashion. This is demonstrated by Program 6-4, which has three functions: `main`, `deep`, and `deeper`.

Program 6-4

```
// This program has three functions: main, deep, and deeper.
#include <iostream>
using namespace std;

/*************************************
 *                deeper             *
 * This function displays a message. *
 *************************************/
void deeper()
{
   cout << "I am now inside the function deeper.\n";
}

/*************************************
 *                 deep              *
 * This function displays a message. *
 *************************************/
void deep()
{
   cout << "I am now inside the function deep.\n";
   deeper();  // Call function deeper
   cout << "Now I am back in deep.\n";
}

/*************************************
 *                 main              *
 *************************************/
int main()
{
   cout << "I am starting in function main.\n";
   deep();    // Call function deep
   cout << "Back in function main again.\n";
   return 0;
}
```

Program Output

```
I am starting in function main.
I am now inside the function deep.
I am now inside the function deeper.
Now I am back in deep.
Back in function main again.
```

In Program 6-4, function `main` only calls the function `deep`. In turn, `deep` calls `deeper`. The paths taken by this program are shown in Figure 6-5.

Figure 6-5

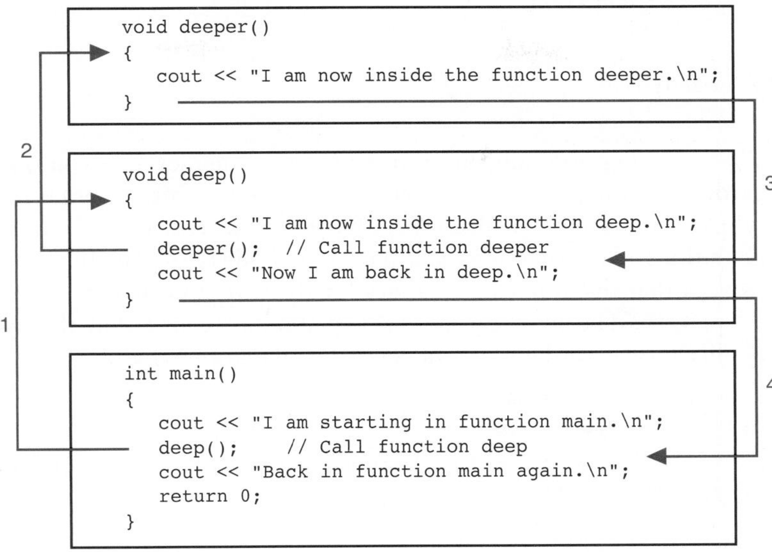

Checkpoint

6.1 Is the following a function header or a function call?

```
calcTotal();
```

6.2 Is the following a function header or a function call?

```
void showResults()
```

6.3 What will the output of the following program be if the user enters 10?

```
#include <iostream>
using namespace std;

void func1()
{
   cout << "Able was I\n";
}

void func2()
{
   cout << "I saw Elba\n";
}

int main()
{
   int input;
   cout << "Enter a number: ";
   cin  >> input;
   if (input < 10)
   {
      func1();
      func2();
   }
```

```
    else
    {
       func2();
       func1();
    }
    return 0;
}
```

6.4 The following program skeleton determines whether a person qualifies for a credit card. To qualify, the person must have worked on his or her current job for at least two years and make at least $17,000 per year. Finish the program by writing the definitions of the functions `qualify` and `noQualify`. The function `qualify` should explain that the applicant qualifies for the card and that the annual interest rate is 12 percent. The function `noQualify` should explain that the applicant does not qualify for the card and give a general explanation why.

```
#include <iostream>
using namespace std;

// You must write definitions for the two functions qualify
// and noQualify.

int main()
{
   double salary;
   int years;


   cout << "This program will determine if you qualify\n";
   cout << "for our credit card.\n";
   cout << "What is your annual salary? ";
   cin  >> salary;
   cout << "How many years have you worked at your ";
   cout << "current job? ";
   cin  >> years;

   if (salary >= 17000.0 && years >= 2)
       qualify();
   else
       noQualify();
   return 0;
}
```

6.3 Function Prototypes

CONCEPT: A function prototype eliminates the need to place a function definition before all calls to the function.

Before the compiler encounters a call to a particular function, it must already know certain things about the function. In particular, it must know the number of parameters the function uses, the type of each parameter, and the return type of the function. Parameters allow information to be sent to a function. Certain return types allow information to be returned from a function. You will learn more about parameters and return types in later sections of this chapter. For now, the functions we will use will have no parameters and, except for `main`, will have a return type of `void`.

One way of ensuring that the compiler has this required information is to place the function definition before all calls to that function. This was the approach taken in Programs 6-1 through 6-4. Another method is to declare the function with a *function prototype*. Here is a prototype for the `displayMessage` function in Program 6-1:

```
void displayMessage();
```

This prototype looks similar to the function header, except there is a semicolon at the end. The statement tells the compiler that the function `displayMessage` uses no parameters and has a `void` return type, meaning it doesn't return a value.

NOTE: Function prototypes are also known as *function declarations*.

WARNING! You must either place the function definition or the function prototype ahead of all calls to the function. Otherwise the program will not compile.

Function prototypes are usually placed near the top of a program so the compiler will "see" them before any function calls. Program 6-5 is a modification of Program 6-3. The definitions of the functions `first` and `second` have been placed after `main`, and their function prototypes have been placed above `main`, directly after the `using namespace std` statement.

Program 6-5

```
// This program has three functions: main, first, and second.
// It uses function prototypes.
#include <iostream>
using namespace std;

// Function prototypes
void first();
void second();

int main()
{
   cout << "I am starting in function main.\n";
   first();    // Call function first
   second();   // Call function second
   cout << "Back in function main again.\n";
   return 0;
}

/*************************************
 *               first               *
 * This function displays a message. *
 *************************************/
void first()
{
   cout << "I am now inside the function first.\n";
}
```

(program continues)

Program 6-5 *(continued)*

```
27
28 /**************************************
29  *                 second              *
30  * This function displays a message.   *
31  **************************************/
32 void second()
33 {
34    cout << "I am now inside the function second.\n";
35 }
```

Program Output is the same as the output of Program 6-3.

When the compiler is reading Program 6-5, it encounters the calls to the functions `first` and `second` in lines 13 and 14 before it has read the definition of those functions. Because of the function prototypes, however, the compiler already knows the return type and parameter information of `first` and `second`. There should be a prototype for each function in a program except `main`. A prototype is never needed for `main` because it is the starting point of the program.

NOTE: Although some programmers make `main` the last function in the program, many prefer it to be first because it is the program's starting point.

6.4 Sending Data into a Function

CONCEPT: When a function is called, the program may send values into the function.

Values that are sent into a function are called *arguments*. You're already familiar with how to use arguments in a function call. In the following statement the function `pow` is being called with two arguments, 2.0 and 4.0 passed to it:

```
result = pow(2.0, 4.0);
```

Using Function Arguments

A *parameter* is a special variable that holds a value being passed as an argument into a function. By using parameters, you can design your own functions that accept data this way. Here is the definition of a function that has a parameter. The parameter is `num`.

```
void displayValue(int num)
{
   cout << "The value is " << num << endl;
}
```

Notice that the parameter variable is defined inside the parentheses `(int num)`. Because it is declared to be an integer, the function `displayValue` can accept an integer value as an argument. Program 6-6 is a complete program that uses this function.

Program 6-6

```
1 // This program demonstrates a function with a parameter.
2 #include <iostream>
3 using namespace std;
4
5 // Function prototype
6 void displayValue(int num);
7
8 int main()
9 {
10    cout << "I am passing 5 to displayValue.\n";
11    displayValue(5);  // Call displayValue with argument 5
12    cout << "Now I am back in main.\n";
13    return 0;
14 }
15
16 /*********************************************
17  *                displayValue               *
18  *  This function uses an integer parameter *
19  *  whose value is displayed.               *
20  *********************************************/
21 void displayValue(int num)
22 {
23    cout << "The value is " << num << endl;
24 }
```

Program Output

```
I am passing 5 to displayValue.
The value is 5
Now I am back in main.
```

Notice the function prototype for `displayValue` in line 6:

```
void displayValue(int num);     // Function prototype
```

It lists both the data type and the name of the function's parameter variable. However, it is not actually necessary to list the name of the parameter variable inside the parentheses. Only the data type of the variable is required. The function prototype could have been written like this:

```
void displayValue(int);         // Function prototype
```

Because some instructors prefer that you list only the data type for each parameter in a function prototype, while others prefer that you list both the data type and name, we use both versions throughout this book. Your instructor will tell you which version to use.

NOTE: Your instructor will also tell you what to call the function parameters. In this text, the values that are passed into a function are called arguments, and the variables that receive those values are called parameters. However, there are several variations of these terms in use. Some call the arguments *actual parameters* and the parameters *formal parameters*. Others use the terms *actual arguments* and *formal arguments*. Regardless of which set of terms you use, it is important to be consistent.

In Program 6-6 the `displayValue` function is called in line 11 of `main` with the argument 5 inside the parentheses. The number 5 is passed into `num`, which is `displayValue's` parameter. This is illustrated in Figure 6-6.

Figure 6-6

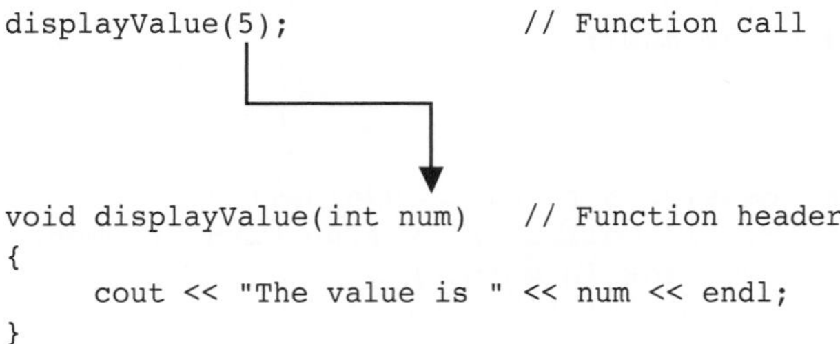

Any argument listed inside the parentheses of a function call is copied into the function's parameter variable. In essence, parameter variables are initialized to the value of the corresponding arguments passed to them when the function is called. Program 6-7 shows the function `displayValue` being called several times with a different argument passed each time.

Program 6-7

```
// This program demonstrates a function with a parameter.
#include <iostream>
using namespace std;

// Function prototype
void displayValue(int num);

int main()
{
   cout << "I am passing several values to displayValue.\n";
   displayValue(5);         // Call displayValue with argument 5
   displayValue(10);        // Call displayValue with argument 10
   displayValue(2);         // Call displayValue with argument 2
   displayValue(16);        // Call displayValue with argument 16
   cout << "Now I am back in main.\n";
   return 0;
}

/*********************************************
 *                displayValue               *
 *  This function uses an integer parameter  *
 *  whose value is displayed.                *
 *********************************************/
void displayValue(int num)
{
   cout << "The value is " << num << endl;
}
```

(program continues)

Program 6-7 *(continued)*

Program Output

```
I am passing several values to displayValue.
The value is 5
The value is 10
The value is 2
The value is 16
Now I am back in main.
```

In lines 11–14 of Program 6-7 the `displayValue` function is called four times, and each time `num` takes on a different value. Any expression whose value could normally be assigned to `num` may be used as an argument. For example, the following function call would pass the value 8 into `num`:

```
displayValue(3 + 5);
```

When a function is called, it is best if each argument passed to it has the same data type as the parameter receiving it. However, it is possible to send an argument with a different data type. In this case, the argument will be promoted or demoted to match the data type of the parameter receiving it. Be very careful if you do this, as you may introduce a hard to find bug. For example, the `displayValue` function in Program 6-7 has an integer parameter, which means it expects to receive an integer value. If the function is called as shown here,

```
displayValue(4.7);
```

the argument will be truncated and the integer 4 will be stored in the parameter `num`.

Often it is useful to pass several arguments into a function. Program 6-8 includes a function that has three parameters. Look carefully at how these parameters are defined in the function header in line 27, as well as in the function prototype in line 6. In this case the prototype lists variable names along with the data types of the function's parameters. This makes the prototype look exactly like the function header except that the prototype *must* end with a semicolon and the function header *must not* end with a semicolon.

```
// Prototype
   void showSum(int num1, int num2, int num3);  // Ends with ;

// Function header
   void showSum(int num1, int num2, int num3)   // NO ;
```

Notice also that the call to the function in line 18 must now send three arguments to the function.

```
showSum(value1, value2, value3);
```

Program 6-8

```
// This program demonstrates a function with three parameters.
#include <iostream>
using namespace std;

// Function prototype
void showSum(int num1, int num2, int num3);

int main()
{
   int value1, value2, value3;

   // Get 3 integers
   cout << "Enter three integers and I will display ";
   cout << "their sum: ";
   cin  >> value1 >> value2 >> value3;

   // Call showSum, passing 3 arguments
   showSum(value1, value2, value3);
   return 0;
}

/****************************************
 *              showSum                 *
 *  This function displays the sum of the   *
 *  3 integers passed into its parameters.  *
 ****************************************/
void showSum(int num1, int num2, int num3)
{
   cout << "The sum is " << (num1 + num2 + num3) << endl;
}
```

Program Output with Example Input Shown in Bold

```
Enter three integers and I will display their sum: 4 8 7[Enter]
The sum is 19
```

One important point to mention about Program 6-8 is how the `showSum` parameter variables are defined in its function header.

```
void showSum(int num1, int num2, int num3)
```

As you might expect they are each preceded by their data type and they are separated by commas. However, unlike regular variable definitions, they cannot be combined into a single definition even if they all have the same data type. That is, even though all three parameter variables are integers, they *cannot* be defined like this:

```
void showSum(int num1, num2, num3)    // Error!
```

Another point to notice is that whereas the function prototype and function header *must* list the data type of each parameter, the call to the function *must not* list any data types. Each argument in the function call must be a value or something that can be evaluated to produce a value. If `value1`, `value2`, and `value3` hold the values `4`, `8`, and `7` respectively, as they did in the sample run for Program 6-8, the following three function calls would all be legal and would cause the `showSum` function to display the same thing.

```
showSum(value1, value2, value3);      // Legal The sum is 19
showSum(4, 8, 7);                     // Legal The sum is 19
showSum(3+1, 16/2, 7);                // Legal The sum is 19
```

But the following function call would cause an error.

```
showSum(int value1, int value2, int value3);     // Error!
```

Figure 6-7 shows the difference in the syntax between the function call and the function header when variables are used as arguments. It also illustrates that when a function with multiple parameters is called, the arguments are passed to the parameters in order.

Figure 6-7

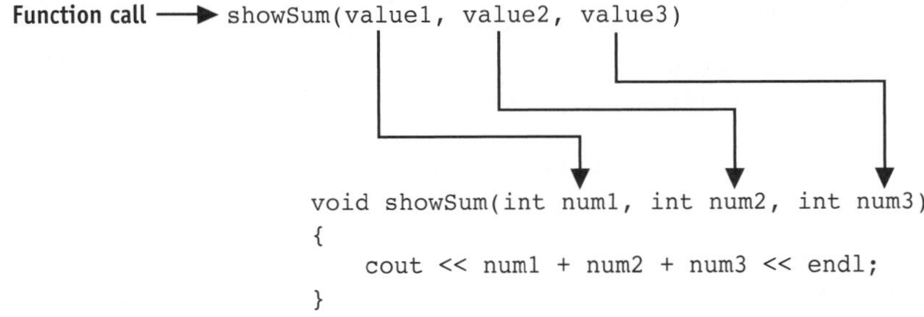

The following function call will cause 4 to be passed into the `num1` parameter, 8 to be passed into `num2`, and 7 to be passed into `num3`:

```
showSum(4, 8, 7);
```

NOTE: Like all variables, parameters have a scope. The scope of a parameter is limited to the body of the function which uses it.

6.5 Passing Data by Value

CONCEPT: When an argument is passed into a parameter by value, only a copy of the argument's value is passed. Changes to the parameter do not affect the original argument.

As you have seen in this chapter, parameters are special-purpose variables that are defined inside the parentheses of a function definition. Their purpose is to hold the information passed to them by the arguments, which are listed inside the parentheses of a function call. Normally when information is passed to a function it is *passed by value*. This means the parameter receives a copy of the value that is passed to it. If a parameter's value is changed inside a function, it has no effect on the original argument. Program 6-9 demonstrates this concept.

Program 6-9 also illustrates that when a function prototype lists variable names along with data types, the names it uses are just *dummy names*. They are not actually used by the compiler and do not have to agree with the names used in the function header. The `changeMe` function prototype in line 7 and the `changeMe` function header in line 29 both specify that the function has one `int` parameter, but they use different names for it.

Program 6-9

```
 1 // This program demonstrates that changes to a function
 2 // parameter have no effect on the original argument.
 3 #include <iostream>
 4 using namespace std;
 5
 6 // Function Prototype
 7 void changeMe(int aValue);
 8
 9 int main()
10 {
11    int number = 12;
12
13    // Display the value in number
14    cout << "In main number is " << number << endl;
15
16    // Call changeMe, passing the value in number as an argument
17    changeMe(number);
18
19    // Display the value in number again
20    cout << "Back in main again, number is still " << number << endl;
21    return 0;
22 }
23
24 /**************************************
25  *               changeMe             *
26  *  This function changes the value   *
27  *  stored in its parameter myValue   *
28  **************************************/
29 void changeMe(int myValue)
30 {
31    // Change the value of myValue to 0
32    myValue = 0;
33
34    // Display the value in myValue
35    cout << "In changeMe, the value has been changed to "
36         << myValue << endl;
37 }
```

Program Output

```
In main number is 12
In changeMe, the value has been changed to 0
Back in main again, number is still 12
```

Even though the parameter variable `myValue` is changed in the `changeMe` function, the argument `number` is not modified. This occurs because the `myValue` variable contains only a copy of the `number` variable. Just this copy is changed, not the original. The `changeMe` function does not have access to the original argument.

Figure 6-8 illustrates that a parameter variable's storage location in memory is separate from that of the original argument.

Figure 6-8

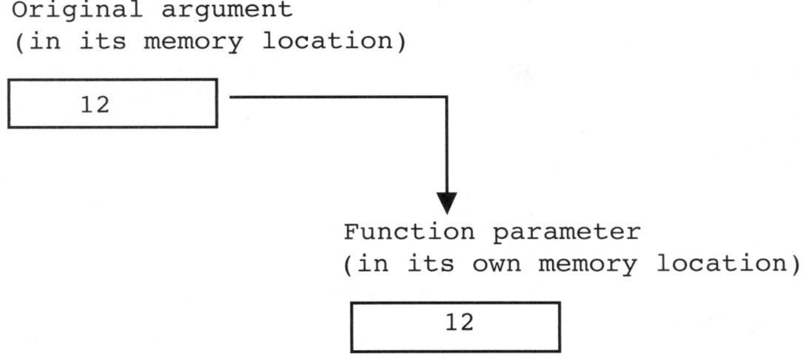

NOTE: Later in this chapter you will learn ways to give a function access to its original arguments.

Checkpoint

6.5 Indicate which of the following is the function prototype, the function header, and the function call:

```
void showNum(double num)
void showNum(double);
showNum(45.67);
```

6.6 Write a function named `timesTen`. The function should have an integer parameter named `number`. When `timesTen` is called, it should display the product of `number` times 10. (Note: just write the function. Do not write a complete program.)

6.7 Write a function prototype for the `timesTen` function you wrote in question 6.6.

6.8 What is the output of the following program?

```
#include <iostream>
using namespace std;

void showDouble(int value); // Function prototype

int main()
{
   int num;

   for (num = 0; num < 10; num++)
      showDouble(num);
   return 0;
}
// Definition of function showDouble
void showDouble(int value)
{
   cout << value << "   " << (value * 2) << endl;
}
```

6.9 What is the output of the following program?

```
#include <iostream>
using namespace std;

void func1(double, int); // Function prototype

int main()
{
   int x = 0;
   double y = 1.5;

   cout << x << " " << y << endl;
   func1(y, x);
   cout << x << " " << y << endl;
   return 0;
}
void func1(double a, int b)
{
   cout << a << " " << b << endl;
   a = 0.0;
   b = 10;
   cout << a << " " << b << endl;
}
```

6.10 The following program skeleton asks for the number of hours you've worked and your hourly pay rate. It then calculates and displays your wages. The function `showDollars`, which you are to write, formats the output of the wages.

```
#include <iostream>
#include <iomanip>
using namespace std;

void showDollars(double pay); // Function prototype

int main()
{
   double payRate, hoursWorked, wages;

   cout << "How many hours have you worked? "
   cin  >> hoursWorked;
   cout << "What is your hourly pay rate? ";
   cin  >> payRate;
   wages = hoursWorked * payRate;
   showDollars(wages);
   return 0;
}

// Write the definition of the showDollars function here.
// It should have one double parameter and display the message
// "Your wages are $" followed by the value of the parameter.
```

6.6 The return Statement

CONCEPT: The return statement causes a function to end immediately.

When the last statement in a function has finished executing, the function terminates. The program returns to the module that called it and continues executing from the point immediately following the function call. It is possible, however, to force a function to return to where it was called from before its last statement has been executed. This can be done with the `return` statement, as illustrated in Program 6-10. In this program, the function `divide` shows the quotient of `arg1` divided by `arg2`. If `arg2` is set to zero, however, the function returns back to `main` without performing the division.

Program 6-10

```
// This program uses a function to perform division.
// It illustrates the return statement.
#include <iostream>
using namespace std;

// Function prototype
void divide(double arg1, double arg2);

int main()
{
   double num1, num2;

   cout << "Enter two numbers and I will divide the first\n";
   cout << "number by the second number: ";
   cin  >> num1 >> num2;
   divide(num1, num2);
   return 0;
}

/***************************************************************
 *                           divide                            *
 *  This function uses two parameters, arg1 and arg2.          *
 *  If arg2 does not = zero, the function displays the         *
 *  result of arg1/arg2. Otherwise it returns without          *
 *  performing the division.                                   *
 ***************************************************************/
void divide(double arg1, double arg2)
{
   if (arg2 == 0.0)
   {
      cout << "Sorry, I cannot divide by zero.\n";
      return;
   }
   cout << "The quotient is " << (arg1 / arg2) << endl;
}
```

(program continues)

Program 6-10 *(continued)*

Program Output with Example Input Shown in Bold
```
Enter two numbers and I will divide the first
number by the second number: 12 0[Enter]
Sorry, I cannot divide by zero.
```

In the example running of the program, the user entered 12 and 0 as input. These were stored as double values as variables `num1` and `num2`. In line 16 the `divide` function was called, passing 12.0 into the `arg1` parameter and 0.0 into the `arg2` parameter. Inside the `divide` function, the `if` statement in line 29 executes. Because `arg2` is equal to 0.0, the code in lines 31 and 32 execute. When the `return` statement in line 32 executes, the `divide` function immediately ends. This means the `cout` statement in line 34 does not execute. The program resumes at line 17 in the `main` function.

6.7 Returning a Value from a Function

CONCEPT: A function may send a value back to the part of the program that called the function.

You've seen that data may be passed into a function by way of parameter variables. Data may also be returned from a function back to the statement that called it. Functions that return a value are known as *value-returning functions.*

VideoNote
Value-Returning Functions

The `pow` function, which you have already used, is an example of a value-returning function. Here is an example:

```
double x;
x = pow(4.0, 2.0);
```

This code calls the `pow` function, passing 4.0 and 2.0 as arguments. The function calculates the value of 4.0 raised to the power of 2.0 and *returns* that value. The value, which is 16.0, is assigned to the `x` variable by the = operator.

Although several arguments can be passed into a function, only one value can be returned from it. Think of a function as having multiple communication channels for receiving data (parameters), but only one channel for sending data (the return value). This is illustrated in Figure 6-9.

Figure 6-9

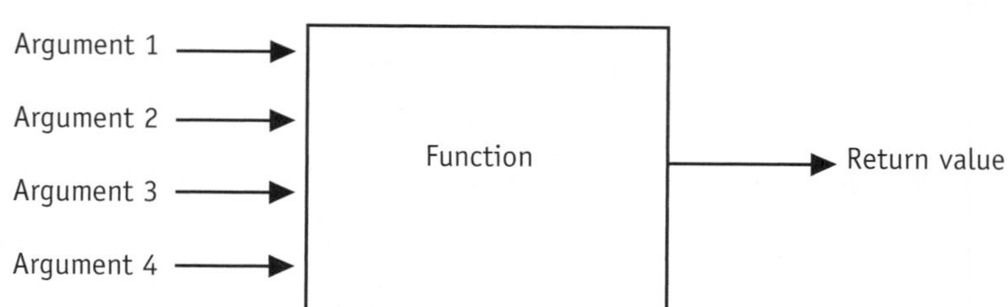

NOTE: In order to return multiple values from a function, they must be "packaged" in such a way that they are treated as a single value. You will learn to do this in Chapter 7.

Defining a Value-Returning Function

When you are writing a value-returning function, you must decide what type of value the function will return. This is because you must specify the data type of the return value in the function header and function prototype. Up until now all the functions we have written have been `void` functions. This means they do not return a value. These functions use the key word `void` as the return type in their function header and function prototype. A value-returning function, on the other hand, uses `int`, `double`, `bool`, or any other valid data type in its header. Here is an example of a function that returns an `int` value:

```
int sum(int num1, int num2)
{
   int result;

   result = num1 + num2;
   return result;
}
```

The name of this function is `sum`. Notice in the function header that the return type is `int`, as illustrated in Figure 6-10.

Figure 6-10


```
int sum(int num1, int num2)
```

This code defines a function named `sum` that accepts two `int` arguments. The arguments are passed into the parameter variables `num1` and `num2`. Inside the function, the variable `result` is defined. Variables that are defined inside a function are called *local variables*. After the variable definition, the values of the parameter variables `num1` and `num2` are added, and their sum is assigned to the `result` variable. The last statement in the function is:

```
return result;
```

This statement causes the function to end, and it sends the value of the `result` variable back to the statement that called the function. A value-returning function must have a `return` statement written in the following general format:

```
return expression;
```

In the general format, *`expression`* is the value to be returned. It can be any expression that has a value, such as a variable, literal, or mathematical expression. The value of the expression is converted to the data type that the function returns and is sent back to the statement that called the function. In this case, the `sum` function returns the value in the `result` variable.

However, we could have eliminated the `result` variable entirely and returned the expression `num1 + num2`, as shown in the following code:

```
int sum(int num1, int num2)
{
   return num1 + num2;
}
```

The prototype for a value-returning function follows the same conventions that we covered earlier. Here is the prototype for the `sum` function:

```
int sum(int num1, int num2);
```

Calling a Value-Returning Function

Program 6-11 shows an example of how to call the `sum` function.

Program 6-11

```
// This program uses a function that returns a value.
#include <iostream>
using namespace std;

// Function prototype
int sum(int num1, int num2);

int main()
{
   int value1 = 20,    // The first value
       value2 = 40,    // The second value
       total;          // Holds the returned total

   // Call the sum function, passing the contents of
   // value1 and value2 as arguments. Assign the return
   // value to the total variable.
   total = sum(value1, value2);

   // Display the sum of the values
   cout << "The sum of " << value1 << " and "
        << value2 << " is " << total << endl;
   return 0;
}

/*********************************************************
 *                          sum                          *
 *  This function returns the sum of its two parameters. *
 *********************************************************/
int sum(int num1, int num2)
{
   return num1 + num2;
}
```

Program Output

```
The sum of 20 and 40 is 60
```

Here is the statement in line 17, which calls the sum function, passing value1 and value2 as arguments.

```
total = sum(value1, value2);
```

This statement assigns the value returned by the sum function to the total variable. In this case, the function will return 60. Figure 6-11 shows how the arguments are passed into the function and how a value is passed back from the function.

Figure 6-11

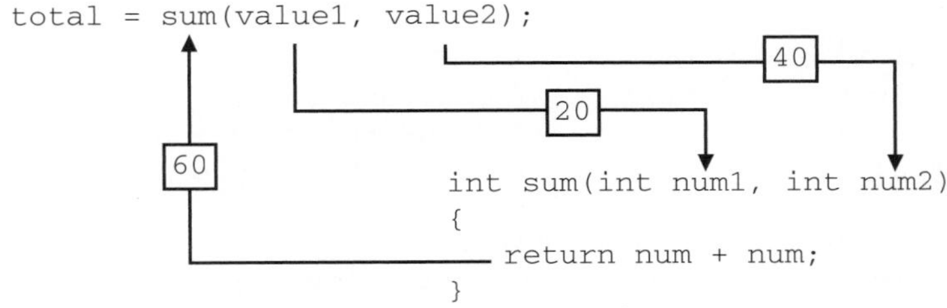

When you call a value-returning function, you usually want to do something meaningful with the value it returns. Program 6-11 shows a function's return value being assigned to a variable. This is commonly how return values are used, but you can do many other things with them as well. For example, the following code shows a math expression that uses a call to the sum function:

```
int x = 10, y = 15;
double average;
average = sum(x, y) / 2.0;
```

In the last statement, the sum function is called with x and y as its arguments. The function's return value, which is 25, is divided by 2.0. The result, 12.5, is assigned to average. Here is another example:

```
int x = 10, y = 15;
cout << "The sum is " << sum(x, y) << endl;
```

This code sends the sum function's return value to cout so it can be displayed on the screen. The message "The sum is 25" will be displayed.

Remember, a value-returning function returns a value of a specific data type. You can use the function's return value anywhere that you can use a regular value of the same data type. This means that anywhere an int value can be used, a call to an int value-returning function can be used. Likewise, anywhere a double value can be used, a call to a double value-returning function can be used. The same is true for all other data types.

Let's look at another example. Program 6-12, which calculates the area of a circle, has two functions in addition to main. One of the functions is named square, and it returns the square of any number passed to it as an argument. The square function is called in a mathematical statement. The program also has a function named getRadius, which prompts the user to enter the circle's radius. The value entered by the user is returned from the function.

Program 6-12

```
// This program demonstrates two value-returning functions.
// The square function is called in a mathematical statement.
#include <iostream>
#include <iomanip>
using namespace std;

//Function prototypes
double getRadius();
double square(double number);

int main()
{
   const double PI = 3.14159;    // Constant for pi
   double radius;                // Holds the circle's radius
   double area;                  // Holds the circle's area

   // Set the numeric output formatting
   cout << fixed << showpoint << setprecision(2);

   // Get the radius of the circle
   cout << "This program calculates the area of a circle.\n";
   radius = getRadius();

   // Caclulate the area of the circle
   area = PI * square(radius);

   // Display the area
   cout << "The area is " << area << endl;
   return 0;
}

/*******************************************
 *               getRadius                 *
 * This function returns the circle radius *
 * input by the user.                      *
 *******************************************/
double getRadius()
{
   double rad;

   cout << "Enter the radius of the circle: ";
   cin  >> rad;
   return rad;
}

/********************************************
 *                   square                 *
 * This function returns the square of the  *
 * double argument sent to it               *
 ********************************************/
double square(double number)
{
   return number * number;
}
```

Program 6-12 *(continued)*

Program Output with Example Input Shown in Bold

```
This program calculates the area of a circle.
Enter the radius of the circle: 10[Enter]
The area is 314.16
```

First, look at the `getRadius` function which is defined in lines 37 through 44. Notice that there is nothing inside the parentheses of the function header on line 37. This means the function has no parameters, so no arguments are sent to it when it is called. The purpose of this function is to get the circle radius from the user. In line 39 the function defines a local variable, `rad`. Line 41 displays a prompt and line 42 accepts the user's input for the circle's radius, which is stored in the `rad` variable. In line 43 the value of the `rad` variable is returned. The `getRadius` function is called in line 22 of the `main` function. When the value is returned from the `getRadius` function it is assigned to the `radius` variable.

Next look at the `square` function, which is defined in lines 51 through 54. When the function is called, a `double` argument is passed to it. The function stores the argument in its `number` parameter. The `return` statement in line 53 returns the value of the expression `number * number`, which is the square of the value in the `number` parameter. The `square` function is called in line 25 of the `main` function, with the value of `radius` passed as an argument. The `square` function will return the square of the `radius` variable, and that value will be used in the mathematical expression that computes the circle's area.

Assuming the user has entered 10.0 as the radius, and this value is passed as an argument to the `square` function, the function will return the value 100.0. Figure 6-12 illustrates how this value is passed back to be used in the mathematical expression.

Figure 6-12

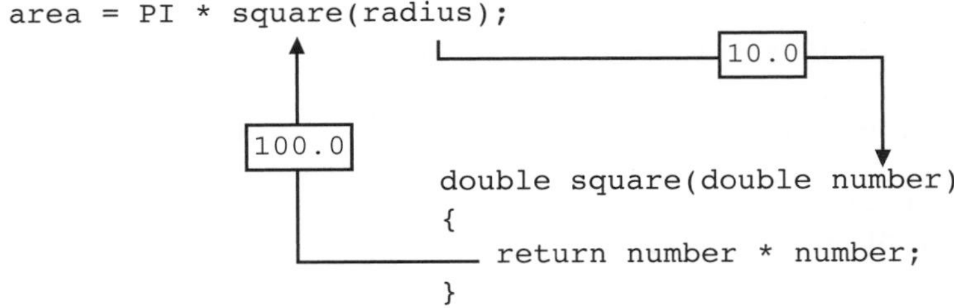

Functions can return values of any type. Both the `getRadius` and `square` functions in Program 6-12 return a `double`. The `sum` function you saw in Program 6-11 returned an `int`. When a statement calls a value-returning function, it should properly handle the return value. For example, if you assign the return value of the `square` function to a variable, the variable should be a `double`. If the return value of the function has a fractional portion and you assign it to an `int` variable, the value will be truncated.

6.8 Returning a Boolean Value

CONCEPT: Functions may return `true` or `false` values.

Frequently there is a need for a function that tests an argument and returns a `true` or `false` value indicating whether or not a condition is satisfied. Such a function would return a `bool` value. For example, the `isValid` function shown below accepts an `int` argument and returns `true` if the argument is within the range of 1 through 100, or `false` otherwise.

```
bool isValid(int number)
{
   bool status;

   if (number >= 1 && number <= 100)
      status = true;
   else
      status = false;
   return status;
}
```

The following code shows an `if/else` statement that makes a call to the function:

```
int value = 20;
if (isValid(value))
   cout << "The value is within range.\n";
else
   cout << "The value is out of range.\n";
```

Because `value` equals 20, this code will display the message "The value is within range." when it executes.

Program 6-13 shows another example of a function whose return type is `bool`. This program has a function named `isEven`, which returns `true` if its argument is an even number. Otherwise, the function returns `false`.

Program 6-13

```
// This program uses a function that returns true or false.
#include <iostream>
using namespace std;

// Function prototype
bool isEven(int);

int main()
{
   int val;        // the value to be tested

   // Get a number from the user
   cout << "Enter an integer and I will tell you ";
   cout << "if it is even or odd: ";
   cin  >> val;

```

(program continues)

Program 6-13 *(continued)*

```
17    // Indicate whether it is even or odd
18    if (isEven(val))
19       cout << val << " is even.\n";
20    else
21       cout << val << " is odd.\n";
22    return 0;
23 }
24
25 /*****************************************************
26  *                       isEven                        *
27  * This Boolean function tests if the integer argument *
28  * it receives is even or odd. It returns true if the  *
29  * argument is even and false if it is odd.            *
30  *****************************************************/
31 bool isEven(int number)
32 {
33    if (number % 2 == 0)
34        return true;  // The number is even if there's no remainder
35    else
36        return false; // Otherwise, the number is odd
37 }
```

Program Output with Example Input Shown in Bold

```
Enter an integer and I will tell you if it is even or odd: 5[Enter]
5 is odd.
```

Notice how the `isEven` function is called in line 18 with the following statement:

```
if (isEven(val))
```

Recall from Chapter 4 that this is asking if the function call `isEven(val)` returned the value `true`. When the `if` statement executes, `isEven` is called with `val` as its argument. If `val` is even, `isEven` returns `true`, otherwise it returns `false`.

Notice also how the `isEven` function that begins on line 31 uses an `if` statement to return either the value `true` or the value `false`. There are several other ways this function could have been written. Let's compare three different ways to write it.

```
// Program 6-13 code
bool isEven(int number)
{
   if (number % 2 == 0)
      return true;
   else
      return false;
}
```

```
// Version 2
bool isEven(int number)
{  bool answer;

   if (number % 2 == 0)
      answer = true;
   else
      answer = false;

   return answer;
}
```

```
// Version 3
bool isEven(int number)
{  bool answer = false;

   if (number % 2 == 0)
      answer = true;

   return answer;
}
```

Although the code used in Program 6-13 is short and clear, it has two different `return` statements. Many instructors prefer that a value-returning function have only a single `return` statement, placed at the end of the function. Versions 2 and 3 do this. Your instructor will let you know which method you should use.

Checkpoint

6.11 How many return values may a function have?

6.12 Write a header for a function named `distance`. The function should return a `double` and have two `double` parameters: `rate` and `time`.

6.13 Write a header for a function named `days`. The function should return an `int` and have three `int` parameters: `years`, `months`, and `weeks`.

6.14 Write a header for a function named `getKey`. The function should return a `char` and use no parameters.

6.15 Write a header for a function named `lightYears`. The function should return a `long` and have one `long` parameter: `miles`.

6.9 Using Functions in a Menu-Driven Program

CONCEPT: Functions are ideal for use in menu-driven programs. When the user selects an item from a menu, the program can call the appropriate function.

In Chapters 4 and 5 you saw a menu-driven program that calculates the charges for a health club membership. Program 6-14 is an improved modular version of that program.

Program 6-14

```
// This is a modular, menu-driven program that computes
// health club membership fees.
#include <iostream>
#include <iomanip>
#include <string>
using namespace std;

// Function prototypes
void displayMenu();
int getChoice();
void showFees(string category, double rate, int months);

int main()
{
   // Constants for monthly membership rates
   const double ADULT_RATE  = 120.0,
                CHILD_RATE  =  60.0,
                SENIOR_RATE = 100.0;
```

(program continues)

Program 6-14 *(continued)*

```
   int choice,                       // Holds the user's menu choice
       months;                       // Number of months being paid

   // Set numeric output formatting
   cout << fixed << showpoint << setprecision(2);

    do
    {  displayMenu();
       choice = getChoice(); // Assign choice the value returned
                             // by the getChoice function
       if (choice != 4)      // If user does not want to quit, proceed
       {
          cout << "For how many months? ";
          cin  >> months;

          switch (choice)
          {
             case 1:  showFees("Adult", ADULT_RATE, months);
                      break;
             case 2:  showFees("Child", CHILD_RATE, months);
                      break;
             case 3:  showFees("Senior", SENIOR_RATE, months);
          }
       }
   } while (choice != 4);
   return 0;
}

/**********************************************
 *                 displayMenu                *
 * This function clears the screen and then   *
 * displays the menu choices.                 *
 **********************************************/
void displayMenu()
{
   system("cls");          // Clear the screen.
   cout << "\n  Health Club Membership Menu\n\n";
   cout << "1.  Standard Adult Membership\n";
   cout << "2.  Child Membership\n";
   cout << "3.  Senior Citizen Membership\n";
   cout << "4.  Quit the Program\n\n";
}

/**************************************************
 *                  getChoice                     *
 *  This function inputs, validates, and returns  *
 *  the user's menu choice.                       *
 **************************************************/
```

(program continues)

Program 6-14 *(continued)*

```
int getChoice()
{
   int choice;

   cin >> choice;
   while (choice < 1 || choice > 4)
   {  cout << "The only valid choices are 1-4.  Please re-enter. ";
      cin  >> choice;
   }
   return choice;
}

/**************************************************************
 *                           showFees                         *
 * This function uses the membership type, monthly rate, and  *
 * number of months passed to it as arguments to compute and  *
 * display a member's total charges. It then holds the screen *
 * until the user presses the ENTER key. This is necessary    *
 * because after returning from this function the displayMenu *
 * function will be called, and it will clear the screen.     *
 **************************************************************/
void showFees(string memberType, double rate, int months)
{
   cout << endl
        << "Membership Type : "  << memberType << "     "
        << "Number of months: "  << months << endl
        << "Total charges   : $" << (rate * months) << endl;

   // Hold the screen until the user presses the ENTER key.
   cout << "\nPress the Enter key to return to the menu. ";
   cin.get();     // Clear the previous \n out of the input buffer
   cin.get();     // Wait for the user to press ENTER
}
```

Program Output with Example Input Shown in Bold

```
     Health Club Membership Menu
1.  Standard Adult Membership
2.  Child Membership
3.  Senior Citizen Membership
4.  Quit the Program

1[Enter]
For how many months? 3[Enter]

Membership Type : Adult    Number of months: 3
Total charges   : $360.00

Press the Enter key to return to the menu.
```

Notice how each function, or module, of Program 6-14 is designed to perform a specific task.

- `displayMenu`, as its name suggests, displays the menu of choices.
- `getChoice` gets the user's menu choice and validates it before returning it to the main function. The main function can then use the value, knowing it is good, without having to validate it itself.
- `showFees` computes and displays membership information and fees.

Notice, in particular, the versatility of the `showFees` function, which is called in three different places within the `switch` statement. It is passed three arguments: a string holding the membership type, a `double` holding the monthly fee for that membership type, and an `int` holding the number of months being billed. Without these arguments, we would need a whole set of functions: one to compute adult membership fees, another to compute child membership fees, and a third to compute senior membership fees. Because we can vary the information passed as arguments to the function, however, we are able to create a single general-purpose function that works for all three cases.

Clearing the Screen

Sometimes in a program you want to clear the screen and place the cursor back up at the top. This is particularly useful when you are writing a menu-driven program. After the user has made a menu selection and the function to carry out that choice has been executed, it would be nice to be able to clear the screen before redisplaying the menu. This can be accomplished by inserting a command in your program that asks the operating system to clear the screen for you. Here is the command for Unix-based operating systems, such as Linux and Mac OS:

```
system("clear");
```

And here is the command for Windows operating systems. You may have noticed that it appears in line 54 of Program 6-14, just before the menu is displayed.

```
system("cls");
```

This removes the previous report from the screen before the user selects a new one to be displayed. However, it is important not to clear the screen too quickly after a report displays, or it will disappear before the user has a chance to look at it. Take a look at lines 95 through 98 of Program 6-14. These lines hold the report screen until the user presses the [Enter] key to signal readiness to return to the menu and begin something new.

6.10 Local and Global Variables

CONCEPT: A local variable is defined inside a function and is not accessible outside the function. A global variable is defined outside all functions and is accessible to all functions in its scope.

Local Variables

Variables defined inside a function are *local* to that function. They are hidden from the statements in other functions, which normally cannot access them. Program 6-15 shows that because the variables defined in a function are hidden, other functions may have separate, distinct variables with the same name.

Program 6-15

```
// This program shows that variables defined in a function
// are hidden from other functions.
#include <iostream>
using namespace std;}

void anotherFunction();     // Function prototype

int main()
{
   int num = 1;             // Local variable

   cout << "In main, num is " << num << endl;
   anotherFunction();
   cout << "Back in main, num is still " << num << endl;
   return 0;
}

/*****************************************************************
 *                       anotherFunction                         *
 * This function displays the value of its local variable num.  *
 *****************************************************************/
void anotherFunction()
{
   int num = 20;            // Local variable

   cout << "In anotherFunction, num is " << num << endl;
}
```

Program Output

```
In main, num is 1
In anotherFunction, num is 20
Back in main, num is still 1
```

Even though there are two variables named num, the program can only "see" one of them at a time because they are in different functions. When the program is executing in main, the num variable defined in main is visible. When anotherFunction is called, however, only variables defined inside it are visible, so the num variable in main is hidden. Figure 6-13 illustrates the closed nature of the two functions. The boxes represent the scope of the variables.

Figure 6-13

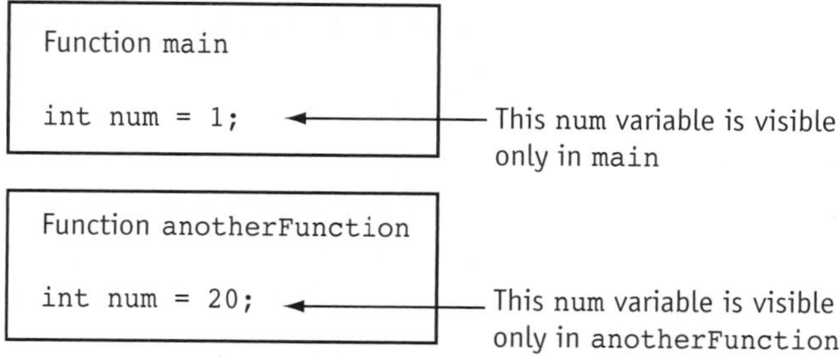

Local Variable Lifetime

A local variable exists only while the function it is defined in is executing. This is known as the *lifetime* of a local variable. When the function begins, its parameter variables and any local variables it defines are created in memory, and when the function ends, they are destroyed. This means that any values stored in a function's parameters or local variables are lost between calls to the function.

Initializing Local Variables with Parameter Values

It is possible to use parameter variables to initialize local variables. Sometimes this simplifies the code in a function. Here is a modified version of the `sum` function we looked at earlier. In this version, the function's parameters are used to initialize the local variable `result`.

```
int sum(int num1, int num2)
{
   int result = num1 + num2;
   return result;
}
```

Global Variables

A global variable is any variable defined outside all the functions in a program, including `main`. The scope of a global variable is the portion of the program from the variable definition to the end of the entire program. This means that a global variable can be accessed by all functions that are defined after the global variable is defined. Program 6-16 shows two functions, `main` and `anotherFunction`, which access the same global variable, `num`.

Program 6-16

```
// This program shows that a global variable is visible to all functions
// that appear in a program after the variable's definition.
#include <iostream>
using namespace std;

void anotherFunction();     // Function prototype
int num = 2;                // Global variable

int main()

{
   cout << "In main, num is " << num << endl;
   anotherFunction();
   cout << "Back in main, num is " << num << endl;
   return 0;
}
/***************************************************************
 *                     anotherFunction                        *
 * This function changes the value of the global variable num. *
 ***************************************************************/
```

(program continues)

Program 6-16 *(continued)*

```
void anotherFunction()
{
   cout << "In anotherFunction, num is " << num << endl;
   num = 50;
   cout << "But, it is now changed to " << num << endl;
}
```

Program Output

```
In main, num is 2
In anotherFunction, num is 2
But, it is now changed to 50
Back in main, num is 50
```

In Program 6-16, `num` is defined outside of all the functions. Because its definition appears before the definitions of `main` and `anotherFunction`, both functions have access to it.

In C++, unless you explicitly initialize numeric global variables, they are automatically initialized to zero. Global character variables are initialized to NULL.* In Program 6-17 the variable `globalNum` is never set to any value by a statement, but because it is global it is automatically set to zero.

Program 6-17

```
// This program has an uninitialized global variable.
#include <iostream>
using namespace std;

int globalNum;          // Global variable automatically set to zero

int main()
{
   cout << "globalNum is " << globalNum << endl;
   return 0;
}
```

Program Output

```
globalNum is 0
```

NOTE: Remember that local variables are not automatically initialized as global variables are. The programmer must handle this.

Although global variables can be useful, you should restrict your use of them. When beginning students first learn to write programs with multiple functions, they are sometimes tempted to make all their variables global. This is usually because global variables can be accessed by any function in the program without being passed as arguments. Although this approach might make a program easier to create, it usually causes problems later.

* The NULL character is stored as ASCII 0.

The reasons are as follows:

- *Global variables make debugging difficult.* Any statement in a program can change the value of a global variable. If you find that the wrong value is being stored in a global variable, you have to track down every statement that accesses it to determine where the bad value is coming from. In a program with thousands of lines of code, this can be difficult.
- *Functions that use global variables are usually dependent on those variables.* If you want to use such a function in a different program, most likely you will have to redesign it so it does not rely on the global variable.
- *Global variables make a program hard to understand.* A global variable can be modified by any statement in the program. So to understand any part of the program that uses a global variable, you have to be aware of all the other parts of the program that access it.

Because of this, you should not use global variables for the conventional purposes of storing, manipulating, and retrieving data. In most cases, you should declare variables locally and pass them as arguments to the functions that need to access them.

Global Constants

Although you should try to avoid the use of global variables, it is generally permissible to use global constants in a program. A *global constant* is a named constant that is available to every function in a program. Because a global constant's value cannot be changed during the program's execution, you do not have to worry about the potential hazards associated with the use of global variables.

Global constants are typically used to represent unchanging values that are needed throughout a program. For example, suppose a banking program uses a named constant to represent an interest rate. If the interest rate is used in several functions, it is easier to create a global constant, rather than a local named constant in each function. This also simplifies maintenance. If the interest rate changes, only the declaration of the global constant has to be changed, instead of several local declarations.

Program 6-18 shows an example of how global constants might be used. The program calculates gross pay, including overtime, for a company's management trainees. All trainees earn the same amount per hour. In addition to `main`, this program has two functions: `getBasePay` and `getOvertimePay`. The `getBasePay` function accepts the number of hours worked and returns the amount of pay for the non-overtime hours. The `getOvertimePay` function accepts the number of hours worked and returns the amount of pay for the overtime hours, if any.

Program 6-18

```
// This program calculates gross pay. It uses global constants.
#include <iostream>
#include <iomanip>
using namespace std;

```

(program continues)

Program 6-18 *(continued)*

```
// Global constants
const double PAY_RATE = 22.55;      // Hourly pay rate
const double BASE_HOURS = 40.0;     // Max non-overtime hours
const double OT_MULTIPLIER = 1.5;   // Overtime multiplier

// Function prototypes
double getBasePay(double);
double getOvertimePay(double);

int main()
{
   double hours,                 // Hours worked
          basePay,               // Base pay
          overtimePay = 0.0,     // Overtime pay
          totalPay;              // Total pay

   // Get the number of hours worked
   cout << "How many hours did you work? ";
   cin  >> hours;

   // Get the amount of base pay
   basePay = getBasePay(hours);

   // Get overtime pay, if any
   if (hours > BASE_HOURS)
       overtimePay = getOvertimePay(hours);

   // Calculate the total pay
   totalPay = basePay + overtimePay;

   // Display the pay
   cout << setprecision(2) << fixed << showpoint;
   cout << "Base pay     $" << setw(7) << basePay     << endl;
   cout << "Overtime pay $" << setw(7) << overtimePay << endl;
   cout << "Total pay    $" << setw(7) << totalPay    << endl;
   return 0;
}

/****************************************************************
 *                            getBasePay                        *
 * This function uses the hours worked value passed in to      *
 * compute and return an employee's pay for non-overtime hours.*
 ***************************************************************/
double getBasePay(double hoursWorked)
{
   double basePay;

   if (hoursWorked > BASE_HOURS)
      basePay = BASE_HOURS * PAY_RATE;
   else
      basePay = hoursWorked * PAY_RATE;

   return basePay;
}
```

(program continues)

Program 6-18 *(continued)*

```
60
61 /*****************************************************
62  *                  getOvertimePay                   *
63  * This function uses the hours worked value passed in  *
64  * to compute and return an employee's overtime pay.    *
65  *****************************************************/
66 double getOvertimePay(double hoursWorked)
67 {
68    double overtimePay;
69
70    if (hoursWorked > BASE_HOURS)
71    {
72       overtimePay =
73          (hoursWorked - BASE_HOURS) * PAY_RATE * OT_MULTIPLIER;
74    }
75    else
76       overtimePay = 0.0;
77
78    return overtimePay;
79 }
```

Program Output with Example Input Shown in Bold

```
How many hours did you work? 48[Enter]
Base pay     $ 902.00
Overtime pay $ 270.60
Total pay    $1172.60
```

Let's take a closer look at the program. Three global constants are defined in lines 7, 8, and 9. The `PAY_RATE` constant is set to the employee's hourly pay rate, which is 22.55. The `BASE_HOURS` constant is set to 40.0, which is the number of hours an employee can work in a week without getting paid overtime. The `OT_MULTIPLIER` constant is set to 1.5, which is the pay rate multiplier for overtime hours. This means that the employee's hourly pay rate is multiplied by 1.5 for all overtime hours.

Because these constants are global and are defined before all of the functions in the program, all the functions may access them. For example, the `getBasePay` function accesses the `BASE_HOURS` constant in lines 53 and 54 and accesses the `PAY_RATE` constant in lines 54 and 56. The `getOvertimePay` function accesses the `BASE_HOURS` constant in line 70 and all three constants in line 73.

Local and Global Variables with the Same Name

You cannot have two local variables with the same name in the same function. This applies to parameter variables as well. A parameter variable is, in essence, a local variable. So, you cannot give a parameter variable and a local variable in the same function the same name.

However, you can have a parameter or local variable with the same name as a global variable or constant. When you do this, the name of the parameter or local variable *shadows* the name of the global variable or constant. This means that the global variable or constant's name is hidden by the name of the parameter or local variable. So, the global variable or constant can't be seen or used in this part of the program. Program 6-19 illustrates this. It has a global constant named `BIRDS` set to 500 and a local constant in the `california` function named `BIRDS` set to 10000.

Program 6-19

```
1 // This program demonstrates how a local variable or constant
2 // can shadow the name of a global variable or constant.
3 #include <iostream>
4 using namespace std;
5
6 void california();        // Function prototype
7
8 const int BIRDS = 500;    // Global constant
9
10 int main()
11 {
12    cout << "In main there are " << BIRDS << " birds.\n";
13    california();
14    return 0;
15 }
16
17 /******************************
18  *          california        *
19  ******************************/
20 void california()
21 {
22    const int BIRDS = 10000;
23
24    cout << "In california there are " << BIRDS << " birds.\n";
25 }
```

Program Output

```
In main there are 500 birds.
In california there are 10000 birds.
```

When the program is executing in the `main` function, the global constant `BIRDS`, which is set to 500, is visible. The `cout` statement in line 12 displays "In main there are 500 birds." (My apologies to folks living in Maine for the difference in spelling.) When the program is executing in the `california` function, however, the local constant `BIRDS` shadows the global constant `BIRDS`. When the `california` function accesses `BIRDS`, it accesses the local constant. That is why the `cout` statement in line 24 displays "In california there are 10000 birds."

6.11 Static Local Variables

If a function is called more than once in a program, the values stored in the function's local variables do not persist between function calls. This is because local variables are destroyed when a function terminates and are then re-created when the function starts again. This is shown in Program 6-20.

Program 6-20

```
1 // This program shows that local variables do not retain
2 // their values between function calls.
3 #include <iostream>
4 using namespace std;
5
6 void showLocal();      // Function prototype
7
8 int main()
9 {
10    showLocal();
11    showLocal();
12    return 0;
13 }
14
15 /*******************************************************
16  *                    showLocal                        *
17  * This function sets, displays, and then changes the *
18  * value of local variable localNum before returning. *
19  *******************************************************/
20 void showLocal()
21 {
22    int localNum = 5;   // Local variable
23
24    cout << "localNum is " << localNum << endl;
25    localNum = 99;
26 }
```

Program Output

```
localNum is 5
localNum is 5
```

Even though in line 25 the last statement in the `showLocal` function stores 99 in `localNum`, the variable is destroyed when the function terminates. The next time the function is called, `localNum` is re-created and initialized to 5 all over again.

Sometimes, however, it's desirable for a program to "remember" what value is stored in a local variable between function calls. This can be accomplished by making the variable `static`. Static local variables are not destroyed when a function returns. They exist for the entire lifetime of the program, even though their scope is only the function in which they are defined. Program 6-21 uses a static local variable to count how many times a function is called.

Program 6-21

```
 1 // This program uses a static local variable.
 2 #include <iostream>
 3 using namespace std;
 4
 5 void showStatic();    // Function prototype
 6
 7 int main()
 8 {
 9    // Call the showStatic function five times
10    for (int count = 0; count < 5; count++)
11       showStatic();
12    return 0;
13 }
14
15 /*********************************************
16  *                  showStatic               *
17  * This function keeps track of how many times it *
18  * has been called by incrementing a static local *
19  * variable, numCalls, each time it is called.    *
20  *********************************************/
21 void showStatic()
22 {
23    static int numCalls = 0;   // Static local variable
24
25    cout << "This function has been called "
26         << ++numCalls << " times. " << endl;
27 }
```

Program Output

```
This function has been called 1 times.
This function has been called 2 times.
This function has been called 3 times.
This function has been called 4 times.
This function has been called 5 times.
```

In Program 6-21 `numCalls` is defined and initialized to 0 in line 23. It is incremented in line 26 once each time the `showStatic` function is called, and because it is a static variable, it retains its value between calls. You might think that every time the function is called, `numCalls` would be reinitialized to 0. But this does not happen because a variable is only initialized when it is first created, and static variables are only created once during the running of the program. If we had not initialized `numCalls`, it would automatically have been initialized to 0 because numeric static local variables, like global variables, are initialized to 0 if the programmer does not initialize them.

Checkpoint

6.16 What is the difference between a static local variable and a global variable?

6.17 What is the output of the following program?

```
#include <iostream>
using namespace std;

void myFunc();  // Function prototype

int main()
{  int var = 100;

   cout << var << endl;
   myFunc();
   cout << var << endl;
   return 0;
}
// Definition of function myFunc
void myFunc()
{  int var = 50;

   cout << var << endl;
}
```

6.18 What is the output of the following program?

```
#include <iostream>
using namespace std;

void showVar(); // Function prototype

int main()
{  for (int count = 0; count < 10; count++)
      showVar();
   return 0;
}
// Definition of function showVar
void showVar()
{  static int var = 10;

   cout << var << endl;
   var++;
}
```

6.12 Default Arguments

CONCEPT: Default arguments are passed to parameters automatically if no argument is provided in the function call.

It's possible to assign *default arguments* to function parameters. A default argument is passed to the parameter when the actual argument is left out of the function call. The default arguments are usually listed in the function prototype. Here is an example:

```
void showArea(double length = 20.0, double width = 10.0);
```

Because parameter names are not required in function prototypes, the example prototype could also be declared like this:

```
void showArea(double = 20.0, double = 10.0);
```

In either case, the default arguments, which must be literal values or constants, have an = operator in front of them.

Notice that in both example prototypes, the function `showArea` has two `double` parameters. The first is assigned the default argument 20.0 and the second is assigned the default argument 10.0. Here is the definition of the function:

```
void showArea(double length, double width)
{
   double area = length * width;
   cout << "The area is " << area << endl;
}
```

The default argument for `length` is 20.0, and the default argument for `width` is 10.0. Because both parameters have default arguments, they may optionally be omitted in the function call, as shown here:

```
showArea();
```

In this function call, both default arguments will be passed to the parameters. Parameter `length` will receive the value 20.0, and `width` will receive the value 10.0. The output of the function will be

```
The area is 200
```

The default arguments are only used when the actual arguments are omitted from the function call. In the following call, the first argument is specified, but the second is omitted:

```
showArea(12.0);
```

The value 12.0 will be passed to `length`, while the default value 10.0 will be passed to `width`. The output of the function will be

```
The area is 120
```

Of course, all the default arguments may be overridden. In the following function call, arguments are supplied for both parameters:

```
showArea(12.0, 5.5);
```

The output of this function call will be

```
The area is 66
```

NOTE: A function's default arguments should be assigned in the earliest occurrence of the function name. This will usually be the function prototype. However, if a function does not have a prototype, default arguments may be specified in the function header. The `showArea` function could be defined as follows:

```
void showArea(double length = 20.0, double width = 10.0)
{
     double area = length * width;
     cout << "The area is " << area << endl;
}
```

Program 6-22 illustrates the use of default function arguments. It has a function that displays asterisks on the screen. This function receives arguments specifying how many rows of asterisks to display and how many asterisks to print on each row. Default arguments are provided to display 1 row of 10 asterisks.

Program 6-22

```
// This program demonstrates the use of default function arguments.
#include <iostream>
using namespace std;

// Function prototype with default arguments
void displayStars(int starsPerRow = 10, int numRows = 1);

int main()
{
   displayStars();      // starsPerRow & numRows use defaults (10 & 1)
   cout << endl;
   displayStars(5);     // starsPerRow 5. numRows uses default value 1
   cout << endl;
   displayStars(7, 3); // starsPerRow 7. numRows 3. No defaults used.
   return 0;
}

/*********************************************************
 *                      displayStars                     *
 *  This function displays a rectangle made of asterisks.  *
 *  If arguments are not passed to it, it uses the default *
 *  arguments 10 for starsPerRow and 1 for numRows.        *
 *********************************************************/
void displayStars(int starsPerRow, int numRows)
{
   // Nested loop. The outer loop controls the rows and
   // the inner loop controls the number of stars per row.
   for (int row = 1; row <= numRows; row++)
   {
      for (int star = 1; star <= starsPerRow; star++)
         cout << '*';
      cout << endl;
   }
}
```

Program Output

```
**********

*****

*******
*******
*******
```

Although C++'s default arguments are very convenient, they are not totally flexible in their use. When an argument is left out of a function call, all arguments that come after it must be left out as well. In the `displayStars` function in Program 6-22, it is not possible to omit the argument for `starsPerRow` without also omitting the argument for `numRows`. For example, the following function call would be illegal:

```
displayStars(, 3);      // Illegal function call!
```

It is possible, however, for a function to have some parameters with default arguments and some without. For example, in the following function, only the last parameter has a default argument:

```
// Function prototype
void calcPay(int empNum, double payRate, double hours = 40.0);

// Definition of function calcPay
void calcPay(int empNum, double payRate, double hours)
{
   double wages;

   wages = payRate * hours;

   cout << "Gross pay for employee number ";
   cout << empNum << " is " << wages << endl;
}
```

When calling this function, arguments must always be specified for the first two parameters (`empNum` and `payRate`) because they have no default arguments. Here are examples of valid calls:

```
calcPay(769, 15.75);      // Uses default argument for hours
calcPay(142, 12.00, 20);  // Specifies number of hours
```

When a function uses a mixture of parameters with and without default arguments, the parameters with default arguments must be declared last. In the `calcPay` function, `hours` could not have been declared before either of the other parameters. The following prototypes are illegal:

```
// Illegal prototype
void calcPay(int empNum, double hours = 40.0, double payRate);

// Illegal prototype
void calcPay(double hours = 40.0, int empNum, double payRate);
```

Here is a summary of the important points about default arguments:

- The value of a default argument must be a literal value or a named constant.
- When an argument is left out of a function call (because it has a default value), all the arguments that come after it must also be left out.
- When a function has a mixture of parameters both with and without default arguments, the parameters with default arguments must be defined last.

6.13 Using Reference Variables as Parameters

CONCEPT: A reference variable is a variable that references the memory location of another variable. Any change made to the reference variable is actually made to the one it references. Reference variables are sometimes used as function parameters.

Earlier you saw that arguments are normally passed to a function by value. This means that parameters receive only a copy of the value sent to them, which they store in the function's local memory. Any changes made to the parameter's value do not affect the value of the original argument.

Sometimes, however, we want a function to be able to change a value in the calling function (i.e., the function that called it). This can be done by making the parameter a reference variable.

You learned in Chapter 1 that variables are the names of memory locations that may hold data. When we use a variable we are accessing data stored in the memory location assigned to it. A *reference variable* is an alias for another variable. Instead of having its own memory location for storing data, it accesses the memory location of another variable. Any change made to the reference variable's data is actually made to the data stored in the memory location of the other variable. When we use a reference variable as a parameter, it becomes an alias for the corresponding variable in the argument list. Any change made to the parameter is actually made to the variable in the calling function. When data is passed to a parameter in this manner, the argument is said to be *passed by reference.*

Reference variables are defined like regular variables, except there is an ampersand (`&`) between the data type and the name. For example, the following function definition makes the parameter `refVar` a reference variable:

```
void doubleNum(int &refVar)
{
   refVar *= 2;
}
```

You may place the space either before or after the ampersand. The `doubleNum` function heading could also have been written like this:

```
void doubleNum(int& refVar)
```

NOTE: The variable `refVar` is called "a reference to an `int`."

This function doubles `refVar` by multiplying it by 2. Because `refVar` is a reference variable, this action is actually performed on the variable that was passed to the function as an argument.

The prototype for a function with a reference parameter must have an ampersand as well. As in the function header, it goes between the data type and the variable name. If the variable name is omitted from the prototype, the ampersand simply follows the data type. All of the following prototypes for the `doubleNum` function are correct.

```
void doubleNum(int &refVar);
void doubleNum(int& refVar);
void doubleNum(int &);
void doubleNum(int&);
```

Your instructor will let you know which form to use.

NOTE: The ampersand must appear in both the prototype and the header of any function that uses a reference variable as a parameter. It does not appear in the function call.

Program 6-23 demonstrates the use of a parameter that is a reference variable.

Program 6-23

```
// This program uses a reference variable as a function parameter.
#include <iostream>
using namespace std;

// Function prototype. The parameter is a reference variable.
void doubleNum(int &refVar);

int main()
{
   int value = 4;

   cout << "In main, value is " << value << endl;
   cout << "Now calling doubleNum..." << endl;
   doubleNum(value);
   cout << "Now back in main, value is " << value << endl;
   return 0;
}

/**********************************************************
 *                        doubleNum                       *
 * This function's parameter is a reference variable. The &  *
 * tells us that. This means it receives a reference to the  *
 * original variable passed to it, rather than a copy of that *
 * variable's data. The statement refVar *= 2 is doubling the *
 * data stored in the value variable defined in main.      *
 **********************************************************/
void doubleNum (int &refVar)
{
   refVar *= 2;
}
```

Program Output

```
In main, value is 4
Now calling doubleNum...
Now back in main, value is 8
```

The parameter `refVar` in Program 6-23 "points" to the `value` variable in function `main`. When a program works with a reference variable, it is actually working with the variable it references, or points to. This is illustrated in Figure 6-14.

Figure 6-14

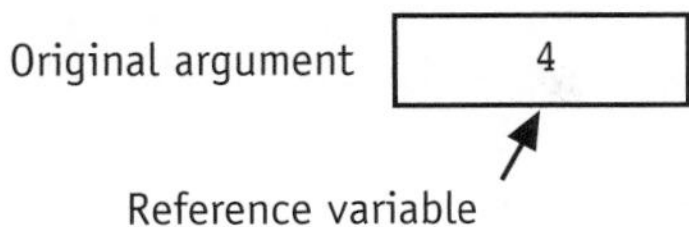

Using reference variables as function parameters is especially useful when the purpose of the function is to accept input values to be stored in variables of the calling function. Another use of reference parameters is when multiple values must be sent back from the function. If the function is computing and sending back a single value, it is generally considered more appropriate to use a value-returning function and send the value back with a `return` statement.

Program 6-24 is a modification of Program 6-23. It adds a function `getNum`, which accepts an input from the user and stores it in `userNum`. However, the parameter `userNum` is a reference to `main's` variable `value`, so that is where the input data is actually stored. Program 6-24 also rewrites the function `doubleNum` as a value-returning function. Notice in line 19 how `main` must now store the value when `doubleNum` returns it.

Program 6-24

```
 1 // This program uses 2 functions: a void function with a reference
 2 // variable as a parameter, and a value-returning function.
 3 #include <iostream>
 4 using namespace std;
 5 
 6 // Function prototypes
 7 void getNum(int &);
 8 int doubleNum(int);
 9 
10 int main()
11 {
12    int value;
13 
14    // Call getNum to get a number and store it in value
15    getNum(value);
16 
17    // Call doubleNum, passing it the number stored in value
18    // Assign value the number returned by the function
19    value = doubleNum(value);
20 
21    // Display the resulting number
22    cout << "That value doubled is " << value << endl;
23    return 0;
24 }
25 
```

(program continues)

Program 6-24 *(continued)*

```
/*********************************************************
 *                          getNum                       *
 * This function stores user input data in main's value  *
 * variable by using a reference variable as a parameter. *
 *********************************************************/
void getNum(int &userNum)
{
   cout << "Enter a number: ";
   cin  >> userNum;
}

/**********************************************************
 *                         doubleNum                      *
 * This function doubles the number it receives as an     *
 * argument and returns it to main thru a return statement.*
 **********************************************************/
int doubleNum (int number)
{
   return number * 2;
}
```

Program Output with Example Input Shown in Bold

```
Enter a number: 12[Enter]
That value doubled is 24
```

NOTE: Only variables may be passed by reference. If you attempt to pass a non-variable argument, such as a literal, a constant, or an expression, into a reference parameter, an error will result.

If a function has more than one parameter that is a reference variable, you must use an ampersand for each of them in both the prototype and the function header. Here is the prototype for a function that uses four reference variable parameters:

```
void addThree(int& num1, int& num2, int& num3, int& sum);
```

and here is the function definition:

```
void addThree(int& num1, int& num2, int& num3, int& sum)
{
   cout << "Enter three integer values: ";
   cin  >> num1 >> num2 >> num3;
   sum = num1 + num2 + num3;
}
```

Notice, however, that the `addThree` function really only needed one reference parameter, `sum`. The other three parameters could have received their arguments by value, because the function was not changing them.

WARNING! Don't get carried away with using reference variables as function parameters. Only use them where absolutely needed. Any time you allow a function to alter a variable that's outside the function, you are creating potential debugging problems.

When to Pass Arguments by Reference and When to Pass Arguments by Value

New programmers often have a problem determining when an argument should be passed to a function by reference and when it should be passed by value. The problem is further compounded by the fact that if a value must be "sent back" to the calling function there are two ways to do it: by using a reference parameter or by using a `return` statement. Here are some general guidelines.

- When an argument is a constant, it must be passed by value. Only variables can be passed by reference.
- When a variable passed as an argument should not have its value changed, it should be passed by value. This protects it from being altered.
- When exactly one value needs to be "sent back" from a function to the calling routine, it should generally be returned with a `return` statement rather than through a reference parameter.
- When two or more variables passed as arguments to a function need to have their values changed by that function, they should be passed by reference.
- When a copy of an argument cannot reasonably or correctly be made, such as when the argument is a file stream object, it must be passed by reference.

Here are three common instances when reference parameters are used.

- When data values being input in a function need to be known by the calling function.
- When a function must change existing values in the calling function.
- When a file stream object is passed to a function.

Program 6-25 illustrates the first two of these uses. The `getNums` function uses reference variables as parameters so that it can store the values it inputs into the `main` function's `small` and `big` variables. The `orderNums` function uses reference variables as parameters so that when it swaps the two items passed to it, the values will actually be swapped in the `main` function.

Program 6-25

```
// This program illustrates two appropriate uses
// of passing arguments by reference.
#include <iostream>
using namespace std;

// Function prototypes
void getNums (int&, int&);    // Uses reference parameters to input
                              // values in the function, but to actually
                              // store them in variables defined in main

void orderNums(int&, int&);   // Uses reference parameters to change the
                              // values of existing values stored in main
```

(program continues)

Program 6-25 *(continued)*

```
int main()
{
   int small, big;

   // Call getNums to input the two numbers
   getNums(small, big);

   // Call orderNums to put the numbers in order
   orderNums(small, big);

   // Display the new values
   cout  << "The two input numbers ordered smallest to biggest are "
         << small << " and " << big << endl;
   return 0;
}

/**********************************************************
 *                        getNums                         *
 * The arguments passed into input1 and input2 are passed *
 * by reference so that the values entered into them will *
 * actually be stored in the memory space of main's small *
 * and big variables.                                     *
 **********************************************************/
void getNums(int &input1, int &input2)
{
   cout << "Enter an integer: ";
   cin  >> input1;
   cout << "Enter a second integer: ";
   cin  >> input2;
}

/**********************************************************
 *                       orderNums                        *
 * The arguments passed into num1 and num2 are passed by  *
 * reference so that if they are out of order main's      *
 * variables small and big can be swapped. Just swapping  *
 * num1 and num2 in orderNum's local memory would not     *
 * accomplish the desired result.                         *
 **********************************************************/
void orderNums (int &num1, int &num2)
{
   int temp;

   if (num1 > num2)  // If the numbers are out of order, swap them
   {   temp = num1;
       num1 = num2;
       num2 = temp;
   }
}
```

(program continues)

Program 6-25 *(continued)*

Program Output With Example Input Shown in Bold

```
Enter an integer: 10[Enter]
Enter a second integer: 5[Enter]
The two input numbers ordered smallest to biggest are 5 and 10
```

Passing Files to Functions

As mentioned previously, reference parameters should always be used when a file stream object is passed to a function. Program 6-26 illustrates how to pass a file to a function. The `weather.dat` file used by the program contains the following seven values: 72 83 71 69 75 77 70.

Program 6-26

```
// This program reads a set of daily high temperatures from a file
// and displays them. It demonstrates how to pass a file to a
// function. The function argument, which is a file stream object,
// must be passed by reference.
#include <iostream>
#include <fstream>
using namespace std;

void readFile(ifstream&);        // Function prototype

int main()
{
   ifstream dataIn;

   dataIn.open("weather.dat");
   if (dataIn.fail())
      cout << "Error opening data file.\n";
   else
   {  readFile(dataIn);
      dataIn.close();
   }
   return 0;
}

/*******************************************************
 *                      readFile                       *
 * This function reads and displays the contents of the *
 * input file whose file stream object is passed to it. *
 *******************************************************/
```

(program continues)

Program 6-26 *(continued)*

```
void readFile(ifstream &someFile)
{
   int temperature;

   while (someFile >> temperature)
      cout << temperature << "  ";
   cout << endl;
}
```

Program Output

```
72  83  71  69  75  77  70
```

Checkpoint

6.19 What kinds of values may be specified as default arguments?

6.20 Write the prototype and header for a function called `compute`. The function should have three parameters: an `int`, a `double`, and a `long` (not necessarily in that order). The `int` parameter should have a default argument of 5, and the `long` parameter should have a default argument of 65536. The `double` parameter should not have a default argument.

6.21 Write the prototype and header for a function called `calculate`. The function should have three parameters: an `int`, a reference to a `double`, and a `long` (not necessarily in that order.) Only the `int` parameter should have a default argument, which is 47.

6.22 What is the output of the following program?

```
#include <iostream>
using namespace std;

void test(int = 2, int = 4, int = 6);

int main()
{
   test();
   test(6);
   test(3, 9);
   test(1, 5, 7);
   return 0;
}

void test (int first, int second, int third)
{
   first += 3;
   second += 6;
   third += 9;
   cout << first << "  " << second << "  " << third << endl;
}
```

6.23 The following program asks the user to enter two numbers. What is the output of the program if the user enters 12 and 14?

```
#include <iostream>
using namespace std;

void func1(int &, int &);
void func2(int &, int &, int &);
void func3(int, int, int);

int main()
{
   int x = 0, y = 0, z = 0;
   cout << x << " " << y << z << endl;
   func1(x, y);
   cout << x << " " << y << z << endl;
   func2(x, y, z);
   cout << x << " " << y << z << endl;
   func3(x, y, z);
   cout << x << " " << y << z << endl;
   return 0;
}

void func1(int &a, int &b)
{  cout << "Enter two numbers: ";
   cin  >> a >> b;
}

void func2(int &a, int &b, int &c)
{  b++;
   c--;
   a = b + c;
}

void func3(int a, int b, int c)
{  a = b - c;
}
```

6.14 Overloading Functions

CONCEPT: Two or more functions may have the same name, as long as their parameter lists are different.

Sometimes you will create two or more functions that perform the same operation, but use a different set of parameters, or parameters of different data types. For instance, in Program 6-12 there is a `square` function that uses a `double` parameter. But suppose you also wanted a `square` function that works exclusively with integers and accepts an `int` as its argument. Both functions would do the same thing, return the square of their argument. The only difference is the data type involved in the operation. If you were to use both these functions in the same program, you could assign a unique name to each function. For example, the function that squares an `int` might be named `squareInt`, and the one that squares a `double` might be named `squareDouble`. C++, however, allows you to *overload* function names. That means you may assign the same name to multiple functions, as long as their parameter lists are different. Program 6-27 uses two overloaded `square` functions.

Program 6-27

```
// This program uses overloaded functions.
#include <iostream>
#include <iomanip>
using namespace std;

// Function prototypes
int square(int);
double square(double);

int main()
{
   int userInt;
   double userReal;

   // Get an int and a double
   cout << "Enter an integer and a floating-point value: ";
   cin  >> userInt >> userReal;

   // Display their squares
   cout << "Here are their squares: ";
   cout << fixed << showpoint << setprecision(2);
   cout << square(userInt) << " and " << square(userReal) << endl;
   return 0;
}

/***************************************************
 *            overloaded function square           *
 * This function returns the square of the value   *
 * passed into its int parameter.                  *
 ***************************************************/
int square(int number)
{
   return number * number;
}

/***************************************************
 *            overloaded function square           *
 * This function returns the square of the value   *
 * passed into its double parameter.               *
 ***************************************************/
double square(double number)
{
   return number * number;
}
```

Program Output with Example Input Shown in Bold

```
Enter an integer and a floating-point value: 12 4.2[Enter]
Here are their squares: 144 and 17.64
```

Here are the headers for the square functions used in Program 6-27:

```
int square(int number)
double square(double number)
```

In C++, each function has a signature. The *function signature* is the name of the function and the data types of the function's parameters in the proper order. The square functions in Program 6-27 would have the following signatures:

```
square(int)
square(double)
```

When an overloaded function is called, C++ uses the function signature to distinguish it from other functions with the same name. In Program 6-27, when an int argument is passed to square, the version of the function that has an int parameter is called. Likewise, when a double argument is passed to square, the version with a double parameter is called.

Note that the function's return value is not part of the signature. The following functions could *not* be used in the same program because their parameter lists aren't different.

```
int square(int number)
{
   return number * number
}

double square(int number)  // Wrong! Parameter lists must differ
{
   return number * number
}
```

Overloading is also convenient when there are similar functions that use a different number of parameters. For example, consider a program with functions that return the sum of integers. One returns the sum of two integers, another returns the sum of three integers, and yet another returns the sum of four integers. Here are their function headers:

```
int sum(int num1, int num2)
int sum(int num1, int num2, int num3)
int sum(int num1, int num2, int num3, int num4)
```

Because the number of parameters is different in each, they may all be used in the same program. Program 6-28 uses two functions, each named calcWeeklyPay, to determine an employee's gross weekly pay. One version of the function uses an int and a double parameter, while the other version only uses a double parameter.

Program 6-28

```
// This program demonstrates overloaded functions to calculate
// the gross weekly pay of hourly-wage or salaried employees.
#include <iostream>
#include <iomanip>
using namespace std;

```

(program continues)

Program 6-28 *(continued)*

```
// Function prototypes
char getChoice();
double calcWeeklyPay(int, double);
double calcWeeklyPay(double);

int main()
{
   char selection;              // Menu selection
   int worked;                  // Weekly hours worked
   double rate,                 // Hourly pay rate
          yearly;               // Annual salary

   // Set numeric output formatting
   cout << fixed << showpoint << setprecision(2);

   // Display the menu and get a selection
   cout << "Do you want to calculate the weekly pay of\n";
   cout << "(H) an hourly-wage employee, or \n";
   cout << "(S) a salaried employee? ";
   selection = getChoice();

   // Process the menu selection
   switch (selection)
   {
      // Hourly employee
      case 'H' :
      case 'h' :  cout << "How many hours were worked? ";
                  cin  >> worked;
                  cout << "What is the hourly pay rate? ";
                  cin  >> rate;
                  cout << "The gross weekly pay is $";
                  cout << calcWeeklyPay(worked, rate) << endl;
                  break;

      // Salaried employee
      case 'S' :
      case 's' :     cout << "What is the annual salary? ";
                     cin  >> yearly;
                     cout << "The gross weekly pay is $";
                     cout << calcWeeklyPay(yearly) << endl;
   }
   return 0;
}

/*****************************************************
 *                     getChoice                     *
 * Accepts and returns user's validated menu choice. *
 *****************************************************/
char getChoice()
{
   char letter;          // Holds user's letter choice

```

(program continues)

Program 6-28 *(continued)*

```
   // Get the user's choice
   cin >> letter;

   // Validate the choice
   while (letter != 'H' && letter != 'h'
       && letter != 'S' && letter != 's')
   {
      cout << "Enter H or S: ";
      cin  >> letter;
   }
   // Return the choice
   return letter;
}

/*************************************************************
 *             overloaded function calcWeeklyPay             *
 * This function calculates and returns the gross weekly pay *
 * of an hourly-wage employee. Parameters hours and payRate  *
 * hold the number of hours worked and the hourly pay rate.  *
 *************************************************************/
double calcWeeklyPay(int hours, double payRate)
{
   return hours * payRate;
}

/*************************************************************
 *             overloaded function calcWeeklyPay             *
 * This function calculates and returns the gross weekly pay *
 * of a salaried employee. The parameter annSalary holds the *
 * employee's annual salary.                                 *
 *************************************************************/
double calcWeeklyPay(double annSalary)
{
   return annSalary / 52.0;
}
```

Program Output with Example Input Shown in Bold

```
Do you want to calculate the weekly pay of
(H) an hourly-wage employee, or
(S) a salaried employee? H[Enter]
How many hours were worked? 40[Enter]
What is the hourly pay rate? 18.50[Enter]
The gross weekly pay is $740.00
```

Program Output with Other Example Data Shown in Bold

```
Do you want to calculate the weekly pay of
(H) an hourly-wage employee, or
(S) a salaried employee? S[Enter]
What is the annual salary? 48000.00[Enter]
The gross weekly pay is $923.08
```

6.15 The `exit()` Function

CONCEPT: The `exit()` function causes a program to terminate, regardless of which function or control mechanism is executing.

A C++ program stops executing when a `return` statement in function `main` is encountered. When other functions end, however, the program does not stop. Control of the program goes back to the place immediately following the function call. Sometimes, however, rare circumstances make it necessary to terminate a program in a function other than `main`. To accomplish this, the `exit` function is used.

When the `exit` function is called, it causes the program to stop, regardless of which function contains the call. Program 6-29 demonstrates this.

Program 6-29

```
// This program shows how the exit function causes a program
// to stop executing.
#include <iostream>
#include <cstdlib>    // Needed to use the exit function
using namespace std;

// Function prototype
void someFunction();

int main()
{
   someFunction();
   return 0;
}

/*****************************************************************
 *                        someFunction                           *
 * This function demonstrates that exit() can be used to end    *
 * a program from a function other than main. This is not       *
 * considered good programming practice and should normally     *
 * be done only to signal that an error condition has occurred. *
 *****************************************************************/
void someFunction()
{
   cout << "This program terminates with the exit function.\n";
   cout << "Bye!\n";
   exit(0);
   cout << "This message will never be displayed\n";
   cout << "because the program has already terminated.\n";
}
```

Program Output

```
This program terminates with the exit function.
Bye!
```

To use the exit function, you must include the cstdlib header file. Notice the function takes an integer argument. This argument is the exit code you wish the program to pass back to the computer's operating system. This code is sometimes used outside of the program to indicate whether the program ended successfully or as the result of a failure. In Program 6-29, the exit code zero is passed. This code, which is also normally used in the return statement at the end of a program's main function, indicates a successful program termination. Another way to signal this is to use the C++ named constant EXIT_SUCCESS. This constant, which is defined in cstdlib, is used with the exit function like this:

```
exit(EXIT_SUCCESS);
```

However, because it is considered good programming practice to always terminate a program at the end of the main function where possible, many programmers use exit() only to handle error conditions. In this case, the error code should indicate that a problem has occurred. This can be done by using another C++ named constant, EXIT_FAILURE. This named constant, also defined in cstdlib, is defined as the termination code that commonly represents an unsuccessful exit under the current operating system. Here is an example of its use:

```
exit(EXIT_FAILURE);
```

WARNING! The exit() function unconditionally shuts down your program. Because it bypasses a program's normal logical flow, you should use it with caution.

Checkpoint

6.24 Is it required that overloaded functions have different return types, different parameter lists, or both?

6.25 What is the output of the following program?

```
#include <iostream>
#include <cstdlib>
using namespace std;

void showVals(double, double);

int main()
{
   double x = 1.2, y = 4.5;

   showVals(x, y);
   return 0;
}

void showVals(double p1, double p2)
{
   cout << p1 << endl;
   exit(0);
   cout << p2 << endl;
}
```

6.26 What is the output of the following program?

```
#include <iostream>
using namespace std;
int manip(int);
int manip(int, int);
int manip(int, double);

int main()
{
   int x = 2, y= 4, z;
   double a = 3.1;

   z = manip(x) + manip(x, y) + manip(y, a);
   cout << z << endl;
   return 0;
}

int manip(int val)
{
   return val + val * 2;
}

int manip(int val1, int val2)
{
   return (val1 + val2) * 2;
}

int manip(int val1, double val2)
{
   return val1 * static_cast<int>(val2);
}
```

6.16 Stubs and Drivers

Stubs and drivers are very helpful tools for testing and debugging programs that use functions. They allow you to test the individual functions in a program, in isolation from the parts of the program that call the functions.

A *stub* is a dummy function that is called instead of the actual function it represents. It usually displays a test message acknowledging that it was called, and nothing more. For example, if a stub were used for the `showFees` function in Program 6-14 (the modular health club membership program), it might look like this:

```
// Stub for the showFees function
void showFees(string memberType, double rate, int months)
{
   cout << "The function showFees was called with arguments:\n"
        << "Member type: "  << memberType << endl
        << "rate: " << rate << endl
        << "months: " << months << endl;
}
```

Here is example output of the program if it were run with this stub instead of with the actual `showFees` function. Input is shown in bold.

```
        Health Club Membership Menu

    1. Standard Adult Membership
    2. Child Membership
    3. Senior Citizen Membership
    4. Quit the Program

    1[Enter]
    For how many months? 3[Enter]
    The function showFees was called with arguments:
    Member type: Adult
    rate: 120.00
    months: 3

        Health Club Membership Menu

    1. Standard Adult Membership
    2. Child Membership
    3. Senior Citizen Membership
    4. Quit the Program

    4[Enter]
```

As you can see, by replacing an actual function with a stub, you can concentrate your testing efforts on the parts of the program that call the function. Primarily, the stub allows you to determine whether your program is calling a function when you expect it to and confirm that valid values are being passed to the function. If the stub represents a function that returns a value, then the stub should return a test value. This helps you confirm that the return value is being handled properly. When the parts of the program that call a function are debugged to your satisfaction, you can move on to testing and debugging the actual functions themselves. This is where drivers become useful.

A *driver* is a program that tests a function by simply calling it. If the function accepts any arguments, the driver passes test data. If the function returns a value, the driver displays the return value on the screen. This allows you to see how the function performs in isolation from the rest of the program it will eventually be part of. Program 6-30 is a driver for testing the `showFees` function in the health club membership program.

Program 6-30

```
// This program is a driver for testing the showFees function.
#include <iostream>
#include <string>
using namespace std;

// Function prototype
void showFees(string, double, int);

```

(program continues)

Program 6-30 *(continued)*

```
int main()
{
   cout << "Calling the showFees function with arguments "
        << "Adult, 120.0, 3.\n";
   showFees("Adult", 120.0, 3);

   cout << "Calling the showFees function with arguments "
        << "Child, 60.0, 2.\n";
   showFees("Child", 60.0, 2);

   cout << "Calling the showFees function with arguments "
        << "Senior, 100.0, 4.\n";
   showFees("Senior", 100.0, 4);

   return 0;
}

/*****************************************************
 *                    showFees                       *
 * This function uses the membership type, monthly   *
 * rate and number of months passed to it as arguments *
 * to compute and print a member's total charges.    *
 *****************************************************/
void showFees(string memberType, double rate, int months)
{
   cout << endl
        << "Membership Type : " << memberType << "    "
        << "Monthly rate $"     << rate   << endl
        << "Number of months: " << months << endl
        << "Total charges   : $"<< (rate * months)
        << endl << endl;
}
```

Program Output

```
Calling the showFees function with arguments Adult, 120.0, 3.

Membership Type : Adult    Monthly rate $120
Number of months: 3
Total charges   : $360

Calling the showFees function with arguments Child, 60.0, 2.

Membership Type : Child    Monthly rate $60
Number of months: 2
Total charges   : $120

Calling the showFees function with arguments Senior, 100.0, 4.

Membership Type : Senior    Monthly rate $100
Number of months: 4
Total charges   : $400
```

As shown in Program 6-30, a driver can be used to thoroughly test a function. It can repeatedly call the function with different test values as arguments. When the function performs as desired, it can be placed into the actual program it will be part of.

Little Lotto Case Study

Problem Statement

The mathematics department of Jefferson Junior High School wants a program developed that will illustrate basic probability for their students in an entertaining way. In particular they want a program called "Little Lotto" that simulates a lottery. In this program students can specify the number of numbers in the selection set (1–12) and the number of numbers patrons must pick and match to the winning numbers (between 1 and the size of the selection set). The order of the selected numbers is not significant. It will report the patron's chances of winning as both a number and a probability.

Example Output

This example output clarifies exactly what the department wants the program to do.

```
This program will tell you your probability of winning "Little Lotto".

How many numbers (1-12) are there to pick from? 12
How many numbers must you pick to play? 5

Your chance of winning the lottery is 1 chance in 792.
This is a probability of 0.0013
```

Program Design

Program Steps

The program must carry out the following general steps:

1. Get and validate how many numbers there are to choose from (`n`).
2. Get and validate how many of these numbers must be selected (`k`).
3. Compute the number of ways a set of `k` items can be selected from a set of `n` items.
4. Report to the player his chance of winning and his probability of winning.

Program Modules

The program will be designed as a set of modules, each having a specific function. Table 6-1 describes the modules that will be used:

Table 6-1 Little Lotto Program Modules

Function	Description
`main`	This function explains the "game", organizes calls to other functions, and reports results.
`getLotteryInfo`	This function gets and validates the number of numbers to select from (n) and the number that must be chosen (k).
`computeWays`	This function computes the number of different sets of size k that can be chosen from n numbers.
`factorial`	This function computes factorials. It is used by `computeWays`.

Program Organization

In previous chapters hierarchy charts were used to illustrate the relationship of actions that a program must carry out. However, they are more commonly used to illustrate the relationship of program modules in a program that is organized into a set of functions. The hierarchy chart in Figure 6-15 illustrates the organization of the Little Lotto program. Notice that it clarifies which functions call which other functions.

Figure 6-15

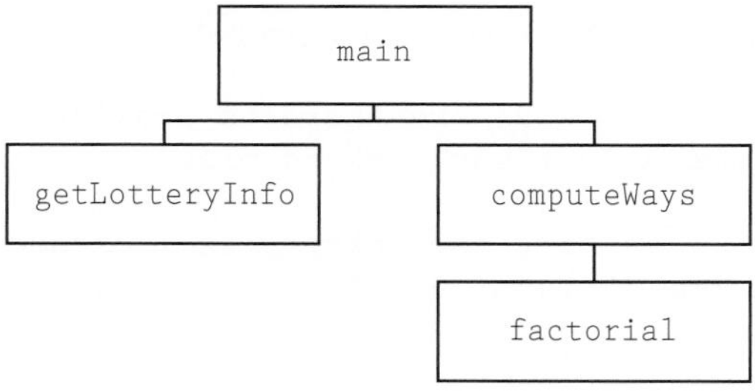

Variables whose values will be input

```
int  pickFrom        // Number of numbers available to select from
int  numPicks        // Number of numbers that must be chosen
```

Variables and values whose values will be output

```
long int ways        // Number of different possible selections
                     // Only 1 of these can "win"
1.0 / ways           // Probability of winning
```

Detailed Pseudocode for Each Module

In a modular program, a separate pseudocode routine should be created to capture the logic of each function. Here is the pseudocode for each function in the Little Lotto program.

```
main
   Display information on what the program does
   Call getLotteryInfo  // Puts value in pickFrom and numPicks variables
   Call computeWays     // Returns number of ways numbers can be selected
   Store the returned result in the ways variable
   Display ways and 1 / ways
End main

getLotteryInfo          // Places inputs in reference variables
   Input pickFrom
   While pickFrom < 1 or pickFrom > 12
      Display an error message
      Input pickFrom
   End while
   Input numPicks
   While numPicks < 1 or numPicks > pickFrom
      Display an error message
      Input pickFrom
   End while
End getLotteryInfo

computeWays             // Receives pickFrom as n and numPicks as k
   Call factorial 3 times to get information for its calculations
   Return  ________factorial(n)__________
           factorial(k) *  factorial (n-k)
End computeWays

factorial      // Receives number whose factorial is to be calculated
   factTotal = 1
   Loop for count = number down to 1
      factTotal = factTotal * count
   End Loop
   Return factTotal
End factorial
```

The Program

The next step, after the pseudocode has been checked for logic errors, is to expand the pseudocode into the final program. This is shown in Program 6-31.

Program 6-31

```
// This program finds the probability of winning a "mini" lottery when
// the user's set of numbers must exactly match the set drawn by the
// lottery organizers. In addition to main, it uses three functions.
#include <iostream>
#include <iomanip>
using namespace std;

// Function prototypes
void getLotteryInfo(int&, int&);
long int computeWays(int, int);
long int factorial(int);

```

(program continues)

Program 6-31 *(continued)*

```
int main()
{
   int pickFrom,           // The number of numbers to pick from
       numPicks;           // The number of numbers to select
   long int ways;          // The number of different possible
                           // ways to pick the set of numbers

   cout << "This program will tell you your probability of "
        << "winning \"Little Lotto\". \n";
   getLotteryInfo(pickFrom, numPicks);
   ways = computeWays(pickFrom, numPicks);

   cout << fixed << showpoint << setprecision(4);
   cout << "\nYour chance of winning the lottery is "
        << "1 chance in " << ways << ".\n";
   cout << "This is a probability of " << (1.0 / ways)    << "\n";
   return 0;
}

/*******************************************************************
 *                        getLotteryInfo                           *
 * Gets and validates lottery info. from the user and places it in *
 * reference parameters referencing variables in the main function.*
 *******************************************************************/
void getLotteryInfo(int &pickFrom, int &numPicks)
{
   cout << "\nHow many numbers (1-12) are there to pick from? ";
   cin  >> pickFrom;
   while (pickFrom < 1 || pickFrom > 12)
   {
      cout << "There must be between 1 and 12 numbers.\n"
           << "How many numbers (1-12) are there to pick from? ";
      cin  >> pickFrom;
   }
   cout << "How many numbers must you pick to play? ";
   cin  >> numPicks;
   while (numPicks < 1 || numPicks > pickFrom)
   {
      if (numPicks < 1)                          // too few picks
         cout << "You must pick at least one number.\n";
      else                                       // too many picks
         cout << "You must pick " << pickFrom << " or fewer numbers.\n";

      cout << "How many numbers must you pick to play? ";
      cin  >> numPicks;
   }
}

```

(program continues)

Program 6-31 *(continued)*

```
/*******************************************************************
 *                       computeWays                               *
 * Computes and returns the number of different possible sets      *
 * of k numbers that can be chosen from a set of n numbers.        *
 * The formula for this is   n!                                    *
 *                        --------                                 *
 *                        k!(n-k)!                                 *
 *******************************************************************/
// Note that the computation is done in a way that does not require
// multiplying two factorials together. This is done to prevent any
// intermediate result becoming so large that it causes overflow.
long int computeWays(int n, int k)
{
   return ( factorial(n) / factorial(k) / factorial (n-k) );
}

/*******************************************************************
 *                          factorial                              *
 * Computes and returns the factorial of the non-negative integer  *
 * passed to it. n! means n * (n-1) * (n-2) ... * 1                *
 * 0! is a special case and is defined to be 1.                    *
 *******************************************************************/
// Notice that if number equals 0, the loop condition will
// initially be false and the loop will never be executed.
// This will, correctly, leave factTotal = 1.

long int factorial(int number)
{
   long int factTotal = 1;

   for (int count = number; count >= 1; count--)
   {
      factTotal *= count;
   }
   return factTotal;
}
```

Program Output with Example Input Shown in Bold

```
This program will tell you your probability of winning "Little Lotto".

How many numbers (1-12) are there to pick from? 10[Enter]
How many numbers must you pick to play? 3[Enter]

Your chance of winning the lottery is 1 chance in 120.
This is a probability of 0.0083
```

High Adventure Travel Agency Case Study

The following additional case study, which contain applications of material introduced in Chapter 6, can be found on the book's companion website. It demonstrates all the steps needed to develop a modular program that calculates and itemizes charges for the vacation packages offered by the High Adventure Travel Agency.

6.18 Tying It All Together: *Glowing Jack-o-lantern*

Functions are not just practical. They are fun. True, they let you simplify programs by breaking them into smaller modules. And they minimize repetitive code. If you need to do the same thing in several different places in your program, you can just write a function to do it, then call that function from different places in the program instead of writing the same block of code more than once. But they also let you do new and fun things. This is because even though the function code is the same, it will behave differently every time it is called with different arguments.

For example, we could write the following `printSpaces` function and each time it will print a different number of spaces depending on the value passed in to its parameter `n`.

```
void printSpaces(int n)
{
   for (int space = 1; space <= n; space++)
      cout << " ";
}
```

Now that may not sound like fun, but let's see how we can use it and other functions to enhance the smiley face we created in Chapter 2 and the colored alphabet program we created in Chapter 5. We will start with the alphabet program and use the simple `printSpaces` function shown above to make the letters appear to "climb down a set of stairs" by moving them across the screen as they are displayed. So that they will all fit on one screen, we will print them in pairs.

Recall from Chapter 5, however, that the function we are using to display output in color uses a Windows operating system function, so this program will only run on Windows systems.

Program 6-32

```
// This program writes the ABCs in green, red, and yellow,
// displaying them diagonally across the screen so they
// appear to be climbing down a staircase.
#include <iostream>
#include <windows.h>      // Needed to display colors and call Sleep
using namespace std;

// Prototype
void printSpaces(int n);

int main()
{
   // Bright Green = 10   Bright Red = 12   Bright Yellow = 14

   // Get the handle to standard output device (the console)
   HANDLE screen = GetStdHandle(STD_OUTPUT_HANDLE);

   // Write the ABCs using 3 colors
   // Display 2 per line, stair stepping across the screen
   int color = 10;      // Starting color = green
```

(program continues)

Program 6-32 *(continued)*

```
   for (char letter = 'A'; letter <= 'Z'; letter+=2)
   {
      SetConsoleTextAttribute (screen, color);    // Set the color
      printSpaces(letter-'A');                    // Indent
      cout << letter                              // Print 2 letters
           << static_cast<char>(letter+1) << endl;
      color +=2;                                  // Choose next color
      if (color > 14)
         color = 10;

      Sleep(280);  // Pause between characters to watch them appear
   }
   // Restore normal text attribute (i.e. white)
   SetConsoleTextAttribute(screen, 7);
   return 0;
}

/*******************************************
 *                printSpaces              *
 * Prints n spaces where n is passed as an  *
 * argument to the function.               *
 *******************************************/
void printSpaces(int n)
{
   for (int space = 1; space <= n; space++)
      cout << " ";
}
```

Run the program and view the results. The output display should look like the one below, but in color of course.

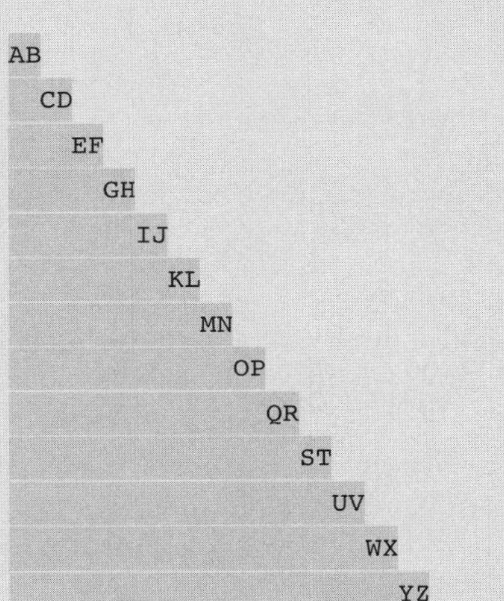

Now, can you modify the program to make the letters appear to climb UP the stairs? The program will still print starting with the top line and move down the screen, but the final display should look like this:

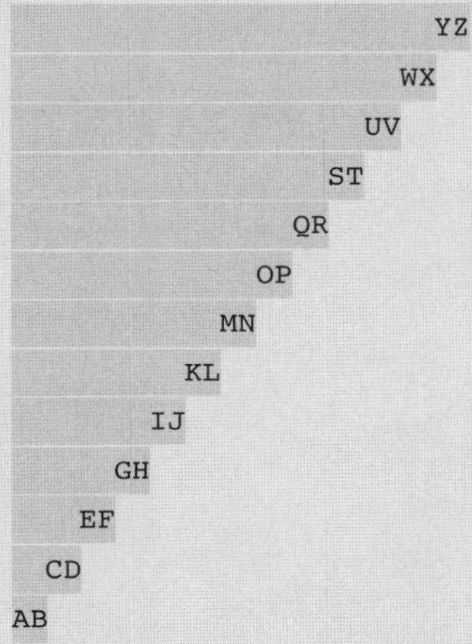

If you have trouble figuring this out, the solution can be found in the Program 6-32B. cpp file on the book's companion website.

Now let's use a function to turn the Smiley Face we created in Chapter 2's Tying It All Together into a spooky Jack-o-lantern glowing in the dark. We'll let the user pick what color to display it in.

Program 6-33

```
// This program displays a Jack-o-lantern glowing in the dark.
// It lets the user select what color it should be.
#include <iostream>
#include <windows.h>     // Needed to display colors
using namespace std;

// Function prototypes
void displayMenu();
int getChoice();
void makeJackOLantern();

// Global constants
const int QUIT = 6, MAX_CHOICE = 6;

int main()
{
   int colorChoice;
   // Get the handle to standard output device (the console)
   HANDLE screen = GetStdHandle(STD_OUTPUT_HANDLE);

   do
   {  SetConsoleTextAttribute(screen, 7);   // Set to white on black
      displayMenu();                        // for menu display
      colorChoice = getChoice();

      if (colorChoice != QUIT)
      {  SetConsoleTextAttribute(screen, colorChoice + 9);
         makeJackOLantern();
      }
   } while (colorChoice != QUIT);
   return 0;
}

/*****************************************************
 *                    displayMenu                    *
 * This function displays the menu of color choices.*
 *****************************************************/
void displayMenu()
{  system("cls");                 // Clear the screen
   cout << "I will draw a Jack-o-lantern. What color should it be?\n\n"
        << "Enter 1 for Green      2 for Blue      3 for Red \n"
        << "      4 for Purple     5 for Yellow    6 to quit: ";
}

```

(program continues)

Program 6-33 *(continued)*

```
/*******************************************************
 *                       getChoice                      *
 *  This function inputs, validates, and returns        *
 *  the user's menu choice.                             *
 *******************************************************/
int getChoice()
{
   int choice;

   cin >> choice;
   while (choice < 1 || choice > MAX_CHOICE)
   {  cout << "\nThe only valid choices are 1-" << MAX_CHOICE
           << ". Please re-enter. ";
      cin  >> choice;
   }
   return choice;
}

/************************************************
 *               makeJackOLantern                *
 *  This function draws a Jack-o-lantern         *
 *  in whatever color the user selected.         *
 ************************************************/
void makeJackOLantern()
{
   cout << "\n\n";
   cout << "                             ^   ^   \n";
   cout << "                               *     \n";
   cout << "                             \\___/    " << endl;
   cout << "\n\n            Press ENTER to return to the menu." ;
   cin.get();     // Clear the previous \n out of the input buffer
   cin.get();     // Wait for the user to press ENTER
}
```

Review Questions and Exercises

Fill-in-the-Blank and Short Answer

1. The _________ is the part of a function definition that shows the function name, return type, and parameter list.
2. If a function doesn't return a value, the word _________ will appear as its return type.
3. If function `showValue` has the following header: `void showValue(int quantity)` you would use the statement _________ to call it with the argument 5.
4. Either a function's _________ or its _________ must precede all calls to the function.
5. Values that are sent into a function are called _________.
6. Special variables that hold copies of function arguments are called _________.

7. When only a copy of an argument is passed to a function, it is said to be passed by _________.
8. A(n)_________ eliminates the need to place a function definition before all calls to the function.
9. A(n)_________ variable is defined inside a function and is not accessible outside the function.
10. _________ variables are defined outside all functions and are accessible to any function within their scope.
11. _________ variables provide an easy way to share large amounts of data among all the functions in a program.
12. Unless you explicitly initialize numeric global variables, they are automatically initialized to _________.
13. If a function has a local variable with the same name as a global variable, only the _________ variable can be seen by the function.
14. _________ local variables retain their value between function calls.
15. The _________ statement causes a function to end immediately.
16. _________ arguments are passed to parameters automatically if no argument is provided in the function call.
17. When a function uses a mixture of parameters with and without default arguments, the parameters with default arguments must be defined _________.
18. The value of a default argument must be a(n)_________.
19. When used as parameters, _________ variables allow a function to access the parameter's original argument.
20. Reference variables are defined like regular variables, except there is a(n) _________ in front of the name.
21. Reference variables allow arguments to be passed by ____________.
22. The _________ function causes a program to terminate immediately.
23. Two or more functions may have the same name, as long as their _________ are different.
24. What is the advantage of breaking your application's code into several small functions?
25. What is the difference between an argument and a parameter variable?
26. When a function accepts multiple arguments, does it matter what order the arguments are passed in?
27. What does it mean to overload a function?
28. If you are writing a function that accepts an argument and you want to make sure the function cannot change the value of the argument, what should you do?
29. Give an example where an argument should be passed by reference.
30. How do you return a value from a function?
31. Can a function have a local variable with the same name as a global variable?
32. When should a `static` local variable be used?

Algorithm Workbench

33. The following statement calls a function named `half`, which returns a value that is half that of the argument passed to it. Assume that `result` and `number` have both been defined to be `double` variables. Write the `half` function.

```
result = half(number);
```

34. A program contains the following function.

```
int cube(int num)
{
    return num * num * num;
}
```

Write a statement that passes the value 4 to this function and assigns its return value to the variable `result`.

35. Write a function, named `timesTen`, that accepts an integer argument. When the function is called, it should display the product of its argument multiplied times 10.

36. A program contains the following function.

```
void display(int arg1, double arg2, char arg3)
{
   cout << "Here are the values: "
        << arg1 << " " << arg2 << " " << arg3 << endl;
}
```

Write a statement that calls the function and passes the following variables to it:

```
int age;
double income;
char initial;
```

37. Write a function named `getNumber`, which uses a reference parameter to accept an integer argument. The function should prompt the user to enter a number in the range of 1 through 100. The input should be validated and stored in the parameter variable.

38. Write a function named `biggest` that receives three integer arguments and returns the largest of the three values.

Find the Errors

39. Each of the following functions has errors. Locate as many errors as you can.

A)
```
void total(int value1, value2, value3)
{
   return value1 + value2 + value3;
}
```

B)
```
double average(int value1, int value2, int value3)
{
   double average;

   average = value1 + value2 + value3 / 3;
}
```

C)
```
void area(int length = 30, int width)
{
   return length * width;
}
```

D)
```
void getValue(int value&)
{
   cout << "Enter a value: ";
   cin  >> value&;
}
```

E)
```
// Overloaded functions
int getValue()
{
   int inputValue;
   cout << "Enter an integer: ";
   cin  >> inputValue;
   return inputValue;
}
double getValue()
{
   double inputValue;

   cout << "Enter a floating-point number: ";
   cin  >> inputValue;
   return inputValue;
}
```

Soft Skills

Programmers need to develop the ability to break a large problem into a set of manageable components, or modules, each of which can focus on handling one specific task. If these tasks are large, they may be divided even further into a set of subtasks. Each component can then be programmed as a separate function. Often there is more than one acceptable way to divide a program into modules and to organize the modules. However, in general, if module A calls module B then module B should carry out some subtask that helps module A perform its function.

40. Read the following program statement and then come to class prepared to discuss how you would design the program. How many modules would you use? What task would each module handle? How would you organize the modules? That is, which modules would call which other modules? Be prepared to state the advantages of the design you have chosen.

Artistic Solutions Paint Job Estimator

Artistic Solutions, a painting company, has determined that for every 160 square feet of wall space, one gallon of paint and three hours of labor are required. The company charges $28.00 per hour for labor. Design a modular program that allows the user to enter the number of rooms that are to be painted, the approximate square feet of wall space in each room (it may differ from room to room), and the price of the paint per gallon. It should then create a report that includes a fancy company header and displays the following information:

- The number of gallons of paint required (rounded up to the next full gallon)
- The hours of labor required

- The cost of the paint
- The labor charges
- The total cost of the paint job

Input validation: The program should not accept a value less than 1 or more than 12 for the number of rooms or a value less than 100 for the square footage of a room. It should also not accept a value less than $10.00 or more than $25.00 for the price of a gallon of paint.

Programming Challenges

1. Markup

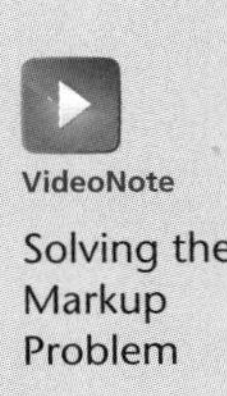

VideoNote

Solving the Markup Problem

Write a program that asks the user to enter an item's wholesale cost and its markup percentage. It should then display the item's retail price. For example:

- If an item's wholesale cost is 5.00 and its markup percentage is 100%, then the item's retail price is 10.00.
- If an item's wholesale cost is 5.00 and its markup percentage is 50%, then the item's retail price is 7.50.

The program should have a function named `calculateRetail` that receives the wholesale cost and the markup percentage as arguments and returns the retail price of the item.

2. Celsius Temperature Table

The formula for converting a temperature from Fahrenheit to Celsius is

$$C = \frac{5}{9}(F - 32)$$

where F is the Fahrenheit temperature and C is the Celsius temperature. Write a function named `celsius` that accepts a Fahrenheit temperature as an argument. The function should return the temperature, converted to Celsius. Demonstrate the function by calling it in a loop that displays a table of the Fahrenheit temperatures 0 through 20 and their Celsius equivalents.

3. Falling Distance

The following formula can be used to determine the distance an object falls due to gravity in a specific time period:

$$d = \frac{1}{2} gt^2$$

The variables in the formula are as follows: d is the distance in meters, g is 9.8, and t is the time in seconds that the object has been falling.

Write a function named `fallingDistance` that accepts an object's falling time (in seconds) as an argument. The function should return the distance, in meters, that the object has fallen during that time interval. Write a program that demonstrates the function by calling it in a loop that passes the values 1 through 10 as arguments and displays the return value.

4. Kinetic Energy

In physics, an object that is in motion is said to have kinetic energy. The following formula can be used to determine a moving object's kinetic energy:

$$KE = \frac{1}{2} mv^2$$

The variables in the formula are as follows: KE is the kinetic energy in joules, m is the object's mass in kilograms, and v is the object's velocity in meters per second.

Write a function named `kineticEnergy` that accepts an object's mass (in kilograms) and velocity (in meters per second) as arguments. The function should return the amount of kinetic energy that the object has. Demonstrate the function by calling it in a program that asks the user to enter values for mass and velocity.

5. Winning Division

Write a program that determines which of a company's four divisions (Northeast, Southeast, Northwest, and Southwest) had the greatest sales for a quarter. It should include the following two functions, which are called by `main`.

- `double getSales()` is passed the name of a division. It asks the user for a division's quarterly sales figure, validates that the input is not less than 0, then returns it. It should be called once for each division.
- `void findHighest()` is passed the four sales totals. It determines which is the largest and prints the name of the high grossing division, along with its sales figure.

6. String Compare

You know that the `==` operator can be used to test if two `string` objects are equal. However, you will recall that they are not considered equal, even when they hold the exact same letters, if the cases of any letters are different. So, for example, if `name1 = "Jack"` and `name2 = "JACK"`, they are not considered the same. Write a program that asks the user to enter two names and stores them in `string` objects. It should then report whether or not, ignoring case, they are the same.

To help the program accomplish its task, it should use two functions in addition to `main`, `upperCaseIt()` and `sameString()`. Here are their function headers.

```
string upperCaseIt(string s)
Boolean sameString (string s1, string s2)
```

The `sameString` function, which receives the two strings to be compared, will need to call `upperCaseIt` for each of them before testing if they are the same. The `upperCaseIt` function should use a loop so that it can call the `toupper` function for every character in the string it receives before returning it back to the `sameString` function.

7. Lowest Score Drop

- Write a program that calculates the average of a group of test scores, where the lowest score in the group is dropped. It should use the following functions:
- `void getScore()` should ask the user for a test score, store it in a reference parameter variable, and validate that it is not lower than 0 or higher than 100. This function should be called by `main` once for each of the five scores to be entered.

- `void calcAverage()` should calculate and display the average of the four highest scores. This function should be called just once by `main` and should be passed the five scores.
- `int findLowest()` should find and return the lowest of the five scores passed to it. It should be called by `calcAverage`, which uses the function to determine which one of the five scores to drop.

8. Star Search

A particular talent competition has 5 judges, each of whom awards a score between 0 and 10 to each performer. Fractional scores, such as 8.3, are allowed. A performer's final score is determined by dropping the highest and lowest score received, then averaging the 3 remaining scores. Write a program that uses these rules to calculate and display a contestant's score. It should include the following functions:

- `void getJudgeData()` should ask the user for a judge's score, store it in a reference parameter variable, and validate it. This function should be called by `main` once for each of the 5 judges.
- `double calcScore()` should calculate and return the average of the 3 scores that remain after dropping the highest and lowest scores the performer received. This function should be called just once by `main` and should be passed the 5 scores.

Two additional functions, described below, should be called by `calcScore`, which uses the returned information to determine which of the scores to drop.

- `int findLowest()` should find and return the lowest of the 5 scores passed to it.
- `int findHighest()` should find and return the highest of the 5 scores passed to it.

9. `isPrime` Function

A prime number is an integer greater than 1 that is evenly divisible by only 1 and itself. For example, the number 5 is prime because it can only be evenly divided by 1 and 5. The number 6, however, is not prime because it can be divided by 1, 2, 3, and 6.

Write a Boolean function named `isPrime`, which takes an integer as an argument and returns `true` if the argument is a prime number, and `false` otherwise. Demonstrate the function in a complete program.

TIP: Recall that the % operator divides one number by another and returns the remainder of the division. In an expression such as num1 % num2, the % operator will return 0 if num1 is evenly divisible by num2.

10. Present Value

Suppose you want to deposit a certain amount of money into a savings account and then leave it alone to draw interest for the next 10 years. At the end of 10 years you would like to have $10,000 in the account. How much do you need to deposit today to make that happen? To find out you can use the following formula, which is known as the present value formula:

$$P = \frac{F}{(1 + r)^n}$$

The terms in the formula are as follows:

- P is the **present value**, or the amount that you need to deposit today.
- F is the **future value** that you want in the account (in this case, $10,000).
- r is the **annual interest rate** (expressed in decimal form, such as .042).
- n is the **number of years** that you plan to let the money sit in the account.

Write a program with a function named `presentValue` that performs this calculation. The function should accept the future value, annual interest rate, and number of years as arguments. It should return the present value, which is the amount that you need to deposit today. Demonstrate the function in a program that lets the user experiment with different values for the formula's terms.

11. Stock Profit

The profit from the sale of a stock can be calculated as follows:

$$\text{Profit} = ((NS \times SP) - SC) - ((NS \times PP) + PC)$$

where NS is the number of shares, SP is the sale price per share, SC is the sale commission paid, PP is the purchase price per share, and PC is the purchase commission paid. If the calculation yields a positive value, then the sale of the stock resulted in a profit. If the calculation yields a negative number, then the sale resulted in a loss.

Write a function that accepts as arguments the number of shares, the purchase price per share, the purchase commission paid, the sale price per share, and the sale commission paid. The function should return the profit (or loss) from the sale of stock.

Demonstrate the function in a program that asks the user to enter the necessary data and displays the amount of the profit or loss.

12. Multiple Stock Sales

Use the function that you wrote for Programming Challenge 11 (Stock Profit) in a program that calculates the total profit or loss from the sale of multiple stocks. The program should ask the user for the number of stock sales, and the necessary data for each stock sale. It should accumulate the profit or loss for each stock sale and then display the total.

13. Order Status

The Middletown Wholesale Copper Wire Company sells spools of copper wiring for $100 each and ships them for $10 apiece. Write a program that displays the status of an order. It should use two functions. The first function asks for the following data and stores the input values in reference parameters.

- The number of spools ordered.
- The number of spools in stock.
- Any special shipping and handling charges (above the regular $10 rate).

The second function receives as arguments any values needed to compute and display the following information:

- The number of ordered spools ready to ship from current stock.
- The number of ordered spools on backorder (if the number ordered is greater than what is in stock).

- Total selling price of the portion ready to ship (the number of spools ready to ship times $100).
- Total shipping and handling charges on the portion ready to ship.
- Total of the order ready to ship.

The shipping and handling parameter in the second function should have the default argument 10.00.

14. Overloaded Hospital

Write a program that computes and displays the charges for a patient's hospital stay. First, the program should ask if the patient was admitted as an in-patient or an out-patient. If the patient was an in-patient the following data should be entered:

- The number of days spent in the hospital
- The daily rate
- Charges for hospital services (lab tests, etc.)
- Hospital medication charges.

If the patient was an out-patient the following data should be entered:

- Charges for hospital services (lab tests, etc.)
- Hospital medication charges.

Use a single, separate function to validate that no input is less than zero. If it is, it should be re-entered before being returned.

Once the required data has been input and validated, the program should use two overloaded functions to calculate the total charges. One of the functions should accept arguments for the in-patient data, while the other function accepts arguments for out-patient data. Both functions should return the total charges.

15. Population

In a population, the birth rate is the percentage increase of the population due to births, and the death rate is the percentage decrease of the population due to deaths. Write a program that asks for the following:

- The starting size of a population (minimum 2)
- The annual birth rate
- The annual death rate
- The number of years to display (minimum 1)

The program should then display the starting population and the projected population at the end of each year. It should use a function that calculates and returns the projected new size of the population after a year. The formula is

```
N = P(1 + B)(1 - D)
```

where `N` is the new population size, `P` is the previous population size, `B` is the birth rate, and `D` is the death rate. Annual birth rate and death rate are the typical number of births and deaths in a year per 1000 people, expressed as a decimal. So, for example, if there are normally about 32 births and 26 deaths per 1000 people in a given population, the birth rate would be .032 and the death rate would be .026.

16. Transient Population

Modify Programming Challenge 15 to also consider the effect on population caused by people moving into or out of a geographic area. Given as input a starting population size, the annual birth rate, the annual death rate, the number of individuals that typically move into the area each year, and the number of individuals that typically leave the area each year, the program should project what the population will be `numYears` from now. You can either prompt the user to input a value for `numYears`, or you can set it within the program.

17. Using Files—Hospital Report

Modify Programming Challenge 14, Overloaded Hospital, to write the report it creates to a file. Print the contents of the file to hand in to your instructor.

Group Project

18. Using Files—Travel Expenses

This program should be designed and written by a team of students. Here are some suggestions:

- One student should design function `main`, which will call the other functions in the program. The rest of the functions should be designed by other team members.
- Analyze the program requirements so each student is given about the same workload.
- Decide on the function names, parameters, and return types in advance.
- Use stubs and drivers to test and debug the program.
- The program can be implemented either as a multi-file program, or all the functions can be cut and pasted into the main file.

Here is the assignment. Write a program that calculates and displays the total travel expenses of a businessperson on a trip. The program should have functions that ask for and return the following:

- The total number of days spent on the trip
- The time of departure on the first day of the trip, and the time of arrival back home on the last day of the trip
- The amount of any round-trip airfare
- The amount of any car rentals
- Miles driven, if a private vehicle was used. Vehicle allowance is $0.58 per mile.
- Parking fees. (The company allows up to $12 per day. Anything in excess of this must be paid by the employee.)
- Taxi fees. (The company allows up to $40 per day for each day a taxi was used. Anything in excess of this must be paid by the employee.)
- Conference or seminar registration fees
- Hotel expenses. (The company allows up to $90 per night for lodging. Anything in excess of this must be paid by the employee.)
- The cost of each meal eaten. On the first day of the trip, breakfast is allowed as an expense if the time of departure is before 7 a.m. Lunch is allowed if the time of departure is before noon. Dinner is allowed if the time of departure is before 6 p.m. On the last day of the trip, breakfast is allowed if the time of arrival is after 8 a.m. Lunch is allowed if the time of arrival is after 1 p.m. Dinner is allowed if the time of

arrival is after 7 p.m. The program should only ask for the costs of allowable meals. (The company allows up to $18 for breakfast, $12 for lunch, and $20 for dinner. Anything in excess of this must be paid by the employee.)

The program should perform the necessary calculations to determine the total amount spent by the business traveler in each category (mileage charges, parking, hotel, meals, etc.) as well as the maximum amount allowed in each category. It should then create a well laid out expense report that includes the amount spent and the amount allowed in each category, as well as the total amount spent and total amount allowed for the entire trip. This report should be written to a file.

Input Validation: The program should not accept negative numbers for any dollar amount or for miles driven in a private vehicle. It should also ensure that the number of days is at least 1 and that the time of departure and the time of arrival are valid.

CHAPTER 7

Introduction to Classes and Objects

TOPICS

7.1 Abstract Data Types

CONCEPT: An abstract data type (ADT) is a data type that specifies the values the data type can hold and the operations that can be done on them without the details of how the data type is implemented.

Abstraction

An *abstraction* is a general model of something. It is a definition that includes only the general characteristics of an object without the details that characterize specific instances of the object.

An automobile provides an illustration of abstraction. Most people understand what an automobile is, and many people know how to drive one. Yet few people understand exactly how an automobile works or what all its parts are. This is a feature of abstraction.

Details of the internal components, organization, and operations of an object are kept separate from the description of what it can do and how to operate it. We are surrounded in our everyday lives with such examples of abstraction, from our microwaves and washing machines to our DVD players and computers. We know what these objects can do, and we understand how to operate them, but most of us do not know, or care, how they work inside. We do not need to be concerned with this information.

The Use of Abstraction in Software Development

Abstraction occurs in programming as well. In order to focus on the bigger picture of creating a working application, a programmer needs to be able to use certain objects and routines without having to be concerned with the details of their implementation. You have been doing this since the beginning of this text when you used objects such as `cin` and `cout` and functions such as `sqrt` and `pow`. All you need to know to use the objects or functions is what they do and the interface for using them. For example, to use the `sqrt` function you only have to know its name and that it must be called with one numeric argument, the value whose square root is to be returned. To use the `pow` function you only have to know its name and that it must be called with two numeric arguments. The first is the value to be raised to a power, and the second is the exponent. In neither case do you need to know what algorithm is used by the function to compute the result it returns.

Abstraction applies to data too. To use any data type you need to know just two things about it: what values it can hold and what operations apply to it. For example, to use a `double` you need to know that it can only hold numeric values, such as `5.0` or `–5.1`, and not strings, such as `"5.1"`. To use a `double` you also need to know what operations can be performed on it. It can be used with the addition, subtraction, multiplication, and division operators, but not with the modulus operator (which only works with integer operands, as in the expression `8 % 3`). You do not have to know anything else about a `double` to use it. You do not have to know how it is stored in memory or how the arithmetic operations that can be performed on it are carried out by the computer. This separation of a data type's logical properties from its implementation details is known as *data abstraction.*

Abstract Data Types

The term *abstract data type* (*ADT*) describes any data type whose implementation details are kept separate from the logical properties needed to use it. Normally though, the term is used to refer to data types created by the programmer. Often these data types can hold more than one value, as with classes, which you will learn about in this chapter. The programmer defines a set of values the data type can hold, defines a set of operations that can be performed on the data, and creates a set of functions to carry out these operations. In C++ and other object-oriented languages, programmer created ADTs are normally implemented as classes.

7.2 Object-Oriented Programming

CONCEPT: Object-oriented programming is centered around objects that encapsulate both data and the functions that operate on them.

There are two common programming methods in practice today: procedural programming and object-oriented programming (OOP). Up to this chapter, you have learned to write procedural programs.

Procedural programming is a method of writing software centered on the procedures, or functions, that carry out the actions of the program. The program's data, typically stored in variables, is separate from these procedures. So you must pass the variables to the functions that need to work with them. Object-oriented programming, on the other hand, is centered on objects. You will learn about objects in this chapter.

Procedural programming has worked well for software developers for many years. However, as programs become larger and more complex, the separation of a program's data from the code that operates on it can lead to problems. For example, quite often a program's specifications change, resulting in the need to change the format of the data or the design of a data structure. When the structure of the data changes, the code that operates on the data must also be changed to accept the new format. Finding all the code that needs changing results in additional work for programmers and an opportunity for bugs to be introduced into the code.

This problem has helped influence the shift from procedural programming to object-oriented programming. OOP is centered on creating and using objects. An *object* is a software entity that combines both data and the procedures that work with it in a single unit. An object's data items, also referred to as its *attributes*, are stored in *member variables*. The procedures that an object performs are called its *member functions*. This bundling of an object's data and procedures together is called *encapsulation*.

NOTE: In some object-oriented programming languages, the procedures that an object performs are called *methods*.

Figure 7-1 shows a representation of what a `Circle` object might look like. It has just one member variable to hold data and two member functions. The `Circle` object's member variable is `radius`. Its `setRadius` member function sets the radius, and its `getArea` member function calculates and returns the area.

Figure 7-1

`Circle`

Member variables (Attributes)
`double radius;`

Member functions
`void setRadius(double r)`
`double getArea()`

The member variable and the member functions are all members of the `Circle` object, bound together in a single unit. When an operation needs to be performed, such as calculating the area of the circle, a message is passed to the object telling it to execute the `getArea` function. Because `getArea` is a member of the `Circle` object, it automatically has access to the object's member variables. Therefore, there is no need to pass `radius` to the `getArea` function.

In addition to bundling associated data and functions together, objects also permit data hiding. *Data hiding* refers to an object's ability to hide its data from code outside the object. Only the object's member functions can directly access and make changes to its data. An object typically hides its data, but allows outside code to access it through some of its member functions. As Figure 7-2 illustrates, the object's member functions provide programming statements outside the object with a way to indirectly access the object's data.

Figure 7-2

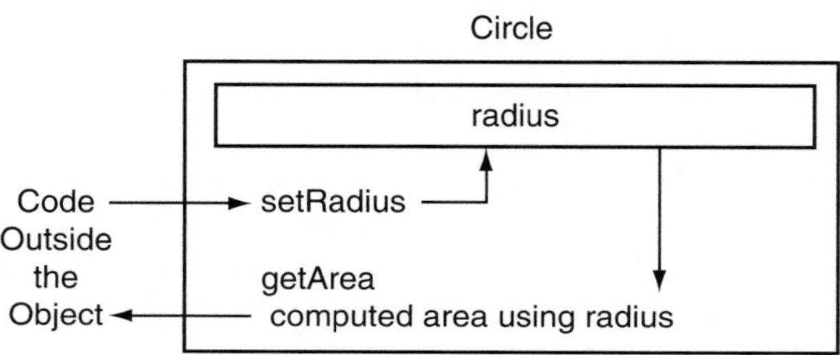

Why is hiding information a good thing? When an object's internal data is hidden from outside code, and that data can only be accessed by going through the object's member functions, the data is protected from accidental or intentional corruption. In addition, the programming code outside the object does not need to know about the format or internal structure of the object's data. The code only needs to interact with the object's functions. When a programmer changes the structure of an object's internal data, the object's member functions are also modified so they will still properly operate on it. These changes, however, are hidden from code outside the object. That code does not have to be changed. It can call and use the member functions exactly the same way as it did before.

Earlier we used the automobile as an example of an abstract object that can be used without having to understand the details of how it works. It has a rather simple interface that consists of an ignition switch, steering wheel, gas pedal, brake pedal, and a gear selector. (Vehicles with manual transmissions also provide a clutch pedal). If you want to drive an automobile, you only have to learn to operate these elements of its interface. To start the motor, you simply turn the key in the ignition switch. What happens internally is irrelevant to the driver. If you want to steer the auto to the left, you rotate the steering wheel left. The movements of all the linkages connecting the steering wheel to the front tires occur without your awareness. If the manufacturer redesigns the vehicle to perform one of the behind-the-scenes operations differently, the driver does not need to learn a new interface.

Because automobiles have simple user interfaces, they can be driven by people who have no mechanical knowledge. This is good for the makers of automobiles because it means more people are likely to become customers. It's good for the users of automobiles because they can learn just a few simple procedures and operate almost any vehicle.

These are also valid concerns in software development. A program is rarely written by only one person. Even the small programs you have created so far weren't written entirely by you. If you incorporated C++ library functions, or objects like `cin` and `cout`, you used code written by someone else. In the world of professional software development, programmers commonly work in teams, buy and sell their code, and collaborate on projects. With OOP, programmers can create objects with powerful engines tucked away "under the hood," but simple interfaces that safeguard the object's algorithms and data.

7.3 Introduction to Classes

CONCEPT: In C++, the class is the construct primarily used to create objects.

Before we can create and use an object, there must be a description of what member variables and member functions it will have. This is done by defining a class. A *class* is a programmer-defined data type that describes what objects of the class will look like when they are created. Shortly, you will see how to define your own classes, but first let's look at a class you are already familiar with.

Using a Class You Already Know

You have been using the `string` class to create and use `string` objects since almost the beginning of this book. Recall that you must have the following `#include` directive in any program that uses the `string` class:

```
#include <string>
```

This is necessary because the `string` header file is where the `string` class is defined. With this header file included in your program, you can now define as many `string` objects as you wish. To do this you simply name the class, followed by the names you wish to give the objects. Here is an example:

```
string city,
       state;
```

This statement creates two `string` objects. One is named `city` and the other is named `state`. Both objects are instances of the `string` class, and although they can be assigned different data values, both objects essentially *look* the same. That is, both will have a member variable that can hold a string, and both will have the same set of functions that can operate on strings.

Once a `string` object has been created, you can store data in it. Because the `string` class is designed to work with the assignment operator, you can assign a string literal to a `string` object. Here is an example:

```
city  = "Chicago";
state = "Illinois";
```

These statements store `"Chicago"` in the `city` object's member variable and `"Illinois"` in the `state` object's member variable.

The `string` class includes numerous member functions that perform operations on the data that a `string` object holds. In earlier chapters you were introduced to several of these. One is a member function named `length`, which returns the length of the string stored in a `string` object. The following code demonstrates this:

```
cout << city.length()    << endl;    // This prints 7
cout << state.length()   << endl;    // This prints 8
```

These statements both call their same member function, but in each case it works with the object's own data. The data stored in `city` is a string of length 7. The data stored in `state` is a string of length 8.

It is important to note that in order to create and use `string` objects, we do not need to know anything about how the `string` class is implemented. We just have to know what kind of data it can hold and what functions we can call to operate on the data.

Creating Your Own Class

To create your own class, you must write a class declaration. Here is the general format of a class declaration.

```
class ClassName              // Class declaration begins with
{                            // the key word class and a name.

   Declarations for class member variables
   and member functions go here.

};                           // Notice the required semicolon.
```

VideoNote
Creating a Class

We will learn how to implement a class by building one step by step. Our example will be the simple `Circle` class depicted in Figure 7-1. The first step is to determine what member variables and member functions the class should have. In this case we have determined, as already described, that the class needs a member variable to hold the circle's radius and two member functions: `setRadius` and `getArea`.

> **NOTE:** This information, along with other design information, is sometimes expressed using visual modeling tools that are part of an object-oriented modeling "language" known as the Unified Modeling Language, or UML. Figure 7-1 illustrated a commonly used type of UML diagram called a *class diagram*. You will see more examples of these later in this chapter, and more detailed examples can be found in Appendix F (Using UML in Class Design).

Once the class has been designed, the next step is to write the class declaration. This tells the compiler what the class includes. Here is the declaration for our `Circle` class. Notice that the class name begins with a capital letter. Although this is not strictly required, it is conventional to always begin class names with an uppercase letter.

```
class Circle
{  private:
       double radius;

   public:
      void setRadius(double r)
      {   radius = r; }

      double getArea()
      {   return 3.14 * pow(radius, 2);  }
};
```

Access Specifiers

The class declaration looks very much like Figure 7-1 with the addition of the actual code for each member function and two key words, `private` and `public`. These are called *access specifiers* because they designate who can access various members of the class. Notice that each access specifier is followed by a colon. A public member variable can be accessed by functions outside the class, and a public member function can be called by functions outside the class. A private member variable, on the other hand, can only be accessed by a function that is a member of the same class, and a private member function can only be called by other functions that are members of the class. If we had omitted the words `public` and `private` altogether, everything would have defaulted to being private. This would not have been very useful because then, except in special circumstances, no functions outside the class could ever use the class.

In our `Circle` class, the member variable `radius` is declared to be private, and the member functions are declared to be public. This is common. Member data is usually made private to safeguard it. Public functions are then created to allow carefully controlled access to this data from outside the class. For now, all our class member variables will be declared as private and all our member functions will be declared as public. Later you will see cases where private member functions are used.

NOTE: If a program statement outside a class attempts to access a private member, a compiler error will result. Later you will learn how outside functions may be given special permission to access private class members.

Placement of `private` and `public` Members

It does not matter whether we list the private or public members first. In fact, it is not even required that all members of the same access specification be declared together. Both examples below are legal declarations of the `Circle` class.

```
class Circle
{public:
   void setRadius(double r)
   { radius = r; }

   double getArea()
   { return 3.14 * pow(radius, 2); }

private:
   double radius;
};
```

```
    class Circle
{   public:
      void setRadius(double r)
      { radius = r; }

  private:
      double radius;

  public:
      double getArea()
      { return 3.14 * pow
      (radius, 2); }
 };
```

However, most programmers consider it more orderly to separate private and public members, and most instructors prefer that you do this. In this text we follow the standard practice of listing private members together first, followed by the public members, as shown in the initial `Circle` declaration.

7.4 Creating and Using Objects

CONCEPT: Objects are instances of a class. They are created with a definition statement after the class has been declared.

Creating and Using Class Objects

A class declaration is similar to the blueprint for a house. The blueprint itself is not a house, but is a detailed description of a house. When we use the blueprint to build an actual house, we could say we are constructing an instance of the house described by the blueprint. If we wish, we can construct several identical houses from the same blueprint. Each house is a separate instance of the house described by the blueprint. This idea is illustrated in Figure 7-3.

Figure 7-3

Blueprint that describes a house.

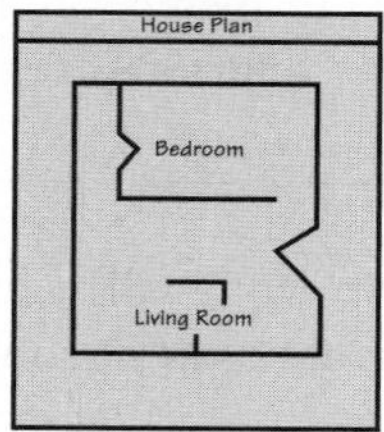

Instances of the house described by the blueprint.

A class declaration serves a similar purpose. It describes what the objects created from the class will look like when they are constructed. Each object created from it is called an *instance* of the class, and defining a class object is called *instantiating* the class.

Class objects for classes you define are created with simple definition statements, just like objects of classes defined in header files and just like variables. For example, the following statement defines `circle1` and `circle2` to be two objects of the `Circle` class:

```
Circle circle1,
       circle2;
```

They are two distinct instances of the `Circle` class, with different memory assigned to hold the values stored in their member variables.

Accessing an Object's Members

Public members of a class object are accessed with the dot operator. You saw this in the previous section when we called the `length` function for the `string` object `city` with the following statement:

```
cout << city.length() << endl;
```

The following statements call the `setRadius` function of `circle1` and `circle2`.

```
circle1.setRadius(1.0);     // This sets circle1's radius to 1.0
circle2.setRadius(2.5);     // This sets circle2's radius to 2.5
```

Notice that member functions, just like regular functions, can be passed arguments when they are called if they have been defined to accept arguments. We defined `setRadius` to accept one `double` argument.

As mentioned earlier, an object's member variables are usually declared to be private. However, if one were declared to be public, it also could be accessed from outside the class by using the dot operator. If the `circle` class `radius` variable was public, we could just set it like this:

```
circle1.radius = 1.0;
circle2.radius = 2.5;
```

Now that the radii have been set, we can call the `getArea` member function to return the area of the `Circle` objects:

```
cout << "The area of circle1 is " << circle1.getArea() << endl;
cout << "The area of circle2 is " << circle2.getArea() << endl;
```

Program 7-1 is a complete program that demonstrates the `Circle` class. Notice that the statements to create and use `Circle` objects are in `main`, not in the class declaration.

Program 7-1

```
// This program demonstrates a simple class.
#include <iostream>
#include <cmath>
using namespace std;

// Circle class declaration
class Circle
{  private:
      double radius;

   public:
      void setRadius(double r)
      {  radius = r; }

      double getArea()
      {  return 3.14 * pow(radius, 2); }
};

```

(program continues)

Program 7-1 *(continued)*

```
19 int main()
20 {
21    // Define 2 Circle objects
22    Circle circle1,
23           circle2;
24
25    // Call the setRadius function for each circle
26    circle1.setRadius(1);    // This sets circle1's radius to 1.0
27    circle2.setRadius(2.5);  // This sets circle2's radius to 2.5
28
29    // Call the getArea function for each circle and
30    // display the returned result
31    cout << "The area of circle1 is " << circle1.getArea() << endl;
32    cout << "The area of circle2 is " << circle2.getArea() << endl;
33
34    return 0;
35 }
```

Program Output

```
The area of circle1 is 3.14
The area of circle2 is 19.625
```

Accessors and Mutators

Notice in lines 13 and 16 of Program 7-1 how the class member functions `setRadius` and `getArea` use the member variable `radius`. They do not need to use the dot operator to reference it because member functions of a class can access member variables of the same class like regular variables, without any extra notation. Notice also that the class member function `getArea` only uses, but does not modify, the member variable `radius`. A function like this, that uses the value of a class variable but does not change it, is known as an *accessor*. The function `setRadius`, on the other hand, modifies the contents of `radius`. A member function like this, which stores a value in a member variable or changes its value, is known as a *mutator*. Some programmers refer to mutators as *set functions* or *setter functions* because they set the value of a class variable and refer to accessors as *get functions* or *getter functions* because they just retrieve or use the value.

7.5 Defining Member Functions

CONCEPT: Class member functions can be defined either inside or outside the class declaration.

Class member functions are defined similarly to regular functions. Except for a few special cases we will look at later, they have a function header that includes a return type (which may be `void`), a function name, and a parameter list (which may possibly be empty). The statements that carry out the actions of the function are contained within a pair of braces that follow the function header.

When we defined the `Circle` class in the previous section, we defined its two member functions within the class declaration itself. When a class function is defined there, it is called an *inline function*. Inline functions provide a convenient way to contain function information within a class declaration, but they can only be used when a function body is very short, usually a single line. When a function body is longer, we place a prototype for the function in the class declaration, instead of the function definition itself. We then put the function definition outside the class declaration, either following it or in a separate file.

Even though the two functions in our `Circle` class are short enough to be written as inline functions, we will rewrite them as regular functions, defined outside the class declaration, to illustrate how this is done. Inside the class declaration the functions will be replaced by the following prototypes:

```
void setRadius(double);
double getArea();
```

Following the class declaration we will place a *function implementation* section containing the following function definitions:

```
void Circle::setRadius(double r)
{   radius = r;
}

double Circle::getArea()
{   return 3.14 * pow(radius, 2);
}
```

Notice that these look like ordinary functions except that the class name and a double colon (`::`) are placed after the function return type, just before the function name. The `::` symbol is called the *scope resolution operator*. It is needed to indicate that these are class member functions and to tell the compiler which class they belong to.

WARNING! The class name and scope resolution operator are an extension of the function name. When a function is defined outside the class declaration, these must be present and must be located immediately before the function name in the function header.

Here are some additional examples to illustrate how the scope resolution is used when a class function is defined outside the class declaration.

```
double getArea()           // Wrong! The class name and scope
                           // resolution operator are missing.

Circle::double getArea()   // Wrong! The class name and scope
                           // resolution operator are misplaced.

double Circle::getArea()   // Correct!
```

Program 7-2 revises Program 7-1 to define the class member functions outside the class.

Program 7-2

```
// This program demonstrates a simple class with member functions
// defined outside the class declaration.
#include <iostream>
#include <cmath>
using namespace std;

// Circle class declaration
class Circle
{  private:
      double radius;            // This is a member variable.

   public:
      void  setRadius(double);  // These are just prototypes
      double getArea();         // for the member functions.
};

// The member function implementation section follows. It contains the
// actual function definitions for the Circle class member functions.

/*******************************************************************
 *                        Circle::setRadius                        *
 *  This function copies the argument passed into the parameter to *
 *  the private member variable radius.                            *
 *******************************************************************/
void Circle::setRadius(double r)
{  radius = r;
}

/*******************************************************************
 *                         Circle::getArea                         *
 * This function calculates and returns the Circle object's area. *
 * It does not need any parameters because it already has access  *
 * to the member variable radius.                                  *
 *******************************************************************/
double Circle::getArea()
{  return 3.14 * pow(radius, 2);
}

/*******************************************************************
 *                              main                               *
 *******************************************************************/
int main()
{
   Circle circle1,          // Define 2 Circle objects
          circle2;

   circle1.setRadius(1);    // This sets circle1's radius to 1.0
   circle2.setRadius(2.5);  // This sets circle2's radius to 2.5

```

(program continues)

Program 7-2 *(continued)*

```
                              // Get and display each circle's area
   cout << "The area of circle1 is " << circle1.getArea() << endl;
   cout << "The area of circle2 is " << circle2.getArea() << endl;

   return 0;
}
```

Program Output is the same as for Program 7-1.

Naming Conventions for Class Member Functions

Program 7-3 provides another example using classes and objects. It declares and implements a `Rectangle` class that has two private member variables and five public member functions. Notice that the names of the member functions in Program 7-3 all begin with the word *set* or the word *get*. Functions `setLength` and `setWidth` are mutator, or set, functions. It is common to name a mutator with the word *set* followed by the name of the member variable whose value it is setting. As you would expect, the `setLength` function sets the value of the `length` member variable and the `setWidth` function sets the value of the `width` member variable.

Member functions `getLength` and `getWidth` are accessor, or get, functions. It is common to name an accessor with the word *get* followed by the name of the member variable whose value it is getting. Function `getLength` returns the value stored in the `length` member variable, while `getWidth` returns the value stored in the `width` member variable. The member function `getArea` also has a name that begins with *get* because it gets and returns the area, even though it calculates this value rather than retrieving it from a member variable.

Program 7-3

```
// This program implements a Rectangle class.
#include <iostream>
using namespace std;

// Rectangle class declaration
class Rectangle
{
   private:
      double length;
      double width;
   public:
      void setLength(double);
      void setWidth(double);
      double getLength();
      double getWidth();
      double getArea();
};

```

(program continues)

Program 7-3 *(continued)*

```
// Member function implementation section

/*****************************************************************
 *                      Rectangle::setLength                      *
 * This function sets the value of the member variable length.    *
 * If the argument passed to the function is zero or greater, it is *
 * copied into length. If it is negative, 1.0 is assigned to length.*
 *****************************************************************/
void Rectangle::setLength(double len)
{
   if (len >= 0.0)
      length = len;
   else
   {   length = 1.0;
       cout << "Invalid length. Using a default value of 1.0\n";
   }
}

/*****************************************************************
 *                      Rectangle::setWidth                       *
 * This function sets the value of the member variable width.     *
 * If the argument passed to the function is zero or greater, it is *
 * copied into width. If it is negative, 1.0 is assigned to width.  *
 *****************************************************************/
void Rectangle::setWidth(double w)
{
   if (w >= 0.0)
      width = w;
   else
   {   width = 1.0;
       cout << "Invalid width. Using a default value of 1.0\n";
   }
}

/**********************************************************
 *                 Rectangle::getLength                    *
 * This function returns the value in member variable length. *
 **********************************************************/
double Rectangle::getLength()
{
   return length;
}

/**********************************************************
 *                 Rectangle::getWidth                     *
 * This function returns the value in member variable width.  *
 **********************************************************/
double Rectangle::getWidth()
{
   return width;
}

```

(program continues)

Program 7-3 *(continued)*

```
/*****************************************************************
 *                        Rectangle::getArea                     *
 * This function calculates and returns the area of the rectangle. *
 *****************************************************************/
double Rectangle::getArea()
{
   return length * width;
}

/*******************************************************
 *                        main                         *
 *******************************************************/
int main()
{
   Rectangle box;          // Declare a Rectangle object
   double boxLength, boxWidth;

   // Get box length and width
   cout << "This program will calculate the area of a rectangle.\n";
   cout << "What is the length? ";
   cin  >> boxLength;
   cout << "What is the width? ";
   cin  >> boxWidth;

   // Call member functions to set box dimensions
   box.setLength(boxLength);
   box.setWidth(boxWidth);

   // Call member functions to get box information to display
   cout << "\nHere is the rectangle's data:\n";
   cout << "Length: " << box.getLength() << endl;
   cout << "Width : " << box.getWidth()  << endl;
   cout << "Area  : " << box.getArea()   << endl;
   return 0;
}
```

Program Output with Example Input Shown in Bold

```
This program will calculate the area of a rectangle.
What is the length? 3[Enter]
What is the width? -1[Enter]
Invalid width. Using a default value of 1.0

Here is the rectangle's data:
Length: 3
Width : 1
Area  : 3
```

Program Output with Different Example Input Shown in Bold

```
This program will calculate the area of a rectangle.
What is the length? 10.1[Enter]
What is the width? 5[Enter]

Here is the rectangle's data:
Length: 10.1
Width : 5
Area  : 50.5
```

We mentioned earlier that when designing a class it is common practice to make all member variables private and to provide public set and get functions for accessing those variables. This safeguards the data. Functions outside the class can only access the member data through calls to the public member functions, and these functions can be written to prevent the data from being corrupted or modified in a way that might adversely affect the behavior of an object of the class. Notice in Program 7-3 how the two set functions are written to filter out invalid data. Rather than allowing an invalid value to be stored in a member variable, they use a default value if the data passed to them is not acceptable.

Avoiding Stale Data

In the `Rectangle` class, the `getLength` and `getWidth` member functions return the values stored in the `length` and `width` member variables, but the `getArea` member function returns the result of a calculation. You might wonder why the area of the rectangle is not also stored in a member variable. The area is not stored because it could potentially become stale. When the value of an item is dependent on other data and that item is not updated when the other data is changed, we say that the item has become *stale*. If the area of the rectangle were stored in a member variable, its value would become incorrect as soon as either the `length` or `width` member variables changed.

When designing a class, you should normally not use a member variable to store a calculated value that could potentially become stale. Instead, provide a member function that calculates the value, using the most current data, and then returns the result of the calculation.

More on Inline Functions

When designing a class, you will need to decide which member functions to write as inline functions within the class declaration and which ones to define outside the class. Inline functions are handled completely differently by the compiler than regular functions are. An understanding of this difference may help you decide which to use when.

A lot goes on behind the scenes each time a regular function is called. A number of special items, such as the address to return to when the function has finished executing and the values of the function arguments, must be stored in a section of memory called the *stack*. In addition, local variables are created and a location is reserved to hold the function's return value. All this overhead, which sets the stage for a function call, takes CPU time. Although the time needed is small, it can add up if a function is called many times, as in a loop.

An inline function, on the other hand, is not called in the conventional sense at all. Instead, in a process known as *inline expansion*, the compiler replaces every call to the function with the actual code of the function itself. This means that if the function is called from multiple places in the program, the entire body of its code will be inserted multiple times, increasing the size of the program. This is why only a function with very few lines of code should be written as an inline function. In fact, if the function is too large to make the inline expansion practical, the compiler will ignore the request to handle the function this way. However, when a member function is small, it can improve performance to write it as an inline function because there is less overhead when you don't make actual function calls.

Checkpoint

7.1 Which of the following shows the correct use of the scope resolution operator in a member function definition?

A) `InvItem::void setOnHand(int units)`

B) `void InvItem::setOnHand(int units)`

7.2 An object's private member variables can be accessed from outside the object by

A) public member functions

B) any function

C) the dot operator

D) the scope resolution operator

7.3 Assuming that `soap` is an instance of the `Inventory` class, which of the following is a valid call to the `setOnHand` member function?

A) `setOnHand(20);`

B) `soap::setOnHand(20);`

C) `soap.setOnHand(20);`

D) `Inventory.setOnHand(20);`

7.4 Complete the following code skeleton to declare a class called `Date`. The class should contain member variables and functions to store and retrieve the month, day, and year components of a date.

```
class Date
{  private:
   public:
}
```

7.6 Constructors

CONCEPT: A constructor is a member function that is automatically called when a class object is created.

A *constructor* is a special public member function that is automatically called to *construct* a class object when it is created. If the programmer does not write a constructor, C++ automatically provides one. You never see it, but it runs silently in the background each time your program defines an object. Often, however, programmers write their own constructor when they create a class. If they do this, in addition to constructing each newly created object of the class, it will execute whatever code the programmer has included in it. Most often programmers use a constructor to initialize an object's member variables. However, it can do anything a normal function can do.

NOTE: Appendix F shows how to denote a constructor in UML.

A constructor looks like a regular function except that its name must be the same as the name of the class it is a part of. This is how the compiler knows that a particular member function is a constructor. Also, a constructor is not allowed to have a return type.

Program 7-4 includes a class called `Demo` with a constructor that does nothing except print a message. It was written this way to demonstrate when the constructor executes. Because the `Demo` object is created between two `cout` statements, the constructor will print its message between the output lines produced by those two statements.

Program 7-4

```
// This program demonstrates when a constructor executes.
#include <iostream>
using namespace std;

class Demo
{
 public:
   Demo()              // Constructor
   {
      cout << "Now the constructor is running.\n";
   }
};

int main()
{
   cout << "This is displayed before the object is created.\n";

   Demo demoObj;     // Define a Demo object

   cout << "This is displayed after the object is created.\n";
   return 0;
}
```

Program Output

```
This is displayed before the object is created.
Now the constructor is running.
This is displayed after the object is created.
```

In Program 7-4 we defined the constructor as an inline function inside the class declaration. However, like any other class member function, we could have just put its prototype in the class declaration and then defined it outside the class. In that case, we would need to add the name of the class the function belongs to and the scope resolution operator in front of the function name. But the name of the constructor function is the *same* as the class name, so the name would appear twice. Here is how the function header for the `Demo` constructor would look if we defined it outside the class.

```
Demo::Demo()              // Constructor
{
    cout << "Now the constructor is running.\n";
}
```

Program 7-5 modifies Program 7-2 to include a constructor that initializes an object's member data. The constructor is defined outside of the class.

Program 7-5

```
// This program uses a constructor to initialize a member variable.
#include <iostream>
#include <cmath>
using namespace std;

// Circle class declaration
class Circle
{  private:
      double radius;

   public:              // Member function prototypes
      Circle();
      void setRadius(double);
      double getArea();
};

// Circle member function implementation section

/*******************************************
 *               Circle::Circle            *
 * This is the constructor. It initializes *
 * the radius class member variable.       *
 *******************************************/
Circle::Circle()
{  radius = 1.0;
}

/*******************************************
 *               Circle::setRadius         *
 * This function validates the value passed *
 * to it before assigning it to the radius  *
 * member variable.                         *
 *******************************************/
void Circle::setRadius(double r)
{  if (r >= 0.0)
      radius = r;
   // else leave it set to its previous value
}

/*********************************************
 *               Circle::getArea             *
 * This function calculates and returns the  *
 * Circle object's area. It does not need any *
 * parameters because it can directly access  *
 * the member variable radius.                *
 *********************************************/
```

(program continues)

Program 7-5 *(continued)*

```
double Circle::getArea()
{  return 3.14 * pow(radius, 2);
}

/*************************************
 *               main                *
 * The main function creates and uses *
 * 2 Circle objects.                 *
 *************************************/
int main()
{
   // Define a Circle object. Because the setRadius function
   // is never called for it, it will keep the value set
   // by the constructor.
   Circle circle1;

   // Define a second Circle object and set its radius to 2.5
   Circle circle2;
   circle2.setRadius(2.5);

   // Get and display each circle's area
   cout << "The area of circle1 is " << circle1.getArea() << endl;
   cout << "The area of circle2 is " << circle2.getArea() << endl;

   return 0;
}
```

Program Output

```
The area of circle1 is 3.14
The area of circle2 is 19.625
```

Overloading Constructors

Recall from Chapter 6 that when two or more functions share the same name, the function name is said to be overloaded. Multiple functions with the same name may exist in a C++ program, as long as their parameter lists are different.

Any class member function may be overloaded, including the constructor. One constructor might take an integer argument, for example, while another constructor takes a `double`. There could even be a third constructor taking two integers. As long as each constructor has a different list of parameters, the compiler can tell them apart.

Program 7-6 declares and uses a class named `Sale`, which has two constructors. The first has a parameter that accepts a sales tax rate. The second, which is for tax-exempt sales, has no parameters. It sets the tax rate to 0. A constructor like this, which has no parameters, is called a *default constructor.*

Program 7-6

```
// This program demonstrates the use of overloaded constructors.
#include <iostream>
#include <iomanip>
using namespace std;

// Sale class declaration
class Sale
{
 private:
   double taxRate;

 public:
    Sale(double rate)        // Constructor with 1 parameter
    {  taxRate = rate;       // handles taxable sales
    }

    Sale()                   // Default constructor
    {  taxRate = 0.0         // handles tax-exempt sales
    }

    double calcSaleTotal(double cost)
    {  double total = cost + cost*taxRate;
       return total;
    }
};

int main()
{
   Sale cashier1(.06);       // Define a Sale object with 6% sales tax
   Sale cashier2;            // Define a tax-exempt Sale object

   // Format the output
   cout << fixed << showpoint << setprecision(2);

   // Get and display the total sale price for two $24.95 sales
   cout << "With a 0.06 sales tax rate, the total\n";
   cout << "of the $24.95 sale is $";
   cout << cashier1.calcSaleTotal(24.95) << endl;

   cout << "\nOn a tax-exempt purchase, the total\n";
   cout << "of the $24.95 sale is, of course, $";
   cout << cashier2.calcSaleTotal(24.95) << endl;
   return 0;
}
```

Program Output

```
With a 0.06 sales tax rate, the total
of the $24.95 sale is $26.45

On a tax-exempt purchase, the total
of the $24.95 sale is, of course, $24.95
```

Notice on lines 29 and 30 of Program 7-6 how the two `Sale` objects are defined.

```
Sale cashier1(.06);
Sale cashier2;
```

There is a pair of parentheses after the name `cashier1` to hold the value being sent to the 1-parameter constructor. However, there are no parentheses after the name `cashier2`, which sends no arguments. In C++ when an object is defined using the default constructor, instead of passing arguments, there must *not* be any parentheses.

```
Sale cashier2();         // Wrong!
Sale cashier2;           // Correct
```

Default Constructors

The `Sale` class needed a default constructor to handle tax-free sales. Other classes may appear not to need one—for example, if objects created from them are always expected to pass arguments to the constructors. Yet, any time you design a class that will have constructors, it is considered good programming practice to include a default constructor. If you do not have one, and the program tries to create an object without passing any arguments, it will not compile. This is because there must be a constructor to create an object. In order to create an object that passes no arguments, there must be a constructor that expects no arguments—a default constructor. If the programmer doesn't write any constructors for a class, the compiler automatically creates a default constructor for it. However, when the programmer writes one or more constructors, even ones that all have parameters, the compiler does not create a default constructor. So it is the responsibility of the programmer to do this.

A class may have many constructors, but can only have one default constructor. This is because if multiple functions have the same name, the compiler must be able to determine from their parameter lists which one is being called at any given time. It uses the number and type of arguments passed to the function to determine which of the overloaded functions to invoke. Because there can be only one function with the class name that is able to accept no arguments, there can be only one default constructor.

Normally, as in the `Sale` class, default constructors have no parameters. However, it is possible to have a default constructor with parameters if all of its parameters have default values, so that it can be called with no arguments. It would be an error to create one constructor that accepts no arguments and another that has arguments but allows default values for all of them. This would essentially create two "default" constructors. The following class declaration illegally does this.

```
class Sale                  // Illegal declaration!
{ private:
     double taxRate;

  public:
     Sale()                 // Default constructor with no arguments
     {  taxRate = 0.05; }

     Sale(double r = 0.05) // Default constructor with a default argument
     {  taxRate = r; }

     double calcSaleTotal(double cost)
     {  double total = cost + cost * taxRate;
        return total;
};
```

As you can see, the first constructor has no parameters. The second constructor has one parameter, but it has a default argument. If an object is defined with no argument list, the compiler will not be able to tell which constructor to execute.

7.7 Destructors

CONCEPT: A destructor is a member function that is automatically called when an object is destroyed.

Destructors are public member functions with the same name as the class, preceded by a tilde character (~). For example, the destructor for the `Rectangle` class would be named `~Rectangle`.

Destructors are automatically called when an object is destroyed. In the same way that constructors can be used to set things up when an object is created, destructors are used to perform shutdown procedures when an object ceases to exist. This happens, for example, when a program with an object stops executing or when you return from a function that created an object.

NOTE: Appendix F shows how to denote a destructor in UML.

Program 7-7 shows a simple class with a constructor and a destructor. It illustrates when each is called during the program's execution.

Program 7-7

```
// This program demonstrates a destructor.
#include <iostream>
using namespace std;

class Demo
{
   public:
      Demo();         // Constructor prototype
     ~Demo();         // Destructor prototype
};

Demo::Demo()          // Constructor function definition
{  cout << "An object has just been defined, so the constructor"
        << " is running.\n";
}

Demo::~Demo()         // Destructor function definition
{  cout << "Now the destructor is running.\n";
}

```

(program continues)

Program 7-7 *(continued)*

```
int main()
{
   Demo demoObj;     // Declare a Demo object;

   cout << "The object now exists, but is about to be destroyed.\n";
   return 0;
}
```

Program Output

```
An object has just been defined, so the constructor is running.
The object now exists, but is about to be destroyed.
Now the destructor is running.
```

In addition to the fact that destructors are automatically called when an object is destroyed, the following points should be mentioned:

- Like constructors, destructors have no return type.
- Destructors cannot accept arguments, so they never have a parameter list.
- Because destructors cannot accept arguments, there can only be one destructor.

Destructors are most useful when working with objects that are dynamically allocated. You will learn about this in Chapter 10.

Checkpoint

7.5 Briefly describe the purpose of a constructor.

7.6 Constructor functions have the same name as the
   A) class
   B) class instance
   C) program
   D) none of the above

7.7 A constructor that requires no arguments is called
   A) a default constructor
   B) an inline constructor
   C) a null constructor
   D) none of the above

7.8 Assume the following is a constructor:

```
ClassAct::ClassAct(int x)
{
   item = x;
}
```

Define a `ClassAct` object called `sally` that passes the value 25 to the constructor.

7.9 True or false: Like any C++ function, a constructor may be overloaded, providing each constructor has a unique parameter list.

7.10 True or false: A class may have a constructor with no parameter list, and an overloaded constructor whose parameters all take default arguments.

7.11 A destructor function name always starts with
A) a number
B) the tilde character (~)
C) a data type name
D) the name of the class

7.12 True or false: Just as a class can have multiple constructors, it can also have multiple destructors.

7.13 What will the following program display on the screen?

```
#include <iostream>
using namespace std;

class Tank
{
private:
   int gallons;
public:
   Tank()
      { gallons = 50; }
   Tank(int gal)
      { gallons = gal; }
   int getGallons()
      { return gallons; }
};

int main()
{  Tank storage1, storage2, storage3(20);

   cout << storage1.getGallons() << endl;
   cout << storage2.getGallons() << endl;
   cout << storage3.getGallons() << endl;
   return 0;
}
```

7.14 What will the following program display on the screen?

```
#include <iostream>
using namespace std;

class Package
{
private:
   int value;
public:
   Package()
      { value = 7; cout << value << endl; }
   Package(int v)
      { value = v; cout << value << endl; }
   ~Package()
      { cout << "goodbye" << endl; }
};
```

```
int main()
{  Package obj1(4);
   Package obj2;
   return 0;
}
```

7.8 Private Member Functions

CONCEPT: Private member functions may only be called from a function that is a member of the same class.

Until now all of the class member functions you have seen have been public functions. This means they can be called by code in programs outside the class. Often, however, a class needs functions for internal processing that should not be called by code outside the class. These functions should be made private.

NOTE: Appendix F shows how to denote private and public members in UML.

Program 7-8 shows an example of a class with a private function. The `SimpleStat` class is designed to find and report information, such as the average and the largest number, from a set of non-negative integers sent to it. However, once a number has been received and added to a running total, it is not kept. So the class cannot later determine which number was the biggest. It must do this by examining each number it reads in to see if it is bigger than any number it previously read. The private `isNewLargest` function does this.

Program 7-8

```
// This program uses a private Boolean function to determine if
// a new value sent to it is the largest value received so far.
#include <iostream>
using namespace std;

class SimpleStat
{
  private:
   int largest;             // The largest number received so far
   int sum;                 // The sum of the numbers received
   int count;               // How many numbers have been received

   bool isNewLargest(int); // This is a private class function
```

(program continues)

Program 7-8 *(continued)*

```

  public:

   SimpleStat();            // Default constructor
   bool addNumber(int);
   double getAverage();

   int getLargest()
   {  return largest; }

   int getCount()
   {  return count; }
};

// SimpleStat Class Implementation Code

/************************************
 *  SimpleStat Default Constructor   *
 ************************************/
SimpleStat::SimpleStat()
{
   largest = sum = count = 0;
}

/************************************
 *      SimpleStat::addNumber        *
 ************************************/
bool SimpleStat::addNumber(int num)
{   bool goodNum = true;
   if (num >= 0)             // If num is valid
   {
      sum += num;            // Add it to the sum
      count++;               // Count it
      if(isNewLargest(num))  // Find out if it is
         largest = num;      // the new largest
   }
   else                      // num is invalid
      goodNum = false;

   return goodNum;
}

/************************************
 *     SimpleStat::isNewLargest      *
 ************************************/
bool SimpleStat::isNewLargest(int num)
{
   if (num > largest)
      return true;
   else
      return false;
}
```

(program continues)

Program 7-8 *(continued)*

```

/**********************************
 *      SimpleStat::getAverage      *
 **********************************/
double SimpleStat::getAverage()
{
   if (count > 0)
      return static_cast<double>(sum) / count;
   else
      return 0;
}

// Client Program

/**********************************
 *               main               *
 **********************************/
int main()
{
   int num;
   SimpleStat statHelper;

   cout << "Please enter the set of non-negative integer \n";
   cout << "values you want to average. Separate them with \n";
   cout << "spaces and enter -1 after the last value. \n\n";

   cin >> num;
   while (num >= 0)
   {
      statHelper.addNumber(num);
      cin >> num;
   }
   cout << "\nYou entered " << statHelper.getCount() << " values. \n";
   cout << "The largest value was " << statHelper.getLargest() << endl;
   cout << "The average value was " << statHelper.getAverage() << endl;

  return 0;
}
```

Program Output with Example Input Shown in Bold

```
Please enter the set of non-negative integer
values you want to average. Separate them with
spaces and enter -1 after the last value.

7 6 8 8 9 7 7 8 9 7 -1[Enter]

You entered 10 values.
The largest value was 9
The average value was 7.6
```

In Program 7-8 the private function `isNewLargest` was written to create a more modular class with code that is easy to follow. The program could have been written without this function. However, in that case, the `addNumber` function itself would have to handle the additional work of comparing the new value with `largest`. In later chapters you will encounter many examples where the use of private functions is essential.

7.9 Passing Objects to Functions

CONCEPT: Class objects may be passed as arguments to functions.

In Chapter 6 you learned how to use variables as function arguments. Class objects can also be passed as arguments to functions. For example, the following function has a parameter that receives a `Rectangle` object.

```
void displayRectangle(Rectangle r)
{
   cout << "Length = " << r.getLength() << endl;
   cout << "Width  = " << r.getWidth()  << endl;
   cout << "Area   = " << r.getArea()   << endl;
}
```

The following lines of code create a `Rectangle` object with length 15 and width 10, and then pass it to the `displayRectangle` function.

```
Rectangle box(15, 10);
displayRectangle(box);
```

Assuming the `Rectangle` class includes the member functions used in this example, the `displayRectangle` function will output the following information:

```
Length = 15
Width  = 10
Area   = 150
```

As with regular variables, objects can be passed to functions by value or by reference. In the `Rectangle` example, `box` is passed to the `displayRectangle` function by value. This means that `displayRectangle` receives a copy of `box`. If `displayRectangle` called any `Rectangle` class mutator functions, they would only change the copy of `box`, not the original. If a function needs to store or change data in an object's member variables, the object must be passed to it by reference.

Program 7-9 illustrates this. It has two functions that receive an `InventoryItem` object. The object is passed to `storeValues` by reference because this function needs to call a class mutator function that stores new values into the object. The object is passed to `showValues` by value because this function only needs to use accessor functions that retrieve and use values stored in the object's data members. Notice in Program 7-9 that the `InventoryItem` class declaration appears *before* the prototype for the `storeValues` and showValues functions. This is important. Because both functions have an InventoryItem object as a parameter, the compiler must know what an InventoryItem is before it encounters anything that refers to it. Otherwise an error will occur.

Program 7-9

```
// This program passes an object to a function. It passes it
// to one function by reference and to another by value.
#include <iostream>
#include <iomanip>
#include <string>
using namespace std;

class InventoryItem
{
 private:
   int partNum;          // Part number
   string description;   // Item description
   int onHand;           // Units on hand
   double price;         // Unit price

 public:

   void storeInfo(int p, string d, int oH, double cost); // Prototype

   int getPartNum()
   {  return partNum; }

   string getDescription()
   {  return description; }

   int getOnHand()
   {  return onHand; }

   double getPrice()
   {  return price; }
};

// Implementation code for InventoryItem class function storeInfo
void InventoryItem::storeInfo(int p, string d, int oH, double cost)
{  partNum = p;
   description = d;
   onHand = oH;
   price = cost;
}

// Function prototypes for client program
void storeValues(InventoryItem&);  // Receives an object by reference
void showValues (InventoryItem);   // Receives an object by value

```

(program continues)

Program 7-9 *(continued)*

```
//*************** main *****************
int main()
{
   InventoryItem part;             // part is an InventoryItem object

   storeValues(part);
   showValues(part);
   return 0;
}

/*******************************************************
 *                    storeValues                      *
 * This function stores user input data in the members of *
 * an InventoryItem object passed to it by reference.     *
 * *****************************************************/
void storeValues(InventoryItem &item)
{
   int partNum;                 // Local variables to hold user input
   string description;
   int qty;
   double price;

   // Get the data from the user
   cout << "Enter data for the new part number \n";
   cout << "Part number: ";
   cin  >> partNum;
   cout << "Description: ";
   cin.get();                   // Move past the '\n' left in the
                                // input buffer by the last input
   getline(cin, description);
   cout << "Quantity on hand: ";
   cin  >> qty;
   cout << "Unit price: ";
   cin  >> price;

   // Store the data in the InventoryItem object
   item.storeInfo(partNum, description, qty, price);
}

/*****************************************************
 *                    showValues                     *
 * This function displays the member data stored in the *
 * InventoryItem object passed to it by value.          *
 *****************************************************/
void showValues(InventoryItem item)
{
   cout << fixed << showpoint << setprecision(2) << endl;;
   cout << "Part Number  : "  << item.getPartNum() << endl;
   cout << "Description  : "  << item.getDescription() << endl;
   cout << "Units On Hand: "  << item.getOnHand() << endl;
   cout << "Price        : $" << item.getPrice() << endl;
}
```

(program continues)

Program 7-9 *(continued)*

Program Output with Example Input Shown in Bold

```
Enter data for the new part number

Part number: 175[Enter]
Description: Hammer[Enter]
Quantity on hand: 12[Enter]
Unit price: 7.49[Enter]

Part Number  : 175
Description  : Hammer
Units On Hand: 12
Price        : $7.49
```

Constant Reference Parameters

In Program 7-9 `part`, the `InventoryItem` object, was passed by value to the `showValues` function. However, passing an object by value requires making a copy of all of the object's members. This can slow down a program's execution time, particularly if it has many members. When an object is passed by reference, on the other hand, no copy has to be made because the function has access to the original object. For this reason it is generally preferable to pass objects by reference.

There is a disadvantage to passing an object by reference, however. Because the function has access to the original object, it can call its mutator functions and alter its member data. This is why we normally do not pass variables by reference when we want to safeguard their contents. Luckily there is a solution. To protect an object when it is passed as an argument, without having to make a copy, it can be passed as a *constant reference*. This means that a reference to the original object is passed to the function, but it cannot call any mutator functions or change any of the object's member data. It can only call accessor functions that have themselves been designated as *constant functions*.

To declare a parameter to be a constant reference parameter, we must put the key word `const` in the parameter list of both the function prototype and function header. Here is what the function prototype and header of the `showValues` function from Program 7-9 would look like if we changed it to use a constant reference parameter.

```
void showValues (const InventoryItem&)        // Function prototype
void showValues (const InventoryItem &item)   // Function header
```

Now the `showValues` function can only call `InventoryItem` functions that also have the key word `const` listed in their function prototype and header, like this:

```
double getPrice() const
```

If showValues tried to call any other InventoryItem functions, a compiler error would occur. Notice that when showValues is modified to have a constant reference parameter, only the function prototypes and headers are changed to include the word const. The body of the showValues function and the call to showValues do not change.

Returning an Object from a Function

Just as functions can be written to return an int, double, or other data type, they can also be designed to return an object. In fact, you have done this before when you returned a string from a function, since a string is an object. When a function returns an object it normally creates a local instance of the class, sets its data members, and then returns it. Here is an example of how the InventoryItem object used in Program 7-9 could be created in the storeValues function and then returned to the calling function. Notice that this new version of the storeValues function does not accept any arguments, and its return type is now InventoryItem rather than void.

```
InventoryItem storeValues()
{
   InventoryItem tempItem;    // Local InventoryItem object
   int partNum;               // Local variables to hold user input
   string description;
   int qty;
   double price;

   // Code to get the data from the user goes here.

   // Store the data in the InventoryItem object and return it.
   tempItem.storeInfo(partNum, description, qty, price);
   return tempItem;
}
```

The main function could then create part like this:

```
InventoryItem part = storeValues();
```

Program 7-10 revises Program 7-9 to incorporate the techniques we have just discussed. The function previously named storeValues is renamed createItem, as it now creates an InventoryItem object and returns it to main. The showValues function now receives part as a constant reference, instead of having it passed by value, as before.

Program 7-10

```
// This program uses a constant reference parameter.
// It also shows how to return an object from a function.
#include <iostream>
#include <iomanip>
#include <string>
using namespace std;

```

(program continues)

Program 7-10 *(continued)*

```
class InventoryItem
{
 private:
   int partNum;                    // Part number
   string description;             // Item description
   int onHand;                     // Units on hand
   double price;                   // Unit price

 public:

   void storeInfo(int p, string d, int oH, double cost); // Prototype

   int getPartNum() const          // The get functions have all been made
   {  return partNum; }            // const functions. This ensures they
                                   // cannot alter any class member data.
   string getDescription() const
   {  return description; }

   int getOnHand() const
   {  return onHand; }

    double getPrice() const
   {  return price; }
};

// Implementation code for InventoryItem class function storeInfo
void InventoryItem::storeInfo(int p, string d, int oH, double cost)
{  partNum = p;
   description = d;
   onHand = oH;
   price = cost;
}

// Function prototypes for client program
InventoryItem createItem();                  // Returns an InventoryItem object
void showValues (const InventoryItem&);      // Receives a reference to an
                                             // InventoryItem object

//*************** main *****************
int main()
{
   InventoryItem part = createItem();
   showValues(part);
   return 0;
}

```

(program continues)

Program 7-10 *(continued)*

```
/*******************************************************
 *                      createItem                     *
 * This function stores user input data in the members of a *
 * locally defined InventoryItem object, then returns it.   *
 *******************************************************/
InventoryItem createItem()
{
   InventoryItem tempItem;   // Local InventoryItem object
   int partNum;              // Local variables to hold user input
   string description;
   int qty;
   double price;

   // Get the data from the user
   cout << "Enter data for the new part number \n";
   cout << "Part number: ";
   cin  >> partNum;
   cout << "Description: ";
   cin.get();                // Move past the '\n' left in the
                             // input buffer by the last input
   getline(cin, description);
   cout << "Quantity on hand: ";
   cin  >> qty;
   cout << "Unit price: ";
   cin  >> price;

   // Store the data in the InventoryItem object and return it
   tempItem.storeInfo(partNum, description, qty, price);
   return tempItem;
}

/***********************************************************
 *                       showValues                        *
 * This function displays the member data in the InventoryItem *
 * object passed to it. Because it was passed as a constant    *
 * reference, showValues accesses the original object, not a   *
 * copy, but it can only call member functions declared to be  *
 * const. This prevents it from calling any mutator functions. *
 ***********************************************************/
void showValues(const InventoryItem &item)
{
   cout << fixed << showpoint << setprecision(2) << endl;;
   cout << "Part Number  : "  << item.getPartNum() << endl;
   cout << "Description  : "  << item.getDescription() << endl;
   cout << "Units On Hand: "  << item.getOnHand() << endl;
   cout << "Price        : $" << item.getPrice() << endl;
}
```

Program Output is the Same as for Program 7-9.

Checkpoint

7.15 A private class member function can be called by
- A) any other function
- B) only public functions in the same class
- C) only private functions in the same class
- D) any function in the same class

7.16 When an object is passed to a function, a copy of it is made if the object is
- A) passed by value
- B) passed by reference
- C) passed by constant reference
- D) any of the above

7.17 If a function receives an object as an argument and needs to change the object's member data, the object should be
- A) passed by value
- B) passed by reference
- C) passed by constant reference
- D) none of the above

7.18 True or false: Objects can be passed to functions, but they cannot be returned by functions.

7.19 True or false: When an object is passed to a function, but the function is not supposed to change it, it is best to pass it by value.

7.10 Object Composition

CONCEPT: It is possible for a class to have a member variable that is an instance of another class.

Sometimes it's helpful to nest an object of one class inside another class. For example, consider the following declarations:

```
class Rectangle
{
   private:
      double length;
      double width;
   public:
      void setLength(double);
      void setWidth(double);
      double getLength();
      double getWidth();
      double getArea();
};
```

```
class Carpet
{
   private:
      double pricePerSqYd;
      Rectangle size;          // size is an instance of
                               // the Rectangle class
   public:
      void setPricePerYd(double p);
      void setDimensions(double l, double w);
      double getTotalPrice();
};
```

Notice that the `Carpet` class has a member variable named `size`, which is an instance of the `Rectangle` class. The `Carpet` class can use this object to store the room dimensions and to compute the area for a carpet purchase. Figure 7-4 illustrates how the two classes are related. When one class is nested inside another like this, it is called *object composition.*

Figure 7-4

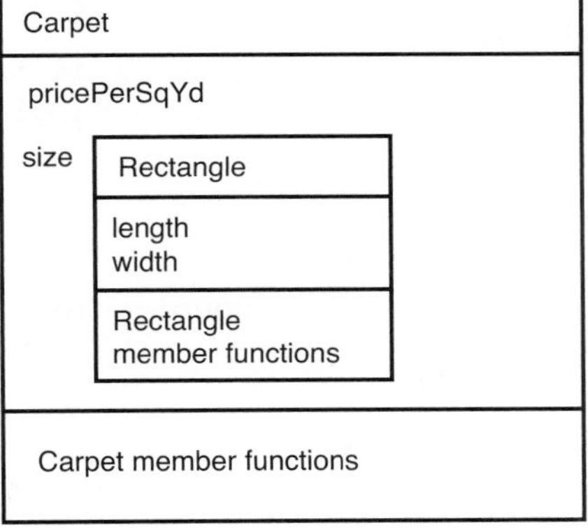

Program 7-11 uses these two classes to create an application that computes carpet sale prices.

Program 7-11

```
// This program nests one class inside another. It has a class
// with a member variable that is an instance of another class.
#include <iostream>
using namespace std;

class Rectangle
{
   private:
      double length;
      double width;
```

(program continues)

Program 7-11 *(continued)*

```
   public:
      void setLength(double len)
      {  length = len; }

      void setWidth(double wid)
      {  width = wid; }

      double getLength()
      {  return length; }

      double getWidth()
      {  return width; }

      double getArea()
      {  return length * width; }
};

class Carpet
{
   private:
      double pricePerSqYd;
      Rectangle size;              // size is an instance of
                                   // the Rectangle class
   public:
      void setPricePerYd(double p)
      { pricePerSqYd = p; }

      void setDimensions(double len, double wid)
      {  size.setLength(len/3);    // Convert feet to yards
         size.setWidth (wid/3);
      }

      double getTotalPrice()
      { return (size.getArea() * pricePerSqYd); }
};

// ************** Client Program *****************
int main()
{
   Carpet purchase;            // This variable is a Carpet object
   double pricePerYd;
   double length;
   double width;

   cout << "Room length in feet: ";
   cin  >> length;
   cout << "Room width in feet : ";
   cin  >> width;
   cout << "Carpet price per sq. yard: ";
   cin  >> pricePerYd;
```

(program continues)

Program 7-11 *(continued)*

```
61
62     purchase.setDimensions(length, width);
63     purchase.setPricePerYd(pricePerYd);
64
65     cout << "\nThe total price of my new " << length << " x " << width
66          << " carpet is $" << purchase.getTotalPrice() << endl;
67
68     return 0;
69 }
```

Program Output with Example Input Shown in Bold

```
Room length in feet: 16.5[Enter]
Room width in feet : 12[Enter]
Carpet price per sq. yard: 22.49[Enter]

The total price of my new 16.5 x 12 carpet is $494.78
```

Let's take a closer look at Program 7-11. Notice that the client program, which defines `purchase`, a `Carpet` object, only uses it to call `Carpet` class functions, not `Rectangle` class functions. It does not even know that the `Carpet` class has a `Rectangle` object inside it. Notice also, in lines 39, 40, and 44, how `Carpet` class functions call `Rectangle` functions. Just as the user program calls `Carpet` functions through the name of its `Carpet` object, the `Carpet` class functions must call `Rectangle` functions through the name of its `Rectangle` object. The `Rectangle` object, defined in line 32, is named `size`. That is why the `Carpet` functions make calls like this:

```
size.getArea()
```

Checkpoint

7.20 Assume a `Map` class has a member variable named `position` that is an instance of the `Location` class. The `Location` class has a private member variable named `latitude` and a public member function called `getLatitude`. Which of the following lines of code would correctly get and return the value stored in `latitude`?

A) `return Location.latitude;`
B) `return Location.getLatitude();`
C) `return position.latitude;`
D) `return position.getLatitude();`

7.21 Write a class declaration for a class named `Circle`, which has the data member `radius`, a `double`, and member functions `setRadius` and `getArea`. Write the code for these as inline functions.

7.22 Write a class declaration for a class named `Pizza` that has the data members `price`, a `double`, and `size`, a `Circle` object (declared in question 7.21). It also has member functions: `setPrice`, `setSize`, and `costPerSqIn`. Write the code for these as inline functions.

7.23 Write 4 lines of code that might appear in a client program using the `Pizza` class to do the following:
Define an instance of the `Pizza` class named `myPizza`.
Call a `Pizza` function to set the price.
Call a `Pizza` function to set the size (i.e., the radius).
Call a `Pizza` function to return the price per square inch and then print it.

7.11 Focus on Software Engineering: *Separating Class Specification, Implementation, and Client Code*

CONCEPT: Usually class declarations are stored in their own header files and member function definitions are stored in their own `.cpp` files.

In the programs we've looked at so far, the class declaration, the member function definitions, and the application program that uses the class are all stored in one file. A more conventional way of designing C++ programs is to store these in three separate files. Typically, program components are stored in the following fashion:

- Class declarations are stored in their own header files. A header file that contains a class declaration is called a *class specification file*. The name of the class specification file is usually the same as the name of the class, with a `.h` extension. For example, the `Rectangle` class would be declared in the file `Rectangle .h`.
- Any program that uses the class should `#include` this header file.
- The member function definitions for a class are stored in a separate `.cpp` file, which is called the *class implementation file*. The file usually has the same name as the class, with the `.cpp` extension. For example the `Rectangle` class member functions would be defined in the file `Rectangle.cpp`.
- The class `.cpp` file should be compiled and linked with the application program that uses the class. This program, also known as the *client program*, or *client code*, is the one that includes the `main` function. This process can be automated with a `project` or `make` utility. Integrated development environments such as Visual Studio also provide the means to create multi-file projects.

Let's see how we could rewrite Program 7-3, the rectangle program, using this design approach. First, the `Rectangle` class declaration would be stored in the following `Rectangle.h` file.

Contents of `Rectangle.h`

```
 1 // Rectangle.h is the Rectangle class specification file.
 2 #ifndef RECTANGLE_H
 3 #define RECTANGLE_H
 4
 5 // Rectangle class declaration
 6 class Rectangle
 7 {
 8    private:
 9       double length;
10       double width;
11    public:
12       bool setLength(double);
13       bool setWidth(double);
14       double getLength();
15       double getWidth();
16       double getArea();
17 };
18 #endif
```

This is the specification file for the `Rectangle` class. It contains only the declaration of the `Rectangle` class. It does not contain any member function definitions. When we write other programs that use the `Rectangle` class, we can have an `#include` directive that includes this file. That way, we won't have to write the class declaration in every program that uses the `Rectangle` class.

This file also introduces two new preprocessor directives: `#ifndef` and `#endif`. The `#ifndef` directive that appears in line 2 is called an *include guard*. It prevents the header file from accidentally being included more than once. When your main program file has an `#include` directive for a header file, there is always the possibility that the header file will have an `#include` directive for a second header file. If your main program file also has an `#include` directive for the second header file, the preprocessor will include the second header file twice. Unless an include guard has been written into the second header file, an error will occur because the compiler will process the declarations in the second header file twice. Let's see how an include guard works.

The word `ifndef` stands for "if not defined". It is used to determine whether or not a specific constant has already been defined with another `#define` directive. When the `Rectangle.h` file is being compiled, the `#ifndef` directive checks for the existence of a constant named `RECTANGLE_H`. If this constant has not been defined yet, it is immediately defined in line 3, and the rest of the file is included. However, if the constant has already been defined, it means that this file has already been included. In that case, it is not included a second time. Instead, everything between the `#ifndef` and `#endif` directives is skipped. Note that the constant used in the `#infdef` and `#define` directives should be written in all capital letters and is customarily named `FILENAME_H`, where `FILENAME` is the name of the header file.

Next we need an implementation file that contains the class member function definitions. The implementation file for the `Rectangle` class is `Rectangle.cpp`.

Contents of `Rectangle.cpp`

```
// Rectangle.cpp is the Rectangle class function implementation file.
#include "Rectangle.h"

/*******************************************************************
 *                       Rectangle::setLength                      *
 * If the argument passed to the setLength function is zero or     *
 * greater, it is copied into the member variable length, and true *
 * is returned. If the argument is negative, the value of length   *
 * remains unchanged and false is returned.                        *
 *******************************************************************/
bool Rectangle::setLength(double len)
{
   bool validData = true;

   if (len >= 0)               // If the len is valid
      length = len;            // copy it to length
   else
      validData = false;       // else leave length unchanged

   return validData;
}

/*******************************************************************
 *                       Rectangle::setWidth                       *
 * If the argument passed to the setWidth function is zero or      *
 * greater, it is copied into the member variable width, and true  *
 * is returned. If the argument is negative, the value of width    *
 * remains unchanged and false is returned.                        *
 *******************************************************************/
bool Rectangle::setWidth(double w)
{
   bool validData = true;

   if (w >= 0)                 // If w is valid
      width = w;               // copy it to width
   else
      validData = false;       // else leave width unchanged

   return validData;
}

/**************************************************************
 *                       Rectangle::getLength                 *
 * This function returns the value in member variable length. *
 **************************************************************/
double Rectangle::getLength()
{
   return length;
}

```

```
51 /***************************************************************
52  *                         Rectangle::getWidth                   *
53  * This function returns the value in member variable width.   *
54  ***************************************************************/
55 double Rectangle::getWidth()
56 {
57    return width;
58 }
59
60 /*******************************************************************
61  *                           Rectangle::getArea                     *
62  * This function calculates and returns the area of the rectangle. *
63  *******************************************************************/
64 double Rectangle::getArea()
65 {
66    return length * width;
67 }
```

Look at the code for the five functions. Notice that the three accessor functions, `getLength`, `getWidth`, and `getArea`, are the same as those that appeared in Program 7-3. However, a change has been made to the two mutator functions, `setLength` and `setWidth`, to illustrate another way that public class functions can safeguard private member data. In Program 7-3, the `setLength` and `setWidth` functions use a default value for `length` and `width` if invalid data is passed to them. In the `Rectangle.cpp` code, these two functions return a Boolean value indicating whether or not the value received was stored in the member variable. If a valid argument is received, it is stored in the member variable and `true` is returned. If an invalid argument is received, the member variable is left unchanged and `false` is returned. The client program that uses this class must test the returned Boolean value to determine how to proceed.

Now look at line 2, which has the following `#include` directive:

```
#include "Rectangle.h"
```

This directive includes the `Rectangle.h` file, which contains the `Rectangle` class declaration. Notice that the name of the header file is enclosed in double-quote characters (`" "`) instead of angled brackets (< >). When you are including a C++ system header file, such as `iostream`, you enclose the name of the file in angled brackets. This indicates that the file is located in the compiler's *include file directory*. That is the directory or folder where all of the standard C++ header files are located. When you are including a header file that you have written, such as a class specification file, you enclose the name of the file in double quote marks. This indicates that the file is located in the current project directory.

Any file that uses the `Rectangle` class must have an `#include` directive for the `Rectangle.h` file. We need to include `Rectangle.h` in the class specification file because the functions in this file belong to the `Rectangle` class. Before the compiler can process a function with `Rectangle::` in its name, it must have already processed the `Rectangle` class declaration.

With the `Rectangle` class stored in its own specification and implementation files, we can see how to use them in a program. Program 7-12 is a modified version of Program 7-3. Notice that Program 7-12 is much shorter than Program 7-3 because it does not contain the `Rectangle` class declaration or member function definitions. Instead, it is designed to be compiled and linked with the class specification and implementation files. Program 7-12 only needs to contain the client code that creates and uses a `Rectangle` object.

Program 7-12

```
 1 // This program uses the Rectangle class.
 2 // The Rectangle class declaration is in file Rectangle.h.
 3 // The Rectangle member function definitions are in Rectangle.cpp
 4 // These files should all be combined into a project.
 5 #include <iostream>
 6 #include "Rectangle.h"          // Contains Rectangle class declaration
 7 using namespace std;
 8 
 9 int main()
10 {
11    Rectangle box;               // Declare a Rectangle object
12    double boxLength, boxWidth;
13 
14    //Get box length and width
15    cout << "This program will calculate the area of a rectangle.\n";
16    cout << "What is the length? ";
17    cin  >> boxLength;
18    cout << "What is the width? ";
19    cin  >> boxWidth;
20 
21    // Call member functions to set box dimensions.
22    // If the function call returns false, it means the
23    // argument sent to it was invalid and not stored.
24    if (!box.setLength(boxLength))                // Store the length
25       cout << "Invalid box length entered.\n";
26    else if (!box.setWidth(boxWidth))             // Store the width
27       cout << "Invalid box width entered.\n";
28    else                                          // Both values were valid
29    {
30       // Call member functions to get box information to display
31       cout << "\nHere is the rectangle's data:\n";
32       cout << "Length: " << box.getLength() << endl;
33       cout << "Width : " << box.getWidth()  << endl;
34       cout << "Area  : " << box.getArea()   << endl;
35    }
36    return 0;
37 }
```

Notice that line 6 of Program 7-12 has an `#include` directive for the `Rectangle.h` file. This is needed so the `Rectangle` class declaration will be included in the file.

Now that we have created the three files for this program, the following steps must be taken to create an executable program.

- First, the implementation file, `Rectangle.cpp`, should be compiled to create an object file. This file would typically be named `Rectangle.obj`.
- Next, the main program file, located in file `pr7-12.cpp`, must be compiled to create an object file. This file would typically be named `pr7-12.obj`.
- Finally, the object files `pr7-12.obj` and `Rectangle.obj` are linked together to create an executable file, which would be named something like `pr7-12.exe`.

Table 7-1 summarizes how the different files of Program 7-12 are organized and compiled on a typical Windows computer.

Table 7-1 Files Used in Program 7-12

`Rectangle.h`	Contains the `Rectangle` class declaration. This file is included by `Rectangle.cpp` and `pr7-12.cpp`.
`Rectangle.cpp`	Contains the definitions of the `Rectangle` class member functions. This file is compiled to create an object file, such as `Rectangle.obj`.
`pr7-12.cpp`	Contains the application program that uses the class. In this case, the application program consists of just the function `main`. This file is compiled to create an object file, such as `pr7-12.obj`.
`Linking the .obj files`	The two object code files created by compiling `Rectangle.cpp` and `pr7-12.cpp` are linked to make the executable file `pr7-12.exe`

Figure 7-5 further illustrates this process.

Figure 7-5

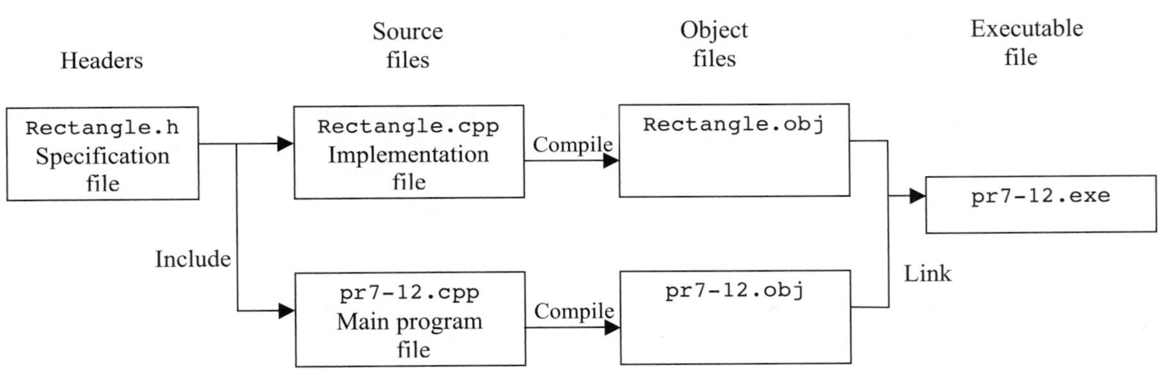

The exact details on how these steps take place are different for each C++ development system. Fortunately, most systems perform all of these steps automatically for you. For example, in Microsoft Visual C++ you create a project, and then you simply add all of the files to the project. When you compile the project, the steps are done for you and an executable file is generated. Once the executable file has been created, you can run the program. When valid values are entered for `boxLength` and `boxWidth` the output should be identical to that shown for Program 7-3.

> **NOTE:** Appendix G, Multi-Source File Programs, provides additional information on creating multifile projects.

Advantages of Using Multiple Files

Separating a client program from the details of a class it uses is considered good programming practice. A class is an example of an abstract data type and, as you learned earlier in this chapter, the only thing a programmer writing an application that uses the class needs to know is what the class does, what kind of data it can hold, what functions it provides, and how to call them. Programmers, and any programs using the class, do not need to know anything about the implementation of the class. In addition, often many different programs use a particular class. If the implementation code that defines the class member functions is in its own separate file, this code does not have to be in all of these programs. They can each simply `#include` the file containing the defintions.

Separating a class into a specification file and an implementation file is also considered good programming practice. If you wish to give your class to other programmers, you don't have to share all of your source code. You can just provide a copy of the specification file and the compiled object file for the class's implementation. The other programmers simply insert the necessary `#include` directive into their programs, compile them, and link them with your class object file. This prevents other programmers, who might not understand all the details of your code, from making changes that introduce bugs.

Separating a class into specification and implementation files also makes things easier when class member functions must be modified. It is only necessary to modify the implementation file and recompile it to create a new object file. Programs that use the class don't have to be recompiled. They just have to be linked with the new object file.

Performing Input/Output in a Class Object

You may have noticed in Program 7-12 that we avoided doing any I/O inside the `Rectangle` class. In general is it considered good design to have class member functions avoid using `cin` and `cout`. This is so anyone writing a program that uses the class will not be locked into the particular way the class performs input or output. Unless a class is specifically designed to perform I/O, it is best to leave operations such as user input and output to the person designing the application. As a general rule, classes should provide member functions for retrieving data values without displaying them on the screen. Likewise, they should provide member functions that store data into private member variables without using `cin`. Program 7-12 follows both of these practices.

NOTE: There are instances where it is appropriate for a class to perform I/O. For example, a class might be designed to display a menu on the screen and get the user's selection. Another example is a class designed to handle a program's file I/O. Classes that hold and manipulate data, however, should not be tied to any particular I/O routines. This allows them to be more versatile.

Checkpoint

7.24 Assume the following class components exist in a program:

`BasePay` class declaration
`BasePay` member function definitions
`Overtime` class declaration
`Overtime` member function definitions

What files would you store each of the above components in?

7.25 What header files should be included in the client program that uses the `BasePay` and `Overtime` classes?

7.12 Structures

CONCEPT: C++ allows a set of variables to be combined together into a single unit called a structure.

A *structure* is a programmer-defined data type that can hold many different data values. In the past, before the use of object-oriented programming became common, programmers typically used these to group logically connected data together into a single unit. Once a structure type is declared and its data members identified, multiple variables of this type can be created, just as multiple objects can be created for the same class.

Although structures are less commonly used today, it is important that you know what they are and how to use them. Not only may you encounter them in older programs, but there are actually some instances in which classes will not work and structures must be used. You will see an example of this later in this chapter.

The way a structure is declared is similar to the way a class is declared, with the following differences:

- The key word `struct` is used instead of the key word `class`.
- Although structures *can* include member functions, they rarely do. So normally a structure declaration only declares member variables.
- Structure declarations normally do not include the access specifiers `public` or `private`.
- Unlike class members, which are private by default, members of a structure default to being public. Programmers normally want them to remain public and simply use the default.

Here is an example of a declaration for a structure that bundles together five variables holding payroll data for an employee. The name of this particular structure is `PayRoll`. Notice that it begins with a capital letter. The convention is to begin structure names, just like class names, with an uppercase letter. Notice also that, like a class declaration, there must be a semicolon after the closing brace of the declaration.

```
struct PayRoll
{
   int     empNumber;
   string  name;
   double  hours,
           payRate,
           grossPay;
};
```

Just as a class declaration is not instantiated until objects of the class are created, a structure declaration does not create any instances of the structure. The structure declaration in our example simply tells the compiler what a `Payroll` structure looks like. It in essence creates a new data type named `Payroll`.

You define variables that are `Payroll` structures the way you define any variable, by first listing the data type, and then the variable name. The following definition creates three variables that are `Payroll` structures.

```
Payroll deptHead, foreman, associate;
```

Each is an instance of a `Payroll` structure, with its own memory allocated to hold its member data. Notice that although the three structure variables have *distinct* names, each contains members with the *same* name. Figure 7.6 illustrates this.

Figure 7-6

deptHead
empNumber
name
hours
payRate
grossPay

foreman
empNumber
name
hours
payRate
grossPay

associate
empNumber
name
hours
payRate
grossPay

Accessing Structure Members

Creating and Using Structures

Members of a structure are accessed just like public members of a class, with the dot operator. However, the data members of a class are normally private and must be accessed through functions. Because structure data members are public, they are accessed directly and can be used like regular variables. The following statements assign values to the `empNumber` member of each of the `Payroll` variables we created.

```
deptHead.empNumber = 475;
foreman.empNumber = 897;
associate.empNumber = 729;
```

And the following statements display the contents of all the `deptHead`'s members.

```
cout << deptHead.empNumber << endl;
cout << deptHead.name << endl;
cout << deptHead.hours << endl;
cout << deptHead.payRate << endl;
cout << deptHead.grossPay << endl;
```

Program 7-13 is a complete program that uses the `PayRoll` structure. Notice how the individual structure members are used just like regular variables in `cin` statements, in `cout` statements, and in mathematical operations.

Program 7-13

```
// This program demonstrates the use of a structure.
#include <iostream>
#include <iomanip>
#include <string>
using namespace std;

```

(program continues)

Program 7-13 *(continued)*

```
struct PayRoll
{
   int    empNumber;  // Employee number
   string name;       // Employee name
   double hours,      // Hours worked
          payRate;    // Hourly pay rate
};

int main()
{
   PayRoll employee;  // Employee is a PayRoll structure
   double grossPay;   // Gross amount the employee earned this week

   //Get the employee's data
   cout << "Enter the employee's number: ";
   cin  >> employee.empNumber;

   cout << "Enter the employee's name: ";
   cin.ignore();      // Skip the '\n' character left in the input buffer
   getline(cin, employee.name);

   cout << "Hours worked this week: ";
   cin  >> employee.hours;

   cout << "Employee's hourly pay rate: ";
   cin  >> employee.payRate;

   // Calculate the employee's gross pay
   grossPay = employee.hours * employee.payRate;

   // Display the results
   cout << "\nHere is the employee's payroll data:\n";
   cout << "Name:            " << employee.name << endl;
   cout << "Employee number: " << employee.empNumber << endl;
   cout << "Hours worked:    " << employee.hours << endl;
   cout << "Hourly pay rate: " << employee.payRate << endl;
   cout << fixed << showpoint  << setprecision(2);
   cout << "Gross pay:      $" << grossPay << endl;
   return 0;
}
```

Program Output with Example Input Shown in Bold

```
Enter the employee's number: 2214[Enter]
Enter the employee's name: Jack Smith[Enter]
Hours worked this week: 40[Enter]
Employee's hourly pay rate: 12.50[Enter]

Here is the employee's payroll data:
Name:            Jack Smith
Employee number: 2214
Hours worked:    40
Hourly pay rate: 12.5
Gross pay:      $500.00
```

In Program 7-13 the variable `employee` is defined in line 17 to be an instance of a `Payroll` structure. Its five data members can then be accessed with the dot operator through the name of the variable. For example, in line 22 the following statement reads a value into the variable's `empNumber` member.

```
cin  >> employee.empNumber;          // Correct
```

It would have been wrong to try to access this member through the name of the structure type.

```
cin  >> Payroll.empNumber;           // Wrong!
```

Displaying and Comparing Structure Variables

In Program 7-13 each member of the `employee` structure variable was displayed separately. This is necessary because the entire contents of a structure variable cannot be displayed by simply passing the whole variable to `cout`. For example, the following statement will *not* work.

```
cout << employee << endl;                    // Error!
```

Likewise, while it is possible to compare the contents of two individual structure members, you cannot perform comparison operations on entire structures. For example, if `employee1` and `employee2` are both `Payroll` structure variables, this comparison will cause an error.

```
if (employee1 == employee2)                  // Error!
```

The following comparison, on the other hand, is perfectly legal.

```
if (employee1.hours == employee2.hours) // Legal
```

Initializing a Structure

There are two ways a structure variable can be initialized when it is defined: with an initialization list or with a constructor.

The simplest way to initialize the members of a structure variable is to use an initialization list. An *initialization list* is a list of values used to initialize a set of memory locations. The items in the list are separated by commas and surrounded by braces. Suppose, for example, the following `Date` structure has been declared:

```
struct Date
{  int day,
       month,
       year;
};
```

A `Date` variable can now be defined and initialized by following the variable name with the assignment operator and an initialization list, as shown here:

```
Date birthday = {23, 8, 1983};
```

This statement defines `birthday` to be a variable which is a `Date` structure. The values inside the curly braces are assigned to its members in order. So the data members of `birthday` have been initialized as shown in Figure 7-7.

Figure 7-7

birthday.day	23
birthday.month	8
birthday.year	1983

It is also possible to initialize just some of the members of a structure variable. For example, if we know the birthday to be stored is August 23, but do not know the year, the variable could be defined and initialized like this:

```
Date birthday = {23, 8};
```

Only the `day` and `month` members are initialized here. The `year` member is not initialized. If you leave a structure member uninitialized, however, you must leave all the members that follow it uninitialized as well. C++ does not provide a way to skip members when using an initialization list. The following statement attempts to skip the initialization of the `month` member. It is *not* legal.

```
Date birthday = {23, , 1983};     // Illegal!
```

It is important to note that you cannot initialize a structure member in the declaration of the structure because the structure declaration just creates a new data type. No variables of this type exist yet. For example, the following declaration is illegal:

```
// Illegal structure declaration
struct Date
{  int day   = 23,
       month = 8,
       year  = 1983;
};
```

Because a structure declaration only declares what a structure "looks like", the member variables are not created in memory until the structure is instantiated by defining a variable of that structure type. Until then there is no place to store an initial value.

Although an initialization list is easy to use, it has two drawbacks:

1. It does not allow you to leave some members uninitialized and still initialize others that follow.
2. It will not work on many compilers if the structure includes any objects, such as strings.

In these cases you can initialize structure member variables the same way you initialize class member variables—by using a constructor. As with a class constructor, a constructor for a structure must be a public member function with the same name as the structure and no return type. Because all structure members are public by default, however, the key word `public` does not need to be used. Here is a structure declaration for a structure named `Employee`. It includes a 2-argument constructor that provides default values in case an `Employee` variable is created without passing any arguments to the constructor.

```
struct Employee
{
   string name;                // Employee name
   int vacationDays,           // Vacation days allowed per year
       daysUsed;               // Vacation days used so far

   Employee(string n = "", int d = 0)  // Constructor
   {  name = n;
      vacationDays = 10;
      daysUsed = d;
   }
};
```

Nested Structures

Just as objects of one class can be nested within another class, instances of one structure can be nested within another structure. For example, consider the following declarations:

```
struct Costs
{
   double wholesale;
   double retail;
};

struct Item
{
   string partNum;
   string description;
   Costs pricing;
};
```

The `Costs` structure has two `double` members, `wholesale` and `retail`. The `Item` structure has three members. The first two, `partNum` and `description`, are `string` objects. The third, `pricing`, is a nested `Costs` structure. If `widget` is defined to be an `Item` structure, Figure 7-8 illustrates its members.

Figure 7-8

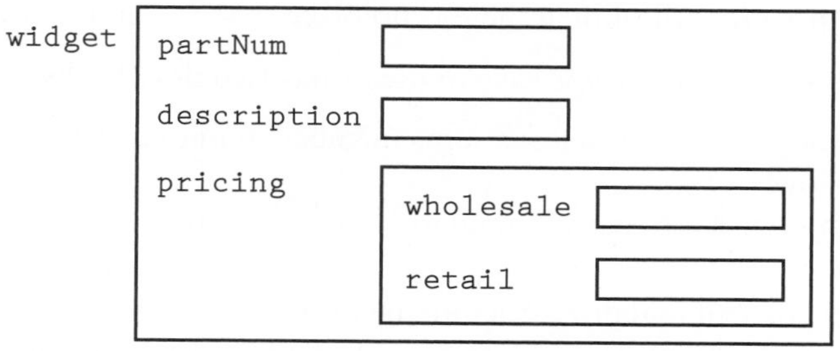

They would be accessed as follows:

```
widget.partnum = "123A";
widget.description = "iron widget";
widget.pricing.wholesale = 100.0;
widget.pricing.retail = 150.0;
```

Notice that `wholesale` and `retail` are not members of `widget`; `pricing` is. To access `wholesale` and `retail`, `widget`'s `pricing` member must first be accessed and then, because it is a `Costs` structure, its `wholesale` and `retail` members can be accessed. Notice also, as with all structures, it is the *member* name, not the *structure* name, that must be used in accessing a member. The following statements would not be legal.

```
cout << widget.retail;              // Wrong!
cout << widget.Costs.wholesale;     // Wrong!
```

When you are deciding whether to use nested structures or not, think about how various members are related. A structure bundles together items that logically belong together. Normally the members of a structure are attributes describing some object. In our example, the object was a widget, and its part number, description, and wholesale and retail prices were its attributes. When some of the attributes are related and form a logical subgroup of the object's attributes, it makes sense to bundle them together and use a nested structure. Notice the relatedness of the attributes in the inner structure of Program 7-14, which uses a nested structure.

Program 7-14

```
// This program demonstrates the use of a nested structure.
#include <iostream>
#include <iomanip>
#include <string>
using namespace std;

struct CostInfo
{
   double food,       // Food costs
          medical,    // Medical costs
          license,    // License fee
          misc;       // Miscellaneous costs
};

struct PetInfo
{
   string name;       // Pet name
   string type;       // Pet type
   int    age;        // Pet age

   CostInfo cost;     // A PetInfo structure has a CostInfo structure
                      // nested inside as one of its members

   PetInfo()          // Default constructor
   {  name = "unknown";
      type = "unknown";
      age = 0;
      cost.food = cost.medical = cost.license = cost.misc = 0.00;
   }
};
```

(program continues)

Program 7-14 *(continued)*

```
int main()
{
   // Define a PetInfo structure variable called pet
   PetInfo pet;

   // Assign values to the pet member variables.
   // Notice that cost.misc is not assigned a value,
   // so it remains 0, as set by the constructor.
   pet.name = "Sassy";
   pet.type = "cat";
   pet.age = 5;
   pet.cost.food = 300.00;
   pet.cost.medical = 200.00;
   pet.cost.license = 7.00;

   // Display the total annual costs for the pet
   cout << fixed << showpoint << setprecision(2);
   cout << "Annual costs for my " << pet.age << "-year-old "
        << pet.type << " " << pet.name  << " are $"
        << (pet.cost.food + pet.cost.medical +
            pet.cost.license + pet.cost.misc) << endl;
   return 0;
}
```

Sample Output

```
Annual costs for my 5-year-old cat Sassy are $507.00
```

Checkpoint

7.26 Write a structure declaration for a structure named `Student` that holds the following data about a student:

- ID (`int`)
- entry year (`int`)
- GPA (`double`)

Then write definition statements that create the following two `Student` variables and initialize them using initialization lists.

- Variable `s1` should have ID number 1234, entry year 2008, and GPA 3.41.
- Variable `s2` should have ID number 5678 and entry year 2010. The GPA member should be left uninitialized.

7.27 Write a structure declaration for a structure named `Account` that holds the following data about a savings account. Include a constructor that allows data values to be passed in for all four members.

- Account number (`string`)
- Account balance (`double`)
- Interest rate (`double`)
- Average monthly balance (`double`)

Now write a definition statement for an `Account` variable that initializes the members with the following data:

Account number: ACZ42137
Account balance: $4512.59
Interest rate: 4%
Average monthly balance: $4217.07

7.28 The following program skeleton, when complete, asks the user to enter the following information about his or her favorite movie:

Name of the movie
Name of the movie's director
The year the movie was released

Complete the program by declaring the structure that holds this information, defining a structure variable, and writing the required individual statements.

```
#include <iostream>
#include <string>
using namespace std;

// Write the structure declaration to hold the movie information.

int main()
{
   // Define the structure variable here.

   cout << "Enter the following information about your "
        << " favorite movie.\n" << "Name: ";
   // Write a statement here that lets the user enter a movie name.
   // Store it in the appropriate structure member.

   cout << "Director: ";
   // Write a statement here that lets the user enter the director's
   // name. Store it in the appropriate structure member.

   cout << "Year of Release: ";
   // Write a statement here that lets the user enter the movie
   // release year. Store it in the appropriate structure member.

   cout << "\nHere is information on your favorite movie:\n";
   // Write statements here that display the information
   // just entered into the structure variable.
   return 0;
}
```

7.29 Write a declaration for a structure named `Location`, with the following three `double` member variables: `latitude`, `longitude`, and `height`.

7.30 Write a declaration for a structure named `City`, which has the members `cityName`, a `string`, and `position`, a `Location` structure (declared above). Then define a variable named `destination` that is an instance of the `City` structure.

7.31 Write assignment statements that store the following information in `destination`.

city name	:	Tupelo	
latitude	:	34.28	// 34.28 degrees north
longitude	:	–88.77	// 88.77 degrees west
height	:	361.0	// feet above sea level

Passing Structures to Functions

Structure variables, just like class objects, can be passed to functions by value, by reference, and by constant reference. By default, they are passed by value. This means that a copy of the entire original structure is made and passed to the function. Because it is not desirable to take the time to copy an entire structure, unless it is quite small, structures are normally passed to functions by reference. This, however, gives the function access to the member variables of the original structure, allowing it to change them. If you do not want a function to change any member variable values, the structure variable should be passed to it as a constant reference.

Program 7-15 is a modification of Program 7-9 that defines a structure variable and passes it to two functions.

Program 7-15

```
// This program passes a structure variable to one function
// by reference and to another as a constant reference.
#include <iostream>
#include <iomanip>
#include <string>
using namespace std;

struct InvItem                  // Holds data for an inventory item
{
   int partNum;                 // Part number
   string description;          // Item description
   int onHand;                  // Units on hand
   double price;                // Unit price
};

// Function prototypes
void getItemData(InvItem &);    // Function getItemData will receive an
                                // InvItem structure passed to it by
                                // reference so new values can be stored
                                // in its member variables.

void showItem(const InvItem &);
                                // Function showItem will receive an
                                // InvItem structure passed to it as a
                                // constant reference because showItem
                                // just needs display member variable
                                // values, not change them.
int main()
{
   InvItem part;                // Define an InvItem structure variable.

   getItemData(part);
   showItem(part);
   return 0;
}
```

(program continues)

Program 7-15 *(continued)*

```

/*******************************************************************
 *                          getItemData                            *
 * This function stores data input by the user in the members of an *
 * InvItem structure variable passed to the function by reference.  *
 * ******************************************************************/
void getItemData(InvItem &item)
{
   cout << "Enter the part number: ";
   cin  >> item.partNum;
   cout << "Enter the part description: ";
   cin.get();                    // Move past the '\n' left in the
                                 // input buffer by the last input.
   getline(cin, item.description);
   cout << "Enter the quantity on hand: ";
   cin  >> item.onHand;
   cout << "Enter the unit price: ";
   cin  >> item.price;
}

/*******************************************************************
 *                             showItem                            *
 * This function displays the data stored in the members of an     *
 * InvItem structure variable passed to it as a constant reference. *
 * ******************************************************************/
void showItem(const InvItem &item)
{
   cout << fixed << showpoint << setprecision(2) << endl;;
   cout << "Part Number  : "  << item.partNum << endl;
   cout << "Description  : "  << item.description << endl;
   cout << "Units On Hand: "  << item.onHand << endl;
   cout << "Price        : $" << item.price << endl;
}
```

Program Output with Example Input Shown in Bold

```
Enter the part number: 800[Enter]
Enter the part description: Screwdriver[Enter]
Enter the quantity on hand: 135[Enter]
Enter the unit price: 1.25[Enter]

Part Number  : 800
Description  : Screwdriver
Units On Hand: 135
Price        : $1.25
```

Returning a Structure from a Function

A structure variable can also be returned from a function. In this case the return type of the function is the name of the structure. Program 7-15 could have been written to allow the `getItemData` function to create a local instance of an `InvItem` structure, place data values into its member variables, and then pass it back to `main`, instead of receiving it from `main` as a reference variable. This is what the revised `getItemData` function would look like.

```
/***************************************************************
 *                        getItemData                          *
 * This function stores data input by the user in the members  *
 * of a local InvItem structure variable and then returns it.  *
 * *************************************************************/

InvItem getItemData()
{
   InvItem item;           // Create a local InvItem variable
                           // to hold data until it can be returned.
   cout << "Enter the part number: ";
   cin  >> item.partNum;
   cout << "Enter the part description: ";
   cin.get();              // Move past the '\n' left in the
                           // input buffer by the last input.
   getline(cin, item.description);
   cout << "Enter the quantity on hand: ";
   cin  >> item.onHand;
   cout << "Enter the unit price: ";
   cin  >> item.price;

   return item;
}
```

And here is how it would be called from `main`.

```
part = getItemData();
```

This version of Program 7-15 can be found in the Chapter 7 folder on the book's companion website as Program 7-15B.

NOTE: In Chapter 6 you learned that C++ only allows you to return a single value from a function. Structures, however, provide a way around this limitation. Even though a structure may have several members, it is technically a single object. By packaging multiple values inside a structure, you can return as many values as you need from a function.

Checkpoint

Use the following structure declaration to answer the questions in this section.

```
struct Rectangle
{
   int length;
   int width;
};
```

7.32 Write a function that accepts the `Rectangle` structure defined above as its argument and displays the structure's contents on the screen.

7.33 Write a function that uses a `Rectangle` structure reference variable as its parameter and stores the user's input in the structure's members.

7.34 Write a function that returns a `Rectangle` structure. The function should create a local `Rectangle` variable, store the user's input in its members, and then return it.

Unions

A union is like a structure, except all the member variables occupy the *same* memory area, so only one member can be used at a time. A union might be used in an application where the program needs to work with two or more values (of different data types), but only needs to use one of the values at a time. Unions conserve memory by storing all of their members in the same memory location.

Unions are declared just like structures, except the key word `union` is used instead of `struct`. Here is an example:

```
union PaySource
{
   short hours;
   float sales;
};
```

A union variable of the data type shown can then be defined like this:

```
PaySource employee1;
```

The `PaySource` union variable defined here has two members: `hours` (a `short`) and `sales` (a `float`). The entire variable will only take up as much memory as the largest member (in this case, a `float`). The way this variable is stored on a typical computer is illustrated in Figure 7-9.

Figure 7-9

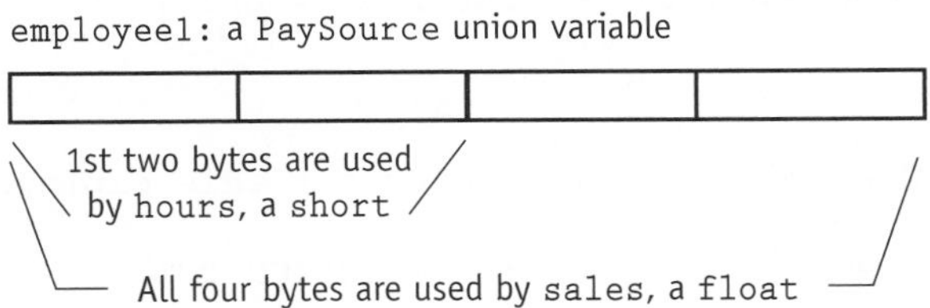
employee1: a PaySource union variable
1st two bytes are used
by hours, a short
All four bytes are used by sales, a float

As shown in Figure 7-9, this union uses four bytes on a typical computer. It can store a `short` or a `float`, depending on which member is used. When a value is stored in the `sales` member, all four bytes are needed to hold the data. When a value is stored in the `hours` member, only the first two bytes are used. Obviously, both members can't hold values at the same time. This union is demonstrated in Program 7-16.

Program 7-16

```
// This program demonstrates a union.
#include <iostream>
#include <iomanip>
using namespace std;

union PaySource                 // Declare a union
{
   short hours;                 // These two variables share
   float sales;                 // the same memory space
};

int main()
{
   const double COMMISSION_PCT = .10;

   PaySource employee1;         // employee1 is a PaySource union
                                // This employee can have hours or
                                // sales, but not both at once

   char  hourlyType;            // 'y' if hourly, 'n' if on commission
   float payRate, grossPay;

   cout << fixed << showpoint << setprecision(2);
   cout << "This program calculates either hourly wages or "
        << "sales commission.\n";
   cout << "Is this an hourly employee (y or n)? ";
   cin  >> hourlyType;

   if (hourlyType == 'y' || hourlyType == 'Y')   // Hourly employee
   {
      cout << "What is the hourly pay rate? ";
      cin  >> payRate;
      cout << "How many hours were worked? ";
      cin  >> employee1.hours;
      grossPay = employee1.hours * payRate;
      cout << "Gross pay: $" << grossPay << endl;
   }
   else                                          // Commission employee
   {
      cout << "What are the total sales for this employee? ";
      cin  >> employee1.sales;
      grossPay = employee1.sales * COMMISSION_PCT;
      cout << "Gross pay: $" << grossPay << endl;
   }
   return 0;
}
```

(program continues)

Program 7-16 *(continued)*

Program Output with Example Input Shown in Bold
```
This program calculates either hourly wages or sales commission.
Is this an hourly employee (y or n)? y[Enter]
What is the hourly pay rate? 20[Enter]
How many hours were worked? 40[Enter]
Gross pay: $800.00
```

Program Output with Other Example Input Shown in Bold
```
This program calculates either hourly wages or sales commission.
Is this an hourly employee (y or n)? n[Enter]
What are the total sales for this employee? 5000[Enter]
Gross pay: $500.00
```

Everything else you already know about structures applies to unions.

7.13 Home Software Company OOP Case Study

You are a programmer for the Home Software Company assigned to develop a class that models the basic workings of a bank account. The class should perform the following tasks:

- Save the account balance.
- Save the number of transactions performed on the account.
- Allow deposits to be made to the account.
- Allow withrawals to be taken from the account.
- Calculate interest for the period.
- Report the current account balance at any time.
- Report the current number of transactions at any time.

Private Member Variables

Table 7-2 lists the private member variables needed by the class.

Table 7-2 Private Member Variables of the Account Class

Variable	Description
`balance`	A `double` that holds the current account balance
`intRate`	A `double` that holds the interest rate for the period
`interest`	A `double` that holds the interest earned for the current period
`transactions`	An integer that holds the current number of transactions

Public Member Functions

Table 7-3 lists the public member functions in the class.

Table 7-3 Public Member Functions of the Account Class

Function	Description
constructor	Takes arguments to be initially stored in the `balance` and `intRate` members. The default value for the balance is zero and the default value for the interest rate is 0.045.
`makeDeposit`	Takes a `double` argument that is the amount of the deposit. This argument is added to `balance`.
`withdraw`	Takes a `double` argument that is the amount of the withdrawal. This value is subtracted from the balance, unless the withdrawal amount is greater than the balance. If this happens, the function reports an error.
`calcInterest`	Takes no arguments. This function calculates the amount of interest for the current period, stores this value in the `interest` member, and then adds it to the `balance` member.
`getBalance`	Returns the current balance (stored in the `balance` member).
`getInterest`	Returns the interest earned for the current period (stored in the `interest` member).
`getTransactions`	Returns the number of transactions for the current period (stored in the `transactions` member).

The Class Declaration

The following listing shows the class declaration.

Contents of `Account.h`

```
// Account.h is the Account class specification file.
class Account
{
 private:
   double balance;
   double intRate;
   double interest;
   int transactions;

 public:

   // Constructor
   Account(double rate = 0.045, double bal = 0.0)
   {  balance = bal;  intRate = rate;
      interest = 0.0; transactions = 0;
   }

   void makeDeposit(double amount)
   {  balance += amount;
      transactions++;
   }

   bool withdraw(double amount);   // Defined in account.cpp
```

```

   void calcInterest()
   {  interest = balance * intRate;
      balance += interest;
   }

   double getBalance()
   {  return balance;
   }

   double getInterest()
   {  return interest;
   }

   int getTransactions()
   {  return transactions;
   }
};
```

The `withdraw` Member Function

The only member function not defined inline in the class declaration is `withdraw`. The purpose of that function is to subtract the amount of a withdrawal from the `balance` member. If the amount to be withdrawn is greater than the current balance, however, no withdrawal is made. The function returns true if the withdrawal is made or false if there is not enough in the account.

Contents of `Account.cpp`

```
// Account.cpp is the Account class function implementation file.
#include "Account.h"

bool Account::withdraw(double amount)
{
   if (balance < amount)
      return false;   // Not enough in the account
   else
   {
      balance -= amount;
      transactions++;
      return true;
   }
}
```

The Class Interface

The `balance`, `intRate`, `interest`, and `transactions` member variables are private, so they are hidden from the world outside the class. This is because a programmer with direct access to these variables might unknowingly commit any of the following errors:

- A deposit or withdrawal might be made without the `transactions` member being incremented.
- A withdrawal might be made for more than is in the account. This will cause the `balance` member to have a negative value.

- The interest rate might be calculated and the `balance` member adjusted, but the amount of interest might not get recorded in the `intRate` member.
- The wrong interest rate might be used.

Because of the potential for these errors, the class contains public member functions that ensure the proper steps are taken when the account is manipulated.

Implementing the Class

Program 7-17 shows an implementation of the `Account` class. It presents a menu for displaying a savings account's balance, number of transactions, and interest earned. It also allows the user to deposit an amount into the account, make a withdrawal from the account, and calculate the interest earned for the current period.

Program 7-17

```
// This client program uses the Account class to perform simple
// banking operations. This file should be combined into a
// project along with the Account.h and Account.cpp files.
#include <iostream>
#include <iomanip>
#include "Account.h"
using namespace std;

// Function prototypes
void displayMenu();
char getChoice(char);
void makeDeposit(Account &);
void withdraw(Account &);

int main()
{
   const char MAX_CHOICE = '7';
   Account savings;              // Account object to model savings account
   char choice;

   cout << fixed << showpoint << setprecision(2);
   do
   {
      displayMenu();
      choice = getChoice(MAX_CHOICE);  // This returns only '1' - '7'
      switch(choice)
      {
         case '1': cout << "The current balance is $";
                   cout << savings.getBalance() << endl;
                   break;
         case '2': cout << "There have been ";
                   cout << savings.getTransactions()
                        << " transactions.\n";
                   break;
```

(program continues)

Program 7-17 *(continued)*

```
         case '3': cout << "Interest earned for this period: $";
                   cout << savings.getInterest() << endl;
                   break;
         case '4': makeDeposit(savings);
                   break;
         case '5': withdraw(savings);
                   break;
         case '6': savings.calcInterest();
                   cout << "Interest added.\n";
      }
   } while(choice != '7');
   return 0;
}

/*****************************************************************
 *                           displayMenu                         *
 * This function displays the user's menu on the screen.         *
 *****************************************************************/
void displayMenu()
{
   cout << "\n\n                MENU\n\n";
   cout << "1) Display the account balance\n";
   cout << "2) Display the number of transactions\n";
   cout << "3) Display interest earned for this period\n";
   cout << "4) Make a deposit\n";
   cout << "5) Make a withdrawal\n";
   cout << "6) Add interest for this period\n";
   cout << "7) Exit the program\n\n";
   cout << "Enter your choice: ";
}

/*****************************************************************
 *                           getChoice                           *
 * This function gets, validates, and returns the user's choice. *
 *****************************************************************/
char getChoice(char max)
{
   char choice = cin.get();
   cin.ignore();            // Bypass the '\n' in the input buffer

   while (choice < '1' || choice > max)
   {
      cout << "Choice must be between 1 and " << max << ". "
           << "Please re-enter choice: ";
      choice = cin.get();
      cin.ignore();       // Bypass the '\n' in the input buffer
   }
   return choice;
}
```

(program continues)

Program 7-17 *(continued)*

```
/*************************************************************
 *                        makeDeposit                        *
 * This function accepts a reference to an Account object.   *
 * The user is prompted for the dollar amount of the deposit, *
 * and the makeDeposit member of the Account object is       *
 * then called.                                              *
 *************************************************************/
void makeDeposit(Account &account)
{
   double dollars;

   cout << "Enter the amount of the deposit: ";
   cin  >> dollars;
   cin.ignore();
   account.makeDeposit(dollars);
}

/*************************************************************
 *                        withdraw                           *
 * This function accepts a reference to an Account object.   *
 * The user is prompted for the dollar amount of the withdrawal,*
 * and the withdraw member of the Account object is then called.*
 *************************************************************/
void withdraw(Account &account)
{
   double dollars;

   cout << "Enter the amount of the withdrawal: ";
   cin  >> dollars;
   cin.ignore();
   if (!account.withdraw(dollars))
      cout << "ERROR: Withdrawal amount too large.\n\n";
}
```

Program Output with Example Input Shown in Bold

```
                 Menu
1) Display the account balance
2) Display the number of transactions
3) Display interest earned for this period
4) Make a deposit
5) Make a withdrawal
6) Add interest for this period
7) Exit the program

Enter your choice: 4[Enter]
Enter the amount of the deposit: 500[Enter]

                 Menu
1) Display the account balance
2) Display the number of transactions
3) Display interest earned for this period
4) Make a deposit
5) Make a withdrawal
6) Add interest for this period
7) Exit the program

Enter your choice: 1[Enter]
The current balance is $500.00
```

(program output continues)

Program 7-17 *(continued)*

```
                  Menu
1) Display the account balance
2) Display the number of transactions
3) Display interest earned for this period
4) Make a deposit
5) Make a withdrawal
6) Add interest for this period
7) Exit the program

Enter your choice: 5[Enter]
Enter the amount of the withdrawal: 700[Enter]
ERROR: Withdrawal amount too large.

                  Menu
1) Display the account balance
2) Display the number of transactions
3) Display interest earned for this period
4) Make a deposit
5) Make a withdrawal
6) Add interest for this period
7) Exit the program

Enter your choice: 5[Enter]
Enter the amount of the withdrawal: 200[Enter]

                  Menu
1) Display the account balance
2) Display the number of transactions
3) Display interest earned for this period
4) Make a deposit
5) Make a withdrawal
6) Add interest for this period
7) Exit the program

Enter your choice: 6[Enter]
Interest added.

                  Menu
1) Display the account balance
2) Display the number of transactions
3) Display interest earned for this period
4) Make a deposit
5) Make a withdrawal
6) Add interest for this period
7) Exit the program

Enter your choice: 1[Enter]
The current balance is: $313.50

                  Menu
1) Display the account balance
2) Display the number of transactions
3) Display interest earned for this period
4) Make a deposit
5) Make a withdrawal
6) Add interest for this period
7) Exit the program

Enter your choice: 7[Enter]
```

7.14 Introduction to Object-Oriented Analysis and Design

CONCEPT: Object-oriented analysis determines the requirements for a system to clarify what it must be able to do, what classes are needed, and how those classes are related. Object-oriented design then designs the classes and specifies how they will carry out their responsibilities.

So far you have learned the basics of writing a class, creating an object from the class, and using the object to perform operations. This knowledge is necessary to create an object-oriented application, but it is not the first step in designing the application. First a programmer or analyst must carefully analyze the problem to be solved to determine exactly what the program must be able to do. In OOP terminology, this phase of program development is known as the *object-oriented analysis phase*. During this time it is determined what classes are needed.

The process of object-oriented analysis typically includes the following steps:

1. Identify the classes and objects to be used in the program.
2. Define the attributes for each class.
3. Define the behaviors for each class.
4. Define the relationships between classes.

Let's look at each step more closely.

1. Identify the Classes and Objects.

Remember, a class is a package that consists of data and procedures that perform operations on the data. In order to determine the classes that will appear in a program, the programmer should think of the major data elements and decide what procedures or actions are required for each class. For example, consider a restaurant that uses an object-oriented program to enter customer orders. A customer order is a list of menu items with their respective prices. The restaurant uses this list to charge the customer, so a class could be created to model it. Also, the restaurant's menu has several main entrees, appetizers, side dishes, and beverages to choose from. A class could be designed to represent menu items as well.

Classes can be easily designed to model real-world objects, such as customer orders and a restaurant's menu items. Here are some other types of items that may be candidates for classes in a program:

- User-interface components, such as windows, menus, and dialog boxes
- Input/output devices, such as the keyboard, mouse, display, and printer
- Physical objects, such as vehicles, machines, or manufactured products
- Recordkeeping items, such as customer histories, and payroll records
- A role played by a human (employee, client, teacher, student, and so forth).

2. Define Each Class's Attributes.

A class's *attributes* are the data elements used to describe an object instantiated from the class. They are the values needed for the object to function properly in the program.

Using the restaurant example, here is the beginning of a possible specification for a `menuItem` class.

```
Class name:  MenuItem
Attributes:  itemName
             price
             category    // 1 = appetizer, 2 = salad,   3 = entrée
                         // 4 = side dish, 5 = dessert, 6 = beverage
```

And here is the beginning of a possible specification for a `CustomerOrder` class.

```
Class name:  CustomerOrder
Attributes:  orderNumber
             tableNumber
             serverNumber
             date
             items       // a list of MenuItem objects
             totalPrice
             tip
```

3. Define Each Class's Behaviors.

Once the class's attributes have been defined, the programmer must identify the activities, or *behaviors*, each class must be capable of performing. For example, some of the the activities the `MenuItem` class should be able to perform include

- changing a price
- displaying a price

Some of the activities the `CustomerOrder` class should be able to perform include

- accepting the information for a new order
- adding an item to an existing order
- returning any information on a previously stored order
- calculating the total price of all items on an order
- printing a list of ordered items for the kitchen
- printing a bill for the patron.

In C++, a class's behaviors are its *member functions*.

4. Define the Relationships Between Classes.

The last step in our object-oriented analysis phase is to define the relationships that exist between and among the classes in a program. The possible relationships may be formally stated as

- Access
- Ownership (Composition)
- Inheritance.

Informally, these three relationships can be described as

- Uses-a
- Has-a
- Is-a.

The first relationship, access, allows an object to modify the attributes of another object. Normally, an object has attributes not accessible to parts of the program outside the object. These are known as private attributes. An access relationship between two objects means that one object will have access to the other object's private attributes. When this relationship exists, it can be said that one object *uses* the other.

The second relationship, ownership, means that one object has another object as one of its members. For example, in our restaurant example, the `CustomerOrder` class has a list of `MenuItem` objects as one of its attributes. In OOP terminology, this type of relationship is also called *composition*.

The third relationship is inheritance. Sometimes a class is based on another class. This means that one class is a specialized case of the other. For example, consider a program that uses classes representing cars, trucks, and jet planes. Although those three types of classes in the real world are very different, they have many common characteristics: They are all modes of transportation, and they all carry some number of passengers. So each of the three classes could be based on a Vehicle class that has attributes and behaviors common to them all. This is illustrated in Figure 7-10.

Figure 7-10

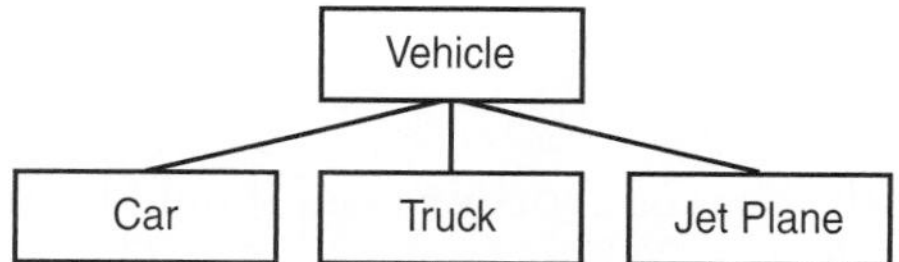

In OOP terminology, the Vehicle class is the *base class* and the Car, Truck and Jet Plane classes are *derived* classes. All of the attributes and behaviors of the Vehicle class are inherited by the Car, Truck, and Jet Plane classes. The relationship implies that a car *is a* vehicle, a truck *is a* vehicle and a jet plane *is a* vehicle.

In addition to inheriting the attributes and behaviors of the base class, derived classes add their own. For example, the Car class might have attributes and behaviors that set and indicate whether it is a sedan or a coupe and the type of engine it has. The Truck class might have attributes and behaviors that set and indicate the maximum amount of weight it can carry, and how many miles it can travel between refuelings. The Jet Plane class might have attributes and behaviors that set and indicate its altitude and heading. These added components of the derived classes make them more specialized than the base class.

These three types of relationships between classes, *access*, *ownership*, and *inheritance*, are discussed further in Chapter 11.

Once an enterprise and its operations have been analyzed, each class can be designed, and a set of programs can be developed to automate some of these operations.

Finding the Classes

Let's look further at step 1 in the analysis process: identifying the classes. Over the years, software professionals have developed numerous techniques for doing this, but they all involve identifying the different types of real-world objects present in the problem, so that classes can be created for them. One simple and popular technique involves the following steps:

1. Get a written description of the problem domain.
2. Identify all the nouns (including pronouns and noun phrases) in the description. Each of these is a potential class.
3. Refine the list to include only the classes that are relevant to the problem.

Let's take a closer look at each of these steps.

Write a Description of the Problem Domain

The *problem domain* is the set of real-world objects, parties, and major events related to the problem. If you understand the nature of the problem you are trying to solve, you can write a description of the problem domain yourself. If you do not thoroughly understand it, you should have an expert write the description for you.

For example, suppose we are programming an application that the manager of Joe's Automotive Shop will use to print service quotes for customers. Here is a description that an expert, perhaps Joe himself, might have written:

Joe's Automotive Shop services foreign cars and specializes in servicing cars made by Mercedes, Porsche, and BMW. When a customer brings a car to the shop, the manager gets the customer's name, address, and telephone number. The manager then determines the make, model, and year of the car, and gives the customer a service quote. The service quote shows the estimated parts charges, estimated labor charges, sales tax, and total estimated charges.

The problem domain description should include any of the following:

- Physical objects such as vehicles, machines, or products
- Any role played by a person, such as manager, employee, customer, teacher, or student
- The results of a business event, such as a customer order, or in this case a service quote
- Record-keeping items, such as customer histories and payroll records

Identify All of the Nouns

The next step is to identify all of the nouns and noun phrases. (If the description contains pronouns, include them too.) Here's another look at the previous problem domain description. This time the nouns and noun phrases appear in bold.

> **Joe's Automotive Shop** services **foreign cars,** and specializes in servicing **cars** made by **Mercedes, Porsche,** and **BMW.** When a **customer** brings a **car** to the **shop,** the **manager** gets the **customer's name, address,** and **telephone number.** The **manager** then determines the **make, model,** and **year** of the **car,** and gives the **customer** a **service quote.** The **service quote** shows the **estimated parts charges, estimated labor charges, sales tax,** and **total estimated charges.**

Notice that some of the nouns are repeated. The following lists all of the nouns without duplicating any of them.

address	foreign cars	Porsche
BMW	Joe's Automotive Shop	sales tax
car	make	service quote
cars	manager	shop
customer	Mercedes	telephone number
estimated labor charges	model	total estimated charges
estimated parts charges	name	year

Refine the List of Nouns

The nouns that appear in the problem description are merely candidates to become classes. It might not be necessary to make classes for them all. The next step is to refine the list to include only the classes that are necessary to solve the particular problem at hand. Here are the common reasons that a noun can be eliminated from the list of potential classes.

Some of the nouns really mean the same thing.

In this example, the following sets of nouns refer to the same thing:

- **cars** and **foreign cars** both refer to the general concept of a car.
- **Joe's Automotive Shop** and **shop** both refer to the same shop.

We can settle on a single class for each of these. In this example we will arbitrarily eliminate **foreign cars** from the list, and use the word **cars**. Likewise we will eliminate **Joe's Automotive Shop** from the list and use the word **shop**. The updated list of potential classes is:

address	~~foreign cars~~	Porsche
BMW	~~Joe's Automotive Shop~~	sales tax
car	make	service quote
cars	manager	shop
customer	Mercedes	telephone number
estimated labor charges	model	total estimated charges
estimated parts charges	name	year

Some nouns might represent items that we do not need to be concerned with in order to solve the problem.

A quick review of the problem description reminds us of what the application should do: print a service quote. To do this, two of the potential classes we have listed are not needed.

- We can cross **shop** off the list because our application only needs to be concerned with individual service quotes. It doesn't need to work with or determine any company-wide information. If the problem description asked us to keep a total of all the service quotes, then it would make sense to have a class for the shop.
- We will also not need a class for the **manager** because the problem statement does not ask us to process any information about the manager. If there were multiple shop managers, and the problem description asked us to record which manager wrote each service quote, it would make sense to have a class for the manager.

The updated list of potential classes at this point is:

address	~~foreign cars~~	Porsche
BMW	~~Joe's Automotive Shop~~	sales tax
car	make	service quote
cars	~~manager~~	~~shop~~
customer	Mercedes	telephone number
estimated labor charges	model	total estimated charges
estimated parts charges	name	year

Some of the nouns might represent objects, not classes.

We can eliminate **Mercedes, Porsche,** and **BMW** as classes because, in this example, they all represent specific cars, and can be considered instances of a single **cars** class. Also, we can eliminate the word **car** from the list. In the description it refers to a specific car brought to the shop by a customer. Therefore, it would also represent an instance of a **cars** class. At this point the updated list of potential classes is:

address	~~foreign cars~~	~~Porsche~~
~~BMW~~	~~Joe's Automotive Shop~~	sales tax
~~car~~	make	service quote
cars	~~manager~~	~~shop~~
customer	~~Mercedes~~	telephone number
estimated labor charges	model	total estimated charges
estimated parts charges	name	year

Some of the nouns might represent simple values that can be stored in a variable and do not require a class.

Remember, a class contains attributes and member functions. Attributes are related items stored within a class object that define its state. Member functions are actions or behaviors the class object can perform. If a noun represents a type of item that would not have any identifiable attributes or member functions, then it can probably be eliminated from the list. To help determine whether a noun represents an item that would have attributes and member functions, ask the following questions about it:

- Would you use a group of related values to represent the item's state?
- Are there any obvious actions to be performed by the item?

If the answers to both of these questions are no, then the noun probably represents a value that can be stored in a simple variable. If we apply this test to each of the nouns that remain in our list, we can conclude that the following are probably not classes: **address, estimated labor charges, estimated parts charges, make, model, name, sales tax, telephone number, total estimated charges** and **year**. These are all simple string or numeric values that can be stored in variables.

Here is the updated list of potential classes:

~~address~~	~~foreign cars~~	~~Porsche~~
~~BMW~~	~~Joe's Automotive Shop~~	~~sales tax~~
~~car~~	~~make~~	service quote
cars	~~manager~~	~~shop~~
customer	~~Mercedes~~	~~telephone number~~
~~estimated labor charges~~	~~model~~	~~total estimated charges~~
~~estimated parts charges~~	~~name~~	~~year~~

As you can see from the list, we have eliminated everything except **cars, customer**, and **service quote.** This means that in our application, we will need classes to represent cars, customers, and service quotes. Ultimately, we will write a `Car` class, a `Customer` class, and a `ServiceQuote` class.

Identifying Class Responsibilities

Once the classes have been identified, the next task is to identify each class's responsibilities. Class *responsibilities* are

- the things that the class is responsible for knowing
- the actions that the class is responsible for doing

When you have identified the things that a class is responsible for knowing, then you have identified the class's attributes. Likewise, when you have identified the actions that a class is responsible for doing, you have identified its member functions.

It is often helpful to ask the questions "In the context of this problem, what must the class know? What must the class do?" The first place to look for the answers is in the description of the problem domain. Many of the things that a class must know and do will be mentioned. Some class responsibilities, however, might not be directly mentioned in the problem domain, so additional analysis is often required. Let's apply this methodology to the classes we previously identified from our problem domain.

The `Customer` Class

In the context of our problem domain, what must any object of the `Customer` class know? The description mentions the following items, which are all attributes of a customer:

- the customer's name
- the customer's address
- the customer's telephone number.

These are all values that can be represented as strings and stored in the class's member variables. The `Customer` class can potentially know many other things also. One mistake that can be made at this point is to identify too many things that an object is responsible for knowing. In some applications, for example, a `Customer` class might know the customer's email address. However, this particular problem domain does not mention that the customer's email address is used for any purpose, so it is not the responsibility of this class to know it, and we should not include it as an attribute.

Now let's identify the class's member functions. In the context of our problem domain, what must the `Customer` class do? The only obvious actions are:

- create an object of the `Customer` class
- set and get the customer's name
- set and get the customer's address
- set and get the customer's telephone number.

From this list we can see that the `Customer` class will need a constructor, as well as accessor and mutator functions for each of its attributes.

Figure 7-11 shows a UML class diagram for the `Customer` class. Notice that the diagram looks like a simple rectangle with three parts. The top section holds the name of the class. The middle section lists the class attributes, that is, its member variables. The bottom section lists its member functions. The minus sign to the left of each attribute indicates that it is private. The plus sign to the left of each function indicates that it is public. Each attribute name is followed by a colon and its data type. Each function name is followed by a set of parentheses. If the function accepts any arguments, its parameters will be listed inside these parentheses, along with the data type of each one. After the parentheses is a colon, followed by the function's return type. More information on class UML diagrams can be found in Appendix F.

Figure 7-11

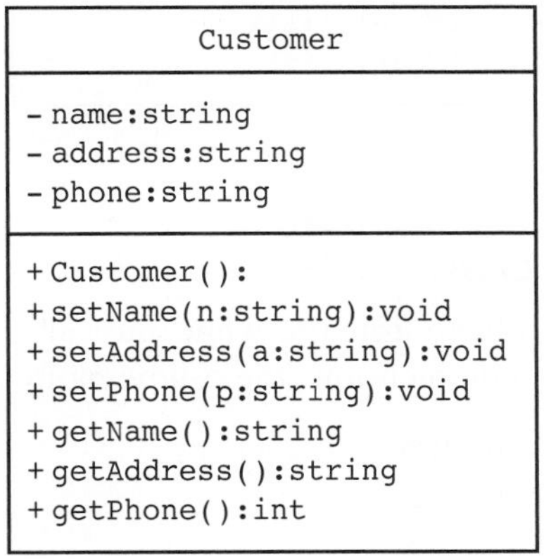

```
Customer
--------------------------------
- name:string
- address:string
- phone:string
--------------------------------
+ Customer():
+ setName(n:string):void
+ setAddress(a:string):void
+ setPhone(p:string):void
+ getName():string
+ getAddress():string
+ getPhone():int
```

The `Car` Class

In the context of our problem domain, what must an object of the `Car` class know? The following items are all attributes of a car, and are mentioned in the problem domain:

- the car's make
- the car's model
- the car's year

Now let's identify the class member functions. In the context of our problem domain, what must the `Car` class do? Once again, the only obvious actions are the standard member functions we find in most classes: constructors, accessors, and mutators. Specifically, the actions are:

- create an object of the `Car` class
- set and get the car's make
- set and get the car's model
- set and get the car's year

Figure 7-12 shows a UML class diagram for the `Car` class at this point.

Figure 7-12

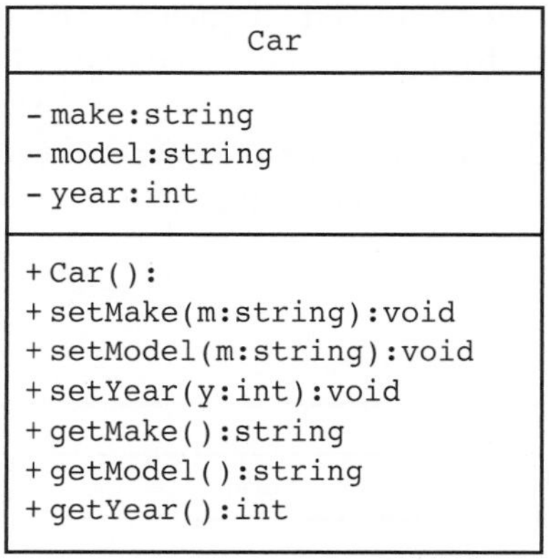

```
Car
-----------------------------
- make:string
- model:string
- year:int
-----------------------------
+ Car():
+ setMake(m:string):void
+ setModel(m:string):void
+ setYear(y:int):void
+ getMake():string
+ getModel():string
+ getYear():int
```

The `ServiceQuote` Class

In the context of our problem domain, what must an object of the `ServiceQuote` class know? The problem domain mentions the following items:

- the estimated parts charges
- the estimated labor charges
- the sales tax
- the total estimated charges.

Careful thought will reveal that two of these items are the results of calculations: sales tax and total estimated charges. These items are dependent on the values of the estimated parts and labor charges. In order to avoid the risk of holding stale data, we will not store these values in member variables. Rather, we will provide member functions that calculate these values and return them. The other member functions that we will need for this class are a constructor and the accessors and mutators for the estimated parts charges and estimated labor charges attributes.

Figure 7-13 shows a UML class diagram for the `ServiceQuote` class.

Figure 7-13

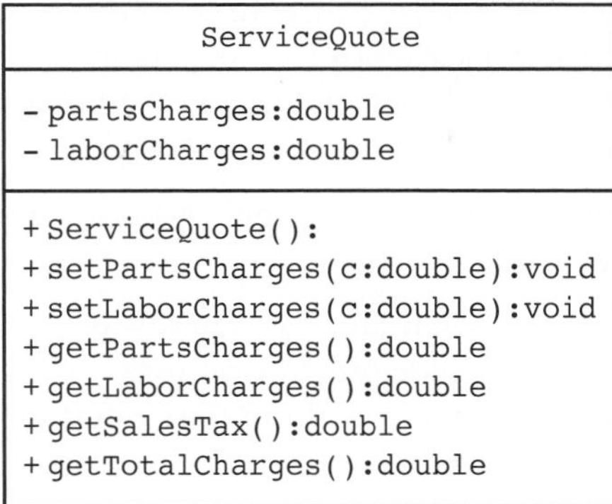

ServiceQuote
- partsCharges:double
- laborCharges:double
+ ServiceQuote():
+ setPartsCharges(c:double):void
+ setLaborCharges(c:double):void
+ getPartsCharges():double
+ getLaborCharges():double
+ getSalesTax():double
+ getTotalCharges():double

This Is Only the Beginning

You should look at the process that we have discussed in this section as merely a starting point. It's important to realize that designing an object-oriented application is an iterative process. It may take you several attempts to identify all of the classes that you will need, and to determine all of their responsibilities. As the design process unfolds, you will gain a deeper understanding of the problem, and consequently you will see ways to improve the design.

Object Reusability

We have mentioned several advantages offered by object-oriented programming. Still another is *object reusability.* A class is not a stand-alone program. It is a mechanism for creating objects used by programs that need its service. Ideally, a class created for use in one program can be made general enough to be used by other programs as well. For example, the `Customer` class can be designed to create objects used by many different applications that have customers. The `Car` class can be designed to create objects used by many different programs that involve vehicles.

Object-Oriented vs. Object-Based Programming

Although classes and objects form the basis of object-oriented programming, by themselves they are not sufficient to constitute true object-oriented programming. Using them might more correctly be referred to as object-based programming. When we add the ability to define relationships among different classes of objects, to create classes of objects from other classes (inheritance) and to determine the behavior of a member function depending on which object calls it (polymorphism), it becomes true object-oriented programming. You will learn about these more advanced object-oriented programming features later in the book.

Checkpoint

7.35 What is a problem domain?

7.36 When designing an object-oriented application, who should write a description of the problem domain?

7.37 How do you identify the potential classes in a problem domain description?

7.38 What two questions should you ask to determine a class's responsibilities?

7.39 Look at the following description of a problem domain:

A doctor sees patients in her practice. When a patient comes to the practice, the doctor performs one or more procedures on the patient. Each procedure performed has a description and a standard fee. As patients leave, they receive a statement that shows their name and address, as well as the procedures that were performed, and the total charge for the procedures.

Assume that you are creating an application to generate a statement that can be printed and given to the patient.

A) Identify all of the potential classes in this problem domain.
B) Refine the list to include only the necessary class or classes for this problem.
C) Identify the responsibilities of the class or classes that you identified in step B.

7.15 Screen Control

CONCEPT: Operating system functions allow you to control how output appears on the console screen.

Positioning the Cursor on the Screen

In Chapter 5's Tying It All Together section you learned that C++ compilers provide special libraries for calling on operating system functions. So far, in Chapters 5 and 6, we have used the Windows `SetConsoleTextAttribute` function to display screen output in color. Now we will look at a Windows operating system function for positioning the cursor on the screen. This function is `SetConsoleCursorPosition`.

> **NOTE:** Recall from Chapter 5 that operating system functions are tailored to specific operating systems. So programs that use them will only run on the system for which they were written. The functions described here work with Windows 2000 and newer operating systems. If you are using Linux or Mac OS, your instructor may be able to provide you with similar functions that work on those systems.

Until now, all the programs you have created display output beginning on the top line of the screen. They then move down the screen, one line at a time, when the user presses the [Enter] key or when the program outputs an `endl` or `"\n"`. But what if you are writing on the fifth row of the screen and want to go back to the second row? Or what if you want to display something in the very middle of the screen? You can do these things on a Windows system by using the `SetConsoleCursorPosition` function to move the cursor to the desired location before writing the output.

To use this function, you will need to do the same two things you did in Chapters 5 and 6 to use color. You must

- `#include <windows.h>` in your program.
- Create a *handle* to the standard output screen by including the following definition in your program.

```
HANDLE screen = GetStdHandle(STD_OUTPUT_HANDLE);
```

A typical text screen has 25 rows, or lines, with 80 print positions per row. Each of these positions is called a cell. A *cell* is a little block that can display a single character and it is identified by its row number and its position on that row. The rows range from 0 to 24, with 0 being the top row of the screen. The print positions on each row, usually referred to as columns, range from 0 to 79, with 0 being at the far left-hand side. The row and column of a cell, which identifies its location on the screen, are called its *coordinates*.

To place the cursor in a specific screen cell, you must specify its cell coordinates by setting two variables in a `COORD` structure that is already defined in Windows. This structure has two member variables named `X` and `Y`, with `X` holding the column and `Y` holding the row. Here is what the structure looks like.

```
struct COORD
{
   short int X;   // Column position
   short int Y;   // Row position
};
```

Here is how you use it. The following code segment writes the word `Hello` centered on the standard output screen.

```
HANDLE screen = GetStdHandle(STD_OUTPUT_HANDLE);
COORD position;     // position is a COORD structure

position.X = 38;    // Set column near screen center
position.Y = 11;    // Set row near screen center
                    // Place cursor there, then print
SetConsoleCursorPosition(screen, position);
cout << "Hello" << endl;
```

NOTE: When you set a screen position, you must follow all output that your program writes there with an `endl`. This is necessary to ensure that the output is actually displayed at this location. If you do not use an `endl`, the output may be buffered and written to the screen much later, after the cursor position has changed. Following your output with the new line character `'\n'` does not work because it does not flush the screen buffer like `endl` does.

Program 7.18 positions the cursor to display a set of nested boxes near the center of the screen. Notice that it uses the `Sleep` function, previously seen in Chapter 5 and Chapter 6's Tying It All Together programs. This function pauses the program execution for part of a second so things do not happen too fast for the user to see them. The argument passed to the function tells it how many milliseconds it should pause. A *millisecond* is a thousandth of a second. So, for example, to pause execution of a program for a half second the following function call would work.

```
Sleep(500);
```

Program 7.18 uses the command `Sleep(750)` to pause the program execution for $\frac{3}{4}$ of a second after each box displays.

Program 7-18

```
// This program demonstrates the use of Windows functions
// for positioning the cursor. It displays a series of nested
// boxes near the center of the screen.
#include <iostream>
#include <windows.h>    // Needed to set cursor positions & call Sleep
using namespace std;

void placeCursor(HANDLE, int, int);   // Function prototypes
void printStars(int);

int main()
{
   const int midRow = 12,
             midCol = 40,
             numBoxes = 3;
   int width, startRow, endRow;

   // Get the handle to standard output device (the console)
    HANDLE screen = GetStdHandle(STD_OUTPUT_HANDLE);

   // Each loop prints one box
   for (int box = 1, height = 1; box <= numBoxes; box++, height+=2)
   {  startRow = midRow - box;
      endRow = midRow + box;
      width = box*5 + (box+1)%2;  // Adds 1 if box*5 is an even number

      // Draw box top
      placeCursor(screen, startRow, midCol-width/2);
      printStars(width);

      // Print box sides
      for (int sideRow = 1; sideRow <= height; sideRow++)
      {  placeCursor(screen, startRow + sideRow, midCol-width/2);
         cout << '*' << endl;
         placeCursor(screen, startRow + sideRow, midCol+width/2);
         cout << '*' << endl;
      }
      // Draw box bottom
      placeCursor(screen, endRow, midCol-width/2);
      printStars(width);

      Sleep(750);   // Pause 3/4 second between boxes displayed
   }

   placeCursor(screen, 20, 0);   // Move cursor out of the way
   return 0;
}

/*****************************************************
 *                    placeCursor                     *
 *****************************************************/
```

(program continues)

Program 7-18 *(continued)*

```
void placeCursor(HANDLE screen, int row, int col)
{                         // COORD is a defined C++ structure that
   COORD position;        // holds a pair of X and Y coordinates
   position.Y = row;
   position.X = col;
   SetConsoleCursorPosition(screen, position);
}

/*******************************************************
 *                     printStars                      *
 *******************************************************/
void printStars(int numStars)
{
   for (int star = 1; star <= numStars; star++)
      cout << '*';
   cout << endl;
}
```

Program Output

```
***************
* *********** *
* *  *****  * *
* *  *   *  * *
* *  *****  * *
* *********** *
***************
```

Creating a Screen Input Form

Program 7-18 is fun to run, but Program 7-19 demonstrates a more practical application of positioning the cursor on the screen. Instead of prompting the user to input a series of entries one prompt at a time, we can design a *screen input form*. This more professional looking way of getting input from the user involves creating and displaying a screen that shows all the prompts at once. The cursor is then placed beside a particular prompt the user is expected to respond to. When the user enters the data for this prompt and presses [Enter], the cursor moves to the next prompt.

Program 7-19

```
// This program creates a screen form for user input.
// from the user.
#include <iostream>
#include <windows.h>      // Needed to set cursor positions
#include <string>
using namespace std;

struct UserInfo
{  string name;
   int age;
   char gender;
};
```

(program continues)

Program 7-19 *(continued)*

```

void placeCursor(HANDLE, int, int);    // Function prototypes
void displayPrompts(HANDLE);
void getUserInput(HANDLE, userInfo&);
void displayData (HANDLE, userInfo);

int main()
{
   userInfo input;            // input is a UserInfo structure
                              // that has 3 member variables

   // Get the handle to standard output device (the console)
   HANDLE screen = GetStdHandle(STD_OUTPUT_HANDLE);

   displayPrompts(screen);
   getUserInput(screen, input);
   displayData (screen, input);

   return 0;
}

/*******************************************************
 *                    placeCursor                      *
 *******************************************************/
void placeCursor(HANDLE screen, int row, int col)
{                       // COORD is a defined C++ structure that
   COORD position;      // holds a pair of X and Y coordinates
   position.Y = row;
   position.X = col;
   SetConsoleCursorPosition(screen, position);
}

/*******************************************************
 *                   displayPrompts                    *
 *******************************************************/
void displayPrompts(HANDLE screen)
{
   placeCursor(screen, 3, 25);
   cout << "******* Data Entry Form *******" << endl;
   placeCursor(screen, 5, 25);
   cout << "Name: " << endl;
   placeCursor(screen, 7, 25);
   cout << "Age:            Gender (M/F): " << endl;
}

/*******************************************************
 *                    getUserInput                     *
 *******************************************************/
void getUserInput(HANDLE screen, userInfo &input)
{
   placeCursor(screen, 5, 31);
   getline(cin, input.name);
```

(program continues)

Program 7-19 *(continued)*

```
   placeCursor(screen, 7, 30);
   cin >> input.age;
   placeCursor(screen, 7, 55);
   cin >> input.gender;
}

/*****************************************************
 *                    displayData                    *
 *****************************************************/
void displayData(HANDLE screen, userInfo input)
{
   placeCursor(screen, 10, 0);
   cout << "Here is the data you entered.\n";
   cout << "Name  : " << input.name   << endl;
   cout << "Age   : " << input.age    << endl;
   cout << "Gender: " << input.gender << endl;
}
```

Initial Screen Display

```
                ******* Data Entry Form *******

                Name:

                Age:            Gender (M/F):
```

Program Output with Example Input Shown in Bold

```
                 ******* Data Entry Form *******

                 Name: Mary Beth Jones[Enter]

                 Age: 19[Enter]  Gender (M/F): F[Enter]

Here is the data you entered.
Name  : Mary Beth Jones
Age   : 19
Gender: F
```

7.16 Tying It All Together: *Yoyo Animation*

With what you have learned in this chapter you can now create simple *text-based graphics*. To do that, simply arrange characters in different patterns to form images on the screen. Then *animate* those images, giving the illusion of motion, by erasing them from their old position and redisplaying them somewhere else on the screen. To erase a character from the screen simply write a blank " " on top of it.

Program 7-20 uses Windows operating system functions to simulate a yoyo unwinding and then winding back up. The `Sleep` function is used to pause execution between moves, so that the user can watch the motion taking place.

Program 7-20

```
// This program creates a simple animation using Windows
// functions to simulate a yoyo moving down and up.
#include <iostream>
#include <windows.h>    // Needed to set cursor positions
using namespace std;

int main()
{
   HANDLE screen = GetStdHandle(STD_OUTPUT_HANDLE);
   COORD pos = {40, 3};     // Start position
   SetConsoleCursorPosition(screen, pos);
   cout << "O" << endl;
   Sleep(500);

   // Watch the yoyo go down & back up 3 times
   for (int tossIt = 1; tossIt <= 3; tossIt++)
   {
      // Yoyo unwinds
      while (pos.Y <= 20)  // pos.Y is the row
      {
         // Move the yoyo down 1 position and then pause
         SetConsoleCursorPosition(screen, pos);
         cout << "|" << endl;
         pos.Y++;
         SetConsoleCursorPosition(screen, pos);
         cout << "O" << endl;
         Sleep(100);
      }

      // Yoyo winds back up
      while (pos.Y > 3)
      {
         // Erase character at current position
         // Move yoyo up one position, then pause
         SetConsoleCursorPosition(screen, pos);
         cout << " " << endl;
         pos.Y --;
         SetConsoleCursorPosition(screen, pos);
         cout << "O" << endl;
         Sleep(100);
      }
   }
   return 0;
}
```

You will need to run the program to see the animation as the yoyo unwinds and then winds back up on its string.

```
:
:
:
:
0
```

Review Questions and Exercises

Fill-in-the-Blank and Short Answer

1. What does ADT stand for?
2. Which of the following must a programmer know about an ADT to use it?
   A) What values it can hold
   B) What operations it can perform
   C) How the operations are implemented
3. The two common programming methods in practice today are _________ and _________.
4. ____________ programming is centered around functions, or procedures, whereas ____________ programming is centered around objects.
5. An object is a software entity that combines both __________ and ____________in a single unit.
6. An object is a(n) ______________ of a class.
7. Creating a class object is often called _____________ the class.
8. Once a class is declared, how many objects can be created from it?
   A) 1
   B) 2
   C) Many
9. An object's data items are stored in its ___________________________________.
10. The procedures, or functions, an object performs are called its ________________.
11. Bundling together an object's data and procedures is called ___________________.
12. An object's members can be declared `public` or `private`.
    A public member can be accessed by ___________________________________.
    A private member can be accessed by ___________________________________.
13. Normally a class's ______________________________ are declared to be private and its ____ are declared to be public.
14. A class member function that uses, but does not change, the value of a member variable is called a(n) ___________.
15. A class member function that changes the value of a member variable is called a(n) ____________.
16. When a member function's body is written inside a class declaration, the function is a(n) _________ function.
17. A class constructor is a member function with the same name as the _________.
18. A constructor is automatically called when an object is _________.
19. Constructors cannot have a(n) _________ type.
20. A(n) _________ constructor is one that requires no arguments.

21. A destructor is a member function that is automatically called when an object is _________.
22. A destructor has the same name as the class, but is preceded by a(n) _________ character.
23. A constructor whose parameters all have default values is a(n) _________ constructor.
24. A class may have more than one constructor, as long as each has a different _________.
25. A class may only have one default _________ and one _________.
26. In general it is considered good practice to have member functions avoid doing _________.
27. When a member function forms part of the interface through which a client program can use the class, the function must be _____________.
28. When a member function performs a task internal to the class and should not be called by a client program, the function should be made ___________.
29. True or false: A class object can be passed to a function, but cannot be returned by a function.
30. True or false: C++ class objects are always passed to functions by reference.
31. It is considered good programming practice to store the declaration for a class, its function definitions, and the client program that uses the class in _________________ files.
32. If you were writing a class declaration for a class named `Canine` and wanted to place it in its own file, what should you name the file? ___________________
33. If you were writing the definitions for the `Canine` class member functions and wanted to place these in their own file, what should you name the file? ___________________
34. A structure is like a class, but normally only contains member variables and no _______________________.
35. By default, are the members of a structure public or private? ___________________
36. Before a structure variable can be created, the structure must be _________________.
37. When a structure variable is created its members can be initialized with either a(n) _______________________ or a(n) _________________________.
38. The __________ operator is used to access structure members.
39. An `Inventory` structure is declared as follows:

```
struct Inventory
{
   int itemCode;
   int qtyOnHand;
};
```

Write a definition statement that creates an `Inventory` variable named `trivet` and initializes it with an initialization list so that its code is 555 and its quantity is 110.

40. A `Car` structure is declared as follows:

```
struct Car
{
   string make,
          model;
   int    year;
   double cost;

   Car(string mk, string md, int y, double c)
   {  make = mk; model = md; year = y; cost = c; }
};
```

Write a definition statement that defines a `Car` structure variable initialized with the following information:

Make: Ford Model: Mustang
Year: 2010 Cost: $22,495

41. Declare a structure named `TempScale`, with the following members:

```
fahrenheit: a double
celsius: a double
```

Next, declare a structure named `Reading`, with the following members:

```
windSpeed: an int
humidity: a double
temperature: a TempScale structure variable
```

Next, define a `Reading` structure variable named `today`.

Now write statements that will store the following data in the `Reading` variable.

Wind speed: 37 mph
Humidity: 32%
Fahrenheit temperature: 32 degrees
Celsius temperature: 0 degrees

42. Write a function called `showReading`. It should have a parameter that accepts a `Reading` structure variable (see question 41) and should display the values of the structure's member variables on the screen.

43. Write a function called `inputReading` that has a parameter to accept a `Reading` structure reference variable (see question 41). The function should ask the user to enter values for each member of the structure.

44. Write a function called `getReading`, which returns a `Reading` structure (see question 41). The function should ask the user to enter values for each member of a `Reading` structure, and then return the structure.

45. Write the declaration of a union called `Items` with the following members. Then define an `Items` union variable named `anItem`.

```
alpha: a character        // 1 byte
num: an integer           // 4 bytes
bigNum: a long integer    // 4 bytes
real: a double            // 8 bytes
```

46. How many bytes of memory will be allocated for `anItem`?

Algorithm Workbench

47. Assume a class named `Inventory` keeps track of products in stock for a company. It has member variables `prodID`, `prodDescription`, and `qtyInStock`. Write a constructor that initializes a new `Inventory` object with the values passed as arguments, but which also includes a reasonable default value for each parameter.

48. Write a `remove` member function that accepts an argument for a number of units and removes that number of units of an item from inventory. If the operation is completed successfully it should return the number of units remaining in stock for that item. However, if the number of units passed to the function is less than the number of units in stock, it should not make the removal and should return –1 as an error signal.

Find the Errors

Each of the following declarations, programs, and program segments has errors. Locate as many as you can.

49. A)
```
struct
{  int x;
   double y;
};
```
B)
```
struct Values
{  string name;
   int age;
}
```

50. A)
```
struct TwoVals
{
   int a, b;
};
int main()
{
   TwoVals.a = 10;
   TwoVals.b = 20;
   return 0;
}
```
B)
```
#include <iostream>
using namespace std;

struct ThreeVals
{
   int a, b, c;
   void ThreeVals()
   {a = 1; b = 2; c = 3;}
};
int main()
{
   ThreeVals vals;
   cout << vals << endl;
   return 0;
}
```

51. A)
```
struct Names
{  string first;
   string last;
};
int main()
{
   Names customer ("Smith", "Orley");
   cout << Names.first << endl;
   cout << Names.last << endl;
   return 0;
}
```

B)
```
struct TwoVals
{
   int a = 5;
   int b = 10;
};

int main()
{
   TwoVals v;
   cout << v.a << " " << v.b;
   return 0;
}
```

52. A)
```
class Circle:
{
 private
   double centerX;
   double centerY;
   double radius;
 public
   setCenter(double, double);
   setRadius(double);
}
```

B)
```
#include <iostream>
using namespace std;
Class Moon;
{
 Private;
   double earthWeight;
   double moonWeight;
 Public;
   moonWeight(double ew);// Constructor
   { earthWeight = ew; moonWeight = earthWeight / 6; }
   double getMoonWeight();
   { return moonWeight; }
}
```

```
int main()
{
   double earth;

   cout >> "What is your weight? ";
   cin  << earth;
   Moon lunar(earth);
   cout << "On the moon you would weigh "
        <<lunar.getMoonWeight() << endl;
   return 0;
}
```

53. A)

```
#include <iostream>
using namespace std;

class DumbBell;
{
   int weight;
 public:
   void setWeight(int);
};
void setWeight(int w)
{  weight = w; }

int main()
{
   DumBell bar;

   DumbBell.setWeight(200);
   cout << "The weight is " << bar.weight << endl;
   return 0;
}
```

B)

```
class Change
{
 private:
   int pennies;
   int nickels;
   int dimes;
   int quarters;
   Change()
      { pennies = nickels = dimes = quarters = 0; }
   Change(int p = 100, int n = 50, d = 50, q = 25);
};
void Change::Change(int p, int n, d, q)
{
   pennies = p;
   nickels = n;
   dimes = d;
   quarters = q;
}
```

54. If the items on the following list appeared in a problem domain description, which would be potential classes?

Animal	Medication	Nurse
Inoculate	Operate	Advertise
Doctor	Invoice	Measure
Patient	Client	Customer

55. Look at the following description of a problem domain:

    The bank offers the following types of accounts to its customers: savings accounts, checking accounts, and money market accounts. Customers are allowed to deposit money into an account (thereby increasing its balance), withdraw money from an account (thereby decreasing its balance), and earn interest on the account. Each account has an interest rate.

    Assume that you are writing an application that will calculate the amount of interest earned for a bank account.

    A) Identify the potential classes in this problem domain.
    B) Refine the list to include only the necessary class or classes for this problem.
    C) Identify the responsibilities of the class or classes.

Soft Skills

Working in a team can often help individuals better understand new ideas related to programming. Others can explain things that you do not understand. Also, you will find that by explaining something to someone else, you actually understand it better.

56. Write down one question you have about the object-oriented programming material from Chapter 7. For example, you could mention something you want explained about how classes are designed and created, about how objects are related to classes, or about how overloaded constructors work. Then form a group with three to four other students. Each person in the group should participate in answering the questions posed by the other members of the group.

Programming Challenges

1. Date

Design a class called `Date` that has integer data members to store month, day, and year. The class should have a three-parameter default constructor that allows the date to be set at the time a new `Date` object is created. If the user creates a `Date` object without passing any arguments, or if any of the values passed are invalid, the default values of 1, 1, 2001 (i.e., January 1, 2001) should be used. The class should have member functions to print the date in the following formats:

```
3/15/13
March 15, 2013
15 March 2013
```

Demonstrate the class by writing a program that uses it. Be sure your program only accepts reasonable values for month and day. The month should be between 1 and 12. The day should be between 1 and the number of days in the selected month.

2. Report Heading

Design a class called `Heading` that has data members to hold the company name and the report name. A two-parameter default constructor should allow these to be specified at the time a new `Heading` object is created. If the user creates a `Heading` object without passing any arguments, "`ABC Industries`" should be used as a default value for the company name and "`Report`" should be used as a default for the report name. The class should have member functions to print a heading in either one-line format, as shown here:

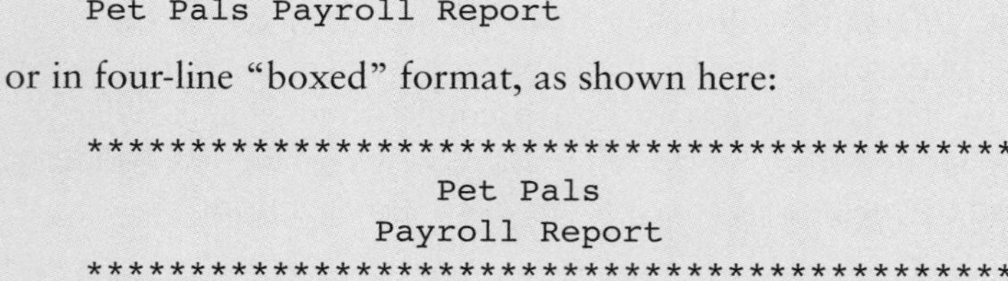

```
Pet Pals Payroll Report
```

or in four-line "boxed" format, as shown here:

```
********************************************
                 Pet Pals
              Payroll Report
********************************************
```

Try to figure out a way to center the headings on the screen, based on their lengths. Demonstrate the class by writing a simple program that uses it.

3. Widget Factory

Design a class for a widget manufacturing plant. Assuming that 10 widgets may be produced each hour, the class object will calculate how many days it will take to produce any number of widgets. (The plant operates two 8-hour shifts per day.) Write a program that asks the user for the number of widgets that have been ordered and then displays the number of days it will take to produce them. Think about what values your program should accept for the number of widgets ordered.

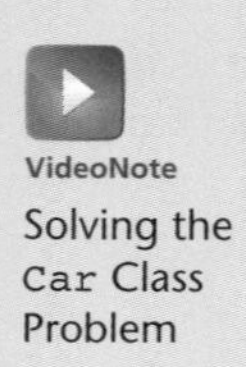

VideoNote
Solving the `Car` Class Problem

4. `Car` Class

Write a class named `Car` that has the following member variables:

- **`year`.** An `int` that holds the car's model year.
- **`make`.** A `string` object that holds the make of the car.
- **`speed`.** An `int` that holds the car's current speed.

In addition, the class should have the following member functions.

- **`Constructor`.** The constructor should accept the car's `year` and `make` as arguments and assign these values to the object's `year` and `make` member variables. The constructor should initialize the `speed` member variable to 0.
- **`Accessors`.** Appropriate accessor functions should be created to allow values to be retrieved from an object's `year`, `make`, and `speed` member variables.
- **`accelerate`.** The `accelerate` function should add 5 to the `speed` member variable each time it is called.
- **`brake`.** The `brake` function should subtract 5 from the `speed` member variable each time it is called.

Demonstrate the class in a program that creates a `Car` object, and then calls the `accelerate` function five times. After each call to the `accelerate` function, get the current speed of the car and display it. Then, call the `brake` function five times. After each call to the `brake` function, get the current speed of the car and display it.

5. Population

In a population, the birth rate and death rate are calculated as follows:

Birth Rate = Number of Births ÷ Population
Death Rate = Number of Deaths ÷ Population

For example, in a population of 100,000 that has 8,000 births and 6,000 deaths per year,

Birth Rate = 8,000 ÷ 100,000 = 0.08
Death Rate = 6,000 ÷ 100,000 = 0.06

Design a `Population` class that stores a current population, annual number of births, and annual number of deaths for some geographic area. The class should allow these three values to be set in either of two ways: by passing arguments to a three-parameter constructor when a new `Population` object is created or by calling the `setPopulation`, `setBirths`, and `setDeaths` class member functions. In either case, if a population figure less than 2 is passed to the class, use a default value of 2. If a birth or death figure less than 0 is passed in, use a default value of 0. The class should also have `getBirthRate` and `getDeathRate` functions that compute and return the birth and death rates. Write a short program that uses the `Population` class and illustrates its capabilities.

6. Gratuity Calculator

Design a `Tips` class that calculates the gratuity on a restaurant meal. Its only class member variable, `taxRate`, should be set by a one-parameter constructor to whatever rate is passed to it when a `Tips` object is created. If no argument is passed, a default tax rate of .065 should be used. The class should have just one public function, `computeTip`. This function needs to accept two arguments, the total bill amount and the tip rate. It should use this information to compute what the cost of the meal was before the tax was added. It should then apply the tip rate to just the meal cost portion of the bill to compute and return the tip amount. Demonstrate the class by creating a program that creates a single `Tips` object, then loops multiple times to allow the program user to retrieve the correct tip amount using various bill totals and desired tip rates.

7. Inventory Class

Design an `Inventory` class that can hold information for an item in a retail store's inventory. The class should have the following private member variables.

Variable Name	Description
`itemNumber`	An `int` that holds the item's number.
`quantity`	An `int` that holds the quantity of the item on hand.
`cost`	A `double` that holds the wholesale per-unit cost of the item

The class should have the following public member functions.

Member Function	Description
default constructor	Sets all the member variables to 0.
constructor #2	Accepts an item's number, quantity, and cost as arguments. Calls other class functions to copy these values into the appropriate member variables. Then calls the `setTotalCost` function.

Member Function	Description
`setItemNumber`	Accepts an `int` argument and copies it into the `itemNumber` member variable.
`setQuantity`	Accepts an `int` argument and copies it into the `quantity` member variable.
`setCost`	Accepts a `double` argument and copies it into the `cost` member variable.
`getItemNumber`	Returns the value in `itemNumber`.
`getQuantity`	Returns the value in `quantity`.
`getCost`	Returns the value in `cost`.
`getTotalCost`	Computes and returns the `totalCost`.

Demonstrate the class by writing a simple program that uses it. This program should validate the user inputs to ensure that negative values are not accepted for item number, quantity, or cost.

8. Movie Data

Write a program that uses a structure named `MovieData` to store the following information about a movie:

Title
Director
Year Released
Running time (in minutes)

Include a constructor that allows all four of these member data values to be specified at the time a `MovieData` variable is created. The program should create two `MovieData` variables and pass each one in turn to a function that displays the information about the movie in a clearly formatted manner. Pass the `MovieData` variables to the display function by value.

9. Movie Profit

Modify the Movie Data program written for Programming Challenge 8 to include two more members that hold the movie's production costs and first-year revenues. The constructor should be modified so that all six member values can be specified when a `MovieData` variable is created. Modify the function that displays the movie data to display the title, director, release year, running time, and first year's profit or loss. Also, improve the program by having the `MovieData` variables passed to the display function as constant references.

10. Corporate Sales Data

Write a program that uses a structure named `CorpData` to store the following information on a company division:

Division name (such as East, West, North, or South)
First quarter sales
Second quarter sales
Third quarter sales
Fourth quarter sales

Include a constructor that allows the division name and four quarterly sales amounts to be specified at the time a `CorpData` variable is created.

The program should create four `CorpData` variables, each representing one of the following corporate divisions: East, West, North, and South. These variables should be passed one at a time, as constant references, to a function that computes the division's annual sales total and quarterly average, and displays these along with the division name.

11. Monthly Budget Screen Form

A student has established the following monthly budget:

Housing	500.00
Utilities	150.00
Household expenses	65.00
Transportation	50.00
Food	250.00
Medical	30.00
Insurance	100.00
Entertainment	150.00
Clothing	75.00
Miscellaneous	50.00

Write a modular program that declares a `MonthlyBudget` structure with member variables to hold each of these expense categories. The program should create two `MonthlyBudget` structure variables. The first will hold the budget figures given above. The second will hold the user-enter amounts actually spent during the past month. Using Program 7-19 as a model, the program should create a screen form that displays each category name and its budgeted amount, then positions the cursor next to it for the user to enter the amount actually spent in that category. Once the user data has all been entered, the program should compute and display the amount over or under budget the student's expenditures were in each category, as well as the amount over or under budget for the entire month.

12. Ups and Downs

Write a program that displays the word UP on the bottom line of the screen a couple of inches to the left of center and displays the word DOWN on the top line of the screen a couple of inches to the right of center. Moving about once a second, move the word UP up a line and the word DOWN down a line until UP disappears at the top of the screen and DOWN disappears at the bottom of the screen.

13. Wrapping Ups and Downs

Modify the program you wrote for Programming Challenge 12, so that after disappearing off of the screen, the word UP reappears at the bottom of the screen and the word DOWN reappears at the top of the screen. Have these words each traverse the screen three times before the program terminates.

14. Left and Right

Modify the program you wrote for Programming Challenge 12 to display the words LEFT (starting at the right-hand side of the screen a row or two down from the middle) and RIGHT (starting at the left-hand side of the screen a row or two up from the middle). Moving about 6 moves per second, move LEFT to the left and RIGHT to the right until both words disappear off the screen.

15. Moving Inchworm

Write a program that displays an inchworm on the left-hand side of the screen, facing right. Then slowly move him across the screen, until he disappears off the right-hand side. You may wish to do this in a loop so that after disappearing to the right, the worm appears again on the left. The diagram below shows how he may look at various points on the screen.

```
         \/              \/              \/              \/            \/
         OO          O   OO          OOO OO          O   OO            OO
~OOOOOOOOO      ~OOOO OOOO      ~OOO    OOO      ~OOOO OOOO      ~OOOOOOOOO
```

Group Project

16. Patient Fees

This program should be designed and written by a team of students. Here are some suggestions:

- One or more students may work on a single class.
- The requirements of the program should be analyzed so each student is given about the same workload.
- The names, parameters, and return types of each function and class member function should be decided in advance.
- The program will be best implemented as a multifile program.

Write a program that computes a patient's bill for a hospital stay. The different components of the program are

- The `PatientAccount` class will keep a total of the patient's charges. It will also keep track of the number of days spent in the hospital. The group must decide on the hospital's daily rate.
- The `Surgery` class will have stored within it the charges for at least five types of surgery. It can update the `charges` variable of the `PatientAccount` class.
- The `Pharmacy` class will have stored within it the price of at least five types of medication. It can update the `charges` variable of the `PatientAccount` class.
- The `main` program.

The student who designs the main program will design a menu that allows the user to enter a type of surgery, enter one or more types of medication, and check the patient out of the hospital. When the patient checks out, the total charges should be displayed.

CHAPTER

8 Arrays

TOPICS

8.1 Arrays Hold Multiple Values

CONCEPT: An array allows you to store and work with multiple values of the same data type.

The variables you have worked with so far are designed to hold only one value at a time. Each of the variable definitions in Figure 8-1 cause only enough memory to be reserved to hold one value of the specified data type.

Figure 8-1

`int count;`	12314	Enough memory for 1 `int`
`double price;`	56.981	Enough memory for 1 `double`
`char letter;`	A	Enough memory for 1 `char`

An array works like a variable that can store a group of values, all of the same type. The values are stored together in consecutive memory locations. Here is a definition of an array of integers:

```
int hours[6];
```

The name of this array is `hours`. The number inside the brackets is the array's *size declarator.* It indicates the number of *elements*, or values, the array can hold. The `hours` array can store six elements, each one an integer. This is depicted in Figure 8-2.

Figure 8-2

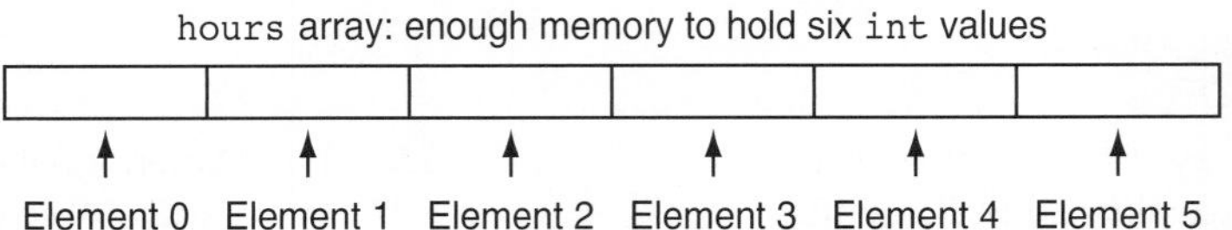

An array's size declarator must be a constant integer expression with a value greater than zero. It can be either a literal, as in the previous example, or a named constant, as shown here:

```
const int SIZE = 6;
int hours[SIZE];
```

Arrays of any data type can be defined. The following are all valid array definitions:

```
float temperature[100];     // Array of 100 floats
char letter[26];            // Array of 26 characters
double size[1200];          // Array of 1200 doubles
string name[10];            // Array of 10 string objects
```

Memory Requirements of Arrays

The amount of memory used by an array depends on the array's data type and the number of elements. The `age` array, defined here, is an array that holds six `short int` values.

```
short age[6];
```

On a typical PC, a `short int` uses 2 bytes of memory, so the `age` array would occupy 12 bytes. This is shown in Figure 8-3.

Figure 8-3

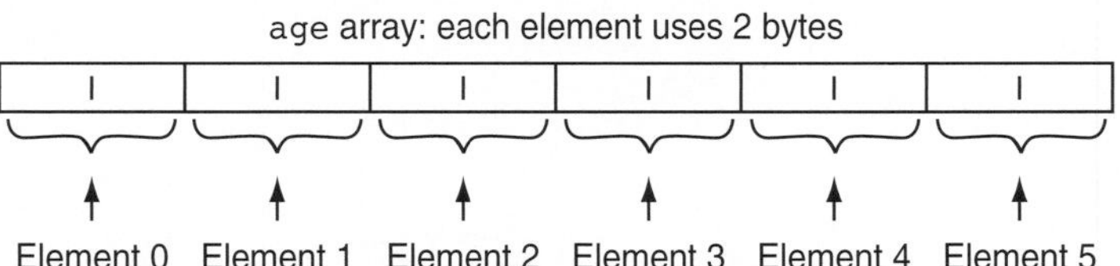

The size of an array can be calculated by multiplying the number of bytes needed to store an individual element by the number of elements in the array. Table 8-1 shows the sizes of various arrays on a typical system.

Table 8-1 Example Array Size Declarators

Array declaration	Number of elements	Size of each element	Size of the array
`char letter[26];`	26	1 byte	26 bytes
`short ring[100];`	100	2 bytes	200 bytes
`int mile[84];`	84	4 bytes	336 bytes
`float temp[12];`	12	4 bytes	48 bytes
`double distance[1000];`	1000	8 bytes	8,000 bytes

8.2 Accessing Array Elements

CONCEPT: The individual elements of an array are assigned unique subscripts. These subscripts are used to access the elements.

VideoNote Accessing Array Elements

Even though an entire array has only one name, the elements may be accessed and used as individual variables. This is possible because each element is assigned a number known as a *subscript*. A subscript is used as an index to pinpoint a specific element within an array. The first element is assigned the subscript 0, the second element is assigned 1, and so forth. The six elements in the `hours` array we defined in the previous section would have the subscripts 0 through 5. This is shown in Figure 8-4.

Figure 8-4

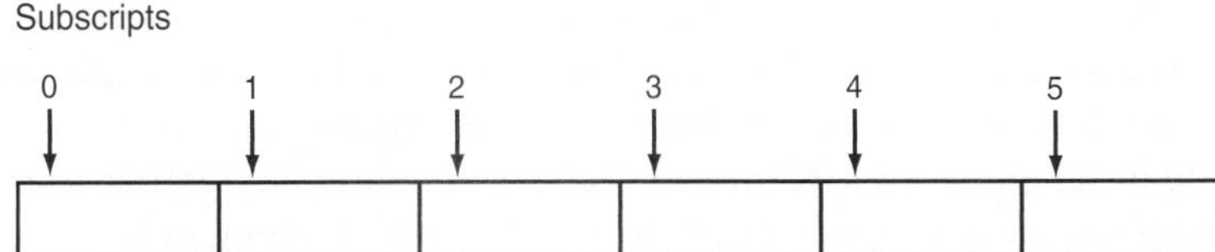

> **NOTE:** Subscript numbering in C++ always starts at zero. The subscript of the last element in an array is one less than the total number of elements in the array. This means that in the array shown in Figure 8-4, the element `hours[6]` does not exist. The last element in the array is `hours[5]`.

Each element in the `hours` array, when accessed by its subscript, can be used as an `int` variable. Here is an example of a statement that stores the number 20 in the first element of the array:

```
hours[0] = 20;
```

> **NOTE:** The expression `hours[0]` is pronounced "hours sub zero." You would read this assignment statement as "hours sub zero is assigned twenty."

Figure 8-5 shows the contents of the hours array after the statement assigns 20 to `hours[0]`.

Figure 8-5

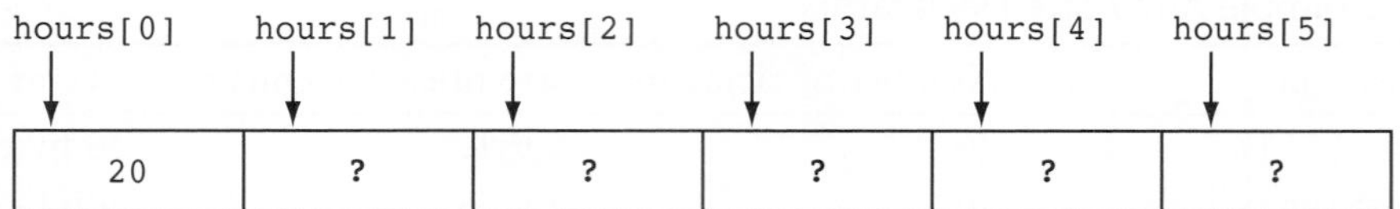

NOTE: Because values have not been assigned to the other elements of the array, question marks are used to indicate that the contents of those elements are unknown. If an array holding numeric values is defined globally, all of its elements are initialized to zero by default. Local arrays, however, have no default initialization value.

The following statement stores the integer 30 in `hours[3]`. Note that this is the fourth array element.

```
hours[3] = 30;
```

Figure 8-6 shows the contents of the array after this statement executes.

Figure 8-6

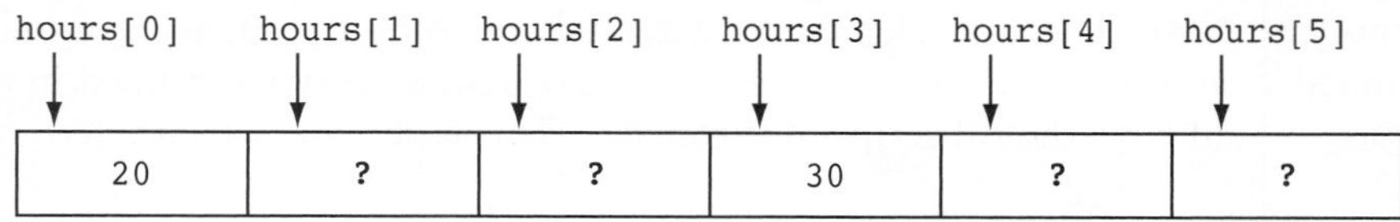

NOTE: It is important to understand the difference between the array size declarator and a subscript. The number inside the brackets in an array definition is the size declarator. It specifies how many elements the array holds. The number inside the brackets in an assignment statement or any statement that works with the contents of an array is a subscript. It specifies which element is being accessed.

Array elements may receive values with assignment statements just like other variables. However, entire arrays may not receive values for all their elements at once. Assume the following two arrays have been defined.

```
int doctorA[5];      // Holds the number of patients seen by Dr. A
                     // on each of 5 days.
int doctorB[5];      // Holds the number of patients seen by Dr. B
                     // on each of 5 days.
```

The following are all legal assignment statements.

```
doctorA[0] = 31;            // doctorA[0] now holds 31.
doctorA[1] = 40;            // doctorA[1] now holds 40.
doctorA[2] = doctorA[0];    // doctorA[2] now also holds 31.
doctorB[0] = doctorA[1];    // doctorB[0] now holds 40.
```

However, the following statements are not legal.

```
doctorA = 152;       // Illegal! An array as a whole may not
doctorB = doctorA;   // be assigned a value. This must be done
                     // one element at a time, using a subscript.
```

8.3 Inputting and Displaying Array Contents

Array elements may also have information read into them using the `cin` object and have their values displayed with the `cout` object, just like regular variables, as long as it is done one element at a time. Program 8-1 shows the `hours` array, discussed in the last section, being used to store and display values entered by the user.

Program 8-1

```
// This program stores employee work hours in an int array.
#include <iostream>
using namespace std;

int main()
{
   const int NUM_EMPLOYEES = 6;
   int hours[NUM_EMPLOYEES];    // Holds hours worked for 6 employees

   // Input the hours worked by each employee
   cout << "Enter the hours worked by " << NUM_EMPLOYEES
        << " employees: ";
   cin  >> hours[0];
   cin  >> hours[1];
   cin  >> hours[2];
   cin  >> hours[3];
   cin  >> hours[4];
   cin  >> hours[5];

   // Display the contents of the array
   cout << "The hours you entered are:";
   cout << "  " << hours[0];
   cout << "  " << hours[1];
   cout << "  " << hours[2];
   cout << "  " << hours[3];
   cout << "  " << hours[4];
   cout << "  " << hours[5] << endl;
   return 0;
}
```

Program Output with Example Input Shown in Bold

Enter the hours worked by 6 employees: **20 12 40 30 30 15[Enter]**
The hours you entered are: 20 12 40 30 30 15

Figure 8-7 shows the contents of the hours array with the example values entered by the user for Program 8-1.

Figure 8-7

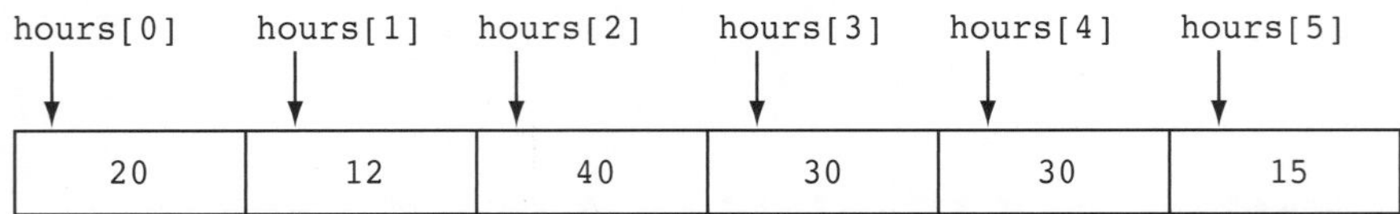

Even though most C++ compilers require the size declarator of an array definition to be a constant or a literal, subscript numbers can be stored in variables. This makes it possible to use a loop to "cycle through" an entire array, performing the same operation on each element. For example, Program 8-1 could be simplified by using two loops: one to input the values into the array and another to display the contents of the array. This is shown in Program 8-2.

Program 8-2

```
// This program stores employee work hours in an int array. It uses
// one loop to input the hours and another loop to display them.
#include <iostream>
using namespace std;

int main()
{
   const int NUM_EMPLOYEES = 6;
   int hours[NUM_EMPLOYEES];       // Holds hours worked for 6 employees
   int count;                      // Loop counter

   // Input the hours worked by each employee
   cout << "Enter the hours worked by " << NUM_EMPLOYEES
        << " employees: ";

   for (count = 0; count < NUM_EMPLOYEES; count++)
      cin >> hours[count];

   // Display the contents of the array
   cout << "The hours you entered are:";

   for (count = 0; count < NUM_EMPLOYEES; count++)
      cout << " " << hours[count];

   cout << endl;
   return 0;
}
```

Program Output with Example Input Shown in Bold

```
Enter the hours worked by 6 employees: 20 12 40 30 30 15[Enter]
The hours you entered are: 20 12 40 30 30 15
```

Let's look at Program 8-2 more carefully. In line 9, the `hours` array is defined using the named constant `NUM_EMPLOYEES` as the size declarator. This creates the `hours` array with six elements, `hours[0]` through `hours[5]`. In lines 16 and 17 a `for` loop is used to input a value into each array location. Notice that `count`, the loop control variable, is also used as the subscript for the `hours` array. Each time the loop iterates, `count` will have a different value, so a different array element will be accessed.

Because the `for` loop initializes `count` to 0, the first time the loop iterates, the user input value is read into `hours[0]`. The next time the loop iterates, `count` equals 1, so this time the user input value is read into `hours[1]`. This continues until, on the last iteration, `count` equals 5, and the final user input value is read into `hours[5]`. The `for` loop test condition is written so that when `count` reaches `NUM_EMPLOYEES`, which equals 6, the loop will stop.

The program's second `for` loop appears in lines 22 and 23. It works in a similar fashion, except that this loop is using `cout` to display each array element's value, rather than `cin` to read a value into each array element. In line 22 the `count` variable is re-initialized to 0, so the first time the loop iterates, the value stored in `hours[0]` is displayed. The next time the loop iterates, `count` equals 1, so this time the value stored in `hours[1]` is displayed. This continues until, on the final iteration, `count` equals 5 and the value stored in `hours[5]` is displayed.

Reading Data from a File into an Array

Sometimes you will need to read data from a file and store it in an array. The process is straightforward. Simply open the file and use a loop to read each item from the file, storing each item in an array element. The loop should iterate until either the array is filled or the end of the file is reached. Program 8-3 modifies Program 8-2 to read the data from a file.

Program 8-3

```
// This program reads employee work hours from a file
// and stores them in an int array. It uses one loop
// to input the hours and another to display them.
#include <iostream>
#include <fstream>
using namespace std;

int main()
{
   const int NUM_EMPLOYEES = 6;  // Sets number of employees
   int hours[NUM_EMPLOYEES];     // Holds each employee's hours
   int count = 0;                // Loop control variable counts
                                 // how many data items have been read in
   ifstream datafile;            // Input file stream object

   // Open the data file.
   datafile.open("work.dat");
   if (!datafile)
      cout << "Error opening data file\n";
```

(program continues)

Program 8-3 *(continued)*

```
20      else
21      {  // Read the numbers from the file into the array. When we exit
22         // the loop, count will hold the number of items read in.
23         while (count < NUM_EMPLOYEES && datafile >> hours[count] )
24            count++;
25
26         // Close the file.
27         datafile.close();
28
29         // Display the contents of the array.
30         cout << "The hours worked by each employee are\n";
31         for (int employee = 0; employee < count; employee++)
32         {   cout << "Employee " << employee+1 << ": ";
33             cout << hours[employee] << endl;
34         }
35      }
36      return 0;
37  }
```

Program Output

```
The hours worked by each employee are
Employee 1: 20
Employee 2: 12
Employee 3: 40
Employee 4: 30
Employee 5: 30
Employee 6: 15
```

Notice in Program 8-3 that the contents of the `hours` array were input and displayed one element at a time. The following statements would have been incorrect.

```
cin  >> hours;         // Incorrect!
cout << hours;         // Incorrect!
datafile >> hours;     // Incorrect!
```

Notice also that when we displayed a worker's data in line 33 we used the loop control variable, `employee`, as the subscript to access that worker's data in the `hours` array.

```
cout << hours[employee] << endl;
```

However, when we displayed that same worker's number in line 32 we added 1 to the value of the loop control variable, like this:

```
cout << "Employee " << employee+1 << ": ";
```

This is because the data for employee 1 is stored in `hours[0]`, the data for employee 2 is stored in `hours[1]`, and so forth.

Writing the Contents of an Array to a File

Writing the contents of an array to a file is also a straightforward matter. First open an output file pointed to by an `ofstream` object, as you learned to do in Chapter 5. Then simply use a loop to step through each element of the array and direct the output to the file instead of to the computer screen.

No Bounds Checking in C++

Historically, one of the reasons for C++'s popularity has been the freedom it gives programmers to work with the computer's memory. However, this means that many of the safeguards provided by other languages to prevent programs from unsafely accessing memory are absent in C++. For example, C++ does not perform array bounds checking. This means you could write a program that accidentally allows an array's subscript to go beyond its boundaries. This is why line 23 of Program 8-3 tested the value of the loop control variable to make sure it was less than `NUM_EMPLOYEES`, which was the size of the array, before it allowed the loop to continue iterating and reading in values. If the program tried to read in all the items in a file that contained more items than the array could hold, it could cause serious problems. What exactly occurs depends on how your system manages memory. On many systems it causes other nearby variables to have their contents overwritten, losing their correct value. On some systems it can even cause the computer to crash.

Program 8-4 demonstrates what occurs on the authors' computer when an array subscript goes out of bounds. It shows that data stored into one array overwrites the data in another array. It also shows, in line 10, how to initialize an array with data when it is defined. This technique is discussed further in the following section.

Program 8-4

```
1  // This program unsafely stores values beyond an array's boundary.
2  // What happens depends on how your computer manages memory.
3  // It MAY overwrite other memory variables. It MAY crash your computer.
4  #include <iostream>
5  using namespace std;
6
7  int main()
8  {
9     const int SIZE = 3;
10    int A[SIZE] = {1, 1, 1}; // Define A as a 3-element int array
11                             // holding the values 1, 1, 1
12    int B[SIZE];             // Define B as another 3-element int array
13
14    // Here is what is stored in array A
15    cout << "Here are the original numbers in 3-element array A:  ";
16    for (int count = 0; count < 3; count++)
17       cout << A[count] << "   ";
18
19    // Attempt to store seven numbers in the 3-element array
20    cout << "\n\nNow I'm storing 7 numbers in 3-element array B.";
21    for (int count = 0; count < 7; count++)
22       B[count] = 5;
23
24    // If the program is still running, display the numbers
25    cout << "\nIf you see this message, the computer did not crash.";
26    cout << "\n\nHere are the 7 numbers in array B  : ";
27    for (int count = 0; count < 7; count++)
28       cout << B[count] << "  ";
29
```

(program continues)

Program 8-4 *(continued)*

```
30    cout << "\nHere are the numbers now in array A: ";
31    for (int count = 0; count < 3; count++)
32       cout << A[count] << "   ";
33
34    cout << "\n\nArray A's values were overwritten by \n"
35         << "the values that did not fit in Array B.\n";
36    return 0;
37 }
```

Program Output

```
Here are the original numbers in 3-element array A:  1    1    1

Now I'm storing 7 numbers in 3-element array B.
If you see this message, the computer did not crash.

Here are the 7 numbers in array B  : 5   5   5   5   5   5   5
Here are the numbers now in array A: 5   5   5

Array A's values were overwritten by
the values that did not fit in Array B.
```

Let's look more closely at what occurred. Notice that array A started out with the values 1, 1, 1, but ended up with the values 5, 5, 5. This occurred because the loop in lines 21 and 22 of the program stored the value 5 in seven array B elements, even though array B only had enough memory assigned to it to store three values. The rest of the values were stored in adjacent memory locations that did not belong to array B. In this case, some of them belonged to array A, so its contents were overwritten and destroyed. Figure 8-8 illustrates this.

Figure 8-8

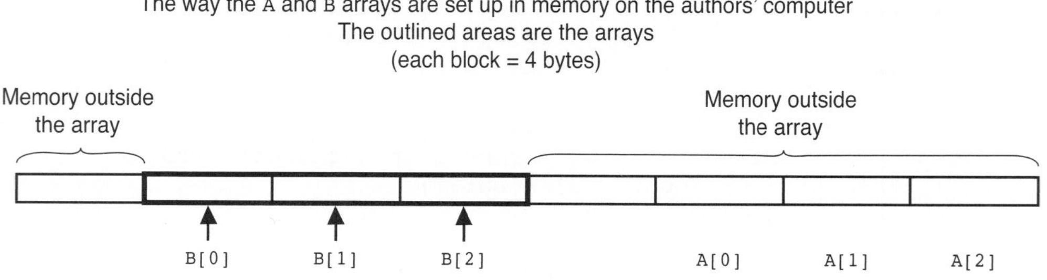
The way the A and B arrays are set up in memory on the authors' computer
The outlined areas are the arrays
(each block = 4 bytes)
Memory outside the array
Memory outside the array
B[0]
B[1]
B[2]
A[0]
A[1]
A[2]
How the numbers assigned to array B elements overflow the array's boundaries

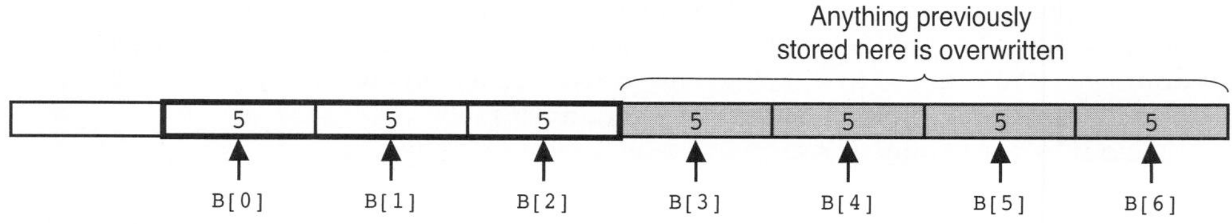
Anything previously stored here is overwritten
5
5
5
5
5
5
5
B[0]
B[1]
B[2]
B[3]
B[4]
B[5]
B[6]

You can see why it's important to make sure that any time you assign values to array elements, the values are written within the array's boundaries.

Watch for Off-By-One Errors

When working with arrays, a common type of mistake is the *off-by-one error*. This is an easy mistake to make because array subscripts start at 0 rather than 1. For example, look at the following code:

```
// This code has an off-by-one error
const int SIZE = 100;
int numbers[SIZE];
for (int count = 1; count <= SIZE; count++)
   numbers[count] = 0;
```

The intent of this code is to create an array of integers with 100 elements, and store the value 0 in each element. However, this code has an off-by-one error. The loop uses its counter variable, `count`, as a subscript with the `numbers` array. During the loop's execution, the variable `count` takes on the values 1 through 100, when it should take on the values 0 through 99. As a result, the first element, which is at subscript 0, is skipped. In addition, the loop attempts to use 100 as a subscript during the last iteration. Because 100 is an invalid subscript, the program will write data beyond the array's boundaries.

Checkpoint

8.1 Define the following arrays:

A) `empNum`, a 100-element array of `int`s

B) `payRate`, a 25-element array of `double`s

C) `miles`, a 14-element array of `long`s

D) `stateCapital`, a 50-element array of `string` objects.

E) `lightYears`, a 1,000-element array of `double`s

8.2 What's wrong with the following array definitions?

```
int readings[-1];
double measurements[4.5];
int size;
string name[size];
```

8.3 What would the valid subscript values be in a four-element array of `double`s?

8.4 What is the difference between an array's size declarator and a subscript?

8.5 What is "array bounds checking"? Does C++ perform it?

8.6 What is the output of the following code?

```
int values[5], count;

for (count = 0; count < 5; count++)
   values[count] = count + 1;

for (count = 0; count < 5; count++)
   cout << values[count] << endl;
```

8.7 Complete the following program skeleton so it will have a 10-element array of `int` values called `fish`. When completed, the program should ask how many fish were caught by fishermen 1 through 10, and store this information in the array. Then it should display the data.

```
#include <iostream>
using namespace std;

int main ()
{
   const int NUM_MEN = 10;
   // Define an array named fish that can hold 10 int values.

   // You must finish this program so it works as
   // described above.
   return 0;
}
```

8.4 Array Initialization

CONCEPT: Arrays may be initialized when they are defined.

Sometimes it is more appropriate to set variable values within a program than to input them. However, writing separate assignment statements for the individual elements of an array can mean a lot of typing, especially for large arrays. For example, consider Program 8-5.

Program 8-5

```
// This program displays the number of days in each month.
#include <iostream>
#include <iomanip>
using namespace std;

int main()
{
   const int NUM_MONTHS = 12;
   int days[NUM_MONTHS];

   days[0]  = 31;  // January
   days[1]  = 28;  // February
   days[2]  = 31;  // March
   days[3]  = 30;  // April
   days[4]  = 31;  // May
   days[5]  = 30;  // June
   days[6]  = 31;  // July
   days[7]  = 31;  // August
   days[8]  = 30;  // September
   days[9]  = 31;  // October
   days[10] = 30;  // November
   days[11] = 31;  // December

```

(program continues)

Program 8-5 *(continued)*

```
    for (int month = 0; month < NUM_MONTHS; month++)
    {
       cout << "Month " << setw(2) << (month+1) << " has ";
       cout << days[month] << " days.\n";
    }
    return 0;
}
```

Program Output

```
Month  1 has 31 days.
Month  2 has 28 days.
Month  3 has 31 days.
Month  4 has 30 days.
Month  5 has 31 days.
Month  6 has 30 days.
Month  7 has 31 days.
Month  8 has 31 days.
Month  9 has 30 days.
Month 10 has 31 days.
Month 11 has 30 days.
Month 12 has 31 days.
```

Fortunately, there is an alternative. As you saw briefly in Program 8-4, C++ allows you to initialize arrays when you define them. By using an initialization list, all the elements of the array can be easily initialized when the array is created. The following statement defines the `days` array and initializes it with the same values established by the set of assignment statements in Program 8-5:

```
int days[NUM_MONTHS] = {31, 28, 31, 30, 31, 30, 31, 31, 30, 31, 30, 31};
```

These values are stored in the array elements in the order they appear in the list. (The first value, 31, is stored in `days[0]`, the second value, 28, is stored in `days[1]`, and so forth). Figure 8-9 shows the contents of the array after the initialization.

Figure 8-9

Subscripts

0	1	2	3	4	5	6	7	8	9	10	11
31	28	31	30	31	30	31	31	30	31	30	31

Program 8-6 is a modification of Program 8-5. It initializes the `days` array at the time it is created rather than by using separate assignment statements. Notice that the initialization list is spread across multiple lines. The program also adds an array of `string` objects to hold the month names.

Program 8-6

```
// This program displays the number of days in each month. It uses an
// array of string objects to hold the month names and an int array
// to hold the number of days in each month. Both are initialized with
// initialization lists at the time they are created.
```

(program continues)

Program 8-6 *(continued)*

```
#include <iostream>
#include <iomanip>
#include <string>
using namespace std;

int main()
{
   Const int NUM_MONTHS = 12;
   string name[NUM_MONTHS] =
              { "January",   "February", "March",    "April",
                "May",       "June",     "July",     "August",
                "September", "October",  "November", "December" };

   int days[NUM_MONTHS] = {31, 28, 31, 30,
                           31, 30, 31, 31,
                           30, 31, 30, 31};

   for (int month = 0; month < NUM_MONTHS; month++)
   {
      cout << setw(9) << left << name[month] << " has ";
      cout << days[month] << " days.\n";
   }
   return 0;
}
```

Program Output

```
January   has 31 days.
February  has 28 days.
March     has 31 days.
April     has 30 days.
May       has 31 days.
June      has 30 days.
July      has 31 days.
August    has 31 days.
September has 30 days.
October   has 31 days.
November  has 30 days.
December  has 31 days.
```

So far we have demonstrated how to fill an array with values and then display all the values. Sometimes, however, we want to retrieve one specific value from the array. Program 8-7 is a variation of Program 8-6 that displays how many days are in the month the user selects.

Program 8-7

```
// This program allows the user to select a month and then
// displays how many days are in that month. It does this
// by "looking up" information it has stored in arrays.
#include <iostream>
```

(program continues)

Program 8-7 *(continued)*

```
#include <iomanip>
#include <string>
using namespace std;

int main()
{
   const int NUM_MONTHS = 12;
   int choice;
   string name[NUM_MONTHS] =
            { "January",   "February", "March",    "April",
              "May",       "June",     "July",     "August",
              "September", "October",  "November", "December" };

   int days[NUM_MONTHS] = {31, 28, 31, 30,
                           31, 30, 31, 31,
                           30, 31, 30, 31};

   cout << "This program will tell you how many days are "
        << "in any month.\n\n";

   // Display the months
   for (int month = 1; month <= NUM_MONTHS; month++)
      cout << setw(2) << month << "  " << name[month-1] << endl;

   cout << "\nEnter the number of the month you want: ";
   cin  >> choice;

   // Use the choice the user entered to get the name of
   // the month and its number of days from the arrays.
   cout << "The month of " << name[choice-1] << " has "
        << days[choice-1]  << " days.\n";
   return 0;
}
```

Program Output with Example Input Shown in Bold

```
This program will tell you how many days are in any month.

 1  January
 2  February
 3  March
 4  April
 5  May
 6  June
 7  July
 8  August
 9  September
10  October
11  November
12  December

Enter the number of the month you want: 4[Enter]
The month of April has 30 days.
```

Starting with Array Element 1

Some instructors prefer that you not use array element 0 and, instead, begin storing the actual data in element 1 when you are modeling something in the real world that logically begins with 1. The months of the year are a good example. In this case you would declare the name and days arrays to each have 13 elements and would initialize them like this:

```
string name[NUM_MONTHS+1] =
           { " ", "January",   "February", "March",    "April",
                  "May",       "June",     "July",     "August",
                  "September", "October",  "November", "December" };

int days[NUM_MONTHS+1] = {0, 31, 28, 31, 30,
                             31, 30, 31, 31,
                             30, 31, 30, 31};
```

Notice that array element 0 is not used. It just holds a dummy value. This allows the name of the first month, January, to be stored in name[1], the name of the second month, February, to be stored in name[2], and so on. Likewise, the number of days in January is found in days[1], the number of days in February in days[2], and so on.

Here is what the loop found in lines 22 through 26 of Program 8-6 would look like if the arrays were defined and initialized as we have done here. It displays the contents of array elements 1 through 12, instead of elements 0 through 11 as before.

```
for (int month = 1; month <= NUM_MONTHS; month++)
{
   cout << setw(9) << left << name[month] << " has ";
   cout << days[month] << " days.\n";
}
```

If the actual data is stored beginning with element 1, it is also not necessary to offset array subscripts by 1 to locate a particular piece of data. Here is what the loop in lines 26 and 27 of Program 8-7 that lists each month number with its name would look like:

```
for (int month = 1; month <= NUM_MONTHS; month++)
   cout << setw(2) << month << "   " << name[month] << endl;
```

And lines 34 and 35 of Program 8-7 that display the number of days in a month selected by the user would look like this:

```
cout << "The month of " << name[choice] << " has "
     << days[choice]  << " days.\n";
```

Versions of Programs 8-5, 8-6, and 8-7 that store data values beginning with element 1 can be found in the Chapter 8 folder of the book's companion website in files pr8-05B.cpp, pr8-06B.cpp, and pr8-07B.cpp, respectively.

Partial Array Initialization

When an array is being initialized, C++ does not require a value for every element. It's possible to only initialize part of an array, like this:

```
int numbers[7] = {1, 2, 4, 8};
```

This definition only initializes the first four elements of a seven-element array, as illustrated in Figure 8-10.

Figure 8-10

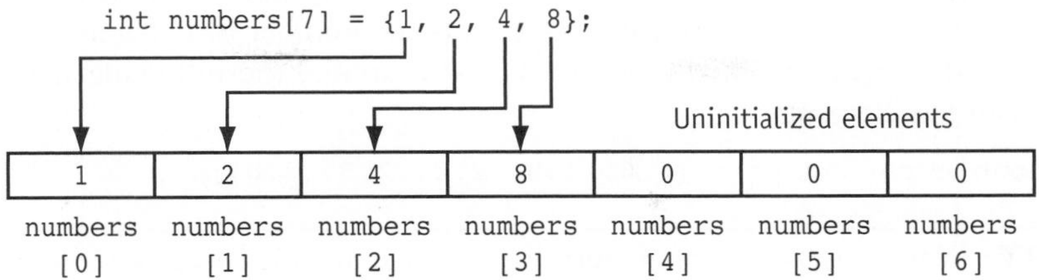

Notice in Figure 8-10 that the uninitialized elements have all been set to zero. This is what happens when a numeric array is partially initialized. When an array of `string` objects is partially initialized, the uninitialized elements will all contain empty strings, that is, strings of length 0. This is true even if the partially initialized array is defined locally. If a local array is *completely* uninitialized, however, its elements will contain "garbage," just like other local variables. Program 8-8 shows the contents of the `numbers` array after it is partially initialized.

Program 8-8

```
// This program has a partially initialized array.
#include <iostream>
using namespace std;

int main ()
{
   const int SIZE = 7;
   int numbers[SIZE] = {1, 2, 4, 8}; // Initialize the first 4 elements

   cout << "Here are the contents of the array:\n";
   for (int index = 0; index < SIZE; index++)
      cout << numbers[index] << " ";
   cout << endl;
   return 0;
}
```

Program Output

```
Here are the contents of the array:
1 2 4 8 0 0 0
```

Although an array initialization list can have fewer values than the array has elements, it is not allowed to have *more* values than the array can hold. The following statement would be illegal because the `numbers` array can only hold 7 values, but the initialization list contains 8 values.

```
int numbers[7] = {1, 2, 4, 8, 3, 5, 7, 9}; // NOT legal!
```

Also, if you leave an element uninitialized, you must leave all the elements that follow it uninitialized as well. C++ does not provide a way to skip elements in the initialization list. Here is another example that is illegal.

```
int numbers[7] = {1, , 4, , 3, 5, 7};      // NOT legal!
```

Implicit Array Sizing

You can define an array without specifying its size by providing an initialization list that includes a value for every element. C++ counts the number of items in the initialization list and gives the array that many elements. For example, the following definition creates an array with five elements:

```
double ratings[] = {1.0, 1.5, 2.0, 2.5, 3.0};
```

NOTE: You *must* specify an initialization list if you leave out the size declarator. Otherwise, C++ doesn't know how large to make the array.

8.5 Processing Array Contents

CONCEPT: Individual array elements are processed like any other type of variable.

Processing array elements is no different than processing other variables. For example, the following statement multiplies `hours[3]` by the variable `rate`:

```
pay = hours[3] * rate;
```

And the following are examples of pre-increment and post-increment operations on array elements:

```
int score[5] = {7, 8, 9, 10, 11};
++score[2];       // Pre-increment operation on the value in score[2]
score[4]++;       // Post-increment operation on the value in score[4]
```

NOTE: When using increment and decrement operators, be careful not to confuse the subscript with the array element. The following example illustrates the difference.

```
amount[count]--;  // This decrements the value stored in amount[count]
amount[count--];  // This decrements the variable count, but does
                  // nothing to the value stored in amount[count]
```

Program 8-9 demonstrates the use of array elements in a simple mathematical statement. A loop steps through each element of the array, using the elements to calculate the gross pay of five employees.

Program 8-9

```
// This program uses an array to store the hours worked by
// a set of employees who all make the same hourly wage.
#include <iostream>
#include <iomanip>
using namespace std;

```

(program continues)

Program 8-9 *(continued)*

```
int main()
{
   const int NUM_WORKERS = 5;  // Set the number of employees
   int hours[NUM_WORKERS];     // Array to hold each employee's hours
   double payRate;             // Hourly pay rate for all employees

   // Input hours worked by each employee
   cout << "Enter the hours worked by \n";
   for (int worker = 0; worker < NUM_WORKERS; worker++)
   {
      cout << "Employee #" << (worker+1) << ": ";
      cin  >> hours[worker];
   }

   // Input the hourly pay rate for all employees
   cout << "\nEnter the hourly pay rate for all the employees: ";
   cin  >> payRate;

   // Display each employee's gross pay
   cout << "\nHere is the gross pay for each employee:\n";
   cout << fixed << showpoint << setprecision(2);
   for (int worker = 0; worker < NUM_WORKERS; worker++)
   {
      double grossPay = hours[worker] * payRate;
      cout << "Employee #" << (worker + 1);
      cout << ": $" << setw(7) << grossPay << endl;
   }
   return 0;
}
```

Program Output with Example Input Shown in Bold

```
Enter the hours worked by
Employee #1: 5[Enter]
Employee #2: 10[Enter]
Employee #3: 15[Enter]
Employee #4: 20[Enter]
Employee #5: 40[Enter]

Enter the hourly pay rate for all the employees: 12.75[Enter]

Here is the gross pay for each employee:
Employee #1: $  63.75
Employee #2: $ 127.50
Employee #3: $ 191.25
Employee #4: $ 255.00
Employee #5: $ 510.00
```

Array elements can be used in all the same ways regular variables can. You have seen how to read in a value and store it in an array element, how to assign a value to an array element, and how to display an element's value.

Array elements can also be used in relational expressions. For example, the following `if` statement tests `cost[20]` to determine whether it is less than `cost[0]`:

```
if (cost[20] < cost[0])
```

And this line begins a `while` loop that iterates as long as `value[place]` does not equal 0:

```
while (value[place] != 0)
```

Copying One Array to Another

We have already discussed that you cannot simply assign one array to another array. To copy the contents of one array to another, you must assign each element of the first array, one at a time, to the corresponding element of the second array. The following code segment uses a `for` loop to do this.

```
const int SIZE = 6;
int arrayA[SIZE] = {10, 20, 30, 40, 50, 60};
int arrayB[SIZE] = { 2,  4,  6,  8, 10, 12};
for (int index = 0; index < SIZE; index++)
   arrayA[index] = arrayB[index];
```

On the first iteration of the loop, `index = 0`, so `arrayA[0]` is assigned the value stored in `arrayB[0]`. On the second iteration, `index = 1`, so `arrayA[1]` is assigned the value stored in `arrayB[1]`. This continues until, one by one, all the elements of `arrayB` are copied to `arrayA`. When the loop is finished executing, both arrays will contain the values 2, 4, 6, 8, 10, 12.

This code can be found in the program `ArrayCopy.cpp` in the Chapter 8 folder on the book's companion website.

Comparing Two Arrays

Just as you cannot copy one array to another with a single statement, you also cannot compare the contents of two arrays with a single statement. That is, you cannot use the == operator with the names of two arrays to determine whether the arrays are equal. The following code appears to compare the contents of two arrays, but in reality does not.

```
int arrayA[] = { 5, 10, 15, 20, 25 };
int arrayB[] = { 5, 10, 15, 20, 25 };

if (arrayA == arrayB)       // This is a mistake
   cout << "The arrays are the same.\n";
else
   cout << "The arrays are not the same.\n";
```

When you use the == operator with array names, the operator compares the beginning memory addresses of the arrays, not the contents of the arrays. The two arrays in this code will obviously have different memory addresses. Therefore, the result of the expression `arrayA == arrayB` is false and the code reports that the arrays are not the same.

To compare the contents of two arrays, you must compare their individual elements. For example, look at the following code.

```
const int SIZE = 5;
int arrayA[SIZE] = { 5, 10, 15, 20, 25 };
int arrayB[SIZE] = { 5, 10, 15, 20, 25 };
bool arraysEqual = true;  // Flag variable
int count = 0;            // Loop counter variable
```

```
// Determine whether the elements contain the same data
while (arraysEqual && count < SIZE)
{
      if (arrayA[count] != arrayB[count])
         arraysEqual = false;
      count++;
}
// Display the appropriate message
if (arraysEqual)
   cout << "The arrays are equal.\n";
else
   cout << "The arrays are not equal.\n";
```

This code determines whether `arrayA` and `arrayB` contain the same values. A `bool` variable `arraysEqual`, which is initialized to `true`, signals whether or not the arrays are equal. Another variable `count`, which is initialized to 0, is used as a loop counter.

Then a `while` loop begins. The loop executes as long as `arraysEqual` is `true` and the counter variable `count` is less than `SIZE`. During each iteration, it compares a different pair of corresponding elements in the arrays. If it finds two corresponding elements that have different values, the `arraysEqual` variable is set to `false`, which allows the loop to be exited without examining any more values. After the loop finishes, an `if` statement tests the `arraysEqual` variable. If the variable is still `true`, then no differences were found. The arrays are equal, and a message indicating this is displayed. Otherwise, they are not equal, so a different message is displayed. This code can be found in the program `ArrayCompare.cpp` in the Chapter 8 folder on the book's companion website.

Summing the Values in a Numeric Array

To sum the values in an array, you must use a loop with an accumulator variable. The loop adds the value in each array element to the accumulator. For example, assume that the following statements appear in a program.

```
const int NUM_UNITS = 6;
int units[NUM_UNITS] = {16, 20, 14, 8, 6, 10};
int total = 0;                // Initialize accumulator
```

The following loop adds the values of each element in the array to the `total` variable. When the code is finished, `total` will contain the sum of the `units` array's elements.

```
for (int count = 0; count < NUM_UNITS; count++)
   total += units[count];
```

NOTE: Notice that `total` is initialized to 0. Recall from Chapter 5 that an accumulator variable must be set to 0 before it is used to keep a running total or the sum will not be correct.

Finding the Average of the Values in a Numeric Array

The first step in calculating the average of all the values in an array is to sum the values. The second step is to divide the sum by the number of elements in the array. Assume that the following statements appear in a program.

```
const int NUM_SCORES = 5;
double scores[NUM_SCORES] = {90, 88, 91, 82, 95};
```

The following code calculates the average of the values in the `scores` array and stores the result in the `average` variable.

```
double total = 0;          // Initialize accumulator
double average;            // Will hold the average

for (int count = 0; count < NUM_SCORES; count++)
   total += scores[count];
average = total / NUM_SCORES;
```

Notice that the last statement, which divides `total` by `NUM_SCORES`, is not inside the loop. This statement should only execute once, after the loop has finished all its iterations.

Finding the Highest and Lowest Values in a Numeric Array

The algorithms for finding the highest and lowest values in an array are very similar. First, let's look at code for finding the highest value in an array. Assume that the following lines appear in a program.

```
const int SIZE = 10;
int numbers[SIZE] = {15, 6, 3, 11, 22, 4, 0, 1, 9, 12};
```

The code to find the highest value in the array is as follows.

```
int count;
int highest;

highest = numbers[0];
for (count = 1; count < SIZE; count++)
{
   if (numbers[count] > highest)
      highest = numbers[count];
}
```

First we copy the value in the first array element to the variable named `highest`. Then the loop compares all of the remaining array elements, beginning at subscript 1, to the value stored in `highest`. Each time it finds a value in the array that is greater than `highest`, it copies it to `highest`. When the loop has finished, `highest` will contain the highest value in the array.

The following code finds the lowest value in the array. As you can see, it is nearly identical to the code for finding the highest value.

```
int count;
int lowest;

lowest = numbers[0];
for (count = 1; count < SIZE; count++)
{
   if (numbers[count] < lowest)
      lowest = numbers[count];
}
```

When the loop has finished, `lowest` will contain the lowest value in the array.

Program 8-10, which creates a monthly sales report, demonstrates the algorithms for finding the sum, average, highest, and lowest values in an array. It combines the algorithms to find the highest and the lowest value into a single loop. The sales data used to fill the array is read in from the `sales.dat` file, which contains the following values

62458 81598 98745 53460 35678 86322
89920 78960 124569 43550 45679 98750

Program 8-10

```
// This program uses an array to store monthly sales figures
// for a company's regional offices. It then finds and displays
// the total, average, highest, and lowest sales amounts.
// The data to fill the array is read in from a file.
#include <iostream>
#include <fstream>             // Needed to use files
#include <iomanip>
using namespace std;

int main()
{
   const int NUM_OFFICES = 12;
   ifstream dataIn;
   int office;                 // Loop counter
   double sales[NUM_OFFICES],  // Array to hold the sales data
          totalSales = 0.0,    // Accumulator initialized to zero
          averageSales,
          highestSales,
          lowestSales;

   // Open the data file
   dataIn.open("sales.dat");
   if (!dataIn)
      cout << "Error opening data file.\n";
   else
   {  // Fill the array with data from the file
      for (office = 0; office < NUM_OFFICES; office++)
         dataIn >> sales[office];
      dataIn.close();

      // Sum all the array elements
      for (office = 0; office < NUM_OFFICES; office++)
         totalSales += sales[office];

      // Calculate average sales
      averageSales = totalSales / NUM_OFFICES;

      // Find highest and lowest sales amounts
      highestSales = lowestSales = sales[0];
      for (office = 1; office < NUM_OFFICES; office++)
      {
         if (sales[office] > highestSales)
            highestSales = sales[office];
         else if (sales[office] < lowestSales)
            lowestSales = sales[office];
      }
```

(program continues)

Program 8-10 *(continued)*

```
      // Display results
      cout << fixed << showpoint << setprecision(2);
      cout << "Total sales   $" << setw(9) << totalSales   << endl;
      cout << "Average sales $" << setw(9) << averageSales << endl;
      cout << "Highest sales $" << setw(9) << highestSales << endl;
      cout << "Lowest sales  $" << setw(9) << lowestSales  << endl;
   }
   return 0;
}
```

Program Output

```
Total sales   $899689.00
Average sales $ 74974.08
Highest sales $124569.00
Lowest sales  $ 35678.00
```

Partially-Filled Arrays

Sometimes you need to store a series of items in an array, but you do not know the number of items that there are. As a result, you do not know the exact number of elements needed for the array. One solution is to make the array large enough to hold the largest possible number of items. This can lead to another problem, however. If the actual number of items stored in the array is less than the number of elements, the array will be only partially filled. When you process a partially-filled array, you must only process the elements that contain valid data items.

A partially-filled array is normally used with an accompanying integer variable that tells how many items are currently stored in the array. For example, suppose a program uses the code shown below to create a 100-element array, and an `int` variable named `numValues` which will hold the number of items stored in the array. Notice that `numValues` is initialized to zero because no values have been stored in the array yet.

```
const int SIZE = 100;
int array[SIZE];
int numValues = 0;
```

Each time we add an item to the array, we must increment `numValues`. The following code demonstrates.

```
int number;

cout << "Enter a number or -1 to quit: ";
cin  >> number;
while (number != -1 && numValues < SIZE)
{
   array[numValues] = number;
   numValues++;
   cout << "Enter a number or -1 to quit: ";
   cin  >> number;
}
```

Each iteration of this sentinel-controlled loop allows the user to enter a number to be stored in the array, or –1 to quit. After each value is stored in the array, `numValues` is incremented to hold the subscript of the next available element in the array. When the user enters –1, or when `numValues` exceeds 99, the loop stops. The following code displays all of the valid items in the array.

```
for (int index = 0; index < numValues; index++)
{
   cout << array[index] << endl;
}
```

Why Use an Array?

Program 8-10 stored a set of numbers in an array in order to sum the numbers and find the average, largest, and smallest values. However, this could have been done without using an array at all. The sales figures could have just been placed one at a time into a simple variable, added to a sum, and compared to the largest and smallest values as they were read in. This is illustrated by the following code segment.

```
dataIn >> salesAmt;      // Input the data from the first office
totalSales = highestSales = lowestSales = salesAmt;
for (office = 2; office <= numOffices; office++)
{  dataIn >> salesAmt;
   totalSales += salesAmt;
   if (salesAmt > highestSales)
      highestSales = salesAmt;
   else if (salesAmt < lowestSales)
      lowestSales = salesAmt;

}
averageSales = totalSales / numOffices;
```

Then why use an array at all? There are many reasons. One of the most important is that once the data is in the array it can be used more than once without having to be input again. For example, suppose that instead of finding the highest and lowest sales figures we want to create a report that tells which offices have below-average sales figures. Program 8-11 modifies Program 8-10 to do this. Note that it requires looking at each piece of data twice. First each value is input and summed to find and display the average. Then each data value is examined again, so it can be compared to the average, and any below-average value can be displayed. Program 8-11 also illustrates the use of a partially-filled array. It allows the `sales` array to hold up to 20 values, then uses the loop control variable of a `while` loop to count the actual number of values stored in it as they are read in from the file. The data is read in from the same `sales.dat` file used by Program 8-10.

Program 8-11

```
// This program uses a partially-filled array to store monthly sales
// figures for a set of offices. It then finds and displays the total
// sales amount, the average sales amount, and a listing of the offices
// with sales below the average. The data to fill the array is read
// in from a file and the number of data values are counted.
#include <iostream>
```

(program continues)

Program 8-11 *(continued)*

```
#include <fstream>           // Needed to use files
#include <iomanip>
using namespace std;

int main()
{
   const int SIZE = 20;
   ifstream dataIn;           // Object to read file input
   int numOffices,            // Number of data values read in
       count;                 // Loop counter
   double sales[SIZE],        // Array to hold the sales data
          totalSales = 0.0,   // Accumulator initialized to zero
          averageSales;       // Average sales for all offices

   // Open the data file
   dataIn.open("sales.dat");
   if (!dataIn)
      cout << "Error opening the data file.\n";
   else
   {  // Read values from the file and store them in the array,
      // counting them and summing them as they are read in
      count = 0;
      while (count < SIZE && dataIn >> sales[count])
      {  totalSales += sales[count];
         count++;
      }
      numOffices = count;
      dataIn.close();

      // Calculate average sales
      averageSales = totalSales / numOffices;

      // Display total and average
      cout << fixed << showpoint << setprecision(2);
      cout << "The total sales are   $"
           << setw(9) << totalSales << endl;
      cout << "The average sales are $"
           << setw(9) << averageSales << endl;

      // Display figures for offices performing below the average
      cout << "\nThe following offices have below-average "
           << "sales figures.\n";
      for (int office = 0; office < numOffices; office++)
      {  if (sales[office] < averageSales)
            cout << "Office "     << setw(2) << (office + 1)
                 << " $" << sales[office] << endl;
      }
   }
   return 0;
}
```

(program continues)

Program 8-11 *(continued)*

Program Output

```
The total sales are   $899689.00
The average sales are $ 74974.08

The following offices have below-average sales figures.
Office  1 $62458.00
Office  4 $53460.00
Office  5 $35678.00
Office 10 $43550.00
Office 11 $45679.00
```

Let's look at a couple of key points in Program 8-11. First, look at line 29. This line controls the `while` loop and reads in the data.

```
while (count < SIZE && dataIn >> sales[count])
```

The loop repeats as long as `count` is less than the size of the array *and* a data value is successfully read in from the file (i.e., the end of the file has not been encountered). The first part of the `while` loop's test expression, `count < SIZE`, prevents the loop from writing outside the array boundaries. The second part of the test expression stops the loop if there is no more data in the file to read. Recall from Chapter 4 that the `&&` operator performs short-circuit evaluation, so the second part of the `while` loop's test expression, `dataIn >> sales[count]`, will be executed only if `count` is less than `SIZE`. The `sales` array defined in line 17 has room to store up to 20 values, but because the data file contains only 12 values, the `while` loop terminates after reading in these 12 items.

Notice how `count`, the loop control variable, serves two purposes in addition to controlling execution of the loop. Because it is initialized to zero and is incremented on line 31 once each time the loop iterates, it keeps count of which array position the next item read should be stored in, correctly allowing the 12 values from the `sales.dat` file to be stored in array positions 0 through 11. It also keeps count of how many values are read in. When the loop terminated in our sample run, `count` was 12, which equaled the number of items read in.

We said that using an array is particularly helpful when data values need to be looked at more than once. That is exactly what happens in Program 8-11. The statement in line 30 adds each piece of stored data to a total it is accumulating of all the values. This total is later used in line 37 to compute an average. Then, inside the `for` loop on lines 49 through 53, each stored data item is again examined to compare it to the average and to display it if it is below the average

As you continue to program you will encounter many additional algorithms that require examining data values more than once and you will discover many cases where arrays are a particularly useful way to organize and store data.

Processing Strings

Strings are internally stored as arrays of characters. They are different from other arrays in that the elements can either be treated as a set of individual characters or can be used as a single entity. The following sample code defines a `string` object and treats it as a single entity, inputting it and displaying it as a single unit.

```
string name;
cout << "Enter your name: ";
cin  >> name;
cout << "Hello, " << name << endl;
```

This is, in fact, how strings are normally treated and processed—as single entities. However, C++ provides the ability to index them with a subscript, like an array, so they can be processed character by character. If `"Warren"` were entered for the name in the previous code segment, it would be stored in the `name string` object as shown in Figure 8-11.

Figure 8-11

'W'	'a'	'r'	'r'	'e'	'n'
name [0]	name [1]	name [2]	name [3]	name [4]	name [5]

NOTE: Both `string` objects and C-strings are stored as characters in contiguous bytes of memory, as shown in Figure 8-11. String literals and C-strings are terminated by placing a `'\0'`, which represents the null terminator, in the byte of memory following the last character of the string. There is no guarantee, however, how `string` objects will be implemented. Many versions of C++ do terminate `string` objects with the null terminator, but it is never safe to assume they will be terminated this way.

If we wanted to process the string character by character, like a regular array, we could do so. For example the statement

```
cout << name[0];     would print the letter W,
cout << name[1];     would print the letter a, and so forth
```

Program 8-12 illustrates character by character string processing. It reads in a string and then counts the number of vowels in the string. The `string` class member function `length` is used to determine how many characters are in the string.

Program 8-12

```
// This program illustrates how a string can be processed as an array
// of individual characters. It reads in a string, then counts the
// number of vowels in the string. It uses the toupper function to
// uppercase each letter in the string and the string class member
// function length() to determine how many characters are in the string.
#include <iostream>
#include <string>          // Needed to use string objects
#include <cctype>          // Needed for the toupper function
using namespace std;

int main()
{
   char ch;
   int vowelCount = 0;
   string sentence;
```

(program continues)

Program 8-12 *(continued)*

```

   cout << "Enter any sentence you wish and I will \n"
        << "tell you how many vowels are in it.\n";
   getline(cin, sentence);

   for (int pos = 0; pos < sentence.length(); pos++)
   {
      // Uppercase a copy of the next character and assign it to ch
      ch = toupper(sentence[pos]);

      // If the character is a vowel, increment vowelCount
      switch(ch)
      {  case 'A':
         case 'E':
         case 'I':
         case 'O':
         case 'U': vowelCount++;
      }
   }
   cout << "There are " << vowelCount << " vowels in the sentence.\n";
   return 0;
}
```

Program Output with Example Input Shown in Bold

```
Enter any sentence you wish and I will
tell you how many vowels are in it.
The quick brown fox jumped over the lazy dog.[Enter]
There are 12 vowels in the sentence.
```

Additional examples of string processing are introduced in Chapter 12.

8.6 Using Parallel Arrays

CONCEPT: By using the same subscript, you can build relationships between data stored in two or more arrays.

Sometimes it is useful to store related data in two or more arrays. It's especially useful when the related data is of different data types. We did this in Programs 8-6 and 8-7, where the `name` array stored the names of the 12 months and the `days` array stored the number of days in a given month. A month name and its number of days were related by having the same subscript. For example, `days[3]` stored the number of days in the month whose name was stored in `month[3]`. When data items stored in two or more arrays are related in this fashion, the arrays are called *parallel arrays*. Program 8-13, which is a variation of the payroll program, uses parallel arrays. An `int` array stores the hours worked by each employee, and a `double` array stores each employee's hourly pay rate.

Program 8-13

```
// This program stores employee hours worked
// and hourly pay rates in two parallel arrays.
#include <iostream>
#include <iomanip>
using namespace std;

int main()
{
   const int NUM_EMPS = 5;
   int index;
   int hours[NUM_EMPS];        // Define 2 parallel arrays
   double payRate[NUM_EMPS];
   double grossPay;

   // Get employee work data
   cout << "Enter the hours worked and hourly pay rates of "
        << NUM_EMPS << " employees. \n";

   for (index = 0; index < NUM_EMPS; index++)
   {
      cout << "Hours worked by employee #" << (index + 1) << ": ";
      cin  >> hours[index];
      cout << "Hourly pay rate for employee #" << (index + 1) << ": ";
      cin  >> payRate[index];
   }
   // Display the data
   cout << "\nHere is the gross pay for each employee:\n";
   cout << fixed << showpoint << setprecision(2);
   for (index = 0; index < NUM_EMPS; index++)
   {
      grossPay = hours[index] * payRate[index];
      cout << "Employee #" << (index + 1);
      cout << ": $" << setw(7) << grossPay << endl;
   }
   return 0;
}
```

Program Output with Example Input Shown in Bold

```
Enter the hours worked and hourly pay rates of 5 employees.
Hours worked by employee #1: 10[Enter]
Hourly pay rate for employee #1: 9.75[Enter]
Hours worked by employee #2: 15[Enter]
Hourly pay rate for employee #2: 8.62[Enter]
Hours worked by employee #3: 20[Enter]
Hourly pay rate for employee #3: 10.50[Enter]
Hours worked by employee #4: 40[Enter]
Hourly pay rate for employee #4: 18.75[Enter]
Hours worked by employee #5: 40[Enter]
Hourly pay rate for employee #5: 15.65[Enter]
```

(program output continues)

Program 8-13 *(continued)*

```
Here is the gross pay for each employee:
Employee #1: $  97.50
Employee #2: $ 129.30
Employee #3: $ 210.00
Employee #4: $ 750.00
Employee #5: $ 626.00
```

Notice in the loops that the same subscript is used to access both arrays. That's because the data for a particular employee is stored in the same relative position in each array. For example, the hours worked by employee #1 are stored in `hours[0]`, and the same employee's pay rate is stored in `payRate[0]`. The subscript relates the data in both arrays. This concept is illustrated in Figure 8-12.

Figure 8-12

10	15	20	40	40
hours[0]	hours[1]	hours[2]	hours[3]	hours[4]
↑	↑	↑	↑	↑
Employee #1	Employee #2	Employee #3	Employee #4	Employee #5
↓	↓	↓	↓	↓
9.75	8.62	10.50	18.75	15.65
payRate[0]	payRate[1]	payRate[2]	payRate[3]	payRate[4]

Checkpoint

8.8 Define the following arrays:

A) `ages`, a 10-element array of `int`s initialized with the values 5, 7, 9, 14, 15, 17, 18, 19, 21, and 23

B) `temps`, a 7-element array of `double`s initialized with the values 14.7, 16.3, 18.43, 21.09, 17.9, 18.76, and 26.7

C) `alpha`, an 8-element array of `char`s initialized with the values 'J', 'B', 'L', 'A', '*', '$', 'H', and 'M'

8.9 Indicate if each of the following array definitions is valid or invalid. (If a definition is invalid, explain why.)

A) `int numbers[10] = {0, 0, 1, 0, 0, 1, 0, 0, 1, 1};`

B) `int matrix[5] = {1, 2, 3, 4, 5, 6, 7};`

C) `double radii[10] = {3.2, 4.7};`

D) `int table[7] = {2, , , 27, , 45, 39};`

E) `char codes[] = {'A', 'X', '1', '2', 's'};`

F) `int blanks[];`

G) `string suit[4] = {"Clubs", "Diamonds", "Hearts", "Spades"};`

8.10 Given the following array definitions

```
double array1[4] = {1.2, 3.2, 4.2, 5.2};
double array2[4];
```

will the following statement work? If not, why?

```
array2 = array1;
```

8.11 Given the following array definition:

```
int values[] = {2, 6, 10, 14};
```

what do each of the following display?

A) `cout << values[2];`
B) `cout << ++values[0];`
C) `cout << values[1]++;`
D)
```
x = 2;
cout << values[++x];
```

8.12 Given the following array definition

```
int nums[5] = {1, 2, 3};
```

what will the following statement display?

```
cout << nums[3];
```

8.13 What is the output of the following code?

```
double balance[5] = {100.0, 250.0, 325.0, 500.0, 1100.0};
const double INT_RATE = 0.1;

cout << fixed << showpoint << setprecision(2);
for (int count = 0; count < 5; count++)
   cout << (balance[count] * INT_RATE) << endl;
```

8.14 What is the output of the following code?

```
const int SIZE 5;
int count;
int time[SIZE] =  {1, 2, 3, 4, 5},
    speed[SIZE] = {18, 4, 27, 52, 100},
    dist[SIZE];

for (count = 0; count < SIZE; count++)
   dist[count] = time[count] * speed[count];

for (count = 0; count < SIZE; count++)
{
   cout << time[count] << "  ";
   cout << speed[count] << "  ";
   cout << dist[count] << endl;
}
```

8.7 The typedef Statement

CONCEPT: The `typedef` statement allows an alias to be associated with a simple or structured data type.

The `typedef` statement allows the programmer to create an alias, or synonym, for an existing data type. This can be a simple data type, like an `int`, or a more complicated data type such as an array. The simplest form of the statement is

```
typedef  <existing data type> <alias>;
```

For example, the following statements declare `examScore` to be another name for an `int` and then define two variables of type `examScore`.

```
typedef int examScore;
examScore score1, score2;  // score1 and score2 are of type examScore
```

The declaration emphasizes that variables of type `examScore` are integers that will hold exam scores.

One of the most common uses of the `typedef` statement is to provide a descriptive alias for an array of a specific purpose. When used with arrays, the `[]` holding the array size is written next to the alias name, not next to the data type name. The following statement creates an alias named `score` for a `double` array of size 100.

```
typedef double score[100];
```

This means that anything defined to be a `score` is an array of 100 `double` elements intended to hold scores. The following two statements now do the same thing.

```
double finalExam[100];
score finalExam;
```

Sometimes it is desirable to create an alias for an array of a specific data type without specifying its size. The following statement creates an alias, named `arrayType` for an `int` array of unspecified size.

```
typedef int arrayType[];
```

In the next section, when you learn how to pass arrays as function arguments, it will become apparent why it is convenient to set up a `typedef` for an array type.

8.8 Arrays as Function Arguments

CONCEPT: Individual elements of arrays and entire arrays can both be passed as arguments to functions.

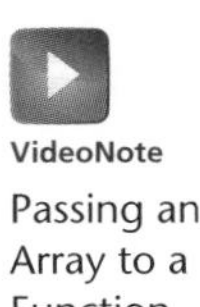

VideoNote
Passing an Array to a Function

Quite often you'll want to write functions that process the data in arrays. For example, functions can be written to put values in an array, display an array's contents on the screen, total all of an array's elements, or calculate their average. Usually, such functions accept an array as an argument.

When a single element of an array is passed to a function, it is handled like any other variable. For example, Program 8-14 shows a loop that passes one element of the `collection` array to the `showValue` function each time the loop is executed. Because the elements of the `collection` array are `int`s, a single `int` value is passed to the `showValue` function each time it is called. Notice how this is specified in the `showValue` function prototype and function header. All `showValue` knows is that it is receiving an `int`. It does not matter that it happens to be coming from an array.

Program 8-14

```
// This program demonstrates that an array element
// can be passed to a function like any other variable.
#include <iostream>
using namespace std;

void showValue(int);     // Function prototype

int main()
{
   const int ARRAY_SIZE = 8;
   int collection[ARRAY_SIZE] = {5, 10, 15, 20, 25, 30, 35, 40};

   for (int index = 0; index < ARRAY_SIZE; index++)
      showValue(collection[index]);
   cout << endl;
   return 0;
}

/***************************************
 *              showValue              *
 * This function displays the integer *
 * value passed to its num parameter. *
 ***************************************/
void showValue(int num)
{
   cout << num << " ";
}
```

Program Output

```
5 10 15 20 25 30 35 40
```

Because the `showValue` function simply displays the contents of `num` and doesn't need to work directly with the array elements themselves, the array elements are passed to it by value. If the function needed to access the original array elements, they would be passed by reference.

If the function were written to accept the entire array as an argument, the parameter would be set up differently. In the following function definition, the parameter `nums` is followed by an empty set of brackets. This indicates that the argument will be an entire array, not a single value.

```
void showValues (int nums[], int size)
{
   for (int index = 0; index < size; index++)
      cout << nums[index] << " ";
   cout << endl;
}
```

Notice that along with the array containing the values, the size of the array is also passed to `showValues`. This is so it will know how many values there are to process.

Notice also that there is no size declarator inside the brackets of `nums`. This is because `nums` is not actually an array—it's a special variable that accepts the *address* of an array. When an entire array is passed to a function, it is not passed by value. Imagine the CPU time and memory that would be necessary if a copy of a 10,000-element array were created each time it was passed to a function! Instead, only the starting memory address of the array is passed. This is similar to passing a variable to a function by reference, except that in this case no `&` is used. Program 8-15 illustrates how function `showValues` receives the address of an entire array so it can access and display the contents of all its elements.

Program 8-15

```
// This program shows how to pass an entire array to a function.
#include <iostream>
using namespace std;

void showValues(int intArray[], int size); // Function prototype

int main()
{
   const int ARRAY_SIZE = 8;
   int collection[ARRAY_SIZE] = {5, 10, 15, 20, 25, 30, 35, 40};

   cout << "The array contains the values\n";
   showValues(collection, ARRAY_SIZE);
   return 0;
}

/**************************************************************
 *                          showValues                        *
 * This function displays the contents of an integer array    *
 * when passed the array's address and its size as arguments.*
 **************************************************************/
void showValues (int nums[], int size)
{
   for (int index = 0; index < size; index++)
      cout << nums[index] << "  ";
   cout << endl;
}
```

Program Output

```
The array contains the values
5  10  15  20  25  30  35  40
```

Look closely at the showValues prototype in line 5 and function header in line 22. In both cases a pair of braces follows the first parameter name. This lets the program know that this parameter accepts the address of an array. If the function prototype had not used parameter names, it would have looked like this:

```
void showValues(int [], int);
```

This would still have indicated that the first showValues parameter receives the address of an integer array and the second parameter receives a single integer value.

Look also at how the showValues function is called in line 13 of the program with the following statement:

```
showValues(collection, ARRAY_SIZE);
```

The first argument is the name of the array being passed to the function. Remember, in C++ the name of an array without brackets and a subscript is actually the beginning address of the array. In this function call, the address of the collection array is being passed to the function. The second argument is the size of the array.

In the showValues function, the beginning address of the collection array is copied into the nums parameter variable. The nums variable is then used to reference the collection array. Figure 8-13 illustrates the relationship between the collection array and the nums parameter variable. When nums[0] is displayed, it is actually the contents of collection[0] that appears on the screen.

Figure 8-13

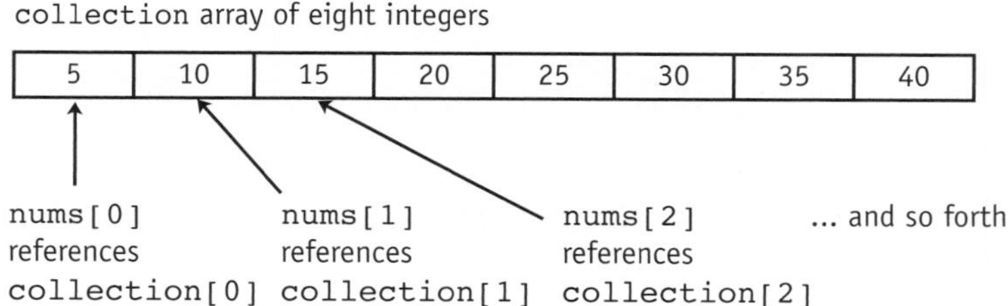

NOTE: Although nums is not a reference variable, it works like one.

The nums parameter variable in the showValues function can accept the address of any integer array and can use it to reference that array. So, we can use the showValues function to display the contents of any integer array by passing the name of the array and its size as arguments. Program 8-16 uses this function to display the contents of two different arrays. Notice that they do not have to be the same size. Notice also the use of the typedef statement in this program. It makes the name arrayType an alias for an array of integers. This name is then used in the showValues prototype and function header, instead of using int[], to indicate that the first parameter receives the starting address of an int array.

Program 8-16

```
1 // This program demonstrates passing different arrays to a function.
2 #include <iostream>
3 using namespace std;
4
5 // Declare arrayType to be an alias for an array of ints
6 typedef int arrayType[];
7
8 void showValues(arrayType, int);  // Function prototype
9
10 int main()
11 {
12    const int SIZE1 = 8;
13    const int SIZE2 = 5;
14    int set1[] = {5, 10, 15, 20, 25, 30, 35, 40};
15    int set2[] = {2, 4, 6, 8, 10};
16
17    cout << "Here are the values stored in array set1: ";
18    showValues(set1, SIZE1);       // Pass set 1 to showValues
19
20    cout << "Here are the values stored in array set2: ";
21    showValues(set2, SIZE2);       // Pass set 2 to showValues
22    return 0;
23 }
24
25 /**************************************************************
26  *                         showValues                          *
27  * This function displays the contents of an integer array    *
28  * when passed the array's address and its size as arguments.*
29  **************************************************************/
30 void showValues (arrayType nums, int size)
31 {
32    for (int index = 0; index < size; index++)
33       cout << nums[index] << " ";
34    cout << endl;
35 }
```

Program Output

```
Here are the values stored in array set1: 5 10 15 20 25 30 35 40
Here are the values stored in array set2: 2 4 6 8 10
```

Notice that when `set1` and `set2` are declared in lines 14 and 15, no size declarator is used. We could have used one, but recall that a size declarator is not required when an initialization list is used.

Recall also, from Chapter 6, that when a reference variable is used as a parameter, it gives the function access to the original argument. Any changes made to the reference variable are actually performed on the argument referenced by the variable. Array parameters work very much like reference variables. They give the function direct access to the original array. Any changes made to the array parameter are actually made to the original array used as the argument. The function `doubleArray` in Program 8-17 uses this capability to double the contents of each element in the array.

Program 8-17

```
// This program uses a function to double the value of
// each element of an array.
#include <iostream>
using namespace std;

// Declare arrayType to be an alias for an array of ints
typedef int arrayType[];

// Function prototypes
void doubleArray(arrayType, int);
void showValues (arrayType, int);

int main()
{
   const int ARRAY_SIZE = 7;
   arrayType set = {1, 2, 3, 4, 5, 6, 7};

   // Display the original values
   cout << "The arrays values are:\n";
   showValues(set, ARRAY_SIZE);

   // Double the values in the array
   doubleArray(set, ARRAY_SIZE);

   // Display the new values
   cout << "\nAfter calling doubleArray, the values are:\n";
   showValues(set, ARRAY_SIZE);
   cout << endl;
   return 0;
}

/****************************************************
 *                    doubleArray                   *
 * This function doubles the value of each element *
 * in the array whose address is passed to it.      *
 ****************************************************/
void doubleArray(arrayType nums, int size)
{
   for (int index = 0; index < size; index++)
      nums[index] *= 2;
}

/**********************************************************
 *                       showValues                       *
 * This function displays the contents of an int array   *
 * when passed the array's address and size as arguments.*
 **********************************************************/
void showValues (arrayType nums, int size)
{
   for (int index = 0; index < size; index++)
      cout << nums[index] << " ";
   cout << endl;
}
```

(program continues)

Program 8-17 *(continued)*

Program Output

```
The array values are:
1 2 3 4 5 6 7

After calling doubleArray, the values are:
2 4 6 8 10 12 14
```

Notice that in line 16 of Program 8-17 the `set` array is defined to be type `arrayType` rather than `int set[]` or `int set[ARRAY_SIZE]`, although it could be defined either of these ways also. As in Program 8-16, it is not necessary to indicate the size of the array because it is initialized with an initialization list at the time it is created.

Notice also that in the `typedef` statement in line 7, the `showValues` prototype in line 11, and the `showValues` function header in line 48, there is no `&`. Remember, when you pass an array to a function you do not use an `&`.

NOTE: In C++ when a regular variable is passed to a function and an `&` precedes its name, it means that the function is receiving a reference to the memory address where a variable is stored. An array name, however, is already a memory address. That is, instead of holding a value, it holds the starting address of where the array is located in memory. Therefore, an `&` should *not* be used with it.

Using `const` Array Parameters

Sometimes you want a function to be able to modify the contents of an array that is passed to it as an argument, but other times you don't. In Program 8-17, for example, we needed the `doubleArray` function to be able to change the values in the array, but we did not want the `showValues` function to change them. You can prevent a function that should not change an array passed to it from accidentally making changes to it by using the `const` key word. Here is what the `showValues` prototype and function header would look like with a `const` array parameter:

```
void showValues(const arrayType, int)            // Function prototype
void showValues(const arrayType nums, int size)  // Function header
```

Nothing in the call to the function or in the function code changes when you use a `const` array parameter. Only the function prototype and header are affected. When an array parameter is declared as `const`, the function is not allowed to make changes to the array's contents. If a statement in the function attempts to modify the array, an error will occur at compile time. As a precaution, it is a good idea to always use a `const` array parameter in any function that is not intended to modify its array argument.

Some Useful Array Functions

Section 8.5 introduced you to algorithms such as summing an array and finding the highest and lowest values in an array. Now we can write general-purpose functions that perform these operations. Program 8-18, which is a modification of Program 8-10, uses the functions `sumArray`, `getHighest`, and `getLowest`. Because none of these functions should make changes to the array, they all have `const` array parameters.

Program 8-18

```
// This program passes an array filled with sales data
// to functions which find and return its total, highest,
// and lowest values. The functions should not change the
// array, so they each use a const array parameter.
#include <iostream>
#include <iomanip>
using namespace std;

// Function prototypes
double sumArray  (const double[], int);
double getHighest(const double[], int);
double getLowest (const double[], int);

int main()
{
   const int NUM_DAYS = 5;     // Number of days
   double sales[NUM_DAYS],     // Holds the daily sales amounts
          total,               // Holds the week's total sales
          average,             // Holds the average daily sales
          highest,             // Holds the highest daily sales
          lowest;              // Holds the lowest daily sales

   // Get the sales data
   cout << "Enter the sales for this week.\n";
   for (int day = 0; day < NUM_DAYS; day++)
   {  cout << "Day " << (day+1) <<": ";
      cin  >> sales[day];
   }

   // Get total sales and compute average sales
   total = sumArray(sales, NUM_DAYS);
   average = total / NUM_DAYS;

   // Get highest and lowest sales amounts
   highest = getHighest(sales, NUM_DAYS);
   lowest = getLowest(sales, NUM_DAYS);

   // Display results
   cout << fixed << showpoint << setprecision(2) << endl;
   cout << "The total sales are          $"
        << setw(9) << total   << endl;
   cout << "The average sales amount is $"
        << setw(9) << average << endl;
```

(program continues)

Program 8-18 *(continued)*

```
   cout << "The highest sales amount is $"
        << setw(9) << highest << endl;
   cout << "The lowest sales amount  is $"
        << setw(9) << lowest  << endl;
   return 0;
}

/****************************************************
 *                   sumArray                       *
 * This function computes and returns the sum of the  *
 * values in the array whose address is passed to it. *
 ****************************************************/
double sumArray(const double array[], int size)
{
   double total = 0.0;  // Accumulator

   for (int count = 0; count < size; count++)
      total += array[count];
   return total;
}

/****************************************************
 *                  getHighest                      *
 * This function finds and returns the largest value  *
 * in the array whose address is passed to it.        *
 ****************************************************/
double getHighest(const double array[], int size)
{
   double highest = array[0];

   for (int count = 1; count < size; count++)
   {  if (array[count] > highest)
         highest = array[count];
   }
   return highest;
}

/****************************************************
 *                  getLowest                       *
 * This function finds and returns the smallest value *
 * in the array whose address is passed to it.        *
 ****************************************************/
double getLowest(const double array[], int size)
{
   double lowest = array[0];

   for (int count = 1; count < size; count++)
   {  if (array[count] < lowest)
         lowest = array[count];
   }
   return lowest;
}
```

(program continues)

Program 8-18 *(continued)*

Program Output with Example Input Shown in Bold
```
Enter the sales for this week.
Day 1: 2698.72[Enter]
Day 2: 3757.29[Enter]
Day 3: 1109.67[Enter]
Day 4: 2498.65[Enter]
Day 5: 1489.87[Enter]
The total sales are          $ 11554.20
The average sales amount is $  2310.84
The highest sales amount is $  3757.29
The lowest sales amount  is $  1109.67
```

Checkpoint

8.15 Write a `typedef` statement that makes the name `TenInts` an alias for an array that holds 10 integers.

8.16 When an array name is passed to a function, what is actually being passed?

8.17 What is the output of the following program? (You may need to consult the ASCII table in Appendix A.)

```
#include <iostream>
using namespace std;

// Function prototypes
void fillArray(char [], int)
void showArray(const char [], int)

int main ()
{  char prodCode[8] = {'0', '0', '0', '0', '0', '0', '0', '0'};

   fillArray(prodCode,8);
   showArray(prodCode,8);
   return 0;
}

// Definition of function fillArray
// (Hint: 65 is the ASCII code for 'A'.)
void fillArray(char arr[], int size)
{  char code = 65;
   for (int k = 0; k < size; code++, k++)
      arr[k] = code;
}

// Definition of function showArray
void showArray(const char codes[], int size)
{  for (int k = 0; k < size; k++)
      cout << codes[k];
}
```

8.18 The following program skeleton, when completed, will ask the user to enter 10 integers, which are stored in an array. The function `avgArray`, which you must write, should calculate and return the average of the numbers entered.

```
#include <iostream>
using namespace std;

// Write the avgArray function prototype here.
// It should have a const array parameter.

int main()
{
   const int SIZE = 10;
   int userNums[SIZE];

   cout << "Enter 10 numbers: ";
   for (int count = 0; count < SIZE; count++)
   {
      cout << "#" << (count + 1) << " ";
      cin  >> userNums[count];
   }
   cout << "The average of those numbers is ";
   cout << avgArray(userNums, SIZE) << endl;
   return 0;
}

// Write the avgArray function here.
```

8.9 Two-Dimensional Arrays

CONCEPT: A two-dimensional array is like several identical arrays put together. It is useful for storing multiple sets of data.

VideoNote
Two-Dimensional Arrays

An array is useful for storing and working with a set of data. Sometimes, though, it's necessary to work with multiple sets of data. For example, in a grade-averaging program a teacher might record all of one student's test scores in an array of `doubles`. If the teacher has 30 students, that means 30 arrays of `doubles` will be needed to record the scores for the entire class. Instead of defining 30 individual arrays, however, it would be better to define a two-dimensional array.

The arrays that you have studied so far are called *one-dimensional arrays* because they can only hold one set of data. *Two-dimensional arrays*, which are also called *2D arrays*, can hold multiple sets of data. It's best to think of a two-dimensional array as a table having rows and columns of elements, as shown in Figure 8-14. This figure shows an array of test scores that has three rows and four columns. Notice that the three rows are numbered 0 through 2 and the four columns are numbered 0 through 3. There are a total of 12 elements in the array.

Figure 8-14

	Column 0	Column 1	Column 2	Column 3
Row 0	score[0][0]	score[0][1]	score[0][2]	score[0][3]
Row 1	score[1][0]	score[1][1]	score[1][2]	score[1][3]
Row 2	score[2][0]	score[2][1]	score[2][2]	score[2][3]

To define a two-dimensional array, two size declarators are required. The first one is for the number of rows and the second one is for the number of columns. Here is an example definition of a two-dimensional array with three rows and four columns:

```
double score[3][4];
```

Rows Columns

Notice that each number is enclosed in its own set of brackets.

For processing the information in a two-dimensional array, each element has two subscripts, one for its row and another for its column. In the `score` array, the elements in row 0 are referenced as

```
score[0][0]
score[0][1]
score[0][2]
score[0][3]
```

The elements in row 1 are

```
score[1][0]
score[1][1]
score[1][2]
score[1][3]
```

And the elements in row 2 are

```
score[2][0]
score[2][1]
score[2][2]
score[2][3]
```

The subscripted references are used in a program just like the references to elements in a one-dimensional array. For example, the following statement assigns the value 92.25 to the element at row 2, column 1 of the `score` array:

```
score[2][1] = 92.25;
```

And the following statement displays the element at row 0, column 2:

```
cout << score[0][2];
```

Programs that cycle through each element of a two-dimensional array usually do so with nested loops. Program 8-19 shows an example.

Program 8-19

```
// This program uses a two-dimensional array. The
// data stored in the array is read in from a file.
#include <iostream>
#include <fstream>
#include <iomanip>
using namespace std;

int main()
{
   const int NUM_DIVS = 3:             // Number of divisions
   const int NUM_QTRS = 4:             // Number of quarters
   double sales[NUM_DIVS][NUM_QTRS];  // 2D array with 3 rows & 4 columns
   double totalSales = 0;             // Accumulates total sales
   int div, qtr;                      // Loop counters
   ifstream datafile;                 // Used to read data from a file

   datafile.open("sales2.dat");
   if (!datafile)
      cout << "Error opening data file.\n";
   else
   {
      cout << fixed << showpoint << setprecision(2);
      cout << "Quarterly Sales by Division\n\n";

      // Nested loops are used to fill the array with quarterly
      // sales figures for each division and to display the data
      for (div = 0; div < NUM_DIVS; div++)
      {  for (qtr = 0; qtr < NUM_QTRS; qtr++)
         {
            cout << "Division "  << (div + 1)
                 << ", Quarter " << (qtr + 1) << ": $";
            datafile >> sales[div][qtr];
            cout << sales[div][qtr] << endl;
         }
         cout << endl;                // Print blank line
      }
      datafile.close();

      // Nested loops are used to add all the elements
      for (div = 0; div < NUM_DIVS; div++)
      {  for (qtr = 0; qtr < NUM_QTRS; qtr++)
            totalSales += sales[div][qtr];
      }
      // Display the total
      cout << "The total sales for the company are: $";
      cout << totalSales << endl;
   }
   return 0;
}
```

(program continues)

Program 8-19 *(continued)*

Program Output

```
Quarterly Sales by Division

Division 1, Quarter 1: $31569.45
Division 1, Quarter 2: $29654.23
Division 1, Quarter 3: $32982.54
Division 1, Quarter 4: $39651.21

Division 2, Quarter 1: $56321.02
Division 2, Quarter 2: $54128.63
Division 2, Quarter 3: $41235.85
Division 2, Quarter 4: $54652.33

Division 3, Quarter 1: $29654.35
Division 3, Quarter 2: $28963.32
Division 3, Quarter 3: $25353.55
Division 3, Quarter 4: $32615.88

The total sales for the company are: $456782.34
```

As with one-dimensional arrays, two-dimensional arrays can be initialized when they are created. When initializing a two-dimensional array, it helps to enclose each row's initialization list in a set of braces. Here is an example:

```
int hours[3][2] = {{8, 5}, {7, 9}, {6, 3}};
```

The same statement could also be written as

```
int hours[3][2] = {{8, 5},
                   {7, 9},
                   {6, 3}};
```

In either case, the values are assigned to hours in the following manner:

```
hours[0][0] is set to 8
hours[0][1] is set to 5
hours[1][0] is set to 7
hours[1][1] is set to 9
hours[2][0] is set to 6
hours[2][1] is set to 3
```

Figure 8-15 illustrates the initialization.

Figure 8-15

	Column 0	Column 1
Row 0	8	5
Row 1	7	9
Row 2	6	3

The extra braces that enclose each row's initialization list are optional. The following statements both perform the same initialization:

```
int hours[3][2] = {{8, 5}, {7, 9}, {6, 3}};
int hours[3][2] = {8, 5, 7, 9, 6, 3};
```

Because the extra braces visually separate each row, however, it's a good idea to use them. In addition, the braces give you the ability to leave out initializers within a row without omitting the initializers for the rows that follow it. For instance, look at the following array definition:

```
int table[3][2] = {{1}, {3, 4}, {5}};
```

`table[0][0]` is initialized to 1, `table[1][0]` is initialized to 3, `table[1][1]` is initialized to 4, and `table[2][0]` is initialized to 5. The uninitialized elements (in this case `table[0][1]` and `table[2][1]`) are automatically set to zero.

Passing Two-Dimensional Arrays to Functions

Program 8-20 illustrates how to pass a two-dimensional array to a function. When a two-dimensional array is passed to a function, the parameter type must contain a size declarator for the number of columns. C++ needs this information to correctly translate a subscripted array reference, such as `table[2][1]`, to the address in memory where that element is stored. Here is the header for the function `showArray`, from Program 8-20:

```
void showArray(const int array[][NUM_COLS], int numRows)
```

The `showArray` function can accept any two-dimensional integer array, as long as it has four columns. In Program 8-20, the contents of two separate arrays are displayed by this function.

Program 8-20

```
// This program demonstrates how to pass
// a two-dimensional array to a function.
#include <iostream>
#include <iomanip>
using namespace std;

const int NUM_COLS  = 4;     // Number of columns in each array
const int TBL1_ROWS = 3;     // Number of rows in table1
const int TBL2_ROWS = 4;     // Number of rows in table2

void showArray(const int [][NUM_COLS], int); // Function prototype

int main()
{
   int table1[TBL1_ROWS][NUM_COLS] = { {1,  2,  3,  4},
                                       {5,  6,  7,  8},
                                       {9, 10, 11, 12} };
```

(program continues)

Program 8-20 *(continued)*

```
   int table2[TBL2_ROWS][NUM_COLS] = { { 10,  20,  30,  40},
                                       { 50,  60,  70,  80},
                                       { 90, 100, 110, 120},
                                       {130, 140, 150, 160} };

   cout << "The contents of table1 are:\n";
   showArray(table1, TBL1_ROWS);
   cout << "\nThe contents of table2 are:\n";
   showArray(table2, TBL2_ROWS);
   return 0;
}

/*****************************************************************
 *                          showArray                            *
 * This function displays the contents of a 2-D integer array.  *
 * Its first parameter receives the address of the array, which *
 * has NUM_COLS columns. The second parameter receives the      *
 * number of rows in the array.                                 *
 *****************************************************************/
void showArray(int const array[][NUM_COLS], int numRows)
{
   for (int row = 0; row < numRows; row++)
   {  for (int col = 0; col < NUM_COLS; col++)
      {
         cout << setw(5) << array[row][col] << " ";
      }
      cout << endl;
   }
}
```

Program Output

```
The contents of table1 are:
    1     2     3     4
    5     6     7     8
    9    10    11    12

The contents of table2 are:
   10    20    30    40
   50    60    70    80
   90   100   110   120
  130   140   150   160
```

C++ requires the columns to be specified in the function prototype and header because of the way two-dimensional arrays are stored in memory. One row actually follows another, as shown in Figure 8-16.

Figure 8-16

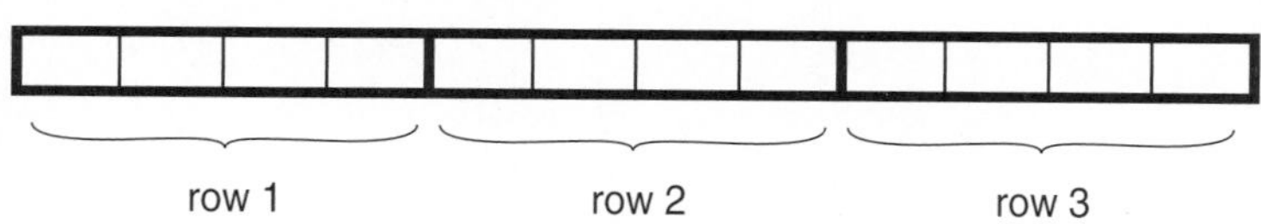

When the compiler generates code for accessing the elements of a two-dimensional array, it needs to know how many bytes separate the rows in memory. The number of columns is a critical factor in this calculation.

This required column information can also be provided with a `typedef` statement. Here is how a `typedef` declaration for a two-dimensional array might look:

```
typedef int intTable[][4];
```

This statement makes `intTable` an alias for a two-dimensional array with any number of rows and four columns. If this `typedef` statement had been included in Program 8-20, the prototype for the `showArray` function could then have been written as

```
void showArray(intTable, int);
```

and its function header could have been written as

```
void showArray(intTable array, int numRows)
```

Summing All the Elements of a Two-Dimensional Array

In Program 8-19 we summed all the data in a two-dimensional array by using a nested loop and adding the contents of each array element to an accumulator. You will recall that the code to sum the array elements looked like this:

```
for (div = 0; div < NUM_DIVS; div++)
{  for (qtr = 0; qtr < NUM_QTRS; qtr++)
      totalSales += sales[div][qtr];
}
```

`NUM_DIVS` was the number of rows in the array and `NUM_QTRS` was the number of columns. The outer loop iterates once for each row in the array and the inner loop iterates once for each column in the row.

Summing the Rows of a Two-Dimensional Array

Sometimes, however, you need to calculate separately the sum of each row in a two-dimensional array. For example, suppose a two-dimensional array is used to hold a set of test scores for a group of students. Each row in the array is a set of scores for one student. To sum the scores for each student, you again use a pair of nested loops. The inner loop is used to add all the scores in a row, that is, all the scores for one student. The outer loop is executed once for each student. But now the accumulator must be set back to 0 for *each* row, before you begin accumulating its values. Also the sum of the row needs to be stored somewhere or displayed before beginning a new row. Here is an example.

```
const int NUM_STUDENTS = 3;       // Number of students
const int NUM_SCORES = 5;         // Number of test scores
double total;                     // Accumulator
double average;                   // Holds a given student's average
double scores[NUM_STUDENTS][NUM_SCORES] = {{88, 97, 79, 86, 94},
                                           {86, 91, 78, 79, 84},
                                           {82, 73, 77, 82, 89}};
```

```
// Sum each student's test scores so his or her
// average can be calculated and displayed
for (int row = 0; row < NUM_STUDENTS; row ++)
{
   // Reset accumulator to 0 for this student
   total = 0;

   // Sum a row
   for (int col = 0; col < NUM_SCORES; col++)
      total += scores[row][col];

   // Compute and display the average for this student
   average = total / NUM_SCORES;
   cout << "Score average for student "
        << (row + 1) << " is " << average << endl;
}
```

Summing the Columns of a Two-Dimensional Array

Sometimes you may need to calculate the sum of each column in a two-dimensional array. Using the array of test scores from the previous example, suppose you wish to calculate the class average for each of the tests, rather that for each student. To do this, you must calculate the average of each column in the array. As in the previous example, this is accomplished with a set of nested loops. However, now the order of the two loops is reversed. The inner loop is used to add all the scores in a column, that is, all the scores for one test. The outer loop is executed once for each test. The following code illustrates this.

```
const int NUM_STUDENTS = 3;    // Number of students
const int NUM_SCORES = 5;      // Number of test scores
double total;                  // Accumulator
double average;                // Holds average score on a given test
double scores[NUM_STUDENTS][NUM_SCORES] = {{88, 97, 79, 86, 94},
                                           {86, 91, 78, 79, 84},
                                           {82, 73, 77, 82, 89}};
// Calculate and display the class
// average for each test
for (int col = 0; col < NUM_SCORES; col++)
{
   // Reset accumulator to 0 for this test
   total = 0;

   // Sum a column
   for (int row = 0; row < NUM_STUDENTS; row++)
       total += scores[row][col];
   // Compute and display the class average for this test
   average = total / NUM_STUDENTS;
   cout << "Class average for test " << (col + 1)
        << " is " << average << endl;
}
```

8.10 Arrays with Three or More Dimensions

CONCEPT: C++ permits arrays to have multiple dimensions.

C++ allows you to create arrays with virtually any number of dimensions. Here is an example of a three-dimensional (3D) array definition:

```
double seat[3][5][8];
```

This array can be thought of as three sets of five rows, with each row having eight elements. The array might be used, for example, to store the price of seats in an auditorium that has three sections of seats, with five rows of eight seats in each section.

Figure 8-17 illustrates the concept of a three-dimensional array as "pages" of two-dimensional arrays.

Figure 8-17

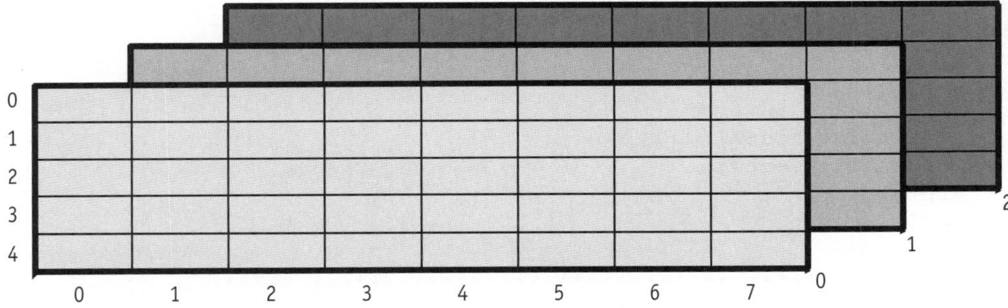

Arrays with more than three dimensions are difficult to visualize but can be useful in some programming problems.

When writing functions that accept multidimensional arrays as arguments, you must explicitely state all but the first dimension in the parameter list. If the `seat` array, defined here, were passed to a `displaySeats` function, its prototype and function header might look like the following:

```
// Function prototype
void displaySeats(double [][5][8], int);

// Function header
void displaySeats(double array[][5][8], int numGroups);
```

As with one-dimensional and two-dimensional arrays, the parameter lists can be simplified if a `typedef` statement is used to create an alias for the array type. This is demonstrated in Program 8-21, which uses the `seat` array to store theater seat prices. The information to populate the array is read in from a file. The information on number of sections, number of rows in a section, and number of seats in a row is stored in global constants, rather than being passed to the functions.

Program 8-21

```
// This program stores and displays theater seat prices.
// It demonstrates how to pass a 3-dimensional array to a function.
// The data is read in from a file.
#include <iostream>
#include <fstream>
#include <iomanip>
using namespace std;

const int NUM_SECTIONS = 3,
          ROWS_IN_SECTION = 5,
          SEATS_IN_ROW = 8;

typedef double seatTable[][ROWS_IN_SECTION][SEATS_IN_ROW];

// Function prototypes
void fillArray(seatTable);
void showArray(const seatTable);

int main()
{
   // Define 3-D array to hold seat prices
   double seats[NUM_SECTIONS][ROWS_IN_SECTION][SEATS_IN_ROW];

   fillArray(seats);
   showArray(seats);
   return 0;
}

/*****************************************************
 *                    fillArray                      *
 * This function receives the address of a 3-D array *
 * and fills it with data read in from a file.       *
 *****************************************************/
void fillArray(seatTable array)
{
   ifstream dataIn;
   dataIn.open("seats.dat");

   if (!dataIn)
      cout << "Error opening file.\n";
   else
   {  for (int section = 0; section < NUM_SECTIONS; section++)
         for (int row = 0; row < ROWS_IN_SECTION; row++)
            for (int seat = 0; seat < SEATS_IN_ROW; seat++)
               dataIn >> array[section][row][seat];

      dataIn.close();
   }
}
```

(program continues)

Program 8-21 *(continued)*

```
/****************************************************
 *                  showArray                       *
 * This function displays the contents of the 3-D   *
 * array of doubles whose address is passed to it.  *
 ****************************************************/
void showArray(const seatTable array)
{
   cout << fixed << showpoint << setprecision(2);

   for (int section = 0; section < NUM_SECTIONS; section++)
   {
      cout << "\n\nSection" << (section+1);
      for (int row = 0; row < ROWS_IN_SECTION; row++)
      {
         cout << "\nRow " << (row+1) << ": ";
         for (int seat = 0; seat < SEATS_IN_ROW; seat++)
            cout << setw(7) << array[section][row][seat];
      }
   }
   cout << endl;
}
```

Program Output

```
Section1
Row 1:   18.00  18.00  18.00  18.00  18.00  18.00  18.00  18.00
Row 2:   15.00  15.00  15.00  15.00  15.00  15.00  15.00  15.00
Row 3:   15.00  15.00  15.00  15.00  15.00  15.00  15.00  15.00
Row 4:   15.00  15.00  15.00  15.00  15.00  15.00  15.00  15.00
Row 5:   12.00  12.00  12.00  12.00  12.00  12.00  12.00  12.00

Section2
Row 1:   12.00  12.00  12.00  12.00  12.00  12.00  12.00  12.00
Row 2:   12.00  12.00  12.00  12.00  12.00  12.00  12.00  12.00
Row 3:   12.00  12.00  12.00  12.00  12.00  12.00  12.00  12.00
Row 4:   10.00  10.00  10.00  10.00  10.00  10.00  10.00  10.00
Row 5:   10.00  10.00  10.00  10.00  10.00  10.00  10.00  10.00

Section3
Row 1:    8.00   8.00  10.00  10.00  10.00  10.00   8.00   8.00
Row 2:    8.00   8.00  10.00  10.00  10.00  10.00   8.00   8.00
Row 3:    5.00   5.00   8.00   8.00   8.00   8.00   5.00   5.00
Row 4:    5.00   5.00   8.00   8.00   8.00   8.00   5.00   5.00
Row 5:    5.00   5.00   8.00   8.00   8.00   8.00   5.00   5.00
```

Checkpoint

8.19 Define a two-dimensional array of `int`s named `grades`. It should have 30 rows and 10 columns.

8.20 How many elements are in the following array?

```
double sales[6][4];
```

8.21 Write a statement that assigns the value 56893.12 to the first column of the first row of the `sales` array defined in question 8.20.

8.22 Write a statement that displays the contents of the last column of the last row of the `sales` array defined in question 8.20.

8.23 Define a two-dimensional array named `settings` large enough to hold the table of information below. Initialize the array with the values in the table.

12	24	32	21	42
14	67	87	65	90
19	1	24	12	8

8.24 Fill in the empty table below so it shows the contents of the following array:

```
int table[3][4] = {{2, 3}, {7, 9, 2}, {1}};
```


8.25 Write a function called `displayArray7`. The function should accept a two-dimensional array as an argument and display its contents on the screen. The function should work with any of the following arrays:

```
int hours[5][7];
int stamps[8][7];
int autos[12][7];
```

8.26 A DVD rental store keeps DVDs on 50 racks with 10 shelves each. Each shelf holds 25 DVDs. Define a 3D array to represent this storage system.

8.11 Vectors

CONCEPT: The Standard Template Library includes a data type called a `vector`. It is similar to a one-dimensional array, but has some advantages compared to a standard array.

The *Standard Template Library* (STL) is a collection of *programmer-defined* data types and algorithms that are available for you to use in your C++ programs. These data types and algorithms are not part of the C++ language, but were created in addition to the built-in data types. If you plan to continue your studies in the field of computer science, you should become familiar with the STL. This section introduces one of the STL data types, the `vector`.

> **NOTE:** To use vectors your program header must indicate that you are using `namespace std`, since vectors are contained within that namespace. Many older compilers do not allow namespaces or support the STL.

The data types that are defined in the STL are commonly called *containers*. They are called containers because they store and organize data. There are two types of containers in the STL: sequence containers and associative containers. A *sequence container* organizes data in a sequential fashion, similar to an array. *Associative containers* organize data with keys, which allow rapid, random access to elements stored in the container.

The `vector` data type is a sequence container that is like a one-dimensional array in the following ways:

- A vector holds a sequence of values, or elements.
- A vector stores its elements in contiguous memory locations.
- You can use the array subscript operator `[]` to access individual elements in the vector.

However, a vector offers several advantages over arrays. Here are just a few:

- You do not have to declare the number of elements that the vector will have.
- If you add a value to a vector that is already full, the vector will automatically increase its size to accommodate the new value.
- Vectors can report the number of elements they contain.

Defining a Vector

To use vectors in your program, you must include the `vector` header file with the following statement:

```
#include <vector>
```

To create a vector object you must use a statement whose syntax is somewhat different from the syntax used in defining a regular variable or array. Here is an example:

```
vector<int> numbers;
```

This statement defines `numbers` as a vector of `int`s. Notice that the data type is enclosed in angled brackets, immediately after the word `vector`. Because a vector expands in size as you add values to it, there is no need to declare a size. However, you can declare a starting size, if you prefer. Here is an example:

```
vector<int> numbers(10);
```

This statement defines `numbers` as a vector of 10 `int`s, but this is only a starting size. Its size will expand if you add more than 10 values to it.

NOTE: Notice that if you specify a starting size for a vector, the size declarator is enclosed in parentheses, not square brackets.

When you specify a starting size for a vector, you may also specify an initialization value. The initialization value is copied to each element. Here is an example:

```
vector<int> numbers(10, 2);
```

In this statement, `numbers` is defined as a vector of 10 `int`s. Each element in `numbers` is initialized to the value 2.

You may also initialize a vector with the values in another vector. For example, if set1 is a vector of ints that already has values in it, the following statement will create a new vector, named set2, which is an exact copy of set1.

```
vector<int> set2(set1);
```

After this statement executes, the vector set2 will have the same number of elements and hold the same set of values as set1.

Table 8-2 summarizes the vector definition procedures we have discussed.

Table 8-2 Example Vector Definitions

Definition Format	Description
`vector<double> values2(values1);`	Defines values2 as a vector of doubles. All the elements of values1, which is also a vector of doubles, are copied to value2.
`vector<int> scores(15);`	Defines scores as a vector of 15 ints.
`vector<char> letters(25, 'A');`	Defines letters as a vector of 25 characters. Each element is initialized with 'A'.
`vector<string> names;`	Defines names as an empty vector of string objects.

Storing and Retrieving Values in a Vector

To store a value in an element that already exists in a vector, you may use the array subscript operator [ ]. Program 8-22, which is a modification of Program 8-13, illustrates this.

Program 8-22

```
// This program stores employee hours worked and hourly pay rates
// in vectors.
#include <iostream>
#include <iomanip>
#include <vector>                     // Needed to use vectors
using namespace std;

int main()
{
   const int NUM_EMPS = 5;            // Number of employees
   vector <int> hours(NUM_EMPS);      // Define a vector of integers
   vector <double> payRate(NUM_EMPS); // Define a vector of doubles
   double grossPay;
   int index;                         // Loop counter

   // Get employee work data
   cout << "Enter the hours worked and hourly pay rates of "
        << NUM_EMPS << " employees. \n";

```

(program continues)

Program 8-22 *(continued)*

```
20     for (index = 0; index < NUM_EMPS; index++)
21     {
22        cout << "Hours worked by employee #" << (index + 1) << ": ";
23        cin  >> hours[index];
24        cout << "Hourly pay rate for employee #" << (index + 1) << ": ";
25        cin  >> payRate[index];
26     }
27     // Display each employee's gross pay
28     cout << "\nHere is the gross pay for each employee:\n";
29     cout << fixed << showpoint << setprecision(2);
30     for (index = 0; index < NUM_EMPS; index++)
31     {
32        grossPay = hours[index] * payRate[index];
33        cout << "Employee #" << (index + 1);
34        cout << ": $" << setw(7) << grossPay << endl;
35     }
36     return 0;
37  }
```

Program Output with Example Input Shown in Bold

```
Enter the hours worked and hourly pay rates of 5 employees.
Hours worked by employee #1: 10[Enter]
Hourly pay rate for employee #1: 9.75[Enter]
Hours worked by employee #2: 15[Enter]
Hourly pay rate for employee #2: 8.62[Enter]
Hours worked by employee #3: 20[Enter]
Hourly pay rate for employee #3: 10.50[Enter]
Hours worked by employee #4: 40[Enter]
Hourly pay rate for employee #4: 18.75[Enter]
Hours worked by employee #5: 40[Enter]
Hourly pay rate for employee #5: 15.65[Enter]

Here is the gross pay for each employee:
Employee #1: $  97.50
Employee #2: $ 129.30
Employee #3: $ 210.00
Employee #4: $ 750.00
Employee #5: $ 626.00
```

Notice that Program 8-22 uses the following statements in lines 11 and 12 to define two vectors:

```
vector<int> hours(NUM_EMPS);         // Define a vector of integers
vector<double> payRate(NUM_EMPS);    // Define a vector of doubles
```

Because the named constant `NUM_EMPS` equals 5, both vectors are defined with the starting size 5. The program uses the following loop in lines 20 through 26 to store a value in each element of both vectors:

```
for (index = 0; index < NUM_EMPS; index++)
{
   cout << "Hours worked by employee #" << (index + 1) << ": ";
   cin  >> hours[index];
   cout << "Hourly pay rate for employee #" << (index + 1) << ": ";
   cin  >> payRate[index];
}
```

Because the values entered by the user are being stored in vector elements that already exist, the program uses the array subscript operator `[]`, as shown in the following statements which appear in lines 23 and 25:

```
cin >> hours[index];
cin >> payRate[index];
```

Using the `push_back` Member Function

You cannot, however, use the `[]` operator to access a vector element that does not yet exist. To store a value in a vector that does not have a starting size, or that is already full, you should use the `push_back` member function. This function accepts a value as an argument, and stores it in a new element placed at the end of the vector. (It "pushes" the value at the "back" of the vector.) Here is an example that uses the `push_back` function to add an element to a vector of `int`s named `numbers`.

```
numbers.push_back(25);
```

This statement creates a new element holding 25 and places it at the end of `numbers`. If `numbers` previously had no elements, the new element becomes its single element.

Program 8-23 is a modification of Program 8-22. This version, however, allows the user to specify the number of employees. The two vectors, `hours` and `payRate`, are defined without starting sizes. Because these vectors have no starting elements, the `push_back` member function is used to store values in them.

Program 8-23

```
// This program stores employee hours worked and hourly pay rates
// in two vectors. It demonstrates the use of the push_back member
// function to add new elements to the vectors.
#include <iostream>
#include <iomanip>
#include <vector>                    // Needed to use vectors
using namespace std;

int main()
{
   vector<int> hours;                // hours is an empty integer vector
   vector<double> payRate;           // payRate is an empty double vector
   double grossPay;
   int numEmployees;                 // Number of employees
   int index;                        // Loop counter

   // Get the number of employees
   cout << "How many employees do you have? ";
   cin  >> numEmployees;

```

(program continues)

Program 8-23 *(continued)*

```
21     // Input the payroll data
22     cout << "Enter the hours worked and hourly pay rates of the "
23          << numEmployees << " employees. \n";
24 
25     for (index = 0; index < numEmployees; index++)
26     {
27        int tempHours;                       // Number of hours entered
28        double tempRate;                     // Pay rate entered
29 
30        cout << "Hours worked by employee #" << (index + 1) << ": ";
31        cin  >> tempHours;
32        hours.push_back(tempHours);          // Add an element to hours
33        cout << "Hourly pay rate for employee #" << (index + 1) << ": ";
34        cin  >> tempRate;
35        payRate.push_back(tempRate);         // Add an element to payRate
36     }
37     // Display each employee's gross pay
38     cout << "\nHere is the gross pay for each employee:\n";
39     cout << fixed << showpoint << setprecision(2);
40     for (index = 0; index < numEmployees; index++)
41     {
42        grossPay = hours[index] * payRate[index];
43        cout << "Employee #" << (index + 1);
44        cout << ": $" << setw(7) << grossPay << endl;
45     }
46     return 0;
47 }
```

Program Output with Example Input Shown in Bold

```
How many employees do you have? 3[Enter]
Enter the hours worked by 3 employees and their hourly rates.
Hours worked by employee #1: 40[Enter]
Hourly pay rate for employee #1: 12.63[Enter]
Hours worked by employee #2: 25[Enter]
Hourly pay rate for employee #2: 10.35[Enter]
Hours worked by employee #3: 45[Enter]
Hourly pay rate for employee #3: 22.65[Enter]

Here is the gross pay for each employee:
Employee #1: $ 505.20
Employee #2: $ 258.75
Employee #3: $1019.25
```

Notice that the Program 8-23 loop in lines 40 through 45, which calculates and displays each employee's gross pay, uses the `[]` operator to access the elements of the `hours` and `payRate` vectors. This is possible because the first loop in lines 25 through 36 already used the `push_back` member function to create the elements in the two vectors.

Determining the Size of a Vector

Unlike arrays, vectors can report the number of elements they contain. This is accomplished with the `size` member function. Here is an example of a statement that uses the `size` member function:

```
numValues = set.size();
```

In this statement, assume that `numValues` is an `int` and `set` is a vector. After the statement executes, `numValues` will contain the number of elements in `set`.

The `size` member function is especially useful when you are writing functions that accept vectors as arguments. For example, look at the following code for the `showValues` function:

```
void showValues(vector<int> vect)
{
   for (int count = 0; count < vect.size(); count++)
      cout << vect[count] << endl;
}
```

Because the vector can report its size, this function does not need a second argument indicating the number of elements in the vector. Program 8-24 demonstrates this function.

Program 8-24

```
// This program demonstrates the vector size member function.
#include <iostream>
#include <vector>
using namespace std;

// Function prototype
void showValues(vector<int>);

int main()
{
   vector<int> values;

   // Store a series of numbers in the vector
   for (int count = 0; count < 7; count++)
      values.push_back(count * 2);

   // Display the numbers
   showValues(values);

   return 0;
}

```

(program continues)

Program 8-24 *(continued)*

```
/*****************************************************************
 *                          showValues                          *
 * This function accepts an int vector as its sole argument, and *
 * displays the value stored in each of the vector's elements.   *
 *****************************************************************/
void showValues(vector<int> vect)
{
   for (int count = 0; count < vect.size(); count++)
      cout << vect[count] << "  ";
   cout << endl;
}
```

Program Output

```
0  2  4  6  8  10  12
```

Removing Elements from a Vector

To remove the last element from a vector you can use the `pop_back` member function. The following statement removes the last element from a vector named `collection`.

```
collection.pop_back();
```

Program 8-25 demonstrates the `pop_back` function.

Program 8-25

```
// This program demonstrates the vector size,
// push_back, and pop_back member functions.
#include <iostream>
#include <vector>
using namespace std;

int main()
{
   vector<int> values;

   // Store values in the vector
   values.push_back(1);
   values.push_back(2);
   values.push_back(3);
   cout << "The size of values is " << values.size() << endl;

   // Remove a value from the vector
   cout << "Popping a value from the vector...\n";
   values.pop_back();
   cout << "The size of values is now " << values.size() << endl;

```

(program continues)

Program 8-25 *(continued)*

```
    // Now remove another value from the vector
    cout << "Popping a value from the vector...\n";
    values.pop_back();
    cout << "The size of values is now " << values.size() << endl;

    // Remove the last value from the vector
    cout << "Popping a value from the vector...\n";
    values.pop_back();
    cout << "The size of values is now " << values.size() << endl;
    return 0;
}
```

Program Output

```
The size of values is 3
Popping a value from the vector...
The size of values is now 2
Popping a value from the vector...
The size of values is now 1
Popping a value from the vector...
The size of values is now 0
```

NOTE: The `pop_back` function is a `void` function that does not return the value being removed from the vector. The following line of code will *not* work:

```
cout << "The value being removed from the vector is "
     << values.pop_back() << endl;     // Error!
```

Clearing a Vector

To completely clear the contents of a vector, use the `clear` member function, as shown in the following example:

```
numbers.clear();
```

After this statement executes, `numbers` will be cleared of all its elements. Program 8-26 demonstrates the function.

Program 8-26

```
// This program demonstrates the vector clear member function.
#include <iostream>
#include <vector>
using namespace std;

```

(program continues)

Program 8-26 *(continued)*

```
int main()
{
   vector<int> values(100);

   cout << "The values vector has "
        << values.size() << " elements.\n";
   cout << "I will call the clear member function...\n";
   values.clear();
   cout << "Now the values vector has "
        << values.size() << " elements.\n";
   return 0;
}
```

Program Output

```
The values vector has 100 elements.
I will call the clear member function...
Now the values vector has 0 elements.
```

Detecting an Empty Vector

To determine if a vector is empty, use the `empty` member function. The function returns `true` if the vector is empty, and `false` if the vector has elements stored in it. Assuming `set` is a vector, here is an example of its use:

```
if (set.empty())
   cout << "No values in set.\n";
```

Program 8-27 uses a function named `avgVector`, which demonstrates the `empty` member function.

Program 8-27

```
// This program demonstrates the vector empty member function.
#include <iostream>
#include <vector>
using namespace std;

// Function prototype
double avgVector(vector<int>);

int main()
{
   vector<int> values;      // Define a vector to hold int values
   int numValues;           // Number of values to be averaged
   double average;          // Average of the stored values

   // Get the number of values to average
   cout << "How many values do you wish to average? ";
   cin  >> numValues;

```

(program continues)

Program 8-27 *(continued)*

```
   // Get the values and store them in a vector
   for (int count = 0; count < numValues; count++)
   {  int tempValue;

      cout << "Enter an integer value: ";
      cin  >> tempValue;
      values.push_back(tempValue);
   }
   // Get the average of the values and display it
   average = avgVector(values);
   cout << "Average: " << average << endl;
   return 0;
}

/*************************************************************
 *                        avgVector                          *
 * This function accepts an int vector as its argument. If   *
 * the vector contains values, the function returns the      *
 * average of those values. Otherwise, an error message is   *
 * displayed and the function returns 0.0.                   *
 *************************************************************/
double avgVector(vector<int> vect)
{
   int total = 0;          // Accumulator
   double avg = 0.0;

   if (vect.empty())       // Determine if the vector is empty
       cout << "No values to average.\n";
   else
   {  for (int count = 0; count < vect.size(); count++)
         total += vect[count];
      avg = static_cast<double>(total)/vect.size();
   }
   return avg;
}
```

Program Output with Example Input Shown in Bold

```
How many values do you wish to average? 4[Enter]
Enter an integer value: 12[Enter]
Enter an integer value: 3[Enter]
Enter an integer value: 7[Enter]
Enter an integer value: 9[Enter]
Average: 7.75
```

Program Output with Different Example Input Shown in Bold

```
How many values do you wish to average? 0[Enter]
No values to average.
Average: 0
```

Summary of Vector Member Functions

Table 8-3 provides a summary of the `vector` member functions we have discussed, as well as some additional ones.

Table 8-3 Vector Member Functions

Member Function	Description
`at(`*`position`*`)`	Returns the value of the element located at *position* in the vector. *Example:* `x = vect.at(5);` // Assigns the value of `vect[5]` to `x`.
`capacity()`	Returns the maximum number of elements that may be stored in the vector without additional memory being allocated. (This is not the same value as returned by the `size` member function). *Example*: `x = vect.capacity();` // Assigns the capacity of `vect` to `x`.
`clear()`	Clears a vector of all its elements. *Example*: `vect.clear();` // Removes all the elements from `vect`.
`empty()`	Returns `true` if the vector is empty. Otherwise, it returns `false`. *Example*: `if (vect.empty();` // If the vector is empty `cout << "The vector is empty.";` // the message is displayed.
`pop_back()`	Removes the last element from the vector. *Example*: `vect.pop_back();` // Removes the last element of `vect`, thus // reducing its size by 1.
`push_back(`*`value`*`)`	Stores a value in the last element of the vector. If the vector is full or empty, a new element is created. *Example*: `vect.push_back(7);` // Stores 7 in the last element of `vect`.
`reverse()`	Reverses the order of the elements in the vector (the last element becomes the first element, and the first element becomes the last element). *Example*: `vect.reverse();` // Reverses the order of the element in `vect`.

`resize(n)`
 	
`resize(n, value)`
	Resizes a vector to have `n` elements, where `n` is greater than the vector's current size. If the optional `value` argument is included, each of the new elements will be initialized with that value.
	Example where `vect` *currently has 4 elements:*
	`vect.resize(6,99);` // Adds two elements to the end of the vector, // each initialized to 99.

`size()`	Returns the number of elements in the vector. *Example:* `numElements = vect.size();`
`swap(`*`vector2`*`)`	Swaps the contents of the vector with the contents of *vector2*. *Example*: `vect1.swap(vect2);` // Swaps the contents of `vect1` and `vect2`.

Checkpoint

8.27 What header file must you `#include` in order to define vector objects?

8.28 Write definition statements for the following three vector objects: `frogs` (an empty vector of `int`s), `lizards` (a vector of 20 `double`s), and `toads` (a vector of 100 `char`s, with each element initialized to `'Z'`).

8.29 Define `gators` to be an empty vector of `int`s and `snakes` to be a 10-element vector of `double`s. Then write a statement that stores the value 27 in `gators` and a statement that stores the value 12.897 in element 4 of `snakes`.

8.12 Arrays of Objects*

CONCEPT: Elements of arrays can be class objects.

Earlier in this chapter you learned that all the elements in an array must be of the same data type. So far we have only used arrays of simple data types, like `int` arrays and `string` arrays. However, arrays can also hold more complex data types, such as programmer-defined structures or objects. All that is required is that each element hold a structure of the same type or an object of the same class.

Let's look at arrays of objects. You define an array of objects the same way you define any array. If, for example, a class named `Circle` has been defined, here is how you would create an array that can hold four `Circle` objects:

```
Circle circle[4];
```

The four objects are `circle[0]`, `circle[1]`, `circle[2]`, and `circle[3]`.

Notice that the name of the class is `Circle`, with a capital C. The name of the array is `circle`, with a lowercase c. You will recall from Chapter 7, that the convention is to begin the name of a class with a capital letter and the name of a variable or object with a lowercase letter. Calling a class function for one of these objects is just like calling a class function for any other object, except that a subscript must be included to identify which of the objects in the array is being referenced. For example, the following statement would call the `findArea` function of `circle[2]`.

```
circle[2].findArea();
```

Program 8-28 illustrates these ideas by creating and using an array of `Circle` class objects. Here is the definition of the `Circle` class it uses. It is a variation of the `Circle` class introduced in Chapter 7.

* This section should be skipped if Chapter 7 has not yet been covered.

Circle.h

```
// This header file contains the Circle class declaration.
#ifndef CIRCLE_H
#define CIRCLE_H
#include <cmath>

class Circle
{  private:
      double radius;                        // Circle radius
      int centerX, centerY;                 // Center coordinates

   public:
      Circle()                              // Default constructor
      {  radius = 1.0;                      // accepts no arguments
         centerX = centerY = 0;
      }

      Circle(double r)                      // Constructor 2
      {  radius = r;                        // accepts 1 argument
         centerX = centerY = 0;
      }

      Circle(double r, int x, int y)        // Constructor 3
      {  radius = r;                        // accepts 3 arguments
         centerX = x;
         centerY = y;
      }

      void setRadius(double r)
      {  radius = r;
      }

      int getXcoord()
      {  return centerX;
      }

      int getYcoord()
      {  return centerY;
      }

      double findArea()
      {  return 3.14 * pow(radius, 2);
      }
}; // End Circle class declaration
#endif
```

Program 8-28 creates an array of four `Circle` objects in line 12, then uses a loop in lines 15 through 20 to call the `setRadius` method for each object. A second loop is used in lines 26 through 29 to call the `findArea` method for each object and display the result.

Program 8-28

```
// This program uses an array of objects.
// The objects are instances of the Circle class.
#include <iostream>
#include <iomanip>
#include "Circle.h"            // Circle class declaration file
using namespace std;

const int NUM_CIRCLES = 4;

int main()
{
   Circle circle[NUM_CIRCLES];  // Define an array of Circle objects

   // Use a loop to initialize the radius of each object
   for (int index = 0; index < NUM_CIRCLES; index++)
   {  double r;
      cout << "Enter the radius for circle " << (index+1) << ": ";
      cin  >> r;
      circle[index].setRadius(r);
   }

   // Use a loop to get and print out the area of each object
   cout  << fixed << showpoint << setprecision(2);
   cout  << "\nHere are the areas of the " << NUM_CIRCLES
         << " circles.\n";
   for (int index = 0; index < NUM_CIRCLES; index++)
   {  cout  << "circle " << (index+1) << setw(8)
            << circle[index].findArea() << endl;
   }
   return 0;
}
```

Program Output with Example Input Shown in Bold

```
Enter the radius for circle 1: 0[Enter]
Enter the radius for circle 2: 2[Enter]
Enter the radius for circle 3: 2.5[Enter]
Enter the radius for circle 4: 10[Enter]

Here are the areas of the 4 circles.
circle 1    0.00
circle 2   12.56
circle 3   19.63
circle 4  314.00
```

NOTE: Whenever an array of objects is created with no constructor arguments, the default constructor, if one exists, runs for every object in the array. This occurred in Program 8-28.

When the array of `Circle` objects was first created, the default constructor executed for each object in the array and assigned its radius the value 1.0. We never saw this because the call made to the `setRadius` member function of each object replaced its 1.0 with the new value passed to `setRadius`. If we commented out lines 15 through 20 of Program 8-28, no calls would be made to `setRadius`. So every object in the array would still have a radius of 1.0 when the loop on lines 26 through 29 gets and prints the area. The output would look like this:

```
Here are the areas of the 4 circles.
circle 1    3.14
circle 2    3.14
circle 3    3.14
circle 4    3.14
```

This version of Program 8-28 can be found in the Chapter 8 folder on the book's companion website with the name `pr8-28B.cpp`.

It is also possible to create an array of objects and have another constructor called for each object. To do this you must use an initialization list. The following array definition and initialization list creates four `Circle` objects and initializes them to the same four values that were input in the original Program 8-28 sample run.

```
Circle circle[NUM_CIRCLES] = {0.0, 2.0, 2.5, 10.0};
```

This invokes the constructor that accepts one `double` argument and sets the radii shown here.

Object	radius
`circle[0]`	0.0
`circle[1]`	2.0
`circle[2]`	2.5
`circle[3]`	10.0

If the initialization list had been shorter than the number of objects, any remaining objects would have been initialized by the default constructor. For example, the following statement invokes the constructor that accepts one `double` argument for the first three objects and causes the default constructor to run for the fourth object. The fourth object is assigned a default radius of 1.0.

```
Circle circle[NUM_CIRCLES] = {0.0, 2.0, 2.5};
```

This is illustrated in Program 8-29.

Program 8-29

```
// This program demonstrates how an overloaded constructor
// that accepts an argument can be invoked for multiple objects
// when an array of objects is created.
#include <iostream>
#include <iomanip>
#include "Circle.h"          // Circle class declaration file
using namespace std;

const int NUM_CIRCLES = 4;

```

(program continues)

Program 8-29 *(continued)*

```
int main()
{
   // Define an array of 4 Circle objects. Use an initialization list
   // to call the 1-argument constructor for the first 3 objects.
   // The default constructor will be called for the final object.
   Circle circle[NUM_CIRCLES] = {0.0, 2.0, 2.5};

   // Display the area of each object
   cout  << fixed << showpoint << setprecision(2);
   cout  << "\nHere are the areas of the " << NUM_CIRCLES
         << " circles.\n";

   for (int index = 0; index < NUM_CIRCLES; index++)
   {  cout  << "circle " << (index+1) << setw(8)
            << circle[index].findArea() << endl;
   }
   return 0;
}
```

Program Output

```
Here are the areas of the 4 circles.
circle 1     0.00
circle 2    12.56
circle 3    19.63
circle 4     3.14
```

To use a constructor that requires more than one argument, the initializer must take the form of a function call. For example, look at the following definition statement. It invokes the 3-argument constructor for each of three `Circle` objects.

```
Circle circle[3] = { Circle(4.0, 2,  1),
                     Circle(2.0, 1,  3),
                     Circle(2.5, 5, -1) };
```

`circle[0]` will have its `radius` variable set to 4.0, its `centerX` variable set to 2, and its `centerY` variable set to 1. `circle[1]` will have its `radius` variable set to 2.0, its `centerX` variable set to 1, and its `centerY` variable set to 3. `circle[2]` will have its `radius` variable set to 2.5, its `centerX` variable set to 5, and its `centerY` variable set to –1.

It isn't necessary to call the same constructor for each object in an array. For example, look at the following statement:

```
Circle circle[3] = { 4.0,
                     Circle(2.0, 1,  3),
                     2.5 };
```

This statement invokes the 1-argument constructor for `circle[0]` and `circle[2]` and the 3-argument constructor for `circle[1]`.

In summary, there are seven key points to remember about arrays of objects.

1. The elements of arrays can be objects.
2. If you do not use an initialization list when an array of objects is created, the default constructor will be invoked for each object in the array.
3. It is not necessary that all objects in the array use the same constructor.
4. If you do use an initialization list when an array of objects is created, the correct constructor will be called for each object, depending on the number and type of arguments used.
5. If a constructor requires more than one argument, the initializer must take the form of a constructor function call.
6. If there are fewer initializer calls in the list than there are objects in the array, the default constructor will be called for all the remaining objects.
7. It is best to always provide a default constructor; but if there is none you must be sure to furnish an initializer for every object in the array.

These seven statements also apply to arrays of structures, which we will look at more closely in the next few pages.

Checkpoint

8.30 True or false: The default constructor is the only constructor that may be called for objects in an array of objects.

8.31 True or false: All elements in an array of objects must use the same constructor.

8.32 What will the following program display on the screen?

```
#include <iostream>
using namespace std;

class Tank
{
private:
   int gallons;
public:
   Tank()
     { gallons = 50; }
   Tank(int gal)
     { gallons = gal; }
   int getGallons()
     { return gallons; }
};

int main ()
{
   Tank storage[3] = { 10, 20 };

   for (int index = 0; index < 3; index++)
      cout << storage[index].getGallons() << endl;
   return 0;
}
```

8.33 Complete the following program so it defines an array of 10 `Yard` objects. The program should use a loop to ask the user for the length and width of each yard. Then it should use a second loop to display the length and width of each yard. To do this you will need to add two member functions to the `Yard` class.

```
#include <iostream>
using namespace std;

class Yard
{
private:
   int length, width;
public:
   Yard()
      { length = 0; width = 0; }
   void  setLength(int l)
     { length = l; }
   void  setWidth(int w)
     { width = w; }
};

int main ()
{
   // Finish this program.
}
```

Arrays of Structures

As mentioned earlier in this section, array elements can also be structures. This is useful when you want to store a collection of records that hold multiple data fields, but you aren't using objects. Program 8-13, which we saw earlier in this chapter, showed how related information of different data types can be stored in parallel arrays. These are two or more arrays with a relationship established between them through their subscripts. Because structures can hold multiple items of varying data types, a single array of structures can be used in place of several arrays of regular variables.

An array of structures is defined like any other array. Assume the following structure declaration exists in a program:

```
struct BookInfo
{
   string title;
   string author;
   string publisher;
   double price;
};
```

The following statement defines an array, `bookList`, which has 20 elements. Each element is a `BookInfo` structure.

```
BookInfo bookList[20];
```

Each element of the array may be accessed through a subscript. For example, `bookList[0]` is the first structure in the array, `bookList[1]` is the second, and so forth. Because members of structures are public by default, you do not need to use a function, as you do with class objects, to access them. You can access a member of any element by simply placing the dot operator and member name after the subscript. For example, the following expression refers to the `title` member of `bookList[5]`:

```
bookList[5].title
```

The following loop steps through the array, displaying the information stored in each element:

```
for (int index = 0; index < 20; index++)
{
   cout << bookList[index].title << endl;
   cout << bookList[index].author << endl;
   cout << bookList[index].publisher << endl;
   cout << bookList[index].price << endl << endl;
}
```

Because the members `title`, `author`, and `publisher` are `string` objects the individual characters making up the string can be accessed as well. The following statement displays the first character of the `title` member of `bookList[10]`:

```
cout << bookList[10].title[0];
```

And the following statement stores the character 't' in the fourth position of the `publisher` member of `bookList[2]`:

```
bookList[2].publisher[3] = 't';
```

Program 8-30 is a modification of Program 8-13 which calculates and displays payroll information for a set of employees. The original program used two parallel arrays to hold the hours and pay rates of the employees. This modified version uses a single array of structures.

Program 8-30

```
// This program uses an array of structures to hold payroll data.
#include <iostream>
#include <iomanip>
using namespace std;

struct PayInfo
{
   int hours;                  // Hours worked
   double payRate;             // Hourly pay rate
};

int main ()
{
   const int NUM_EMPS = 3;     // Number of employees
   int index;
   PayInfo workers[NUM_EMPS];  // Define an array of structures
   double grossPay;

   // Get payroll data
   cout  << "Enter the hours worked and hourly pay rates of "
         << NUM_EMPS << " employees.";
```

(program continues)

Program 8-30 *(continued)*

```
    for (index = 0; index < NUM_EMPS; index++)
    {
       cout << "\n Hours worked by employee #" << (index + 1);
       cout << ": ";
       cin  >> workers[index].hours;
       cout << "Hourly pay rate for employee #";
       cout << (index + 1) << ": ";
       cin  >> workers[index].payRate;
    }

    // Display each employee's gross pay
    cout << "\nHere is the gross pay for each employee:\n";
    cout << fixed << showpoint << setprecision(2);
    for (index = 0; index < NUM_EMPS; index++)
    {
       grossPay = workers[index].hours * workers[index].payRate;
       cout << "Employee #" << (index + 1);
       cout << ": $" << setw(7) << grossPay << endl;
    }
    return 0;
}
```

Program Output with Example Input Shown in Bold

```
Enter the hours worked and hourly pay rates of 3 employees.
Hours worked by employee #1: 10[Enter]
Hourly pay rate for employee #1: 9.75[Enter]

Hours worked by employee #2: 20[Enter]
Hourly pay rate for employee #2: 10.00[Enter]

Hours worked by employee #3: 40[Enter]
Hourly pay rate for employee #3: 20.00[Enter]

Here is the gross pay for each employee:
Employee #1: $  97.50
Employee #2: $ 200.00
Employee #3: $ 800.00
```

You can initialize an array of structures the same way you initialize an array of class objects, with a constructor. Here is the structure declaration from Program 8-30 modified to include a constructor. It accepts two arguments, but also has default values in case a structure variable is created without passing any values to the constructor.

```
struct PayInfo
{
   int hours;                               // Hours worked
   double payRate;                          // Hourly pay rate

   PayInfo(int h = 0, double p = 0.0)  // Constructor
   {  hours = h;
      payRate = p;
   }
};
```

Using this structure declaration, the array in Program 8-30 could now be initialized as follows:

```
PayInfo workers[NUM_EMPS] = { PayInfo(10,  9.75),
                              PayInfo(20, 10.00),
                              PayInfo(40, 20.00) };
```

Notice that the syntax for initializing members in an array of structures is the same as for initializing members in an array of objects. It is different from the syntax presented in Chapter 7 for initializing a single structure.

Checkpoint

For questions 8.34–8.38, assume the `Product` structure is declared as follows:

```
struct Product
{
   string description;  // Product description
   int partNum;         // Part number
   double cost;         // Product cost
};
```

8.34 Add two constructors to the `Product` structure declaration. The first should be a default constructor that sets the `description` member to the null string and the `partNum` and `cost` members to zero. The second constructor should have three parameters: a `string`, an `int`, and a `double`. It should copy the values of the arguments into the `description`, `partNum`, and `cost` members.

8.35 Write a definition for an array named `items` that can hold 100 `Product` structures.

8.36 Write statements that store the following information in the first element of the `items` array you defined in question 8.35.

Description: Claw Hammer
Part Number: 547
Part Cost: $8.29

8.37 Write a loop that displays the contents of the entire `items` array you created in question 8.35.

8.38 Write the definition for an array of five `Product` structures, initializing the first three elements with the following information:

Description	Part Number	Cost
Screwdriver	621	$ 1.72
Socket set	892	18.97
Claw hammer	547	8.29

8.39 Write a structure declaration called `Measurement`, with the following members:

`miles`, an `int`
`hours`, a `double`

8.40 Write a structure declaration called `Destination`, with the following members:

`city`, a `string` object
`travelTime`, a `Measurement` structure (declared in Checkpoint 8.39)

8.41 Define an array of 20 `Destination` structures (see Checkpoint 8.40). Write statements that store the following information in the fifth array element:

City: Tupelo
Miles: 375
Hours: 7.5

National Commerce Bank Case Study

The National Commerce Bank has hired you as a contract programmer. Your first assignment is to write a function that will be used by the bank's automated teller machines (ATMs) to validate a customer's personal identification number (PIN).

Your function will be incorporated into a larger program that asks the customer to input his or her PIN on the ATM's numeric keypad. (PINs are four-digit numbers. The program stores each digit in an element of an `int` array.) The program also retrieves a copy of the customer's actual PIN from a database. (The PINs are also stored in the database as four element arrays.) If these two numbers match, then the customer's identity is validated. Your function should compare the two arrays and determine whether they contain the same numbers.

Here are the specifications your function must meet.

Parameters The function should accept three arguments. The first is an array holding the digits entered by the customer. The second is an array holding the digits of the customer's correct PIN, retrieved from the bank's database. The final argument indicates the number of digits in a PIN. This is set in the program to 4. However, by passing this argument to the function it makes the program easier to update in the future if the bank decides to change the PIN size.

Return value The function should return a Boolean `true` value if the two arrays are identical. Otherwise, it should return `false`.

Here is the pseudocode for the function:

```
For each element in the first array
    Compare the element with the corresponding one in the 2nd array
    If the two elements contain different values
        Return false
    End If
End For   // If we made it this far the values are the same
Return true
```

You have only been asked to write a function that performs the comparison between the customer's input and the PIN that was retrieved from the database, however, code must also be written to test it. Program 8-31 is a complete program that includes both the function and a test driver.

Program 8-31

```
// This program tests a function that compares the contents of two arrays.
#include <iostream>
using namespace std;

// Function prototype
bool testPIN(const int set1[], const int set2[], int size);

int main()
{
   const int NUM_DIGITS = 4;
   int pin1[NUM_DIGITS] = {2, 4, 1, 8};  // Base set of values

   int pin2[NUM_DIGITS] = {2, 4, 6, 8};  // One element is
                                         // different from PIN1.
   int pin3[NUM_DIGITS] = {1, 2, 3, 4};  // All elements are
                                         // different from PIN1.
   if (testPIN(pin1, pin2, NUM_DIGITS))
      cout << "ERROR: pin1 and pin2 are reported to be the same.\n";
   else
      cout << "SUCCESS: pin1 and pin2 are correctly identified "
           << "as different.\n";

   if (testPIN(pin1, pin3, NUM_DIGITS))
      cout << "ERROR: pin1 and pin3 are reported to be the same.\n";
   else
      cout << "SUCCESS: pin1 and pin3 are correctly identified "
           << "as different.\n";

   if (testPIN(pin1, pin1, NUM_DIGITS))
      cout << "SUCCESS: pin1 and pin1 are correctly reported "
           << "to be the same.\n";
   else
      cout << "ERROR: pin1 and pin1 are erroneously identified "
           << "as different.\n";
   return 0;
}

/*******************************************************************
 *                            testPIN                              *
 * This Boolean function accepts and compares the values stored in *
 * two int arrays. If they both have exactly the same set of values, *
 * true is returned. If there are any differences, false is returned.*
 *******************************************************************/
bool testPIN(const int custPIN[], const int databasePIN[], int size)
{
   for (int index = 0; index < size; index++)
   {
      if (custPIN[index] != databasePIN[index])
         return false;            // We've found two different values
   }
   return true;                   // If we make it this far,
                                  // all values are the same
}
```

(program continues)

Program 8-31 *(continued)*

Program Output

```
SUCCESS: pin1 and pin2 are correctly identified as different.
SUCCESS: pin1 and pin3 are correctly identified as different.
SUCCESS: pin1 and pin1 are correctly reported to be the same.
```

Additional Case Studies

The following additional case studies, which contain applications of material introduced in Chapter 8, can be found in the Chapter 8 folder of the book's companion website.

Set Intersection Case Study

In algebra, the intersection of two sets is defined as a new set that contains those values common to the two original sets. This case study, which utilizes three one-dimensional arrays, finds and displays the intersection of two sets.

Creating an Abstract Array Data Type—Part 1

The lack of bounds checking in C++ can lead to problems. This object-oriented case study develops a simple integer list class with array-like characteristics that provides bounds checking.

8.14 Tying It All Together: *Rock, Paper, Scissors*

Now that you have learned to use arrays, you can create more advanced computer games, like Rock, Paper, Scissors. You have probably played this game before. Here is how it works. Simultaneously, two players form their hand to represent one of three objects. A fist represents a rock. A flat palm represents a sheet of paper. Two extended fingers represent a pair of scissors. If the two players choose the same object, the round is a tie. Otherwise, someone wins the round. Rock beats scissors because it can break a pair of scissors. Scissors beats paper because it can cut a sheet of paper. Paper beats rock because it can wrap itself around the rock.

In this section we will create a program that lets a user play a game of Rock, Paper, Scissors with the computer. Notice how in line 9 of the Rock, Paper, Scissors program shown here, the strings holding the names of the choices are stored in an array. In line 28 the program randomly generates a 1, 2, or 3 for the computer's choice. Then, in lines 31 and 32, the human player's choice is entered:

```
cout << "Pick 1 (rock), 2 (paper), or 3 (scissors): ";
cin  >> playerChoice;
```

Notice how, for both the computer and the player, the choice number matches the array element holding the name of the object they chose. Therefore, the choice number can be used as a subscript to get the string to be displayed. With this ability, the program can easily display information for each round of the game about who chose what, what beats what, and who wins that round.

Try running the program to see if you can beat the computer.

Program 8-32

```
// This program lets the user play a game of rock, paper, scissors
// with the computer. The computer's choices are randomly generated.
#include <iostream>
#include <ctime>
#include <cstdlib>
#include <string>
using namespace std;

const string name[4] = {" ", "rock", "paper", "scissors"};

int main()
{
   int computerChoice,
       playerChoice,
       computerPoints = 0,   // Point accumulators
       playerPoints = 0;

   srand(time(NULL));        // Give the random generator
                             // a seed to start with
   playerPoints = 0;
   computerPoints = 0;

   cout << "Let's play Rock-Paper-Scissors!\n";
   cout << "The first player to score 5 points wins.\n\n";

   do
   {  // Generate a random number 1 to 3 to simulate computer choice
      computerChoice = 1 + rand() % 3;

      // Get player's choice
      cout << "Pick 1 (rock), 2 (paper), or 3 (scissors): ";
      cin  >> playerChoice;

      if (computerChoice == playerChoice)                     // Tie
      {   cout << "I chose " << name[computerChoice]
               << " too, so we tied.\n\n";
      }
      else if ((playerChoice == 1 && computerChoice == 2) ||  // Computer
               (playerChoice == 2 && computerChoice == 3) ||  // wins
               (playerChoice == 3 && computerChoice == 1) )
      {   cout << "I chose " << name[computerChoice] << ", so I win! "
               << name[computerChoice] << " beats "
               << name[playerChoice] << ".\n\n";
          computerPoints++;
      }                                                       // Player
      else                                                    // wins
      {   cout << "I chose " << name[computerChoice] << ", so you win! "
               << name[playerChoice] << " beats "
               << name[computerChoice] << ".\n\n";
          playerPoints++;
      }
   } while (playerPoints < 5 && computerPoints < 5);
```

(program continues)

Program 8-32 *(continued)*

```

   cout << "Let's see how you did :\n"
        << "You won " << playerPoints << " points and I won "
        << computerPoints << " points.\n";

   if (playerPoints == 5)
      cout << "Congratulations! You're the champ!\n";
   else
      cout << "Hurray for me! I'm the champ!\n";

   return 0;
}
```

Review Questions and Exercises

Fill-in-the-Blank and Short Answer

1. The _________ indicates the number of elements, or values, an array can hold.
2. The size declarator must be a(n) _________ with a value greater than _________.
3. Each element of an array is accessed and indexed by a number known as a(n) _________.
4. Subscript numbering in C++ always starts at _________.
5. The number inside the brackets of an array definition is the _________, but the number inside an array's brackets in an assignment statement, or any other statement that works with the contents of the array, is the _________.
6. C++ has no array _________ checking, which means you can inadvertently store data past the end of an array.
7. Starting values for the elements of an array may be specified with a(n) _________ list.
8. If a numeric array is partially initialized, the uninitialized elements will bet set to _________.
9. If the size declarator of an array definition is omitted, C++ counts the number of items in the _________ to determine how large the array should be.
10. To allow an array of structures or an array of objects to be initialized, the `struct` or `class` declaration should include a(n) _________.
11. By using the same _________ for multiple arrays, you can build relationships between the data stored in the arrays. These arrays are referred to as parallel arrays.
12. You cannot use the _________ operator to copy data from one array to another in a single statement.
13. Arrays are never passed to functions by _________ because there would be too much overhead in copying all the elements.
14. To pass an array to a function, pass the _________ of the array.
15. A(n) _________ array is like several arrays of the same type put together.

16. It's best to think of a two-dimensional array as having ________ and ________.
17. To define a two-dimensional array, ________ size declarators are required.
18. When initializing a two-dimensional array, it helps to enclose each row's initialization list in ________.
19. When a two-dimensional array is passed to a function, the number of ________ must be specified.
20. To print out all elements of a two-dimensional array you would normally use a(n) ________ loop.
21. Look at the following array definition.

```
int values[10];
```

A) How many elements does the array have?
B) What is the subscript of the first element in the array?
C) What is the subscript of the last element in the array?
D) If an `int` uses four bytes of memory, how much memory does the array use?

22. Given the following array definition:

```
int values[5] = { 4, 7, 6, 8, 2 };
```

What does the following statement display?

```
cout << values[4] << "   " << (values[2] + values[3])
     << "   " << ++values[1] << endl;
```

23. Look at the following array definition.

```
int numbers[5] = { 1, 2, 3 };
```

A) What value is stored in `numbers[2]`?
B) What value is stored in `numbers[4]`?

24. Assume that `array1` and `array2` are both 25-element integer arrays. Indicate whether each of the following statements is legal or illegal.

A) `array1 = array2;`
B) `cout << array1;`
C) `cin  >> array2;`

25. When you pass an array name as an argument to a function, what is actually being passed?
26. How do you establish a parallel relationship between two or more arrays?
27. Look at the following array definition.

```
double sales[8][10];
```

A) How many rows does the array have?
B) How many columns does the array have?
C) How many elements does the array have?
D) Write a statement that stores 3.52 in the last column of the last row in the array.

Use the following Car structure declaration to answer questions 28–30.

```
struct Car
{
   string make,
          model;
   int    year;
   double cost;

   // Constructors
   Car()
   { make = model = ""; year = cost = 0; }

   Car(string mk, string md, int yr, double c)
   {  make = mk;  model = md;  year = yr;  cost = c; }
};
```

28. Define an array named `collection` that holds 25 `Car` structures.
29. Define an array named `forSale` that holds 35 `Car` structures. Initialize the first three elements with the following data:

Make	Model	Year	Cost
Ford	Taurus	2006	$21,000
Honda	Accord	2004	$11,000
Jeep	Wrangler	2007	$24,000

30. Write a loop that will step through the array you defined in question 29, displaying the contents of each element.

Algorithm Workbench

31. The arrays `array1` and `array2` each hold 25 integer elements. Write code that copies the values in `array1` to `array2`.
32. The following code totals the values in each of two arrays described in question 31. Will the code print the correct total for both arrays? Why or why not?

```
int total = 0;      // Accumulator
int count;          // Loop counter
// Calculate and display the total of the first array.
for (count = 0; count <= 25; count++)
   total += array1[count];

cout << "The total for array1 is " << total << endl;

// Calculate and display the total of the second array.
for (count = 0; count <= 25; count++)
   total += array2[count];

cout << "The total for array2 is " << total << endl;
```

33. In a program you need to store the identification numbers of 10 employees (as `int`s) and their weekly gross pay (as `double`s).
    A) Define two arrays that may be used in parallel to store the 10 employee identification numbers and 10 weekly gross pay amounts.
    B) Write a loop that uses these arrays to print each employee's identification number and weekly gross pay.

34. Revise your answer for question 33 to define and use an array of `Payroll` structures, instead of two parallel arrays. A `Payroll` structure should hold an employee ID and weekly gross pay amount.

35. In a program you need to store the names and populations of 12 countries. Create an appropriate array to store this information and then write the code needed to read the information into the array from a file named `pop.dat`.

36. A weather analysis program uses the following array to store the temperature for each hour of the day on each day of a week.

```
int temp[7][24];
```

Each row represents a day (0 = Sunday, 1 = Monday, etc.) and each column represents a time (0 = midnight, 1 = 1 a.m., ... , 12 = noon, 13 = 1 p.m., etc.).

A) Write code to find Tuesday's average temperature.
B) Write code to find the average weekly noon temperature.

Find the Errors

37. Each of the following definitions has errors. Locate as many as you can.

A)
```
int size;
double values[size];
```
B)
```
int collection[-20];
```
C)
```
int hours[3] = 8, 12, 16;
```

38. Each of the following definitions has errors. Locate as many as you can.

A)
```
int numbers[8] = {1, 2, , 4, , 5};
```
B)
```
double ratings[];
```
C)
```
values[3] = {6, 8.2, 'A'};
```

39. Each of the following functions contains errors. Locate as many as you can.

A)
```
void showValues(int nums)
{
    for (int count = 0; count < 8; count++)
        cout << nums[count];
}
```
B)
```
void showValues(int nums[4][])
{
    for (rows = 0; rows < 4; rows++)
        for (cols = 0; cols < 5; cols++)
            cout << nums[rows][cols];
}
```

Soft Skills

Diagrams are an important means of clarifying many programming concepts. You have seen them used throughout this book to illustrate such things as how the flow of control works for various programming constructs, how a program is broken into modules and those modules related, how data is stored in memory, and how data is organized.

40. Here is a set of declarations that define how the data for a set of poker hands is organized. Create a neat diagram that illustrates this organization. The diagram in Section 7.12 of Chapter 7 on nested structures might give you an idea of how to begin.

```
struct CardStruct
{  int  face;
   char suit;      // 's', 'h', 'd', or 'c'
};

struct PlayerStruct
{  int playerNum;
   CardStruct card[5];
}

PlayerStruct player[4];
```

Programming Challenges

Programming Challenges 1–7 allow you to practice working with arrays without using classes or structures. Most of the problems beginning with Programming Challenge 8 use arrays with classes or structures.

1. Perfect Scores

Write a modular program that accepts up to 20 integer test scores in the range of 0 to 100 from the user and stores them in an array. Then `main` should report how many perfect scores were entered (i.e., scores of 100), using a value-returning `countPerfect` function to help it.

2. Roman Numeral Converter

Write a program that displays the roman numeral equivalent of any decimal number between 1 and 20 that the user enters. The roman numerals should be stored in an array of strings and the decimal number that the user enters should be used to locate the array element holding the roman numeral equivalent. The program should have a loop that allows the user to continue entering numbers until an end sentinel of 0 is entered.

3. Chips and Salsa

VideoNote
Solving the Chips and Salsa Problem

Write a program that lets a maker of chips and salsa keep track of their sales for five different types of salsa they produce: mild, medium, sweet, hot, and zesty. It should use two parallel five-element arrays: an array of strings that holds the five salsa names and an array of integers that holds the number of jars sold during the past month for each salsa type. The salsa names should be stored using an initialization list at the time the `name` array is created. The program should prompt the user to enter the number of jars sold for each type. Once this sales data has been entered, the program should produce a report that displays sales for each salsa type, total sales, and the names of the highest selling and lowest selling products.

4. Monkey Business

A local zoo wants to keep track of how many pounds of food each of its three monkeys eats each day during a typical week. Write a program that stores this information in a two-dimensional 3 × 7 array, where each row represents a different monkey and each column represents a different day of the week. The program should first have the user input the data for each monkey. Then it should create a report that includes the following information:

- Average amount of food eaten per day by the whole family of monkeys.
- The least amount of food eaten during the week by any one monkey.
- The greatest amount of food eaten during the week by any one monkey.

5. Rain or Shine

An amateur meteorologist wants to keep track of weather conditions during the past year's three month summer season and has designated each day as either rainy ('R'), cloudy ('C'), or sunny ('S'). Write a program that stores this information in a 3 × 30 array of characters, where the row indicates the month (0 = June, 1 = July, 2 = August) and the column indicates the day of the month. Note that data is not being collected for the 31st of any month. The program should begin by reading the weather data in from a file. Then it should create a report that displays for each month and for the whole three-month period, how many days were rainy, how many were cloudy, and how many were sunny. It should also report which of the three months had the largest number of rainy days. Data for the program can be found in the `RainOrShine.dat` file.

6. Lottery

Write a program that simulates a lottery. The program should have an array of 5 integers named `winningDigits`, with a randomly generated number in the range of 0 through 9 for each element in the array. The program should ask the user to enter 5 digits and should store them in a second integer array named `player`. The program must compare the corresponding elements in the two arrays and count how many digits match. For example, the following shows the `winningDigits` array and the `Player` array with sample numbers stored in each. There are two matching digits, elements 2 and 4.

`WinningDigits`	7	4	9	1	3
`player`	4	2	9	7	3

Once the user has entered a set of numbers, the program should display the winning digits and the player's digits and tell how many digits matched.

7. Rainfall Statistics

Write a modular program that analyzes a year's worth of rainfall data. In addition to `main`, the program should have a `getData` function that accepts the total rainfall for each of 12 months from the user and stores it in a `double` array. It should also have four value-returning functions that compute and return to `main` the `totalRainfall`, `averageRainfall`, `driestMonth`, and `wettestMonth`. These last two functions return the *number* of the month with the lowest and highest rainfall amounts, not the amount of rain that fell those months. Notice that this month number can be used to obtain the amount of rain that fell those months. This information should be used either by `main` or by a `displayReport` function called by `main` to print a summary rainfall report similar to the following:

```
        2010 Rain Report for Neversnows County

    Total rainfall: 23.19 inches
    Average monthly rainfall: 1.93 inches
    The least rain fell in January with 0.24 inches.
    The most rain fell in April with 4.29 inches.
```

8. Chips and Salsa Version 2

Revise Programming Challenge 3 to use an array of `Product` objects instead of two parallel arrays. The `Product` class will need member variables to hold a product name and a quantity.

9. `Stats` Class and Rainfall Statistics

Create a `Stats` class whose member data includes an array capable of storing 30 `double` data values, and whose member functions include `total`, `average`, `lowest`, and `highest` functions for returning information about the data to the client program. These are general versions of the same functions you created for Programming Challenge 7, but now they belong to the `Stats` class, not the application program. In addition to these functions, the `Stats` class should have a Boolean `storeValue` function that accepts a `double` value from the client program and stores it in the array. It is the job of this function to keep track of how many values are currently in the array, so it will know where to put the next value it receives and will know how many values there are to process when it is carrying out its other functions. It is also the job of this function to make sure that no more than 30 values are accepted. If the `storeValue` function is able to successfully store the value sent to it, it should return `true` to the client program. However, if the client program tries to store a thirty-first value, the function should *not* store the value and should return `false` to the client program.

The client program should create and use a `Stats` object to carry out the same rainfall analysis requested by Programming Challenge 7. Notice that the `Stats` object does no I/O. All input and output is done by the client program.

10. `Stats` Class and Track Statistics

Write a client program that uses the `Stats` class you created for Programming Challenge 9 to store and analyze "best" 100-yard dash times for each of the 15 runners on a track team. As in Programming Challenge 8, all I/O is done by the client program. In addition to `main`, the client program should have two other functions: a `getData` function to accept input from the user and send it to the `Stats` object and a `createReport` function that creates and displays a report similar to the one shown here,

```
           Tulsa Tigers Track Team

    Average 100 yard-dash time: 11.16 seconds
    Slowest runner: Jack        13.09 seconds
    Fastest runner: Will        10.82 seconds
```

11. Character Converter Class

Create a `CharConverter` class that performs various operations on strings. It should have the following two public member functions to start with. Your instructor may ask you to add additional functions to the class.

- The `uppercase` member function accepts a string and returns a copy of it with all lowercase letters converted to uppercase. If a character is already uppercase, or is not a letter, it should be left alone.
- The `properWords` member function accepts a string of words separated by spaces and returns a copy of it with the first letter of each word converted to uppercase.

Write a simple program that uses the class. It should prompt the user to input a string. Then it should call the `properWords` function and display the resulting string. Finally, it should call the `uppercase` function and display this resulting string. The program should loop to allow additional strings to be converted and displayed until the user chooses to quit.

12. Driver's License Exam

The State Department of Motor Vehicles (DMV) has asked you to write a program that grades the written portion of the driver's license exam, which has 20 multiple choice questions. Here are the correct answers:

1. B	5. C	9. C	13. D	17. C
2. D	6. A	10. D	14. A	18. B
3. A	7. B	11. B	15. D	19. D
4. A	8. A	12. C	16. C	20. A

To do this you should create a `TestGrader` class. The class will have an `answers` array of 20 characters, which holds the correct test answers. It will have two public member functions that enable user programs to interact with the class: `setKey` and `grade`. The `setKey` function receives a 20-character string holding the correct answers and copies this information into its `answers` array. The `grade` function receives a 20-character array holding the test taker's answers and compares each of their answers to the correct one. An applicant must correctly answer 15 or more of the 20 questions to pass the exam. After "grading" the exam, the grade function should create and return to the user a string that includes the following information:

- a message indicating whether the applicant passed or failed the exam
- the number of right answers and the number of wrong answers
- a list of the question numbers for all incorrectly answered questions.

The client program that creates and uses a `TestGrader` object should first make a single call to `setKey`, passing it a string containing the 20 correct answers. Once this is done it should allow a test taker's 20 answers to be entered, making sure only answers of A–D are accepted, and store them in a 20-character array. Then it should call the `grade` function to grade the exam and should display the string the function returns. The program should loop to allow additional tests to be entered and graded until the user indicates a desire to quit.

13. Array of `Payroll` Objects

Design a `PayRoll` class that has data members for an employee's hourly pay rate and number of hours worked. Write a program with an array of seven `PayRoll` objects. The program should read the number of hours each employee worked and their hourly pay rate from a file and call class functions to store this information in the appropriate objects. It should then call a class function, once for each object, to return the employee's gross pay, so this information can be displayed. Sample data to test this program can be found in the `payroll.dat` file.

14. Drink Machine Simulator

Create a class that simulates and manages a soft drink machine. Information on each drink type should be stored in a structure that has data members to hold the drink name, the drink price, and the number of drinks of that type currently in the machine.

The class should have an array of five of these structures, initialized with the following data.

Drink Name	Cost	Number in Machine
Cola	1.00	20
Root beer	1.00	20
Orange soda	1.00	20
Grape soda	1.00	20
Bottled water	1.50	20

The class should have two public member functions, `displayChoices` (which displays a menu of drink names and prices) and `buyDrink` (which handles a sale). The class should also have at least two private member functions, `inputMoney`, which is called by `buyDrink` to accept, validate, and return (to `buyDrink`) the amount of money input, and `dailyReport`, which is called by the destructor to report how many of each drink type remain in the machine at the end of the day and how much money was collected. You may want to use additional functions to make the program more modular.

The client program that uses the class should have a main processing loop which calls the `displayChoices` class member function and allows the patron to either pick a drink or quit the program. If the patron selects a drink, the `buyDrink` class member function is called to handle the actual sale. This function should be passed the patron's drink choice. Here is what the `buyDrink` function should do:

- Call the `inputMoney` function, passing it the patron's drink choice.
- If the patron no longer wishes to make the purchase, return all input money.
- If the machine is out of the requested soda, display an appropriate "sold out" message and return all input money.
- If the machine has the soda and enough money was entered, complete the sale by updating the quantity on hand and money collected information, calculating any change due to be returned to the patron, and delivering the soda. This last action can be simulated by printing an appropriate "here is your beverage" message.

Input Validation: Only accept valid menu choices. Do not deliver a beverage if the money inserted is less than the price of the selected drink.

15. Bin Manager Class

Design and write an object-oriented program for managing inventory bins in a warehouse. To do this you will use two classes: `InvBin` and `BinManager`. The `InvBin` class holds information about a single bin. The `BinManager` class will own and manage an array of `InvBin` objects. Here is a skeleton of what the `InvBin` and `BinManager` class declarations should look like:

```
class InvBin
{
   private:
      string description;                        // Item name
      int qty;                                    // Quantity of items
                                                  // in this bin

   public:
      InvBin (string d = "empty", int q = 0)     // 2-parameter constructor
      {   description = d;  qty = q; }           // with default values

      // It will also have the following public member functions. They
      // will be used by the BinManager class, not the client program.
      void setDescription(string d)
      string getDescription()
      void setQty(int q)
      int getQty( )
};

class BinManager
{
   private:
      InvBin bin[30];                             // Array of InvBin objects
      int numBins;                                // Number of bins
                                                  // currently in use

   public:
      BinManager()                                // Default constructor
      {   numBins = 0; }

      BinManager(int size, string d[], int q[])   // 3-parameter constructor
      {   // Receives number of bins in use and parallel arrays of item names
          // and quantities. Uses this info. to store values in the elements
          // of the bin array. Remember, these elements are InvBin objects.
      }

      // The class will also have the following public member functions:
      string getDescription(int index)          // Returns name of one item
      int getQuantity(int index)                // Returns qty of one item
      bool addParts(int binIndex, int q)        // These return true if the
      bool removeParts(int binIndex, int q)     // action was done and false
                                                // if it could not be done—
                                                // see validation information
};
```

Client Program

Once you have created these two classes, write a menu-driven client program that uses a `BinManager` object to manage its warehouse bins. It should initialize it to use 9 of the bins, holding the following item descriptions and quantities. The bin index where the item will be stored is also show here.

1. regular pliers 25	2. n. nose pliers 5	3. screwdriver 25
4. p. head screw driver 6	5. wrench-large 7	6. wrench-small 18
7. drill 51	8. cordless drill 16	9. hand saw 12

The modular client program should have functions to display a menu, get and validate the user's choice, and carry out the necessary activities to handle that choice. This includes adding items to a bin, removing items from a bin, and displaying a report of all bins. Think about what calls the `displayReport` client function will need to make to the `BinManager` object to create this report. When the user chooses the "Quit" option from the menu, the program should call its `displayReport` function one last time to display the final bin information. All I/O should be done in the client class. The `BinManager` class only accepts information, keeps the array of `InvBin` objects up to date, and returns information to the client program.

Input Validation in the `BinManager` class: The class functions should not accept numbers less than 1 for the number of parts being added or removed from a bin. They should also not allow the user to remove more items from a bin than it currently holds.

Group Projects

16. Tic-Tac-Toe Game

Write a modular program that allows two players to play a game of tic-tac-toe. Use a two-dimensional `char` array with 3 rows and 3 columns as the game board. Each element of the array should be initialized with an asterisk (*). The program should display the initial board configuration and then start a loop that does the following:

- Allow player 1 to select a location on the board for an X by entering a row and column number. Then redisplay the board with an X replacing the * in the chosen location.
- If there is no winner yet and the board is not yet full, allow player 2 to select a location on the board for an O by entering a row and column number. Then redisplay the board with an O replacing the * in the chosen location.

The loop should continue until a player has won or a tie has occurred, then display a message indicating who won, or reporting that a tie occurred.

- Player 1 wins when there are three Xs in a row, a column, or a diagonal on the game board.
- Player 2 wins when there are three Os in a row, a column, or a diagonal on the game board.
- A tie occurs when all of the locations on the board are full, but there is no winner.

Input Validation: Only allow legal moves to be entered. The row must be 1, 2, or 3. The column must be 1, 2, or 3. The (row, column) position entered must currently be empty (i.e., still have an asterisk in it).

17. Theater Ticket Sales

Create a `TicketManager` class and a program that uses it to sell tickets for a single performance theater production. This project is intended to be designed and written by a team of 2–4 students. Here are some suggestions:

- One student might design and write the client program that uses the class, while other team members design and write the `TicketManager` class and all of its functions.
- Each student should be given about the same workload.
- The class design and the names, parameters, and return types of each function should be decided in advance.
- The project can be implemented either as a multi-file program, or all the functions can be cut and pasted into a single file.

Here are the specifications:

- The theater's auditorium has 15 rows, with 30 seats in each row. To represent the seats, the `TicketManager` class should have a two-dimensional array of `SeatStructures`. Each of these structures should have data members to keep track of the seat's price and whether or not it is available or already sold.
- The seat prices should be read in from the `SeatPrices.dat` file. It contains 15 values representing the price for each row. All seats in a given row are the same price, but different rows have different prices. The seat availability information should be read in from the `SeatAvailability.dat` file. It contains 450 characters (15 rows with 30 characters each), indicating which seats have been sold (`'*'`) and which are available (`'#'`). Initially all seats are available. However, once the program runs and the file is updated, some of the seats will have been sold. The obvious function to read in the data from these files and set up the array is the constructor that runs when the `TicketManager` object is first created.
- The client program should be a menu-driven program that provides the user with a menu of box office options, accepts and validates user inputs, and calls appropriate class functions to carry out desired tasks. The menu should have options to display the seating chart, request tickets, print a sales report, and exit the program.
- When the user selects the *display seats* menu option, a `TicketManager` function should be called that creates and returns a string holding a chart, similar to the one shown here. It should indicate which seats are already sold (`*`) and which are still available for purchase (`#`). The client program should then display the string.

```
                         Seats
              123456789012345678901234567890
    Row  1    ***###***###*########*****####
    Row  2    ####*************####*******##
    Row  3    **##***********########****###
    Row  4    **######**************##******
    Row  5    ********#####*********########
    Row  6    ##############************####
    Row  7    #######************###########
    Row  8    ************##****############
    Row  9    #########*****############****
    Row 10    #####*************############
    Row 11    #**********#################**
    Row 12    #############********########*
    Row 13    ###***********########**######
    Row 14    ##############################
    Row 15    ##############################
```

- When the user selects the *request tickets* menu option, the program should prompt for the number of seats the patron wants, the desired row number, and the desired starting seat number. A `TicketManager` ticket request function should then be called and passed this information so that it can handle the ticket request. If any of the requested seats do not exist, or are not available, an appropriate message should be returned to be displayed by the client program. If the seats exist and are available, a string should be created and returned that lists the number of requested seats, the price per seat in the requested row, and the total price for the seats. Then the user program should ask if the patron wishes to purchase these seats.
- If the patron indicates they do want to buy the requested seats, a `TicketManager` purchase tickets module should be called to handle the actual sale. This module must be able to accept money, ensure that it is sufficient to continue with the sale, and if it is, mark the seat(s) as sold, and create and return a string that includes a ticket for each seat sold (with the correct row, seat number, and price on it).
- When the user selects the *sales report* menu option, a `TicketManager` report module should be called. This module must create and return a string holding a report that tells how many seats have been sold, how many are still available, and how much money has been collected so far for the sold seats. Think about how your team will either calculate or collect and store this information so that it will be available when it is needed for the report.
- When the day of ticket sales is over and the *quit* menu choice is selected, the program needs to be able to write the updated seat availability data back out to the file. The obvious place to do this is in the `TicketManager` destructor.

CHAPTER

9 Searching, Sorting, and Algorithm Analysis

TOPICS

9.1 Introduction to Search Algorithms

CONCEPT: A search algorithm is a method of locating a specific item in a collection of data.

It's very common for programs not only to store and process data stored in arrays, but to search arrays for specific items. This section will show you two methods of searching an array: the linear search and the binary search. Each has its advantages and disadvantages.

The Linear Search

The *linear search* is a very simple algorithm. Sometimes called a *sequential search,* it uses a loop to sequentially step through an array, starting with the first element. It compares each element with the value being searched for, and stops when either the value is found or the end of the array is encountered. If the value being searched for is not in the array, the algorithm will search to the end of the array.

Here is the pseudocode for a function that performs the linear search:

```
Set found to false
Set position to -1
Set index to 0
While index < number of elements and found is false
   If list[index] is equal to search value
      found = true
      position = index
   End If
   Add 1 to index
End While
Return position
```

The function `searchList`, which follows, is an example of C++ code used to perform a linear search on an integer array. The array `list`, which has a maximum of `size` elements, is searched for an occurrence of the number stored in `value`. If the number is found, its array subscript is returned. Otherwise, –1 is returned, indicating the value did not appear in the array.

```
int searchList(const int list[], int size, int value)
{
   int index = 0;          // Used as a subscript to search array
   int position = -1;      // Used to record position of search value
   bool found = false;     // Flag to indicate if the value was found

   while (index < size && !found)
   {
      if (list[index] == value)     // If the value is found
      {
          found = true;             // Set the flag
          position = index;         // Record the value's subscript
      }
      index++;                      // Go to the next element
   }
   return position;                 // Return the position, or -1
}
```

NOTE: The reason –1 is chosen to indicate that the search value was not found in the array is that –1 is not a valid subscript. Any other nonvalid subscript value could also have been used to signal this.

Program 9-1 is a complete program that uses the `searchList` function. It searches the five-element `tests` array to find a score of 100.

Program 9-1

```
// This program demonstrates the searchList function,
// which performs a linear search on an integer array.
#include <iostream>
using namespace std;

```

(program continues)

Program 9-1 *(continued)*

```
// Function prototype
int searchList(const int [], int, int);

const int SIZE = 5;

int main()
{
   int tests[SIZE] = {87, 75, 98, 100, 82};
   int results;         // Holds the search results

   // Search the array for the value 100
   results = searchList(tests, SIZE, 100);

   // If searchList returned -1, 100 was not found
   if (results == -1)
      cout << "You did not earn 100 points on any test.\n";
   else
   {  // Otherwise results contains the subscript of
      // the first 100 found in the array
      cout << "You earned 100 points on test ";
      cout << (results + 1) << ".\n";
   }
   return 0;
}

/*****************************************************************
 *                           searchList                          *
 * This function performs a linear search on an integer array.   *
 * The list array, which has size elements, is searched for      *
 * the number stored in value. If the number is found, its array *
 * subscript is returned. Otherwise, -1 is returned.             *
 *****************************************************************/
int searchList(const int list[], int size, int value)
{
   int index = 0;          // Used as a subscript to search array
   int position = -1;      // Used to record position of search value
   bool found = false;     // Flag to indicate if the value was found

   while (index < size && !found)
   {
      if (list[index] == value)  // If the value is found
      {
         found = true;           // Set the flag
         position = index;       // Record the value's subscript
      }
      index++;                   // Go to the next element
   }
   return position;              // Return the position, or -1
}
```

Program Output

```
You earned 100 points on test 4.
```

Inefficiency of the Linear Search

The advantage of the linear search is its simplicity. It is very easy to understand and implement. Furthermore, it doesn't require the data in the array to be stored in any particular order. Its disadvantage, however, is its inefficiency. If the array being searched contained 20,000 elements, the algorithm would have to look at all 20,000 elements in order to find a value stored in the last element or to determine that a desired element was not in the array.

In a typical case, an item is just as likely to be found near the beginning of the array as near the end. On average, for an array of N items, the linear search will locate an item in N/2 attempts. If an array has 20,000 elements, the linear search will make a comparison with 10,000 of them on average. This is assuming, of course, that the search item is consistently found in the array. (N/2 is the average number of comparisons. The maximum number of comparisons is always N.)

When the linear search fails to locate an item, it must make a comparison with every element in the array. As the number of failed search attempts increases, so does the average number of comparisons. When it can be avoided the linear search should not be used on large arrays if speed is important.

The Binary Search

VideoNote

Performing a Binary Search

The *binary search* is a clever algorithm that is much more efficient than the linear search. Its only requirement is that the values in the array be in order. Instead of testing the array's first element, this algorithm starts with the element in the middle. If that element happens to contain the desired value, then the search is over. Otherwise, the value in the middle element is either greater than or less than the value being searched for. If it is greater than the desired value then the value (if it is in the list) will be found somewhere in the first half of the array. If it is less than the desired value then the value (again, if it is in the list) will be found somewhere in the last half of the array. In either case, half of the array's elements have been eliminated from further searching.

If the desired value wasn't found in the middle element, the procedure is repeated for the half of the array that potentially contains the value. For instance, if the last half of the array is to be searched, the algorithm immediately tests *its* middle element. If the desired value isn't found there, the search is narrowed to the quarter of the array that resides before or after that element. This process continues until the value being searched for is either found or there are no more elements to test.

Here is the pseudocode for a function that performs a binary search on an array whose elements are stored in ascending order.

```
Set first to 0
Set last to the last subscript in the array
Set found to false
Set position to -1
```

```
While found is not true and first is less than or equal to last
   Set middle to the subscript halfway between first and last
   If array[middle] equals the desired value
       Set found to true
       Set position to middle
   Else If array[middle] is greater than the desired value
       Set last to middle - 1
   Else
       Set first to middle + 1
   End If
End While
Return position
```

This algorithm uses three index variables: `first`, `last`, and `middle`. The `first` and `last` variables mark the boundaries of the portion of the array currently being searched. They are initialized with the subscripts of the array's first and last elements. The subscript of the element approximately halfway between `first` and `last` is calculated and stored in the `middle` variable. If there is no precisely central element, the integer division used to calculate `middle` will select the element immediately preceding the midpoint. If the element in the middle of the array does not contain the search value, the `first` or `last` variables are adjusted so that only the top or bottom half of the array is searched during the next iteration. This cuts the portion of the array being searched in half each time the loop fails to locate the search value.

The function `binarySearch` in the following example C++ code is used to perform a binary search on an integer array. The first parameter, `array`, which has `size` elements, is searched for an occurrence of the number stored in `value`. If the number is found, its array subscript is returned. Otherwise, –1 is returned indicating the value did not appear in the array.

```
int binarySearch(const int array[], int size, int value)
{
   int  first = 0,                        // First array element
        last = size - 1,                  // Last array element
        middle,                           // Midpoint of search
        position = -1;                    // Position of search value
   bool found = false;                    // Flag

   while (!found && first <= last)
   {
      middle = (first + last) / 2;        // Calculate midpoint
      if (array[middle] == value)         // If value is found at mid
      {
         found = true;
         position = middle;
      }
      else if (array[middle] > value)     // If value is in lower half
         last = middle - 1;
      else
         first = middle + 1;              // If value is in upper half
   }
   return position;
}
```

Program 9-2 is a complete program using the `binarySearch` function. It searches an array of employee ID numbers for a specific value.

Program 9-2

```
// This program performs a binary search on an integer
// array whose elements are in ascending order.
#include <iostream>
using namespace std;

// Function prototype
int binarySearch(const int [], int, int);

const int SIZE = 20;

int main()
{
   // Create an array of ID numbers sorted in ascending order
   int IDnums[SIZE] = {101, 142, 147, 189, 199, 207, 222,
                       234, 289, 296, 310, 319, 388, 394,
                       417, 429, 447, 521, 536, 600 };

   int empID,          // Holds the ID to search for
       results;        // Holds the search results

   // Get an employee ID to search for
   cout << "Enter the employee ID you wish to search for: ";
   cin  >> empID;

   // Search for the ID
   results = binarySearch(IDnums, SIZE, empID);

   // If binarySearch returned -1, the ID was not found
   if (results == -1)
      cout << "That number does not exist in the array.\n";
   else
   {  // Otherwise results contains the subscript of
      // the specified employee ID in the array
      cout << "ID " << empID << " was found in element "
           << results << " of the array.\n";
   }
   return 0;
}
```

(program continues)

Program 9-2 *(continued)*

```
/*****************************************************************
 *                     binarySearch                              *
 * This function performs a binary search on an integer array    *
 * with size elements whose values are stored in ascending       *
 * order. The array is searched for the number stored in the     *
 * value parameter. If the number is found, its array subscript  *
 * is returned. Otherwise, -1 is returned.                       *
 *****************************************************************/
int binarySearch(const int array[], int size, int value)
{
   int  first = 0,                     // First array element
        last = size - 1,               // Last array element
        middle,                        // Midpoint of search
        position = -1;                 // Position of search value
   bool found = false;                 // Flag

   while (!found && first <= last)
   {
      middle = (first + last) / 2;     // Calculate midpoint
      if (array[middle] == value)      // If value is found at mid
      {
         found = true;
         position = middle;
      }
      else if (array[middle] > value) // If value is in lower half
         last = middle - 1;
      else
         first = middle + 1;           // If value is in upper half
   }
   return position;
}
```

Program Output with Example Input Shown in Bold

```
Enter the employee ID you wish to search for: 199[Enter]
ID 199 was found in element 4 of the array.
```

The Efficiency of the Binary Search

Obviously, the binary search is much more efficient than the linear search. Every time it makes a comparison and fails to find the desired item, it eliminates half of the remaining portion of the array that must be searched. For example, consider an array with 20,000 elements. If the binary search fails to find an item on the first attempt, the number of elements that remains to be searched is 10,000. If the item is not found on the second attempt, the number of elements that remains to be searched is 5,000. This process continues until the binary search locates the desired value or determines that it is not in the array. With 20,000 elements in the array, this takes a maximum of 15 comparisons. (Compare this to the linear search, which would make an average of 10,000 comparisons!)

Powers of 2 are used to calculate the maximum number of comparisons the binary search will make on an array of any size. (A power of 2 is 2 raised to some integer exponent.) Simply find the smallest power of 2 that is greater than the number of elements in the array. That will tell you the maximum number of comparisons needed to find an element, or to determine that it is not present. For example, a maximum of 16 comparisons will be made to find an item in an array of 50,000 elements ($2^{16} = 65,536$), and a maximum of 20 comparisons will be made to find an item in an array of 1,000,000 elements ($2^{20} = 1,048,576$).

Searching an Array of Objects

CONCEPT: Linear and binary searches can also be used to search for a specific entry in an array of objects or structures.

In Programs 9-1 and 9-2 we searched for a particular value in an array of integers. We can just as easily search through an array holding values of some other data type, such as `double` or `string`. We can even search an array of objects or structures. In this case, however, the search value is not the entire object or structure we are looking for, but rather a value in a particular member variable of that object or structure. The member variable being examined by the search is sometimes called the *key field*, and the particular value being looked for is called the *search key*.

Assume we have a class named `Inventory` that includes the following member variables

```
string itemCode;
string description;
double price;
```

as well as methods to *set* and *get* the value of each of these. Assume also that we have set up an array of `Inventory` objects. We might want to search for a particular object in the array, say the object whose `itemCode` is K33, so that we can then call the `getPrice` method for that object. Program 9-3 illustrates how to do this. It searches the array of `Inventory` objects using a `search` function similar to the `searchList` function we used earlier in this chapter. However, it has been modified to work with an array of `Inventory` objects.

Program 9-3

```
// This program searches an array of Inventory objects to get
// the price of a particular object. It demonstrates how to
// perform a linear search using an array of objects.
#include <iostream>
#include <string>
using namespace std;

// Inventory class declaration
class Inventory
{   private:
      string itemCode;
      string description;
      double price;

```

(program continues)

Program 9-3 *(continued)*

```
  public:
     Inventory()                                 // Default constructor
     {  itemCode = "XXX";  description = " ";  price = 0.0; }

     Inventory(string c, string d, double p) // 3 argument constructor
     {  itemCode = c;
        description = d;
        price = p;
     }

     // Add methods setCode, setDescription, and setPrice here.

     // Get functions to retrieve member variable values
     string getCode() const
     {  string code = itemCode;
        return code;
     }

     string getDescription() const
     {  string d = description;
        return d;
     }

     double getPrice() const
     {  return price;
     }

}; // End Inventory class declaration

// Program that uses the Inventory class

// Function prototype
int search(const Inventory[], int, string);

/*******************************************************
 *                      main                           *
 *******************************************************/
int main()
{
   const int SIZE = 6;

   // Create and initialize the array of Inventory objects
   Inventory silverware[SIZE] =
                              { Inventory("S15", "soup spoon",  2.35),
                                Inventory("S12", "teaspoon",    2.19),
                                Inventory("F15", "dinner fork", 3.19),
                                Inventory("F09", "salad fork" , 2.25),
                                Inventory("K33", "knife",       2.35),
                                Inventory("K41", "steak knife", 4.15) };

   string desiredCode;      // The itemCode to search for
   int pos;                 // Position of desired object in the array
   char doAgain;            // Look up another price (Y/N)?
```

(program continues)

Program 9-3 *(continued)*

```

   do
   {   // Get the itemCode to search for
       cout << "\nEnter an item code: ";
       cin  >> desiredCode;

       // Search for the object
       pos = search(silverware, SIZE, desiredCode);

       // If pos = -1, the code was not found
       if (pos == -1)
          cout << "That code does not exist in the array\n";
       else
       {  // The object was found, so use pos to get the
          // description and price
          cout << "This "    << silverware[pos].getDescription()
               << " costs $" << silverware[pos].getPrice() << endl;
       }

       // Does the user want to look up another price?
       cout << "\nLook up another price (Y/N)? ";
       cin  >> doAgain;

   } while (doAgain == 'Y' || doAgain == 'y');
   return 0;
}// End main

/***************************************************************
 *                          search                             *
 * This function performs a linear search on an array of       *
 * Inventory objects, using itemCode as the key field.         *
 * If the desired code is found, its array subscript is        *
 * returned. Otherwise, -1 is returned.                        *
 ***************************************************************/
int search(const Inventory object[], int size, string value)
{
   int index = 0;          // Used as a subscript to search array
   int position = -1;      // Used to record position of search value
   bool found = false;     // Flag to indicate if the value was found

   while (index < size && !found)
   {
      if (object[index].getCode() == value) // If the value is found
      {
         found = true;            // Set the flag
         position = index;        // Record the value's subscript
      }
      index++;                    // Go to the next element
   }
   return position;               // Return the position, or -1
}// End search
```

(program continues)

Program 9-3 *(continued)*

Program Output with Example Input Shown in Bold
```
Enter an item code: F15[Enter]
This dinner fork costs $3.19

Look up another price (Y/N)? n[Enter]
```

Recall from Chapter 7 that when an object is passed to a function as a constant reference, any of the object's member functions that the receiving function will call must also be defined with the key word `const`. This is also the case when an array of objects is passed to a function. In Program 9-3 the `search` function uses a `const` array parameter to receive the array of `Inventory` objects in order to safeguard it from any changes being made to it. Therefore, the `Inventory` class member functions it calls are also declared to be `const`.

Checkpoint

9.1 Describe the difference between the linear search and the binary search.

9.2 On average, with an array of 20,000 elements, how many comparisons will the linear search perform? (Assume the items being search for are consistently found in the array.)

9.3 With an array of 20,000 elements, what is the maximum number of comparisons the binary search will perform?

9.4 If a linear search is performed on an array, and it is known that some items are searched for more frequently than others, how can the contents of the array be reordered to improve the average performance of the search?

9.3 Introduction to Sorting Algorithms

CONCEPT: Sorting algorithms are used to arrange data into some order.

VideoNote
Sorting a Set of Data

Often the data in an array must be sorted in some order. Customer lists, for instance, are commonly sorted in alphabetical order. Student grades might be sorted from highest to lowest. Mailing label records could be sorted by ZIP code. To sort the data in an array, the programmer must use an appropriate *sorting algorithm*. A sorting algorithm is a technique for scanning through an array and rearranging its contents in some specific order. This section will introduce two simple sorting algorithms: the *bubble sort* and the *selection sort*.

The Bubble Sort

The bubble sort is an easy way to arrange data in *ascending* or *descending order*. Sorting data in ascending order means placing the values in order from lowest to highest. Sorting in descending order means placing them in order from highest to lowest. Bubble sort works by comparing each element in the array with its neighbor and swapping them if they are not in the desired order. Let's see how it arranges the following array's elements in ascending order:

7	2	3	8	9	1
Element 0	Element 1	Element 2	Element 3	Element 4	Element 5

The bubble sort starts by comparing the first two elements in the array. If element 0 is greater than element 1, they are exchanged. After the exchange, the array appears as

2	7	3	8	9	1
Element 0	Element 1	Element 2	Element 3	Element 4	Element 5

This process is repeated with elements 1 and 2. If element 1 is greater than element 2, they are exchanged. The array now appears as

2	3	7	8	9	1
Element 0	Element 1	Element 2	Element 3	Element 4	Element 5

Next, elements 2 and 3 are compared. However, in this array, these two elements are already in the proper order (element 2 is less than element 3), so no exchange takes place.

As the cycle continues, elements 3 and 4 are compared. Once again, because they are already in the proper order, no exchange is necessary. When elements 4 and 5 are compared, however, an exchange must take place because element 4 is greater than element 5. The array now appears as

2	3	7	8	1	9
Element 0	Element 1	Element 2	Element 3	Element 4	Element 5

At this point, the entire array has been scanned. This is called the first *pass* of the sort. Notice that the largest value is now correctly placed in the last array element. However, the rest of the array is not yet sorted. So the sort starts over again with elements 0 and 1. Because they are in the proper order, no exchange takes place. Elements 1 and 2 are compared next, but once again, no exchange takes place. This continues until elements 3 and 4 are compared. Because element 3 is greater than element 4, they are exchanged. The array now appears as

2	3	7	1	8	9
Element 0	Element 1	Element 2	Element 3	Element 4	Element 5

Notice that this second pass over the array elements has placed the second largest number in the next to the last array element. This process will continue, with the sort repeatedly passing through the array and placing at least one number in order on each pass, until the array is fully sorted. Ultimately, the array will appear as

1	2	3	7	8	9
Element 0	Element 1	Element 2	Element 3	Element 4	Element 5

Here is the bubble sort in pseudocode. Notice that it uses a pair of nested loops. The outer loop, a `do-while` loop, iterates once for each pass of the sort. The inner loop, a `for` loop, holds the code that does all the comparisons and needed swaps during a pass. If two elements are exchanged, the `swap` flag variable is set to `true`. The outer loop continues iterating, causing additional passes to be made, until it finds the `swap` flag `false`, meaning that no elements were swapped on the previous pass. This indicates that the array is now fully sorted.

```
Do
   Set swap flag to false
   For count = 0 to the next-to-last array subscript
      If array[count] is greater than array[count + 1]
         Swap the contents of array[count] and array[count + 1]
         Set swap flag to true
      End If
   End For
While the swap flag is true    // A swap ocurred on the previous pass.
```

The following C++ code implements the bubble sort as a function. The parameter `array` references an integer array to be sorted. The parameter `size` contains the number of elements in `array`.

```
void sortArray(int array[], int size)
{
   int temp;
   bool swap;

   do
   {  swap = false;
      for (int count = 0; count < (size - 1); count++)
      {
         if (array[count] > array[count + 1])
         {
            temp = array[count];
            array[count] = array[count + 1];
            array[count + 1] = temp;
            swap = true;
         }
      }
   } while (swap);    // Loop again if a swap occurred on this pass.
}
```

Let's look more closely at the `for` loop that handles the comparisons and exchanges during a pass. Here is its starting line:

```
for (int count = 0; count < (size - 1); count++)
```

The variable `count` holds the array subscripts. It starts at zero and is incremented as long as it is less than `size - 1`. The value of `size` is the number of elements in the array, and `count` stops just short of reaching this value because the following line compares each element with the one after it:

```
if (array[count] > array[count + 1])
```

When `array[count]` is the next-to-last element, it will be compared to the last element. If the `for` loop were allowed to increment `count` past `size - 1`, the last element in the array would be compared to a value outside the array.

Here is the `if` statement in its entirety:

```
if (array[count] > array[count + 1])
{
   temp = array[count];
   array[count] = array[count + 1];
   array[count + 1] = temp;
   swap = true;
}
```

If `array[count]` is greater than `array[count + 1]`, the two elements must be exchanged. First, the contents of `array[count]` is copied into the variable `temp`. Then the contents of `array[count + 1]` is copied into `array[count]`. The exchange is made complete when `temp` (which holds the previous contents of `array[count]`) is copied to `array[count + 1]`. Last, the `swap` flag variable is set to `true`. This indicates that an exchange has been made.

Program 9-4 demonstrates the bubble sort function in a complete program.

Program 9-4

```
// This program uses the bubble sort algorithm to sort an array
// of integers in ascending order.
#include <iostream>
using namespace std;

// Function prototypes
void sortArray(int [], int);
void showArray(const int [], int);

int main()
{
   const int SIZE = 6;

   // Array of unsorted values
   int values[SIZE] = {7, 2, 3, 8, 9, 1};

   // Display the values
   cout << "The unsorted values are:\n";
   showArray(values, SIZE);

   // Sort the values
   sortArray(values, SIZE);

   // Display them again
   cout << "The sorted values are:\n";
   showArray(values, SIZE);
   return 0;
}

```

(program continues)

Program 9-4 *(continued)*

```
/*********************************************************
 *                     sortArray                          *
 * This function performs an ascending-order bubble sort on *
 * array. The parameter size holds the number of elements   *
 * in the array.                                            *
 **********************************************************/
void sortArray(int array[], int size)
{
   int  temp;
   bool swap;

   do
   {   swap = false;
      for (int count = 0; count < (size - 1); count++)
      {
         if (array[count] > array[count + 1])
         {
            temp = array[count];
            array[count] = array[count + 1];
            array[count + 1] = temp;
            swap = true;
         }
      }
   } while (swap);   // Loop again if a swap occurred on this pass.
}

/**********************************************************
 *                     showArray                            *
 * This function displays the contents of array. The        *
 * parameter size holds the number of elements in the array. *
 **********************************************************/
void showArray(const int array[], int size)
{
   for (int count = 0; count < size; count++)
      cout << array[count] << " ";
   cout << endl;
}
```

Program Output

```
The unsorted values are:
7 2 3 8 9 1
The sorted values are:
1 2 3 7 8 9
```

The Selection Sort

The bubble sort is inefficient for large arrays because repeated data swaps are often required to place a single item in its correct position. The selection sort, like the bubble sort, places just one item in its correct position on each pass. However, it usually performs fewer exchanges because it moves items immediately to their correct position in the array.

Like any sort, it can be modified to sort in either ascending or descending order. An ascending sort works like this: The smallest value in the array is located and moved to element 0. Then the next smallest value is located and moved to element 1. This process continues until all of the elements have been placed in their proper order.

Let's see how the selection sort works when arranging the elements of the following array:

5	7	2	8	9	1
Element 0	Element 1	Element 2	Element 3	Element 4	Element 5

The selection sort scans the array, starting at element 0, and locates the element with the smallest value. The contents of this element are then swapped with the contents of element 0. In this example, the 1 stored in element 5 is the smallest value, so it is swapped with the 5 stored in element 0. This completes the first pass and the array now appears as

1	7	2	8	9	5
Element 0	Element 1	Element 2	Element 3	Element 4	Element 5

The algorithm then repeats the process, but because element 0 already contains the smallest value in the array, it can be left out of the procedure. For the second pass, the algorithm begins the scan at element 1. It locates the smallest value in the unsorted part of the array, which is the 2 in element 2. Therefore, element 2 is exchanged with element 1. The array now appears as

1	2	7	8	9	5
Element 0	Element 1	Element 2	Element 3	Element 4	Element 5

Once again the process is repeated, but this time the scan begins at element 2. The algorithm will find that element 5 contains the next smallest value and will exchange this element's contents with that of element 2, causing the array to appear as

1	2	5	8	9	7
Element 0	Element 1	Element 2	Element 3	Element 4	Element 5

Next, the scanning begins at element 3. Its contents is exchanged with that of element 5, causing the array to appear as

1	2	5	7	9	8
Element 0	Element 1	Element 2	Element 3	Element 4	Element 5

At this point there are only two elements left to sort. The algorithm finds that the value in element 5 is smaller than that of element 4, so the two are swapped. This puts the array in its final arrangement:

1	2	5	7	8	9
Element 0	Element 1	Element 2	Element 3	Element 4	Element 5

Here is the selection sort algorithm in pseudocode:

```
For startScan = 0 to the next-to-last array subscript
   Set index to startScan
   Set minIndex to startScan
   Set minValue to array[startScan]
   For index = (startScan + 1) to the last subscript in the array
      If array[index] is less than minValue
         Set minValue to array[index]
         Set minIndex to index
      End If
      Increment index
   End For
   Set array[minIndex] to array[startScan]
   Set array[startScan] to minValue
End For
```

The following function uses the selection sort to arrange the values in an integer array in ascending order. It accepts two arguments. The first parameter, `array`, receives the array to be sorted and the second, `size`, indicates how many values are stored in the array.

```
void selectionSort(int array[], int size)
{
    int startScan, minIndex, minValue;

    for (startScan = 0; startScan < (size - 1); startScan++)
    {
       minIndex = startScan;
       minValue = array[startScan];

       for (int index = startScan + 1; index < size; index++)
       {
          if (array[index] < minValue)
          {
             minValue = array[index];
             minIndex = index;
          }
       }
       array[minIndex] = array[startScan];
       array[startScan] = minValue;
    }
}
```

As with bubble sort, selection sort uses a pair of nested loops, in this case two `for` loops. The inner loop sequences through the array, starting at `array[startScan + 1]`, searching for the element with the smallest value. When the element is found, its subscript is stored in the variable `minIndex`, and its value is stored in `minValue`. The outer loop then exchanges the contents of this element with `array[startScan]` and increments `startScan`. This procedure repeats until the contents of every element have been moved to their proper location. For N pieces of data this requires N-1 passes.

Program 9-5 demonstrates the selection sort function in a complete program.

Program 9-5

```
// This program uses the selection sort algorithm to sort
// an array in ascending order.
#include <iostream>
using namespace std;

// Function prototypes
void selectionSort(int [], int);
void showArray(const int [], int);

int main()
{
   const int SIZE = 6;

   // Array of unsorted values
   int values[SIZE] = {5, 7, 2, 8, 9, 1};

   // Display the values
   cout << "The unsorted values are\n";
   showArray(values, SIZE);

   // Sort the array
   selectionSort(values, SIZE);

   // Display the values again
   cout << "The sorted values are\n";
   showArray(values, SIZE);
   return 0;
}

/**************************************************************
 *                        selectionSort                       *
 * This function performs an ascending-order selection sort   *
 * on array. The parameter size holds the number of elements  *
 * in the array.                                              *
 **************************************************************/
void selectionSort(int array[], int size)
{
   int startScan, minIndex, minValue;

```

(program continues)

Program 9-5 *(continued)*

```
   for (startScan = 0; startScan < (size - 1); startScan++)
   {
      minIndex = startScan;
      minValue = array[startScan];
      for(int index = startScan + 1; index < size; index++)
      {
         if (array[index] < minValue)
         {
            minValue = array[index];
            minIndex = index;
         }
      }
      array[minIndex] = array[startScan];
      array[startScan] = minValue;
   }
}

/************************************************************
 *                        showArray                         *
 * This function displays the contents of array. The       *
 * parameter size holds the number of elements in the array. *
 ************************************************************/
void showArray(const int array[], int size)
{
   for (int count = 0; count < size; count++)
      cout << array[count] << " ";
   cout << endl;
}
```

Program Output

```
The unsorted values are
5 7 2 8 9 1
The sorted values are
1 2 5 7 8 9
```

Checkpoint

9.5 True or false: Any sort can be modified to sort in either ascending or descending order.

9.6 What one line of code would need to be modified in the bubble sort to make it sort in descending, rather than ascending order? How would the revised line be written?

9.7 After one pass of bubble sort, which value is in order?

9.8 After one pass of selection sort, which value is in order?

9.9 Which sort usually requires fewer data values to be swapped, bubble sort or selection sort?

9.4 Sorting an Array of Objects

CONCEPT: Sorting algorithms can also be used to order elements in an array of objects or structures.

Programs 9-4 and 9-5 illustrated how to sort an array of integers using bubble sort and selection sort. These sorts could just as easily be used to sort array elements of any other data type. Program 9-6 uses a bubble sort to sort `Inventory` objects, using the `Inventory` class introduced earlier in this chapter. When sorting objects or structures, one must decide which data item to sort on. For example, we could arrange `Inventory` objects in order by `itemCode`, by `description`, or by `price`. To determine if two elements are out of order and should be swapped, we compare *only* the values in the data member we are sorting on. However, if the two array elements are found to be out of order, we swap the *entire* two elements. This is illustrated in Program 9-6.

Program 9-6

```
// This program uses bubble sort to sort an array of objects.
// It places Inventory objects in ascending order by their itemCode.
#include <iostream>
#include <iomanip>
#include <string>
using namespace std;

// Inventory class declaration
class Inventory
{   private:
       string itemCode;
       string description;
       double price;

  public:
     Inventory()                                  // Default constructor
     {  itemCode = "XXX";  description = " ";  price = 0.0; }

     Inventory(string c, string d, double p) // 3 argument constructor
     {  itemCode = c;
        description = d;
        price = p;
     }

     // Add methods setCode, setDescription, and setPrice here.

     // Get functions to retrieve member variable values
     string getCode() const
     {  string code = itemCode;
        return code;
     }

```

(program continues)

Program 9-6 *(continued)*

```
    string getDescription() const
    {  string d = description;
       return d;
    }

    double getPrice() const
    {  return price;
    }

}; // End Inventory class declaration

// Program that uses the Inventory class

// Function prototype
void displayInventory(const Inventory[], int);
void bubbleSort(Inventory[], int);

/*******************************************************
 *                      main                           *
 *******************************************************/
int main()
{
   const int SIZE = 6;

   // Create and initialize the array of Inventory objects
   Inventory silverware[SIZE] =
                          { Inventory("S15", "soup spoon",  2.35),
                            Inventory("S12", "teaspoon",    2.19),
                            Inventory("F15", "dinner fork", 3.19),
                            Inventory("F09", "salad fork" , 2.25),
                            Inventory("K33", "knife",       2.35),
                            Inventory("K41", "steak knife", 4.15) };

   // Display the inventory
   cout << "Here is the original data\n";
   displayInventory(silverware, SIZE);

   // Sort the objects by their itemCode
   bubbleSort(silverware, SIZE);

   // Display the inventory again
   cout << "\nHere is the sorted data\n";
   displayInventory(silverware, SIZE);

   return 0;
} //End main

```

(program continues)

Program 9-6 *(continued)*

```
/*****************************************************
 *                  displayInventory                 *
 * This function displays the entire array.          *
 *****************************************************/
void displayInventory(const Inventory object[], int size)
{
   for (int index = 0; index < size; index++)
   {  cout << setw(5)  << left  << object[index].getCode()
           << setw(13) << left  << object[index].getDescription()
           << "$"      << right << object[index].getPrice() << endl;
   }
}// End displayInventory

/*****************************************************
 *                      bubbleSort                   *
 * This function performs a bubble sort on Inventory *
 * objects, arranging them in ascending itemCode order. *
 *****************************************************/
void bubbleSort(Inventory array[], int size)
{
   Inventory temp;    // Holds an Inventory object
   bool swap;

   do
   {  swap = false;
      for (int count = 0; count < (size - 1); count++)
      {
         if (array[count].getCode() > array[count + 1].getCode())
         {
            temp = array[count];
            array[count] = array[count + 1];
            array[count + 1] = temp;
            swap = true;
         }
      }
   } while (swap);
}// End bubbleSort
```

Program Output

```
Here is the original data
S15  soup spoon   $2.35
S12  teaspoon     $2.19
F15  dinner fork  $3.19
F09  salad fork   $2.25
K33  knife        $2.35
K41  steak knife  $4.15

Here is the sorted data
F09  salad fork   $2.25
F15  dinner fork  $3.19
K33  knife        $2.35
K41  steak knife  $4.15
S12  teaspoon     $2.19
S15  soup spoon   $2.35
```

Let's take a closer look at the `bubbleSort` function. Line 107 contains the code that compares the objects stored in two array elements. Notice that only the `itemCode` values of the objects are compared and that these values are retrieved by using each object's `getCode` method.

Next look at lines 109 through 111 where the actual swap takes place when two objects are out of order. Notice that the entire objects are swapped and that an entire object can be moved in a single statement. It isn't necessary to move each of the member variables one by one.

Finally, notice in line 100 that `temp` is defined as an `Inventory` object. Because it will be used to temporarily hold an array element during each swap, and because the array elements in this case are `Inventory` objects, `temp` must also be defined as an `Inventory` object.

9.5 Sorting and Searching Vectors

CONCEPT: The sorting and searching algorithms you have studied in this chapter can be applied to STL vectors as well as to arrays.

In the previous chapter you learned about the vector class that is part of the Standard Template Library (STL). Once you have properly defined an STL `vector` and populated it with values, you may sort and search the vector with the algorithms presented in this chapter. Simply substitute the vector syntax for the array syntax when necessary.

Program 9-7 modifies Program 9-4 to use a STL `vector` instead of an array.

Program 9-7

```
// This program uses the bubble sort algorithm to sort
// a vector of integers in ascending order.
#include <iostream>
#include <vector>               // Needed to use vectors
using namespace std;

// Function prototypes
void displayVector(vector<int>);
void sortVector(vector<int> &);

int main()
{
   const int SIZE = 6;

   // Create a vector to hold a set of unsorted integers
   vector<int> values(SIZE);

   // Prompt the user to enter the values to be stored.
   cout << "Please enter " << SIZE << " integers separated by spaces.\n";

   for (int i = 0; i < SIZE; i++)
      cin >> values[i];

```

(program continues)

Program 9-7 *(continued)*

```
   // Display the values
   cout << "\nThe unsorted values entered are:\n";
   displayVector(values);

   // Sort the values
   sortVector(values);

   // Display them again
   cout << "The sorted values are:\n";
   displayVector(values);
   return 0;
}

/************************************************************
 *                        sortVector                        *
 * This function performs an ascending-order bubble sort on *
 * numbers, a vector of integers.                           *
 ************************************************************/
void sortVector(vector<int> &numbers)
{  int  temp;
   bool swap;

   do
   {  swap = false;
      for (unsigned count = 0; count < numbers.size()-1; count++)
      {
         if (numbers[count] > numbers[count + 1])
         {
            temp = numbers[count];
            numbers[count] = numbers[count + 1];
            numbers[count + 1] = temp;
            swap = true;
         }
      }
   } while (swap);
}

/*************************************************************
 *                     displayVector                         *
 * This function displays the contents of numbers, a         *
 * vector of integers.                                       *
 *************************************************************/
void displayVector(vector<int> numbers)
{
   for (unsigned count = 0; count < numbers.size(); count++)
      cout << numbers[count] << " ";
   cout << endl;
}
```

Program 9-7 *(continued)*

Program Output With Example Input Shown in Bold

```
Please enter 6 integers separated by spaces.
9 4 8 6 3 1[Enter]

The unsorted values entered are:
9 4 8 6 3 1
The sorted values are:
1 3 4 6 8 9
```

Notice the similarities and differences between Program 9-7 and Program 9-4. The code in Program 9-7 that sorts vectors is almost identical to the code in Program 9-4 that sorts arrays. The differences lie in some details of initialization and argument passing.

First, notice that in Program 9-4 the array data is provided in an initialization list when the array is created, but in Program 9-7 the data to be stored in the vector is input by the user. This is done because vectors do not accept initialization lists. Second, notice that in Program 9-7 the vector is passed by reference to the `sortVector` function. This is necessary because, unlike arrays, vectors are passed by value unless the programmer uses a reference variable as a parameter. Finally, notice that in Program 9-7 we don't have to pass the size of the vector to the functions that work with it because the vector's `size` member function can tell us how many elements it holds. You may have noticed that the loop control variables in lines 48 and 68 of Program 9-7 are declared to be `unsigned`. This is because they are compared to the value returned by the `size` function, and it returns an `unsigned` value. Some compilers complain if an `int` variable is compared to an `unsigned` value.

9.6 Introduction to Analysis of Algorithms

CONCEPT: We can estimate the efficiency of an algorithm by counting the number of steps it requires to solve a problem.

An algorithm is a mechanical step-by-step procedure for solving a problem and is the basic strategy used in designing a program. There is often more than one algorithm that can be used to solve a given problem. For example, we saw earlier in this chapter that the problem of searching a sorted array can be solved by two different methods: *sequential search* and *binary search.*

How can we decide which of two algorithms for solving a problem is better? To answer this question, we need to establish criteria for judging the "goodness" or efficiency of an algorithm. The two criteria most often used are space and time. The *space* criterion refers to the amount of memory the algorithm requires to solve the problem, while the *time* criterion refers to the length of execution time. In this chapter, we will use the time criterion to evaluate the efficiency of algorithms.

One possibility for comparing two algorithms is to code them and then time the execution of the resulting C++ programs. This experimental approach can yield useful information, but it has the following shortcomings:

- It measures the efficiency of programs rather than algorithms.

- The results depend on the programming language used to code the algorithms, and on the quality of the compiler used to generate machine code. The programs may run faster or slower if they are coded in a different language, or compiled by a different compiler.
- The results depend on how the operating system executes programs, and on the nature of the hardware on which the programs are executing. The execution times may be different if we run the programs on a different computer and a different operating system.
- The results apply only to those inputs that were part of the execution runs and may not be representative of the performance of the algorithms using a different set of inputs.

A better approach is to count the number of basic steps an algorithm requires to process an input of a given size. To make sense of this approach, we need more precise definitions of what we mean by computational problem, problem input, input size, and basic step.

Computational Problems and Basic Steps

A *computational problem* is a problem to be solved using an algorithm. Such a problem is a collection of *instances*, with each instance specified by input data given in some prescribed format. For example, if the problem P is to sort an array of integers, then an instance of P is a specific integer array to be sorted. The *size* of an instance refers to the amount of memory needed to hold the input data. The input size is usually given as a number that allows us to infer the total number of bits occupied by the input data. If the number of bits occupied by each entry of the array is fixed, say at 64 bits, then the length of the array is a good measure of input size. In contrast, the length of the array is not a good measure of input size if the size of array elements can vary and there is no fixed upper bound on the size of these elements.

A step executed by an algorithm is a *basic step* (also called a *basic operation*) if the algorithm can execute the step in time bounded by a constant regardless of the size of the input. In sorting an array of integers, the step

Swap the elements in positions k and k+1

is basic because the time required to swap two array elements remains constant even if the length of the array increases. In contrast, a step such as

Find the largest element of the array

is not basic because the time required to complete the step depends on the length of the array. Intuitively, a basic step is one that could conceivably be built into the hardware of some physical computer.

The definition of a basic step does not specify the size of the constant that bounds the time required to execute the step. Ignoring the exact value of these constants reflects the reality that the same operation may be executed with different speeds on different hardware, and that an operation that can be executed with one hardware instruction on one computer may require several hardware instructions on another computer. A consequence of this definition is that we can count any constant number of basic steps as one basic step. For example, an algorithm that executes $5n$ basic steps can accurately be described as executing n basic steps.

It is important to realize that ordinary arithmetic and logic operations such as addition and comparison are not basic unless a constant bound is put on the size of the numbers being added or compared. The size of the bound does not matter as long as the bound is constant. It may be 32, 64, 128, 1024 bits, or even larger, and these operations will still be basic. In the following discussion, we assume that all the numbers used in our algorithms as inputs, outputs, or computed intermediate results are bounded in size. This allows us to consider operations on them as basic.

It only makes sense to describe an algorithm after we have described the problem it is supposed to solve. A computational problem is described by stating what the input will look like, how big it is, and what output the algorithm solving the problem is supposed to produce. These must be described clearly, so there is no ambiguity, and generally, so the algorithm can work with any data set that fits the description.

Let's look at an example. Suppose the problem P is to sum all the integer values in a one-dimensional array. We could describe the problem by saying that the input data is an array of n integer values and that the output to be produced is the integer sum of these values. Formally, this is written as follows:

INPUT: an integer array `a[]` of size n
SIZE OF INPUT: The number n of array entries
OUTPUT: An integer *sum* representing the sum total of the values stored in the array

Notice that the word INPUT used this way does not mean a set of data entered by the user, but rather means the form of the data used by the algorithm solving the problem. Likewise, the word OUTPUT used this way does not mean something displayed on the computer screen by a program. It means the result created by the algorithm that solves the problem. Because we have assumed all the array entries are of some fixed size, such as 32 or 64 bits, the number n of elements in the array is a good measure of input size.

Once a computational problem has been described, there can be many different algorithms designed to solve it. Some, of course, are better than others, as we will soon see. Here is one possible algorithm for solving the computational problem just described. Notice that it is expressed in pseudocode, rather than in C++ or any other particular programming language.

Algorithm 1:

```
1: sum = 0
2: k = 0 //array index
3: While k < n do
4:     sum = sum + a[k]
5:     k = k + 1
6: End While
```

Complexity of Algorithms

We can measure the complexity of an algorithm that solves a computational problem by determining the number of basic steps it requires for an input of size n. Let's count the number of steps required by Algorithm 1. The algorithm consists of two statements on lines 1 and 2 that are each executed once and two statements inside a loop on lines 4 and 5 that will execute once each time the loop iterates. Recall that because the statements on lines 1 and 2 perform basic operations they can be grouped together and counted as one basic operation. Let's call this operation A.

Also, because both statements in the loop execute in constant time, independently of the size of n, they are also basic operations. Since the loop body contains only basic operations, the amount of time the algorithm takes to execute a *single* iteration of the loop is also constant, and not dependent on the size of n. This allows us to count each loop iteration as a single basic operation. Let's call this operation B.

Operation A executes only one time, regardless of how big n is. Operation B executes once each time the loop iterates. Because the loop iterates n times, operation B is executed n times. Thus, the total number of operations performed is $1 + n$. When $n = 10$, for example, 11 operations are performed. When $n = 1000$, 1001 operations are performed. When $n = 10{,}000$ the number of operations performed is 10,001. Notice that as n becomes large, the 1 becomes insignificant and the number of operations performed is approximately n. We thus say that the algorithm requires execution time proportional to n to process an input set of size n.

There is another way we could look at Algorithm 1 and determine how many operations it requires. The crucial operation in summing the values in an array is the addition of each value to the variable accumulating the sum. This occurs in line 4, and there are as many additions of array values as there are loop iterations.

Thus, we could get the same result by just counting additions of array elements. It turns out that for most algorithms, it is sufficient to identify and count only one or two basic operations that are in some way crucial to the problem being solved. For example, in many array searching and sorting algorithms, it is sufficient to just count the number of comparisons between array elements.

The array-summing algorithm just considered is particularly simple to analyze because it performs the same amount of work for all input sets of a given size.

This is not the case with all algorithms. Consider the linear search algorithm introduced earlier in this chapter. It searches through an array of values, looking for one that matches a search key. Let's call the key X. The input to the algorithm is the array of n values and the key value X. The output of the algorithm is the subscript of the array location where the value was located or, if it is not found, the determination that the loop control variable has become larger than the subscript of the last array element. Formally, the problem can be stated like this:

INPUT: An integer array $a[\,]$ of size n, and an integer X
SIZE OF INPUT: The number n of array entries
OUTPUT: An integer k in the range $0 \le k \le n - 1$ such that $a[k] = X$, or $k = n$

Algorithm 2, shown here, uses the linear search algorithm to solve the problem.

Algorithm 2:

```
k = 0
While k < n and a[k] ≠ X do
    k = k + 1
End While
```

This algorithm starts at one end and searches sequentially through the array. The algorithm stops as soon as it encounters X, but will search the entire array if X is not in the array. The algorithm may stop after making only one comparison (X is found in the first entry examined), or it may not stop until it has made n comparisons (X is found in the last place examined or is not in the array). In fact, the algorithm may perform m comparisons where m is any value from 1 to n. In cases where an algorithm may perform different amounts of work for different inputs of the same size, it is common to measure the efficiency of the algorithm by the work done on an input of size n that requires the *most* work. This is called measuring the algorithm by its worst-case complexity function.

Worst-Case Complexity of Algorithms

The *worst-case complexity function* $f(n)$ of an algorithm is the number of steps it performs on an input of size n that requires the most work. It gives an indication of the longest time the algorithm will ever take to solve an instance of size n and is a good measure of efficiency to use when we are looking for a performance guarantee.

Let's determine the worst-case complexity of binary search, which was introduced earlier in this chapter. This algorithm is used to locate an item X in an array sorted in ascending order. The worst case occurs when X is not found in the array. In this case, as we will see, the algorithm performs $L + 1$ steps, where L is the number of loop iterations.

Here is the binary search algorithm to search an array of n elements.

Algorithm 3:

```
first = 0
last = n - 1     // n - 1 is the subscript of the last element.
found = false
position = -1
While found is not true and first <= last
   middle = (first + last) / 2
   If a[middle] = X
      found = true
      position = middle
   Else if a[middle] > X
      last = middle - 1
   Else
      first = middle + 1
   End If
End While
// When the loop terminates, position holds the subscript
// where the value matching X was found, or holds –1 if
// the value was not found.
```

The algorithm consists of some initialization of variables followed by a loop. The initialization requires constant time and can therefore be considered to be one basic operation. Likewise, each iteration of the loop is a basic step because increasing the number of entries in the array does not increase the amount of time required by a single iteration of the loop. This shows that the number of steps required by binary search is $L + 1$. Now L is approximately equal to the integer part of $\log_2 n$, the logarithm of n to the base 2. To see this, notice that the size of the array to be searched is initially n, and each iteration reduces the size of the remaining portion of the array by approximately one half. Because each loop iteration performs at most two comparisons, binary search performs a total of $2 \log_2 n$ comparisons. We can summarize our findings as follows:

In the worst case, binary search requires time proportional to $\log_2 n$.

Let's look at one more algorithm to determine its worst-case complexity. The computational problem to be solved is to arrange a set of n integers into ascending order.

INPUT: An array $a[\,]$ of n integers
SIZE OF INPUT: The number n of array entries
OUTPUT: The array $a[\,]$ rearranged so that $a[0] \leq a[1] \leq \ldots \leq a[n-1]$

The algorithm we will use is a modification of the selection sort algorithm introduced earlier in this chapter. This version scans for the largest element (instead of the smallest) and moves it to the end in each pass.

Algorithm 4:

```
1:  For (k = n-1; k ≥ 1; k --)
2:      // a[0..k] is what remains to be sorted
3:      Determine position p of largest entry in a[0..k]
4:          Swap a[p] with a[k]
5:  End For
```

To analyze the complexity of this algorithm, let's begin by determining the number of array entry comparisons it makes when sorting an array of n entries. These comparisons occur in step 3. Step 3 is clearly not a basic step, as it requires time proportional to k, and k varies with each iteration of the loop. To better see what is going on, let's restate step 3 using operations that are basic.

INPUT: array $a[0..k]$ of $k + 1$ entries
SIZE OF INPUT: number $k + 1$ of array entries

```
3.0:  p = 0 //Position of largest value in unsorted part of the array
3.1:  For (m = 1; m ≤ k; m ++)
3.2:      If a[m] > a[p] Then
3.3:         p = m
3.4:    End if
3.5:  End For
```

We can see that the loop in lines 3.1 through 3.5 iterates k times and on line 3.2 makes one comparison each time it iterates. Therefore this algorithm requires k comparisons between array entries.

Now returning to the main sorting algorithm, we observe that there will be $n - 1$ iterations of the loop that starts at line 1 and ends at line 5, one iteration for each value of k in the range $n - 1$ to 1. On the first iteration, k equals $n - 1$, so step 3, as we learned from the analysis of lines 3.0 through 3.5, performs $n - 1$ comparisons between array elements. On the second iteration, k equals $n - 2$, so step 3 performs $n - 2$ comparisons. This continues until, on the final iteration, k equals 1, and step 3 performs 1 comparison. Here is what it looks like:

$k = n - 1$: step 3 performs $n - 1$ comparisons
$k = n - 2$: step 3 performs $n - 2$ comparisons
$\vdots$
$k = 1$: step 3 performs 1 comparison

Generalizing, we can thus say that for every value of k from $n - 1$ to 1, on the kth iteration, the step on line 3 will perform k comparisons.

Thus the total number of comparisons performed by this simple sorting algorithm is given by the expression

$1 + 2 + 3 + \ldots + (n - 1) = (n - 1)n/2$

For large n, this expression is very close to $n^2 / 2$. So we say that:

In the worst case, selection sort requires time proportional to n^2.

Average-Case Complexity

The worst-case complexity does not, however, give a good indication of how an algorithm will perform in practical situations where inputs that yield worst-case performance are rare. Often we are more interested in determining the complexity of the typical, or average case. The *average-case complexity function* can be used when we know the relative frequencies with which different inputs are likely to occur in practice. The average-case complexity function uses these frequencies to form a weighted average of the number of steps performed on each input. Unfortunately, although it yields a good measure of the expected performance of an algorithm, accurate estimates of input frequencies may be difficult to obtain.

Asymptotic Complexity and the Big O Notation

We can compare two algorithms F and G for solving a problem by comparing their complexity functions. More specifically, if $f(n)$ and $g(n)$ are the complexity functions for the two algorithms, we can compare the algorithms against each other by looking at what happens to the ratio $f(n)/g(n)$ when n gets large. This is easiest to understand if this ratio tends to some limit. Let us consider some specific examples. Throughout, we assume that $f(n) \geq 1$ and $g(n) \geq 1$ for all $(n) \geq 1$.

- $f(n) = 3n^2 + 5n$ and $g(n) = n^2$. In this case

$$\frac{f(n)}{g(n)} = \frac{3n^2 + 5n}{n^2} = 3 + \frac{5}{n} \rightarrow 3 \text{ as } n \rightarrow \infty$$

That is, the value of $f(n)/g(n)$ gets closer and closer to 3 as n gets large. What this means is that for very large input sizes F performs three times as many basic operations as G. However, because the two algorithms differ in performance only by a constant factor, we consider them to be equivalent in efficiency.

- $f(n) = 3n^2 + 5n$ and $g(n) = 100n$. In this case

$$\frac{f(n)}{g(n)} = \frac{3n^2 + 5n}{100n} = \frac{3n}{100} + \frac{5}{100} \rightarrow \infty \text{ as } n \rightarrow \infty$$

Here, the ratio $f(n)/g(n)$ gets larger and larger as n gets large. This means F does a lot more work than G on large input sizes. This makes G the better algorithm for large inputs.

- $f(n) = 3n^2 + 5n$ and $g(n) = n^3$. In this case

$$\frac{f(n)}{g(n)} = \frac{3n^2 + 5n}{n^3} = \frac{3}{n} + \frac{5}{n^2} \rightarrow 0 \text{ as } n \rightarrow \infty$$

This means that for large inputs the algorithm *G* is doing a lot more work than *F*, making *F* the more efficient algorithm.

In general, we can compare two complexity functions $f(n)$ and $g(n)$ by looking at what happens to $f(n)/g(n)$ as n gets large. Although thinking in terms of a limit of this ratio is helpful in comparing the two algorithms, we cannot assume that such a limit will always exist. It turns out that a limit does not have to exist for us to gain useful information from this ratio. We can usefully compare the two complexity functions if we can find a positive constant *K* such that

$$\frac{f(n)}{g(n)} \leq K \text{ for all } n \geq 1$$

If this can be done, it means that the algorithm *F* is no worse than *K* times *G* for large problems. In this case, we say that $f(n)$ is in $O(g(n))$, pronounced "*f* is in Big O of *g*." The condition that defines $f(n)$ is in $O(g(n))$ is often written like this

$$f(n) \leq Kg(n) \text{ whenever } n \geq 1.$$

Showing that $f(n)$ is in $O(g(n))$ is usually straightforward. You look at the ratio $f(n)/g(n)$ and try to find a positive constant *K* that makes $f(n)/g(n) \leq K$ for all $n \geq 1$. For example, to show that $3n^2 + 5n$ is in $O(n^2)$, look at the ratio

$$\frac{3n^2 + 5n}{n^2} = 3 + \frac{5}{n}$$

and notice that $5/n$ will be at most 5 for all $n \geq 1$. So $3 + 5/n \leq 8$. Therefore for $K = 8$, $f(n) / g(n) \leq K$.

To show that $f(n)$ is not in $O(g(n))$, you have to show that there is no way to find a positive *K* that will satisfy $f(n) / g(n) \leq K$ for all $n \geq 1$. For example, the function $3n^2 + 5n$ is not in $O(n)$ because there is no constant *K* that satisfies

$$\frac{3n^2 + 5n}{n} = 3n + 5 \leq K \text{ for all } n \geq 1.$$

Although defined for functions, the "Big O" notation and terminology is also used to characterize algorithms and computational problems. Thus, we say that an algorithm *F* is in $O(g(n))$ for some function $g(n)$ if the worst-case complexity function $f(n)$ of *F* is in Big O of $g(n)$. Accordingly, sequential search of an array is in $O(n)$ whereas binary search is in $O(\log_2 n)$.

Similarly, a computational problem is said to be in $O(g(n))$ if there exists an algorithm for the problem whose worst-case complexity function is in $O(g(n))$. Thus, the problem of sorting an array is in $O(n^2)$, whereas the problem of searching a sorted array is in $O(\log_2 n)$.

If $g(n)$ is a function, $O(g(n))$ can be regarded as a family of functions that grow no faster than $g(n)$. These families are called *complexity classes*, and a few of them are important enough to merit specific names. We list them here in order of their rate of growth.

1. O(1): A function $f(n)$ is in this class if there is a constant $K > 0$ such that $f(n) \leq K$ for all $n \geq 1$. An algorithm whose worst-case complexity function is in this class is said to run in *constant time.*
2. $O(\log_2 n)$: Algorithms in this class run in *logarithmic time*. Because log n grows much slower than n, a huge increase in the size of the problem results in only a small increase in the running time of the algorithm. This complexity is characteristic of search problems that eliminate half of the search space with each basic operation. The *binary search* algorithm is in this class.
3. $O(n)$: Algorithms in this class run in *linear time*. Any increase in the size of the problem results in a proportionate increase in the running time of the algorithm. This complexity is characteristic of algorithms like *sequential search* that make a single pass, or a constant number of passes, over their input.
4. $O(n \log_2 n)$: This class is called "n log n" *time*. An increase in the size of the problem results in a slight increase in the running time of the algorithm. The average case complexity of *Quicksort,* a sorting algorithm you will learn about in Chapter 14, is in this class.
5. $O(n^2)$: This class is called *quadratic time*. This performance is characteristic of algorithms that make multiple passes over the input data using two nested loops. An increase in the size of the problem causes a much greater increase in the running time of the algorithm. The worst-case complexity functions of *bubble sort, selection sort,* and *Quicksort* all lie in this class.

Checkpoint

9.10 What is a basic operation?

9.11 What is the worst-case complexity function of an algorithm?

9.12 One algorithm needs $10n$ basic operations to process an input of size n, and another algorithm needs $25n$ basic operations to process the same input. Which of the two algorithms is more efficient? Or are they equally efficient?

9.13 What does it mean to say that $f(n)$ is in $O(g(n))$?

9.14 Show that $100n^3 + 50n^2 + 75$ is in $O(20n^3)$ by finding a positive K that satisfies the equation $(100n^3 + 50n^2 + 75) / 20n^3 \leq K$.

9.15 Assuming $g(n) \geq 1$ for all $n \geq 1$, show that every function in $O(g(n) + 100)$ is also in $O(g(n))$.

9.7 Case Studies

The following case studies, which contain applications of material introduced in Chapter 9, can be found on the book's companion website.

Demetris Leadership Center—Parts 1 & 2

Chapter 9 included programs illustrating how to search and sort arrays, including arrays of objects. These two case studies illustrate how to search and sort arrays of structures. Both studies develop programs for DLC, Inc., a fictional company that publishes books, DVDs, and audio CDs. DLC's inventory data, used by both programs, is stored in an array of structures.

Creating an Abstract Array Data Type—Part 2

The `IntList` class, begun as a case study in Chapter 8, is extended to include array searching and sorting capabilities.

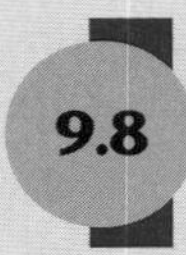

9.8 Tying It All Together: *Secret Messages*

Now that you know how to search through an array to locate a desired item, we can write a program to encode and decode secret messages. We will use a simple substitution cipher. This means that for each character in a message, a different character will be substituted. For example, if we substitute `f` for `c`, `t` for `a`, and `x` for `t`, then the word `cat` would be written `ftx`. Can you guess what this message says?

```
*>P;HMAyJHyJH9|[3Lf
```

You'll know if you run the message through the program decoder.

For this program we'll create a `CodeMaker` class that has `encode` and `decode` functions. When a `CodeMaker` object is created, the constructor will open the `code.dat` file that contains the character substitutions to be used. This file is located, along with the program source code file, in the Chapter 9 folder on the book's companion website. Be sure to place it in the project directory so the program can open and use it. There is one substitution character for each of the printable ASCII characters, which are represented by the decimal numbers 32 through 126. The program will read in these characters and store them in a one-dimensional array of characters, using the ASCII code of the original character, minus 32, as the index for the stored substitution character. So, for example, the substitution for ASCII character 32, a blank, will be stored in array element 0. The substitution for ASCII character 33, an exclamation point, will be in array element 1, and so forth.

The code will be hard to break because even the blank space will be represented by another character. So someone trying to read the code will not know where one word ends and the next one begins.

When the `encode` method is called, it is passed a string holding the message to be encoded. The method simply uses the ASCII code of each character in the string to compute the array index where its replacement character is located. Once each character in the string has been replaced, the string is returned.

When the `decode` method is called, it is passed a string holding an encoded message to be turned back into its original, or *plain text*, form. However, this method cannot compute an index to reverse the code. Instead, for each character in the string, it must do a search of the array to locate it. When the character is found, its array subscript can be used to compute the ASCII value of the original character. Once each character in the encoded string has been translated back to its original form, the string is returned.

In addition to creating the `CodeMaker` class, we will also write a client program that does the following:

- Creates a `CodeMaker` object.
- Has the user input a message and store it as a string.
- Calls the `encode` function, passing it the string.
- Displays the returned `encoded` string.
- Calls the `decode` function, passing it the encoded string.
- Displays the returned decoded string. This should equal the original message.

Program 9-8 does all of this.

Program 9-8

```
// This program encodes and decodes secret messages.
#include <iostream>
#include <fstream>
#include <string>
using namespace std;

class CodeMaker
{
   private:
      int size;
      char codeChar[94];      // Array to hold the substitutions
                              // for the 94 printable ASCII chars
      int findIt(char[], int, char);

   public:
      CodeMaker();
      string encode(string);
      string decode(string);
};

// Member function implementation section

/*****************************************************
 *     CodeMaker::CodeMaker - the Constructor        *
 * This method reads the substitution characters in  *
 * from a file and stores them it the codeChar array.*
 * It also sets member variable size.                *
 *****************************************************/
CodeMaker::CodeMaker()
{
   size = 94;
   ifstream inFile;
   inFile.open("code.dat");                      // Open the file

   for (int ascii = 32; ascii < 127; ascii++)  // Read in data
      inFile >> codeChar[ascii - 32];
   inFile.close();                               // Close the file
}

/******************************************************
 *                   CodeMaker::encode                *
 * This method encodes and returns a clear text string.*
 ******************************************************/
string CodeMaker::encode(string s)
{
   int ascii;
   char newChar;
   string newString = "";   // Will hold the encoded string

```

(program continues)

Program 9-8 *(continued)*

```
   for (unsigned pos = 0; pos < s.length(); pos++)
   {
      // Get the original character's ASCII code
      ascii = s[pos];

      // Get the new replacement character
      newChar = codeChar[ascii - 32];

      // Concatenate it onto the end of the new string
      newString += newChar;
   }
   return newString;
}

/**********************************************
 *                  CodeMaker::decode             *
 * This method converts an encoded string back to  *
 * clear text and returns it.                       *
 **********************************************/
string CodeMaker::decode(string s)
{
   int index;
   char nextChar;
   char originalChar;
   string decodedText = "";

   for (unsigned pos = 0; pos < s.length(); pos++)
   {
      // Get the next character from the string
      nextChar = s[pos];

      // Call findIt to find it in the array and return its index
      index = findIt(codeChar, size, nextChar);

      // Get the original character by computing its ASCII code
      originalChar = index + 32;

      // Concatenate this character onto the end of the
      // decoded text string being constructed
      decodedText += originalChar;
   }
   return decodedText;
}

/****************************************
 *            CodeMaker::findIt             *
 * This method performs a linear search on  *
 * a character array looking for value.     *
 ****************************************/
```

(program continues)

Program 9-8 *(continued)*

```
int CodeMaker::findIt (char A[], int size, char value)
{
   int index = 0;
   int position = -1;
   bool found = false;

   while (index < size && !found)
   {
      if (A[index] == value)   // If the value is found
      {  found = true;         // Set the flag
         position = index;     // Record the value's subscript
      }
      index++;                 // Go to the next element
   }
   return position;            // Return the position, or -1
}

/*******************************************************
 *                         main                        *
 * The client "program" that uses the CodeMaker class.*
 *******************************************************/
int main()
{
  string originalText, secretCode, finalText;
  CodeMaker myCoder;

  // Get text from the user
  cout << "Enter the message to be encoded.\n";
  getline(cin, originalText);

  // Send the text to be encoded and display the result
  secretCode = myCoder.encode(originalText);
  cout << "\nHere is the encoded message\n" << secretCode << endl;

  // Send the encoded text back to be decoded
  // and display the result
  finalText = myCoder.decode(secretCode);
  cout << "\nHere is the decoded message\n" << finalText << endl;

  return 0;
}
```

Program Output with Example Input Shown in Bold

```
Enter the message to be encoded.
I can write a secret message.[Enter]

Here is the encoded message.
xH43DHP|yL[H3HJ[4|[LH=[JJ39[f

Here is the decoded message.
I can write a secret message.
```

Review Questions and Exercises

Fill-in-the-Blank and Short Answer

1. The _________ search algorithm steps sequentially through an array, comparing each item with the search value.
2. The _________ search algorithm repeatedly divides the portion of an array being searched in half.
3. The _________ search algorithm is adequate for small arrays but not large arrays.
4. The _________ search algorithm requires that the array's contents be sorted.
5. The *average* number of comparisons performed by linear search to find an item in an array of N elements is _________.
6. The *maximum* number of comparisons performed by linear search to find an item in an array of N elements is _________.
7. A linear search will find the value it is looking for with just one comparison if that value is stored in the _________ array element.
8. A binary search will find the value it is looking for with just one comparison if that value is stored in the _________ array element.
9. In a binary search, after three comparisons have been made, only ________ of the array will be left to search.
10. The maximum number of comparisons that a binary search function will make when searching for a value in a 2,000-element array is ________.
11. If an array is sorted in ________ order, the values are stored from lowest to highest.
12. If an array is sorted in ________ order, the values are stored from highest to lowest.
13. Bubble sort places ________ number(s) in place on each pass through the data.
14. Selection sort places ________ number(s) in place on each pass through the data.
15. To sort N numbers, bubble sort continues making passes through the array until ________.
16. To sort N numbers, selection sort makes ________ passes through the data.
17. Why is selection sort more efficient than bubble sort on large arrays?
18. Which sort, bubble sort or selection sort, would require fewer passes to sort a set of data that is already in the desired order?
19. Complete the following table by calculating the average and maximum number of comparisons the linear search will perform, and the maximum number of comparisons the binary search will perform.

Array Size →	50 Elements	500 Elements	10,000 Elements	100,000 Elements	10,000,000 Elements
Linear Search (Average Comparisons)					
Linear Search (Maximum Comparisons)					
Binary Search (Maximum Comparisons)					

Algorithm Workbench

20. Assume that `empName` and `empID` are two parallel arrays of size `numEmp` that hold employee data. Write a pseudocode algorithm that sorts the `empID` array in ascending ID number order (using any sort you wish), such that the two arrays remain parallel. That is, after sorting, for all indexes in the arrays, `empName[index]` must still be the name of the employee whose ID is in `empID[index]`.
21. Assume an array of structures is in order by the customerID field of the record, where customer IDs go from 101 to 500.
    A) Write the most efficient pseudocode algorithm you can to find the record with a specific customerID if every single customer ID from 101 to 500 is used and the array has 400 elements.
    B) Write the most efficient pseudocode algorithm you can to find a record with a customer ID near the end of the IDs, say 494, if not every single customer ID in the range of 101 to 500 is used and the array size is only 300.

Soft Skills

Deciding how to organize and access data is an important part of designing a program. You are already familiar with many structures and methods that allow you to organize data. These include one-dimensional arrays, vectors, multidimensional arrays, parallel arrays, structures, classes, arrays of structures, and arrays of class objects. You are also now familiar with some techniques for arranging (i.e., sorting) data and for locating (i.e., searching for) data items.

22. Team up with two to three other students and jointly decide how you would organize, order, and locate the data used in the following application. Be prepared to present your group's design to the rest of the class.

    The program to be developed is a menu-driven program that will keep track of parking tickets issued by the village that is hiring you. When a ticket is issued the program must be able to accept and store the following information: ticket number, officer number, vehicle license plate state and number, location, violation code (this indicates which parking law was violated), and date and time written. The program must store information on the amount of the fine associated with each violation code. When a ticket is paid the program must be able to accept and store the information that it has been paid, the amount of the payment, and the date the payment was received. The program must be able to accept inquiries such as displaying the entire ticket record when a ticket number is entered. The program must also be able to produce the following reports:

    - A list of all tickets issued on a specific date, ordered by ticket number
    - A list of all tickets for which payment was received on a specific date and the total amount of money collected that day
    - A report of all tickets issued in a one-month period, ordered by officer number, with a count of how many tickets each officer wrote
    - A report of all tickets that have not yet been paid, or for which payment received was less than payment due, ordered by vehicle license number

Programming Challenges

These programming challenges can all be written either with or without the use of classes. Your instructor will tell you which approach you should use.

1. Charge Account Validation

Write a program that lets the user enter a charge account number. The program should determine if the number is valid by checking for it in the following list:

5658845	4520125	7895122	8777541	8451277	1302850
8080152	4562555	5552012	5050552	7825877	1250255
1005231	6545231	3852085	7576651	7881200	4581002

Initialize a one-dimensional array with these values. Then use a simple linear search to locate the number entered by the user. If the user enters a number that is in the array, the program should display a message saying the number is valid. If the user enters a number not in the array, the program should display a message indicating it is invalid.

2. Lottery Winners

Solving the Lottery Winners Problem

A lottery ticket buyer purchases ten tickets a week, always playing the same ten five-digit "lucky" combinations. Write a program that initializes an array with these numbers and then lets the player enter this week's winning five-digit number. The program should perform a linear search through the list of the player's numbers and report whether or not one of the tickets is a winner this week. Here are the numbers:

13579	26791	26792	33445	55555
62483	77777	79422	85647	93121

3. Lottery Winners Modification

Modify the program you wrote for Programming Challenge 2 (Lottery Winners) so it performs a binary search instead of a linear search.

4. Annual Rainfall Report

Write a program that displays the name of each month in a year and its rainfall amount, sorted in order of rainfall from highest to lowest. The program should use an array of structures, where each structure holds the name of a month and its rainfall amount. Use a constructor to set the month names. Make the program modular by calling on different functions to input the rainfall amounts, to sort the data, and to display the data.

5. Hit the Slopes

Write a program that can be used by a ski resort to keep track of local snow conditions for one week. It should have a seven-element array of structures, where each structure holds a date and the number of inches of snow in the base on that date. The program should have the user input the name of the month, the starting and ending date of the seven-day period being measured, and then the seven base snow depths. The program should then sort the data in ascending order by base depth and display the results. Here is a sample report.

```
Snow Report December 12 — 18
   Date  Base
    13   42.3
    12   42.5
    14   42.8
    15   43.1
    18   43.1
    16   43.4
    17   43.8
```

6. String Selection Sort

Modify the `selectionSort` function presented in this chapter so it sorts an array of strings instead of an array of `int`s. Test the function with a driver program. Use Program 9-9 as a skeleton to complete.

Program 9-9

```
// Include needed header files here.

int main()
{
   const int SIZE = 20;

   string name[SIZE] =
   {"Collins, Bill",  "Smith, Bart",  "Michalski, Joe", "Griffin, Jim",
    "Sanchez, Manny", "Rubin, Sarah", "Taylor, Tyrone", "Johnson, Jill",
    "Allison, Jeff",  "Moreno, Juan", "Wolfe, Bill",    "Whitman, Jean",
    "Moretti, Bella", "Wu, Hong",     "Patel, Renee",   "Harrison, Rose",
    "Smith, Cathy",   "Conroy, Pat",  "Kelly, Sean",    "Holland, Beth"};

   // Insert your code to complete this program.
}
```

7. Binary String Search

Modify the `binarySearch` function presented in this chapter so it searches an array of strings instead of an array of `int`s. Test the function with a driver program. Use Program 9-8 as a skeleton to complete. (The array must be sorted before the binary search will work.)

8. Search Benchmarks

Write a program that has an array of at least 20 integers. It should call a function that uses the linear search algorithm to locate one of the values. The function should keep a count of the number of comparisons it makes until it finds the value. The program then should call a function that uses the binary search algorithm to locate the same value. It should also keep count of the number of comparisons it makes. Display these values on the screen.

9. Sorting Benchmarks

Write a program that uses two identical arrays of at least 20 integers. It should call a function that uses the bubble sort algorithm to sort one of the arrays in ascending order. The function should count the number of exchanges it makes. The program should then call a function that uses the selection sort algorithm to sort the other array. It should also count the number of exchanges it makes. Display these values on the screen.

10. Sorting Orders

Write a program that uses two identical arrays of eight integers. It should display the contents of the first array, then call a function to sort it using an ascending order bubble sort, modified to print out the array contents after each pass of the sort. Next the program should display the contents of the second array, then call a function to sort it using an ascending order selection sort, modified to print out the array contents after each pass of the sort.

11. Ascending Circles

Program 8-28 from Chapter 8 creates an array of four `Circle` objects, then displays the area of each object. Using a copy of that program as a starting point, modify it to create an array of eight `Circle` objects initialized with the following radii: 2.5, 4.0, 1.0, 3.0, 6.0, 5.5, 3.5, 2.0. Then use a bubble sort to arrange the objects in ascending order of radius size before displaying the area of each object.

12. Modified Bin Manager Class

Modify the `BinManager` class you wrote for Programming Challenge 15 in Chapter 8 to overload its `getQuantity`, `addParts`, and `removeParts` functions as shown here:

```
bool addParts(string itemDescription, int q);
bool removeParts(string itemDescription, int q)
int getQuantity(string itemDescription);
```

These new functions allow parts to be added, parts to be removed, and the quantity in stock for a particular item to be retrieved by using an *item description*, rather than a bin number, as an argument. In addition to writing the three overloaded functions, you will need to create a `private BinManager` class function that uses the item description as a search key to locate the index of the desired bin.

Test the new class functions with the same client program you wrote for Programming Challenge 15 in Chapter 8, modifying it to call the new functions. Be sure to use some descriptions that match bins in the array and some that do not.

As you did in the previous Bin Manager program, if an add or remove operation is successfully carried out, make the function return `true`. If it cannot be done—for example, because the string passed to it does not match any item description in the array—make the function return `false`. If the `getQuantity` function cannot locate any item whose description matches the one passed to it, make it return –1.

13. Using Files—String Selection Sort Modification

Modify the program you wrote for Programming Challenge 6 so it reads in the 20 strings from a file. The data can be found in the `names.dat` file.

14. Using Vectors—String Selection Sort Modification

Modify the program you wrote for Programming Challenge 13 so it stores the names in a vector of strings, rather than in an array of strings. Create the vector without specifying a size and then use the `push_back` member function to add an element holding each string to the vector as it is read in from a file. Instead of assuming there are always 20 strings, read in the strings and add them to the vector until there is no data left in the file. The data can be found in the `names.dat` file.

CHAPTER

10 Pointers

TOPICS

10.1 Pointers and the Address Operator

CONCEPT: **Every variable is assigned a memory location whose address can be retrieved using the address operator &. The address of a memory location is called a *pointer.***

Every variable in an executing program is allocated a section of memory large enough to hold a value of that variable's type. Current C++ compilers that run on PCs usually allocate a single byte to variables of type `char`, two bytes to variables of type `short`, four bytes to variables of type `float` and `long`, and 8 bytes to variables of type `double`.

Each byte of memory has a unique address. A variable's address is the address of the first byte allocated to that variable. Suppose that the following variables are defined in a program:

```
char letter;
short number;
float amount;
```

Figure 10-1 illustrates how they might be arranged in memory and shows their addresses.

Figure 10-1

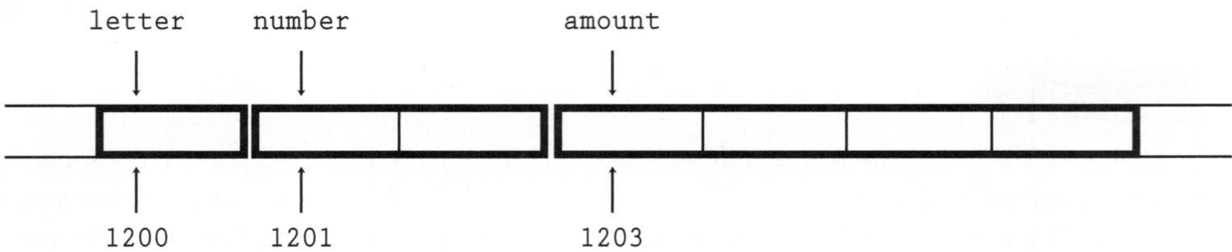

In Figure 10-1, the variable `letter` is shown at address 1200, `number` is at address 1201, and `amount` is at address 1203.

The addresses of the variables shown in Figure 10.1 are somewhat arbitrary and are used for illustrative purposes only. In fact, most compilers allocate space in such a way that individual variables are always assigned even addresses. This is because current computer hardware can access data that resides at even addresses faster than data that resides at odd addresses.

C++ has an *address operator* & that can be used to retrieve the address of any variable. To use it, place it before the variable whose address you want. Here is an expression that returns the address of the variable `amount`:

```
&amount
```

And here is a statement that displays the variable's address to the screen:

```
cout << long(&amount);
```

By default, C++ prints addresses in hexadecimal. Here we have used a function-style cast to `long` to make the address print in the usual decimal format. Program 10-1 demonstrates the use of the address operator to display addresses of variables.

Program 10-1

```
// This program uses the & operator to determine a
// variable's address.
#include <iostream>
using namespace std;

char letter;
short number;
float amount
```

(program continues)

Program 10-1 *(continued)*

```
double profit;
char ch;

int main()
{
   // Print address of each variable
   // The cast to long makes addresses print in decimal
   // rather than in hexadecimal
   cout << "Address of letter is:   "
        << long(&letter) << endl;
   cout << "Address of number is:   "
        << long(&number) << endl;
   cout << "Address of amount is:   "
        << long(&amount) << endl;
   cout << "Address of profit is:   "
        << long(&profit) << endl;
   cout << "Address of ch is:       "
        << long(&ch) << endl;
   return 0;
}
```

Program Output

```
Address of letter is:  4468752
Address of number is:  4468754
Address of amount is:  4468756
Address of profit is:  4468760
Address of ch is:      4468768
```

The value `&amount` specifies the location of the variable `amount` in the computer's memory: in a sense, it points to `amount`. A value that represents the address of a memory location, or holds the address of some variable, is called a *pointer*.

10.2 Pointer Variables

CONCEPT: A pointer variable is a variable that holds addresses of memory locations.

Like other data values, memory addresses, or pointer values, can be stored in variables of the appropriate type. A variable that stores an address is called a *pointer variable*, but is often simply referred to as just a *pointer*. The definition of a pointer variable, say `ptr`, must specify the type of data that `ptr` will point to. Here is an example:

VideoNote Pointer Variables

```
int *ptr;
```

The asterisk before the variable name indicates that `ptr` is a pointer variable, and the `int` data type indicates that `ptr` can only be used to point to, or hold addresses of, integer variables. This definition is read as "`ptr` is a pointer to `int`." It is also useful to think of `*ptr` as the "variable that `ptr` points to." With this view, the definition of `ptr` just given can be read as "the variable that `ptr` points to has type `int`." Because the asterisk (`*`) allows you to pass from a pointer to the variable being pointed to, it is called the *indirection operator*.

Some programmers prefer to declare pointers with the asterisk next to the type name, rather than the variable name. For example, the declaration shown above could be written as:

```
int* ptr;
```

This style of declaration might visually reinforce the fact that `ptr`'s data type is not `int`, but pointer-to-`int`. Both declaration styles are correct.

Program 10-2 demonstrates a very simple usage of a pointer: storing and printing the address of another variable.

Program 10-2

```
// This program stores the address of a variable in a pointer.
#include <iostream>
using namespace std;

int main()
{
   int x = 25;   // int variable
   int *ptr;     // Pointer variable, can point to an int

   ptr = &x;     // Store the address of x in ptr
   cout << "The value in x is " << x << endl;
   cout << "The address of x is " << ptr << endl;
   return 0;
}
```

Program Output

```
The value in x is 25
The address of x is 0x7e00
```

In Program 10-2, two variables are defined: `x` and `ptr`. The variable `x` is an `int`, while `ptr` is a pointer to an `int`. The variable `x` is initialized with `25`, while `ptr` is assigned the address of `x` with the following statement:

```
ptr = &x;
```

Figure 10-2 illustrates the relationship between `ptr` and `x`.

Figure 10-2

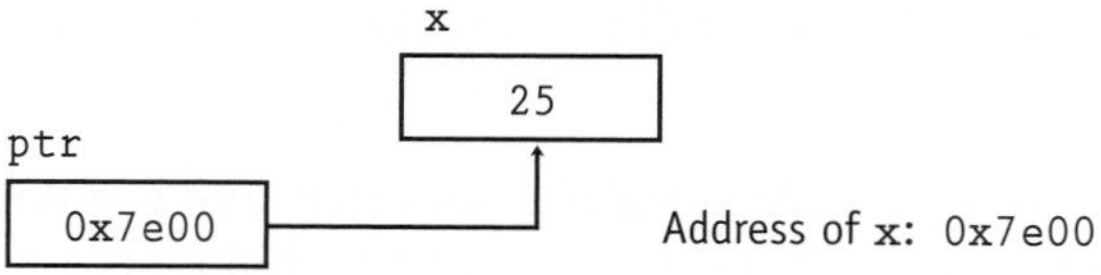

As shown in Figure 10-2, the variable `x` is located at memory address `0x7e00` and contains the number `25`, while the pointer `ptr` contains the address `0x7e00`. In essence, `ptr` "points" to the variable `x`.

You can use a pointer to indirectly access and modify the variable being pointed to. In Program 10-2, for instance, `ptr` could be used to change the contents of the variable `x`. When the indirection operator is placed in front of a pointer variable name, it *dereferences* the pointer. When you are working with a dereferenced pointer, you are actually working with the value the pointer is pointing to. This is demonstrated in Program 10-3.

Program 10-3

```
// This program demonstrates the use of the indirection
// operator.
#include <iostream>
using namespace std;

int main()
{
   int x = 25;       // int variable
   int *ptr;         // Pointer variable, can point to an int

   ptr = &x;         // Store the address of x in ptr

   // Use both x and ptr to display the value in x
   cout << "Here is the value in x, printed twice:\n";
   cout << x << "  " << *ptr << endl;

   // Assign 100 to the location pointed to by ptr
   // This will actually assign 100 to x.
   *ptr = 100;

   // Use both x and ptr to display the value in x
   cout << "Once again, here is the value in x:\n";
   cout << x << "  " << *ptr << endl;
   return 0;
}
```

Program Output

```
Here is the value in x, printed twice:
25  25
Once again, here is the value in x:
100  100
```

Every time the expression `*ptr` appears in Program 10-3, the program indirectly uses the variable `x`. The following `cout` statement displays the value in `x` twice:

```
cout << x << "  " << *ptr << endl;
```

And the following statement stores 100 in `x`:

```
*ptr = 100;
```

With the indirection operator, `ptr` can be used to indirectly access the variable it is pointing to. Program 10-4 demonstrates that pointers can point to different variables.

Program 10-4

```
// This program demonstrates the ability of a pointer to
// point to different variables.
#include <iostream>
using namespace std;

int main()
{
   int x = 25, y = 50, z = 75;        // Three int variables
   int *ptr;                          // Pointer variable

   // Display the contents of x, y, and z
   cout << "Here are the values of x, y, and z:\n";
   cout << x << "  " << y << "  " << z << endl;

   // Use the pointer to manipulate x, y, and z

   ptr = &x;          // Store the address of x in ptr
   *ptr *= 2;         // Multiply value in x by 2

   ptr = &y;          // Store the address of y in ptr
   *ptr *= 2;         // Multiply value in y by 2

   ptr = &z;          // Store the address of z in ptr
   *ptr *= 2;         // Multiply value in z by 2

   // Display the contents of x, y, and z
   cout  << "Once again, here are the values "
         << "of x, y, and z:\n";
   cout  << x << "  " << y << "  " << z << endl;
   return 0;
}
```

Program Output

```
Here are the values of x, y, and z:
25  50  75
Once again, here are the values of x, y, and z:
50  100  150
```

NOTE: So far you've seen three different uses of the asterisk in C++:

- As the multiplication operator, in statements such as

```
distance = speed * time;
```

- In the definition of a pointer variable, such as

```
int *ptr;
```

- As the indirection operator, in statements such as

```
*ptr = 100;
```

10.3 The Relationship Between Arrays and Pointers

CONCEPT: Array names can be used as pointer constants, and pointers can be used as array names.

You learned earlier that an array name, without brackets and a subscript, actually represents the starting address of the array. This means that an array name is really a pointer. Program 10-5 illustrates this by showing an array name being used with the indirection operator.

Program 10-5

```
// This program shows an array name being dereferenced with the *
// operator.
#include <iostream>
using namespace std;

int main()
{
   short numbers[] = {10, 20, 30, 40, 50};

   cout << "The first element of the array is ";
   cout << *numbers << endl;
   return 0;
}
```

Program Output

```
The first element of the array is 10
```

Because `numbers` works like a pointer to the starting address of the array in Program 10-5, the first element is retrieved when `numbers` is dereferenced. So, how could the entire contents of an array be retrieved using the indirection operator? Remember, array elements are stored together in memory, as illustrated in Figure 10-3.

Figure 10-3

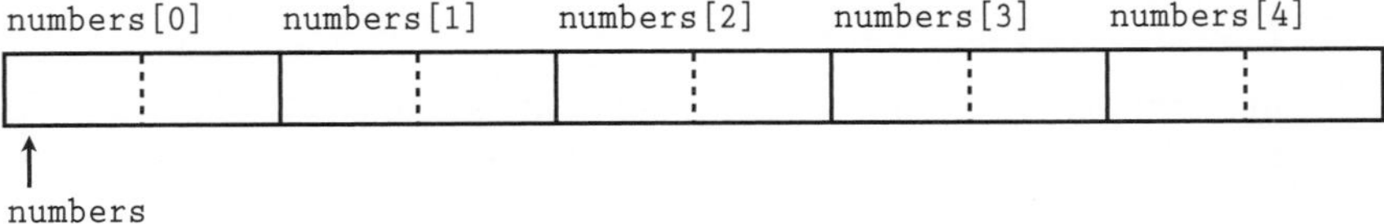

It makes sense that if `numbers` is the address of `numbers[0]`, values could be added to `numbers` to get the addresses of the other elements in the array. It's important to know, however, that pointers do not work like regular variables when used in mathematical statements. In C++, when you add a value to a pointer, you are actually adding that value *times the size of the data type being referenced by the pointer.* In other words, if you add one to `numbers`, you are actually adding `1 * sizeof(short)` to `numbers`. If you add two to `numbers`, the result is `numbers + 2 * sizeof(short)`, and so forth. On a PC, this means the following are true, because `short` integers typically use 2 bytes:

`*(numbers + 1)` is the value at address `numbers + 1 * 2`
`*(numbers + 2)` is the value at address `numbers + 2 * 2`
`*(numbers + 3)` is the value at address `numbers + 3 * 2`

and so forth.

This automatic conversion means that an element in an array can be retrieved by using its subscript or by adding its subscript to a pointer to the array. If the expression `*numbers`, which is the same as `*(numbers + 0)`, retrieves the first element in the array, then `*(numbers + 1)` retrieves the second element. Likewise, `*(numbers + 2)` retrieves the third element, and so forth. Figure 10-4 shows the equivalence of subscript notation and pointer notation.

Figure 10-4

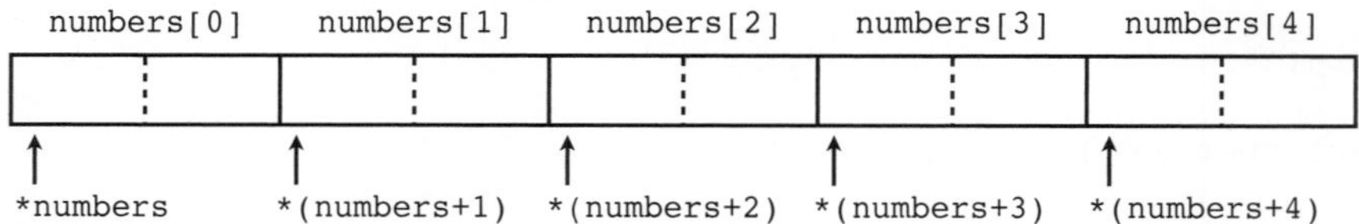

NOTE: The parentheses are critical when adding values to pointers. The `*` operator has precedence over the `+` operator, so the expression `*numbers + 1` is not equivalent to `*(numbers + 1)`. The expression `*numbers + 1` adds one to the contents of the first element of the array, while `*(numbers + 1)` adds one to the address in `numbers`, then dereferences it.

Program 10-6 shows the entire contents of the array being accessed, using pointer notation.

Program 10-6

```
// This program processes an array using pointer notation.
#include <iostream>
using namespace std;

int main()
{
   const int SIZE = 5;     // Size of the array
   int numbers[SIZE];      // Array of integers

   // Get values to store in the array
   // Use pointer notation instead of subscripts
   cout << "Enter " << SIZE << " numbers: ";
   for (int count = 0; count < SIZE; count++)
      cin >> *(numbers + count);

```

(program continues)

Program 10-6 *(continued)*

```
   // Display the values in the array
   // Use pointer notation instead of subscripts
   cout << "Here are the numbers you entered:\n";
   for (int count = 0; count < SIZE; count++)
      cout << *(numbers + count) << " ";
   cout << endl;
   return 0;
}
```

Program Output with Example Input Shown in Bold

```
Enter 5 numbers: 5 10 15 20 25[Enter]
Here are the numbers you entered:
5 10 15 20 25
```

When working with arrays, remember the following rule:

`array[index]` is equivalent to `*(array + index)`

WARNING! Remember that C++ performs no bounds checking with arrays. When stepping through an array with a pointer, it's possible to give the pointer an address outside of the array.

To demonstrate just how close the relationship is between array names and pointers, look at Program 10-7. It defines an array of `doubles` and a `double` pointer, which is assigned the starting address of the array. Not only is pointer notation then used with the array name, but subscript notation is used with the pointer!

Program 10-7

```
// This program uses subscript notation with a pointer
// variable and pointer notation with an array name.
#include <iostream>
#include <iomanip>
using namespace std;

int main()
{
   const int NUM_COINS = 5;
   double coins[NUM_COINS] = {0.05, 0.1, 0.25, 0.5, 1.0};
   double *doublePtr;   // Pointer to a double

   // Assign the address of the coins array to doublePtr
   doublePtr = coins;

   // Display the contents of the coins array
   // Use subscripts with the pointer!
   cout << setprecision(2);
   cout << "Here are the values in the coins array:\n";
   for (int count = 0; count < NUM_COINS; count++)
      cout << doublePtr[count] << " ";

```

(program continues)

Program 10-7 *(continued)*

```
    // Display the contents of the coins array again, but
    // this time use pointer notation with the array name!
    cout << "\nAnd here they are again:\n";
    for (int count = 0; count < NUM_COINS; count++)
       cout << *(coins + count) << " ";
    cout << endl;
    return 0;
}
```

Program Output

```
Here are the values in the coins array:
0.05 0.1 0.25 0.5 1
And here they are again:
0.05 0.1 0.25 0.5 1
```

Notice that the address operator is not needed when an array's address is assigned to a pointer. Since the name of an array is already an address, use of the `&` operator would be incorrect. You can, however, use the address operator to get the address of an individual element in an array. For instance, `&numbers[1]` gets the address of `numbers[1]`. This technique is used in Program 10-8.

Program 10-8

```
// This program uses the address of each element in the array.
#include <iostream>
#include <iomanip>
using namespace std;

int main()
{
   const int NUM_COINS = 5;
   double coins[NUM_COINS] = {0.05, 0.1, 0.25, 0.5, 1.0};
   double *doublePtr; // Pointer to a double

   // Use the pointer to display the values in the array
   cout << setprecision(2);
   cout << "Here are the values in the coins array:\n";
   for (int count = 0; count < NUM_COINS; count++)
   {
      doublePtr = &coins[count];
      cout << *doublePtr << " ";
   }
   cout << endl;
   return 0;
}
```

Program Output

```
Here are the values in the coins array:
0.05 0.1 0.25 0.5 1
```

The only difference between array names and pointer variables is that you cannot change the address an array name points to. For example, given the following definitions:

```
double readings[20], totals[20];
double *dptr;
```

These statements are legal:

```
dptr = readings; // Make dptr point to readings
dptr = totals;   // Make dptr point to totals
```

But these are illegal:

```
readings = totals;    // ILLEGAL! Cannot change readings
totals = dptr;        // ILLEGAL! Cannot change totals
```

Array names are *pointer constants*. You can't make them point to anything but the array they represent.

10.4 Pointer Arithmetic

CONCEPT: Some mathematical operations may be performed on pointers.

The contents of pointer variables may be changed with mathematical statements that perform addition or subtraction. This is demonstrated in Program 10-9. The first loop increments the pointer variable, stepping it through each element of the array. The second loop decrements the pointer, stepping it through the array backwards.

Program 10-9

```
// This program uses a pointer to display
// the contents of an array.
#include <iostream>
using namespace std;

int main()
{
   const int SIZE = 8;
   int set[ ] = {5, 10, 15, 20, 25, 30, 35, 40};
   int *numPtr;    // Pointer

   // Make numPtr point to the set array
   numPtr = set;

   // Use the pointer to display the array elements
   cout << "The numbers in set are:\n";
   for (int index = 0; index < SIZE; index++)
   {
      cout << *numPtr << " ";
      numPtr++;
   }

```

(program continues)

Program 10-9 *(continued)*

```
   // Display the array elements in reverse order
   cout << "\nThe numbers in set backwards are:\n";
   for (int index = 0; index < SIZE; index++)
   {
      numPtr--;
      cout << *numPtr << " ";
   }
   return 0;
}
```

Program Output

```
The numbers in set are:
5 10 15 20 25 30 35 40
The numbers in set backwards are:
40 35 30 25 20 15 10 5
```

NOTE: Because `numPtr` is a pointer, the increment operator adds the size of one integer to `numPtr`, so it points to the next element in the array. Likewise, the decrement operator subtracts the size of one integer from the pointer.

Not all arithmetic operations may be performed on pointers. For example, you cannot use multipication or division with pointers. The following operations are allowable:

- The ++ and -- operators may be used to increment or decrement a pointer variable.
- An integer may be added to or subtracted from a pointer variable. This may be performed with the + and - operators, or the += and -= operators.
- A pointer may be subtracted from another pointer.

10.5 Initializing Pointers

CONCEPT: Pointers may be initialized with the address of an existing object.

Remember that a pointer is designed to point to an object of a specific data type. When a pointer is initialized with an address, it must be the address of an object the pointer can point to. For instance, the following definition of `pint` is legal because `myValue` is an integer:

```
int myValue;
int *pint = &myValue;
```

The following is also legal because `ages` is an array of integers:

```
int ages[20];
int *pint = ages;
```

But the following definition of `pint` is illegal because `myFloat` is not an `int`:

```
float myFloat;
int *pint = &myFloat;   // Illegal!
```

Pointers may be defined in the same statement as other variables of the same type. The following declaration defines an integer variable, `myValue`, and then defines a pointer, `pint`, which is initialized with the address of `myValue`:

```
int myValue, *pint = &myValue;
```

And the following definition defines an array, `readings`, and a pointer, `marker`, which is initialized with the address of the first element in the array:

```
double readings[50], *marker = readings;
```

Of course, a pointer can only be initialized with the address of an object that has already been defined. The following is illegal because `pint` is being initialized with the address of an object that does not exist yet:

```
int *pint = &myValue;    // Illegal!
int myValue;
```

In most computers, memory at address 0 is inaccessible to user programs because it is occupied by operating system data structures. This fact allows programmers to signify that a pointer variable does not point to a memory location accessible to the program by initializing the pointer to 0. For example, if `ptrToint` is a pointer to `int`, and `ptrTofloat` is a pointer to `float`, we can indicate that neither of them points to a legitimate address by assigning 0 to both:

```
int *ptrToint = 0;
float *ptrTofloat = 0;
```

Many header files, including `iostream`, `fstream`, and `cstdlib`, define a constant named `NULL` whose value is zero. Thus, assuming one of these header files has been included, the code can be written as

```
int *ptrToint = NULL;
float *ptrTofloat = NULL;
```

A pointer whose value is the address 0 is often called a *null* pointer.

Checkpoint

10.1 Write a statement that displays the address of the variable `count`.

10.2 Write a statement defining a variable `dPtr`. The variable should be a pointer to a `double`.

10.3 List three uses of the `*` symbol in C++.

10.4 What is the output of the following program?

```
#include <iostream>
using namespace std;
int main()
{
   int x = 50, y = 60, z = 70;
   int *ptr;

   cout << x << "   " << y << "   " << z << endl;
   ptr = &x;
```

```
    *ptr *= 10;
    ptr = &y;
    *ptr *= 5;
    ptr = &z;
    *ptr *= 2;
    cout << x << "   " << y << "   " << z << endl;
    return 0;
}
```

10.5 Rewrite the following loop so it uses pointer notation (with the indirection operator) instead of subscript notation.

```
for (int x = 0; x < 100; x++)
    cout << array[x] << endl;
```

10.6 Assume `ptr` is a pointer to an `int` and holds the address 12000. On a system with 4-byte integers, what address will be in `ptr` after the following statement?

```
ptr += 10;
```

10.7 Assume `pint` is a pointer variable. For each of the following statements, determine whether the statement is valid or invalid. For those that are invalid, explain why.

A) `pint++;`
B) `--pint;`
C) `pint /= 2;`
D) `pint *= 4;`
E) `pint += x;   // Assume x is an int.`

10.8 For each of the following variable definitions, determine whether the statement is valid or invalid. For those that are invalid, explain why.

A)
```
int ivar;
int *iptr = &ivar;
```
B) `int ivar, *iptr = &ivar;`
C)
```
float fvar;
int *iptr = &fvar;
```
D) `int nums[50], *iptr = nums;`
E)
```
int *iptr = &ivar;
int ivar;
```

10.6 Comparing Pointers

CONCEPT: C++'s relational operators may be used to compare pointer values.

Pointers may be compared by using any of C++'s relational operators:

```
> < == != >= <=
```

If one address comes before another address in memory, the first address is considered "less than" the second. In an array, all the elements are stored in consecutive memory locations, so the address of element 1 is greater than the address of element 0. This is illustrated in Figure 10-5.

Figure 10-5

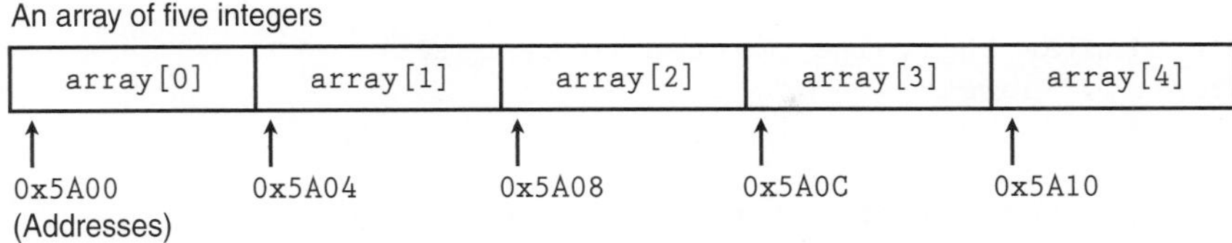

Because the addresses grow larger for each subsequent element in the array, the following boolean expressions are all true:

```
&array[1] > &array[0]
array < &array[4]
array == &array[0]
&array[2] != &array[3]
```

NOTE: Comparing two pointers is not the same as comparing the values the two pointers point to. For example, the following `if` statement compares the addresses stored in the pointer variables `ptr1` and `ptr2`:

```
if (ptr1 < ptr2)
```

The following statement, however, compares the values that `ptr1` and `ptr2` point to:

```
if (*ptr1 < *ptr2)
```

The capability of comparing addresses gives you another way to be sure a pointer does not go beyond the boundaries of an array. Program 10-10 initializes the pointer `numPtr` with the starting address of the array `set`. The pointer `numPtr` is then stepped through the array `set` until the address it contains is equal to the address of the last element of the array. Then the pointer is stepped backwards through the array until it points to the first element.

Program 10-10

```
// This program uses a pointer to display the contents
// of an integer array. It illustrates the comparison of
// pointers.
#include <iostream>
using namespace std;

int main()
{
   const int SIZE = 8;
   int set[ ] = {5, 10, 15, 20, 25, 30, 35, 40};
   int *numPtr = set;          // Make numPtr point to set

   cout << "The numbers in set are:\n";
   cout << *numPtr << " ";    // Display first element
```

(program continues)

Program 10-10 *(continued)*

```
    while (numPtr < &set[SIZE-1])
    {
       // Advance numPtr to the next element
       numPtr++;
       // Display the value pointed to by numPtr
       cout << *numPtr << " ";
    }

    // Display the numbers in reverse order
    cout << "\nThe numbers in set backwards are:\n";
    cout << *numPtr << " "; // Display last element
    while (numPtr > set)
    {
       // Move backward to the previous element
       numPtr--;
       // Display the value pointed to by numPtr
       cout << *numPtr << " ";
    }
    return 0;
}
```

Program Output

```
The numbers in set are:
5 10 15 20 25 30 35 40
The numbers in set backwards are:
40 35 30 25 20 15 10 5
```

Most comparisons involving pointers compare a pointer to 0 (`NULL`) to determine whether the pointer points to a legitimate address. For example, assuming that `ptrToInt` has been defined as a pointer to `int`, the code

```
if (ptrToInt != 0)
   cout << *ptrToInt;
else
   cout << "null pointer";
```

prints the integer pointed to by the pointer only after checking that the pointer is not 0. Many programmers, when checking to see if the value of a pointer such as `ptrToInt` is different from 0, omit the comparison to 0 and simply write

```
if (ptrToInt)
   cout << *ptrToInt;
else
   cout << "null pointer";
```

The two ways of writing the test turn out to be equivalent because when

```
ptrToInt != 0
```

is true, the value `ptrToInt` is nonzero, and nonzero values are interpreted as being true. This means that the expressions `ptrToInt != 0` and `ptrToInt` have the same truth value.

10.7 Pointers as Function Parameters

CONCEPT: A pointer can be used as a function parameter. It gives the function access to the original argument, much like a reference parameter does.

In Chapter 6 you were introduced to the concept of reference variables being used as function parameters. A reference variable acts as an alias to the original variable used as an argument. This gives the function access to the original argument variable, allowing it to change the variable's contents. When a variable is passed into a reference parameter, the argument is said to be passed by reference.

An alternative to passing an argument by reference is to use a pointer variable as the parameter. Admittedly, reference variables are much easier to work with than pointers. Reference variables hide all the "mechanics" of dereferencing and indirection. You should still learn to use pointers as function arguments, however, because some tasks, especially when dealing with C-strings, are best done with pointers.* Also, the C++ library has many functions that use pointers as parameters.

Here is the definition of a function that uses a pointer parameter:

```
void doubleValue(int *val)
{
   *val *= 2;
}
```

The purpose of this function is to double the variable pointed to by `val` with the following statement:

```
*val *= 2;
```

When `val` is dereferenced, the `*=` operator works on the variable pointed to by `val`. This statement multiplies the original variable, whose address is stored in `val`, by two. Of course, when the function is called, the address of the variable that is to be doubled must be used as the argument, not the variable itself.

Here is an example of a call to the `doubleValue` function:

```
doubleValue(&number);
```

This statement uses the address operator (`&`) to pass the address of `number` into the `val` parameter. After the function executes, the contents of `number` will have been multiplied by two.

The use of this function is illustrated in Program 10-11.

* It is also important to learn the technique in case you ever have to write a C program. In C, the only way to get the effect of pass by reference is to use a pointer.

Program 10-11

```
// This program uses two functions that accept
// addresses of variables as arguments.
#include <iostream>
using namespace std;

// Function prototypes
void getNumber(int *);
void doubleValue(int *);

int main()
{
   int number;

   // Call getNumber and pass the address of number
   getNumber(&number);

   // Call doubleValue and pass the address of number
   doubleValue(&number);

   // Display the value in number
   cout << "That value doubled is " << number << endl;
   return 0;
}

//****************************************************
// Definition of getNumber. The parameter, input, is a *
// pointer. This function asks the user for a number.  *
// The value entered is stored in the variable         *
// pointed to by input.                                *
//****************************************************

void getNumber(int *input)
{
   cout << "Enter an integer number: ";
   cin >> *input;
}

//****************************************************
// Definition of doubleValue. The parameter, val, is a *
// pointer. This function multiplies the variable      *
// pointed to by val by two.                           *
//****************************************************

void doubleValue(int *val)
{
   *val *= 2;
}
```

Program Output with Example Input Shown in Bold

```
Enter an integer number: 10[Enter]
That value doubled is 20
```

Program 10-11 has two functions that use pointers as parameters. Notice the function prototypes:

```
void getNumber(int *);
void doubleValue(int *);
```

Each one uses the notation `int *` to indicate the parameter is a pointer to an `int`. As with all other types of parameters, it isn't necessary to specify the name of the variable in the prototype. The `*` is required, though.

The `getNumber` function asks the user to enter an integer value. The following `cin` statement stores the value entered by the user in memory:

```
cin >> *input;
```

The indirection operator causes the value entered by the user to be stored, not in `input`, but in the variable pointed to by `input`.

WARNING! It's critical that the indirection operator be used in the previous statement. Without it, `cin` would store the value entered by the user in `input`, as if the value were an address. If this happens, `input` will no longer point to the `number` variable in function `main`. Subsequent use of the pointer will result in erroneous, if not disastrous, results.

When the `getNumber` function is called, the address of the `number` variable in function `main` is passed as the argument. After the function executes, the value entered by the user is stored in `number`. Next, the `doubleValue` function is called, with the address of `number` passed as the argument. This causes `number` to be multiplied by two.

Pointer variables can also be used to accept array addresses as arguments. Either subscript or pointer notation may then be used to work with the contents of the array. This is demonstrated in Program 10-12.

Program 10-12

```
// This program demonstrates that a pointer may be used as a
// parameter to accept the address of an array. Either subscript
// or pointer notation may be used.
#include <iostream>
#include <iomanip>
using namespace std;

// Function prototypes
void getSales(double *sales, int size);
double totalSales(double *sales, int size);

int main()
{
   const int QUARTERS = 4;
   double sales[QUARTERS];

```

(program continues)

Program 10-12 *(continued)*

```
    getSales(sales, QUARTERS);
    cout << setprecision(2);
    cout << fixed << showpoint;
    cout << "The total sales for the year are $";
    cout << totalSales(sales, QUARTERS) << endl;
    return 0;
}

//****************************************************************
// Definition of getSales. This function uses a pointer to accept *
// the address of an array of doubles. The number of elements in  *
// in the array is passed as a separate integer parameter. The    *
// The function asks the  user to enter the sales figures for     *
// four quarters, then stores those figures in the array using    *
// subscript notation.                                            *
//****************************************************************
void getSales(double *array, int size)
{
   for (int count = 0; count < size; count++)
   {
      cout << "Enter the sales figure for quarter ";
      cout << (count + 1) << ": ";
      cin >> array[count];
   }
}

//**************************************************************
// Definition of totalSales. This function uses a pointer to    *
// accept the address of an array of doubles whose size is      *
// is passed as a separate parameter. The function uses pointer *
// notation to sum the elements of the array.                   *
//**************************************************************
double totalSales(double *array, int size)
{
    double sum = 0.0;

    for (int count = 0; count < size; count++)
    {
       sum += *array;
       array++;
    }
    return sum;
}
```

Program Output with Example Input Shown in Bold

Enter the sales figure for quarter 1: **10263.98[Enter]**
Enter the sales figure for quarter 2: **12369.69[Enter]**
Enter the sales figure for quarter 3: **11542.13[Enter]**
Enter the sales figure for quarter 4: **14792.06[Enter]**
The total sales for the year are $48967.86

Notice that in the getSales function in Program 10-12, even though the parameter array is defined as a pointer, subscript notation is used in the cin statement:

```
cin >> array[count];
```

In the totalSales function, array is used with the indirection operator in the following statement:

```
sum += *array;
```

And in the next statement, the address in array is incremented to point to the next element:

```
array++;
```

NOTE: The two previous statements could be combined into the following statement:

```
sum += *array++;
```

The * operator will first dereference array, then the ++ operator will increment the address in array.

10.8 Pointers to Constants and Constant Pointers

CONCEPT: A pointer to a constant may not be used to change the value it points to; a constant pointer may not be changed after it has been initialized.

Pointers to Constants

You have seen how an item's address can be passed into a pointer parameter, and the pointer can be used to modify the item that was passed as an argument. Sometimes it is necessary to pass the address of a const item into a pointer. When this is the case, the pointer must be defined as a pointer to a const item. For example, consider the following array definition:

```
const int SIZE = 6;
const double payRates[SIZE] = { 18.55, 17.45,
                                12.85, 14.97,
                                10.35, 18.89 };
```

In this code, payRates is an array of const doubles. This means that each element in the array is a const double, and the compiler will not allow us to write code that changes the array's contents. If we want to pass the payRates array into a pointer parameter, the parameter must be declared as a pointer to const double. The following function shows such an example:

```
void displayPayRates(const double *rates, int size)
{
   // Set numeric output formatting
   cout << setprecision(2) << fixed << showpoint;

   // Display all the pay rates
   for (int count = 0; count < size; count++)
   {
      cout << "Pay rate for employee " << (count + 1)
           << " is $" << *(rates + count) << endl;
   }
}
```

In the function header, notice that the `rates` parameter is defined as a pointer to `const double`. It should be noted that the word `const` is applied to the thing that rates points to, not `rates` itself. This is illustrated in Figure 10-6.

Figure 10-6

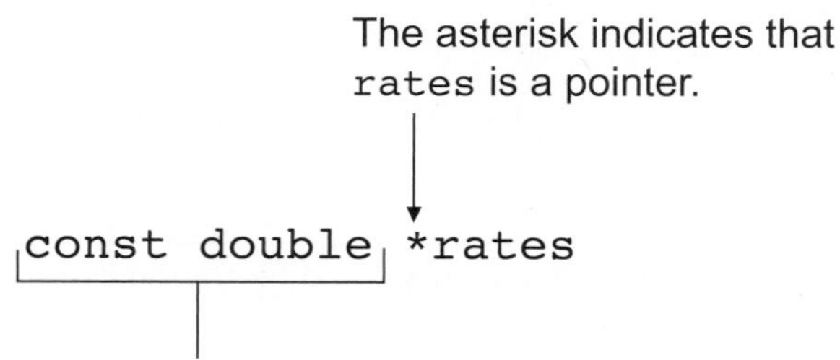
The asterisk indicates that
rates is a pointer.
const double *rates
This is what rates points to.

Because `rates` is a pointer to a `const`, the compiler will not allow us to write code that changes the thing that `rates` points to.

When passing the address of a constant into a pointer variable, the variable must be defined as a pointer to a constant. If the word `const` has been left out of the definition of the `rates` parameter, a compiler error would have resulted.

Passing a Non-Constant Argument into a Pointer to a Constant

Although a constant's address can be passed only to a pointer to `const`, a pointer to `const` can also receive the address of a non-constant item. For example, look at Program 10-13.

Program 10-13

```
// This program demonstrates a pointer to const parameter
#include <iostream>
using namespace std;

void displayValues(const int *numbers, int size);

int main()
{
   // Array sizes
   const int SIZE = 6;

   // Define an array of const ints
   const int array1[SIZE] = { 1, 2, 3, 4, 5, 6 };

   // Define an array of non-const ints
   int array2[SIZE] = { 2, 4, 6, 8, 10, 12 };

   // Display the contents of the const array
   displayValues(array1, SIZE);

```

(program continues)

Program 10-13 *(continued)*

```
   // Display the contents of the non-const array
   displayValues(array2, SIZE);
   return 0;
}

//**************************************************
// The displayValues function uses a pointer to     *
// parameter to display the contents of an array.   *
//**************************************************

void displayValues(const int *numbers, int size)
{
   // Display all the values
   for (int count = 0; count < size; count++)
   {
      cout << *(numbers + count) << " ";
   }
   cout << endl;
}
```

Program Output

```
1 2 3 4 5 6
2 4 6 8 10 12
```

NOTE: When writing a function that uses a pointer parameter, and the function is not intended to change the data the parameter points to, it is always a good idea to make the parameter a pointer to `const`. Not only will this protect you from writing code in the function that accidentally changes the argument, but the function will be able to accept the addresses of both constant and non-constant arguments.

Constant Pointers

In the previous section we discussed pointers to `const`. That is, pointers that point to `const` data. You can also use the `const` key word to define a constant pointer. Here is the difference between a pointer to `const` and a `const` pointer:

- A pointer to `const` points to a constant item. The data that the pointer points to cannot change, but the pointer itself can change.
- With a `const` pointer, it is the pointer itself that is constant. Once the pointer is initialized with an address, it cannot point to anything else.

The following code shows an example of a `const` pointer.

```
int value = 22;
int * const ptr = &value;
```

Notice in the definition of `ptr` the word `const` appears after the asterisk. This means that `ptr` is a `const` pointer. This is illustrated in Figure 10-7. In the code, `ptr` is initialized with the address of the `value` variable. Because `ptr` is a constant pointer, a compiler error will result if we write code that makes ptr point to anything else. An error will not result, however, if we use ptr to change the contents of value. This is because value is not constant, and ptr is not a pointer to const.

Figure 10-7

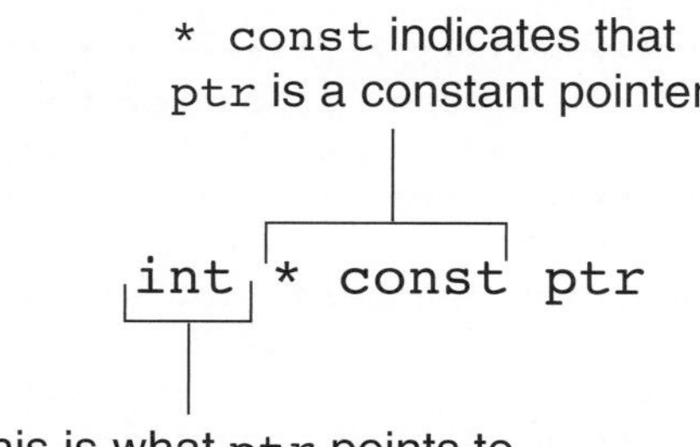

Constant pointers must be initialized with a starting value, as shown in the previous example code. If a constant pointer is used as a function parameter, the parameter will be initialized with the address that is passed as an argument into it and cannot be changed to point to anything else while the function is executing. Here is an example that attempts to violate this rule:

```
void setToZero(int * const ptr)
{
   ptr = 0;  // ERROR!! Cannot change the contents of ptr.
}
```

This function's parameter, ptr, is a const pointer. It will not compile because we cannot have code in the function that changes the contents of ptr. However, ptr does not point to a const, so we can have code that changes the data that ptr points to. Here is an example of the function that will compile:

```
void setToZero(int * const ptr)
{
   *ptr = 0;
}
```

Although the parameter is const pointer, we can call the function multiple times with different arguments. The following code will successfully pass the addresses of x, y, and z to the setToZero function:

```
int x, y, z;
// Set x, y, and z to 0.
setToZero(&x);
setToZero(&y);
setToZero(&z);
```

Constant Pointers to Constants

So far, when using const with pointers we've seen pointers to constants and we've seen constant pointers. You can also have constant pointers to constants. For example, look at the following code:

```
int value = 22;
const int * const ptr = &value;
```

In this code `ptr` is a `const` pointer to a `const int`. Notice the word `const` appears before `int`, indicating that `ptr` points to a `const int`, and it appears after the asterisk, indicating that `ptr` is a constant pointer. This is illustrated in Figure 10-8.

Figure 10-8

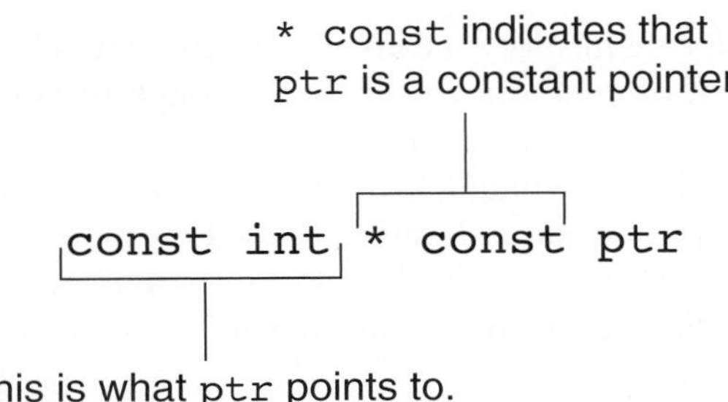

In the code, `ptr` is initialized with the address of `value`. Because `ptr` is a `const` pointer, we cannot write code that makes `ptr` point to anything else. Because `ptr` is a pointer to `const`, we cannot use it to change the contents of `value`. The following code shows one more example of a `const` pointer to a `const`. This is another version of the `displayValues` function in Program 10-13.

```
void displayValues(const int * const numbers, int size)
{
   // Display all the values.
   for (int count = 0; count < size; count++)
   {
      cout << *(numbers + count) << " ";
   }
   cout << endl;
}
```

In this code, the parameter `numbers` is a `const` pointer to a `const int`. Although we can call the function with different arguments, the function itself cannot change what `numbers` points to, and it cannot use `numbers` to change the contents of an argument.

10.9 Focus on Software Engineering: *Dynamic Memory Allocation*

CONCEPT: Variables may be created and destroyed while a program is running.

As long as you know how many variables you will need during the execution of a program, you can define those variables up front. For example, a program to calculate the area of a rectangle will need three variables: one for the rectangle's length, one for the rectangle's width, and one to hold the area. If you are writing a program to compute the payroll for 30 employees, you'll probably create an array of 30 elements to hold the amount of pay for each person.

But what about those times when you don't know how many variables you need? For instance, suppose you want to write a test-averaging program that will average any number of tests. Obviously the program would be very versatile, but how do you store the individual test scores in memory if you don't know how many variables to define? Quite simply, you allow the program to create its own variables "on the fly." This is called *dynamic memory allocation* and is only possible through the use of pointers.

To dynamically allocate memory means that a program, while running, asks the computer to set aside a chunk of unused memory large enough to hold a variable of a specific data type. Let's say a program needs to create an integer variable. It will make a request to the computer that it allocate enough bytes to store an `int`. When the computer fills this request, it finds and sets aside a chunk of unused memory large enough for the variable. It then gives the program the starting address of the chunk of memory. The program can only access the newly allocated memory through its address, so a pointer is required to use those bytes.

The way a C++ program requests dynamically allocated memory is through the `new` operator. Assume a program has a pointer to an `int` defined as

```
int *iptr;
```

Here is an example of how this pointer may be used with the `new` operator:

```
iptr = new int;
```

This statement is requesting that the computer allocate enough memory for a new `int` variable. The operand of the new operator is the data type of the variable being created. This is illustrated in Figure 10-9. Once the statement executes, `iptr` will contain the address of the newly allocated memory. A value may be stored in this new variable by dereferencing the pointer:

```
*iptr = 25;
```

Figure 10-9

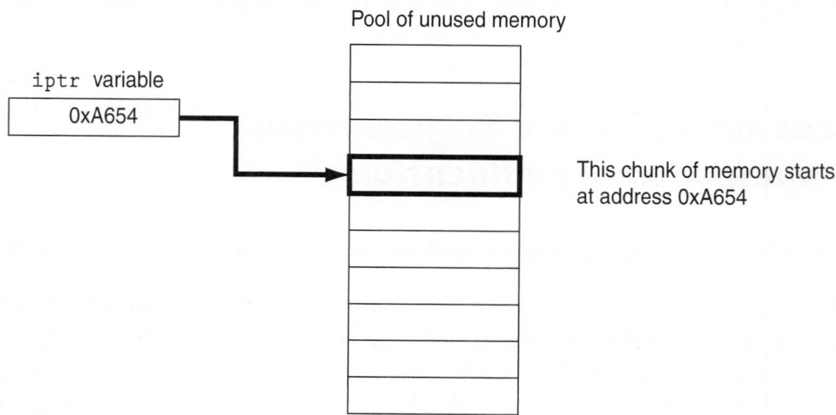

Any other operation may be performed on the new variable by simply using the dereferenced pointer. Here are some example statements:

```
cout << *iptr;          // Display the contents of the new variable.
cin >> *iptr;           // Let the user input a value.
total += *iptr;         // Use the new variable in a computation.
```

Although these statements illustrate the use of the new operator, there's little purpose in dynamically allocating a single variable. A more practical use of the new operator is to dynamically create an array. Here is an example of how a 100-element array of integers may be allocated:

```
iptr = new int[100];
```

VideoNote
Dynamically Allocating an Array

Once the array is created, the pointer may be used with subscript notation to access it. For instance, the following loop could be used to store the value 1 in each element:

```
for (int count = 0; count < 100; count++)
   iptr[count] = 1;
```

Every call to new allocates storage from a special area of the program's memory called the *heap*. If a program makes a lot of requests for dynamic memory, the heap will eventually become depleted, and additional calls to new will fail. When this happens, the C++ runtime system will *throw* a bad_alloc exception to notify the calling program that the requested memory cannot be allocated. An *exception* is a mechanism for notifying a program that something has gone drastically wrong with the operation that was being executed and that the results of the operation cannot be trusted. The default action of an exception is to force the executing program to terminate.

Older C++ compilers do not throw bad_alloc. Instead, they indicate memory-allocation failure by returning the address 0 (NULL) from the call to new. Memory-allocation code written for these compilers should check the returned address to make sure it is not 0 before using it, as in the following code fragment:

```
// For older versions of C++
iptr = new int[100];
if (iptr == NULL)
{
   cout << "Memory allocation error.";
   exit(1);
}
// Rest of code to use the allocated array
```

A program that has finished using a dynamically allocated block of memory should *free* the memory and return it to the heap to make it available for future use. This is accomplished by calling the delete operator and passing it the address of the memory to be deallocated. Here is an example of how delete is used to free up a single variable pointed to by iptr:

```
delete iptr;
iptr = 0;
```

If iptr points to a dynamically allocated array, a pair of square brackets must be placed between delete and iptr:

```
delete [] iptr;
iptr = 0;
```

Dangling Pointers and Memory Leaks

A pointer is said to be *dangling* if it is pointing to a memory location that has been freed by a call to `delete`. When you access a dangling pointer, you are trying to use memory that has already been freed and returned to the heap. In fact, such memory may already be reallocated by another call to `new`. The use of dangling pointers can cause errors in your program that are difficult to trace. You can avoid the use of dangling pointers by setting pointers to 0 as soon as they are freed, as shown in the examples above.

A *memory leak* is said to occur in your program if after you have finished using a block of memory allocated by `new`, you forget to free it via `delete`. The leaked block of memory remains unavailable for use until the program terminates. Memory leaks are especially serious when they occur in loops. They are even more serious in programs such as Web servers and other network programs that are expected to run for months or even years without being shut down. Over time, a Web server with a memory leak will exhaust all memory in the computer on which it is running, requiring both it and the computer to be shut down and restarted.

WARNING! Only use pointers with `delete` that were previously used with `new`. If you use a pointer with `delete` that does not reference dynamically allocated memory, unexpected problems could result!

Program 10-14 demonstrates the use of `new` and `delete`. It asks for sales figures for any number of days. The figures are stored in a dynamically allocated array and then totaled and averaged.

Program 10-14

```
// This program totals and averages the sales figures for
// any number of days. The figures are stored in a
// dynamically allocated array.
#include <iostream>
#include <iomanip>
using namespace std;

int main()
{
   double *sales,         // To dynamically allocate an array
          total = 0.0,    // Accumulator
          average;        // To hold average sales
   int numDays;           // To hold number of days of sales

   // Get number of days of sales
   cout << "How many days of sales figures do you wish ";
   cout << "to process? ";
   cin >> numDays;

   // Dynamically allocate an array large enough
   // to hold that many days of sales amounts
   sales = new double[numDays];  // Allocate memory

```

(program continues)

Program 10-14 *(continued)*

```
24      // Get the sales figures for each day
25      cout << "Enter the sales figures below.\n";
26      for (int count = 0; count < numDays; count++)
27      {
28         cout << "Day " << (count + 1) << ": ";
29         cin >> sales[count];
30      }
31
32      // Calculate the total sales
33      for (int count = 0; count < numDays; count++)
34      {
35         total += sales[count];
36      }
37
38      // Calculate the average sales per day
39      average = total / numDays;
40
41      // Display the results
42      cout << setprecision(2) << fixed << showpoint;
43      cout << "\n\nTotal Sales: $" << total << endl;
44      cout << "Average Sales: $" << average << endl;
45
46      // Free dynamically allocated memory
47      delete [] sales;
48      sales = 0;
49      return 0;
50  }
```

Program Output with Example Input Shown in Bold

```
How many days of sales figures do you wish to process? 5[Enter]
Enter the sales figures below.
Day 1: 898.63[Enter]
Day 2: 652.32[Enter]
Day 3: 741.85[Enter]
Day 4: 852.96[Enter]
Day 5: 921.37[Enter]

Total Sales: $4067.13
Average Sales: $813.43
```

The statement in line 23 dynamically allocates memory for an array of `doubles`, using the value in `numDays` as the number of elements. The `new` operator returns the starting address of the memory allocated, and this address is assigned to the `sales` pointer variable. The `sales` variable is then used throughout the program to store the sales amounts in the array and perform the necessary calculations. In line 48 the `delete` operator is used to free the allocated memory.

Notice that in line 49 the value 0 is assigned to the `sales` pointer. It is good practice to store 0 in a pointer variable after using `delete` on it. First, it prevents code from inadvertently using the pointer to access the area of memory that was freed. Second, it prevents errors from occurring if `delete` is accidentally called on the pointer again. The `delete` operator is designed to have no effect when used on a null pointer.

10.10 Focus on Software Engineering: *Returning Pointers from Functions*

CONCEPT: Functions can return pointers, but you must be sure the item the pointer references still exists.

It is often useful for a function to dynamically allocate storage for an object, fill the object with data, and return its address. Consider a function that returns for a given positive integer *n* the sequence of the first *n* integer squares. For example, if the function is passed the value 4, it returns an array whose elements are 1, 4, 9, and 16.

When called, the function allocates an array of the given size, sets the elements of the array to the required values, and returns the address of the base of the array.

```
int *squares(int n)
{
   // Allocate an array of size n
   int *sqarray = new int[n];

   // Fill the array with squares
   for (int k = 0; k < n; k++)
      sqarray[k] = (k+1) * (k+1);

   // Return base address of allocated array
   return sqarray;
}
```

Program 10-15 shows another example. This program contains a function that returns a pointer to an array of random numbers. The function accepts an integer size, dynamically allocates an array of the given size, and then populates the array with random values. The function uses the system clock to seed the random number generator. Notice that the array containing the random numbers is only deleted *after* the function `main` is done with it.

Program 10-15

```
// This program demonstrates a function that returns
// a pointer.
#include <iostream>
#include <cstdlib>   // For rand and srand
#include <ctime>     // For the time function
using namespace std;

// Function prototype
int *getRandomNumbers(int);

```

(program continues)

Program 10-15 *(continued)*

```
int main()
{
   int *numbers;  // To point to the numbers

   // Get an array of five random numbers
   numbers = getRandomNumbers(5);

   // Display the numbers
   for (int count = 0; count < 5; count++)
      cout << numbers[count] << endl;

   // Free the memory
   delete [] numbers;
   numbers = 0;
   return 0;
}

//**************************************************
// The getRandomNumbers function returns a pointer *
// to an array of random integers. The parameter   *
// indicates the number of numbers requested.      *
//**************************************************

int *getRandomNumbers(int size)
{
   int *array;    // Array to hold the numbers

   // Return null if size is zero or negative
   if (size <= 0)
      return NULL;

   // Dynamically allocate the array
   array = new int[size];

   // Seed the random number generator by passing
   // the return value of time(0) to srand
   srand( time(0) );

   // Populate the array with random numbers
   for (int count = 0; count < size; count++)
      array[count] = rand();

   // Return a pointer to the array
   return array;
}
```

Program Output with Example Input Shown in Bold

```
2712
9656
24493
12483
7633
```

A function can safely return a pointer to dynamically allocated storage that has not yet been deleted. In contrast, functions should not return pointers to local variables because the storage for such variables is automatically deallocated upon return. Consider the following function, which returns the address of a local array:

```
int *errSquares(int n)
{
   // Assume n is less than 100, use local array
   int array[100];

   // Fill the array with squares
   for (int k = 0; k < n; k++)
      array[k] = (k+1) * (k+1);

   // Return base address of local array
   return array;
}
```

A call such as

```
int * arr = errSquares(5);
```

will return the address of an array that has already been deallocated. Trying to access an element of such an array, as in

```
cout << arr[0];
```

will result in a reference to non-existent storage and cause an error.

NOTE: Storage for a static local variable is not deallocated upon return, so a function returning a pointer to such a variable will not trigger the kind of error we are talking about here. Such a function, however, may cause other types of errors whose discussion is beyond the scope of this book.

Checkpoint

10.9 Assuming `array` is an array of `int`s, which of the following program segments will display "True" and which will display "False"?

A)
```
if (array < &array[1])
   cout << "True";
else
   cout << "False";
```

B)
```
if (&array[4] < &array[1])
   cout << "True";
else
   cout << "False";
```

C)
```
if (array != &array[2])
   cout << "True";
else
   cout << "False";
```

D)
```
if (array != &array[0])
   cout << "True";
else
   cout << "False";
```

10.10 Give an example of the proper way to call the following function in order to negate the variable `int num = 7;`

```
void makeNegative(int *val)
{
   if (*val > 0)
       *val = -(*val);
}
```

10.11 Complete the following program skeleton. When finished, the program should ask the user for a length (in inches), convert that value to centimeters, and display the result. You are to write the function `convert`. (Note: 1 inch = 2.54 cm. Do not modify function `main`.)

```
#include <iostream>
#include <iomanip>
using namespace std;

// Write your function prototype here.

int main()
{
   double measurement;

   cout << "Enter a length in inches, and I will convert\n";
   cout << "it to centimeters: ";
   cin >> measurement;
   convert(&measurement);
   cout << setprecision(4);
   cout << fixed << showpoint;
   cout << "Value in centimeters: " << measurement << endl;
   return 0;
}
//
// Write the function convert here.
//
```

10.12 Look at the following array definition:

```
const int numbers[SIZE] = { 18, 17, 12, 14 };
```

Suppose we want to pass the array to the function `processArray` in the following manner:

```
processArray(numbers, SIZE);
```

Which of the following function headers is the correct one for the `processArray` function?

A) `void processArray(const int *array, int size)`
B) `void processArray(int * const array, int size)`

10.13 Assume `ip` is a pointer to an `int`. Write a statement that will dynamically allocate an integer variable and store its address in `ip`, then write a statement that will free the memory allocated in the statement you just wrote.

10.14 Assume `ip` is a pointer to an `int`. Write a statement that will dynamically allocate an array of 500 integers and store its address in `ip`, then write a statement that will free the memory allocated in the statement you just wrote.

10.15 What is a null pointer?

10.16 Give an example of a function that correctly returns a pointer.

10.17 Give an example of a function that incorrectly returns a pointer.

10.11 Pointers to Class Objects and Structures

CONCEPT: Pointers and dynamic memory allocation can be used with class objects and structures.

Declaring a pointer to a class is the same as declaring any other pointer type. For example, if `Rectangle` is defined as

```
class Rectangle
{
   int width, height;
};
```

you can declare a pointer to `Rectangle` and create a `Rectangle` object by writing

```
Rectangle *pRect; // Pointer to Rectangle
Rectangle rect;   // Rectangle object
```

and you can assign the address of `rect` to `pRect` as follows:

```
pRect = &rect;
```

Now suppose that you want to access the members of the `Rectangle` object through the pointer `pRect`. Because `*pRect` is just another way of accessing `rect`, you might think that the expression

```
*pRect.width
```

will access `rect.width`, but this is not so. The reason is that the dot selector has higher priority than the `*` operator, so `*pRect.width` is equivalent to `*(pRrect.width)`. This last expression is a type error. To get it right, you must use parentheses to force the indirection operator `*` to be applied first, as shown here:

```
(*pRect).width
```

The following statements will correctly set the dimensions of the rectangle to 10 and 20.

```
(*pRect).width = 10;
(*pRect).height = 20;
```

The combined use of parentheses, the indirection operator, and the dot selector to access members of class objects via pointers can result in expressions that are hard to read. To solve this problem, C++ provides the *structure pointer operator* -> to use when you want to access a member of a class object through a pointer. It consists of a hyphen – and a greater-than symbol > written next to each other to look like an arrow. Using this operator, you can set the dimensions of the rectangle with these statements:

```
pRect->width = 10;
pRect->height = 20;
```

Member functions of class objects can be called through a pointer. In particular, if `ptr` is a pointer to an object that has a member function `fun()`, then the function can be called with either one of these two (equivalent) expressions:

```
(*ptr).fun();
ptr->fun();
```

Dynamic Allocation of Class Objects

Dynamically allocated class objects are used in programs that build and manage advanced data structures such as lists (studied in Chapter 17) and binary trees (studied in Chapter 19). The `new` operator is used to allocate such objects in the same way that it is used to allocate variables of other types. For example, the following statements allocate a single `Rectangle` object and set its dimensions

```
pRect = new Rectangle;
pRect->width = 10;
pRect->height = 3;
```

If `Rectangle` has a constructor that takes two integer parameters, then you can simultaneously allocate the object and invoke the constructor like this:

```
pRect = new Rectangle(10, 30);
```

Program 10-16 illustrates these concepts.

Program 10-16

```
// This program uses pointers to dynamically allocate
// structures and class objects.
#include <iostream>
#include <string>
using namespace std;

// Person class
class Person
{
private:
    string name;
    int  age;
public:
    Person(string name1, int age1)
    {
        name = name1;
        age = age1;
    }
    int getAge() { return age; }
    string getName(){ return name; }
};

// Rectangle structure
struct Rectangle
{
```

(program continues)

Program 10-16 *(continued)*

```
    int width, height;
};

int main()
{
    Rectangle *pRect;    // Pointer to Rectangle
    Person *pPerson;     // Pointer to Person

    // Create a rectangle object and access it through a pointer
    Rectangle rect;
    pRect = &rect;
    (*pRect).height = 12;
    pRect->width = 10;
    cout << "Area of the first rectangle is "
         << pRect->width * pRect->height;

    // Allocate a Rectangle object and access it through a pointer
    pRect = new Rectangle;
    pRect->height = 6;
    pRect->width = 5;
    cout << "\nArea of the second rectangle is "
        << pRect->width * pRect->height;

    // Allocate a Person object and call its methods through a pointer
    pPerson = new Person("Miguel E. Gonzalez", 23);
    cout << "\n\nThe person's name is " << pPerson->getName();
    cout << "\nThe person's age is " << pPerson->getAge() << endl;

    return 0;
}
```

Program Output

```
Area of the first rectangle is 120
Area of the second rectangle is 30

The person's name is Miguel E. Gonzalez
The person's age is 23
```

Pointers to Class Objects as Function Parameters

Pointers to structures and class variables can be passed to functions as parameters. The function receiving the pointer can then use it to access or modify members of the structure. This is shown in Program 10-17.

Program 10-17

```
// This program illustrates pointers to class objects
// and structures as parameters of functions.
#include <iostream>
#include <string>
```

(program continues)

Program 10-17 *(continued)*

```
using namespace std;

// Person class
class Person
{
private:
    string name;
    int  age;
public:
    Person(string name1, int age1)
    {
        name = name1;
        age = age1;
    }
    int getAge() { return age; }
    string getName(){ return name; }
};

// Rectangle structure
struct Rectangle
{
    int width, height;
};

// Prototypes
void magnify(Rectangle *pRect, int mfactor);
int lengthOfName(Person *p);
void output(Rectangle *pRect);

int main()
{
    // Create, then magnify a Rectangle by a factor of 3
    Rectangle rect;
    rect.width = 4;
    rect.height = 2;
    cout << "Initial size of  rectangle is ";
    output(&rect);
    magnify(&rect, 3);
    cout << "Size of Rectangle after magnification is ";
    output(&rect);

    // Create a Person and find the length of the person's name
    Person *pPerson = new Person("Susan Wu", 32);
    cout << "The name " << pPerson->getName()
         << " has length " << lengthOfName(pPerson) << endl;

    return 0;
}

//*********************************************
// Output the dimensions of a rectangle       *
//*********************************************
```

(program continues)

Program 10-17 *(continued)*

```
void output(Rectangle *pRect)
{
    cout << "width: " << pRect->width << " height: "
         << pRect->height << endl;
}

//****************************************************
// Returns the number of characters in a person's name *
//****************************************************
int lengthOfName(Person *p)
{
    string name = p->getName();
    return name.length();
}

//****************************************************
// Stretch the width and height of a rectangle by     *
// a specified factor                                 *
//****************************************************
void magnify(Rectangle *pRect, int factor)
{
    pRect->width = pRect->width * factor;
    pRect->height = pRect->height * factor;
}

```

Program Output

```
Initial size of rectangle is width: 4 height: 2
Size of Rectangle after magnification is width: 12 height: 6
The name Susan Wu has length 8
```

Stopping Memory Leaks

It is important for programs that use dynamically allocated memory to ensure that each call to new is eventually followed by a call to `delete` that frees the allocated memory and returns it to the heap. A program that fails to do this will suffer from *memory leaks,* a condition in which the program loses track of dynamically allocated storage and therefore never calls `delete` to free the memory. There are two rules of the thumb that can be used to avoid memory leaks:

- The function that invokes `new` to allocate storage should also be the function that invokes `delete` to deallocate the storage.
- A class that needs to dynamically allocate storage should invoke `new` in its constructors and invoke the corresponding `delete` in its destructor. Because the destructor is automatically called by the system whenever an object is deleted or goes out of scope, a `delete` statement placed in a destructor will always be called.

By following these rules, you will always be able to find the `delete` operation that corresponds to a given call to `new`, thereby verifying that a particular call to `new` does not result in a memory leak. Program 10-18 is an example of a program that follows these rules. Note that the `Squares` class allocates dynamic memory in its constructor and has a `delete` statement in its destructor. The program is garnished with output statements in strategic places to show when the `new` and `delete` operators in constructors and destructors are called.

Program 10-18

```
// This program illustrates the use of constructors
// and destructors in the allocation and deallocation of memory.
#include <iostream>
#include <string>
using namespace std;

class Squares
{
private:
    int length;  // How long is the sequence
    int *sq;     // Dynamically allocated array
public:
    // Constructor allocates storage for sequence
    // of squares and creates the sequence
    Squares(int len)
    {
        length = len;
        sq = new int[length];
        for (int k = 0; k < length; k++)
        {
            sq[k] = (k+1)*(k+1);
        }
        // Trace
        cout << "Construct an object of size " << length << endl;
    }
    // Print the sequence
    void print()
    {
        for (int k = 0; k < length; k++)
            cout << sq[k] << "  ";
        cout << endl;
    }
    // Destructor deallocates storage
    ~Squares()
    {
        delete [ ] sq;
        // Trace
        cout << "Destructor for object of size " << length <<  endl;
    }
};

//*********************************************
// Outputs the sequence of squares in a       *
// Squares object                             *
//*********************************************
```

(program continues)

Program 10-18 *(continued)*

```
void outputSquares(Squares *sqPtr)
{
    cout << "The list of squares is: ";
    sqPtr->print();

}
int main()
{
    Squares sqs(5);
    cout << "The first 5 squares are: ";
    sqs.print();

    // Main allocates a Squares object
    Squares *sqPtr = new Squares(3);
    outputSquares(sqPtr);
    // Main deallocates the Squares object
    delete sqPtr;

    return 0;
}
```

Program Output

```
Construct an object of size 5
The first 5 squares are: 1   4   9   16   25
Construct an object of size 3
The list of squares is: 1   4   9
Destructor for object of size 3
Destructor for object of size 5
```

Everything we have said in this section applies to structures as well.

10.12 Focus on Software Engineering: *Selecting Members of Objects*

Sometimes structures and classes contain pointers as members. For example, the following structure declaration has an `int` pointer member:

```
struct GradeInfo
{
   string name;     // Student name
   int *testScores;// Dynamically allocated array
   double average; // Test average
};
```

It's important to remember that the structure pointer operator (`->`) is used to dereference a pointer to a structure or class object, not a pointer that is a member of a structure or class. If a program dereferences the `testScores` pointer in the structure in the example, the indirection operator must be used. For example, assuming the following variable has been defined:

```
GradeInfo student1;
```

The following statement will display the value pointed to by the `testScores` member:

```
cout << *student1.testScores;
```

It's still possible to define a pointer to a structure that contains a pointer member. For instance, the following statement defines `stPtr` as a pointer to a `GradeInfo` structure:

```
GradeInfo *stPtr;
```

Assuming `stPtr` points to a valid `GradeInfo` variable, the following statement will display the value pointed to by its `testScores` member:

```
cout << *stPtr->testScores;
```

In this statement, the `*` operator dereferences `stPtr->testScores`, while the `->` operator dereferences `stPtr`. It might help to remember that the expression

```
stPtr->testScores
```

is equivalent to

```
(*stPtr).testScores
```

So, the expression

```
*stPtr->testScores
```

is the same as

```
*(*stPtr).testScores
```

The awkwardness of this expression shows the necessity of the `->` operator. Table 10-1 lists some expressions using the `*`, `->`, and `.` operators, and describes what each references. The table is easier to understand if you remember that the operators `->` and `.` for selecting members of structures have higher precedence than the dereferencing operator `*`.

Table 10-1 Dereferencing Pointers to Structures

Expression	Description
`s->m`	`s` is a pointer to a structure variable or class object, and `m` is a member. This expression accesses the `m` member of the structure or class object pointed to by `s`.
`*a.p`	`a` is a structure variable or class object and `p`, a pointer, is a member of `a`. This expression accesses the value pointed to by `a.p`.
`(*s).m`	`s` is a pointer to a structure variable or class object, and `m` is a member. The `*` operator dereferences `s`, causing the expression to access the `m` member of the object `*s`. This expression is the same as `s->m`.
`*s->p`	`s` is a pointer to a structure variable or class object and `p`, a pointer, is a member of the object pointed to by `s`. This expression accesses the value pointed to by `s->p`.
`*(*s).p`	`s` is a pointer to a structure variable or class object and `p`, a pointer, is a member of the object pointed to by `s`. This expression accesses the value pointed to by `(*s).p`. This expression is the same as `*s->p`.

Checkpoint

Assume the following structure declaration exists for questions 10.18 through 10.20:

```
struct Rectangle
{
   int length;
   int width;
};
```

10.18 Write the definition of a pointer to a `Rectangle` structure.

10.19 Assume the pointer you defined in question 10.18 points to a valid `Rectangle` structure. Write the statement that displays the structure's members through the pointer.

10.20 Assume `rptr` is a pointer to a `Rectangle` structure. Which of the expressions, A, B, or C, is equivalent to the expression:

```
rptr->width
```

A) `*rptr.width`
B) `(*rptr).width`
C) `rptr.(*width)`

10.13 United Cause Relief Agency Case Study

CONCEPT: This case study demonstrates how an array of pointers can be used to display the contents of a second array in sorted order, without sorting the second array.

The United Cause, a charitable relief agency, solicits donations from businesses. The local United Cause office received the following donations from the employees of CK Graphics, Inc:

$5, $100, $5, $25, $10, $5, $25, $5, $5, $100, $10, $15, $10, $5, $10

The donations were received in the order they appear. The United Cause manager has asked you to write a program that displays the donations in ascending order, as well as in their original order.

You decide to create a class, `DonationList`, that will hold and process the donation data. The class declaration is

```
class DonationList
{
private:
      int numDonations;
      double *donations;
      double **arrPtr;
      void selectSort();
```

```
public:
      DonationList(int num, double gifts[]);
      ~DonationList();
      void show();
      void showSorted();
};
```

Table 10-2 lists and describes the class's member variables.

Table 10-2 Description of Member Variables

Member Variable	Description
`numDonations`	An integer that will hold the number of donations received. This value will be used to dynamically allocate arrays for holding and processing the donation values.
`donations`	A pointer that will point to a dynamically allocated array of `doubles` containing the donation amounts.
`arrPtr`	A pointer that will point to an array of pointers. The array of pointers will be dynamically allocated. Each element of the array will point to an element of the `donations` array.

In this class, the donation values will be stored in their original order in a dynamically allocated array of `doubles`. The `donations` member will point to the array. We will refer to this array as the `donations` array. The following statement shows how the `donations` member will be defined.

```
double *donations;
```

The `arrPtr` member will also point to a dynamically allocated array. Its array, however, will be an array of pointers. The elements of the array are pointers to `doubles`. The following statement shows how the `arrPtr` member will be declared.

```
double **arrPtr;
```

Since the `arrPtr` member will point to an array of pointers, it is a *pointer-to-a-pointer*. That is why two asterisks appear in the declaration statement. The pointer that `arrPtr` points to is a pointer to a `double`. Figure 10-10 illustrates `arrPtr` as a pointer to an array of pointers-to-`doubles`.

Figure 10-10

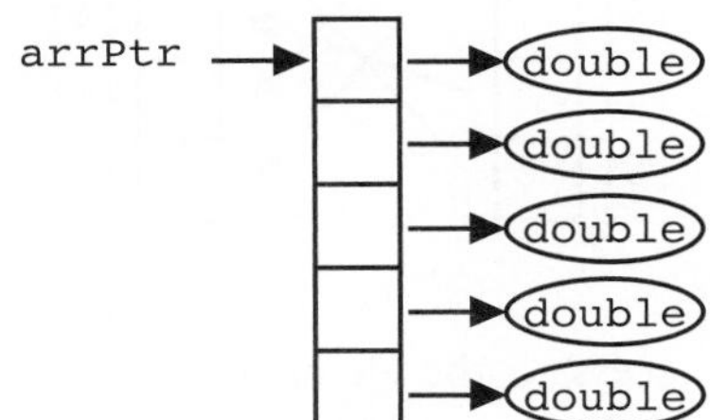

We will refer to the array of pointers as the `arrPtr` array. Once the `arrPtr` array is allocated in memory, its elements will be initialized so they point to the elements of the `donations` array, as illustrated in Figure 10-11.

Figure 10-11

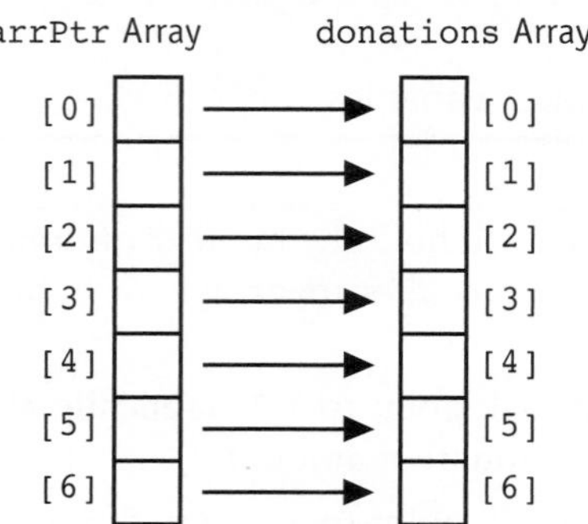

The elements of the `arrPtr` array will initially point to the elements of the `donations` array in their natural order (as shown in Figure 10-11). In other words, `arrPtr[0]` will point to `donations[0]`, `arrPtr[1]` will point to `donations[1]`, and so forth. In that arrangement, the following statement would cause the contents of `donations[5]` to be displayed:

```
cout << *(arrPtr[5]) << endl;
```

After the `arrPtr` array is sorted, however, `arrPtr[0]` will point to the smallest value in the `donations` array, `arrPtr[1]` will point to the next-to-smallest value in the `donations` array, and so forth. This is illustrated in Figure 10-12.

Figure 10-12

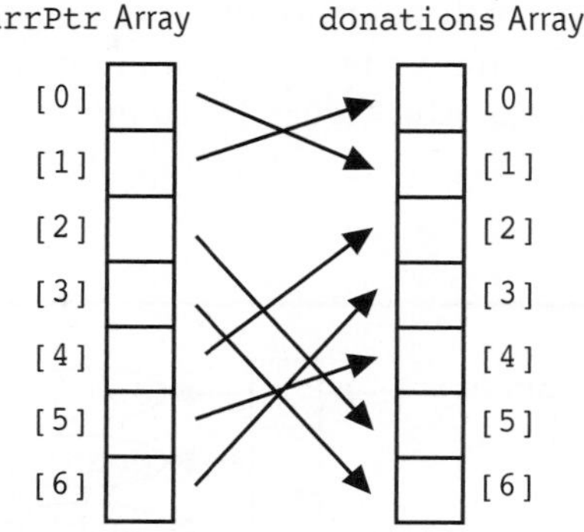

This technique gives us access to the elements of the `donations` array in a sorted order without actually disturbing the contents of the `donations` array itself.

Table 10-3 lists the class's member functions.

Table 10-3 Description of Member Functions

Member Function	Description
Constructor	The constructor accepts as arguments an integer, which indicates the number of donations received, and an array of `doubles`, which holds the list of donation values. When the constructor is finished, the `donations` member will point to a dynamically allocated array holding the list of donation values (in their original order), and the `arrPtr` member will point to a dynamically allocated array of pointers. The elements of the `arrPtr` array will point, in ascending order, to the elements of the `donations` array.
Destructor	Deletes the storage that was allocated by the constructor.
`selectSort`	This function, which performs an ascending-order selection sort on `arrPtr`, is called by the constructor. Before the sort, `arrPtr [0]`points to `donations [0]`, `arrPtr [1]` points to `donations [1]`, and so forth. After the sort, `arrPtr` will point to the elements of the `donations` array in ascending order.
`show`	Displays the contents of the `donations` array. (This function displays the donations in their original order.)
`showSorted`	Displays the contents of what each element of the `arrPtr` array points to. (This function displays the contents of the `donations` array in sorted order.)

Let's look at each member function in more detail.

The Constructor

The constructor's code is as follows:

```
DonationList::DonationList(int num, double gifts[])
{
   numDonations = num;
   if (num > 0)
   {
      // Allocate an array of doubles
      donations = new double[num];
      // Allocate an array of pointers-to-doubles.
      arrPtr = new double*[num];
      // Initialize the arrays
      for (int count = 0; count < numDonations; count++)
      {
         donations[count] = gifts[count];
         arrPtr[count] = &donations[count];
      }
      // Now sort the array of pointers
      selectSort();
   }
}
```

The `num` argument (which is copied to `numDonations`) holds the number of donations, and the `gifts` array contains the list of donation values.

If the value in `num` is greater than 0, the constructor allocates and initializes the elements of the `donations` and `arrPtr` arrays. The elements of the `gifts` array are copied to the elements of the `donations` array, and the elements of the `arrPtr` array are set to point to the elements of the `donations` array.

The `selectSort` Member Function

The `selectSort` function is a modified version of the selection sort algorithm. The only difference is that this function sorts an array of pointers. Instead of sorting on the contents of the array's elements, the array is sorted on the contents of what its elements point to. Here is the pseudocode.

```
For scan is set to the values 0 up to (but not including) the next-
to-last subscript in arrPtr
   Set minIndex variable to scan
   Set minElem pointer to arrPtr[scan]
   For index variable is set to the values from (scan + 1) through
   the next-to-last subscript in arrPtr
      If *(arrPtr[index]) is less than *minElem
         Set minElem to arrPtr[index]
         Set minIndex to index
      End If
   End For
   Set arrPtr[minIndex] to arrPtr[scan]
   Set arrPtr[scan] to minElem
End For
```

Here is the C++ code for the function:

```
void DonationList::selectSort()
{
   int minIndex;
   double *minElem;

   for (int scan = 0; scan < (numDonations - 1); scan++)
   {
      minIndex = scan;
      minElem = arrPtr[scan];
      for(int index = scan + 1; index < numDonations; index++)
      {
         if (*(arrPtr[index]) < *minElem)
         {
            minElem = arrPtr[index];
            minIndex = index;
         }
      }
      arrPtr[minIndex] = arrPtr[scan];
      arrPtr[scan] = minElem;
   }
}
```

The `show` Member Function

The `show` member function simply displays the contents of the `donations` array sequentially. Here is its pseudocode:

```
For every element in donations Array
   Display the element's contents
End For
```

Here is the function's actual C++ code:

```
void DonationList::show()
{
   for (int count = 0; count < numDonations; count++)
      cout << donations[count] << " ";
   cout << endl;
}
```

The `showSorted` Member Function

The `showSorted` function displays the values pointed to by the elements of the `arrPtr` array. Here is its pseudocode:

```
For every element in the arrPtr array
   Dereference the element and display what it points to
End For
```

Here is the function's C++ code:

```
void DonationList::showSorted()
{
   for (int count = 0; count < numDonations; count++)
      cout << *(arrPtr[count]) << " ";
   cout << endl;
}
```

The Entire `Class` Listing

The class in its entirety is shown here.

Contents of `donlist.h`

```
#ifndef DONLIST_H
#define DONLIST_H

class DonationList
{
private:
   int numDonations;
   double *donations;
   double **arrPtr;
   void selectSort();
public:
   DonationList(int num, double gifts[]);
   ~DonationList();
   void show();
   void showSorted();
};
#endif
```

Contents of donlist.cpp

```
#include <iostream>   //needed for cout
#include "donlist.h"
using namespace std;

//***********************************************************
// Constructor.                                             *
// The argument passed to num indicates the number of       *
// elements in array passed to gifts. The gifts array       *
// holds the list of donation values. The constructor       *
// allocates the donations and arrPtr arrays. The gifts     *
// array is copied to the donations array. The elements     *
// of the arrPtr array are made to point to the elements    *
// of the donations array, and then sorted in ascending     *
// order by the selectSort function.                        *
//***********************************************************
DonationList::DonationList(int num, double gifts[])
{
   numDonations = num;
   if (num > 0)
   {
      // Allocate an array of doubles
      donations = new double[num];
      // Allocate an array of pointers-to-doubles
      arrPtr = new double*[num];
      // Initialize the arrays
      for (int count = 0; count < numDonations; count++)
      {
         donations[count] = gifts[count];
         arrPtr[count] = &donations[count];
      }
      // Now, sort the array of pointers
      selectSort();
   }
}

//***********************************************************
// Destructor frees the memory allocated by the constructor*
//***********************************************************
DonationList::~DonationList()
{
   if (numDonations > 0)
   {
      delete [ ] donations;
      donations = 0;
      delete [ ] arrPtr;
      arrPtr = 0;
   }
}

//*************************************************************
// The selecSort function performs a selection sort on the   *
```

```
// arrPtr array of pointers. The array is sorted on the      *
// values its elements point to.                             *
//************************************************************
void DonationList::selectSort()
{
   int minIndex;
   double *minElem;

   for (int scan = 0; scan < (numDonations - 1); scan++)
   {
      minIndex = scan;
      minElem = arrPtr[scan];
      for(int index = scan + 1; index < numDonations; index++)
      {
         if (*(arrPtr[index]) < *minElem)
         {
            minElem = arrPtr[index];
            minIndex = index;
         }
      }
      arrPtr[minIndex] = arrPtr[scan];
      arrPtr[scan] = minElem;
   }
}

//*******************************************************
// The show function uses cout to display the donations *
// array in sequential order.                           *
//*******************************************************
void DonationList::show()
{
   for (int count = 0; count < numDonations; count++)
        cout << donations[count] << " ";
        cout << endl;
}

//*********************************************************
// The showSorted function uses cout to display the values*
// pointed to by the elements of the arrPtr array. Since  *
// arrPtr is sorted, this function displays the elements  *
// of the donations array in ascending order.             *
//*********************************************************
void DonationList::showSorted()
{
   for (int count = 0; count < numDonations; count++)
      cout << *(arrPtr[count]) << " ";
   cout << endl;
}
```

Implementing the Class

Program 10-19 shows how the class is used. The funds array is initialized with the 15 donation values.

Program 10-19

```
// This program shows the donations made to the United Cause
// by the employees of CK Graphics, Inc. It displays
// the donations in order from lowest to highest
// and in the original order they were received.
#include <iostream>
#include "donlist.h"
using namespace std;

int main()
{
   double funds[] = {5,  100, 5,  25, 10,
                     5,  25,  5,  5,  100,
                     10, 15,  10, 5,  10 };
   DonationList ckGraphics(15, funds);
   cout << "The donations sorted in ascending order are:\n";
   ckGraphics.showSorted();
   cout << "The donations in their original order are:\n";
   ckGraphics.show();
   return 0;
}
```

Program Output

```
The donations sorted in ascending order are:
5 5 5 5 5 5 10 10 10 10 15 25 25 100 100
The donations in their original order are:
5 100 5 25 10 5 25 5 5 100 10 15 10 5 10
```

When the `ckGraphics` object is defined, the value 15 is passed to the constructor's `num` parameter, and the `funds` array is passed to the `gifts` parameter. The `showSorted` member function is called to display the donation values in ascending order (by using the `arrPtr` array to display them), and the `show` member function is called to display the values in their original order.

10.14 Tying It All Together: *Pardon Me, Do You Have the Time?*

Professor Susan Gonzalez wants to have her students take some of their tests online and has asked you to write a program to administer the tests. For each student, the program must record the student's starting time, the student's answer for each question, and the student's ending time. Before you write the program, you want to make sure that you can write code to accurately capture a student's start and end time. You decide to write a short program that experiments with the C++ library functions for telling time.

C++ libraries provide a number of data types and functions that can be used to determine the current calendar time. By convention, many computers mark calendar time by the number of seconds that have elapsed since a point in time that has come to be known among computer scientists as *the epoch*. In case you want to know, the epoch is midnight January 1, 1970.

The C++ data type `time_t` is used to represent the number of seconds since the epoch. The library function

```
time_t time (time_t * epSecs);
```

takes as parameter a pointer to a `time_t` object that will hold the value representing the current time. Program 10-20 illustrates the use of this function.

Program 10-20

```
// This program illustrates the use of the time function.
#include <iostream>
#include <ctime>    // Needed to use the time functions and types
using namespace std;

int main()
{
    time_t epSeconds;
    time(&epSeconds);
    cout << "The number of seconds since the epoch is "
         << epSeconds << endl;
    return 0;
}
```

Program Output

```
The number of seconds since the epoch is 1247930628
```

Somewhat redundantly, the value stored in the parameter `epSecs` is also returned by the `time` function. This allows the programmer to pass `NULL` for the parameter to `time()` and use the returned value instead. The following program is equivalent to Program 10-20.

Program 10-21

```
// This program illustrates the use of the time function.
#include <iostream>
#include <ctime>    // Needed to use the time functions and types
using namespace std;

int main()
{
    time_t epSeconds;
    epSeconds = time(NULL);
    cout << "Number of seconds since the epoch is "
         << epSeconds << endl;
    return 0;
}
```

Program Output

```
Number of seconds since the epoch is 1247930807
```

As useful as `time()` is, it does not solve all time-related problems. First, Professor Gonzalez would much prefer that chronological times be stated in a form such as

```
Friday June 6, 2009, 4:29PM
```

instead of as so many seconds after the epoch. Second, she wants the program to take differences in time zones into account and always give the correct local time. The C++ function

```
tm * localtime(const time_t *eps)
```

is exactly what is needed: it takes a `time_t` value, converts it into a structure of type `tm`, and returns the address of that structure. The members of `tm` are integers and have the meanings shown here:

```
int tm_min;  // Minutes after the hour (0..59)
int tm_hour; // Hours after midnight (0..23)
int tm_mday; // Day of the month (1..31)
int tm_mon;  // Month since January (0..11)
int tm_year; // Years since 1900
int tm_wday; // Weekday (Sunday=0, Monday=1, .. Saturday=6)
```

The following is an example of how to use `time()` in conjunction with `localtime()` to print the number of the current month:

```
time_t epSecs;        // Seconds since epoch
tm *pCalendarTime;    // Pointer to calendar time
// Get seconds since epoch
epSecs = time(NULL);
// Convert to local time
pCalendarTime = localtime(&epSecs);
// Print number of current month
cout << pCalendarTime->tm_mon;
```

The following program determines and prints the day of the week, month, and year of the time of its execution:

Program 10-22

```
// This program prints "today's" date
#include <iostream>
#include <ctime>
#include <string>
using namespace std;

int main()
{
    time_t epSeconds;          // Seconds since epoch
    tm *pCalendarTime;         // Pointer to calendar time
    // Array of weekday names
    string wDay[] = {"Sunday", "Monday", "Tuesday", "Wednesday",
                     "Thursday", "Friday", "Saturday"
                    };
    // Array of month names
    string month[] = {"January", "February", "March", "April",
                      "May", "June", "July", "August", "September",
                      "October", "November", "December"
                     };

```

(program continues)

Program 10-22 *(continued)*

```
    epSeconds = time(NULL);                  // Seconds since epoch
    pCalendarTime = localtime(&epSeconds); // Convert to local time

    // Print day of month and day of week
    cout << "Today is " << wDay[pCalendarTime->tm_wday]
         << " " << month[pCalendarTime->tm_mon]
         << " " << pCalendarTime->tm_mday
         << ", " << 1900 + pCalendarTime->tm_year << endl;

    return 0;
}
```

Program Output

```
Today is Friday September 20, 2013
```

Review Questions and Exercises

Fill-in-the-Blank and Short Answer

1. Each byte in memory is assigned a unique __________.
2. The __________ operator can be used to determine a variable's address.
3. __________ variables are designed to hold addresses.
4. The __________ operator can be used to work with the variable a pointer points to.
5. Array names can be used as __________ and vice versa.
6. Creating variables while a program is running is called __________.
7. The __________ operator is used to dynamically allocate memory.
8. If the `new` operator cannot allocate the amount of memory requested, it throws __________.
9. A pointer that contains the address 0 is called a(n) __________ pointer.
10. When a program is finished with a chunk of dynamically allocated memory, it should free it with the __________ operator.
11. You should only use the `delete` operator to deallocate memory that was dynamically acquired with the __________ operator.
12. What does the indirection operator do?
13. Look at the following code.

    ```
    int x = 7;
    int *ptr = &x;
    ```

    What will be displayed if you send the expression `*iptr` to `cout`? What happens if you send the expression `ptr` to `cout`?

14. Name two different uses for the C++ operator *.
15. Which arithmetic operations can be applied to pointers?
16. Assuming that `ptr` is a pointer to an `int`, what happens when you add 4 to it?
17. Look at the following array definition.

    ```
    int numbers [] = {2, 4, 6, 8, 10};
    ```

    What will the following statement display?

    ```
    cout << *(numbers + 3) << endl;
    ```

18. What is the purpose of the new operator?
19. What happens when a program uses the `new` operator to allocate a block of memory, but the amount of requested memory isn't available? How do programs written with older compilers handle this?
20. Under what circumstances can you successfully return a pointer from a function?
21. What is the purpose of the `delete` operator?
22. What is the difference between a pointer to a constant and a constant pointer?
23. Show C++ code for defining a variable `ptr` that is a pointer to a constant `int`.
24. Show C++ code for defining a variable `ptr` that is a constant pointer to `int`.

C++ Language Elements

25. Consider the function

    ```
    void change(int *p)
    {
       *p = 20;
    }
    ```

    Show how to call the `change` function so that it sets the integer variable

    ```
    int i;
    ```

    to 20.

26. Consider the function

    ```
    void modify(int & x)
    {
       x = 10;
    }
    ```

    Show how to call the `modify` function so that it sets the integer

    ```
    int i;
    ```

    to 10.

Algorithm Workbench

27. Write a function whose prototype is

    ```
    void exchange(int *p, int *q);
    ```

    that takes two pointers to integer variables and exchanges the values in those variables.

28. Write a function

```
void switchEnds(int *array, int size);
```

that is passed the address of the beginning of an array and the size of the array. The function swaps the values in the first and last entries of the array.

Predict the Output

29. Given the variable initializations

```
int a[5] = {0, 10, 20, 30, 40};
int k = 3;
int *p = a + 1;
```

determine the output from each of the following statements:

A) `cout << a[k];`
B) `cout << *(a + k);`
C) `cout << *a;`
D) `cout << a[*a];`
E) `cout << a[*a + 2];`
F) `cout << *p;`
G) `cout << p[0];`
H) `cout << p[1];`

Find the Error

30. Each of the following declarations and program segments has errors. Locate as many as you can.

A)
```
int ptr*;
```
B)
```
int x, *ptr;
&x = ptr;
```
C)
```
int x, *ptr;
*ptr = &x;
```
D)
```
int x, *ptr;
ptr = &x;
ptr = 100; // Store 100 in x
cout << x << endl;
```
E)
```
int numbers[] = {10, 20, 30, 40, 50};
cout << "The third element in the array is ";
cout << *numbers + 3 << endl;
```
F)
```
int values[20], *iptr;
iptr = values;
iptr *= 2;
```
G)
```
double level;
int dPtr = &level;
```
H)
```
int *iptr = &ivalue;
int ivalue;
```
I)
```
void doubleVal(int val)
{
    *val *= 2;
}
```

J)
```
int *pint;
new pint;
```
K)
```
int *pint;
pint = new int;
pint = 100;
```
L)
```
int *pint;
pint = new int[100]; // Allocate memory
   .
   .
Process the array
   .
   .
delete pint;// Free memory
```
M)
```
int *getNum()
{
    int wholeNum;

    cout << "Enter a number: ";
    cin >> wholeNum;
    return &wholeNum;
}
```

Soft Skills

31. Suppose that you are a manager of a programming team. To facilitate project development and maintenance, you have decided to establish some programming and coding guidelines. Make a list of pointer-related programming guidelines you think will improve program readability and decrease pointer-related bugs.

Programming Challenges

1. Test Scores #1

Write a program that dynamically allocates an array large enough to hold a user-defined number of test scores. Once all the scores are entered, the array should be passed to a function that sorts them in ascending order. Another function should be called that calculates the average score. The program should display the sorted list of scores and averages with appropriate headings. Use pointer notation rather than array notation whenever possible.

Input Validation: Do not accept negative numbers for test scores.

2. Test Scores #2

Modify the program of Programming Challenge 1 to allow the user to enter name–score pairs. For each student taking a test, the user types a string representing the name of the student, followed by an integer representing the student's score. Modify both the sorting and average-calculating functions so they take arrays of structures, with each structure containing the name and score of a single student. In traversing the arrays, use pointers rather than array indices.

3. Money Money Money #1

Modify Program 10-19 (the *United Cause* case study program) so it can be used with any set of donations. The program should dynamically allocate the `donations` array and ask the user to input its values.

4. Money Money Money #2

Modify Program 10-19 (the *United Cause* case study program) so the `arrPtr` array is sorted in descending order instead of ascending order.

5. Pie a la Mode

In statistics the *mode* of a set of values is the value that occurs most often. Write a program that determines how many pieces of pie most people eat in a year. Set up an integer array that can hold responses from 30 people. For each person, enter the number of pieces they say they eat in a year. Then write a function that finds the mode of these 30 values. This will be the number of pie slices eaten by the most people. The function that finds and returns the mode should accept two arguments, an array of integers, and a value indicating how many elements are in the array.

6. Median Function

In statistics the median of a set of values is the value that lies in the middle when the values are arranged in sorted order. If the set has an even number of values, then the median is taken to be the average of the two middle values. Write a function that determines the median of a sorted array. The function should take an array of numbers and an integer indicating the size of the array and return the median of the values in the array. You may assume the array is already sorted. Use pointer notation whenever possible.

7. Movie Statistics

Write a program that can be used to gather statistical data about the number of movies college students see in a month. The program should ask the user how many students were surveyed and dynamically allocate an array of that size. The program should then allow the user to enter the number of movies each student has seen. The program should then calculate the average, median, and mode of the values entered.

8. Days in Current Month

Solving the Days in Current Month Problem

Write a program that can determine the number of days in a month for a specified month and year. The program should allow a user to enter two integers representing a month and a year, and it should determine how many days are in the specified month. The integers 1 through 12 will be used to identify the months of January through December. The user indicates the end of input by entering 0 0 for the month and year. At that point, the program prints the number of days in the current month and terminates.

Use the following criteria to identify leap years:

1. A year *Y* is divisible by 100. Then *Y* is a leap year if and if only it is divisible by 400. For example, 2000 is a leap year but 2100 is not.
2. A year *Y* is not divisible by 100. Then *Y* is a leap year if and if only it is divisible by 4. For example, 2008 is a leap year but 2009 is not.

Here is sample run of the program:

```
Enter month and year: 2 2008[Enter]
29 days
Enter month and year: 0 0[Enter]

The current month, September 2009, has 30 days.
```

9. Age

Write a program that asks for the user's name and year of birth, greets the user by name, and declares the user's age in years. Users are assumed to be born between the years 1800 and 2099, and should enter the year of birth in one of the three formats 18XX, 19XX, or 20XX. A typical output should be “Hello Caroline, you are 23 years old.”

CHAPTER

11 More About Classes and Object-Oriented Programming

TOPICS

11.1 The `this` Pointer and Constant Member Functions

CONCEPT: By default, the compiler provides each member function of a class with an implicit parameter that points to the object through which the member function is called. The implicit parameter is called **`this`**. A constant member function is one that does not modify the object through which it is called.

The `this` Pointer

Consider the class

```
class Example
{
   int x;
   public:
      Example(int a){ x = a;}
      void setValue(int);
      int getValue();
};
```

with the member function

```
int Example::getValue()
{
   return x;
}
```

that simply returns the value in an object of the class. As an example, the `getValue` function might be invoked in a program such as

```
int main()
{
   Example ob1(10), ob2(20);
   cout << ob1.getValue() << " " << ob2.getValue();
   return 0;
}
```

in which case the program would print out the values `10    20`.

You learned in an earlier chapter that the different objects of a structure or class type are called *instances* of that class, and that each instance of a class has its own copy of the data members listed in the class. These data members, called *instance members* because they belong to instances of the class, can have different values in different objects. Thus in the preceding example, the instance member `x` in the `ob1` object has a value of `10` while `x` in `ob2` has a value of `20`.

Now consider again the code for the member function

```
int Example::getValue()
{
   return x;
}
```

This function is supposed to return the `x` member of some object of the `Example` class, but how does it know which object to use? What happens is that by default, the compiler provides each member function of every class with an implicit parameter that is a pointer to an object of the class. Thus for example, the `getValue` function is equipped with a single parameter of type pointer to `Example`. Similarly, the member function

```
void Example::setValue(int a)
{
   x = a;
}
```

although written by the programmer to take a single parameter of type `int`, in reality has two parameters: an pointer to an object of the class `Example`, and the

```
int a
```

parameter specified by the programmer. In all cases, the actual parameter for the implicit object parameter is the address of the object through which the member function is being called. Thus in the call

```
ob1.getValue()
```

the implicit parameter passed to `getValue` is the address of `ob1`, whereas in the call

```
ob2.setValue(78)
```

the implicit parameter passed to `setValue` is `&ob2`.

The implicit pointer passed by the compiler to a member function can be accessed by code inside that function by using the reserved key word `this`. So for example, a member function of the `Example` class could access the object through which it is called by using the expression

```
*this
```

and it could also access any of the members of that object through the same pointer. Program 11-1 illustrates these concepts. It modifies the `Example` class to include a member function that uses the `this` pointer to print the address of the object through which it is called as well as the value of the instance member `x` in the same object.

Program 11-1

Contents of `ThisExample.h`

```
class Example
{
   int x;
 public:
   Example(int a){ x = a;}
   void setValue(int);
   void printAddressAndValue();
};
```

Contents of `ThisExample.cpp`

```
#include "ThisExample.h"
#include <iostream>
using namespace std;

//***************************************
// Set value of object.                 *
//***************************************
void Example::setValue(int a)
{
   x = a;
}
//***************************************
// Print address and value.             *
//***************************************
void Example::printAddressAndValue()
{
   cout << "The object at address " << this << " has "
        << "value " << (*this).x << endl;
}
```

Contents of main program, `pr11-1.cpp`

```
// This program illustrates the this pointer.
#include <iostream>
#include "ThisExample.h"
using namespace std;

int main()
{
   Example ob1(10), ob2(20);

```

(program continues)

Program 11-1 *(continued)*

```
    // Print the addresses of the two objects
    cout << "Addresses of objects are " << &ob1
         << " and " << &ob2 << endl;

    // Print the addresses and values from within
    // the member function
    ob1.printAddressAndValue();
    ob2.printAddressAndValue();

    return 0;
}
```

Program Output

```
Addresses of objects are 0x241ff5c and 0x241ff58
The object at address 0x241ff5c has value 10
The object at address 0x241ff58 has value 20
```

As an example of a common use of the `this` pointer, consider the member function

```
void Example::setValue(int a)
{
   x = a;
}
```

It is natural to name the parameter to be used to set the value of the member `x` using an identifier that makes its connection to `x` explicit, perhaps `xValue` or even `x` itself. However, a formal parameter of a member function with the same identifier as a member of the class will hide the class member, making it inaccessible inside the function. The `this` pointer can be used to qualify the name of the class member and make it visible again. Here is the `setValue` member function rewritten in this manner:

```
void Example::setValue(int x)
{
   this->x = x;
}
```

Recall from Chapter 10 that the notation `this->x` is equivalent to `(*this).x`.

Constant Member Functions

A parameter that is passed to a function by reference or through a pointer may be modified by that function. The `const` key word is used with a parameter to prevent the called function from modifying it. For example, a function declared as

```
void fun(const string *str);
```

takes a pointer to a string object as a parameter, but will not be able to modify the object. There is a similar mechanism that can be used to protect the implicit parameter `*this` from being modified by a member function. When placed right after the parameter list in the definition of a member function, the `const` key word serves as an indication to the compiler that the member function should not be allowed to modify its object. If the member function is defined outside the class, both the in-class declaration and the definition must have the `const`. Here is an example

```
class ConstExample
{
   int x;
public:
   ConstExample(int a){ x = a;}
   void setValue(int);
   int getValue() const;
};
```

The definition of the getValue function would be

```
int ConstExample::getValue() const
{
   return x;
}
```

A function with a constant parameter x cannot turn around and pass x as a non-constant parameter to another function. In other words, a function that promises not to modify x may not pass x to another function unless that second function also promises not to modify x . This can sometimes occur in ways that are not obvious. The following program uses a function with a constant parameter to print the first element of an array. It does not compile because it is not consistent in its use of const.

```
#include <iostream>
using namespace std;

class K
{
public:
    void output()   // Missing const!
    {
        cout << "Output of a K object" << endl;
    }
};

void outputFirst(const K arr[])
{
   arr[0].output();
}

int main(int argc, char** argv)
{
    K arr[] = { K() };
    outputFirst(arr);
    return 0;
}
```

The program does not compile because the compiler cannot guarantee that an element of the const array will not be modified when passed as the implicit this parameter to the output member function:

```
arr[0].output();
```

You can get the program to compile by making `output()` a `const` member function to signify that it has a constant `this` parameter:

```
class K
{
public:
    void output() const
    {
        cout << "Output of a K object" << endl;
    }
};
```

11.2 Static Members

CONCEPT: If a member variable is declared `static`, all objects of that class have access to that variable. If a member function is declared `static`, it may be called before any instances of the class are defined.

Each class object (an instance of a class) has its own copy of the class's member variables. An object's member variables are separate and distinct from the member variables of other objects of the same class. For example, consider the following declaration:

```
class Widget
{
   private:
      double price;
      int quantity;
   public:
      Widget(double p, int q)
          { price = p; quantity = q; }
      double getPrice() const
          { return price; }
      int getQuantity() const
          { return quantity; }
};
```

Assume that in a program, two separate instances of the `Widget` class are created by the following declaration:

```
Widget w1(14.50, 100), w2(12.75, 500);
```

This statement creates `w1` and `w2`, two distinct objects. Each has its own `price` and `quantity` member variables. This is illustrated by Figure 11-1.

Figure 11-1

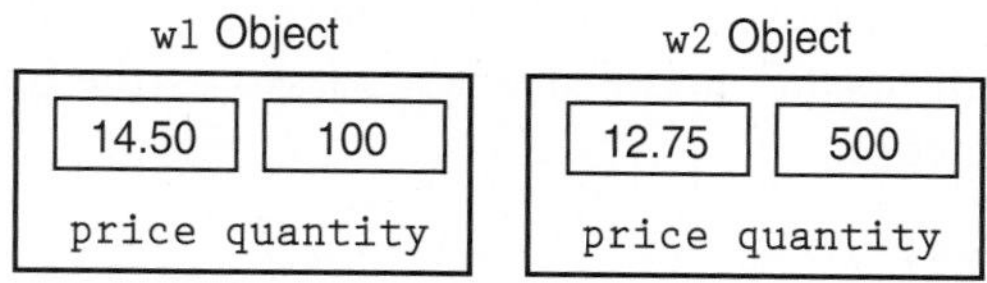

When the `getQuantity` member function of either instance is called, it returns the value stored in the calling object's `quantity` variable. Based on the values initially stored in the objects, the statement

```
cout << w1.getQuantity() << " " << w2.getQuantity();
```

will cause `100 500` to be displayed.

Static Member Variables

It's possible to create a member variable that is shared by all the objects of the same class. To create such a member, simply place the key word `static` in front of the variable declaration, as shown in the following class:

```
class StatDemo
{
  private:
     static int x;
     int y;
  public:
     void setx(int a) const { x = a; }
     void sety(int b) const { y = b; }
     int getx() { return x; }
     int gety() { return y; }
};
```

Next, place a separate definition of the variable outside the class, such as:

```
int StatDemo::x;
```

In this example, the member variable `x` will be shared by all objects of the `StatDemo` class. When one class object puts a value in `x`, it will appear in all other `StatDemo` objects. For example, assume the following statements appear in a program:

```
StatDemo obj1, obj2;
obj1.setx(5);
obj1.sety(10);
obj2.sety(20);
cout << "x: " << obj1.getx() << " " << obj2.getx() << endl;
cout << "y: " << obj1.gety() << " " << obj2.gety() << endl;
```

The `cout` statements shown will display

```
x: 5 5
y: 10 20
```

The value `5` is stored in the static member variable `x` by the object `obj1`. Since `obj1` and `obj2` share the variable `x`, the value 5 shows up in both objects. This is illustrated by Figure 11-2.

Figure 11-2

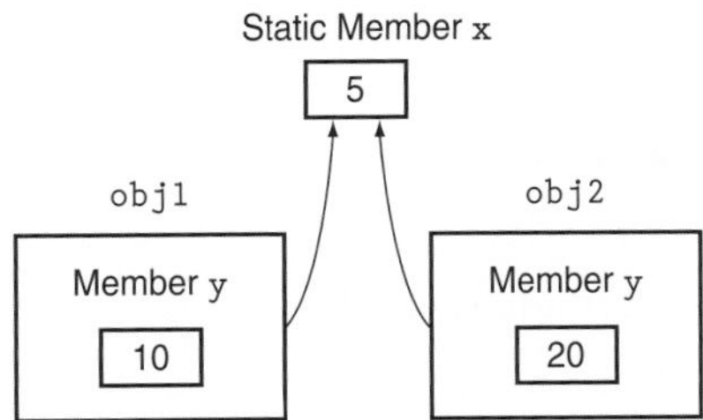

Both `obj1` and `obj2` share the static member `x`

A more practical use of a static member variable is demonstrated in Program 11-2. The `Budget` class is used to gather the budget requests for all the divisions of a company. The class uses a static member, `corpBudget`, to hold the amount of the overall corporate budget. When the member function `addBudget` is called, its argument is added to the current contents of `corpBudget`. By the time the program is finished, `corpBudget` will contain the total of all the values placed there by all the `Budget` class objects.

Program 11-2

Contents of `budget.h`

```
#ifndef BUDGET_H
#define BUDGET_H

class Budget
{
private:
   static double corpBudget;
   double divBudget;
public:
   Budget() { divBudget = 0; }
   void addBudget(double b)
      { divBudget += b; corpBudget += divBudget; }
   double getDivBudget() const { return divBudget; }
   double getCorpBudget() const { return corpBudget; }
};
#endif
```

Contents of main program, `pr11-2.cpp`

```
// This program demonstrates a static class member variable.
#include <iostream>
#include <iomanip>
#include "budget.h"          // For Budget class declaration
using namespace std;

// Definition of the static member of the Budget class
double Budget::corpBudget = 0;

int main()
{
   const int N_DIVISIONS = 4;
   Budget divisions[N_DIVISIONS];

   // Get the budget request for each division
   for (int count = 0; count < N_DIVISIONS; count++)
   {
      double bud;

      cout << "Enter the budget request for division ";
      cout << (count + 1) << ": ";
      cin >> bud;
      divisions[count].addBudget(bud);
   }

```

(program continues)

Program 11-2 *(continued)*

```
    // Display the budget request for each division
    cout << setprecision(2);
    cout << showpoint << fixed;
    cout << "\nHere are the division budget requests:\n";
    for (int count = 0; count < N_DIVISIONS; count++)
    {
      cout << "Division " << (count + 1) << "\t$ ";
      cout << divisions[count].getDivBudget() << endl;
    }

    // Display the total budget request
    cout << "Total Budget Requests:\t$ ";
    cout << divisions[0].getCorpBudget() << endl;

    return 0;
}
```

Program Output with Example Input Shown in Bold

```
Enter the budget request for division 1: 102000[Enter]
Enter the budget request for division 2: 201000[Enter]
Enter the budget request for division 3: 570000[Enter]
Enter the budget request for division 4: 100100[Enter]

Here are the division budget requests:
Division 1      $ 102000.00
Division 2      $ 201000.00
Division 3      $ 570000.00
Division 4      $ 100100.00
Total Budget Requests:  $ 973100.00
```

NOTE: Static member variables furnish a good example of the distinction between C++ declarations and C++ definitions. A *declaration* provides information about the existence and type of a variable or function. A *definition* provides all the information contained in a declaration, and in addition, causes memory to be allocated for the variable or function being defined. Static member variables must be *declared* inside the class and *defined* outside of it.

In general, we can divide the member variables and functions of a class into two groups: *instance members* and *static members*. An instance member is one whose use must be associated with a particular instance of the class. In particular, an instance variable of a class must be accessed through a specific instance of its class, and an instance member function must be called through a specific instance of its class.

In contrast, the use of a static member variable, or the call of a static member function, does not need to be associated with any instance. Only the class of the static member needs to be specified.

Static Member Functions

A member function of a class can be declared static by prefixing its declaration with the key word `static`. Here is the general form:

```
static <return type><function name>(<parameter list>)
```

Static member functions are normally used to work with static member variables of the class. In fact, member functions that do not access any nonstatic members of their class, such as `getCorpBudget()` in Program 11-2, should be made static.

Program 11-3, a modification of Program 11-2, demonstrates this. It asks the user to enter the main office's budget request before any division requests are entered. The `Budget` class has been modified to include a static member function named `mainOffice`. This function adds its argument to the static `corpBudget` variable and is called before any instance of the `Budget` class is defined. The `getCorpBudget()` function has also been made static.

Program 11-3

Contents of `budget2.h`

```
#ifndef BUDGET_H
#define BUDGET_H

class Budget
{
private:
   static double corpBudget;
   double divBudget;
public:
   Budget() { divBudget = 0; }
   void addBudget(double b)
      { divBudget += b; corpBudget += divBudget; }
   double getDivBudget() const { return divBudget; }
   static double getCorpBudget() { return corpBudget; }
   static void mainOffice(double);
};
#endif
```

Contents of `budget2.cpp`

```
#include "budget2.h"

// Definition of the static member of Budget class.
double Budget::corpBudget = 0;

//**********************************************************
// Definition of static member function mainOffice         *
// This function adds the main office's budget request to  *
// the corpBudget variable.                                *
//**********************************************************
void Budget::mainOffice(double budReq)
{
   corpBudget += budReq;
}
```

Contents of main program, `pr11-3.cpp`

```
// This program demonstrates a static class member function.
#include <iostream>
#include <iomanip>
#include "budget2.h"        // For Budget class declaration
using namespace std;

```

(program continues)

Program 11-3 *(continued)*

```
int main()
{
   const int N_DIVISIONS = 4;

   // Get the budget requests for each division
   cout << "Enter the main office's budget request: ";
   double amount;
   cin >> amount;
   // Call the static member function of the Budget class
   Budget::mainOffice(amount);
   // Create instances of the Budget class
   Budget divisions[N_DIVISIONS];
   for (int count = 0; count < N_DIVISIONS; count++)
   {
      double bud;

      cout << "Enter the budget request for division ";
      cout << (count + 1) << ": ";
      cin >> bud;
      divisions[count].addBudget(bud);
   }

   // Display the budget for each division
   cout << setprecision(2);
   cout<< showpoint << fixed;
   cout << "\nHere are the division budget requests:\n";
   for (int count = 0; count < N_DIVISIONS; count++)
   {
      cout << "\tDivision " << (count + 1) << "\t$ ";
      cout << divisions[count].getDivBudget() << endl;
   }

   // Print total budget requests
   cout << "Total Requests (including main office): $ ";
   cout << Budget::getCorpBudget() << endl;
   return 0;
}
```

Program Output with Example Input Shown in Bold

```
Enter the main office's budget request: 400000[Enter]
Enter the budget request for division 1: 102000[Enter]
Enter the budget request for division 2: 210000[Enter]
Enter the budget request for division 3: 240000[Enter]
Enter the budget request for division 4: 105000[Enter]

Here are the division budget requests:
        Division 1      $ 102000.00
        Division 2      $ 210000.00
        Division 3      $ 240000.00
        Division 4      $ 105000.00
Total Requests (including main office): $ 1057000.00
```

Notice the statement that calls the static function `mainOffice`:

```
Budget::mainOffice(amount);
```

Calls to static member functions are normally made by connecting the function name to the class name with the scope resolution operator. If objects of the class have been defined, static member functions can also be called by connecting their names to the object with the dot operator. Thus the last output statement of Program 11-3 could be written as

```
cout << divisions[0].getCorpBudget() << endl;
```

The `this` pointer cannot be used in a static member function, because static member functions are not called through any instance of their class. Moreover, a static member function cannot access an instance member of its class unless it specifies what instance the member belongs to. For example, in the class

```
class StatAccess
{
   private:
      int x;
   public:
   static void output()
      {
         cout << x;  // Incorrect access of non-static member
      }
   StatAccess(int x) { this->x = x; }
};
```

The attempt to access `x` in the statement `cout << x` is incorrect because it is tantamount to an implicit use of the `this` pointer, which the static function `output` does not have. In contrast, in the following modified example of the same class, the static member function `print` correctly accesses the nonstatic member `x` because it qualifies it with the name of a class object passed to it as a parameter.

```
class StatAccess
{
   private:
      int x;
   public:
      static void print(StatAccess a)
      {
         cout << a.x;
      }
   StatAccess(int x) { this->x = x; }
};
```

An advantage of static member functions is they can be called before any instances of the class have been created. This allows them to be used to perform complex initialization tasks that have to be done before objects of the class have been created.

11.3 Friends of Classes

CONCEPT: A friend is a function that is not a member of a class, but has access to the private members of the class.

Private members are hidden from all parts of the program outside the class, and accessing them requires a call to a public member function. Sometimes you will want to create an exception to that rule. A *friend* function is a function that is not a member of a class, but that has access to the class's private members. In other words, a friend function is treated as if it were a member of the class. A friend function can be a regular stand-alone function, or it can be a member of another class. (In fact, an entire class can be declared a friend of another class.)

In order for a function or class to become a friend of another class, it must be declared as such by the class granting it access. Classes keep a "list" of their friends, and only the external functions or classes whose names appears in the list are granted access. A function is declared a friend by placing the key word `friend` in front of a prototype of the function. Here is the general format:

```
friend <return type><function name>(<parameter type list>);
```

In the following declaration of the `Budget` class, the `addBudget` function of another class, `Aux`, has been declared a friend:

```
class Budget
{
private:
   static double corpBudget;
   double divBudget;
public:
   Budget() { divBudget = 0; }
   void addBudget(double b)
      { divBudget += b; corpBudget += divBudget; }
   double getDivBudget() const { return divBudget; }
   static double getCorpBudget() { return corpBudget; }
   static void mainOffice(double);
   friend void Aux::addBudget(double);    // A friend
};
```

Let's assume another class `Aux` represents a division's auxiliary office, perhaps in another country. The auxiliary office makes a separate budget request, which must be added to the overall corporate budget. The friend declaration of the `Aux::addBudget` function tells the compiler that the function is to be granted access to `Budget`'s private members. The function takes an argument of type `double` representing an amount to be added to the corporate budget:

```
class Aux
{
private:
   double auxBudget;
```

```
public:
   Aux() { auxBudget = 0; }
   void addBudget(double);
   double getDivBudget() { return auxBudget; }
};
```

And here is the definition of the `Aux` `addBudget` member function:

```
void Aux::addBudget(double b)
{
   auxBudget += b;
   Budget::corpBudget += auxBudget;
}
```

The parameter `b` is added to the corporate budget, which is accessed by using the expression `Budget::corpBudget`. Program 11-4 demonstrates the classes in a complete program.

Program 11-4

Contents of `auxil.h`

```
#ifndef AUXIL_H
#define AUXIL_H

// Aux class declaration.
class Aux
{
private:
   double auxBudget;
public:
   Aux() { auxBudget = 0; }
   void addBudget(double);
   double getDivBudget() const { return auxBudget; }
};
#endif
```

Contents of `budget3.h`

```
#ifndef BUDGET3_H
#define BUDGET3_H
#include "auxil.h"    // For Aux class declaration

// Budget class declaration.
class Budget
{
private:
   static double corpBudget;
   double divBudget;
public:
   Budget() { divBudget = 0; }
   void addBudget(double b)
      { divBudget += b; corpBudget += divBudget; }
   double getDivBudget() const { return divBudget; }
   static double getCorpBudget() { return corpBudget; }
   static void mainOffice(double);
   friend void Aux::addBudget(double);
};
#endif
```

(program continues)

Program 11-4 *(continued)*

Contents of budget3.cpp

```
#include "budget3.h"

// Definition of static member.
double Budget::corpBudget = 0;

//*********************************************************
// Definition of static member function mainOffice        *
// This function adds the main office's budget request to *
// the corpBudget variable.                               *
//*********************************************************
void Budget::mainOffice(double budReq)
{
   corpBudget += budReq;
}
```

Contents of auxil.cpp

```
#include "auxil.h"
#include "budget3.h"

//*********************************************************
// Definition of member function addBudget                *
// This function is declared a friend by the Budget class *
// It adds the value of argument b to the static corpBudget *
// member variable of the Budget class.                   *
//*********************************************************

void Aux::addBudget(double b)
{
   auxBudget += b;
   Budget::corpBudget += auxBudget;
}
```

Contents of main program pr11-4.cpp

```
// This program demonstrates a static class member variable.
#include <iostream>
#include <iomanip>
#include "budget3.h"
using namespace std;

int main()
{
   const int N_DIVISIONS = 4;

   // Get the budget requests for the divisions and
   // offices
   cout << "Enter the main office's budget request: ";
   double amount;
   cin >> amount;
   Budget::mainOffice(amount);

```

(program continues)

Program 11-4 *(continued)*

```
    // Create the division and auxiliary offices
    Budget divisions[N_DIVISIONS];
    Aux auxOffices[N_DIVISIONS];

    cout << "\nEnter the budget requests for the divisions and  "
         << "\ntheir auxiliary offices as prompted:\n";
    for (int count = 0; count < N_DIVISIONS; count++)
    {
        double bud;
        cout <<  "Division " << (count + 1) << ": ";
        cin >> bud;
        divisions[count].addBudget(bud);
        cout << "Division " << (count + 1) << "'s auxiliary office: ";
        cin >> bud;
        auxOffices[count].addBudget(bud);
    }

    // Print the budgets
    cout << setprecision(2);
    cout << showpoint << fixed;
    cout << "Here are the division budget requests:\n";
    for (int count = 0; count < N_DIVISIONS; count++)
    {
        cout << "\tDivision: " << (count + 1) << "\t\t\t$ ";
        cout << setw(7);
        cout << divisions[count].getDivBudget() << endl;
        cout << "\tAuxiliary Office of Division " << (count+1);
        cout << "\t$  ";
        cout << auxOffices[count].getDivBudget() << endl;
    }
    // Print total requests
    cout << "\tTotal Requests (including main office): $ ";
    cout << Budget::getCorpBudget() << endl;
    return 0;
}
```

Program Output with Example Input Shown in Bold

```
Enter the main office's budget request: 100000[Enter]

Enter the budget requests for the divisions and
their auxiliary offices as prompted:
Division 1: 100000[Enter]
Division 1's auxiliary office: 500000[Enter]
Division 2: 200000[Enter]
Division 2's auxiliary office: 40000[Enter]
Division 3: 300000[Enter]
Division 3's auxiliary office: 700000[Enter]
Division 4: 400000[Enter]
Division 4's auxiliary office: 650000[Enter]
```

(program output continues)

Program 11-4 *(continued)*

```
Here are the division budget requests:
        Division: 1                       $ 100000.00
        Auxiliary Office of Division 1    $  50000.00
        Division: 2                       $ 200000.00
        Auxiliary Office of Division 2    $  40000.00
        Division: 3                       $ 300000.00
        Auxiliary Office of Division 3    $  70000.00
        Division: 4                       $ 400000.00
        Auxiliary Office of Division 4    $  65000.00
        Total Requests (including main office): $ 1325000.00
```

NOTE: As mentioned before, it is possible to make an entire class a friend of another class. The `Budget` class could make the `Aux` class its friend with the following declaration:

```
friend class Aux;
```

This may not be a good idea, however. Every member function of `Aux` (including ones that may be added later) would have access to the private members of `Budget`. The best practice is to declare as friends only those functions that must have access to the private members of the class.

Checkpoint

11.1 What is the difference between an instance member variable and a static member variable?

11.2 Static member variables are declared inside the class declaration. Where are static member variables defined?

11.3 Does a static member variable come into existence in memory before, at the same time as, or after any instances of its class?

11.4 What limitation does a static member function have?

11.5 What action is possible with a static member function that isn't possible with an instance member function?

11.6 If class `X` declares function `f` as a friend, does function `f` become a member of class `X`?

11.7 Suppose that class `Y` is a friend of class `X`, meaning that the member functions of class `Y` have access to all the members of class `X`. Should the friend key word appear in class `Y`'s declaration or in class `X`'s declaration?

11.4 Memberwise Assignment

CONCEPT: The = operator may be used to assign one object to another, or to initialize one object with another object's data. By default, each member of one object is copied to its counterpart in the other object.

Like other variables (except arrays), objects may be assigned to each other using the = operator. As an example, consider Program 11-5, which uses a `Rectangle` class similar to the one discussed in Chapter 7:

Program 11-5

```
// This program demonstrates object assignment.
#include <iostream>
using namespace std;

class Rectangle
{
private:
    double width, length;
public:
    Rectangle(double width, double length)
    {
        this->width = width;
        this->length = length;
    }
    double getWidth() const { return width; }
    double getLength() const { return length; }
    void output() const
    {
        cout << "Width is " << width << ", "
             << "Length is " << length << endl;
    }
};

int main()
{
   // Set up two rectangle objects
   Rectangle box1(10, 20), box2(5, 10);

   // Display the rectangle objects
   cout << "Before the assignment:\n";
   cout << "Box 1 data:\t";  box1.output();
   cout << "Box 2 data:\t";  box2.output();

   // Assignment
   box2 = box1;

   // Display the rectangle objects
   cout << "\nAfter the assignment:\n";
```

(program continues)

Program 11-5 *(continued)*

```
    cout << "Box 1 data:\t"; box1.output();
    cout << "Box 2 data:\t"; box2.output();
    return 0;
}
```

Program Output

```
Before the assignment:
Box 1 data:     Width is 10, Length is 20
Box 2 data:     Width is 5, Length is 10

After the assignment:
Box 1 data:     Width is 10, Length is 20
Box 2 data:     Width is 10, Length is 20
```

As you can see, the statement

```
box2 = box1
```

copied the `width` and `length` variables of `box1` directly into the `width` and `length` variables of `box2`.

Memberwise assignment also occurs when one object is initialized with another object's values. Remember the difference between assignment and initialization: assignment occurs between two objects that already exist, and initialization happens to an object being created. Consider the following program segment:

```
Rectangle box1(10, 50);
Rectangle box2 = box1;
```

The second statement defines a `Rectangle` object `box2` and initializes it to the values stored in `box1`. Because memberwise assignment takes place, the `box2` object will contain the same values as the `box1` object.

11.5 Copy Constructors

CONCEPT: A copy constructor is a special constructor that is called whenever a new object is created and initialized with the data of another object of the same class.

Many times it makes sense to create an object and have it start out with its data being the same as that of another, previously created object. For example, if Mary and Joan live in the same house and an address object for Mary has already been created, it makes sense to initialize Joan's address object to a copy of Mary's. In particular, suppose we have the following class to represent addresses:

```
class Address
{
private:
   string street;
```

```
public:
   Address() { street = ""; }
   Address(string st) { setStreet(st); }
   void setStreet(string st) { street = st; }
   string getStreet() const { return street; }
};
```

We could then create Mary's address and then initialize Joan's address to a copy of Mary's using the following code:

```
Address mary("123 Main St");
Address joan = mary;
```

Recall that a constructor must execute whenever an object is being created. When an object is created and initialized with another object of the same class, the compiler automatically calls a special constructor, called a *copy constructor*, to perform the initialization using the existing object's data. This copy constructor can be specified by the programmer, as we will shortly show.

The Default Copy Constructor

If the programmer does not specify a copy constructor for the class, then the compiler automatically calls a *default copy constructor*. This default copy constructor simply copies the data of the existing object to the new object using memberwise assignment.

Most of the time, the default copy constructor provides the kind of behavior that we want. For example, if after initializing Joan's address with Mary's, Joan later moves out and gets her own place, we can change Joan's address without affecting Mary's. This is illustrated in Program 11-6.

Program 11-6

```
// This program demonstrates the operation of the
// default copy constructor.
#include <iostream>
#include <string>
using namespace std;

class Address
{
private:
  string street;
public:
  Address() { street = ""; }
  Address(string st) { setStreet(st); }
  void setStreet(string st) { street = st; }
  string getStreet() const { return street; }
};

int main()
{
  // Mary and Joan live at same address
```

(program continues)

Program 11-6 *(continued)*

```
    Address mary("123 Main St");
    Address joan = mary;
    cout << "Mary lives at " << mary.getStreet() << endl;
    cout << "Joan lives at " << joan.getStreet() << endl;

    // Now Joan moves out
    joan.setStreet("1600 Pennsylvania Ave");
    cout << "Now Mary lives at " << mary.getStreet() << endl;
    cout << "Now Joan lives at " << joan.getStreet() << endl;

    return 0;
}
```

Program Output

```
Mary lives at 123 Main St
Joan lives at 123 Main St
Now Mary lives at 123 Main St
Now Joan lives at 1600 Pennsylvania Ave
```

Deficiencies of Default Copy Constructors

There are times, however, when the behavior of the default copy constructor is not what we expect. Consider a class

```
class NumberArray
{
private:
   double *aPtr;
   int arraySize;
public:
   NumberArray(int size, double value);
   // ~NumberArray(){ if (arraySize > 0) delete [] aPtr;}
   void print() const;
   void setValue(double value);
};
```

that encapsulates an array of numbers of type `double` (in practice there may be other members of the class as well). To allow flexibility for different size arrays, the class contains a pointer to the array instead of directly containing the array itself. The constructor of the class, whose code is shown below, allocates an array of a specified size, then sets all the entries of the array to a given value. The class has member functions for printing the array and for setting the entries of the array to a given (possibly different) value. The class's destructor uses the delete `[]` statement to deallocate the array (see Chapter 10) but is currently commented out to avoid problems caused by the default copy constructor. We shall shortly point out the specific nature of these problems.

Program 11-7 creates an object of the class, creates and initializes a second object with the data of the first, and then changes the array in the second object. As shown by the output of the program, changing the second object's data changes the data in the first object. In many cases, this is undesirable and leads to bugs.

Program 11-7

Contents of `NumberArray.h`

```
#include <iostream>
using namespace std;

class NumberArray
{
private:
   double *aPtr;
   int arraySize;
public:
   NumberArray(int size, double value);
   // ~NumberArray(){ if (arraySize > 0) delete [ ] aPtr;}
   // Commented out to avoid problems with the
   // default copy constructor
   void print() const;
   void setValue(double value);
};
```

Contents of `NumberArray.cpp`

```
#include <iostream>
#include "NumberArray.h"
using namespace std;

//*******************************************
//Constructor allocates an array of the      *
//given size and sets all its entries to the *
//given value.                               *
//*******************************************
NumberArray::NumberArray(int size, double value)
{
   arraySize = size;
   aPtr = new double[arraySize];
   setValue(value);
}

//*****************************************************
//Sets all the entries of the array to the same value. *
//*****************************************************
void NumberArray::setValue(double value)
{
   for(int index = 0; index < arraySize; index++)
      aPtr[index] = value;
}

//**************************************
//Prints all the entries of the array.  *
//**************************************
void NumberArray::print()
{
   for(int index = 0; index < arraySize; index++)
      cout << aPtr[index] << "  ";
}
```

(program continues)

Program 11-7 *(continued)*

Contents of `Pr11-7.cpp`

```
// This program demonstrates the deficiencies of
// the default copy constructor.
#include <iostream>
#include <iomanip>
#include "NumberArray.h"
using namespace std;

int main()
{
   // Create an object
   NumberArray first(3, 10.5);

   // Make a copy of the object
   NumberArray second = first;

   // Display the values of the two objects
   cout << setprecision(2) << fixed << showpoint;
   cout << "Value stored in first object is ";
   first.print();
   cout << endl << "Value stored in second object is ";
   second.print();
   cout << endl << "Only the value in second object "
        << "will be changed."  << endl;

   // Now change the  value stored in the second object
   second.setValue(20.5);

   // Display the values stored in the two objects
   cout << "Value stored in first object is ";
   first.print();
   cout << endl << "Value stored in second object is ";
   second.print();

   return 0;
}
```

Program Output

```
Value stored in first object is 10.50  10.50  10.50
Value stored in second object is 10.50  10.50  10.50
Only the value in second object will be changed.
Value stored in first object is 20.50  20.50  20.50
Value stored in second object is 20.50  20.50  20.50
```

The reason changing the data in one object changes the other object is that the memberwise assignment performed by the default copy constructor copies the value of the pointer in the first object to the pointer in the second object, *leaving both pointers pointing to the same data*. Thus when one of the objects changes its data through its pointer, it affects the other object as well. This is illustrated in Figure 11-3.

Figure 11-3

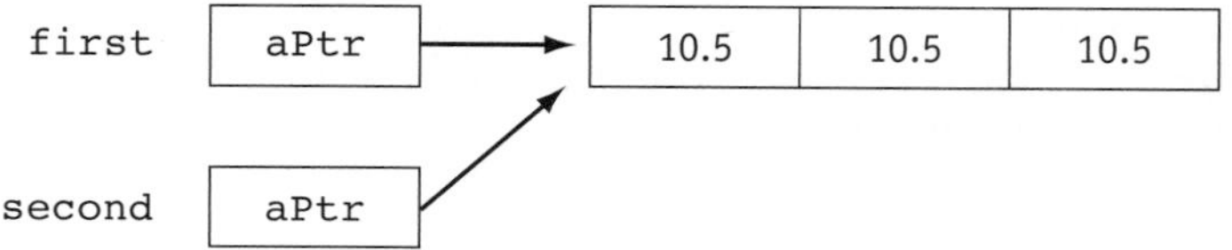

The fact that the two pointers point to the same memory location will also cause problems when the destructors for the two objects try to deallocate the same memory (that is why the destructor code in the above class is commented out). In general, classes with pointer members will not behave correctly under the default copy constructor provided by the compiler. They must be provided with a copy constructor written by the programmer.

Programmer-Defined Copy Constructors

A programmer can define a copy constructor for a class. A programmer-defined copy constructor must have a single parameter that is a reference to the *same* class. Thus in the case of the previous example, the prototype for the copy constructor would be

```
NumberArray::NumberArray(NumberArray &obj)
```

This copy constructor avoids the problems of the default copy constructor by allocating separate memory for the pointer of the new object before doing the copy:

```
NumberArray::NumberArray(NumberArray &obj)
{
   arraySize = obj.arraySize;
   aPtr = new double[arraySize];
   for(int index = 0; index < arraySize; index++)
      aPtr[index] = obj.aPtr[index];
}
```

Program 11-8 demonstrates the use of the `NumberArray` class modified to have a copy constructor. The class declaration is in the `NumberArray2.h` file, with the implementations of its member functions being given in `NumberArray2.cpp`.

Program 11-8

Contents of `NumberArray2.h`

```
#include <iostream>
using namespace std;

class NumberArray
{
private:
  double *aPtr;
  int arraySize;
public:
  NumberArray(NumberArray &);
  NumberArray(int size, double value);
```

(program continues)

Program 11-8 *(continued)*

```
  ~NumberArray() { if (arraySize > 0) delete [] aPtr; }
  void print() const;
  void setValue(double value);
};
```

Contents of `NumberArray2.cpp`

```
#include <iostream>
#include "NumberArray2.h"
using namespace std;

//*****************************************
//Copy constructor allocates a new        *
//array and copies into it the entries    *
//of the array in the other object.       *
//*****************************************
NumberArray::NumberArray(NumberArray &obj)
{
   arraySize = obj.arraySize;
   aPtr = new double[arraySize];
   for(int index = 0; index < arraySize; index++)
     aPtr[index] = obj.aPtr[index];
}

//*********************************************
//Constructor allocates an array of the       *
//given size and sets all its entries to the  *
//given value.                                *
//*********************************************
NumberArray::NumberArray(int size, double value)
{
   arraySize = size;
   aPtr = new double[arraySize];
   setValue(value);
}

//******************************************************
//Sets all the entries of the array to the same value. *
//******************************************************
void NumberArray::setValue(double value)
{
   for(int index = 0; index < arraySize; index++)
      aPtr[index] = value;
}

//**************************************
//Prints all the entries of the array. *
//**************************************
void NumberArray::print() const
{
   for(int index = 0; index < arraySize; index++)
   cout << aPtr[index] << "  ";
}
```

(program continues)

Program 11-8 *(continued)*

Contents of `Pr11-8.cpp`

```
// This program demonstrates the use of copy constructors.
#include <iostream>
#include <iomanip>
#include "NumberArray2.h"

using namespace std;

int main()
{
   NumberArray first(3, 10.5);

   //Make second a copy of first object
   NumberArray second = first;

   // Display the values of the two objects
   cout << setprecision(2) << fixed << showpoint;
   cout << "Value stored in first object is ";
   first.print();
   cout << "\nValue stored in second object is ";
   second.print();
   cout <<  "\nOnly the value in second object will "
        <<  "be changed.\n";

   //Now change value stored in second object
   second.setValue(20.5);

   // Display the values stored in the two objects
   cout << "Value stored in first object is ";
   first.print();
   cout << endl << "Value stored in second object is ";
   second.print();
   return 0;
}
```

Program Output

```
Value stored in first object is 10.50  10.50  10.50
Value stored in second object is 10.50  10.50  10.50
Only the value in second object will be changed.
Value stored in first object is 10.50  10.50  10.50
Value stored in second object is 20.50  20.50  20.50
```

NOTE: A copy constructor must have a single parameter that is a reference to the same class. Forgetting the `&` that identifies reference parameters will result in compiler errors.

The copy constructor is also automatically called by the compiler to create a copy of an object whenever an object is being passed by *value* in a function call. It is for this reason that the parameter to the copy constructor must be passed by reference; if it was passed by value when the constructor was called, then the constructor would immediately have to be called again to create the copy to be passed by value, leading to an endless chain of calls to the constructor.

The copy constructor is also called to create a copy of an object to be returned from a function.

Using `const` Parameters

Because copy constructors are required to use reference parameters, they have access to their argument's data. Since the purpose of a copy constructor is to make a copy of the argument, there is no reason the constructor should modify the argument's data. With this in mind, it's a good idea to make a copy constructor's parameter constant by specifying the `const` key word in the parameter list. Here is an example:

```
NumberArray::NumberArray(const NumberArray &obj)
{
   arraySize = obj.arraySize;
   aPtr = new double[arraySize];
   for(int index = 0; index < arraySize; index++)
      aPtr[index] = obj.aPtr[index];
}
```

Invocation of Copy Constructors

Copy constructors are automatically called by the system whenever an object is being created by initializing it with another object of the same class. For example, the copy constructor for the `Rectangle` class is called for each of the following initialization statements:

```
Rectangle box(5, 10);
Rectangle b = box;     // Initialization statement
Rectangle b1(box);     // Initialization statement
```

Copy constructors are also automatically called when a function call receives a value parameter of the class type. For example, for a function of the form

```
void fun(Rectangle rect)
{
}
```

a call such as

```
fun(box);
```

will cause the `Rectangle` copy constructor to be called. Finally, copy constructors are automatically called whenever a function returns an object of the class by value. Thus, in the function

```
Rectangle makeRectangle()
{
    Rectangle rect(12, 3);
    return rect;

}
```

the copy constructor will be called when the return statement is executed. This is because the return statement must create a nonlocal copy of the object that will be available to the caller after the function is done executing. To summarize, a class copy constructor is called when

- A variable is being initialized from an object of the same class
- A function is called with a value parameter of the class
- A function is returning a value that is an object of the class

NOTE: Copy constructors are not called when a parameter of the class is passed by reference or through a pointer, nor are they called when a function returns a reference or pointer to an object of the class.

Checkpoint

11.8 Briefly describe what is meant by memberwise assignment.

11.9 Describe two scenarios in which memberwise assignment occurs.

11.10 Describe a situation in which memberwise assignment should not be used.

11.11 When is a copy constructor called?

11.12 How does the compiler know that a member function is a copy constructor?

11.13 What action is performed by a class's default copy constructor?

11.6 Operator Overloading

CONCEPT: C++ allows you to redefine how standard operators work when used with class objects.

Overloading the = Operator

VideoNote
Operator Overloading

As we have seen, copy constructors are designed to solve problems that arise when an object containing a pointer is initialized with the data of another object of the same class using memberwise assignment. Similar problems arise in object assignment. For example, with the `NumberArray` class of the previous section, we may have a program that has defined two objects of that class:

```
NumberArray first(3, 10.5);
NumberArray second(5, 20.5);
```

Now, because C++ allows the assignment operator to be used with class objects, we may execute the statement

```
first = second;
```

if we want to set the first object to exactly the same value as the second. At this point, C++ will once again perform a memberwise copy from the second to the first object, leaving pointers in both objects pointing to the same memory.

Because the default object assignment encounters the same problem as the default copy constructor, we might think that a programmer-defined copy constructor can be used to solve the problem caused by the default assignment, but this is not so. Copy constructors only come into play when an object is being *initialized* at creation time. In particular, copy constructors are not called in an *assignment*. To see the difference between initialization and assignment, suppose that the object `first` has already been created. Then the statement

```
NumberArray second = first;     // copy constructor called
```

which creates `second` and initializes it with the value of `first`, is an *initialization* and causes the copy constructor to be called to perform the initialization. However, the statement

```
second = first;                 // copy constructor not called
```

which assumes that both objects have previously been created, is an *assignment*, and therefore no constructor is invoked.

To address the problems that result from memberwise assignment of objects, we need to modify the behavior of the assignment operator so that it does something other than memberwise assignment when it is applied to objects of classes that have pointer members. In effect we are supplying a different version of the assignment operator to be used for objects of that class. In so doing, we say that we are *overloading* the assignment operator.

One way to overload the assignment operator for a given class is to define an *operator function* called `operator=` as a member function of the class. To do this for the `NumberArray` class, we would write the class declaration as follows:

```
class NumberArray
{
private:
   double *aPtr;
   int arraySize;
public:
   void operator=(const NumberArray &right); // Overloaded operator
   NumberArray(const NumberArray &);
   NumberArray(int size, double value);
   ~NumberArray() { if (arraySize > 0) delete [ ] aPtr; }
   void print() const;
   void setValue(double value);
};
```

Let's take a look at the function header, or prototype, before we look at how the operator function itself is implemented. We break the header down into its main parts, as shown in Figure 11-4.

Figure 11-4

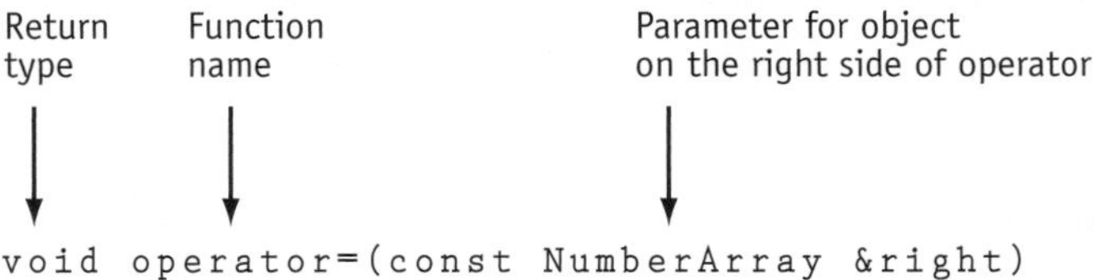

The name of the function is `operator=`. Since the operator function is an instance member of a class, it can only be called through an object of the class. The object of the class through which it is called is considered the left operand of the assignment operator, while the parameter passed to the function is considered the right operand of the assignment operator. To illustrate, let us suppose that two objects, `left` and `right`, have been defined in a program:

```
NumberArray left(3,10.5);
NumberArray right(5, 20.5);
```

To assign the value of `right` to `left`, we call the member function `operator=` through the `left` object, and pass it the `right` object as parameter:

```
left.operator=(right);
```

While you can call operator functions this way, the compiler will also let you use the more conventional notation

```
left = right;
```

NOTE: Parameters to operator functions do not have to be passed by reference, nor do they have to be declared `const`. In this example we have used a reference parameter for efficiency reasons: Reference parameters avoid the overhead of copying the object being passed as parameter. The `const` is used to protect the parameter from change.

Let us now consider the implementation of the above operator function. The function starts out by deleting memory allocated to pointers in the object being assigned to, then makes a copy of the other object in pretty much the same way as the copy constructor for the class. Here is the code for the function (we have used the name `right` for the object that is the right parameter of the assignment, but any other name could have been used).

```
void NumberArray::operator=(const NumberArray &right)
{
   if (arraySize > 0) delete [] aPtr;
   arraySize = right.arraySize;
   aPtr = new double[arraySize];
   for (int index = 0; index < arraySize; index++)
      aPtr[index] = right.aPtr[index];
}
```

In general, the assignment operator should be overloaded whenever a nondefault copy constructor is used. In particular, classes allocating dynamic memory to a pointer member in any constructor should define both a copy constructor and an overloaded assignment operator. In addition, they should also provide a destructor to deallocate the storage allocated in the constructor.

The class `NumberArray`, with modifications to include both a copy constructor and an overloaded assignment operator, is demonstrated in Program 11-9.

Program 11-9

Contents of `overload.h`

```
#include <iostream>
using namespace std;

class NumberArray
{
private:
```

(program continues)

Program 11-9 *(continued)*

```
  double *aPtr;
  int arraySize;
public:
  // Overloaded operator function
  void operator=(const NumberArray &right);

  // Constructors and other member functions
  NumberArray(const NumberArray &);
  NumberArray(int size, double value);
  ~NumberArray() { if (arraySize > 0) delete [ ] aPtr; }
  void print() const;
  void setValue(double value);
};
```

Contents of `overload.cpp`

```
#include <iostream>
#include "overload.h"
using namespace std;

//*****************************************************
//The overloaded operator function for assignment.   *
//*****************************************************
void NumberArray::operator=(const NumberArray &right)
{
   if (arraySize > 0) delete [] aPtr;
   arraySize = right.arraySize;
   aPtr = new double[arraySize];
   for (int index = 0; index < arraySize; index++)
    aPtr[index] = right.aPtr[index];
}

//********************************************
//Copy constructor.                          *
//********************************************
NumberArray::NumberArray(const NumberArray &obj)
{
   arraySize = obj.arraySize;
   aPtr = new double[arraySize];
   for(int index = 0; index < arraySize; index++)
     aPtr[index] = obj.aPtr[index];
}

//********************************************
//Constructor.                               *
//********************************************
NumberArray::NumberArray(int size1, double value)
{
   arraySize = size1;
   aPtr = new double[arraySize];
   setValue(value);
}

```

(program continues)

Program 11-9 *(continued)*

```
//*************************************************
//Sets the value stored in all entries of the array. *
//*************************************************
void NumberArray::setValue(double value)
{
   for(int index = 0; index < arraySize; index++)
      aPtr[index] = value;
}

//*************************************
//Print out all entries in the array.   *
//*************************************
void NumberArray::print() const
{
   for(int index = 0; index < arraySize; index++)
     cout << aPtr[index] << "  ";
}
```

Contents of `Pr11-9.cpp`

```
// This program demonstrates overloading of
// the assignment operator.
#include <iostream>
#include <iomanip>
#include "overload.h"
using namespace std;

int main()
{
   NumberArray first(3, 10.5);
   NumberArray second(5, 20.5);

   // Display the values of the two objects
   cout << setprecision(2) << fixed << showpoint;
   cout << "First object's data is ";
   first.print();
   cout << endl << "Second object's data is ";
   second.print();

   // Call the overloaded operator
   cout << "\nNow we will assign the second object "
        << "to the first." << endl;
   first = second;

   // Display the new values of the two objects
   cout << "First object's data is ";
   first.print();
   cout << endl << "The second object's data is ";
   second.print();

   return 0;
}
```

(program continues)

Program 11-9 *(continued)*

Program Output
```
First object's data is 10.50  10.50  10.50
Second object's data is 20.50  20.50  20.50  20.50  20.50
Now we will assign the second object to the first.
First object's data is 20.50  20.50  20.50  20.50  20.50
The second object's data is 20.50  20.50  20.50  20.50  20.50
```

The = Operator's Return Value

There is only one problem with the overloaded = operator shown in Program 11-8: It has a `void` return type. C++'s built-in assignment operator allows multiple assignment statements such as

```
a = b = c;
```

Multiple assignment statements work because the built-in assignment operator is implemented so that it returns the value of its left operand *after* the assignment has been performed. Thus in this statement, the expression `b = c` causes `c` to be assigned to `b` and then returns the value of `b`. The return value is then stored in `a`.

To make an overloaded assignment operator behave similarly, we must redefine the operator function so that it also returns the value of its left operand after the assignment has been performed. In particular, we need to declare the operator function to have a return type of the same type as the class. This is shown in our final modification of the `NumberArray` class:

```
class NumberArray
{
private:
   double *aPtr;
   int arraySize;
public:
   NumberArray operator=(const NumberArray &right);
   NumberArray(const NumberArray &);
   NumberArray(int size, double value);
   ~NumberArray() { if (arraySize > 0) delete [] aPtr; }
   void print() const;
   void setValue(double value);
};
```

The only modification we need to make to the assignment operator function is to add a statement at the very end returning the value of its left operand. Since the assignment is equivalent to the statement

```
left.operator=(right);
```

returning the value of the left operand is accomplished by the operator function returning the value of the object through which it is called. Recall that C++ makes available to each call of a non-static member function, the address of the object through which the call is being made, and that the address of that object is accessed through the pointer `this`. The value of the object itself can be obtained and returned by dereferencing the `this` pointer:

```
return *this;
```

The code for the modified assignment operator function is

```
NumberArray NumberArray::operator=(const NumberArray &right)
{
   if (arraySize > 0)  delete [] aPtr;
   arraySize = right.arraySize;
   aPtr = new double[arraySize];
   for (int index = 0; index < arraySize; index++)
      aPtr[index] = right.aPtr[index];
   return *this;
}
```

Overloading Other Operators

C++ allows the programmer to overload other operators besides assignment. There are many times when it is natural to overload some of C++'s built-in operators to make them work with classes that the programmer has defined. For example, assume that a class named `Date` exists, and that objects of the `Date` class hold the day, month, and year in member variables. Suppose the `Date` class has a member function named `add`. The `add` member function adds a number of days to the date and adjusts the member variables if the date goes to another month or year. For example, the following statement adds five days to the date stored in the `today` object:

```
today.add(5);
```

Although it might be obvious that the statement is adding five days to the date stored in `today`, the use of an operator might be more intuitive. For example, look at the following statement:

```
today += 5;
```

This statement uses the standard += operator to add 5 to `today`. This behavior does not happen automatically, however. The += operator must be overloaded for this action to occur. In this section, you will learn to overload many of C++'s operators to perform specialized operations on class objects.

NOTE: You have already experienced the behavior of an overloaded operator. The / operator performs two types of division: floating-point and integer. If one of operator's operands is a floating-point type, the result will be a floating-point value. If both of the / operator's operands are integers, however, a different behavior occurs: the result is an integer, and the fractional part is thrown away.

Some General Issues of Operator Overloading

Now that you have had an introduction to operator overloading, let's look at some of the general issues involved in this programming technique.

First, you can change an operator's entire meaning, if that's what you wish to do. There is nothing to prevent you from changing the = symbol from an assignment operator to a "display" operator. For instance, the following class does just that:

```
class Weird
{
private:
   int value;
```

```
public:
   Weird(int v)
      {value = v; }
   void operator=(const Weird &right)
      { cout << right.value << endl; }
};
```

Although the `operator=` function overloads the assignment operator, the function doesn't perform an assignment. All the overloaded operator does is display the contents of `right.value`. Consider the following program segment:

```
Weird a(5), b(10);
a = b;
```

Although the statement `a = b` looks like an assignment statement, it actually causes the contents of `b`'s `value` member to be displayed on the screen:

```
10
```

Another operator overloading issue is that you cannot change the number of operands taken by an operator. The = symbol must always be a binary operator. Likewise, ++ and -- must always be unary operators.

The last issue is that although you may overload most of the C++ operators, you cannot overload all of them. Table 11-1 shows all of the C++ operators that may be overloaded.

NOTE: Some of the operators in Table 11-1 are beyond the scope of this book and are not covered.

Table 11-1 Operators That Can Be Overloaded

+	-	*	/	%	^	&	|	~	!	=	<
>	+=	-=	*=	/=	%=	^=	&=	|=	<<	>>	>>=
<<=	==	!=	<=	>=	&&	||	++	--	->*	,	->
[]	()	new	delete								

The only operators that cannot be overloaded are

```
?:    .    .*    ::    sizeof
```

Approaches to Operator Overloading

There are two approaches you can take to overload an operator:

1. *Make the overloaded operator a member function of the class.* This allows the operator function access to private members of the class. It also allows the function to use the implicit `this` pointer parameter to access the calling object.
2. *Make the overloaded member function a separate, stand-alone function.* When overloaded in this manner, the operator function must be declared a friend of the class to have access to the private members of the class.

Some operators, such as the stream input and output operators >> and <<, must be overloaded as stand-alone functions. Other operators may be overloaded either as member functions or stand-alone functions. Consider a class

```
class Length
{
private:
    int len_inches;
public:
    Length(int feet, int inches)
    {
        setLength(feet, inches);
    }
    Length(int inches) { len_inches = inches; }
    int getFeet() const { return len_inches / 12; }
    int getInches() const { return len_inches % 12; }
    void setLength(int feet, int inches)
    {
        len_inches = 12 *feet + inches;
    }

};
```

designed to represent length measurements. The class internally represents the length of an item in inches, but allows its clients to specify measurements in feet and inches via a `setLength()` function. The class also provides member functions `getFeet()` and `getInches()` to allow the feet and inch components of a measurement to be separately retrieved.

Overloading the Arithmetic and Relational Operators

Clients of the class must be able to add and subtract measurements. In addition, they should be able to compare two measurements to see if they are equal, or if one of them is less or greater than the other. We will provide all these capabilities by overloading the operators +, -, <, and == as stand-alone functions. We start by adding the following declarations to the `Length` class:

```
friend Length operator+(Length a, Length b);
friend Length operator-(Length a, Length b);
friend bool operator<(Length a, Length b);
friend bool operator==(Length a, Length b);
```

To see how we arrive at these declarations, consider the *addition* and *less-than* operators. Addition needs to take two `Length` objects `a` and `b` as parameters and produce a third `Length` object that is the sum of `a` and `b`. Similarly, the less-than operator needs to take two `Length` objects as parameters and return a Boolean value.

To see how to write the code that implements these functions, consider again the addition operator. Given two input parameters `a` and `b`, it needs to return a `Length` object whose `len_inches` member is the sum of the `len_inches` members of `a` and `b`. This can be done by writing

```
Length operator+(Length a, Length b)
{
    Length result(a.len_inches + b.len_inches);
    return result;
}
```

or more succinctly:

```
Length operator+(Length a, Length b)
{
    return Length(a.len_inches + b.len_inches);
}
```

We can reason in a similar manner to work out the definitions of the operator functions -, <, and ==. Here is a complete program showing the class and its overloaded operators and illustrating their use.

Contents of `Length.h`

```
#ifndef _LENGTH_H
#define _LENGTH_H
#include <iostream>
using namespace std;

class Length
{
private:
    int len_inches;
public:
    Length(int feet, int inches)
    {
        setLength(feet, inches);
    }
    Length(int inches){ len_inches = inches; }
    int getFeet() const { return len_inches / 12; }
    int getInches() const { return len_inches % 12; }
    void setLength(int feet, int inches)
    {
        len_inches = 12 *feet + inches;
    }
    friend Length operator+(Length a, Length b);
    friend Length operator-(Length a, Length b);
    friend bool operator< (Length a, Length b);
    friend bool operator== (Length a, Length b);
};
#endif
```

Contents of `Length.cpp`

```
#include "Length.h"

//*************************************
// Overloaded operator +              *
//*************************************
Length operator+(Length a, Length b)
{
    return Length(a.len_inches + b.len_inches);
}

//*************************************
// Overloaded  operator -             *
//*************************************
Length operator-(Length a, Length b)
{
```

```
    return Length(a.len_inches - b.len_inches);
}

//**********************************
// Overloaded operator ==          *
//**********************************
bool operator==(Length a, Length b)
{
    return a.len_inches == b.len_inches;
}

//**********************************
// Overloaded operator <           *
//**********************************
bool operator<(Length a, Length b)
{
    return a.len_inches < b.len_inches;
}
```

Program 11-10

```
// This program demonstrates the Length class's overloaded
// +, -, ==, and < operators.
#include <iostream>
#include "Length.h"
using namespace std;

int main()
{
    Length first(0), second(0), third(0);
    int f, i;
    cout << "Enter a distance in feet and inches: ";
    cin  >> f >> i;
    first.setLength(f, i);
    cout << "Enter another distance in feet and inches: ";
    cin  >> f >> i;
    second.setLength(f, i);

    // Test the + and - operators
    third = first + second;
    cout << "first + second = ";
    cout << third.getFeet() << " feet, ";
    cout << third.getInches() << " inches.\n";
    third = first - second;
    cout << "first - second = ";
    cout << third.getFeet() << " feet, ";
    cout << third.getInches() << " inches.\n";

    // Test the relational operators
    cout << "first == second = ";
    if (first == second) cout << "true"; else cout << "false";
    cout << "\n";
```

(program continues)

Program 11-10 *(continued)*

```
    cout << "first < second = ";
    if (first < second) cout << "true"; else cout << "false";
    cout << "\n";

    return 0;
}
```

Program Output with Example Input Shown in Bold

```
Enter a distance in feet and inches: 6 5[Enter]
Enter another distance in feet and inches: 3 10[Enter]
first + second = 10 feet, 3 inches.
first - second = 2 feet, 7 inches.
first == second = false
first < second = false
```

Choosing Between Stand-Alone and Member-Function Operators

Given the stand-alone overloads we have written, the code

```
Length a(4, 2), b(1, 8), c(0);
c = a + b;
```

is interpreted by the compiler as being

```
Length a(4, 2), b(1, 8), c(0);
c = operator+(a, b);
```

The compiler allows the programmer to use the friendly infix notation. Internally, however, it sees the operator as just an ordinary function whose name is `operator+`. This has an implication that is not immediately obvious. The statement

```
c = 2 + a;
```

is equivalent to

```
c = operator+(2, b);
```

Both of these statements compile and execute correctly because the *convert constructor* of the `Length` class is able to create a `Length` object out of the integer parameter 2. You will learn about convert constructors in Section 11.8.

We could just as easily have overloaded the arithmetic and relational operators as member functions. Here is how to do so for the addition operator. First, modify the in-class declaration to make the operator a member function:

```
class Length
{
private:
    int len_inches;
public:
    // Modified declaration of operator+
    Length operator+(Length b);
    // Rest of class not shown
};
```

Notice that the operator is now declared as taking a single operator of type `Length`. This is because as a member function, the operator is automatically passed a `Length` object through the implicit parameter `this`. When we write

```
Length a(4, 2), b(1, 8), c(0);
c = a + b;
```

The compiler sees this as

```
Length a(4, 2), b(1, 8), c(0);
c = a.operator+(b);
```

When you write `a + b`, the left operand of the overloaded + operator becomes the object through which the member function is called, and the right operand becomes the explicit parameter. With these changes, the body of the operator is written as follows:

```
Length Length::operator+(Length b)
{
    return Length(this->len_inches + b.len_inches);
}
```

To sum up, the addition operator (as well as other arithmetic and relational operators) can be overloaded equally well as member functions or as stand-alone functions. It is generally better to overload binary operators that take parameters of the same type as stand-alone functions. This is because, unlike stand-alone operator overloading, member-function overloading introduces an artificial distinction between the two parameters by making the left parameter implicit. This allows convert constructors to apply to the right parameter but not to the left, creating situations where changing the order of parameters causes a compiler error in an otherwise correct program:

```
Length a(4, 2), c(0);
c = a + 2;  // Compiles, equivalent to c = a.operator+(2)
c = 2 + a;  // Does not compile: equivalent to c = 2.operator+(a);
```

Overloading the Prefix ++ Operator

We want to overload the prefix operator for the `Length` class so that the expression `++b` increments the object `b` by adding 1 inch to its length and returns the resulting object. We overload this operator as a member function. This makes its single parameter implicit, so the overloaded operator needs no parameters. Here is the portion of the `Length` class that shows the operator declaration:

```
class Length
{
private:
    int len_inches;
public:
    // Declaration of prefix ++
    Length operator++();
    // Rest of class not shown
};
```

Here is the implementation of the operator—it increases the number of inches by 1 and returns the modified object:

```
Length Length::operator++()
{
   len_inches ++;
   return *this;
}
```

Given this overload, the user-friendly notation `++b` is equivalent to the call `b.operator++()`. Either notation may be used in your program.

Overloading the Postfix ++ Operator

The postfix increment operator `b++` also increments the length of `b`, but differs from the prefix version in that it returns the value that the object had *prior* to being incremented. Overloading the postfix operator is only slightly different from overloading the prefix version. Here is the function that overloads the postfix operator for the `Length` class:

```
Length Length::operator++(int)
{
    Length temp = *this;
    len_inches ++;
    return temp;
}
```

The first difference you will notice is that the function has a *dummy parameter* of type `int` that is never used in the body of the function. This is a convention that tells the compiler that the increment operator is being overloaded in postfix mode. The second difference is the use of a temporary local variable `temp` to capture the value of the object before it is incremented. This value is saved and is later returned by the function.

Overloading the Stream Insertion and Extraction Operators

Overloading the stream insertion operator << is convenient because it allows values of objects to be converted into text and output to `cout`, to a file object, or to any object of a class that derives from `ostream`. In the presence of appropriate overloads, the statements

```
Length b(4, 8), c(2, 5);
cout << b;
cout << b + c;
```

appear to the compiler as

```
Length b(4, 8), c(2, 5);
operator<<(cout, b);
operator(cout, b + c);
```

This equivalence has the following implications:

1. The overloaded operator << takes two parameters, the first of which is an `ostream` object and the second of which is an object of the class for which the operator is being overloaded. For the `Length` class, the prototype would be `operator<<(ostream &strm, Length a)`.

2. To allow expressions (such as `b + c`) in the second parameter, the second parameter should be passed by value. The first parameter should be passed by reference because `ostream` parameters should never be passed by value.

In addition, the stream insertion operator should return its stream parameter so that several output expressions can be chained together, as in

```
Length b(4, 8), c(2, 5);
cout << b << "   " << b + c;
```

Putting all of this together, we see that the stream insertion operator should be written as

```
ostream &operator<<(ostream& out, Length a)
{
    out << a.getFeet() << " feet, " << a.getInches() << " inches";
    return out;
}
```

Overloading the stream output operator is useful because it allows for the various fields of a complex class to be labeled during output.

Overloading the stream input operator is similar, except that the class parameter signifying the object to be read into must be passed by reference. Thus the header for the stream input operator looks like this:

```
istream &operator>>(istream &in, Length &a);
```

The full implementation of this function can be found in lines 3–18 of the following listing of `Length1.cpp`. At first glance, the function appears to be useful in that it relieves the programmer of the necessity of issuing prompts for the different parts of the object when the user is entering data at the screen and keyboard. Notice, however, that the prompts become an irritating distraction if the operator is being used to read `Length` objects from a non-keyboard source such as a file or network connection.

Contents of `Length1.h`

```
#ifndef _LENGTH1_H
#define _LENGTH1_H
#include <iostream>
using namespace std;

class Length
{
private:
    int len_inches;
public:
    Length(int feet, int inches)
    {
        setLength(feet, inches);
    }
    Length(int inches){ len_inches = inches; }
    int getFeet() const { return len_inches / 12; }
    int getInches() const { return len_inches % 12; }
    void setLength(int feet, int inches)
```

```
    {
        len_inches = 12 *feet + inches;
    }
    // Overloaded arithmetic and relational operators
    friend Length operator+(Length a, Length b);
    friend Length operator-(Length a, Length b);
    friend bool operator<(Length a, Length b);
    friend bool operator==(Length a, Length b);
    Length operator++();
    Length operator++(int);

    // Overloaded stream input and output operators
    friend ostream &operator<<(ostream &out, Length a);
    friend istream &operator>>(istream &in, Length &a);
};
#endif
```

Contents of `Length1.cpp`

```
#include "Length1.h"

//*********************************************
// Overloaded stream extraction operator >>    *
//*********************************************
istream &operator>>(istream &in, Length &a)
{
    // Prompt for and read the object data
    int feet, inches;
    cout << "Enter feet: ";
    in >> feet;
    cout << "Enter inches: ";
    in >> inches;

    // Modify the object a with the data and return
    a.setLength(feet, inches);
    return in;
}

//*********************************************
// Overloaded stream insertion operator <<    *
//*********************************************
ostream &operator<<(ostream& out, Length a)
{
    out << a.getFeet() << " feet, " << a.getInches() << " inches";
    return out;
}

//***********************************
// Overloaded prefix ++ operator    *
//***********************************
Length Length::operator++()
{
    len_inches ++;
    return *this;
}
```

```

//***********************************
// Overloaded postfix ++ operator   *
//***********************************
Length Length::operator++(int)
{
    Length temp = *this;
    len_inches ++;
    return temp;
}

//*************************************
// Overloaded operator -              *
//*************************************
Length operator+(Length a, Length b)
{
    return Length(a.len_inches + b.len_inches);
}

//*************************************
// Overloaded  operator -             *
//*************************************
Length operator-(Length a, Length b)
{
    return Length(a.len_inches - b.len_inches);
}

//************************************
// Overloaded operator ==            *
//************************************
bool operator==(Length a, Length b)
{
    return a.len_inches == b.len_inches;
}

//************************************
// Overloaded operator <             *
//************************************
bool operator<(Length a, Length b)
{
    return a.len_inches < b.len_inches;
}
```

Program 11-11

```
// This program demonstrates the Length class's overloaded
// prefix ++, postfix ++, and stream operators.
#include <iostream>
#include "Length1.h"
using namespace std;

int main()
```

(program continues)

Program 11-11 *(continued)*

```
{
    Length first(0), second(1, 9), c(0);

    cout << "Demonstrating prefix ++ operator and output operator.\n";
    for (int count = 0; count < 4; count++)
    {
        first = ++second;
        cout << "First: " << first <<  ". Second: " << second << ".\n";
    }
    cout << "\nDemonstrating postfix ++ operator and output operator.\n";
    for (int count = 0; count < 4; count++)
    {
        first = second++;
        cout << "First: " << first <<  ". Second: " << second << ".\n";
    }

    cout << "\nDemonstrating input and output operators.\n";
    cin >> c;
    cout << "You entered " << c << "." << endl;
    return 0;
}
```

Program Output with Example Input Shown in Bold

```
Demonstrating prefix ++ operator and output operator.
First: 1 feet, 10 inches. Second: 1 feet, 10 inches.
First: 1 feet, 11 inches. Second: 1 feet, 11 inches.
First: 2 feet, 0 inches. Second: 2 feet, 0 inches.
First: 2 feet, 1 inches. Second: 2 feet, 1 inches.

Demonstrating postfix ++ operator and output operator.
First: 2 feet, 1 inches. Second: 2 feet, 2 inches.
First: 2 feet, 2 inches. Second: 2 feet, 3 inches.
First: 2 feet, 3 inches. Second: 2 feet, 4 inches.
First: 2 feet, 4 inches. Second: 2 feet, 5 inches.

Demonstrating input and output operators.
Enter feet: 3[Enter]
Enter inches: 4[Enter]
You entered 3 feet, 4 inches.
```

Overloading the `[]` Operator

In addition to the traditional operators, C++ allows you to change the way the `[]` symbols work. This gives you the ability to write classes that have array-like behaviors. For example, the `string` class overloads the `[]` operator so you can access the individual characters stored in `string` class objects. Assume the following definition exists in a program:

```
string name = "William";
```

The first character in the string, `W`, is stored at `name[0]`, so the following statement will display `W` on the screen.

```
cout << name[0];
```

Program 11-12 further demonstrates the `string` class's overloaded `[]` operator.

Program 11-12

```
// This program demonstrates the string class's
// overloaded [] operator.
#include <iostream>
#include <string>
using namespace std;

int main()
{
   string name = "William";

   cout << "Here are the letters in your name: \n";
   for (int x=0; x < name.length(); x++)
     cout << name[x] << ' ';
   cout << "\nEnter a character and press Enter: ";
   cin >> name[2];
   cout << "Now, here are the letters in your name:\n";
   for (int x=0; x < name.length(); x++)
     cout << name[x] << ' ';

   return 0;
}
```

Program Output with Output Shown in Bold

```
Here are the letters in your name:
W i l l i a m
Enter a character and press Enter: x[Enter]
Now, here are the letters in your name:
W i x l i a m
```

You can use the `overloaded[]`operator to create an array class, like the following one. The class behaves like a regular array but performs the bounds checking that C++ lacks. It also has several other enhancements over regular integer arrays.

```
class IntArray
{
   private:
      int *aptr;
      int arraySize;
      void subError();              // Handles subscripts out of range
   public:
      IntArray(int);                // Constructor
      IntArray(const intArray &); // Copy constructor
      ~IntArray();                  // Destructor
      int size() const
          { return arraySize; }
      int &operator[](int) const; // Overloaded [] operator
};
```

Before focusing on the overloaded operator, let's look at the constructors and the destructor. The code for the first constructor is

```
IntArray::IntArray(int s)
{
   arraySize = s;
   aptr = new int [s];
   for (int count = 0; count < size; count++)
      *(aptr + count) = 0;
}
```

When an instance of the class is defined, the number of elements the array is to have is passed into the constructor's parameter `s`. This value is copied to the `arraySize` member, then used to dynamically allocate enough memory for the array. The constructor's final step is to store zeros in all of the array's elements:

```
for (int count = 0; count < size; count++)
   *(aptr + count) = 0;
```

The class also has a copy constructor, which is used when a class object is initialized with another object's data:

```
IntArray::IntArray(const IntArray &obj)
{
   arraySize = obj.arraySize;
   aptr = new int [arraySize];
   for(int count = 0; count < arraySize; count++)
      *(aptr + count) = *(obj.aptr + count);
}
```

A reference to the initializing object is passed into the parameter `obj`. Once the memory is successfully allocated for the array, the constructor copies all the values in `obj`'s array into the calling object's array.

The destructor simply frees the memory allocated by the class's constructors. First, however, it checks the value in `arraySize` to be sure the array has at least one element:

```
IntArray::~IntArray()
{
   if (arraySize > 0)
      delete [] aptr;
}
```

The `[]` operator is overloaded similarly to other operators. Here is the definition of the `operator[]` function for the `IntArray` class:

```
int &IntArray::operator[](int sub) const
{
   if (sub < 0 || sub >= arraySize)
      subError();
   return aptr[sub];
}
```

The `operator[]` function can only have a single parameter. The one shown here uses an integer parameter. This parameter holds the value placed inside the brackets in an expression. For example, if `table` is an `IntArray` object, the number 12 will be passed into the `sub` parameter in the following statement:

```
cout << table[12];
```

Inside the function, the value in the `sub` parameter is tested by the following `if` statement:

```
if (sub < 0 || sub >= arraySize)
   subError();
```

This statement determines whether `sub` is within the range of the array's subscripts. If `sub` is less than zero or greater than or equal to `arraySize`, it's not a valid subscript, so the `subError` function is called. If `sub` is within range, the function uses it as an offset into the array and returns a reference to the value stored at that location.

One critically important aspect of the function shown is its return type. It's crucial that the function not simply return an integer, but a *reference* to an integer. The reason for this is that expressions such as the following must be possible:

```
table[5] = 27;
```

Remember, the built-in = operator requires the object on its left to be an lvalue. An lvalue must represent a modifiable memory location, such as a variable. The integer return value of a function is not an lvalue. If the `operator[]` function merely returns an integer, it cannot be used to create expressions placed on the left side of an assignment operator.

A reference to an integer, however, is an lvalue. If the `operator[]` function returns a reference, the statement above causes the `operator[]` function to be called with 5 being passed as its argument. Assuming 5 is within range, the function returns a reference to the integer stored at `(aptr + 5)`. In essence, the statement is equivalent to

```
*(aptr + 5) = 27;
```

Because the `operator[]` function returns actual integers stored in the array, it is not necessary for math or relational operators to be overloaded. Even the stream operators << and >> will work just as they are with the `IntArray` class.

Here is the complete listing of `intarray.h` and `intarray.cpp`:

Contents of `intarray.h`

```
#ifndef INTARRAY_H
#define INTARRAY_H
#include <iostream>
using namespace std;

class IntArray
{
private:
   int *aptr;
   int arraySize;
   void subError() const;   // Handles subscripts out of range
public:
   IntArray(int);                     // Constructor
   IntArray(const IntArray &);        // Copy constructor
   ~IntArray();                       // Destructor
   int size() const { return arraySize; }
   int &operator[](int) const;        // Overloaded [] operator
};
#endif
```

Contents of `intarray.cpp`

```
#include "intarray.h"
#include <cstdlib>
//*************************************************
// Constructor for IntArray class. Sets the size of  *
// the array and allocates memory for it.            *
//*************************************************
IntArray::IntArray(int s)
{
   arraySize = s;
   aptr = new int [s];
   for (int count = 0; count < arraySize; count++)
      *(aptr + count) = 0;
}

//*************************************************
// Copy constructor for IntArray class.              *
//*************************************************
IntArray::IntArray(const IntArray &obj)
{
   arraySize = obj.arraySize;
   aptr = new int [arraySize];
   for(int count = 0; count < arraySize; count++)
      *(aptr + count) = *(obj.aptr + count);
}

 //*************************************************
// Destructor for IntArray class.                    *
//*************************************************
IntArray::~IntArray()
{
   if (arraySize > 0)
      delete [] aptr;
}

//**************************************************
// subError function. Displays an error message and   *
// exits the program when a subscript is out of range.*
//**************************************************
void IntArray::subError() const
{
   cout << "ERROR: Subscript out of range.\n";
   exit(0);
}

//***************************************************
// Overloaded [] operator. The argument is a subscript *
// This function returns a reference to the element    *
// in the array indexed by the subscript.              *
//***************************************************
int &IntArray::operator[](int sub) const
```

```
{
   if (sub < 0 || sub >= arraySize)
      subError();
   return aptr[sub];
}
```

Program 11-13 demonstrates how the class works.

Program 11-13

```
// This program demonstrates a class that behaves
// like an array.
#include <iostream>
#include "intarray.h"
using namespace std;

int main()
{
   IntArray table(10);

   // Store values in the array
   for (int x = 0; x < table.size(); x++)
      table[x] = (x * 2);

   // Display the values in the array
   for (int x = 0; x < table.size(); x++)
      cout << table[x] << " ";
   cout << endl;

   // Use the built-in + operator on array elements
   for (int x = 0; x < table.size(); x++)
      table[x] = table[x] + 5;

   // Display the values in the array
   for (int x = 0; x < table.size(); x++)
      cout << table[x] << " ";
   cout << endl;

   // Use the built-in ++ operator on array elements
   for (int x = 0; x < table.size(); x++)
      table[x]++;

   // Display the values in the array
   for (int x = 0; x < table.size(); x++)
      cout << table[x] << " ";

   cout << endl;
   return 0;
}
```

Program Output

```
0 2 4 6 8 10 12 14 16 18
5 7 9 11 13 15 17 19 21 23
6 8 10 12 14 16 18 20 22 24
```

Program 11-14 demonstrates the `IntArray` class's bounds-checking capability.

Program 11-14

```
// This program demonstrates the bounds-checking
// capabilities of the IntArray class.
#include <iostream>
#include "intarray.h"
using namespace std;

int main()
{
   IntArray table(10);

   // Store values in the array
   for (int x = 0; x < table.size(); x++)
      table[x] = x;

   // Display the values in the array
   for (int x = 0; x < table.size(); x++)
      cout << table[x] << " ";
   cout << endl;

   cout << "Attempting to store outside the array bounds:\n";
   table[table.size()] = 0;

   return 0;
}
```

Program Output

```
0 1 2 3 4 5 6 7 8 9
Attempting to store outside the array bounds:
ERROR: Subscript out of range.
```

Checkpoint

11.14 Assume there is a class named `Pet`. Write the prototype for a member function of `Pet` that overloads the = operator.

11.15 Assume that `dog` and `cat` are instances of the `Pet` class, which has overloaded the = operator. Rewrite the following statement so it appears in function call notation instead of operator notation:

```
dog = cat;
```

11.16 What is the disadvantage of an overloaded = operator returning `void`?

11.17 Describe the purpose of the `this` pointer.

11.18 The `this` pointer is automatically passed to what type of functions?

11.19 Assume there is a class named `Animal`, which overloads the = and + operators. In the following statement, assume `cat`, `tiger`, and `wildcat` are all instances of the `Animal` class:

```
wildcat = cat + tiger;
```

Of the three objects, `wildcat`, `cat`, and `tiger`, which is calling the `operator+` function? Which object is passed as an argument into the function?

11.20 What does the use of a dummy parameter in a unary operator function indicate to the compiler?

11.21 Describe the values that should be returned from functions that overload relational operators.

11.22 What is the advantage of overloading the << and >> operators?

11.23 What type of object should an overloaded << operator function return?

11.24 What type of object should an overloaded >> operator function return?

11.25 If an overloaded << or >> operator accesses a private member of a class, what must be done in that class's declaration?

11.26 Assume the class `NumList` has overloaded the `[]` operator. In the expression below, `list1` is an instance of the `NumList` class:

```
list1[25]
```

Rewrite this expression to explicitly call the function that overloads the [] operator.

11.27 When overloading a binary operator such as + or - as an instance member function of a class, what object is passed into the operator function's parameter?

11.28 Explain why overloaded prefix and postfix ++ and -- operator functions should return a value.

11.29 How does C++ tell the difference between an overloaded prefix and postfix ++ or -- operator function?

11.30 Overload the function call `operator () (int i, int j)` for the `IntArray` class of Program 11-13 to return the sum of all array entries in positions `i` through `j`.

11.7 Type Conversion Operators

CONCEPT: Special operator functions may be written to convert a class object to any other type.

As you've already seen, operator functions allow classes to work more like built-in data types. Another capability that operator functions can give classes is automatic type conversion.

Data type conversion happens "behind the scenes" with the built-in data types. For instance, suppose a program uses the following variables:

```
int i;
double d;
```

The following statement automatically converts the value in `i` to a double and stores it in `d`:

```
d = i;
```

Likewise, the following statement converts the value in `d` to an integer (truncating the fractional part) and stores it in `i`:

```
i = d;
```

The same functionality can also be given to class objects. For example, assuming `distance` is a `Length` object and `d` is a `double`, the following statement would conveniently store distance into a floating-point number stored in `d`, if `Length` is properly written:

```
d = distance;
```

To be able to use a statement such as this, an operator function must be written to perform the conversion. Here is an operator function for converting a `Length` object to a `double`:

```
Length::operator double() const
{
   return len_inches /12 + (len_inches %12) / 12.0;
}
```

This function computes the real decimal equivalent of a length measurement in feet. For example, a measurement of 4 feet 6 inches would be converted to the real number 4.5.

NOTE: No return type is specified in the function header because the return type is inferred from the name of the operator function. Also, because the function is a member function, it operates on the calling object and requires no other parameters.

Program 11-15 demonstrates a modified version of the `Length` class with both a `double` and an `int` conversion operator. The `int` operator simply returns the number of inches of the `Length` object.

Contents of `Length2.h`

```
#ifndef _LENGTH1_H
#define _LENGTH1_H
#include <iostream>
using namespace std;

class Length
{
private:
  int len_inches;
public:
  Length(int feet, int inches)
  {
      setLength(feet, inches);
  }
  Length(int inches){ len_inches = inches; }
  int getFeet() const { return len_inches / 12; }
  int getInches() const { return len_inches % 12; }
  void setLength(int feet, int inches)
  {
      len_inches = 12 *feet + inches;
  }
  // Type conversion operators
  operator double() const;
  operator int() const { return len_inches;  }

  // Overloaded stream output operator
  friend ostream &operator<<(ostream &out, Length a);
};
#endif
```

Contents of `Length2.cpp`

```
#include "Length2.h"

//*********************************************
// Operator double converts Length to a double  *
//*********************************************
Length::operator double() const
{
   return len_inches /12 + (len_inches %12) / 12.0;
}

//*****************************************
// Overloaded stream insertion operator <<  *
//*****************************************
ostream &operator<<(ostream& out, Length a)
{
   out << a.getFeet() << " feet, " << a.getInches() << " inches";
   return out;
}
```

Program 11-15

```
// This program demonstrates the type conversion operators for
// the Length class.
#include "Length2.h"

#include <iostream>
#include <string>
using namespace std;

int main()
{
   Length distance(0);
   double feet;
   int inches;
   distance.setLength(4, 6);
   cout << "The Length object is " << distance <<  "." << endl;

   // Convert and print
   feet = distance;
   inches = distance;
   cout << "The Length object measures " << feet << " feet." << endl;
   cout << "The Length object measures " << inches << " inches."
        << endl;
   return 0;
 }
```

Program Output

```
The Length object is 4 feet, 6 inches.
The Length object measures 4.5 feet.
The Length object measures 54 inches.
```

11.8 Convert Constructors

CONCEPT: In addition to providing a means for the creation of objects, convert constructors provide a way for the compiler to convert a value of a given type to an object of the class.

A constructor that takes a single parameter of a type other than its class type can be regarded as converting its parameter into an object of its class. Such a constructor is called a *convert constructor.*

In addition to the function of creating objects of its class, a convert constructor provides the compiler with a way of performing implicit type conversions. Such type conversions will be performed by the compiler whenever a value of the constructor's parameter type is given where a value of the class type is expected.

As a simple example, consider the class

```
class IntClass
{
private:
   int value;
public:
   // Convert constructor from int
   IntClass(int intValue)
   {
      value = intValue;
   }
   int getValue() const { return value; }
};
```

Since the constructor `IntClass(int)` takes a single parameter of a type other than `IntClass`, it is a convert constructor.

Convert constructors are automatically invoked by the compiler whenever the context demands a class object but a value of constructor's parameter type is provided. This occurs in four different contexts:

1. An object of the class is initialized with a value of the convert constructor's parameter type: for example

   ```
   IntClass intObject = 23;
   ```

2. An object of the class is assigned a value of the convert constructor's parameter type: for example

   ```
   intObject = 24;
   ```

3. A function expecting a value parameter of the class type is instead passed a value of the constructor's parameter type. For example, we may define a function

   ```
   void printValue(IntClass x)
   {
       cout << x.getValue();
   }
   ```

and then pass it an `int` when we call it:

```
printValue(25);
```

The compiler will use the convert constructor to convert the integer `25` into an object of the `IntClass` class and will then pass the object to the function. The compiler will not invoke the convert constructor if the formal parameter is a pointer or a reference to an `IntClass` object: *convert constructors are only invoked when the formal parameter uses pass by value.*

4. A function that declares a return value of the class type actually returns a value of the convert constructor's parameter type. For example, the compiler will accept the following function:

```
IntClass f(int intValue)
{
    return intValue;
}
```

Note that the function returns a value of type integer, even though `IntClass` is declared as its return type. Again, the compiler will implicitly call the convert constructor to convert the integer `intValue` to an `IntClass` object. It is this object which is returned from the function.

The following program illustrates the action of convert constructors.

Contents of `Convert.h`

```
#include <iostream>
using namespace std;

class IntClass
{
private:
  int value;
public:
  // Convert constructor from int
  IntClass(int intValue)
  {
    value = intValue;
  }
  int getValue() const { return value; }
};
```

Contents of `Convert.cpp`

```
#include "Convert.h"
//******************************************
// This function returns an int even though *
// an IntClass object is declared as the    *
// return type.                             *
//******************************************
IntClass f(int intValue)
{
   return intValue;
}

```

```
//*****************************************
// Prints the int value inside an IntClass   *
// object.                                   *
//*****************************************
void printValue(IntClass x)
{
   cout << x.getValue();
}
```

Program 11-16

```
// This program demonstrates the action of
// convert constructors.
#include "Convert.h"

// Function prototypes.
void printValue(IntClass);
IntClass f(int);

int main()
{
   // Initialize with an int
   IntClass intObject = 23;
   cout << "The value is " << intObject.getValue() << endl;

   // Assign an int
   intObject = 24;
   cout  << "The value is " << intObject.getValue()  << endl;

   // Pass an int to a function expecting IntClass
   cout << "The value is ";
   printValue(25);
   cout << endl;

   // Demonstrate conversion on a return
   intObject = f(26);
   cout << "The value is ";
   printValue(intObject);

   return 0;
}
```

Program Output

```
The value is 23
The value is 24
The value is 25
The value is 26
```

You should consider the use of a convert constructor whenever it makes sense to have automatic conversions from some type to the class type. A practical example of the use of convert constructors can be found in the C++ `string` class. That class provides a convert constructor from C-strings:

```
class string
{
   // Only the convert constructor is shown
   public:
      string(char *);
};
```

The presence of this convert constructor allows programmers to pass C-strings to functions that expect `string` object parameters, assign C-strings to `string` objects, and use C-strings as initial values of `string` objects:

```
string str = "Hello";
str = "Hello There!";
```

In a way, convert constructors work in a way that is the opposite of the type conversion operators covered in a previous section: whereas type conversion operators convert an object to a value of another type, convert constructors convert a value of a given type to an object of the class.

Checkpoint

11.31 What are the benefits of having operator functions that perform object conversion?

11.32 Why is it not necessary to specify a return type for an operator function that performs data type conversion?

11.33 Assume that there is a class named `BlackBox`. Write a prototype for a member function that converts `BlackBox` to `int`.

11.34 Assume there are two classes, `Big` and `Small`.Write a prototype for the convert constructor that converts objects of type `Small` to objects of type `Big`.

11.9 Aggregation and Composition

CONCEPT: Class aggregation occurs when an object of one class owns an object of another class. Class composition is a form of aggregation where the owner class controls the lifetime of objects of the owned class.

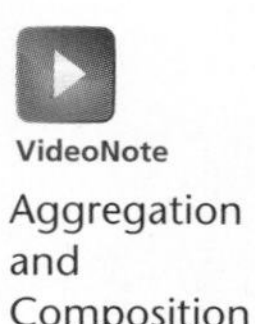

VideoNote
Aggregation and Composition

In Chapter 7, you learned that a class can contain members that are themselves objects of other classes. When a class C contains a member that is an object of another class D, every object of C will have inside it an object of the class D. This creates a *has-a* relationship between C and D. In this type of relationship, every instance of C *has*, or *owns*, an instance of the class D. In C++, such ownership usually occurs as result of C having a member of type D, but it can also occur as result of C having a pointer to an object of D. The term *aggregation* is often broadly used to describe situations in which objects of one class own objects of other classes.

Member Initialization Lists

Consider the following `Person` and `Date` classes.

```
class Date
{
   string month;
   int day, year;
public:
   Date(string m, int d, int y)
   {
      month = m;
      day = d;
      year = y;
   }
};
```

```
class Person
{
   String name;
   Date dateOfBirth;
public:
   Person(string name, string month, int day, int year)
   {
      // Pass month, day and year to the
      // dateOfBirth constructor
      this->name = name;
   }
};
```

The `Person` constructor receives parameters `month`, `day`, and `year` that it needs to pass to the `Date` constructor of its `dateOfBirth` member. C++ provides a special notation, called a *member initialization list*, that allows constructors of classes to pass arguments to constructors of member objects. A member initialization list is a list of comma-separated calls to member object constructors. It is prefixed with a colon and is placed just after the header, but before the body, of the constructor of the containing class:

```
class Person
{
   String name;
   Date dateOfBirth;
public:
   Person(string name, string month, int day, int year):
   dateOfBirth(month, day, year) // Member initialization list
   {
      this->name = name;
   }
};
```

Notice the colon at the end of the constructor header, and notice that in invoking the constructor of the contained `Date` object, it is the *name of the object* (`dateOfBirth`) rather than the *class of the object* (`Date`) that is used. This allows constructors of different objects of the same class to be invoked in the same initialization list.

Although the member initialization list is usually used to invoke constructors on member objects, it can be used to initialize member variables of any type. Thus, the `Person` and `Date` class can be written as follows:

```
class Date
{
   string month;
   int day, year;
```

```
public:
   Date(string m, int d, int y):
   month(m), day(d), year(y)  // Member Initialization list
   {
   }
};

class Person
{
   String name;
   Date dateOfBirth;
public:
   Person(string name, string month, int day, int year):
   name(name),
   dateOfBirth(month, day, year)
   {
   }
};
```

Notice that the bodies of the `Date` and `Person` constructors are now empty. This is because the assignment of values to member variables normally performed there is now accomplished by the initialization lists. Many programmers prefer the use of member initialization lists to assignment inside of the body of the constructor because it allows the compiler to generate more efficient code in certain situations. When using member initialization lists, it is good programming practice to list the members in the initialization list in the same order that they are declared in the class.

Finally, notice the occurrence of `name(name)` in the initialization list of the `Person` constructor. The compiler is able to determine that the first occurrence of `name` refers to the member variable, and that its second occurrence refers to the parameter.

Aggregation Through Pointers

Now let's suppose that in addition to having a date of birth, each person has a country of residence. A country has a name, and possibly many other attributes:

```
class Country
{
   string name;
   // Additional fields
};
```

Because many people will "have" the same country, the has-a relationship between `Person` and `Country` should not be implemented by embedding an instance of the `Country` class inside every `Person` object. Because many people share the same country of residence, implementing the has-a relation by containment will result in unnecessary duplication of data and waste memory. In addition, it would require many `Person` objects to be updated whenever a country has a change in any of its data. Using a pointer to implement the has-a relation avoids these problems. Here is a version of the `Person` class, modified to include a pointer to the country of residence:

```
class Person
{
   string name;
   Date dateOfBirth;
   Country *pCountry;  // Pointer to country of residence
```

```
public:
   Person(string name, string month, int day, int year, Country *pC):
   dateOfBirth(month, day, year), name(name), pCountry(pC)
   {
   }
};
```

Aggregation, Composition, and Object Lifetimes

Composition is a term used to describe special cases of aggregation in which the lifetime of the owned object coincides with the lifetime of its owner. A good example of composition is when a class C contains a member that is an object of another class D. The contained D object is created at the same time that the C object is created and is destroyed when the containing C object is destroyed or goes out of scope. Another example of composition is when a class C contains a pointer to a D object, and the D object is created by the C constructor and destroyed by the C destructor.

The following program features modified versions of the above classes designed to illustrate aggregation, composition, and object lifetimes. Each class has a constructor to announce the creation of its objects and a destructor to announce their demise. The `Person` class has a static member

```
int Person::uniquePersonID;
```

that is used to generate numbers assigned to `Person` objects as they are created. These numbers serve as a sort of universal personal identification number, much as social security numbers are used to identify people in the United States. The numbers are stored in a `personID` field of the `Person` and `Date` classes and are used to identify objects being created or destroyed. Each `dateOfBirth` object carries the same `personID` number as the `Person` object that contains it.

Program 11-17

```
// This program illustrates aggregation, composition
// and object lifetimes.
#include <iostream>
#include <string>
using namespace std;

class Date
{
   string month;
   int day, year;
   int personID;  // ID of person whose birthday this is
public:
   Date(string m, int d, int y, int id):
   month(m), day(d), year(y), personID(id)
   {
      cout << "Date-Of-Birth object for person "
           << personID  << " has been created.\n";
   }
   ~Date()
```

(program continues)

Program 11-17 *(continued)*

```
   {
      cout << "Date-Of-Birth object for person "
           << personID  << " has been destroyed.\n";
   }
};

class Country
{
   string name;
public:
   Country(string name) : name(name)
   {
      cout << "A Country object has been created.\n";
   }
   ~Country()
   {
      cout << "A Country object has been destroyed.\n";
   }
};

class Person
{
   string name;
   Date dateOfBirth;
   int personID;         // Person identification number (PID)
   Country *pCountry;
public:
   Person(string name, string month, int day, int year, Country *pC):
   name(name),
   dateOfBirth(month, day, year, Person::uniquePersonID),
   personID(Person::uniquePersonID),
   pCountry(pC)
   {
      cout << "Person object "
           << personID << " has been created.\n";
      Person::uniquePersonID ++;
   }
   ~Person()
   {
      cout << "Person object "
           << personID << " has been destroyed.\n";
   }
   static int uniquePersonID;  // Used to generate PIDs
};

// Define the static class variable
int Person::uniquePersonID = 1;

int main()
{
   // Create a Country object
```

(program continues)

Program 11-17 *(continued)*

```
    Country usa("USA");
    // Create a Person object
    Person *p = new Person("Peter Lee", "January", 1, 1985, &usa);
    // Create another Person object
    Person p1("Eva Gustafson", "May", 15, 1992, &usa);
    cout << "Now there are two people.\n";
    // Delete the first person
    delete p;
    cout << "Now there is only one.\n";
    // The second person will go out of scope when main returns
    return 0;
}
```

Program Output

```
A Country object has been created.
Date-Of-Birth object for person 1 has been created.
Person object 1 has been created.
Date-Of-Birth object for person 2 has been created.
Person object 2 has been created.
Now there are two people.
Person object 1 has been destroyed.
Date-Of-Birth object for person 1 has been destroyed.
Now there is only one.
Person object 2 has been destroyed.
Date-Of-Birth object for person 2 has been destroyed.
A Country object has been destroyed.
```

The relationship between the `dateOfBirth` objects and the `Person` objects that contain them is an example of composition. As you can see from the program output, those `Date` objects are created at the same time, and die at the same time, as the `Person` objects that own them. Aggregation in its more general form is exemplified by the has-a relationship between `Person` and `Country`.

By looking at the `print` member function, you can see an example of how the member functions of the enclosing class can access the member functions of the contained class.

The Has-A Relation

When one class contains an instance of a second class, the first class is said to sustain a *has-a* relation to the second. For example, the `Acquaintance` class has-a `Date` class in the form of its `dob` member, while the `Date` class has-a `string` object in the form of its `month` member. The has-a relation is important in modeling relationships among classes and objects during the design of an object-oriented system. Another important relation between classes in a program is the is-a relation, which we will discuss in a later section after we have discussed the concept of inheritance. Thus object composition realizes the has-a relation, while, as we will see later, inheritance is a way of realizing the is-a relation.

11.10 Inheritance

Generalization and Specialization

In the real world you can find many objects that are specialized versions of other more general objects. For example, the term "insect" describes a very general type of creature with numerous characteristics. Because grasshoppers and bumblebees are insects, they have all the general characteristics of an insect. In addition, they have special characteristics of their own. For example, the grasshopper has its jumping ability, and the bumblebee has its stinger. Grasshoppers and bumblebees are specialized versions of an insect. This is illustrated in Figure 11-5.

Figure 11-5

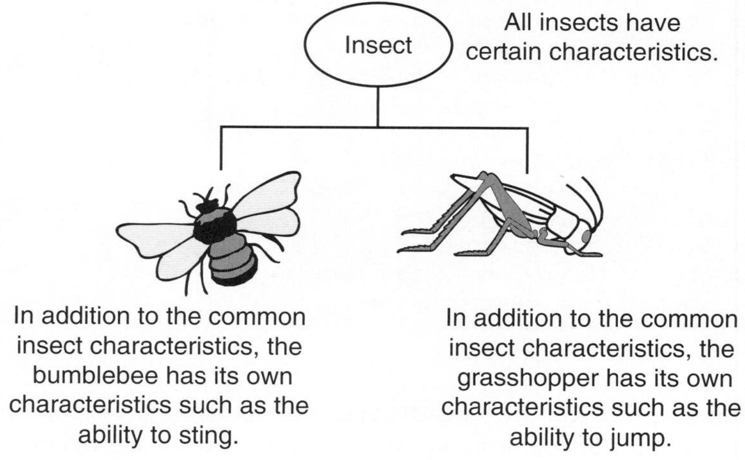

Insect
All insects have certain characteristics.
In addition to the common insect characteristics, the bumblebee has its own characteristics such as the ability to sting.
In addition to the common insect characteristics, the grasshopper has its own characteristics such as the ability to jump.

Inheritance and the Is-a Relationship

When one object is a specialized version of another object, there is an *is-a relationship* between them. For example, a grasshopper *is an* insect. Here are a few other examples of the is-a relationship.

- A poodle *is a* dog.
- A car *is a* vehicle.
- A rectangle *is a* shape.

When an is-a relationship exists between objects, it means that the specialized object has all of the characteristics of the general object, plus additional characteristics that make it special. In object-oriented programming, *inheritance* is used to create an is-a relationship between classes.

Inheritance involves a base class and a derived class. The *base class* is the general class and the *derived class* is the specialized class. The derived class is based on, or derived from, the base class. You can think of the base class as the parent and the derived class as the child. This is illustrated in Figure 11-6.

Figure 11-6

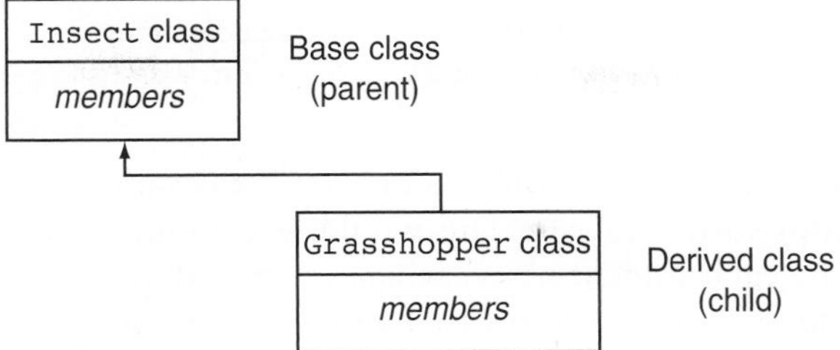

The derived class inherits the member variables and member functions of the base class without any of them being rewritten. Furthermore, new member variables and functions may be added to the derived class to make it more specialized than the base class. To take a specific example, consider a college or university environment where there are both students and faculty personnel. Suppose that we have a class `Person` with a `name` data member and member functions for working with the `name` member:

```
class Person{
private:
   string name;
public:
   Person(){ setName(""); }
   Person(string pName) { setName(pName);}
   void setName(string pName) { name = pName; }
   string getName() const { return name;}
};
```

Assuming the enumerated types

```
enum Discipline {
   ARCHEOLOGY, BIOLOGY, COMPUTER_SCIENCE
};
enum Classification {
   FRESHMAN, SOPHOMORE, JUNIOR, SENIOR
};
```

to define the range of disciplines in which studies are offered and the classification of students, we can define both the `Student` and `Faculty` classes as classes that inherit from the `Person` class. This makes sense because a `Student` is a `Person`, and a `Faculty` member is also a `Person`.

To define a class by inheritance, we need to specify the base class plus the additional members that the derived class adds to the base class. Let's say that in addition to having all the characteristics of a `Person`, a `Student` must declare a major in some discipline and have an academic advisor who is a `Person`. The `Student` class can be defined as follows:

```
class Student : public Person
{
private:
   Discipline major;
   Person *advisor;
```

```
public:
   void setMajor(Discipline d) { major = d; }
   Discipline getMajor() const { return major;  }
   void setAdvisor(Person *p) { advisor = p; }
   Person *getAdvisor() const { return advisor; }
};
```

We assume that many different students may have the same advisor. Having each `Student` object store a copy of the advisor data would lead to unnecessary duplication and would force us to update each student object whenever the advisor data is updated. The `Student` object stores a pointer to the advisor to avoid these and other problems.

The first part of the first line of the class declaration specifies `Student` as the name of the class being defined and specifies the existing class `Person` as its base class:

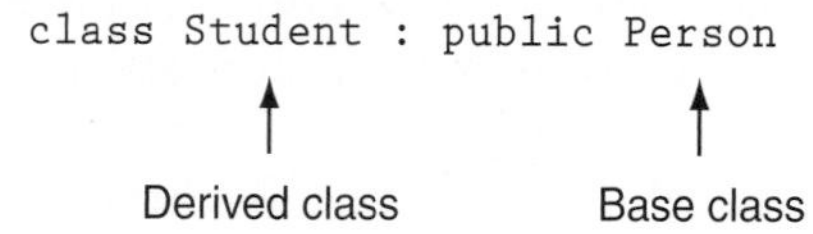

The key word `public` that precedes the name of the base class is the *base class access specification*. It affects how the members of the base class will be accessed by the member functions of the derived class, and by code outside of the two classes. We will discuss the base class access specification in greater detail in a later section.

A class can be used as the base class for more than one derived class. In particular, a `Faculty` class can also be derived from the `Person` class as follows:

```
class Faculty : public Person
{
private:
  Discipline department;
public:
  void setDepartment(Discipline d) { department = d; }
  Discipline getDepartment( ) const { return department;  }
};
```

Thus a `Faculty` object is a `Person` object that has a home department in some discipline. It is also important to note that each object of the derived class will contain all members of the base class. This is illustrated by Figure 11-7 in the case of the `Student` and `Person` classes.

Figure 11-7

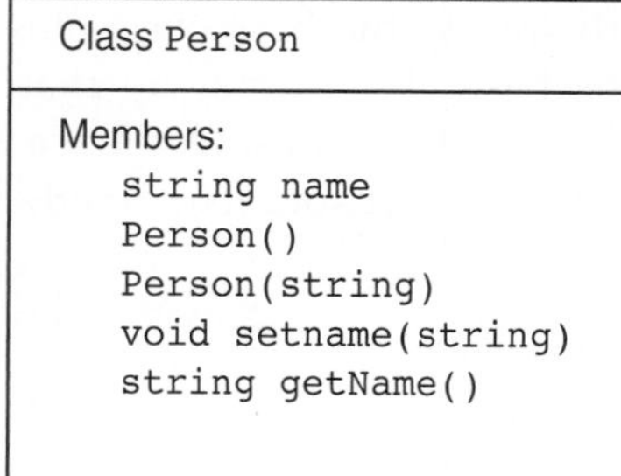

Class `Student`

Members inherited from `Person`:
```
string name
Person()
Person(string)
void setname(string)
string getName()
```
New Members added by `Student`:
```
Discipline major
Person *advisor
```

Program 11-18 demonstrates the creation and use of an object of a derived class by creating a `Faculty` object. The program uses arrays of strings that map values of enumerated types to strings to enable printing of values of enumerated types in the form of strings. The included "`inheritance.h`" file contains declarations of the `Person`, `Student`, and `Faculty` classes, as well as the enumerated types `Discipline` and `Classification`.

Contents of `Inheritance.h`

```
#include <string>
using namespace std;

enum Discipline { ARCHEOLOGY, BIOLOGY, COMPUTER_SCIENCE };
enum Classification { FRESHMAN, SOPHOMORE, JUNIOR, SENIOR };

class Person
{
private:
  string name;
public:
  Person() { setName(""); }
  Person(string pName) { setName(pName); }
  void setName(string pName) { name = pName; }
  string getName() const { return name; }
};

class Student:public Person
{
private:
  Discipline major;
  Person *advisor;
public:
  void setMajor(Discipline d) { major = d; }
  Discipline getMajor() const { return major; }
  void setAdvisor(Person *p) { advisor = p; }
  Person *getAdvisor() const { return advisor; }
};

class Faculty:public Person
{
private:
  Discipline department;
public:
  void setDepartment(Discipline d) { department = d; }
  Discipline getDepartment( ) { return department; }
};
```

Program 11-18

```
// This program demonstrates the creation and use
// of objects of derived classes.
#include <iostream>
#include "inheritance.h"

using namespace std;
```

(program continues)

Program 11-18 *(continued)*

```

// These arrays of string are used to print the
// enumerated types.
const string dName[] = {
  "Archeology", "Biology", "Computer Science"
};

const string cName[] = {
  "Freshman", "Sophomore", "Junior", "Senior"
};

int main()
{
   // Create a  Faculty object
   Faculty prof;

   // Use a Person member function
   prof.setName("Indiana Jones");

   // Use a Faculty member function
   prof.setDepartment(ARCHEOLOGY);
   cout << "Professor " << prof.getName()
        << " teaches in the " << "Department of ";

   // Get department as an enumerated type
   Discipline dept = prof.getDepartment();

   // Print out the department in string form
   cout << dName[dept] << endl;

   return 0;
}
```

Program Output

```
Professor Indiana Jones teaches in the Department of Archeology
```

Superclasses and Subclasses

We can think of a class as describing the set of all objects that have certain characteristics. An object of a derived class inherits all the characteristics of the base class, so it can be regarded as belonging to the base class. Thus objects of the derived class are just specialized objects of the base class. For this reason, the derived class is often called a *subclass* of the base class, and the base class is called a *superclass* of the derived class.

Multiple Inheritance

C++ supports *multiple inheritance*, in which a derived class simultaneously derives from two or more base classes. Although interesting, multiple inheritance can lead to programs that are very difficult to understand, and is rarely useful in practice. You can find a discussion of it in Appendix H on the book's companion website.

Appendix F on the book's companion website shows how to represent inheritance using UML.

11.11 Protected Members and Class Access

CONCEPT: Protected members of a base class are like private members, except they may be accessed by derived classes. The base class access specification determines how private, protected, and public base class members are accessed when they are inherited by the derived class.

Until now you have used two access specifications within a class: `private` and `public`. C++ provides a third access specification, `protected`. Protected members of a base class are like private members, except they may be accessed by member functions of a derived class. Protected members are inaccessible to all other code in the program.*

Let us suppose we want to add to the `Faculty` class a constructor that takes as parameter the name and department of a professor. The best way to accomplish this is to have the constructor call the `setName()` member function inherited from the `Person` class. To illustrate the use of protected members, however, we will change the access specification of the `name` field of the `Person` class to `protected` and have the `Faculty` constructor access it directly. We make similar changes to the `Student` class, adding a constructor that takes parameters and sets the protected member `name`. The resulting code is stored in the `inheritance1.h` file:

Contents of `Inheritance1.h`

```
#include <string>
using namespace std;

enum Discipline { ARCHEOLOGY, BIOLOGY, COMPUTER_SCIENCE };
enum Classification { Freshman, Sophomore, Junior, Senior };

class Person
{
protected:
  string name;
public:
  Person() { setName("");}
  Person(string pName) { setName(pName);}
  void setName(string pName) { name = pName; }
  string getName() const { return name; }
};

class Student:public Person
{
private:
  Discipline major;
  Person *advisor;
```

* Friend functions and friend classes have access to both private and protected members.

```
public:
  // Constructor
  Student(string sname, Discipline d, Person *adv);

  void setMajor(Discipline d) { major = d; }
  Discipline getMajor() const {return major; }
  void setAdvisor(Person *p){advisor = p;}
  Person *getAdvisor() const { return advisor; }
 };

class Faculty:public Person
{
private:
  Discipline department;
public:
  // Constructor
  Faculty(string fname, Discipline d)
  {
     // Access the protected base class member
     name = fname;
     department = d;
   }
   // Other member functions
   void setDepartment(Discipline d) { department = d; }
   Discipline getDepartment( ) const { return department; }
};
```

Contents of `inheritance1.cpp`

```
#include "inheritance1.h"
//*********************************************
// Constructor for the Student class.         *
//*********************************************
Student::Student(string sname, Discipline d, Person *adv)
{
   // Access the  protected member name
   name = sname;

   // Access the other members
   major = d;
   advisor = adv;
}
```

Program 11-19 demonstrates the use of these classes.

Program 11-19

```
//This program demonstrates the use of
//objects of derived classes.
#include "inheritance1.h"
#include <iostream>
using namespace std;

// These arrays of string are used to print
// values of enumerated types
```

(program continues)

Program 11-19 *(continued)*

```
const string dName[] =
      {"Archeology", "Biology", "Computer Science"};

const string cName[] =
  {"Freshman", "Sophomore", "Junior", "Senior"};

int main()
{
   // Create Faculty and Student objects
   Faculty prof("Indiana Jones", ARCHEOLOGY);
   Student st("Sean Bolster", ARCHEOLOGY, &prof);
   cout << "Professor " << prof.getName() << " teaches "
        << dName[prof.getDepartment()] << "." << endl;

   // Get student's advisor
   Person *pAdvisor = st.getAdvisor();
   cout << st.getName() <<"\'s advisor is "
        << pAdvisor->getName() << ".";

   return 0;
}
```

Program Output

```
Professor Indiana Jones teaches Archeology.
Sean Bolster's advisor is Indiana Jones.
```

Although our example does not show it, member functions of a base class can be declared protected as well. Protected member functions can be called by member functions of derived classes, and by friend functions and friend classes.

Base Access Specifications

In addition to public, C++ permits the use of protected and private as base access specifications, as illustrated in the following (incompletely specified) examples

```
class Cat : protected Feline
{

};

class Dog : private Canine
{

};
```

Be careful not to confuse base access specification with member access specification. Member access specification determines the type of access for members *defined* in the class, whereas base access specification determines the type of access for *inherited* members. Table 11-2 and Figure 11-8 show the interplay between member access specification in the base class and base class specification that determines access to the inherited member.

Table 11-2 Base Class Access Specifications

Base Class Access Specification	How Members of the Base Class Appear in the Derived Class
`private`	• Private members of the base class are inaccessible to the derived class. • Protected members of the base class become private members of the derived class. • Public members of the base class become private members of the derived class.
`protected`	• Private members of the base class are inaccessible to the derived class. • Protected members of the base class become protected members of the derived class. • Public members of the base class become protected members of the derived class.
`public`	• Private members of the base class are inaccessible to the derived class. • Protected members of the base class become protected members of the derived class. • Public members of the base class become public members of the derived class.

Figure 11-8

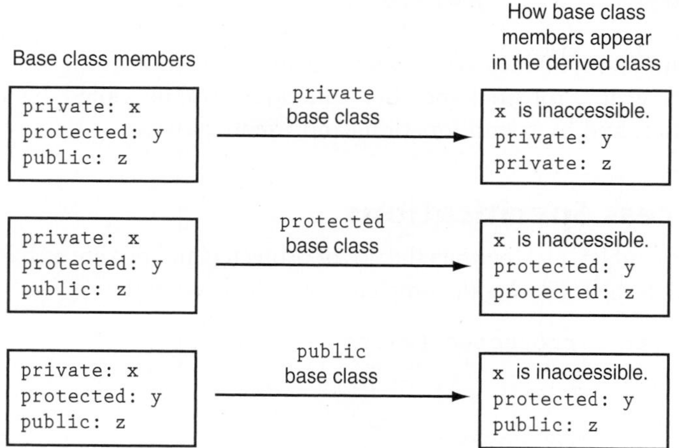

11.35 What type of relationship between classes is realized by inheritance?

11.36 Why does it make sense to think of a base class as a superclass of its derived class?

11.37 What is a base class access specification?

11.38 Think of an example of two classes where one class is a special case of the other, and write declarations for both classes, with the special case being written as a derived class.

11.39 What is the difference between private members and protected members?

11.40 What is the difference between member access specification and base class access specification?

11.41 Suppose a program has the following class declaration:

```
class CheckPoint
{
   private:
      int a;
   protected:
      int b;
      int c;
      void setA(int x) { a = x;}
   public:
      void setB(int y) { b = y;}
      void setC(int z) { c = z;}
};
```

Answer the following questions.

A) Suppose another class, `Quiz`, is derived from the `CheckPoint` class. Here is the first line of its declaration:

```
class Quiz : private CheckPoint
```

Indicate whether each member of the `CheckPoint` class is `private`, `protected`, `public`, or inaccessible:

```
a
b
c
setA
setB
setC
```

B) Suppose the `Quiz` class, derived from the `CheckPoint` class, is declared as

```
class Quiz : protected Checkpoint
```

Indicate whether each member of the `CheckPoint` class is `private`, `protected`, `public`, or inaccessible:

```
a
b
c
setA
setB
setC
```

C) Suppose the `Quiz` class, derived from the `CheckPoint` class, is declared as

```
class Quiz : public Checkpoint
```

Indicate whether each member of the `CheckPoint` class is `private`, `protected`, `public`, or inaccessible:

```
a
b
c
setA
setB
setC
```

D) Suppose the `Quiz` class, derived from the `CheckPoint` class, is declared as

```
class Quiz : Checkpoint
```

Is the `CheckPoint` class a `private`, `public`, or `protected` base class?

11.12 Constructors, Destructors, and Inheritance

CONCEPT: When an object of a derived class is being instantiated, the base class constructor is called before the derived class constructor. When the object is destroyed, the derived class destructor is called before the base class destructor.

Recall that constructors are automatically called by the compiler whenever an object of a class is being created. Because every object of a derived class can be regarded as having an object of the base class embedded within it, the creation of a derived class object involves the creation of the embedded base class object. The compiler will always call the base class constructor before it calls the derived class constructor. This order is reversed upon destruction of a derived class object; the destructor in the derived class is called before the destructor in the base class. This order permits the derived class constructors and destructors to use data or member functions of the base class in doing their work.

Program 11-20 illustrates this behavior in a simple program.

Program 11-20

```
// This program demonstrates the order in which base and
// derived class constructors and destructors are called.
// For the sake of simplicity, all the class declarations
// are in this file.
#include <iostream>
using namespace std;

// Base class
class BaseDemo
{
public:
   BaseDemo()   // Constructor
      { cout << "This is the BaseDemo constructor.\n"; }
   ~BaseDemo() // Destructor
      { cout << "This is the BaseDemo destructor.\n"; }
};
```

(program continues)

Program 11-20 *(continued)*

```

// Derived class
class DeriDemo : public BaseDemo
{
public:
   DeriDemo()   // Constructor
      { cout << "This is the DeriDemo constructor.\n"; }
   ~DeriDemo()  // Destructor
      { cout << "This is the DeriDemo destructor.\n"; }
};

int main()
{
   cout << "We will now create a DeriDemo object.\n";
   DeriDemo object;
   cout << "The program is now going to end.\n";
   return 0;
}
```

Program Output

```
We will now create a DeriDemo object.
This is the BaseDemo constructor.
This is the DeriDemo constructor.
The program is now going to end.
This is the DeriDemo destructor.
This is the BaseDemo destructor.
```

Passing Arguments to Base Class Constructors

As already mentioned, the compiler will automatically call a base class constructor before executing the derived class constructor. The compiler's default action is to call the default constructor in the base class. Some classes, however, may not have a default constructor. Also, the programmer may want to specify which of several base class constructors should be called during the creation of a derived class object.

In these cases, the programmer must explicitly specify which base class constructor should be called by the compiler. This is done by specifying the arguments to the selected base class constructor in the definition of the derived class constructor.

The syntax for passing arguments to base class constructors is simple: the header for the derived class constructor is followed by a colon, an indication of which base class constructor to call, and the arguments to be passed. To illustrate, we will modify the constructor for the `Faculty` class so that it invokes a constructor in the `Person` class.

The constructor in its previous form was

```
Faculty(string fname, Discipline d)
{
   name = fname;
   department = d;
}
```

It now becomes

```
Faculty(string fname, Discipline d) : Person(fname)
{
   department = d;
}
```

Notice that one of the arguments passed to the derived class constructor is passed to the base class constructor. In general, the argument passed to the base class constructor may be any expression and may involve any variables that are in scope at the point of the call to the derived class constructor. For example, a string literal, or even a global string variable, could have been passed as the argument to the `Person` constructor. If for example, it was desired that the name of a faculty member default to that of the ubiquitous "Dr. Staff," the following constructor would be just what we want:

```
Faculty(Discipline d) : Person("Staff")
{
   department = d;
}
```

In general, the base class constructor may take any number of parameters.

Contents of `inheritance2.h`

```
#include <string>
using namespace std;

enum Discipline { ARCHEOLOGY, BIOLOGY, COMPUTER_SCIENCE };
enum Classification { FRESHMAN, SOPHOMORE, JUNIOR, SENIOR };

class Person
{
protected:
  string name;
public:
  Person() {setName(""); }
  Person(string pName) { setName(pName); }
  void setName(string pName) { name = pName; }
  string getName() const { return name; }
};

class Student:public Person
{
private:
  Discipline major;
  Person *advisor;
public:
  // Constructor
  Student(string sname, Discipline d, Person *adv);

  void setMajor(Discipline d) { major = d; }
  Discipline getMajor() const { return major; }
  void setAdvisor(Person *p) { advisor = p; }
  Person *getAdvisor() const { return advisor; }
```

```
31 };
32
33 class Faculty:public Person
34 {
35 private:
36   Discipline department;
37 public:
38   // Constructor
39   Faculty(string fname, Discipline d) : Person(fname)
40   {
41      department = d;
42   }
43
44   void setDepartment(Discipline d) { department = d; }
45   Discipline getDepartment( ) const { return department; }
46 };
```

Contents of `inheritance2.cpp`

```
 1 #include "inheritance2.h"
 2 //*******************************************
 3 // Constructor for the Student class.       *
 4 //*******************************************
 5 Student::Student(string sname, Discipline d, Person *adv)
 6 : Person(sname) // Base constructor initialization
 7 {
 8    major = d;
 9    advisor = adv;
10 }
```

The new constructors are demonstrated in Program 11-21App on the book's companion website, which is virtually the same as Program 11-19. The only difference is that Program 11-21App includes `inheritance2.h` rather than `inheritance1.h`, and must be compiled and linked with `inheritance2.cpp`. It can be found in the file Pr11-21App.cpp on the book's companion website.

It is important to remember that the arguments to the base class constructor must be specified in the *definition* of the derived class constructor, and not in its *declaration*. In the case of the `Student` class, the declaration of the constructor occurs at line 25 of the `inheritance.h` file. The corresponding definition starts at line 5 of the `inheritance.cpp` file, and specifies the argument to pass to the `Person` superclass in line 6.

Checkpoint

11.42 What is the reason that base class constructors are called before derived class constructors?

11.43 Why do you think the arguments to a base class constructor are specified in the definition of the derived class constructor rather than in the declaration?

11.44 Passing arguments to base classes constructors solves the problem of selecting a base class constructor in inheritance. Can the same problem arise with composition? That is, might there be a case where a constructor of a class might have to pass arguments to the constructor of a contained class? If so, guess the syntax that would be used to pass the parameters, and construct a simple example to verify your guess.

11.45 What will the following program display?

```
#include <iostream>
using namespace std;
class Base
{
    public:
       Base() { cout << "Entering the base.\n"; }
       ~Base() { cout << "Leaving the base.\n"; }
};

class Camp : public Base
{
public:
   Camp() { cout << "Entering the camp.\n"; }
   ~Camp() { cout << "Leaving the camp.\n"; }
};
int main()
{
   Camp outpost;
   return 0;
}
```

11.46 What will the following program display?

```
#include <iostream>
#include <string>
using namespace std;

class Base
{
public:
   Base(){cout << "Entering the base.\n";}
   Base(string str)
   {
      cout << "This base is " << str << ".\n";
   }
   ~Base() {cout << "Leaving the base.\n";}
};
class Camp : public Base
{
public:
   Camp(){cout << "Entering the camp.\n";}
   Camp(string str1, string str2) : Base(str1)
   {
      cout << "The camp is " << str2 << ".\n";
   }
};

int main()
{
   Camp outpost("secure", "secluded");
   return 0;
}
```

11.13 Overriding Base Class Functions

CONCEPT: A derived class can override a member function of its base class by defining a derived class member function with the same name and parameter list.

It is often useful for a derived class to define its own version of a member function inherited from its base class. This may be done to specialize the member function to the needs of the derived class. When this happens, the base class member function is said to be *overridden*, or *redefined*, by the derived class.

VideoNote
Overriding Base Class Functions

As a simple example, suppose that we want to have a class `Tfaculty` that will allow us to associate with each member of the faculty a title such as “Dr.”, “Professor”, or “Dean.” To accomplish this, we derive the new class from the `Faculty` class by adding a `title` data member, an appropriate constructor, a member function to set the title, and then overriding the inherited `getName()` member function to return a “titled” name.

```
class TFaculty: public Faculty
{
private:
  string title;
public:
  // This Constructor allows the specification of a title
  TFaculty(string fname, Discipline d, string title)
  : Faculty(fname, d)
  {
    setTitle(title);
  }

  void setTitle(string title) { this->title = title; }

  // Override the getName function
  string getName( ) const { return title + " " + name; }
};
```

Program 11-21 illustrates the use of this class and its overridden member function. It uses the files `inheritance3.h` and `inheritance3.cpp`. The `inheritance3.h` file is just `inheritance2.h` with the class declaration of `TFaculty` added, and `inheritance3.cpp` is the same as `inheritance2.cpp`. Code listings of `inheritance2.h` and `inheritance2.cpp` can be found at the end of Section 11.12. Copies of all these files are included on the book’s companion website.

Program 11-21

```
// This program illustrates member function overriding.
#include "inheritance3.h"
#include <iostream>
using namespace std;

```

(program continues)

Program 11-21 *(continued)*

```
// These arrays of string are used to output
// values of enumerated types
const string dName[] =
    { "Archeology", "Biology", "Computer Science" };

const string cName[] =
    { "Freshman", "Sophomore", "Junior", "Senior" };

int main()
{
   // New constructor allows specification of title
   TFaculty prof("Indiana Jones", ARCHEOLOGY, "Dr.");
   Student st("Sean Bolster", ARCHEOLOGY, &prof);

   // Use the new TFaculty version of getName
   cout << prof.getName() << " teaches "
        << dName[prof.getDepartment()] << "." << endl;

   // This call uses the Person version of getName
   Person *pAdvisor = st.getAdvisor();
   cout << st.getName() <<"\'s advisor is "
        << pAdvisor->getName() << ".";

   return 0;
}
```

Program Output

```
Dr. Indiana Jones teaches Archeology.
Sean Bolster's advisor is Indiana Jones.
```

Choosing Between Base and Derived Class Versions of an Overriden Function

An object of a derived class that has overridden a base class member function contains more than one version of the member function. The compiler will determine which of the several versions to call by using type information in the expression used to make the call to the member function. For example, in Program 11-21, there are two calls to `getName()`:

1. The call `prof.getName()` returns `Dr. Indiana Jones` because the function is called through `prof`, which has type `TFaculty`. The compiler calls the `TFaculty` version `getName()`.
2. The call `pAdvisor->getName()` returns `Indiana Jones` without the "Dr." because the function is called through the pointer `pAdvisor`, which is a pointer to `Person`. The compiler calls the Person version of `getName()`.

The Difference Between Overloading and Overriding

Both overloading and overriding involve the definition of different functions with the same name. There are differences between the two concepts, however. Overriding can only be done in the context of inheritance and refers to the defining of a member function by a derived class when the base class already has a member function of the same name and parameter list. Overloading refers to the definition of different functions within the same class with the same name and *different* parameter lists. Overloading can also refer to the definition of different functions with different parameter lists at the global level.

Gaining Access to an Overridden Member Function

If a derived class overrides a base class member function, member functions of the derived class that would have otherwise called the overridden base class member function will now call the version in the derived class. It is occasionally useful to be able to call the overridden version. In fact, the new member function of the derived class may want to call the base class member function that it is overriding. This is done by using the scope resolution operator to specify the class of the overridden member function being accessed. For example, a member function of `TFaculty` that is to call the `getName` function of `Person` can do so in this fashion:

```
Person::getName();
```

Thus, a better version of the `TFaculty` class is the following. Note that the overriding function does not need to access any protected members of `Person`, but instead calls the public member function `getName`.

```
class TFaculty : public Faculty
{
private:
   string title;
public:
   TFaculty(string fname, Discipline d, string title)
   : Faculty(fname, d)
   {
      setTitle(title);
   }
   void setTitle(string title) { this->title = title; }
   // Override getName() by calling Person::getName
   string getName( ) const
   {
      return title + " " + Person::getName();
   }
};
```

Code for the program demonstrating this can be found in files `Pr11-22App.cpp`, `inheritance4.h`, and `inheritance4.cpp` on the book's companion website.

11.14 Tying It All Together: *Putting Data on the World Wide Web*

The ability to generate output formatted in HTML (Hypertext Markup Language) is important to programs that interact with users via the World Wide Web. These applications include Web servers and Web-based E-commerce applications such as Amazon and eBay. Often the information displayed by these programs must be formatted using *HTML tables*.

HTML tables are quite simple. They consist of *rows* of cells where each cell holds a unit of information referred to as *table data*. The information comprising the table is marked with HTML *tags* as shown in Table 11-3.

Table 11-3 HTML Tags for Formatting Tables

`<table>`	Marks the beginning of the table
`</table>`	Marks the end of the table
`<tr>`	Marks the beginning of a row in the table
`</tr>`	Marks the end of a row in the table
`<td>`	Marks the beginning of data in a single cell of the table
`</td>`	Marks the end of data in a single cell of the table
`<th>`	Marks the beginning of the header for a single column of the table
`</th>`	Marks the end of the header for a single column of the table

The `<table>` tag normally causes a browser to display tables with no borders. To display tables with borders, the *border* attribute can be used. For example, the data table shown in Table 11-4 can be displayed using the following HTML markup, identified here as the contents of a file named `table.html`. The file can be found on the book's companion website.

Table 11-4 Sample Input Data for the HTML Table Program

Name	Address	Phone
Mike Sane	1215 Mills St	630-555-1293
Natasha Upenski	513 Briarcliff Ln	412-555-1004

Contents of `table.html`

```
<table border = "1">
  <tr>
       <th> Name    </th>
       <th> Address </th>
       <th> Phone   </th>
  </tr>
  <tr>
       <td> Mike Sane     </td>
       <td> 1215 Mills St </td>
       <td> 630-728-1293  </td>
  </tr>
  <tr>
      <td> Natasha Upenski   </td>
      <td> 513 Briarcliff Ln </td>
      <td> 412-672-1004      </td>
  </tr>
</table>
```

If you use Microsoft Windows, you can display this table in your browser by double-clicking on the file table.html in Windows Explorer, or by using *Open* in the *File* menu of your browser.

Let's write a program that converts a two-dimensional array of strings into an HTML table capable of being displayed in a Web browser. The centerpiece of our program is an HTMLTable class with two member variables

```
vector<string> headers;
vector<vector<string> > rows;
```

that represent the *headers* and the *rows* of the table. The headers constitute a single vector of strings, while the rows of the table are represented by a vector of vectors. Note the blank character between the closing > > characters at the end of the definition of a vector of vectors: it is needed to avoid confusion with the >> operator. The HTMLTable class has a member function setHeaders() for setting the headers and a member function addRow() for adding rows to the table. The class also has an overloaded stream output operator

```
ostream & operator <<(ostream &out, HTMLTable hTable);
```

that is used to convert the table data stored in the headers and rows vectors into HTML markup and write that markup onto an output stream. If the stream receiving the markup is a file, you can open the file in a browser for viewing. Alternatively, if your system has established a default browser for opening files with an .html extension, you can use the C++ library function

```
system("file_location.html");
```

to make the operating system open the HTML file using the default browser. This, of course, assumes that the HTML markup is stored in a file named "file_location.html."

We learned in this chapter that a derived class object can be used wherever a base class object is expected. We use this fact to allow for more flexibility in the data that is passed as parameters to functions. We build this flexibility into an overloaded stream output operator and into a convert constructor for a class derived from the STL vector class. The overloaded stream output operator is able to write the standard output object cout because cout is an ostream object. It is also able to write to an ofstream object because ofstream inherits from ostream.

C++ programmers often face a dilemma: Although vectors are preferable to arrays in many ways, arrays are more convenient to initialize. The solution we adopt is to use vectors as parameters to functions, but use arrays for initialization. To bridge the gap, we write a StringVector class that has a convert constructor that takes an array of strings as parameter. Because StringVector derives from a vector of string, it can be used wherever a vector of string is expected. At the same time, its convert constructor allows for the use of arrays of strings, as shown in lines 91–100 of Program 11-22.

Program 11-22

```
// This program demonstrates the use of classes
// to put tabular data on the World Wide Web.
#include <iostream>
#include <fstream>
#include <string>
#include <vector>
using namespace std;

// This is a convenience class used to convert
// an array of strings into a vector of strings.
// The array of strings must be (sentinel)-terminated
// by a string of length 0.

class StringVector : public vector<string>
{
public:
     StringVector(string s[])
     {
         int k = 0;
         while (s[k].length() != 0)
         {
             this->push_back(s[k]);
             k++;
         }
     }
 };

// This class allows a 2-dimensional table expressed as
// a vectors of vector of strings to be transformed into
// HTML form.

class HTMLTable
{
private:
     vector<string> headers;
     vector<vector<string> > rows;
     // Helper method for writing an HTML row in a table
     void writeRow(ostream &out, string tag, vector<string> row);
public:
     // Set headers for the table columns
     void setHeaders(const vector<string> &headers)
     {  this->headers = headers; }
     // Add rows to the table
     void addRow(const vector<string> &row)
     {  rows.push_back(row);  }
     // Write the table into HTML form onto an output stream
    friend ostream & operator<<(ostream & out, HTMLTable htmlTable);
 };

```

(program continues)

Program 11-22 *(continued)*

```
//*****************************************************************
// Writes a row of the table, using the given tag for the table    *
// data. The tag may be td for table data or th for table header.  *
//*****************************************************************
void HTMLTable::writeRow(ostream &out, string tag, vector<string> row)
{
    out << "<tr>\n";
    for (unsigned int k = 0; k < headers.size(); k++)
     {
         out << "<" << tag << "> "
             << row[k] << " </" << tag << "> ";
     }
    out << "\n</tr>\n";
 }

//*****************************************************
// Overloaded stream output operator <<               *
//*****************************************************
ostream & operator<<(ostream &out, HTMLTable htmlTable)
{
     out << "<table border = \"1\">\n";
     // Write the headers
     htmlTable.writeRow(out, "th", htmlTable.headers);
     // Write the rows of the table
     for (unsigned int r = 0; r < htmlTable.rows.size(); r++)
     {
         htmlTable.writeRow(out, "td", htmlTable.rows[r]);
     }
     // Write end tag for table
     out << "</table>\n";
     return out;
}

int main()
{
     // Hard-coded data for table column headers
     // The arrays must have empty string sentinels
     string headers [] = {"Name", "Address", "Phone", ""};

     // Hard-coded data for the two rows of the table
     // The arrays must have empty string sentinels
     string person1 [] =
        {"Mike Sane", "1215 Mills St", "630-728-1293", ""};
     string person2 [] =
        {"Natasha Upenski", "513 Briarcliff Ln", "412-672-1004", ""};

     // Create the HTML table object and set its members
     HTMLTable hTable;
     hTable.setHeaders(StringVector(headers));
```

(program continues)

Program 11-22 *(continued)*

```
        hTable.addRow(StringVector(person1));
        hTable.addRow(StringVector(person2));

        // Open a file and write the HTML code to the file
        ofstream outFile("c:\\temp\\table.html");
        outFile << hTable;
        outFile.close();

        // Write the same HTML code to the screen for ease of viewing
        cout << hTable;
        // Use the default browser to view generated HTML table
        system("c:\\temp\\table.html");

        return 0;
}
```

Program Output as Displayed in Browser

Name	Address	Phone
Mike Sane	1215 Mills St	630-555-1293
Natasha Upenski	513 Briarcliff Ln	412-555-1004

Review Questions and Exercises

Fill-in-the-Blank and Short Answer

1. If a member variable is declared __________, all objects of that class share that variable.
2. Static member variables are defined __________ the class.
3. A(n) __________ member function cannot access any nonstatic member variables in its own class.
4. A static member function may be called __________ any instances of its class are defined.
5. A(n) __________ function is not a member of a class, but has access to the private members of the class.
6. A(n) __________ tells the compiler that a specific class will be declared later in the program.
7. __________ is the default behavior when an object is assigned the value of another object of the same class.
8. A(n)__________ is a special constructor, called whenever a new object is initialized with another object's data.
9. __________ is a special built-in pointer that is automatically passed as a hidden argument to all nonstatic member functions.

10. An operator may be __________ to work with a specific class.
11. When the __________ operator is overloaded, its function must have a dummy parameter.
12. Making an instance of one class a member of another class is called __________.
13. Object composition is useful for creating a(n) __________ relationship between two classes.
14. A constructor that takes a single parameter of a type different from the class type is a __________ constructor.
15. The class `Stuff` has both a copy constructor and an overloaded = operator. Assume that `blob` and `clump` are both instances of the `Stuff` class. For each of the statements, indicate whether the copy constructor or the overloaded = operator will be called.

```
Stuff blob = clump;
clump = blob;
blob.operator=(clump);
showValues(blob);    // Blob is passed by value.
```

16. Explain the programming steps necessary to make a class's member variable static.
17. Explain the programming steps necessary to make a class's member function static.
18. Consider the following class declaration:

```
class Thing
{
   private:
      int x;
      int y;
      static int z;
   public:
      Thing()
         { x = y = z; }
      static void putThing(int a)
         { z = a; }
};
int Thing:: z = 0:
```

Assume a program containing the class declaration defines three `Thing` objects with the following statement:

```
Thing one, two, three;
```

A) How many separate instances of the `x` member exist?
B) How many separate instances of the `y` member exist?
C) How many separate instances of the `z` member exist?
D) What value will be stored in the `x` and `y` members of each object?
E) Write a statement that will call the `putThing` member function *before* the `Thing` objects are defined.

19. Describe the difference between making a class a member of another class (object composition) and making a class a friend of another class.
20. What is the purpose of a forward declaration of a class?

21. Explain why memberwise assignment can cause problems with a class that contains a pointer member.
22. Explain why a class's copy constructor is called when an object of that class is passed by value into a function.
23. Explain why the parameter of a copy constructor must be a reference.
24. Assume a class named `Bird` exists. Write the header for a member function that overloads the = operator for that class.
25. Assume a class named `Dollars` exists. Write the headers for member functions that overload the prefix and postfix ++ operators for that class.
26. Assume a class named `Yen` exists. Write the header for a member function that overloads the < operator for that class.
27. Assume a class named `Length` exists. Write the header for a member function that overloads the stream insertion << operator for that class.
28. Assume a class named `Collection` exists. Write the header for a member function that overloads the `[]` operator for that class.
29. Explain why a programmer would want to overload operators rather than use regular member functions to perform similar operations.

Find the Error

30. Each of the following class declarations has errors. Locate as many as you can.

A)
```
class Box
{
    private:
       double width;
       double length;
       double height;
    public:
       Box(double w, l, h)
          { width = w; length = l; height = h; }
       Box(Box b) // Copy constructor
          { width = b.width;
            length = b.length;
            height = b.height; }

  ... Other member functions follow ...
};
```

B)
```
class Circle
{
    private:
        double diameter;
        int centerX;
        int centerY;
    public:
        Circle(double d, int x, int y)
            { diameter = d; centerX = x; centerY = y;   }
        // Overloaded = operator
        void Circle=(Circle &right)
```

```
            { diameter = right.diameter;
              centerX = right.centerX;
              centerY = right.centerY; }
```

... Other member functions follow ...

```
    };
```

C)
```
class Point
  {
      private:
          int xCoord;
          int yCoord;
      public:
          Point (int x, int y)
              { xCoord = x; yCoord = y; }
          // Overloaded + operator
          void operator+(const &Point Right)
             { xCoord += right.xCoord;
               yCoord += right.yCoord;
             }
```

... Other member functions follow ...

```
};
```

D)
```
class Box
  {
      private:
         double width;
         double length;
         double height;
      public:
         Box(double w, l, h)
             { width = w; length = l; height = h; }
         // Overloaded prefix ++ operator
         void operator++()
            {   ++width; ++length; }
         // Overloaded postfix ++ operator
         void operator++()
            {width++; length++; }
```

... Other member functions follow ...

```
  };
```

E)
```
class Yard
  {
     private:
        double length;
     public:
         Yard(double l)
            { length = l; }
         // double conversion function
         void operator double()
            { return length; }
```

... Other member functions follow ...

```
  };
```

Fill-in-the-Blank

31. A derived class inherits the __________ of its base class.

32. The base class named in the following line of code is __________ .

```
class Pet : public Dog
```

33. The derived class named in the following line of code is __________ .

```
class Pet : public Dog
```

34. In the following line of code, the class access specification for the base class is __________.

```
class Pet : public Dog
```

35. In the following line of code, the class access specification for the base class is __________.

```
class Pet : Fish
```

36. Protected members of a base class are like __________ members, except they may be accessed by derived classes.

37. Complete the following table by filling in private, protected, public, or inaccessible in the right-hand column:

In a private base class, this base class MEMBER access specification...	**...becomes this access specification in the derived class.**
private	
protected	
public	

38. Complete the following table by filling in private, protected, public, or inaccessible in the right-hand column:

In a protected base class, this base class MEMBER access specification...	**...becomes this access specification in the derived class.**
private	
protected	
public	

39. Complete the following table by filling in private, protected, public, or inaccessible in the right-hand column:

In a public base class, this base class MEMBER access specification...	**...becomes this access specification in the derived class.**
private	
protected	
public	

40. When both a base class and a derived class have constructors, the base class's constructor is called __________ (first/last).
41. When both a base class and a derived class have destructors, the base class's destructor is called __________ (first/last).
42. An overridden base class function may be called by a function in a derived class by using the __________ operator.

Find the Errors

43. Each of the following class declarations and/or member function definitions has errors. Find as many as you can.

A)
```
class Car, public Vehicle
{
   public:
      Car();
      ~Car();
    protected:
      int passengers;
}
```

B)
```
class Truck, public : Vehicle, public
{
   private:
      double cargoWeight;
   public:
      Truck();
      ~Truck();
};
```

Soft Skills

44. Your company's software is a market leader, but is proving difficult to maintain because it was written in C without using object-oriented concepts. Customers have identified problems with the software that must be fixed immediately and have pointed out features in competitors' products that they want you to support. The best solution will require a complete OOP redesign and subsequent implementation, but will take three years. Write a memo to company management outlining your recommendation for the course of action the company should pursue.

Programming Challenges

1. Check Writing

Design a class `Numbers` that can be used to translate whole dollar amounts in the range 0 through 9999 into an English description of the number. For example, the number 713 would be translated into the string *seven hundred thirteen*, and 8203 would be translated into *eight thousand two hundred three*.

The class should have a single integer member variable

```
int number;
```

and a collection of static string members that specify how to translate key dollar amounts into the desired format. For example, you might use static strings such as

```
string lessThan20[ ] =
    {"zero", "one", …, "eighteen", "nineteen" };
string hundred = "hundred";
string thousand = "thousand";
```

The class should have a constructor that accepts a nonnegative integer and uses it to initialize the `Numbers` object. It should have a member function `print()` that prints the English description of the `Numbers` object. Demonstrate the class by writing a main program that asks the user to enter a number in the proper range and then prints out its English description.

2. Day of the Year

Assuming that a year has 365 days, write a class named `DayOfYear` that takes an integer representing a day of the year and translates it to a string consisting of the month followed by day of the month. For example,

Day 2 would be *January 2*

Day 32 would be *February 1*

Day 365 would be *December 31*.

The constructor for the class should take as parameter an integer representing the day of the year, and the class should have a member function `print()` that prints the day in the month-day format. The class should have an integer member variable to represent the day and should have static member variables of type `string` to assist in the translation from the integer format to the month–day format.

Test your class by inputting various integers representing days and printing out their representation in the month–day format.

3. Day of the Year Modification

Modify the `DayOfYear` class, written in an earlier Programming Challenge, to add a constructor that takes two parameters: a string representing a month and an integer in the range 0 through 31 representing the day of the month. The constructor should then initialize the integer member of the class to represent the day specified by the month and day of month parameters. The constructor should terminate the program with an appropriate error message if the number entered for a day is outside the range of days for the month given.

Add the following overloaded operators:

++ prefix and postfix increment operators. These operators should modify the `DayOfYear` object so that it represents the next day. If the day is already the end of the year, the new value of the object will represent the first day of the year.

-- prefix and postfix decrement operators. These operators should modify the `DayOfYear` object so that it represents the previous day. If the day is already the first day of the year, the new value of the object will represent the last day of the year.

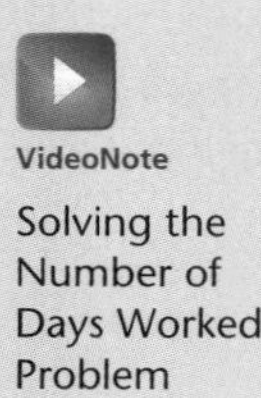

Solving the Number of Days Worked Problem

4. Number of Days Worked

Design a class called `NumDays`. The class's purpose is to store a value that represents a number of work hours and convert it to a number of days. For example, 8 hours would be converted to 1 day, 12 hours would be converted to 1.5 days, and 18 hours would be converted to 2.25 days. The class should have a constructor that accepts a number of hours, as well as member functions for storing and retrieving the hours and days. The class should also have the following overloaded operators:

- *The addition operator* `+`. The number of hours in the sum of two objects is the sum of the number of hours in the individual objects.
- *The subtraction operator* `-`. The number of hours in the difference of two objects X and Y is the number of hours in X minus the number of hours in Y.
- *Prefix and postfix increment operators* `++`. The number of hours in an object is incremented by 1.
- *Prefix and postfix decrement operators* `--`. The number of hours in an object is decremented by 1.

5. Palindrome Testing

A palindrome is a string that reads the same backward as forward. For example, the words *mom*, *dad*, *madam* and *radar* are all palindromes. Write a class `Pstring` that is derived from the STL `string` class. The `Pstring` class adds a member function

```
bool isPalindrome( )
```

that determines whether the string is a palindrome. Include a constructor that takes an STL `string` object as parameter and passes it to the `string` base class constructor. Test your class by having a main program that asks the user to enter a string. The program uses the string to initialize a `Pstring` object and then calls `isPalindrome()` to determine whether the string entered is a palindrome.

You may find it useful to use the subscript operator `[]` of the string class: if `str` is a string object and `k` is an integer, then `str[k]` returns the character at position `k` in the string.

6. String Encryption

Write a class `EncryptableString` that is derived from the STL `string` class. The `Encryptable` string class adds a member function

```
void encrypt( )
```

That encrypts the string contained in the object by replacing each letter with its successor in the ASCII ordering. For example, the string *baa* would be encrypted to *cbb*. Assume that all characters that are part of an `EncryptableString` object are letters `a`, .., `z` and `A`, .., `Z`, and that the successor of `z` is `a` and the successor of `Z` is `A`. Test your class with a program that asks the user to enter strings that are then encrypted and printed.

7. Corporate Sales

A corporation has six divisions, each responsible for sales to different geographic locations. Design a `DivSales` class that keeps sales data for a division, with the following members:

- An array with four elements for holding four quarters of sales figures for the division
- A private static variable for holding the total corporate sales for all divisions for the entire year.

- A member function that takes four arguments, each assumed to be the sales for a quarter. The value of the arguments should be copied into the array that holds the sales data. The total of the four arguments should be added to the static variable that holds the total yearly corporate sales.
- A function that takes an integer argument within the range of 0 to 3. The argument is to be used as a subscript into the division quarterly sales array. The function should return the value of the array element with that subscript.

Write a program that creates an array of six `DivSales` objects. The program should ask the user to enter the sales for four quarters for each division. After the data is entered, the program should display a table showing the division sales for each quarter. The program should then display the total corporate sales for the year.

8. Rational Arithmetic I

A *rational number* is a quotient of two integers. For example, 12/5, 12/–4, –3/4, and 4/6 are all rational numbers. A rational number is said to be in *reduced form* if its denominator is positive and its numerator and denominator have no common divisor other than 1. For example, the reduced forms of the rational numbers given above are 12/5, –3/1, –3/4, and 2/3.

Write a class called `Rational` with a constructor `Rational(int, int)` that takes two integers, a numerator and a denominator, and stores those two values in reduced form in corresponding private members. The class should have a private member function `void reduce()` that is used to accomplish the transformation to reduced form. The class should have an overloaded insertion operator << that will be used for output of objects of the class.

9. Rational Arithmetic II

Modify the class `Rational` of Programming Challenge 8 to add overloaded operators +, -, *, and / to be used for addition, subtraction, multiplication, and division. Test the class by reading and processing from the keyboard (or from a file) a series of rational expressions such as

```
2 / 3 + 2 / 8
2 / 3 * – 2 / 8
2 / 3 – 2/ 8
2 / 3 / 2 / 8
```

To facilitate parsing of the input, you may assume that numbers and arithmetic operators are separated by whitespace.

10. HTML Table of Names and Scores

Write a class whose constructor takes a vector of `Student` objects, where the each `Student` has a name of type `string` and a score of type `int`. The class internally stores the data passed to it in its constructor. The class should have an overloaded output operator that outputs its data in the form of an HTML table. Make up suitable input and use it to test your class.

CHAPTER 12

More on C-Strings and the string Class

TOPICS

12.1 C-Strings

CONCEPT: A C-string is a sequence of characters stored in consecutive memory locations and terminated by a null character.

In C++, a C-string is a sequence of characters stored in consecutive memory locations and terminated by a null character. Recall that the null character is the character whose ASCII code is 0. In a program, the null character is usually written '\0'. It is also common to use the integer 0 or the constant `NULL` to denote the null character in a program. Thus, all of the following statements store the null character into a character variable:

```
char ch1, ch2, ch3;
ch1 = '\0';
ch2 = 0;
ch3 = NULL;
```

Because an array is a sequence of consecutive memory locations that store values of the same type, a C-string is really a null-terminated array of characters. C-strings can appear in a program in one of three forms:

- "Hard-coded" string literals
- Programmer-defined arrays of character
- Pointers to character

Regardless of which one of the three forms a C-string appears in a program, a C-string is always a null-terminated array of characters and is represented in the program by a pointer to the first character in the array. In other words, the type of a C-string is

```
char *
```

that is, the type of a C-string is *pointer to char.*

String Literals

String literals, also called *string constants*, are written directly into the program as a sequence of characters enclosed in double quotes: For example,

```
"What is your name?"
"Bailey"
```

are both string literals.

When the compiler encounters a string literal such as `"Bailey"`, it allocates an array of seven characters, stores the six characters of `"Bailey"` in the first six entries of the array, and then stores the null character in the last entry, as shown in Figure 12-1. The compiler then treats the address of the first character of the array (which has type `char *`) as the value of the string literal.

Figure 12-1

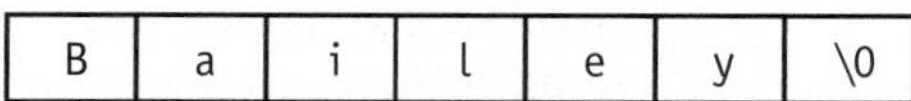

Program 12-1 illustrates the fact that a string literal is regarded by the compiler as a value of type `const char *`. The key word `const` indicates that the compiler does not expect the programmer to alter the contents of the string literal.

Program 12-1

```
//This program demonstrates that string literals
//are pointers to char.
#include <iostream>
using namespace std;

int main()
{
```

(program continues)

Program 12-1 *(continued)*

```
    // Define variables that are pointers to char
    const char *p, *q;

    // Assign string literals to the pointers to char
    p = "Hello ";
    q = "Bailey";

    // Print the pointers as C-strings!
    cout << p << q << endl;

    // Print the pointers as C-strings and as addresses
    cout << p  << " is stored at " << int(p) << endl;
    cout << q  << " is stored at " << int(q) << endl;

    // A string literal can be treated as a pointer!
    cout << "String literal stored at " << int("literal");
    return 0;
}
```

Program Output

```
Hello Bailey
Hello is stored at 4206692
Bailey is stored at 4206699
String literal stored at 4206721
```

The first two assignments of Program 12-1 show that string literals are pointers to `char` by assigning them to variables of type `char *`. The pointers `p` and `q` then hold the addresses of the two string literals. By casting the pointers to `int`, we can see where in memory the string literals are stored. Notice that in this case, the compiler has stored all string literals in the program in consecutive memory locations.

Programmer-Defined Arrays of Character

String literals can only hold C-strings that are hard-coded into the program. To have a C-string whose characters are read from the keyboard or a file, you must explicitly define an array to hold the characters of the C-string. In doing this, you should make sure that you allocate an additional entry in the array for the terminating null character. For example, if your C-string will be at most 19 characters long, you will need to allocate an array of 20 characters, as in

```
const int SIZE = 20;
char company[SIZE];
```

As in the case of literals, the compiler will represent the C-string by the address of the first character of the string, in this case, the array identifier. Recall from Chapter 8 that an array identifier without the brackets is interpreted by the compiler to be the address of the first entry of the array.

A C-string defined as an array can be given its value by initializing it with a string literal, by reading characters into it from the keyboard or a file, or by copying characters into the array one character at a time. Here are some examples of initialization:

```
const int SIZE = 20;
char company[SIZE] = “Robotic Systems, inc.”;
char corporation[] = “C. K. Graphics”;
```

When initializing an array with a string literal in this manner, the size of the array in the array definition is optional. If not specified, the compiler will set the size to one more than the number of characters in the initializing literal string (thus allowing room for the null terminator).

As described in Chapter 3, C-strings defined as arrays can be read and written using the various objects, operators, and member functions of the input and output stream classes. A C-string stored as a programmer-defined array can be processed using standard subscript notation. Program 12-2 is an example. It outputs a string one character at a time, and stops when it finds the null terminator. It uses the `getline` member function, covered in Chapter 3, to read the string to be output.

Program 12-2

```
// This program cycles through a character array, displaying
// each element until a null terminator is encountered.
#include <iostream>
using namespace std;

int main()
{
   const int LENGTH = 80;    // Maximum length for string
   char line[LENGTH];        // Array of char

   // Read a string into the character array
   cout  << "Enter a sentence of no more than "
         <<  LENGTH-1 << " characters:\n";
   cin.getline(line, LENGTH);
   cout  << "The sentence you entered is:\n";

   // Loop through the array printing each character
   for(int index = 0; line[index] != '\0'; index++)
   {
      cout << line[index];
   }
   return 0;
}
```

Program Output with Example Input Shown in Bold

```
Enter a sentence of no more than 79 characters:
C++ is challenging but fun![Enter]
The sentence you entered is:
C++ is challenging but fun!
```

(In the printed output, the line "C++ is challenging but fun![Enter]" is the example input shown in bold.)

Pointers to `char`

As we have seen, C-strings can be represented as string literals or as arrays of characters. Both of these methods allocate an array and then use the address of the array as a pointer to `char` to actually represent the string. The difference between the two is that in the first case, the array used to store the string is allocated implicitly by the compiler, whereas in the second, the array is explicitly allocated by the programmer.

The third method of representing a C-string uses a pointer to `char` to point to a C-string whose storage has already been allocated by one of the other two methods. Here are some examples of using C-strings in this way:

```
char name[] = "John Q. Public";
char *p;
p = name;                 // Point to an existing C-string
cout << p << endl;        // Print
p = "Jane Doe";           // Point to another C-string
cout << p << endl;        // Print
```

A major advantage in using a pointer variable to represent a C-string is the ability to make the pointer point to different C-strings.

Another way to use a pointer to a `char` as a C-string is to define the pointer and then set it to point to dynamically allocated storage returned by the `new` operator. This is illustrated in Program 12-3.

Program 12-3

```
// This program illustrates dynamic allocation
// of storage for C-strings.
#include <iostream>
using namespace std;

int main()
{
   const int NAME_LENGTH = 50;  // Maximum length
   char *pname;                 // Address of array

   // Allocate the array
   pname = new char[NAME_LENGTH];

   // Read a string
   cout << "Enter your name: ";
   cin.getline(pname, NAME_LENGTH);

   // Display the string
   cout << "Hello " << pname;
   return 0;
}
```

Program Output with Example Input Shown in Bold

```
Enter your name: George[Enter]
Hello George
```

A common mistake when using pointers to char as C-strings is using the pointer when it does not point to a properly allocated C-string. For example, the code

```
char *pname;
cout << "Enter your name: ";
cin  >> pname;
```

is erroneous because the program tries to read a string into the memory location pointed to by pname, when pname has not been properly initialized.

12.2 Library Functions for Working with C-Strings

CONCEPT: The C++ library provides many functions for working with C-strings.

The C++ library provides many functions that can be used to work with C-strings. There are functions for determining the length of a string, for concatenating two strings, for comparing two strings, and for searching for the occurrence of one string within another. You must include the cstring header file to use these functions.

The strlen Function

The strlen function is passed a C-string as its argument and returns the length of the string. This is the number of characters up to, but not including, the null terminator. For example, in the code segment

```
char str[] = "Hello";
int length = strlen(str);
```

the variable length will have the number 5 stored in it.

The length of a string should not be confused with the size of the array holding it. Remember, the only information passed to strlen is the beginning of the C-string. It doesn't know where the array ends, so it looks for the null terminator to indicate the end of the string.

Passing C-String Arguments

Because C-strings are pointers to char, C-string handling functions take parameters that are arrays of char, or equivalently, pointers to char. The C-string can be passed to the function in any one of the three forms that a C-string can take:

- A string literal
- The name of an array that stores the C-string
- A pointer variable holding the address of the C-string

The strcat Function

Another example of a C-string handling function is strcat. The strcat function takes two strings as parameters and concatenates them, returning a single string that consists of all the characters of the first string followed by the characters of the second string. Here is an example of its use:

```
const int SIZE = 13;
char string1[SIZE] = "Hello ";
char string2[] = "World!";
cout << string1 << endl;
cout << string2 << endl;
strcat(string1, string2);
cout << string1 << endl;
```

These statements will produce the following output:

```
Hello
World!
Hello World!
```

The `strcat` function copies the contents of `string2` to the end of `string1`. In this example, `string1` contains the string "Hello " before the call to `strcat`. After the call, it contains the string "Hello World!". Figure 12-2 shows the contents of both arrays before and after the function call.

Figure 12-2

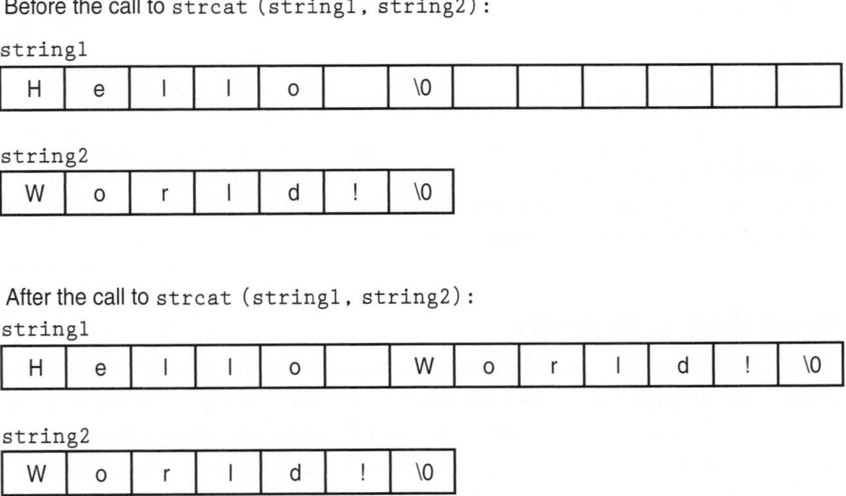

Notice the last character in `string1` (before the null terminator) is a space. The `strcat` function doesn't insert a space, so it's the programmer's responsibility to make sure one is already there, if needed. It's also the programmer's responsibility to make sure the array holding `string1` is large enough to hold `string1` plus `string2` plus a null terminator. Here is a program segment that uses the `sizeof` operator to test an array's size before `strcat` is called:

```
if (sizeof(string1) >= (strlen(string1) + strlen(string2) + 1))
    strcat(string1, string2);
else
    cout << "String1 is not large enough for both strings.\n";
```

WARNING! If the array holding the first string isn't large enough to hold both strings, `strcat` will overflow the boundaries of the array.

The `strcpy` Function

Recall from Chapter 8 that one array cannot be assigned to another with the = operator. Each individual element must be assigned, usually inside a loop. The `strcpy` function, which you have already encountered in Chapter 3, can be used to copy one string to another. Here is an example of its use:

```
const int SIZE = 20;
char name[SIZE];
strcpy(name, "Albert Einstein");
```

The `strcpy` function's arguments are both C-strings. The second C-string is copied to the address specified by the first C-string argument.

If anything is already stored in the location referenced by the first argument, it is overwritten, as shown in the following program segment:

```
char string1[] = "Hello ";
cout << string1 << endl;
strcpy(string1, "World!");
cout << string1;
```

Here is the output:

```
Hello
World!
```

WARNING! Being true to C++'s nature, `strcpy` performs no bounds checking. The array specified by the first argument will be overflowed if it isn't large enough to hold the string specified by the second argument.

Comparing C-Strings

The assignment and relational operators work with the C++ `string` class because they have been overloaded to work with that class. However, just as the assignment operator cannot be used to assign to C-strings, the relational operators <=, <, >, >=, `!=`, and `==` cannot be used to compare C-strings. This is because when used with C-strings, these operators compare the addresses at which the C-strings are stored instead of comparing the actual sequence of characters that comprise the C-strings. Program 12-4 shows the incorrect result of trying to compare C-strings using the equality operator.

Program 12-4

```
// This program illustrates that you cannot compare
// C-strings with relational operators. Although it
// appears to test the strings for equality, that is
// not what happens.
#include <iostream>
using namespace std;

```

(program continues)

Program 12-4 *(continued)*

```
int main()
{
   // Two arrays for holding two strings
   const int LENGTH = 40;
   char firstString[LENGTH], secondString[LENGTH];

   // Read two strings
   cout << "Enter a string: ";
   cin.getline(firstString, LENGTH);
   cout << "Enter another string: ";
   cin.getline(secondString, LENGTH);

   // Attempt to compare the two strings using ==
   if    (firstString == secondString)
         cout << "You entered the same string twice.\n";
   else
         cout << "The strings are not the same.\n";

   return 0;
}
```

Program Output with Example Input Shown in Bold

```
Enter a string: Alfonso[Enter]
Enter another string: Alfonso[Enter]
The strings are not the same.
```

Although two identical strings may be entered, Program 12-4 will always report that they are not equal. This is because the expression

```
firstString == secondString
```

used in the `if` statement compares the memory addresses of the two arrays instead of comparing the strings of characters stored at those addresses. Because these addresses are different, the comparison yields a result of false. In fact, in C++, even the comparison

```
"abc" == "abc"
```

will usually yield a result of false. This is because most compilers do not check to see if a string literal has been encountered before and will store the two strings at different memory addresses. The compiler will then compare the two different addresses, giving a value of false for the result.

The `strcmp` Function

To properly compare C-strings, you should use the library function `strcmp`. This function takes two C-strings as parameters and returns an integer that indicates how the two strings compare to each other. Its prototype,

```
int strcmp(char *string1, char *string2);
```

indicates that the function takes two C-strings as parameters (recall that `char *` is the type of C-string) and returns an integer result. The value of the result is set according to the following convention:

- The result is *zero* if the two strings are *equal* on a character by character basis
- The result is *negative* if `string1` comes *before* `string2` in alphabetical order
- The result is *positive* if `string1` comes *after* `string2` in alphabetical order

Here is an example of the use of `strcmp` to determine if two strings are equal:

```
if (strcmp(string1, string2) == 0)
    cout << "The strings are equal";
else
    cout << "The strings are not equal";
```

Program 12-4, which incorrectly tested two C-strings with a relational operator, can be correctly rewritten with the `strcmp` function, as shown in Program 12-5.

Program 12-5

```
// This program correctly tests two C-strings for
// equality with the strcmp function.
#include <iostream>
#include <cstring>
using namespace std;

int main()
{
   // Two arrays for two strings
   const int LENGTH = 40;
   char firstString[LENGTH], secondString[LENGTH];

   // Read two strings
   cout << "Enter a string: ";
   cin.getline(firstString, LENGTH);
   cout << "Enter another string: ";
   cin.getline(secondString, LENGTH);

   // Compare the strings for equality with strcmp
   if  (strcmp(firstString, secondString) == 0)
       cout << "You entered the same string twice.\n";
   else
       cout << "The strings are not the same.\n";

   return 0;
}
```

Program Output with Example Input Shown in Bold

Enter a string: **Alfonso[Enter]**
Enter another string: **Alfonso[Enter]**
You entered the same string twice.

The function `strcmp` is case sensitive when it compares strings. If the user enters "Dog" and "dog" in Program 12-5, it will report they are not the same. Some compilers provide nonstandard versions of strcmp that perform case-insensitive comparisons. Such functions work identically to strcmp except the case of the characters is ignored.

Program 12-6 is a more practical example of how strcmp can be used. It asks the user to enter the number of the computer part they wish to purchase. The part number contains digits, letters, and a hyphen, so it must be stored as a string. Once the user enters the part number, the program displays its price.

Program 12-6

```
// This program uses strcmp to compare the string entered
// by the user with the valid part numbers.
#include <iostream>
#include <cstring>
#include <iomanip>
using namespace std;

int main()
{
   // Price of items
   const double A_PRICE = 49.0, B_PRICE = 69.95;

   // Character array for part number
   const int PART_LENGTH = 8;
   char partNum[PART_LENGTH];

   // Instruct the user to enter a part number
   cout << "The computer part numbers are:\n";
   cout << "\tBlu-ray Disk Drive, part number S147-29A\n";
   cout << "\tWireless Router, part number S147-29B\n";
   cout << "Enter the part number of the item you\n";
   cout << "wish to purchase: ";

   // Read a part number of at most 8 characters
   cin >> setw(9);
   cin >> partNum;

   // Determine what user entered using strcmp
   // and print its price
   cout << showpoint << fixed << setprecision(2);
   if (strcmp(partNum, "S147-29A") == 0)
      cout << "The price is $" << A_PRICE << endl;
   else if (strcmp(partNum, "S147-29B") == 0)
      cout << "The price is $" << B_PRICE << endl;
   else
      cout << partNum << " is not a valid part number.\n";

   return 0;
}
```

(program continues)

Program 12-6 *(continued)*

Program Output with Example Input Shown in Bold

```
The computer part numbers are:
     Blu-ray Disk Drive, part number S147-29A
     Wireless Router, part number S147-29B
Enter the part number of the item you
wish to purchase: S147-29A[Enter]
The price is $49.00
```

Using ! with `strcmp`

Some programmers prefer to use the logical NOT operator with `strcmp` when testing strings for equality. Since 0 is considered logically `false`, the `!` operator converts that value to `true`. The expression `!strcmp(string1, string2)` will return `true` when both strings are the same and `false` when they are different. The two following statements have exactly the same effect when executed.

```
if(strcmp(str1, str2) == 0) cout << "equal";
if(!strcmp(str1, str2)) cout << "equal";
```

Sorting Strings

Because `strcmp` returns information on the relative alphabetic order of the two strings being compared, it can be used to sort lists of C-strings. Program 12-7 is a simple illustration of this: it asks the user to enter two names, which are then printed in ascending alphabetic order.

Program 12-7

```
// This program uses the return value of strcmp to
// alphabetically order two strings entered by the user.
#include <iostream>
#include <cstring>
using namespace std;

int main()
{
   // Two arrays to hold two strings
   const int NAME_LENGTH = 30;
   char name1[NAME_LENGTH], name2[NAME_LENGTH];

   // Read two strings
   cout << "Enter a name (last name first): ";
   cin.getline(name1, NAME_LENGTH);
   cout << "Enter another name: ";
   cin.getline(name2, NAME_LENGTH);

```

(program continues)

Program 12-7 *(continued)*

```
    // Print the two strings in alphabetical order
    cout << "Here are the names sorted alphabetically:\n";
    if  (strcmp(name1, name2) < 0)
        cout << name1 << endl << name2 << endl;
    else if (strcmp(name1, name2) > 0)
        cout << name2 << endl << name1 << endl;
    else
        cout << "You entered the same name twice!\n";

    return 0;
}
```

Program Output with Example Input Shown in Bold

```
Enter a name (last name first): **Smith, Richard[Enter]**
Enter another name: **Jones, John[Enter]**
Here are the names sorted alphabetically:
Jones, John
Smith, Richard
```

Table 12-1 summarizes the string-handling functions discussed here, as well as others. (All the functions listed require the `cstring` header file.)

Table 12-1 (See your C++ reference manual for more information on these functions.)

Function	Description
`strlen`	Accepts a C-string as an argument. Returns the length of the C-string (not including the null terminator). *Example Usage:* `len = strlen(name);`
`strcat`	Accepts two C-strings as arguments. The function appends the contents of the second string to the first C-string. (The first string is altered, the second string is left unchanged.) *Example Usage:* `strcat(string1, string2);`
`strcpy`	Accepts two C-strings as arguments. The function copies the second C-string to the first C-string. The second C-string is left unchanged. *Example Usage:* `strcpy(string1, string2);`
`strncpy`	Copies at most `n` characters of `string2` to `string1`. If `string2` has fewer than `n` characters, then `string1` is padded with '\0' characters until a total of `n` characters have been written to it. If `string2` has `n` or more characters, then the first `n` characters are copied and `string1` is not null-terminated. *Example Usage:* `strncpy(string1, string2, n);`
`strcmp`	Accepts two C-string arguments. If `string1` and `string2` are the same, this function returns 0. If `string2` is alphabetically greater than `string1`, it returns a negative number. If `string2` is alphabetically less than `string1`, it returns a positive number. *Example Usage:* `if (strcmp(string1, string2))`
`strstr`	Searches for the first occurrence of `string2` in `string1`. If an occurrence of `string2` is found, the function returns a pointer to it. Otherwise, it returns a `NULL` pointer (address 0). *Example Usage:* `cout << strstr(string1, string2);`

The `strstr` Function

The last function in Table 12-1 is `strstr`, which searches for a string inside of a string. For instance, it could be used to search for the string "seven" inside the larger string "Four score and seven years ago." The function's first argument is the string to be searched, and the second argument is the string to look for. If the function finds the second string inside the first, it returns the address of the occurrence of the second string within the first string. Otherwise it returns the address 0, or the `NULL` address. Here is an example:

```
char array[] = "Four score and seven years ago";
char *strPtr;
cout << array << endl;
strPtr = strstr(array, "seven");  // search for "seven"
cout << strPtr << endl;
```

In the preceding program segment `strstr` will locate the string "seven" inside the string "Four score and seven years ago." It will return the address of the first character in "seven", which will be stored in the pointer variable `strPtr`. If run as part of a complete program, the segment will display the following:

```
Four score and seven years ago
seven years ago
```

The `strstr` function can be useful in any program that must locate information inside one or more strings. Program 12-8, for example, stores a database of product numbers and descriptions in an array of C-strings. It allows the user to look up a product description by entering all or part of its product number.

Program 12-8

```
// This program uses the strstr function to search an array
// of strings for a name.
#include <iostream>
#include <cstring> // For strstr
using namespace std;

int main()
{
   const int   N_ITEMS = 5,    // Maximum number of items
               S_LENGTH = 31; // maximum length of description

   // Array of product descriptions
   char prods[N_ITEMS][S_LENGTH] = {"TV327  31 inch Television",
                                    "CD257  CD Player",
                                    "TA677  Answering Machine",
                                    "CS109  Car Stereo",
                                    "PC955  Personal Computer"};
```

(program continues)

Program 12-8 *(continued)*

```
20     char lookUp[S_LENGTH];  // For user input
21     char *strPtr = NULL;    // Result from strstr
22 
23     // Get user input
24     cout << "\tProduct Database\n\n";
25     cout << "Enter a product number to search for: ";
26     cin.getline(lookUp, S_LENGTH);
27 
28     // Search for the string
29     int index = 0;
30     while(index < N_ITEMS)
31     {
32        strPtr = strstr(prods[index], lookUp);
33        if (strPtr != NULL)
34           break;
35        index++;
36     }
37 
38     // Output the result of the search
39     if (strPtr == NULL)
40        cout << "No matching product was found.\n";
41     else
42        cout << prods[index] << endl;
43 
44     return 0;
45 }
```

Program Output with Example Input Shown in Bold

```
        Product Database

Enter a product to search for: CD257[Enter]
CD257   CD Player
```

Program Output with Other Example Input Shown in Bold

```
        Product Database

Enter a product to search for: CS[Enter]
CS109   Car Stereo
```

Program Output with Other Example Input Shown in Bold

```
        Product Database

Enter a product to search for: AB[Enter]
No matching product was found.
```

In Program 12–8, the loop in lines 29–36 cycles through each C-string in the array calling the following statement:

```
strPtr = strstr(prods[index], lookUp);
```

The `strstr` function searches the string referenced by `prods[index]` for the name entered by the user, which is stored in `lookUp`. If `lookUp` is found inside `prods[index]`, the function returns its address. In that case, the following `if` statement causes the loop to terminate:

```
if (strPtr != NULL)
       break;
```

Outside the loop, the following `if-else` statement determines if the string entered by the user was found in the array. If not, it informs the user that no matching product was found. Otherwise, the product number and description are displayed:

```
if (strPtr == NULL)
   cout << "No matching product was found.\n";
else
   cout << prods[index] << endl;
```

Checkpoint

12.1 Write a short description of each of the following functions:
A) `strlen`
B) `strcat`
C) `strcpy`
D) `strncpy`
E) `strcmp`
F) `strstr`

12.2 What will the following program segment display?

```
char dog[] = "Fido";
cout << strlen(dog) << endl;
```

12.3 Assume the constant `SIZE` has value 16. What will the following program segment display?

```
char string1[SIZE] = "Have a ";
char string2[] = "nice day";
strcat(string1, string2);
cout << string1 << endl;
cout << string2 << endl;
```

12.4 Write a statement that will copy the string "Beethoven" to the array `composer`.

12.5 When complete, the following program skeleton will search for the string "`Windy`" in the array `place`. If `place` contains "`Windy`" the program will display the message "`Windy found.`" Otherwise it will display "`Windy not found.`"

```
#include <iostream>
// include any other necessary header files
int main()
{
   char place[] = "The Windy City";
   // Complete the program. It should search the array place
   // for the string "Windy" and display the message "Windy
   // found" if it finds the string. Otherwise, it should
   // display the message "Windy not found."
}
```

12.6 Indicate whether the following `strcmp` function calls will return 0, a negative number, or a positive number. Refer to the ASCII table in Appendix A if necessary.

A) `strcmp("ABC", "abc");`
B) `strcmp("Jill", "Jim");`
C) `strcmp("123", "ABC");`
D) `strcmp("Sammy", "Sally");`

12.7 Complete the `if` statements in the following program skeleton.

```
#include <iostream>
using namespace std;

int main()
{
   const int LENGTH = 20;
   char iceCream[LENGTH];
   cout << "What flavor of ice cream do you like best? ";
   cout << "Chocolate, Vanilla, or Pralines and Pecan? ";
   cin.getline(iceCream, LENGTH);
   cout << "Here is the number of fat grams for a half ";
   cout << "cup serving:\n";
   //
   // Finish the following if-else statement
   // so the program will select the ice cream entered
   // by the user
   //
   if (/* insert your code here */)
      cout << "Chocolate: 9 fat grams.\n";
   else if (/* insert your code here */)
      cout << "Vanilla: 10 fat grams.\n";
   else if (/* insert your code here */)
      cout << "Pralines and Pecan: 14 fat grams.\n";
   else
      cout << "That's not one of our flavors!\n";
   return 0;
}
```

12.3 Conversions Between Numbers and Strings

CONCEPT: The C++ libraries provide classes that can be used to convert a string representation of a number to numeric form and vice versa.

There is a difference between a number that is stored as a string and one stored as a numeric value. The string "2679" isn't a number: it is a sequence of ASCII codes of the characters that form the individual digits of the number 2679. Because the string "2679" is not a number, the compiler will not allow arithmetic operations such as addition, multiplication, and division to be applied to it. Strings that represent numbers must first be converted to numeric form before they can be used with arithmetic operators.

String representations of numbers arise naturally in computing, most often during input and output of numbers. When a user enters a number at a keyboard, the number is entered in its string form as a sequence of characters (digits) typed by the user. In C++, such a number is usually read via the stream extraction operator >>. This operator automatically performs conversions as needed before storing into a variable of numeric type. During output, the reverse conversion from numeric to string is performed by the stream output operator <<.

There are times when a string such as "2679" that is already stored in memory as a C-string or string object needs to be converted to numeric form. There are also times when a number already stored in numeric form in memory needs to be converted into its string representation. C++ has two classes, `ostringstream` and `istringstream`, that can be used to perform string/numeric conversions. The class `ostringstream` is a subclass of `ostream` (the class that `cout` belongs to) and uses the stream insertion operator << to convert numeric values to string. Objects of type `ostringstream` work the same way that `cout` and file objects do, except that instead of writing to the screen or to a file, `ostringstream` writes its data to a string object contained inside it. Each time you use << on the `ostringstream` object, it performs any numeric-to-string conversions necessary and appends the result to the end of its string. In addition to supporting all the member functions and operators of the `ostream` class, `ostringstream` objects support the `str` member functions shown in Table 12-2.

VideoNote
Converting Strings to Numbers

The `istringstream` class derives from `istream`. It contains a string object inside it that functions as an input stream that can be "read" from. The input stream can be set by the `istringstream` constructor when the object is created, or can be set by calling the `str(string s)` function after the object has been created. The stream extraction operator >> reads from the enclosed string and converts from string to numeric where necessary. Member functions of `istringstream` are also listed in Table 12-2. You must include the `sstream` header file in your programs to use these classes.

Table 12-2 Member Functions of `ostringstream` and `istringstream` Classes

Member Function	Description
`istringstream(string s)`	Constructor for `istringstream`: sets the initial value of the input stream for the object. Example: `istringstream istr("50 64 28");`
`ostringstream(string s)`	Constructor for `ostringstream`: sets the initial value of the output stream for the object. Example: `ostringstream ostr("50 64 28");`
`string str()`	Returns the string contained in the `ostringstream` or `istringstream` object. Example: `string is = istr.str();` `string os = ostr.str();`
`void str(string &s)`	Sets the string that serves as the input or output stream for the object. Example: `ostr.str("50 64 28");` `istr.str("50 64 28");`

Program 12-9 demonstrates the use of these classes.

Program 12-9

```
// This program illustrates the use of sstream objects.
#include <sstream>
#include <iostream>
#include <string>
using namespace std;

int main()
{
    string str = "John  20 50";          // String to read from
    const char *cstr = "Amy 30 42";      // Cstring to read from
    istringstream istr1(str);            // istr1 will read from str
    istringstream istr2;                 // istr2 will read from cstr
    ostringstream ostr;                  // The ostringstream object

    string name;
    int score1, score2, average_score;

    // Read name and scores and compute average then write to ostr
    istr1 >> name >> score1 >> score2;
    average_score = (score1 + score2)/2;
    ostr <<  name << " has average score " << average_score << "\n";

    // Set istr2 to read from the C string and repeat the above
    istr2.str(cstr);
    istr2 >> name >> score1 >> score2;
    average_score = (score1 + score2)/2;
    ostr <<  name << " has average score " << average_score << "\n";

    // Switch to hexadecimal output on ostr
    ostr << hex;

    // Write Amy's scores in hexadecimal
    ostr << name << "'s scores in hexadecimal are: " << score1
         << " and " << score2 << "\n";

    // Extract the string from ostr and print it to the screen
    cout << ostr.str();

    return 0;
}
```

Program Output

```
John has average score 35
Amy has average score 36
Amy's scores in hexadecimal are: 1e and 2a
```

Notice that these classes have the full power of `ostream` and `istream` objects, including the ability to convert numbers to string using different bases such as octal and hexadecimal. Although these classes are the preferred way to convert between numeric and string forms, you should also be aware of the C++ library functions shown in Table 12-3. These functions work on C-strings only.

Table 12-3 (See your C++ reference manual for more information on these functions.)

Function	Description
`atoi`	Accepts a C-string as an argument. The function converts the C-string to an integer and returns that value. *Example Usage:* `num = atoi("4569");`
`atol`	Accepts a C-string as an argument. The function converts the C-string to a `long` integer and returns that value. *Example Usage:* `lnum = atol("500000");`
`atof`	Accepts a C-string as an argument. The function converts the C-string to a `double` and returns that value. Use this function to convert a C-string to a `float` or `double`. *Example Usage:* `fnum = atof("3.14159");`
`itoa`	Converts an integer to a C-string. The first argument, `value`, is the integer. The result will be stored at the location pointed to by the second argument, `string`. The third argument, `base`, is an integer. It specifies the numbering system that the converted integer should be expressed in (8 = octal, 10 = decimal, 16 = hexadecimal, etc.). *Example Usage:* `itoa(value, string, base);`

The `atoi` function converts a string to an integer. It accepts a C-string argument and returns the converted integer value. Here is an example of how to use it:

```
int num;
num = atoi("1000");
```

In these statements, `atoi` converts the string "1000" into the integer 1000. Once the variable `num` is assigned this value, it can be used in mathematical operations or any task requiring a numeric value.

NOTE: The `atoi` function as well as the others discussed in this section require that the `cstdlib` header file be included.

The `atol` function works just like `atoi`, except the return value is a `long` integer. Here is an example:

```
long bigNum;
bigNum = atol("500000");
```

As expected, the `atof` function accepts a C-string argument and converts it to a `double`. The numeric `double` value is returned, as shown here:

```
double fnum;
fnum = atof("12.67");
```

NOTE: If a string that cannot be converted to a numeric value is passed to any of these functions, the function's behavior is undefined by C++. Many compilers, however, will perform the conversion process until an invalid character is encountered. For example, `atoi("123x5")` might return the integer 123. It is possible that these functions will return 0 if they cannot successfully convert their argument.

The `itoa` function is similar to `atoi`, but it works in reverse. It converts a numeric integer into a string representation of the integer. The `itoa` function accepts three arguments: the integer value to be converted, a pointer to the location in memory where the string is to be stored, and a number that represents the base of the converted value. Here is an example:

```
const int SIZE = 15;
char numArray[SIZE];
itoa(1200, numArray, 10);
cout << numArray << endl;
```

This program segment converts the integer value 1200 to a string. The string is stored in the array `numArray`. The third argument, 10, means the number should be written in decimal, or base 10 notation. The output of the `cout` statement is

```
1200
```

WARNING! As always, C++ performs no array bounds checking. Make sure the array whose address is passed to `itoa` is large enough to hold the converted number, including the null terminator.

Now let's look at Program 12-10, which uses a string-to-number conversion function, `atoi`. It allows the user to enter a series of values, or the letters Q or q to quit. The average of the numbers is then calculated and displayed.

Program 12-10

```
// This program demonstrates the strcmp and atoi functions.
#include <iostream>
#include <cstring> // For strcmp
#include <cstdlib> // For atoi
using namespace std;

int main()
{
   // Array used to read numbers in string form
   const int LENGTH = 20;
   char input[LENGTH];

   int   total = 0;  // Running total
         count = 0;  // Number of numbers read
   double average;   // Average

   // Read numbers and computer total of numbers
   cout << "This program will average a series of numbers.\n";
   cout << "Enter the first number or Q to quit: ";
   cin.getline(input, LENGTH);
   while((strcmp(input,"Q")!= 0)&&(strcmp(input,"q")!= 0))
   {
      // Keep a running total
      total += atoi(input);

      // Keep track of how many numbers are entered
      count++;

```

(program continues)

Program 12-10 *(continued)*

```
      // Are there more?
      cout << "Enter the next number or Q to quit: ";
      cin.getline(input,LENGTH);}
   }

   // Compute and print average
   if (count != 0)
   {
      average = double(total) / count;
      cout << "average: " << average << endl;
   }

   return 0;
}
```

Program Output with Example Input Shown in Bold

```
This program will average a series of numbers.
Enter the first number or Q to quit: 74[Enter]
Enter the next number or Q to quit: 98[Enter]
Enter the next number or Q to quit: 23[Enter]
Enter the next number or Q to quit: 54[Enter]
Enter the next number or Q to quit: Q[Enter]
Average: 62.25
```

Recall that `strcmp` compares two C-strings. If they are identical, it returns 0. Otherwise a nonzero value is returned. The following `while` statement uses `strcmp` to determine if the string in `input` is either “`Q`” or “`q`”.

```
while ((strcmp(input, "Q") != 0)&&(strcmp(input, "q") != 0))
```

If the user hasn't entered “`Q`” or “`q`” the program uses `atoi` to convert the string in `input` to an integer and adds its value to `total` with the following statement:

```
total += atoi(input);   // Keep a running total
```

The user is then asked for the next number. When all the numbers are entered, the user terminates the loop by entering “`Q`” or “`q`”. If one or more numbers are entered, their average is displayed.

Checkpoint

12.8 Write a short description of each of the following functions.

A) `atoi`
B) `atol`
C) `atof`
D) `itoa`

12.9 Write a statement that will convert the C-string “`10`” to an integer and store the result in the variable `num`.

12.10 Write a statement that will convert the C-string “`100000`” to a `long` and store the result in the variable `num`.

12.11 Write a statement that will convert the string "7.2389" to a `double` and store the result in the variable `num`.

12.12 Write a statement that will convert the integer 127 to a string, stored in base 10 notation in the array `value`.

12.4 Writing Your Own C-String Handling Functions

CONCEPT: You can design your own specialized functions for manipulating strings.

By being able to pass arrays as arguments, you can write your own functions for processing C-strings. For example, Program 12-11 uses a function to copy a C-string from one array to another.

Program 12-11

```
// This program uses a function to copy
// a string into an array.
#include <iostream>
using namespace std;

// Function prototype
void stringCopy(char [], const char []);

int main()
{
   // Define two arrays of char
   const int S_LENGTH = 30;
   char dest[S_LENGTH], source[S_LENGTH];

   // Read a string into a source array
   cout  << "Enter a string with no more than "
         << S_LENGTH - 1 << " characters:\n";
   cin.getline(source, S_LENGTH);

   // Copy it into a destination array and print
   stringCopy(dest, source);
   cout << "The string you entered is:\n" << dest << endl;
   return 0;
}

//**************************************************
// Definition of the stringCopy function.          *
// This function accepts two character arrays as   *
// arguments. The function assumes the two arrays  *
// contain C-strings. The contents of the second   *
// array are copied to the first array.            *
//**************************************************
```

(program continues)

Program 12-11 *(continued)*

```
void stringCopy(char destStr[], const char sourceStr[])
{
   int index = 0;

   // Copy one character at a time till we come to
   // the null terminator
   while (sourceStr[index] != '\0')
   {
      destStr[index] = sourceStr[index];
      index++;
   }
   destStr[index] = '\0';
}
```

Program Output with Example Input Shown in Bold

```
Enter a string with no more than 29 characters:
Thank goodness it's Friday![Enter]
The string you entered is:
Thank goodness it's Friday!
```

Notice the function `stringCopy` in Program 12-11 does not accept an argument indicating the size of the arrays. It simply copies the characters from the source string to the destination until it encounters a null terminator in the source string. When the null terminator is found, the loop has reached the end of the C-string. The last statement in the function assigns a null terminator (the `'\0'` character) to the end of `string2`, so it is properly terminated.

WARNING! Since the `stringCopy` function doesn't know the size of the destination array, it's the programmer's responsibility to make sure the destination array is large enough to hold the source string array.

Program 12-12 uses another C-string handling function: `nameSlice`. The program asks the user to enter his or her first and last names, separated by a space. The function searches the string for the space and replaces it with a null terminator. In effect, this cuts off the last name of the string.

Program 12-12

```
// This program uses the function nameSlice
// to "cut" off the last name of a string that
// contains the user's first and last names.
#include <iostream>
using namespace std;

void nameSlice(char []);   // Function prototype

int main()
{

// Define array of char to hold name
   const int NAME_LENGTH = 41;
```

(program continues)

Program 12-12 *(continued)*

```
   char name[NAME_LENGTH];

   // Get user's first and last names
   cout << "Enter your first and last names, separated ";
   cout << "by a space:\n";
   cin.getline(name, NAME_LENGTH);

   // Slice off the last name and print what is left
   nameSlice(name);
   cout << "Your first name is: " << name << endl;
   return 0;
}

//****************************************************
// Definition of function nameSlice. This function    *
// accepts a character array as its argument. It      *
// scans the array looking for a space. When it finds *
// one, it replaces it with a null terminator.        *
//****************************************************
void nameSlice(char userName[])
{
   // Look for the end of the first name, indicated
   // by a space or a null terminator
   int k = 0;
   while (userName[k] != ' ' && userName[k] != '\0')
      k++;

   // Insert null terminator
   if (userName[k] == ' ')
      userName[k] = '\0';
}
```

Program Output with Example Input Shown in Bold

```
Enter your first and last names, separated by a space:
Jimmy Jones[Enter]
Your first name is: Jimmy
```

The following loop in `nameSlice` starts at the first character in the array and scans the string, searching for either a space or a null terminator:

```
while (userName[k] != ' ' && userName[k] != '\0')
   k++;
```

If the character in `userName[k]` isn't a space or the null terminator, `k` is incremented, and the next character is examined. With the example input "`Jimmy Jones`," the loop finds the space separating "`Jimmy`" and "`Jones`" at `userName[5]`. When the loop stops, `k` is set to 5. This is illustrated in Figure 12-3.

NOTE: The loop stops if it encounters a null terminator so it will not go beyond the boundary of the array if the user didn't enter a space.

Once the loop has finished, `userName[k]` will either contain a space or a null terminator. If it contains a space, the following `if` statement, whose action is illustrated in Figure 12-4, replaces it with a null terminator:

```
if (userName[k] == ' ')
   userName[k] = '\0';
```

The new null terminator now becomes the end of the string.

Figure 12-3

The loop stops when `k` reaches 5 because `userName[5]` contains a space

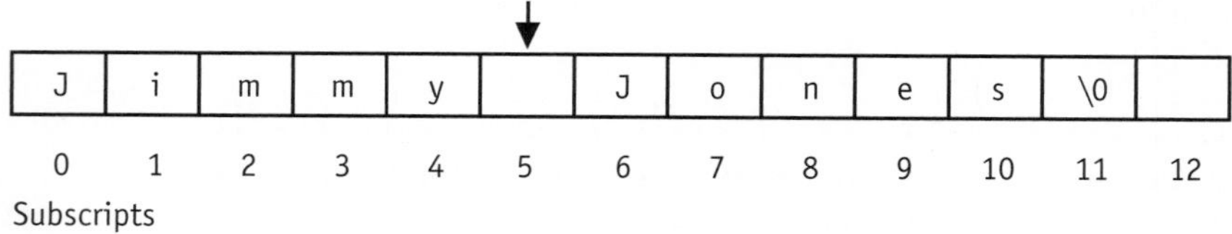

Figure 12-4

The space is replaced with a null terminator. This now becomes the end of the string.

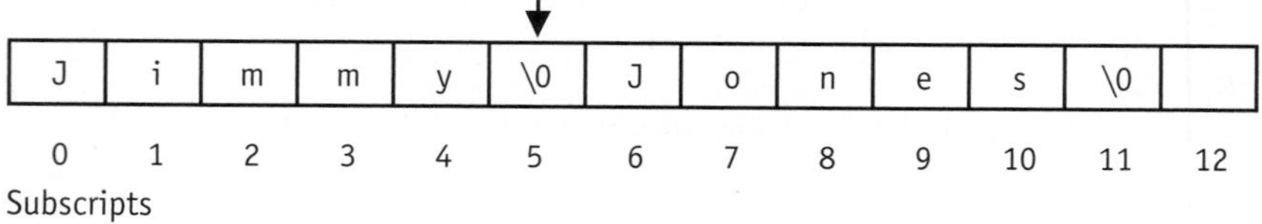

Using Pointers to Pass C-String Arguments

Pointers are extremely useful for writing functions that process C-strings. If the starting address of a string is passed into a pointer parameter variable, it can be assumed that all the characters, from that address up to the byte that holds the null terminator are part of the string. (It isn't necessary to know the length of the array that holds the string.)

Program 12-13 demonstrates a function, `countChars`, that uses a pointer to count the number of times a specific character appears in a C-string.

Program 12-13

```
// This program demonstrates a function, countChars,
// that counts the number of times a specific
// character appears in a string.
#include <iostream>
using namespace std;

// Function prototype
int countChars(const char *, char);

```

(program continues)

Program 12-13 *(continued)*

```
int main()
{
   // Define array to hold the string
   const int S_LENGTH = 51;
   char userString[S_LENGTH];

   char letter;   // User input

   // Read the string and the letter to count
   cout  << "Enter a string (up to "
         << S_LENGTH-1 << " characters): ";
   cin.getline(userString, S_LENGTH);
   cout << "Enter a character and I will tell you how many\n;
   cout << "times it appears in the string: ";
   cin >> letter;

   // Output the results of the letter count
   cout << letter << " appears ";
   cout << countChars(userString, letter) << " times.\n";
   return 0;
}

//*****************************************************
// Definition of countChars. The parameter strPtr is    *
// a pointer that points to a string. The parameter     *
// ch is a character that the function searches for     *
// in the string. The function returns the number of    *
// times the character appears in the string.           *
//*****************************************************
int countChars(const char *strPtr, char ch)
{
   int count = 0;
   while (*strPtr != '\0')
   {
      if (*strPtr == ch)
         count++;
      strPtr++;
   }
   return count;
}
```

Program Output with Example Input Shown in Bold

```
Enter a string (up to 50 characters): Starting Out With C++[Enter]
Enter a character and I will tell you how many
times it appears in the string: t[Enter]
t appears 4 times.
```

In the function `countChars`, `strPtr` points to the C-string that is to be searched and `ch` contains the character to look for. The `while` loop repeats as long the character `strPtr` points to is not the null terminator:

```
while (*strPtr != '\0')
```

Inside the loop, the following `if` statement compares the character that `strPtr` points to with the character in `ch`:

```
if (*strPtr == ch)
```

If the two are equal, the variable `count` is incremented. (`count` keeps a running total of the number of times the character appears.) The last statement in the loop is

```
strPtr++;
```

This statement increments the address in `strPtr`. This causes `strPtr` to point to the next character in the string. Then the loop starts over. When `strPtr` finally reaches the null terminator, the loop terminates and the function returns the value in `count`.

Checkpoint

12.13 What is the output of the following program?

```
#include <iostream>
using namespace std;

// Function prototype
void mess(char []);

int main()
{
   char stuff[] = "Tom Talbert Tried Trains";

   cout << stuff << endl;
   mess(stuff);
   cout << stuff << endl;
   return 0;
}

// Definition of function mess
void mess(char str[])
{
   int step = 0;

   while (str[step] != '\0')
   {
      if (str[step] == 'T')
         str[step] = 'D';
      step++;
   }
}
```

12.5 More About the C++ string Class

From an ease-of-programming point of view, the standard library `string` class offers several advantages over C-strings. As you have seen throughout this text, the `string` class has several member functions and overloaded operators. These simplify tasks, such as locating a character or string within a string, that are difficult and tedious to perform with C-strings. In this section we review some basic operations with `string`s, then discuss more of the `string` class's member functions.

Any program using the `string` class must `#include` the `string` header file. String objects may then be created using any of several constructors. Program 12-14 demonstrates two string class constructors: the default constructor, and, the convert constructor that converts a C-string into a string object.

Program 12-14

```
// This program demonstrates some C++ string class constructors.
#include <iostream>
#include <string>
using namespace std;

int main()
{
   string greeting;              // Default constructor
   string name("William Smith"); // Convert constructor

   greeting = "Hello ";
   cout << greeting << name << endl;
   return 0;
}
```

Program Output

```
Hello William Smith
```

Other examples of the use of `string` constructors are given in Table 12-4.

Table 12-4 String Constructors

Definition	Description
`string()`	Default constructor: Creates an empty string. Example: `string str();`
`string(const char *s)`	Convert constructor: creates a string object from a C-string s. Example: `string name("William Smith");`
`string(const string &s)`	Copy constructor: creates a new string from an existing string s. Example: `string name1(name);`
`string(const char *s, int n)`	Creates a string initialized to the first `n` characters of the C-string `s`.
`string(int n, char ch)`	Creates a string object by concatenating `n` copies of the character `ch`.
`string(const string &s, int p, int n)`	Creates a string by taking the substring of `s` that starts at position `p` and is `n` characters long.

Notice in Program 12-14 the use of the = operator to assign a value to the string object. The string class overloads several operators, which are described in Table 12-5.

Table 12-5 String Class Operators

Overloaded Operator	Description
>>	Extracts characters from a stream and inserts them into the string. Characters are copied until a whitespace or the end of the input is encountered.
<<	Inserts the string into a stream.
=	Assigns the string on the right to the string object on the left.
+=	Appends a copy of the string on the right to the string object on the left.
+	Returns a string that is the concatenation of the two string operands.
[ ]	Implements array-subscript notation, as in `name[x]`. A reference to the character in the `x` position is returned.
Relational Operators	Each of the relational operators are implemented: < > <= >= == !=

The string class also has several member functions. For example, the `size` function returns the length of the string. Table 12-6 lists many of the `string` class member functions and their overloaded variations. In some cases, the arguments passed to a member function may be such that the operation being requested is impossible. In those cases, the member function will signal the occurrence of an error by *throwing an exception*. Exceptions are discussed in Chapter 16.

Table 12-6 `string` Class Member Functions

Member Function Example	Description
`theString.append(str);`	Appends `str` to `theString`. The argument `str` can be a string object or character array.
`theString.append(str, p, n);`	`n` number of characters from `str`, starting at position `p`, are appended to `theString`. An exception is thrown if the substring of `str` that begins at `p` has fewer than `n` characters.
`theString.append(str, n);`	The first `n` characters of the C-string `str` are appended to `theString`.
`theString.append(n, ch);`	Appends `n` copies of character `ch` to `theString`.
`theString.assign(str);`	Assigns `str` to `theString`. The parameter `str` can be a string object or a C-string.
`theString.assign(str, p, n);`	`n` number of characters from `str`, starting at position `p`, are assigned to `theString`. An exception is thrown if the substring of `str` the begins at `p` has fewer than `n` characters.

(table continues)

Table 12-6 `string` Class Member Functions *(continued)*

Member Function Example	Description
`theString.assign(str, n);`	The first n characters of the C-string str are assigned to theString.
`theString.assign(n, ch);`	Assigns n copies of the character ch to theString.
`theString.at(p);`	Returns the character at position p in the string.
`theString.begin();`	Returns an iterator pointing to the first character in the string. (For more information on iterators, see Chapter 16.)
`theString.capacity();`	Returns the size of the storage allocated for the string.
`theString.clear();`	Clears the string by deleting all the characters stored in it.
`theString.compare(str);`	Compare theString to str in the manner of the strcmp. The str argument may be another string object, or may be a C-string.
`theString.copy(str, p, n);`	Copies the substring of length n that begins at position p of theString into the character array str. An exception is thrown if theString has fewer than n characters after the given position p.
`theString.c_str():`	Returns the C-string value of the string object.
`theString.data();`	Returns a character array containing a null terminated string, as stored in theString.
`theString.empty();`	Returns true if theString is empty.
`theString.end();`	Returns an iterator pointing to the last character of the string in theString. (For more information on iterators, see Chapter 16.)
`theString.erase(p, n);`	Erases n characters from theString, beginning at position p.
`theString.find(str, p);`	Returns the first position at or beyond position p where the string str is found in theString. The parameter str may be a string object or a C-string. If str is not found, the static member string::npos of thestring class is returned.
`theString.find(ch, p);`	Returns the first position at or beyond position p where the character ch is found in theString. Returns string::npos if the character is not found.
`theString.insert(p, str);`	Inserts a copy of str into theString, beginning at position p. The argument str may be a string object or a character array.
`theString.insert(p, n, ch);`	Inserts the character ch, n times into theString at position p.
`theString.length();`	Returns the length of the string in theString.

(table continues)

Table 12-6 `string` Class Member Functions *(continued)*

Member Function Example	Description
`theString.replace(p, n, str);`	Replaces the `n` characters in `theString` beginning at position `p` with the characters in string object `str`.
`theString.resize(n, ch);`	Changes the size of the allocation in `theString` to `n`. If `n` is less than the current size of the string, the string is truncated to `n` characters. If `n` is greater, the string is expanded and the character `ch` is appended at the end enough times to fill the new spaces.
`theString.size();`	Returns the length of the string in `theString`.
`theString.substr(p, n);`	Returns a copy of a substring. The substring is `n` characters long and begins at position `p` of `theString`.
`theString.swap(str);`	Swaps the contents of `theString` with `str`.

12.6 Creating Your Own String Class

CONCEPT: This section demonstrates some of the programming techniques used to create the C++ `string` class.

The C++ `string` class automatically handles many of the tedious tasks involved in using strings, such as dynamic memory allocation and bounds checking. It also overloads operators such as + and = and offers many member functions that ease the job of working with strings. In this section, we create a string data type with much of the functionality of the C++ class. In the process, we see examples of copy constructors and overloaded operators in full action, as well as examples of programming techniques that are useful in the solution of many problems.

The `MyString` Class

The `MyString` class defined in this section is an abstract data type for handling strings. It has many of the advantages possessed by the C++ `string` class provided by the Standard Template Library:

- Memory is dynamically allocated for any string stored in a `MyString` object. The programmer using this class doesn't need to be concerned with how large to make an array.
- Strings may be assigned to a `MyString` object with the = operator. The programmer using this class does not have to call the `strcpy` function.
- One string may be concatenated to another with the += operator. This eliminates the need for the `strcat` function.
- Strings may be tested for equality with the == operator. The programmer using this class doesn't have to call the `strcmp` function.

The following program listings show the class implementation.

Contents of `mystring.h`

```
#ifndef MYSTRING_H
#define MYSTRING_H

#include <iostream>
#include <cstring>  // For string library functions
#include <cstdlib>  // For exit() function
using namespace std;
const int SIZE = 256;
class MyString {
private:
    char *str;
    int len;
public:
    // Constructors
    MyString() { str = new char[1]; str[0] = '\0'; len = 0; }
    MyString(char *);
    MyString(const MyString &);

    // Destructor
    ~MyString() { if (len != 0) delete [] str; }

    // Various member functions and operators
    int length() const { return len; }
    char *data() { return str; };
    MyString operator+=(MyString );
    MyString operator=(MyString );

    // Various overloaded operators
    friend bool operator==(MyString, MyString);
    friend bool operator!=(MyString, MyString);
    friend bool operator>(MyString, MyString);
    friend bool operator<(MyString, MyString);
    friend bool operator>=(MyString, MyString);
    friend bool operator<=(MyString, MyString);
    friend ostream & operator<<(ostream &, MyString );
    friend istream & operator>>(istream &, MyString &);
};
#endif
```

Contents of `mystring.CPP`

```
#include "mystring.h"

//***********************************************
// Constructor to initialize the str member     *
// with a C-string constant.                    *
//***********************************************
MyString::MyString(const char *sptr)
{
    len = strlen(sptr);
    str = new char[len + 1];
    strcpy(str, sptr);
}
```

```

//*************************************************
// Copy constructor.                              *
//*************************************************
MyString::MyString(const MyString &right)
{
    str = new char[right.len + 1];
    strcpy(str, right.str);
    len = right.len;
}

//************************************************
// Overloaded = operator.                        *
//************************************************
MyString MyString::operator=(MyString right)
{
    if (len != 0) delete [] str;
    str = new char[right.len + 1];
    strcpy(str, right.str);
    len = right.len;
    return *this;
}

//**************************************************
// Overloaded += operator.                         *
// Concatenates the str member of right to the     *
// str member of the calling object.               *
// Returns the calling object.                     *
//**************************************************
MyString MyString::operator+=(MyString right)
{
    char *temp = str;
    str = new char[len + right.len + 1];
    strcpy(str, temp);
    strcat(str, right.str);
    if (len != 0) delete [] temp;
    len += right.len;
    return *this;
}

//*********************************************************
// Overloaded == operator.                                *
//*********************************************************
bool operator==(MyString left, MyString right)
{
    return strcmp(left.str, right.str) == 0;
}

//*********************************************************
// Overloaded != operator.                                *
//*********************************************************
bool operator!=(MyString left, MyString right)
{
    return strcmp(left.str, right.str) != 0;
}
```

```
//****************************************************
// Overloaded > operator.                            *
//****************************************************
bool operator>(MyString left, MyString right)
{
    return (strcmp(left.str, right.str) > 0);
}

//****************************************************
// Overloaded < operator.                            *
//****************************************************
bool operator<(MyString left, MyString right)
{
    return (strcmp(left.str, right.str) < 0);
}

//***************************************************
// Overloaded >= operator.                          *
//***************************************************
bool operator>=(MyString left, MyString right)
{
    return (strcmp(left.str, right.str) >= 0);
}

//***************************************************
// Overloaded <= operator.                          *
//***************************************************
bool operator<=(MyString left, MyString right)
{
   return  (strcmp(left.str, right.str) <= 0);
}

//***********************************************
// Overloaded stream insertion operator (<<).    *
//***********************************************
ostream &operator<<(ostream &strm, MyString obj)
{
    strm << obj.str;
    return strm;
}

//***********************************************
// Overloaded stream extraction operator (>>).   *
//***********************************************
istream &operator>>(istream &strm, MyString &obj)
{
   // Read the string
   char buffer[SIZE];
   strm.getline(buffer, SIZE);
   // Invoke the convert constructor and overloaded assignment
   obj = buffer;
   return strm;
}
```

Constructors and Destructors

Because the MyString class has a pointer that is used to dynamically allocate memory, it requires a programmer-defined copy constructor, assignment operator, and destructor. In addition to the copy constructor, there is a default constructor that initializes a MyString object to an empty string and a convert constructor that allows C-strings to be used in place of MyString objects in assignment statements. The convert constructor also allows C-strings to be passed to functions and operators that would otherwise require MyString objects as parameters. An example of this is line 119 in the MyString.cpp file, where in the statement

```
obj = buffer;
```

obj is a MyString object being assigned the value of the C-string variable buffer.

The Overloaded = Operator

The overloaded assignment operator is invoked whenever one MyString object is being assigned to another, as in

```
MyString x("Hello");
MyString y;
y = x;
```

It is also called whenever a C-string is assigned to a MyString object, as in

```
MyString x;
x = "hello";
```

In this second example, the convert constructor will automatically be called to convert the C-string "hello" to a MyString object, which is then assigned to the object x.

The Overloaded += Operator

This operator concatenates the Mystring object on its right to the object on its left. The right operand may be a MyString object, or it may be a C-string:

```
MyString x("Hello ");
x += "World";
```

The Overloaded Relational Operators ==, !=, <, <=, >, >=

These operators are overloaded as nonmember functions to preserve the symmetry between the left and right operands and to allow the convert constructor to be called when a C-string is passed for the left operand (parameter). These functions return a Boolean value that is exactly the Boolean value that is obtained when the contained C-strings are passed to strcmp and the result is compared to 0. As an example, here is code for operator < :

```
bool operator<(MyString left, MyString right)
{
    return (strcmp(left.str, right.str) < 0);
}
```

Program 12-15 demonstrates the use of the += operator and various other features of the `MyString` class.

Program 12-15

```
// This program demonstrates the MyString class. Be sure to
// compile this program with mystring.cpp.
#include <iostream>
#include "mystring.h"
using namespace std;

int main()
{
   MyString object1("This"), object2("is");
   MyString object3("a test.");
   MyString object4 = object1;  // Call copy constructor
   MyString object5("is only a test.");
   char string1[] = "a test.";

   cout << "Object1: " << object1 << endl;
   cout << "Object2: " << object2 << endl;
   cout << "Object3: " << object3 << endl;
   cout << "Object4: " << object4 << endl;
   cout << "Object5: " << object5 << endl;
   cout << "String1: " << string1 << endl;
   object1 += " ";
   object1 += object2;
   object1 += " ";
   object1 += object3;
   object1 += " ";
   object1 += object4;
   object1 += " ";
   object1 += object5;
   cout << "object1: " << object1 << endl;
   return 0;
}
```

Program Output

```
Object1: This
Object2: is
Object3: a test.
Object4: This
Object5: is only a test.
String1: a test.
object1: This is a test. This is only a test.
```

Program 12-16 shows how `MyString`'s relational operators can be used to compare strings with the same ease that numeric data types are compared.

Program 12-16

```
// This program demonstrates the MyString class. Be sure to
// compile this program with mystring.cpp.
#include <iostream>
#include "mystring.h"
using namespace std;

int main()
{
   MyString name1("Billy"), name2("Sue");
   MyString name3("Joe");
   MyString string1("ABC"), string2("DEF");

   cout << "name1: " << name1.getValue() << endl;
   cout << "name2: " << name2.getValue() << endl;
   cout << "name3: " << name3.getValue() << endl;
   cout << "string1: " << string1.getValue() << endl;
   cout << "string2: " << string2.getValue() << endl;
   if (name1 == name2)
      cout << "name1 is equal to name2.\n";
   else
      cout << "name1 is not equal to name2.\n";
   if (name3 == "Joe")
      cout << "name3 is equal to Joe.\n";
   else
      cout << "name3 is not equal to Joe.\n";
   if (string1 > string2)
      cout << "string1 is greater than string2.\n";
   else
      cout << "string1 is not greater than string2.\n";
   if (string1 < string2)
      cout << "string1 is less than string2.\n";
   else
      cout << "string1 is not less than string2.\n";
   if (string1 >= string2)
      cout << "string1 is greater than or equal to "
           << "string2.\n";
   else
      cout << "string1 is not greater than or equal to "
           << "string2.\n";
   if (string1 >= "ABC")
      cout << "string1 is greater than or equal to "
           << "ABC.\n";
   else
      cout << "string1 is not greater than or equal to "
           << "ABC.\n";
   if (string1 <= string2)
      cout << "string1 is less than or equal to "
           << "string2.\n";
   else
      cout << "string1 is not less than or equal to "
           << "string2.\n";
   if (string2 <= "DEF")
```

(program continues)

Program 12-16 *(continued)*

```
        cout << "string2 is less than or equal to "
             << "DEF.\n";
    else
        cout << "string2 is not less than or equal to "
        << "DEF.\n";
    return 0;
}
```

Program Output

```
name1: Billy
name2: Sue
name3: Joe
string1: ABC
string2: DEF
name1 is not equal to name2.
name3 is equal to Joe.
string1 is not greater than string2.
string1 is less than string2.
string1 is not greater than or equal to string2.
string1 is greater than or equal to ABC.
string1 is less than or equal to string2.
string2 is less than or equal to DEF.
```

12.7 Advanced Software Enterprises Case Study

You are a summer intern at Advanced Software Enterprises, and your boss has asked you to develop a function that can format string representations of dollar amounts. Specifically, he wants you to add commas and a dollar sign ($) at appropriate places in the string. For example, when the function is given the string object or C-string with a value of "1084567.89", it should return the string "$1,084,567.89".

After reviewing the `String` class members listed in Table 12-6 and giving the problem some thought, you decide to use the `find` method. This will let you find the index of the decimal point in the input string. Beginning at that point, you can back up in the string, inserting a comma at every third location. You then finish it off by inserting a $ sign at the beginning. In no time at all, you have the solution and the demonstration program shown in the listing for Program 12-17.

Program 12-17

```
// This program demonstrates the use of the string find
// and insert member functions.
#include <iostream>
#include <string>
using namespace std;

string dollarFormat(string );  // Prototype

```

(program continues)

Program 12-17 *(continued)*

```
int main(void)
{
   string input;    // User input

   // Get the dollar amount from the user
   cout << "Enter a dollar amount in the form nnnnn.nn : ";
   cin >> input;

   // Display the formatted dollar amount
   cout << "Formatted amount:    " << dollarFormat(input) << endl;
   return 0;
}

//*************************************************
// Returns a $-formatted version of the input string *
//*************************************************
string dollarFormat(string original)
{
    string formatted = original;
    int dp = formatted.find('.');  // Position of decimal point
    int pos = dp;                  // Search for comma position
    while (pos > 3)
    {
       pos = pos - 3;
       formatted.insert(pos, ",");
    }
    formatted.insert(0, "$");
    return formatted;
}
```

Program Output with Example Input Shown in Bold

```
Enter a dollar amount in the form nnnnn.nn : 1084567.89[Enter]
Here is the amount formatted:   $1,084,567.89
```

12.8 Tying It All Together: *Program Execution Environments*

Most operating systems provide every executing program with an *execution environment* consisting of a set of strings of the form

name=value

The *name* part of this equation is called an *environment variable*, and the *value* part is used to specify a string value for that particular environment variable. As an example, look at this partial listing of the execution environment of a C++ program running on one of the authors' machines:

```
COMPUTERNAME=GCM-RED
ComSpec=C:\Windows\system32\cmd.exe
```

```
 3 HOMEDRIVE=C:
 4 HOMEPATH=\Users\gcm
 5 LOGONSERVER=\\GCM-RED
 6 NUMBER_OF_PROCESSORS=4
 7 OS=Windows_NT
 8 SESSIONNAME=Console
 9 SystemDrive=C:
10 SystemRoot=C:\Windows
11 USERDOMAIN=gcm-Red
12 USERNAME=gcm
13 windir=C:\Windows
```

In line 1, `COMPUTERNAME` is the environment variable and `GCM-VISTA1` is the associated value.

A program that examines its execution environment can obtain information about the user currently logged in and about the machine on which it is running. Depending on the operating system, the program can also gather information about the network to which the machine is connected. For example, by examining the above listing, we can tell that the user's login name is `gcm` (line 12), that the user's home folder is `\Users\gcm` (line 4), and that the machine's operating system is a version of Microsoft Windows (line 7). Furthermore, we can tell that the computer has four central processing units (line 6) and that the network name of the machine is `GCM-RED` (line 1).

The operating system stores the program's environment as an array of pointers to C-strings. To mark the end of the array, the system sets the last entry in the array to 0. It then passes the base address of this array to the program. When the program starts executing, the C++ runtime system sets a variable

```
char **environ;
```

to point to the beginning of the environment array.

Basically, the `environ` variable is a global variable defined in library code that is linked with the executable code of your program. In C++, a function can access a global variable defined in a separate file by declaring the variable and prefixing the declaration with the key word `extern`. This means that you can gain access to the environment by including this declaration in your program:

```
extern char ** environ;
```

In Chapter 10 you learned that if `environ` is a pointer to the beginning of an array of items, you can use the notation

```
environ[k]
```

to access the various components of that array. By starting a variable `k` at 0 and repeatedly incrementing `k`, you can step through the array and examine each environment string, as shown in Program 12-18.

Program 12-18

```
// This program prints its environment variables.
#include <iostream>
using namespace std;

int main(int argc, char** argv)
{
    extern char **environ;    // Needed to access the environment

    int k = 0;
    while(environ[k] != 0)    // Is  it last C-string in environment?
    {
        // Print the string
        cout << environ[k] << "\n";
        k++;
    }
    return 0;
}
```

The output from this program will vary depending on the user running the program and the machine on which the program is running. It will be similar to what is shown at the beginning of this section.

Review Questions and Exercises

Fill-in-the-Blank

1. A(n) __________ is represented in memory as an array of characters with a null terminator.
2. The __________ statement is required before the C-string library functions can be used in a program.
3. A(n) __________ is written in your program as a sequence of characters surrounded by double quotes.
4. The type __________ is used by the compiler as the type of a string literal.
5. The __________ is used to mark the end of a C-string.
6. The __________ class can be used to read input from an in-memory string object.
7. The __________ class can be used to write output to an in-memory string object.
8. The __________ function returns the length of a string.
9. To __________ two strings means to append one string to the other.
10. The __________ function concatenates two strings.
11. The __________ function copies one string to another.
12. The __________ function searches for a string inside of another one.
13. The __________ function compares two strings.

14. The ________ function copies, at most, n number of characters from one string to another.
15. The ________ function returns the value of a string converted to an integer.
16. The ________ function returns the value of a string converted to a `long` integer.
17. The ________ function returns the value of a string converted to a `double`.
18. The ________ function converts an integer to a string.

Algorithm Workbench

19. Write a function whose prototype is

```
char lastChar(const char *str)
```

that takes a nonempty C-string as parameter and returns the last character in the string. For example, the call `lastChar("abc")` will return the character `c`.

Predict the Output

20.
```
#include <iostream>
using namespace std;
int main()
{
    cout << ("hello")[1];
    return 0;
}
```
21.
```
#include <iostream>
using namespace std;
int main()
{
    cout << *("hello");
    return 0;
}
```
22.
```
#include <iostream>
using namespace std;
int main()
{
    cout << *("C++ is fun" + 5);
    return 0;
}
```
23.
```
#include <iostream>
#include <string>
using namespace std;
int main()
{
    cout << string("fantastic").size();
    return 0;
}
```
24.
```
#include <iostream>
#include <cstring>
using namespace std;
int main()
{
    cout << strcmp("a", "b");
    return 0;
}
```

25.
```
#include <iostream>
using namespace std;
int main()
{
    if ("a" == "a")
       cout << "equal";
    else
       cout << "not equal";
    return 0;
}
```

26.
```
#include <iostream>
#include <string>
using namespace std;
int main()
{
    string s(5, 'a');
    s.append(3, 'b');
    s.insert(6, "xyz");
    cout << s;
    return 0;
}
```

27.
```
#include <iostream>
#include <cstring>
using namespace std;
int main()
{
    char name[20] = "abracadabra";
    strcpy(name+4, "sion");
    cout << name;
    return 0;
}
```

28.
```
#include <iostream>
#include <cstring>
using namespace std;
int main()
{
    char name[20] = "John ";
    *name = '\0';
    strcat(name, "Smith");
    cout << name;
    return 0;
}
```

Find the Errors

29. Each of the following programs or program segments has errors. Find as many as you can.

A)
```
char string[] = "Stop";
if (isupper(string) == "STOP")
   exit(0);
```

B)
```
char numeric[5];
int x = 123;
numeric = atoi(x);
```

C)
```
char string1[] = "Billy";
char string2[] = " Bob Jones";
strcat(string1, string2);
```

D)
```
char x = 'a', y = 'a';
if (strcmp(x, y) == 0)
    exit(0);
```

Soft Skills

30. You are a member of a standardization committee for a new C++ standard, and there is a proposal on the table to drop C-strings from the language and support only the C++ string class. State whether you would oppose or support the proposal and explain why.

Programming Challenges

1. Word Counter

Write a function that accepts a C-string as an argument and returns the number of words contained in the string. For instance, if the string argument is "Four score and seven years ago" the function should return the number 6. Demonstrate the function in a program that asks the user to input a string and then passes it to the function. The number of words in the string should be displayed on the screen.

2. Average Number of Letters

Modify the program you wrote for problem 1 (Word Counter), so it also displays the average number of letters in each word.

3. Sentence Capitalizer

Write a function that accepts a C-string as an argument and capitalizes the first character of each sentence in the string. For instance, if the string argument is "`hello. my name is Joe. what is your name?`" the function should manipulate the string so it contains "`Hello. My name is Joe. What is your name?`" Demonstrate the function in a program that asks the user to input a string and then passes it to the function. The modified string should be displayed on the screen.

4. Vowels and Consonants

Write a function that accepts a C-string as its argument. The function should count the number of vowels appearing in the string and return that number.

Write another function that accepts a C-string as its argument. This function should count the number of consonants appearing in the string and return that number.

Demonstrate the two functions in a program that performs the following steps:

1. The user is asked to enter a string.
2. The program displays the following menu:
   A) Count the number of vowels in the string
   B) Count the number of consonants in the string
   C) Count both the vowels and consonants in the string
   D) Enter another string
   E) Exit the program
3. The program performs the operation selected by the user and repeats until the user selects E, to exit the program.

5. Name Arranger

Write a program that asks for the user's first, middle, and last names. The names should be stored in three different character arrays. The program should then store in a fourth array the name arranged in the following manner: the last name followed by a comma and a space, followed by the first name and a space, followed by the middle name. For example, if the user entered "`Carol Lynn Smith`", it should store "`Smith, Carol Lynn`" in the fourth array. Display the contents of the fourth array on the screen.

6. Sum of Digits in a String

Write a program that asks the user to enter a series of single-digit numbers with nothing separating them. Read the input as a C-string or a `string` object. The program should display the sum of all the single-digit numbers in the string. For example, if the user enters 2514, the program should display 12, which is the sum of 2, 5, 1, and 4. The program should also display the highest and lowest digits in the string.

7. Most Frequent Character

Write a function that accepts either a pointer to a C-string, or a `string` object, as its argument. The function should return the character that appears most frequently in the string. Demonstrate the function in a complete program.

8. `replaceSubstring` Function

Write a function named `replaceSubstring`. The function should accept three C-string or `string` object arguments. Let's call them *`string1`*, *`string2`*, and *`string3`*. It should search *`string1`* for all occurrences of *`string2`*. When it finds an occurrence of *`string2`*, it should replace it with *`string3`*. For example, suppose the three arguments have the following values:

```
string1:    "the dog jumped over the fence"
string2:    "the"
string3:    "that"
```

With these three arguments, the function would return a `string` object with the value "that dog jumped over that fence". Demonstrate the function in a complete program.

9. Case Manipulator

VideoNote
Solving the Case Manipulator Problem

Write a program with three functions: `upper`, `lower`, and `flip`. The `upper` function should accept a C-string as an argument. It should step through all the characters in the string, converting each to uppercase. The `lower` function, too, should accept a pointer to a C-string as an argument. It should step through all the characters in the string, converting each to lowercase. Like `upper` and `lower`, `flip` should also accept a C-string. As it steps through the string, it should test each character to determine whether it is upper- or lowercase. If a character is uppercase, it should be converted to lowercase. If a character is lowercase, it should be converted to uppercase.

Test the functions by asking for a string in function `main`, then passing it to them in the following order: `flip`, `lower`, and `upper`.

10. Password Verifier

Imagine you are developing a software package that requires users to enter their own passwords. Your software requires that user's passwords meet the following criteria:

- The password should be at least six characters long.
- The password should contain at least one uppercase and at least one lowercase letter.
- The password should have at least one digit.

Write a program that asks for a password and then verifies that it meets the stated criteria. If it doesn't, the program should display a message telling the user why.

11. Phone Number List

Write a program that has an array of at least 10 string objects that hold people's names and phone numbers. You may make up your own strings or use the following:

```
"Becky Warren, 678-1223"
"Joe Looney, 586-0097"
"Geri Palmer, 223-8787"
"Lynn Presnell, 887-1212"
"Holly Gaddis, 223-8878"
"Sam Wiggins, 486-0998"
"Bob Kain, 586-8712"
"Tim Haynes, 586-7676"
"Warren Gaddis, 223-9037"
"Jean James, 678-4939"
"Ron Palmer, 486-2783"
```

The program should ask the user to enter a name or partial name to search for in the array. Any entries in the array that match the string entered should be displayed. For example, if the user enters "`Palmer`" the program should display the following names from the list:

```
Geri Palmer, 223-8787
Ron Palmer, 486-2783
```

12. Check Writer

Write a program that displays a simulated paycheck. The program should ask the user to enter the date, the payee's name, and the amount of the check. It should then display a simulated check with the dollar amount spelled out, as shown here:

```
                                    Date: 12/24/2012


Pay to the Order of: John Phillips           $1920.85

One thousand nine hundred twenty and 85 cents
```

You may assume the amount is no greater than $10000. Be sure to format the numeric value of the check in fixed-point notation with two decimal places of precision. Be sure the decimal place always displays, even when the number is zero or has no fractional part. Use either C-strings or string class objects in this program.

13. Digit Sums of Squares and Cubes

If you add up all the digits in 468, you get 4 + 6 + 8 = 18. The square and cube of 468 are 219024 and 102503232, respectively. Interestingly, if you add up the digits of the square or cube, you get 18 again. Are there other integers that share this property? Write a program that lists all positive integers k less than 1000 such that the three numbers k, k^2, and k^3 have digits that add up to the same number.

14. Dollar Amount Formatter

Modify Program 12-17 by adding a function

```
string dollarFormat(double amount)
```

that takes a dollar amount in numeric form and returns a string formatted in currency notation, with a $ sign and commas inserted at the appropriate locations. Test your function using suitable inputs.

15. Word Separator

Write a program that accepts as input a sentence in which all of the words are run together, but the first character of each word is uppercase. Convert the sentence to a string in which the words are separated by spaces and only the first word starts with an uppercase letter. For example the string "StopAndSmellTheRoses." would be converted to "Stop and smell the roses."

16. Pig Latin

Write a program that reads a sentence as input and converts each word to "Pig Latin." In one version, to convert a word to Pig Latin you remove the first letter and place that letter at the end of the word. Then you append the string "ay" to the word. Here is an example:

English: I SLEPT MOST OF THE NIGHT

Pig Latin: IAY LEPTSAY OSTMAY FOAY HETAY IGHTNAY

17. I before e except after c

A friend of yours who is an educator is conducting research into the effectiveness of teaching the spelling rule "I before e except after c" to students. She wishes to analyze writing samples from two groups of students, only one of which was taught the rule. Write a program that will take a file containing a writing sample and print a list of all words in the file that contain at least one of the strings "ie" or "ei". Write two versions of the program: one version should use the `strstr` function on C-strings, the other version should use only `string` class methods.

18. User Name

Write a program that queries its environment, determines the user's login name, and then greets the user by name. For example, if the login name of the user is `gcm`, then the program prints

```
Hello, gcm
```

when it is executed.

CHAPTER 13 Advanced File and I/O Operations

TOPICS

13.1 Input and Output Streams

CONCEPT: `ifstream` objects are used for file input, `ofstream` objects are used for file output, and `fstream` objects are used for both input and output.

An *input stream* is a sequence from which data can be read; an *output stream* is a sequence to which data can be written; and an *input-output* stream is a sequence of data that allows both reading and writing. The keyboard is the standard example of an input stream, and the monitor screen is the standard example of an output stream.

C++ provides various classes for working with streams. These include `istream` and `ostream` for standard input and output; `ifstream`, `ofstream`, and `fstream` for file IO; and `istringstream` and `ostringstream` for reading and writing strings. To read from the keyboard, you use `cin`, which is a predefined object of the `istream` class. To write to the screen, you use `cout`, a predefined object of the `ostream` class. In Chapter 5 you learned how to use an `ifstream` object to read a file and how to use an `ofstream` object to write to a disk file. In Chapter 12, you learned how to read and write in-memory string objects through the use of `istringstream` and `ostringstream` objects. In this chapter we will discuss the `fstream` class, which allows a file to be used for both input and output. We will also cover additional material related to output formatting, error testing, binary files, random access files, and data serialization.

The File Stream Classes

The `ifstream`, `ofstream`, and `fstream` classes are very similar. All three have a default constructor that allows instances of the class to be created:

```
ifstream inFile;
ofstream outFile;
fstream inOutFile;
```

These classes have an `open` member function that is used to open a disk file and connect it to the stream object so the program can read or write the file. They also have a `close` member function that is used to sever the connection when the program is done using the file:

```
void open(const char *filename);
void close();
```

Open files use resources in the operating system, so it is important to close files as soon as you are done using them. Also, data that your program writes to the file stream object is often buffered within the operating system and is not immediately written to disk. When you close the file, the operating system writes this data to the disk in a process known as *flushing the buffer*. Closing the file will ensure that buffered data is not lost in the event of a power failure or some other circumstances that causes your program to terminate abnormally.

The `fstream` class combines in itself the capabilities of both `ifstream` and `ofstream`. Therefore, `fstream` has every member function and operator possessed by those two classes. In particular, you can use the extraction operator >> and the insertion operator << to read and write data on `fstream` objects.

By default, `ifstream` objects open files for input, `ofstream` objects open files for output, and `fstream` objects open files for both input and output. Program 13-1 gives a simple (albeit not very useful) example of using an `fstream` object to open a file for both reading and writing. It opens the file, reads and prints its contents, and then writes the word "Hello" at the end of the file. If you start with an empty file named "inout.txt," repeated execution of this program will result in the word "Hello" being added to the file each time the program is run.

Program 13-1

```
//This program demonstrates reading and writing
//a file through an fstream object.
#include <iostream>
#include <fstream>
#include <string>
using namespace std;

int main()
{
   fstream inOutFile;
   string word;          // Used to read a word from the file
```

(program continues)

Program 13-1 *(continued)*

```
12
13     // Open the file
14     inOutFile.open("inout.txt");
15     if (inOutFile.fail())
16     {
17         cout << "The file was not found." << endl;
18         return 1;
19     }
20
21     // Read and print every word already in the file
22     while (inOutFile >> word)
23     {
24         cout << word << endl;
25     }
26
27     // Clear end of file flag to allow additional file operations
28     inOutFile.clear();
29
30     // Write a word to the file and close the file
31     inOutFile << "Hello" << endl;
32     inOutFile.close();
33
34     return 0;
35 }
```

Program Output (Sample)

```
Hello
Hello
Hello
```

In Program 13-1, the loop of lines 22–25 terminates only when the extraction operator fails to read the next word at the end of the file. File stream objects set a number of error flags whenever an input or output operation fails. Once an error flag is set, the stream will not allow further operations to be performed on it until the error flags have been cleared. The call to the `clear` function in line 28 clears these flags, allowing the statements in lines 31 and 32 to succeed.

File Open Modes

The open member function has an optional second parameter that specifies a file open mode:

```
void open(const char *filename, ios::openmode mode);
```

A *file open mode* is a setting that determines how the file can be used. The type `openmode` is defined in a stream-related class called `ios`. Values of this type are static constant members of the ios class. Each such value represents a flag or an option that can be set when the file is opened. Table 13-1 lists the mode flags together with their meanings.

Table 13-1 File Mode Flags

File Mode Flag	Meaning
`ios::app`	Append: output will always take place at the end of the file.
`ios::ate`	At end: output will initially take place at the end of the file.
`ios::binary`	Binary: data read or written to the file is in binary form.
`ios::in`	Input: the file will allow input operations. If the file does not exist, the open will fail.
`ios::out`	Output: the file will allow output operations. If the file does not exist, an empty file of the given name is created.
`ios::trunc`	Truncate: if the file being opened exists, its contents are discarded and its size is truncated to zero.

The *binary or* operator | can be used to combine the effect of two or more flags. For example, the open mode

```
ios::in | ios::out | ios::ate
```

causes the file to be opened for both input and output, with output initially taking place at the end of the file. Here is an example of opening three files for input, output, and input-output using `fstream`:

```
fstream inFile, outFile, inOutFile;
inFile.open("in.txt", ios::in);
outFile.open("out.txt", ios::out);
outFile.open("inout.txt", ios::in | ios::out);
```

NOTE: When used by itself, the `ios::out` flag causes the contents of an existing file to be deleted, the assumption being that the programmer wants to overwrite the file. If `ios::out` is combined with `ios::app`, the contents of the existing file are preserved, and all new data is appended to the end of the file.

Using Constructors to Open Files

Each of the three stream classes `ifstream`, `ofstream`, and `fstream` has a constructor that takes the name of a file and a file mode and opens the file when the object is created. This allows you to create the stream object and open the file in a single statement:

```
fstream outFile("inout.txt", ios::in | ios::out);
```

Output Formatting and I/O Manipulators

The I/O manipulators you learned about in Chapter 3 can be used on stream objects. In particular, the manipulators

```
setw(n)                         fixed
showpoint                       setprecision(n)
left                            right
```

can be used on `fstream`, `ofstream`, and `ostringstream` objects. To illustrate, consider the need for a function that takes an argument of type `double` representing the price of an item in dollars and returns a string that starts with the dollar sign `$` and represents the value of the price to two decimal places. For example, an amount of `12.5` passed as parameter would result in the function returning the string `$12.50`. We can easily write this function using our knowledge of `ostringstream` gained from Chapter 12:

```
string dollarFormat(double amount)
{
  // Create ostringstream object
  ostringstream outStr;

  // Set up format information and write to outStr.
  outStr << showpoint << fixed << setprecision(2);
  outStr << '$' << amount;

  // Extract and return the string inside outStr.
  return outStr.str();
}
```

Program 13-2 uses the `dollarFormat` function to write a neatly formatted table of prices. The prices are given in a two dimensional array. The program formats each price and prints a table of all prices, with each price being right-justified in a column of width 10.

Program 13-2

```
// This program demonstrates the use of an ostringstream
// object to do sophisticated formatting.
#include <iostream>
#include <iomanip>
#include <sstream>
using namespace std;

string dollarFormat(double); // Function Prototype

int main()
{
  const int ROWS = 3, COLS = 2;
  double amount[ROWS][COLS] = {184.45,    7, 59.13,
                                64.32, 7.29,  1289};

  // Format table of dollar amounts right justified
  // in columns of width 10
  cout << right;
  for (int row = 0; row< ROWS; row++)
    {
      for (int column = 0; column < COLS; column++)
       {
         cout << setw(10)
              << dollarFormat(amount[row][column]);
```

(program continues)

Program 13-2 *(continued)*

```
        }
      cout << endl;
    }
  return 0;
}

//*************************************************
// formats a dollar amount                        *
//*************************************************
string dollarFormat(double amount)
{
  // Create ostringstream object
  ostringstream outStr;

  // Set up format information and write to outStr.
  outStr << showpoint << fixed << setprecision(2);
  outStr << '$' << amount;

  // Extract and return the string inside outStr.
  return outStr.str();
}
```

Program Output

```
$184.45     $7.00
 $59.13    $64.32
  $7.29  $1289.00
```

Table 13-2 shows a list of I/O manipulators that can be used with C++ stream objects and gives a brief description of their meanings.

Table 13-2 I/O Manipulators

Manipulator	Description
`dec`	Displays subsequent numbers in decimal format.
`endl`	Writes new line and flushes output stream.
`fixed`	Uses fixed notation for floating-point numbers.
`flush`	Flushes output stream.
`hex`	Inputs or outputs in hexadecimal.
`left`	Left justifies output.
`oct`	Inputs or outputs in octal.
`right`	Right justifies output.
`scientific`	Uses scientific notation for floating-point numbers.
`setfill(ch)`	Makes `ch` the fill character.
`setprecision(n)`	Sets floating-point precision to `n`.
`setw(n)`	Set width of output field to `n`.

(table continues)

Table 13-2 I/O Manipulators *(continued)*

Manipulator	Description
`showbase`	Show the base when printing numbers.
`noshowbase`	Do not show the base when printing numbers.
`showpoint`	Forces decimal point and trailing zeros to be displayed.
`noshowpoint`	Prints no trailing zeros and drops decimal point if possible.
`showpos`	Prints a + with nonnegative numbers.
`noshowpos`	Prints no + with nonnegative numbers.

You have already encountered some of these manipulators in Chapter 3. The `oct`, `dec`, and `hex` manipulators can be used with both input and output streams; they allow numbers to be read or written using the octal, decimal, or hexadecimal number systems. Program 13-3 demonstrates how to use `cin` and `cout` to read and write decimal, hexadecimal, and octal values.

Program 13-3

```
//This program demonstrates input and output of numbers
//using the octal, decimal, and hexadecimal number systems.
#include <iostream>
#include <iomanip>
using namespace std;

int main()
{
    int a, b;
    // Read two decimals and print hex and octal equivalents
    cout << "Enter two decimal numbers: ";
    cin  >> a >> b;
    cout << "The numbers in decimal: " << a << '\t' << b << endl;
    cout << "The numbers in hexadecimal: " <<  hex
         << showbase << a << '\t' << b << endl;
    cout << "The numbers in octal: " << oct
         <<  a << '\t' << b << endl;

    // Read some hexadecimals and print their decimal equivalents
    cout << "Enter two hexadecimal numbers: ";
    cin  >> hex >> a >> b;
    cout << "You entered decimal " << dec
         << a << '\t' << b << endl;

    // Read some octals and print their decimal equivalents
    cout << "Enter two octal numbers: ";
    cin  >> oct >>  a >> b;
    cout << "You entered decimal " << dec
         << a << '\t' << b << endl;

    return 0;
}
```

(program continues)

Program 13-3 *(continued)*

Program Output With Sample Input Shown in Bold

```
Enter two decimal numbers: 23 45[Enter]
The numbers in decimal: 23       45
The numbers in hexadecimal: 0x17         0x2d
The numbers in octal: 027        055
Enter two hexadecimal numbers: 17 2d[Enter]
You entered decimal 23  45
Enter two octal numbers: 27 55
You entered decimal 23  45
```

Recall that when a program writes data to an open file, the data does not go directly to the file. Instead, the data is stored in an output buffer associated with the file and is later transferred to the file in a process known as flushing the buffer. Usually the buffer is only flushed if it is full or when the file is closed. The `endl` and `flush` manipulators allow the programmer to flush the buffer at any time, hence forcing transfer of buffered data to the file. For example, the following statement flushes the buffer of an output stream:

```
outFile << flush;
```

The `scientific` manipulator causes floating-point numbers to be written out in scientific notation, that is, in the form d.dddEdd. The *fill* character is the character that is written when a printed number does not fill the entire field it is printed in. By default, the fill character is a blank. The programmer can specify a different fill character by using the `setfill` manipulator. For example,

```
outFile << setfill('%');
```

will make the percent character (`%`) the fill character.

Checkpoint

13.1 Name three different C++ classes that can be used to create input streams.

13.2 Name three different C++ classes that can be used to create output streams.

13.3 What is the purpose of the second parameter to the file stream member function `open`?

13.4 Why is it important for a program to close an open file as soon as it is done using the file? Give two reasons.

13.5 Which file open flag causes all output to take place at the end of the file?

13.6 Which file open flag causes the contents of an existing file to be discarded and the file size reduced to zero?

13.7 What happens if `ios::out` is used by itself to open a file that does not exist?

13.8 What happens if `ios::out` is used by itself to open an existing file?

13.9 Write a sequence of C++ statements that reads in two numbers entered in octal format and separated by whitespace and prints their sum in octal.

13.10 Write a sequence of C++ statements that reads in two hexadecimal numbers and prints the sum of the numbers twice, once in decimal and the second time in hexadecimal.

13.11 Show how to use the constructor of the `fstream` class to open a file for input without having to call the open function.

13.12 Consider two parallel arrays of the same size, one containing strings and the second containing integers. Write C++ statements to output the information in the two arrays as a table of names and numbers. The first column of the table will contain the names left-justified in a field of 20, and the second column will contain the integers right-justified in a field of 10. Here is an example of the data when the size of the array is 2.

```
const int SIZE = 2;
string names[SIZE] = {"Catherine", "Bill"};
int numbers[SIZE] = {12, 2005};
```

13.2 More Detailed Error Testing

CONCEPT: All stream objects have error state bits that indicate the condition of the stream.

All stream objects contain a set of bits that act as flags. These flags indicate the current state of the stream. Table 13-3 lists these bits.

Table 13-3 Files Condition Bit Flags

Bit	Description
`ios::eofbit`	Set when the end of an input stream is encountered.
`ios::failbit`	Set when an attempted operation has failed.
`ios::hardfail`	Set when an unrecoverable error has occurred.
`ios::badbit`	Set when an invalid operation has been attempted.
`ios::goodbit`	Set when all the flags above are not set. Indicates the stream is in good condition.

These bits can be tested by the member functions listed in Table 13-4. One of the functions listed in the table, `clear()`, can be used to set a status bit.

Table 13-4 Member Functions That Report on the Bit Flags

Function	Description
`eof()`	Returns true (nonzero) if the `eofbit` flag is set; otherwise returns false.
`fail()`	Returns true (nonzero) if the `failbit` or `hardfail` flags are set; otherwise returns false.
`bad()`	Returns true (nonzero) if the `badbit` flag is set; otherwise returns false.
`good()`	Returns true (nonzero) if the `goodbit` flag is set; otherwise returns false.
`clear()`	When called with no arguments, clears all the flags listed above. Can also be called with a specific flag as an argument.

The function `showState`, shown here, accepts a file stream reference as its argument. It shows the state of the file by displaying the return values of the `eof()`, `fail()`, `bad()`, and `good()` member functions:

```
void showState(fstream &file)
{
   cout << "File Status:\n";
   cout << "  eof bit: " << file.eof() << endl;
   cout << "  fail bit: " << file.fail() << endl;
   cout << "  bad bit: " << file.bad() << endl;
   cout << "  good bit: " << file.good() << endl;
   file.clear();         // Clear any bad bits
}
```

Program 13-4 uses the `showState` function to display `testFile`'s status after various operations. First, the file is created and the integer value 10 is stored in it. The file is then closed and reopened for input. The integer is read from the file, and then a second read operation is performed. Since there is only one item in the file, the second read operation will result in an error.

Program 13-4

```
// This program demonstrates the return value of
// the stream object error testing member functions.
#include <iostream>
#include <fstream>
using namespace std;

// Function prototype
void showState(fstream &);

int main()
{
   // Open a file, write a number, and show file status
   fstream testFile("stuff.dat", ios::out);
   if (testFile.fail())
   {
      cout << "cannot open the file.\n";
      return 0;
   }
   int num = 10;
   cout << "Writing to the file.\n";
   testFile << num;
   showState(testFile);
   testFile.close();

   // Open the same file, read the number, show status
   testFile.open("stuff.dat", ios::in);
   if (testFile.fail())
   {
      cout << "cannot open the file.\n";
      return 0 ;
   }
```

(program continues)

Program 13-4 *(continued)*

```
   cout << "Reading from the file.\n";
   testFile >> num;
   showState(testFile);

   // Attempt an invalid read, and show status
   cout << "Forcing a bad read operation.\n";
   testFile >> num;
   showState(testFile);

   // Close file and quit
   testFile.close();
   return 0;
}

//*********************************************************
// Definition of function showState. This function uses   *
// an fstream reference as its parameter. The return      *
// values of the eof(), fail(), bad(), and good() member  *
// functions is displayed. The clear() function is called *
// before the function returns.                           *
//*********************************************************
void showState(fstream &file)
{
   cout << "File Status:\n";
   cout << "  eof bit: " << file.eof() << endl;
   cout << "  fail bit: " << file.fail() << endl;
   cout << "  bad bit: " << file.bad() << endl;
   cout << "  good bit: " << file.good() << endl;
   file.clear();  // Clear any bad bits.
}
```

Program Screen Output

```
Writing to the file.
File Status:
  eof bit: 0
  fail bit: 0
  bad bit: 0
  good bit: 1
Reading from the file.
File Status:
  eof bit: 1
  fail bit: 0
  bad bit: 0
  good bit: 0
Forcing a bad read operation.
File Status:
  eof bit: 1
  fail bit: 1
  bad bit: 0
  good bit: 0
```

For the purpose of error testing, a stream object behaves as a Boolean expression that is *true* when no error flags are set and is *false* otherwise. To check whether the last operation performed on a stream `dataFile` succeeded, you can write

```
if (dataFile)
{
   cout << "Success!";
}
```

To check whether the operation failed due to some error, you can call the `fail()` member function, or alternatively, you can write

```
if (!dataFile)
{
   cout << "Failure!";
}
```

13.3 Member Functions for Reading and Writing Files

CONCEPT: File stream objects have member functions for more specialized file reading and writing.

If whitespace characters are part of the information in a file, a problem arises when the file is read by the >> operator. Since the operator considers whitespace characters as delimiters, it does not read them. For example, consider the file `murphy.txt` that contains the following information:

Jayne Murphy
47 Jones Circle
Almond, NC 28702

Figure 13-1 shows the way the information is recorded in the file.

Figure 13-1

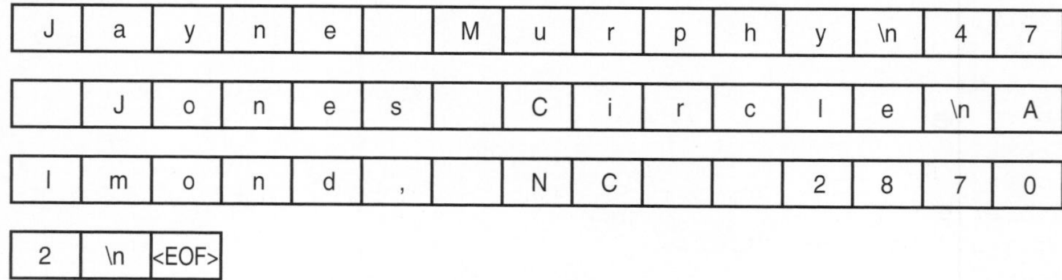

The problem that arises from the use of the >> operator is evident in the output of Program 13-5.

Program 13-5

```
// This program shows the behavior of the >> operator
// on files that contain spaces as part of the information.
// The program reads the contents of the file and transfers
// those contents to standard output.
#include <iostream>
#include <string>
#include <fstream>
using namespace std;

int main()
{
   // variables needed to read file
   fstream file;
   string input;

   // Open the file
   file.open("murphy.txt", ios::in);
   if (!file)
   {
      cout << "File open error!" << endl;
      return 0;
   }

   // Read the file and echo to screen
   file >> input;
   while (!file.fail())
   {
      cout << input;
      file >> input;
   }

   // Close the file
   file.close();
   return 0;
}
```

Program Screen Output

```
JayneMurphy47JonesCircleAlmond,NC28702
```

The `getline` function

One way to get around the problem in Program 13-5 is to use a function that reads an entire line of text. There is a global function that is part of the string library that you can use for this purpose:

```
istream& getline (istream& is, string& str, char delim = '\n');
```

This function reads a line of text from a stream `is` and stores it into a string variable `str`. The function has an optional parameter `delim` that marks the end of the line to be read. The delimiting character is removed from the stream and discarded. If `getline` is called without the third parameter, the delimiter is assumed to be the end of line character `'\n'`.

The first parameter, `is`, must be an object of the class `istream`. It can also be any object of the classes `istringstream`, `ifstream`, or `fstream` (if an `fstream` object is passed, it must have been opened for input). The value returned is a reference to the input stream that was just read. This allows the return value to be tested to ascertain the success or failure of the call as in this code fragment:

```
string str;
if (getline(inputstream, str))
{
    // A line was read and stored in str
    cout << str << endl;
}
else
{
   // An error occurred or we reached end of file
}
```

Alternatively, you can ignore the return value and test the stream in a statement after the call:

```
string str;
getline(inputstream, str);
if (inputstream)
{
    // A line was read and stored in str
    cout << str << endl;
}
else
{
    // An error occurred or we reached end of file
}
```

Program 13-6 is a modification of Program 13-5 that uses the `getline` function to read the file line by line, thereby preserving the whitespace between words.

Program 13-6

```
// This program uses the getline function to read
// a line of information from the file.
#include <iostream>
#include <string>
#include <fstream>
using namespace std;

int main()
{
    // Variables needed for file input
```

(program continues)

Program 13-6 *(continued)*

```
    fstream nameFile;
    string input;

    // Open the file
    nameFile.open("murphy.txt", ios::in);
    if (!nameFile)
    {
        cout << "File open error!" << endl;
        return 0;
    }

    // Read first line of the file
    getline(nameFile, input);
    while (nameFile)
    {
        // If successful, print line and read another line
        cout << input << endl;
        getline(nameFile, input);
    }

    // Close the file
    nameFile.close();
    return 0;
}
```

Program Screen Output

```
Jayne Murphy
47 Jones Circle
Almond, NC 28702
```

Because the third argument of the `getline` function was left out in Program 13-6, its default value is `\n`. Sometimes you might want to specify another delimiter. For example, consider a file that contains multiple names and addresses internally formatted in the following manner:

Contents of `addresses.txt`

```
Jayne Murphy$47 Jones Circle$Almond, NC 28702\n$Bobbie Smith$
217 Halifax Drive$Canton, NC 28716\n$Bill Hammet$PO Box 121$
Springfield, NC 28357\n$
```

Think of this file as consisting of three records. A record is a complete set of information about a single item. Also, the records in the file are made of three fields. The first field is the person's name. The second field is the person's street address or PO box number. The third field contains the person's city, state, and ZIP code. Notice that each field ends with a `$` character, and each record ends with a `\n` character. Program 13-7 demonstrates how a `getline` function can be used to detect the `$` characters.

Program 13-7

```
// This file demonstrates the getline function with a
// user-specified delimiter.
#include <iostream>
#include <string>
#include <fstream>
using namespace std;

int main()
{
    // Variable needed to read file
    string input;

    // Open the file
    fstream dataFile("addresses.txt", ios::in);
    if (!dataFile)
    {
        cout << "Error opening file.";
        return 0;
    }

    // Read lines terminated by '$' sign and output
    getline(dataFile, input, '$');
    while (!dataFile.fail())
    {
        cout << input << endl;
        getline(dataFile, input, '$');
    }

    // Close the file.
    dataFile.close();
    return 0;
}
```

Program Output

```
Jayne Murphy
47 Jones Circle
Almond, NC 28702

Bobbie Smith
217 Halifax Drive
Canton, NC 28716

Bill Hammet
PO Box 121
Springfield, NC 28357
```

Notice that the \n characters, which mark the end of each record, are also part of the output. They cause an extra blank line to be printed on the screen, separating the records.

NOTE: When using a printable character such as `$` to delimit information in a file, be sure to select a character that will not actually appear in the information itself. Since it's doubtful that anyone's name or address contains a `$` character, it's an acceptable delimiter. If the file contained dollar amounts, however, another delimiter would have been chosen.

The `get` Family of Member Functions

VideoNote
The `get` Family of Member Functions

Each of the input classes `ifstream` , `fstream` , and `istringstream` has a family of `get` member functions that can be used to read single characters:

```
int get();
istream& get(char& c);
```

The first version reads a single character. If successful, returns an integer code representing the character that was read. If unsuccessful, it sets the error codes on the stream and returns the special value `EOF`. The following program uses the `get` function to copy a file to the screen. The loop of lines 27–32 terminates when `get()` returns `EOF`.

Program 13-8

```
1 // This program demonstrates the use of the get member
2 // functions of the istream class
3 #include <iostream>
4 #include <string>
5 #include <fstream>
6 using namespace std;
7
8 int main()
9 {
10     // Variables needed to read file one character at a time
11     string fileName;
12     fstream file;
13     char ch;     // character read from the file
14
15     // Get file name and open file
16     cout << "Enter a file name: ";
17     cin >> fileName;
18
19     file.open(fileName.c_str(), ios::in);
20     if (!file)
21     {
22         cout << fileName << " could not be opened.\n";
23         return 1;
24     }
25
```

(program continues)

Program 13-8 *(continued)*

```
26     // Read file one character at a time and echo to screen
27     ch = file.get();
28     while (ch != EOF)
29     {
30         cout << ch;
31         ch = file.get();
32     }
33
34     // Close file
35     file.close();
36     return 0;
37 }
```

Program 13-8 will display the contents of any file. Because the get function does not skip whitespaces, all the characters will be shown exactly as they appear in the file.

The second version of `get` takes a reference to a character variable to read into and returns the stream that was read from. If you use this version of the function, you must test the stream to determine whether the operation was successful. The behavior of Program 13-8 will not change if you replace lines 27–32 with following code:

```
27     file.get(ch);
28     while (!file.fail())
29     {
30         cout << ch;
31         file.get(ch);
32     }
```

The peek Member Function

The `peek` member function is similar to `get`, but there is an important difference. When the `get` function is called, it returns the next character available from the input stream and removes that character from the stream. In contrast, the `peek` function returns a copy of the next character available without removing it from the stream. Thus `get()`reads a character from the file, but `peek()` just "looks" at the next character without actually reading it. To see the difference, suppose that a newly opened file contains the string `"abc"`. Then the sequence of statements

```
char ch = inFile.get();   // Read a character
cout << ch;               // Output the character
ch = inFile.get();        // Read another character
cout << ch;               // Output the character
```

will print the two characters `"ab"` on the screen. However, the statements

```
char ch = inFile.peek(); // Return the next character without reading it
cout << ch;              // Output the character
ch = inFile.get();       // Now read the next character
cout << ch;              // Output the character
```

will print the two characters `"aa"` on the screen.

The `peek` function is useful when you need to know what kind of data you are about to read before you actually read it, so you can decide on the best input method to use. If the data is numeric, it is best read with the stream extraction operator >>, but if the data is a non-numeric sequence of characters, then it should be read with `get` or `getline`. The following program uses the `peek` function in making a modified copy of a file by incrementing the value of each integer number appearing in the file by one.

Program 13-9

```
// This program demonstrates the peek member function.
#include <iostream>
#include <string>
#include <fstream>
using namespace std;

int main()
{
    // Variables needed to read characters and numbers
    char ch;
    int number;

    // Variables for file handling
    string fileName;
    fstream inFile, outFile;

    // Open the file to be modified
    cout << "Enter a file name: ";
    cin >> fileName;
    inFile.open(fileName.c_str(), ios::in);
    if (!inFile)
    {
       cout << "Cannot open file " <<  fileName;
       return 1;
    }
    // Open the file to receive the modified copy
    outFile.open("modified.txt", ios::out);
    if (!outFile)
    {
        cout << "Cannot open the output file.";
        return 2;
    }
    // Copy the input file one character at a time
    // except numbers in the input file must have 1
    // added to them

    // Peek at the first character
    ch = inFile.peek();
    while (ch != EOF)
    {
        // Examine current character
        if (isdigit(ch))
        {
```

(program continues)

Program 13-9 *(continued)*

```
44              // Numbers should be read with >>
45              inFile >> number;
46              outFile << number + 1;
47          }
48          else
49          {
50              // Just a simple character, read it and copy it
51              ch = inFile.get();
52              outFile << ch;
53          }
54          // Peek at the next character from input file
55          ch = inFile.peek();
56      }
57      // Close the files
58      inFile.close();
59      outFile.close();
60      return 0;
61  }
```

Sample Input File

```
Amy is 23 years old. Robert is 50 years old. The
difference between their ages is 27 years. Amy was born
in 1986.
```

Program Ouput for the Given Sample Input File

```
Amy is 24 years old. Robert is 51 years old. The
difference between their ages is 28 years. Amy was born
in 1987.
```

The program cannot tell beforehand whether the next character to be read is a digit that starts a number (in which case the entire number should be read using the stream extraction operator >>) or just an ordinary nondigit character (in which case the character should be read using a call to the `get()` member function). The program therefore uses `peek()`to examine characters without actually reading them (lines 38 and 55). If a character is a digit, the extraction operator is called to read the number that starts with that character (lines 44–46). Otherwise, the character is read using a call to `get()`(lines 50–52) and copied to the target file.

The `put` Member Function

Each of the output stream classes `ofstream`, `fstream`, and `ostringstream` has a member function

```
ostream& put(int c);
```

that takes the integer code of a character and writes the corresponding character to the stream. You can think of `put` as the output stream counterpart to the input stream `get` functions. As an example, the following simple program prints `AB` on the screen.

```
#include <iostream>
using namespace std;
int main()
{
    char ch = 'A';
    cout.put(ch);
    cout.put(ch + 1);
}
```

Rewinding a File

VideoNote
Rewinding a File

Many times it is useful to open a file, process all the data in it, rewind the file back to the beginning, and process it again, perhaps in a slightly different fashion. For example, a user may ask the program to search a database for all records of a certain kind, and when those are found, the user may want to search the database for all records of some other kind.

File stream classes offer a number of different member functions that can be used to move around in a file. One such method is the

```
seekg(offset, place);
```

member function of the input stream classes (the file "seeks" to a certain place in the file; the 'g' is for "get" and denotes that the function works on an input stream, because we "get" data from an input stream). The new location in the file to seek to is given by the two parameters: the new location is at an offset of `offset` bytes from the starting point given by `place`. The offset parameter is a `long` integer, while `place` can be one of three values defined in the `ios` class. The starting place may be the beginning of the file, the current place in the file, or the end of the file. These places are indicated by the constants `ios:beg`, `ios::cur`, and `ios::end`, respectively.

More information on moving around in files will be given in a later section. Here we are interested in moving to the beginning of the file. To move to the beginning of a file, use the call

```
seekg(0L, ios::beg);
```

to move 0 bytes relative to the beginning of the file.

NOTE: If you are already at the end of the file, you must clear the end of file flag *before* calling this function. Thus, to move to the beginning of a file stream `dataIn` that you have just read to the end, you need the two statements

```
dataIn.clear();
dataIn.seekg(0L, ios::beg);
```

Program 13-10 illustrates how to rewind a file. It creates a file, writes some text to it, and closes the file. The file is then opened for input, read once to the end, rewound, and then read again.

Program 13-10

```
// Program shows how to rewind a file. It writes a
// text file and opens it for reading, then rewinds
// it to the beginning and reads it again.
#include <iostream>
#include <fstream>
using namespace std;

int main()
{
   // Variables needed to read or write file one
   // character at a time
   char ch;
   fstream ioFile("rewind.txt", ios::out);

   // Open file
   if (!ioFile)
   {
      cout << "Error in trying to create file";
      return 0;
   }

   // Write to file and close
   ioFile << "All good dogs " << endl
          << "growl, bark, and eat." << endl;
   ioFile.close();

   // Open the file
   ioFile.open("rewind.txt", ios::in);
   if (!ioFile)
   {
      cout << "Error in trying to open file";
      return 0;
   }

   // Read the file and echo to screen
   ioFile.get(ch);
   while (!ioFile.fail())
   {
      cout.put(ch);
      ioFile.get(ch);
   }

   // Rewind the file
   ioFile.clear();
   ioFile.seekg(0, ios::beg);

   // Read file again and echo to screen
   ioFile.get(ch);
   while (!ioFile.fail())
   {
      cout.put(ch);
      ioFile.get(ch);
```

(program continues)

Program 13-10 *(continued)*

```
    }
    return 0;
}
```

Program Output

```
All good dogs
growl, bark, and eat.
All good dogs
growl, bark, and eat.
```

Checkpoint

13.13 Make the required changes to the following program so it writes its output to the file `output.txt` instead of to the screen.

```
#include <iostream>
using namespace std;

int main()
{
   cout << "Today is the first day\n";
   cout << "of the rest of your life.\n";
   return 0;
}
```

13.14 Describe the purpose of the `eof` member function.

13.15 Assume the file `input.txt` contains the following characters:

R	u	n		S	p	o	t		r	u	n	\n	S	e

e		S	p	o	t		r	u	n	\n	<EOF>

What will the following program display on the screen?

```
#include <iostream>
#include <string>
#include <fstream>
using namespace std;

int main()
{
   fstream inFile("input.txt", ios::in);
   string item;
   inFile >> item;
   while (!inFile.fail())
   {
      cout << item << endl;
      inFile >> item;
   }
   return 0;
}
```

13.16 Describe the difference between reading a file with the >> operator and with the `getline` function.

13.17 Describe the difference between the `getline` function and the `get` member functions.

13.18 Describe the purpose of the `put` member function.

13.19 What will be stored in the file `out.dat` after the following program runs?

```
#include <iostream>
#include <fstream>
#include <iomanip>
using namespace std;

int main()
{
   const int SIZE = 5;
   ofstream outFile("out.dat");
   double nums[ ] = {100.279, 1.719, 8.602, 7.777, 5.099};
   outFile << setprecision(2);
   for (int count = 0; count < SIZE; count++)
   {
      outFile << setw(8) << nums[count];
   }
   outFile.close();
   return 0;
}
```

13.20 The following program skeleton, when complete, will allow the user to store names and telephone numbers in a file. Complete the program.

```
#include <iostream>
#include <fstream>
#include <cctype>  // Needed for toupper
using namespace std;

int main()
{
   // Define a file stream object here and use
   // the file stream to open the file phones.dat
   string name, phone;
   char add;
   cout << "This program allows you to add names and phone\n";
   cout << "numbers to phones.dat.\n";
   do
   {
      cout << "Do you wish to add an entry? ";
      cin >> add;
      if (toupper(add) == 'Y')
      {
         // Write code here that asks the user for a name
         // and phone number, then stores it in the file
      }
```

```
    } while (toupper(add) == 'Y');
    // Don't forget to close the file.
    return 0;
}
```

13.4 Binary Files

CONCEPT: Values of numeric data types such as `int` and `double` must be formatted for output before being written to text files. No such formatting takes place when numbers are written to binary files.

A short integer number such as 1297 has both a string representation "1297" (shown in Figure 13-2) and a binary numeric representation (shown in Figure 13-3). Both representations can be viewed as sequences of bytes. The string representation depends on the type of encoding used to represent individual characters and is 4 bytes long when the ASCII encoding is used. The number of bytes in the binary numeric representation depends on the type of the number and is 2 bytes long when the number is a `short int`. The conversion of string representation to numeric is called *parsing*, while the reverse conversion from numeric to string is called *formatting*.

Although people find it natural to work with numbers in their string representation, computer hardware is better adapted to processing numbers in their binary form. This is why numbers must be parsed when input from the keyboard or from a file that has been edited by a person. It is also the reason why numbers must be formatted when being output in a form that will be viewed by humans. There are times, however, when a program is outputting data to a file that will only be read by other programs and will never be viewed by humans. In those cases, formatting of numeric data during output and the parsing of numbers during input can be omitted. When data is written in unformatted form, it is said to be written in *binary*, and files written in this way are called *binary files*. In contrast, files that hold formatted data are called *text files*.

As a convenience to programmers, the stream insertion operator << provides automatic formatting of numbers during output. Likewise, the stream extraction operator >> provides parsing of numeric input. For example, consider the following program fragment:

```
ofstream file("num.dat");
short x = 1297;
file << x;
```

The last statement writes the contents of `x` to the file. When the number is written, however, it is stored as the characters `'1'`, `'2'`, `'9'`, and `'7'`. This is illustrated in Figure 13-2.

Figure 13-2

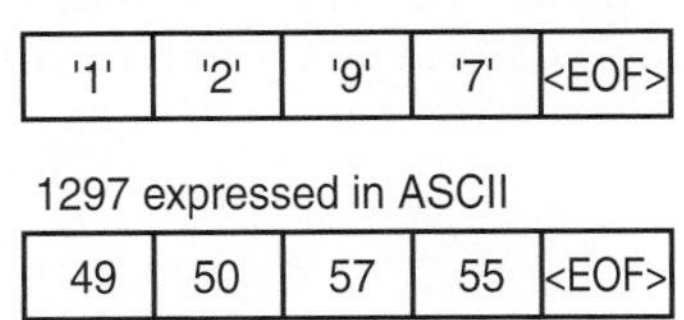

The number 1297 isn't stored in memory (in the variable `x`) in the fashion depicted in Figure 13-2, however. It is formatted as a binary number, occupying 2 bytes on a typical PC. Figure 13-3 shows how the number is represented in memory, using binary or hexadecimal.

Figure 13-3

1297 as a short integer, in binary

00000101	00010001

1297 as a short integer, in hexadecimal

05	11

The unformatted representation of the number shown in Figure 13-3 is the way the "raw" data is stored in memory. Information can be stored in a file in its pure, binary format. The first step is to open the file in binary mode. This is accomplished by using the `ios::binary` flag. Here is an example:

```
file.open("stuff.dat", ios::out | ios::binary);
```

Notice the `ios::out` and `ios::binary` flags are joined in the statement with the `|` operator. This causes the file to be opened in both output and binary modes.

NOTE: By default, files are opened in text mode.

The `write` member function of the `ostream` and `ofstream` classes can be used to write binary data to a file or other output stream. To call this function, you specify the address of a buffer containing an array of bytes to be written and an integer indicating how many bytes are to be written:

```
write(addressOfBuffer, numberOfBytes);
```

The `write` member function does not distinguish between integers, floats, or some other type in the buffer; it just treats the buffer as an array of bytes. Because C++ does not support a pointer to a byte, the prototype of `write` specifies that the address of a buffer be a pointer to a `char`:

```
write(char *addressOfBuffer, int numberOfBytes);
```

This means that when we call `write`, we need to tell the compiler to interpret the address of the buffer as a pointer to `char`. We do this by using a special form of type casting called a `reinterpret_cast`. Briefly, `reinterpret_cast` is used to force the compiler to interpret the bits of one type as if they defined a value of a different type. Here is an example of using `reinterpet_cast` to convert a pointer to a `double` into a pointer to a `char`.

```
double d = 45.9;
double *pd = &d;
```

```
char *pChar;
// convert pointer to double to pointer to char
pChar = reinterpret_cast<char *>(pd);
```

In general, to convert a value to some target type, use the expression

```
reinterpret_cast<TargetType>(value);
```

Here are examples of using `write` to write a `double` and an array of `double` to a file.

```
double dl = 45.9;
double dArray[3] = { 12.3, 45.8, 19.0 };
ofstream outFile("stuff.dat", ios::binary);
outFile.write(reinterpret_cast<char *>(&dl), sizeof(dl));
outFile.write(reinterpret_cast<char *>(dArray),
                                       sizeOf(dArray));
```

Notice that in writing a single variable such as `dl`, we treat the variable itself as the buffer and pass its address (in this case the address is `&dl`). However, in using an array as the buffer, we just pass the array because the array is already an address.

If the data we are writing happens to be character data, there is no need to use the cast. Here are some examples of writing character data.

```
char ch = 'X';
char charArray[5] = "Hello";
outFile.write(&ch, sizeof(ch));
outFile.write(charArray, sizeof(charArray));
```

There is a `read` member function in the `istream` and `ifstream` classes that can be used to read binary data written by `write`. It takes as parameters the address of a buffer in which the bytes read are to be stored, and the number of bytes to read:

```
read(addressOfBuffer, numberOfBytes)
```

The address of the buffer must be interpreted as a pointer to `char` using `reinterpret_cast`. You can find out if the specified number of bytes was successfully read by calling the `fail()` member function on the input stream.

Program 13-11 demonstrates the use of `write` and `read`. The program initializes an array of integers and then stores the number of array entries in the array using the statements

```
int buffer[ ] = {1, 2, 3, 4, 5, 6, 7, 8, 9, 10};
int size = sizeof(buffer)/sizeof(buffer[0]);
```

Recall that the `sizeof` operator can be used on variables to determine the number of bytes occupied by the variable. Here `sizeof(buffer)` returns the number of bytes allocated to the array by the initialization statement, and `sizeof(buffer[0])` returns the number of bytes occupied by a single array entry. By dividing the former by the latter, we obtain the number of array entries, which we then store in `size`.

Program 13-11

```
//This program uses the write and read functions.
#include <iostream>
#include <fstream>
using namespace std;

int main()
{
   // File object used to access file
   fstream file("nums.dat", ios::out | ios::binary);
   if (!file)
   {
      cout << "Error opening file.";
      return 0;
   }

   // Integer data to write to binary file
   int buffer[ ] = {1, 2, 3, 4, 5, 6, 7, 8, 9, 10};
   int size = sizeof(buffer)/sizeof(buffer[0]);

   // Write the data and close the file
   cout << "Now writing the data to the file.\n";
   file.write(reinterpret_cast<char *>(buffer),
              sizeof(buffer));
   file.close();

   // Open the file and use a binary read to read
   // contents of the file into an array
   file.open("nums.dat", ios::in);
   if (!file)
   {
      cout << "Error opening file.";
      return 0;
   }

   cout << "Now reading the data back into memory.\n";
   file.read(reinterpret_cast<char *>(buffer),
             sizeof(buffer));

   // Write out the array entries
   for (int count = 0; count < size ; count++)
      cout << buffer[count] << " ";

   // Close the file
   file.close();
   return 0;
}
```

Program Screen Output

```
Now writing the data to the file.
Now reading the data back into memory.
1 2 3 4 5 6 7 8 9 10
```

13.5 Creating Records with Structures

CONCEPT: Structures may be used to store fixed-length records to a file.

Earlier in this chapter the concept of fields and records was introduced. A field is an individual piece of information pertaining to a single item. A record is made up of fields and is a complete set of information about a single item. For example, a set of fields might be a person's name, age, address, and phone number. Together, all those fields that pertain to one person make up a record.

In C++, structures provide a convenient way to organize information into fields and records. For example, the following structure declaration could be used to create a record containing information about a person.

```
const int NAME_SIZE = 51, ADDR_SIZE = 51, PHONE_SIZE = 14;
struct Info
{
   char name[NAME_SIZE];
   int age;
   char address1[ADDR_SIZE];
   char address2[ADDR_SIZE];
   char phone[PHONE_SIZE];
};
```

Besides providing an organizational structure for information, structures also package information into a single unit. For example, assume the structure variable `person` is declared as

```
Info person;
```

Once the members (or fields) of `person` are filled with information, the entire variable may be written to a file using the `write` function:

```
file.write(reinterpret_cast<char*>(&person), sizeof(person));
```

The first argument is the address of the `person` variable. The `reinterpret_cast<char*>` cast operator is necessary because `write` expects the first argument to be a pointer to a `char`. When you pass the address of anything other than a `char` to the `write` function, you must make it look like a pointer to a `char` with the cast operator. The second argument is the `sizeof` operator. It tells `write` how many bytes to write to the file. Program 13-12 demonstrates this technique.

NOTE: Since structures can contain a mixture of data types, you should always use the `ios::binary` mode when opening a file to store them.

Program 13-12 allows you to build a file by filling the members of the `person` variable, then writing the variable to the file. To read a C-string into an array, the program first reads a string object using the `getline` function, and then uses `strcpy` to move the C-string into a character array. Program 13-13 opens the file and reads each record into the `person` variable, then displays the information on the screen.

Program 13-12

```
//This program demonstrates the use of a structure variable
//to store a record of information to a file.
#include <iostream>
#include <fstream>
#include <cstring>
#include <cctype>  // for toupper
using namespace std;

const int NAME_SIZE = 51, ADDR_SIZE = 51, PHONE_SIZE = 14;
struct Info
{
    char name[NAME_SIZE];
    int age;
    char address1[ADDR_SIZE];
    char address2[ADDR_SIZE];
    char phone[PHONE_SIZE];
};

int main() {
    Info person;   // Store information about a person
    char response; // User response

        string input;  // Used to read strings

    // Create file object and open file
    fstream people("people.dat", ios::out | ios::binary);
    if (!people)
    {
        cout << "Error opening file. Program aborting.\n";
        return 0;
    }

    // Keep getting information from user and writing it
    // to the file in binary mode
    do
    {
        cout << "Enter person information:\n";
        cout << "Name: ";
        getline(cin, input);
        strcpy(person.name, input.c_str());
        cout << "Age: ";
        cin >> person.age;
        cin.ignore(); // Skip over remaining newline
        cout << "Address line 1: ";
        getline(cin, input);
        strcpy(person.address1, input.c_str());
        cout << "Address line 2: ";
        getline(cin, input);
        strcpy(person.address2, input.c_str());
        cout << "Phone: ";
        getline(cin, input);
```

(program continues)

Program 13-12 *(continued)*

```
        strcpy(person.phone, input.c_str());
        people.write(reinterpret_cast<char *>(&person),
                     sizeof(person));
        cout << "Do you want to enter another record? ";
        cin >> response;
        cin.ignore();
    } while (toupper(response) == 'Y');

    // Close file
    people.close();
    return 0;
}
```

Program Screen Output with Example Input Shown in Bold

```
Enter person information:
Name: Charlie Baxter[Enter]
Age: 42[Enter]
Address line 1: 67 Kennedy Bvd.[Enter]
Address line 2: Perth, SC  38754[Enter]
Phone: (803)555-1234[Enter]
Do you want to enter another record? Y[Enter]
Enter person information:
Name: Merideth Murney[Enter]
Age: 22[Enter]
Address line 1: 487 Lindsay Lane[Enter]
Address line 2: Hazelwood, NC  28737[Enter]
Phone: (704)453-9999[Enter]
Do you want to enter another record? N[Enter]
```

Program 13-13

```
// This program demonstrates the use of a structure
// variable to read a record of information from a file.
#include <iostream>
#include <fstream>
using namespace std;

const int NAME_SIZE = 51, ADDR_SIZE = 51, PHONE_SIZE = 14;
struct Info
{
    char name[NAME_SIZE];
    int age;
    char address1[ADDR_SIZE];
    char address2[ADDR_SIZE];
    char phone[PHONE_SIZE];
};

int main()
{
```

(program continues)

Program 13-13 *(continued)*

```
    Info person; // Store person information
    char response; // User response

    // Create file object and open file for binary reading
    fstream people("people.dat", ios::in | ios::binary);
    if (!people)
    {
        cout << "Error opening file. Program aborting.\n";
        return 0;
    }

    // Label the output
    cout << "Here are the people in the file:\n\n";

    // Read one structure at a time and echo to screen
    people.read(reinterpret_cast<char *>(&person),
                sizeof (person));
    while (!people.eof())
    {
        cout << "Name: ";
        cout << person.name << endl;
        cout << "Age: ";
        cout << person.age << endl;
        cout << "Address line 1: ";
        cout << person.address1 << endl;
        cout << "Address line 2: ";
        cout << person.address2 << endl;
        cout << "Phone: ";
        cout << person.phone << endl;
        cout << "\nStrike any key to see the next record.\n";
        cin.get(response);
        people.read(reinterpret_cast<char *>(&person),
                    sizeof(person));
    }
    cout << "That's all the information in the file!\n";
    people.close();
    return 0;
}
```

Program Screen Output (Using the same file created by Program 13-12 as input)

```
Here are the people in the file:

Name: Charlie Baxter
Age: 42
Address line 1: 67 Kennedy Bvd.
Address line 2: Perth, SC  38754
Phone: (803)555-1234
```

(program output continues)

Program 13-13 *(continued)*

```
Strike any key to see the next record.
Name: Merideth Murney
Age: 22
Address line 1: 487 Lindsay Lane
Address line 2: Hazelwood, NC  28737
Phone: (704)453-9999

Strike any key to see the next record.
That's all the information in the file!
```

NOTE: Structures containing pointers cannot be correctly stored to disk using the techniques of this section. This is because if the structure is read into memory on a subsequent run of the program, it cannot be guaranteed that all program variables will be at the same memory locations. Because `string` class objects contain implicit pointers, they cannot be a part of a structure that has to be stored.

Checkpoint

13.21 Write a short program that opens two files `data1.txt` and `data2.txt` and then creates a third file `data3.txt` that consists of all the characters in `data1.txt` followed by all the characters in `data2.txt`.

13.22 How would the number 479 be stored in a text file? (Show the character and ASCII code representation.)

13.23 Describe the differences between the `write` member function and the << operator.

13.24 What are the purposes of the two arguments needed for the `write` member function?

13.25 What are the purposes of the two arguments needed for the `read` member function?

13.26 Describe the relationship between fields and records.

13.27 Assume the following structure declaration, variable, and file stream object definition exist in a program:

```
const int NAME_SIZE = 51;
struct Data
{
   char customer[NAME_SIZE];
   int num;
   double balance;
};
Data cust;
fstream file("stuff", ios::out | ios::binary);
```

Write a statement that uses the `write` member function to store the contents of `cust` in the file.

13.6 Random-Access Files

CONCEPT: Random access means nonsequentially accessing information in a file.

All of the programs created so far in this chapter have performed *sequential file access*. When a file is opened, the position where reading and/or writing will occur is at the file's beginning (unless the `ios::app` mode is used, which causes data to be written to the end of the file). If the file is opened for output, bytes are written to it one after the other. If the file is opened for input, data is read beginning at the first byte. As the reading or writing continues, the file stream object's read/write position advances sequentially through the file's contents.

The problem with sequential file access is that in order to read a specific byte from the file, all the bytes that precede it must be read first. For instance, if a program needs information stored at the 100th byte of a file, it will have to read the first 99 bytes to reach it. If you've ever searched for a song on a cassette tape, you understand sequential access. To find a song, you have to listen to all the songs that come before it, or fast-forward over them. There is no way to immediately jump to that particular song.

Although sequential file access is useful in many circumstances, it can slow a program down tremendously. If the file is very large, locating information buried deep inside it can take a long time. Alternatively, C++ allows a program to perform *random file access*. In random file access, a program may immediately jump to any byte in the file without first reading the preceding bytes. The difference between sequential and random file access is like the difference between a cassette tape and a compact disc. When listening to a CD, there is no need to listen to or fast-forward over unwanted songs. You simply jump to the track that you want to listen to. This is illustrated in Figure 13-4.

Figure 13-4

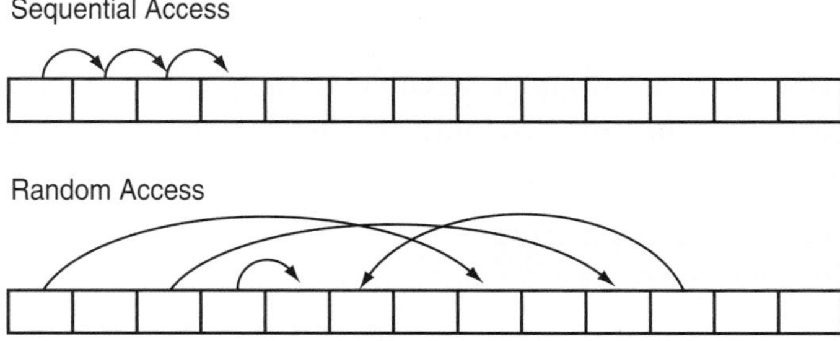

The `seekp` and `seekg` Member Functions

File stream objects have two member functions that are used to move the read/write position to any byte in the file. They are `seekp` and `seekg`. The `seekp` function is used with files opened for output and `seekg` is used with files opened for input. (It makes sense if you remember that "p" stands for "put" and "g" stands for "get." `seekp` is used with files that you put information into, and `seekg` is used with files you get information out of.)

Here is an example of seekp's usage:

```
file.seekp(20L, ios::beg);
```

The first argument is a long integer representing an offset into the file. This is the number of the byte you wish to move to. In this example, 20L is used. (Remember, the L suffix forces the compiler to treat the number as a long integer.) This statement moves the file's write position to byte number 20. (All numbering starts at 0, so byte number 20 is actually the 21st byte.)

The second argument is called the mode flag, and it designates where to calculate the offset from. The flag ios::beg means the offset is calculated from the beginning of the file. Alternatively, the offset can be calculated from the end of the file or the current position in the file. Table 13-5 lists the flags for all three of the random-access modes.

Table 13-5 File Positioning Flags

Mode Flag	Description
ios::beg	The offset is calculated from the beginning of the file.
ios::end	The offset is calculated from the end of the file.
ios::cur	The offset is calculated from the current position.

Table 13-6 shows examples of seekp and seekg using the various mode flags.

Table 13-6 File Seek Operations

Statement	How It Affects the Read/Write Position
file.seekp(32L, ios::beg);	Sets the write position to the 33rd byte (byte 32) from the beginning of the file.
file.seekp(-10L, ios::end);	Sets the write position to the 11th byte (byte 10) from the end of the file.
file.seekp(120L, ios::cur);	Sets the write position to the 121st byte (byte 120) from the current position.
file.seekg(2L, ios::beg);	Sets the read position to the 3rd byte (byte 2) from the beginning of the file.
file.seekg(-100L, ios::end);	Sets the read position to the 101st byte (byte 100) from the end of the file.
file.seekg(40L, ios::cur);	Sets the read position to the 41st byte (byte 40) from the current position.
file.seekg(0L, ios::end);	Sets the read position to the end of the file.

Notice that some of the examples in Table 13-6 use a negative offset. Negative offsets result in the read or write position being moved backward in the file, while positive offsets result in a forward movement.

Assume the file letters.txt contains the following data:

```
abcdefghijklmnopqrstuvwxyz
```

Program 13-14 uses the seekg function to jump around to different locations in the file, retrieving a character after each stop.

Program 13-14

```
// This program demonstrates the seekg function.
#include <iostream>
#include <fstream>
using namespace std;

int main()
{
   // Variable to access file
   char ch;

   // Open the file for reading
   fstream file("letters.txt", ios::in);
   if (!file)
   {
     cout << "Error opening file.";
     return 0;
   }

   // Get fifth byte from beginning of alphabet file
   file.seekg(5L, ios::beg);
   file.get(ch);
   cout << "Byte 5 from beginning: " << ch << endl;

   // Get tenth byte from end of alphabet file
   file.seekg(-10L, ios::end);
   file.get(ch);
   cout << "Byte 10 from end: " << ch << endl;

   // Go forward three bytes from current position
   file.seekg(3L, ios::cur);
   file.get(ch);
   cout << "Byte 3 from current: " << ch << endl;

   // Close file
   file.close();
   return 0;
}
```

Program Screen Output

```
Byte 5 from beginning: f
Byte 10 from end: q
Byte 3 from current: u
```

Program 13-15 shows another example of the seekg function. It opens the people.dat file created by Program 13-12. The file contains two records. Program 13-15 displays record 1 (the second record) first, then displays record 0.

Program 13-15

```
// This program demonstrates the use of a structure
// variable to read a record of information from a file.
#include <iostream>
#include <fstream>
using namespace std;

const int NAME_SIZE = 51, ADDR_SIZE = 51, PHONE_SIZE = 14;

// Declare a structure for the record
struct Info
{
   char name[NAME_SIZE];
   int age;
   char address1[ADDR_SIZE];
   char address2[ADDR_SIZE];
   char phone[PHONE_SIZE];
};

// Function Prototypes
long byteNum(int);
void showRec(Info);

int main()
{
   // Person information
   Info person;

   // Create file object and open the file
   fstream people("people.dat", ios::in | ios::binary);
   if (!people)
   {
      cout << "Error opening file. Program aborting.\n";
      return 0;
   }

   // Skip forward and read record 1 in the file
   cout << "Here is record 1:\n";
   people.seekg(byteNum(1), ios::beg);
   people.read(reinterpret_cast<char *>(&person),
               sizeof(person));
   showRec(person);

   // Skip backwards and read record 0 in the file
   cout << "\nHere is record 0:\n";
   people.seekg(byteNum(0), ios::beg);
   people.read(reinterpret_cast<char *>(&person),
               sizeof(person));
   showRec(person);

   // Close the file
   people.close();
```

(program continues)

Program 13-15 *(continued)*

```
   return 0;
}


//**********************************************************
// Definition of function byteNum. Accepts an integer as    *
// its argument. Returns the byte number in the file of the *
// record whose number is passed as the argument.           *
//**********************************************************
long byteNum(int recNum)
{
   return sizeof(Info) * recNum;
}

//**********************************************************
// Definition of function showRec. Accepts an Info structure *
// as its argument, and displays the structure's contents.   *
//**********************************************************
void showRec(Info record)
{
   cout << "Name: ";
   cout << record.name << endl;
   cout << "Age: ";
   cout << record.age << endl;
   cout << "Address line 1: ";
   cout << record.address1 << endl;
   cout << "Address line 2: ";
   cout << record.address2 << endl;
   cout << "Phone: ";
   cout << record.phone << endl;
}
```

Program Screen Output (Using the same file created by Program 13-12 as input)

```
Here is record 1:
Name: Merideth Murney
Age: 22
Address line 1: 487 Lindsay Lane
Address line 2: Hazelwood, NC  28737
Phone: (704)453-9999

Here is record 0:
Name: Charlie Baxter
Age: 42
Address line 1: 67 Kennedy Bvd.
Address line 2: Perth, SC  38754
Phone: (803)555-1234
```

The program has two important functions other than `main`. The first, `byteNum`, takes a record number as its argument and returns that record's starting byte. It calculates the record's starting byte by multiplying the record number by the size of the `Info` structure. This returns the offset of that record from the beginning of the file. The second function, `showRec`, accepts an `Info` structure as its argument and displays its contents on the screen.

The `tellp` and `tellg` Member Functions

File stream objects have two more member functions that may be used for random file access: `tellp` and `tellg`. Their purpose is to return, as a `long` integer, the current byte number of a file's read and write position. As you can guess, `tellp` is used to return the write position and `tellg` is used to return the read position. Assuming `pos` is a `long` integer, here is an example of the functions' usage:

```
pos = outFile.tellp();
pos = inFile.tellg();
```

Program 13-16 demonstrates the `tellg` function. It opens the `letters.txt` file, which was also used in Program 13-14. The file contains the following characters:

```
abcdefghijklmnopqrstuvwxyz
```

Program 13-16

```
// This program demonstrates the tellg function.
#include <iostream>
#include <fstream>
#include <cctype>       // For toupper
using namespace std;

int main()
{
    // Variables used to read the file
    long offset;
    char ch;
    char response; //User response

    // Create the file object and open the file
    fstream file("letters.txt", ios::in);
    if (!file)
    {
        cout << "Error opening file.";
        return 0;
    }
    // Work with the file
    do
    {
        // Where in the file am I?
        cout << "Currently at position "
             << file.tellg() << endl;

        // Get a file offset from the user.
        cout << "Enter an offset from the "
             <<  "beginning of the file: ";
        cin >> offset;

```

(program continues)

Program 13-16 *(continued)*

```
        // Read the character at the given offset
        file.seekg(offset, ios::beg);
        file.get(ch);
        cout << "Character read: " << ch << endl;
        cout << "Do it again? ";
        cin >> response;
    } while (toupper(response) == 'Y');
    file.close();
    return 0;
}
```

Program Output with Example Input Shown in Bold

```
Currently at position 0
Enter an offset from the beginning of the file: 5[Enter]
Character read: f
Do it again? y[Enter]
Currently at position 6
Enter an offset from the beginning of the file: 0[Enter]
Character read: a
Do it again? y[Enter]
Currently at position 1
Enter an offset from the beginning of the file: 20[Enter]
Character read: u
Do it again? n[Enter]
```

13.7 Opening a File for Both Input and Output

CONCEPT: You may perform input and output on an `fstream` file without closing it and reopening it.

There are times when you need to update data stored in a file. To do this, you need to open the file, copy some of the data into memory, modify it, write the data back to the file, and then close the file. A file can be opened for both input and output by combining the `ios::in` and `ios::out` flags with the | operator:

```
fstream file("data.dat", ios::in | ios::out)
```

The same operation may be accomplished with the open member function:

```
file.open("data.dat", ios::in | ios::out);
```

You can also specify the `ios::binary` flag if binary data is to be written to the file. Here is an example:

```
file.open("data.dat", ios::in | ios::out | ios::binary);
```

When an `fstream` file is opened with both the `ios::in` and `ios::out` flags, the file's current contents are preserved, and the read/write position is initially placed at the beginning of the file. If the file does not exist, it is created (unless the `ios::nocreate` is also used).

Programs 13-17, 13-18, and 13-19 demonstrate many of the techniques we have discussed. Program 13-17 sets up a file with five blank inventory records. Each record is a structure with members for holding a part description, quantity on hand, and price. Program 13-18 displays the contents of the file on the screen. Program 13-19 opens the file in both input and output modes and allows the user to change the contents of a specific record.

Program 13-17

```
// This program sets up a file of blank inventory records.
#include <iostream>
#include <fstream>
using namespace std;

const int DESC_SIZE = 31, NUM_RECORDS = 5;
// Declaration of Invtry structure.
struct Invtry
{
   char desc[DESC_SIZE];
   int qty;
   double price;
};

int main()
{
   // Variables needed to write the file
   Invtry record = { "", 0, 0.0 };

   // Create file object and open file
   fstream inventory("invtry.dat", ios::out | ios::binary);
   if (!inventory)
   {
      cout << "Error opening file.";
      return 0;
   }

   // Now write the blank records
   for (int count = 0; count < NUM_RECORDS; count++)
   {
      cout << "Now writing record " << count << endl;
      inventory.write(reinterpret_cast<char *>(&record),
                      sizeof(record));
   }

   // Close the file
   inventory.close();
   return 0;
}
```

(program continues)

Program 13-17 *(continued)*

Program Screen Output

```
Now writing record 0
Now writing record 1
Now writing record 2
Now writing record 3
Now writing record 4
```

Program 13-18 simply displays the contents of the inventory file on the screen. It can be used to verify that Program 13-17 successfully created the blank records and that Program 13-19 correctly modified the designated record.

Program 13-18

```
// This program displays the contents of the inventory file.
#include <iostream>
#include <fstream>
using namespace std;

const int DESC_SIZE = 31;

// Declaration of Invtry structure
struct Invtry
{
   char desc[DESC_SIZE];
   int qty;
   double price;
};

int main()
{
   // Buffer used for reading
   Invtry record;

   // Create and open the file for reading
   fstream inventory("invtry.dat", ios::in | ios::binary);
   if (!inventory)
   {
      cout << "Error in opening the file.";
      return 0;
   }

   // Now read and display the records
   inventory.read(reinterpret_cast<char *>(&record),
                  sizeof(record));
   while (!inventory.eof())
   {
      cout << "Description: ";
      cout << record.desc << endl;
```

(program continues)

Program 13-18 *(continued)*

```
        cout << "Quantity: ";
        cout << record.qty << endl;
        cout << "Price: ";
        cout << record.price << endl << endl;
        inventory.read(reinterpret_cast<char *>(&record),
                       sizeof(record));
    }
    inventory.close();
    return 0;
}
```

Here is the screen output of Program 13-18 if it is run immediately after Program 13-17 sets up the file of blank records.

Program Screen Output

```
Description:
Quantity: 0
Price: 0.0

Description:
Quantity: 0
Price: 0.0

Description:
Quantity: 0
Price: 0.0

Description:
Quantity: 0
Price: 0.0

Description:
Quantity: 0
Price: 0.0
```

Program 13-19 allows the user to change the contents of an individual record in the inventory file.

Program 13-19

```
// This program allows the user to edit a specific
// record in the inventory file.
#include <iostream>
#include <fstream>
using namespace std;

const int DESC_SIZE = 31;
// Declaration of Invtry structure
struct Invtry
{
```

(program continues)

Program 13-19 *(continued)*

```
   char desc[DESC_SIZE];
   int qty;
   double price;
};

int main()
{
   // Variables needed to read the file
   Invtry record;
   long recNum;

   // Open the file
   fstream inventory("invtry.dat", ios::in | ios::out |
                     ios::binary);
   if (!inventory)
   {
      cout << "Error opening file.";
      return 0;
   }

   // Move to the desired record and read it into record
   cout << "Which record do you want to edit?";
   cin >> recNum;
   inventory.seekg(recNum * sizeof(record), ios::beg);
   inventory.read(reinterpret_cast<char *>(&record),
                  sizeof(record));

   // Get new data from user and edit in-memory record
   cout << "Description: ";
   cout << record.desc << endl;
   cout << "Quantity: ";
   cout << record.qty << endl;
   cout << "Price: ";
   cout << record.price << endl;
   cout << "Enter the new data:\n";
   cout << "Description: ";
   cin.ignore();
   cin.getline(record.desc, DESC_SIZE);
   cout << "Quantity: ";
   cin >> record.qty;
   cout << "Price: ";
   cin >> record.price;

   // Move to the right place in file and write the record
   inventory.seekp(recNum * sizeof(record), ios::beg);
   inventory.write(reinterpret_cast<char *>(&record),
                   sizeof(record));

   // Close the file
   inventory.close();
   return 0;
}
```

(program continues)

Program 13-19 *(continued)*

Program Screen Output with Example Input Shown in Bold

```
Which record do you want to edit? 2[Enter]
Description:
Quantity: 0
Price: 0.0
Enter the new data:
Description: Wrench[Enter]
Quantity: 10[Enter]
Price: 4.67[Enter]
```

Checkpoint

13.28 Describe the difference between the `seekg` and the `seekp` functions.

13.29 Describe the difference between the `tellg` and the `tellp` functions.

13.30 Describe the meaning of the following file access flags.

```
ios::beg
ios::end
ios::cur
```

13.31 What is the number of the first byte in a file?

13.32 Briefly describe what each of the following statements does.

```
file.seekp(100L, ios::beg);
file.seekp(-10L, ios::end);
file.seekg(-25L, ios::cur);
file.seekg(30L, ios::cur);
```

13.33 Describe the mode that each of the following statements causes a file to be opened in.

```
file.open("info.dat", ios::in | ios::out);
file.open("info.dat", ios::in | ios::app);
file.open("info.dat", ios::in | ios::out | ios::ate);
file.open("info.dat", ios::in | ios::out | ios::binary);
```

13.8 Online Friendship Connections Case Study: *Object Serialization*

Online Friendship Connections is an online service that helps people meet and make new friends. People who want to join the club and use its services fill out a registration form, stating their names, age, contact information, gender, hobbies, personal interests, and other pertinent information about themselves. They also specify the qualities they are looking for in a new friend. The service will then try to get two people together if the personal information submitted indicates that there is a high probability of a good match.

Object Serialization

Online Friendship Connections will store information about its members in files. Member information will be manipulated by a C++ program and will be stored in objects of appropriately designed classes. These objects may involve pointers to other objects, forming a network of objects whose structure must somehow be preserved when the data are stored to a file. This structure is then reconstructed when the data is read back from the file at a later time. The process of transforming complex networks of objects interconnected through pointers into a form that can be stored in a disk file (or on some other medium outside of central memory) is called *object serialization*.

In this section, we will illustrate some of the techniques used in serializing objects by looking at a simple case in which an object containing a C++ `string` object is serialized. Recall that C++ strings are normally implemented using pointers to dynamically allocated array of `char`.

Designing the Classes Needed by the Program

A simple class that stores a portion of the information submitted by members of Online Friendship Connections might include a first name, middle initial, last name, and the age of a member. In addition to the usual getter and setter functions, we need member functions for *serializing* the object: that is, a member function that converts the object into data stored in a file:

```
void store(ofstream &outFile);
```

We also need a member function for *deserializing* an object: that is, one that reads from a file data previously placed there by `store`, recovers its structure, and sets the data members of the object correctly:

```
void load(ifstream &inFile);
```

After adding a constructor and a `display` member function, we come up with the following class:

Contents of `serialization.h`

```
#include <iostream>
#include <fstream>
#include <string>
using namespace std;

class Person
{
  string fname, lname;
  char mi;
  int age;
public:
  string getFname() const {return fname;}
  string getLname() const {return lname;}
  char getMi() const {return mi;}
  int getAge() const {return age;}

  void setFname(string name){fname = name;}
```

```
   void setLname(string name){lname = name;}
   void setMi(char ch){mi = ch;}

   // Read data from file
   void load(ifstream &inFile);
   // store data to file
   void store(ofstream  &outFile);

   // Constructor
   Person(string fname = "", char mi = 0,
          string lname = "", int age = 0);

   void display()
   {
     cout << fname << " " << mi << " " << lname << endl
          << "Age : " << age << endl;
   }
};
```

Determining a Serialization Scheme

We cannot just write the contents of a `Person` object to a disk file because the string members contain pointers to arrays of characters which need to be stored so that the string objects can be reconstructed at a later time when the object is deserialized. Because strings have varying lengths, `Person` objects will occupy varying amounts of space on the disk when they are deserialized. A simple but effective serialization scheme is to first write all the members of the object that take up constant space, and then write each member whose space requirement may vary on the disk, preceded by the number of bytes that the member occupies. For the `Person` class, we can use the scheme shown in Figure 13-5.

Figure 13-5

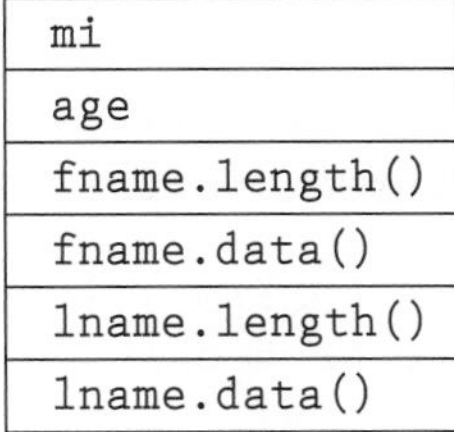

mi
age
fname.length()
fname.data()
lname.length()
lname.data()

The code for the `store` function is then very straightforward and can be seen in the listing of the file `serialization.cpp`. To design the `load` function, we note that we need to reconstruct the `fname` and `lname` strings by first reading their data portions into an in-memory `buffer` that is an array of character. To do this for `fname`, we first read the number of bytes occupied by its data portion from the file:

```
int firstNameLength;
inFile.read(addr(&firstNameLength), sizeof(int));
```

We must then read that many bytes into a buffer and null terminate the buffer to turn it into a C-string:

```
inFile.read(buffer, firstNameLength);
buffer[firstNameLength] = '\0';
```

Finally, we convert the C-string to a string object by assigning it to the `fname` member. The C++ string has a convert constructor that automatically converts C-strings to string objects to make such assignments possible.

```
frame = buffer;
```

The `buffer` array is used as a temporary holding place. Making it an instance member of the class would allocate space for it in every object and would waste a lot of memory. A better idea to make it a static member of the class, so that the scratch space can be shared by all members of the object. However, we note that it is only used by the `load` member function. For this reason, we make it local static. That way, space for the buffer is allocated once instead of being allocated anew for each call to `load`. Static local variables were described in Chapter 6.

The rest of the member functions needed to implement the `Person` class are shown in the listing of the `serialization.cpp` file.

Contents of `serialization.cpp`

```
#include "serialization.h"

Person::Person(string fname,  char mi,
               string lname,  int age)
{
   this->fname = fname;
   this->lname = lname;
   this->mi = mi;
   this->age = age;
}

//*******************************************
// Stores mi, age, then length of fname,     *
// then data for fname, then length of lname, *
// then data for lname                        *
//*******************************************
void Person::store(ofstream &outFile)
{
   outFile.write(&mi, sizeof(mi));
   outFile.write(reinterpret_cast<char *>(&age),
                 sizeof(age));

   // Write length and data for fname and lname
   int firstNameLength = fname.length();
   outFile.write(reinterpret_cast<char *>(&firstNameLength),
                 sizeof(int));
   outFile.write(fname.data(), firstNameLength);
   int lastNameLength = lname.length();
   outFile.write(reinterpret_cast<char *>(&lastNameLength),
                 sizeof(int));
   outFile.write(lname.data(), lastNameLength);
}

```

```
//******************************************
// Reads the data in the format written by     *
// Person::store                                *
//******************************************
void Person::load(ifstream &inFile)
{
   const int BUFFER_SIZE = 256;
   static char buffer[256]; //used to read names

   inFile.read(&mi, sizeof(mi));
   inFile.read(reinterpret_cast<char *>(&age), sizeof(age));

   // First get length and data for fname
   int firstNameLength;
   inFile.read(reinterpret_cast<char *>(&firstNameLength),
               sizeof(int));

   // Read the data for fname into a local buffer
   inFile.read(buffer, firstNameLength);

   // Null terminate the buffer
   buffer[firstNameLength] = '\0';
   fname = buffer;  //take advantage of convert constructor

   // Do the same thing for length and data for lname
   int lastNameLength;
   inFile.read(reinterpret_cast<char *>(&lastNameLength),
               sizeof(int));
   inFile.read(buffer, lastNameLength);
   buffer[lastNameLength] = '\0';
   lname = buffer;
}
```

We need two separate programs to demonstrate the serialization capabilities of the `Person` class. Program 13-20, which generates no screen output, creates an array of two objects, serializes them, and writes them to a file.

Program 13-20

```
// This program demonstrates object serialization.
#include "serialization.h"
int main()
{
   // Array of objects to store in file
   Person people[ ] =
       { Person("Joseph", 'X', "Puff", 32),
         Person("Louise", 'Y', "Me", 28)
       };
   // Open a file and store the array of people
   ofstream outFile("MorePeople.dat", ios::binary);
   if(!outFile)
   {
     cout << "The output file cannot be opened";
```

(program continues)

Program 13-20 *(continued)*

```
      exit(1);
    }

    // Store the people data in the file
    people[0].store(outFile);
    people[1].store(outFile);
    cout << "Data has been written to the file "
         << " 'Morepeople.dat'";

   // Close file
   outFile.close();
   return 0;
}
```

Program 13-21 opens the file created by Program 13-20, deserializes the two objects in the file, and displays them on the screen.

Program 13-21

```
//This program demonstrates object deserialization.
#include "serialization.h"
int main()
{
   const int NUM_PEOPLE = 2;
   Person people[NUM_PEOPLE];
   // Open a file and load the array of people
   ifstream inFile("MorePeople.dat", ios::binary);
   if(!inFile)
   {
     cout << "The input file cannot be opened";
     exit(1);
   }

   // Read the data from the file
   for (int k = 0; k < NUM_PEOPLE; k++)
      people[k].load(inFile);

   // Display the data
   for (int k = 0; k < NUM_PEOPLE; k++)
      people[k].display();

   // Close the file
   inFile.close();
   return 0;
}
```

Program Output

```
Joseph X Puff
Age : 32
Louise Y Me
Age : 28
```

13.9 Tying It All Together: *File Merging and Color-Coded HTML*

Suppose that you have two files, with each file containing a sorted list of names and each name occurring on a line by itself, as illustrated in Table 13-7.

Table 13-7

Black File	Blue File
Abrams, Elaine	Avon, Martha
Bostrom, Andy	Gomez, Diane
Potus, Nicholas	Pistachio, Mary
Radon, Joseph	Rhodes, Peter
Williams, Nancy	Wilson, Zelda
	Zazinski, Pete

You want to merge the contents of the two files into one file in such a way that the merged file is sorted in alphabetic order. You also want people to be able to tell at a glance which of the two original files a given line in the merged file came from. One way to do this is to color-code the original files and then display each line of the merged file in the color of the originating file:

Abrams, Elaine
Avon, Martha
Bostrom, Andy
Gomez, Diane
Pistachio, Mary
Potus, Nicholas
Radon, Joseph
Rhodes, Peter
Williams, Nancy
Wilson, Zelda
Zazinski, Pete

To accomplish this, we code the output file in HTML and arrange for the browser to display each line with the appropriate color. This can be done via what are called CSS styles. We will use the HTML span elements to enclose a line and then color the content of the span element using the CSS style attribute. For the two files shown above, our program will produce the following output:

```
<span style = "color:black"> Abrams, Elaine <br/> </span>
<span style = "color:blue"> Avon, Martha <br/> </span>
<span style = "color:black"> Bostrom, Andy <br/> </span>
<span style = "color:blue"> Gomez, Diane <br/> </span>
<span style = "color:blue"> Pistachio, Mary <br/> </span>
<span style = "color:black"> Potus, Nicholas <br/> </span>
<span style = "color:black"> Radon, Joseph <br/> </span>
```

```
<span style = "color:blue"> Rhodes, Peter <br/> </span>
<span style = "color:black"> Williams, Nancy <br/> </span>
<span style = "color:blue"> Wilson, Zelda <br/> </span>
<span style = "color:blue"> Zazinski, Pete <br/> </span>
```

The `<br/>` HTML element signifies a line break.

Our solution to this problem will use a subclass of `fstream` that has a member function for writing a string inside of an HTML span element. The span element will specify the color the browser should use to display the string:

```
class ColorCodedStream : public fstream
{
public:
    void writeInColor(string str, string  aColor)
    {
        *this << "<span style = \"color:" + aColor + "\"> ";
        *this << str << " <br/> ";
        *this << "</span>\n";
    }
};
```

Our program will need to open two files for reading and a third file for writing. To avoid repetition of code, we write a function

```
void openFile(fstream &file, string descr);
```

that takes a file object and a description (`"black"`, `"blue"`, or `"output"`), prompts the user for the name of a file, and then opens the file. A file described as `"black"` or `"blue"` is opened for input, while a file described as `"output"` is opened for output.

Our program also uses the library function

```
getline(istream &in, string &str);
```

to read strings from the input file one line at a time. The program has two variables

```
string blackInput, blueInput
```

that are used to hold the line that was last read from the corresponding file. Because a read may be unsuccessful, the program tests each file object for errors before using the input last read from it. For example, the code

```
if (blackFile && !blueFile)
 {
     // Only blackInput is good
     outputFile.writeInColor(blackInput, "black");
     getline(blackFile, blackInput);
 }
```

determines that the last read from the black file was good while the read from the blue file failed, so it processes the input from the black file. After the input from the black file has been written out, the black file is read again to prepare for the next iteration of the loop. When the program cannot read any more data from either file (this is checked at the top of the loop that begins at line 39) the program terminates.

Program 13-22

```
// This program demonstrates file merging and the use
// of CSS to determine text colors in HTML documents.
#include <stdlib.h>
#include <iostream>
#include <fstream>
#include <string>
using namespace std;

// This subclass of fstream adds the ability to
// write a string that is automatically embedded
// in an HTML span element with a color specification
// style
class ColorCodedStream : public fstream
{
public:
     void writeInColor(string str, string  aColor)
     {
         *this << "<span style = \"color:" + aColor + "\"> ";
         *this << str << " <br/> ";
         *this << "</span>\n";
     }
};

void openFile(fstream &file, string descr); // Prototype

int main()
{
     ColorCodedStream outputFile;
     fstream blackFile, blueFile;
     openFile(blackFile, "black");
     openFile(blueFile, "blue");
     openFile(outputFile, "output");

     string blackInput, blueInput;
     // read the first line from each file
     getline(blackFile, blackInput);   // Read black file into buffer
     getline(blueFile, blueInput); // Read blue file into buffer

     while (blackFile || blueFile)
     {
         if (blackFile &&  blueFile)
         {
             // Both buffers have fresh data
             if (blackInput <= blueInput)
             {
                 outputFile.writeInColor(blackInput, "black");
                 getline(blackFile, blackInput);
             }
             else
             {
```

(program continues)

Program 13-22 *(continued)*

```
                outputFile.writeInColor(blueInput, "blue");
                getline(blueFile, blueInput);
            }
        }
        if (blackFile && !blueFile)
        {
            // Only blackInput is good
            outputFile.writeInColor(blackInput, "black");
            getline(blackFile, blackInput);
        }
        if (blueFile && !blackFile)
        {
            // Only blueInput is good
            outputFile.writeInColor(blueInput, "blue");
            getline(blueFile, blueInput);
        }
    }
    return 0;
}
//*******************************************************************
// Opens a specified file for reading or writing. The descr argument *
// is used in prompting for the name of the file.                     *
//*******************************************************************
void openFile(fstream &file, string descr)
{
    string fileName;
    cout << "Enter the  name of the " << descr << " file: ";
    cin >> fileName;

    // Determine whether the file should be opened for reading
    // or writing based on the description (descr)
    if (descr == "output")
        file.open(fileName.data(), ios::out);
    else
        file.open(fileName.data(), ios::in);

    // Check if file open was successful
    if (!file)
    {
        cout << "Cannot open the file " << fileName;
        exit(1);
    }
}
```

Sample Program Interaction with User Input Shown in Bold

```
Enter the name of the black file: blackfile.txt[Enter]
Enter the name of the blue file: bluefile.txt[Enter]
Enter the name of the output file: mergedfile.html[Enter]
```

The contents of the output file can be viewed in a browser.

Review Questions and Exercises

Fill-in-the-Blank and Short Answer

1. All files are assigned a(n)__________ that is used for identification purposes by the operating system and the user.
2. Before a file can be used, it must first be __________.
3. When a program is finished using a file, it should __________ it.
4. The __________ header file is required for file I/O operations.
5. The three file stream data types are __________, __________, and __________.
6. The __________ file stream data type is for output files.
7. The __________ file stream data type is for input files.
8. The __________ file stream data type is for output files, input files, or files that perform both input and output.
9. Write a statement that defines a file stream object named `people`. The object will be used for file output.
10. Write a statement that defines a file stream object named `pets`. The object will be used for file input.
11. Write a statement that defines a file stream object named `places`. The object will be used for both output and input.
12. Write two statements that use the `people` file stream object to open a file named `people.dat`. (Show how to open the file with a member function and at definition.) The file should be opened for output.
13. Write two statements that use the `pets` file stream object to open a file named `pets.dat`. (Show how to open the file with a member function and at definition.) The file should be opened for input.
14. Write two statements that use the `places` file stream object to open a file named `places.dat`. (Show how to open the file with a member function and at definition.) The file should be opened for both input and output.
15. If a file fails to open, the file stream object will be set to __________.
16. Write a program segment that defines a file stream object named `employees`. The file should be opened for both input and output (in binary mode). If the file fails to open, the program segment should display an error message.
17. The same formatting techniques used with __________ may also be used when writing information to a file.
18. The __________ member function reports when the end of the file has been encountered.
19. The __________ function reads a line of text from a file.
20. The __________ member function reads a single character from a file.
21. The __________ member function writes a single character to a file.

22. __________ files contain data that is unformatted and not necessarily stored as ASCII text.
23. __________ files contain information formatted as ASCII text.
24. A record is a complete set of information about a single item and is made up of __________.
25. In C++, __________ provide a convenient way to organize information into fields and records.
26. The __________ member function writes "raw" binary data to a file.
27. The __________ member function reads "raw" binary data from a file.
28. The __________ operator is necessary if you pass anything other than a pointer to `char` as the first argument of the two functions mentioned in questions 26 and 27.
29. In __________ file access, the contents of the file are read in the order they appear in the file, from the file's start to its end.
30. In __________ file access, the contents of a file may be read in any order.
31. The __________ member function moves a file's read position to a specified byte in the file.
32. The __________ member function moves a file's write position to a specified byte in the file.
33. The __________ member function returns a file's current read position.
34. The __________ member function returns a file's current write position.
35. The __________ mode flag causes an offset to be calculated from the beginning of a file.
36. The __________ mode flag causes an offset to be calculated from the end of a file.
37. The __________ mode flag causes an offset to be calculated from the current position in the file.
38. A negative offset causes the file's read or write position to be moved __________ in the file from the position specified by the mode.

Algorithm Workbench

39. Give a pseudocode algorithm for determining the length of a file: that is, the number of bytes that are stored in the file.
40. Give a pseudocode algorithm for comparing two files to see if their contents are identical.
41. Design a pseudocode algorithm for reversing the contents of a text file into another file. Assume that the amount of memory is limited, so that you cannot read the entire source file into memory before you start writing it to a second file in reverse order.
42. Suppose that you have two text files that contain sequences of integers separated by white space (blank space, tabs, and line breaks). The integers in both files appear in sorted order, with smaller values near the beginning of the file and large values closer to the end. Write a pseudocode algorithm that merges the two sequences into a single sorted sequence that is written to a third file.

Find the Error

43. Each of the following programs or program segments has errors. Find as many as you can.

A)
```
fstream file(ios::in | ios::out);
file.open("info.dat");
if (!file)
{
   cout << "Could not open file.\n";
}
```

B)
```
ofstream file;
file.open("info.dat", ios::in);
if (file)
{
   cout << "Could not open file.\n";
}
```

C)
```
fstream file("info.dat");
if (!file)
{
   cout << "Could not open file.\n";
}
```

D)
```
fstream dataFile("info.dat", ios:in | ios:binary);
int x = 5;
dataFile << x;
```

E)
```
fstream dataFile("info.dat", ios:in);
int x;
while (dataFile.eof())
{
   dataFile >> x;
   cout << x << endl;
}
```

F)
```
fstream dataFile("info.dat", ios:in);
char line[81];
dataFile.get(line);
```

G)
```
fstream dataFile("info.dat", ios:in);
char stuff[81];
dataFile.get(stuff);
```

H)
```
fstream dataFile("info.dat", ios:in);
char stuff[81] = "abcdefghijklmnopqrstuvwxyz";
dataFile.put(stuff);
```

I)
```
fstream dataFile("info.dat", ios:out);
struct Date
{
   int month;
   int day;
   int year;
};
Date dt = { 4, 2, 98 };
dataFile.write(&dt, sizeof(int));
```

J)
```
fstream inFile("info.dat", ios:in);
int x;
inFile.seekp(5);
inFile >> x;
```

Soft Skills

44. Learning to look beyond the symptoms of a problem to identify the root cause is an important skill. Bugs in a program are sometimes the result of careless mistakes, but at other times, they reflect a fundamental misunderstanding of some concept.

    Suppose that a friend has been trying to determine why his file processing program is not working correctly. You notice that he is passing file objects to functions by value. In addition to simply telling your friend that file parameters need to be passed by reference, what can you tell him that will help him understand *why* files need to be passed by reference?

    Suppose now that you need to demonstrate this bug to other people. Bugs usually occur in the context of a larger program, which can make it difficult for a person unfamiliar with the program to understand what is happening. Write a program that is as short as possible, but still has the file-passing bug.

Programming Challenges

1. File Previewer

Write a program that asks the user for the name of a text file. The program should display the first 10 lines of the file on the screen. If the file has fewer than 10 lines, the entire file should be displayed along with a message indicating the entire file has been displayed.

2. File Display Program

Write a program that asks the user for the name of a file. The program should display the contents of the file on the screen. If the file's contents won't fit on a single screen, the program should display 24 lines of output at a time, and then pause. Each time the program pauses, it should wait for the user to type a key before the next 24 lines are displayed.

3. Punch Line

Write a program that reads and prints a joke and its punch line from two different files. The first file contains a joke, but not its punch line. The second file has the punch line as its last line, preceded by "garbage." The main function of your program should open the two files and then call two functions, passing each one the file it needs. The first function should read and display each line in the file it is passed (the joke file). The second function should display only the last line of the file it is passed (the punch line file). It should find this line by seeking to the end of the file and then backing up to the beginning of the last line. Data to test your program can be found in the `joke.dat` and `punchline.dat` files.

4. Tail of a File

Write a program that asks the user for the name of a text file. The program should display the last 10 lines of the file on the screen (the "tail" of the file). If the file has less than 10 lines, the entire file is displayed, with a message that the entire file has been displayed. The program should do this by seeking to the end of the file and then backing up to the tenth line from the end.

5. String Search

Write a program that asks the user for the name of a file and a string to search for. The program will search the file for all occurrences of the specified string and display all lines that contain the string. After all occurrences have been located, the program should report the number of times the string appeared in the file.

6. Sentence Filter

A program that processes an input file and produces an output file is called a *filter*. Write a program that asks the user for two file names. The first file will be opened for input, and the second file will be opened for output. (It will be assumed that the first file contains sentences that end with a period.) The program will read the contents of the first file and change all the letters other than the first letter of sentences to lowercase. First letter of sentences should be made uppercase. The revised contents should be stored in the second file.

7. File Encryption Filter

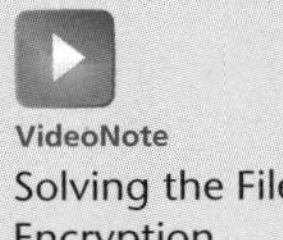

VideoNote
Solving the File Encryption Filter Problem

File encryption is the science of writing the contents of a file in a secret code. Your encryption program should work like a filter, reading the contents of one file, modifying the information into a code, and then writing the coded contents out to a second file. The second file will be a version of the first file, but written in a secret code.

Although there are complex encryption techniques, you should come up with a simple one of your own. For example, you could read the first file one character at a time and add 10 to the ASCII code of each character before it is written to the second file.

8. File Decryption Filter

Write a program that decrypts the file produced by the program in Programming Challenge 7. The decryption program should read the contents of the coded file, restore the information to its original state, and write it to another file.

9. Letter Frequencies

The letter *e* is the most frequently used letter in English prose, and the letter *z* is the least frequently used. A friend of yours doing a sociology experiment believes that this may not necessarily be true of the writings of first-year college students. To test his theory, he asks you to write a program that will take a text file and print, for each letter of the English alphabet, the number of times the letter appears in the file.

Hint: Use an integer array of size 128, and use the ASCII values of letters to index into the array to store and retrieve counts for the letters.

10. Put It Back

C++ input stream classes have two member functions, `unget()` and `putback()`, that can be used to "undo" an operation performed by the `get()` function. Research these functions on the Internet, and then use one of them to rewrite Program 13-9 without using the `peek()` function.

11. Insertion Sort on a File I

Write a program that uses an initially empty file to store a sorted list of integers entered by the user. The integers are stored in binary form. Each time the program is run, it opens the file and outputs the list of stored integers onto the screen. The program then asks the user to enter a new integer X. The program then looks at the integer at the end of the file. If that integer is less or equal to X, the program stores X at the end of the file and closes the file. Otherwise, the program starts at the end of the file and works toward the beginning, moving each value in the file that is greater than X up by one until it reaches the position in the file where X should be stored. The program then writes X at that position and closes the file.

12. Insertion Sort on a File II

Modify the program written for Programming Challenge 11 so that the file contains records of people. Each record should contain an array of 10 characters to hold the name of a person and an integer to hold the person's age. The file should be sorted by alphabetic order of the names.

13. Corporate Sales Data Output

Write a program that uses a structure to store the following information on a company division:

Division name (such as East, West, North, or South)
Quarter (1, 2, 3, or 4)
Quarterly sales

The user should be asked for the four quarters' sales figures for the East, West, North, and South divisions. The information for each quarter for each division should be written to a file.

14. Corporate Sales Data Input

Write a program that reads the information in the file created by the program in Programming Challenge 13. The program should calculate and display the following figures:

- Total corporate sales for each quarter
- Total yearly sales for each division
- Total yearly corporate sales
- Average quarterly sales for the divisions
- The highest and lowest quarters for the corporation

15. Inventory Program

Write a program that uses a structure to store the following inventory information in a file:

Item description
Quantity on hand
Wholesale cost
Retail cost
Date added to inventory

The program should have a menu that allows the user to perform the following tasks:

- Add new records to the file
- Display any record in the file
- Change any record in the file

16. Inventory Screen Report

Write a program that reads the information in the file created by the program in Programming Challenge 14. The program should calculate and display the following information:

- The total wholesale value of the inventory
- The total retail value of the inventory
- The total quantity of all items in the inventory

Group Project

17. Customer Accounts

This program should be designed and written by a team of students. Here are some suggestions:

- One student should design function `main`, which will call other program functions or class member functions. The remainder of the functions will be designed by other members of the team.
- The requirements of the program should be analyzed so each student is given about the same workload.

Write a program that uses a structure to store the following information about a customer account:

- Name
- Address
- City, state, and ZIP
- Telephone number
- Account balance
- Date of last payment

The structure should be used to store customer account records in a file. The program should have a menu that lets the user perform the following operations:

- Enter new records into the file
- Search for a particular customer's record and display it
- Search for a particular customer's record and delete it
- Search for a particular customer's record and change it
- Display the contents of the entire file

Input Validation: When the information for a new account is entered, be sure the user enters data for all the fields. No negative account balances should be entered.

CHAPTER

14 Recursion

TOPICS

14.1 Introduction to Recursion

CONCEPT: A recursive function is one that calls itself.

You have seen instances of functions calling other functions. Function *A* can call function *B*, which can then call Function *C*. It's also possible for a function to call itself. A function that calls itself is a *recursive function*. Look at this `message` function:

```
void message()
{
   cout << "This is a recursive function.\n";
   message();
}
```

This function displays the string `"This is a recursive function.\n"`, and then calls itself. Each time it calls itself, the cycle is repeated. Can you see a problem with the function? There's no way to stop the recursive calls. This function is like an infinite loop because there is no code to stop it from repeating.

To be useful, a recursive function must have a way of controlling the number of recursive calls. The following is a modification of the `message` function. It passes an integer argument that holds the number of times the function is to call itself.

```
void message(int times)
{
   if (times > 0)
   {
      cout << "This is a recursive function.\n";
      message(times - 1);
   }
}
```

This function contains an `if` statement that controls the recursion. As long as the `times` argument is greater than zero, it will display the message and call itself again. Each time it calls itself, it passes `times - 1` as the argument. For example, let's say a program calls the function with the following statement:

```
message(3);
```

The argument, 3, will cause the function to be called four times. The first time the function is called, the `if` statement will display the message and call itself with 2 as the argument. Figure 14-1 illustrates this.

Figure 14-1

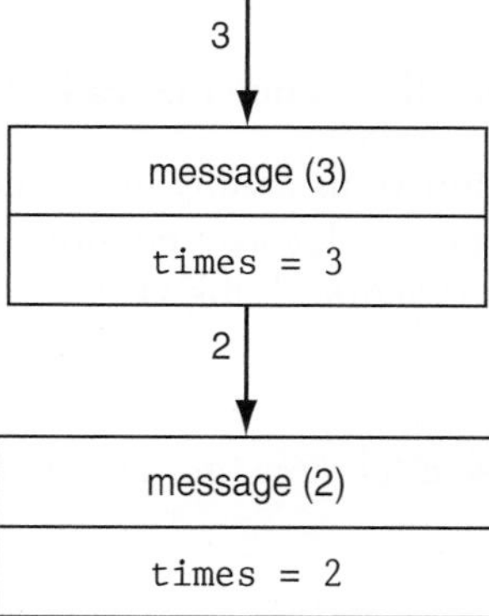

The diagram in Figure 14-1 illustrates two separate calls of the `message` function. Each time the function is called, a new instance of the `times` parameter is created in memory. The first time the function is called, the `times` parameter is set to 3. When the function calls itself, a new instance of `times` is created, and the value 2 is passed into it. This cycle repeats until zero is passed to the function. This is illustrated in Figure 14-2.

As you can see from Figure 14-2, the function will be called four times, so the *depth of recursion* is four. When the function reaches the fourth call, the `times` parameter will be set to 0. At that point, the `if` statement will stop the recursive chain of calls, and the

Figure 14-2

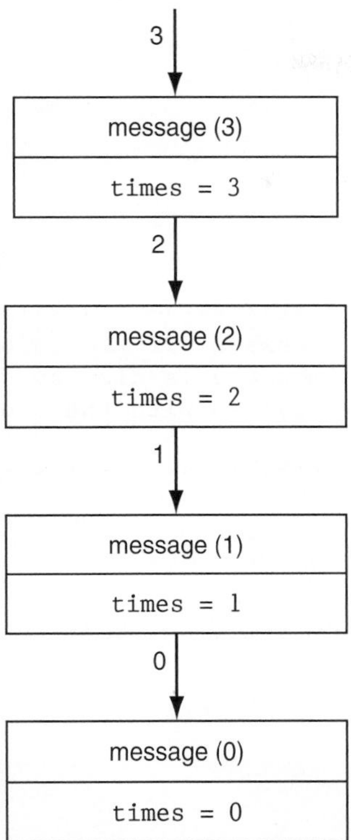

fourth instance of the function will return. Control of the program will return from the fourth instance of the function to the point in the third instance directly after the recursive function call:

```
if (times > 0)
{
   cout << "This is a recursive function.\n";
   message(times - 1);
}
```

Control returns here.

Because there are no more statements to be executed after the function call, the third instance of the function returns control of the program back to the second instance. This repeats until all instances of the function return. Program 14-1 demonstrates the recursive `message` function, modified to show the value of the parameter to each call.

Program 14-1

```
// This program demonstrates a simple recursive function.
#include <iostream>
using namespace std;

```

(program continues)

Program 14-1 *(continued)*

```
// Function prototype
void message(int);

int main()
{
   message(3);
   return 0;
}

//**********************************************************
// Definition of function message. If the value in times    *
// is greater than 0, the message is displayed and the      *
// function is recursively called with the argument         *
// times - 1.                                               *
//**********************************************************
void message(int times)
{
   if (times > 0)
   {
      cout << "Message " << times << "\n";
      message(times - 1);
   }
}
```

Program Output

```
Message 3
Message 2
Message 1
```

To further illustrate the inner workings of this recursive function, let's look at another version of the program. In Program 14-2, a message is displayed each time the function is entered, and another message is displayed just before the function returns.

Recursive functions work by breaking a complex problem down into subproblems of the same type. This breaking down process stops when it reaches a *base case*, that is, a subproblem that is simple enough to be solved directly. For example, in the recursive `message` function of the preceding examples, the base case is when the parameter `times` is 0.

Program 14-2

```
// This program demonstrates a simple recursive function.
#include <iostream>
using namespace std;

// Function prototype
void message(int);
```

(program continues)

Program 14-2 *(continued)*

```
int main()
{
   message(3);
   return 0;
}

//*********************************************************
// Definition of function message. If the value in times    *
// is greater than 0, the message is displayed and the      *
// function is recursively called with the argument         *
// times - 1.                                                *
//*********************************************************
void message(int times)
{
   cout << "Message " << times << ".\n";
   if (times > 0)
   {
      message(times - 1);
   }
   cout << "Message " << times << " is returning.\n";
}
```

Program Output

```
Message 3.
Message 2.
Message 1.
Message 0.
Message 0 is returning.
Message 1 is returning.
Message 2 is returning.
Message 3 is returning.
```

You should consider the use of recursion when there is a way to express the solution of a problem in terms of solutions of simpler, or smaller, problems of the same type. As an example, one can envision sorting a long list of names by splitting the list into two sublists and assigning the two sublists to two different people to sort. Once the sublists are sorted, they can be merged into a sorted version of the original list by a suitable collating process. In this case, the problems of sorting the sublists are the simpler problems of the same type, and the base cases occur when the sublists consist of a single name.

Let's look at a simple example of recursion that performs a useful task. The function `frequency` counts the number of times a specific character appears in a string.

```
int frequency(char ch, string inputString, int position)
{
   if (position == inputString.length())   //base case
      return 0;
   if (inputString[position] == ch)
```

```
      return 1 + frequency(ch, inputString, position+1);
   else
      return frequency(ch, inputString, position+1);
}
```

The function's parameters are

- `ch`: the character to be searched for and counted
- `inputString`: the string to be searched
- `position`: the starting subscript for the search

The first `if` statement determines whether the base case, that is, the end of the string, has been reached:

```
if (position == inputString.length())
    return 0;
```

If the end of the string has been reached, the function returns 0, indicating there are no more characters to count. Otherwise, the following `if` statement is executed:

```
if (inputString[position] == ch)
   return 1 + frequency(ch, inputString, position+1);
else
   return frequency(ch, inputString, position+1);
```

If `inputString[position]` is the search character, the function performs a recursive call. The return statement returns `1` + the number of times the search character appears in the string, starting at `position + 1`. If `inputString[position]` is not the search character, a recursive call is made to search the remainder of the string. Program 14-3 demonstrates the program.

Program 14-3

```
// This program demonstrates a recursive function for
// counting the number of times a character appears
// in a string.
#include <iostream>
#include <string>
using namespace std;

// Function prototype
int frequency(char ch, string inputString , int pos);

int main()
{
   string inputString = "abcddddef";

   cout << "The letter d appears "
        << frequency('d', inputString, 0) << " times.\n";
   return 0;
}
```

(program continues)

Program 14-3 *(continued)*

```

//*********************************************
// Function frequency. This recursive function   *
// counts the number of times the character      *
// ch appears in inputString. The search begins  *
// at index position in the string.              *
//*********************************************
int frequency(char ch, string inputString, int position)
{
   if (position == inputString.length()) //base case
      return 0;
   if (inputString[position] == ch)
      return 1 + frequency(ch, inputString, position+1);
   else
      return frequency(ch, inputString, position+1);
}
```

Program Output

```
The letter d appears 4 times.
```

Direct and Indirect Recursion

The examples we have discussed so far show recursive functions that directly call themselves. This is known as *direct recursion*. There is also the possibility of creating *indirect recursion* in a program. This occurs when function A calls function B, which in turn calls function A. There can even be several functions involved in the recursion. For example, function A could call function B, which could call function C, which calls function A.

Checkpoint

14.1 What is a recursive function's base case?

14.2 What happens if a recursive function does not handle base cases correctly?

14.3 What will the following program display?

```
#include <iostream>
using namespace std;

// Function prototype
void showMe(int arg);

int main()
{
   int num = 0;

   showMe(num);
   return 0;
}
```

```
void showMe(int arg)
{
   if (arg < 10)
    showMe(++arg);
   else
    cout << arg << endl;
}
```

14.4 What is the difference between direct and indirect recursion?

14.2 The Recursive Factorial Function

CONCEPT: The recursive factorial function accepts an argument and calculates its factorial. Its base case is when the argument is 0.

Let's use an example from mathematics to examine an application of recursion. In mathematics, the notation *n!* represents the *factorial* of the number *n*. The factorial of an integer *n* is defined as

$$n! = 1 \times 2 \times 3 \times \ldots \times n; \text{ if } n > 0$$
$$= 1; \text{ if } n = 0$$

The rule states that when n is greater than 0, its factorial is the product of all the positive integers from 1 up to n. For instance, 6! can be calculated as $1 \times 2 \times 3 \times 4 \times 5 \times 6$. The rule also specifies the base case: the factorial of 0 is 1.

We can define the factorial of a number using recursion as follows:

$$\text{factorial}(n) = n \times \text{factorial}(n - 1) \text{ if } n > 0$$
$$= 1; \text{ if } n = 0$$

The C++ implementation of this recursive definition is

```
int factorial(int num)
{
   if (num == 0) // base case
      return 1;
   else
      return num * factorial(num – 1);
}
```

Consider a program that displays the value of 3! with the following statement:

```
cout << factorial(3) << endl;
```

The first time the function is called, num is set to 3. The if statement will execute the following line:

```
return num * factorial(num - 1);
```

Although this is a return statement, it does not immediately return. Before the return value can be determined, the value of factorial(num - 1) must be determined. The function is called recursively until the fourth call, in which the num parameter will be set to zero. The diagram in Figure 14-3 illustrates the value of num and the return value during each call of the function.

Figure 14-3

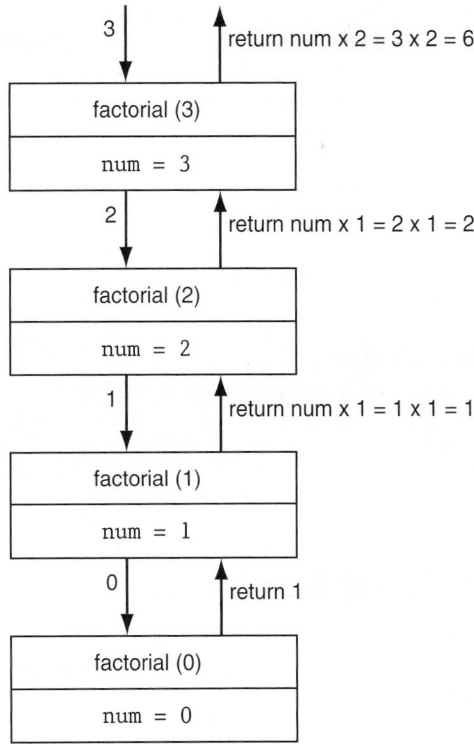

Program 14-4 demonstrates the `factorial` function.

Program 14-4

```
// This program demonstrates a recursive function
// to calculate the factorial of a number.
#include <iostream>
using namespace std;

// Function prototype
int factorial(int);

int main()
{
   int number;

   cout << "Enter an integer value and I will display\n";
   cout << "its factorial: ";
   cin  >> number;
   cout << "The factorial of " << number << " is ";
   cout << factorial(number)   << endl;
   return 0;
   }

```

(program continues)

Program 14-4 *(continued)*

```
//***************************************************
// Definition of factorial. A recursive function to  *
// calculate the factorial of the parameter, num.    *
//***************************************************
int factorial(int num)
{
   if (num == 0)  //base case
      return 1;
   else
      return num * factorial(num - 1);
}
```

Program Output with Example Input

```
Enter an integer value and I will display
its factorial: 4
The factorial of 4 is 24
```

14.3 The Recursive gcd Function

CONCEPT: There is a recursive method for finding the greatest common divisor (gcd) of two numbers.

Our next example of recursion is the calculation of the greatest common divisor, or gcd, of two numbers. Using Euclid's algorithm, the gcd of two positive integers, x and y, is

$$\begin{aligned} \gcd(x, y) &= y && \text{if } y \text{ divides } x \text{ with no remainder} \\ &= \gcd(y, \text{remainder of } x/y); && \text{otherwise} \end{aligned}$$

This definition states that the gcd of x and y is y if x/y has no remainder. Otherwise, the answer is the gcd of y and the remainder of x/y. Program 14-5 shows the recursive C++ implementation:

Program 14-5

```
// This program demonstrates a recursive function to
// calculate the greatest common divisor (gcd) of two
// numbers.
#include <iostream>
using namespace std;

// Function prototype
int gcd(int, int);

int main()
{
   int num1, num2;

```

(program continues)

Program 14-5 *(continued)*

```
   cout << "Enter two integers: ";
   cin >> num1 >> num2;
   cout << "The greatest common divisor of " << num1;
   cout << " and " << num2 << " is ";
   cout << gcd(num1, num2) << endl;
   return 0;
}

//*****************************************************
// Definition of gcd. This function uses recursion to     *
// calculate the greatest common divisor of two integers, *
// passed into the parameters x and y.                    *
//*****************************************************
int gcd(int x, int y)
{
   if (x % y == 0)    //base case
      return y;
   else
      return gcd(y, x % y);
}
```

Program Output with Example Input Shown in Bold

```
Enter two integers: 49 28
The greatest common divisor of 49 and 28 is 7
```

14.4 Solving Recursively Defined Problems

CONCEPT: **Some problems naturally lend themselves to recursive solutions.**

Some problems naturally lend themselves to recursive solutions. One well-known example is the calculation of *Fibonacci numbers*. The Fibonacci numbers, named after the Italian mathematician Leonardo Fibonacci (born circa 1170), form the following sequence:

0, 1, 1, 2, 3, 5, 8, 13, 21, 34, 55, 89, 144, 233, ...

Notice that after the second number, each number in the sequence is the sum of the two previous numbers. The Fibonacci sequence can be defined as:

$$F_0 = 0,$$
$$F_1 = 1,$$
$$F_N = F_{N-1} + F_{N-2} \quad \text{for all } N \geq 2.$$

It is clear that the problem of computing a Fibonacci number other than the first two can be reduced to the problems of computing the two preceding Fibonacci numbers. Thus this problem makes a good candidate for a recursive solution. The problems of computing the first two Fibonacci numbers are the base cases. Here is the recursive C++ function for computing the *n*th number in the Fibonacci sequence:

```
int fib(int n)
{
   if (n <= 0)        // base case
      return 0;
   else if (n == 1)   // base case
      return 1;
   else
      return fib(n - 1) + fib(n - 2);
}
```

The function is demonstrated in Program 14-6, which displays the first 10 numbers in the Fibonacci sequence.

Program 14-6

```
// This program demonstrates a recursive function
// that calculates Fibonacci numbers.
#include <iostream>
using namespace std;

// Function prototype
int fib(int);

int main()
{
   cout << "The first 10 Fibonacci numbers are:\n";
   for (int x = 0; x < 10; x++)
       cout << fib(x) << " ";
   cout << endl;
   return 0;
}

//*****************************************
// Function fib. Accepts an int argument   *
// in n. This function returns the nth     *
// Fibonacci number.                       *
//*****************************************

int fib(int n)
{
   if (n <= 0)          //base case
      return 0;
   else if (n == 1)     //base case
      return 1;
   else
      return fib(n - 1) + fib(n - 2);
}
```

Program Output

```
The first 10 Fibonacci numbers are:
0 1 1 2 3 5 8 13 21 34
```

Another such example is Ackermann's function. A Programming Challenge at the end of this chapter asks you to write a recursive function that calculates Ackermann's function.

14.5 A Recursive Binary Search Function

CONCEPT: The binary search algorithm can be defined as a recursive function.

In Chapter 9 you learned about the binary search algorithm and how it can be used to search a sorted array for a given value. Let us look to see how the binary search algorithm can be formulated using recursion. Suppose that we want to write the function so that it has prototype

VideoNote
Recursive Binary Search

```
int binarySearch(const int array[], int first, int last, int value)
```

where the parameter `array` is the array to be searched; the parameter `first` holds the subscript of the first element in the search range (the portion of the array to be searched); the parameter `last` holds the subscript of the last element in the search range; and the parameter `value` holds the value to be searched for. The function will return the subscript of `value` if it is found within the array, and will return –1 otherwise.

In order to use recursion, we need to find a way of breaking down the problem of searching a range of a sorted array for a given value into smaller problems of the same type. We start by comparing value to the middle element of the search range. If `value` is equal to the middle element, we are done and we return the subscript of the middle element. Otherwise, if `value` is smaller than the middle element, then we must search for it in the lower half of the original range (a recursive call on a smaller problem of the same type); but if `value` is larger than the middle element, we must search for it in the upper half of the original range. Notice that every time we make a recursive call, the search range will be smaller. The base case is when the search range is empty. Here is the function:

```
int binarySearch(const int array[], int first, int last, int value)
{
   int middle;        // mid point of search

   if (first > last)  // base case
      return -1;
   middle = (first + last) / 2;
   if (array[middle] == value)
      return middle;
   if (array[middle] < value)
      return binarySearch(array, middle+1,last,value);
   else
      return binarySearch(array, first,middle-1,value);
}
```

This function is demonstrated in Program 14-7.

Program 14-7

```
// This program demonstrates a recursive function that
// performs a binary search on an integer array.
#include <iostream>
using namespace std;

// Function prototype
```

(program continues)

Program 14-7 *(continued)*

```
int binarySearch(const int [], int, int, int);

const int SIZE = 20;

int main()
{
   int tests[SIZE] = { 101, 142, 147, 189, 199, 207, 222,
                       234, 289, 296, 310, 319, 388, 394,
                       417, 429, 447, 521, 536, 600};
   int result; // Result of the search
   int  empID; // What to search for

   cout << "Enter the Employee ID you wish to search for: ";
   cin >> empID;
   result = binarySearch(tests, 0, SIZE - 1, empID);
   if (result == -1)
      cout << "That number does not exist in the array.\n";
   else
   {
      cout << "That ID is found at element " << result;
      cout << " in the array\n";
   }
return 0;
}

//*****************************************************
// The binarySearch function performs a recursive binary   *
// search on a range of elements of an integer array. The  *
// parameter first holds the subscript of the range's      *
// starting element, and last holds the subscript of the   *
// ranges's last element. The parameter value holds the    *
// the search value. If the search value is found, its     *
// array subscript is returned. Otherwise, -1 is returned  *
// indicating the value was not in the array.              *
//*****************************************************
int binarySearch(const int array[], int first, int last, int value)
{
   int middle;          // Mid point of search

   if (first > last)    // Base case
      return -1;
   middle = (first + last)/2;
   if (array[middle]==value)
      return middle;
   if (array[middle]<value)
      return binarySearch(array, middle+1,last,value);
   else
      return binarySearch(array, first,middle-1,value);
}
```

Program Output with Example Input Shown in Bold

```
Enter the Employee ID you wish to search for: 521 [Enter]
That ID is found at element 17 in the array
```

14.6 Focus on Problem Solving and Program Design: *The QuickSort Algorithm*

CONCEPT: The QuickSort algorithm uses recursion to sort lists efficiently.

VideoNote
QuickSort

QuickSort is a recursive sorting algorithm that was invented in 1960 by C. A. R. Hoare. It is very efficient and is often used to sort lists of items stored in arrays. QuickSort is usually written as a recursive function with three parameters that define a portion of an array to be sorted. The three parameters are an array `arr` containing a list of items, and two subscripts `start` and `end` denoting the beginning and end of the segment of `arr` that is to be sorted. Let us write `arr[start..end]` for these three parameters. To sort the entire array, you call QuickSort with `start` set to 0 and `end` set to the size of the array minus 1.

QuickSort works as follows. If `start` is greater than or equal to `end`, then the segment of `arr` to be sorted has at most one element and is therefore already sorted. In this case, QuickSort returns immediately. Otherwise, QuickSort *partitions* `arr[start..end]` by selecting one of the elements in `arr[start..end]` to be a *pivot* element and then rearranging `arr[start..end]` so that all entries that are less than the pivot are to the left of the pivot, and all entries greater than or equal to the pivot are to the right of the pivot. In effect, the partition step rearranges `arr[start..end]` so that it consists of a sublist 1, the pivot element, and a sublist 2 as shown in Figure 14-4.

Figure 14-4

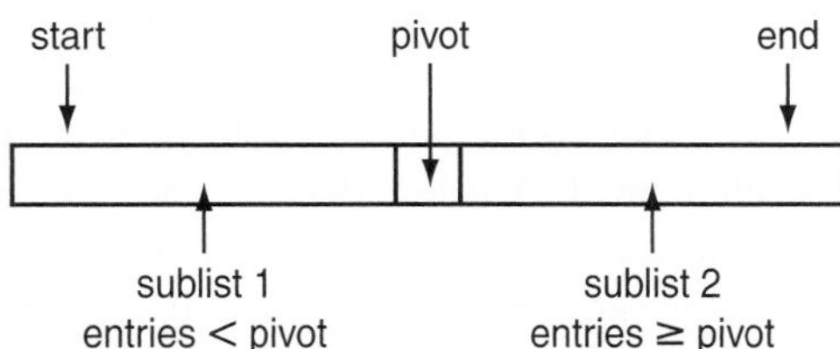

Depending on the value selected to be the pivot element, one or the other of the two sublists may be empty. For example, if the pivot element happens to be the minimum array element, there will be no array entries less than the pivot, and sublist 1 will be empty.

Notice that once the partition stage is completed and we have the situation shown in Figure 14-4, the pivot element will be in the right place. By recursively applying the QuickSort procedure to the two sublists, each of the sublists will be partitioned, putting whatever element was selected to be the pivot for that sublist in its right place. The process continues until the length of the sublists is at most one. At that point, the original array will be sorted.

Let us assume that we have a function

```
int partition(int arr[], int start, int end)
```

which when called will

1. select a pivot element from `arr[start..end]`

2. rearrange `arr[start..end]` into sublist 1, the pivot element, and sublist 2 (see Figure 14-4) so that the pivot element is at position `p` and sublist 1 and sublist 2 are respectively `arr[start . . p-1]` and `arr[p+1..end]`,
3. return the position `p` of the pivot.

We can then implement QuickSort in C++ as follows:

```
void quickSort(int arr[], int start, int end)
{
   if (start < end)
   {
      // Partition the array and get the pivot point
      int p = partition(arr, start, end);

      // Sort the portion before the pivot point
      quickSort(arr, start, p - 1);

      // Sort the portion after the pivot point
      quickSort(arr, p + 1, end);
   }
}
```

Now let us consider the process of partitioning the array segment `arr[start..end]`. The partitioning algorithm selects `arr[start]` to be the pivot element and then builds the two sublists on the left and right of the pivot element in stages. Initially, the portion of the array that has been partitioned consists of just the pivot element by itself. In effect, the initial situation will be as shown in Figure 14-4, with sublist 1 and sublist 2 being empty and all the array entries that have not yet been added to the partitioned part lying to the right of sublist 2.

The main idea is to extend the partitioned portion of the array one element at a time by considering the element *X* that is just to the right of sublist 2. If such an *X* is greater than or equal to the pivot, it is added to the end of sublist 2 by leaving it where it is and moving on to consider the next element. If *X* is less than the pivot element, it is added to the end of sublist 1 by placing it just to the left of the pivot element. One way to do this is to store *X* in a temporary location, move every element in sublist 2 up one position, move the pivot element up one position, and then drop *X* into the array position just vacated by the pivot element. This simplistic strategy moves too many array elements and does not result in an efficient algorithm. Instead, we can put *X* to the left of the pivot more efficiently by first exchanging *X* with the array item *Y* that is just to the right of the pivot element and then exchanging *X* with the pivot element. The first exchange puts *Y*, which is greater or equal to the pivot element, at the end of sublist 2 while putting *X* in a position that is adjacent to the pivot. The second exchange then puts *X* to the left of the pivot. This is repeated until the entire list has been partitioned. The code for the partition function is

```
int partition(int arr[], int start, int end)
{
   // The pivot element is taken to be the element at
   // the start of the subrange to be partitioned
   int pivotValue = arr[start];
   int pivotPosition = start;

   // Rearrange the rest of the array elements to
   // partition the subrange from start to end
   for (int pos = start + 1; pos <= end; pos++)
```

```
      {
         if (arr[pos] < pivotValue)
         {
            // arr[scan] is the "current" item
            // Swap the current item with the item to the
            // right of the pivot element
            swap(arr[pivotPosition + 1], arr[pos]);
            // Swap the current item with the pivot element
            swap(arr[pivotPosition], arr[pivotPosition + 1]);
            // Adjust the pivot position so it stays with the
            // pivot element
            pivotPosition ++;
         }
      }
      return pivotPosition;
   }
```

The swap function used in `partition` is part of the standard template library. You need to include the `algorithm` header file to use it.

Program 14-8 demonstrates the QuickSort algorithm in action.

Program 14-8

```
// This program demonstrates the QuickSort algorithm.
#include <iostream>
#include <algorithm>   //needed for swap function
using namespace std;

// Function prototypes
void quickSort(int [], int, int);
int partition(int [], int, int);

int main()
{
   // Array to be sorted
   const int SIZE = 10;
   int array[SIZE] = {17, 53, 9, 2, 30, 1, 82, 64, 26, 5};

   // Echo the array to be sorted
   for (int k = 0; k < SIZE; k++)
      cout << array[k] << " ";
   cout << endl;

   // Sort the array using Quicksort
   quickSort(array, 0, SIZE-1);

   // Print the sorted array
   for (int k = 0; k < SIZE; k++)
      cout << array[k] << " ";
   cout << endl;

   return 0;
}

```

(program continues)

Program 14-8 *(continued)*

```
//*********************************************
// quickSort uses the QuickSort algorithm to     *
// sort arr from arr[start] through arr[end].    *
//*********************************************
void quickSort(int arr[], int start, int end)
{
   if (start < end)
   {
     // Partition the array and get the pivot point
     int p = partition(arr, start, end);

     // Sort the portion before the pivot point
     quickSort(arr, start, p - 1);

     // Sort the portion after the pivot point
     quickSort(arr, p + 1, end);
   }
}

//*********************************************************
// partition rearranges the entries in the array arr from   *
// start to end so all values greater than or equal to the  *
// pivot are on the right of the pivot and all values less  *
// than are on the left of the pivot.                        *
//*********************************************************
int partition(int arr[], int start, int end)
{
   // The pivot element is taken to be the element at
   // the start of the subrange to be partitioned
   int pivotValue = arr[start];
   int pivotPosition = start;

   // Rearrange the rest of the array elements to
   // partition the subrange from start to end
   for (int pos = start + 1; pos <= end; pos++)
   {
      if (arr[pos] < pivotValue)
      {
         // arr[scan] is the "current" item.
         // Swap the current item with the item to the
         // right of the pivot element
         swap(arr[pivotPosition + 1], arr[pos]);
         // Swap the current item with the pivot element
         swap(arr[pivotPosition], arr[pivotPosition + 1]);
         // Adjust the pivot position so it stays with the
         // pivot element
         pivotPosition ++;
      }
  }
  return pivotPosition;
}
```

Program Output

```
17 53 9 2 30 1 82 64 26 5
1 2 5 9 17 26 30 53 64 82
```

14.7 The Towers of Hanoi

CONCEPT: There are problems that have simple recursive solutions, but which are otherwise very difficult to solve.

The Towers of Hanoi is a game that is often used in computer science textbooks to illustrate the power of recursion. The game uses three pegs and a set of disks of different sizes with holes through their centers. The game begins with all of the disks stacked on the first of the three pegs as shown in Figure 14-5.

Figure 14-5 The pegs and disks in the Towers of Hanoi game

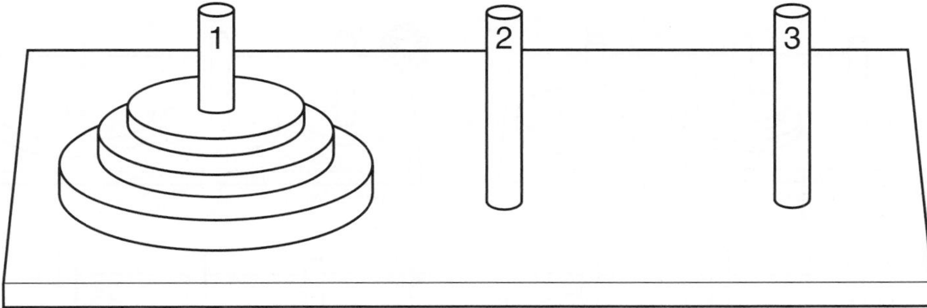

The object of the game is to move all the disks from the first peg to the third, while abiding by the following rules:

- All disks must rest on a peg except while being moved.
- Only one disk may be moved at a time.
- No disk may be placed on top of a smaller disk.

Let us look at some examples of how the game is played. The simplest case is when there is only one disk: in this case, you solve the game in one move, by moving the disk from peg 1 to peg 3.

If you have two disks, you can solve the game with three moves:

1. Move a disk from peg 1 to peg 2 (it must be the top one.)
2. Move a disk from peg 1 to peg 3.
3. Move a disk from peg 2 to peg 3.

Notice that although the object of the game is to move the disks from peg 1 to peg 3, it is necessary to use peg 2 as a temporary resting place for some of the disks. The complexity of the solution increases rapidly as the number of disks to be moved increases. Moving three disks requires seven moves as shown in Figure 14-6.

Figure 14-6

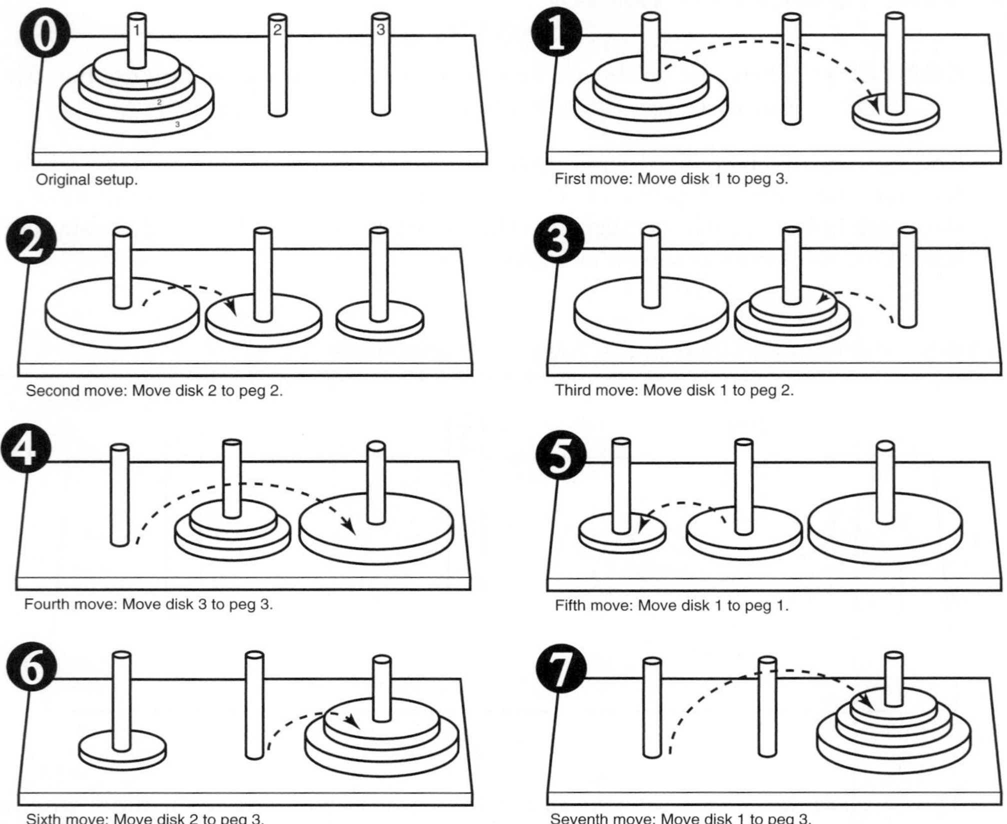

1
2
3
Original setup.
First move: Move disk 1 to peg 3.
Second move: Move disk 2 to peg 2.
Third move: Move disk 1 to peg 2.
Fourth move: Move disk 3 to peg 3.
Fifth move: Move disk 1 to peg 1.
Sixth move: Move disk 2 to peg 3.
Seventh move: Move disk 1 to peg 3.

There is a charming legend associated with this game. According to this legend, there is a group of monks in a temple in Hanoi who have a set of pegs with 64 disks. The monks are busy moving the 64 disks, initially stacked on the first peg, to the third peg. When the monks complete their task the world will come to an end.

Let us now return to the problem and consider its solution in the general case when we can have any number of disks. The problem can be stated as:

Move n disks from peg 1 to peg 3 using peg 2 as a temporary peg.

It is very difficult to see how this problem can be solved using loops. Happily, it is not difficult to envision a recursive solution: If we can (recursively) move $n - 1$ disks from peg 1 to peg 2 while using peg 3 as the temporary peg, then the largest disk will be left sitting alone on peg 1. We can then move the large disk from peg 1 to peg 3 in one move. We can then (recursively) move the $n - 1$ disks from peg 2 to peg 3, this time using peg 1 as the temporary peg. This plan can be formulated in pseudocode as follows:

To move n disks from peg 1 to peg 3, using peg 2 as a temporary peg:
    If n > 0 Then
        Move n − 1 disks from peg 1 to peg 2, using peg 3 as a temporary peg.

Move a disk from peg 1 to peg 3.
Move n − 1 disks from peg 2 to peg 3, using peg 1 as a temporary peg.
End If

We will now write a function that implements this solution by printing a sequence of moves that solves the game. We will also use names rather than numbers to describe the pegs. The object of the function is then to move a stack of disks from a source peg (peg 1) to a destination peg (peg 2) using a temporary peg (peg 3). Here is the code for the function:

```
void moveDisks(int n, string source, string dest, string temp)
{
   if (n > 0)
   {
      // Move n - 1 disks from source to temp
      // using dest as the temporary peg
      moveDisks(n - 1, source, temp, dest);

      // Move a disk from source to dest
      cout << "Move a disk from " << source
           << " to " << dest << endl;

      // Move n - 1 disks from temp to dest
      // using source as the temporary peg
      moveDisks(n - 1, temp, dest, source);
   }
}
```

The base case occurs when $n = 0$ and there are no disks to be moved. In this case the function call returns without doing anything. The function is demonstrate7d in Program 14-9.

Program 14-9

```
// This program displays a solution to the Towers of
// Hanoi game.

#include <iostream>
using namespace std;

// Function prototype
void moveDisks(int, string, string, string);

int main()
{
   // Play the game with 3 disks
   moveDisks(3, "peg 1", "peg 3", "peg 2");
   cout << "All the disks have been moved!"

   return 0;
}

```

(program continues)

Program 14-9 *(continued)*

```
//**************************************************
// The moveDisks function displays disk moves used  *
// to solve the Towers of Hanoi game.               *
// The parameters are:                              *
//    n      : The number of disks to move.         *
//    source : The peg to move from.                *
//    dest   : The peg to move to.                  *
//    temp   : The temporary peg.                   *
//**************************************************
void
moveDisks(int n, string source, string dest, string temp)
 {
     if (n > 0)
     {
         // Move n - 1 disks from source to temp
         // using dest as the temporary peg
         moveDisks(n - 1, source, temp, dest);

         // Move a disk from source to dest
         cout << "Move a disk from " << source
              << " to " << dest << endl;

        // Move n - 1 disks from temp to dest
        // using source as the temporary peg
         moveDisks(n - 1, temp, dest, source);
     }
}
```

Program Output

```
Move a disk from peg 1 to peg 3
Move a disk from peg 1 to peg 2
Move a disk from peg 3 to peg 2
Move a disk from peg 1 to peg 3
Move a disk from peg 2 to peg 1
Move a disk from peg 2 to peg 3
Move a disk from peg 1 to peg 3
All the disks have been moved!
```

NOTE: You can find many animations on the World Wide Web and on YouTube. Type "Towers of Hanoi Animation" into your favorite search engine.

14.8 Focus on Problem Solving: *Exhaustive and Enumeration Algorithms*

CONCEPT: An enumeration algorithm is one that generates all possible combinations of items of a certain type; an exhaustive algorithm is one that searches through such a set of combinations to find the best one.

Many problems can only be solved by examining all possible combinations of items of a certain type and then choosing the best one. For example, consider the problem of making change for $1.00 using the U.S. system of coins. A few of the solutions to this problem are:

one dollar coin
two fifty-cent coins
four quarters
one fifty-cent coin and two quarters
three quarters, two dimes, and one nickel.

In fact, there are 293 ways to make change for $1.00, so we need to have a systematic method for generating them. Suppose we want to make change for a given amount using the fewest coins. A strategy for this problem that almost immediately suggests itself is to give as many of the largest coin as possible, then as many of the second largest coin as possible, and so on, until you have made change for the complete amount. It turns out that for the U.S. system of coins, this procedure, which is called the *greedy strategy,* always finds the best solution. However, the procedure does not work for other systems of coins. For example, if there are only three coin sizes,

1, 20, 25

and one has to make change for 44 cents, the greedy strategy will give one quarter and 19 pennies, for a total of 20 coins. The best solution uses six coins: two twenty-cent pieces and four pennies. In general, one would have to try all possible ways of making change to determine the best one. An algorithm that searches through all possible combinations to solve a problem is called an *exhaustive* algorithm; an algorithm that generates all possible combinations is an *enumeration* algorithm.

Recursive techniques are often useful in exhaustive and enumeration algorithms. In this section, we look at a recursive algorithm that counts the number of different ways to make change for a given amount. With some modification, the algorithm can be adapted to keep track of the different combinations and either enumerate the list of all such combinations or report which combination is best. Although the algorithm works for any system that includes a one-cent piece among its coins, we will assume the American system with the six coin values: 1, 5, 10, 25, 50, and 100.

The main idea is this. Suppose we want to calculate the number of ways to make change for 24 cents using coins in the set 1, 5, 10, 25, 50, 100. Since there is no way to make change for 24 cents that uses coins in the set 25, 50, 100, the largest usable coin is a dime, and we can just calculate the number of ways to make change for 24 cents using coins in the set 1, 5, 10. Moreover, we cannot use more than two 10-cent pieces in making change for 24 cents, so we only need to count the number of ways to make change that use zero, one, or two 10-cent pieces and add them all together to get our answer. Table 14-1 lists these possibilities, shows how each possibility can be decomposed into a smaller problem of the same type, and shows the call to the recursive `mkChange` function that would be invoked to solve the subproblem. The parameters for the `mkChange` function will be explained shortly.

Table 14-1

number of ways to make change for 24 cents using no dimes	=	number of ways to make change for 24 cents using coins in the set 1, 5	=	`mkChange(24,1);`
number of ways to make change for 24 cents using one dime	=	number of ways to make change for 14 cents using coins in the set 1, 5	=	`mkChange(14,1);`
number of ways to make change for 24 cents using two dimes	=	number of ways to make change for 4 cents using coins in the set 1, 5	=	`mkChange(4,1);`

We are now ready to present the implementation of the algorithm. The set of possible coin values is given by an array

```
const int coinValues[] = {1, 5, 10, 25, 50, 100};
```

and the algorithm itself is embodied in the recursive function

```
int mkChange(amount, largestIndex)
```

where the first parameter is the amount to make change for, the second is the index of the largest coin in the `coinValues` array to be used in making that amount, and the integer returned is the number of combinations possible to make the specified amount of change using the specified maximum coin value. Thus the call to make change for 24 cents using coin values 1, 5 is

```
mkChange(24,1);
```

In this case, the second parameter `1` is the index of the largest coin to be used, that is the index of the nickel in the `coinValues` array. Likewise, the call to make change for 14 cents using the same coin values is

```
mkChange(14,1);
```

Program 14-10 implements this algorithm for the U.S. system of coins. It would work for any other coin system by simply changing the coin set size and the values in the `coinValues` array. The algorithm assumes that the `coinValues` array lists its values in increasing order.

Notice how the function handles the base case in lines 23–24. It returns 1 when the amount equals 0, so that when the calling function deducts coins that equal the desired amount exactly in line 34, `nWays` will be incremented by 1 in line 38. The function also returns 1 when `largestIndex` equals 0 to indicate that any amount can be composed in just 1 way using pennies (this wouldn't necessarily be true if the smallest coin were not 1).

Program 14-10

```
1 // This program demonstrates a recursive function that finds
2 // and counts all possible combinations of coin values to
3 // make a specified amount of change.
4
5 #include <iostream>
6 using namespace std;
7
```

(program continues)

Program 14-10 *(continued)*

```
const int COIN_SET_SIZE = 6;
const int coinValues[ ] = {1, 5, 10, 25, 50, 100};

//*******************************************************
// This function returns the number of ways to make change  *
// for an amount if we can only use coinValues in the array *
// positions 0 through largestIndex                         *
//*******************************************************

int mkChange(int amount, int largestIndex)
{
   // Don't use coin values bigger than amount
   while(coinValues[largestIndex] > amount)
      largestIndex--;

   if (amount == 0 || largestIndex == 0)
      return 1;

   // Number of ways to make change for amount
   int nWays = 0;
   // Number of coins of largest index to use
   int nCoins = 0 ;

   while (nCoins <= amount/coinValues[largestIndex])
   {
      int amountLeft;
      amountLeft = amount - nCoins * coinValues[largestIndex];

      // Add the number of ways to make change with nCoins
      // of the largest index
      nWays = nWays + mkChange(amountLeft, largestIndex-1);

      nCoins++;
   }
   return nWays;
}

int main( )
{
   // Display possible coin values
   cout << "Here are the valid coin values, in cents: ";
   for (int index = 0; index < COIN_SET_SIZE; index ++)
      cout << coinValues[index] << " ";
   cout << endl;

   // Get input from user
   int amount;
   cout << "Enter the amount of cents to make change for: ";
   cin  >> amount;

```

(program continues)

Program 14-10 *(continued)*

```
    // Compute and display number of ways to make change
    cout << "Number of possible combinations is "
         << mkChange(amount, COIN_SET_SIZE-1)
         << endl;
    return 0;
}
```

Program Output with Example Input Shown in Bold

```
Here are the valid coin values, in cents: 1 5 10 25 50 100
Enter (as an integer) the amount of cents to make change for: 11[Enter]
Number of possible combinations: 4
```

14.9 Focus on Software Engineering: *Recursion versus Iteration*

CONCEPT: Recursion and iteration are equivalent in expressive power.

Recursion and iteration are equivalent in expressive power in the sense that whatever can be done with one can also be done with the other. In any program, any recursive function can be replaced with an equivalent function that uses loops and no recursion, and conversely, any function that uses loops can be replaced with an equivalent recursive function that uses no loops.

In general, programs that use recursion incur more overhead than equivalent programs that use iteration. This is because recursion typically involves the making of several function calls. For each such call, the machine must pass parameters to the call, keep track of the return address, create the function's local variables, and finally, destroy the local variables when the fuction returns. Current computers are fast enough that for many problems people would not notice this difference in efficiency between an algorithm that uses recursion and one that does not. In such cases, it does not make much difference whether one uses recursion or iteration.

There are, however, some recursive algorithms (like the one used to compute the Fibonacci sequence) that in the course of solving a problem recompute solutions to the same subproblems over and over again. Such algorithms tend to be extremely inefficient and should always be avoided in favor of iteration.

In general, recursion should be used whenever the problem has a natural recursive solution that does not unncessarily recompute solutions to subproblems and the equivalent solution based on iteration either is not obvious or is difficult.

14.10 Tying It All Together: *Infix and Prefix Expressions*

A binary operator is said to be *infix* if it is written between its operands, as in the expression x + y. It is said to *prefix* if it is written before its operands, as in the expression + x y. Finally, it is said to be *postfix* if it is written after its operands as in x y +. An arithmetic expression consisting of numbers, variables, and operators is called *infix* if it uses only infix operators, *prefix* if it uses only prefix operators, and *postfix* if all of its operators are postfix. Table 14-2 shows the infix, prefix, and postfix forms of five different expressions.

Table 14-2

Infix Expression	Prefix Expression	Postfix Expression
2	2	2
x	x	x
x + 2	+ x 2	x 2 +
x + 23 * y	+ x * 23 y	x 23 y * +
(x + 23) * y	* + x 23 y	x 23 + y *

An infix expression with more than one operator can be evaluated in different ways yielding different results. Consider the expression 2 + 5 *3. If we add before multiplying, the result is 21, but if we multiply and then add, we get 17. Infix expressions depend on elaborate rules of operator precedence to determine how the expression is evaluated. In addition, parentheses must sometimes be used with infix expressions to override the precedence rules.

Prefix and postfix expressions do not suffer from these drawbacks and need neither parentheses nor rules of precedence. Instead, their operators are simply applied in the order in which they are encountered. The omission of parentheses allows prefix and postfix expressions to be stored in very compact forms, leading to savings in the amount of memory used. Because algorithms that work with prefix and postfix expressions do not need to process the parentheses or deal with precedence, they are often simpler.

Most programming languages, however, use infix expressions because that is what people are accustomed to. Many compilers and interpreters internally translate infix expressions to prefix or postfix so they can take advantage of the resulting efficiencies in storage and processing.

It is useful, when working with prefix expressions, to know they can be defined recursively:

1. A simple variable such as x, or a number such as 23, is a prefix expression.
2. Any operator followed by two prefix expressions is a prefix expression.

Based on this recursive definition, we will develop a strategy for converting a fully parenthesized infix expression to its prefix equivalent. First, note that an infix expression that involves no operators (it is an identifier or a number) is already in prefix form, in which case there is nothing to do. Otherwise, place the outermost operator of the fully parenthesized infix expression before its operands and then recursively apply this strategy to the subexpressions (the operands of the outermost operator). Continue this until all subexpressions have been converted to prefix. Here is an example of this process:

1. Original infix expression is (x + 23)* y.
2. Place the outermost operator before its operands to give the result * (x + 23) y.
3. Recursively apply the same strategy to the inner subexpression x + 23 by placing + before x and 23 to give the result * + x 23 y.
4. Recursively apply the strategy to x, 23, and y. However, these are all base cases so they remain unchanged. The procedure terminates with the result * + x 23 y.

Having gained some practice working with prefix expressions, let's write a program that reads in prefix expressions, evaluates them, and prints the results. We assume that the prefix expressions contain no variables.

We use a recursive strategy. The base case is when the prefix expression is a single number. In that case, we just read the number and return its value. A prefix expression that is not a single number must consist of an operator followed by two prefix expressions. To evaluate such an expression, we read and store the operator, recursively evaluate the two prefix expressions to get two results, and then apply the operator to the two results. The recursive function `prefixExpr()` shown in Program 14-11 implements this strategy.

The `prefixExpr()` function uses the `peek()` member function of the `istream` class to skip whitespace and locate the beginning of the prefix expression. The `peek()` function returns the next available character from the stream without actually reading it and removing it from the stream. We use `peek()` to ensure that we do not skip a character that is part of the expression while we are skipping leading whitespace. We also use the `peek()` function to check if the first non-space character is a digit: if it is, we know the prefix expression is a number and we read it using the extraction operator in line 50:

```
exprStream >> number;
```

A non-space character that begins a prefix expression but is not a digit must be an operator. In that case, we read the character using the `get()` member function in line 42:

```
ch = exprStream.get();
```

The main function of this program just reads one line at a time, transforms the string retrieved into an `istringstream` object, and calls the `prefixExpr()` function. The user can enter multiple infix expressions with each expression being entered on its own line. The program terminates when the user enters a blank line.

Program 14-11

```
1  // This program evaluates prefix expressions.
2  #include <stdlib.h>
3  #include <string>
4  #include <sstream>
5  #include <iostream>
6  using namespace std;
7
8  int prefixExpr(istream &exprStream); //Prototype
9
10 int main()
```

(program continues)

Program 14-11 *(continued)*

```
{
    string input;
    cout << "Enter prefix expressions to evaluate.\n"
         << "Press enter after each expression,\n"
         << "and press enter on a blank line to quit.\n\n" ;
    cout << "Enter a prefix expression to evaluate: ";
    getline(cin, input);
    while (input.size() != 0)
    {
        // Convert string to istringstream
        istringstream exprStream(input);
        // Evaluate the prefix expression
        cout << prefixExpr(exprStream) << endl;
        // Get next line of input
        cout << "Enter a prefix expression to evaluate: ";
        getline(cin, input);
    }
    return 0;
}

//*****************************************************************
// Takes an istream that contains a single prefix expression p   *
// and returns the integer value of p                            *
//*****************************************************************
int prefixExpr(istream &exprStream)
{

   // Peek at first non-space character in prefix expression
   char ch = exprStream.peek();
   while (isspace(ch))
   {
       ch = exprStream.get();   // Read the space character
       ch = exprStream.peek();  // Peek again
   }

   if (isdigit(ch))
   {
       // The prefix expression is a  single number
       int number;
       exprStream >> number;
       return number;
   }
   else
   {
       // The prefix expression is an operator followed
       // by two prefix expressions: Compute values of
       // the prefix expressions

       // Read the operator
       ch = exprStream.get();

```

(program continues)

Program 14-11 *(continued)*

```
        // Recursively evaluate the two subexpressions
        int value1 = prefixExpr(exprStream);
        int value2 = prefixExpr(exprStream);

        // Apply the operator
        switch(ch)
        {
            case '+': return value1 + value2;
            case '-': return value1 - value2;
            case '*': return value1 * value2;
            case '/': return value1 / value2;
            default:  cout << "Bad input expression";
                      exit(1);
        }
    }
}
```

Program Output with Example Input Shown in Bold

```
Enter prefix expressions to evaluate.
Press enter after each expression,
and press enter on a blank line to quit.

Enter a prefix expression to evaluate: 34[Enter]
34
Enter a prefix expression to evaluate: + 23 5[Enter]
28
Enter a prefix expression to evaluate: * +23 5 2[Enter]
56
Enter a prefix expression to evaluate:[Enter]
```

Review Questions and Exercises

Fill-in-the-Blank and Short Answer

1. What type of recursive function do you think would be more difficult to debug; one that uses direct recursion, or one that uses indirect recursion? Why?
2. Which repetition approach is less efficient; a loop or a recursive function? Why?
3. When should you choose a recursive algorithm over an iterative algorithm?
4. The __________ of recursion is the number of times a function calls itself.
5. __________ recursion is when a function explicitly calls itself.
6. __________ recursion is when function A calls function B, which in turn calls function A.

Predict the Output

7. What is the output of the following programs?

A)
```
#include <iostream>
using namespace std;

int function(int);
int main()
{
   int x = 10;

   cout << function(x) << endl;
   return 0;
}

int function(int num)
{
   if (num <= 0)
      return 0;
   else
      return function(num - 1) + num;
}
```

B)
```
#include <iostream>
using namespace std;

void function(int);

int main()
{
   int x = 10;

   function(x);
   return 0;
}

void function(int num)
{
   if (num > 0)
   {
      for (int x = 0; x < num; x++)
         cout << '*';
      cout << endl;
      function(num - 1);
   }
}
```

C)
```
#include <cstdlib>
#include <string>
#include <iostream>
using namespace std;
void function(string str, int pos);

int main(int argc, char** argv)
```

```
{
    string names = "Adam and Eve";
    function(names, 0);
    return 0;
}
void function (string str, int pos)
{
    if (pos < str.length())
    {
        function(str, pos+1);
        cout << str[pos];
    }
}
```

Soft Skills

8. Programming is communication; the programmer "explains" to a computer how to carry out a task, with the explanation being the program. Can you think of any cases where communication directed to people uses direct or indirect recursion? Are there cases where such a use of recursion is indispensable?

Programming Challenges

1. Iterative Factorial

Write an iterative version (using a loop instead of recursion) of the factorial function shown in this chapter. Demonstrate the use of the function in a program that prints the factorial of a number entered by the user.

2. Recursive Conversion

Convert the following function to one that uses recursion.

```
void sign(int n)
{
   while (n > 0)
   {
      cout << "No Parking\n";
      n--;
   }
}
```

Demonstrate the function with a driver program.

3. QuickSort Template

Create a template version of the `quickSort` algorithm that will work with any data type that overloads the comparison operators. Demonstrate the template with a driver function.

4. Recursive Array Sum

Write a function that accepts two arguments, an array of integers and a number indicating the number of elements in the array. The function should recursively calculate the sum of all the numbers in the array. Demonstrate the use of the function in a program that asks the user to enter an array of numbers and prints its sum.

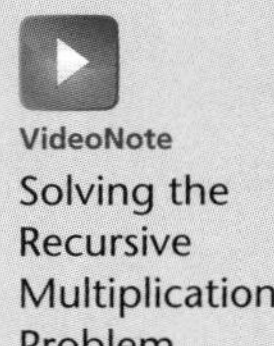

Solving the Recursive Multiplication Problem

5. Recursive Multiplication

Write a recursive function that accepts two arguments into the parameters `x` and `y`. The function should return the value of `x` times `y`. Remember, multiplication can be performed as repeated addition:

$$7 * 4 = 4 + 4 + 4 + 4 + 4 + 4 + 4$$

6. Recursive Member Test

Write a recursive Boolean function named `isMember`. The function should accept three parameters: an array of integers, an integer indicating the number of elements in the array, and an integer value to be searched for. The function should return `true` if the value is found in the array, or `false` if the value is not found. Demonstrate the use of the function in a program that asks the user to enter an array of numbers and a value to be searched for.

7. String Reverser

Write a recursive function that accepts a string as its argument and prints the string in reverse order. Demonstrate the function in a driver program.

8. Ackermann's Function

Ackermann's function is a recursive mathematical algorithm that can be used to test how well a computer performs recursion. Write a function `A(m, n)` that solves Ackermann's function. Use the following logic in your function:

```
If m = 0 then   return n + 1
If n = 0 then   return A(m-1, 1)
Otherwise,      return A(m-1, A(m, n-1))
```

Test your function in a driver program that displays the following values:

A(0, 0)   A(0, 1)   A(1, 1)   A(1, 2)   A(1, 3)   A(2, 2)   A(3, 2)

9. Prefix to Postfix

Write a program that reads prefix expressions and converts them to postfix. Each prefix expression should be entered on a separate line. The program should keep reading prefix expressions and converting them to postfix until a blank line is entered.

10. Prefix to Infix

Write a program that reads prefix expressions and converts them to infix. The infix expressions should be fully parenthesized to show the order of application of the operators. Each prefix expression should be entered on a separate line. The program should keep reading prefix expressions and converting them to infix until a blank line is entered.

11. Ancestral Trees

Assume the following arrays are globally defined.

```
const string people[] = {"Al", "Beth", "Bob", "Carol", "Chuck",
                         "Candy", "Cain", "Debbie", "Doug",
                         "Diane", "Dwayne", "Delores", "Dwight"
                        };
const string mother[] = {"Beth", "Carol", "Charity", "Debbie",
                         "Diane", "", "Delores"
                        };
const string father[] = {"Bob", "Charley", "Cain", "Douglas",
                         "Dwayne", "", "Dwight"
                        };
const int mom[] = {1, 3, 5, 7, 9, -1, 11, -1, -1, -1, -1, -1, -1};
const int pop[] = {2, 4, 6, 8, 10, -1, 12, -1, -1, -1, -1, -1, -1};
```

The `people` array establishes a correspondence between a name and its position in the array: Al is assigned the index 0, Beth is assigned the index 1, and so on. The `mother` and `father` arrays specify parental information. Al, who has index 0, has Beth (`mother[0]`) for his mother and Bob (`father[0]`) for his father. Similarly, the mother and father of Beth are Carol and Charley respectively. The mother and father of Candy (index 5) are not known, so they are indicated by empty strings.

The `mom` and `pop` arrays give the same information in integer rather than string format. Values of -1 denote unknown information. For example, the mother of the person at index 4 has index `mom[4]= 9`, and the father has index `pop[4]= 10`.

The ancestral lineage of a person is a list that begins with that person, and includes all of his or her ancestors. For example, the ancestral lineage of Al (index 0) is given by the `people` array, while the ancestral lineage of Cain (index 6) is `Cain`, `Delores`, `Dwight`.

Write a function `void ancestors(int index)` that prints a list of names that comprises the ancestral lineage of the person with the given index.

CHAPTER 15 Polymorphism and Virtual Functions

TOPICS

15.1 Type Compatibility in Inheritance Hierarchies

CONCEPT: Objects of a derived class can be used wherever objects of a base class object are expected.

Hierarchies of Inheritance

As you learned in Chapter 11, it often makes sense to create a new class based on an existing class if the new class is a special version of the existing one. The derived class can then itself serve as the base class for other classes, resulting in an *inheritance hierarchy*. For example, in Chapter 11, we used the process of inheritance to create a hierarchy of several classes: `Person`, `Student`, `Faculty`, and `TFaculty`. The relationship of inheritance is normally depicted using rectangles to represent the classes and arrows pointing from the derived class to the base class, as shown in Figure 15-1.

This hierarchy may of course be extended. For example, the `Student` class might itself be used as a base class for two other derived classes, `CStudent` and `RStudent`. These last two classes might be used to represent a type of student that commutes and another type of student that is resident on campus.

Figure 15-1

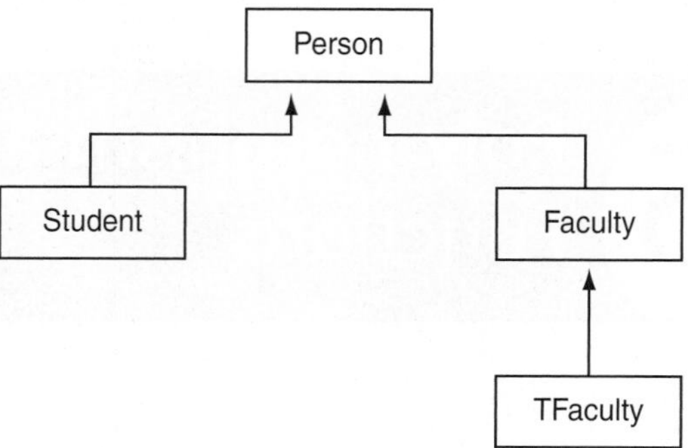

Type Compatibility in Inheritance

Certain type compatibility relationships hold among different classes in an inheritance hierarchy. Because objects in an inheritance hierarchy are commonly accessed through pointers, we state these rules in terms of pointers:

- *A derived class pointer can always be assigned to a base class pointer.* This means that base class pointers can point to derived class objects.
- *A type cast is required to perform the opposite assignment of a base class pointer to a derived class pointer.* An error may result at run time if the base class pointer does not actually point to a derived class object.

Let us illustrate the use of these rules with a simple example.

```
class Base
{
public:
   int i;
   Base(int k){i = k;}
};
class Derived : public Base
{
public:
   double d;
   Derived(int k, double g) : Base(k){ d = g ;}
};

Base *pb = new Base(5);
Derived *pd = new Derived(6, 10.5);
```

The first rule says we can assign derived class pointers to base class pointers. Thus we can write:

```
Base *pb1 = pd;
Base *pb2 = new Derived(7, 11.5);
```

The second rule says we can assign a base class pointer to a derived class pointer if we use a type cast. Thus we can write:

```
Derived *pd1 = static_cast<Derived *>(pb1);
```

This assignment leaves `pd1`, (which is a pointer to `Derived`) pointing to a `Derived` class object, and allows subsequent accesses to `Derived` class members through `pd1` to execute correctly:

```
cout << pd1->d;
```

Consider now the scenario in which a `Base` class pointer `pb` pointing to a `Base` class object is assigned to a `Derived` class pointer using a type cast.

```
pd = static_cast<Derived *>pb;
```

The statement compiles correctly, but when it is executed, it leaves a `Derived` class pointer pointing to a `Base` class object. A subsequent access to `Derived` class members through `pd` will cause a runtime error:

```
cout << pd->d;    // Error
```

The error occurs because the `Base` class object pointed to by `pd` does not have a member `d`.

These types of compatibility rules hold even for deep inheritance hierarchies. For example, if as in Figure 15-1 `Person` is a base class for `Faculty` which is in turn a base class for `TFaculty`, then you can assign a `TFaculty` pointer to a `Person` pointer:

```
TFaculty  *tF = new TFaculty(name, disc);
Person *p ;
p = tF;
```

The assignment in the reverse direction, however, requires a type cast:

```
tF = static_cast<TFaculty *>(p);
```

To give further illustration of these concepts, consider the following program which uses modified versions of classes first encountered in Section 12 of Chapter 11.

Contents of `Inheritance4.h`

```
#include <string>
using namespace std;

enum Discipline { ARCHEOLOGY, BIOLOGY, COMPUTER_SCIENCE };
enum Classification { FRESHMAN, SOPHOMORE, JUNIOR, SENIOR };

class Person
{
protected:
  string name;
public:
  Person() { setName(""); }
  Person(string pName) { setName(pName); }
  void setName(string pName) { name = pName; }
  string getName() const { return name; }
};
```

```

class Student:public Person
{
private:
  Discipline major;
  Person *advisor;
public:

  Student(string sname, Discipline d, Person *adv)
  : Person(sname)
  {
    major = d;
    advisor = adv;
  }
  void setMajor(Discipline d) { major = d; }
  Discipline getMajor() const { return major; }
  void setAdvisor(Person *p) { advisor = p; }
  Person *getAdvisor() const { return advisor; }
};

class Faculty:public Person
{
private:
  Discipline department;
public:
  Faculty(string fname, Discipline d) : Person(fname)
  {
     department = d;
  }
  void setDepartment(Discipline d) { department = d; }
  Discipline getDepartment( ) const { return department; }
};

class TFaculty : public Faculty
{
private:
  string title;
public:
  TFaculty(string fname, Discipline d, string title)
  : Faculty(fname, d)
  {
    setTitle(title);
  }
  void setTitle(string title) { this->title = title; }

  // Override getName()
  string getName( ) const
   {
     return title + " " + Person::getName();
   }
};
```

Here are other examples of assigning derived class pointers to base classes:

```
Person *ptp;
TFaculty *ptf;
// Pointer to Derived class is assigned to Base class
// pointer
ptp = new TFaculty("Indiana Jones", ARCHEOLOGY, "Dr.");
// Assigning a base class pointer to a derived class
// pointer requires a typecast
ptf = static_cast<TFaculty *>(ptp);
```

In this section of code, the `new` operator returns a pointer to the derived class `TFaculty`, which is assigned to the base class pointer `ptp`. The base class pointer `ptp` is then assigned to `ptf` using a type cast.

These type compatibility rules apply in two other cases. A function that is declared as taking a pointer to a base class will accept a pointer to a derived class object as an actual parameter. Also, a function that declares a return type of a pointer to a particular class *C* may actually return a pointer to on object of a class derived from *C*.

Using Type Casts with Base Class Pointers

We have seen that a pointer to a particular class *C* may actually be pointing an object of a class derived from *C*. In this case, the class type of the pointer will be different from the class type of the object, and C++ defaults to using the class of the pointer to determine access to the members of the object. As an example, consider the statement

```
Person *pPerson = new Faculty("Donald Knuth", COMPUTER_SCIENCE);
```

Even though this assignment is legal, it does not make the pointer `pPerson` aware of additional members of the `Faculty` class that are not in the `Person` class. Consequently, an attempt to access members of the `Faculty` class through `pPerson`, such as

```
pPerson->setDepartment(BIOLOGY); //  compiler error!
```

is rejected by the compiler. If we do know that `pPerson` actually points to a `Faculty` object, we can use a type cast to get the compiler to accept the statement:

```
static_cast<Faculty *>(pPerson)->setDepartment(BIOLOGY);
```

The type cast informs the compiler that `pPerson` is actually pointing to a `Faculty` object derived from the `Person` base class. Alternatively, we can first cast `pPerson` to a pointer to `Faculty`, and then use the new pointer:

```
Faculty *pFaculty = static_cast<Faculty *>(pPerson);
pFaculty->setDepartment(BIOLOGY);
```

In general, a pointer to a base class that actually points to a derived class object must first be appropriately cast before the additional features of the derived class can be used.

Recall from Chapter 11 that a derived class may override member functions that are defined in its base class. When a pointer to a base class is being used to access a member function that has been overridden by the derived class, the default C++ behavior is to use the version of the function that is defined in the class of the pointer rather than in the class of the object. For example, the code

```
Person *pP = new TFaculty("Indiana Jones", ARCHEOLOGY);
```

sets pP, which is a pointer to the base class Person, to point to a TFaculty object. Note that TFaculty overrides the getName function defined in Person. In executing the statement

```
cout << pP->getName();
```

the compiler is not aware that the actual class type of the object is TFaculty. The compiler sees the class type of the pointer and assumes that the class type of the object is the same as that of the pointer. Therefore, it calls the version of getName defined in the Person class. Program 15-1 illustrates these concepts.

Program 15-1

```
// This program demonstrates type compatibility within
// an inheritance hierarchy.
#include "inheritance4.h"
#include <iostream>
using namespace std;

int main()
{
   Person *pp;
   Faculty *pf;
   TFaculty *ptf;
   ptf = new TFaculty("Indiana Jones", ARCHEOLOGY, "Dr.");

   // Calling getName through a pointer to TFaculty uses
   // the version of getName in TFaculty
   cout << "Get name through a pointer to TFaculty: ";
   cout << ptf->getName() << endl;

   // Assignment of derived to base needs no cast
   pf = ptf;

   // Calling getName through a pointer to Faculty uses the
   // version of getName in Faculty
   cout << "Get name through a pointer to Faculty: ";
   cout << pf->getName() << endl;

   // Assignment of derived to base needs no cast
   pp = ptf;

   // Derived class members can be accessed using a cast
   cout << "Get name through a cast to pointer to TFaculty: ";
   cout << static_cast<TFaculty *>(pp)->getName() << endl;

   // Assigment from base to derived needs a cast
   TFaculty *ptf1;
   ptf1 = static_cast<TFaculty *>(pp);

   // Access getName through a pointer to TFaculty
   cout << "Get name through a pointer to TFaculty: ";
   cout << ptf1->getName();

   return 0;
}
```

(program continues)

Program 15-1 *(continued)*

Program Output
```
Get name through a pointer to TFaculty: Dr. Indiana Jones
Get name through a pointer to Faculty: Indiana Jones
Get name through a cast to pointer to TFaculty: Dr. Indiana Jones
Get name through a pointer to TFaculty: Dr. Indiana Jones
```

15.2 Polymorphism and Virtual Member Functions

CONCEPT: Virtual functions allow the most specific version of a member function in an inheritance hierarchy to be selected for execution. Virtual functions make polymorphism possible.

VideoNote Polymorphism

A piece of code is said to be *polymorphic* if executing the code with different types of data produces different behavior. For example, a function would be called polymorphic if it executes differently when it is passed different types of parameters.

To illustrate polymorphism, consider the following program. The program creates an array of (pointers to) `Person` objects of type `Student`, `Faculty`, and `TFaculty`. It then prints the names in all the objects using the same code. Because an array can only hold elements of one type, we must use an array of pointers to the base class.

Program 15-2

```
// This exhibits the default non-polymorphic behavior of C++.
#include "inheritance4.h"
#include <iostream>
using namespace std;

int main()
{
   // Create an array of pointers to Person objects
   const int NUM_PEOPLE = 5;
   Person *arr[NUM_PEOPLE] =
    {
      new TFaculty("Indiana Jones", ARCHEOLOGY, "Dr."),
      new Student("Thomas Cruise", COMPUTER_SCIENCE, NULL),
      new Faculty("James Stock", BIOLOGY),
      new TFaculty("Sharon Rock", BIOLOGY, "Professor"),
      new TFaculty("Nicole Eweman", ARCHEOLOGY, "Dr.")
    };
   // Print the names of the Person objects
   for (int k = 0; k < NUM_PEOPLE; k++)
   {
      cout << arr[k]->getName() << endl;
   }
   return 0;
}
```

(program continues)

Program 15-2 *(continued)*

Program Output

```
Indiana Jones
Thomas Cruise
James Stock
Sharon Rock
Nicole Eweman
```

Notice that the program calls the `Person` version of the `getName` function for all objects in the array, even though the `TFaculty` objects have their own, more specialized version. This code is obviously not polymorphic, for it executes the same member function for each object, regardless of its type. In other words, it does not behave differently for different types of objects.

To better understand what is happening, we need to take a closer look at each of the five calls

```
arr[k]->getName()
```

used to retrieve the name to be printed. In each of these calls, a pointer `arr[k]` to the base class `Person` is used to invoke the `getName` function in objects of different derived classes. Some of these classes, like `TFaculty`, override `getName` to provide a more specialized version of that function. When `arr[k]` is pointing to a `TFaculty` object, the compiler must choose between the `getName` defined in `Person`, the class of the pointer, and the `getName` defined in `TFaculty`, the class that the object actually belongs to. The default C++ behavior is to use the class type of the pointer rather than that of the object to determine which version of an overridden function to call.

The scenario of invoking a member function of a derived class object through a base class pointer is a common occurrence in object-oriented programming. Let us say that we have a base class `B` with a member function `mfun()` and a base class pointer `ptr` that is pointing to an object of a derived class `D`.

```
class B
{
public:
   void mfun()
   {
      cout << "Base class version";
   }
};
class D : public B
{
public:
   void mfun()
   {
      cout << "Derived class version";
   }
};
Base *ptr = new D();
```

We want to tell the compiler that whenever we write

```
ptr->mfun()
```

the compiler should select the more specialized version of `mfun()` in the derived class. We can do this in C++ by declaring `mfun()` to be a *virtual* function in the base class. Virtual functions are used in C++ to support polymorphic behavior. Thus, to achieve polymorphic behavior for `mfun()` in the class B and all of its derived classes, we must modify the definition of B as follows:

```
class B
{
public:
   virtual void mfun()
   {
      cout << "Base class version";
   }
};
```

The virtual characteristic is inherited: that is, if a member function of a derived class overrides a virtual function in the base class, then that member function is automatically virtual itself. Thus the declaration of `mfun` as virtual in `B` makes `mfun` virtual in `D` and in all classes derived from `D`.

Although it is not necessary, many programmers tag all virtual functions with the key word `virtual` to make it easer to identify them. This is good practice, and accordingly, the definition of `D` should be written as follows:

```
class D : public B
{
public:
   virtual void mfun()
   {
      cout << "Derived class version";
   }
};
```

The following program is a modification of Program 15-2. In it, the `getName` function of the `Person` class has been declared virtual. It includes the `inheritance5.h` file, which is the just the `inheritance4.h` file modified to make the `getName` function in the `Person` class virtual.

Program 15-3

Contents of `Inheritance5.h`

```
#include <string>
using namespace std;

enum Discipline { ARCHEOLOGY, BIOLOGY, COMPUTER_SCIENCE };
enum Classification { FRESHMAN, SOPHOMORE, JUNIOR, SENIOR };

// The Person class is modified to make getName
```

(program continues)

Program 15-3 *(continued)*

```
// a virtual function
class Person{
protected:
  string name;
public:
  Person() { setName(""); }
  Person(string pName) { setName(pName); }
  void setName(string pName) { name = pName; }

  // Virtual function
  virtual string getName() const { return name; }
};

class Student:public Person
{
private:
  Discipline major;
  Person *advisor;
public:
  Student(string sname, Discipline d, Person *adv)
  : Person(sname)
  {
    major = d;
    advisor = adv;
  }
  void setMajor(Discipline d) { major = d; }
  Discipline getMajor() const { return major; }
  void setAdvisor(Person *p) { advisor = p; }
  Person *getAdvisor() const { return advisor; }
};

class Faculty:public Person
{
private:
  Discipline department;
public:
  Faculty(string fname, Discipline d) : Person(fname)
  {
     department = d;
  }
  void setDepartment(Discipline d) { department = d; }
  Discipline getDepartment( ) const { return department; }
};

class TFaculty : public Faculty
{
private:
  string title;
public:
  TFaculty(string fname, Discipline d, string title)
  : Faculty(fname, d)
```

(program continues)

Program 15-3 *(continued)*

```
  {
    setTitle(title);
  }

  void setTitle(string title) { this->title = title; }

  // Virtual function
  virtual string getName( ) const
  {
    return title + " " + Person::getName();
  }
};

```

Contents of Main Program, `pr15-03.cpp`

```
// This demonstrates the polymorphic behavior
// of classes with virtual functions.
#include "inheritance5.h"
#include <iostream>
using namespace std;

int main()
{
   // Create an array of Person objects
   const int NUM_PEOPLE = 5;
   Person *arr[NUM_PEOPLE] =
       {
         new TFaculty("Indiana Jones", ARCHEOLOGY, "Dr."),
         new Student("Thomas Cruise", COMPUTER_SCIENCE, NULL),
         new Faculty("James Stock", BIOLOGY),
         new TFaculty("Sharon Rock", BIOLOGY, "Professor"),
         new TFaculty("Nicole Eweman", ARCHEOLOGY, "Dr.")
       };
   // Print the names of the Person objects
   for (int k = 0; k < NUM_PEOPLE; k++)
   {
     cout << arr[k]->getName() << endl;
   }
   return 0;
}
```

Program Output

```
Dr. Indiana Jones
Thomas Cruise
James Stock
Professor Sharon Rock
Dr. Nicole Eweman
```

Dynamic and Static Binding

The compiler is said to *bind* the name of a function when it selects the code that should be executed when the function name is invoked. In other words, the compiler binds the name to a function definition when the function is called.

Static binding happens at compile time and binds the name to a fixed function definition, which is then executed each time the name is invoked. For example, in Program 15-2 of the previous section, the compiler used static binding to bind `getName` in the statement

```
for (int k = 0; k < NUM_PEOPLE; k++)
{
   cout << arr[k]->getName() << endl;
}
```

to the definition of `getName` in the `Person` class.

In static binding, the compiler uses type information available at compile time. If the code is operating on objects of different classes within an inheritance hierarchy, the only type information available to the compiler will be the base class pointer type used to access all the objects. Consequently, static binding will always use the base class version of a member function.

In contrast, *dynamic binding* occurs at run time. Dynamic binding works only if the compiler can determine at run time the exact class that a subclass object belongs to. The compiler then uses this run-time type information to call the version of the function defined in that class. To make dynamic binding possible, the compiler stores run-time type information in every object of a class with a virtual function. Dynamic binding always uses the version of the member function in the actual class of the object, regardless of the class of the pointer used to access the object.

More information on dynamic binding and run-time type information can be found in Appendix K on the book's companion website.

15.3 Abstract Base Classes and Pure Virtual Functions

CONCEPT: Abstract classes and pure virtual functions can be used to define an interface that must be implemented by derived classes.

It is often convenient to have a base class for an inheritance hierarchy that defines a member function that must be implemented in every derived class, but which cannot be implemented by the base class itself because the details needed for a reasonable implementation can only be found in the derived classes. If this is the case, the C++ language permits the programmer to declare the function a *pure virtual function*, that is, a member function for which the class provides no implementation. The C++ way of declaring a pure virtual function is to put the expression `= 0` in the class declaration where the body of the function would otherwise have gone. For example, if a member function `void draw()` is being declared pure virtual, then its declaration in its class looks like

```
void draw() = 0;
```

A pure virtual function is sometimes called an *abstract* function, and a class with at least one pure virtual function is called an *abstract* class. The C++ compiler will not allow you to instantiate an abstract class. Abstract classes can only be subclassed: that is, you can only use them as base classes from which to derive other classes.

A class derived from an abstract class inherits all functions in the base class and will itself be an abstract class unless it overrides all the abstract functions it inherits. The usefulness of abstract classes lies in the fact that they define an interface that will then have to be supported by objects of all classes derived from it.

You can think of an abstract class as a class which has no instances other than those that belong to some subclass. There are many examples of abstract classes in real life. For example, in the animal kingdom, the class "Animal" of all animals is an abstract class. There are instances of animals that do not actually belong to some subclass. There are animals that are dogs, or chickens, or foxes, but there no animals that are just animals.

Consider a graphics system that consists of a collection of shapes that must be drawn at certain locations on the screen. Each shape object would have some member variables to keep track of its position and a member function for drawing the shape at the right position. The different shapes supported by the system might include rectangles, hexagons, and others. Because a rectangle is a shape, and a hexagon is a shape, it makes sense to have a `Shape` class and have both `Rectangle` and `Hexagon` be classes derived from `Shape`. The `Shape` class will have a member function `setPosition` for setting the position of the shape, as well as a member function `draw` for drawing the shape. However, because `Shape` is an abstract class (there is no shape that is just a "shape," it must be a rectangle, a hexagon, a triangle, or other) the logic for drawing a particular shape must be delegated to an appropriate subclass. Thus the `draw()` function cannot have an implementation in the `Shape` class and must be made a pure virtual function.

Program 15-4 shows a `Shape` class with two derived classes: `Rectangle` and `Hexagon`. The class declares a pure virtual function `draw()` that is implemented by its two subclasses. The `main` function maintains a collection of `Shape` objects using an array of pointers.

Program 15-4

```
// This program demonstrates abstract base
// classes and pure virtual functions.
#include <iostream>
using namespace std;

class Shape
{
protected:
   int posX, posY;
public:
   virtual void draw() const = 0;
   void setPosition(int pX, int pY)
   {
     posX = pX;
     posY = pY;
   }
};

class Rectangle : public Shape
{
```

(program continues)

Program 15-4 *(continued)*

```
public:
  virtual void draw() const
  {
    cout << "Drawing rectangle at "  << posX << "  "
         <<  posY << endl;
  }
};

class Hexagon : public Shape
{
public:
  virtual void draw() const
  {
     cout << "Drawing hexagon at "  << posX << "  "
          <<  posY << endl;
  }
};

int main()
 {
   // Create array of pointers to Shapes of various types
   const int NUM_SHAPES = 3;
   Shape * shapeArray[] = { new Hexagon(),
                            new Rectangle(),
                            new Hexagon()
                          };
   // Set positions of all the shapes
   int posX = 5, posY = 15;
   for (int k = 0; k < NUM_SHAPES; k++)
   {
     shapeArray[k]->setPosition(posX, posY);
     posX += 10;
     posY += 10;
   };

   // Draw all the shapes at their positions
   for (int j = 0; j < NUM_SHAPES; j++)
   {
     shapeArray[j]->draw();
   }
   return 0;
 }
```

Program Output

```
Drawing hexagon at 5  15
Drawing rectangle at 15  25
Drawing hexagon at 25  35
```

Program 15-4 affords another demonstration of dynamic binding and polymorphism. Consider in particular the statement

```
shapeArray[j]->draw();
```

which is executed a number of different times in the loop

```
for (int j = 0; j < NUM_SHAPES; j++)
{
   shapeArray[j]->draw();
}
```

The first time the statement is executed, it invokes the `draw` function on a hexagon object, while the second time, it invokes the `draw` function on a rectangle object. Because the two `draw` functions are in different classes, they produce different behavior.

Remember the following points about abstract base classes and pure virtual functions:

- When a class contains a pure virtual function, it is an abstract base class.
- Abstract base classes cannot be instantiated.
- Pure virtual functions are declared with the `= 0` notation, and have no body, or definition.
- Pure virtual functions *must* be overridden in derived classes that need to be instantiated.

Checkpoint

15.1 Explain the difference between static binding and dynamic binding.

15.2 Are virtual functions statically bound or dynamically bound?

15.3 What will the following program display?

```
#include <iostream>
using namespace std;
class First
{
   protected:
      int a;
   public:
      First(int x = 1) { a = x; }
      int getVal() const { return a; }
};
class Second : public First
{
   private:
      int b;
   public:
      Second(int y = 5) { b = y; }
      int getVal() const { return b; }
};
int main()
{
   First object1;
   Second object2;
   cout << object1.getVal() << endl;
   cout << object2.getVal() << endl;
   return 0;
}
```

15.4 What will the following program display?

```
#include <iostream>
using namespace std;
class First
```

```
{
   protected:
      int a;
   public:
      First(int x = 1) { a = x; }
      void twist() { a *= 2; }
      int getVal() { twist(); return a; }
};
class Second : public First
{
   private:
      int b;
   public:
      Second(int y = 5) { b = y; }
      void twist() { b *= 10; }
};
int main()
{
   First object1;
   Second object2;
   cout << object1.getVal() << endl;
   cout << object2.getVal() << endl;
   return 0;
}
```

15.5 What will the following program display?

```
#include <iostream>
using namespace std;
class First
{
   protected:
      int a;
   public:
      First(int x = 1) { a = x; }
      virtual void twist() { a *= 2; }
      int getVal() { twist(); return a; }
};
class Second : public First
{
   private:
      int b;
   public:
      Second(int y = 5) { b = y; }
      virtual void twist() { b *= 10; }
};
int main()
{
   First object1;
   Second object2;
   cout << object1.getVal() << endl;
   cout << object2.getVal() << endl;
   return 0;
}
```

15.6 What will the following program display?

```
#include <iostream>
using namespace std;
class Base
{
   protected:
      int baseVar;
   public:
      Base(int val = 2) { baseVar = val; }
      int getVar() const { return baseVar; }
};
class Derived : public Base
{
   private:
      int deriVar;
   public:
      Derived(int val = 100) { deriVar = val; }
      int getVar() const { return deriVar; }
};

int main()
{
   Base *optr;
   Derived object;

   optr = &object;
   cout << optr->getVar() << endl;
   return 0;
}
```

15.7 How can you tell from looking at a class declaration that a virtual member function is pure?

15.8 What makes an abstract class different from other classes?

15.9 Examine the following classes. The table lists the variables that are members of the `Third` class (some are inherited). Complete the table by filling in the access specification each member will have in the `Third` class. Write "inaccessible" if a member is inaccessible to the `Third` class.

```
class First
{
   private:
      int a;
   protected:
      double b;
   public:
      long c;
};

class Second : protected First
{
   private:
      int d;
```

```
   protected:
      double e;
   public:
      long f;
};

class Third : public Second
{
   private:
      int g;
   protected:
      double h;
   public:
      long i;
}
```

Member Variable	Access Specification in `Third` class
a	
b	
c	
d	
e	
f	
g	
h	
i	

15.4 Focus on Object-Oriented Programming: *Composition versus Inheritance*

CONCEPT: Inheritance should model an "is -a" relation, rather than a "has -a" relation, between the derived and base classes.

VideoNote Composition versus Inheritance

Class inheritance in an object-oriented language should be used to model the fact that the type of the derived class is a special case of the type of the base class. Actually, a class can be considered to be the *set* of all objects that can be created from it. Because the derived class is a special case of the base class, the set of objects that correspond to the derived class will be a *subset* of the set of objects that correspond to the base class. Thus, every object of the derived class is also an object of the base class. In other words, each derived class object *is a* base class object.

Class composition occurs whenever a class contains an object of another class as one of its member variables. Composition was discussed in Chapter 11, where it was pointed out that composition models a *has-a* relation between classes.

Because a derived class inherits all the members of its base class, a derived class effectively contains an object of its base class. Because of this, it is possible to use inheritance where a correct design would call for composition. As an example, consider a program that needs to represent data for a person, say the person's name and street address. The street address might consist of two lines:

123 Main Street
Hometown, 12345

Now suppose we had a class for representing a street address:

```
class StreetAddress
{
   private:
      string line1, line2;
   public:
      void setLine1(string);
      void setLine2(string);
      string getLine1();
      string getLine2();
};
```

Because a person's data has a name and a street address, the proper formulation of a class to represent a person's data would use composition in the following way:

```
class PersonData
{
   private:
      string name;
      StreetAddress address;
   public:
      ...
};
```

We have left off the rest of the class declaration for `PersonData` because we don't need it for our purposes.

It is possible to define this class using inheritance instead of composition. For example, we could define a class `PersonData1` as follows:

```
class PersonData1:public StreetAddress
{
   private:
      string name;
   public:
      ...
};
```

While this new definition would compile correctly, it is conceptually the wrong thing to do because it regards a person's data as a special kind of `StreetAddress`, which it is not. This type of conceptual error in design can result in a program that is confusing to understand and difficult to maintain. It is a good design practice to prefer composition to inheritance whenever possible. One reason is that inheritance breaks the encapsulation of the base class by exposing the base class's protected members to the methods of the derived class.

Let us next consider an example where it makes sense to use inheritance rather than composition. Suppose that we have a class `Dog` that represents the set of all dogs. Assuming that each `Dog` object has a member variable `weight` of type `double` and a member function `void bark()`, we might have the following class:

```
class Dog
{
   protected:
      double weight;
   public:
      Dog(double w)
         { weight = w; }
      virtual void bark() const
         {
              cout << "I am dog weighing "
                   << weight << " pounds." << endl;
         }
};
```

The class also has a constructor to allow `Dog` objects to be initialized. Note that we have declared the `bark()` member function as virtual to allow it to be overridden in a derived class.

Suppose that we need to have a class that represents the set of all sheep dogs. Since every sheep dog is also a dog, it makes sense to derive the new `SheepDog` class from the `Dog` class. That way, a `SheepDog` object will inherit every member of the `Dog` class. In addition to having every characteristic that every dog has, a sheep dog can be expected to have other characteristics peculiar to sheep dogs, for example, an integer member `numberSheep` that indicates the maximum number of sheep the dog is trained to herd. In addition, a sheep dog might have a way of barking different from that of a generic dog, perhaps one adapted to the tending of sheep. This is accounted for by overriding the `bark()` member function of the `Dog` class.

```
class SheepDog:public Dog
{
   private:
      int numberSheep;
   public:
      SheepDog(double w, int nSheep) : Dog(w)
      {
         numberSheep = nSheep;
      }
      void bark() const
      {
         cout << "I am a sheepdog weighing "
```

```
                << weight << " pounds \n   and guarding "
                << numberSheep << " sheep." << endl;
        }
   };
```

To demonstrate this class, we will set up an array of dogs with some of the dogs in the array being sheep dogs. To get around the fact that an array cannot hold two different types, we will use an array of pointers to `Dog`. Recall from Section 15.1 that a pointer to a base class (in this case, `Dog`) can point to any derived class object (in this case, `SheepDog`). We can therefore create an array of pointers to `Dog` and have some of those pointers point to `Dog` objects while others point to `SheepDog` objects:

```
Dog *kennel[3] = { new Dog(40.5),
                   new SheepDog(45.3, 50),
                   new Dog(24.7)
                 };
```

Finally, we can use a loop to call the `bark()`member function of each `Dog` object in the array.

```
for (int k = 0; k < 3; k++)
   {
      cout << k+1 << ": ";
      kennel[k]->bark();
   }
```

Because of polymorphism, and because the `bark()` function was declared virtual, the same line of code inside the loop will call the original `bark()` function for a regular dog, but will call the specialized `bark()` function for a sheep dog. The complete program is given in Program 15-5.

Program 15-5

```
// This program demonstrates the is-a
// relation in inheritance.
#include <iostream>
using namespace std;

// Base class
class Dog
{
  protected:
    double weight;
  public:
    Dog(double w)
     { weight = w; }
    virtual void bark( ) const
     {
       cout << "I am a dog weighing "
            << weight << " pounds." << endl;
     }
};

```

(program continues)

Program 15-5 *(continued)*

```
// A SheepDog is a special type of Dog
class SheepDog:public Dog
{
    int numberSheep;
  public:
    SheepDog(double w, int nSheep) : Dog(w)
    {
      numberSheep = nSheep;
    }
    void bark( ) const
    {
      cout << "I am a sheepdog weighing "
           << weight << " pounds \n   and guarding "
           << numberSheep << " sheep." << endl;
    }
};

int main( )
{
   // Create an array of dogs
   const int NUM_DOGS = 3;
   Dog *kennel[ ] = { new Dog(40.5),
                      new SheepDog(45.3, 50),
                      new Dog(24.7)
                    };

   // Walk by each kennel and make the dog bark
   for (int k = 0; k < NUM_DOGS; k++)
   {
     cout << k+1 << ": ";
     kennel[k]->bark( );
   }
   return 0;
}
```

Program Output

```
1: I am a dog weighing 40.5 pounds.
2: I am a sheepdog weighing 45.3 pounds
   and guarding 50 sheep.
3: I am a dog weighing 24.7 pounds.
```

Inheritance is a better choice than composition in this example, since to use composition would be tantamount to saying that a sheep dog *has a* dog, instead of saying that a sheep dog *is a* dog.

There is a third relationship between classes that some authors talk about: the *uses implementation of* relation. Basically, one class uses the implementation of a second class if it calls a member function of an object of the second class.

How can you know when to use inheritance and when to use composition? Suppose that you have an existing class `C1` and you need to write a definition for another class `C2` that will need the services of an associated `C1` object. Should you derive `C2` from `C1`, or should you give `C2` a member variable of type `C1`? In general, you should prefer composition to inheritance. To help determine if inheritance may be appropriate, you might ask the following questions:

- Is it natural to think of a `C2` object as a special type of `C1` object? If so, then you should use inheritance.
- Will objects of class `C2` need to be used in places where objects of class `C1` are used? For example, will they need to be passed to functions that take reference parameters of type `C1`, or pointers to `C1`? If so, then you should make `C2` a derived class of `C1`.

15.5 Secure Encryption Systems, Inc., Case Study

Secure Encryption Systems is a recently founded consulting company that advises business and corporations on how to protect their data from unauthorized access. The company is interested in developing a framework that enables the rapid evaluation and testing of different encryption and decryption algorithms to determine their effectiveness and the level of security they offer.

In this section, we will consider the use of virtual functions and abstract classes to build application frameworks. An *application framework* can be regarded as an application in skeletal form: it only needs the user to specify the definition of a few functions to transform the framework into a useful application.

Understanding the Problem

In Chapter 9's *Tying It All Together* section you were introduced to the idea of encoding a message so that it could only be read by someone possessing the right information to decode it. More formally, *encryption* is the process of transforming a message, called *plain text*, into *cipher text*, a form that disguises its true meaning. The encryption algorithm used in Chapter 9 involved substituting a new character for each original character. There are many other methods of encrypting text. For example, a simple encryption algorithm might remove all punctuation and spacing from a message and then mix up all the letters in some predetermined way. The message can later be "unmixed" to allow it to be read. For example, the plain text message

```
attack at dawn
```

might be transformed into the cipher text

```
aadakntwctta
```

The "mixing" scheme is an example of an *encryption key*, while the "unmixing" scheme would be a corresponding *decryption key*. *Decryption* is the process of reversing the encryption transformation that has been performed on a message. Decryption is applied to cipher text to yield the original plain text.

A Simple Encryption / Decryption Framework

To provide a framework for testing encryption and decryption algorithms, we will implement a class that provides all the functionality needed to test such an algorithm, but leaves the function that is used to transform the letters unspecified. The framework will be realized as a class, and the transformation function will be a pure virtual member function of the class. Specific encryption algorithms can then be easily tested by forming a derived class of the framework class and overriding the virtual transformation function.

We use a really simple character transformation algorithm: it just shifts up the character by one in the ASCII code: it does not even wrap around to the beginning of the alphabet when it shifts the letters 'z' or 'Z'. The major part of the program is the `Encryption` class:

```
class Encryption
{
 protected:
   ifstream inFile;
   ofstream outFile;
 public:
   Encryption(char *inFileName, char *outFileName);
   ~Encryption();
   // Pure virtual function
   virtual char transform(char ch) = 0;
   // Do the actual work
   void encrypt();
};
```

This class contains the file objects that will be used to access the input and output files. The constructor is passed the names of the two files and does the work of opening the files. The destructor closes the files. The `encrypt` function will read characters from the input file, call the virtual function `transform` to transform the single character, and write the character to the output file.

Because the `transform` function is pure virtual, the `Encryption` class is abstract and cannot be instantiated. All a subclass of `Encryption` needs to do is implement a suitable `transform` function and pass the file names as parameters to its base class constructor. The complete program follows.

Application frameworks are used in many areas of software development to simplify the creation of software. Most application frameworks rely heavily on virtual functions and abstract classes.

Program 15-6

```
// This program demonstrates an application
// of pure virtual functions.
#include <iostream>
#include <fstream>
```

(program continues)

Program 15-6 *(continued)*

```
using namespace std;

class Encryption
{
 protected:
   ifstream inFile;
   ofstream outFile;
 public:
   Encryption(char *inFileName, char *outFileName);
   ~Encryption();
   // Pure virtual function
   virtual char transform(char ch) const = 0;
   // Do the actual work
   void encrypt();
};

//**********************************************
// Constructor opens the input and output file.    *
//**********************************************
Encryption::Encryption(char *inFileName, char *outFileName)
{
   inFile.open(inFileName);
   outFile.open(outFileName);
   if (!inFile)
     {
       cout <<  "The file " << inFileName
            << " cannot be opened.";
       exit(1);
     }
   if (!outFile)
    {
      cout << "The file " << outFileName
           << " cannot be opened.";
      exit(1);
    }
}

//**********************************************
//Destructor closes files.                         *
//**********************************************
Encryption::~Encryption()
{
   inFile.close();
   outFile.close();
}

```

(program continues)

Program 15-6 *(continued)*

```
//*************************************************
//Encrypt function uses the virtual transform      *
//member function to transform individual characters. *
//*************************************************
void Encryption::encrypt()
{
   char ch;
   char transCh;
   inFile.get(ch);
   while (!inFile.fail())
     {
       transCh = transform(ch);
       outFile.put(transCh);
       inFile.get(ch);
     }
}

// The subclass simply overides the virtual
// transformation function
class SimpleEncryption : public Encryption
{
public:
   char transform(char ch) const
   {
     return ch + 1;
   }
   SimpleEncryption(char *inFileName, char *outFileName)
   : Encryption(inFileName, outFileName)
   {
   }
};

int main()
{
  char inFileName[80], outFileName[80];
  cout << "Enter name of file to encrypt: ";
  cin >> inFileName;
  cout << "Enter name of file to receive "
       << "the encrypted text: ";
  cin >> outFileName;
  SimpleEncryption obfuscate(inFileName, outFileName);
  obfuscate.encrypt();
  return 0;
}
```

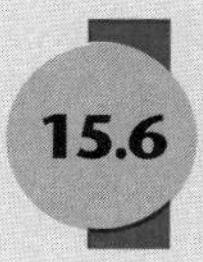

15.6 Tying It All Together: *Let's Move It*

Video game programmers often have to maintain a collection of figures that are simultaneously moving in various directions on the screen. Let's devise a solution to a simplifed version of this problem. We will maintain a collection of geometric shapes and simultaneously animate those shapes. The functions used to directly access the screen and manage the timer are peculiar to Microsoft Windows, but the principles used are very general and are applicable to all operating systems.

We begin with a class that represents a shape that is able to move in any of eight different directions, with each direction being specified by a pair of integer (X, Y) coordinates. Upward or downward motion is indicated by a Y component of ±1, and likewise, motion in a left or rightward direction is indicated by an X component of ±1. A value of 0 for an X or Y coordinate indicates lack of motion in that direction. Thus, a value of (0, 1) for (X, Y) indicates motion straight up, a value of (–1, 0) indicates motion to the left, and (1, 1) is motion that is simultaneously downward and to the right. The `Shape` class can be seen in lines 13–23 of the `ShapeAnimator.h` file.

The `Shape` class has a `move()` function that is pure virtual. This is because a shape is moved by erasing it at its current position and redrawing it at a new position, and it is not possible to know how to draw a shape without knowing what type of shape it is.

Our solution for representing the different shapes will use the five classes `Shape`, `ComplexShape`, `SimpleShape`, `Box`, and `Tent`. These classes form the inheritance hierarchy shown in Figure 15-2.

Figure 15-2

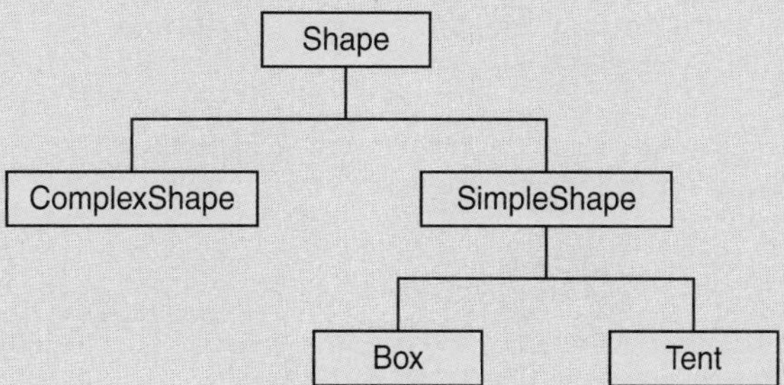

The `SimpleShape` class represents objects that can be drawn at a given position in a specified color. Accordingly, it has member variables for representing position and color and member functions for setting and accessing those values. The `SimpleShape` class appears in lines 26–44 of the `ShapeAnimator.h` file. Notice that the `SimpleShape` class is still abstract because it provides no implementation for the `draw()` method. The class does implement the `move()` method, though. This is because the `move()` method works the same way for all subclasses of SimpleShape: erase the shape at its current position, compute its new position, and draw the shape at the new position. The `draw()` method, however, works differently for each concrete subclass that implements it. Because `draw()` is virtual, the `move()` method will always call the appropriate version of `draw()`, even when the call to `draw()` is through a pointer to the abstract class `Shape`.

The `Box` and `Tent` classes are the concrete classes at the tip of the inheritance hierarchy. They define a specific concrete shape and implement the member function `draw()` that draws the shape at its current position using the shape's specified color. The `Box` class defines a rectangular shape by specifying the position of its top left-hand corner together with its width and height. The `Tent` class defines a triangle with a horizontal base whose two other sides are equal in length and whose height is half the length of the base. A `Tent` object is specified by giving the position of the left end point of its base together with the length of the base. For example, a tent whose base has length 5 would look like this:

```
  *
 ***
*****
```

The `Box` and `Tent` classes can be seen in Lines 46–66 of `ShapeAnimator.h`.

The `ComplexShape` class provides a mechanism for assembling a collection of simple shapes to form a single shape that can be moved using a single command. The class maintains a vector of pointers to `Shape` objects, and implements its `move()` method is by calling the `move()` methods of all the `Shape` objects in its collection. Likewise, `ComplexShape` has a `setDirection()` method that can be used to cause all of its constituent shapes to move in the same direction. The class itself is found in lines 70–78 of the `ShapeAnimator.h` file, and its `move()` method is implemented in lines 124–128 of `ShapeAnimator.cpp`.

Contents of `SortAnimator.h`

```
 1 #include <iostream>
 2 #include <string>
 3 #include <vector>
 4 #include <windows.h>
 5 using namespace std;
 6
 7 // A global constant can be included in more than one cpp file.
 8 // This is the handle to the output console.
 9 const HANDLE outHandle = GetStdHandle(STD_OUTPUT_HANDLE);
10
11 // A shape has a direction and is able to move in that direction.
12 // The move is a virtual member function
13 class Shape
14 {
15 public:
16     virtual void setDirection(int drow, int dcol) const
17       {dRow = drow; dCol = dcol;}
18     void getDirection(int &drow, int &dcol)
19       {drow = dRow; dcol = dCol;}
20     virtual void move()= 0;
21 private:
22     int dRow, dCol; // Direction of motion
23 };
24
25 // A SimpleShape is drawn at a given position in a specified color
26 class SimpleShape : public Shape
```

```
{
public:
    virtual void draw() const = 0;
    void getPosition(int &row, int &col) const
    {
        row = rowPos; col = colPos;
    }
    void setPosition(int row, int col)
    {
        rowPos = row; colPos = col;
    }
    void setColor(int c){ color = c; }
    int getColor() const {return color; }
    virtual void move();
private:
    int color;
    int rowPos, colPos;
};

// A Box is a rectangular type of shape
class Box : public SimpleShape
{
public:
    virtual void draw() const;
    Box(int rowPos, int colPos, int width, int height);
private:
    int width, height;
};

// A Tent is an isosceles triangle whose horizontal base has a
// given length and whose height is half the length of the base
// The position of the triangle is the left end point of the base
class Tent : public SimpleShape
{
public:
    virtual void draw() const;
    Tent(int baseRowPos, int baseColPos, int baseLength);
private:
    int baseLength;
};

// A ComplexShape is made up of simpler shapes. It is represented
// as a vector of pointers to the simpler shapes that make it up
class ComplexShape : public Shape
{
public:
    ComplexShape(Shape ** shapeCollection, int shapesCount);
    virtual void move();
    virtual void setDirection(int dRow, int dCol);
private:
    vector<Shape *> shapes;
};
```

Contents of `ShapeAnimator.cpp`

```
#include "ShapeAnimator.h"

//**************************************************************
// Moves a simple shape one step by erasing the shape          *
// at its current position, changing its position, and then    *
// redrawing the shape at its new position.                    *
//**************************************************************
void SimpleShape::move()
{
    int dRow, dCol; // Direction of motion
    int savedColor = color;
    color = 0;      // Drawing in color 0 erases the shape
    draw();
    // Compute the new position for the shape by adding a step in
    // the proper direction to the current position
    getDirection(dRow, dCol);
    rowPos += dRow;
    colPos += dCol;
    // Draw the shape at its new position in its specified color
    color = savedColor;
    draw();
}
//*************************************
// Draws a tent at its position       *
//*************************************
void Tent:: draw() const
{
    int rowPos, colPos;
    COORD pos;
    int currentLength = baseLength;
    // Set the color attribute
    SetConsoleTextAttribute(outHandle, getColor());
    getPosition(rowPos, colPos);
    pos.Y = rowPos; pos.X = colPos;

    // Draw the lines that form the tent beginning with
    // the base and moving up toward the point
    for (int r = 0; r < (baseLength + 1)/2; r++)
    {
        SetConsoleCursorPosition(outHandle,pos);
        // Draw a horizontal line of a given length
        for (int k = 0; k < currentLength; k++)
        {
            cout << "*";
        }
        cout << endl;
        pos.Y--;
        pos.X ++;
        currentLength -= 2;
    }
    // Restore normal attribute
    SetConsoleTextAttribute(outHandle, 7);
}
```

```
//*********************************
// Draws a box shape             *
//*********************************
void Box::draw() const
{
    int rowPos, colPos;
    COORD pos;

    // Set the color attribute for the box
    SetConsoleTextAttribute(outHandle, getColor());
    getPosition(rowPos, colPos);
    pos.X = colPos; pos.Y = rowPos;

    // Draw the lines that make up the  box
    for (int r = 0; r < height; r++)
    {
        SetConsoleCursorPosition(outHandle, pos);
        for (int c = 0; c < width; c++)
        {
            cout << "*";
        }
        cout << endl;
        pos.Y++;
    }
    // Restore normal text attribute
    SetConsoleTextAttribute(outHandle, 7);
}
//**********************************************
// Constructor sets the color, position, and    *
// dimensions for a box shape, and draws        *
// the box at its initial position              *
//**********************************************
Box::Box(int rowPos, int colPos, int width, int height)
{
    setColor(4);
    setPosition(rowPos, colPos);
    this->width = width;
    this->height = height;
    draw();
}
//**********************************************
// Constructor sets the color for a Tent shape, *
// sets the position of the tent as well as the *
// length of its base and draws it at its       *
// initial position                             *
//**********************************************
Tent::Tent(int baseRowPos, int baseColPos, int baseLength)
{
    setColor(2);
    setPosition(baseRowPos, baseColPos);
    this->baseLength = baseLength;
    draw();
}
```

```
//*****************************************************************
// Constructor builds a complex shape by assembling a vector of    *
// constituent shapes                                               *
//*****************************************************************
ComplexShape::ComplexShape(Shape ** shapeCollection, int shapesCount)
{
    Shape *p;
    for (int k = 0; k < shapesCount; k++)
    {
        p = shapeCollection[k];
        shapes.push_back(p);
    }
}
//*************************************
// Moves a complex shape by moving the *
// constituent shapes                  *
//*************************************
void ComplexShape::move()
{
    for (int k = 0; k < shapes.size(); k++)
        shapes[k]->move();
}
//*****************************************************
// Sets the direction of a complex shape by setting the  *
// direction of all constituent shapes                   *
//*****************************************************
 void ComplexShape::setDirection(int dRow, int dCol)
 {
     // Set direction for the ComplexShape object so
     // getDirection() will work correctly
     Shape::setDirection(dRow, dCol);

     // Set the directions for the constituent shapes so
     // move() will work correctly
     for (int k = 0; k < shapes.size(); k++)
         shapes[k]->setDirection(dRow, dCol);
 }
```

Program 15-7, which follows, illustrates the use of these classes. The program starts out by creating two simple shapes, a tent and a box, in lines 7–8. The tent is created at the left edge of the screen while the box is near the right edge. In lines 14–26, the program moves the tent to the right at the same time that it is moving the box to the left, stopping the motion when the two shapes are within a few coordinates of each other. Lines 27–39 create a complex shape out of the two simple shapes, and then moves the complex shape diagonally downward and to the right. Finally, in lines 40–46, the program moves the box horizontally to the right.

Program 15-7

```
// This program illustrates the use of the various Shape
// classes and subclasses to do graphic animation.
#include "ShapeAnimator.h"
int main()
{
    // Create a tent and a box
    Tent tent(11, 5, 13);
    Box box(5, 65, 4, 7);

    // Draw the tent and the box
    tent.draw();
    box.draw();

    // Set initial direction of motion for the two shapes
    tent.setDirection(0, 1);    // Tent moves horizontally to the right
    box.setDirection(0, -1);    // Box moves horizontally to the left

    // Simultaneously move the tent and the box, this makes them
    // move toward each other
    for (int k = 0; k <= 20; k++)
    {
        Sleep(75);
        tent.move();
        box.move();
    }

    // Create a complex shape composed of the tent and the box
    Shape *myShapes[] = {&tent, &box};
    ComplexShape cS(myShapes, 2);

    // Set direction for the complex shape and  move the
    // complex shape: this moves both the tent and the box
    // diagonally to the right
    cS.setDirection(1, 1);
    for (int k = 0; k < 12; k++)
    {
        Sleep(75);
        cS.move();
    }
    // Move the box by itself horizontally to the right
    box.setDirection(0, 1);
    for (int k = 0; k < 10; k ++)
    {
        Sleep(75);
        box.move();
    }
    return 0;
}
```

Review Questions and Exercises

Fill-in-the-Blank

1. A class that cannot be instantiated is a(n) _________.
2. A member function of a class that is not implemented is called a(n) _________ function.
3. A class with at least one pure virtual member function is called a(n) _________ class.
4. In order to use dynamic binding, a member function of a class needs to be declared as a(n) _________ function.
5. Static binding takes place at _________ time.
6. Dynamic binding takes place at _________ time.
7. The ability of code to execute differently depending on the type of data is called _________.
8. A base class pointer needs a(n) _________ to be assigned to a derived class pointer.
9. The *is-a* relation between classes is best implemented using the mechanism of class _________.
10. The *has-a* relation between classes is best implemented using the mechanism of class _________.
11. If *every* `C1` class object can be used as a `C2` class object, the relationship between the two classes should be implemented using _________.
12. A collection of abstract classes defining an application in skeletal form is called a(n) _________.

C++ Language Elements

Suppose that the classes `Dog` and `Cat` derive from `Animal`, which in turn derives from `Creature`. Suppose further that `pDog`, `pCat`, `pAnimal`, and `pCreature` are pointers to the respective classes. Suppose that `Animal` and `Creature` are both abstract classes.

13. Will the statement

```
Animal a;
```

compile?

14. Will the statement

```
pAnimal = new Cat;
```

compile?

15. Will the statement

```
pCreature = new Dog;
```

compile?

16. Will the statement

```
pCat = new Animal;
```

compile?

17. Rewrite the following two statements to get them to compile correctly.

```
pAnimal = new Dog;
pDog = pAnimal;
```

Algorithm Workbench

18. Write a C++ class that has an array of integers as a member variable, a pure virtual member function

```
bool compare(int x, int y) = 0;
```

that compares its two parameters and returns a boolean value, and a member function

```
void sort()
```

that uses the comparison defined by the compare virtual function to sort the array. The sort function will swap a pair of array elements `a[k]` and `a[j]` if

```
compare (a[k], a[j])
```

returns true. Explain how you can use this class to produce classes that sort arrays in ascending order and descending order.

Find the Errors

19. Find all errors in the following fragment of code.

```
class MyClass
{
public:
   virtual myFun() = 0;
   { cout << "Hello";}
};
```

Soft Skills

20. Suppose that you need to have a class that can sort an array in ascending order or descending order upon request. If an array is already sorted in ascending or descending order, you can easily sort it the other way by reversing it. Now suppose you have two different classes that encapsulate arrays. One provides a member function to reverse its array, while the other provides a member function to sort its array. Can you use multiple inheritance to obtain a quick solution to your problem? Should you? Write a couple of paragraphs explaining whether using multiple inheritance will or will not work to solve this problem, and, if it can, whether this is a good way to solve the problem.

Programming Challenges

1. Analysis of Sorting Algorithms

Design a class `AbstractSort` that can be used to analyze the number of comparisons performed by a sorting algorithm. The class should have a member function compare that is capable of comparing two array elements, and a means of keeping track of the number of comparisons performed. The class should be an abstract class with a pure virtual member function

```
void sort(int arr[ ], int size)
```

which, when overridden, will sort the array by calling the compare function to determine the relative order of pairs of numbers. Create a subclass of `AbstractSort` that uses a simple sorting algorithm to implement the `sort` function. The class should have a member function that can be called after the sorting is done to retrieve the number of comparisons performed.

2. Analysis of Quicksort

Create a subclass of the `AbstractSort` class of Programming Challenge 1 that uses the `Quicksort` algorithm to implement the `sort` function.

3. Sequence Sum

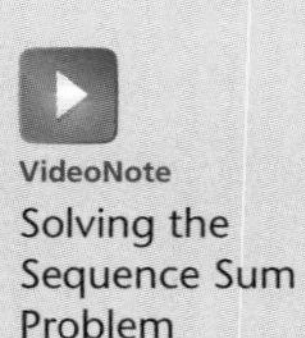

Solving the Sequence Sum Problem

A sequence of integers such as 1, 3, 5, 7, … can be represented by a function that takes a nonnegative integer as parameter and returns the corresponding term of the sequence. For example, the sequence of odd numbers just cited can be represented by the function

```
int odd(int k) {return 2 * k + 1;}
```

Write an abstract class `AbstractSeq` that has a pure virtual member function

```
virtual int fun(int k) = 0;
```

as a stand-in for an actual sequence, and two member functions

```
void printSeq(int k, int m);
int sumSeq(int k, int m)
```

that are passed two integer parameters k and m, where k < m. The function `printSeq` will print all the terms `fun(k)` through `fun(m)` of the sequence, and likewise, the function `sumSeq` will return the sum of those terms. Demonstrate your `AbstractSeq` class by creating subclasses that you use to sum the terms of at least two different sequences. Determine what kind of output best shows off the operation of these classes, and write a program that produces that kind of output.

4. Flexible Encryption

Write a modification of the encryption program of Section 15.5 whose transform function uses an integer key to transform the character passed to it. The function transforms the character by adding the key to it. The key should be represented as a member of the `Encryption` class, and the class should be modified so that it has a member function that sets the encryption key. When the program runs, the main function should ask the user for the input file, the output file, and an encryption key.

Show that with these modifications, the same program can be used for both encryption and decryption.

5. File Filter

A file filter reads an input file, transforms it in some way, and writes the results to an output file. Write an abstract file filter class that defines a pure virtual function for transforming a character. Create one subclass of your file filter class that performs encryption, another that transforms a file to all uppercase, and another that creates an unchanged copy of the original file.

The class should have a member function

```
void doFilter(ifstream &in, ofstream &out)
```

that is called to perform the actual filtering. The member function for transforming a single character should have the prototype

```
char transform(char ch)
```

The encryption class should have a constructor that takes an integer as an argument and uses it as the encrytion key.

6. File Double Spacer

Create a subclass of the abstract filter class of Programming Challenge 5 that double spaces a file: that is, it inserts a blank line between any two lines of the file.

7. Bumper Shapes

Write a program that creates two rectangular shapes and then animates them. The two shapes should start on opposite ends of the screen and then move toward each other. When they meet in the middle of the screen, each shape reverses course and moves toward the edge of the screen. The two shapes keep oscillating and bouncing off of each other in the middle of the screen. The program terminates when the shapes meet each other in the middle for the tenth time.

8. Bow Tie

In this chapter's Tying It All Together we defined a *tent* to be a certain type of triangular shape. Define a *wedge* to be a tent that has been rotated 90 degrees clockwise, and a *reverse wedge* to be a tent rotated 90 degrees counterclockwise. Write a program that creates a wedge and a reverse wedge at the left and right edges of the screen, respectively, and then moves them toward each other until they meet in the middle. The two shapes should form a bow tie when they meet.

CHAPTER 16

Exceptions, Templates, and the Standard Template Library (STL)

TOPICS

16.1 Exceptions

CONCEPT: Exceptions are used to signal errors or unexpected events that occur while a program is running.

Error testing is usually a straightforward process involving `if` statements or other control mechanisms. For example, the following code segment will trap a division-by-zero error before it occurs:

```
if (denominator == 0)
   cout << "ERROR: Cannot divide by zero.\n";
else
   quotient = numerator / denominator;
```

But what if similar code is part of a function that returns the quotient as in the following example:

```
// An unreliable division function
double divide(double numerator, double denominator)
```

```
{
   if (denominator == 0)
   {
      cout << "ERROR: Cannot divide by zero.\n";
      return 0;
   }
   else
      return numerator / denominator;
}
```

Functions commonly signal error conditions by returning a predetermined value. In this example, the function returns 0 when division by zero has been attempted. This is unreliable, however, because 0 is a valid result of a division operation. Even though the function displays an error message, the part of the program that calls the function will not know when an error has occurred. Problems like these require more sophisticated error-handling techniques.

Throwing an Exception

One way of handling complex error conditions is with *exceptions*. An exception is a value or an object that signals an error. When the error occurs, an exception is said to be "thrown" because control will pass to a part of the program that catches and handles that type of error. For example, the following code shows the `divide` function, modified to throw an exception when division by zero has been attempted.

```
double divide(double numerator, double denominator)
{
   if (denominator == 0)
      throw string("ERROR: Cannot divide by zero.\n");
   else
      return numerator / denominator;
}
```

The following statement causes the exception to be thrown.

```
throw string("ERROR: Cannot divide by zero.\n");
```

The `throw` key word is followed by an argument, which can be any value. As you will see, the type of the argument is used to determine the nature of the error. The function above simply throws a string object containing a descriptive error message.

The line containing a throw statement is known as the *throw point*. When a `throw` statement is executed, control is passed to another part of the program known as an *exception handler*.

Handling an Exception

To handle an exception, a program must have a *try/catch* construct. The general format of the try/catch construct is

VideoNote
Throwing and Handling Exceptions

```
try
{
   // code here calls functions or object member
   // functions that might throw an exception.
}
```

```
catch(exception parameter)
{
   // code here handles the exception
}
// Repeat as many catch blocks as needed.
```

The first part of the construct is the *try block*. This starts with the key word `try` and is followed by a block of code executing any statements that might directly or indirectly cause an exception to be thrown. The try block is immediately followed by one or more *catch blocks*, which are the exception handlers. A catch block starts with the key word `catch`, followed by a set of parentheses containing the declaration of an exception parameter. For example, here is a try/catch construct that can be used with the `divide` function:

```
try
{
   quotient = divide(num1, num2);
   cout << "The quotient is " << quotient << endl;
}
catch (string exceptionString)
{
   cout << exceptionString;
}
```

Because the `divide` function throws an exception whose type is a string, there must be an exception handler that catches a string. The catch block shown catches the error message in the `exceptionString` parameter, then displays it with `cout`.

Now let's look at an entire program to see how `throw`, `try`, and `catch` work together. In the first sample run of Program 16-1, valid data is given. This shows how the program should run with no errors. In the second sample run, a denominator of 0 is given. This shows the result of the exception being thrown.

Program 16-1

```
// This program illustrates exception handling.
#include <iostream>
#include <string>
using namespace std;

// Function prototype
double divide(double, double);

int main()
{
   int num1, num2;
   double quotient;

   cout << "Enter two numbers: ";
   cin >> num1 >> num2;
   try
```

(program continues)

Program 16-1 *(continued)*

```
   {
      quotient = divide(num1, num2);
      cout << "The quotient is " << quotient << endl;
   }
   catch (string exceptionString)
   {
      cout << exceptionString;
   }
   cout << "End of the program.\n";
   return 0;
}

double divide(double numerator, double denominator)
{
   if (denominator == 0)
        throw string("ERROR: Cannot divide by zero.\n");
   else
      return numerator / denominator;
}
```

Program Output with Example Input Shown in Bold

```
Enter two numbers: 12 2[Enter]
The quotient is 6
End of the program.
```

Program Output with Example Input Shown in Bold

```
Enter two numbers: 12 0[Enter]
ERROR: Cannot divide by zero.
End of the program.
```

As you can see from the second output screen, the exception caused the program to jump out of the `divide` function and into the catch block. After the catch block has finished, the program resumes with the first statement after the try/catch construct.

What If an Exception Is Not Caught?

There are two possible ways for a thrown exception to go uncaught. The first possibility is for the program to contain no catch blocks with an exception parameter of the right data type. The second possibility is for the exception to be thrown from outside a try block. In either case, the exception will cause the entire program to abort execution.

Object-Oriented Exception Handling with Classes

Now that you have an idea of how the exception mechanism in C++ works, we will examine an object-oriented approach to exception handling. Let's begin by looking at the `IntRange` class:

Contents of `IntRange.h`

```
#ifndef INTRANGE_H
#define INTRANGE_H

#include <iostream>
using namespace std;

class IntRange
{
private:
   int input;  // For user input
   int lower;  // Lower limit of range
   int upper;  // Upper limit of range
public:
   // Exception class
   class OutOfRange
      { };     // Empty class declaration
   // Member functions
   IntRange(int low, int high)   // Constructor
   {
      lower = low;
      upper = high;
   }
   int getInput()
   {
      cin >> input;
      if (input < lower || input > upper)
         throw OutOfRange();
      return input;
   }
};
#endif
```

`IntRange` is a simple class whose member function, `getInput`, lets the user enter an integer value. The value is compared against the member variables `lower` and `upper` (which are initialized by the class constructor). If the value entered is less than `lower` or greater than `upper`, an exception is thrown indicating the value is out of range. Otherwise, the value is returned from the function.

Instead of throwing a string or some value of a primitive type, this function throws an *exception class*. Notice the empty class declaration that appears in the public section:

```
class OutOfRange
   { };  // Empty class declaration
```

Notice that the class has no members. The only important part of this class is its name, which will be used by the exception handling code. Look at the `if` statement in the `getinput` function:

```
if (input < lower || input > upper)
   throw OutOfRange();
```

The throw statement's argument, `OutOfRange()`, causes an instance of the `OutOfRange` class to be created and thrown as an exception. All that remains is for a catch block to handle the exception. Here is an example:

```
catch (IntRange::OutOfRange)
{
   cout << "That value is out of range.\n";
}
```

All that must appear inside the catch block's parentheses is the name of the exception class. The exception class is empty, so there is no need to declare an actual parameter. All the catch block needs to know is the type of the exception.

Since the `OutOfRange` class is declared in the `IntRange` class, its name must be fully qualified with the scope resolution operator. Program 16-2 shows the class at work in a driver program.

Program 16-2

```
// This program demonstrates the use of object-oriented
// exception handling.
#include <iostream>
#include "IntRange.h"
using namespace std;

int main()
{
   IntRange range(5, 10);
   int userValue;

   cout << "Enter a value in the range 5 - 10: ";
   try
   {
      userValue = range.getInput();
      cout << "You entered " << userValue << endl;
   }
   catch (IntRange::OutOfRange)
   {
      cout << "That value is out of range.\n";
   }
   cout << "End of the program.\n";
   return 0;
}
```

Program Output with Example Input Shown in Bold

```
Enter a value in the range 5 - 10: 12[Enter]
That value is out of range.
End of the program.
```

Multiple Exceptions

The programs we have studied so far test only for a single type of error and throw only a single type of exception. In many cases a program will need to test for several different types of errors and signal which one has occurred. C++ allows you to throw and catch multiple exceptions. The only requirement is that each different exception be of a different type. You then code a separate catch block for each type of exception that may be thrown in the try block.

For example, suppose we wish to expand the `IntRange` class so it throws one type of exception if the user enters a value that is too low, and another type if the user enters a value that is too high. First, we declare two different exception classes, such as

```
// Exception classes
class TooLow
   { };
class TooHigh
   { };
```

An instance of the `TooLow` class will be thrown when the user enters a low value, and an instance of the `TooHigh` class will be thrown when a high value is entered.

Next we modify the `getInput` member function to perform the two error tests and throw the appropriate exception:

```
if (input < lower)
   throw TooLow();
else if (input > upper)
   throw TooHigh();
```

The entire modified class, which is named `IntRange2`, is shown here:

Contents of `IntRange2.h`

```
#ifndef INTRANGE2_H
#define INTRANGE2_H

#include <iostream>
using namespace std;

class IntRange2
{
private:
   int input;   // For user input
   int lower;   // Lower limit of range
   int upper;   // Upper limit of range
public:
   // Exception classes
   class TooLow
      { };
   class TooHigh
      { };
   // Member functions
   IntRange2(int low, int high)  // Constructor
   {
        lower = low;
        upper = high;
   }
   int getInput()
```

```
      {
         cin >> input;
         if (input < lower)
            throw TooLow();
         else if (input > upper)
            throw TooHigh();
         return input;
      }
};
#endif
```

Program 16-3 is a simple driver that demonstrates this class.

Program 16-3

```
// This program demonstrates the IntRange2 class.
#include <iostream>
#include "IntRange2.h"
using namespace std;

int main()
{
   IntRange2 range(5, 10);
   int userValue;

   cout << "Enter a value in the range 5 - 10: ";
   try
   {
      userValue = range.getInput();
      cout << "You entered " << userValue << endl;
   }
   catch (IntRange2::TooLow)
   {
      cout << "That value is too low.\n";
   }
   catch (IntRange2::TooHigh)
   {
      cout << "That value is too high.\n";
   }

   cout << "End of the program.\n";
   return 0;
}
```

Program Output with Example Input Shown in Bold

```
Enter a value in the range 5 - 10: 3[Enter]
That value is too low.
End of the program.
```

Extracting Information from the Exception Class

Sometimes we might want an exception to pass information back to the exception handler. For example, suppose we would like the `IntRange` class not only to signal when an invalid value has been entered, but to pass the value back. This can be accomplished by giving the exception class members in which information can be stored.

`IntRange3`, our next modification of the `IntRange` class, again uses a single exception class: `OutOfRange`. This version of `OutOfRange`, however, has a member variable and a constructor that initializes it:

```
// Exception class
class OutOfRange
{  public:
      int value;
      OutOfRange(int i)
      {  value = i; }
};
```

When we throw this exception, we want to pass the value entered by the user to `OutOfRange`'s constructor. This is done with the following statement:

```
throw OutOfRange(input);
```

This `throw` statement creates an instance of the `OutOfRange` class and passes a copy of the `input` variable to the constructor. The constructor then stores this number in `OutOfRange`'s member variable `value`. The class instance carries this member variable to the catch block that intercepts the exception.

Back in the catch block, the value is extracted:

```
catch (IntRange3::OutOfRange ex)
{
   cout << "That value " << ex.value
        << " is out of range.\n";
}
```

Notice that the catch block declares a parameter object named `ex`. This is necessary, because the exception has a member variable that we want to examine. The entire `IntRange3` class is as follows, and Program 16-4 is a driver that demonstrates it.

Contents of `IntRange3.h`

```
#ifndef INTRANGE3_H
#define INTRANGE3_H

#include <iostream>
using namespace std;

class IntRange3
{
private:
   int input;   // For user input
   int lower;   // Lower limit of range
   int upper;   // Upper limit of range
public:
   // Exception class
   class OutOfRange
   {
      public:
```

```
         int value;
         OutOfRange(int i)
         {  value = i; }
      };
      // Member functions
      IntRange3(int low, int high)  // Constructor
      {
         lower = low;
         upper = high;
      }
      int getInput()
      {
         cin >> input;
         if (input < lower || input > upper)
            throw OutOfRange(input);
         return input;
      }
};
#endif
```

Program 16-4

```
 // This program demonstrates the IntRange3 class.
#include <iostream>
#include "IntRange3.h"
using namespace std;

int main()
{
   IntRange3 range(5, 10);
   int userValue;

   cout << "Enter a value in the range 5 - 10: ";
   try
   {
      userValue = range.getInput();
      cout << "You entered " << userValue << endl;
   }
   catch (IntRange3::OutOfRange ex)
   {
      cout << "That value " << ex.value
           << " is out of range.\n";
   }
   cout << "End of the program.\n";
   return 0;
}
```

Program Output with Example Input Shown in Bold

```
Enter a value in the range 5 - 10: 12[Enter]
That value 12 is out of range.
End of the program.
```

Handling the `bad_alloc` Exception Thrown by `new`

The `new` operator throws a system-defined exception of type `bad_alloc` if it is unable to allocate the requested storage. For example, the following program attempts to allocate an array of two integers using the `new` operator inside a try block. If the allocation fails, the resulting `bad_alloc` exception is caught in the attached catch block and the program is terminated with an appropriate error message. If the allocation succeeds, the program proceeds on to print the two numbers 10 and 20. The `bad_alloc` type is defined in the header file `new`, which must be included in programs that refer to it.

Program 16-5

```
// This program demonstrates the use of the bad_alloc
// exception.
#include <iostream>
#include <cstdlib>
#include <new>          // Needed to use bad_alloc
using namespace std;

int main()
{
   int *p;
   try
   {
      p = new int[2];
      p[0] = 10;
      p[1] = 20;
   }
   catch(bad_alloc)
   {
      cout << "Memory cannot be allocated.";
      exit(1);
   }
   cout << p[0] << "  " << p[1];
   return 0;
}
```

Program Output

```
10 20
```

Unwinding the Stack

If an exception is thrown in a try block that has a catch block capable of handling the exception, control transfers from the throw point to the catch block. Assuming that the catch block executes to completion without throwing further exceptions, returning from the function, or terminating the program, execution will continue at the first statement after the sequence of catch blocks attached to the try block.

If the function does not contain a catch block capable of handling the exception, control passes out of the function, and the exception is automatically rethrown at the point of the call in the calling function. By this process, an exception can propagate backwards along the chain of function calls until the exception is thrown out of a try block that has a catch block that can handle it. If no such try block is ever found, the exception will eventually be thrown out of the main function, causing the program to be terminated. This process of propagating uncaught exceptions from a function to its caller is called *unwinding the stack* of function calls.

Rethrowing an Exception

It is possible for try blocks to be nested. For example, look at this code segment:

```
void main()
{
   try
   {
      doSomething();
   }
   catch(exception1)
   {
      Code to handle exception 1
   }
   catch(exception2)
   {
      Code to handle exception 2
   }
}
```

In this try block the function `doSomething` is called. There are two catch blocks, one that handles `exception1`, and another that handles `exception2`. If the `doSomething` function contains a try block, then it is nested inside the one shown.

With nested try blocks, it is sometimes necessary for an inner exception handler to pass an exception to an outer exception handler. Sometimes, both an inner and an outer catch block must perform operations when a particular exception is thrown. These situations require that the inner catch block *rethrow* the exception so the outer catch block can catch it.

A catch block can rethrow an exception with the `throw;` statement with no parameter. For example, suppose the `doSomething` function (called in the try block above) executes code that potentially can throw `exception1` or `exception3`. Suppose we do not want to handle the `exception1` error in `doSomething`, but instead want to rethrow it to the outer block. The following code segment illustrates how this is done.

```
void doSomething()
{
   try
   {
      Code that can throw exceptions 1 and 3
   }
   catch(exception1)
   {
      throw; // Rethrow the exception
   }
   catch(exception3)
   {
      Code to handle exception 3
   }
}
```

When the first catch block catches `exception1`, the `throw;` statement simply throws the exception again. The catch block in the outer try/catch construct, in this case the one in the `main` function, will then handle the exception.

Checkpoint

16.1 What is the difference between a try block and a catch block?

16.2 What happens if an exception is thrown, but not caught?

16.3 If multiple exceptions can be thrown, how does the catch block know which exception to catch?

16.4 After the catch block has handled the exception, where does program execution resume?

16.5 How can an exception pass information to the exception handler?

16.2 Function Templates

CONCEPT: A function template is a "generic" function that can work with different data types. The programmer writes the specifications of the function, but substitutes parameters for data types. When the compiler encounters a call to the function, it generates code to handle the specific data type(s) used in the call.

Overloaded functions make programming convenient because only one function name must be remembered for a set of functions that perform similar operations. Each of the functions, however, must still be written individually. For example, consider the following overloaded `square` functions.

```
int square(int number)
{
   return number * number;
}

double square(double number)
{
   return number * number;
}
```

The only differences between these two functions are the data types of their return values and their parameters. In situations like this, it is more convenient to write a *function template* than an overloaded function. Function templates allow you to write a single function definition that works with many different data types, instead of having to write a separate function for each data type used.

A function template is not an actual function, but a "mold" the compiler uses to generate one or more functions. When writing a function template, you do not have to specify actual types for the parameters, return value, or local variables. Instead, you use a *type parameter* to specify a generic data type. When the compiler encounters a call to the function, it examines the data types of its arguments and generates the function code that will work with those data types.

Here is a function template for the square function:

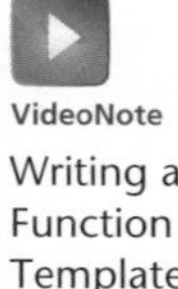

Writing a Function Template

```
template <class T>
T square(T number)
{
   return number * number;
}
```

The beginning of a function template is marked by a *template prefix*, which begins with the key word `template`. Next is a set of angled brackets that contains one or more generic data types used in the template. A generic data type starts with the key word `class`, followed by a parameter name that stands for the data type. The example just given only uses one, which is named `T`. (If there were more, they would be separated by commas.) After this, the function definition is written as usual, except the type parameters are substituted for the actual data type names. In the example the function header reads

```
T square(T number)
```

`T` is the type parameter, or generic data type. The header defines `square` as a function that returns a value of type `T` and uses a parameter, `number`, which is also of type `T`.

As mentioned before, the compiler examines each call to `square` and fills in the appropriate data type for `T`. For example, the following call uses an `int` argument:

```
int y, x = 4;
y = square(x);
```

This code will cause the compiler to generate the function:

```
int square(int number)
{
   return number * number;
}
```

while the statements

```
double y, d = 6.2
y = square(d);
```

will result in the generation of the function

```
double square(double number)
{
   return number * number;
}
```

Program 16-6 demonstrates how this function template is used.

Program 16-6

```
// This program uses a function template.
#include <iostream>
#include <iomanip>
using namespace std;
```

(program continues)

Program 16-6 *(continued)*

```

// Template definition for square function
template <class T>
T square(T number)
{
   return number * number;
}

int main()
{
   cout << setprecision(5);

   // Get an integer and compute its square
   cout << "Enter an integer: ";
   int iValue;
   cin >> iValue;

   // The compiler creates int square(int) at the first
   // occurrence of a call to square with an int argument
   cout << "The square is " <<  square(iValue);

   // Get a double and compute its square
   cout << "\nEnter a double: ";
   double dValue;
   cin >> dValue;

   // The compiler creates double square(double)at the first
   // occurrence of a call to square with a double argument
   cout << "The square is " << square(dValue) << endl;

   return 0;
}
```

Program Output with Example Input Shown in Bold

```
Enter an integer: 3[Enter]
The square is 9
Enter a double: 8.3[Enter]
The square is 68.89
```

NOTE: All type parameters defined in a function template must appear at least once in the function parameter list.

Since the compiler encountered two calls to `square` in Program 16-6, each with different parameter types, it generated the code for two instances of the function: one with an `int` parameter and `int` return type, the other with a `double` parameter and `double` return type. This is illustrated in Figure 16-1.

Figure 16-1

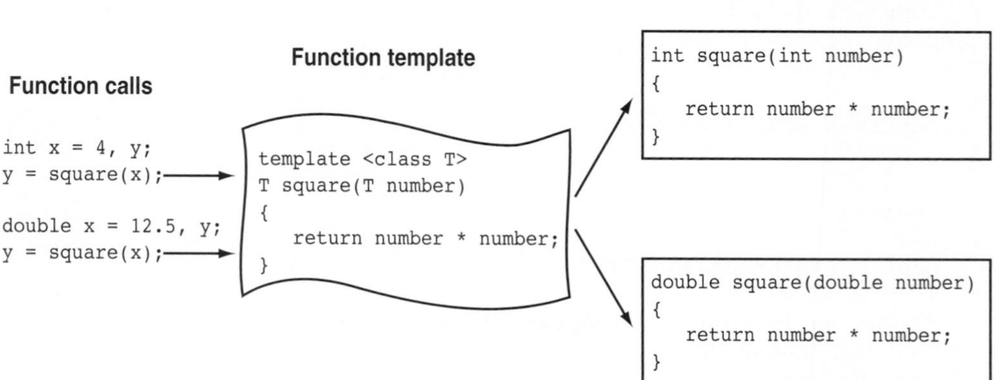

Notice in Program 16-6 that the template appears before all calls to `square`. As with regular functions, the compiler must already know the template's contents when it encounters a call to the template function. Templates, therefore, should be placed near the top of the program or in a header file.

NOTE: A function template is merely the specification of a function and by itself does not cause memory to be used. An actual instance of the function is created in memory when the compiler encounters a call to the template function.

The `swap` Function Template

In many applications, there is a need for swapping the contents of two variables of the same type. For example, while sorting an array of integers, there would be a need for the function

```
void swap(int &a, int &b)
{
   int temp = a;
   a = b;
   b = temp;
}
```

whereas while sorting an array string objects, there would be a need for the function

```
void swap(string &a, string &b)
{
   string temp = a;
   a = b;
   b = temp;
}
```

Because the only difference in the coding of these two functions is the type of the variables being swapped, the logic of both functions and all others like them can be captured with one template function:

```
template<class T>
void swap(T &a, T &b)
```

```
{
   T temp = a;
   a = b;
   b = temp;
}
```

Such a template function is available in the libraries that come with standard C++ compilers. The function is declared in the `algorithm` header file. Program 16-7 demonstrates the use of this library template function to swap contents of pairs of variables.

Program 16-7

```
// This program demonstrates the use of the swap
// function template.
#include <iostream>
#include <string>
#include <algorithm>  // Needed for swap
using namespace std;

int main()
{
   // Get and swap two chars
   char firstChar, secondChar;
   cout << "Enter two characters: ";
   cin >> firstChar >> secondChar;
   swap(firstChar, secondChar);
   cout << firstChar << " " << secondChar << endl;

   // Get and swap two ints
   int firstInt, secondInt;
   cout << "Enter two integers: ";
   cin >> firstInt >> secondInt;
   swap(firstInt, secondInt);
   cout << firstInt << " " << secondInt << endl;

   // Get and swap two strings
   cout << "Enter two strings: ";
   string firstString, secondString;
   cin >> firstString >> secondString;
   swap(firstString, secondString);
   cout << firstString << " " << secondString << endl;
   return 0;
}
```

Program Output With Example Input Shown in Bold

Enter two characters: **a b[Enter]**
b a
Enter two integers: **12 45[Enter]**
45 12
Enter two strings: **Ronald Reagan[Enter]**
Reagan Ronald

Using Operators in Function Templates

The `square` function template shown earlier in this section applies the operator `*` to its parameter. The `square` template will work correctly as long as the type of the parameter passed to it supports the `*` operator. For example, it works for numeric types such as `int`, `long`, and `double`, because all these types have a multiplication operator `*`. In addition, the `square` template will work with any user-defined class type that overloads the operator `*`. Errors will result if `square` is used with types that do not support the operator `*`.

Always remember that templates will only work with types that support the operations used by the template. For example, a class can only be used with a template that applies the relational operators such as <, <=, and != to its type parameter if the class overloads those operators.

For example, because the string class overloads all the relational operators, it can be used with template functions that compute the minimum of an array of items. Program 16-8 illustrates this.

Program 16-8

```
// This program illustrates the use of function templates.
#include <string>
#include <iostream>
using namespace std;

// Template for minimum of an array
template <class T>
T minimum(T arr[ ], int size)
{
   T smallest = arr[0];
   for (int k = 1; k < size; k++)
   {
      if (arr[k] < smallest)
         smallest = arr[k];
   }
   return smallest;
}

int main()
{
   // The compiler creates int minimum(int [], int)
   // when you pass an array of int
   int arr1[] = {40, 20, 35};
   cout << "The minimum number is " << minimum(arr1, 3)
        << endl;

   // The compiler creates string minimum(string [], int)
   // when you pass an array of string
   string arr2[] = {"Zoe", "Snoopy", "Bob", "Waldorf"};
   cout << "The minimum string is " << minimum(arr2, 4)
        << endl;

   return 0;
}
```

(program continues)

Program 16-8 *(continued)*

Program Output
```
The minimum number is 20
The minimum string is Bob
```

Function Templates with Multiple Types

More than one generic type may be used in a function template. Here is an example of a function that takes as parameters a list of three values of any printable type, prints out the list in order, and then prints out the list in reverse. The type parameters for the template function are represented using the identifiers `T1`, `T2` and `T3`.

Program 16-9

```
// This program illustrates the use of function templates
// with multiple types.
#include <iostream>
#include <string>
using namespace std;

// Template function
template <class T1, class T2, class T3>
void echoAndReverse(T1 a1, T2 a2, T3 a3)
{
   cout << "Original order is: "
        << a1 << "  " << a2 << "  " << a3 << endl;
   cout << "Reversed order is: "
        << a3 << "  " << a2 << "  " << a1 << endl;
}

int main()
{
   echoAndReverse("Computer", 'A', 18);
   echoAndReverse("One", 4, "All");
   return 0;
}
```

Program Output
```
Original order is: Computer  A  18
Reversed order is: 18  A  Computer
Original order is: One  4  All
Reversed order is: All  4  One
```

NOTE: Each type parameter declared in the template prefix must be used somewhere in the template definition.

Overloading with Function Templates

Function templates may be overloaded. As with regular functions, function templates are overloaded by having different parameter lists. For example, there are two overloaded versions of the sum function in Program 16-10. The first version accepts two arguments, and the second version accepts three.

Program 16-10

```
// This program demonstrates an overloaded function template.
#include <iostream>
using namespace std;

template <class T>
T sum(T val1, T val2)
{
   return val1 + val2;
}

template <class T>
T sum(T val1, T val2, T val3)
{
   return val1 + val2 + val3;
}

int main()
{
   double num1, num2, num3;

   cout << "Enter two values: ";
   cin >> num1 >> num2;
   cout << "Their sum is " << sum(num1, num2) << endl;
   cout << "Enter three values: ";
   cin >> num1 >> num2 >> num3;
   cout << "Their sum is " << sum(num1, num2, num3) << endl;
   return 0;
}
```

Program Output with Example Input Shown in Bold

```
Enter two values: 12.5 6.9[Enter]
Their sum is 19.4
Enter three values: 45.76 98.32 10.51[Enter]
Their sum is 154.59
```

There are other ways to perform overloading with function templates as well. For example, a program might contain a regular (non-template) version of a function as well as a template version. As long as each has a different parameter list, they can coexist as overloaded functions.

Defining Template Functions

In defining template functions, it may be helpful to start by writing a non-template version of the function, and then converting it to a template after it has been tested. The conversion is then achieved by prefixing the function definition with an appropriate template header, say

```
template <class T>
```

and then systematically replacing the relevant type with the generic type T. We followed a similar procedure in defining the template for the swap function.

16.6 When does the compiler actually generate code for a function template?

16.7 The function

```
int minPosition(int arr[ ], int size)
```

takes an array of integers of the given size and returns the index of the smallest element of the array. Define a template that works like this function, but permits as parameter arrays of any type that can be compared using the less-than operator <.

16.8 What must you be sure of when passing a class object to a function template that uses an operator, such as `*` or >?

16.9 What is a good method for writing a function template?

16.3 Class Templates

CONCEPT: Templates may also be used to create generic classes and abstract data types.

Function templates are used whenever we need several different functions with the same problem-solving logic, but which differ only in the types of the parameters they work with. Class templates can be used whenever we need several classes that only differ in the types of some of their data members, or in the types of the parameters of their member functions.

Declaring a class template is similar to declaring a function template: you write the class using identifiers such as `T`, `T1`, `T2` (or whatever other identifier you choose) as generic types, and then prefix the class declaration with an appropriately written template header. For example, suppose that we wish to define a class similar to the `NumberArray` class studied in Chapter 11, that represents an array of a generic type, and adds an overloaded operator `[]` that performs bounds checking. Calling our class `SimpleVector`, and putting in the appropriate data members and constructors, we arrive at the template:

```
template <class T>
class SimpleVector
{
private:
   T *aptr;
   int arraySize;
   void subError() const;    // Handles subscripts out of range
public:
   SimpleVector()
     { aptr = 0; arraySize = 0;}          // Default Constructor
   SimpleVector(int);                     // Constructor
   SimpleVector(const SimpleVector &);    // Copy constructor
   ~SimpleVector();                       // Destructor
   int size() const
     { return arraySize; }
   T &operator[](int);                  // Overloaded [] operator
   void print() const;                  // Output array
};
```

This class template will store elements of type `T` in a dynamically generated array. This explains why the pointer `aptr`, which will point to the base of this array, is declared to be of type `T*`, a pointer to `T`. Likewise, the overloaded array subscription operator returns a value of type `T`. Notice, however, that the `size` member function and the member `arraySize` that represents the number of elements stored in the array are both of type `int`. This makes sense because the number of elements in an array is always an integer, regardless of the type of element the array stores.

You can think of the `SimpleVector` template as a generic pattern that can be specialized to create classes of `SimpleVector` that hold `double`, `long`, `string`, or any other type that you can define. The rule is that you form the name of such an actual class by appending a list of the actual types, enclosed in angled brackets, to the name of the class template:

- `SimpleVector<double>` is the name of a class that stores arrays of `double`.
- `SimpleVector<string>` is the name of a class that stores arrays of `string`.
- `SimpleVector<char>` is the name of a class that stores arrays of `char`.

Let us look at some examples of defining objects:

```
SimpleVector<int>  iTable1;
SimpleVector<double> dTable1;
SimpleVector<double> dTable2(10);
```

The first two statements use default constructors to create `iTable1` and `dTable1`, which are respectively arrays of `int` and `double` of size 0. The last statement uses the convert constructor to create an array of 10 elements of type `double`.

Defining a member function of a template class inside the class is straightforward: an example is furnished by the definition of the default constructor in the `SimpleVector` class. To define a member function outside the class, you must prefix the definition of the member function with a template header that specifies the list of type parameters, and then within the definition, use the name of the class template followed by a list of the type parameters in angled brackets whenever you need the *name of the class*.

Let us use the operator `[ ]` function to illustrate the definition of a member function outside the class.

```
template <class T>
T &SimpleVector<T>::operator[](int sub)
{
   if (sub < 0 || sub >= arraySize)
      subError();
   return aptr[sub];
}
```

In this definition, the name of the class is needed just before the scope resolution operator, so we have `SimpleVector<T>` at that place. As another example, consider the definition of the convert constructor:

```
template <class T>
SimpleVector<T>::SimpleVector(int s)
{
   arraySize = s;
   aptr = new T [s];
   for (int count = 0; count < arraySize; count++)
         aptr[count] = T();
}
```

Here, we need to have `SimpleVector<T>` before the scope resolution operator, but only `SimpleVector`, without the `<T>`, after. This is because what is needed after the scope resolution operator is not the name of the class, but the name of a member function, which in this case happens to be a constructor.

There is an exception to the rule of attaching the list of type parameters to the name of template class. The list, and the angled brackets that enclose it, can be omitted whenever the name of the class is within the scope of the template class. Thus the list can be omitted when the name of a class is being used anywhere within the class itself, or within the local scope of a member function that is being defined outside of the class. For example, the copy constructor

```
template <class T>
SimpleVector<T>::SimpleVector(const SimpleVector &obj)
{
   arraySize = obj.arraySize;
   aptr = new T [arraySize];
   for(int count = 0; count < arraySize; count++)
      aptr[count] = obj[count];
}
```

does not need to append the `<T>` to the `SimpleVector` that denotes the type of its argument.

The convert constructor for `SimpleVector` assumes that the type parameter `T` has a default constructor `T()` when it executes the assignment `aptr[count] = T();`. If `T` is a primitive type, the C++ compiler will use the default value of 0 in place of `T()`. For example, if `T` were `int`, the assignment is equivalent to `aptr[count] = int();` and a value of 0 will be stored in `aptr[count]`.

The code for the `SimpleVector` template is listed in the `SimpleVector.h` file.

Contents of `SimpleVector.h`

```
#ifndef SIMPLEVECTOR_H
#define SIMPLEVECTOR_H

#include <iostream>
#include <cstdlib>
using namespace std;

template <class T>
class SimpleVector
{
private:
   T *aptr;
   int arraySize;
   void subError() const;       // Handles subscripts out of range
public:
   SimpleVector(int);                      // Constructor
   SimpleVector(const SimpleVector &);     // Copy constructor
   ~SimpleVector();                        // Destructor
   int size() const
      { return arraySize; }
   T &operator[](int);      // Overloaded [] operator
   void print() const;            // Output array
};

```

```
//*******************************************************
// Constructor for SimpleVector class. Sets the size    *
// of the array and allocates memory for it.           *
//*******************************************************
template <class T>
SimpleVector<T>::SimpleVector(int s)
{
   arraySize = s;
   aptr = new T [s];
   for (int count = 0; count < arraySize; count++)
      aptr[count] = T();
}
//******************************************************
// Copy Constructor for SimpleVector class.            *
//******************************************************
template <class T>
SimpleVector<T>::SimpleVector(const SimpleVector &obj)
{
   arraySize = obj.arraySize;
   aptr = new T [arraySize];
   for(int count = 0; count < arraySize; count++)
      aptr[count] = obj[count];
}
//*****************************************************
// Destructor for SimpleVector class.                 *
//*****************************************************
template <class T>
SimpleVector<T>::~SimpleVector()
{
   if (arraySize > 0)
      delete [] aptr;
}

//******************************************************
// subError function. Displays an error message and    *
// terminates the program when a subscript is out of   *
// range.                                              *
//******************************************************
template <class T>
void SimpleVector<T>::subError() const
{
   cout << "ERROR: Subscript out of range.\n";
   exit(0);
}
//*******************************************************
// Overloaded [] operator. The argument is a subscript. *
// This function returns a reference to the element     *
// in the array indexed by the subscript.               *
//*******************************************************
template <class T>
T &SimpleVector<T>::operator[](int sub)
{
   if (sub < 0 || sub >= arraySize)
      subError();
```

```
   return aptr[sub];
}
//****************************************************
// prints all the entries in the array.              *
//****************************************************
template <class T>
void SimpleVector<T>::print( ) const
{
   for (int k = 0; k < arraySize; k++ )
      cout << aptr[k] << "  ";
   cout << endl;
}
#endif
```

Program 16-11 demonstrates the `SimpleVector` template.

Program 16-11

```
// This program demonstrates the SimpleVector template.
#include <iostream>
#include "SimpleVector.h"
using namespace std;

int main()
{
   const int SIZE = 10;

   SimpleVector<int> intTable(SIZE);
   SimpleVector<double> doubleTable(SIZE);

   // Store values in the arrays
   for (int x = 0; x < SIZE; x++)
   {
      intTable[x] = (x * 2);
      doubleTable[x] = (x * 2.14);
   }

   // Display the values in the arrays
   cout << "These values are in intTable:\n";
   intTable.print();
   cout << "These values are in doubleTable:\n";

   doubleTable.print();

   // Use the built-in + operator on array elements
   for (int x = 0; x < SIZE; x++)
   {
      intTable[x] = intTable[x] + 5;
      doubleTable[x] = doubleTable[x] + 1.5;
   }
   // Display the values in the array
   cout << "These values are in intTable:\n";
   intTable.print();
```

(program continues)

Program 16-11 *(continued)*

```
    cout << "These values are in doubleTable:\n";
    doubleTable.print();

    // Use the built-in ++ operator on array elements
    for (int x = 0; x < SIZE; x++)
    {
       intTable[x]++;
       doubleTable[x]++;
    }
    // Display the values in the array
    cout << "These values are in intTable:\n";
    intTable.print();
    cout << "These values are in the doubleTable:\n";
    doubleTable.print();
    cout << endl;
    return 0;
}
```

Program Output

```
These values are in intTable:
0  2  4  6  8  10  12  14  16  18
These values are in doubleTable:
0  2.14  4.28  6.42  8.56  10.7  12.84  14.98  17.12  19.26
These values are in intTable:
5  7  9  11  13  15  17  19  21  23
These values are in doubleTable:
1.5  3.64  5.78  7.92  10.06  12.2  14.34  16.48  18.62  20.76
These values are in intTable:
6  8  10  12  14  16  18  20  22  24
These values are in the doubleTable:
2.5  4.64  6.78  8.92  11.06  13.2  15.34  17.48  19.62  21.76
```

NOTE: The file that contains the template code has been included in the file that contains the driver code to avoid the complexities of linking separately compiled files that use templates.

16.4 Class Templates and Inheritance

Inheritance can be applied to class templates. For example, in the following template, `SearchableVector` is derived from the `SimpleVector` class.

Contents of `SearchVect.h`

```
#ifndef SEARCHABLEVECTOR_H
#define SEARCHABLEVECTOR_H

```

```
#include "SimpleVector.h"

template <class T>
class SearchableVector : public SimpleVector<T>
{
public:
   // Constructor
   SearchableVector(int s) : SimpleVector<T>(s)
      { }
   // Copy constructor
   SearchableVector(SearchableVector &);
   // Additional constructor
   SearchableVector(SimpleVector<T> &obj):
           SimpleVector<T>(obj)
      { }
   int findItem(T);
};

//*******************************************
// Definition of the copy constructor.      *
//*******************************************
template <class T>
SearchableVector<T>::
SearchableVector(SearchableVector &obj) :
SimpleVector<T>(obj)
{
}

//*******************************************
// findItem takes a parameter of type T     *
// and searches for it within the array.    *
//*******************************************
template <class T>
int SearchableVector<T>::findItem(T item)
{
   for (int count = 0; count < this->size(); count++)
   {
      if (this->operator[](count) == item)
         return count;
   }
   return -1;
}
#endif
```

Let us use this example to take a closer look at the derivation of a class from a template base class. First, we have to indicate to the compiler that we are defining a new class template based on an another, already existing class template:

```
template <class T>
class SearchableVector : public SimpleVector<T>
{
   // Members of the class will go here
};
```

Here the new class template being defined is `SearchableVector`, while the existing base class template is `SimpleVector<T>`. The class has three constructors. The first constructor, shown here,

```
SearchableVector(int size) : SimpleVector<T>(size){ }
```

is designed to dynamically allocate an array of `size` elements of type `T`, which it does by invoking the base class constructor and passing it the parameter `size`. This constructor will create an array of the specified size with all elements initialized to default values of type `T`. The class has another constructor,

```
SearchableVector(SimpleVector<T> &obj): SimpleVector<T>(obj){ }
```

which takes as parameter a base class object, a copy of which is to be searched. The constructor simply passes its parameter to the base class copy constructor. The remaining constructor is the copy constructor for the `SearchableVector` class,

```
SearchableVector(SearchableVector<T> &obj): SimpleVector<T>(obj){ }
```

Because the initialization of a `SearchableVector` is the same as that of a `SimpleVector`, the `SearchableVector` copy constructor simply passes its argument to the copy constructor of its base class. The member function `findItem` takes an item of type `T` as its argument and returns the position of the item within the array. If the item is not found in the array, a value of –1 is returned.

Program 16-12 demonstrates the class by storing values in two `SearchableVector` objects and then searching for a specific value in each.

Program 16-12

```
// This program demonstrates the SearchableVector template.
#include <iostream>
#include "searchvect.h"
using namespace std;

int main()
{
   const int SIZE = 10;
   SearchableVector<int> intTable(SIZE);
   SearchableVector<double> doubleTable(SIZE);

   // Store values in the vectors
   for (int x = 0; x < SIZE; x++)
   {
      intTable[x] = (x * 2);
      doubleTable[x] = (x * 2.14);
   }
   // Display the values in the vectors
   cout << "These values are in intTable:\n";
   for (int x = 0; x < SIZE; x++)
      cout << intTable[x] << " ";
```

(program continues)

Program 16-12 *(continued)*

```
   cout << endl;
   cout << "These values are in doubleTable:\n";
   for (int x = 0; x < SIZE; x++)
      cout << doubleTable[x] << " ";
   cout << endl;

   // Now search for values in the vectors
   int result;
   cout << "Searching for 6 in intTable.\n";
   result = intTable.findItem(6);
   if (result == -1)
      cout << "6 was not found in intTable.\n";
   else
      cout << "6 was found at subscript "
           << result << endl;

   cout << "Searching for 12.84 in doubleTable.\n";
   result = doubleTable.findItem(12.84);
   if (result == -1)
      cout << "12.84 was not found in doubleTable.\n";
   else
      cout << "12.84 was found at subscript "
           << result << endl;
   return 0;
}
```

Program Output

```
These values are in intTable:
0 2 4 6 8 10 12 14 16 18
These values are in doubleTable:
0 2.14 4.28 6.42 8.56 10.7 12.84 14.98 17.12 19.26
Searching for 6 in intTable.
6 was found at subscript 3
Searching for 12.84 in doubleTable.
12.84 was found at subscript 6
```

The `SearchableVector` class demonstrates that a class template may be derived from another class template. In addition, class templates may be derived from ordinary classes, and ordinary classes may be derived from class templates.

Checkpoint

16.10 Suppose your program uses a class template named `List`, which is defined as

```
template<class T>
class List
{
   // Members are declared here...
};
```

Give an example of how you would use `int` as the data type in the declaration of a `List` object. (Assume the class has a default constructor.)

16.11 In the following `Rectangle` class declaration, the `width`, `length`, and `area` members are of type `double`. Rewrite the class as a template that will accept any numeric type for these members.

```
class Rectangle
{
   private:
     double width;
     double length;
     double area;
   public:
     void setData(double w, double l)
            { width = w; length = l;}
     void calcArea()
            { area = width * length; }
     double getWidth()
            { return width; }
     double getLength()
            { return length; }
     double getArea()
            { return area; }
};
```

16.5 Introduction to the Standard Template Library

CONCEPT: The Standard Template Library contains many templates for useful algorithms and data structures.

In addition to its run-time library, which you have used throughout this book, C++ also provides a library of templates. The *Standard Template Library* (or *STL*) contains numerous templates for implementing data types and algorithms.

The most important data structures in the STL are the *containers* and *iterators*. A container is a class that stores data and organizes it in some fashion. An iterator is an object that works like a pointer and allows access to items stored in containers.

Sequential Containers

There are two types of container classes in the STL: *sequential* containers and *associative* containers. Sequential containers store items in the form of *sequences*, meaning that there is a natural way to order the items by their position within the container. An array is an example of a sequential container. The STL provides the three sequential containers shown in Table 16-1.

Table 16-1 STL Sequential Containers

Container Name	Description
`vector`	A sequence of items implemented as an array that can automatically grow as needed during program execution. Items can be efficiently added and removed from the vector at its end. Insertions and removals from the middle or beginning of the vector are not as efficient.
`deque`	A sequence of items that has a front and back: items can be efficiently added or removed from the front and back. Insertions and removals in the middle of a deque are not as efficient.
`list`	A sequence of items that allows quick additions and removals from any position.

Because a sequential container organizes the items it stores as a sequence, it can be said to have a *front* and a *back*. A container is said to provide *random access* to its contents if it is possible to specify a position of an item within the container and then jump directly to that item without first having to go through all the items that precede it in the container.

Positions used in random access are usually specified by giving an integer specifying the position of the desired item within the container. The integer may specify a position relative to the beginning of the container, the end of the container, or relative to some other position. Arrays and vectors are examples of sequential containers that provide random access.

Associative Containers

Sequential containers use the position of an item within the sequence to access their data. In contrast, associative containers associate a *key* with each item stored, and then use the key to retrieve the stored item. A telephone book is an example of an associative container; the values stored are telephone numbers, and each telephone number is associated with a name. The name can later be used as a key to look up, or retrieve, the telephone number. The STL provides four associative containers, as shown in Table 16-2.

Table 16-2 STL Associative Containers

Container Name	Description
`set`	Stores a set of keys. No duplicate values are allowed.
`multiset`	Stores a set of keys. Duplicates are allowed.
`map`	Maps a set of keys to data elements. Each key is associated with a unique data element, and duplicate keys are not permitted.
`multimap`	Maps a set of keys to data elements. The same key may be associated with multiple values.

A *map* is a container that requires each value stored to be associated with a key. Each key may be associated with only one value; once a key is used, no other value with the same key may be added to the map. A *multimap* is like a map, except a key may be associated with multiple values.

A *set* is like a map in which only keys are stored, with no associated values. No item may be stored twice in a set: that is, duplicates are not permitted. A *multi set* is like a set in which duplicates are permitted.

Iterators

VideoNote
Iterators

Iterators are objects that behave like pointers. They are used to access items stored in containers. A typical iterator is an object of a class declared inside a container class. The iterator overloads pointer operators such as the increment operator ++ , the decrement operator --, and the dereferencing operator * in order to provide pointer-like behavior.

Each STL container object provides member functions `begin()` and `end()` that return the beginning and ending iterators for the object. The `begin()` iterator points to the item at the beginning of the container if the container is nonempty, while the `end()` iterator points to just past the end of the container. More details on the use of these iterators will be given later.

Table 16-3 shows the different types of iterators available for use with various STL containers.

Table 16-3 Iterator Types

Iterator Type	Description
Forward	Can only move forward in a container (uses the ++ operator).
Bidirectional	Can move forward or backward in a container (uses the ++ and -- operators).
Random-access	Can move forward and backward, and can jump to a specific data element in a container.
Input	Can be used with `cin` to read information from an input device or a file.
Output	Can be used with `cout` to write information to an output device or a file.

The Use of Iterators

Let us consider the use of iterators, including `begin()` and `end()`, to access items stored in an STL container.

Because an iterator is an object of an inner class called `iterator` that is defined inside a container class, the use of the scope resolution operator is necessary to obtain an iterator for a given container. For example, to define an iterator object `iter` that will work with a class of type `vector<int>`, we write:

```
vector<int>::iterator iter;
```

To define an iterator for a vector of `int` and have it initialized to the beginning of the container `vect`, we write:

```
vector<int> vect;
vector<int>::iterator iter = vect.begin();
```

Once an iterator is defined and made to point to the beginning of the container, the items in the container at the position of the iterator can be accessed by dereferencing the iterator. An iterator can be made to move to the next item in the container by incrementing it, and if the iterator is bidirectional, it can be made to move to the previous element by decrementing it. For example, the statements

```
cout << *iter;
iter++;
```

print the value of an element in the container and then move the iterator to the next element.

Because the end iterator does not point to a legitimate element, an iterator whose value is `end()` should not be dereferenced. Program 16-13 illustrates the use of iterators with vector containers.

Program 16-13

```
// This program provides a simple demonstration of the
// vector STL template.
#include <iostream>
#include <vector>  // Needed to use vectors
using namespace std;

int main()
{
   vector<int> vect;   // Create a vector of int

   for (int x = 0; x < 10; x++)
       vect.push_back(x*x);

   // Print everything using iterators
   vector<int>::iterator iter = vect.begin();
   while (iter != vect.end())
   {
      cout <<  *iter << " ";
      iter ++;
   }
   return 0;
}
```

Program Output

```
0 1 4 9 16 25 36 49 64 81
```

Notice in Program 16-13 the inclusion of the `vector` header file, which is required for the `vector` container. The vector container is one of the simplest types of containers in the STL. In the following chapters, you will see examples using other types of containers.

The `vector` Container

Table 16-4 lists a selection of member functions of the vector class template. Some of these accept iterators as parameters, and some of them return iterators as results.

Table 16-4 Selected Member Functions of the Vector Class

Member Function	Description
`at(position)`	Returns the value of the element located at `position` in the vector. Example: `x = vect.at(5);` This statement assigns the value of the element in position 5 of `vect` to `x`.
`back()`	Returns a reference to the last element in the vector. Example: `cout << vect.back() << endl;`
`begin()`	Returns an iterator pointing to the vector's first element. Example: `iter = vect.begin();`
`capacity()`	Returns the maximum number of elements that may be stored in the vector without additional memory being allocated. (This is not the same value as returned by the `size` member function). Example: `x = vect.capacity();` This statement assigns the capacity of `vect` to `x`.
`clear()`	Clears a vector of all its elements. Example: `vect.clear();` This statement removes all the elements from `vect`.

`empty()`	Returns true if the vector is empty. Otherwise, it returns false.
	Example:
	`if (vect.empty())`
	`    cout << "The vector is empty.";`

`end()`	Returns an iterator pointing to just after the last element of the vector. Example: `iter = vect.end();`
`erase(iter)`	Causes the vector element pointed to by the iterator `iter` to be removed. Example: `vect.erase(iter);`
`erase(iter1, iter2)`	Removes all vector elements in the range specified by the iterators `iter1` and `iter2`. Example: `vect.erase(iter1, iter2);`
`front()`	Returns a reference to the vector's first element. Example: `cout << vector.front() << endl;`
`insert(iter, value)`	Inserts an element into the vector. Example: `vect.insert(iter, x);` This statement inserts the value `x` just before the element pointed to by the iterator `iter`.

(table continues)

Table 16-4 Selected Member Functions of the Vector Class *(continued)*

Member Function	Description
`insert(iter, n, value)`	Inserts `n` copies of `value` into the vector, starting just before the position pointed to by the iterator `iter`. Example: `vect.insert(iter, 7, x);` This statement inserts 7 copies of the value `x` just before the element pointed to by the iterator `iter`.
`pop_back()`	Removes the last element from the vector. Example: `vect.pop_back();` This statement removes the last element of `vect`, thus reducing its size by one.
`push_back(value)`	Stores `value` as the new last element of the vector. If the vector is already filled to capacity, it is automatically resized. Example: `vect.push_back(7);` This statement stores 7 as the new last element of `vect`.
`reverse()`	Reverses the order of the elements in the vector (the last element becomes the first element, and the first element becomes the last element.) Example: `vect.reverse();.`
`resize(n)` `resize(n, value)`	Resizes a vector to have `n` elements, where `n` is greater than the vector's current size. If the optional `value` argument is included, each of the new elements will be initialized with that value. Example where `vect` currently has 4 elements: `vect.resize(6,99);` adds two elements to the end of the vector, each initialized to 99.
`size()`	Returns the number of elements in the `vector`. Example: `cout << vector.size() << endl;`
`swap(vector2)`	Swaps the contents of the vector with the contents of `vector2`. Example: `vect1.swap(vect2);` The statement above swaps the contents of `vect1` and `vect2`.

Algorithms

The algorithms provided by the STL are implemented as function templates and perform various operations on elements of containers. There are many algorithms in the STL; Table 16-5 lists a few of them. (The table gives only general descriptions.)

Table 16-5 STL Algorithms

Algorithm	Description
`binary_search`	Performs a binary search for an object and returns `true` if the object is found, `false` if not. Example: `binary_search(iter1, iter2, value);` In this statement, `iter1` and `iter2` define a range of elements within the container. (`iter1` points to the first element in the range, and `iter2` points to just after the last element in the range.) The statement performs a binary search on the range of elements, searching for `value`. The `binary_search` function returns `true` if the element was found and `false` if the element was not found.
`count`	Returns the number of times a value appears in a range. Example: `number = count(iter1, iter2, value);` In this statement, `iter1` and `iter2` define a range of elements within the container. (`iter1` points to the first element in the range, and `iter2` points to just after the last element in the range.) The statement returns the number of times `value` appears in the range of elements.
`for_each`	Executes a function for each element in a container. Example: `for_each(iter1, iter2, func);` In this statement, `iter1` and `iter2` define a range of elements within the container. (`iter1` points to the first element in the range, and `iter2` points to just after the last element in the range.) The third argument, `func`, is the name of a function. The statement calls the function `func` for each element in the range, passing the element as an argument.
`find`	Finds the first object in a container that matches a value and returns an iterator to it. Example: `iter3 = find(iter1, iter2, value);` In this statement, `iter1` and `iter2` define a range of elements within the container. (`iter1` points to the first element in the range, and `iter2` points to just after the last element in the range.) The statement searches the range of elements for `value`. If `value` is found, the function returns an iterator to the element containing it, otherwise, it returns the iterator `iter2`.
`max_element`	Returns an iterator to the largest object in a range. Example: `iter3 = max_element(iter1, iter2);` In this statement, `iter1` and `iter2` define a range of elements within the container. (`iter1` points to the first element in the range, and `iter2` points to just after the last element in the range.) The statement returns an iterator to the element containing the largest value in the range.

(table continues)

Table 16-5 STL Algorithms *(continued)*

Algorithm	Description
`min_element`	Returns an iterator to the smallest object in a range. Example: `iter3 = min_element(iter1, iter2);` In this statement, `iter1` and `iter2` define a range of elements within the container. (`iter1` points to the first element in the range, and `iter2` points to just after the last element in the range.) The statement returns an iterator to the element containing the smallest value in the range.
`random_shuffle`	Randomly shuffles the elements of a container. Example: `random_shuffle(iter1, iter2);` In this statement, `iter1` and `iter2` define a range of elements within the container. (`iter1` points to the first element in the range, and `iter2` points to just after the last element in the range.) The statement randomly reorders the elements in the range.
`sort`	Sorts a range of elements. Example: `sort(iter1, iter2);` In this statement, `iter1` and `iter2` define a range of elements within the container. (`iter1` points to the first element in the range, and `iter2` points to just after the last element in the range.) The statement sorts the elements in the range in ascending order.

NOTE: The STL algorithms require the inclusion of the `algorithm` header file.

Program 16-14 demonstrates the use of the `random_shuffle`, `sort`, and `binary_search` algorithm templates.

Program 16-14

```
// This program provides a simple demonstration of the
// STL algorithms.

#include <iostream>
#include <vector>     // Include the vector header
#include <algorithm>  // Required for STL algorithms
using namespace std;

int main()
{
   vector<int> vect;    // Define a vector object

   // Use push_back to push values into the vector
```

(program continues)

Program 16-14 *(continued)*

```
   for (int x = 0; x < 10; x++)
      vect.push_back(x*x);

   // Display the vector's elements
   cout << "The collection has " << vect.size()
        << " elements. Here they are:\n";
   for (int x = 0; x < vect.size(); x++)
                 cout << vect[x] << " ";
   cout << endl;

   // Randomly shuffle the vector's contents
   random_shuffle(vect.begin(), vect.end());

   // Display the vector's elements
   cout << "The elements have been shuffled:\n";
   for (int x = 0; x < vect.size(); x++)
      cout << vect[x] << " ";
   cout << endl;

   // Now sort them
   sort(vect.begin(), vect.end());

   // Display the vector's elements again
   cout << "The elements have been sorted:\n";
   for (int x = 0; x < vect.size(); x++)
      cout << vect[x] << " ";
   cout << endl;

   // Now search for an element
   int val = 49;
   if (binary_search(vect.begin(), vect.end(), val))
   cout << "The value " << val
        << " was found in the vector.\n";
   else
       cout << "The value " << val
            << " was not found in the vector.\n";
   return 0;
}
```

Program Output

```
The collection has 10 elements. Here they are:
0 1 4 9 16 25 36 49 64 81
The elements have been shuffled:
64 1 81 4 0 25 49 9 16 36
The elements have been sorted:
0 1 4 9 16 25 36 49 64 81
The value 49 was found in the vector.
```

NOTE: Your run of this program will generate a different random shuffle.

The `random_shuffle` function rearranges the elements of a container. In Program 16-14, it is called in the following manner:

```
random_shuffle(vect.begin(), vect.end());
```

The function takes two arguments, which together represent a range of elements within a container. The first argument is an iterator to the first element in the range. In this case, `vect.begin()` is used. The second argument is an iterator to just after the last element in the range. Here we have used `vect.end()`. These arguments tell `random_shuffle` to rearrange all the elements from the beginning to the end of the `vect` container.

The `sort` algorithm also takes iterators to a range of elements. Here is the function call that appears in Program 16-14:

```
sort(vect.begin(), vect.end());
```

All the elements within the range are sorted in ascending order.

The `binary_search` algorithm searches a range of elements for a value. If the value is found, the function returns `true`. Otherwise, it returns `false`. For example, the following function call searches all the elements in `vect` for the value 7.

```
binary_search(vect.begin(), vect.end(), 7)
```

Program 16-15 demonstrates the `count` algorithm.

Program 16-15

```
// This program demonstrates the STL count algorithm.
#include <iostream>
#include <vector> // Needed to declare the vector
#include <algorithm> // Needed for the for_each algorithm
using namespace std;

int main()
{
   vector<int> values;
   vector<int>::iterator iter;

   // Store some values in the vector
   values.push_back(1);
   values.push_back(2);
   values.push_back(2);
   values.push_back(3);
   values.push_back(3);
   values.push_back(3);

   // Display the values in the vector
   cout << "The values in the vector are:\n";
   for (iter = values.begin(); iter != values.end(); iter++)
      cout << *iter << " ";
   cout << endl << endl;

```

(program continues)

Program 16-15 *(continued)*

```
    // Display the count of each number
    cout << "The number of 1s in the vector is ";
    cout << count(values.begin(), values.end(), 1) << endl;
    cout << "The number of 2s in the vector is ";
    cout << count(values.begin(), values.end(), 2) << endl;
    cout << "The number of 3s in the vector is ";
    cout << count(values.begin(), values.end(), 3) << endl;
    return 0;
}
```

Program Output

```
The values in the vector are:
1 2 2 3 3 3

The number of 1s in the vector is 1
The number of 2s in the vector is 2
The number of 3s in the vector is 3
```

Program 16-16 demonstrates the `max_element` and `min_element` algorithms.

Program 16-16

```
// This program demonstrates the STL max_element
// and min_element algorithms.
#include <iostream>
#include <vector>             // Needed to declare the vector
#include <algorithm>          // Needed for the algorithms
using namespace std;

int main()
{
    vector<int> numbers;
    vector<int>::iterator iter;

    // Store some numbers in the vector
    for (int x = 0; x < 10; x++)
        numbers.push_back(x);

    // Shuffle things up just for fun
    random_shuffle(numbers.begin(), numbers.end());

    // Display the numbers in the vector
    cout << "The numbers in the vector are:\n";
    for (iter = numbers.begin(); iter != numbers.end(); iter++)
        cout << *iter << " ";
    cout << endl;

    // Find the largest value in the vector
    iter = max_element(numbers.begin(), numbers.end());
    cout << "The largest value in the vector is "
         << *iter << endl;
```

(program continues)

Program 16-16 *(continued)*

```

   // Find the smallest value in the vector
   iter = min_element(numbers.begin(), numbers.end());
   cout << "The smallest value in the vector is "
        << *iter << endl;

   return 0;
}
```

Program Output

```
The values in the vector are:
8 1 9 2 0 5 7 3 4 6
The largest value in the vector is 9
The smallest value in the vector is 0
```

Program 16-17 demonstrates the `find` algorithm.

Program 16-17

```
// This program demonstrates the STL find algorithm.
#include <iostream>
#include <vector>    // Needed to declare the vector
#include <algorithm> // Needed for the find algorithm
using namespace std;

int main()
{
   vector<int> numbers;
   vector<int>::iterator iter;

   // Store some numbers in the vector
   for (int x = 0; x < 10; x++)
      numbers.push_back(x);

   // Display the numbers in the vector
   cout << "The numbers in the vector are:\n";
   for (iter = numbers.begin(); iter != numbers.end(); iter++)
      cout << *iter << " ";
   cout << endl << endl;

   // Find 7 in the vector
   iter = find(numbers.begin(), numbers.end(), 7);
   cout << "The value searched for is " << *iter << endl;
   return 0;
}
```

Program Output

```
The numbers in the vector are:
0 1 2 3 4 5 6 7 8 9

The value searched for is 7
```

Program 16-18 demonstrates the `for_each` algorithm.

Program 16-18

```
// This program demonstrates the for_each find algorithm.

#include <iostream>
#include <vector>        // Needed to declare the vector
#include <algorithm>     // Needed for the for_each algorithm
using namespace std;

// Function prototype
void doubleValue(int &);

int main()
{
   vector<int> numbers;
   vector<int>::iterator iter;

   // Store some numbers in the vector
   for (int x = 0; x < 10; x++)
      numbers.push_back(x);

   // Display the numbers in the vector
   cout << "The numbers in the vector are:\n";
   for (iter = numbers.begin(); iter != numbers.end(); iter++)
      cout << *iter << " ";
   cout << endl;

   // Double the values in the vector
   for_each(numbers.begin(), numbers.end(), doubleValue);

   // Display the numbers in the vector again
   cout << "Now the numbers in the vector are:\n";
   for (iter = numbers.begin(); iter != numbers.end(); iter++)
      cout << *iter << " ";
   cout << endl;
   return 0;
}

//*****************************************************
// Function doubleValue. This function accepts an int    *
// reference as its argument. The value of the argument  *
// is doubled.                                            *
//*****************************************************
void doubleValue(int &val)
{
   val *= 2;
}
```

Program Output

```
The numbers in the vector are:
0 1 2 3 4 5 6 7 8 9
Now the numbers in the vector are:
0 2 4 6 8 10 12 14 16 18
```

In Program 16-18, the following statement calls `for_each`:

```
for_each(numbers.begin(), numbers.end(), doubleValue);
```

The first and second arguments specify a range of elements. In this case, the range is the entire vector. The third argument is the name of a function. The `for_each` algorithm calls the function once for each element in the range, passing the element as an argument to the function.

The programs in this section give you a brief introduction to using the STL by demonstrating simple operations on a `vector`. In the remaining chapters you will be given specific examples of how to use other STL containers, iterators, and algorithms.

16.6 Tying It All Together: *Word Transformers Game*

A software entrepreneur is designing an educational word game for children. A child playing the game is given two words and must determine if it is possible to rearrange the letters in the first word to form the second. What the program does next depends on the relation between the two words and on the correctness of the player's answer.

When given two words, *the child may claim that transformation of the first word into the second is possible.* In this case, the program asks the child to demonstrate the correctness of the answer by typing a sequence of words starting with the first and ending with the second. Such a sequence is an *acceptable proof sequence* if each word is obtained from its predecessor by swapping a single pair of adjacent letters. For example, the sequence

tops, *tosp*, *tsop*, *stop*, *sotp*, *sopt*, *spot*

proves that the word *tops* can be transformed into spot. If the proof sequence is accepted, the child earns a point and play proceeds to the next round with a fresh pair of words.

A proof sequence is *rejected* if a word cannot be obtained from its predecessor by swapping an adjacent pair of letters, or if the first word in the sequence is not the first word of the pair of words being tested, or if the last word is not the second word in the given pair. When a sequence is rejected, play proceeds to the next round, but the child earns no points.

The child may observe that transformation is not possible. If the child's answer is correct, he or she receives a point and play proceeds to the next round. If the child's answer is incorrect and the transformation is indeed possible, the child receives no points. In this case, however, the program displays a correct proof sequence before moving on to the next round of the game.

A program at the heart of this game must perform several tasks.

1. The program must be able to determine if one of a given pair of words can be transformed into another.
2. The program must be able to determine if one word results from another by swapping an adjacent pair of letters.
3. The program must be able to produce a proof sequence when transformation of one word into another is possible.

How can we write a program for producing proof sequences for a pair of words? One idea is to start with the first word as the current word. Then, swap an adjacent pair of letters to obtain a new current word. Repeating this strategy will generate a sequence of words. If the current word ever turns out to be the target word, we know we have a proof sequence.

Although the approach we have just outlined is easy to think of, it is difficult to implement. An alternative approach involves sorting. If a transformation between the two words is possible, sorting them will yield the same word. If in addition, we use a sorting method that works by swapping adjacent letters, the sorting process will yield a proof sequence from each of the original words to the same word. For example, sorting *tops* and *spot* yields the same word *opst* with the corresponding sequences

tops, *otps*, *opts*, *opst*

and

spot, *psot*, *post*, *opst*.

Notice that the second sequence is a sequence from *opst* to *spot* in reverse. By concatenating this last sequence to the first and eliminating the duplicate entry in the middle, we obtain the proof sequence from *tops* to *spot*:

tops, *otps*, *opts*, *opst*, *spot*, *psot*, *post*, *spot*

Let us consider some details related to the implementation of this plan. Rather than keep a list of intermediate words generated during the sort, we can keep a list of swaps or *transpositions* performed by the sort. We do this by storing the index i for each pair $(i, i+1)$ of positions of characters swapped by the transposition. Our program uses the well known Bubblesort sorting algorithm. A function

```
sort(char str[], int size, vector<int> &tranpose)
```

is used to sort an array of characters of a given size while saving the list of transpositions performed on the array during the sort. Once both words have been sorted, the resulting two lists of transpositions will be applied to a copy of the first word as previously described, and the words resulting from the application of each transposition will be printed. This strategy is implemented in the following program.

Program 16-19

```
// This program solves the word transformation puzzle.
#include <iostream>
#include <string>
#include <vector>
#include <algorithm>
using namespace std;

// Prototype
void sort(char str[], int size, vector<int>& transpositions);

int main()
```

(program continues)

Program 16-19 *(continued)*

```
{
     // The two words and a copy of the first word
     char str1[] = "spot";
     char str1Copy[] = "spot";
     char str2[] = "stop";

     // These vectors hold the list of transpositions
     vector<int> transpose;
     vector<int> reverse_transpose;

     // Sort the two words
     cout << "The first word is " << str1 <<  endl
          << "The second word is " << str2 << endl;
     sort(str1, 4, transpose);
     sort(str2, 4, reverse_transpose);

     // Apply the first list of transpositions
     cout << "The transformation steps are: " << endl;
     cout << str1Copy <<  " ";
     for (int k = 0; k < transpose.size(); k++)
     {
         int index = transpose[k];
         swap(str1Copy[index], str1Copy[index + 1]);
         cout << str1Copy << " ";
     }
     // Apply the second list of transpositions in reverse order
     for (int k = reverse_transpose.size()-1; k >=0 ; k--)
     {
         int index = reverse_transpose[k];
         swap(str1Copy[index], str1Copy[index + 1]);
         cout << str1Copy << " ";
     }
     cout << endl;
     return 0;
}

//*************************************************************
// This is a version of Bubblesort that saves a list of all   *
// transpositions that are needed to sort the list            *
//*************************************************************
void sort(char str[], int size, vector<int>& transpositions)
{
     // Last index of portion yet to be sorted
     int upperBound = size-1;

     while (upperBound  > 0)
     {
         for (int k = 0; k < upperBound; k++ )
         {
             if (str[k] > str[k+1])
```

(program continues)

Program 16-19 *(continued)*

```
            {
                // Save the swap index
                transpositions.push_back(k);
                swap(str[k], str[k+1]);
            }
        }
        upperBound--;
    }
}
```

Program Output

```
The first word is spot
The second word is stop
The transformation steps are:
spot psot post opst ospt sopt sotp stop
```

Review Questions and Exercises

Fill-in-the-Blank

1. The line containing a throw statement is known as the __________.
2. The __________ block should enclose code that directly or indirectly might cause an exception to be thrown.
3. The __________ block handles an exception.
4. When writing function or class templates, you use a(n) __________ to specify a generic data type.
5. The beginning of a template is marked by a(n) __________.
6. When declaring objects of class templates, the __________ you wish to pass into the type parameter must be specified.
7. A(n)__________ container organizes data in a sequential fashion similar to an array.
8. A(n)__________ container uses keys to rapidly access elements.
9. __________ are pointer-like objects used to access information stored in a container.

C++ Language Elements

10. Modify the `SimpleVector` template presented in this chapter to include an overloaded assignment operator.

Algorithm Workbench

11. Write a function template that takes a generic array of a given size as a parameter and reverses the order of the elements in the array. The first parameter of the function should be the array, the second parameter should be the size of the array.
12. Write a function template that is capable of adding any two numeric values and returning the result.

13. Describe what will happen if you call the function of question 11 and pass it an array of `char`.
14. Describe what will happen if you call the function of question 11 and pass it an array of `string`.

Find the Error

15. Each of the following declarations or code segments has errors. Locate as many as possible.

A)
```
catch
{
   quotient = divide(num1, num2);
   cout << "The quotient is " << quotient << endl;
}
try (string exceptionString)
{
   cout << exceptionString;
}
```

B)
```
try
{
   quotient = divide(num1, num2);
}
cout << "The quotient is " << quotient << endl;
catch (string exceptionString)
{
   cout << exceptionString;
}
```

C)
```
template <class T>
T square(T number)
{
   return T * T;
}
```

D)
```
template <class T>
int square(int number)
{
   return number * number;
}
```

E)
```
template <class T1, class T2>
T1 sum(T1 x, T1 y)
{
   return x + y;
}
```

F) Assume the following declaration appears in a program that uses the `SimpleVector` class template presented in this chapter.

```
int <SimpleVector> array(25);
```

G) Assume the following statement appears in a program that has defined `valueSet` as an object of the `SimpleVector` class presented in this chapter. Assume that `valueSet` is a vector of `int`s, and has 20 elements.

```
cout << valueSet<int>[2] << endl;
```

Soft Skills

16. Suppose that you are part of a project team and it becomes clear to you that one of the team members is not "pulling his weight." What should you do if you are the project leader? What should you do if you are not the project leader?

Programming Challenges

1. String Bound Exceptions

Write a class `BCheckString` that is derived from the STL `string` class. This new class will have two member functions:

A) A `BCheckString(string s)` constructor that receives a string object passed by value and passes it on to the base class constructor.

B) An `char operator[](int k)` function that throws a `BoundsException` object if `k` is negative or is greater than or equal to the length of the string. If `k` is within the bounds of the string, this function will return the character at position `k` in the string.

You will need to write the definition of the `BoundsException` class. Test your class with a main function that attempts to access characters that are within and outside the bounds of a suitably initialized `BCheckString` object.

2. Arithmetic Exceptions

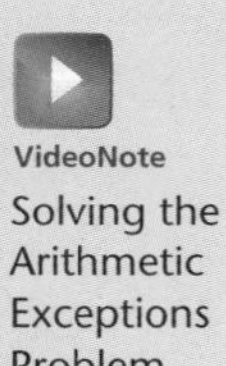
VideoNote
Solving the Arithmetic Exceptions Problem

Write a function that accepts an integer parameter and returns its integer square root. The function should throw an exception if it is passed an integer that is not a perfect square. Demonstrate the function with a suitable driver program.

3. Min/Max Templates

Write templates for the two functions `min` and `max`. `min` should accept two arguments and return the value of the argument that is the lesser of the two. `max` should accept two arguments and return the value of the argument that is the greater of the two. Design a simple driver program that demonstrates the templates with various data types.

4. Sequence Accumulation

Write a function

```
T accum(vector <T>  v)
```

that forms and returns the "sum" of all items in the vector `v` passed to it. For example, if `T` is a numeric type such as int or double, the numeric sum will be returned, and if `T` represents the STL string type, then the result of concatenation is returned.

NOTE: For any type `T`, the expression `T()` yields the value or object created by the default constructor. For example, `T()` yields the empty string object if `T` is the string class. If `T` represents a numeric type such as `int`, then `T()` yields 0. Use this fact to initialize your "accumulator."

Test your function with a driver program that asks the user to enter 3 integers, uses `accum` to compute the sum, and prints out the sum. The program than asks the user to enter 3 strings, uses `accum` to concatenate the strings, and prints the result.

5. Rotate Left

The two sets of output below show the results of successive circular rotations of a vector. One set of data is for a vector of integers, and the second is for a vector of strings.

```
1  3  5  7
3  5  7  1
5  7  1  3
7  1  3  5

a  b  c  d  e
b  c  d  e  a
c  d  e  a  b
d  e  a  b  c
e  a  b  c  d
```

Write two template functions that can be used to rotate and output a vector of a generic type:

```
void rotateLeft(vector <T>& v)
void output(vector <T> v)
```

The first function performs a single circular left rotation on a vector, and the second prints out the vector passed to it as parameter. Write a suitable driver program that will allow you to test the two functions by generating output similar to the above. Verify that the program works with vectors whose element types are `char`, `int`, `double`, and `string`.

6. Template Reversal

Write a template function that takes as parameter a vector of a generic type and reverses the order of elements in the vector, and then add the function to the program you wrote for Programming Challenge 5. Modify the driver program to test the new function by reversing and outputting vectors whose element types are `char`, `int`, `double`, and `string`.

7. `SimpleVector` Modification

Modify the `SimpleVector` class template, presented in this chapter, to include the member functions `push_back` and `pop_back`. These functions should emulate the STL vector class member functions of the same name. (See Table 16-4.) The `push_back` function should throw an exception if the array is full. The `push_back` function should accept an argument and insert its value at the end of the array. The `pop_back` function should accept no argument and remove the last element from the array. Test the class with a driver program.

8. `SearchableVector` Modification

Modify the `SearchableVector` class template, presented in this chapter, so it performs a binary search instead of a linear search. Test the template in a driver program.

9. `SortableVector` Class Template

Write a class template named `SortableVector`. The class should be derived from the `SimpleVector` class presented in this chapter. It should have a member function that sorts the array elements in ascending order. (Use the sorting algorithm of your choice.) Test the template in a driver program.

10. Two-Dimensional Data

Suppose that data representing a list of people and places they would like to visit is stored in a file as follows:

```
3
0 Paul
1 Peter
2 David

0 3 Chicago Boston Memphis
1 1 Boston
2 0
```

The first number *n* in the file indicates how many people there are in the list. Here *n* is 3, so there are 3 people. Each person in the list is assigned a number in the range $0..\ n - 1$ that is used to identify her. For each person, the file lists the numerical identifier of the person, followed by the number of places the person wants to visit, followed by the names of those places. For example, Boston is the only place that Peter cares to visit, while David wants to visit no places.

Write a program that reads in this type of data from a file and stores it in appropriate STL data structure. For example, you might use vectors, as well as vectors of vectors, to represent this information. The program allows users to type in the name of a person whose list of favorite destinations is to be printed out. The program prints an error message if the person is not in the database.

11. Word Transformers Modification

Modify Program 16-19 so that it keeps lists of intermediate words during the two sorts instead of keeping lists of swap indices.

CHAPTER

17 Linked Lists

TOPICS

17.1 Introduction to the Linked List ADT

CONCEPT: Dynamically allocated data structures may be linked together in memory to form a chain.

A linked list is a series of connected *nodes*, where each node is a data structure. The nodes of a linked list are usually dynamically allocated, used, and then deleted, allowing the linked list to grow or shrink in size as the program runs. If new information needs to be added to a linked list, the program simply allocates another node and inserts it into the series. If a particular piece of information needs to be removed from the linked list, the program deletes the node containing that information.

Advantages of Linked Lists over Arrays and Vectors

Although linked lists are more complex to code and manage than arrays, they have some distinct advantages. First, a linked list can easily grow or shrink in size. In fact, the programmer doesn't need to know how many nodes will be in the list. They are simply created in memory as they are needed.

One might argue that linked lists are not superior to vectors (found in the Standard Template Library), because they too can expand or shrink. The advantage that linked lists have over vectors, however, is the speed at which a node may be inserted into or deleted from the list.

To insert a value into the middle of a vector requires all the elements after the insertion point to be moved one position toward the vector's end, thus making room for the new value. Likewise, removing a value from a vector requires all the elements after the removal point to be moved one position toward the vector's beginning. When a node is inserted into or deleted from a linked list, none of the other nodes have to be moved.

The Structure of Linked Lists

Each node in a linked list contains one or more members that hold data. (For example, the data stored in the node may be an inventory record; or it may be a customer information record consisting of the customer's name, address, and telephone number.) In addition to the data, each node contains a *successor* pointer that points to the next node in the list. The makeup of a single node is illustrated in Figure 17-1.

Figure 17-1

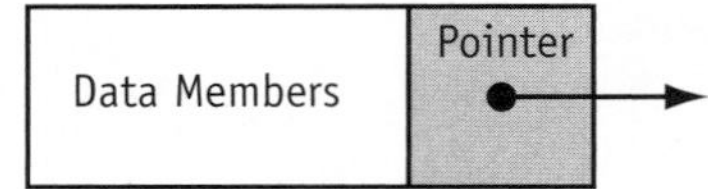

The first node of a nonempty linked list is called the *head* of the list. To access the nodes in a linked list, you need to have a pointer to the head of the list. Beginning with the head, you can access the rest of the nodes in the list by following the successor pointers stored in each node. The successor pointer in the last node is set to NULL to indicate the end of the list.

Because the pointer to the head of the list is used to locate the head of the list, we can think of it as representing the list head. The same pointer can also be used to locate the entire list by starting at the head and following the successor pointers, so it is also natural to think of it as representing the entire list. Figure 17-2 illustrates a linked list of three nodes, showing the pointer to the head, the three nodes of the list, and the NULL pointer that signifies the end of the list.

Figure 17-2

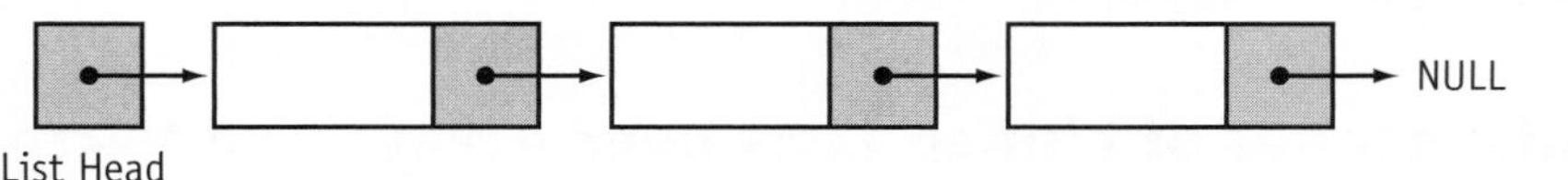

NOTE: Figure 17-2 depicts the nodes in the linked list as being very close to each other, neatly arranged in a row. In reality, the nodes may be scattered around various parts of memory.

C++ Representation of Linked Lists

To represent linked lists in C++, we need to have a data type that represents a single node in the list. Looking at Figure 17-1, we see that it is natural to make this data type a structure that contains the data to be stored, together with a pointer to another node of the same type. Assuming that each node will store a single data item of type `double`, we can declare the following type to hold the node:

```
struct ListNode
{
   double value;
   ListNode *next;
};
```

Here `ListNode` is the type of a node to be stored in the list, the structure member `value` is the data portion of the node, and the structure member `next`, declared as a pointer to `ListNode`, is the successor pointer that points to the next node.

The `ListNode` structure has an interesting property: it contains a pointer to a data structure of the same type and thus can be said to be a type that contains a reference to itself. Such types are called *self-referential data types*, or *self-referential data structures*.

Having declared a data type to represent a node, we can define an initially empty linked list by defining a pointer to be used as the list head and initializing it to NULL:

```
ListNode *head = NULL;
```

We can now create a linked list that consists of a single node storing 12.5 as follows:

```
head = new ListNode;      // allocate new node
head->value = 12.5;       // store the value
head->next = NULL;        // signify end of list
```

Now let's see how we can create a new node, store 13.5 in it, and make it the second node in the list. We can use a second pointer to point to a newly allocated node into which the 13.5 will be stored:

```
ListNode *secondPtr = new ListNode;
secondPtr->value = 13.5;
secondPtr->next = NULL;      // second node is end of list
head->next = secondPtr;      // first node points to second
```

Note that we have now made the second node the end of the list by setting its successor pointer, `secondPtr->next`, to NULL, and we have changed the successor pointer of the list head to point to the second node. Program 17-1 illustrates the creation of a simple linked list.

Program 17-1

```
// This program illustrates the creation
// of linked lists.
#include <iostream>
using namespace std;

struct ListNode
{
   double value;
   ListNode *next;
};

```

(program continues)

Program 17-1 *(continued)*

```
int main()
{
   ListNode *head;

   // Create first node with 12.5
   head = new ListNode;     // Allocate new node
   head->value = 12.5;      // Store the value
   head->next = NULL;       // Signify end of list

   // Create second node with 13.5
   ListNode *secondPtr = new ListNode;
   secondPtr->value = 13.5;
   secondPtr->next = NULL;  // Second node is end of list
   head->next = secondPtr; // First node points to second

   // Print the list
   cout << "First item is " << head->value << endl;
   cout << "Second item is " << head->next->value << endl;
   return 0;
}
```

Program Output

```
First item is 12.5
Second item is 13.5
```

Using Constructors to Initialize Nodes

Recall that C++ structures can have constructors. It is often convenient to provide the structures that define the type for a list node with one or more constructors, to allow nodes to be initialized as soon as they are created. Recall also that just like regular functions, constructors can be defined with default parameters. It is very common to provide a default parameter of NULL for the successor pointer of a node. Here is an alternative definition of the `ListNode` structure:

```
struct ListNode
{
   double value;
   ListNode *next;
   // Constructor
   ListNode(double value1, ListNode *next1 = NULL)
   {
      value = value1;
      next = next1;
   }
};
```

With this declaration, a node can be created in two different ways:

1. by specifying just its `value` part and letting the successor pointer default to NULL, or
2. by specifying both the `value` part and a pointer to the node that is to follow this one in the list.

The first method is useful when we are creating a node to put at the end of a linked list, while the second method is useful when the newly created node is to be inserted at a place in the list where it will have a successor.

Using this new declaration of a node, we can create the previous list of `12.5` followed by `13.5` with much shorter code:

```
ListNode *secondPtr = new ListNode(13.5);
ListNode *head = new ListNode(12.5, secondPtr);
```

We can actually dispense with the second pointer and write the above code as:

```
ListNode *head = new ListNode(13.5);
head = new ListNode(12.5, head);
```

This code is equivalent to what precedes it because the assignment statement

```
head = new ListNode(12.5, head);
```

is evaluated from right to left: first the old value of `head` is used in the constructor, and then the address returned from the new operator is assigned to `head`, becoming its new value.

Building a List

Using the constructor version of `ListNode`, it is very easy to create a list by reading values from a file and adding each newly read value to the beginning of the list of values already accumulated. For example, using `numberList` for the list head, and `numberFile` for the input file object, the following code will read in numbers stored in a text file and arrange them in a list:

```
ListNode *numberList = NULL;
double number;
while (numberFile >> number)
{
   // Create a node to hold this number
   numberList = new ListNode(number, numberList);
}
```

Traversing a List

The process of beginning at the head of a list and going through the entire list while doing some processing at each node is called *traversing* the list. For example, we would have to traverse a list if we needed to print the contents of every node in the list. To traverse a list, say one whose list head pointer is `numberList`, we take another pointer `ptr` and point it to the beginning of the list:

```
ListNode *ptr = numberList;
```

We can then process the node pointed to by `ptr` by working with the expression `*ptr`, or by using the structure pointer operator `->`. For example, if we needed to print the value at the node, we could write the code

```
cout << ptr->value;
```

Once the processing at the node is done, we move the pointer to the next node, if there is one, by writing

```
ptr = ptr->next;
```

thus replacing the pointer to a node by the pointer to the successor of the node. Thus to print an entire list we can use code such as

```
ListNode *ptr = numberList;
while (ptr != NULL)
{
   cout << ptr->value << " ";    // Process node
   ptr = ptr->next;              // Move to next node
}
```

Program 17-2 illustrates these techniques by reading a file of numbers, arranging the numbers in a linked list, and then traversing the list to print the numbers on the screen.

Program 17-2

```
// This program illustrates the building
// and traversal of a linked list.

#include <iostream>
#include <fstream>
using namespace std;

struct ListNode
  {
     double value;
     ListNode *next;
     // Constructor
     ListNode(double value1, ListNode *next1 = NULL)
     {
       value = value1;
       next = next1;
     }
  };

int main()
{
   double number;                   // Used to read the file
   ListNode *numberList = NULL;     // List of numbers

   // Open the file
   ifstream numberFile("numberFile.dat");
   if (!numberFile)
   {
      cout << "Error in opening the file of numbers.";
      exit(1);
   }
   // Read the file into a linked list
   cout << "The contents of the file are: " << endl;
   while (numberFile >> number)
```

(program continues)

Program 17-2 *(continued)*

```
    {
       cout << number << "  ";
       // Create a node to hold this number
       numberList = new ListNode(number, numberList);
    }
    // Traverse the list while printing
    cout << endl << "The contents of the list are: " << endl;
    ListNode *ptr = numberList;
    while (ptr != NULL)
    {
       cout << ptr->value << "  "; // Process node
       ptr = ptr->next;             // Move to next node
    }
    return 0;
}
```

Program Output

```
The contents of the file are:
10  20  30  40
The contents of the list are:
40  30  20  10
```

Checkpoint

17.1 Describe the two parts of a node.

17.2 What is a list head?

17.3 What signifies the end of a linked list?

17.4 What is a self-referential data structure?

17.2 Linked List Operations

CONCEPT: The basic linked list operations are adding an element to a list, removing an element from the list, traversing the list, and destroying the list.

In this section we develop some simple list classes. The first of these, which we call `NumberList`, will store values of type `double`. It is based on the `ListNode` structure defined in the preceding section and is shown here.

Contents of `NumberList.h`

```
#include <iostream>
using namespace std;
class NumberList
{
protected:
     // Declare a class for the list node
     struct ListNode
```

```
     {
        double value;
        ListNode *next;
        ListNode(double value1, ListNode *next1 = NULL)
        {
           value = value1;
           next = next1;
        }
     };
     ListNode *head;                     // List head pointer
public:
     NumberList() { head = NULL;  }      // Constructor
     ~NumberList();                      // Destructor
     void add(double number);
     void remove(double number);
     void displayList() const;
};
```

Because `ListNode` does not need to be accessed by any code outside of `NumberList`, we have declared it inside the `NumberList` class. We have also declared `ListNode` in a protected section to make it accessible to classes that may later be derived from `NumberList`.

Notice that the constructor initializes the `head` pointer to `NULL`, thereby indicating that the list starts out empty. The class has an `add` function that takes a value and adds it to the end of the list, as well as a `displayList` function that prints to the screen all values stored in the list. A destructor function destroys the list by deleting all its nodes. With the exception of `remove()`, all of these functions are defined in `NumberList.cpp`. The `remove()` function will be added later.

Contents of `NumberList.cpp`

```
#include "NumberList.h"
using namespace std;

//*****************************************************
// add adds a new element to the end of the list.     *
//*****************************************************
void NumberList::add(double number)
{
    if (head == NULL)
       head = new ListNode(number);
    else
      {
        // The list is not empty
        // Use nodePtr to traverse the list
        ListNode *nodePtr = head;
        while (nodePtr->next != NULL)
           nodePtr = nodePtr->next;

        // nodePtr->next is NULL so nodePtr points to the last node
        // Create a new node and put it after the last node
        nodePtr->next = new ListNode(number);
      }
}

```

```
//*************************************************
// displayList outputs a sequence of all values     *
// currently stored in the list.                     *
//*************************************************
void NumberList::displayList() const
{
    ListNode *nodePtr = head;   // Start at head of list
    while (nodePtr)
    {
       // Print the value in the current node
       cout << nodePtr->value << "    ";
       // Move on to the next node
       nodePtr = nodePtr->next;
    }
}

//*****************************************************
// Destructor deallocates the memory used by the list. *
//*****************************************************
NumberList::~NumberList()
{
   ListNode *nodePtr = head;  // Start at head of list
   while (nodePtr != NULL)
   {
       // garbage keeps track of node to be deleted
       ListNode *garbage = nodePtr;
       // Move on to the next node, if any
       nodePtr = nodePtr->next;
       // Delete the "garbage" node
       delete garbage;
   }
}
```

Because the `NumberList` class contains pointers to dynamically allocated memory, it needs to be equipped with both a copy constructor and an overloaded assignment operator before it can safely be used in situations that require copies of lists to be made.

Adding an Element to the List

VideoNote

Adding an Element to a Linked List

The `add` member function accepts as an argument a number of type `double`, creates a node containing the number, and adds it to the end of the list. The basic idea is as follows. If the list is empty, the newly created node becomes the only node in the list:

```
head = new ListNode(number);
```

If, on the other hand, the list is not empty, we take a `pointer nodePtr`, set it to the beginning of the list, and walk it down the list until it points to the last node. We will know it is pointing to the last node when `nodePtr->next` equals `NULL`. The code for starting the pointer at the beginning of the list and walking it down to the end is

```
ListNode *nodePtr = head;
while (nodePtr->next != NULL)
      nodePtr = nodePtr->next;
```

Once `nodePtr` is pointing to the last node, we can add the new node after it by using the code

```
nodePtr->next = new ListNode(number);
```

Putting all of this together, we get the `add` function shown in lines 7–23 of `NumberList.cpp`.

Displaying a List

The code for the `displayList` member function, in lines 29–39, is based on the algorithm for traversing a list presented in the last section.

Destroying the List

It is important for the class's destructor to release all the memory used by the list. It does this by stepping through the list, deleting one node at a time. The code for doing so is found in lines 44–56 of the `NumberList.cpp` file. A pointer `nodePtr` starts at the beginning (head) of the list and steps through the list one node at a time. A second pointer, `garbage`, follows in `nodePtr's` wake and is used to delete each node as soon as `nodePtr` has passed on to the node's successor.

Program 17–3 demonstrates the operation of the member functions of the `NumberList` class.

Program 17-3

```
// This program demonstrates the add and
// display linked list operations.

#include "Numberlist.h"
using namespace std;

int main()
{
     NumberList list;
     list.add(2.5);
     list.add(7.9);
     list.add(12.6);
     list.displayList();
     cout << endl;
     return 0;
}
```

Program Output

```
2.5  7.9  12.6
```

Let's step through Program 17-3, observing how the `add` function builds a linked list to store the three argument values used.

The `head` pointer, a member variable of the `NumberList` class, is automatically initialized to NULL by the constructor when the list is created. This indicates that the list is initially empty.

The first call to add passes `2.5` as the argument. Because the list is empty at that time, the code

```
head = new ListNode(num);
```

is executed, resulting in the situation depicted in Figure 17-3:

Figure 17-3

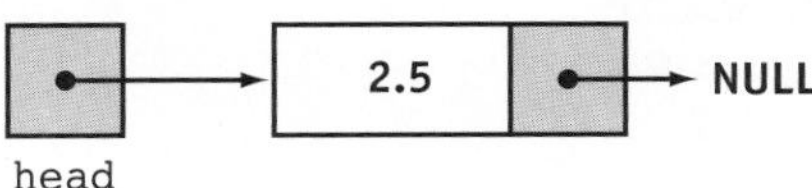

There are no more statements to execute, so control returns to function `main`. In the second call to `add`, `7.9` is passed as the argument. The `else` clause of the `if` statement will be executed, setting `nodePtr` to point to the first node of the list, as illustrated in Figure 17-4.

Figure 17-4

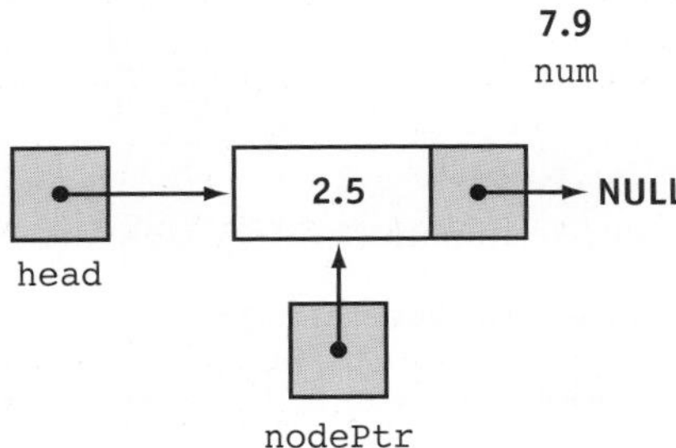

At this point, the pointer `nodePtr->next` has value NULL, and the `while` loop terminates. The statement

```
nodePtr->next = new ListNode(num);
```

which follows the loop, is then executed, giving the situation depicted in Figure 17.5. The function then returns.

Figure 17-5

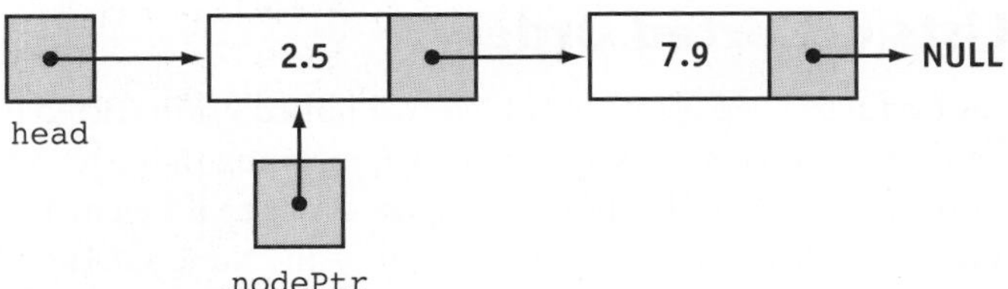

The value `12.6` is passed on the third call to `add`. Again, control will flow to the `else` clause of the `if` statement because the list is nonempty. The pointer `nodePtr` will be set to the beginning of the list as shown in Figure 17-6.

Figure 17-6

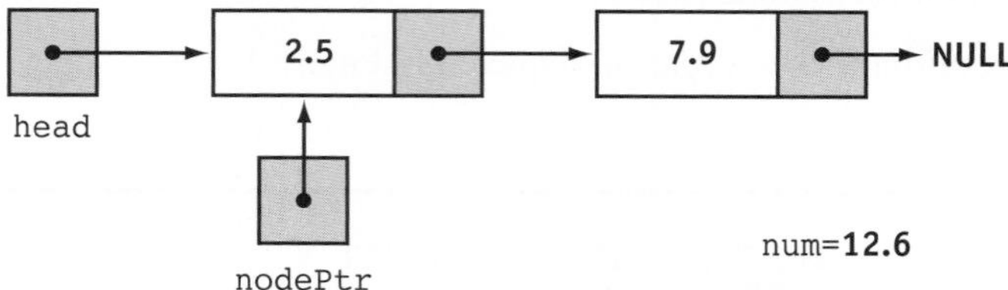

Because `nodePtr->next` is not NULL, the `while` loop executes, resulting in the situation illustrated in Figure 17-7.

Figure 17-7

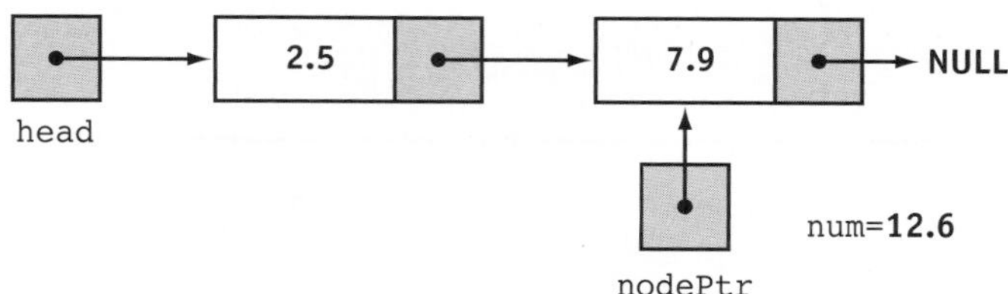

At this point, the `while` loop terminates, and the statement

```
nodePtr->next = new ListNode(num);
```

that comes after the `while` loop is executed. This gives the situation depicted in Figure 17-8.

Figure 17-8

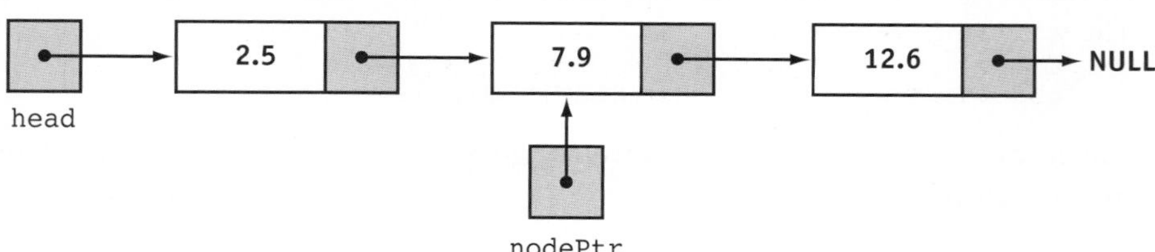

Linked Lists in Sorted Order

It is sometimes useful to keep elements added to a linked list in sorted order. For example, the list may maintain its elements in ascending order, meaning that each element in the list is less than or equal to its successor. In these cases, we cannot add elements to the list by putting them at the end of the list as in the `add` function of the `NumberList` class, because doing so would violate the order of the elements in the list. A different approach is needed.

Consider a class `SortedNumberList` that maintains its elements in ascending order. It is similar to the `NumberList` class, except the `add` function is modified so that it keeps the list in sorted order when placing new elements. Because a sorted list is still a list, it makes sense to use inheritance and derive it from `NumberList`.

Contents of `SortedNumberList.h`

```
#include "NumberList.h"
class SortedNumberList : public NumberList
{
public:
    void add(double number);
};
```

Inserting a Node into a Sorted List

Suppose that we have a linked list of numbers that is sorted in ascending order. We want to write the `add` function so that it inserts its argument `number` in the list at a position that leaves the list sorted.

There are two cases to consider. The first case is when the new number to be inserted should go *before every node already in the list*. This happens when the list is either empty, *or* the first number in the list is greater or equal to `num`:

```
if (head == NULL || head->value >= number)
   head = new ListNode(number, head);
```

Note that the order of these two tests should not be reversed: you should make sure that `head` is not NULL before you try to access `head->value`: trying to evaluate the expression `head->value` will result in a runtime error if `head` is NULL.

The second case that should be considered is when the new number needs to go *after one of the nodes already in the list*. In this case, the new number will need to be placed just *before* the first node that has a value greater or equal to the number. To locate such a node, we use a pointer called `nodePtr`. We will start `nodePtr` at the second node, and then keep moving it forward in the list until it falls off the end of the list (this will happen when `nodePtr` becomes NULL) or it points to a node whose value is greater or equal to `number` (this will happen when the expression `nodePtr->value >= number` becomes true). In order to insert the new node just before `nodePtr`, we will need a pointer to the node that precedes the one that `nodePtr` points to. To this end, we use a pointer `previousNodePtr` that always points to the node previous to the one that `nodePtr` points to. The whole process of finding the insertion point is accomplished by the following code:

```
previousNodePtr = head;
nodePtr = head->next;

// Find the insertion point
while (nodePtr != NULL && nodePtr->value < number)
{
   previousNodePtr = nodePtr;
   nodePtr = nodePtr->next;
}
```

The entire function, including the code for creating a new node and inserting it at the point just after `previousNodePtr` but before `nodePtr`, is given here:

Contents of `SortedNumberList.h`

```
#include "SortedNumberList.h"

//*******************************************
// Adds a number to the sorted list.        *
// This function overrides add in NumberList. *
//*******************************************
```

```
void SortedNumberList::add(double number)
{
   ListNode *nodePtr, *previousNodePtr;

   if (head == NULL || head->value >= number)
   {
      // A new node goes at the beginning of the list
      head = new ListNode(number, head);
   }
   else
   {
      previousNodePtr = head;
      nodePtr = head->next;

      // Find the insertion point
      while (nodePtr != NULL && nodePtr->value < number)
      {
         previousNodePtr = nodePtr;
         nodePtr = nodePtr->next;
      }
      // Insert the new node just before nodePtr
      previousNodePtr->next = new ListNode(number, nodePtr);
   }
}
```

Here is a program that uses the add function. A discussion of how the function works follows the program.

Program 17-4

```
// This program illustrates the NumberList append,
// insert, and displayList member functions.
#include "SortedNumberList.h"

int main()
{
   SortedNumberList list;

   // Add elements in order
   list.add(2.5);
   list.add(7.9);
   list.add(12.6);
   // Add a value that should go in the middle of the list
   list.add(10.5);
   // Display the list
   list.displayList();
   cout << endl;
   return 0;
}
```

Program Output

```
2.5  7.9  10.5  12.6
```

Like Program 17-3, Program 17-4 starts out by building a list with the values 2.5, 7.9, and 12.6. Because of the order of addition to the list, each of these values is handled by the `if` clause in lines 11–15 of `SortedNumberList.cpp`. The `add` function is then called with argument 10.5. This time, the `else` part in lines 16–26 is executed. The statements

```
previousNodePtr = head;
nodePtr = head->next;
```

are executed, giving the situation depicted in Figure 17-9.

Figure 17-9

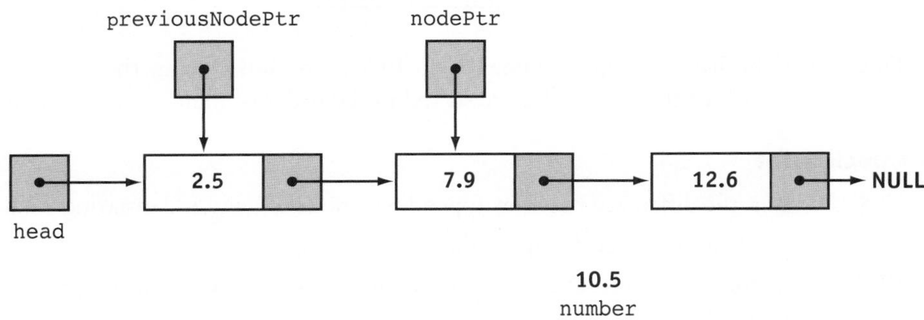

The `while` loop then executes once, leaving the state of the linked list as shown in Figure 17-10.

Figure 17-10

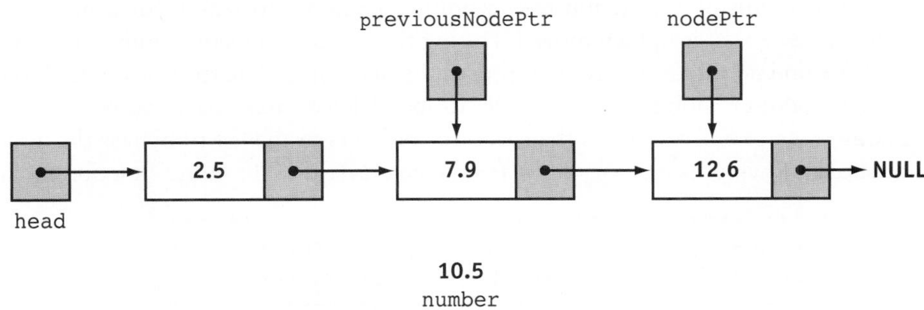

At this point, `nodePtr->value` is greater or equal to `number`, so the loop terminates. The statement after the loop is executed:

```
previousNodePtr->next = new ListNode(number, nodePtr);
```

This final state of the list is illustrated in Figure 17-11.

Figure 17-11

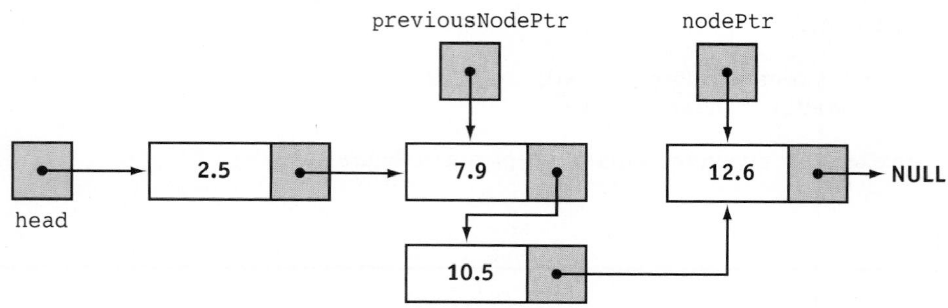

This leaves the list in its final state. If you follow the links, from the `head` pointer to the NULL, you will see that the nodes are stored in the order of their `value` members.

Checkpoint

17.5 What is the difference between appending a node to a list and inserting a node into a list?

17.6 Which is easier to code, appending or inserting?

17.7 Why does the `insertNode` function shown in this section use a `previousNodePtr` pointer?

Removing an Element

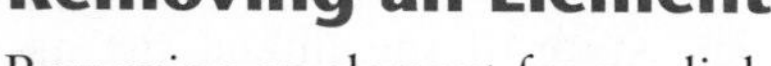

Removing an element from a linked list requires a number of steps:

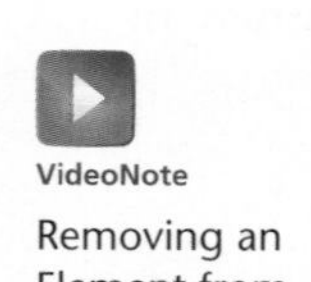

VideoNote
Removing an Element from a Linked List

1. Locating the node containing the element to be removed.
2. Unhooking the node from the list.
3. Deleting the memory allocated to the node.

The `remove` member function uses a pointer `nodePtr` to search for a node containing the value `number` that is to be removed. During this process, a second pointer `previousNodePtr` trails behind `nodePtr`, always pointing to the node preceding the one pointed to by `nodePtr`. When `nodePtr` points to the node to be deleted, `previousNodePtr->next` is set to `nodePtr->next`. This causes the successor pointers in the list to bypass the node containing `number`, allowing its memory to be freed using `delete`. The entire function is shown here:

```
//**********************************************
// Removes a number from a list. The function  *
// does not assume that the list is sorted.    *
//**********************************************
void NumberList::remove(double number)
{
  ListNode *nodePtr, *previousNodePtr;

   // If the list is empty, do nothing
   if (!head) return;

   // Determine if the first node is the one to delete
   if (head->value == number)
```

```
   {
     nodePtr = head;
     head = head->next;
     delete nodePtr;
   }
   else
   {
     // Initialize nodePtr to the head of the list
     nodePtr = head;

     // Skip nodes whose value member is not number
     while (nodePtr != NULL && nodePtr->value != number)
     {
        previousNodePtr = nodePtr;
        nodePtr = nodePtr->next;
     }
     // Link the previous node to the node after
     // nodePtr, then delete nodePtr
     if (nodePtr)
     {
        previousNodePtr->next = nodePtr->next;
        delete nodePtr;
     }
   }
}
```

Notice that the `remove()` function is a member of `NumberList` rather than `SortedNumberList`. Unlike `add()`, the `remove()` function works with both sorted and unsorted lists, and so does not have to be overridden. The file `RNumberList.cpp`, found on the book's companion website, is a simple modification of the `NumberList.cpp`: it simply adds the implementation of `remove()`. Program 17-5 demonstrates this new function by first building a list of three values and then removing the values one by one.

Program 17-5

```
// This program demonstrates the remove member function.
#include "NumberList.h"
using namespace std;

int main()
{
    NumberList list;

    // Build the list
    list.add(2.5);
    list.add(7.9);
    list.add(12.6);

    // Display the list
    cout << "Here are the initial values:\n";
    list.displayList();
    cout << "\n\n";
```

(program continues)

Program 17-5 *(continued)*

```

    // Demonstrate the remove function
    cout << "Now removing the value in the middle.\n";
    list.remove(7.9);
    cout << "Here are the values left.\n";
    list.displayList();
    cout << "\n\n";

    cout << "Now removing the last value.\n";
    list.remove(12.6);
    cout << "Here are the values left.\n";
    list.displayList();
    cout << "\n\n";

    cout << "Now removing the only remaining value.\n";
    list.remove(2.5);
    cout << "Here are the values left.\n";
    list.displayList();
    cout << endl;

    return 0;
}
```

Program Output

```
Here are the initial values:
2.5  7.9  12.6

Now removing the value in the middle.
Here are the values left.
2.5  12.6

Now removing the last value.
Here are the values left.
2.5

Now removing the only remaining value.
Here are the values left.
```

To illustrate how `remove` works, we will step through the first call, the one that removes 7.9 from the list. This is a value that is in the middle of the list.

Look at the `else` part of the second if statement, lines 44–61. This is where the function will perform its action because the list is not empty and the first node does not contain the value 7.9. Just like the sorted list version of `add()`, this function uses `nodePtr` and `previousNodePtr` to traverse the list. The `while` loop terminates when the value 7.9 is located. At this point, the list head and the other pointers will be in the state depicted in Figure 17-12.

Figure 17-12

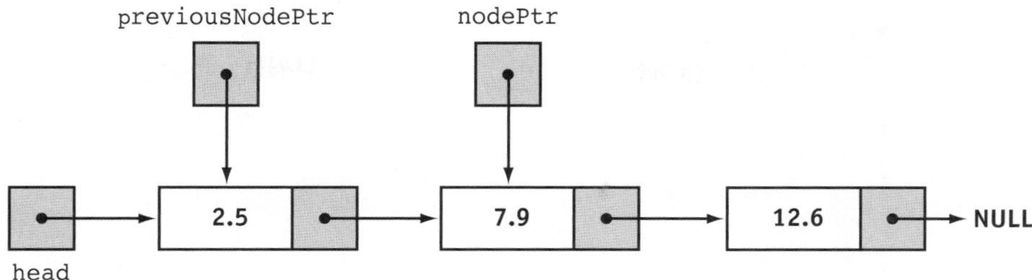

Next, the following statement executes.

```
previousNodePtr->next = nodePtr->next;
```

This statement causes the links in the list to bypass the node that `nodePtr` points to. Although the node still exists in memory, this removes it from the list, as illustrated in Figure 17-13.

Figure 17-13

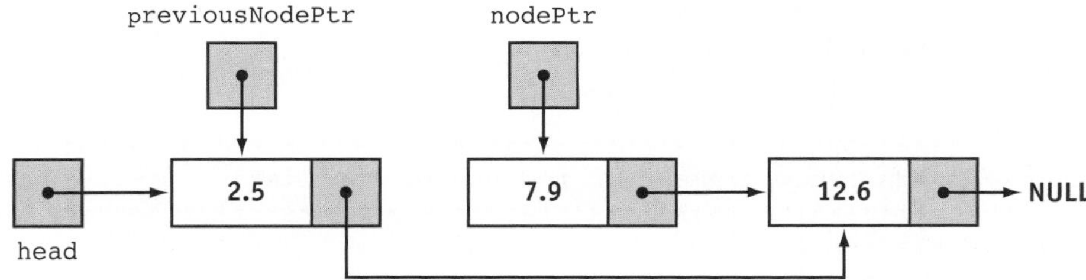

The last statement uses the `delete` operator to free the memory used by the deleted node.

Checkpoint

17.8 What are the two steps involved in deleting a node from a linked list?

17.9 When deleting a node, why can't you just use the `delete` operator to remove it from memory? Why must you take the steps you listed in response to question 17.8?

17.10 In a program that uses several linked lists, what might eventually happen if the class destructor does not destroy its linked list?

17.3 A Linked List Template*

A major limitation of the `NumberList` class is that it can only hold values of type `double`. A list class is most useful when it can be used to hold values of different types. The `LinkedList` class, which we will cover next, uses templates to achieve type flexibility. It uses the same logic as the `NumberList` class.

* Note: This section should be skipped if Chapter 16 has not yet been covered.

Contents of `LinkedList.h`

```
#include <iostream>
using namespace std;
template <class T>
class LinkedList
{
protected:
    // Declare a class for the list node
    struct ListNode
    {
       T value;
       ListNode *next;
       ListNode(T value1, ListNode *next1 = NULL)
       {
          value = value1;
          next = next1;
       }
    };
    ListNode *head;                        // List head pointer
public:
    LinkedList() { head = NULL;  }         // Constructor
    ~LinkedList();                         // Destructor
    void add(T value);
    void remove(T value);
    void displayList() const;
};

//*****************************************************
// Adds a new element to the end of the list.         *
//*****************************************************
template <class T>
void LinkedList<T>::add(T value)
{
   if (head == NULL)
      head = new ListNode(value);
   else
     {
       // The list is not empty
       // Use nodePtr to traverse the list
       ListNode *nodePtr = head;
       while (nodePtr->next != NULL)
          nodePtr = nodePtr->next;

       // nodePtr->next is NULL so nodePtr points to the last node
       // Create a new node and put it after the last node
       nodePtr->next = new ListNode(value);
     }
}

//**********************************************
// Removes a number from a list. The function  *
// does not assume that the list is sorted.    *
//**********************************************
template <class T>
void LinkedList<T>::remove(T value)
```

```
{
  ListNode *nodePtr, *previousNodePtr;

   // If the list is empty, do nothing
   if (!head)  return;

   // Determine if the first node is the one to delete
   if (head->value == value)
   {
     nodePtr = head;
     head = head->next;
     delete nodePtr;
   }
   else
   {
     // Initialize nodePtr to the head of the list
     nodePtr = head;

     // Skip nodes whose value member is not num
     while (nodePtr != NULL && nodePtr->value != value)
     {
        previousNodePtr = nodePtr;
        nodePtr = nodePtr->next;
     }
     // Link the previous node to the node after
     // nodePtr, then delete nodePtr
     if (nodePtr)
     {
        previousNodePtr->next = nodePtr->next;
        delete nodePtr;
     }
   }
}

//*****************************************************
// displayList outputs a sequence of all values      *
// currently stored in the list.                     *
//*****************************************************
template <class T>
void LinkedList<T>::displayList() const
{
   ListNode *nodePtr = head;   // Start at head of list
   while (nodePtr)
   {
      // Print the value in the current node
      cout << nodePtr->value << "    ";
      // Move on to the next node
      nodePtr = nodePtr->next;
   }
}

//*******************************************************
// Destructor deallocates the memory used by the list. *
//*******************************************************
```

```
template <class T>
LinkedList<T>::~LinkedList()
{
  ListNode *nodePtr = head;  // Start at head of list
  while (nodePtr != NULL)
  {
      // garbage keeps track of node to be deleted
      ListNode *garbage = nodePtr;
      // Move on to the next node, if any
      nodePtr = nodePtr->next;
      // Delete the "garbage" node
      delete garbage;
  }
}
```

Notice that the implementation of the class member functions, previously in a separate `.cpp` file, have now been folded into the header file. This has been done to avoid the tremendous complexities of compiling and linking a multifile program that uses templates.

The template class will work for any data type that supports comparison operators such as == and <=. In particular, it will work for all numeric types and for `string`. Program 17-6 shows the template being used as list of strings.

Program 17-6

```
// This program demonstrates the linked list template
// being used to create a linked list of strings.
#include <string>
#include "LinkedList.h"
using namespace std;

int main()
{
      LinkedList<string> list;

      // Build the list
      list.add("Alice");
      list.add("Chuck");
      list.add("Elaine");
      list.add("Fran");

      cout << "Here are the initial names:\n";
      list.displayList();
      cout << "\n\n";

      cout << "Now removing Elaine.\n\n";
      list.remove("Elaine");
      cout << "Here are the remaining elements.\n";
      list.displayList();
      cout << endl;

      return 0;
}
```

(program continues)

Program 17-6 *(continued)*

Program Output

```
Here are the initial names:
Alice  Chuck  Elaine  Fran

Now removing Elaine.

Here are the remaining elements.
Alice  Chuck  Fran
```

17.4 Recursive Linked List Operations

CONCEPT: Recursion is a useful technique for working with linked lists.

Recursion is a useful approach to solving problems that can be broken down into smaller problems of the same type. Some data structures, such as arrays and linked lists, mirror this property of recursion in that a large array can be split into smaller arrays; and likewise, a nonempty linked list can be reduced to a smaller linked list by removing its first node. Because of this, both array and linked list operations are often well suited to a recursive solution. In this section, we will take a look at the recursive implementation of linked list operations.

Let's take a look at some examples of recursive linked list operations. We will first look at the implementation of recursive stand-alone functions, and then later on in the section, we will look at how member functions of a class can be made recursive. We will use for our examples linked lists of numbers based on the node type

```
struct ListNode
{
   double value;
   ListNode *next;
   ListNode(double value1, ListNode *next1 = NULL)
   {
      value = value1;
      next = next1;
   }
};
```

We have used a structure here to represent the node for ease of presentation only, normally, the node would be a class type to restrict access to its private members.

Recall that the *head* of a nonempty list is the first item on the list. The *tail* of a nonempty list is the list that remains after you remove the head. For example, any list with only one item has the empty list for its tail. A list of numbers `2.5, 7.9, 12.6` has the list `7.9, 12.6` as its tail. With a declaration such as `ListNode`, if a nonempty list is represented by a pointer `ptr`, the tail will be represented by `ptr->next`.

Finally, remember that a good recursive solution must be careful to identify and deal with base cases of the problem, that is, the subproblems resulting from the breaking down process that can be directly solved. In the case of linked lists, the process will often involve breaking a list down by separating it into its head and tail, and then recursively solving the problem on the tail. The base case will usually be when the list on which the operation is to be performed is empty, or in some cases, has only one item.

Recursive List Functions

Let's write some recursive linked list functions. The function

```
int size(ListNode *ptr)
```

takes as parameter a pointer to the head node of a linked list and returns the number of elements stored in the list. If the list is empty, its size is zero:

```
if (ptr == NULL) return 0;
```

But if a list is nonempty, its size will be one more than the size of its tail:

```
if (ptr != NULL) return 1 + size(ptr->next);
```

Putting these two observations together, we arrive at the following code for the `size()` function:

```
int size(ListNode *ptr)
{
   if (ptr == NULL)
      return 0;
   else
      return 1 + size(ptr->next);
}
```

Consider now a recursive strategy for a function

```
void displayList(ListNode *ptr)
```

that takes a pointer to the head node of a list and prints the list elements. There is nothing to print if the list is empty. To display a nonempty list, we first display the element stored in the head node

```
cout << ptr->value << "  ";
```

and then recursively display the tail of the list. Because the tail of the list is given by `ptr->next`, we arrive at the following code:

```
void displayList(ListNode *ptr)
{
  if (ptr != NULL)
  {
     cout << ptr-> value << "  ";
     displayList(ptr->next);
  }
}
```

Program 17-7 gathers these two functions together and illustrates their use. The program reads data from a file `Numberfile.dat` that can be found on the book's companion website.

Program 17-7

```
// This program illustrates recursion on linked lists.
#include <iostream>
#include <fstream>
using namespace std;

struct ListNode
  {
     double value;
     ListNode *next;
     // Constructor
     ListNode(double value1, ListNode *next1 = NULL)
     {
       value = value1;
       next = next1;
     }
  };

// Function prototypes
int size(ListNode *);
void displayList(ListNode *);

int main()
{
   ListNode *numberList = NULL;     // List of numbers
   double number;                   // Used to read the file

   // Open the file
   ifstream numberFile("numberFile.dat");
   if (!numberFile)
   {
        cout << "Error in opening the file of numbers.";
        exit(1);
   }
   // Read the file into a linked list
   while (numberFile >> number)
   {
      // Create a node to hold this number
      numberList = new ListNode(number, numberList);
   }
   // Print the list
   cout << endl << "The contents of the list are: " << endl;
   displayList(numberList);

   // Print the size of the list
   cout << endl << "The number of items in the list is: "
        << size(numberList);
   return 0;
}

```

(program continues)

Program 17-7 *(continued)*

```
//****************************************
// length computes the number of nodes in *
// a linked list                          *
//****************************************
int size(ListNode *ptr)
{
  if (ptr == NULL)
    return 0;
  else
   return 1 + size(ptr->next);
}

//******************************************
// displayList prints all the values stored *
// in the list                              *
//******************************************
void displayList(ListNode *ptr)
{
  if (ptr != NULL)
    {
      cout << ptr-> value << "  ";
      displayList(ptr->next);
    }
}
```

Program Output:

```
The contents of the list are:
40  30  20  10
The number of items in the list is: 4
```

Recursive Member Functions

Let's write a new version of the `NumberList` class in which the member functions for adding an element, removing an element, and displaying the list have recursive implementations. The class will also have a `size()` function. Here is the class declaration:

Contents of `NumberList2.h`

```
#include <iostream>
using namespace std;
class NumberList2
{
protected:
    // Declare a class for the list node
    struct ListNode
    {
       double value;
       ListNode *next;
       ListNode(double value1, ListNode *next1 = NULL)
       {
          value = value1;
```

```
14             next = next1;
15         }
16     };
17     ListNode *head;                        // List head pointer
18 public:
19     NumberList2() { head = NULL; }     // Constructor
20     ~NumberList2();                        // Destructor
21     void add(double value) { head = add(head, value);}
22     void remove(double value) {head = remove(head, value);}
23     void displayList() const {displayList(head);}
24     int size() const {return size(head);}
25 private:
26     // Recursive implementations
27     ListNode *add(ListNode *aList, double value);
28     ListNode *remove(ListNode *aList, double value);
29     void displayList(ListNode *aList) const;
30     int size(ListNode *aList) const;
31 };
```

If you look at the class, you will notice that each public member function in lines 20–24 has a corresponding private member function in lines 27–30. The private member functions provide recursive implementations for their public counterparts. Notice that each of the private member functions has a parameter of type `ListNode*`. This parameter is needed for the recursion to work.

You might wonder why we do not make the recursive functions public. The reason is that the parameters of type `ListNode*` are implementation details, and therefore should not be exposed to the users of the class. The user of the public interface of the class does not need to know that the list is internally implemented using a pointer to `ListNode` named `head`.

The Recursive add Member Function

Notice that the recursive `add` member function

```
ListNode *add(ListNode *aList, double value);
```

takes as parameters an input list and a value and returns the list that results from adding the value to the input list. Technically, the function takes as its first parameter a pointer to the head of a linked list and returns a pointer to the head of the resulting list. Line 21 of the code listing of `NumberList2.h` shows how the recursive function is called to add a value to the list.

Let's see how the `add` function works. If the input list is empty (base case), the function creates a new node containing the value and returns a pointer to that node:

```
return new ListNode(value);
```

If the list is not empty, the function proceeds as follows. First, it splits the input list into its constituent head node and tail.

```
ListNode *tail = aList->next;  // Fix the tail
aList->next = null;            // aList now points to the head
```

The tail is shorter than the original input list, and is therefore closer to the base case. Using recursion, the function adds the value to the tail of the list, resulting in a "bigger" tail:

```
ListNode *biggerTail = add(tail, value);
```

Finally, the original head, which is being pointed to by `aList`, is reattached to the bigger tail, and a pointer to the original head is returned:

```
aList->next = biggerTail;  // Reattach the head
return aList;              // Return pointer to augmented list
```

Putting all of this together, we get the following code for the `add` function:

```
42 NumberList2::ListNode *NumberList2::add(ListNode *aList, double value)
43 {
44     if (aList == NULL)
45         return new ListNode(value);
46     else
47     {
48         // Split into constituent head and tail
49         ListNode *tail = aList->next;    // tail
50         aList->next = NULL;              // Detached head
51         // Recursively add value to tail
52         ListNode *biggerTail = add(tail, value);
53         // Reattach the head
54         aList->next = biggerTail;
55         // Return pointer to head of bigger list
56         return aList;
57     }
58 }
```

The code in this function can be shortened. First, notice that line 50 is not needed. The head does not have to be detached before making the recursive call on the tail in line 52, as long as it is "reattached" in line 54. Then, we can eliminate the tail variable and just use `aList->next` in line 52. The code in the else clause then gets shortened to

```
ListNode *biggerTail = add(aList->next, value);
aList->next = biggerTail;
return aList;
```

which can in turn be shortened to

```
aList->next = add(aList->next, value);
return  aList;
```

The `add` function can therefore be written as follows:

```
NumberList2::ListNode *NumberList2::add(ListNode *aList, double value)
{
    if (aList == NULL)
        return new ListNode(value);
    else
    {
        // Add the value to the end of the tail
        aList->next = add(aList->next, value);
        return aList;
    }
}
```

The Recursive `remove` Member Function

The `remove` function

```
ListNode *remove(ListNode *aList, double value)
```

takes as parameter an input list and a value, removes the value from the input list, and returns the resulting list. If the value to be removed is not on the list, the function returns the input list unchanged.

The function works as follows. If the list is empty, the function returns `NULL`.

```
if(aList == NULL) return NULL;
```

Otherwise, the function compares the value to what is stored in the first (head) node of the list. If the value is found there, the head node (pointed to by `aList`) is deleted and the function returns the tail:

```
if (aList->value == value)
{
   ListNode *tail = aList->next;
   delete aList;
   return tail;
}
```

The last case considered is when the list is not empty and the head of the list does not contain the value to be removed. In this case, the function recursively removes the value from the tail of the list, reattaches the original head to the modified tail, and returns a pointer to the head of the (possibly) modified list. Using the same reasoning as in the `add()` function, we can write this case as

```
aList->next = remove(aList->next, value);
return aList;
```

Again putting it all together, we get the complete function as found lines 10–60 of the implementation file `NumberList2.cpp`.

Contents of `NumberList2.cpp`

```
 1 #include "NumberList2.h"
 2 
 3 //*****************************************
 4 // Returns the number of elements in a list *
 5 // ****************************************
 6 int NumberList2::size(ListNode *aList) const
 7 {
 8     if (aList == NULL)
 9         return 0;
10     else
11         return 1 + size(aList->next);
12 }
13 
14 //*****************************************
15 // Prints all elements stored in a list     *
16 //*****************************************
17 void NumberList2::displayList(ListNode *aList) const
```

```
{
    if (aList != NULL)
    {
        cout << aList->value << "  ";
        displayList(aList->next);
    }
}
//*********************************************
// Adds a value at the end of a list           *
//*********************************************
NumberList2::ListNode *NumberList2::add(ListNode *aList, double value)
{
    if (aList == NULL)
        return new ListNode(value);
    else
    {
        // Add the value to the end of the tail
        aList->next = add(aList->next, value);
        return aList;
    }
}

NumberList2::ListNode *NumberList2::remove(ListNode *aList, double value)
{
    if (aList == NULL) return NULL;
    // The list is not empty

    // See if value is first on the list
    // If so, delete the value and return the tail
    if (aList->value == value)
    {
       ListNode *tail = aList->next;
       delete aList;
       return tail;
    }
    else
    {
        // value is not the first on the list
        // Return the list with the value removed
        // from the tail of the list
        aList->next = remove(aList->next, value);
        return aList;
    }
}

NumberList2::~NumberList2()
{
   ListNode *ptr = head;
   while (ptr != NULL)
```

```
    {
        // Point to the node to be deleted
        ListNode *garbage = ptr;
        // Go on to the next node
        ptr = ptr->next;
        // Delete the current node
        delete garbage;
    }
}
```

The following program demonstrates the use of these member functions.

Program 17-8

```
// This program demonstrates the recursive member
// functions of the NumberList2 class.
#include "NumberList2.h"

int main()
{
    NumberList2 list;
    double number;
    list.add(23);
    list.add(17);
    list.add(59);
    cout << "The members of the list are: ";
    list.displayList();
    cout << "\n";
    cout << "Enter a number to add: ";
    cin >> number;
    list.add(number);
    cout << "The members of the list are: ";
    list.displayList();
    cout << "\n";
    cout << "Enter a number to remove: ";
    cin >> number;
    list.remove(number);
    cout << "The members of the list are: ";
    list.displayList();
    cout << "\n";
    return 0;
}
```

Program Output with Example Input Shown in Bold

```
The members of the list are: 23  17  59
Enter a number to add: 89
The members of the list are: 23  17  59  89
Enter a number to remove: 17
The members of the list are: 23  59  89
```

17.5 Variations of the Linked List

CONCEPT: There are many ways to link dynamically allocated data structures together. Two variations of the linked list are the doubly linked list and the circular linked list.

The linked list examples that we have discussed are *singly linked lists*: Each node is linked to a single other node. A variation of this is the *doubly linked list*. In this type of list, each node not only points to the next node, but also to the previous one. This is illustrated in Figure 17-14.

Figure 17-14

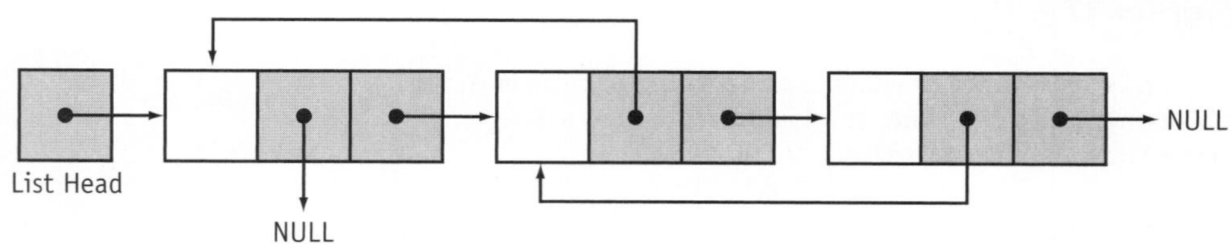

In Figure 17-14, the last node and the first node in the list have pointers to the NULL address. When the program traverses the list it knows when it has reached either end.

Another variation is the *circular linked list*. The last node in this type of list points to the first, as shown in Figure 17-15.

Figure 17-15

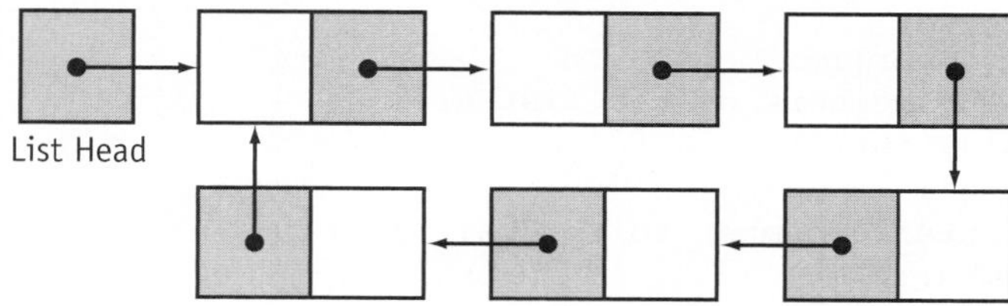

17.6 The STL `list` Container*

CONCEPT: The Standard Template Library provides a linked list container.

The `list` container, found in the Standard Template Library, is a template version of a doubly linked list. STL `lists` can insert elements or add elements within the list more quickly than vectors can, because lists do not have to shift the other elements. Lists are also efficient at adding elements at their back because they have a built-in pointer to the last element in the list (no traversal required).

* Note: This section should be skipped if Chapter 16 has not yet been covered.

Table 17-1 describes some of the list member functions.

Table 17-1 Selected List Member Functions

Member Function	Examples and Description
back	`cout << list.back() << endl;` The back member function returns a reference to the last element in the list.

erase	`list.erase(iter);`
	`list.erase(firstIter, lastIter)`
	The first form causes the list element pointed to by the iterator iter to be removed. The second form causes all of the list elements from firstIter to lastIter to be removed.

empty	`if (list.empty())` The empty member function returns true if the list is empty. It returns false if the list has elements.
end	`iter = list.end();` end returns an iterator to the end of the list.
front	`cout << list.front() << endl;` front returns a reference to the first element of the list.
insert	`list.insert(iter, x)` The insert member function inserts an element into the list. The example inserts an element with the value x, just before the element pointed to by iter.
merge	`list1.merge(list2);` The merge member function expects both list1 and list2 to be already sorted. Every element of list2 will be inserted into list1 in such a way that the expanded list1 remains sorted.
pop_back	`list.pop_back();` pop_back removes the last element of the list.
pop_front	`list.pop_front();` pop_front removes the first element of the list.
push_back	`list.push_back(x);` push_back inserts an element with value x at the end of the list.
push_front	`list.push_front(x);` push_front inserts an element with value x at the beginning of the list.
reverse	`list.reverse();` reverse reverses the order in which the elements appear in the list.
size()	Returns the number of elements in the list.
swap	`list1.swap(list2)` The swap member function swaps the elements stored in two lists. For example, assuming list1 and list2 are lists, the statement shown will exchange the values in the two lists.
unique	`list.unique();` unique eliminates duplicate values by removing any element that has the same value as the element before it.

Program 17-9 demonstrates some simple operations with the STL lists.

Program 17-9

```
// This program demonstrates the STL list container.
#include <iostream>
#include <list>     // Include the list header
using namespace std;

int main()
{
   list<int> myList;
   list<int>::iterator iter;

   // Add values to the list
   for (int x = 0; x < 100; x += 10)
      myList.push_back(x);

   // Display the values
   for (iter = myList.begin(); iter != myList.end(); iter++)
      cout << *iter << " ";
   cout << endl;

   // Now reverse the order of the elements
   myList.reverse();

   // Display the values again
   for (iter = myList.begin(); iter != myList.end(); iter++)
      cout << *iter << " ";
   cout << endl;
   return 0;
}
```

Program Output

```
0 10 20 30 40 50 60 70 80 90
90 80 70 60 50 40 30 20 10 0
```

17.7 Reliable Software Systems, Inc., Case Study

Problem Statement

Reliable Software Systems, Inc., writes and markets C++ class libraries for use by programmers worldwide. One of the company's products is a library package that includes the `NumberList` class introduced in Section 2 of this chapter. Its customers need to use the class in programs in which copies and assignment of `NumberList` objects will occur. You have been asked to modify the class to support a copy constructor and an assignment operator.

Planning for the Changes and Class Design

At least two functions need to be added to the `NumberList` class. Rather than modifying the original class, you opt to use inheritance to create a new class with the requested enhancements. Both copy constructor and assignment need to make a copy of the linked list of nodes inside of the `NumberList` object being copied. To avoid duplication of code, we will add a member function

```
ListNode *copyList(ListNode *aList);
```

that creates and returns a distinct copy of a list of nodes. In addition, the assignment operator, when applied as in the statement

```
x = y;
```

will need to deallocate storage allocated to the linked list in the `NumberList` object `x`. Accordingly, we add a member function

```
void destroyList(ListNode *aList);
```

to the class. The result of this design work is the `ReliableNumberList` class shown in the listing of the `ReliableNumberList.h` file.

Contents of `ReliableNumberList.h`

```
 1 #include "numberlist.h"
 2 
 3 class ReliableNumberList : public NumberList
 4 {
 5 public:
 6     // Copy constructor
 7     ReliableNumberList(const ReliableNumberList& original);
 8     // Now we need a default constructor
 9     ReliableNumberList(){}
10     // Assignment operator
11     ReliableNumberList& operator=(ReliableNumberList right);
12 private:
13     static ListNode* copyList(ListNode *aList);
14     static void destroyList(ListNode *aList);
15 };
```

We have added a default constructor (Line 9) to allow lists that are initially empty to be created. Notice that the auxiliary functions `copyList` and `destroyList` are declared static. This is because they are generic utility functions that do not require access to specific `NumberList` objects to do their job.

Implementation of Class Member Functions

We adopt a recursive strategy for implementing `copyList` and `destroyList`. If a list is empty, `copyList` returns `NULL`. If a list is not empty, then the function creates a copy of the head node, attaches it to recursively created copy of the tail, and returns the resulting list.

Consider now the working of `destroyList`. There is nothing to destroy if the argument list is empty. If the argument list is nonempty, the function recursively destroys the tail and then deallocates the storage for the head node. The coding details for both `copyList` and `destroyList` can be seen in the listing of `ReliableNumberList.cpp` that follows.

Having the `copyList` function makes writing the copy constructor almost trivial: the constructor simply copies the linked list in the existing object and assigns the result to the head pointer of the object being created:

```
head = copylist(original.head);
```

Coding the assignment operator is not much harder. The operator first deallocates the storage for the linked list in the calling object and then assigns a copy of the list in its right operand to the head member of the calling object.

```
destroyList(head);
head = copyList(right.head);
```

You can find the full implementation details and an illustration of the use of this new class in the following listing.

Contents of `ReliableNumberList.h`

```
#include "reliablenumberlist.h"

//***********************************************
// Copy constructor                             *
//***********************************************
ReliableNumberList::
ReliableNumberList(const ReliableNumberList& original)
{
    head = copyList(original.head);
}

//************************************************
// Overloaded Assignment operator                *
//************************************************
ReliableNumberList&
ReliableNumberList::operator=(ReliableNumberList right)
{
    // First destroy the linked list in this object
    destroyList(head);
    // Assign a copy of the linked list in other object
    head = copyList(right.head);
}

//************************************************
// Make a separate copy of the linked list inside *
// a ReliableNumberList object                   *
//************************************************
NumberList::ListNode *
ReliableNumberList::copyList(ListNode *aList)
{
    if (aList == NULL)
        return NULL;
    else
```

```
    {
        // First copy the tail
        ListNode *tailCopy = copyList(aList->next);
        // Return copy of head attached to copy of tail
        return new ListNode(aList->value, tailCopy);
    }
}

//*************************************************
// Destroy a list by deallocating all of its nodes   *
//*************************************************
void ReliableNumberList::destroyList(ListNode *aList)
{
   if (aList != NULL)
   {
      ListNode *tail = aList->next;
      // Deallocate the head and then destroy the tail
      delete aList;
      destroyList(tail);
   }
}
```

Program 17-10

```
// This program demonstrates the copy constructor
// and assignment operator added to NumberList.
#include "reliablenumberlist.h"
int main()
{
    ReliableNumberList squareList, cubeList;
    // Store values in the two lists
    for (int k = 1; k <= 5; k++)
    {
        squareList.add(k*k);
        cubeList.add(k*k*k);
    }

    // Use copy constructor to create a third list
    ReliableNumberList otherList(squareList);
    cout << "Result of the copy constructor is:  ";
    otherList.displayList();
    cout << endl;

    // Use the assignment operator
    otherList = cubeList;
    cout << "Result of assignment is:            ";
    otherList.displayList();
    cout << endl;
    return 0;
}
```

(program continues)

Program 17-10 *(continued)*

Program Output

```
Result of the copy constructor is:  1   4   9   16   25
Result of assignment is:            1   8   27  64   125
```

17.8 Tying It All Together: *More on Graphics and Animation*

In previous chapters you learned how to use text-based graphics to draw and animate simple geometric shapes like straight lines, rectangles, and triangles. The techniques you learned can be extended to more complex shapes and figures.

Before you can draw a shape, you must determine the screen coordinates of the characters that will form both its outline and interior. For example, consider the slanted line segment shown in Figure 17-16.

Figure 17-16

```
*
 *
  *
   *
```

The line starts at (0, 0) and ends at (3, 3) and is drawn by placing asterisks at the screen coordinates (0, 0), (1, 1), (2, 2), and (3, 3).

Representing Shapes with Image Maps

More generally, a figure or shape may consist of several parts. Each of the individual parts making up the figure may be a line segment, a geometric shape such as a rectangle or triangle, or some other type of shape. It is convenient to use an array of coordinates to specify a part of a multi-part figure, and then combine the arrays into a single list that defines the whole figure. We use the term *image map* to refer to the list of coordinates that specifies a shape to be drawn.

Let us design the class that will be used to represent image maps. An image map is a list of coordinates, so we make the class a subclass of the STL type `list<COORD>`. In addition, we define a member function

```
void add(COORD coordArray[]);
```

to allow us to add an array of coordinates to the list. We mark the end of the coordinate array by storing a `COORD` value of $(-1, -1)$ as the last element of the array.

Here is a preliminary declaration of an `ImageMap` class:

```
class ImageMap: list<COORD>
{
public:
    // Add an array of coordinates to the image map
    void add(COORD coordArray[])
```

```
        {
            for(int k = 0; coordArray[k].X != -1; k++)
            {
               push_back(coordArray[k]);
            }
        }
    }
```

As an example, the line from (0, 0) to (3, 3) would be represented by the code

```
ImageMap line;
COORD lineCoords[] = {{0,0}, {1,1}, {2,2}, {3,3}, {-1,-1}};
line.add(lineCoords);
```

Initializing an array of coordinates in this manner and then adding it to the image map is very handy and is a vast improvement over the alternative of using `push_back` to add the coordinates to the image map one at a time:

```
ImageMap line;
COORD pos;
pos.X = 0;
pos.Y = 0;
line.push_back(pos);
pos.X = 1;
pos.Y = 1;
line.push_back(pos);
// Rest of the code is omitted
```

The braces { } that go around a single COORD object in the initialization of the `lineCoords` array are tedious to insert, particularly when the array has a lot of elements. We will therefore consider an alternative notation for initializing the image map. The alternative will allow us to use an array of short integers to initialize an array of coordinates.

An array of two short integers and a `COORD` object both consist of two short integers and C++ compilers store both in memory the *same way*. Once stored in memory, an array of `5 COORD` objects is indistinguishable from an array of 10 short integers. If we write

```
short int lineShorts[] = {0, 0, 1, 1, 2, 2, 3, 3, -1, -1};
```

then the array `lineShorts` is indistinguishable from `lineCoords` in the way the two arrays are stored in memory. We can use this fact to find an alternative way of initializing image maps that does not require as many braces. We add a second `add` member function to `ImageMap`, one that takes an array of `short int` as a parameter. The new `add` function uses a cast to convert its parameter to an array of COORD and then calls the first `add` function.

```
void add(short *coordAsShorts)
{
    COORD *pCoord = reinterpret_cast<COORD *>(coordAsShorts);
    add(pCoord);
}
```

It will help you to understand why this code works if you remember that an array of `COORD`, which is what the member function `add(COORD arr[])` expects, has the same type as a pointer to `COORD`.

Basics of Animation

Now consider a video game in which a person has to run across the screen. The effect of running will be achieved by creating image maps of a person in successive running position as in Figure 17-17.

Figure 17-17

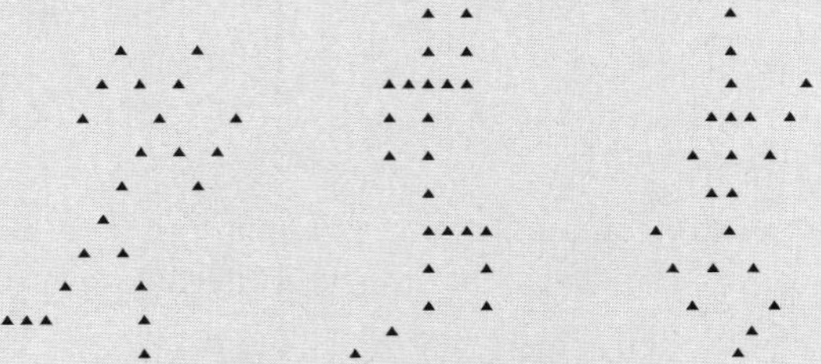

The first image is displayed briefly at a certain position and then erased. Next, the second image is briefly displayed a little to the right of the first position and then erased. By successively displaying and erasing a progression of images at a series of positions in left to right order, we obtain the appearance of a person running.

Implementation Details

Once an `ImageMap` object is created, a programmer can use its `add` methods to incrementally build the list of coordinates that comprises the shape. Starting with an empty image map, the programmer can initialize arrays of short integers to represent different parts of the human body. In this way, arms, legs, torsos, and other parts of the body can be represented and added to the image map to form the shape of a complete person. Two additional methods,

```
void displayAt(char ch, int col, int row);
void displayAt(int col, int row);
```

can be used to display the image map's shape at a given position. The first of the two methods specifies a fill character to be used for the outline and interior of the shape. The second is a convenience method—it calls the first display method and passes it the asterisk as fill character. Finally, the method

```
void eraseAt(int col, int row);
```

is used to erase the image map's shape at a specified position. The full implementation of the ImageMap class, and an illustration of its use to achieve graphics animation, are shown in the listings that follow.

Contents of `Imagemap.h`

```
#include <iostream>
#include <list>
#include <windows.h>
using namespace std;

const HANDLE console = GetStdHandle(STD_OUTPUT_HANDLE);
```

```

class ImageMap:list<COORD>{

public:
    // Add an array of coordinates to the image map
    void add(COORD coordArray[]);
    // Convenience method for adding an array of coordinates
    void add(short *coordAsShorts);
    // Display a given character at a specified position
    void displayAt(char ch, int col, int row);
    // Display an asterisk at a given position
    void displayAt(int col, int row)
    {
        displayAt('*', col, row);
    }
    // Erase whatever character is at a given position
    void eraseAt(int col, int row)
    {
        displayAt(' ', col, row);
    }
};
```

Contents of `Imagemap.cpp`

```
#include "ImageMap.h"

//*************************************************
// Adds an array of coordinates to the image map   *
//*************************************************
void ImageMap::add(COORD coordArray[])
 {
    for(int k = 0; coordArray[k].X != -1; k++)
    {
       push_back(coordArray[k]);
    }
}

//**************************************************
// Allows an array of shorts to be converted to     *
// an array of COORD. That simplifies the           *
// initialization process for an image              *
//**************************************************
 void ImageMap::add(short *coordAsShorts)
 {
    COORD *pCoord = reinterpret_cast<COORD *>(coordAsShorts);
    add(pCoord);
 }

 //****************************************************
 // Shows an image at a given position. The image is    *
 // is drawn using the character ch                     *
 //****************************************************
 void ImageMap::displayAt(char ch, int col, int row)
 {
    list<COORD>::iterator iter = this->begin();
    for (; iter != this->end(); iter++)
```

```
    {
        COORD currentPos;
        currentPos.Y = row + iter->Y;
        currentPos.X = col + iter->X;
        SetConsoleCursorPosition(console, currentPos);
        cout << ch << endl;
    }
}
```

Program 17-11

```
// This program illustrates animation using the
// ImageMap class.
#include "ImageMap.h"

int main()
{
     // Figure 1 - a snapshot of a person running
     ImageMap figure1;

     // Set up the coordinates for the various body parts
     // of the person in the first running position
     short int lowerLeg1[] = { 1, 10, 2, 10, 3, 10, -1, -1};
     short int thigh1[] = { 4, 9, 5, 8, 6, 7, 7, 6, -1, -1};
     short int thigh2[] = { 6, 7, 7, 8, 8, 9, -1, -1};
     short int lowerLeg2[] = {8, 10, 8, 11, -1, -1};
     short int torso[] = { 8, 5, 9, 4, 10, 3, 11, 2, -1, -1};
     short int upperArms[] = { 7, 2, 8, 3, 9,
                               4, 10, 5, 11, 6, -1, -1
                            };
     short int foreArm1[] = { 12, 5, 13, 4, -1, -1};
     short int foreArm2[] = {6, 3, 5, 4, -1, -1};
     short int  * figure1AllParts [ ] =
                 {
                  lowerLeg1, lowerLeg2, thigh1, thigh2, torso,
                  upperArms, foreArm1, foreArm2, 0
                 };
     // Add the coordinates that make up the various body
     // parts to the image map for the first running position
     int k = 0;
     for (int k = 0; figure1AllParts[k] != 0; k++)
         figure1.add(figure1AllParts[k]);

     // Figure 2- a snapshot of the person in a
     //  different running position
     ImageMap figure2;
     short int p2LowerLeg1[] = {1, 11, 2, 10, 3, 9, -1, -1};
     short int p2thigh1[] = {3, 9, 3, 8, 3, 7, -1, -1};
     short int p2thigh2[] = {4, 7, 5, 7, 6, 7, -1, -1};
     short int p2LowerLeg2[] = {6, 8, 6, 9, -1, -1};
```

(program continues)

Program 17-11 *(continued)*

```
    short int p2torso[] = {3, 6, 3, 5, 3, 4, 3, 3,
                            3, 2, 3, 1, -1, -1
                          };
    short int p2UpperArms[] = {1, 3, 2, 3, 4, 3, 5, 3, -1, -1};
    short int p2foreArm1[] = { 1, 4, 1, 5, -1, -1};
    short int p2foreArm2[] = { 5, 2, 5, 1, -1, -1};
    short int *figure2AllParts[] =
              {
                p2LowerLeg1, p2thigh1, p2thigh2, p2LowerLeg2,
                p2torso, p2UpperArms, p2foreArm1, p2foreArm2, 0
               };
    for (int k = 0; figure2AllParts[k] != 0; k++)
        figure2.add(figure2AllParts[k]);

    // Figure 3- a snapshot of a person in
    // yet another running position
    ImageMap figure3;
    short int p3torso[] = {4, 7, 4, 6, 4, 5, 4, 4,
                            4, 3, 4, 2, 4, 1, -1, -1
                          };
    short int p3Thigh1[] = {5, 8, 6, 9, -1, -1};
    short int p3Thigh2[] = {3, 8, 2, 9,  -1, -1};
    short int p3LowerLeg1[] = {6, 10, 6, 11, -1, -1};
    short int p3LowerLeg2[] = {1, 8, 0, 7, -1, -1};
    short int p3UpperArm1[] = {3, 4, 2, 5, -1, -1};
    short int p3UpperArm2[] = {5, 4, 6, 5, -1, -1};
    short int p3ForeArm1[] = {3, 6, 4, 7, -1, -1};
    short int p3ForeArm2[] = {7, 4, 8, 3, -1, -1};
    short int * figure3AllParts[] =
                {
                  p3torso, p3Thigh1, p3Thigh2, p3LowerLeg1,
                  p3LowerLeg2,p3UpperArm1, p3UpperArm2,
                  p3ForeArm1, p3ForeArm2, 0
               };

    for (int k = 0; figure3AllParts[k] != 0; k++)
        figure3.add(figure3AllParts[k]);

    // Ask Microsoft Windows to clear the screen
    system("cls");
    // Form an array of all three figures
    ImageMap *sequence[3] = {&figure1, &figure2, &figure3};

    // Animate to create the appearance of
    // running across the screen
    k = 0;
    int pos = 0;
    while (pos <= 60 )
    {
        // Show the current image at the current position
        sequence[k]->displayAt(pos, 3);
        Sleep(400);
```

(program continues)

Program 17-11 *(continued)*

```
            // Erase the current image
            sequence[k]->eraseAt(pos, 3);
            // Move to next image in the rotation and next position
            k = (k+1) % 3;
            pos = pos + 8;
        }
        sequence[k]->displayAt(pos, 3);
        return 0;
}
```

Review Questions and Exercises

Fill-in-the-Blank

1. The __________ points to the first node in a linked list.
2. A data structure that points to an object of the same type as itself is known as a(n) __________ data structure.
3. To indicate that a linked list is empty, you should set the pointer to its head to the value __________.
4. __________ a node means adding it to the end of a list.
5. __________ a node means adding it to a list, but not necessarily to the end.
6. __________ a list means traveling through the list.
7. In a(n) __________ list, the last node has a pointer to the first node.
8. In a(n) __________ list, each node has a pointer to the one before it and the one after it.

Algorithm Workbench

9. Using the `ListNode` structure introduced in this chapter, write a function

   ```
   void printFirst(ListNode *ptr)
   ```

   that prints the value stored in the first node of a list passed to it as parameter. The function should print an error message and terminate the program if the list passed to it is empty.
10. Write a function

    ```
    void printSecond(ListNode *ptr)
    ```

    that prints the value stored in the second node of a list passed to it as parameter. The function should print an error message and terminate the program if the list passed to it has less than two nodes.
11. Write a function

    ```
    double lastValue(ListNode *ptr)
    ```

    that returns the value stored in the last node of a nonempty list passed to it as parameter. The function should print an error message and terminate the program if the list passed to it is empty.

12. Write a function

```
ListNode *removeFirst(ListNode *ptr)
```

that is passed a linked list as parameter, and returns the tail of the list: that is, it removes the first node and returns what is left. The function should deallocate the storage of the removed node. The function returns NULL if the list passed to it is empty.

13. Write a function

```
ListNode *ListConcat(ListNode *list1, ListNode *list2)
```

That concatenates the items in `list2` to the end of `list1` and returns the resulting list.

Predict the Output

For each of the following program fragments, predict what the output will be.

14.
```
ListNode *p = new ListNode(56.4);
p = new ListNode(34.2, p);
cout << (*p).value <<  endl << p->value;
```

15.
```
ListNode *p = new ListNode(56.4);
p = new ListNode(34.2, p);
ListNode *q = p->next;
cout << q->value;
```

16.
```
ListNode *p = new ListNode(56.4, new ListNode(31.5));
ListNode *q = p;
while (q->next->next != NULL)
q = q->next;
cout << q->value;
```

Find the Errors

17. Each of the following member functions for performing an operation on a linked list of type `NumberList` has at least one error. Explain what is wrong and how to fix it.

A)
```
NumberList::printList( )
{
   while(head)
   {
      cout << head->value;
      head = head->next;
   }
}
```

B)
```
NumberList::printList( )
{
   ListNode *p = head;
   while (p->next)
   {
      cout << p->value;
      p = p->next;
   }
}
```

C)
```
NumberList::printList( )
{
   ListNode *p = head;
   while(p)
   {
      cout << p->value;
      p++;
   }
}
```

D)
```
NumberList::~NumberList()
{
   ListNode *nodePtr, *nextNode;

   nodePtr = head;
   while (nodePtr != NULL)
   {
      nextNode = nodePtr->next;
      nodePtr->next = NULL;
      nodePtr = nextNode;
   }
}
```

Soft Skills

18. You are the leader of a programming team. You want the programmers on your team to attend a two-day workshop on linked lists, stacks, and queues. One of the managers points out that the STL already supplies each one of those data structures, making it unnecessary for your programmers to write their own. Write the manager a short memo that justifies the need for the workshop.

Programming Challenges

1. Simple Linked List Class

Using an appropriate definition of `ListNode`, design a simple linked list class with only two member functions and a default constructor:

```
void add(double x);
boolean isMember(double x);
LinkedList( );
```

The `add` function adds a new node containing `x` to the front (head) of the list, while the `isMember` function tests to see if the list contains a node with the value `x`. Test your linked list class by adding various numbers to the list and then testing for membership.

2. List Copy Constructor

Modify your list class of Programming Challenge 1 to add a copy constructor. Test your class by making a copy of a list and then testing membership on the copy.

3. List Print

Modify the list class you created in the previous programming challenges to add a `print` member function. Test the class by starting with an empty list, adding some elements, and then printing the resulting list out.

4. Recursive Member Check

Modify the list class you created in the previous programming challenges to use a recursive method to check for list membership. Test your class.

5. List Member Deletion

Modify the list class you created in the previous programming challenges by adding a function to remove an item from the list, and by adding a destructor:

```
void remove(double x);
~LinkedList();
```

Test the class by adding by a sequence of instructions that mixes operations for adding items, removing items, and printing the list.

6. List Reverse

Modify the list class you created in the previous programming challenges by adding a member function for reversing the list:

```
void reverse();
```

The member function rearranges the nodes in the list so that their order is reversed. You should do this without creating or destroying nodes.

7. List Search

Modify the list class of Programming Challenge 1 (or later) to include a member function

```
int search(double x)
```

that returns the position of a number `x` on the list. The first node in the list is at position 0, the second node is at position 1, and so on. If `x` is not found on the list, the search should return −1. Test the new member function using an appropriate driver program.

8. Member Insertion By Position

Modify the list class you created in the previous programming challenges by adding a member function for inserting a new item at a specified position:

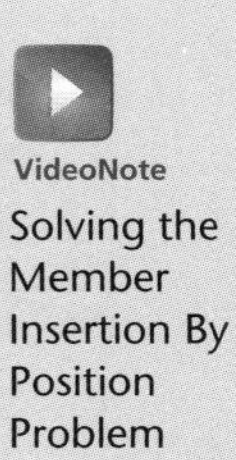

Solving the Member Insertion By Position Problem

```
void insert(double x, int pos);
```

A position of `0` means that `x` will become the first item on the list, a position of 1 means that `x` will become the second item on the list, and so on. A position equal to, or greater than, the length of the list means that the `x` is placed at the end of the list.

9. Member Removal by Position

Modify the list class you created in the previous programming challenges by adding a member function for deleting a node at a specified position:

```
void remove(int pos);
```

A value of 0 for the position means that the first node on the list (the current head) is deleted. The function does nothing if the value passed for `pos` is greater or equal to the length of the list.

10. List Sort

Modify the list class you created in the previous programming challenges by adding a member function that will sort the list into ascending order by the numeric value of the item stored in the node.

```
void sort(  );
```

You should sort the list by moving pointers rather than by copying or swapping the contents of the nodes.

11. Generation of Subsets

Adopt the following strategy to construct the list of all subsets of the set of the integers 1, 2, . . . n. Use an STL vector to represent a single subset of integers, and use an STL list of vectors to represent a list of subsets. Start with a list L_0 of one empty vector; then L_0 represents the list of all subsets of the empty set. Now suppose that you have created the list L_{k-1} of all subsets of 1, 2, . . ., k–1. To form the list L_k of all subsets of 1, 2, . . . k create an empty list L, and then for each vector v in L_{k-1}, add both v and $v + [k]$ to L. Finally, set L_k to L. (Here by $v + [k]$ we mean the result of adding the integer k to the vector v.) Test your program for all values of $n \leq 4$.

12. Recursive Generation of Subsets

Solve the problem of Programming Challenge 11 by using recursion. Do this by writing a recursive function that takes an integer parameter n and returns a list of all subsets of the set 1, 2 . . . , n.

13. Running Back

Program 17-11 makes a person run from across the screen, starting near the left edge of the screen and ending near the right edge. Modify the program so that the person turns around and runs back to the starting point.

CHAPTER

18 Stacks and Queues

TOPICS

18.1 Introduction to the Stack ADT

CONCEPT: A stack is a data structure that stores and retrieves items in a last-in-first-out manner.

Definition

Like an array or a linked list, a stack is a data structure that holds a sequence of elements. Unlike arrays and lists, however, stacks are *last-in-first-out (LIFO)* structures. This means that when a program retrieves elements from a stack, the last element inserted into the stack is the first one retrieved (and likewise, the first element inserted is the last one retrieved).

When visualizing the way a stack works, think of a stack of plates at the beginning of a cafeteria line. When a cafeteria worker replenishes the supply of plates, the first one he or she puts on the stack is the last one taken off. This is illustrated in Figure 18-1.

Figure 18-1

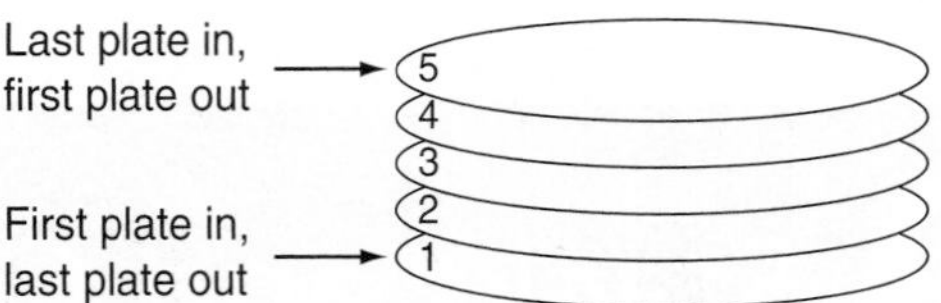

The LIFO characteristic of a stack of plates in a cafeteria is also the primary characteristic of a stack data structure. The last data element placed on the stack is the first data retrieved from the stack.

Applications of Stacks

Stacks are useful data structures for algorithms that work first with the last saved element of a series. For example, computer systems use stacks while executing programs. When a function is called, they save the program's return address on a stack. They also create local variables on a stack. When the function terminates, the local variables are removed from the stack and the return address is retrieved. Also, some calculators use a stack for performing mathematical operations.

Static and Dynamic Stacks

There are two types of stack data structure: static and dynamic. Static stacks have a fixed size and are implemented as arrays. Dynamic stacks grow in size as needed and are implemented as linked lists. In this section you will see examples of both static and dynamic stacks.

Stack Operations

A stack has two primary operations: *push* and *pop*. The push operation causes a value to be stored, or pushed onto the stack. For example, suppose we have an empty integer stack that is capable of holding a maximum of three values. With that stack we execute the following push operations.

```
push(5);
push(10);
push(15);
```

Figure 18-2 illustrates the state of the stack after each of these push operations.

Figure 18-2

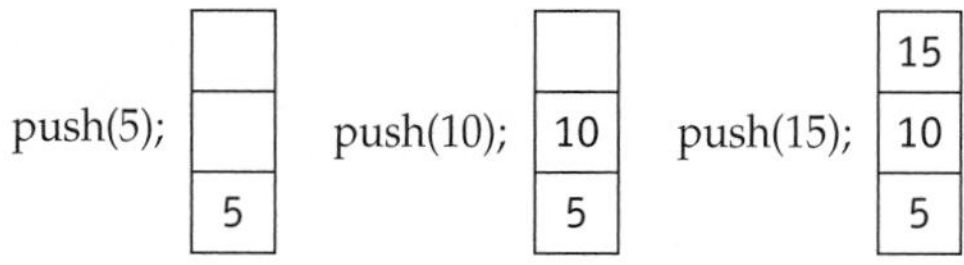

The pop operation retrieves (and hence, removes) a value from the stack. Suppose we execute three consecutive pop operations on the stack shown in Figure 18-2. Figure 18-3 depicts the results.

Figure 18-3

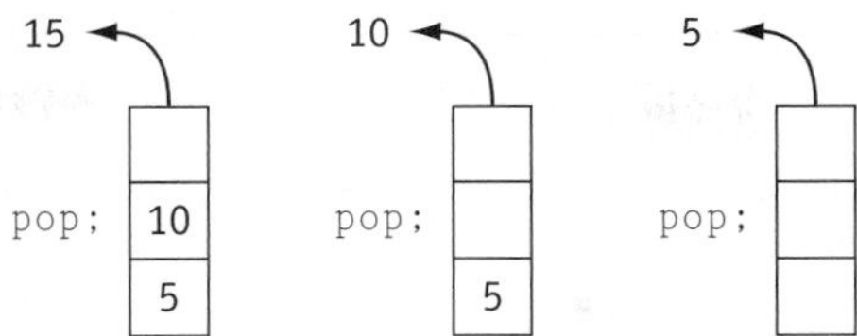

As you can see from Figure 18-3, the last pop operation leaves the stack empty.

For a static stack (one with a fixed size), we will need a Boolean *isFull* operation. The isFull operation returns true if the stack is full and false otherwise. This operation is necessary to prevent a stack overflow in the event a push operation is attempted when all the stack's elements have values stored in them.

For both static and dynamic stacks we will need a Boolean *isEmpty* operation. The isEmpty operation returns true when the stack is empty and false otherwise. This prevents an error from occurring when a pop operation is attempted on an empty stack.

A Static Stack Class

Now we examine a class `IntStack` that stores a static stack of integers and performs the stack operations we have discussed. The class has the member variables described in Table 18-1.

Table 18-1 Members Variables of the Stack Class

Member Variable	Description
`stackArray`	A pointer to `int`. When the constructor is executed, it uses `stackArray` to dynamically allocate an array for storage.
`capacity`	An integer that holds the size of the stack. This is the maximum number of elements the stack can hold, not the number of elements currently in the stack.
`top`	An integer that is used to mark the top of the stack. It specifies the position of the next item that will be added to the stack.

The class's member functions are listed in Table 18-2.

Table 18-2 Members Functions of the Stack Class

Member Functions	Description
Constructor	The class constructor accepts an integer argument, which specifies the size of the stack. An integer array of this size is dynamically allocated and assigned to `stackArray`. Also, the variable `top` is initialized to 0 to indicate that the stack is currently empty.
`push`	The `push` function accepts an integer argument, which is pushed onto the top of the stack.
`pop`	The `pop` function uses an integer reference parameter. The value at the top of the stack is removed and copied into the reference parameter.
`isEmpty`	Returns `true` if the stack is empty, and `false` otherwise. The stack is empty when `top` is set to 0.

> **NOTE:** Even though the constructor dynamically allocates the stack array, it is still considered a static stack since the size of the stack does not change once it is allocated.

The code for the class is shown here:

Contents of `IntStack.h`

```
class IntStack
{
private:
     int *stackArray;
     int capacity;
     int top;
public:
     IntStack(int capacity);  // Constructor
     ~IntStack() { delete[] stackArray; }
     void push(int value);
     void pop(int &value);
     bool isEmpty() const;

     // Stack Exceptions
     class Overflow {};
     class Underflow {};
};
```

In addition to the members of the stack described in Table 18-2, the `IntStack` class defines two inner classes named `Overflow` and `Underflow` to be used as stack exceptions. Exceptions are covered in Chapter 16, but we will briefly explain them here for the benefit of those who may have skipped that chapter. A section of code is said to cause an *exception* when, in the course of execution, it encounters conditions that make it impossible to perform the task the code was designed to do. In the case of a static stack, an *overflow* exception occurs during a call to `push` if there is no more room on the stack. Likewise, an *underflow* exception occurs in a call to `pop` if there is nothing on the stack for `pop` to return.

Code that detects the occurrence of an exception can notify the rest of the program by creating a value that describes the exception and passing that value to the rest of the program using a `throw` statement. For example, the `push` function announces the occurrence of an overflow exception by executing the statement

```
throw InstStack::Overflow();
```

and the `pop` function executes the statement

```
throw IntStack::Underflow();
```

to notify the program that the underflow exception has occurred. By default, a program terminates with an error message when any part of it throws an exception. This default behavior can be changed through a process known as catching the exception. You can learn more about exceptions in Chapter 16.

The `IntStack` constructor allocates an array of a specified capacity and sets the member variable `top` to 0. All stack functions use `top` in such a way that it always points to the next available slot in the stack's array. When `top` equals `capacity`, there are no more slots available to store values, and the next call to `push` throws an exception. Likewise, when `top` is zero, the stack is empty and a call to `pop` throws an exception. Because there are no provisions in the program to catch either exception, the occurrence of either one will terminate the program with an error message. Notice that `push` increments `top` after adding a value to the stack, and `pop` decrements `top` before returning the value stored at `stackArray[top]`.

Contents of `IntStack.cpp`

```
#include "intstack.h"
//************************************
// Constructor                       *
//************************************
IntStack::IntStack(int capacity)
{
     this->capacity = capacity;
     stackArray = new int[capacity];
     top = 0;
}

//***********************************
// Adds a value to the stack        *
//***********************************
void IntStack::push(int value)
{
     if (top == capacity) throw IntStack::Overflow();
     stackArray[top] = value;
     top++;
}

//****************************************
// Determines whether the stack is empty *
//****************************************
bool IntStack::isEmpty() const
{
     if (top == 0)
         return true;
     else
         return false;
}

//************************************************
// Removes a value from the stack and returns it *
//************************************************
void IntStack::pop(int &value)
{
     if (isEmpty()) throw IntStack::Underflow();
     top --;
     value = stackArray[top];
}
```

Program 18-1 illustrates the stack class and its member functions. Notice that the values pushed onto the stack come off in reverse order when they are popped.

Program 18-1

```
// This program illustrates the IntStack class.
#include "intstack.h"
#include <iostream>
using namespace std;
int main()
{
    IntStack  stack(5);
    int values[] = {5, 10, 15, 20, 25};
    int value;

    cout << "Pushing...\n";
    for (int k = 0; k < 5; k++)
    {
        cout << values[k] << "  ";
        stack.push(values[k]);
    }
    cout << "\nPopping...\n";
    while (!stack.isEmpty())
    {
        stack.pop(value);
        cout << value << "  ";
    }
    cout << endl;
    return 0;
}
```

Program Output

```
Pushing...
5  10  15  20  25
Popping...
25  20  15  10  5
```

In Program 18-1, the constructor is called with the argument 5. This sets up the member variables, as shown in Figure 18-4. Since `top` is set to 0, the stack is empty.

Figure 18-4

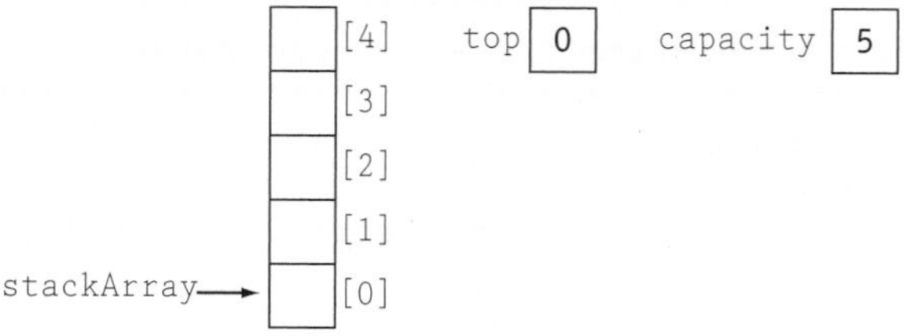

Figure 18-5 shows the state of the member variables after the `push` function is called the first time (with 5 as its argument). The value of `top` is now 1.

Figure 18-5

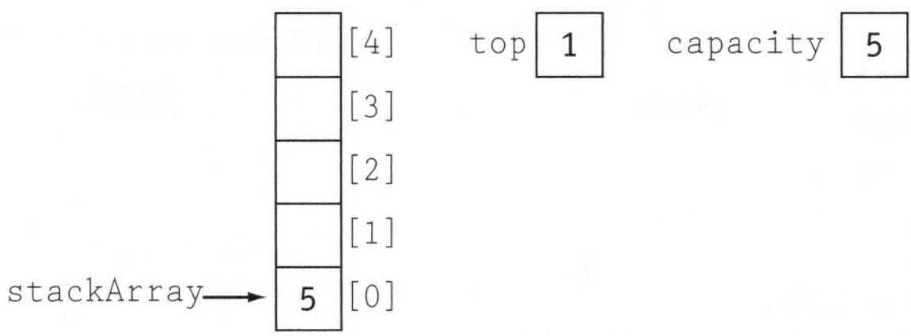

Figure 18-6 shows the state of the member variables after all five calls to the `push` function. Now `top` has value 5, and the stack is full.

Figure 18-6

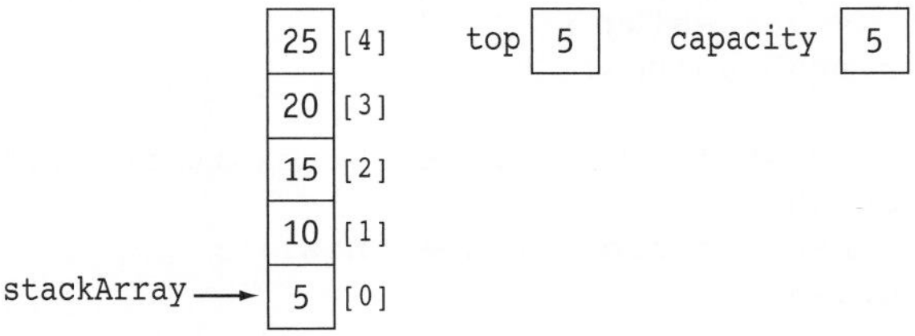

Notice that the `pop` function uses a reference parameter, `value`. The value that is popped off the stack is copied into `value` so it can be used later in the program. Figure 18-7 depicts the state of the class members and the `value` parameter, just after the first value is popped off the stack.

Figure 18-7

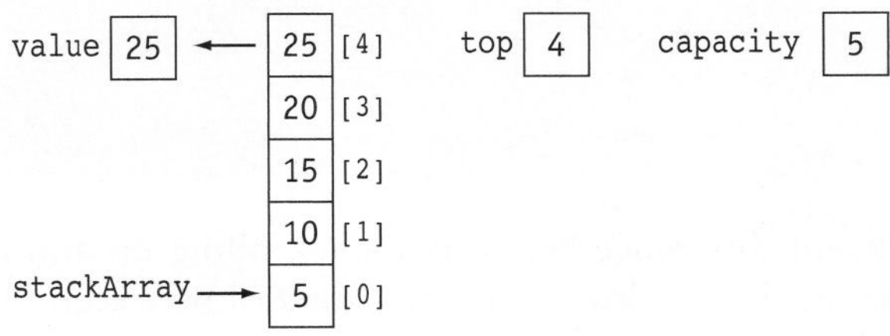

The program continues to call the `pop` function until all the values have been removed from the stack.

Handling Stack Exceptions

As you learned in Chapter 16, the C++ `try/catch` statement can be used to catch and recover from exceptions, thereby allowing the program to avoid being terminated. The following program shows how a program using the `IntStack` class can catch the exceptions that it throws. The program tries to store in the stack more values than the stack can handle, causing push to throw the `Overflow` exception. The main function catches the exception and prints an explanatory error message.

Program 18-2

```
// This program illustrates IntStack exception handling.
#include "intstack.h"
#include <iostream>
using namespace std;
int main()
{
    IntStack  stack(5);
    int values[] = {5, 10, 15, 20, 25};
    int value;
    try
    {
        cout << "Pushing...\n";
        for (int k = 0; k < 5; k++)
        {
            cout << values[k] << "  ";
            stack.push(values[k]);
        }
        cout << "\nPushing value after stack is full..";
        stack.push(30);
        cout << "\nYou should not see this!!";
        cout << endl;
    }
    catch(IntStack::Overflow)
    {
        cout << "\nAn Overflow exception occurred.\n";
    }
    return 0;
}
```

Program Output

```
Pushing...
5  10  15  20  25
Pushing value after stack is full..
An Overflow exception occurred.
```

There is a significant difference between a stack filling up and a stack becoming empty, and between the stack overflow and stack underflow exceptions. In stack overflow, a program has a value to push on a stack, but cannot continue execution because the stack is full. There is a sense in which overflow is unexpected, because a program does not normally expect to use up every slot in the stack. On the other hand, programs are usually written to remove and process all items stored on a stack, so they do expect that the stack will eventually become empty. Indeed, most algorithms that use a stack have a loop that continues to iterate as long as the stack is not empty. This is why a stack always needs an `isEmpty` function, but does not need an `isFull` function. A well-written stack-based algorithm will normally call `isEmpty` to make sure the stack is not empty before calling `pop`.

The difference between overflow and underflow can be summarized as follows. Stack overflow in `push` notifies the caller that the stack has run out of resources, while stack underflow notifies the caller of an error in the program's logic. Unlike overflow, stack underflow can be avoided by careful programming. Therefore, programs should not use `try/catch` to handle underflow. Instead, they should ensure that underflow cannot occur by calling `isEmpty` before calling `pop`.

Stack Templates

The stack classes shown in this chapter work only with integers. A stack template can be easily designed to work with any data type. This is left as a Programming Challenge for you to complete.

18.2 Dynamic Stacks

CONCEPT: A stack may be implemented as a linked list and expand or shrink with each push or pop operation.

A dynamic stack is built on a linked list instead of on an array. A stack based on a linked list offers two advantages over a stack based on an array. First, there is no need to specify the starting size of the stack. A dynamic stack simply starts as an empty linked list, then expands by one node each time a value is pushed. Second, a dynamic stack will never be full, as long as the system has enough free memory.

In this section we will look at a dynamic stack class, `DynIntStack`. This class is a dynamic version of the `IntStack` class previously discussed. The class declaration is shown here:

Contents of `DynIntStack.h`

```
#ifndef DYNINTSTACK_H
#define DYNINTSTACK_H

class DynIntStack
{
private:
   class StackNode
   {
      friend class DynIntStack;
      int value;
      StackNode *next;
      // Constructor
      StackNode(int value1, StackNode *next1 = NULL)
       {
         value = value1;
         next = next1;
       }
   };
   StackNode *top;
public:
   DynIntStack() { top = NULL; }
```

```
      void push(int);
      void pop(int &);
      bool isEmpty() const;
   };
   #endif
```

The `StackNode` class is the data type of each node in the linked list. Because it is easy to add and remove items at the beginning of the list, we make the beginning of the linked list the *top* of the stack and use a pointer `top` to point to the first node in the list. This pointer is initialized to NULL by the stack constructor, to signify that the stack is created empty.

The member functions of this stack class are shown here:

Contents of `DynIntStack.cpp`

```
#include <iostream>
#include "DynIntStack.h"
using namespace std;

//***************************************************
// Member function push pushes the argument onto    *
// the stack.                                       *
//***************************************************
void DynIntStack::push(int num)
{
   top = new StackNode(num, top);
}

//******************************************************
// Member function pop removes the value at the top    *
// of the stack and copies it into the variable        *
// passed as an argument.                              *
//******************************************************
void DynIntStack::pop(int &num)
{
   StackNode *temp;

   if (isEmpty())
   {
      cout << "The stack is empty.\n";
      exit(1);
   }
   else   // Pop value off top of stack
   {
      num = top->value;
      temp = top;
      top = top->next;
      delete temp;
   }
}

//******************************************************
// Member function isEmpty returns true if the stack   *
// is empty, or false otherwise.                       *
//******************************************************
```

```
bool DynIntStack::isEmpty() const
{
   if (!top)
       return true;
   else
       return false;
}
```

The push function is particularly simple. It simply creates a new node whose value is the number to be pushed on the stack and whose successor pointer is the node that is currently the top of the stack, and then makes the newly created node the new top of the stack:

```
top = new StackNode(num, top);
```

Note that this works correctly even if the stack was empty previous to the push operation, because in that case the successor to the new node at the top of the stack will be correctly set to NULL.

Now let's look at the pop function. Just as the push function must insert nodes at the head of the list, pop must delete nodes at the head of the list. First, the function calls `isEmpty` to determine whether there are any nodes in the stack. If not, an error message is displayed, and the program is terminated.

```
if (isEmpty())
{
   cout << "The stack is empty.\n";
   exit(1);
}
```

If `isEmpty` returns `false`, then the following statements are executed.

```
else   // Pop value off top of stack
{
   num = top->value;
   temp = top;
   top = top->next;
   delete temp;
}
```

First, a copy of the `value` member of the node at the top of the stack is saved in the `num` reference parameter. A temporary pointer `temp` is then set to point to the node that is to be deleted, that is, the node currently at the top of the stack. The `top` pointer is then set to point to the node after the one that is currently at the top. The same code will set `top` to NULL if there are no nodes after the one that is currently at the top of the stack. It is then safe to delete the top node through the temporary pointer.

Program 18-3 is a driver that demostrates the `DynIntStack` class.

Program 18-3

```
// This program demonstrates the dynamic stack
// class DynIntStack.
#include <iostream>
#include "DynIntStack.h"
using namespace std;

```

(program continues)

Program 18-3 *(continued)*

```
int main()
{
   DynIntStack stack;
   int catchVar;

   cout << "Pushing 5\n";
   stack.push(5);
   cout << "Pushing 10\n";
   stack.push(10);
   cout << "Pushing 15\n";
   stack.push(15);

   cout << "Popping...\n";
   stack.pop(catchVar);
   cout << catchVar << endl;
   stack.pop(catchVar);
   cout << catchVar << endl;
   stack.pop(catchVar);
   cout << catchVar << endl;

   cout << "\nAttempting to pop again... ";
   stack.pop(catchVar);
   return 0;
}
```

Program Output

```
Pushing 5
Pushing 10
Pushing 15
Popping...
15
10
5

Attempting to pop again... The stack is empty.
```

18.3 The STL `stack` Container*

CONCEPT: The Standard Template Library offers a stack template that may be implemented as a **`vector`**, a **`list`**, or a **`deque`**.

So far, the STL containers you have learned about are `vector`s and `list`s. The STL `stack` container may be implemented as a `vector` or a `list`. (It may also be implemented as a `deque`, which you will learn about later in this chapter.) One class is said to *adapt* another

* This section should be skipped if Chapter 16 has not yet been covered.

class if it provides a new interface for it. The purpose of the new interface is to make it more convenient to use the class for specialized tasks. Because the `stack` container is used to adapt the list, vector, and deque containers, it is often referred to as a *container adapter.*

Here are examples of how to declare a stack of `int`s, implemented as a `vector`, a `list`, and a `deque`.

VideoNote
Storing Objects in an STL Stack

```
stack< int, vector<int> > iStack; // Vector stack
stack< int, list<int> > iStack     // List stack
stack< int > iStack;               // Deque stack (the default)
```

> **NOTE:** Be sure to put spaces between the angled brackets that appear next to each other. This will prevent the compiler from mistaking >> for the stream extraction operator, >>.

Table 18-3 lists and describes some of the stack template's member functions.

Table 18-3 STL Stack Member Fiunctions

Member Function	Examples and Description
`empty`	`if (myStack.empty())` The `empty` member function returns `true` if the stack is empty. It returns `false` if the stack has elements.
`pop`	`myStack.pop();` The pop function removes the element at the top of the stack.
`push`	`myStack.push(x);` The `push` function pushes an element with the value `x` onto the stack.
`size`	`cout << myStack.size() << endl;` The `size` function returns the number of elements currently in the stack.
`top`	`x = myStack.top();` The `top` function returns a reference to the element at the top of the stack.

> **NOTE:** The pop function in the stack template does not retrieve the value from the top of the stack, it only removes it. To retrieve the value, you must call the `top` function first.

Program 18-4 is a driver that demonstrates an STL stack implemented as a vector.

Program 18-4

```
// This program demonstrates the STL stack
// container adapter.
#include <iostream>
#include <vector>
#include <stack>
using namespace std;

int main()
```

(program continues)

Program 18-4 *(continued)*

```
{
   stack< int, vector<int> > iStack;

   for (int x = 2; x < 8; x += 2)
   {
      cout << "Pushing " << x << endl;
      iStack.push(x);
   }

   cout << "The size of the stack is ";
   cout << iStack.size() << endl;

   // Print items and pop until the stack is empty
   while (!iStack.empty())
   {
      cout << "Popping " << iStack.top() << endl;
      iStack.pop();
   }
   return 0;
}
```

Program Output

```
Pushing 2
Pushing 4
Pushing 6
The size of the stack is 3
Popping 6
Popping 4
Popping 2
```

Checkpoint

18.1 Describe what LIFO means.

18.2 What is the difference between static and dynamic stacks? What advantages do dynamic stacks have over static stacks?

18.3 What are the two primary stack operations? Describe them both.

18.4 What STL types does the STL stack container adapt?

18.4 Introduction to the Queue ADT

CONCEPT: A queue is a data structure that stores and retrieves items in a first-in-first-out manner.

Definition

Like a stack, a *queue* (pronounced "cue") is a data structure that holds a sequence of elements. A queue, however, provides access to its elements in *first-in, first-out (FIFO)* order. The elements in a queue are processed like customers standing in a grocery checkout line: The first customer in line is the first one served.

Application of Queues

Queue data structures are commonly used in computer operating systems. They are especially important in multiuser/multitasking environments where several users or tasks may be requesting the same resource simultaneously. Printing, for example, is controlled by a queue because only one document may be printed at a time. A queue is used to hold print jobs submitted by users of the system, while the printer services those jobs one at a time.

Communications software also uses queues to hold information received over networks and dial-up connections. Sometimes information is transmitted to a system faster than it can be processed, so it is placed in a queue when it is received.

Static and Dynamic Queues

Queues, like stacks, can be implemented as arrays or linked lists. Dynamic queues offer the same advantages over static queues that dynamic stacks offer over static stacks. In fact, the primary difference between queues and stacks is the way data elements are accessed in each structure.

Queue Operations

A queue has a front and a rear like a checkout line in a grocery store. This is illustrated in Figure 18-8. When an element is added to a queue, it is added to the rear. When an element is removed from a queue, it is removed from the front. The two primary queue operations are enqueuing and dequeuing. To *enqueue* means to insert an element at the rear of a queue, and to *dequeue* means to remove an element from the front of a queue. There are several algorithms for implementing these operations. We will begin by looking at the simplest.

Figure 18-8

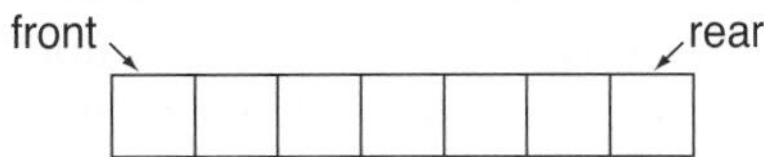

Suppose we have an empty static integer queue that is capable of holding a maximum of three values. With that queue we execute the following enqueue operations:

```
enqueue(3);
enqueue(6);
enqueue(9);
```

Figure 18-9 illustrates the state of the queue after each of these enqueue operations.

Figure 18-9

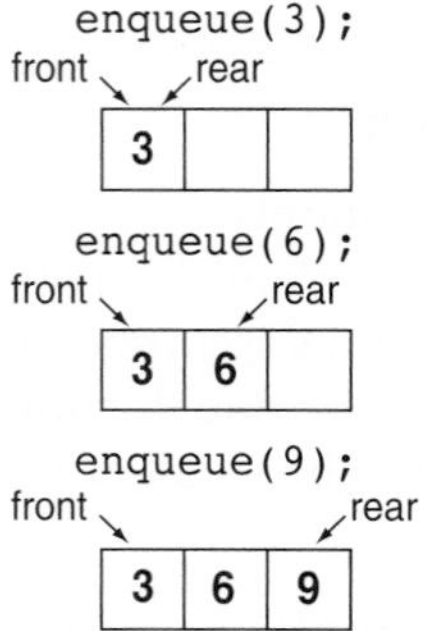

Notice that the front index (which is a variable holding a subscript or perhaps a pointer) always references the same physical element. The rear index moves in the array as items are enqueued. Now let's see how dequeue operations are performed. Figure 18-10 illustrates the state of the queue after each of three consecutive dequeue operations.

Figure 18-10

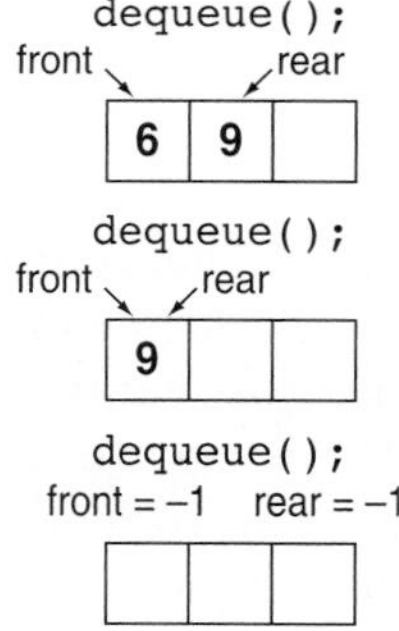

In the dequeuing operation, the element at the front of the queue is removed. This is done by moving all the elements after it forward by one position. After the first dequeue operation, the value 3 is removed from the queue and the value 6 is at the front. After the second dequeue operation, the value 6 is removed and the value 9 is at the front. Notice that when only one value is stored in the queue, that value is at both the front and the rear.

When the last dequeue operation is performed in Figure 18-10, the queue is empty. An empty queue can be signified by setting both front and rear indices to –1.

The problem with this algorithm is its inefficiency. Each time an item is dequeued, the remaining items in the queue are copied forward to their neighboring element. The more items there are in the queue, the longer each successive dequeue operation will take.

Here is one way to overcome the problem: Make both the front and rear indices move in the array. As before, when an item is enqueued, the rear index is moved to make room for it. But in this design, when an item is dequeued, the front index moves by one element toward the rear of the queue. This logically removes the front item from the queue and eleminates the need to copy the remaining items to their neighboring elements.

With this approach, as items are added and removed, the queue gradually “crawls” toward the end of the array. This is illustrated in Figure 18-11. The shaded squares represent the queue elements (between the front and rear).

Figure 18-11

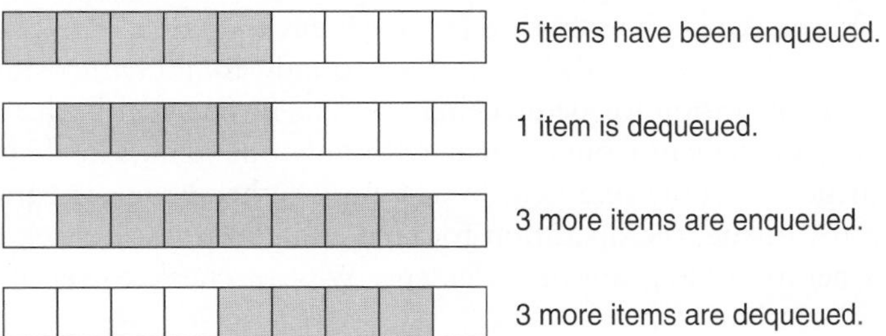

The problem with this approach is that the rear index cannot move beyond the last element in the array. The solution is to think of the array as circular instead of linear. When an item moves past the end of a circular array, it simply wraps around to the beginning. For example, consider the queue depicted in Figure 18-12.

Figure 18-12

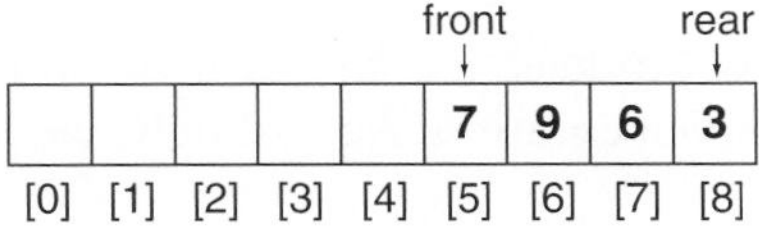

The value 3 is at the rear of the queue, and the value 7 is at the front of the queue. Now, suppose an enqueue operation is performed, inserting the value 4 into the queue. Figure 18-13 shows how the rear of the queue wraps around to the beginning of the array.

Figure 18-13

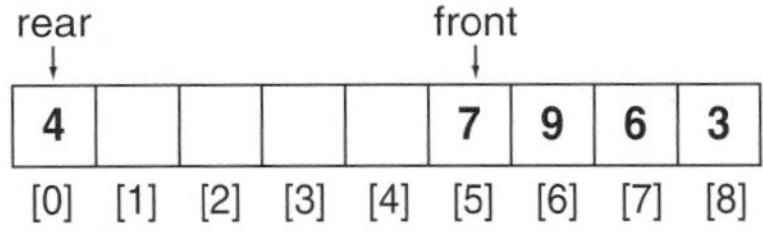

So, what is the code for wrapping the rear marker around to the opposite end of the array? One straightforward approach is to use an `if` statement such as

```
if (rear == queueSize - 1)
   rear = 0;
else
   rear++;
```

Another approach is with modular arithmetic:

```
rear = (rear + 1) % queueSize;
```

This statement uses the `%` operator to adjust the value in `rear` to the proper position. Although this approach appears more elegant, the choice of which code to use is yours.

Detecting Full and Empty Queues with Circular Arrays

In our implementation of a queue using a circular array, we have adopted the convention that the front and rear indices both reference items that are *still in the queue*, and that the front and rear indices will both be set to –1 to indicate an *empty* queue. To preserve this convention, the operation for dequeueing an element must set both `front` and `rear` to –1 after removing an element from a queue with only one item. The dequeuing operation can test for a queue with only one item by testing whether `front` is equal to `rear`. To avoid overflowing the queue, the operation for enqueuing must first check that the queue is not already full before adding another element. We can check to see if the queue is full by testing the expression

```
(rear + 1) % queueSize == front
```

to see if it is true.

There is another way for detecting full and empty queues: A counter variable can be used to keep a count of the number of items currently stored in the queue. With this convention, the counter is incremented with each enqueue operation and decremented with each dequeue operation. The queue is empty when the counter is zero and is full when the counter equals the size allocated for the queue.

Because it might be helpful to keep a count of items in the queue anyway, we will use the second method in our implementation. Accordingly, we introduce the variables

```
int *queueArray;
int queueSize;
int front;
int rear;
int numItems;
```

with `numItems` being the counter variable, and `queueArray` the pointer to a dynamically allocated array of size `queueSize`. We adopt the following two conventions:

- `rear` points to the place in the queue holding the item that was last added to the queue.
- `front` points to the place in the queue that used to hold the item that was last removed from the queue.

Because of the convention on where the rear index is pointing to, the enqueue operation must first (circularly) move `rear` one place to the right before adding a new item `num`:

```
rear =  (rear + 1) % queueSize;
queueArray[rear] = num;
numItems ++;
```

Similarly, because whatever is at `front` has already been removed, the dequeue operation must first move `front` before retrieving a queue item.

A Static Queue Class

The declaration of the `IntQueue` class is as follows:

Contents of `IntQueue.h`

```
#ifndef INTQUEUE_H
#define INTQUEUE_H

class IntQueue
{
private:
   int *queueArray;
   int queueSize;
   int front;
   int rear;
   int numItems;
public:
   IntQueue(int);
   ~IntQueue();
   void enqueue(int);
   void dequeue(int &);
   bool isEmpty() const;
   bool isFull() const;
   void clear();
};
#endif
```

Notice that in addition to the operations discussed in this section, the class also declares a member function named `clear`. This function clears the queue by resetting the `front` and `rear` indices and setting the `numItems` member to 0. The member function definitions are listed here:

Contents of `IntQueue.cpp`

```
#include <iostream>
#include "IntQueue.h"
using namespace std;

//*************************
// Constructor.           *
//*************************
IntQueue::IntQueue(int s)
{
   queueArray = new int[s];
   queueSize = s;
   front = -1;
   rear = -1;
   numItems = 0;
}

//*************************
// Destructor.            *
//*************************
IntQueue::~IntQueue()
```

```
{
   delete [] queueArray;
}

//********************************************
// Function enqueue inserts the value in num *
// at the rear of the queue.                 *
//********************************************
void IntQueue::enqueue(int num)
{
   if (isFull())
      {
         cout << "The queue is full.\n";
         exit(1);
      }
   else
   {
      // Calculate the new rear position
      rear = (rear + 1) % queueSize;
      // Insert new item
      queueArray[rear] = num;
      // Update item count
      numItems++;
   }
}

//**********************************************
// Function dequeue removes the value at the   *
// front of the queue, and copies it into num. *
//**********************************************
void IntQueue::dequeue(int &num)
{
   if (isEmpty())
   {
      cout << "The queue is empty.\n";
      exit(1);
   }
   else
   {
      // Move front
      front = (front + 1) % queueSize;
      // Retrieve the front item
      num = queueArray[front];
      // Update item count
      numItems--;
   }
}

//*********************************************
// Function isEmpty returns true if the queue *
// is empty, and false otherwise.             *
//*********************************************
bool IntQueue::isEmpty() const
{
   if (numItems > 0)
```

```
      return false;
   else
      return true;
}

//********************************************
// Function isFull returns true if the queue *
// is full, and false otherwise.             *
//********************************************
bool IntQueue::isFull() const
{
   if (numItems < queueSize)
      return false;
   else
      return true;
}

//*******************************************
// Function clear resets the front and rear *
// indices, and sets numItems to 0.         *
//*******************************************
void IntQueue::clear()
{
   front =  - 1;
   rear =  - 1;
   numItems = 0;
}
```

Program 18-5 is a driver that demonstrates the `IntQueue` class.

Program 18-5

```
// This program demonstrates the IntQueue class.
#include <iostream>
#include "IntQueue.h"
using namespace std;

int main()
{
   IntQueue iQueue(5);

   cout << "Enqueuing 5 items...\n";

   // Enqueue 5 items
   for (int k = 1; k <= 5; k++)
      iQueue.enqueue(k*k);

   // Deqeue and retrieve all items in the queue
   cout << "The values in the queue were: ";
   while (!iQueue.isEmpty())
   {
      int value;
```

(program continues)

Program 18-5 *(continued)*

```
        iQueue.dequeue(value);
        cout << value << "   ";
    }
    cout << endl;
    return 0;
}
```

Program Output

```
Enqueuing 5 items...
The values in the queue were: 1  4  9  16  25
```

Overflow and Underflow Exceptions in a Static Queue

The `enqueue` and `dequeue` functions in our queue class terminate the calling program when they cannot perform the task they are called to do. But terminating the caller is not always the right thing to do. A better course of action is to throw an exception and allow the caller who is prepared to handle such an exception to take appropriate action. Upon catching such an exception, some callers may indeed decide to terminate the program. Other callers, however, may be able to recover and continue execution. For example, a program that catches a queue overflow exception might be able to create a bigger queue and switch to the new queue.

A better design for a static queue is to have `enqueue` and `dequeue` throw `overflow` and `underflow` exceptions. Having `enqueue` throw `overflow` eliminates the need for a public `isFull` function because the caller can use a `try/catch` block to handle queue overflows if and when they occur. By putting all calls to `enqueue` within the try block, the caller is able to put the code to handle an exception thrown by any of those calls in a single place: the catch block. Without exception handling, every call to `enqueue` would have to be preceded by a call to `isFull` and have code attached to it to recover in the event that `isFull` returns true. One of the programming challenges at the end of this chapter asks you to modify the queue class to use exceptions.

Dynamic Queues

CONCEPT: A queue may be implemented as a linked list and expand or shrink with each enqueue or dequeue operation.

Dynamic queues, which are built around linked lists, are much more intuitive to understand than static queues. A dynamic queue starts as an empty linked list. With the first enqueue operation, a node is added, which is pointed to by the `front` and `rear` pointers. As each new item is added to the queue, a new node is added to the rear of the list, and the `rear` pointer is updated to point to the new node. As each item is dequeued, front is made to point to the next mode in the list, and then the node that was previously at the front of the list is deleted. Figure 18-14 shows the structure of a dynamic queue.

Figure 18-14

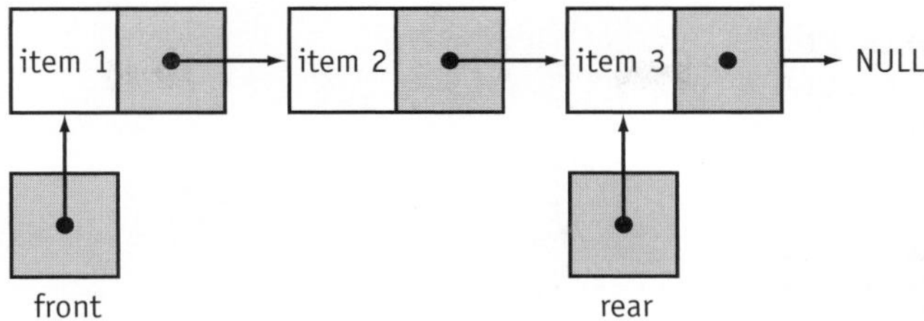

A dynamic integer queue class is listed here:

Contents of `DynIntQueue.h`

```
#ifndef DYNINTQUEUE_H
#define DYNINTQUEUE_H

class DynIntQueue
{
private:
   class QueueNode
   {
      friend class DynIntQueue;
      int value;
      QueueNode *next;
      QueueNode(int value1, QueueNode *next1 = NULL)
      {
         value = value1;
         next = next1;
      }
   };
   // These track the front and rear of the queue
   QueueNode *front;
   QueueNode *rear;
public:
   // Constructor and Destructor
   DynIntQueue();
   ~DynIntQueue();

   // Member functions
   void enqueue(int);
   void dequeue(int &);
   bool isEmpty() const;
   void clear();
};
#endif
```

Contents of `DynIntQueue.cpp`

```
#include <iostream>
#include "DynIntQueue.h"
using namespace std;

//***********************
// Constructor.         *
```

```
//************************
DynIntQueue::DynIntQueue()
{
   front = NULL;
   rear = NULL;
}

//************************
// Destructor.           *
//************************
DynIntQueue::~DynIntQueue()
{
   clear();
}

//********************************************
// Function enqueue inserts the value in num *
// at the rear of the queue.                 *
//********************************************
void DynIntQueue::enqueue(int num)
{
   if (isEmpty())
   {
      front = new QueueNode(num);
      rear = front;
   }
   else
   {
      rear->next = new QueueNode(num);
      rear = rear->next;
   }
}

//**********************************************
// Function dequeue removes the value at the   *
// front of the queue, and copies it into num. *
//**********************************************
void DynIntQueue::dequeue(int &num)
{
   QueueNode *temp;
   if (isEmpty())
   {
      cout << "The queue is empty.\n";
      exit(1);
   }
   else
   {
      num = front->value;
      temp = front;
      front = front->next;
      delete temp;
   }
}

//*********************************************
// Function isEmpty returns true if the queue *
```

```
// is empty, and false otherwise.          *
//*****************************************
bool DynIntQueue::isEmpty() const
{
   if (front == NULL)
      return true;
   else
      return false;
}

//*****************************************
// Function clear dequeues all the elements  *
// in the queue.                             *
//*****************************************
void DynIntQueue::clear()
{
   int value;   // Dummy variable for dequeue

   while(!isEmpty())
      dequeue(value);
}
```

Program 18-6 is a driver that demonstrates the `DynIntQueue` class.

Program 18-6

```
// This program demonstrates the DynIntQeue class.
#include <iostream>
#include "DynIntQueue.h"
using namespace std;

int main()
{
   DynIntQueue iQueue;

   cout << "Enqueuing 5 items...\n";

   // Enqueue 5 items
   for (int k = 1; k < = 5; k++)
      iQueue.enqueue(k*k);

   // Dequeue and retrieve all items in the queue
   cout << "The values in the queue were:\n";
   while (!iQueue.isEmpty())
   {
      int value;
      iQueue.dequeue(value);
      cout << value << "  ";
   }
   return 0;
}
```

Program Ouput

```
Enqueuing 5 items...
The values in the queue were:
1  4  9  16  25
```

18.6 The STL deque and queue Containers*

CONCEPT: The Standard Template Library provides two containers, `deque` and `queue`, for implementing queue-like data structures.

In this section we will examine two ADTs offered by the Standard Template Library: `deque` and `queue`. A deque (pronounced "deck" or "deek") is a double-ended queue. It similar to a vector, but allows efficient access to values at both the front and the rear. The queue ADT is like the stack ADT: It is actually a container adapter.

The deque Container

Think of the `deque` container as a vector that provides quick access to the element at its front as well as at the back. (Like vector, deque also provides access to its elements with the `[]` operator.)

Programs that use the deque ADT must include the `deque` header. Since we are concentrating on its queue-like characteristics, we will focus our attention on the `push_back`, `pop_front`, and `front` member functions. Table 18-4 describes them.

Table 18-4 deque Member Functions

Member Function	Examples and Description
`push_back`	`iDeque.push_back(7);` Accepts as an argument a value to be inserted into the `deque`. The argument is inserted after the last element (pushed onto the back of the `deque`).
`pop_front`	`iDeque.pop_front();` Removes the first element of the `deque` and discards it.
`front`	`cout << iDeque.front() << endl;` `front` returns a reference to the first element of the `deque`.

Program 18-7 demonstrates the deque container.

Program 18-7

```
// This program demonstrates the STL deque
// container.
#include <iostream>
#include <deque>
using namespace std;

int main()
{
   deque<int> iDeque;

```

(program continues)

* Note: This section should be skipped if Chapter 16 has not yet been covered.

Program 18-7 *(continued)*

```
   cout << "I will now enqueue items...\n";
   for (int x = 2; x < 8; x += 2)
   {
      cout << "Pushing " << x << endl;
      iDeque.push_back(x);
   }

   cout << "I will now dequeue items...\n";
   while (!iDeque.empty())
   {
      cout << "Popping " << iDeque.front() << endl;
      iDeque.pop_front();
   }
   return 0;
}
```

Program Output

```
I will now enqueue items...
Pushing 2
Pushing 4
Pushing 6
I will now dequeue items...
Popping 2
Popping 4
Popping 6
```

The queue Container Adapter

The queue container adapter can be built upon vectors, lists, or deques. By default, it uses a deque as its base.

VideoNote

Storing Objects in an STL Queue

The insertion and removal operations supported by `queue` are similar to those supported by the stack ADT: `push`, `pop`, and `front`. There are differences in their behavior, however. The queue version of `push` always inserts an element at the rear of the queue. The queue version of `pop` always removes an element from the structure's front. The `front` function returns the value of the element at the front of the queue.

Program 18-8 demonstrates a queue. Since the declaration of the queue does not specify which type of container is being adapted, the queue will be built on a `deque`.

Program 18-8

```
// This program demonstrates the STL queue
// container adapter.
#include <iostream>
#include <queue>
using namespace std;

```

(program continues)

Program 18-8 *(continued)*

```
int main()
{
   queue<int> iQueue;

   cout << "I will now enqueue items...\n";
   for (int x = 2; x < 8; x += 2)
   {
      cout << "Pushing " << x << endl;
      iQueue.push(x);
   }
   cout << "I will now dequeue items...\n";
   while(!iQueue.empty())
   {
      cout << "Popping " << iQueue.front() << endl;
      iQueue.pop();
   }
   return 0;
}
```

Program Output

```
I will now enqueue items...
Pushing 2
Pushing 4
Pushing 6
I will now dequeue items...
Popping 2
Popping 4
Popping 6
```

18.7 Focus on Problem Solving and Program Design: *Eliminating Recursion*

Although recursion is a very useful programming technique, it carries the overhead of the necessity to make numerous function calls during the process of solving the problem. The efficiency of a recursive solution can often be greatly improved by reformulating a recursive algorithm to eliminate the recursion. In this section, we look at how a stack can be used to eliminate recursion from the Quicksort algorithm.

The main problem in Quicksort is that of sorting a *range*, or a segment of an array `arr`, between two indices `start` and `end`. Naturally, this has to be done only if `start` is less than `end`. As learned in Chapter 14, this is accomplished by calling a procedure `partition`, which determines an integer `pivot` such that

1. All array items in the segment to the left of the pivot are less than the element at the pivot: that is,

   `arr[k] < arr[pivot]` for all `k` in the range `start .. pivot-1`

2. All array items in the segment to the right of the pivot are greater than or equal to the element at the pivot: that is,

   `arr[k] >= arr[pivot]` for all `k` in the range `pivot+1..end`

Once this is done, the array item at the pivot is in its sorted position. Thus an important effect of the `partition` procedure is that it gets the pivot element in its final sorted position. By keeping track of the left and right subranges when we call `partition`, and then later calling `partition` on those subranges, we can sort the entire array without using recursion. We need to keep track of these subranges, and eventually partition them in the order in which the recursive calls to Quicksort would have done them. Because the recursive calls to Quicksort are invoked and return in LIFO (last-in-first-out) order, we use a stack to keep track of the ranges that are waiting to be partitioned.

The main idea of our solution is to define a class

```
class Range
{
   int start;
   int end;
public:
   Range(int s, int e)
   {
      start = s;
      end = e;
   }
};
```

to keep track of the ranges of the array that remain to be partitioned. Accordingly, we use the STL stack class to define a stack of these ranges:

```
stack<Range> qStack;
```

We then use a function `qSort(int arr[ ], int size)` that sorts the array `arr` by initially pushing the range from `0` to `size-1` onto the stack, and then repeatedly removing ranges from the stack, partitioning the range, and putting the left and right subrange back onto the stack. Empty subranges removed from the stack are discarded. The algorithm is

```
push Range(0, size-1) onto stack
While stack not empty
   pop  a range r from the stack
   If r is not empty
      partition the range r into two smaller ranges about the pivot
      push the two smaller ranges onto the stack
   End if
End While
```

The complete solution, which reuses the partition function from Chapter 14, is given in Program 18-9. Notice that we declare the `qSort` function to be a friend of `Range`, to allow access to the private members of `Range`.

NOTE: The statement `qStack.push(Range(0, size-1));` creates a `Range` object by invoking the constructor. The `Range` object is then pushed onto the stack.

Program 18-9

```
// This program illustrates the use of a stack to
// implement a nonrecursive quicksort.
#include <stack>
#include <iostream>
#include <fstream>
#include <algorithm>  // Needed for swap
using namespace std;

// Function prototypes
void qSort(int a[ ], int size);
void outputArray(const int a[ ], int size);
int partition(int a[ ], int, int);

// Range is used to indicate a segment
// of an array that is still to be sorted
class Range
{
   // Make qSort a friend
   friend void qSort(int a[], int);
   int start;
   int end;
public:
   Range(int s, int e)
   {
     start = s;
     end = e;
   }
};

const int MAX = 100;
int main()
{
  ifstream inputFile;
  string filename = "sort.dat" ;
    int array[MAX];
  int size;
  inputFile.open(filename.data());
  if (!inputFile)
    {
      cout << "The file  " << filename << " cannot be "
           << "opened .";
      exit(1);
    }

   // Read the file and count the number of items in the
   // file. Take care not to overrun the array
   size = 0;
   while (inputFile >> array[size])
   {
      size ++;
      if (size == MAX)
         break;
   }
```

(program continues)

Program 18-9 *(continued)*

```
   // Echo the inputted array
   cout << "The original array is :" << endl;
   outputArray(array, size);

   // Perform the sort and output the result
   qSort(array, size);
   cout << "The sorted array is: " << endl;
   outputArray(array, size);
   return 0;
}

//*****************************************
// qSort performs a nonrecursive quicksort   *
// on the array a[ ] of the given size       *
//*****************************************
void qSort(int arr[ ], int size)
{
  // qStack holds segments of the array that have not
  // yet been sorted
  stack<Range> qStack;
  int pivot, start, end;

  qStack.push(Range(0, size-1));
  // As long as there is a range waiting to be sorted,
  // take it off the stack, partition it, and then
  // put the resulting two smaller ranges onto the stack
  while (!qStack.empty())
  {
     Range currentRange = qStack.top();
     qStack.pop();

     // Get the endpoints of the current Range
     // and partition it
     start = currentRange.start;
     end = currentRange.end;
     if (start < end)
     {
        pivot = partition(arr, start, end);
        // Store the resulting smaller ranges for later
        // processing
        qStack.push(Range(start, pivot-1));
        qStack.push(Range(pivot + 1, end));
     }
  }
}

//*************************************************
// partition rearranges the entries in the array arr  *
// from start to end so all values greater than or    *
// equal to the pivot are on the right of the pivot    *
// and all values less than are on the left of the     *
// pivot.                                              *
//*************************************************
```

(program continues)

Program 18-9 *(continued)*

```
int partition(int arr[], int start, int end)
{
   // The pivot element is taken to be the element at
   // the start of the subrange to be partitioned
   int pivotValue = arr[start];
   int pivotPosition = start;

   // Rearrange the rest of the array elements to
   // partition the subrange from start to end
   for (int pos = start + 1; pos <= end; pos++)
   {
      if (arr[pos] < pivotValue)
      {
         // arr[scan] is the "current" item.
         // Swap the current item with the item to the
         // right of the pivot element
         swap(arr[pivotPosition + 1], arr[pos]);
         // Swap the current item with the pivot element
         swap(arr[pivotPosition], arr[pivotPosition + 1]);
         // Adjust the pivot position so it stays with the
         // pivot element
         pivotPosition ++;
      }
   }
   return pivotPosition;
}

//***************************************
// Output an array's elements.          *
//***************************************
void outputArray(const int arr[ ], int size)
{
   for (int k = 0; k < size; k++)
     cout << arr[k] << "   ";
   cout << endl;
}
```

Program Output

```
The original array is :
34  -45  78  32  90  45
The sorted array is:
-45  32  34  45  78  90
```

NOTE: The friend concept should be used with caution, since it circumvents the protection afforded the members of the class by declaring them private. Notice that in our case, the `start` and `end` members of the `Range` class are never modified by the friend function `qSort`.

18.8 Tying It All Together: *Converting Postfix Expressions to Infix*

Stacks can be used to evaluate postfix expressions. Let's see how this can be done. We confine ourselves to postfix expressions that contain only numbers and the binary operators +, −, *, and /.

Recall from Chapter 14 that a postfix expression is either a single number or two postfix expressions followed by an operator. Evaluation of a single-number postfix expression is easy: we just return the number. For the nonsimple case, we must evaluate the two postfix expressions in order and save their values. Then, when we come to the operator, we retrieve the two previously saved values and apply the operator.

To see how the method works consider the example

2 5 −

Because 2 and 5 are single-number postfix expressions, we simply save their values for later use. Then, when we encounter the minus operator, we retrieve the two saved values and apply the operator, yielding −3 as the value of the entire expression. In general, any postfix expression can be evaluated by reading it in left to right order. Whenever a value is encountered, it is pushed onto the stack to await application by an operator at a later stage. Whenever an operator is encountered, its two operands are popped off the stack, and the operator is applied to them to yield a value. This value is in turn pushed onto the stack. The procedure ends when all of the input expression has been read. At that time, there should be only one value on the stack. The value on the stack is the value of the postfix expression.

This same idea can be used to convert postfix expressions to infix. Again, we read the input postfix expression from left to right. This time, though, we use a stack of strings instead of a stack of integer. Any number that is read must be an operand: it is converted to a string and pushed onto the stack. If an operator is encountered, the two strings at the top of the stack are popped and the operator is placed between them. Parentheses are then placed around the resulting string, and the parenthesized string is pushed back onto the stack. Thus, for example, the above input postfix expression would result on the following sequence of pushes of strings onto the stack:

```
"2"
"2"     "5"
"(2 – 5)"
```

These ideas are used in Program 18–10, which follows.

Program 18-10

```
// This program converts postfix expressions to infix.
#include <string>
#include <iostream>
#include <sstream>
```

(program continues)

Program 18-10 *(continued)*

```
#include <stack>

using namespace std;

string postfixExpr(istream & inputStream);

int main()
{
    string input;
    cout << "Enter a postfix expression to convert to infix,"
         << " \nor a blank line to quit the program:";
    getline(cin, input);
    while (input.size() != 0)
    {
        // Convert string to a string stream
        istringstream inputExpr(input);
        cout << "The infix equivalent  is "
             << postfixExpr(inputExpr) << endl;
        cout << "Enter a postfix expression to evaluate: ";
        getline(cin, input);
    }
    return 0;
}

//***************************************************************
// Takes an istream that contains a single postfix expression p *
// and returns a string representing the infix equivalent of p  *
//***************************************************************
string postfixExpr(istream & in)
{
   // Holds intermediate values in computation
   stack<string> infixStack;
   // Used to read characters in the expression
   char ch;
   // Used to read numbers in the expression
   int number;
   // Used to remove infix expressions from the stack
   string lExpr, rExpr;

   ch = in.peek();
   while (ch != EOF)
   {
       // If we have a whitespace character skip it and
       // continue with the next iteration of this loop
       if (isspace(ch))
       {
           ch = in.get();
           ch = in.peek();
           continue;  // Go back to top of loop
       }
```

(program continues)

Program 18-10 *(continued)*

```
        // Nonspace character is next in input stream
        // If the next character is a number, read it, convert
        // to string, and push the string onto the infix stack
        if (isdigit(ch))
        {
           in >> number;
           // Use to convert number to string
           ostringstream numberStr;
           // Convert number to string using stream
           numberStr << number;
           // Push the string representing the expression onto the stack
           infixStack.push(numberStr.str());
           ch = in.peek();
           continue;
        }
        // If the next character is an operator,
        // pop the two top infix expresssions stored on the
        // stack, put the operator between the two infix expressions,
        // and then push the result on the stack

        rExpr = infixStack.top();
        infixStack.pop();
        lExpr = infixStack.top();
        infixStack.pop();
        if (ch == '+' || ch == '-' || + ch == '*' || ch == '/')
            infixStack.push("(" + lExpr + " " + ch + " " + rExpr + ")");
        else
        {
            cout << "Error in the input expression" << endl;
            exit(1);
        }
        ch = in.get();  // Actually read the operator character
        ch = in.peek(); // Prepare for the next iteration of the loop
    }
    return infixStack.top();
}
```

Program Output with Example Input Shown in Bold

```
Enter a postfix expression to convert to infix,
or a blank line to quit the program: 56
The infix equivalent  is 56
Enter a postfix expression to evaluate: 56 2 +
The infix equivalent  is (56 + 2)
Enter a postfix expression to evaluate: 56 2 + 12 9 - *
The infix equivalent  is ((56 + 2) * (12 - 9))
Enter a postfix expression to evaluate: [Enter]
```

Review Questions and Exercises

Short Answer

1. What does LIFO mean?
2. What element is retrieved from a stack by the pop operation?
3. What is the difference between a static stack and a dynamic stack?
4. Describe two operations that all stacks perform.
5. The STL `stack` is considered a container adapter. What does that mean?
6. What types may the STL `stack` be based on? By default, what type is an STL `stack` based on?
7. What does FIFO mean?
8. When an element is added to a queue, where is it added?
9. When an element is removed from a queue, where is it removed from?
10. Describe two operations that all queues perform.
11. What two queue-like containers does the STL offer?
12. Suppose the following operations were performed on an empty stack:

    ```
    push(0);
    push(9);
    push(12);
    push(1);
    ```

    Insert numbers in the following diagram to show what will be stored in the static stack after the operations have executed.

    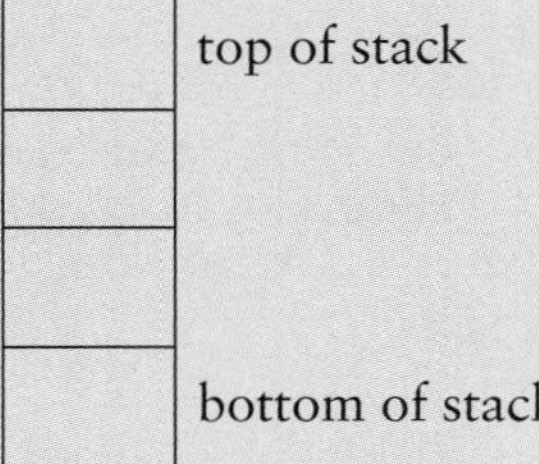

13. Suppose the following operations were performed on an empty stack:

    ```
    push(8);
    push(7);
    pop();
    push(19);
    push(21);
    pop();
    ```

    Insert numbers in the following diagram to show what will be stored in the static stack after the operations have executed.

top of stack

bottom of stack

14. Suppose the following operations are performed on an empty queue:

```
enqueue(5);
enqueue(7);
enqueue(9);
enqueue(12);
```

Insert numbers in the following diagram to show what will be stored in the static queue after the operations have executed.

15. Suppose the following operations are performed on an empty queue:

```
enqueue(5);
enqueue(7);
dequeue();
enqueue(9);
enqueue(12);
dequeue();
enqueue(10);
```

Insert numbers in the following diagram to show what will be stored in the static queue after the operations have executed.

16. What problem is overcome by using a circular array for a static queue?

Algorithm Workbench

17. Give pseudocode that implements a queue using two stacks. The queue operations *enqueue*, *dequeue*, and *empty* must be implemented in terms of the *push*, *pop*, and *empty* stack operations.

Soft Skills

18. A common real-life example used to explain stacks is the stack of plates in a cafeteria. Find at least two other real-life examples in which items are added and removed from a container in last-in-first-out order, and use these examples to explain the concept of a stack.

Programming Challenges

1. Static Stack Template

In this chapter you studied `IntStack`, a class that implements a static stack of integers. Write a template that will create a static stack of any data type. Demonstrate the class with a driver program.

2. Dynamic Stack Template

In this chapter you studied `DynIntStack`, a class that implements a dynamic stack of integers. Write a template that will create a dynamic stack of any data type. Demonstrate the class with a driver program.

3. Static Queue Template

In this chapter you studied `IntQueue`, a class that implements a static queue of integers. Write a template that will create a static queue of any data type. Demonstrate the class with a driver program.

4. Dynamic Queue Template

In this chapter you studied `DynIntQueue`, a class that implements a dynamic queue of integers. Write a template that will create a dynamic queue of any data type. Demonstrate the class with a driver program.

5. Error Testing

The `DynIntStack` and `DynIntQueue` classes shown in this chapter are abstract data types using a dynamic stack and dynamic queue, respectively. The classes do not currently test for memory allocaton errors. Modify the classes so they determine if new nodes cannot be created, and handle the error condition in an appropriate way. (You will need to catch the predefined exception `bad_alloc`.)

NOTE: If you have already done Programming Challenges 2 and 4, modify the templates you created.

6. Dynamic String Queue

Design a class that stores strings on a dynamic queue. The strings should not be fixed in length. Demonstrate the class with a driver program.

7. Queue Exceptions

Modify the static queue class used in Program 18-5 as follows.

1. Make the `isFull` member private.
2. Define a queue *overflow* exception and modify `enqueue` so that it throws this exception when the queue runs out of space.
3. Define a queue *underflow* exception and modify `dequeue` so that it throws this exception when the queue is empty.

4. Rewrite the main program so that it catches overflow exceptions when they occur. The exception handler for queue overflow should print an appropriate error message and then terminate the program.

8. Evaluating Postfix Expressions

Write a program that reads postfix expressions and prints their values. Each input expression should be entered on its own line, and the program should terminate when the user enters a blank line.

Assume only binary operators, and that the expressions contain no variables. Note that you will need to use parentheses to indicate the order of application of the operators in the expression. Here are sample input–output pairs:

```
78                                              78
78 6 +                                          84
78 6 +   9   2 -   /                            12
```

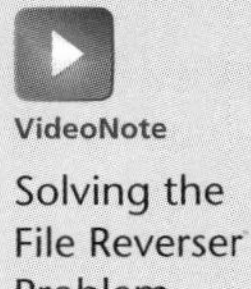

VideoNote

Solving the File Reverser Problem

9. File Reverser

Write a program that opens a text file and reads its contents into a stack of characters. The program should then pop the characters from the stack and save them in a second text file. The order of the characters saved in the second file should be the reverse of their order in the first file.

10. Balanced Parentheses

A string of characters has balanced parentheses if each right parentheses occurring in the string is matched with a preceding left parentheses in the same way each right brace in a C++ program is matched with a preceding left brace. Write a program that uses a stack to determine whether a string entered at the keyboard has balanced parentheses.

11. Balanced Multiple Delimiters

A string may use more than one type of delimiter to bracket information into "blocks." For example, A string may use braces { }, parentheses ( ), and brackets [ ] as delimiters. A string is properly delimited if each right delimiter is matched with a preceding left delimiter of the same type in such a way that the either the resulting blocks of information are disjoint, or one of them is completely nested within the other. Write a program that uses a single stack to check whether a string containing braces, parentheses, and brackets is properly delimited.

12. Stack-based Binary Search

Imitate the technique of Section 18.7 and use a stack to remove recursion from the binary search algorithm.

13. Stack-based Fibonacci Function

Use a stack to remove recursion from the implementation of the Fibonacci function discussed in Section 14.4

CHAPTER 19 Binary Trees

TOPICS

19.1 Definition and Applications of Binary Trees

CONCEPT: Binary trees differ from linked lists in that where a node in a linked list may have at most one successor, a node in a binary tree can have up to two successors.

A *binary tree* is a collection of nodes in which each node is associated with up to two successor nodes, respectively called the *left* and *right child*. Not every node in the binary tree will have two children: one or both nodes may be omitted. A node in a binary tree that has no children is called a *leaf node*.

A node that has children is said to be the *parent* of its children. For a nonempty collection of nodes to qualify as a binary tree, every node must have at most one parent, and there must be exactly one node with no parent. The one node that has no parent is called the *root* of the binary tree. An empty collection of nodes is regarded as constituting an empty binary tree.

There is some similarity between a linked list and a binary tree. The root of a binary tree corresponds to the head of a list, a child of a binary tree node corresponds to a successor node in a list, and the parent of a binary tree node corresponds to the *predecessor* of a node in the list. And of course, the analog of the empty list is the empty binary tree.

Implementation of Binary Trees

Binary trees are used to store values in their nodes. A node in a binary tree will therefore be a structure or class object that contains a member for storing the value, as well as two members that point to nodes that are the left and right children of that node:

```
struct TreeNode
{
   int value;
   TreeNode *left;
   TreeNode *right;
};
```

A binary tree is itself represented by a pointer to the node that is the root of the tree. An example binary tree, with the values stored in the nodes not shown, is illustrated in Figure 19-1. The `left` or `right` pointer in a node is set to NULL if that node does not possess the corresponding child.

Figure 19-1

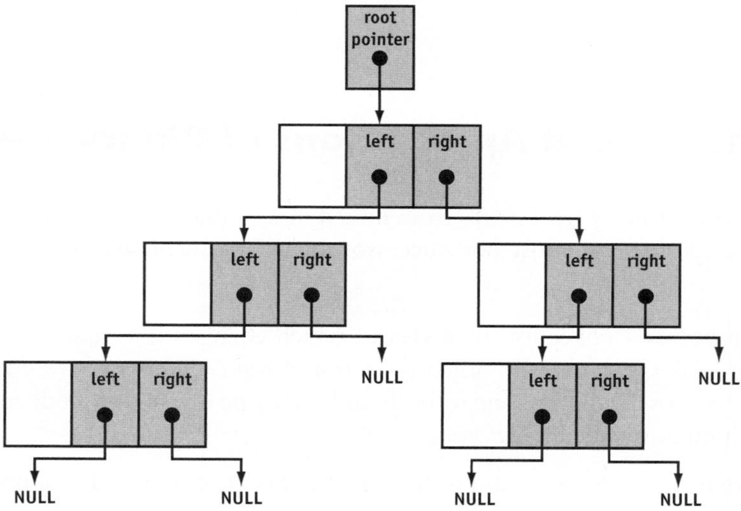

Binary trees are called trees because they resemble an upside-down tree. Any nonempty tree can be partitioned into its root node, its *left subtree*, and its *right subtree*. Intuitively, a subtree is an entire branch of the tree, from one particular node down. Figure 19-2 shows the left subtree of the binary tree shown in Figure 19-1.

Applications of Binary Trees

Searching any linear data structure, such as an array or a standard linked list, is slow when the structure holds a large amount of information. This is because of the sequential nature of linear data structures. Binary trees and their generalizations are excellent data structures for searching large amounts of information. They are commonly used in database applications to organize key values that index database records. When used to facilitate

Figure 19-2

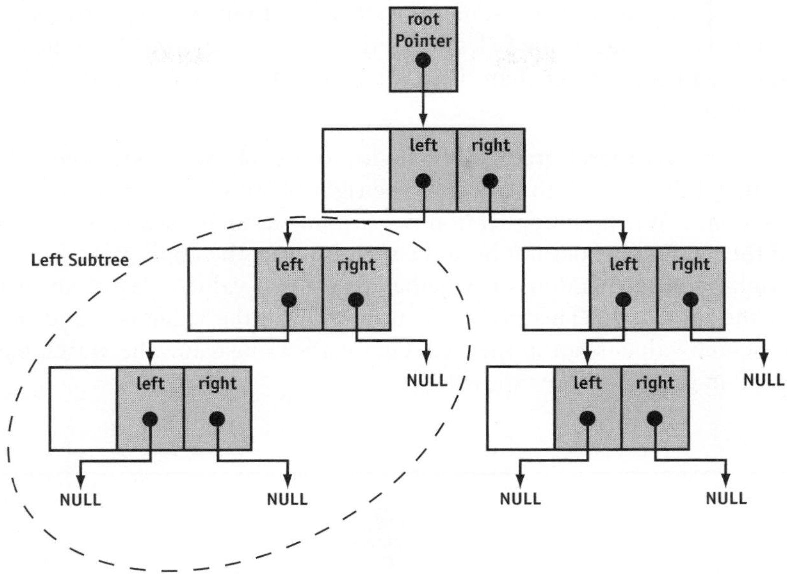

searches, a binary tree is called a *binary search tree*. Binary search trees are the primary focus of this chapter.

Information is stored in binary search trees in a way that makes searching for information in the tree simple. For example, look at Figure 19-3.

Figure 19-3

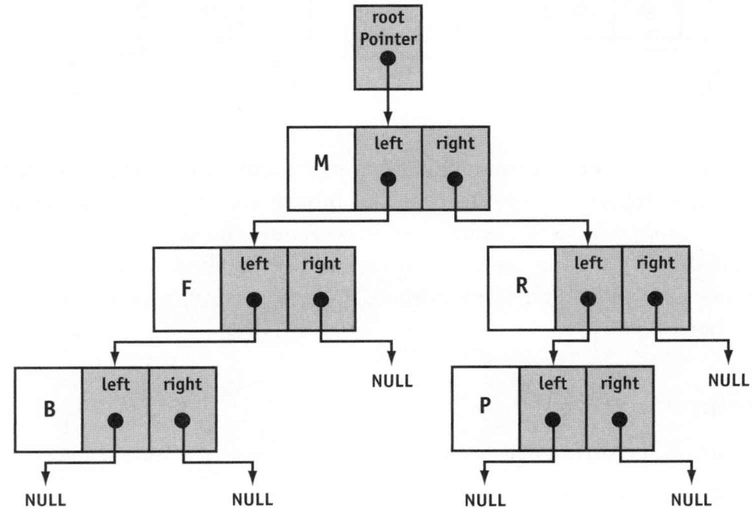

The figure depicts a binary search tree where each node stores a letter of the alphabet. Notice that the root node holds the letter M. The left child of the root node holds the letter F, and the right child holds R. Values are stored in a binary search tree so that a node's left child holds data whose value is less than the node's data, and the node's right child holds data whose value is greater than the node's data. This is true for all nodes in the tree that have children.

In fact, in a binary search tree, *all* the nodes to the left of a node hold values less than the node's value. Likewise, all the nodes to the right of a node hold values that are greater than the node's data. When an application is searching a binary search tree, it starts at the root node. If the root node does not hold the search value, the application branches either to the left or right child, depending on whether the search value is less than or greater than the value at the root node. This process continues until the value is found or it is determined that the search value is not in the tree. Figure 19-4 illustrates the search pattern for finding the letter P in the binary tree shown.

Figure 19-4

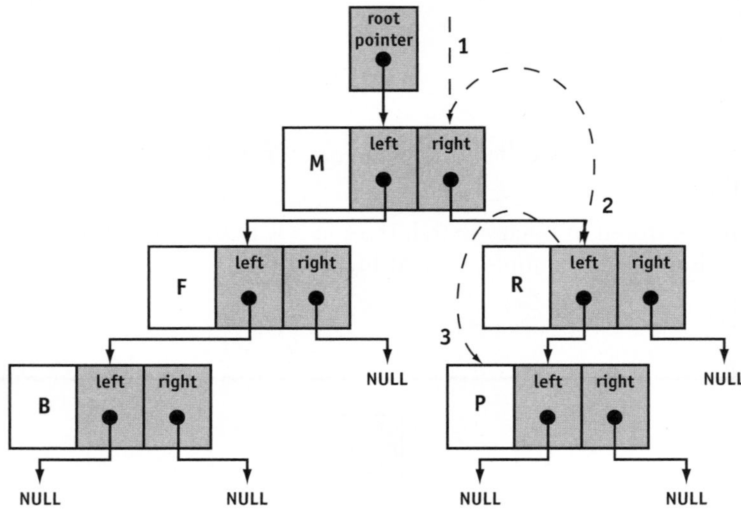

This manner of searching a binary tree is reminiscent of the binary search technique that is used on sorted arrays. Assuming that the binary tree is balanced (meaning that at each node, the left and right subtrees have approximately the same number of nodes), the search will reduce the size of the tree remaining to be searched by one half at each step. This makes it possible to search trees with very large amounts of information in a relatively small number of steps.

Checkpoint

19.1 Describe the difference between a binary tree and a linked list.

19.2 What is a root node?

19.3 What is a child node?

19.4 What is a leaf node?

19.5 What is a subtree?

19.6 Why are binary trees suitable for algorithms that must search large amounts of information?

19.2 Binary Search Tree Operations

CONCEPT: There are many operations that may be performed on a binary search tree, including creating a binary search tree, inserting, finding, and deleting nodes.

In this section you will learn some basic operations that may be performed on a binary search tree. We will study a simple class that implements a binary tree for storing integer values.

Creating a Binary Search Tree

We will demonstrate the fundamental binary tree operations using a simple ADT: the `IntBinaryTree` class. The basis of our binary tree node is the following `class` declaration:

```
class TreeNode
{
   friend class IntBinaryTree;
   int value;
   TreeNode *left;
   TreeNode *right;
   TreeNode(int value1,
          TreeNode *left1 = NULL,
          TreeNode *right1 = NULL
          )
   {
      value = value1;
      left = left1;
      right = right1;
   }
};
```

Notice that each node of the tree has a `value` member, as well as two pointers to keep track of the left and right children of the node. The class will only be used by methods of `IntBinaryTree`, which is declared a friend of `TreeNode` to allow it access to all of the members of `TreeNode`.

The entire `IntBinaryTree` class follows:

Contents of `IntBinaryTree.h`

```
#ifndef INTBINARYTREE_H
#define INTBINARYTREE_H

```

```
class IntBinaryTree
{
private:
   // The TreeNode class is used to build the tree
   class TreeNode
   {
      friend class IntBinaryTree;
      int value;
      TreeNode *left;
      TreeNode *right;
      TreeNode(int value1, TreeNode *left1 = NULL,
                           TreeNode *right1 = NULL)
      {
         value = value1;
         left = left1;
         right = right1;
      }
   };

   TreeNode *root;     // Pointer to the root of the tree

   // Various helper member functions
   void insert(TreeNode *&, int);
   void destroySubtree(TreeNode *);
   void remove(TreeNode *&, int);
   void makeDeletion(TreeNode *&);
   void displayInOrder(TreeNode *) const;
   void displayPreOrder(TreeNode *) const;
   void displayPostOrder(TreeNode *) const;

public:
   // These member functions are the public interface
   IntBinaryTree()      // Constructor
      { root = NULL; }
   ~IntBinaryTree()     // Destructor
      { destroySubtree(root); }
   void insert(int num)
      { insert(root, num); }
   bool search(int) const;
   void remove(int num)
      { remove(root, num);}
   void showInOrder(void) const
      { displayInOrder(root); }
   void showPreOrder() const
      { displayPreOrder(root); }
   void showPostOrder() const
      { displayPostOrder(root); }
};
#endif
```

Besides the `TreeNode` class declaration, the class has a `root` member. This is a pointer to the root node of the binary tree, and plays a role similar to that of the `head` pointer in the linked list class of Chapter 17. In many instances, it is useful to think of the pointer to the node that is the root of a binary tree as the binary tree itself. Thus, we may write

```
TreeNode *tree;
```

or

```
TreeNode *root;
```

and think of both as representing a binary tree because the root provides access to the entire tree. On the other hand, it is also useful to think of an object of the `IntBinaryTree` class as a binary tree, and write

```
IntBinaryTree Tree;
```

To avoid confusion, we will use identifiers with an initial capital letter for a binary tree that is represented by an object of the `IntBinaryTree` class and use identifiers with initial lowercase letters for a binary tree represented by a pointer to its root node.

The public member functions of `IntBinaryTree` include a constructor, a destructor, and member functions for inserting a new number into the tree, for searching a tree to determine whether a given number is in the tree, for removing a number from the tree, and for displaying the numbers stored in the tree according to different orders. All of these member functions are discussed in the sections that follow.

Program 19-1 demonstrates the creation of an `IntBinaryTree` object and the use of the public `insert` member function to build a binary search tree. The implementation code for the member functions are in the `IntBinaryTree.cpp` file; the contents of that file will be discussed later. The tree that results from the execution of Program 19-1 is shown in Figure 19-5.

Program 19-1

```
// This program builds a binary tree with 5 nodes.
#include <iostream>
#include "IntBinaryTree.h"
using namespace std;

int main()
{
   IntBinaryTree tree;

   cout << "Inserting numbers. ";
   tree.insert(5);
   tree.insert(8);
   tree.insert(3);
   tree.insert(12);
   tree.insert(9);
   cout << "Done.\n";
   return 0;
}
```

Figure 19-5

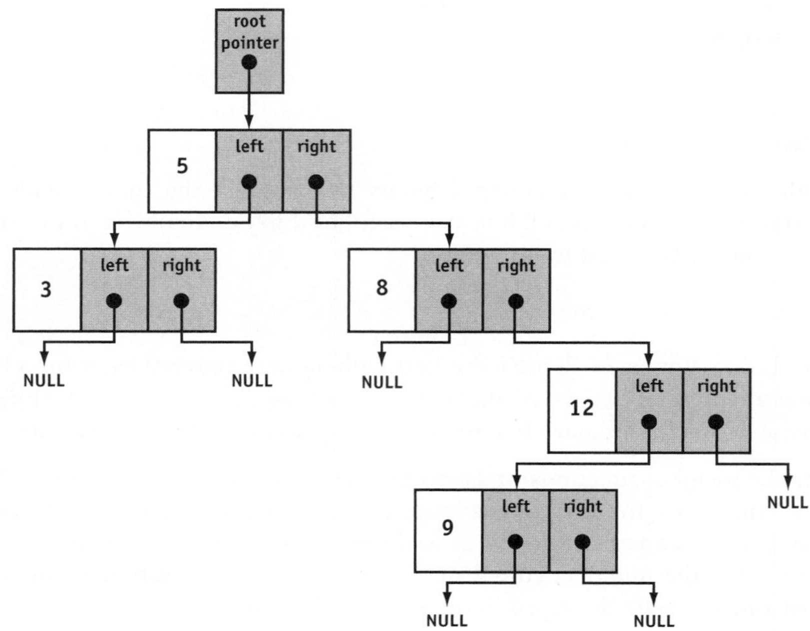

Implementation of the Binary Search Tree Operations

Many binary tree operations have very natural recursive implementations. This is because a binary tree is an inherently recursive data structure: every nonempty binary tree consists of a root node together with the left and right subtrees, which are of course, binary trees. Many binary tree operations can be implemented by performing some processing at the root node and then recursively performing the operation on the left and right subtrees. For example, if the root node is represented by a pointer

```
TreeNode *tree;
```

then the value in the root node will be `tree->value`, and the left and right subtrees will be given by `tree->left` and `tree->right`. A recursive operation might first process `tree->value`, and then the recursively operate on `tree->left` and `tree->right`.

Inserting an Element

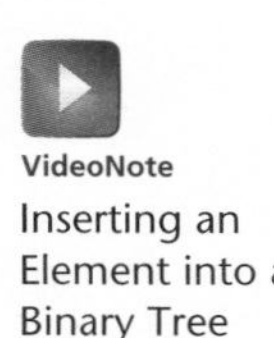

VideoNote
Inserting an Element into a Binary Tree

The work of inserting a number into a binary search tree is performed by the private member function

```
insert(TreeNode *&tree, int num)
```

which is passed a pointer `tree` to the root node of a binary search tree and a number `num` to be inserted into the tree. It uses a recursive strategy: if the binary tree is empty (this is the base case for the recursion), it creates a new `TreeNode` object whose value member is the given number and makes it the root of the tree:

```
if (!tree)
{
   tree = new TreeNode(num);
   return;
}
```

If, however, the binary search tree is not empty, the `insert` function compares `num` to the `tree->value`, the value in the root node. Depending on the outcome of this comparison, the new value is recursively inserted into the left or right subtree:

```
if (num < tree->value)
   insert(tree->left, num);
else
   insert(tree->right, num);
```

The entire function is given here:

```
void IntBinaryTree::insert(TreeNode * &tree, int num)
{
   // If the tree is empty, make a new node and make it
   // the root of the tree
   if (!tree)
      {
        tree = new TreeNode(num);
        return;
      }

   // If num is already in tree: return
   if (tree->value == num)
     return;

   // The tree is not empty: insert the new node into the
   // left or right subtree
   if (num < tree->value)
      insert(tree->left, num);
   else
      insert(tree->right, num);
}
```

Note that the function is passed a reference to a pointer because the pointer passed may need to be modified by the function. This is also the reason the `remove` and `makeDeletion` functions are passed their parameters by reference.

NOTE: The shape of the tree shown in Figure 19-5 is determined by the order in which the values are inserted. The root node holds the value 5 because that was the first value inserted. By stepping through the function, you can see how the other nodes came to appear in their depicted positions.

Traversing the Tree

There are three common methods for traversing a nonempty binary tree and processing the value of each node: *inorder*, *preorder*, and *postorder*. Each of these methods is best implemented as a recursive function. The algorithms are described as follows.

- *Inorder traversal*
  1. The node's left subtree is traversed.
  2. The node's data is processed.
  3. The node's right subtree is traversed.
- *Preorder traversal*
  1. The node's data is processed.
  2. The node's left subtree is traversed.
  3. The node's right subtree is traversed.
- *Postorder traversal*
  1. The node's left subtree is traversed.
  2. The node's right subtree is traversed.
  3. The node's data is processed.

The `IntBinaryTree` class can display all the values in the tree using all three of these algorithms. The algorithms are initiated by the following inline public member functions:

```
void showInOrder(void)
   { displayInOrder(root); }
void showPreOrder()
   { displayPreOrder(root); }
void showPostOrder()
   { displayPostOrder(root); }
```

Each of the public member functions calls a recursive private member function and passes the root pointer as an argument. The recursive functions are very simple and straightforward:

```
void IntBinaryTree::displayInOrder(TreeNode *tree) const
{
   if (tree)
   {
      displayInOrder(tree->left);
      cout << tree->value << "  ";
      displayInOrder(tree->right);
   }
}

void IntBinaryTree::displayPreOrder(TreeNode *tree) const
{
   if (tree)
   {
      cout << tree->value << "  ";
      displayPreOrder(tree->left);
      displayPreOrder(tree->right);
   }
}

void IntBinaryTree::displayPostOrder(TreeNode *tree) const
{
   if (tree)
   {
      displayPostOrder(tree->left);
      displayPostOrder(tree->right);
      cout << tree->value << "  ";
   }
}
```

Program 19-2, which is a modification of Program 19-1, demonstrates each of these traversal methods.

Program 19-2

```
// This program builds a binary tree with 5 nodes.
// The nodes are displayed with inorder, preorder,
// and postorder algorithms.
#include <iostream>
#include "IntBinaryTree.h"
using namespace std;

int main()
{
   IntBinaryTree tree;
   cout << "Inserting the numbers 5 8 3 12 9.\n\n";
   tree.insert(5);
   tree.insert(8);
   tree.insert(3);
   tree.insert(12);
   tree.insert(9);

   cout << "Inorder traversal:  ";
   tree.showInOrder();

   cout << "\n\nPreorder traversal:  ";
   tree.showPreOrder();

   cout << "\n\nPostorder traversal:  ";
   tree.showPostOrder();
   return 0;
}
```

Program Output

```
Inserting the numbers 5 8 3 12 9.

Inorder traversal:  3   5   8   9   12

Preorder traversal:  5   3   8   12   9

Postorder traversal:  3   9   12   8   5
```

Searching the Binary Search Tree

The `IntBinarySearchTree` class has a public member function `search`, which returns `true` if a given value is found in the tree and returns `false` otherwise. The function simply starts out searching the entire tree. The function compares `num`, the value being searched for, to the value in the root of the tree it is currently searching. If the value matches, the function returns `true`. If the value does not match, the function replaces the tree with either its left subtree or its right subtree and continues the search. The search will terminate when the function finds the value or when the tree being searched becomes empty.

```
bool IntBinaryTree::search(int num) const
{
   TreeNode *tree = root;

   while (tree)
   {
      if (tree->value == num)
         return true;
      else if (num < tree->value)
         tree = tree->left;
      else
         tree = tree->right;
   }
   return false;
}
```

Program 19-3 demonstrates this function.

Program 19-3

```
// This program builds a binary tree with 5 nodes.
// The search function determines if the
// value 3 is in the tree.
#include <iostream>
#include "IntBinarytree.h"
using namespace std;

int main()
{
   IntBinaryTree tree;
   cout << "Inserting the numbers 5 8 3 12 9.\n\n";
   tree.insert(5);
   tree.insert(8);
   tree.insert(3);
   tree.insert(12);
   tree.insert(9);

   if (tree.search(3))
      cout << "3 is found in the tree.\n";
   else
      cout << "3 was not found in the tree.\n";
   return 0;
}
```

Program Output

```
Inserting the numbers 5 8 3 12 9.

3 is found in the tree.
```

VideoNote

Removing an Element from a Binary Tree

Removing an Element

To remove an element, we first locate the node containing the element and then delete the node. The procedure for deleting a node X depends on the number of its children. If X has no children, we first find its parent, set the parent's child pointer that links to X to NULL, and then free the memory allocated to X. If X is the root of the tree, the procedure we have just described will not work. In that case, we simply delete X and set the pointer to the root of the tree to NULL.

A procedure for deleting a nonleaf node must ensure that the subtrees that the node links to remain as parts of the tree. The procedure varies according to whether the node being deleted has one or two children. Figure 19-6 shows a tree in which we are about to delete a node with one subtree.

Figure 19-6

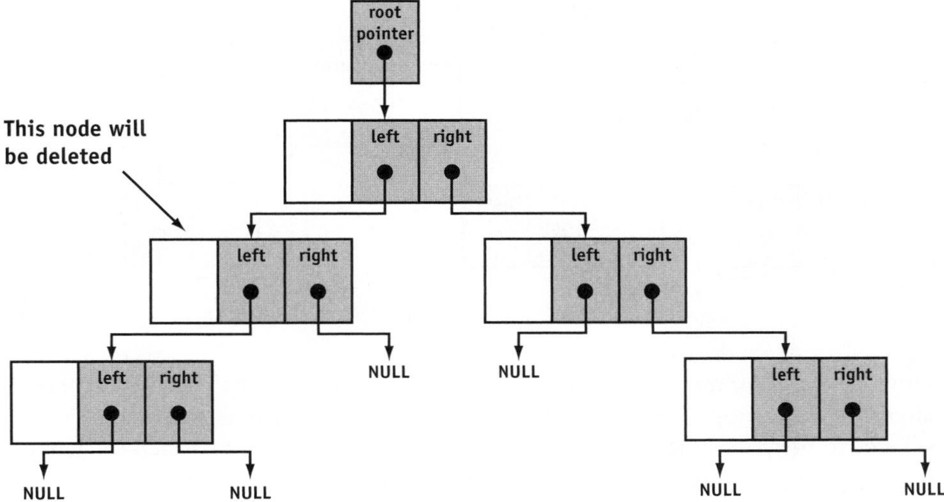

Figure 19-7 shows how we will link the node's subtree with its parent.

Figure 19-7

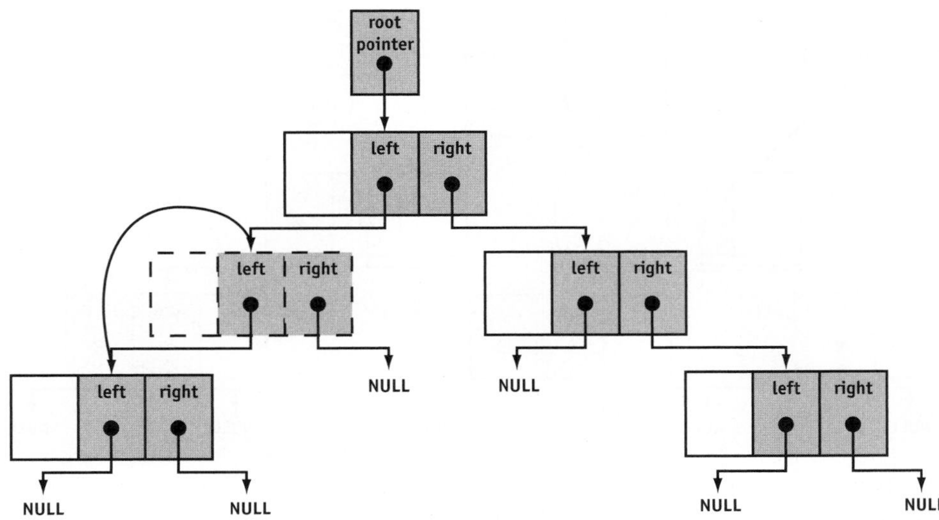

The problem is not as easily solved, however, when the node we are about to delete has two subtrees. For example, look at Figure 19-8.

Figure 19-8

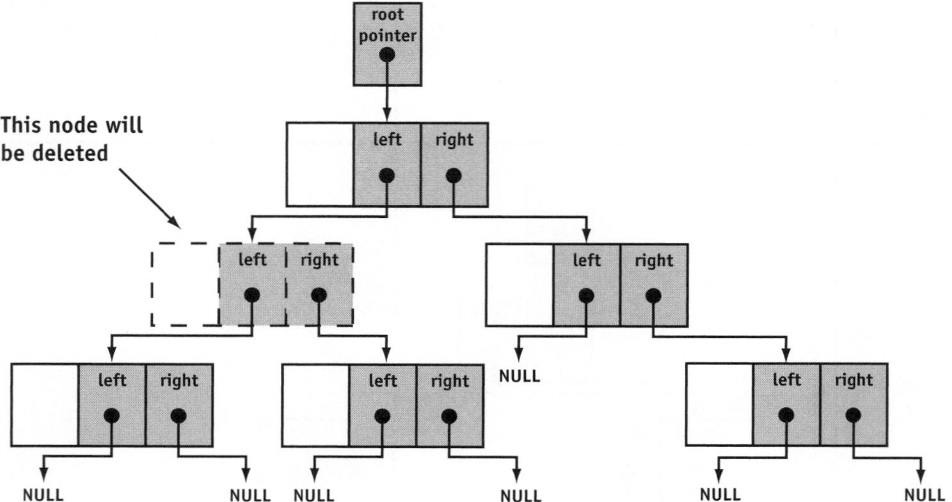

Obviously, we cannot attach both of the node's subtrees to its parent, so there must be an alternative solution. One way of addressing this problem is to attach the node's right subtree to the parent, then find a position in the right subtree to attach the left subtree. The result is shown in Figure 19-9. Note that in attaching the left subtree to the right subtree, we must take care to preserve the binary tree's search property.

Figure 19-9

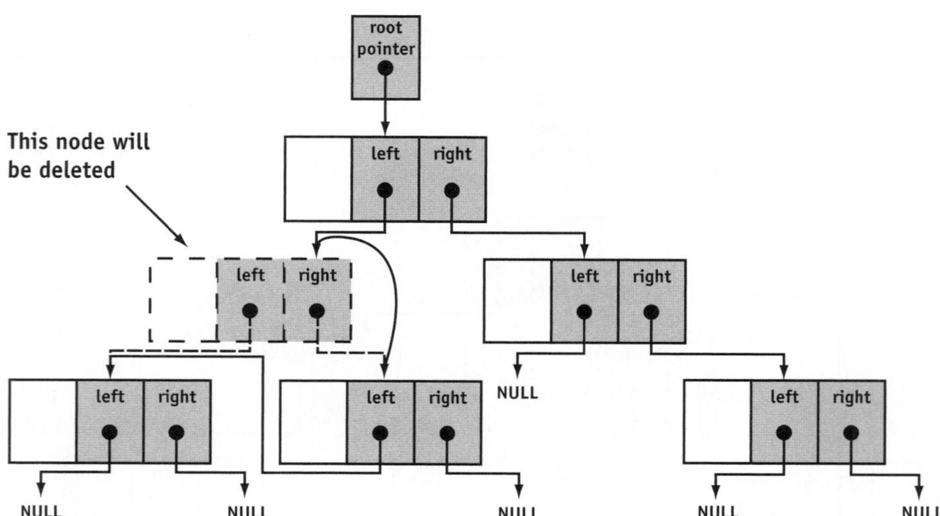

The deletion of a value from an `IntBinaryTree` object is accomplished by calling the public member function `remove`, which in turn calls the private member function of the same name. This latter function is passed (the root of) a binary search tree `tree`, and a value `num` to be removed from the tree:

```
remove(TreeNode *&tree, int num)
```

The function uses a recursive strategy. If the tree is empty, it returns immediately. Otherwise, if `num` is less than the value stored in the root node, the function recursively removes `num` from the left subtree; but if `num` is greater, the function recursively removes `num` from the right subtree. The case where `num` is found in the root node is handed off to a function

```
makeDeletion(TreeNode *&tree)
```

Here is the code for `remove`:

```
void IntBinaryTree::remove(TreeNode *&tree, int num)
{
   if (tree == NULL) return;
   if (num < tree->value)
      remove(tree->left, num);
   else if (num > tree->value)
      remove(tree->right,num);
   else
      // We have found the node to delete.
      makeDeletion(tree);
}
```

The `makeDeletion` function is designed to remove the root node of the binary search tree passed to it as an argument, leaving a binary search tree consisting of the remaining nodes. Let us take a look at the logic behind `makeDeletion`. There are a number of cases to consider:

1. The root of the tree passed to `makeDeletion` has no children. In this case, we delete the root node and replace the tree with NULL.
2. The root of the tree has only one child. In this case we delete the root node and replace the tree with the child of the deleted root:

   ```
   TreeNode *nodeToDelete = tree;
   if (tree->right == NULL)
      tree = tree->left;
   else if (tree->left == NULL)
      tree = tree->right;
   ```

   Note that this code works for the first case as well.
3. The tree passed to `makeDelete` has two children. The deletion of the root node would leave two subtrees, and we need to do something with both of them. The strategy we adopt is to combine the two subtrees into one binary search tree, and then replace the original tree with the tree built from the combined subtrees. As shown in Figure 19-9, we can do this by attaching the left subtree of the original tree as the left subtree of the least node in the right subtree of the original tree. Here is the code for the entire function.

```
void IntBinaryTree::makeDeletion(TreeNode *&tree)
{
   // Used to hold node that will be deleted
   TreeNode *nodeToDelete = tree;

   // Used to locate the  point where the
   // left subtree is attached
   TreeNode *attachPoint;

   if (tree->right == NULL)
   {
      // Replace tree with its left subtree
      tree = tree->left;
   }
   else if (tree->left == NULL)
   {
      // Replace tree with its right subtree
      tree = tree->right;
   }
   else
      //The node has two children
      {
         // Move to right subtree
         attachPoint = tree->right;

         // Locate the smallest node in the right subtree
         // by moving as far to the left as possible
         while (attachPoint->left != NULL)
         attachPoint = attachPoint->left;

         // Attach the left subtree of the original tree
         // as the left subtree of the smallest node
         // in the right subtree
         attachPoint->left = tree->left;

         // Replace the original tree with its right subtree
         tree = tree->right;
      }

      // Delete root of original tree
      delete nodeToDelete;
}
```

Program 19-4 demonstrates these functions.

Program 19-4

```
// This program builds a binary tree with 5 nodes.
// The deleteNode function is used to remove 2 of them.
#include <iostream>
#include "IntBinaryTree.h"
using namespace std;

int main()
```

(program continues)

Program 19-4 *(continued)*

```
{
   IntBinaryTree tree;

   cout << "Inserting the numbers 5 8 3 12 9.";
   tree.insert(5);
   tree.insert(8);
   tree.insert(3);
   tree.insert(12);
   tree.insert(9);

   cout << "\nHere are the values in the tree:\n";
   tree.showInOrder();

   cout << "\nDeleting 8...\n";
   tree.remove(8);

   cout << "Deleting 12...\n";
   tree.remove(12);

   cout << "Now, here are the nodes:\n";
   tree.showInOrder();
   return 0;
}
```

Program Output

```
Inserting the numbers 5 8 3 12 9.
Here are the values in the tree:
3  5  8  9  12
Deleting 8...
Deleting 12...
Now, here are the nodes:
3  5  9
```

For your reference, the entire contents of `IntBinaryTree` file are shown here:

Contents of `IntBinaryTree.cpp`

```
#include <iostream>
#include "IntBinaryTree.h"
using namespace std;

//*************************************************
// This version of insert inserts a number into    *
// a given subtree of the main binary search tree. *
//*************************************************
void IntBinaryTree::insert(TreeNode * &tree, int num)
{
   // If the tree is empty, make a new node and make it
   // the root of the tree
   if (!tree)
      {
        tree = new TreeNode(num);
```

```
         return;
      }

   // If num is already in tree: return
   if (tree->value == num)
      return;

   // The tree is not empty: insert the new node into the
   // left or right subtree
   if (num < tree->value)
      insert(tree->left, num);
   else
      insert(tree->right, num);
}

//*****************************************************
// destroySubTree is called by the destructor. It    *
// deletes all nodes in the tree.                     *
//*****************************************************
void IntBinaryTree::destroySubtree(TreeNode *tree)
{
      if (!tree) return;
      destroySubtree(tree->left);
      destroySubtree(tree->right);
      // Delete the node at the root
      delete tree;
}

//*****************************************************
// searchNode determines if a value is present in    *
// the tree. If so, the function returns true.        *
// Otherwise, it returns false.                       *
//*****************************************************
bool IntBinaryTree::search(int num) const
{
   TreeNode *tree = root;

   while (tree)
   {
      if (tree->value == num)
         return true;
      else if (num < tree->value)
         tree = tree->left;
      else
         tree = tree->right;
   }
   return false;
}

//**********************************************
// remove deletes the node in the given tree *
// that has a value member the same as num.  *
//**********************************************
```

```
void IntBinaryTree::remove(TreeNode *&tree, int num)
{
   if (tree == NULL) return;
   if (num < tree->value)
      remove(tree->left, num);
   else if (num > tree->value)
      remove(tree->right,num);
   else
      // We have found the node to delete
      makeDeletion(tree);
}

//***********************************************************
// makeDeletion takes a reference to a tree whose root      *
// is to be deleted. If the tree has a single child,        *
// the tree is replaced by the single child after the       *
// removal of its root node. If the tree has two children   *
// the left subtree of the deleted node is attached at      *
// an appropriate point in the right subtree, and then      *
// the right subtree replaces the original tree.            *
//***********************************************************
void IntBinaryTree::makeDeletion(TreeNode *&tree)
{
   // Used to hold node that will be deleted
   TreeNode *nodeToDelete = tree;

   // Used to locate the  point where the
   // left subtree is attached
   TreeNode *attachPoint;

   if (tree->right == NULL)
   {
      // Replace tree with its left subtree
      tree = tree->left;
   }
   else if (tree->left == NULL)
   {
      // Replace tree with its right subtree
      tree = tree->right;
   }
   else
      //The node has two children
      {
        // Move to right subtree
        attachPoint = tree->right;

        // Locate the smallest node in the right subtree
        // by moving as far to the left as possible
        while (attachPoint->left != NULL)
           attachPoint = attachPoint->left;

        // Attach the left subtree of the original tree
        // as the left subtree of the smallest node
```

```
         // in the right subtree
         attachPoint->left = tree->left;

         // Replace the original tree with its right subtree
         tree = tree->right;
      }

   // Delete root of original tree
   delete nodeToDelete;
}

//***********************************************************
// This function displays the values  stored in a tree     *
// in inorder.                                              *
//***********************************************************
void IntBinaryTree::displayInOrder(TreeNode *tree) const
{
   if (tree)
   {
      displayInOrder(tree->left);
      cout << tree->value << "  ";
      displayInOrder(tree->right);
   }
}

//***********************************************************
// This function displays the values stored in a tree      *
// in inorder.                                              *
//***********************************************************
void IntBinaryTree::displayPreOrder(TreeNode *tree) const
{
   if (tree)
   {
      cout << tree->value << "  ";
      displayPreOrder(tree->left);
      displayPreOrder(tree->right);
   }
}

//***********************************************************
// This function displays the values  stored  in a tree    *
// in postorder.                                            *
//***********************************************************
void IntBinaryTree::displayPostOrder(TreeNode *tree) const
{
   if (tree)
   {
      displayPostOrder(tree->left);
      displayPostOrder(tree->right);
      cout << tree->value << "  ";
   }
}
```

Checkpoint

19.7 Describe the sequence of events in an inorder traversal.

19.8 Describe the sequence of events in a preorder traversal.

19.9 Describe the sequence of events in a postorder traversal.

19.10 Describe the steps taken in deleting a leaf node.

19.11 Describe the steps taken in deleting a node with one child.

19.12 Describe the steps taken in deleting a node with two children.

19.3 Template Considerations for Binary Search Trees

CONCEPT: Binary search trees may be implemented as templates, but any data types used with them must support the <, >, and == operators.

The actual implementation of a binary tree template has been left as a Programming Challenge for students who have covered Chapters 16 and 19. When designing your template, remember that any data types stored in the binary tree must support the <, >, and == operators. If you use the tree to store class objects, these operators must be overridden.

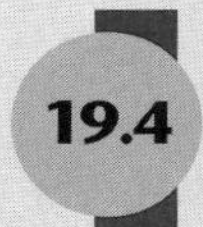

19.4 Tying It All Together: *Genealogy Trees*

Say we want to write a program that will trace peoples' ancestries and build genealogy trees. To keep track of each person's biological parents, we might use a class such as the following:

```
class Person
{
   string name;
   Person *father;
   Person *mother;
};
```

This simple class is very similar to the "node" classes we have been using to build binary trees. In maintaining genealogies, however, we are interested in recording not only a person's ancestors, but their descendants as well. We also want to keep track of gender information to enable people using the program to distinguish between maternal and paternal relatives. The `Person` class, as shown above, is not adequate for these needs. We therefore modify it as shown here:

```
enum Gender {male, female};
class Person
{
   string name;
   Gender gender;
   vector<Person *> parents;
   vector<Person *> children;
};
```

We now have a “node” that can have any number of children and any number of parents. Because each person can have at most two parents, the size of the `parents` vector will never exceed two.

We can make the `Person` class more useful by adding a constructor and several member functions. The method

```
Person *addChild(string name, Gender g);
```

creates a `Person` object with the specified name and gender, adds a pointer `p` to the created object to the `children` of “this” `Person` object, and returns `p` to the caller. Another method,

```
Person *addChild(Person *p);
```

adds a pointer to an already created `Person` object to the `children` vector of `"this"` `Person` object. The following code shows the use of these member functions to record the fact that a father `f` and a mother `m` have a child named `"Charlie"`:

```
Person f("Frank", male);
Person m("Mary", female);
Person *pChild = m.addChild("Charlie", male);
f.addChild(pChild);
```

There is also a method

```
void addParent(Person *p);
```

that is used to record the fact that one person is the parent of another. The class also has an overloaded stream operator that outputs the data in a `Person` object using an XML-like format. Finally, the class has several methods that can be used to access information about various members of the class objects. These additional functions can be seen in lines 29–34 of the program listing.

Program 19-5

```
1 // This program uses a generalization of binary trees to build
2 // genealogy trees.
3 #include <vector>
4 #include <string>
5 #include <iostream>
6 using namespace std;
7 enum Gender{male, female};
8
9 // Person class represents a person participating in a genealogy
10 class Person
11 {
12    string name;
13    Gender gender;
14    vector<Person *> parents;
15    vector<Person *> children;
16    void addParent(Person *p){ parents.push_back(p); }
17 public:
18     Person (string name, Gender g)
```

(program continues)

Program 19-5 *(continued)*

```
    {
        this->name = name;
        gender = g;
    }
   Person *addChild(string name, Gender g);
   Person *addChild(Person *p);

   friend ostream &operator << (ostream &out, Person p);

   // Member functions for getting various Person info
   string getName() const { return name; };
   Gender getGender() const { return gender; };
   int getNumChildren() const { return children.size(); }
   int getNumParents() const { return parents.size(); }
   Person *getChild(int k) const;
   Person *getParent(int k) const;
};

//*************************************************************
// Create a child with specified name and gender, and         *
// set one of the parents to be this person.                  *
// Add the new child to the list of children for this person *
//*************************************************************
Person *Person::addChild(string name, Gender g)
{
    Person *child = new Person(name, g);
    child->addParent(this);     // I am a parent of this child
    children.push_back(child);  // This is one of my children
    return child;
}

//*************************************************************
// Add a child to the list of children for this person       *
//*************************************************************
Person *Person::addChild(Person* child)
{
   child->addParent(this);    // I am a parent of this child
   children.push_back(child); // This is one of my children
   return child;
}

//**********************************************************
// Return a pointer to the specified parent               *
//**********************************************************
Person *Person::getParent(int k) const
{
   if (k < 0 || k >= parents.size())
   {
      cout << "Error indexing parents vector." << endl;
      exit(1);
   }
   return parents[k];
}
```

(program continues)

Program 19-5 *(continued)*

```

//*******************************************************
// Return a pointer to a specified child                *
//*******************************************************
Person *Person::getChild(int k) const
{
   if (k < 0 || k >= children.size())
   {
      cout << "Error indexing children's vector." << endl;
      exit(1);
   }
    return children[k];
}

//***************************************************
// Overloaded stream output operator                *
//***************************************************
ostream & operator<<(ostream & out, Person p)
{
    out << "<person name = " << p.name << ">" << '\n';
    if (p.parents.size() > 0)
        out << "   <parents>" << ' ';
    for (int k = 0; k < p.parents.size(); k++)
    {
        out << " " << p.parents[k]->name << ' ';
    }
    if (p.parents.size() > 0)
       out << " </parents>" << "\n";
    if (p.children.size() > 0)
       out << "   <children>" << ' ';
    for (int k = 0; k < p.children.size(); k++)
    {
        out << " " << p.children[k]->name << ' ';
    }
    if (p.children.size() > 0)
         out << " </children>" << "\n";
    out << "</person>" << "\n";
    return out;
}


int main(int argc, char** argv)
{
    // Here are the people
    Person adam("Adam", male);
    Person eve("Eve", female);
    Person joan("Joan", female);

    // Adam and Eve are parents of Abel
```

(program continues)

Program 19-5 *(continued)*

```
    Person *pAbel = eve.addChild(new Person("Abel", male));
    adam.addChild(pAbel);

    // Abel and Joan are parents of Missy
    Person *pMissy = joan.addChild("Missy", female);
    pAbel->addChild(pMissy);

    // Output all the people
    cout << "Here are all the people:\n\n";
    cout << adam << eve";
    cout << *pAbel << joan;
    cout << *pMissy << "\n";

    // Print parents of Missy
    cout << "Missy's parents are: " << endl;
    for (unsigned int k = 0; k < pMissy->getNumParents(); k++)
    {
        Person * p = pMissy->getParent(k);
        switch(p->getGender())
        {
           case female : cout << "\tMother: "; break;
           case male: cout << "\tFather: "; break;
        }
        cout << p->getName() << endl;
    }
    return 0;
}
```

Program Output

```
Here are all the people:

<person name = Adam>
   <children>  Abel  </children>
</person>
<person name = Eve>
   <children>  Abel  </children>
</person>
<person name = Abel>
   <parents>  Eve  Adam  </parents>
   <children>  Missy  </children>
</person>
<person name = Joan>
   <children>  Missy  </children>
</person>
<person name = Missy>
   <parents>  Joan  Abel  </parents>
</person>

Missy's parents are:
        Mother: Joan
        Father: Abel
```

Review Questions and Exercises

Fill-in-the-Blank and Short Answer

1. The first node in a binary tree is called the __________.
2. A binary tree node's left and right pointers point to the node's __________.
3. A node with no children is called a(n) __________.
4. A(n)__________ is an entire branch of the tree, from one particular node down.
5. The three common types of traversal with a binary tree are __________, __________, and __________.
6. In what ways is a binary tree similar to a linked list?
7. A *ternary* tree is like a binary tree, except each node in a ternary tree may have three children: a left child, a middle child, and a right child. Write an analogue of the `TreeNode` declaration that can be used to represent the nodes of a ternary tree.
8. Imagine a tree in which each node can have up to a hundred children. Write an analog of the `TreeNode` declaration that can be used to represent the nodes of such a tree. A declaration such as

```
TreeNode
{
   int value;
   TreeNode *child1;
   TreeNode *child2;
   TreeNode *child3;
   .
   .
   .
};
```

   that simply lists all the pointers to the hundred children is not acceptable.

Algorithm Workbench

9. Propose a definition of a *preorder traversal* for ternary trees, and give pseudocode for accomplishing such a traversal.
10. Propose a definition of a *postorder traversal* for ternary trees, and give pseudocode for accomplishing such a traversal.
11. What problems do you encounter when you try to define the concept of an *inorder traversal* for ternary trees?
12. Assume that data is stored in a binary tree, but that unlike in the case of binary search tree, no attempt is made to maintain any sort of order in the data stored. Give an algorithm for a function `search` that searches a binary tree for a particular value `num` and returns `true` or `false` according to whether the value `num` is found in the tree.
13. Give an algorithm for a function

```
int largest(TreeNode *tree)
```

   that takes a pointer to a root of a binary search tree as parameter and returns the largest value stored in the tree.

14. Give an algorithm for a function

```
int smallest(TreeNode *tree)
```

that takes a pointer to a root of a binary search tree as parameter and returns the smallest value stored in the tree.

15. Give an algorithm for a function

```
void increment (TreeNode *tree)
```

that increments the value in every node of a binary tree by one.

16. Suppose the following values are inserted into a binary search tree, in the order given:

```
12, 7, 9, 10, 22, 24, 30, 18, 3, 14, 20
```

Draw a diagram of the resulting binary tree.

17. How would the values in the tree you sketched for queston 16 be displayed in an inorder traversal?
18. How would the values in the tree you sketched for queston 16 be displayed in a preorder traversal?
19. How would the values in the tree you sketched for queston 16 be displayed in a postorder traversal?

Soft Skills

20. All three binary tree traversal methods studied in this chapter traverse the left subtree before the right subtree. This is an artifact of Western culture, where people are accustomed to reading material printed on a page from left to right. In a world of increasing globalization, products and services that will be offered in foreign markets must be designed so that they can be easily altered to target different markets. Discuss with your classmates some of the ways these internationalization considerations are affecting the design of computer software and hardware today. Discuss this with a friend who has had a course in International Business, or take such a course yourself, to become better aware of some of the problems businesses face when they enter inter-national markets.

Programming Challenges

1. Simple Binary Search Tree Class

Write a class for implementing a simple binary search tree capable of storing numbers. The class should have member functions

```
void insert(double x)
bool search(double x)
void inorder(vector <double> & v )
```

The insert function should not use recursion directly, or indirectly by calling a recursive function. The search function should work by calling a private recursive member function

```
bool search(double x, BtreeNode *t)
```

The inorder function is passed an initially empty vector v: it fills v with the inorder list of numbers stored in the binary search tree. Demonstrate the operation of the class using a suitable driver program.

2. Tree Size

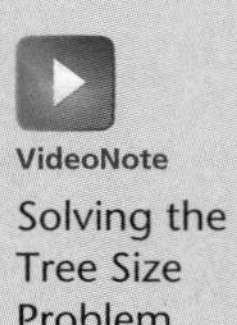

VideoNote

Solving the Tree Size Problem

Modify the binary search tree created in the previous programming challenge to add a member function

```
int size()
```

that returns the number of items (nodes) stored in the tree. Demonstrate the correctness of the new member function with a suitable driver program.

3. Leaf Counter

Modify the binary search tree you created in the preceding programming challenges to add a member function

```
int leafCount()
```

that counts and returns the number of leaf nodes in the tree. Demonstrate that the function works correctly in a suitable driver program.

4. Tree Height

Modify the binary search tree created in the preceding programming challenges by adding a member function that computes and returns the height of the tree.

```
int height()
```

The height of the tree is the number of levels it contains. For example, the tree shown in Figure 19-10 has three levels. Demonstrate the function with a suitable driver program.

Figure 19-10

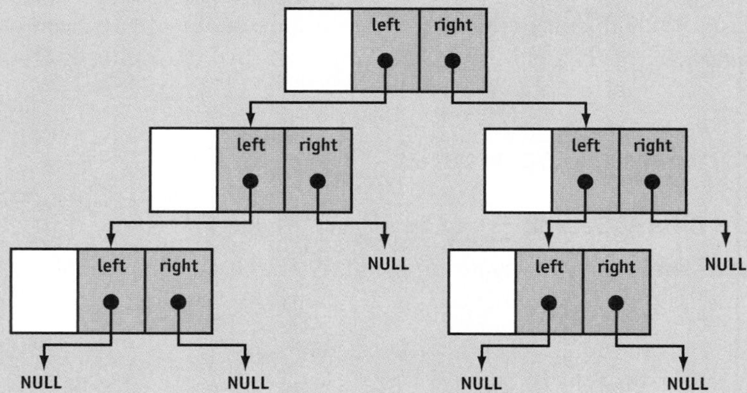

5. Tree Width

Modify the binary search tree created in the preceding programming challenges by adding a member function that computes the width of the tree.

```
int width()
```

The width of a tree is the largest number of nodes at the same level. Demonstrate correctness in a suitable driver program.

6. Tree Copy Constructor

Design and implement a copy constructor for the binary search tree created in the preceding programming challenges. Use a driver program to demonstrate correctness.

7. Tree Assignment Operator

Design and implement an overloaded assignment operator for the binary search tree created in the preceding programming challenges.

8. Employee Tree

Design an `EmployeeInfo` class that holds the following employee information:

Employee ID Number: an integer
Employee Name: a string

Implement a binary tree whose nodes hold an instance of the `EmployeeInfo` class. The nodes should be sorted on the Employee ID number.

Test the binary tree by inserting nodes with the following information.

Employee ID Number	Name
1021	John Williams
1057	Bill Witherspoon
2487	Jennifer Twain
3769	Sophia Lancaster
1017	Debbie Reece
1275	George McMullen
1899	Ashley Smith
4218	Josh Plemmons

Your program should allow the user to enter an ID number, then search the tree for the number. If the number is found, it should display the employee's name. If the node is not found, it should display a message indicating so.

9. Cousins

Building on Program 19-5, write a function that takes a pointer to a `Person` object and produces a list of that person's cousins.

APPENDIX

A The ASCII Character Set

Nonprintable ASCII Characters			
Dec	Hex	Oct	Name of Character
0	0	0	NULL
1	1	1	SOTT
2	2	2	STX
3	3	3	ETY
4	4	4	EOT
5	5	5	ENQ
6	6	6	ACK
7	7	7	BELL
8	8	10	BKSPC
9	9	11	HZTAB
10	a	12	NEWLN
11	b	13	VTAB
12	c	14	FF
13	d	15	CR
14	e	16	SO
15	f	17	SI
16	10	20	DLE
17	11	21	DC1
18	12	22	DC2
19	13	23	DC3
20	14	24	DC4
21	15	25	NAK
22	16	26	SYN
23	17	27	ETB
24	18	30	CAN
25	19	31	EM
26	1a	32	SUB
27	1b	33	ESC
28	1c	34	FS
29	1d	35	GS
30	1e	36	RS
31	1f	37	US
127	7f	177	DEL

Printable ASCII Characters			
Dec	Hex	Oct	Character
32	20	40	(Space)
33	21	41	!
34	22	42	“
35	23	43	#
36	24	44	$
37	25	45	%
38	26	46	&
39	27	47	‘
40	28	50	(
41	29	51	)
42	2a	52	*
43	2b	53	+
44	2c	54	’
45	2d	55	–
46	2e	56	.
47	2f	57	/
48	30	60	0
49	31	61	1
50	32	62	2
51	33	63	3
52	34	64	4
53	35	65	5
54	36	66	6
55	37	67	7
56	38	70	8
57	39	71	9
58	3a	72	:
59	3b	73	;
60	3c	74	<
61	3d	75	=
62	3e	76	>
63	3f	77	?
64	40	100	@

Printable ASCII Characters

Dec	Hex	Oct	Character
65	41	101	A
66	42	102	B
67	43	103	C
68	44	104	D
69	45	105	E
70	46	106	F
71	47	107	G
72	48	110	H
73	49	111	I
74	4a	112	J
75	4b	113	K
76	4c	114	L
77	4d	115	M
78	4e	116	N
79	4f	117	O
80	50	120	P
81	51	121	Q
82	52	122	R
83	53	123	S
84	54	124	T
85	55	125	U
86	56	126	V
87	57	127	W
88	58	130	X
89	59	131	Y
90	5a	132	Z
91	5b	133	[
92	5c	134	\
93	5d	135	]
94	5e	136	^
95	5f	137	_
96	60	140	`
97	61	141	a
98	62	142	b
99	63	143	c
100	64	144	d
101	65	145	e
102	66	146	f
103	67	147	g
104	68	150	h
105	69	151	i
106	6a	152	j
107	6b	153	k
108	6c	154	l
109	6d	155	m
110	6e	156	n
111	6f	157	o
112	70	160	p
113	71	161	q
114	72	162	r
115	73	163	s
116	74	164	t
117	75	165	u
118	76	166	v
119	77	167	w
120	78	170	x

Printable ASCII Characters

Dec	Hex	Oct	Character
121	79	171	y
122	7a	172	z
123	7b	173	{
124	7c	174	|
125	7d	175	}
126	7e	176	~

Extended ASCII Characters

Dec	Hex	Oct	Character
128	80	200	Ç
129	81	201	ü
130	82	202	é
131	83	203	â
132	84	204	ä
133	85	205	à
134	86	206	å
135	87	207	ç
136	88	210	ê
137	89	211	ë
138	8a	212	è
139	8b	213	ï
140	8c	214	î
141	8d	215	ì
142	8e	216	Ä
143	8f	217	Å
144	90	220	É
145	91	221	æ
146	92	222	Æ
147	93	223	ô
148	94	224	ö
149	95	225	ò
150	96	226	û
151	97	227	ù
152	98	230	ÿ
153	99	231	Ö
154	9a	232	Ü
155	9b	233	¢
156	9c	234	£
157	9d	235	ù
158	9e	236	û
159	9f	237	ƒ
160	a0	240	á
161	a1	241	í
162	a2	242	ó
163	a3	243	ú
164	a4	244	ñ
165	a5	245	Ñ
166	a6	246	ª
167	a7	247	º
168	a8	250	¿
169	a9	251	©
170	aa	252	Ñ
171	ab	253	´

Extended ASCII Characters			
Dec	Hex	Oct	Character
172	ac	254	¨
173	ad	255	i
174	ae	256	
175	af	257	»
176	b0	260	∞
177	b1	261	±
178	b2	262	≤
179	b3	263	≥
180	b4	264	¥
181	b5	265	μ
182	b6	266	∂
183	b7	267	∑
184	b8	270	∏
185	b9	271	π
186	ba	272	∫
187	bb	273	a
188	bc	274	o
189	bd	275	Ω
190	be	276	æ
191	bf	277	ø
192	c0	300	¿
193	c1	301	i
194	c2	302	¬
195	c3	303	√
196	c4	304	ƒ
197	c5	305	≈
198	c6	306	∆
199	c7	307	
200	c8	310	»
201	c9	311	…
202	ca	312	_
203	cb	313	À
204	cc	314	Ã
205	cd	315	Õ
206	ce	316	Œ
207	cf	317	œ
208	d0	320	–
209	d1	321	—
210	d2	322	“
211	d3	323	”
212	d4	324	‘
213	d5	325	’

Extended ASCII Characters			
Dec	Hex	Oct	Character
214	d6	326	÷
215	d7	327	◊
216	d8	330	ÿ
217	d9	331	Ÿ
218	da	332	/
219	db	333	
220	dc	334	‹
221	dd	335	›
222	de	336	ﬁ
223	df	337	ﬂ
224	e0	340	‡
225	e1	341	·
226	e2	342	‚
227	e3	343	„
228	e4	344	‰
229	e5	345	Â
230	e6	346	Ê
231	e7	347	Á
232	e8	350	Ë
233	e9	351	È
234	ea	352	Í
235	eb	353	Î
236	ec	354	Ï
237	ed	355	Ì
238	ee	356	Ó
239	ef	357	Ô
240	f0	360	
241	f1	361	Ò
242	f2	362	Ú
243	f3	363	Û
244	f4	364	Ù
245	f5	365	ı
246	f6	366	ˆ
247	f7	367	˜
248	f8	370	¯
249	f9	371	˘
250	fa	372	˙
251	fb	373	·
252	fc	374	¸
253	fd	375	˝
254	fe	376	˛
255	ff	377	

APPENDIX

B Operator Precedence and Associativity

The operators are shown in order of precedence, from highest to lowest.

<table>
<tr><th>Operator</th><th>Associativity</th></tr>
<tr><td><code>::</code></td><td>unary: left to right
binary: right to left</td></tr>
<tr><td><code>() [] -> .</code></td><td>left to right</td></tr>
<tr><td><code>++ -- + - ! ~ (type) * & sizeof</code></td><td>right to left</td></tr>
<tr><td><code>* / %</code></td><td>left to right</td></tr>
<tr><td><code>+ -</code></td><td>left to right</td></tr>
<tr><td><code><< >></code></td><td>left to right</td></tr>
<tr><td><code>< <= > >=</code></td><td>left to right</td></tr>
<tr><td><code>== !=</code></td><td>left to right</td></tr>
<tr><td><code>&</code></td><td>left to right</td></tr>
<tr><td><code>^</code></td><td>left to right</td></tr>
<tr><td><code>|</code></td><td>left to right</td></tr>
<tr><td><code>&&</code></td><td>left to right</td></tr>
<tr><td><code>||</code></td><td>left to right</td></tr>
<tr><td><code>?:</code></td><td>right to left</td></tr>
<tr><td><code>= += -= *= /= %= &= ^= |= <<= >>=</code></td><td>right to left</td></tr>
<tr><td><code>,</code></td><td>left to right</td></tr>
</table>

APPENDIX

C Answers to Checkpoints

Chapter 1

1.1 Because the computer can be programmed to do so many different tasks

1.2 The central processing unit (CPU), main memory (RAM), secondary storage devices, input devices, and output devices

1.3 Arithmetic and logic unit (ALU) and control unit

1.4 Fetch: The CPU's control unit fetches the program's next instruction from main memory.

Decode: The control unit decodes the instruction, which is encoded in the form of a number. An electrical signal is generated.

Execute: The signal is routed to the appropriate component of the computer, which causes a device to perform an operation.

1.5 A memory address is a unique number assigned to each storage location in memory. Its purpose is to allow data stored in RAM to be located.

1.6 Program instructions and data are stored in main memory while the program is running. Main memory is volatile and loses its contents when power is removed from the computer. Secondary storage holds data for long periods of time—even when there is no power to the computer.

1.7 Operating systems and application software

1.8 The operating system

1.9 A utility program

1.10 Application software or application programs

1.11 A set of well-defined steps for performing a task or solving a problem

1.12 To ease the task of programming. Programs may be written in a programming language, then converted to machine language.

1.13 A low-level language is close to the level of the computer and resembles the system's numeric machine language. A high-level language is closer to the level of human readability and resembles natural languages.

1.14 That a program may be written on one type of computer and run on another type

1.15 The preprocessor reads the source file, searching for commands that begin with the # symbol. These are commands that cause the preprocessor to modify the source file in some way. The compiler translates each source code instruction into the appropriate machine language instruction and creates an object file. The linker combines the object file with necessary library routines to create an executable file.

1.16 Source file: Contains program statements written by the programmer.

Object file: Contains machine language instructions generated by the compiler.

Executable file: Contains code ready to run on the computer. Includes the machine language from an object file and the necessary code from library routines.

1.17 A programming environment that includes a text editor, compiler, debugger, and other utilities, integrated into one package

1.18 A key word has a special purpose and is defined as part of a programming language. A programmer-defined symbol is a word or name defined by the programmer.

1.19 Operators perform operations on one or more operands. Punctuation symbols mark the beginning or ending of a statement, or separate items in a list.

1.20 A line is a single line as it appears in the body of a program. A statement is a complete instruction that causes the computer to perform an action. It may be written on 1 or more lines.

1.21 Because their contents may be changed while the program is running.

1.22 It is overwritten by the new value. The old value is "lost".

1.23 The variable must be defined in a declaration.

1.24 Input, processing, and output

1.25 The program's purpose, the information to be input, the processing to take place, and the desired output.

1.26 To imagine what the computer screen looks like while the program is running. This helps define input and output.

1.27 A chart that depicts the logical steps of the program in a hierarchical fashion

1.28 A "language" that is a cross between human language and programming languages that is used to express algorithms.

1.29 High-level psuedocode just lists the steps a program must carry out. Detailed psuedocode shows the variables, logic, and computations needed to create the program.

1.30 It translates each source code statement into the appropriate machine language statements.

1.31 A mistake that causes a program to produce erroneous results. A logic error occurs when what the programmer means for the program to do does not match what the code actually instructs the program to do.

1.32 An error that occurs while the program is running when the system is asked to perform an action it cannot carry out.

1.33 The programmer steps through each statement in the program from beginning to end. The contents of variables are recorded, and screen output is sketched.

Chapter 2

2.1
```
// A crazy mixed up program
#include <iostream>
using namespace std;

int main()
{
   cout << "In 1492 Columbus sailed the ocean blue.";
   return 0;
}
```

2.2
```
// Insert current date here
#include <iostream>
using namespace std;

int main()
{
   cout << "Teresa Jones";
   return 0;
}
```

2.3
```
cout << "red \n" << "blue \n" << "yellow \n" << "green";
```

2.4
```
The works of Wolfgang
include the following:
The Turkish March
and Symphony No. 40 in G minor.
```

2.5
```
#include <iostream>
using namespace std;

int main()
{
   cout << "Teresa Jones\n";
   cout << "127 West 423rd Street\n";
   cout << "San Antonio, TX  78204\n";
   cout << "555-475-1212\n";
   return 0;
}
```

2.6 Only statement **a** is legal. The left-hand side of an assignment statement must be a variable, not a literal.

2.7 Variables: `little` and `big`

Literals: `2`, `2000`, `"The little number is "`, `"The big number is"`, `0`

2.8
```
The little number is 2
The big number is 2000
```

2.9
```
The value is number
```

2.10 `99bottles`: Variable names cannot begin with a number.

`r&d`: Variable names may only use alphabetic letters, digits, and underscores.

2.11 No. Variable names are case sensitive.

2.12 A) `short` or `unsigned short`

B) `int`

C) They both use the same amount of memory.

2.13 `unsigned short`, `unsigned int`, and `unsigned long`

2.14 `int apples 20;`

2.15 `int xCoord = 2, yCoord = -4, zCoord = 6;`

2.16 6.31E17

2.17 3

2.18
```
#include <iostream>
using namespace std;

int main()
{
   int age;
   double weight;

   age = 26;
   weight = 168.5;
   cout << "My age is " << age << "and my weight is " << weight;
   cout << weight << " pounds.\n";
   return 0;
}
```

2.19 67, 70, 87

2.20 'B'

2.21 1 byte, 2 bytes, 6 bytes, 1 byte

2.22 The string literal "`z`" is being stored in the character variable `letter`.

2.23 `string`

2.24
```
// Substitute your name, address, and phone
// number for those shown in this program.
#include <iostream>
#include <string>
using namespace std;

int main()
{
   string name, address, phone;
   name = "George Davis";
   address = "179 Ravenwood Lane";
   phone = "555-6767";
   cout << name << endl;
   cout << address << endl;
   cout << phone << endl;
   return 0;
}
```

2.25 Invalid. The value on the left of the = operator must be an `lvalue`, such as a variable name.

2.26 The variable `critter` is assigned a value before it is declared. You can correct the program by moving the statement `critter = 62.7;` to the line after the variable declaration.

2.27 11, 5, 24, 2

2.28 Integer division. The value 5 will be displayed.

Chapter 3

3.1 `iostream`

3.2 The stream extraction operator

3.3 The console (or keyboard)

3.4 True

3.5 3

3.6 `cin >> miles >> feet >> inches;`

3.7 Include one or more `cout` statements explaining what values the user should enter.

3.8
```
#include <iostream>
using namespace std;

int main()
{
   double pounds, kilograms;

   cout << "Enter your weight in pounds: ";
   cin  >> pounds;
   // The following line does the conversion.
   kilograms = pounds / 2.2;
   cout << "Your weight in kilograms is ";
   cout << kilograms << endl;
   return 0;
}
```

3.9 A) *
B) same
C) same

3.10 *Value*
21
2
31
5
24
2
69
0
30

3.11
```
y = 6 * x;
a = 2 * b + 4 * c;
y = x * x * x;              or  y = pow(x, 3);
g = (x + 2) / (z * z);      or  g = (x + 2) / pow(z, 2);
y = (x * x) / (z * z);      or  y = pow(x, 2) / pow (z, 2);
```

3.12 *If the user enters...* *The program displays...*

If the user enters...	The program displays...
2	6
5	27
4.3	20.49
6	38

3.13
```
#include <iostream>
#include <cmath>
using namespace std;

int main()
{
   double volume, radius, height;
   cout << "This program will tell you the volume of\n";
   cout << "a cylinder-shaped fuel tank.\n";
   cout << "How tall is the tank? ";
   cin  >> height;
   cout << "What is the radius of the tank? ";
   cin  >> radius;
   volume = 3.14159 * pow(radius, 2.0) * height;
   cout << "The volume of the tank is " << volume << endl;
   return 0;
}
```

3.14
A) 2
B) 17.0
C) 2.0
D) 2.4
E) 2.4
F) 2.4
G) 4
H) 27
I) 30
J) 27.0

3.15
```
The ASCII values of uppercase letters are 65 - 90
The ASCII values of lowercase letters are 97 - 122
Enter a letter and I will tell you its ASCII code: B
The ASCII code for B is 66
```

3.16
```
9
9.5
9
```

3.17
```
const double E = 2.71828;
const double MIN_PER_YEAR = 5.256E5;
const double GRAV_ACC_FT_PER_SEC = 32.2;
const double GRAV_ACC_M_PER_SEC = 9.8;
const int METERS_PER_MILE = 1609;
```

3.18
```
#define E 2.71828
#define YEAR_SECS 5.26e5
#define GRAV_ACC_FT_PER_SEC 32.2
#define GRAV_ACC_M_PER_SEC 9.8
#define METERS_PER_MILE 1609
```

3.19
```
This program calculates the number of candy pieces sold.
How many jars of candy have you sold? 6[Enter]
The number of pieces sold: 11160
Candy pieces you get for commission: 2232
```

3.20
```
#include <iostream>
using namespace std;

int main()
{
   const double CONVERSION = 1.467;
   double milesPerHour, feetPerSecond;

   cout << "This program converts miles-per-hour to\n";
   cout << "feet-per-second.\n";
   cout << "Enter a speed in MPH: ";
   cin  >> milesPerHour;
   feetPerSecond = milesPerHour * CONVERSION;
   cout << "That is " << feetPerSecond
        << " feet-per-second.\n";
   return 0;
}
```

3.21
```
total = subtotal = tax = shipping = 0;
```

3.22
A) `x += 6;`
B) `amount -= 4;`
C) `y *= 4;`
D) `total /= 27;`
E) `x %= 7;`
F) `x += (y * 5);`
G) `total -= (discount * 4);`
H) `increase *= (salesRep * 5);`
I) `profit /= (shares – 1000);`

3.23
```
3
11
1
```

3.24
A)
```
cout << fixed << setprecision(2);
cout << setw(9) << 34.789;
```
B)
```
cout << fixed << showpoint
     << setprecision(3);
cout << setw(5) << 7.0;
```
C)
```
cout << fixed << 5.789e12;
```
D)
```
cout << left << setw(7) << 67;
```

3.25
```
#include <iostream>
#include <iomanip>
using namespace std;

int main()
{
   const double PI = 3.14159;
   double degrees, radians;
   cout << "Enter an angle in degrees and I will convert it\n";
   cout << "to radians for you: ";
   cin  >> degrees;
   radians = degrees * PI / 180;
   cout << degrees << " degrees is equal to ";
   cout << fixed << showpoint << setprecision(4);
   cout << left << setw(7) << radians << " radians.\n ";
   return 0;
}
```

3.26 No. Space is needed for a fifth character, to hold the null terminator.

3.27 A) Legal (Though no embedded blanks can be input)
B) Illegal (This works for C-strings only)
C) Legal
D) Legal

3.28 A) Legal (Though no embedded blanks can be input)
B) Legal
C) Legal
D) Illegal (Arrays cannot be assigned to variables like this. Use `strcpy()`.)

3.29 `x = sin(angle1) + cos(angle2);`

3.30 `y = pow(x, 0.2);    // 0.2 is equal to 1/5`

3.31 `luckyNumber = rand() % 100 + 1;`

Chapter 4

4.1 T, T, T, T, T, T, T

4.2 A) Incorrect
B) Incorrect
C) Correct

4.3 A) Yes
B) No
C) No

4.4 0 0 1 0

4.5
```
if (price > 500)
   discountRate = 0.2;
```

4.6
```
if (hours > 40)
   payRate = payRate * 1.5;
```

4.7
```
if (sales > 50000)
{  commissionRate = 0.25;
   bonus = 250;
}
```

4.8 false

4.9
```
if (ticketsSold == 200)
   soldOut = true;
```

4.10
```
if (soldOut)          // Same as if (soldOut == true)
   cout << "The performance is sold out! \n";
```

4.11 A) Error: There is a semicolon after the `if` test condition.

Result: The `cout` statement will execute even though `hours` is not greater than 40.

Output: `12 hours qualifies for over-time.`

B) Error: The `if` test condition uses an assignment operator (=) rather than an equality test (==).

Result: `interestRate` will be assigned the value .07, and the `cout` statement will execute even though it shouldn't.

Output: `This account is earning the maximum rate.`

C) Error: The 2 statements that are supposed to be included in the body of the `if` statement are not surrounded by curly braces.

Result: Only the `cout` statement is in the `if` body. The $10 addition to `balance` will always be done, even when `interestRate` is not greater than .07.

Output: `None`

4.12
```
if (sales >= 50000.00)
   commission = 0.20;
else
   commission = 0.10;
```

4.13
```
if (y == 100)
   x = 1;
else
   x = 0;
```

4.14
```
if (prepaid)          // Same as if (prepaid == true)
   discount = 0.10;
else
   discount = 0.0;
```

4.15 true

4.16 No. When x equals y the two separate `if` statements don't display anything, but the `if/else` statement causes a 2 to display.

4.17 `5  5`

4.18
```
If the customer purchases    This many coupons are given
this many books...
-----------------------------------------------------
      1                            1
      2                            1
      3                            2
      4                            2
      5                            3
      10                           3
```

4.19
```
if (quantityOnHand == 0)
   cout << "Out of stock \n";
else if (quantityOnHand < 10)
   cout << "Reorder \n";
```

4.20
```
if (quantityOnHand == 0)
   cout << "Out of stock \n";
else if (quantityOnHand < 10)
   cout << "Reorder \n";
else
   cout << "Quantity OK \n";
```

4.21 A) Zero
B) Zero Ten
C) Zero Ten Twenty
D) Nothing is displayed

4.22 A) Good luck in the rest of your games.
B) You are the champions.
C) You have won more than 50% of your games.

4.23

Logical Expression	Result (True or False)
true && false	false
true && true	true
false && false	false
true || false	true
true || true	true
false || false	false
!true	false
!false	true

4.24 T, F, T, T, T

4.25 True (`&&` is done before `||`)

4.26
```
if (!activeEmployee)
```

4.27
```
if (speed >= 0 && speed <= 200)
   cout << "The number is valid. \n";
```

4.28
```
if (speed < 0 || speed > 200)
   cout << "The number is not valid.";
```

4.29 The variables `length`, `width`, and `area` should be defined before they are used. There is no prompt for the width.

4.30 A) True
B) False
C) True
D) False
E) False
F) True

4.31 A) False
B) False
C) True
D) False
E) False
F) False
G) True
H) False

4.32
```
if (str1 == str2)
   cout << "Both strings have the value" << str1 << endl;
else if (str1 < str2)
   cout << str1 << endl << str2 << endl;
else
   cout << str2 << endl << str1 << endl;
```

4.33 A) True
B) True
C) False
D) False
E) True
F) False
G) True
H) False

4.34 A) `z = (x > y) ? 1 : 20;`
B) `population = (temp > 45) ? (base * 10) : (base * 2);`
C) `wages *= (hours > 40) ? 1.5 : 1;`
D)
```
cout << ((result >= 0) ? ("The result is positive\n") :
         ("The result is negative.\n"));
```

4.35 A)
```
if (k > 90)
   j = 57;
else
   j = 12;
```
B)
```
if (x >= 10)
   factor = y * 22;
else
   factor = y * 35;
```
C)
```
if (count == 1)
   total += sales;
else
   total += count * sales;
```
D)
```
if (num % 2)
   cout << "Even\n";
else
   cout << "Odd\n";
```

4.36 `2 2`

4.37 Because the `if /else` statement tests several different conditions, consisting of different variables and because it tests values with relational operators other than `equal-to`.

4.38 The case statements must be followed by an integer constant, not a relational expression.

4.39 `That is serious.`

4.40
```
switch (userNum)
{
   case 1 : cout << "One";
            break;
   case 2 : cout << "Two";
            break;
   case 3 : cout << "Three";
            break;
   default: cout << "Enter 1, 2, or 3 please.\n";
}
```

4.41 Here is the converted `if/else if` statement found in the program segment.
```
switch (selection)
{
   case 1   : cout << "Pi times radius squared\n";
              break;
   case 2   : cout << "length times width\n";
              break;
   case 3   : cout << "Pi times radius squared times height\n";
              break;
   case 4   : cout << "Well okay then, good bye!\n";
              break;
   default  : cout << "Not good with numbers, eh?\n";
}
```

4.42 `enum` must be lowercase. There should be no = sign. The symbolic names in the enumeration list should not be in quotes. It should end with a semicolon.

4.43
```
if (color <= yellow)
   cout "primary color \n";
else
   cout "mixed color \n";
```

Chapter 5

5.1 A) 4
B) 0
C) 0. Notice the semicolon after the `while` test expression. This causes an infinite loop that prints nothing.
D) Notice the missing braces. This means the line that increments `count` is not in the loop, so `count` always remains less than 5, causing an infinite loop. The `cout` statement executes over and over again until the user stops the program.

5.2
```
int num = 1;
while (num <= 15)
{  cout << num << endl;
   num += 2;
}
```

5.3 A) 3 2 D) 3 4
B) 3 3 E) `It is true!`
C) 2 3 F) `It is true!`

5.4 A) `Hello World`
B) `5 5 5 5 5 5 5 5` ... (Infinite loop)
C) 8 4

5.5
```
do
{
   cout << "Enter an integer: ";
   cin  >> num;

   if (num % 2 == 0)
      cout << "That integer is even.\n";
   else
      cout << "That integer is odd.\n";

   cout << "Do you want to test another number (y/n)? ";
   cin  >> reply;
} while (reply == 'y' || reply == 'Y');
```

5.6 Change the last line of answer 5.5 to the following:
```
while(toupper(reply) == 'Y')
```

5.7 initialization expression, test expression, and update expression

5.8 A) `count = 1`
B) `count <= 50`
C) `count++`
D)
```
for (count = 1; count <= 50; count++)
   cout << "I love to program.\n";
```

5.9 A) 0 2 4 6 8 10
B) –5 –4 –3 –2 –1 0 1 2 3 4
C) 3 6 9 12

5.10
```
for (int count = 1; count <= 10; count++)
   cout << "Put your name here.\n";
```

5.11
```
for (int num = 1; num < 50; num += 2)
   cout << num << endl;
```

5.12
```
for (int num = 0; num <= 100; num += 5)
   cout << num << endl;
```

5.13 x is the counter, y is the accumulator.

5.14
```
int sum = 0;
for (int num = 1; num <= 10; num++)
   sum += num * num;
cout << "The sum of the squares of the integers \n"
     << "from 1 through 10 is " << sum << endl;
```

5.15
```
int sum = 0;
for (int num = 1; num <= 9; num += 2)
   sum += num * num;
cout << "The sum of the squares of the odd integers \n"
     << "from 1 through 9 is " << sum;
```

5.16
```
int count, number, total = 0;
for (count = 0; count < 7; count++)
{
   cout << "Enter a number: ";
   cin  >> number;
   total += number;
}
cout << "The total is " << total << endl;
```

5.17
```
double x, y, quotient, total = 0.0;
for (x = 1, y = 30; x <= 30; x++, y--)
{
   quotient = x / y;
   total += quotient;
}
cout << "The total is " << total << endl;
```

5.18
```
double total = 0.0;
for (int denom = 2; denom <= 1024; denom *= 2)
   total += 1.0 / denom;
cout << "The total of the series is " << total << endl;
```

5.19
```
int score, numScores = 0;
double total = 0.0;

cout << "Enter the first test score (or -99 to quit): ";
cin  >> score;

while (score != -99)
{  numScores++;
   total += score;
   cout << "Enter the next test score (or -99 to quit): ";
   cin  >> score;
}
if (numScores == 0)
   cout << "No scores were entered." << endl;
else
   cout << "The average of the " << numScores
        << " scores is " << total / numScores << endl;
```

5.20 A) `for`
B) `do-while`
C) `while`
D) `while`
E) `for`

5.21 A) 600 (20 rows with 30 stars in each row)
B) 220 (20 rows with just 11 stars in each row due to the `break` statement)

5.22 1 3 7 12

5.23 A) An output file is one that a program can write output to.
B) In input file is one that a program can read input from.

5.24 `fstream`

5.25 1. Include the `fstream` header file needed to perform file input/output.
2. Define a file stream object.
3. Open the file.
4. Use the file.
5. Close the file.

5.26 A text file contains data that has been encoded as text, so it can be read with a text editor. A binary file contains binary data that has not been converted to text, so it cannot be viewed with a text editor.

5.27 A sequential access file contains data that can only be accessed in sequential order from beginnning to end. A random access file allows direct access to any piece of data without having to read the data that comes before it.

5.28 `ofstream`

5.29 `ifstream`

5.30 C. `dataFile << salary;`

5.31 The open function needs an argument that is a C-string. Change the third line to

```
outputFile.open(filename.c_str());
```

5.32

```
for (int num = 1; num <= 10; num++)
   outfile << num << endl;
```

Chapter 6

6.1 Function call

6.2 Function header

6.3

```
I saw Elba
Able was I
```

6.4

```
void qualify()
{
   cout << "Congratulations, you qualify for\n";
   cout << "the loan. The annual interest rate\n";
   cout << "is 12%\n";
}

void noQualify()
{
   cout << "You do not qualify. In order to\n";
   cout << "qualify you must have worked on\n";
   cout << "your current job for at least two\n";
   cout << "years and you must earn at least\n";
   cout << "$17,000 per year.\n";
}
```

6.5 Header
Prototype
Function call

6.6
```
void timesTen(int number)
{
   cout << (number * 10);
}
```

6.7
```
void timesTen(int);
```

6.8
```
0   0
1   2
2   4
3   6
4   8
5   10
6   12
7   14
8   16
9   18
```

6.9
```
0 1.5
1.5 0
0 10
0 1.5
```

6.10
```
void showDollars(double pay)
{
   cout << fixed << showpoint << setprecision(2);
   cout << "Your wages are $" << pay << endl;
}
```

6.11 One

6.12 `double distance(double rate, double time)`

6.13 `int days(int years, int months, int weeks)`

6.14 `char getKey()`

6.15 `long lightYears(long miles)`

6.16 A static local variable's scope is limited to the function in which it is defined. A global variable's scope is the portion of the program from its definition to the end of the program.

6.17
```
100
50
100
```

6.18
```
10
11
12
13
14
15
16
17
18
19
```

6.19 Literals and Constants

6.20 *Prototype:*

```
void compute(double, int = 5, long = 65536);
```

Header:

```
void compute(double x, int y, long z)
```

6.21 *Prototype:*

```
void calculate(long, &double, int = 47);
```

Header:

```
void calculate(long x, double &y, int z)
```

6.22

```
5 10 15
9 10 15
6 15 15
4 11 16
```

6.23

```
0 00
Enter two numbers: 12 14
12 140
14 15-1
14 15-1
```

6.24 Different parameter lists

6.25 `1.2`

6.26 `30`

Chapter 7

7.1 B

7.2 A

7.3 C

7.4

```
class Date
{
private:
   int month;
   int day;
   int year;
public:
   void setDate(int m, int d, int y)
       { month = m; day = d; year = y; }
   int getMonth()
       { return month; }
   int getDay()
       { return day; }
   int getYear()
       { return year; }
}
```

Alternately these could be separate `setMonth`, `setDay`, and `setYear` member functions to validate and set each component of the date separately.

7.5 A constructor is automatically called when the class object is created. It is useful for initializing member variables or performing setup operations.

7.6 A

7.7 A

7.8 `ClassAct sally(25);`

7.9 True

7.10 False

7.11 B

7.12 False

7.13
```
50
50
20
```

7.14
```
4
7
goodbye
goodbye
```

7.15 D

7.16 A

7.17 B

7.18 False. They can be both passed to functions and returned by functions.

7.19 False. Passing it by value *will* ensure it is not changed, but it is best to pass it as a constant reference.

7.20 D

7.21
```
class Circle
{  private:
      double radius;          // In inches
   public:
      void setRadius(double r)
      {  radius = r; }
      double getArea()        // In sq. in.
      {  return (3.14.159 * radius * radius); }
}
```

7.22
```
class Pizza
{  private:
      double price;
      Circle size;
   public:
      void setPrice(double p)
      {   price = p; }
      void setSize(double r)
      {   size.setRadius(r); }
      double costPerSqIn()
      {   return (price / size.getArea()); }
}
```

7.23 Other prices and sizes could be used.

```
Pizza myPizza;
myPizza.setPrice(12.99);
myPizza.setSize(14);
cout << "Price per square inch $" << myPizza.costPerSqIn();
```

7.24 The `BasePay` class declaration would reside in `Basepay.h`

The `BasePay` member function definitions would reside in `Basepay.cpp`

The `Overtime` class declaration would reside in `Overtime.h`

The `Overtime` member function declarations would reside in `Overtime.cpp`

7.25 `Basepay.h` and `Overtime.h`

7.26

```
struct Student
{  int    id,
          entryYear;
   double gpa;
};
Student s1(1234, 2008, 3.41);
Student s2(5678, 2010);
```

7.27

```
struct Account
{  string acctNum;
   double acctBal,
          intRate,
          avgBal;

   Account(string num, double bal, double rate, double avg)
   {   acctNum = num;  acctBal = bal;
       intRate = rate; avgBal = avg;
   }
};
Account savings("ACZ42137", 4512.59, .04, 4217.07);
```

7.28

```
#include <iostream>
#include <string>
using namespace std;

struct MovieInfo
{
   string name,
          director;
   int    year;
};

int main()
{
   MovieInfo movie;

   cout << "Enter the following information about your "
        << " favorite movie.\n" << "Name: ";
   getline(cin, movie.name);
```

```
   cout << "Director: ";
   getline(cin, movie.director);

   cout << "Year of Release: ";
   cin  >> movie.year;

   cout << "\nHere is information on your favorite movie:\n";
   cout << "Name: " << movie.name << endl;
   cout << "Director: " << movie.director << endl;
   cout << "Year of Release: " << movie.year << endl;
   return 0;
}
```

7.29
```
struct Location
{
   double latitude,
          longitude,
          height;
};
```

7.30
```
struct City
{
   String cityName;
   Location position;
};
City destination;
```

7.31
```
destination.cityName = "Tupelo";
destination.position.latitude  =  34.28;    // degrees north
destination.position.longitude = -88.77;    // degrees west
destination.position.height    =  361.0;    // ft. above sea level
```

7.32
```
void showRect(Rectangle r)
{
   cout << r.length << endl;
   cout << r.width << endl;
}
```

7.33
```
void getRect(Rectangle &r)
{
   cout << "Width: ";
   cin  >> r.width;
   cout << "Length: ";
   cin  >> r.length;
}
```

7.34
```
Rectangle getRect()    // Function return type is a Rectangle structure
{
   Rectangle r;
   cout << "Width: ";
   cin  >> r.width;
   cout << "Length: ";
   cin  >> r.length;
   return r;
}
```

7.35 The problem domain is the set of real-world objects, parties, and major events related to a problem.

7.36 Someone who has an adequate understanding of the problem. If you adequately understand the nature of the problem you are trying to solve, you can write a description of the problem domain yourself. If you do not thoroughly understand the nature of the problem, you should have an expert write the description for you.

7.37 Start by identifying all the nouns (including pronouns and noun phrases) in the problem domain description. Each of these is a potential class. Then, refine the list to include only the classes that are relevant to the problem.

7.38 It is often helpful to ask the questions "In the context of this problem, what must the class know? What must the class do?"

7.39 A) Begin by identifying the nouns: doctor, patients, practice, patient, procedure, description, fee, statement, office manager, name, address, and total charge. After eliminating duplicates, objects, and simple data items that can be stored in variables, the remaining list of potential classes is: *Doctor, Practice, Patient, Procedure, Statement,* and *Office manager.*

B) The necessary classes for this problem are: *Patient, Procedure*, and *Statement.*

C) The *Patient* class knows the patient's name and address. The *Procedure* class knows the procedure description and fee. The *Statement* class knows each procedure that was performed. The *Statement* class can calculate total charges.

Chapter 8

8.1 A) `int empNum[100];`

B) `double payRate[25];`

C) `long miles[14];`

D) `string stateCapital[50];`

E) `double lightYears[1000];`

8.2
```
int readings[-1];          // Size declarator cannot be negative
float measurements[4.5];   // Size declarator must be an integer
int size;                  // This is not an array
string name[size];         // Size declarator must be a constant
```

8.3 0 through 3

8.4 The size declarator is used in the array definition statement. It specifies the number of elements in the array. A subscript is used to access an individual element in an array.

8.5 Array bounds checking is a safeguard provided by some languages. It prevents a program from using a subscript that is beyond the boundaries of an array. C++ does not perform array bounds checking.

8.6
```
1
2
3
4
5
```

8.7
```
#include <iostream>
using namespace std;

int main()
{
   const int NUM_MEN = 10;
   int fish[NUM_MEN], count;

   cout << "Enter the number of fish caught\n";
   cout << "by each fisherman.\n";
   for (int count = 0; count < NUM_MEN; count++)
   {
      cout << "fisherman " << (count+1) << ": ";
      cin  >> fish[count];
   }
   cout << "\n\nFish Report\n\n";
   for (int count = 0; count < NUM_MEN; count++)
   {
      cout << "Fisherman #" << count+1 << " caught "
           << fish[count] << " fish.\n";
   }
   return 0;
}
```

8.8 A) `int ages[10] = {5, 7, 9, 14, 15, 17, 18, 19, 21, 23};`

B) `double temps[7] = {14.7, 16.3, 18.43, 21.09, 17.9, 18.76, 26.7};`

C) `char alpha[8] = {'J', 'B', 'L', 'A', '*', '$', 'H', 'M'};`

8.9 A) `int numbers[10] = {0, 0, 1, 0, 0, 1, 0, 0, 1, 1};`

The definition is valid.

B) `int matrix[5] = {1, 2, 3, 4, 5, 6, 7};`
The definition is invalid because there are too many values in the initialization list.

C) `double radii[10] = {3.2, 4.7};`
The definition is valid. Elements 2 through 9 will be initialized to 0.0.

D) `int table[7] = {2, , , 27, , 45, 39};`
The definition is invalid. Values cannot be skipped in the initialization list.

E) `char codes[] = {'A', 'X', '1', '2', 's'};`
The definition is valid. The `codes` array will be allocated space for five characters.

F) `int blanks[];`
The definition is invalid. An initialization list must be provided when an array is implicitly sized.

G) `string suit[4] = {"Clubs", "Diamonds", "Hearts", "Spades"};`
The definition is valid.

8.10 No. An entire array cannot be copied in a single statement with the = operator. The array must be copied element by element.

8.11 A) `10`

B) `3`

C) `6`

D) `14`

8.12 `0`

8.13
```
10.00
25.00
32.50
50.00
110.00
```

8.14
```
1 18 18
2 4 8
3 27 81
4 52 208
5 100 500
```

8.15 `typedef int TenInts[10];`

8.16 The starting address of the array

8.17 `ABCDEFGH`

8.18 *(The entire program is shown here.)*

```
#include <iostream>
using namespace std;

// Function prototype
double avgArray(const int [], int);

int main()
{
   const int SIZE = 10;
   int userNums[SIZE];

   cout << "Enter 10 numbers: ";
   for (int count = 0; count < SIZE; count++)
   {
      cout << "#" << (count + 1) << " ";
      cin  >> userNums[count];
   }
   cout << "The average of those numbers is ";
   cout << avgArray(userNums, SIZE) << endl;
   return 0;
}

// Function avgArray
double avgArray(const int array[], size)
{
   double total = 0.0, average;
   for (int count = 0; count < size; count++)
      total += array[count];
   average = total / size;
   return average;
}
```

8.19 `int grades[30][10];`

8.20 24

8.21 `sales[0][0] = 56893.12;`

8.22
```
cout << sales[5][3];
```

8.23
```
int settings[3][5] = {{12, 24, 32, 21, 42},
                      {14, 67, 87, 65, 90},
                      {19,  1, 24, 12,  8}};
```

8.24

2	3	0	0
7	9	2	0
1	0	0	0

8.25
```
void displayArray7(int array[][7], int numRows)
{
   for (int row = 0; row < numRows; row ++)
   {
      for (int col = 0; col < 7; col ++)
      {  cout << array[row][col] << " ";
      }
      cout << endl;
   }
}
```

8.26
```
int vidNum[50][10][25];
```

8.27
```
vector
```

8.28
```
vector <int> frogs;
vector <float> lizards(20);
vector <char> toads(100, 'Z');
```

8.29
```
vector <int> gators;
vector <double> snakes(10);
gators.push_back(27);
snakes[4] = 12.897;
```

8.30 False

8.31 False

8.32
```
10
20
50
```

8.33
```
#include <iostream>
using namespace std;

class Yard
{
private:
   int length, width;
public:
   Yard()
      { length = 0; width = 0; }
   void setLength(int len)
      { length = len; }
   void setWidth(int wide)
      { width = wide; }
   int getLength() {return length;}
   int getWidth() {return width;}
};
```

```
int main()
{
   const int SIZE = 10;
   Yard lawns[SIZE];
   cout << "Enter the length and width of "
        << "each yard.\n";

   for (int count = 0; count < SIZE; count++)
   {
      int input;
      cout << "Yard " << (count + 1) << ":\n";
      cout << "length: ";
      cin  >> input;
      lawns[count].setLength(input);
      cout << "width: ";
      cin  >> input;
      lawns[count].setWidth(input);
   }
   cout << "\nHere are the yard dimensions.\n";
   for (int yard = 0; yard < SIZE; yard++)
   {
      cout << "Yard " << (yard+1) << " "
           << lawns[yard].getLength() << " X "
           << lawns[yard].getWidth()  << endl;
   }
   return 0;
}
```

8.34
```
Product()                                // Default constructor
{  description = "";
   partNum = cost = 0;
}
Product(string d, int p, double c)   // Constructor
{  description = d;
   partNum = p;
   cost = c;
}
```

8.35
```
Product items[100];
```

8.36
```
items[0].description = "Claw Hammer";
items[0].partNum = 547;
items[0].cost = 8.29;
```

8.37
```
for (int x = 0; x < 100; x++)
{
   cout << items[x].description << endl;
   cout << items[x].partNum << endl;
   cout << items[x].cost  << endl << endl;
}
```

8.38
```
Product items[5] = { Product("Screw driver", 621,  1.72),
                     Product("Socket set",   892, 19.97),
                     Product("Claw hammer",  547,  8.29) };
```

8.39
```
struct Measurement
{
   int miles;
   double hours;
};
```

8.40
```
struct Destination
{
   string city;
   Measurement travelTime;
};
```

8.41
```
Destination places [20];
places[4].city = "Tupelo";
places[4].travelTime.miles = 375;
places[4].travelTime.hours = 7.5;
```

Chapter 9

9.1 The linear search algorithm simply uses a loop to step through each element of an array, comparing each element's value with the value being searched for. The binary search algorithm, which requires the values in the array to be sorted in order, starts searching at the element in the middle of the array. If the middle element's value is greater than the value being searched for, the algorithm next tests the element in the middle of the first half of the array. If the middle element's value is less than the value being searched for, the algorithm next tests the element in the middle of the last half of the array. Each time the array tests an array element and does not find the value being searched for, it eliminates half of the remaining portion of the array. This method continues until the value is found, or there are no more elements to test. The binary search is more efficient than the linear search.

9.2 10,000

9.3 14

9.4 The items frequently searched for can be stored near the beginning of the array.

9.5 True

9.6 Change the > sign in the `if` statement to a < sign. The line would now read

```
If (array[count] < array[count + 1])
```

9.7 The last value is now in order.

9.8 The first value, in position 0, is now in order.

9.9 selection sort

9.10 A basic operation is one that requires constant time, regardless of the size of the problem that is being solved.

9.11 The worst case complexity function $f(n)$ of an algorithm is a measure of the time required by the algorithm to solve a problem instance of size n that requires the most time.

9.12 Because $10n$ and $25n$ differ by a constant factor and constant factors are not significant, the two algorithms are considered to be equivalent in efficiency.

9.13 To say that $f(n)$ is in $O(g(n))$ means that there exists a positive constant K such that $f(n) \leq Kg(n)$ for all $n \geq 1$. This means that for large problem sizes, an algorithm with complexity function $f(n)$ is no worse than one with complexity function $g(n)$.

9.14 To show that $100n^3 + 50n^2 + 75$ is in $O(20n^3)$, we must show that some constant K exists for which $100n^3 + 50n^2 + 75 \le K(20n^3)$ for all $n \ge 1$.

Observe that for all $n \ge 1$

$$\frac{100n^3 + 50n^2 + 75}{20n^3} = 5 + \frac{5}{2n} + \frac{75}{20n^3} \le 5 + 5 + 75 \le 85$$

Therefore, we have found a constant K that satisfies the inequality, namely $K = 85$.

9.15 Assuming that $g(n) \ge 1$ for all $n \ge 1$, we have $100 \le 100\ g(n)$ for all $n \ge 1$. This implies that $g(n) + 100 \le g(n) + 100g(n) = 101g(n)$ for all $n \ge 1$. Now, if $f(n)$ is in $O(g(n)+100)$, there exists a positive K such that $f(n) \le K(g(n)+100) \le 101Kg(n)$ for all $n \ge 1$. Taking $K_1 = 101K$, we see that $f(n) \le K_1 g(n)$ for all $n \ge 1$.

Chapter 10

10.1
```
cout << &count;
```

10.2
```
double *dPtr;
```

10.3 Multiplication operator, pointer declaration, indirection operator

10.4
```
50  60  70
500  300  140
```

10.5
```
for (int x = 0; x < 100; x++)
      cout << *(array + x) << endl;
```

10.6 12040

10.7 A) Valid
B) Valid
C) Invalid. Only addition and subtraction are valid arithmetic operations with pointers.
D) Invalid. Only addition and subtraction are valid arithmetic operations with pointers.
E) Valid

10.8 A) Valid
B) Valid
C) Invalid. `fvar` is a float, and `iptr` is a pointer to an `int`.
D) Valid
E) Invalid. `ivar` must be defined before it is used.

10.9 A) True
B) False
C) True
D) False

10.10
```
makeNegative (&num);
```

10.11
```
void convert(double *val)
{
   *val *= 2.54;
}
```

10.12 A

10.13
```
ip = new int;
delete ip;
```

10.14
```
ip = new int[500];
delete [] ip;
```

10.15 A pointer whose value is the address 0

10.16
```
char *getname(char *name)
{
   cout << "Enter your name: ";
   cin.getline(name, 81);
   return name;
}
```

10.17
```
char *getname()
{
   char name[81];
   cout << "Enter your name: ";
   cin.getline(name, 81);
   return name;
}
```

10.18 `Rectangle *rptr;`

10.19 `cout << rptr->length << endl << rptr->width << endl;`

10.20 B

Chapter 11

11.1 Each class object (an instance of a class) has its own copy of the class's instance member variables. If a class's member variable is static, however, only one copy of the variable exists in memory. All objects of that class have access to that one variable.

11.2 Outside the class declaration

11.3 Before

11.4 Static member functions cannot access instance members unless they explicitly specify an object of the class.

11.5 You can call a static member function before any instances of the class have been created.

11.6 No, but it has access to all of class X's members, just as if it were a member.

11.7 Class X

11.8 Each member of one object is copied to its counterpart in another object of the same class.

11.9 When one object is copied to another with the = operator, and when one object is initialized with another object's data

11.10 When an object contains a pointer to dynamically allocated memory

11.11 When an object is initialized with another object's data, when an object is passed by value as the argument to a function, and when an object is returned by value.

11.12 The member function has the same name as the class, has no return type, and has a single reference parameter to the same type as the class.

11.13 It performs memberwise assignment.

11.14 `Pet Pet :: operator=(const Pet);`

11.15 `dog.operator=(cat);`

11.16 It cannot be used in multiple assignment statements or other expressions.

11.17 It's a built-in pointer, available to a class's instance member functions, that always points to the instance of the class making the function call.

11.18 Instance member functions

11.19 `cat` is calling the operator+ function. `tiger` is passed as an argument.

11.20 The operator is used in postfix mode.

11.21 They should always return Boolean values.

11.22 The object may be directly used with input stream such as `cin` and output streams such as `cout`.

11.23 An `ostream` object should be returned by reference.

11.24 An `istream` object should be returned by reference.

11.25 The operator function must be declared as a `friend`.

11.26 `list1.operator[](25);`

11.27 The object whose name appears on the right of the operator in the expression

11.28 So statements using the overloaded operators may be used in other expressions

11.29 The postfix version has a dummy parameter.

11.30
```
#ifndef INTARRAY_H
#define INTARRAY_H
#include <iostream>
using namespace std;
// Modified Intarry.h
class IntArray
{
private:
      int *aptr;
      int arraySize;
      void subError();   // Handles subscripts out of range
public:
      IntArray(int);                    // Constructor
      IntArray(const IntArray &); // Copy constructor
      ~IntArray();                          // Destructor
      int size(){ return arraySize; }
      int &operator[](int);       // Overloaded [] operator
      int operator()(int, int); // Overloaded () operator
};
#endif


// Overloaded operator () added to IntArray.cpp
int IntArray::operator()(int i, int j)
{
  int sum = 0;
```

```
    if (i < 0 || j >= arraySize)
        subError();
    for(int k = i; k <= j; k++)
      sum = sum + aptr[k];
    return sum;
}
```

```
#include <iostream>
#include "IntArray.h"

using namespace std;

int main()
{
   IntArray table(10);

   // Store values in the array.
   for (int x = 0; x < table.size(); x++)
      table[x] = x;

   // Print the sum of the values in the range 3..5
   cout << table(3, 5);

   return 0;
}
```

11.31 Objects are automatically converted to other types. This ensures that an object's data is properly converted.

11.32 They always return a value of the data type they are converting to.

11.33 `BlackBox::operator int()`

11.34 `Big::Big(Small sm)`

11.35 The is-a relation

11.36 Because derived class objects can be considered as forming a subset of the set of base class objects. Hence we can think of the base class as a "uperset" or superclass of the derived class.

11.37 The base class access specification determines how members inherited from the base class will be accessed in the derived class.

11.38 A typist is a special case of an employee.

```
class Employee
{
   int yearsOfService;
};
class Typist : public Employee
{
   int wordsPerMinute;
};
```

11.39 Other than to friend functions, private members are only accessible to member functions of the same class. Protected members are accessible to member functions of the class as well as member functions of all derived classes.

11.40 Member access specification determines how a class member is accessible to code outside of the class. Base class access specification determines how members inherited from a base class will be accessed through the derived class.

11.41 A) a is inaccessible; the rest are private.
B) a is inaccessible; the rest are protected.
C) a is inaccessible; b, c, and setA are protected; setB and setC are public.
D) Private

11.42 Derived class constructors can assume members of the base class object have already been initialized.

11.43 Declarations are for typechecking, definitions are for code generation. The compiler needs the arguments to the base class constructor when it is generating code.

11.44 The same situation arises with composition when an outer class object needs to pass arguments to a constructor of an inner class object. The same syntax is used.

11.45
```
Entering the base.
Entering the camp.
Leaving the camp.
Leaving the base.
```

11.46
```
This base is secure.
The camp is secluded.
Leaving the camp.
Leaving the base.
```

Chapter 12

12.1

strlen	Accepts a C-string as an argument. Returns the length of the string (not including the null terminator).
strcat	Accepts two C-strings as arguments. The function appends the contents of the second string to the first string. (The first string is altered, the second string is left unchanged.)
strcpy	Accepts two C-strings as arguments. The function copies the second string to the first string. The second string is left unchanged.
strncpy	Accepts two C-strings and an integer argument. The third argument, an integer, indicates how many characters to copy from the second string to the first string. If the string2 has fewer than n characters, string1 is padded with '\0' characters.
strcmp	Accepts two C-string arguments. If string1 and string2 are the same, this function returns 0. If string2 is alphabetically greater than string1, it returns a negative number. If string2 is alphabetically less than string1, it returns a positive number.
strstr	Searches for the first occurrence of string2 in string1. If an occurrence of string2 is found, the function returns a pointer to it. Otherwise, it returns a NULL pointer (address 0).

12.2 `4`

12.3
```
Have a nice day
nice day
```

12.4 `strcpy(composer, "Beethoven");`

12.5
```
#include <iostream>
#include <cstring>
using namespace std;

int main()
{
   char place[] = "The Windy City";
   if (strstr(place, "Windy"))
      cout << "Windy found.\n";
   else
      cout << "Windy not found.\n";
   return 0;
}
```

12.6
A) negative
B) negative
C) negative
D) positive

12.7
```
if (strcmp(iceCream, "Chocolate") == 0)
       cout << "Chocolate: 9 fat grams.\n";
else if (strcmp(iceCream, "Vanilla") == 0)
       cout << "Vanilla: 10 fat grams.\n";
else if (strcmp(iceCream, "Pralines and Pecan") == 0)
       cout << "Pralines and Pecan: 14 fat grams.\n";
else
       cout << "That's not one of our flavors!\n";
```

12.8

`atoi`	Accepts a C-string as an argument. The function converts the string to an integer and returns that value.
`atol`	Accepts a C-string as an argument. The function converts the string to a long integer and returns that value.
`atof`	Accepts a C-string as an argument. The function converts the string to a double and returns that value.
`itoa`	Converts an integer to a C-string. The first argument is the integer. The result will be stored at the location pointed to by the second argument. The third argument is an integer. It specifies the numbering system that the converted integer should be expressed in. (8 = octal, 10 = decimal, 16 = hexadecimal, etc.)

12.9 `num = atoi("10");`

12.10 `num = atol("10000");`

12.11 `num = atof("7.2389");`

12.12 `itoa(127, strValue, 10);`

12.13
```
Tom Talbert Tried Trains
     Dom Dalbert Dried Drains
```

Chapter 13

13.1 `istream`, `istringstream`, and `ifstream`

13.2 `ostream`, `ostringstream`, and `ofstream`

13.3 To specify a file open mode.

13.4 Closing the file sooner than later frees up operating system resources and prevents loss of data written to the file in the event of an abnormal termination.

13.5 `ios::app`

13.6 `ios::trunc`

13.7 A new file of the given name is created and opened for output.

13.8 The contents of the file are discarded and the file is opened for output.

13.9
```
int a, b;
cout << "Enter two octal numbers " ;
cin >> oct >> a >> b;
cout << "The octal sum is " << oct << a + b;
```

13.10
```
int a, b;
cout << "Enter hexadecimal numbers" ;
cin >> hex >> a >> b;
cout << "The hexadecimal sum is " << hex << a + b << endl;
cout << "The decimal sum is " << dec << a + b;
```

13.11 `fstream fileObj("myfile.txt", ios::in);`

13.12
```
#include <cstdlib>
#include <iostream>
#include <iomanip>

using namespace std;

int main(int argc, char** argv)
{
   const int SIZE = 5;
   string names[SIZE] = {"Alfonso", "Bella", "Clinton",
                         "Dave", "Elaine"};
   int numbers[SIZE] = {12, 56, 23, -45, 9};

   for (int k = 0; k < SIZE; k++)
   {
        cout << left << setw(20) << names[k]
        << right << setw(10) << numbers[k] << endl;
   }
   return 0;
}
```

13.13
```
#include<iostream>
#include <fstream>
using namespace std;

int main()
{
   fstream outFile;
   outFile.open("output.txt", ios::out);
   outFile << "Today is the first day\n";
   outFile << "of the rest of your life.\n";
   return 0;
}
```

13.14 It reports when the end of a file has been encountered.

13.15
```
Run
Spot
run
See
Spot
run
```

13.16 The >> operator considers whitespace characters as delimiters and does not read them. The `getline()` member function does read whitespace characters.

13.17 The `getline` function reads a line of text; the `get` function reads a single character.

13.18 Writes a single character to a file.

13.19 `1e+002      1.7      8.6      7.8      5.1`

13.20
```
#include <cstdlib>
#include <iostream>
#include <fstream>
#include <cctype> // Needed for toupper
using namespace std;
int main()
{
    cout << "This program allows you to add names and phone\n";
    cout << "numbers to phones.dat.\n";
    fstream namesFile("phones.dat", ios::out|ios::app);
    if (!namesFile){ cout << "Error "; return 1;}
    string name, phone;
    char add;
    do
    {
       cout << "Do you wish to add an entry? ";
       cin >> add;
       cin.ignore();
       if (toupper(add) == 'Y')
       {
           cout << "Name: ";
           getline(cin, name);
           namesFile << name << "  ";
           cout << "Phone Number: ";
           getline(cin, phone);
           namesFile << phone << endl;
       }
```

```
    } while (toupper(add) == 'Y');
    namesFile.close();
    return 0;
}
```

13.21
```
#include <cstdlib>
#include <iostream>
#include <fstream>

using namespace std;

int main(int argc, char** argv)
{
   fstream data1("data1.txt", ios::in);
   fstream data2("data2.txt", ios::in);
   fstream data3("data3.txt", ios::out);
   if (!data1 || !data2 || !data2)
   {
       cout << "Trouble opening files.";
       return 1;
   }

   for (char ch = data1.get(); ch != EOF; ch = data1.get())
        data3.put(ch);
   data1.close();
   for (char ch = data2.get(); ch != EOF; ch = data2.get())
        data3.put(ch);
   data2.close();
   data3.close();

   return 0;
}
```

13.22 Character representation: "479"

ASCII codes: 52 55 57

13.23 The << operator writes text to a file. The write member function writes binary data to a file.

13.24 The first argument is the starting address of the section of memory, which is to be written to the file. The second argument is the size, in bytes, of the item being written.

13.25 The first argument is the starting address of the section of memory where information read from the file is to be stored. The second argument is the size, in bytes, of the item being read.

13.26 A filed is an individual piece of information pertaining to a single item. A record is made up of fields and is a complete set of information about a single item.

13.27 `file.write(reinterpret_cast<char> (&cust), sizeof(cust));`

13.28 `seekg` moves the file's read position (for input) and `seekp` moves the file's write position (for output).

13.29 `tellg` reports the file's read position and `tellp` reports the files write position.

13.30 `ios::beg` The offset is calculated from the beginning of the file

`ios::end` The offset is calculated from the end of the file

`ios::curr` The offset is calculated from the current position

13.31 0

13.32 `file.seekp(100L, ios::beg);`

Moves the write position to the one hundred first byte (byte 100) from the beginning of the file.

`file.seekp(-10L, ios::end);`

Moves the write position to 10 bytes before the end of the file.

`file.seekp(-25L, ios::cur);`

Moves the write position 25 bytes backward from the current position.

`file.seekp(30L, ios::cur);`

Moves the write position 30 bytes forward from the current position.

13.33 `file.open("info.dat", ios::in | ios::out);`

Input and output

`file.open("info.dat", ios::in | ios::app);`

Input and output. Output will be appended to the end of the file.

`file.open("info.dat", ios::in | ios::out | ios::ate);`

Input and output. If the file already exists, the program goes immediately to the end of the file.

`file.open("info.dat", ios::in | ios::out | ios::binary);`

Input and output, binary mode

Chapter 14

14.1 A simple case of the problem that can be solved without recursion.

14.2 The function calls itself with no way of stopping. It creates an infinite recursion.

14.3 `10`

14.4 In direct recursion, a recursive function calls itself. In indirect recursion, function A calls function B, which in turn calls function A.

Chapter 15

15.1 Let `p` be a pointer pointing to an object `ob` of a class that is part of an inheritance hierarchy. In general, `p` will be a pointer to some base class `B`, and the object `ob` will be an instance of a class `D` derived from `B`. Let f be a member function of `B` that is overridden in `D`. If the call `p->f()` is being made, static binding will call the version of `f` that is in the class `B`. Static binding will select the function to call based on the type of the pointer and will do so at compile time. Dynamic binding will wait until runtime and will select the version of `f` that is in `D`, the class of the object.

15.2 Dynamically

15.3
```
1
5
```

15.4
```
2
2
```

15.5
```
2
1
```

15.6
```
2
```

15.7 The body of the function is replaced with `= 0;`

15.8 It cannot be used to instantiate objects.

15.9 A) Inaccessible
B) Protected
C) Protected
D) Inaccessible
E) Protected
F) Public
G) Private
H) Protected
I) Public

Chapter 16

16.1 The try block contains one or more statements that may directly or indirectly throw an exception. The catch block contains code that handles, or responds to an exception.

16.2 The entire program will abort execution.

16.3 Each exception must be of a different type. The catch block whose parameter matches the data type of the exception handles the exception.

16.4 With the first statement after the try/catch construct

16.5 By giving the exception class a member variable, and storing the desired information in the variable. The throw statement creates an instance of the exception class, which must be caught by a catch statement. The catch block can then examine the contents of the member variable.

16.6 When it encounters a call to the function

16.7
```
template <class T>
int minPosition(T arr[], int size)
{
   int minPos = 0;
   for (int k = 1; k < size; k++)
   {
      if (arr[k] < arr[minPos])
         minPos = k;
   }
   return minPos;
}
```

16.8 That the operator has been overloaded by the class object

16.9 First write a regular, nontemplated version of the function. Then, after testing the function, convert it to a template.

16.10 `List<int> myList;`

16.11
```
template <class T>
class Rectangle
{
   private:
      T width;
      T length;
      T area;

   public:
      void setData(T W, T L)
         { width = W; length = L;}
      void calcArea()
         { area = width * length; }
      T getWidth()
         { return width; }
      T getLength()
         { return length; }
      T getArea()
         { return area; }
};
```

Chapter 17

17.1 A data member contains the data stored in the node. A successor pointer points to the next node in the list.

17.2 A pointer to the first node in the tree

17.3 The successor pointer in the last node will have a value of NULL.

17.4 A data structure that contains a pointer to an object of the same data structure type

17.5 Appending a node is adding a new node to the end of the list. Inserting a node is adding a new node in a position between two other nodes.

17.6 Appending

17.7 We need a pointer to the previous node so we can set its successor pointer to the new node.

17.8 A) Remove the node from the list without breaking the links created by the `next` pointers.
B) Delete the node from memory.

17.9 Because there is probably a node pointing to the node being deleted. Additionally, the node being deleted probably points to another node. These links in the list must be preserved.

17.10 The unused memory is never freed, so it could eventually be used up.

Chapter 18

18.1 Last-in-first-out. The last item stored in a LIFO data structure is the first item extracted.

18.2 A static stack has a fixed size and is implemented as an array. A dynamic stack grows in size as needed and is implemented as a linked list. Advantages of a dynamic stack: There is no need to specify the starting size of the stack. The stack automatically grows each time an item is pushed and shrinks each time an item is popped. Also, a dynamic stack is never full (as long as the system has free memory).

18.3 Push: An item is pushed onto, or stored in, the stack.

Pop: An item is retrieved (and hence, removed) from the stack.

18.4 Vector, linked list, or deque

Chapter 19

19.1 A standard linked list is a linear data structure in which each node has at most one successor. A binary tree is nonlinear, because each node can have up to two successors.

19.2 The first node in the tree

19.3 A node pointed to by another node in the tree

19.4 A node that points to no other nodes

19.5 A collection of nodes of the binary tree that consists of some node X, together with all the descendants of X. An empty collection of nodes is also a subtree.

19.6 Information can be stored in a binary tree in a way that makes a form of binary search possible.

19.7
1. The node's left subtree is traversed.
2. The node's data is processed.
3. The node's right subtree is traversed.

19.8
1. The node's data is processed.
2. The node's left subtree is traversed.
3. The node's right subtree is traversed.

19.9
1. The node's left subtree is traversed.
2. The node's right subtree is traversed.
3. The node's data is processed.

19.10 The node to be deleted is node D.
1. Find node D's parent and set the child pointer that links the parent to node D, to NULL.
2. Free node D's memory.

19.11 The node to be deleted is node D.
1. Find node D's parent.
2. Link the parent node's child pointer (that points to node D) to node D's child.
3. Free node D's memory.

19.12
1. Attach the node's right subtree to the parent, and then find a position in the right subtree to attach the left subtree.
2. Free the node's memory.

APPENDIX

D Answers to Odd-Numbered Review Questions

Chapter 1

1. programmed
3. arithmetic logic unit (ALU) and control unit
5. operating systems and application software
7. programming language
9. High-level
11. portability
13. programmer-defined symbols
15. Punctuation
17. variable
19. input, processing, output
21. Output
23. Main memory, or RAM, is volatile, which means its contents are erased when power is removed from the computer. Secondary memory, such as a disk or CD, does not lose its contents when power is removed from the computer.
25. A syntax error is the misuse of a key word, operator, punctuation, or other part of the programming language. A logical error is a mistake that tells the computer to carry out a task incorrectly or to carry out tasks in the wrong order. It causes the program to produce the wrong results.
27.
```
Account Balance High Level Pseudocode
   Have user input starting balance
   Have user input total deposits
   Have user input total withdrawals
   Calculate current balance
   Display current balance
```

```
Account Balance Detailed Pseudocode
   Input startBalance            // with prompt
   Input totalDeposits           // with prompt
   Input totalWithdrawals        // with prompt
   currentBalance = startBalance + totalDeposits - totalWithdrawals
   Display currentBalance
```

29. 45
31. 28
33. The error is that the program performs its math operation before the user has entered values for the variables `width` and `length`.

Chapter 2

1. semicolon
3. `main`
5. braces `{}`
7. 9.7865E14
9. B
11. B (C is valid, but prints the contents of variable `Hello`, rather than the string `"Hello"`.)
13. A) 11 B) 14 C) 3 (An integer divide takes place.)
15.
```
double temp,
       weight,
       height;
```
17.
A) `d2 = d1 + 2;`
B) `d1 = d2 * 4;`
C) `c = 'K';`
D) `i = 'K';`
E) `i = i – 1;`
19.
```
cout << "Two mandolins like creatures in the\n\n\n";
cout << "dark\n\n\n";
cout << "Creating the agony of ecstasy.\n\n\n";
cout << "                          - George Barker\n\n\n";
```
21.
```
Input weeks              // with prompt
days = weeks * 7
Display days
```
23.
```
Input speed              // with prompt
Input time               // with prompt
distance = speed * time
Display distance
```

25. A)
```
0
100
```
B)
```
8
2
```
C)
```
I am the incrediblecomputing
machine
and I will
amaze
you.
```

27. The C-style comments symbols are backwards.
`iostream` should be enclosed in angle brackets.
There shouldn't be a semicolon after `int main()`.
The opening and closing braces of function main are reversed.
There should be a semicolon after `int a, b, c`.
The comment `\\ Three integers` should read `// Three integers`.
There should be a semicolon at the end of each of the following lines:
```
a = 3
b = 4
c = a + b
```
`cout` begins with a capital letter.
The stream insertion operator (that appears twice in the `cout` statement) should read << instead of <.
The `cout` statement uses the variable `C` instead of `c`.

Chapter 3

1. A) `cin >> description;`
   B) `getline(cin, description);`
3. A) `cin >> setw(25) >> name;`
   B) `cin.getline(name, 25);`
5. `iostream` and `iomanip`
7. A) `price = 12 * unitCost;`
   B) `cout << setw(12) << 98.7;`
   C) `cout << 12;`
9. A) `a = 12 * x;`
   B) `z = 5 * x + 14 * y + 6 * k;`
   C) `y = pow(x, 4);`
   D) `g = (h + 12) / (4 * k);`
   E) `c = pow(a, 3) / (pow(b, 2) * pow(k, 4));`
11. 8
13. `const int RATE = 12;`
15. `east = west = north = south = 1;`
17. No, a named constant must be initialized at the time it is defined. It cannot be assigned a value at a later time.

19.
```
cout << fixed << showpoint << setprecision(4);
cout << setw(12) << profit;
```

NOTE: Now that you understand that user inputs should *always* be preceded by prompts, the `// with prompt` comment can be omitted from the pseudocode. Beginning with Chapter 3, we have begun omitting it.

21.
```
Input score1
Input score2
Input score3
average = (score1 + score2 + score3) / 3.0
Display average
```

23.
```
Input maxCredit
Input creditUsed
availableCredit = maxCredit – creditUsed
Display availableCredit
```

25. A) `Your monthly wages are 3225`
    B) `6 3 12`
    C) `In 1492 Columbus sailed the ocean blue.`

27. A) `#include <iostream>` is missing.
    Each `cin` and `cout` statement starts with capital C.
    The << operator is mistakenly used with `cin`.
    The assignment statement should read:

    ```
    sum = number1 + number2;
    ```

    The last `cout` statement should have << after `cout`.
    The last `cout` statement is missing a semicolon.
    The body of the main function should be indented within the braces.

    B) The `cin` statement should read:

    ```
    cin >> number1 >> number2;
    ```

    The assignment statement should read:

    ```
    quotient = static_cast<double>(number1) / number2;
    ```

    The last `cout` statement is missing a semicolon.
    There is no `return 0;`

29. A) There shouldn't be a semicolon after the `#include` directive.
    The function header for main should read:

    ```
    int main()
    ```

    The variable `number` is defined, but it is called `number1` in the `cin` statement.
    The combined assignment operator is improperly used. The statement should read:

    ```
    half /= 2;
    ```

There is a logical error. The value divided by 2 should be `number`, not `half`.
The results are never output.
There is no `return 0;`

B) There shouldn't be a semicolon after the `#include` directive.
`name` should be declared as a `string` or a `char` array. If declared as `string`, a `#include <string>` directive is needed.
The statement `cin.getline >> name;` should read

```
cin >> name;
```

The statement `cin >> go;` should read

```
cin.get(go);
```

Chapter 4

1. relational
3. false, true
5. true, false
7. false
9. `!`
11. `&&`
13. block (or local)
15. `break`
17.
```
if (y == 0)
    x = 100;
```
19.
```
if (score >= 90)
   cout << "Excellent";
else if (score >= 80)
   cout << "Good";
else
   cout << "Try Harder";
```
21.
```
if(x < y)
    q = a + b;
else
    q = x * 2;
```
23. T, F, T
25.
```
if (grade >= 0 && grade <= 100)
     cout << "The number is valid.";
```
27.
```
if (hours < 0 || hours > 80)
     cout << "The number is not valid.";
```

29.
```
if(sales < 10000)
   commission = .10;
else if (sales <= 15000)
   commission = .15;
else
   commission = .20;
```

31. It should read

```
if (!(x > 20))
```

33. It should use `||` instead of `&&`.

35. A) The first `cout` statement is terminated by a semicolon too early.
    The definition of `score1`, `score2`, and `score3` should end with a semicolon.
    The following statement:

    ```
    if (average = 100)
    ```

    should read:

    ```
    if (average == 100)
    ```

    `perfectScore` is used before it is declared.
    The following `if` statement should not be terminated with a semicolon:

    ```
    if (perfectScore);
    ```

    The conditionally executed block in the `if` statement shown above should end with a closing brace.

    B) The conditionally executed blocks in the `if/else` construct should be enclosed in braces.
    The following statement:

    ```
    cout << "The quotient of " << num1 <<
    ```

    should end with a semicolon, rather than with a <<.

    C) The trailing `else` statement should come at the end of the `if/else` construct.

    D) A `switch case` construct cannot be used to test relational expressions.
    An `if/else` if statement should be used instead.

Chapter 5

1. increment
3. prefix
5. body
7. pretest
9. infinite (or endless)
11. running total
13. sentinel
15. `do-while`

17. initialization, test, update

19. `break`

21. `fstream`

23. It will be erased and a new file with the same name will be created.

25. It marks the location of the next byte to be read. When an input file is opened, its read position is initially set to the first byte in the file.

27.
```
int num;
cin >> num;
num *=2;
while (num < 50)
{   cout << num << endl;
    num *=2;
}
```

29.
```
for (int x = 0; x <= 1000; x += 10)
    cout << x;
```

31.
```
for (int row = 1; row <= 3; row++)
{   for (int star = 1; star <= 5; star++)
        cout << '*';
    cout << endl;
}
```

33.
```
char doAgain;
int sum = 0;

cout << "This code will increment sum 1 or more times.\n";
do
{   sum++;
        cout << "Sum has been incremented. "
             << "Increment it again(y/n)? ";
        cin  >> doAgain;
} while ((doAgain == 'y') || (doAgain == 'Y'));

cout << "Sum was incremented " << sum << " times.\n";
```

35.
```
for (int count = 0; count < 50; count++)
    cout << "count is " << count << endl;
```

37.
```
ofstream outfile;
outfile.open("numbers.txt");
for (int num = 1; num <= 100; num++)
   outfile << num << "  ";
outfile.close();
```

39. Nothing will print. The erroneous semicolon after the `while` condition causes the `while` loop to end there. Because `x` will continue to remain `1`, `x < 10` will remain true and the infinite loop can never be exited.

41. 2 4 6 8 10

43. A) The statement `result = ++(num1 + num2);` is invalid.
    B) The `while` loop tests the variable `again` before any values are stored in it.
    The `while` loop is missing its opening and closing braces.
45. A) The expression tested by the `do-while` loop should be `choice == 1` instead of `choice = 1`.
    B) The variable `total` is not initialized to 0.
    The `while` loop does not change the value of `count`, so it iterates an infinite number of times.

Chapter 6

1. header
3. `showValue(5);`
5. arguments
7. value
9. local
11. Global
13. local
15. `return`
17. last
19. reference
21. reference
23. parameter lists
25. Arguments appear in the parentheses of a function call. They are the actual values passed to a function. Parameters appear in the parentheses of a function heading. They are the variables that receive the arguments.
27. Function overloading means including more than one function in the same program that has the same name. C++ allows this providing the overloaded functions can be distinguished by having different parameter lists.
29. You want the function to change the value of a variable that is defined in the calling function.
31. Yes, but within that function only the local variable can be "seen" and accessed.
33.
```
double half(double value)
{
    return value / 2;
}
```
35.
```
void timesTen(int num)
{
    cout << num * 10;
}
```

37.
```
void getNumber(int &number)
{
   cout << "Enter an integer between 1 and 100): ";
   cin  >> number;
   while (number < 1 || number > 100)
   {
      cout << "This value is out of the allowed range.\n"
           << "Enter an integer between 1 and 100): ";
   }
}
```

39. A) The data type of `value2` and `value3` must be declared.
    The function is declared `void` but returns a value.
    B) The assignment statement should read:

    ```
    average = (value1 + value2 + value3) / 3.0;
    ```

    The function is declared as a `double` but returns no value.
    C) `width` should have a default argument value.
    The function is declared `void` but returns a value.
    D) The parameter should be declared as:

    ```
    int &value
    ```

    The `cin` statement should read:

    ```
    cin >> value;
    ```

    E) The functions must have different parameter lists.

Chapter 7

1. Abstract Data Type
3. procedural and object-oriented
5. data and procedures (i.e., functions)
7. instantiating
9. member variables
11. encapsulation
13. member variables, member functions
15. mutator
17. class
19. return
21. destroyed
23. default
25. constructor, destructor
27. public
29. False. It can be both passed to a function and returned from a function.

31. separate (i.e., each in their *own* file)

33. `Canine.cpp`

35. public

37. initialization list, constructor

39. `Inventory trivet = {555, 110};`

41.
```
struct TempScale
{   double fahrenheit;
    double celsius;
};
struct Reading
{   int windSpeed;
    double humidity;
    TempScale temperature;
};
Reading today;
today.windSpeed = 37;
today.humidity = .32;
today.temperature.fahrenheit = 32;
today.temperature.celsius = 0;
```

43.
```
void inputReading(Reading &r)
{
    cout << "Enter the wind speed: ";
    cin  >> r.windSpeed;
    cout << "Enter the humidity: ";
    cin  >> r.humidity;
    cout << "Enter the fahrenheit temperature: ";
    cin  >> r.temperature.fahrenheit;
    cout << "Enter the celsius temperature: ";
    cin  >> r.temperature.celsius;
}
```

45.
```
union Items
{
    char  alpha;
    int   num;
    long  bigNum;
    double real;
};
Items anItem;
```

47.
```
Inventory(string id = 0, string descrip = "new", int qty = 0)
{  prodID = id; prodDescription = descrip; qtyInStock = qty; }
```

49. A) The structure declaration has no tag.
    B) The semicolon is missing after the closing brace.

51. A) The `Names` structure needs a constructor that accepts 2 strings.
    B) Structure members cannot be initialized in the structure declaration.

53. A) The semicolon should not appear after the word `DumbBell` in the class declaration.

    Even though the `weight` member variable is private by default, it should be preceded with the `private` access specifier.

    Because the `setWeight` member function is defined outside the class declaration, its function header must appear as:

```
void DumbBell::setWeight(int w)
```

    The line that reads: `DumbBell.setWeight(200);`
    should read: `bar.setWeight(200);`

    Because the `weight` member variable is private, it cannot be accessed outside the class, so the `cout` statement cannot legally output `bar.weight`. There needs to be a public `getWeight()` function that the main program can call.

    B) Constructors must be public, not private.

    Both constructors are considered the default constructor. This is illegal since there can be only one default constructor.

    All the parameters in the `Change` function header should have a data type.

55. A) The nouns are

Bank	Savings Account	Money	Interest rate
Account	Checking Account	Balance	
Customer	Money market account	Interest	

    After eliminating duplicates, objects, and simple values that can be stored in class variables, the potential classes are: `Bank`, `Account`, and `Customer`.

    B) The only class needed for this particular problem is `Account`.

    C) The `Account` class must know its balance and interest rate.

    The `Account` class must be able to handle deposits and withdrawals and calculate interest earned. It is this last capability, calculating interest earned, that this application will use.

Chapter 8

1. size declarator
3. subscript
5. size declarator, subscript
7. initialization
9. initialization list
11. subscript
13. value
15. multidimensional
17. two
19. columns

21. A) 10 B) 0 C) 9 D) 40
23. A) 3 B) 0
25. the starting address of the array
27. A) 8 B) 10 C) 80 D) `sales[7][9] = 3.52;`
29.
```
Car forSale[35] = { Car("Ford", "Taurus",  2006, 21000),
                    Car("Honda","Accord",  2004, 11000),
                    Car("Jeep", "Wrangler",2007, 24000) };
```
31.
```
for (int index = 0; index < 25; index++)
     array2[index] = array1[index]
```
33.
```
int id[10];
double grossPay[10];
for (int emp = 0; emp < 10; emp++)
    cout << id[emp] << "    " << grossPay[emp] << endl;
```
35.
```
struct PopStruct
{  string name;
   long   population;
};
PopStruct country[12];
ifstream dataIn;
dataIn.open("pop.dat");
for (int index = 0; index < 12; index++)
{  getline(dataIn, country[index].name);
   dataIn >> country[index].population;
   dataIn.ignore();
}
dataIn.close();
```
37. A) The size declarator cannot be a variable.
    B) The size declarator cannot be negative.
    C) The initialization list must be enclosed in braces.
39. A) The parameter should be declared as `int nums[]`.
    B) The parameter must specify the number of columns, not the number of rows. Also, a second parameter is needed to specify the number of rows.

Chapter 9

1. linear
3. linear
5. N/2
7. first
9. 1/8
11. ascending
13. one
15. there were no number exchanges on the previous pass

17. Bubble sort normally has to make many data exchanges to place a value in its correct position. Selection sort determines which value belongs in the position currently being filled with the correctly ordered next value and then places that value directly there.

19.

Array Size →	50 Elements	500 Elements	10,000 Elements	100,000 Elements	10,000,000 Elements
Linear Search (Average Comparisons)	25	250	5,000	50,000	5,000,000
Linear Search (Maximum Comparisons)	50	500	10,000	100,000	10,000,000
Binary Search (Maximum Comparisons)	6	9	14	17	24

21. A) Map directly from the desired ID to the array location as follows:
    index = desiredID –101

    B) Do a linear search starting from the last array element and working backwards until the item is found or until a smaller ID is encountered, which means the desired ID is not in the array. Here is the pseudocode:

```
index = 299          // start at the last element
position = -1
found = false
While index >= 0 and array[index].customerID >= desiredID
                 and not found
   If array[index].customerID = desiredID
      found = true
      position = index
   End If
   Decrement index
End While
Return position
```

Chapter 10

1. address
3. pointer
5. pointers
7. new
9. null
11. new
13. Sending `*iptr` to `cout` will display 7. Sending `iptr` to `cout` will display the address of x.
15. You can increment or decrement a pointer using ++ and --, you can add an integer to a pointer, and you can subtract an integer from a pointer.
17. 8

19. If `new` fails to allocate the requested amount of memory, it throws the `bad_alloc` exception. In programs compiled with older compilers, new returns the value 0.
21. `delete` is used to deallocate memory allocated by `new`.
23. `const int *p;`
25. `change(&i);`
27.
```
void exchange(int *p, int *q)
{
    int temp = *p;
    *p = *q;
    *q = temp;
}
```
29. A) 30
    B) 30
    C) 0
    D) 0
    E) 20
    F) 10
    G) 10
    H) 20

Chapter 11

1. static
3. static
5. friend
7. Memberwise assignment
9. this
11. postfix increment (or decrement)
13. has-a
15. copy constructor
    overloaded = operator
    overloaded = operator
    copy constructor
17. Place the static keyword in the function's prototype. Calls to the function are performed by connecting the function name to the *class* name with the scope resolution operator.
19. In object composition, one object is a nested inside another object, which creates a has-a relationship. When a class is a friend of another class, there is no nesting. If a class A is a friend of a class B, member functions of A have access to all of B's members, including the private ones.
21. If a pointer member is used to reference dynamically allocated memory, a memberwise assignment operation will only copy the contents of the pointer, not the section of memory referenced by the pointer. This means that two objects will exist with pointers to the same address in memory. If either object manipulates this area of memory, the changes will show up for both objects. Also, if either object frees the memory, it will no longer contain valid information for either object.

23. If an object were passed to the copy constructor by value, a copy of the argument would have to be created before it can be passed to the copy constructor. But then the creation of the copy would require a call to the copy constructor with the original argument being passed by value. This process will continue indefinitely.

25.
```
Dollars Dollars::operator++();      // Prefix
Dollars Dollars::operator++(int);   // Postfix
```

27.
```
ostream &operator<<(ostream &strm, Length obj);
```

29. The overloaded operators offer a more intuitive way of manipulating objects, similar to the way primitive data types are manipulated.

31. members

33. `Pet`

35. private

37. inaccessible, private, private

39. inaccessible, protected, public

41. last

43. A) The first line of the class declaration should read

```
class Car : public Vehicle
```

Also, the class declaration should end in a semicolon.

B) The first line of the class declaration should read

```
class Truck : public Vehicle
```

Chapter 12

1. `C-string`

3. `string literal`

5. `null terminator`

7. `ostringstream`

9. concatenate

11. `strcpy`

13. `strcmp`

15. `atoi`

17. `atof`

19.
```
char lastChar(const char *str)
{  //go to null terminator at end
   while (*str != 0)
      str++;
   //back up to last character
   str--;
   return *str;
}
```

21. h

23. 9
25. Most compilers will print "not equal". Some compilers store only one copy of each literal string: such compilers will print "equal" because all copies of "a" will be stored at the same address.
27. abrasion
29. A) This is probably a logic error because C-strings should not be compared with the == operator
    B) `atoi` converts a string to an integer, not an integer to a string.
    C) The compiler will not allocate enough space in `string1` to accommodate both strings.
    D) `strcmp` compares C-strings, not characters.

Chapter 13

1. file name
3. close
5. `ifstream`, `ofstream`, `fstream`
7. `ifstream`
9. `ofstream people("people.dat");`
11. `fstream places("places.dat");`
13. `pets.open("pets.dat", ios::in);`
    `fstream pets("pets.dat", ios::in);`
15. null or 0
17. `cout`
19. `getline`
21. `put`
23. text, ASCII text
25. structures
27. `read`
29. sequential
31. `seekg`
33. `tellg`
35. `ios::beg`
37. `ios::cur`
39. Open the file in binary mode, seek to the end, and then call tellg to determine the position of the last byte:

```
ifstream inFile(fileName, ios::binary);
inFile.seekg(0L, ios::end);
long len = inFile.tellg();
```

41. Open the two files in binary mode, the first file for input and the second file for output. Seek to the end of the first file, and then keep backing up in the first file while writing to the second.

```
fstream inFile(file1name, ios::in | ios::binary);
fstream outFile(file2name, ios::out | ios::binary);
char ch;
// seek to end of source file
// and then position just before that last
// character
inFile.seekg(0L, ios::end);
inFile.seekg(-1, ios::cur);
while (true)
{
   // we are positioned before a character we need to read
   inFile.get(ch);
   outFile.put(ch);
   // back up two characters  to skip the character just read
   // and go to the character before it.
   inFile.seekg(-2, ios::cur);
   if (inFile.fail())
      break;
}
```

43. A) File should be opened as

```
fstream file("info.dat", ios::in | ios::out);
```

or

```
fstream file;
file.open("info.dat", ios::in | ios::out);
```

B) Should not specify `ios::in` with an `ofstream` object. Also, the `if` statement should read

```
if (!File)
```

C) File access flags must be specified with `fstream` objects.

D) Should not write to a file opened for input. Also, the << operator should not be used on binary files.

E) The while statement should read

```
while(!dataFile.eof())
```

F) The input stream member function `get` that takes a single parameter requires a single character parameter. There is a version of `get` that reads a string of characters, but that function should be avoided. Use the global `getline` function if you need to read a string.

G) The `get` member function that takes a single parameter cannot be used to read a string: it can only read single characters.

H) The file access flag should be `ios::in`. Also, the `put` member function cannot be used to write a string.

I) The file access flag should be `ios::out`. Also, the last line should read

```
dataFile.write(&dt, sizeof(date));
```

J) The `seekp` member function should not be used since the file is opened for input.

Chapter 14

1. Indirect recursion. There are more function calls to keep up with.
3. When the problem is more easily solved with recursion, and the recursive calls do not repeatedly solve the same subproblems.
5. direct
7. A) 55

   B)
   ```
   **********
   *********
   ********
   *******
   ******
   *****
   ****
   ***
   **
   *
   ```
   C) evE dna madA

Chapter 15

1. abstract class
3. abstract
5. compile
7. polymorphism
9. Inheritance
11. Inheritance
13. yes
15. yes
17. `pAnimal = new Dog; pDog = static_cast<Dog *>(pAnimal);`
19. A pure virtual function cannot have a body, and the function `myFun` has no return type.

Chapter 16

1. throw point
3. catch
5. template prefix
7. vector, list, or any sequence container
9. iterators

11. This solution uses recursion to perform the reversal. It needs the inclusion of the STL algorithm header file to allow use of swap.

```
template<class T>
void reverse(T arr[ ], int size)
{  if (size >= 2)
   {  swap(arr[0], arr[size-1]);
      reverse(arr+1, size-2);
   }
}
```

13. The stiring of characters stored in the array will be reversed.
15. A) The try block must appear before the catch block.
    B) The cout statement should not appear between the try and catch blocks.
    C) The return statement should read `return number * number;`
    D) The type parameter, T, is not used.
    E) The type parameter, T2 is not used.
    F) The declaration should read `SimpleVector<int> array(25);`
    G) The statement should read `cout << valueSet[2] << endl;`

Chapter 17

1. head pointer
3. NULL or 0
5. Inserting
7. circular
9.
```
void printFirst(ListNode *ptr)
{
   if (!ptr) { cout << "Error"; exit(1);}
   cout << ptr->value;
}
```
11.
```
double lastValue(ListNode *ptr)
{
   if (!ptr) { cout << "Error"; exit(1);}
   if (ptr->next == NULL)
      return ptr->value;
   else
      return lastValue(ptr->next);
}
```
13.
```
ListNode *ListConcat(ListNode *list1, ListNode *list2)
{
   if (list1 == NULL)
      return list2;
   // Concatenate list2 to end of list1
   ListNode *ptr = list1;
   while (ptr->next != NULL)
      ptr = ptr->next;
   ptr->next = list2;
   return list1;
}
```

15. 56.4
17. A) The `printList` function should have a return type of `void`. Also, the use of the head pointer to walk down the list destroys the list: use an auxiliary pointer initialized to head instead.
    B) Eventually the pointer `p` becomes `NULL`, at which time the attempt to access `p->next` will result in an error. Replace the test `p->next` in the `while` loop with `p`. Also, the function fails to declare a return type of `void`.
    C) The function should declare a return type of `void`. Also, the function uses `p++` erroneously in place of `p = p->next` when attempting to move to the next node in the list.
    D) Replace `nodeptr->next = NULL;` with `delete nodeptr;`

Chapter 18

1. Last In First Out
3. A static stack has all its storage allocated at once, when the stack is created. A dynamic stack allocates storage for each element as it is added. Normally, static stacks use array-based implementations, whereas dynamic stacks use linked lists.
5. It takes an existing container and implements a new interface on top of it to adapt it to a different use.
7. First In First Out
9. the front of the queue
11. lists and deques
13.

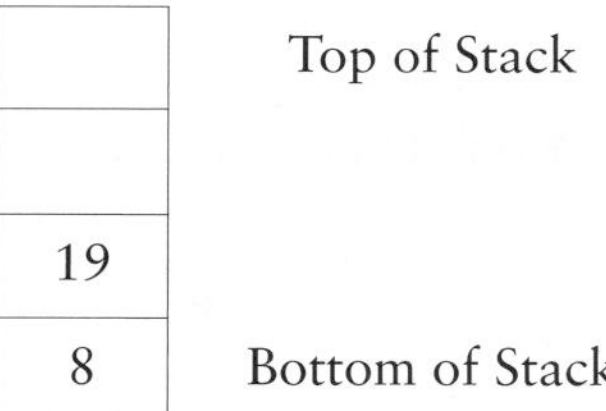

15. Assuming a circular array buffer:

10		9	12
rear		front	

17. Use two stacks, a main stack and an auxiliary stack. The main stack will store all items that are currently enqueued.
    - To enqueue a new item, push it onto the main stack.
    - To dequeue an item, keep popping items from the main stack and pushing them onto the auxiliary stack until the main stack is empty, then pop and store the top element from the auxiliary stack into some variable X. Now keep popping items from the auxiliary stack and pushing them back onto the main stack till the auxiliary stack is empty. Return the stored item X.
    - To check if the queue is empty, see if the main stack is empty.

Chapter 19

1. root node
3. leaf node
5. inorder, preorder, and postorder
7.
```
struct TreeNode
{
   int value;
   TreeNode *left, *middle, *right;
};
```
9. To traverse a ternary tree in preorder, visit the root, then traverse the left, middle, and right subtrees.

```
preorder(ternarytree)
   If (ternarytree != NULL)
      visit the root
      preorder left subtree of ternarytree
      preorder middle subtree of ternarytree
      preorder right subtree of ternarytree
   End If
End preorder
```
11. We must decide whether to visit the root right after the traversal of the left subtree or right after the traversal of the middle subtree.
13.
```
int largest(TreeNode *tree)
   Set a pointer p to the root node of tree
   While node at p has a right child Do
      Set p to the right child of the node at p
   End While
   return value in the node at p
End largest
```
15.
```
int smallest(TreeNode *tree)
   Set a pointer p to the root node of tree
   While node at p has a left child Do
      Set p to the left child of the node at p
   End While
   return value in the node at p
End smallest
```
17. 3 7 9 10 12 14 18 20 22 24 30
19. 3 10 9 7 14 20 18 30 24 22 12

INDEX

Symbols and Numerics

A

B

D

F

Q

R

T

U

V